2025

Survey of Federal Class Action Law

A U.S. SUPREME COURT AND CIRCUIT-BY-CIRCUIT ANALYSIS

CLASS ACTIONS AND DERIVATIVE SUITS COMMITTEE

ABA
AMERICAN BAR ASSOCIATION
Litigation Section

Cover design by ABA Design

Printed in the United States of America.

29 28 27 26 25 5 4 3 2 1

ISBN 978-1-63905-661-3

CONTENTS

2025 Survey of Federal Class Action Law: United States Supreme Court and Circuit-by-Circuit Analysis
A Report of the Class Actions and Derivative Suits Committee
American Bar Association
Litigation Section

Elizabeth J. Cabraser
Executive Editor
Jennifer Rudnick
Jordan Elias
Fabrice N. Vincent
Coordinating Editors
D. Larry Kristinik
Chair, ABA Litigation Section
Tanya Greene
Eric Harlan
Jason Kellogg
Co-Chairs, Class Actions and Derivative Suits Committee

Contributing Authors		
Nina Fields Britt	*Caleb M. Hodge*	*Erin C. Nebbia*
Kenneth S. Byrd	*Beau D. Hollowell*	*Alexis J. Opper*
Keeley O. Cronin	*Jessica Holmes*	*Lucas A. Ritchie*
Nicole E. Crossey	*Paul Karlsgodt*	*Christopher E. Roberts*
Jacob W. Doerr	*Amy E. Keller*	*Elijah Savage*
Catherine Ross Dunham	*McDaniel M. Kelly*	*Angelo A. Stio III*
Joshua D. Dunlap	*James A. King*	*Betsy Sugar*
Jordan Elias	*Adam J. Levitt*	*Trevor Tan*
Daniel R. Ferri	*Margaret Lyle*	*John E. Tangren*
Tyler Harris	*Amy Miller*	*Julia Veeser*
Madeline Hills	*Mark A. Miller*	

INTRODUCTION

In a twenty-first-century America marked by instantaneous communications, increased economic consolidation, and emerging artificial intelligence, the Supreme Court has defined and policed the boundaries of class action litigation with notable vigor. This circuit-by-circuit treatise is intended to serve a need by, in part, examining how the holdings of the Supreme Court have played out, and how the procedural common law of class actions continues to develop, in the lower courts, as they apply both Supreme Court and Circuit-level decisions to new and emerging issues and circumstances. We conceived and developed the treatise with the goal of creating a resource both for newcomers to class actions—welcome to the practice!—and for the veterans among us who may find themselves litigating in unfamiliar circuits.

Our judicial system continues to feel the effects of the Class Action Fairness Act of 2005 (CAFA), which generally expanded original and removal federal subject-matter jurisdiction to cover large class actions. In the years since CAFA's enactment, federal judges have considered a broad range of procedural and case management issues, in addition to substantive questions of state law. The increase in class cases proceeding through federal courts has yielded robust and growing federal class action precedents, prompting this book and its annual updates.

The Supreme Court, for its part, has seized several opportunities to flex its class action muscles since CAFA's enactment.

The Roberts Court's seminal class action decision, *Wal-Mart Stores, Inc. v. Dukes*, overturned certification of a nationwide class of female employees alleging employment discrimination. 564 U.S. 338 (2011). The Court held the statistical evidence proffered by the plaintiffs insufficient to show companywide discrimination in pay and promotion. *Id.* at 356–59. In an important passage, the Court held that the assessment of commonality under Rule 23(a)(2) looks at whether common *answers* are apt to drive the litigation, and whether determination of the truth or falsity of a common contention will, "in one stroke," resolve an issue central to the validity of each of the claims. *Id.* at 350–51. Though often overlooked, the Court's unanimous section addressing injunctive relief classes under Rule 23(b)(2) merits close study as well. *Id.* at 360–63.

The Supreme Court applied another key analytical concept in *Tyson Foods v. Bouaphakeo*, recognizing that a permissible method for submitting evidence in an individual action should generally be available in a corresponding class action. 136 S. Ct. 1036, 1046–47 (2016). *Tyson* is a key resource when considering trial structure and process in class actions and common question trials. In *AT&T Mobility LLC v. Concepcion*, the Court held that the Federal Arbitration Act preempted a California rule disfavoring arbitration provisions with class action waivers. 563 U.S. 333, 352 (2011). In *Comcast Corporation v. Behrend*, the Court reversed an antitrust class certification, holding that a damages model submitted in support of class certification under Rule 23(b)(3) must align with—and cannot sweep beyond—the plaintiff's theory of injury. 133 S. Ct. 1426, 1434 (2013).

In the securities fraud arena, the Supreme Court held in *Amgen Inc. v. Connecticut Retirement Plans and Trust Funds* that investor classes may be certified in the absence of proof that the alleged misrepresentations or omissions were material, recognizing that the issue of materiality itself presented a significant common question of fact for classwide determination. 568 U.S. 455, 459 (2013). The Court clarified that the standard of proof at class certification remains focused on the express requirements of the rule: "the office of a Rule 23(b)(3) certification ruling is not to adjudicate the case," and "Rule 23(b)(3) requires a showing that *questions* common to the class predominate, not that those questions will be answered, on the merits, in favor of the class." 568 U.S. at 459. Also in the area of securities fraud, the Court in 2014 refused to disturb the *Basic* fraud-on-the-market presumption, holding that class certification does not require direct evidence of investor reliance on alleged misrepresentations or omissions. *Halliburton Co. v. Erica P. John Fund, Inc.*, 134 S. Ct. 2398, 2412–14 (2014).

In *Spokeo* and *TransUnion*, the Supreme Court addressed the issue of class action standing and articulated a nuanced test for injury or threatened injury which test is subject to ongoing debate and interpretation in the lower courts, especially in the factual contexts of claimed injuries to privacy and identity rights, granting review of *Ramirez v. TransUnion LLC*, 953 F.3d 1008 (9th Cir. 2020) and *Robins v. Spokeo, Inc.*, 867 F.3d 1108, 1113 (9th Cir. 2017). The lower courts are now addressing the shifting contours of standing in light of *TransUnion LLC v. Ramirez*, 141 S. Ct. 2190 (2021) and *Spokeo v. Robins*, 136 S. Ct. 1540 (2016).

The Supreme Court's recent class action decisions—especially *Wal-Mart, Concepcion, Comcast, Amgen, Spokeo, and TransUnion*—have not only influenced federal class action practice, but also have spawned various differences of opinion among the lower courts, which our distinguished contributors highlight in the chapters that follow. Other doctrinal developments have occurred without much guidance from the high court: as of this writing, the Supreme Court has stayed out of the heated debates among bench and bar regarding the extratextual issues of ascertainability and absent class member standing, as these issues continue to percolate among the Circuits.

In the end, the dual mandates of fairness and efficiency continue to animate the conduct of class actions as modern Rule 23 moves into its second half-century. The courts are beginning to consider and apply the recent 2018 amendments to the notice and settlement approval provisions of Rule 23, updating the concepts of best practicable notice to include electronic alternatives (including email and social media) to first class mail and print publication, and utilizing the new "front-loading" process for class settlement approval. What specifically lies ahead for class action practitioners will, of course, depend on any Congressional legislation and how the Supreme Court and the Circuits, drawing from and adding to the evolving jurisprudence, define the contours of this significant litigation mechanism.

Elizabeth J. Cabraser

EDITORS AND AUTHORS

Nina Fields Britt is a member of the law firm of Rogers, Patrick, Westbrook & Brickman, LLC. She is a graduate of the College of Charleston (B.S., Honors College, cum laude, 1997) and the University of South Carolina, School of Law (J.D., magna cum laude, 2000). During law school, Ms. Britt served as Research Editor for the *South Carolina Law Review* and was awarded membership into the Order of the Coif and the Order of the Wig and Robe. Following law school, Ms. Britt served as a law clerk to The Honorable G. Ross Anderson, Jr., United States District Judge for the District of South Carolina before joining Ness, Motley, Loadholt, Richardson, & Poole, PA, as an associate. Ms. Britt has worked for Rogers, Patrick, Westbrook, & Brickman, LLC, since its inception in 2002. Her primary areas of practice include complex litigation, mutual fund and securities litigation, and class actions on behalf of consumers, homeowners, and businesses. She was named a finalist for Trial Lawyer of the Year by Trial Lawyers for Public Justice in 2003. Ms. Britt is admitted to practice in all courts of South Carolina, the U.S. Supreme Court, the U.S. Courts of Appeals for the Fourth and Eleventh Circuits, and the U.S. District Courts for the Eastern District of Wisconsin and the Northern District of Florida.

Kenneth S. Byrd is a partner and experienced trial attorney at Lieff Cabraser Heimann & Bernstein LLP, obtaining several large jury trial verdicts against Big Tobacco over the past several years. In 2013 and 2014, Kenny was the lead trial attorney in obtaining several substantial jury verdicts for smokers and their families, including a $27 million jury verdict and a $41 million jury verdict. His verdicts paved the way to a $100 million global settlement with Big Tobacco on behalf of hundreds of gravely injured smokers in Florida. He received the Tennessee Association for Justice's 2015 Paladin Award, the group's top honor, for his successful litigation against cigarette manufacturers in Florida federal courts. He represents consumers in consumer class action cases as well as individuals and their loved ones in personal injury lawsuits across the country. Kenny is also a member of Lieff Cabraser's False Claim Act/Fraud on the Government practice group, assisting whistleblowers to stop fraud and the misuse of funds in government contracts and programs. Prior to joining Lieff, Cabraser, Heimann & Bernstein, LLP, Kenneth practiced as a litigation attorney at Harwell, Howard, Hyne, Gabbert & Manner, PC. He also worked as a reporter in Washington D.C., covering church-state and religious liberty matters at the White House, U.S. Supreme Court, and Congress. Covering politicians as a reporter, he learned how to smell out lies and deception and uncover truth.

Elizabeth J. Cabraser is a founding partner of Lieff Cabraser Heimann & Bernstein, with nearly 40 years' experience representing plaintiffs in securities, product, consumer, mass tort, civil rights, and antitrust litigation. She has served in court-appointed leadership roles in scores of federal multidistrict and class proceedings and is presently serving in the plaintiffs' leadership of the Volkswagen "Clean Diesels," Toyota unintended acceleration, GM Ignition, BP Gulf of Mexico oil spill, and Takata airbag litigations. She teaches complex litigation at Berkeley and Columbia law schools, is editor-in-chief of *California Class Action Practice and Procedure*, executive editor of the ABA's *The Law of Class Actions 2013–2014* and writes on class action and complex litigation topics for law reviews and practitioners' publications. Ms. Cabraser was named one of *National Law Journal*'s "75 Outstanding Women Lawyers in America" for 2015 and has four times been recognized by the *NLJ* as one of the "100 Most Influential Lawyers in America." *The Daily Journal* has selected her as one of the "Top 100 Lawyers in California" for an unprecedented eleven years. In 2010, she was appointed to serve on the Federal Rules Advisory Committee.

Keeley O. Cronin is an associate at BakerHostetler, where she focuses her practice on data- and privacy-related class actions. She represents major health care providers, insurance agencies, and private universities, among others. Prior to joining BakerHostetler, she clerked for the Hon. Gregory A. Phillips, U.S. Court of Appeals for the Tenth Circuit, after graduating first in her class, Order of the Coif, with honors from the University of Wyoming College of Law.

Nicole E. Crossey is an associate at Troutman Pepper Locke LLP focusing on commercial litigation, complex business and contract disputes, insurance litigation, higher education law, class actions, data privacy and security law, and construction and real estate law. She represents a diverse clientele, including financial and investment companies, educational institutions, product manufacturers, and IT firms, in U.S. federal and state courts, and in mediations, arbitrations, and SEC investigations. Nicole is actively involved in the Defense Research Institute (DRI) and the American Bar Association (ABA), serving on the Steering Committees for the DRI Women in the Law Committee and the DRI Young Lawyers Committee, and serving as Vice Chair of the First Gen Initiative and Member of the Financial Literacy and Wellness Team within the ABA Young Lawyers Division.

Jacob W. Doerr is an associate in the Litigation Department at Porter Wright Morris & Arthur, LLP, with experience litigating complex commercial, property, and probate disputes. Prior to joining the firm, he completed legal internships at the National Labor Relations Board, Department of Labor, and Federal Trade Commission, where he built a strong foundation in labor law, OSHA and wage and hour litigation, and consumer protection. Jake was an Executive Note Editor for the *Health Matrix Journal of Law-Medicine* and a distinguished member of the Order of the Barristers at Case Western Reserve University School of Law.

Catherine Ross Dunham is a Professor of Law at the Elon University School of Law. She is an expert in the law related to Civil Procedure and Civil Litigation. She teaches and writes about Federal Civil Procedure and is co-author of the text *Skills and Values: Civil Procedure.* In addition to articles on procedural doctrine, class action litigation and evidence, Prof. Dunham has published articles exploring topics related to gender equity and unconscious gender bias. Prof. Dunham regularly teaches Civil Procedure, Complex Civil Litigation, and Evidence. In addition, she serves on the faculty of the National institute for Trial Advocacy (NITA) and teaches in regional, national, and international advocacy programs. She has also served as a trial analyst for several major news outlets, including NBC and CNN. Prof. Dunham is also prior recipient of the ABA Smyth-Gambrell Award for Teaching Professionalism.

Joshua D. Dunlap is a partner in the Portland office of Pierce Atwood LLP and is a member of the firm's Litigation Group and Appellate & Amici team. Mr. Dunlap's trial court practice has focused on class action and other complex commercial litigation, including multidistrict litigation, in federal courts. He also represents clients before state and federal appellate courts, serving as a practice leader for the firm's Appellate & Amici team. Mr. Dunlap is a contributor to his firm's class action blog, www.firstclassdefense.com, and maintains an appellate blog, www.maineappeals.com. Prior to joining Pierce Atwood, Mr. Dunlap clerked for Judge Paul J. Kelly, Jr., on the U.S. Court of Appeals for the Tenth Circuit.

Jordan Elias, a partner at Girard Sharp LLP, has pursued civil claims against pharmaceutical companies, oil and tobacco companies, and the nation's largest banks. He graduated *magna cum* *laude* from Yale College, earned his J.D. from Stanford Law School, serving on the law review, and clerked for the late Judge Cynthia Holcomb Hall of the U.S. Court of Appeals for the Ninth Circuit. In 2016, Mr. Elias received a California Lawyer Attorney of the Year (CLAY) award. He previously served as Chief Arbitrator for the San Francisco Bar Association's attorney-client fee disputes program. An elected member of the American Law Institute, Mr. Elias has published several law review articles, including *Cooperative Federalism in Class Actions*, 86 Tenn. L. Rev. 1 (2019), and *"More Than Tangential": When Does the Public Have a Right to Access Judicial Records?*, 29 J. of Law & Policy 367 (2021). In addition to his case work and contributions to ABA publications, Mr. Elias is responsible for the chapter on antitrust standing, causation, and remedies in *California State Antitrust and Unfair Competition Law* (Matthew Bender).

Daniel R. Ferri is an associate in the Chicago office of DiCello Levitt Gutzler LLP. He litigates class action, commercial, and intellectual property disputes.

Tyler Harris is a 2016 graduate of Vanderbilt University Law School, he served as articles editor of the *Vanderbilt Journal of Transnational Law.*

Madeline Hills is an associate at DiCello Levitt in Chicago. She attended the University of Missouri where she earned a B.A. in Women's and Gender Studies and a minor in Psychology (summa cum laude, 2019), and the University of Wisconsin Law School, where she earned a J.D. (magna cum laude, 2023) and was elected to the Order of the Coif. During law school, Madeline served as a student law clerk to Hon. Judge Duane Benton of the U.S. Court of Appeals for the Eighth Circuit, and to Hon. Justice Ann Walsh Bradley of the Wisconsin Supreme Court. Before joining DiCello Levitt, she served as an Assistant Attorney General for the State of Missouri, Civil Litigation division. She is a member of the state bars of Wisconsin, Missouri, and Illinois.

Caleb M. Hodge, an associate at Rogers, Patrick, Westbrook & Brickman LLC, represents plaintiffs in class actions and complex litigation. He is a graduate of Wake Forest University School of Law, where he was a member of the law review and the American Association for Justice trial team. During law school, he served as a judicial intern to the Chief Judge of the North Carolina Business Court. Mr. Hodge is licensed to practice in South Carolina and West Virginia. He is also admitted to practice in the United States District Court for the District of South Carolina, the United States District Court for the Southern District of West Virginia, and the Fourth Circuit Court of Appeals.

Beau D. Hollowell, of Frantz Ward LLP, focuses his national practice on antitrust, consumer fraud, employment, health benefits, and securities-fraud class-action litigation. He has won multiple bench and jury trials and has successfully argued federal- and state-court appeals. Beau has represented and advised clients in proceedings before state and federal courts in Alabama, California, Delaware, Florida, Hawaii, Illinois, Michigan, Minnesota, New Jersey, New York, Ohio, Oklahoma, Texas, South Carolina, Puerto Rico, Wisconsin, and the U.S. Virgin Islands. After earning his Bachelor of Arts in English from Westminster College, Beau graduated from Case Western Reserve University School of Law. He began his career with a premier trial firm. He next handled complex commercial litigation matters for two sophisticated investor groups with approximately $600 million in assets throughout the United States and Europe. After that, he led a statewide practice group for one of the largest litigation firms in the country. He has also lectured and written extensively, including co-authoring an article that appeared in a national publication and reappeared in a national online journal with 45,000 monthly readers. Beau continues to write articles discussing recent trends, while also presenting seminars on numerous topics at national and regional conferences. He previously served as the chair of Westminster College's Annual Giving Committee.

Paul Karlsgodt is the leader of BakerHostetler's national class action defense practice team. He knows and understands the intricacies of the class action process and is strategic in his work, not only looking at a case from all angles but also knowing which aspects require the most focus and attention. Clients turn to Paul for representation and advice, trusting his experience and knowing that he will be a strong advocate who will keep their long-term business goals in mind. Paul is the Denver office Litigation group coordinator. He is also the editor of and primary contributor to www.ClassActionBlawg.com, which covers global and national class action-related issues such as decisions, trends, best practices, news, and reform.

Amy E. Keller is partner with the law firm of DiCello Levitt Gutzler LLP, where she focuses her practice on class action litigation and consumer protection matters in particular. She has litigated a wide range of product liability, design defect, employment, and food labelling cases and appeals in courts throughout the country. Amy has served in various leadership positions in national class actions as well as in her roles on various organizations, including the Public Justice Foundation, as chair of the Chicago Bar Association's Class Action Committee, and co-chair of the American Bar Association's Litigation Section Rule 23 Subcommittee.

McDaniel M. Kelly is a senior associate in Porter Wright Morris & Arthur LLP's Cleveland office. Prior to joining Porter Wright, he worked for the federal courts at both the appellate and trial levels. Mac began his federal courts career with a two-year appointment as a Staff Attorney for the U.S. Court of Appeals, Eleventh Circuit, in Atlanta, Georgia. Following his service at the Eleventh Circuit, Mac returned to Cleveland as a law clerk to U.S. Magistrate Judge Thomas M. Parker in the Northern District of Ohio. As a law student, Mac served as an extern to U.S. District Judge Christopher A. Boyko in the Northern District of Ohio.

James A. King is a partner in Porter Wright Morris & Arthur LLP's Litigation Department where his practice focuses on complex business and corporate litigation involving class actions, antitrust cases, commercial disputes, securities claims, and regulatory enforcement actions. Mr. King is active in the American Bar Association's Section of Litigation. He is a Fellow of the American College of Trial Lawyers.

Adam J. Levitt is a founding partner of DiCello Levitt Gutzler LLP, resident in the firm's Chicago office. He has successfully led (and is presently leading) numerous class and complex litigation cases in both state and federal courts and he has recovered billions of dollars for his clients, class members, and other claimants. Mr. Levitt is an elected member of the American Law Institute and of the Economic Club of Chicago, an appointed member of the Advisory Council of the Duke Law Center for Judicial Studies, and President of the Class Action Trial Lawyers—a division of the National Trial Lawyers, of which he is an Executive Committee Member. Mr. Levitt speaks and writes on a variety of litigation-related topics and has been widely published, including in the *Yale Law Journal Online* and, most recently, in the *University of Hawaii Law Review* (Adam Levitt and Nicole Negowetti, *Agricultural "Market Touching": Modernizing Trespass to Chattels in Crop Contamination Cases*, 38 U. Haw. L. Rev. 409 (2016)).

Margaret Lyle is of counsel in the Issues and Appeals practice at Jones Day in Dallas, Texas. She defends class actions and represents businesses in complex litigation and appeals. She has successfully defended class actions brought under the Fair Credit Reporting Act, the Magnuson-Moss Warranty Act, the Driver's Privacy Protection Act, the Credit Repair Organizations Act, RICO, and state consumer statutes, as well as class claims for breach of warranty, unjust enrichment, fraud, and product liability. She also has represented industry leaders in federal and state appeals over statutory construction, injunctions, contract interpretation, health care, data privacy, intellectual property, federal jurisdiction, and constitutional protections. Margaret has served as a co-chair of the ABA Litigation Section's Woman Advocate Committee, as a programming chair for the ABA Litigation Section's Class Actions and Derivative Suits Committee, as editor-in-chief of *The Woman Advocate*, and as a practitioner contributor to *Black's Law Dictionary*. She is a frequent author and speaker on class actions and a co-author of *Blockchain for Business Lawyers* (ABA). An American Bar Foundation Fellow, Dallas Bar Foundation Fellow, and a member of Attorneys Serving the Community, Margaret was a founding member of the Texas Law Parents Leadership Association and a founding director of Marshall Lawyers Care.

Amy Miller is of counsel at Cohen Milstein Sellers & Toll PLLC, where she is a member of the firm's Securities Litigation Investor Protection group. Ms. Miller's practice focuses on representing institutional and individual shareholders in derivative lawsuits and securities class actions. Prior to joining Cohen Milstein Sellers & Toll PLLC, Ms. Miller worked at three prominent boutique plaintiffs' law firms over the last decade. Ms. Miller also worked at Cadwalader, Wickersham & Taft LLP for seven years after participating in an externship with the Honorable George B. Daniels of the U.S. District Court for the Southern District of New York during law school.

Mark A. Miller is a partner at Hollingsworth LLP, practicing in the firm's Complex Litigation, Pharmaceutical Products, and Toxic Torts & Products Liability groups. He has extensive experience defending mass pharmaceutical product liability actions, environmental mass toxic torts, and other environmental claims such as property damage and CERCLA actions.

Erin C. Nebbia is an associate at Hollingsworth LLP, practicing in the firm's Complex Litigation and Insurance Coverage groups. Erin received her law degree from the Georgetown University Law Center, and she received her undergraduate degree, cum laude, from the University of Maryland, College Park.

Alexis J. Opper is an associate at BakerHostetler, where she practices class action defense as a member of the Digital Assets and Data Management team. Alexis graduated from the University of Colorado Boulder, Order of the Coif, where she was the Resource Editor for the *Colorado Law Review*.

Lucus A. Ritchie is a partner in Pierce Atwood LLP's Litigation Practice Group. Lucus' practice covers a wide variety of complex commercial disputes, with particular emphasis on class action defense and energy litigation. Lucus regularly appears in federal and state trial courts throughout the U.S., and represents clients in arbitrations, mediations, and contested administrative proceedings. Lucus focuses on developing a detailed understanding of his client's business and its goals and uses advocacy and creativity to obtain favorable results in a practical and efficient manner.

Christopher E. Roberts is a partner at Butsch Roberts & Associates LLC in St. Louis, Missouri. Much of Mr. Roberts's practice is focused on representing consumers in a variety of class action cases. His cases have resulted in tens of millions of dollars being paid to consumers and millions of dollars of debt being eliminated for consumers. His passion for class action litigation stems from his desire to achieve justice for large groups of people and the intellectual challenges presented by class action litigation. Mr. Roberts serves as a co-chair of the Telephone Consumer Practices Act subcommittee for the ABA's Consumer Law Committee. Mr. Roberts is a frequent contributor to the ABA Litigation Section's Class Actions and Derivative Suits Committee and the ABA Litigation Section's Consumer Law Committee. He also presents lectures on class action issues. Mr. Roberts is licensed to practice in Missouri, Illinois, and Kansas. He is also licensed to practice in the Eighth, Ninth, and Tenth Circuit Courts of Appeals, and various federal district courts in Missouri, Illinois, Kansas, Texas, Colorado, and Michigan.

Jennifer Rudnick, *Coordinating Editor*, is a research assistant at Lieff Cabraser Heimann & Bernstein LLP. She holds degrees from Syracuse University, where she earned a B.A. in English and Political Science (2003), and San Jose State University, where she earned a Master of Library and Information Science (2023). Ms. Rudnick was a senior paralegal at Lieff Cabraser for more than 15 years before transitioning to the research team after earning her master's degree.

During graduate school, she served as a peer mentor and she continues to volunteer her time at local school libraries. She is a paralegal member of the American Bar Association.

Elijah Savage is an associate attorney in DiCello Levitt's Chicago office, whose practice focuses on public client, ERISA, and class action litigation. A steadfast advocate for the public interest, Elijah strives to uphold the highest standards of justice and transparency, working to achieve impactful and fair outcomes for those he represents. Elijah earned his law degree from Lewis & Clark Law School, where he was an Associate Editor of *Environmental Law* and served as a judicial extern to a federal judge in the U.S. District Court for the District of Oregon. He also worked as a law clerk for Professor Robert Klonoff, where he gained experience in aggregate and complex litigation.

Angelo A. Stio III is a partner at Troutman Pepper. His practice focuses on financial services issues, higher education law, and data privacy and security. He also has extensive experience handling class actions and complex commercial disputes in each of these areas.

Betsy Sugar is an associate at Lieff Cabraser Heimann & Bernstein. She holds degrees from Davidson College, where she earned a B.A. in English and minor in Economics (magna cum laude, 2021), and Vanderbilt University Law School, where she earned her J.D. (2024) and was awarded membership into the Order of the Coif. In law school, she was Notes Development Editor for the *Vanderbilt Law Review* and published her Note, "Mixed-Up Origins: The Case for a Gestational Presumption in Embryo Mix-Ups." She is co-author of the Tennessee Chapter of *The Law of Class Action: 2024 Fifty-State Survey*, published by the American Bar Association. She is a member of the Tennessee Bar and the Tennessee Trial Lawyers Association.

Trevor Tan is an associate at Girard Sharp LLP in San Francisco, where he focuses on consumer protection and other complex litigation. He previously clerked for the Honorable Fernando M. Olguin of the United States District Court for the Central District of California. Mr. Tan received his law degree from the University of Chicago Law School and graduated magna cum laude from the University of California, Irvine with a B.A. in political science.

John E. Tangren is a partner at DiCello Levitt Gutzler LLP in Chicago. His practice focuses on the prosecution of consumer class action cases, as well as other complex commercial litigation. Mr. Tangren lectures frequently on class action and other litigation issues.

Julia Veeser is an associate attorney at DiCello Levitt LLP, where she focuses most of her time working in the Class Action and Public Client practice groups. She attended Chicago-Kent College of Law and was a notes and comments editor for the *Chicago-Kent Law Review*. While in law school, Julia served as an executive board member for Chicago-Kent's Moot Court Honor Society, was a CALI Award recipient in privacy law, and a Dean's List honoree. Julia also graduated from the University of Michigan with a double major in political science and Spanish. On top of balancing a rigorous academic schedule, Julia participated in varsity athletics, where she won two national cheerleading championships and was a four-time U of M Athletic Academic Achievement Award recipient.

Fabrice N. Vincent, admitted to practice in California, 1992; U.S. District Court, Northern District of California, Central District of California, Eastern District of California, Ninth Circuit Court of Appeals, 1992. *Education*: Cornell Law School (J.D., *cum laude*, 1992); University of California at Berkeley (B.A., 1989). *Awards & Honors:* Selected for inclusion by peers in *The Best Lawyers in America* in fields of "Mass Tort Litigation/Class Actions—Plaintiffs," "Product Liability Litigation—Plaintiffs," and "Personal Injury Litigation—Plaintiffs," 2012–2017; "Super Lawyer for Northern California," *Super Lawyers*, 2006–2017; "Outstanding Subcommittee Chair for the Class Actions & Derivative Suits," *ABA Section of Litigation*, 2013. Former Co-Chair, ABA Litigation Section Class Actions and Derivative Suits Committee.

FEDERAL RULE OF CIVIL PROCEDURE RULE 23[1]

(a) **Prerequisites.** One or more members of a class may sue or be sued as representative parties on behalf of all members only if:[1]
  (1) the class is so numerous that joinder of all members is impracticable;
  (2) there are questions of law or fact common to the class;
  (3) the claims or defenses of the representative parties are typical of the claims or defenses of the class; and
  (4) the representative parties will fairly and adequately protect the interests of the class.

(b) **Types of Class Actions.** A class action may be maintained if Rule 23(a) is satisfied and if:
  (1) prosecuting separate actions by or against individual class members would create a risk of:
    (A) inconsistent or varying adjudications with respect to individual class members that would establish incompatible standards of conduct for the party opposing the class; or
    (B) adjudications with respect to individual class members that, as a practical matter, would be dispositive of the interests of the other members not parties to the individual adjudications or would substantially impair or impede their ability to protect their interests;
  (2) the party opposing the class has acted or refused to act on grounds that apply generally to the class, so that final injunctive relief or corresponding declaratory relief is appropriate respecting the class as a whole; or
  (3) the court finds that the questions of law or fact common to class members predominate over any questions affecting only individual members, and that a class action is superior to other available methods for fairly and efficiently adjudicating the controversy. The matters pertinent to these findings include:
    (A) the class members' interests in individually controlling the prosecution or defense of separate actions;
    (B) the extent and nature of any litigation concerning the controversy already begun by or against class members;
    (C) the desirability or undesirability of concentrating the litigation of the claims in the particular forum; and

---

[1] Proposed Amendments to F.R.C.P. 23 are available at http://www.uscourts.gov/sites/default/files/2016-08-preliminary_draft_of_rules_forms_published_for_public_comment_0.pdf. The public comment period on the Proposed Amendments are now closed. The Standing Committee meets in June 2017 on the proposed revisions. In September 2017, the Judicial Conference meets and the Proposed Amendments may become effective, in whole or in part, in December 2018.

(D) the likely difficulties in managing a class action.

(c) Certification Order; Notice to Class Members; Judgment; Issues Classes; Subclasses.

(1) Certification Order.

(A) *Time to Issue.* At an early practicable time after a person sues or is sued as a class representative, the court must determine by order whether to certify the action as a class action.

(B) *Defining the Class; Appointing Class Counsel.* An order that certifies a class action must define the class and the class claims, issues, or defenses, and must appoint class counsel under Rule 23(g).

(C) *Altering or Amending the Order.* An order that grants or denies class certification may be altered or amended before final judgment.

(2) Notice.

(A) *For (b)(1) or (b)(2) Classes.* For any class certified under Rule 23(b)(1) or (b)(2), the court may direct appropriate notice to the class.

(B) *For (b)(3) Classes.* For any class certified under Rule 23(b)(3), the court must direct to class members the best notice that is practicable under the circumstances, including individual notice to all members who can be identified through reasonable effort. The notice must clearly and concisely state in plain, easily understood language:

(i) the nature of the action;

(ii) the definition of the class certified;

(iii) the class claims, issues, or defenses;

(iv) that a class member may enter an appearance through an attorney if the member so desires;

(v) that the court will exclude from the class any member who requests exclusion;

(vi) the time and manner for requesting exclusion; and

(vii) the binding effect of a class judgment on members under Rule 23(c)(3).

(3) ***Judgment.*** Whether or not favorable to the class, the judgment in a class action must:

(A) for any class certified under Rule 23(b)(1) or (b)(2), include and describe those whom the court finds to be class members; and

(B) for any class certified under Rule 23(b)(3), include and specify or describe those to whom the Rule 23(c)(2) notice was directed, who have not requested exclusion, and whom the court finds to be class members.

(4) ***Particular Issues.*** When appropriate, an action may be brought or maintained as a class action with respect to particular issues.

(5) ***Subclasses.*** When appropriate, a class may be divided into subclasses that are each treated as a class under this rule.

(d) Conducting the Action.

(1) ***In General.*** In conducting an action under this rule, the court may issue orders that:

(A) determine the course of proceedings or prescribe measures to prevent undue repetition or complication in presenting evidence or argument;

(B) require—to protect class members and fairly conduct the action—giving appropriate notice to some or all class members of:

(i) any step in the action;

(ii) the proposed extent of the judgment; or

(iii) the members' opportunity to signify whether they consider the representation fair and adequate, to intervene and present claims or defenses, or to otherwise come into the action;

(C) impose conditions on the representative parties or on intervenors;

(D) require that the pleadings be amended to eliminate allegations about representation of absent persons and that the action proceed accordingly; or

(E) deal with similar procedural matters.

(2) ***Combining and Amending Orders.*** An order under Rule 23(d)(1) may be altered or amended from time to time and may be combined with an order under Rule 16.

(e) **Settlement, Voluntary Dismissal, or Compromise.** The claims, issues, or defenses of a certified class may be settled, voluntarily dismissed, or compromised only with the court's approval. The following procedures apply to a proposed settlement, voluntary dismissal, or compromise:

(1) The court must direct notice in a reasonable manner to all class members who would be bound by the proposal.

(2) If the proposal would bind class members, the court may approve it only after a hearing and on finding that it is fair, reasonable, and adequate.

(3) The parties seeking approval must file a statement identifying any agreement made in connection with the proposal.

(4) If the class action was previously certified under Rule 23(b)(3), the court may refuse to approve a settlement unless it affords a new opportunity to request exclusion to individual class members who had an earlier opportunity to request exclusion but did not do so.

(5) Any class member may object to the proposal if it requires court approval under this subdivision (e); the objection may be withdrawn only with the court's approval.

(f) **Appeals.** A court of appeals may permit an appeal from an order granting or denying class-action certification under this rule if a petition for permission to appeal is filed with the circuit clerk within 14 days after the order is entered. An appeal does not stay proceedings in the district court unless the district judge or the court of appeals so orders.

(g) Class Counsel.

(1) ***Appointing Class Counsel.*** Unless a statute provides otherwise, a court that certifies a class must appoint class counsel. In appointing class counsel, the court:

(A) must consider:

(i) the work counsel has done in identifying or investigating potential claims in the action;

(ii) counsel's experience in handling class actions, other complex litigation, and the types of claims asserted in the action;

(iii) counsel's knowledge of the applicable law; and

(iv) the resources that counsel will commit to representing the class;

(B) may consider any other matter pertinent to counsel's ability to fairly and adequately represent the interests of the class;

(C) may order potential class counsel to provide information on any subject pertinent to the appointment and to propose terms for attorney's fees and nontaxable costs;

(D) may include in the appointing order provisions about the award of attorney's fees or nontaxable costs under Rule 23(h); and

(E) may make further orders in connection with the appointment.

(2) ***Standard for Appointing Class Counsel.*** When one applicant seeks appointment as class counsel, the court may appoint that applicant only if the applicant is adequate under Rule 23(g)(1) and (4). If more than one adequate applicant seeks appointment, the court must appoint the applicant best able to represent the interests of the class.

(3) ***Interim Counsel.*** The court may designate interim counsel to act on behalf of a putative class before determining whether to certify the action as a class action.

(4) ***Duty of Class Counsel.*** Class counsel must fairly and adequately represent the interests of the class.

(h) **Attorney's Fees and Nontaxable Costs.** In a certified class action, the court may award reasonable attorney's fees and nontaxable costs that are authorized by law or by the parties' agreement. The following procedures apply:

(1) A claim for an award must be made by motion under Rule 54(d)(2), subject to the provisions of this subdivision (h), at a time the court sets. Notice of the motion must be served on all parties and, for motions by class counsel, directed to class members in a reasonable manner.

(2) A class member, or a party from whom payment is sought, may object to the motion.

(3) The court may hold a hearing and must find the facts and state its legal conclusions under Rule 52(a).

(4) The court may refer issues related to the amount of the award to a special master or a magistrate judge, as provided in Rule 54(d)(2)(D).

CREDIT(S)

(Amended February 28, 1966, effective July 1, 1966; March 2, 1987, effective August 1, 1987; April 24, 1998, effective December 1, 1998; March 27, 2003, effective December 1, 2003; April 30, 2007, effective December 1, 2007; March 26, 2009, effective December 1, 2009.)

FEDERAL RULE OF CIVIL PROCEDURE 23 ADVISORY COMMITTEE NOTES

ADVISORY COMMITTEE NOTES

1937 Adoption

Note to Subdivision (a). This is a substantial restatement of [former] Equity Rule 38 (Representatives of Class) as that rule has been construed. It applies to all actions, whether formerly denominated legal or equitable. For a general analysis of class actions, effect of judgment, and requisites of jurisdiction see Moore, *Federal Rules of Civil Procedure: Some Problems Raised by the Preliminary Draft*, 25 Georgetown L.J. 551, 570 et seq. (1937); Moore and Cohn, *Federal Class Actions*, 32 Ill.L.Rev. 307 (1937); Moore and Cohn, *Federal Class Actions—Jurisdiction and Effect of Judgment*, 32 Ill.L.Rev. 555–67 (1938); Lesar, *Class Suits and the Federal Rules*, 22 Minn.L.Rev. 34 (1937); cf. Arnold and James, *Cases on Trials, Judgments and Appeals* (1936) 175; and see Blume, *Jurisdictional Amount in Representative Suits*, 15 Minn.L.Rev. 501 (1931).

The general test of [former] Equity Rule 38 (Representatives of Class) that the question should be "one of common or general interest to many persons constituting a class so numerous as to make it impracticable to bring them all before the court," is a common test. For states which require the two elements of a common or general interest and numerous persons, as provided for in [former] Equity Rule 38, see Del.Ch. Rule 113; Fla.Comp.Gen.Laws Ann. (Supp., 1936) § 4918(7); Georgia Code (1933) § 37-1002, and see *English Rules Under the Judicature Act* (The Annual Practice, 1937) O. 16, r. 9. For statutory provisions providing for class actions when the question is one of common or general interest or when the parties are numerous, see Ala.Code Ann. (Michie, 1928) § 5701; 2 Ind.Stat.Ann. (Burns, 1933) § 2-220; N.Y.C.P.A. (1937) 195; Wis.Stat. (1935) § 260.12. These statutes have, however, been uniformly construed as though phrased in the conjunctive. See *Garfein v. Stiglitz, 260 Ky. 430, 86 S.W.2d 155 (1935).* The rule adopts the test of [former] Equity Rule 38, but defines what constitutes a "common or general interest." Compare with code provisions which make the action dependent upon the propriety of joinder of the parties. See Blume, *The "Common Questions" Principle in the Code Provision for Representative Suits*, 30 Mich.L.Rev. 878 (1932). For discussion of what constitutes "numerous persons" see Wheaton, *Representative Suits Involving Numerous Litigants*, 19 Corn.L.Q. 399 (1934); Note, 36 Harv.L.Rev. 89 (1922).

Clause (1), Joint, Common, or Secondary Right. This clause is illustrated in actions brought by or against representatives of an unincorporated association. See *Oster v. Brotherhood of Locomotive Firemen and Enginemen,* 271 Pa. 419, 114 Atl. 377 (1921)*; Pickett v. Walsh,* 192 Mass. 572, 78 N.E. 753, 6 L.R.A., N.S., 1067 (1906); *Colt v. Hicks,* 97 Ind.App. 177, 179 N.E. 335 (1932). Compare Rule 17(b) as to when an unincorporated association has capacity to sue or be sued in its common name; United Mine Workers of America v. Coronado Coal Co., 42 S.Ct. 570, 259 U.S. 344, 66 L.Ed. 975, 27 A.L.R. 762 (1922) (an unincorporated association was sued as an entity for the purpose of enforcing against it a federal substantive right); *Moore, Federal Rules of Civil Procedure: Some Problems Raised by the Preliminary Draft*, 25 Georgetown L.J. 551, 566 (for discussion of jurisdictional requisites when an unincorporated association sues or is sued in its common name and jurisdiction is founded upon diversity of citizenship). For an action brought by representatives of one group against representatives of another group for distribution of a fund held by an unincorporated association, see *Smith v. Swormstedt,* 16 How. 288, 14 L.Ed. 942 (U.S. 1853). Compare *Christopher, et al. v. Brusselback,* 1938, 58 S.Ct. 350, 302 U.S. 500, 82 L.Ed. 388.

For an action to enforce rights held in common by policyholders against the corporate issuer of the policies, see *Supreme Tribe of Ben Hur v. Cauble,* 255 U.S. 356, 41 S.Ct. 338, 65 L.Ed. 673 (1921). See also *Terry v. Little,* 101 U.S. 216, 25 L.Ed. 864 (1880); *John A. Roebling's Sons Co. v. Kinnicutt,* 248 Fed. 596 (D.C.N.Y., 1917) dealing with the right held in common by creditors to enforce the statutory liability of stockholders.

Typical of a secondary action is a suit by stockholders to enforce a corporate right. For discussion of the general nature of these actions see *Ashwander v. Tennessee Valley Authority,* 297 U.S. 288, 56 S.Ct. 466, 80 L.Ed. 688 (1936); *Glenn, The Stockholder's Suit—Corporate and Individual Grievances,* 33 Yale L.J. 580 (1924); McLaughlin, *Capacity of Plaintiff-Stockholder to Terminate a Stockholder's Suit,* 46 Yale L.J. 421 (1937). See also Subdivision (b) of this rule which deals with Shareholder's Action; Note, 15 Minn.L.Rev. 453 (1931).

Clause (2). A creditor's action for liquidation or reorganization of a corporation is illustrative of this clause. An action by a stockholder against certain named defendants as representatives of numerous claimants presents a situation converse to the creditor's action.

Clause (3). See *Everglades Drainage League v. Napoleon Broward Drainage Dist.,* 253 Fed. 246 (D.C.Fla., 1918); *Gramling v. Maxwell,* 52 F.2d 256 (D.C.N.C., 1931), approved in 30 Mich.L.Rev. 624 (1932); *Skinner v. Mitchell,* 108 Kan. 861, 197 Pac. 569 (1921); *Duke of Bedford v. Ellis* (1901) A.C. 1, for class actions when there were numerous persons and there was only a question of law or fact common to them; and see Blume, *The "Common Questions" Principle in the Code Provision for Representative Suits*, 30 Mich.L.Rev. 878 (1932).

Note to Subdivision (b). This is [former] Equity Rule 27 (Stockholder's Bill) with verbal changes. See also *Hawes v. Oakland,* 104 U.S. 450, 26 L.Ed. 827 (1882) and former Equity Rule 94, promulgated January 23, 1882, 104 U.S. IX.

Note to Subdivision (c). See McLaughlin, Capacity of Plaintiff-Stockholder to Terminate a Stockholder's Suit, 46 Yale L.J. 421 (1937).

Supplementary Note

Note. Subdivision (b), relating to secondary actions by shareholders, provides among other things, that in such an action the complainant "shall aver (1) that the plaintiff was a shareholder at the time of the transaction of which he complains or that his share thereafter devolved on him by operation of law * * *."

As a result of the decision in *Erie R. Co. v. Tompkins,* 1938, 304 U.S. 64, 58 S.Ct. 817 (decided April 25, 1938, after this rule was promulgated by the Supreme Court, though before it took effect) a question has arisen as to whether the provision above quoted deals with a matter of substantive right or is a matter of procedure. If it is a matter of substantive law or right, then under *Erie R. Co. v. Tompkins* clause (1) may not be validly applied in cases pending in states whose local law permits a shareholder to maintain such actions, although not a shareholder at the time of the transactions complained of. The Advisory Committee, believing the question should be settled in the courts, proposes no change in Rule 23 but thinks rather that the situation should be explained in an appropriate note.

The rule has a long history. In *Hawes v. Oakland,* 1882, 104 U.S. 450, the Court held that a shareholder could not maintain such an action unless he owned shares at the time of the transactions complained of, or unless they devolved on him by operation of law. At that time the decision in *Swift v. Tyson,* 1842, 16 Peters 1, was the law, and the federal courts considered themselves free to establish their own principles of equity jurisprudence, so the Court was not in 1882 and has not been, until *Erie R. Co. v. Tompkins* in 1938, concerned with the question whether *Hawes v. Oakland* dealt with substantive right or procedure.

Following the decision in *Hawes v. Oakland*, and at the same term, the Court, to implement its decision, adopted [former] Equity Rule 94, which contained the same provision above quoted from Rule 23 F.R.C.P. The provision in [former] Equity Rule 94 was later embodied in [former]

Equity Rule 27, of which the present Rule 23 is substantially a copy.

In *City of Quincy v. Steel,* 1887, 120 U.S. 241, 245, 7 S.Ct. 520, the Court referring to *Hawes v. Oakland* said: "In order to give effect to the principles there laid down, this Court at that term adopted Rule 94 of the rules of practice for courts of equity of the United States."

Some other cases dealing with [former] Equity Rules 94 or 27 prior to the decision in *Erie R. Co. v. Tompkins* are *Dimpfel v. Ohio & Miss. R.R.,* 1884, 3 S.Ct. 573, 110 U.S. 209, 28 L.Ed. 121; *Illinois Central R. Co. v. Adams,* 1901, 21 S.Ct. 251, 180 U.S. 28, 34, 45L.Ed. 410; *Venner v. Great Northern Ry.,* 1908, 28 S.Ct. 328, 209 U.S. 24, 30, 52 L.Ed. 666; *Jacobson v. General Motors Corp.*, S.D.N.Y.1938, 22 F.Supp. 255, 257. These cases generally treat *Hawes v. Oakland* as establishing a "principle" of equity, or as dealing not with jurisdiction but with the "right" to maintain an action, or have said that the defense under the equity rule is analogous to the defense that the plaintiff has no "title" and results in a dismissal "for want of equity."

Those state decisions which held that a shareholder acquiring stock after the event may maintain a derivative action are founded on the view that it is a right belonging to the shareholder at the time of the transaction and which passes as a right to the subsequent purchaser. See *Pollitz v. Gould,* 1911, 202 N.Y. 11, 94 N.E. 1088.

The first case arising after the decision in *Erie R. Co. v. Tompkins*, in which this problem was involved, was *Summers v. Hearst,* S.D.N.Y.1938, 23 F.Supp. 986. It concerned [former] Equity Rule 27, as Federal Rule 23 was not then in effect. In a well-considered opinion Judge Leibell reviewed the decisions and said: "The federal cases that discuss this section of [former] Rule 27 support the view that it states a principle of substantive law." He quoted *Pollitz v. Gould,* 1911, 202 N.Y. 11, 94 N.E. 1088, as saying that the United States Supreme Court "seems to have been more concerned with establishing this rule as one of practice than of substantive law" but that "whether it be regarded as establishing a principle of law or a rule of practice, this authority has been subsequently followed in the United States courts."

He then concluded that, although the federal decisions treat the equity rule as "stating a principle of substantive law," if "[former] Equity Rule 27 is to be modified or revoked in view of *Erie R. Co. v. Tompkins*, it is not the province of this Court to suggest it, much less impliedly to follow that course by disregarding the mandatory provisions of the Rule."

In *Piccard v. Sperry Corporation*, S.D.N.Y.1941, 36 F.Supp. 1006, 1009–10, affirmed without opinion, C.C.A.2d 1941, 120 F.2d 328, a shareholder, not such at the time of the transactions complained of, sought to intervene. The court held an intervenor was as much subject to Rule 23 as an original plaintiff; and that the requirement of Rule 23(b) was "a matter of practice," not substance, and applied in New York where the state law was otherwise, despite *Erie R. Co. v. Tompkins.* In *New York v. Guaranty Trust Co. of New York,* C.C.A.2, 1944, 143 F.2d 503, rev'd on other grounds, 1945, 65 S.Ct. 1464, the court said: "Restrictions on the bringing of stockholders' actions, such as those imposed by F.R.C.P. 23(b) or other state statutes are procedural," citing the Piccard *and other cases.*

Some other federal decisions since 1938 touch the question.

In *Gallup v. Caldwell,* C.C.A.3, 1941, 120 F.2d 90, 95 arising in New Jersey, the point was raised but not decided, the court saying that it was not satisfied that the then New Jersey rule differed from Rule 23(b), and that "under the circumstances the proper course was to follow Rule 23(b)."

In *Mullins v. DeSoto Securities Co.*, W.D.La.1942, 45 F.Supp. 871, 878, the point was not decided, because the court found the Louisiana rule to be the same as that stated in Rule 23(b).

In *Toebelman v. Missouri-Kansas Pipe Line Co.*, D.Del.1941, 41 F.Supp. 334, 340, the court dealt only with another part of Rule 23(b), relating to prior demands on the stockholders and did not discuss *Erie R. Co. v. Tompkins*, or its effect on the rule.

In *Perrott v. United States Banking Corp., D.Del.1944, 53 F.Supp. 953,* it appeared that the Delaware law does not require the plaintiff to have owned shares at the time of the transaction complained of. The court sustained Rule 23(b), after discussion of the authorities, saying:

"It seems to me the rule does not go beyond procedure. * * * Simply because a particu-

> lar plaintiff cannot qualify as a proper party to maintain such an action does not destroy or even whittle at the cause of action. The cause of action exists until a qualified plaintiff can get it started in a federal court."

In *Bankers Nat. Corp. v. Barr*, S.D.N.Y.1945, 9 Fed.Rules Serv. 23b.11, Case 1, the court held Rule 23(b) to be one of procedure, but that whether the plaintiff was a stockholder was a substantive question to be settled by state law.

The New York rule, as stated in *Pollitz v. Gould*, supra, has been altered by an act of the New York Legislature, Chapter 667, Laws of 1944, effective April 9, 1944, General Corporation Law, § 61, which provides that "in any action brought by a shareholder in the right of a * * * corporation, it must appear that the plaintiff was a stockholder at the time of the transaction of which he complains, or that his stock thereafter devolved upon him by operation of law." At the same time a further and separate provision was enacted, requiring under certain circumstances the giving of security for reasonable expenses and attorney's fees, to which security the corporation in whose right the action is brought and the defendants therein may have recourse. (Chapter 668, Laws of 1944, effective April 9, 1944, General Corporation Law, § 61-b.) These provisions are aimed at so-called strike stockholders' suits and their attendant abuses. *Shielcrawt v. Moffett,* Ct.App.1945, 294 N.Y. 180, 61 N.E.2d 435, rev'g 51 N.Y.S.2d 188, aff'g 49 N.Y.S.2d 64; *Noel Associates, Inc. v. Merrill*, Sup.Ct.1944, 184 Misc. 646, 63 N.Y.S.2d 143.

Insofar as § 61 is concerned, it has been held that the section is procedural in nature. *Klum v. Clinton Trust Co.,* Sup.Ct.1944, 183 Misc. 340, 48 N.Y.S.2d 267; *Noel Associates, Inc. v. Merrill*, supra. In the latter case the court pointed out that "The 1944 amendment to Section 61 rejected the rule laid down in the Pollitz case and substituted, in place thereof, in its precise language, the rule which has long prevailed in the Federal Courts and which is now Rule 23(b) * * *." There is, nevertheless, a difference of opinion regarding the application of the statute to pending actions. See *Klum v. Clinton Trust Co.*, supra (applicable); *Noel Associates, Inc. v. Merrill,* supra (inapplicable).

With respect to § 61-b, which may be regarded as a separate problem, *Noel Associates, Inc. v. Merrill*, supra, it has been held that even though the statute is procedural in nature—a matter not definitely decided—the Legislature evinced no intent that the provisions should apply to actions pending when it became effective. *Shielcrawt v. Moffett*, supra. As to actions instituted after the effective date of the legislation, the constitutionality of § 61-b is in dispute. See *Wolf v. Atkinson,* Sup.Ct.1944, 182 Misc. 675, 49 N.Y.S.2d 703 (constitutional); *Citron v. Mangel Stores Corp.,* Sup.Ct.1944, 50 N.Y.S.2d 416 (unconstitutional); Zlinkoff, *The American Investor and the Constitutionality of § 61-b of the New York General Corporation Law,* 1945, 54 Yale L.J. 352.

New Jersey also enacted a statute, similar to Chapters 667 and 668 of the New York law. See P.L.1945, Ch. 131, R.S.Cum.Supp. 14:3–15. The New Jersey provision similar to Chapter 668, *§* 61-b, differs, however, in that it specifically applies retroactively. It has been held that this provision is procedural and hence will not govern a pending action brought against a New Jersey corporation in the New York courts. *Shielcrawt v. Moffett,* Sup.Ct.N.Y.1945, 184 Misc. 1074, 56 N.Y.S.2d 134.

See, also generally, 2 *Moore's Federal Practice*, 1938, 2250–53, and Cum.Supplement § 23.05.

The decisions here discussed show that the question is a debatable one, and that there is respectable authority for either view, with a recent trend toward the view that Rule 23(b)(1) is procedural. There is reason to say that the question is one which should not be decided by the Supreme Court ex parte, but left to await a judicial decision in a litigated case, and that in the light of the material in this note, the only inference to be drawn from a failure to amend Rule 23(b) would be that the question is postponed to await a litigated case.

The Advisory Committee is unanimously of the opinion that this course should be followed.

If, however, the final conclusion is that the rule deals with a matter of substantive right, then the rule should be amended by adding a provision that Rule 23(b)(1) does not apply in jurisdictions where state law permits a shareholder to maintain a secondary action, although he was not a shareholder at the time of the transactions of which he complains.

1966 Amendment

Difficulties with the original rule. The categories of class actions in the original rule were defined in terms of the abstract nature of the rights involved: the so-called true category was defined as involving "joint, common, or secondary rights"; the "hybrid" category, as involving "several" rights related to "specific property"; the "spurious" category, as involving "several" rights affected by a common question and related to common relief. It was thought that the definitions accurately described the situations amenable to the class-suit device, and also would indicate the proper extent of the judgment in each category, which would in turn help to determine the res judicata effect of the judgment if questioned in a later action. Thus the judgments in "true" and "hybrid" class actions would extend to the class (although in somewhat different ways); the judgment in a "spurious" class action would extend only to the parties including intervenors. See Moore, *Federal Rules of Civil Procedure: Some Problems Raised by the Preliminary Draft*, 25 Geo.L.J. 551, 570–76 (1937).

In practice the terms "joint," "common," etc., which were used as the basis of the Rule 23 classification proved obscure and uncertain. See Chafee, *Some Problems of Equity* 245–46, 256–57 (1950); Kalven & Rosenfield, *The Contemporary Function of the Class Suit*, 8 U. of Chi.L.Rev. 684, 707 & n. 73 (1941); Keeffe, Levy & Donovan, *Lee Defeats Ben Hur*, 33 Corn.L.Q. 327, 329–36 (1948); *Developments in the Law: Multiparty Litigation in the Federal Courts*, 71 Harv. L.Rev. 874, 931 (1958); Advisory Committee's Note to Rule 19, as amended. The courts had considerable difficulty with these terms. See, e.g., *Gullo v. Veterans' Coop. H. Assn.*, 13 F.R.D. 11 (D.D.C.1952); *Shipley v. Pittsburgh & L.E.R. Co.*, 70 F.Supp. 870 (W.D.Pa.1947); *Deckert v. Independence Shares Corp.*, 27 F.Supp. 763 (E.D.Pa.1939), rev'd 108 F.2d 51 (3d Cir. 1939), rev'd, 311 U.S. 282 (1940), on remand, 39 F.Supp. 592 (E.D.Pa.1941), rev'd sub nom. *Pennsylvania Co. for Ins. on Lives v. Deckert,* 123 F.2d 979 (3d Cir.1941) (see Chafee, supra, at 264–65).

Nor did the rule provide an adequate guide to the proper extent of the judgments in class actions. First, we find instances of the courts classifying actions as "true" or intimating that the judgments would be decisive for the class where these results seemed appropriate but were reached by dint of depriving the word "several" of coherent meaning. See, e.g., *System Federation No. 91 v. Reed,* 180 F.2d 991 (6th Cir.1950); *Wilson v. City of Paducah,* 100 F.Supp. 116 (W.D.Ky.1951); *Citizens Banking Co. v. Monticello State Bank,* 143 F.2d 261 (8th Cir.1944); *Redmond v. Commerce Trust Co.,* 144 F.2d 140 (8th Cir.1944), cert. denied, 323 U.S. 776 (1944); *United States v. American Optical Co.,* 97 F.Supp. 66 (N.D.Ill.1951); *National Hairdressers' & C. Assn. v. Philad Co.,* 34 F.Supp. 264 (D.Del.1940); 41 F.Supp. 701 (D.Del.1940), aff'd mem., 129 F.2d 1020 (3d Cir.1942). Second, we find cases classified by the courts as "spurious" in which, on a realistic view, it would seem fitting for the judgments to extend to the class. See, e.g., *Knapp v. Bankers Sec. Corp.,* 17 F.R.D. 245 (E.D.Pa.1954), aff'd 230 F.2d 717 (3d Cir.1956); *Giesecke v. Denver Tramway Corp.,* 81 F.Supp. 957 (D.Del.1949); *York v. Guaranty Trust Co.,* 143 F.2d 503 (2d Cir.1944), rev'd on grounds not here relevant, 326 U.S. 99 (1945) (see *Chafee, supra*, at 208); cf. *Webster Eisenlohr, Inc. v. Kalodner*, 145 F.2d 316, 320 (3d Cir.1944), cert. denied, 325 U.S. 867 (1945). But cf. the early decisions, *Duke of Bedford v. Ellis*, [1901] A.C. 1; *Sheffield Waterworks v. Yeomans*, L.R. 2 Ch.App. 8 (1866); *Brown v. Vermuden*, 1 Ch.Cas. 272, 22 Eng.Rep. 796 (1676).

The "spurious" action envisaged by original Rule 23 was in any event an anomaly because, although denominated a "class" action and pleaded as such, it was supposed not to adjudicate the rights or liabilities of any person not a party. It was believed to be an advantage of the "spurious" category that it would invite decisions that a member of the "class" could, like a member of the class in a "true" or "hybrid" action, intervene on an ancillary basis without being required to show an independent basis of Federal jurisdiction, and have the benefit of the date of the commencement of the action for purposes of the statute of limitations. See 3 Moore's *Federal Practice*, pars. 23.10[1], 23.12 (2d ed.1963). These results were attained in some instances but not in others. On the statute of limitations, see *Union Carbide & Carbon Corp. v. Nisley,* 300 F.2d 561 (10th Cir.1961), pet. cert. dism., 371 U.S. 801 (1963); but cf. *P. W. Husserl, Inc. v. Newman,* 25 F.R.D. 264 (S.D.N.Y.1960); *Athas v. Day, 161 F.Supp.* 916 (D.Colo.1958). On ancillary intervention, see *Amen v. Black,* 234 F.2d 12 (10th Cir.1956), cert. granted, 352 U.S. 888 (1956), dism. on stip., 355 U.S. 600 (1958); but cf. *Wagner v. Kemper,* 13 F.R.D. 128 (W.D.Mo.1952). The results, however, can hardly depend upon the mere appearance of a "spurious" category in the rule; they should turn on more basic considerations. See discussion of subdivision (c)(1) below.

Finally, the original rule did not squarely address itself to the question of the measures that might be taken during the course of the action to assure procedural fairness, particularly giving notice to members of the class, which may in turn be related in some instances to the extension of the judgment to the class. See Chafee, supra, at 230–31; Keeffe, Levy & Donovan, supra; *Developments in the law*, supra, 71 Harv.L.Rev. at 937–38; Note, *Binding Effect of Class Actions*, 67 Harv.L.Rev. 1059, 1062–65 (1954); Note, *Federal Class Actions: A Suggested Revision of Rule 23*, 46 Colum.L.Rev. 818, 833–36 (1946); Mich.Gen.Court R. 208.4 (effective Jan. 1, 1963); Idaho R.Civ.P. 23(d); Minn.R.Civ.P. 23.04; N.Dak.R.Civ.P. 23(d).

The amended rule describes in more practical terms the occasions for maintaining class actions; provides that all class actions maintained to the end as such will result in judgments including those whom the court finds to be members of the class, whether or not the judgment is favorable to the class; and refers to the measures which can be taken to assure the fair conduct of these actions.

Subdivision (a) states the prerequisites for maintaining any class action in terms of the numerousness of the class making joinder of the members impracticable, the existence of questions common to the class, and the desired qualifications of the representative parties. See Weinstein, *Revision of Procedure: Some Problems in Class Actions*, 9 Buffalo L.Rev. 433, 458–59 (1960); 2 Barron & Holtzoff, *Federal Practice & Procedure* § 562, at 265, § 572, at 351–52 (Wright ed. 1961). These are necessary but not sufficient conditions for a class action. See, e.g., *Giordano v. Radio Corp. of Am.*, 183 F.2d 558, 560 (3d Cir.1950); *Zachman v. Erwin,* 186 F.Supp. 681 (S.D.Tex.1959); *Baim & Blank, Inc. v. Warren-Connelly Co., Inc.,* 19 F.R.D. 108 (S.D.N.Y.1956). Subdivision (b) describes the additional elements which in varying situations justify the use of a class action.

Subdivision (b)(1). The difficulties which would be likely to arise if resort were had to separate actions by or against the individual members of the class here furnish the reasons for, and the principal key to, the propriety and value of utilizing the class-action device. The considerations stated under clauses (A) and (B) are comparable to certain of the elements which define the persons whose joinder in an action is desirable as stated in Rule 19(a), as amended. See amended Rule 19(a)(2)(i) and (ii), and the Advisory Committee's Note thereto; Hazard, *Indispensable Party: The Historical Origin of a Procedural Phantom*, 61 Colum.L.Rev. 1254, 1259–60 (1961); cf. 3 Moore, supra, par. 23.08, at 3435.

Clause (A): One person may have rights against, or be under duties toward, numerous persons constituting a class, and be so positioned that conflicting or varying adjudications in lawsuits with individual members of the class might establish incompatible standards to govern his conduct. The class action device can be used effectively to obviate the actual or virtual dilemma which would thus confront the party opposing the class. The matter has been stated thus: "The felt necessity for a class action is greatest when the courts are called upon to order or sanction the alteration of the status quo in circumstances such that a large number of persons are in a position to call on a single person to alter the status quo, or to complain if it is altered, and the possibility exists that [the] actor might be called upon to act in inconsistent ways." Louisell & Hazard, *Pleading and Procedure: State and Federal* 719 (1962); see *Supreme Tribe of Ben-Hur v. Cauble*, 255 U.S. 356, 366–67 (1921). To illustrate: Separate actions by individuals against a municipality to declare a bond issue invalid or condition or limit it, to prevent or limit the making of a particular appropriation or to compel or invalidate an assessment, might create a risk of inconsistent or varying determinations. In the same way, individual litigations of the rights and duties of riparian owners, or of landowners' rights and duties respecting a claimed nuisance, could create a possibility of incompatible adjudications. Actions by or against a class provide a ready and fair means of achieving unitary adjudication. See *Maricopa County Mun. Water Con. Dist. v. Looney,* 219 F.2d 529 (9th Cir.1955); *Rank v. Krug*, 142 F.Supp. 1, 154–59 (S.D.Calif.1956), on app., *State of California v. Rank*, 293 F.2d 340, 348 (9th Cir.1961); *Gart v. Cole,* 263 F.2d 244 (2d Cir.1959), cert. denied 359 U.S. 978 (1959); cf. *Martinez v. Maverick Cty. Water Con. & Imp. Dist.,* 219 F.2d 666 (5th Cir.1955); 3 Moore, supra, par. 23.11[2], at 3458–59.

Clause (B): This clause takes in situations where the judgment in a nonclass action by or against an individual member of the class, while not technically concluding the other members, might do so as a practical matter. The vice of an individual action would lie in the fact that the other members of the class, thus practically concluded, would have had no representation in the lawsuit. In an action by policy holders against a fraternal benefit association attacking a financial reorganization of the society, it would hardly have been practical, if indeed it would have been possible, to confine the effects of a validation of the reorganization to the individual plaintiffs. Consequently a class action was called for with adequate representation of all members of the class. See *Supreme Tribe of Ben-Hur v. Cauble,* 255 U.S. 356 (1921); *Waybright v. Columbian Mut. Life Ins. Co.,* 30 F.Supp. 885 (W.D.Tenn.1939); cf. *Smith v. Swormstedt,* 16 How. (57 U.S.) 288 (1853). For much the same reason actions by shareholders to compel the declaration of a dividend[,] the proper recognition and handling of redemption or pre-emption rights, or the like (or actions by the corporation for corresponding declarations of rights), should ordinarily be conducted as class actions, although the matter has been much obscured by the insistence that each shareholder has an individual claim. See *Knapp v. Bankers Securities Corp.,* 17 F.R.D. 245 (E.D.Pa.1954), aff'd, 230 F.2d 717 (3d Cir.1956); *Giesecke v. Denver Tramway Corp.,* 81 F.Supp. 957 (D.Del.1949); *Zahn v. Transamerica Corp.,* 162 F.2d 36 (3d Cir.1947); *Speed v. Transamerica Corp.,* 100 F.Supp. 461 (D.Del.1951); *Sobel v. Whittier Corp.,* 95 F.Supp. 643 (E.D.Mich.1951), app. dism., 195 F.2d 361 (6th Cir.1952); *Goldberg v. Whittier Corp.,* 111 F.Supp. 382 (E.D.Mich.1953); *Dann v. Studebaker-Packard Corp.,* 288 F.2d 201 (6th Cir.1961); *Edgerton v. Armour & Co.,* 94 F.Supp. 549 (S.D.Calif.1950); *Ames v. Mengel Co.,* 190 F.2d 344 (2d Cir.1951). (These shareholders' actions are to be distinguished from derivative actions by shareholders dealt with in new Rule 23.1.) The same reasoning applies to an action which charges a breach of trust by an indenture trustee or other fiduciary similarly affecting the members of a large class of security holders or other beneficiaries, and which requires an accounting or like measures to restore the subject of the trust. See *Boesenberg v. Chicago T. & T. Co.,* 128 F.2d 245 (7th Cir.1942); *Citizens Banking Co. v. Monticello State Bank,* 143 F.2d 261 (8th Cir.1944); *Redmond v. Commerce Trust Co.,* 144 F.2d 140 (8th Cir.1944), cert. denied, 323 U.S. 776 (1944); cf. *York v. Guaranty Trust Co.,* 143 F.2d 503 (2d Cir.1944), rev'd on grounds not here relevant, 326 U.S. 99 (1945).

In various situations an adjudication as to one or more members of the class will necessarily or probably have an adverse practical effect on the interests of other members who should therefore be represented in the lawsuit. This is plainly the case when claims are made by numerous persons against a fund insufficient to satisfy all claims. A class action by or against representative members to settle the validity of the claims as a whole, or in groups, followed by separate proof of the amount of each valid claim and proportionate distribution of the fund, meets the problem. Cf. *Dickinson v. Burnham,* 197 F.2d 973 (2d Cir.1952), cert. denied, 344 U.S. 875 (1952); 3 Moore, supra, at par. 23.09. The same reasoning applies to an action by a creditor to set aside a fraudulent conveyance by the debtor and to appropriate the property to his claim, when the debtor's assets are insufficient to pay all creditors' claims. See *Heffernan v. Bennett & Armour,* 110 Cal.App.2d 564, 243 P.2d 846 (1952); cf. *City & County of San Francisco v. Market Street Ry.,* 95 Cal.App.2d 648, 213 P.2d 780 (1950). Similar problems, however, can arise in the absence of a fund either present or potential. A negative or mandatory injunction secured by one of a numerous class may disable the opposing party from performing claimed duties toward the other members of the class or materially affect his ability to do so. An adjudication as to movie "clearances and runs" nominally affecting only one exhibitor would often have practical effects on all the exhibitors in the same territorial area. Cf. *United States v. Paramount Pictures, Inc.*, 66 F.Supp. 323, 341–46 (S.D.N.Y.1946); 334 U.S. 131, 144–48 (1948). Assuming a sufficiently numerous class of exhibitors, a class action would be advisable. (Here representation of subclasses of exhibitors could become necessary; see subdivision (c)(3)(B).)

Subdivision (b)(2). This subdivision is intended to reach situations where a party has taken action or refused to take action with respect to a class, and final relief of an injunctive nature or of a corresponding declaratory nature, settling the legality of the behavior with respect to the class as a whole, is appropriate. Declaratory relief "corresponds" to injunctive relief when as a practical matter it affords injunctive relief or serves as a basis for later injunctive relief. The subdivision does not extend to cases in which the appropriate final relief relates exclusively or predominantly to money damages. Action or inaction is directed to a class within the meaning of this subdivision even if it has taken effect or is threatened only as to one or a few members of the class, provided it is based on grounds which have general application to the class.

Illustrative are various actions in the civil-rights field where a party is charged with discriminating unlawfully against a class, usually one whose members are incapable of specific enumeration. See *Potts v. Flax,* 313 F.2d 284 (5th Cir. 1963); *Bailey v. Patterson,* 323 F.2d 201 (5th Cir. 1963), cert. denied, 376 U.S. 910, (1964); *Brunson v. Board of Trustees of School District No. 1, Clarendon Cty., S.C.,* 311 F.2d 107 (4th Cir. 1962), cert. denied, 373 U.S. 933 (1963); *Green v. School Bd. of Roanoke, Va.,* 304 F.2d 118 (4th Cir. 1962); *Orleans Parish School Bd. v. Bush,* 242 F.2d 156 (5th Cir. 1957), cert. denied, 354 U.S. 921 (1957); *Mannings v. Board of Public Inst. of Hillsborough County, Fla.,* 277 F.2d 370 (5th Cir. 1960); *Northcross v. Board of Ed. of City of Memphis,* 302 F.2d 818 (6th Cir. 1962), cert. denied, 370 U.S. 944 (1962); *Frasier v. Board of Trustees of Univ. of N.C.,* 134 F.Supp. 589 (M.D.N.C.1955, 3-judge court), aff'd 350 U.S. 979 (1956). Subdivision (b)(2) is not limited to civil-rights cases. Thus an action looking to specific or declaratory relief could be brought by a numerous class of purchasers, say retailers of a given description, against a seller alleged to have undertaken to sell to that class at prices higher than those set for other purchasers, say retailers of another description, when the applicable law forbids such a pricing differential. So also a patentee of a machine, charged with selling or licensing the machine on condition that purchasers or licensees also purchase or obtain licenses to use an ancillary unpatented machine, could be sued on a class basis by a numerous group of purchasers or licensees, or by a numerous group of competing sellers or licensors of the unpatented machine, to test the legality of the "tying" condition.

Subdivision (b)(3). In the situations to which this subdivision relates, class-action treatment is not as clearly called for as in those described above, but it may nevertheless be convenient and desirable depending upon the particular facts. Subdivision (b)(3) encompasses those cases in which a class action would achieve economies of time, effort, and expense, and promote uniformity of decision as to persons similarly situated, without sacrificing procedural fairness or bringing about other undesirable results. Cf. Chafee, supra, at 201.

The court is required to find, as a condition of holding that a class action may be maintained under this subdivision, that the questions common to the class predominate over the questions affecting individual members. It is only where this predominance exists that economies can be achieved by means of the class-action device. In this view, a fraud perpetrated on numerous persons by the use of similar misrepresentations may be an appealing situation for a class action, and it may remain so despite the need, if liability is found, for separate determination of the damages suffered by individuals within the class. On the other hand, although having some common core, a fraud case may be unsuited for treatment as a class action if there was material variation in the representations made or in the kinds or degrees of reliance by the persons to whom they were addressed. See *Oppenheimer v. F. J. Young & Co., Inc.,* 144 F.2d 387 (2d Cir. 1944); *Miller v. National City Bank of N.Y.,* 166 F.2d 723 (2d Cir. 1948); and for like problems in other contexts, see *Hughes v. Encyclopaedia Britannica,* 199 F.2d 295 (7th Cir. 1952); *Sturgeon v. Great Lakes Steel Corp.,* 143 F.2d 819 (6th Cir. 1944). A "mass accident" resulting in injuries to numerous persons is ordinarily not appropriate for a class action because of the likelihood that significant questions, not only of damages but of liability and defenses of liability, would be present, affecting the individuals in different ways. In these circumstances an action conducted nominally as a class action would degenerate in practice into multiple lawsuits separately tried. See *Pennsylvania R.R. v. United States,* 111 F.Supp. 80 (D.N.J.1953); cf. Weinstein, supra, 9 Buffalo L.Rev. at 469. Private damage claims by numerous individuals arising out of concerted antitrust violations may or may not involve predominating common questions. See *Union Carbide & Carbon Corp. v. Nisley,* 300 F.2d 561 (10th Cir. 1961), pet. cert. dism., 371 U.S. 801 (1963); cf. *Weeks v. Bareco Oil Co.,* 125 F.2d 84 (7th Cir. 1941); *Kainz v. Anheuser-Busch, Inc.,* 194 F.2d 737 (7th Cir. 1952); *Hess v. Anderson, Clayton & Co.,* 20 F.R.D. 466 (S.D.Calif.1957).

That common questions predominate is not itself sufficient to justify a class action under subdivision (b)(3), for another method of handling the litigious situation may be available which has greater practical advantages. Thus one or more actions agreed to by the parties as test or model actions may be preferable to a class action; or it may prove feasible and preferable to consolidate actions. Cf. Weinstein, supra, 9 Buffalo L.Rev. at 438–54. Even when several separate actions are proceeding simultaneously, experience shows that the burdens on the parties and the courts can sometimes be reduced by arrangements for avoiding repetitious discovery or the like. Currently the Coordinating Committee on Multiple Litigation in the United States District Courts (a subcommittee of the Committee on Trial Practice and Technique of the Judicial Conference of the United States) is charged with developing methods for expediting such massive litigation. To reinforce the point that the court with the aid of the parties ought to assess the relative advantages of alternative procedures for handling the total controversy, subdivision (b)(3) requires, as a further condition of maintaining the class action, that the court shall find that that procedure is "superior" to the others in the particular circumstances.

Factors (A)–(D) are listed, non-exhaustively, as pertinent to the findings. The court is to consider the interests of individual members of the class in controlling their own litigations and carrying them on as they see fit. See *Weeks v. Bareco Oil Co.*, 125 F.2d 84, 88–90, 93–94 (7th Cir. 1941) (anti-trust action); see also *Pentland v. Dravo Corp.,* 152 F.2d 851 (3d Cir. 1945), and Chafee, supra, at 273–75, regarding policy of Fair Labor Standards Act of 1938, *§* 16(b), 29 U.S.C. *§* 216(b), prior to amendment by Portal-to-Portal Act of 1947, *§* 5(a). [The present provisions of 29 U.S.C. *§* 216(b) are not intended to be affected by Rule 23, as amended.]

In this connection the court should inform itself of any litigation actually pending by or against the individuals. The interests of individuals in conducting separate lawsuits may be so strong as to call for denial of a class action. On the other hand, these interests may be theoretic rather than practical; the class may have a high degree of cohesion and prosecution of the action through representatives would be quite unobjectionable, or the amounts at stake for individuals may be so small that separate suits would be impracticable. The burden that separate suits would impose on the party opposing the class, or upon the court calendars, may also fairly be considered. (See the discussion, under subdivision (c)(2) below, of the right of members to be excluded from the class upon their request.)

Also pertinent is the question of the desirability of concentrating the trial of the claims in the particular forum by means of a class action, in contrast to allowing the claims to be litigated separately in forums to which they would ordinarily be brought. Finally, the court should consider the problems of management which are likely to arise in the conduct of a class action.

Subdivision (c)(1). In order to give clear definition to the action, this provision requires the court to determine, as early in the proceedings as may be practicable, whether an action brought as a class action is to be so maintained. The determination depends in each case on satisfaction of the terms of subdivision (a) and the relevant provisions of subdivision (b).

An order embodying a determination can be conditional; the court may rule, for example, that a class action may be maintained only if the representation is improved through intervention of additional parties of a stated type. A determination once made can be altered or amended before the decision on the merits if, upon fuller development of the facts, the original determination appears unsound. A negative determination means that the action should be stripped of its character as a class action. See subdivision (d)(4). Although an action thus becomes a nonclass action, the court may still be receptive to interventions before the decision on the merits so that the litigation may cover as many interests as can be conveniently handled; the questions whether the intervenors in the nonclass action shall be permitted to claim "ancillary" jurisdiction or the benefit of the date of the commencement of the action for purposes of the statute of limitations are to be decided by reference to the laws governing jurisdiction and limitations as they apply in particular contexts.

Whether the court should require notice to be given to members of the class of its intention to make a determination, or of the order embodying it, is left to the court's discretion under subdivision (d)(2).

Subdivision (c)(2) makes special provision for class actions maintained under subdivision (b)(3). As noted in the discussion of the latter subdivision, the interests of the individuals in pursing their own litigations may be so strong here as to warrant denial of a class action altogether. Even when a class action is maintained under subdivision (b)(3), this individual interest is respected. Thus the court is required to direct notice to the members of the class of the right of each member to be excluded from the class upon his request. A member who does not request exclusion may, if he wishes, enter an appearance in the action through his counsel; whether or not he does so, the judgment in the action will embrace him.

The notice[,] setting forth the alternatives open to the members of the class, is to be the best practicable under the circumstances, and shall include individual notice to the members who can be identified through reasonable effort. (For further discussion of this notice, see the statement under subdivision (d)(2) below.)

Subdivision (c)(3). The judgment in a class action maintained as such to the end will embrace the class, that is, in a class action under subdivision (b)(1) or (b)(2), those found by the court to be class members; in a class action under subdivision (b)(3), those to whom the notice prescribed by subdivision (c)(2) was directed, excepting those who requested exclusion or who are ultimately found by the court not to be members of the class. The judgment has this scope whether it is favorable or unfavorable to the class. In a (b)(1) or (b)(2) action the judgment "describes" the members of the class, but need not specify the individual members; in a (b)(3) action the judgment "specifies" the individual members who have been identified and described the others.

Compare subdivision (c)(4) as to actions conducted as class actions only with respect to particular issues. Where the class-action character of the lawsuit is based solely on the existence of a "limited fund," the judgment, while extending to all claims of class members against the fund, has ordinarily left unaffected the personal claims of nonappearing members against the debtor. See 3 Moore, supra, par. 23.11[4].

Hitherto, in a few actions conducted as "spurious" class actions and thus nominally designed to extend only to parties and others intervening before the determination of liability, courts have held or intimated that class members might be permitted to intervene after a decision on the merits favorable to their interests, in order to secure the benefits of the decision for themselves, although they would presumably be unaffected by an unfavorable decision. See, as to the propriety of this so-called one-way intervention in "spurious" actions, the conflicting views expressed in *Union Carbide & Carbon Corp. v. Nisley,* 300 F.2d 561 (10th Cir. 1961), pet. cert. dism., 371 U.S. 801 (1963); *York v. Guaranty Trust Co.*, 143 F.2d 503, 529 (2d Cir. 1944), rev'd on grounds not here relevant, 326 U.S. 99 (1945); *Pentland v. Dravo Corp.*, 152 F.2d 851, 856 (3d Cir. 1945); *Speed v. Transamerica Corp.*, 100 F.Supp. 461, 463 (D.Del.1951); *State Wholesale Grocers v. Great Atl. & Pac. Tea Co.,* 24 F.R.D. 510 (N.D.Ill.1959); *Alabama Ind. Serv. Stat. Assn. v. Shell Pet. Corp.*, 28 F.Supp. 386, 390 (N.D.Ala.1939); *Tolliver v. Cudahy Packing Co.*, 39 F.Supp. 337, 339 (E.D.Tenn.1941); Kalven & Rosenfield, supra, 8 U. of Chi.L.Rev. 684 (1941); Comment, 53 Nw.U.L.Rev. 627, 632–33 (1958); *Developments in the Law*, supra, 71 Harv.L.Rev. at 935; 2 Barron & Holtzoff, supra, § 568; but cf. *Lockwood v. Hercules Powder Co.*, 7 F.R.D. 24, 28–29 (W.D.Mo.1947); *Abram v. San Joaquin Cotton Oil Co.*, 46 F.Supp. 969, 976–77 (S.D.Calif.1942); Chafee, supra, at 280, 285; 3 Moore, supra, par. 23.12, at 3476. Under proposed subdivision (c)(3), one-way intervention is excluded; the action will have been early determined to be a class or nonclass action, and in the former case the judgment, whether or not favorable, will include the class, as above stated.

Although thus declaring that the judgment in a class action includes the class, as defined, subdivision (c)(3) does not disturb the recognized principle that the court conducting the action cannot predetermine the *res judicata* effect of the judgment; this can be tested only in a subsequent action. See Restatement, Judgments § 86, comment (h), § 116 (1942). The court, however, in framing the judgment in any suit brought as a class action, must decide what its extent or coverage shall be, and if the matter is carefully considered, questions of *res judicata* are less likely to be raised at a later time and if raised will be more satisfactorily answered. See Chafee, supra, at 294; Weinstein, supra, 9 Buffalo L.Rev. at 460.

Subdivision (c)(4). This provision recognizes that an action may be maintained as a class action as to particular issues only. For example, in a fraud or similar case the action may retain its "class" character only through the adjudication of liability to the class; the members of the class may thereafter be required to come in individually and prove the amounts of their respective claims.

Two or more classes may be represented in a single action. Where a class is found to include subclasses divergent in interest, the class may be divided correspondingly, and each subclass treated as a class.

Subdivision (d) is concerned with the fair and efficient conduct of the action and lists some types of orders which may be appropriate.

The court should consider how the proceedings are to be arranged in sequence, and what measures should be taken to simplify the proof and argument. See subdivision (d)(1). The orders resulting from this consideration, like the others referred to in subdivision (d), may be combined with a pretrial order under Rule 16, and are subject to modification as the case proceeds.

Subdivision (d)(2) sets out a non-exhaustive list of possible occasions for orders requiring notice to the class. Such notice is not a novel conception. For example, in "limited fund" cases, members of the class have been notified to present individual claims after the basic class decision. Notice has gone to members of a class so that they might express any opposition to the representation, see *United States v. American Optical Co.,* 97 F.Supp. 66 (N.D.Ill.1951), and 1950–51 CCH Trade Cases 64573–74 (par. 62869); cf. *Weeks v. Bareco Oil Co.*, 125 F.2d 84, 94 (7th Cir. 1941), and notice may encourage interventions to improve the representation of the class. Cf. *Oppenheimer v. F. J. Young & Co.,* 144 F.2d 387 (2d Cir. 1944). Notice has been used to poll members on a proposed modification of a consent decree. See record in *Sam Fox Publishing Co. v. United States,* 366 U.S. 683 (1961).

Subdivision (d)(2) does not require notice at any stage, but rather calls attention to its availability and invokes the court's discretion. In the degree that there is cohesiveness or unity in the class and the representation is effective, the need for notice to the class will tend toward a minimum. These indicators suggest that notice under subdivision (d)(2) may be particularly useful and advisable in certain class actions maintained under subdivision (b)(3), for example, to permit members of the class to object to the representation. Indeed, under subdivision (c)(2), notice must be ordered, and is not merely discretionary, to give the members in a subdivision (b)(3) class action an opportunity to secure exclusion from the class. This mandatory notice pursuant to subdivision (c)(2), together with any discretionary notice which the court may find it advisable to give under subdivision (d)(2), is designed to fulfill requirements of due process to which the class action procedure is of course subject. See *Hansberry v. Lee,* 311 U.S. 32 (1940); *Mullane v. Central Hanover Bank & Trust Co.,* 339 U.S. 306 (1950); cf. *Dickinson v. Burnham*, 197 F.2d 973, 979 (2d Cir. 1952), and studies cited at 979 in 4; see also *All American Airways, Inc. v. Elderd*, 209 F.2d 247, 249 (2d Cir. 1954); *Gart v. Cole*, 263 F.2d 244, 248–49 (2d Cir. 1959), cert. denied, 359 U.S. 978 (1959).

Notice to members of the class, whenever employed under amended Rule 23, should be accommodated to the particular purpose but need not comply with the formalities for service of process. See Chafee, supra, at 230–31; *Brendle v. Smith,* 7 F.R.D. 119 (S.D.N.Y.1946). The fact that notice is given at one stage of the action does not mean that it must be given at subsequent stages. Notice is available fundamentally "for the protection of the members of the class or otherwise for the fair conduct of the action" and should not be used merely as a device for the undesirable solicitation of claims. See the discussion in *Cherner v. Transitron Electronic Corp.*, 201 F.Supp. 934 (D.Mass.1962); *Hormel v. United States*, 17 F.R.D. 303 (S.D.N.Y.1955).

In appropriate cases the court should notify interested government agencies of the pendency of the action or of particular steps therein.

Subdivision (d)(3) reflects the possibility of conditioning the maintenance of a class action, e.g., on the strengthening of the representation, see subdivision (c)(1) above; and recognizes that the imposition of conditions on intervenors may be required for the proper and efficient conduct of the action.

As to orders under subdivision (d)(4), see subdivision (c)(1) above.

Subdivision (e) requires approval of the court, after notice, for the dismissal or compromise of any class action.

1987 Amendment

The amendments are technical. No substantive change is intended.

1998 Amendment

Subdivision (f). This permissive interlocutory appeal provision is adopted under the power conferred by 28 U.S.C. § 1292(e). Appeal from an order granting or denying class certification is permitted in the sole discretion of the court of appeals. No other type of Rule 23 order is covered by this provision. The court of appeals is given unfettered discretion whether to permit the appeal, akin to the discretion exercised by the Supreme Court in acting on a petition for certiorari. This discretion suggests an analogy to the provision in 28 U.S.C. § 1292(b) for permissive appeal on certification by a district court. Subdivision (f), however, departs from the § 1291(b) model in two significant ways. It does not require that the district court certify the certification ruling for appeal, although the district court often can assist the parties and court of appeals by offering advice on the desirability of appeal. And it does not include the potentially limiting requirements of § 1292(b) that the district court order "involve a controlling question of law as to which there is substantial ground for difference of opinion and that an immediate appeal from the order may materially advance the ultimate termination of the litigation.

The courts of appeals will develop standards for granting review that reflect the changing areas of uncertainty in class litigation. The Federal Judicial Center study supports the view that many suits with class-action allegations present familiar and almost routine issues that are no more worthy of immediate appeal than many other interlocutory rulings. Yet several concerns justify expansion of present opportunities to appeal. An order denying certification may confront the plaintiff with a situation in which the only sure path to appellate review is by proceeding to final judgment on the merits of an individual claim that, standing alone, is far smaller than the costs of litigation. An order granting certification, on the other hand, may force a defendant to settle rather than incur the costs of defending a class action and run the risk of potentially ruinous liability. These concerns can be met at low cost by establishing in the court of appeals a discretionary power to grant interlocutory review in cases that show appeal-worthy certification issues.

Permission to appeal may be granted or denied on the basis of any consideration that the court of appeals finds persuasive. Permission is most likely to be granted when the certification decision turns on a novel or unsettled question of law, or when, as a practical matter, the decision on certification is likely dispositive of the litigation.

The district court, having worked through the certification decision, often will be able to provide cogent advice on the factors that bear on the decision whether to permit appeal. This advice can be particularly valuable if the certification decision is tentative. Even as to a firm certification decision, a statement of reasons bearing on the probably benefits and costs of immediate appeal can help focus the court of appeals decision, and may persuade the disappointed party that an attempt to appeal would be fruitless.

The 10-day period for seeking permission to appeal is designed to reduce the risk that attempted appeals will disrupt continuing proceedings. It is expected that the courts of appeals will act quickly in making the preliminary determination whether to permit appeal. Permission to appeal does not stay trial court proceedings. A stay should be sought first from the trial court. If the trial court refuses a stay, its action and any explanation of its views should weigh heavily with the court of appeals.

Appellate Rule 5 has been modified to establish the procedure for petitioning for leave to appeal under subdivision (f).

2003 Amendment

Subdivision (c). Subdivision (c) is amended in several respects. The requirement that the court determine whether to certify a class "as soon as practicable after commencement of an action" is replaced by requiring determination "at an early practicable time." The notice provisions are substantially revised.

Paragraph (1). Subdivision (c)(1)(A) is changed to require that the determination whether to certify a class be made "at an early practicable time." The "as soon as practicable" exaction neither reflects prevailing practice nor captures the many valid reasons that may justify deferring the initial certification decision. See Willging, Hooper & Niemic, *Empirical Study of Class Actions in Four Federal District Courts: Final Report to the Advisory Committee on Civil Rules 26–36* (Federal Judicial Center 1996).

Time may be needed to gather information necessary to make the certification decision. Although an evaluation of the probable outcome on the merits is not properly part of the certification decision, discovery in aid of the certification decision often includes information required to identify the nature of the issues that actually will be presented at trial. In this sense it is appropriate to conduct controlled discovery into the "merits," limited to those aspects relevant to making the certification decision on an informed basis. Active judicial supervision may be required to achieve the most effective balance that expedites an informed certification determination without forcing an artificial and ultimately wasteful division between "certification discovery" and "merits discovery." A critical need is to determine how the case will be tried. An increasing number of courts require a party requesting class certification to present a "trial plan" that describes the issues likely to be presented at trial and tests whether they are susceptible of class-wide proof. See Manual For Complex Litigation Third, § 21.213, p. 44; § 30.11, p. 214; § 30.12, p. 215.

Other considerations may affect the timing of the certification decision. The party opposing the class may prefer to win dismissal or summary judgment as to the individual plaintiffs without certification and without binding the class that might have been certified. Time may be needed to explore designation of class counsel under Rule 23(g), recognizing that in many cases the need to progress toward the certification determination may require designation of interim counsel under Rule 23(g)(2)(A).

Although many circumstances may justify deferring the certification decision, active management may be necessary to ensure that the certification decision is not unjustifiably delayed.

Subdivision (c)(1)(C) reflects two amendments. The provision that a class certification "may be conditional" is deleted. A court that is not satisfied that the requirements of Rule 23 have been met should refuse certification until they have been met. The provision that permits alteration or amendment of an order granting or denying class certification is amended to set the cut-off point at final judgment rather than "the decision on the merits." This change avoids the possible ambiguity in referring to "the decision on the merits." Following a determination of liability, for example, proceedings to define the remedy may demonstrate the need to amend the class definition or subdivide the class. In this setting the final judgment concept is pragmatic. It is not the same as the concept used for appeal purposes, but it should be flexible, particularly in protracted litigation.

The authority to amend an order under Rule 23(c)(1) before final judgment does not restore the practice of "one-way intervention" that was rejected by the 1966 revision of Rule 23. A determination of liability after certification, however, may show a need to amend the class definition. Decertification may be warranted after further proceedings.

If the definition of a class certified under Rule 23(b)(3) is altered to include members who have not been afforded notice and an opportunity to request exclusion, notice—including an opportunity to request exclusion—must be directed to the new class members under Rule 23(c)(2)(B).

Paragraph (2). The first change made in Rule 23(c)(2) is to call attention to the court's authority—already established in part by Rule 23(d)(2)—to direct notice of certification to a Rule 23(b)(1) or (b)(2) class. The present rule expressly requires notice only in actions certified under Rule 23(b)(3). Members of classes certified under Rules 23(b)(1) or (b)(2) have interests that may deserve protection by notice.

The authority to direct notice to class members in a (b)(1) or (b)(2) class action should be exercised with care. For several reasons, there may be less need for notice than in a (b)(3) class action. There is no right to request exclusion from a (b)(1) or (b)(2) class. The characteristics of the class may reduce the need for formal notice. The cost of providing notice, moreover, could easily cripple actions that do not seek damages. The court may decide not to direct notice after balancing the risk that notice costs may deter the pursuit of class relief against the benefits of notice.

When the court does direct certification notice in a (b)(1) or (b)(2) class action, the discretion and flexibility established by subdivision (c)(2)(A) extend to the method of giving notice. Notice facilitates the opportunity to participate. Notice calculated to reach a significant number of class members often will protect the interests of all. Informal methods may prove effective. A simple posting in a place visited by many class members, directing attention to a source of more detailed information, may suffice. The court should consider the costs of notice in relation to the probable reach of inexpensive methods.

If a Rule 23(b)(3) class is certified in conjunction with a (b)(2) class, the (c)(2)(B) notice requirements must be satisfied as to the (b)(3) class.

The direction that class-certification notice be couched in plain, easily understood language is a reminder of the need to work unremittingly at the difficult task of communicating with class members. It is difficult to provide information about most class actions that is both accurate and easily understood by class members who are not themselves lawyers. Factual uncertainty, legal complexity, and the complication of class-action procedure raise the barriers high. The Federal Judicial Center has created illustrative clear-notice forms that provide a helpful starting point for actions similar to those described in the forms.

Subdivision (e). Subdivision (e) is amended to strengthen the process of reviewing proposed class-action settlements. Settlement may be a desirable means of resolving a class action. But court review and approval are essential to assure adequate representation of class members who have not participated in shaping the settlement.

Paragraph (1). Subdivision (e)(1)(A) expressly recognizes the power of a class representative to settle class claims, issues, or defenses.

Rule 23(e)(1)(A) resolves the ambiguity in former Rule 23(e)'s reference to dismissal or compromise of "a class action." That language could be—and at times was—read to require court approval of settlements with putative class representatives that resolved only individual claims. See Manual for Complex Litigation Third, § 30.41. The new rule requires approval only if the claims, issues, or defenses of a certified class are resolved by a settlement, voluntary dismissal, or compromise.

Subdivision (e)(1)(B) carries forward the notice requirement of present Rule 23(e) when the settlement binds the class through claim or issue preclusion; notice is not required when the settlement binds only the individual class representatives. Notice of a settlement binding on the class is required either when the settlement follows class certification or when the decisions on certification and settlement proceed simultaneously.

Reasonable settlement notice may require individual notice in the manner required by Rule 23(c)(2)(B) for certification notice to a Rule 23(b)(3) class. Individual notice is appropriate, for example, if class members are required to take action—such as filing claims—to participate in the judgment, or if the court orders a settlement opt-out opportunity under Rule 23(e)(3).

Subdivision (e)(1)(C) confirms and mandates the already common practice of holding hearings as part of the process of approving settlement, voluntary dismissal, or compromise that would bind members of a class.

Subdivision (e)(1)(C) states the standard for approving a proposed settlement that would bind class members. The settlement must be fair, reasonable, and adequate. A helpful review of many factors that may deserve consideration is provided by *In re: Prudential Ins. Co. America Sales Practice Litigation Agent Actions*, 148 F.3d 283, 316–324 (3d Cir. 1998). Further guidance can be found in the Manual for Complex Litigation.

The court must make findings that support the conclusion that the settlement is fair, reasonable, and adequate. The findings must be set out in sufficient detail to explain to class members and the appellate court the factors that bear on applying the standard.

Settlement review also may provide an occasion to review the cogency of the initial class definition. The terms of the settlement themselves, or objections, may reveal divergent interests of class members and demonstrate the need to redefine the class or to designate subclasses. Redefinition of a class certified under Rule 23(b)(3) may require notice to new class members under Rule 23(c)(2)(B). See Rule 23(c)(1)(C).

Paragraph (2). Subdivision (e)(2) requires parties seeking approval of a settlement, voluntary dismissal, or compromise under Rule 23(e)(1) to file a statement identifying any agreement made in connection with the settlement. This provision does not change the basic requirement that the parties disclose all terms of the settlement or compromise that the court must approve under Rule 23(e)(1). It aims instead at related undertakings that, although seemingly separate, may have influenced the terms of the settlement by trading away possible advantages for the class in return for advantages for others. Doubts should be resolved in favor of identification.

Further inquiry into the agreements identified by the parties should not become the occasion for discovery by the parties or objectors. The court may direct the parties to provide to the court or other parties a summary or copy of the full terms of any agreement identified by the parties. The court also may direct the parties to provide a summary or copy of any agreement not identified by the parties that the court considers relevant to its review of a proposed settlement. In exercising discretion under this rule, the court may act in steps, calling first for a summary of any agreement that may have affected the settlement and then for a complete version if the summary does not provide an adequate basis for review. A direction to disclose a summary or copy of an agreement may raise concerns of confidentiality. Some agreements may include information that merits protection against general disclosure. And the court must provide an opportunity to claim work-product or other protections.

Paragraph (3). Subdivision (e)(3) authorizes the court to refuse to approve a settlement unless the settlement affords class members a new opportunity to request exclusion from a class certified under Rule 23(b)(3) after settlement terms are known. An agreement by the parties themselves to permit class members to elect exclusion at this point by the settlement agreement may be one factor supporting approval of the settlement. Often there is an opportunity to opt out at this point because the class is certified and settlement is reached in circumstances that lead to simultaneous notice of certification and notice of settlement. In these cases, the basic opportunity to elect exclusion applies without further complication. In some cases, particularly if settlement appears imminent at the time of certification, it may be possible to achieve equivalent protection by deferring notice and the opportunity to elect exclusion until actual settlement terms are known. This approach avoids the cost and potential confusion of providing two notices and makes the single notice more meaningful. But notice should not be delayed unduly after certification in the hope of settlement.

Rule 23(e)(3) authorizes the court to refuse to approve a settlement unless the settlement affords a new opportunity to elect exclusion in a case that settles after a certification decision if the earlier opportunity to elect exclusion provided with the certification notice has expired by the time of the settlement notice. A decision to remain in the class is likely to be more carefully considered and is better informed when settlement terms are known.

The opportunity to request exclusion from a proposed settlement is limited to members of a (b)(3) class. Exclusion may be requested only by individual class members; no class member may purport to opt out other class members by way of another class action.

The decision whether to approve a settlement that does not allow a new opportunity to elect exclusion is confided to the court's discretion. The court may make this decision before directing notice to the class under Rule 23(e)(1)(B) or after the Rule 23(e)(1)(C) hearing. Many factors may influence the court's decision. Among these are changes in the information available to class members since expiration of the first opportunity to request exclusion, and the nature of the individual class members' claims.

The terms set for permitting a new opportunity to elect exclusion from the proposed settlement of a Rule 23(b)(3) class action may address concerns of potential misuse. The court might direct, for example, that class members who elect exclusion are bound by rulings on the merits made before the settlement was proposed for approval. Still other terms or conditions may be appropriate.

Paragraph (4). Subdivision (e)(4) confirms the right of class members to object to a proposed settlement, voluntary dismissal, or compromise. The right is defined in relation to a disposition that, because it would bind the class, requires court approval under subdivision (e)(1)(C).

Subdivision (e)(4)(B) requires court approval for withdrawal of objections made under subdivision (e)(4)(A). Review follows automatically if the objections are withdrawn on terms that lead to modification of the settlement with the class. Review also is required if the objector formally withdraws the objections. If the objector simply abandons pursuit of the objection, the court may inquire into the circumstances.

Approval under paragraph (4)(B) may be given or denied with little need for further inquiry if the objection and the disposition go only to a protest that the individual treatment afforded the objector under the proposed settlement is unfair because of factors that distinguish the objector from other class members. Different considerations may apply if the objector has protested that the proposed settlement is not fair, reasonable, or adequate on grounds that apply generally to a class or subclass. Such objections, which purport to represent class-wide interests, may augment the opportunity for obstruction or delay. If such objections are surrendered on terms that do not affect the class settlement or the objector's participation in the class settlement, the court often can approve withdrawal of the objections without elaborate inquiry.

Once an objector appeals, control of the proceeding lies in the court of appeals. The court of appeals may undertake review and approval of a settlement with the objector, perhaps as part of appeal settlement procedures, or may remand to the district court to take advantage of the district court's familiarity with the action and settlement.

Subdivision (g). Subdivision (g) is new. It responds to the reality that the selection and activity of class counsel are often critically important to the successful handling of a class action. Until now, courts have scrutinized proposed class counsel as well as the class representative under Rule 23(a)(4). This experience has recognized the importance of judicial evaluation of the proposed lawyer for the class, and this new subdivision builds on that experience rather than introducing an entirely new element into the class certification process. Rule 23(a)(4) will continue to call for scrutiny of the proposed class representative, while this subdivision will guide the court in assessing proposed class counsel as part of the certification decision. This subdivision recognizes the importance of class counsel, states the obligation to represent the interests of the class, and provides a framework for selection of class counsel. The procedure and standards for appointment vary depending on whether there are multiple applicants to be class counsel. The new subdivision also provides a method by which the court may make directions from the outset about the potential fee award to class counsel in the event the action is successful.

Paragraph (1) sets out the basic requirement that class counsel be appointed if a class is certified and articulates the obligation of class counsel to represent the interests of the class, as opposed to the potentially conflicting interests of individual class members. It also sets out the factors the court should consider in assessing proposed class counsel.

Paragraph (1)(A) requires that the court appoint class counsel to represent the class. Class counsel must be appointed for all classes, including each subclass that the court certifies to represent divergent interests.

Paragraph (1)(A) does not apply if "a statute provides otherwise." This recognizes that provisions of the Private Securities Litigation Reform Act of 1995, Pub. L. No. 104-67, 109 Stat. 737 (1995) (codified in various sections of 15 U.S.C.), contain directives that bear on selection of a lead plaintiff and the retention of counsel. This subdivision does not purport to supersede or to affect the interpretation of those provisions, or any similar provisions of other legislation.

Paragraph (1)(B) recognizes that the primary responsibility of class counsel, resulting from appointment as class counsel, is to represent the best interests of the class. The rule thus establishes the obligation of class counsel, an obligation that may be different from the customary obligations of counsel to individual clients. Appointment as class counsel means that the primary obligation of counsel is to the class rather than to any individual members of it. The class representatives do not have an unfettered right to "fire" class counsel. In the same vein, the class representatives cannot command class counsel to accept or reject a settlement proposal. To the contrary, class counsel must determine whether seeking the court's approval of a settlement would be in the best interests of the class as a whole.

Paragraph (1)(C) articulates the basic responsibility of the court to appoint class counsel who will provide the adequate representation called for by paragraph (1)(B). It identifies criteria that must be considered and invites the court to consider any other pertinent matters. Although couched in terms of the court's duty, the listing also informs counsel seeking appointment about the topics that should be addressed in an application for appointment or in the motion for class certification.

The court may direct potential class counsel to provide additional information about the topics mentioned in paragraph (1)(C) or about any other relevant topic. For example, the court may direct applicants to inform the court concerning any agreements about a prospective award of attorneys' fees or nontaxable costs, as such agreements may sometimes be significant in the selection of class counsel. The court might also direct that potential class counsel indicate how parallel litigation might be coordinated or consolidated with the action before the court.

The court may also direct counsel to propose terms for a potential award of attorneys' fees and nontaxable costs. Attorney fee awards are an important feature of class action practice, and attention to this subject from the outset may often be a productive technique. Paragraph (2)(C) therefore authorizes the court to provide directions about attorneys' fees and costs when appointing class counsel. Because there will be numerous class actions in which this information is not likely to be useful, the court need not consider it in all class actions.

Some information relevant to class counsel appointment may involve matters that include adversary preparation in a way that should be shielded from disclosure to other parties. An appropriate protective order may be necessary to preserve confidentiality.

In evaluating prospective class counsel, the court should weigh all pertinent factors. No single factor should necessarily be determinative in a given case. For example, the resources counsel will commit to the case must be appropriate to its needs, but the court should be careful not to limit consideration to lawyers with the greatest resources.

If, after review of all applicants, the court concludes that none would be satisfactory class counsel, it may deny class certification, reject all applications, recommend that an application be modified, invite new applications, or make any other appropriate order regarding selection and appointment of class counsel.

Paragraph (2). This paragraph sets out the procedure that should be followed in appointing class counsel. Although it affords substantial flexibility, it provides the framework for appointment of class counsel in all class actions. For counsel who filed the action, the materials submitted in support of the motion for class certification may suffice to justify appointment so long as the information described in paragraph (g)(1)(C) is included. If there are other applicants, they ordinarily would file a formal application detailing their suitability for the position.

In a plaintiff class action the court usually would appoint as class counsel only an attorney or attorneys who have sought appointment. Different considerations may apply in defendant class actions.

The rule states that the court should appoint "class counsel." In many instances, the applicant will be an individual attorney. In other cases, however, an entire firm, or perhaps numerous attorneys who are not otherwise affiliated but are collaborating on the action will apply. No rule of thumb exists to determine when such arrangements are appropriate; the court should be alert to the need for adequate staffing of the case, but also to the risk of overstaffing or an ungainly counsel structure.

Paragraph (2)(A) authorizes the court to designate interim counsel during the pre-certification period if necessary to protect the interests of the putative class. Rule 23(c)(1)(B) directs that the order certifying the class include appointment of class counsel. Before class certification, however, it will usually be important for an attorney to take action to prepare for the certification decision. The amendment to Rule 23(c)(1) recognizes that some discovery is often necessary for that determination. It also may be important to make or respond to motions before certification. Settlement may be discussed before certification. Ordinarily, such work is handled by the lawyer who filed the action. In some cases, however, there may be rivalry or uncertainty that makes formal designation of interim counsel appropriate. Rule 23(g)(2)(A) authorizes the court to designate interim counsel to act on behalf of the putative class before the certification decision is made. Failure to make the formal designation does not prevent the attorney who filed the action from proceeding in it. Whether or not formally designated interim counsel, an attorney who acts on behalf of the class before certification must act in the best interests of the class as a whole. For example, an attorney who negotiates a pre-certification settlement must seek a settlement that is fair, reasonable, and adequate for the class.

Rule 23(c)(1) provides that the court should decide whether to certify the class "at an early practicable time," and directs that class counsel should be appointed in the order certifying the class. In some cases, it may be appropriate for the court to allow a reasonable period after commencement of the action for filing applications to serve as class counsel. The primary ground for deferring appointment would be that there is reason to anticipate competing applications to serve as class counsel. Examples might include instances in which more than one class action has been filed, or in which other attorneys have filed individual actions on behalf of putative class members. The purpose of facilitating competing applications in such a case is to afford the best possible representation for the class. Another possible reason for deferring appointment would be that the initial applicant was found inadequate, but it seems appropriate to permit additional applications rather than deny class certification.

Paragraph (2)(B) states the basic standard the court should use in deciding whether to certify the class and appoint class counsel in the single applicant situation—that the applicant be able to provide the representation called for by paragraph (1)(B) in light of the factors identified in paragraph (1)(C).

If there are multiple adequate applicants, paragraph (2)(B) directs the court to select the class counsel best able to represent the interests of the class. This decision should also be made using the factors outlined in paragraph (1)(C), but in the multiple applicant situation the court is to go beyond scrutinizing the adequacy of counsel and make a comparison of the strengths of the various applicants. As with the decision whether to appoint the sole applicant for the position, no single factor should be dispositive in selecting class counsel in cases in which there are multiple applicants. The fact that a given attorney filed the instant action, for example, might not weigh heavily in the decision if that lawyer had not done significant work identifying or investigating claims. Depending on the nature of the case, one important consideration might be the applicant's existing attorney-client relationship with the proposed class representative.

Paragraph (2)(C) builds on the appointment process by authorizing the court to include provisions regarding attorneys' fees in the order appointing class counsel. Courts may find it desirable to adopt guidelines for fees or nontaxable costs, or to direct class counsel to report to the court at regular intervals on the efforts undertaken in the action, to facilitate the court's later determination of a reasonable attorneys' fee.

Subdivision (h). Subdivision (h) is new. Fee awards are a powerful influence on the way attorneys initiate, develop, and conclude class actions. Class action attorney fee awards have heretofore been handled, along with all other attorney fee awards, under Rule 54(d)(2), but that rule is not addressed to the particular concerns of class actions. This subdivision is designed to work in tandem with new subdivision (g) on appointment of class counsel, which may afford an opportunity for the court to provide an early framework for an eventual fee award, or for monitoring the work of class counsel during the pendency of the action.

Subdivision (h) applies to "an action certified as a class action." This includes cases in which there is a simultaneous proposal for class certification and settlement even though technically the class may not be certified unless the court approves the settlement pursuant to review under Rule 23(e). When a settlement is proposed for Rule 23(e) approval, either after certification or with a request for certification, notice to class members about class counsel's fee motion would ordinarily accompany the notice to the class about the settlement proposal itself.

This subdivision does not undertake to create new grounds for an award of attorneys' fees or nontaxable costs. Instead, it applies when such awards are authorized by law or by agreement of the parties. Against that background, it provides a format for all awards of attorneys' fees and nontaxable costs in connection with a class action, not only the award to class counsel. In some situations, there may be a basis for making an award to other counsel whose work produced a beneficial result for the class, such as attorneys who acted for the class before certification but were not appointed class counsel, or attorneys who represented objectors to a proposed settlement under Rule 23(e) or to the fee motion of class counsel. Other situations in which fee awards are authorized by law or by agreement of the parties may exist.

This subdivision authorizes an award of "reasonable" attorneys' fees and nontaxable costs. This is the customary term for measurement of fee awards in cases in which counsel may obtain an award of fees under the "common fund" theory that applies in many class actions, and is used in many fee-shifting statutes. Depending on the circumstances, courts have approached the determination of what is reasonable in different ways. In particular, there is some variation among courts about whether in "common fund" cases the court should use the lodestar or a percentage method of determining what fee is reasonable. The rule does not attempt to resolve the question whether the lodestar or percentage approach should be viewed as preferable.

Active judicial involvement in measuring fee awards is singularly important to the proper operation of the class-action process. Continued reliance on caselaw development of fee-award measures does not diminish the court's responsibility. In a class action, the district court must ensure that the amount and mode of payment of attorneys' fees are fair and proper whether the fees come from a common fund or are otherwise paid. Even in the absence of objections, the court bears this responsibility.

Courts discharging this responsibility have looked to a variety of factors. One fundamental focus is the result actually achieved for class members, a basic consideration in any case in which fees are sought on the basis of a benefit achieved for class members. The Private Securities Litigation Reform Act of 1995 explicitly makes this factor a cap for a fee award in actions to which it applies. See 15 U.S.C. §§ 77z-1(a)(6); 78u-4(a)(6) (fee award should not exceed a "reasonable percentage of the amount of any damages and prejudgment interest actually paid to the class"). For a percentage approach to fee measurement, results achieved is the basic starting point.

In many instances, the court may need to proceed with care in assessing the value conferred on class members. Settlement regimes that provide for future payments, for example, may not result in significant actual payments to class members. In this connection, the court may need to scrutinize the manner and operation of any applicable claims procedure. In some cases, it may be appropriate to defer some portion of the fee award until actual payouts to class members are known. Settlements involving nonmonetary provisions for class members also deserve careful scrutiny to ensure that these provisions have actual value to the class. On occasion the court's Rule 23(e) review will provide a solid basis for this sort of evaluation, but in any event it is also important to assessing the fee award for the class.

At the same time, it is important to recognize that in some class actions the monetary relief obtained is not the sole determinant of an appropriate attorneys fees award. Cf. *Blanchard v. Bergeron*, 489 U.S. 87, 95 (1989) (cautioning in an individual case against an "undesirable emphasis" on "the importance of the recovery of damages in civil rights litigation" that might "shortchange efforts to seek effective injunctive or declaratory relief").

Any directions or orders made by the court in connection with appointing class counsel under Rule 23(g) should weigh heavily in making a fee award under this subdivision.

Courts have also given weight to agreements among the parties regarding the fee motion, and to agreements between class counsel and others about the fees claimed by the motion. Rule 54(d)(2)(B) provides: "If directed by the court, the motion shall also disclose the terms of any agreement with respect to fees to be paid for the services for which claim is made." The agreement by a settling party not to oppose a fee application up to a certain amount, for example, is worthy of consideration, but the court remains responsible to determine a reasonable fee. "Side agreements" regarding fees provide at least perspective pertinent to an appropriate fee award.

In addition, courts may take account of the fees charged by class counsel or other attorneys for representing individual claimants or objectors in the case. In determining a fee for class counsel, the court's objective is to ensure an overall fee that is fair for counsel and equitable within the class. In some circumstances individual fee agreements between class counsel and class members might have provisions inconsistent with those goals, and the court might determine that adjustments in the class fee award were necessary as a result.

Finally, it is important to scrutinize separately the application for an award covering nontaxable costs. If costs were addressed in the order appointing class counsel, those directives should be a presumptive starting point in determining what is an appropriate award.

Paragraph (1). Any claim for an award of attorneys' fees must be sought by motion under Rule 54(d)(2), which invokes the provisions for timing of appeal in Rule 58 and Appellate Rule 4. Owing to the distinctive features of class action fee motions, however, the provisions of this subdivision control disposition of fee motions in class actions, while Rule 54(d)(2) applies to matters not addressed in this subdivision.

The court should direct when the fee motion must be filed. For motions by class counsel in cases subject to court review of a proposed settlement under Rule 23(e), it would be important to require the filing of at least the initial motion in time for inclusion of information about the motion in the notice to the class about the proposed settlement that is required by Rule 23(e). In cases litigated to judgment, the court might also order class counsel's motion to be filed promptly so that notice to the class under this subdivision (h) can be given.

Besides service of the motion on all parties, notice of class counsel's motion for attorneys' fees must be "directed to the class in a reasonable manner." Because members of the class have an interest in the arrangements for payment of class counsel whether that payment comes from the class fund or is made directly by another party, notice is required in all instances. In cases in which settlement approval is contemplated under Rule 23(e), notice of class counsel's fee motion should be combined with notice of the proposed settlement, and the provision regarding notice to the class is parallel to the requirements for notice under Rule 23(e). In adjudicated class actions, the court may calibrate the notice to avoid undue expense.

Paragraph (2). A class member and any party from whom payment is sought may object to the fee motion. Other parties—for example, nonsettling defendants—may not object because they lack a sufficient interest in the amount the court awards. The rule does not specify a time limit for making an objection. In setting the date objections are due, the court should provide sufficient time after the full fee motion is on file to enable potential objectors to examine the motion.

The court may allow an objector discovery relevant to the objections. In determining whether to allow discovery, the court should weigh the need for the information against the cost and delay that would attend discovery. See Rule 26(b)(2). One factor in determining whether to authorize discovery is the completeness of the material submitted in support of the fee motion, which depends in part on the fee measurement standard applicable to the case. If the motion provides thorough information, the burden should be on the objector to justify discovery to obtain further information.

Paragraph (3). Whether or not there are formal objections, the court must determine whether a fee award is justified and, if so, set a reasonable fee. The rule does not require a formal hearing in all cases. The form and extent of a hearing depend on the circumstances of the case. The rule does require findings and conclusions under Rule 52(a).

Paragraph (4). By incorporating Rule 54(d)(2), this provision gives the court broad authority to obtain assistance in determining the appropriate amount to award. In deciding whether to direct submission of such questions to a special master or magistrate judge, the court should give appropriate consideration to the cost and delay that such a process might entail.

2007 Amendment

The language of Rule 23 has been amended as part of the general restyling of the Civil Rules to make them more easily understood and to make style and terminology consistent throughout the rules. These changes are intended to be stylistic only.

Amended Rule 23(d)(2) carries forward the provisions of former Rule 23(d) that recognize two separate propositions. First, a Rule 23(d) order may be combined with a pretrial order under Rule 16. Second, the standard for amending the Rule 23(d) order continues to be the more open-ended standard for amending Rule 23(d) orders, not the more exacting standard for amending Rule 16 orders.

As part of the general restyling, intensifiers that provide emphasis but add no meaning are consistently deleted. Amended Rule 23(f) omits as redundant the explicit reference to court of appeals discretion in deciding whether to permit an interlocutory appeal. The omission does not in any way limit the unfettered discretion established by the original rule.

2009 Amendment

The time set in the former rule at 10 days has been revised to 14 days. See the Note to Rule 6.

Fed. Rules Civ. Proc. Rule 23, 28 U.S.C.A., FRCP Rule 23

Including Amendments Received Through 8-1-17

UNITED STATES SUPREME COURT

1 First Street N.E.
Washington, D.C. 20543

By Jordan Elias*
Girard Sharp LLP

1. INTRODUCTION

Decisions of the Roberts Court apply a strict constructionist approach to the governing class action rules. The Court's opinions reflect different views on how to balance competing but make clear that Rule 23 must be interpreted as written: "[O]f overriding importance, courts must be mindful that the Rule as now composed sets the requirements they are bound to enforce." *Amchem Prods., Inc. v. Windsor*, 521 U.S. 591, 620 (1997). A 2024 concurrence restates this basic point: "A class action allows a named plaintiff to represent others with similar injuries, but it is subject to the many requirements of Federal Rule of Civil Procedure 23." *FDA v. Alliance for Hippocratic Medicine*, 602 U.S. 367, 402 (2024) (Thomas, J., concurring).

Although the Court has issued unanimous opinions on minor points of class action procedure,[2] it has been divided on larger questions. Apart from Rule 23, the Justices have disagreed in recent cases presenting issues of Article III standing and arbitration. Together, these standing and arbitration decisions have had an outsized impact on class action practice, making an introductory study worthwhile.

a. Article III Standing

Just as the Court construes Rule 23 within its textual limits, it shuns "loosen[ing] Article III based on contemporary, evolving beliefs about what kinds of suits should be heard in federal courts." *TransUnion LLC v Ramirez*, 594 U.S. 413, 424–25 (2021). Article III limits the power of the federal judiciary to the resolution of actual cases and controversies, meaning that a plaintiff must have a "personal stake" in the dispute. *Raines v. Byrd*, 521 U.S. 811, 820 (1997). The Court's recent standing decisions in *TransUnion* and *Spokeo* bear on class actions asserting intangible or other harm from invasions of statutory rights—such as those created by the Fair Credit Reporting Act of 1970, 15 U.S.C. § 1681 *et seq.*, the statute at issue in both cases.

In *Spokeo Inc. v. Robins*, the Court held that whether an asserted injury qualifies for Article III standing depends on whether the injury is "'real,' and not 'abstract'"—which raises the question of what injuries are "real" enough to be cognizable. 578 U.S. 330, 340 (2016) (citations omitted). The Court gave only a partial answer. It advised that "intangible injuries can neverthe-

* J.D., Stanford Law School, 2003; B.A. *magna cum laude*, Yale College, 1998. The views and research in this chapter are my own.

[2] For example, in *China Agritech, Inc. v. Resh*, the Justices agreed that the tolling of statutes of limitations by a class action filing does not apply to class—as opposed to individual—claims filed after a denial of class certification. 584 U.S. 732 (2018) (distinguishing American Pipe & Constr. Co. v. Utah, 414 U.S. 538 (1974)). And in *Microsoft Corporation v. Baker*, the Court unanimously held (with three Justices concurring in the judgment) that class plaintiffs cannot create a final judgment subject to immediate appellate review by voluntarily dismissing their claims upon a denial of certification. 582 U.S. 23 (2017).

less be concrete" and that "both history and the judgment of Congress play important roles" in determining whether an alleged intangible harm confers standing. *Id.* at 340–41. Congress can "define injuries and articulate chains of causation that will give rise to a case or controversy where none existed before," and "the violation of a procedural right granted by statute can be sufficient in some circumstances to constitute injury in fact." *Id.* at 341 (emphasis added) (citation omitted). But the inquiry into concreteness also considers whether the plaintiff has sufficiently pleaded or proved harm similar to what is traditionally actionable in American courts. *Id.* So "Congress' role in identifying and elevating intangible harms does not mean that a plaintiff automatically satisfies the injury-in-fact requirement whenever a statute grants a person a statutory right and purports to authorize that person to sue to vindicate that right." *Id.* In other words, the mere violation of a statutory right, "divorced from any concrete harm," does not "satisfy the injury-in-fact requirement of Article III." *Id.* Before remanding for further proceedings, the Court offered an example of a "bare" or illusory harm: "It is difficult to imagine the dissemination of an incorrect zip code, without more, could work any concrete harm." *Id.* at 342.

In a dissent joined by Justice Sotomayor, Justice Ginsburg opined that the plaintiff experienced concrete harm by having his job prospects diminished by the posting of inaccurate information about him on the Spokeo website.[3] Earlier law, the dissent recalls, holds that courts should not attempt to resolve "abstract, intellectual problems, but adjudicate concrete, living contests between adversaries" and that "whether the conflicting contentions of the parties present a real, substantial controversy between parties having adverse legal interests is a question "of degree" that is "not discernable by any precise test." *Spokeo*, 578 U.S. at 352–53 (Ginsburg, J., dissenting) (citations omitted).

TransUnion picks up where *Spokeo* left off, applying the Article III standing limitation based upon illusory harm. Individuals whose credit reports mistakenly said they were on a governmental watch list for potential terrorists, drug traffickers, or other serious criminals, and who requested a copy of their report, could not recover out of a class-wide verdict, the 5–4 majority held, because they had not demonstrated a concrete injury. The Court reiterated that the constitutional limitation on judicial power means the plaintiff must have sustained a real or definite harm to seek or obtain relief. *TransUnion*, 594 U.S. at 424–25.

In *Spokeo*, the Court stated that "the judgment of Congress"—in addition to legal tradition—is "important" in determining whether an asserted injury is sufficiently concrete to give rise to Article III standing. 578 U.S. at 340. But in *TransUnion*, the Court held that although Congress can define new rights, a cause of action for violating them still requires a "harm 'traditionally' recognized as providing a basis for a lawsuit in American courts." 594 U.S. at 424–26. Hence the "*[c]entral*" question is whether there is a "close historical or common-law analogue for the[] asserted injury," with allowance that standing "does not require an exact duplicate in American history and tradition." *Id.* at 417, 424 (emphasis added).

The Court concluded that those who were sent the erroneous credit reports without evidence of any further distribution had not established concrete harm. Defamation requires publication of the falsehoods, but there was no evidence that certain of the credit reports were sent to a third party. *Id.* at 432–37. Nor was there evidence that the class members who requested those reports "were independently harmed by their exposure to the risk itself—that is, that they suffered some other injury (such as an emotional injury) from the mere risk that their credit reports would be provided to third-party businesses." *Id.* at 437. Thus, of the 8,185 individuals who were incorrectly classified as a potential threat, only the 1,853 class members whose credit reports were demonstrably provided to third parties suffered an injury in fact. The other 6,332 class members—whose reports were not shown to have been sent to lenders, employers, or others—could not recover under the judgment. *Id.* at 438–39. The Court accordingly applied its holding that "[e]very class member must have Article III standing in order to recover individual

[3] On remand, the Ninth Circuit held that the plaintiff sufficiently alleged a concrete injury, and the Supreme Court denied a subsequent certiorari petition. Robins v. Spokeo, Inc., 867 F.3d 1108 (9th Cir. 2017), cert. denied, 583 U.S. 1102 (2018).

damages," leaving open whether a class containing uninjured members can be certified prior to judgment. *Id.* at 431 & n.4.

Dissenting and joined by Justices Breyer, Sotomayor, and Kagan, Justice Thomas would have found standing because "TransUnion unlawfully withheld from each class member the [misleading] version of his or her credit report that the class member requested. And TransUnion unlawfully failed to send a summary of rights." *Id.* at 454 (Thomas, J., dissenting). Congress can create new private rights that confer standing even without a showing of actual damage, consistent with tradition, the dissent maintains: "Where an individual sought to sue someone for a violation of his private rights, such as trespass on his land, the plaintiff needed only to allege the violation" and "[n]ever before has this Court declared that legal injury is *inherently* insufficient to support standing." *Id.* at 447, 453–54 & n.5 (Thomas, J., dissenting).

Justice Kagan filed a separate dissent that refers to the majority opinion as "so mistaken," commenting that "this case should be easy. . . . TransUnion willfully violated [the FCRA] by preparing credit files that falsely called the plaintiffs potential terrorists, and by obscuring that fact when the plaintiffs requested copies of their files. To say, as the majority does, that the resulting injuries did not 'exist in the real world' is to inhabit a world I don't know." *Id.* at 461 (Kagan, J., dissenting). Further, "Congress is better suited than courts to determine when something causes a harm or risk of harm in the real world. . . . Overriding an authorization to sue is appropriate when but only when Congress could not reasonably have thought that a suit will contribute to compensating or preventing the harm at issue." *Id.* at 462–63 (Kagan, J., dissenting).

b. Arbitration

While these standing rulings continue to play out in class actions asserting statutory violations, the Court's arbitration jurisprudence has transformed class litigation by limiting suits arising out of form contracts used in the mass economy, including in online commerce. A series of decisions starting with *AT&T Mobility LLC v. Concepcion*, 563 U.S. 333 (2011), holds that these contracts must be enforced as written to preclude class action lawsuits. Dissenting Justices responded that enforcing compulsory arbitration clauses inhibits access to the courts, giving violators a free pass. This line of cases culminated in *Epic Systems Corporation v. Lewis*, where the 5-4 majority held that employers can condition employment on arbitration agreements that prevent employees from maintaining a class action in court against the company or its managers. 584 U.S. 497 (2018).

The Court concluded that the National Labor Relations Act's guarantee of workers' right to engage in "concerted activities for the purpose of collective bargaining or other mutual aid or protection" does not justify invalidating provisions that waive workers' right to bring class claims because the "concerted activities" Congress had in mind were collective bargaining and formation of labor unions, rather than litigation. *Id.* at 511–13. A dissent from Justice Ginsburg and joined by Justices Breyer, Sotomayor, and Kagan asserts that the Court's arbitration case law has taken "many wrong turns" and serves to exculpate wrongdoers because "[e]xpenses entailed in mounting individual claims will often far outweigh potential recoveries." *Id.* at 547–50 (Ginsburg, J., dissenting).

Sharp disagreement also marks the Court's 5–3 decision in *American Express Co. v. Italian Colors Restaurant*, 570 U.S. 228 (2013), which like *Epic Systems* weighs the policies of the Federal Arbitration Act against arguments for enforcement of a coordinate federal statute. A restaurant alleging an antitrust tying violation filed a class action against American Express on behalf of similarly situated merchants. Justice Scalia's opinion for the Court held that the restaurant could not nullify a provision in its contract with American Express mandating that all disputes between them be decided in individual arbitration. Rejecting the argument that enforcing this clause would grant immunity, the Court held that "courts must 'rigorously enforce' arbitration agreements according to their terms." 570 U.S. at 233 (citation omitted). Only if an arbitration agreement waives a party's right to *pursue* statutory remedies may the agreement be invalidated, the Court reasoned, and the class waiver "no more eliminates [the contracting] parties' right to pursue their statutory remedy than did federal law before its adoption of the class action . . . in 1938." *Id.* at 236. Moreover, the Federal Arbitration Act's "command to enforce arbitration agreements trumps any interest in ensuring the prosecution of low-value claims." *Id.* at 238 n.5.

Finding this reasoning excessively formalistic, Justice Kagan, joined by Justices Ginsburg and Breyer, opined in dissent that for the restaurant to pursue its claim individually in arbitration would be a "fool's errand" as "[n]o rational actor would bring a claim worth tens of thousands of dollars if doing so meant incurring costs in the hundreds of thousands." *Id.* at 240, 245 (Kagan, J., dissenting). The dissent also colorfully comments that the majority—"bent on diminishing the usefulness of Rule 23"—had reasoned as if it were still "ye olde glory days." *Id.* at 251–52 (Kagan, J., dissenting).

c. Chapter Overview

In keeping with how class action issues that reach the Supreme Court are often analyzed, this chapter focuses more on public policy than do the circuit-by-circuit chapters that show how the Court's decisions have been applied. After a short detour into the origins and development of class actions in our legal system, the chapter examines how the Court has approached dueling policies embedded in Rule 23, such as efficiency, economy, and procedural fairness. The discussion then shifts gears, delving more deeply into *Amchem* and two other leading decisions from the class action's formative years, *Hansberry v. Lee*, 311 U.S. 32 (1940), and *Phillips Petroleum Co. v. Shutts*, 472 U.S. 797 (1985). The chapter proceeds to consider how class action jurisprudence has evolved in the first quarter of the twenty-first century. The conclusion frames some open questions of class action law that the Supreme Court may address in years to come.

2. CLASS ACTION ORIGINS AND DEVELOPMENT

With roots in medieval group litigation, representative suits took their place in early American legal practice. *See* Stephen C. Yeazell, *Group Litigation and Social Context: Toward a History of the Class Action*, 77 Colum. L. Rev. 866 (1977) (describing seventeenth century chancery suits by English lords and clergy against groups of rural tenants or parishioners for tithes and other property); Zechariah Chafee, Jr., *Bills of Peace with Multiple Parties*, 45 Harv. L. Rev. 1297, 1303–07 (1932) (reviewing the early history of bills of peace with multiple parties). In the fledgling republic, old Equity Rule 48, amended in 1912 as Equity Rule 38, recognized a precursor to the class action. In the antebellum era the Supreme Court articulated what remains the core rationale for representative litigation: "Where the parties interested in the suit are numerous . . . it would not be possible, without very great inconvenience, to make all of them parties, and would oftentimes prevent the prosecution of the suit to a hearing. For convenience, therefore, and to prevent a failure of justice, a court of equity permits a portion of the parties in interest to represent the entire body, and the decree binds all of them the same as if all were before the court." *Smith v. Swormstedt*, 57 U.S. (16 How.) 288, 303 (1853). The Court, citing Justice Story's commentaries on equity pleadings, deemed it "well established" that "where the parties interested are numerous, and the suit is for an object common to them all, some of the body may maintain a bill on behalf of themselves and of the others; and a bill may also be maintained against a portion of a numerous body of defendants, representing a common interest." *Id.* at 302; *see also Hartford Life Ins. Co. v. Ibs*, 237 U.S. 662, 672 (1915); *Beatty v. Kurtz*, 27 U.S. (2 Pet.) 566, 585 (1829) (Story, J.) ("certain persons . . . having a common interest, may sue in behalf of themselves and others having the like interest, as part of the same society; for purposes common to all, and beneficial to all"); *West v. Randall*, 29 F. Cas. 718, 722–23 (C.C.D.R.I. 1820) (Story, J.) (in certain "cases of general right" the court may "dispense with having all the parties, who claim the same right, before it, from the manifest inconvenience, if not impossibility of doing it, and is satisfied with bringing so many before it, as may be considered as fairly representing that right, and honestly contesting in behalf of the whole, and therefore binding, in a sense, that right"). Such cases, the Court pronounced in *Swormstedt*, embody an exception to the general rule that all interested parties must be joined[4]—and "care must be taken that persons are brought on the record fairly representing the interest or right involved, so that it may be fully and honestly tried." 57 U.S. at 303. Hence the twin concerns of efficiency and fundamental fairness have animated the American class action. *See, e.g.*, Deborah R. Hensler, *Happy 50th Anniversary, Rule 23! Shouldn't We Know You Better After All This Time?*, 165 U. Pa. L. Rev. 1599, 1600 (2017) ("The joining of group litigation with a legal regime based on individual autonomy was long considered mainly a marriage of convenience, justified by the inefficiency of resolving large numbers of claims arising out of the same facts and law in individual proceedings.").

Toward the end of the nineteenth century, three "'Old Settlers,' or 'Western Cherokee,' Indians" sued the federal government on behalf of the tribe. *United States v. "Old Settlers,"* 148 U.S. 427, 427–28 (1893). The Supreme Court dismissed "the suggestion that these so-called 'commissioners' d[id] not bring themselves as strictly within the rule [of *Swormstedt*] as they should," affirming a money judgment for the tribe as modified and concluding that the plaintiffs did "so far represent the interests or rights involved that the case may be allowed to proceed to judgment." *Id.* at 480. Further, there was no need for individual beneficiaries "to come in and establish their right to share in the fund"; the Court instead approved a process by which a committee of five would ascertain the beneficiaries and disburse awards on a *per capita* basis. *Id.* at 480–81.

Class actions in the nineteenth century did not bind absent parties unless the court so ordered.[5] But in 1921, the Supreme Court held that a federal diversity judgment permitting a fraternal benefit society's reorganization precluded a subsequent state court action challenging that reorganization. *Supreme Tribe of Ben Hur v. Cauble*, 255 U.S. 356 (1921). Under *Swormstedt* and Equity Rule 38, the earlier decree bound the class, including its Indiana members, since "their rights were duly represented by those before the court" and "[i]f the decree is to be effective and conflicted judgments are to be avoided, all of the class must be concluded by the decree." *Supreme Tribe of Ben Hur*, 255 U.S. at 366–67.

Among the innovations of the New Deal was the merger of law and equity, intended to simplify legal practice, and to that end the Federal Rules of Civil Procedure supplanted the old code pleading system. The original 1938 version of Rule 23, however, was formalistically framed according to legal categories. It provided that:

> If persons constituting a class are so numerous as to make it impracticable to bring them all before the court, such of them, one or more, as will fairly insure the adequate representation of all may, on behalf of all, sue or be sued when the character of the right sought to be enforced for or against the class is (1) joint, or common, or secondary in the sense that an owner of a primary right refuses to enforce that right and a member of the class thereby becomes entitled to enforce it; or (2) several, and the object of the action is the adjudication of claims which do or may affect specific property involved in the action; or (3) several, and there is a common question of law or fact affecting the several rights and a common relief is sought.

A subdivision governing shareholder derivative suits followed, and then a subdivision requiring court approval for any dismissal or compromise of a class action with corresponding notice required to the members of a class certified under subdivision (a)(1). The three types

[4] *See* Fed. R. Civ. P. 12(b)(7), 19 (a civil action may be dismissed for failure to join an indispensable party).

[5] *See* Geoffrey C. Hazard, Jr. et al., *An Historical Analysis of the Binding Effect of Class Suits*, 146 U. Pa. L. Rev. 1849 (1998); George M. Strickler, Jr., *Protecting the Class: The Search for the Adequate Representative in Class Action Litigation*, 34 DePaul L. Rev. 73, 78 (1984).

of classes defined in the rule were known as "true," "hybrid," and "spurious," respectively. The 1938 rule's "silence . . . on the matter of who would be bound by a judgment was thought to be a necessary concession to the requirement that the rules not determine substantive rights." John G. Harkins, Jr., *Federal Rule 23—The Early Years*, 39 Ariz. L. Rev. 705, 708 (1997) (citation omitted).

Predictably, Rule 23 spurred an expansion of class litigation in the federal courts. Many of the new cases filed mid-century alleged securities fraud or overtime pay violations, complex subject matter not previously litigated in class cases. *See* Zechariah Chafee, *Some Problems of Equity* 200 (1950). And in practice, the asymmetric quality of the "spurious" class action proved unjust. Class members in such an action could wait until after entry of judgment to decide whether to intervene and be bound by the outcome. *See* James W. Moore, *Federal Rules of Civil Procedure: Some Problems Raised by the Preliminary Draft*, 25 Geo. L.J. 551, 574–76 (1937) (the architect of Rule 23 described the spurious class action as a permissive joinder device—"an invitation to become a fellow traveller in the litigation, which might or might not be accepted"). The rule consequently gave class members an incentive to intervene only upon entry of a judgment favorable to them. The 1966 amendments removed this nonmutual procedure, providing that a judgment in an action for money damages under subdivision (b)(3) binds the class members, who are, however, entitled to notice of the action and the opportunity to opt out to avoid the judgment's binding effect.

The 1966 overhaul cast the rule in functional rather than formal terms, eliminating "Moore's accursed labels" for the various types of class actions. Harry Kalven, Jr. & Maurice Rosenfield, *The Contemporary Function of the Class Suit*, 8 U. Chi. L. Rev. 684, 707 n.73 (1941); *see Snyder v. Harris*, 394 U.S. 332, 343 (1969) (Fortas, J., dissenting) (the amended rule "replaced the metaphysics of conceptual analysis of the 'character of the right sought to be enforced' by a pragmatic, workable definition of when class actions might be maintained"). In addition to all four Rule 23(a) subdivisions, a plaintiff must satisfy at least one Rule 23(b) subdivision to maintain a class action, and "[i]n drafting Rule 23(b), the Advisory Committee sought to catalogue . . . 'those recurrent life patterns which call for mass litigation through representative parties.'" *Ortiz v. Fibreboard Corp.*, 527 U.S. 815, 833 (1999) (quoting Benjamin Kaplan, *A Prefatory Note*, 10 B.C. Indus. & Com. L. Rev. 497, 497 (1969)). Rule 23(b)(1) applies to mandatory class actions—examined in *Ortiz*—while Rule 23(b)(3) replaced the "spurious" opt-in class action. *See Amchem*, 521 U.S. at 614. Rule 23(b)(2) governs class actions for injunctive or declaratory relief, requires that the relief sought be unitary, and may apply in actions for an injunction to enforce civil rights laws. *See Wal-Mart Stores, Inc. v. Dukes*, 564 U.S. 338, 360–63 (2011); Fed. R. Civ. P. 23(b)(2) advisory committee's note (1966).[6]

3. COMPETING POLICIES IN CLASS ACTIONS

Supreme Court law recognizes that class actions serve important needs but are also subject to abuse and demand careful oversight. The Justices return to the text of Rule 23 for ultimate guidance. Chief Justice Burger summed up the rule's purpose as "promot[ing] judicial economy by allowing for litigation of common questions of law and fact at one time. We have

[6] Notice to the class is optional in actions for injunctive or declaratory relief, which do not carry the opt-out right. *See* Fed. R. Civ. P. 23(c)(2)(A); *Wal-Mart*, 564 U.S. at 360–63; Fed. R. Civ. P. 23(c)(2) advisory committee's note (2003). For a discussion of issues relating to declaratory relief class actions, *see* Andrew Bradt, "*Much to Gain and Nothing to Lose": Implications of the History of the Declaratory Judgment for the (b)(2) Class Action*, 58 Ark. L. Rev. 767 (2006). In a recent 23(b)(2) case brought on behalf of the "involuntary homeless" in an Oregon city, lower courts struck down a local law that prohibited camping in public areas. The Supreme Court reversed in a 6–3 decision, holding that the ordinance and its penalties did not amount to cruel and unusual punishment. *City of Grants Pass, Oregon v. Johnson*, 144 S. Ct. 2202 (2024).

stressed that strict attention to the requirements of Rule 23 is indispensable." *General Tel. Co. of Sw. v. Falcon*, 457 U.S. 147, 161 (1982) (Burger, C.J., concurring in part and dissenting in part) (citations omitted); *see also East Texas Motor Freight Sys. Inc. v. Rodriguez*, 431 U.S. 395, 405 (1977) (instructing courts to pay "careful attention to the requirements of" Rule 23). "[A] district court has both the duty and the broad authority to exercise control over a class action and to enter appropriate orders governing the conduct of counsel and parties. But this discretion is not unlimited, and indeed is bounded by the relevant provisions of the Federal Rules." *Gulf Oil Co. v. Bernard*, 452 U.S. 89, 100 (1981). Thus, for example, because Rule 23 refers to a class action being "maintained," rather than merely "permitted," a district court lacks discretion to deny class certification if the rule is satisfied. *Shady Grove Orthopedic Assocs., P.A. v. Allstate Ins. Co.*, 559 U.S. 393, 399–401 (2010). A class certification decision is reviewed for an abuse of discretion. *Califano*, 442 U.S. at 703.

Importantly, "the right of a litigant to employ Rule 23 is a procedural right only, ancillary to the litigation of substantive claims." *Deposit Guar. Nat'l Bank, Jackson, Miss. v. Roper*, 445 U.S. 326, 332 (1980). The Rules Enabling Act limits the scope of class litigation through its command that procedural rules "shall not abridge, enlarge or modify any substantive right." 28 U.S.C. § 2072(b); *see Ortiz*, 527 U.S. at 845 ("As we said in *Amchem*, no reading of the Rule can ignore the [Rules Enabling] Act's mandate"); *Principles of the Law of Aggregate Litigation* § 2.02 cmt. d (Am. Law. Inst. 2010) ("Aggregate treatment thus is possible when a trial would allow for the presentation of evidence sufficient to demonstrate the validity or invalidity of all claims with respect to a common issue under applicable substantive law, without altering the substantive standards that would be applied were each claim to be tried independently and without compromising the ability of the defendant to dispute the allegations made by claimants or to raise pertinent substantive defenses.").

The fairness considerations of Rule 23 protect the due process rights of the plaintiff, class members, and defendant.[7] The rule's efficiency rationale includes several aims—not just relieving the justice system of duplicative litigation[8] but also delivering relief to numerous persons at once;[9] not just deterring violations by allowing pursuit of relatively small claims[10] but also ensuring that defendants can take repose in a preclusive classwide judgment.[11] The below chart suggested by the Supreme Court's class action precedents depicts

[7] **Fairness:** Eisen v. Carlisle & Jacquelin, 417 U.S. 156, 173 (1974) ("[O]f course" the class action procedure is subject to "requirements of due process") (quoting Fed. R. Civ. P. 23(d)(2) advisory committee's note (1966)); *Wal-Mart*, 564 U.S. at 367 ("Because the Rules Enabling Act forbids interpreting Rule 23 to 'abridge, enlarge or modify any substantive right,' a class cannot be certified on the premise that [the defendant] will not be entitled to litigate its statutory defenses to individual claims.") (internal citations omitted); *see also* S. REP. NO. 109-14, at 14 (2005), *reprinted in* 2005 U.S.C.C.A.N. 3, 14 ("[T]he strict requirements of Rule 23 . . . are intended to protect the due process rights of both unnamed class members and defendants.").

[8] **Economy:** Califano v. Yamasaki, 442 U.S. 682, 690 (1979) ("[U]nnecessary duplication of actions" is "the evil that Rule 23 was designed to prevent."); Cooper v. Federal Reserve Bank of Richmond, 467 U.S. 867, 881 (1984) ("Indeed, Rule 23 is carefully drafted to provide a mechanism for the expeditious decision of common questions.").

[9] **Access/Redress:** *Amchem*, 521 U.S. at 617 ("The policy at the very core of the class action mechanism is to overcome the problem that small recoveries do not provide the incentive for any individual to bring a solo action.") (citation omitted); *Roper*, 445 U.S. at 338–39 ("Where it is not economically feasible to obtain relief within the traditional framework of a multiplicity of small individual suits for damages, aggrieved persons may be without any effective redress unless they may employ the class-action device.").

[10] **Deterrence:** Reiter v. Sonotone Corp., 442 U.S. 330, 344 (1979) ("[P]rivate suits provide a significant supplement to the limited resources available to the Department of Justice for enforcing the antitrust laws and deterring violations."); Amgen Inc. v. Connecticut Ret. Plans & Tr. Funds, 568 U.S. 455, 475–78 (2013) (similar conclusion regarding deterrence of securities fraud) (citing, *inter alia*, Tellabs, Inc. v. Makor Issues & Rights, Ltd., 551 U.S. 308, 313 (2007)).

[11] **Finality:** Phillips Petroleum Co. v. Shutts, 472 U.S. 797, 805 (1985) ("Whether it wins or loses on the merits, [the defendant] has a distinct and personal interest in seeing the entire plaintiff class bound by res judicata"); *Cooper*, 467

how this policy triad of efficiency, fairness, and finality interacts with the rule over the life of a case.

CONTROVERSY
(Preexisting commonality/generally applicable conduct)
⇩

	EFFICIENCY	FAIRNESS
<u>All cases</u>	Joinder impracticable	<u>To class</u>: Adequacy of representation <u>To defendant</u>: Class claims fairly encompassed; Rules Enabling Act
<u>Money damages</u>	Superior means	<u>To class</u>: Notice and opt-out right <u>To defendant</u>: Predominating common questions

⇩
FINALITY
(Collateral attack)

The efficiency and fairness interests codified in Rule 23(b)(3) permeate the rule. The order must define the class—the group that will be bound by the judgment in the case—using precise, objective criteria tailored to the operative facts. *See* Fed. R. Civ. P. 23(c)(1)(B), (c)(3).[12] The court in any class action is expressly empowered to "prescribe measures to prevent undue repetition or complication in presenting evidence or argument." Fed. R. Civ. P. 23(d)(1)(A). The inquiries under the last three subdivisions of Rule 23(a) "tend to merge," looking at whether the putative class claims are "fairly encompassed" by the named plaintiff's claims based on common questions, interests, and evidence, such that binding aggregate litigation is advantageous and just. *Falcon*, 457 U.S. at 158 n.13, 156–58.[13] Where class treatment is unfair it may also be inefficient. *See, e.g.*, *Falcon*, 457 U.S. at 159. If the defendant acted on grounds generally applicable to the class, such that injunctive-relief certification is appropriate under Rule 23(b)(2), "[p]redominance and superiority are self-evident." *Wal-Mart*, 564 U.S. at 363. Impracticability of joinder relates both to superiority and to the numerosity requirement for all class actions. *See Eisen*, 417 U.S. at 182; Fed. R. Civ. P. 23(a)(1), (b)(3)(A). The manageability and subclassing provisions modify each other, and the flexibility to amend class-related determinations allows courts to fashion suitably tailored remedies. *See* Fed. R. Civ. P. 23(b)(3)(D), (c)(5), (c)(1)(C), (c)(3). So although the Rule 23 analysis proceeds element by element, the inquiries overlap and are subject to the primary rule of statutory construction that all provisions must be read together and applied in light of one another.[14] Rule 23 also stands *in pari materia* with the other procedural rules providing for adjudication of multiple claims in a single proceeding—Rules 19, 20, and 42[15]—and with Rule 1, providing for the just, speedy, and inexpensive disposi-

U.S. at 874 ("[U]nder elementary principles of prior adjudication a judgment in a properly entertained class action is binding on class members in any subsequent litigation.").

[12] *See also* Jordan Elias, *The Ascertainability Landscape and the Modern Affidavit*, 84 Tenn. L. Rev. 1, 4–12 (2016).

[13] *See also* In re General Motors Corp. Pick-Up Truck Fuel Tank Prods. Liab. Litig., 55 F.3d 768, 785 (3d Cir. 1995) ("The drafters designed the procedural requirements of Rule 23, especially the requisites of subsection (a), so that the court can assure, to the greatest extent possible, that the actions are prosecuted on behalf of the actual class members in a way that makes it fair to bind their interests.").

[14] Oklahoma v. New Mexico, 501 U.S. 221, 246 (1991); Kohlsaat v. Murphy, 96 U.S. 153, 159–60 (1877).

[15] *See, e.g.*, *Snyder*, 394 U.S. at 337–40; *see also* Sprint Commc'ns Co. v. APCC Servs., Inc., 554 U.S. 269, 291 (2008)

tion of every civil action.

The policies underlying the class action can be understood as revolving around a series of dichotomies, discussed below.

a. Merits vs. Case Structure

The class action procedure cannot be used to abridge any party's substantive rights; by the same token, the procedural determination of whether a suit may proceed as a class action cannot adjudicate any claim or defense. The Supreme Court's *Wal-Mart* and *Amgen* decisions provide guidance on the distinction—and overlap—between the inquiries into how a case should be organized and its substantive merits.

Some confusion resulted from the Court's 1974 decision in *Eisen*, which held that a district judge erred in imposing nearly all of the notice costs on the defendants after conducting a preliminary minitrial and concluding that the class was "more than likely" to prevail. 417 U.S. at 177. The plaintiff "must pay for the cost of notice," the Supreme Court held, and "nothing in either the language or history of Rule 23 . . . gives a court any authority to conduct a preliminary inquiry into the merits of a suit in order to determine whether it may be maintained as a class action." *Id.* at 177–79.

In *Wal–Mart* and *Amgen*, the Court reconciled this holding with the reality that an analysis under Rule 23 of whether claim elements are subject to common proof may require examining that proof. *Wal–Mart* thus accepts that the "rigorous analysis" of whether the plaintiff has satisfied Rule 23 "[f]requently . . . will entail some overlap with the merits of the plaintiff's underlying claim." 564 U.S. at 350–51 (internal citations omitted). But while the proof at trial goes to who should prevail, the proof at class certification goes to how the case should be structured. Given this distinction, *Amgen* clarifies that courts have "no license to engage in free-ranging merits inquiries at the certification stage. Merits questions may be considered to the extent—but only to the extent—that they are relevant to determining whether the Rule 23 prerequisites . . . are satisfied." 568 U.S. at 466; *see Tyson Foods, Inc. v. Bouaphakeo*, 577 U.S. 442, 453 (2016) (the predominance inquiry of Rule 23(b)(3) "asks whether the common, aggregation-enabling, issues in the case are more prevalent or important than the non-common, aggregation-defeating, individual issues.") (quoting 2 William B. Rubenstein, *Newberg on Class Actions* § 4:49 (5th ed. 2012)).[16]

A minor rule change in 2003 anticipated the Supreme Court's focus on the burden of a plaintiff seeking certification to show that Rule 23 is satisfied by the preponderance of the evidence. By requiring courts to make certification decisions "at an early practicable time," instead of "as soon as practicable," the rule allows breathing room for parties to develop the evidentiary record to enable an informed determination. Fed. R. Civ. P. 23(c)(1)(A); *see* Fed. R. Civ. P. 23(c)(1) advisory committee's note (2003) (advising that, "[a]lthough an evaluation of the probable outcome on the merits is not properly part of the certification decision, discovery in aid of the certification decision often includes information required to identify the nature of the issues that actually will be presented at trial. . . . A critical need is to determine how the case will be tried.").

(class actions "are but one of several methods by which multiple similarly situated parties get similar claims resolved at one time and in one federal forum").

[16] *See also* Erica P. John Fund, Inc. v. Halliburton Co., 563 U.S. 804, 809 (2011) (*Halliburton I*) (the predominance inquiry "begins, of course, with the elements of the underlying cause of action"); Krakauer v. Dish Network, L.L.C., 925 F.3d 643, 655 (4th Cir. 2019) ("Efficient and manageable classes require common proof, and the availability of such proof turns on what exactly needs to be proven."); Rutstein v. Avis Rent-A-Car Sys., Inc., 211 F.3d 1228, 1234 (11th Cir. 2000) ("Whether an issue predominates can only be determined after considering what value the resolution of the class-wide issue will have in each class member's underlying cause of action.").

b. Small-Claim Vindication vs. Settlement Pressure

Trials are the exception rather than the rule in class action practice. *See* Richard A. Nagareda, *Class Certification in the Age of Aggregate Proof*, 84 N.Y.U. L. Rev. 97, 99 (2009). Justice Gorsuch's opinion for the Court in *Epic Systems Corporation v. Lewis* states that, "[w]hile . . . class actions can enhance enforcement by spreading the costs of litigation, it's also well known that they can unfairly place pressure on the defendant to settle even unmeritorious claims." Similarly, Justice Alito's dissent in *Home Depot U.S.A., Inc. v. Jackson* characterizes consumer class actions as "important (and often costly)." 587 U.S. 435, 447 (2019) (Alito, J., dissenting). 584 U.S. 497, 524 (2018) (internal quotation marks, citations, and alterations omitted).

Advancing small-claim aggregation, Rule 23(b)(3) calls for consideration of "the class members' interests in individually controlling the prosecution or defense or separate actions." Fed. R. Civ. P. 23(b)(3)(A). In enacting this provision the rulemakers "had dominantly in mind vindication of 'the rights of groups of people who individually would be without effective strength to bring their opponents into court at all.'" *Amchem*, 521 U.S. at 617 (quoting Kaplan, *A Prefatory Note*, 10 B.C. Indus. & Com. L. Rev. at 497); *see also* Fed. R. Civ. P. 23(b)(3) advisory committee's note (1966) ("[T]he amounts at stake for individuals may be so small that separate suits would be impracticable."). A class action, then, can "overcome the problem that small recoveries do not provide the incentive for any individual to bring a solo action prosecuting his or her rights." *Amchem*, 521 U.S. at 617 (citation omitted).

The Court has stressed this policy of combining low-value claims to promote access to justice. At one oral argument, Justice Gorsuch said, "I don't think anybody questions the importance of that—that function of the rule." Transcript of Oral Argument at 39, *China Agritech v. Resh*, No. 17-432, 2018 WL 1471037 (Mar. 26, 2018); *see, e.g.*, *Shutts*, 472 U.S. at 809 (recognizing that "most of the plaintiffs would have no realistic day in court if a class action were not available."); *Roper*, 445 U.S. at 339 (commenting that "aggrieved persons may be without any effective redress unless they may employ the class-action device"); *Exxon Shipping Co. v. Baker*, 554 U.S. 471, 515 n.28 (2008) (noting, in a discussion of punitive damages, that "the class option . . . facilitates suit" when individual "compensation may not be enough to encourage suit" and "large numbers of potential plaintiffs are involved"); *Eisen*, 417 U.S. at 161 ("Economic reality dictates that [plaintiff's] suit proceed as a class action or not at all."); *cf.* 2 William B. Rubenstein, *Newberg on Class Actions* § 4:88 (5th ed. 2012) (to the extent individual claims are larger, a class action is less likely to be superior).

At the same time, the Court recognizes that class certification may induce an unfair settlement. Justice Kavanaugh expressed concern during oral arguments about defendants being "coerced into a massive settlement because of the discovery" and, writing for the Court, quoted Judge Friendly's phrase "blackmail settlements." *Coinbase, Inc. v. Bielski*, 599 U.S. 736, 743 (2023); Transcript of Oral Argument at 69, No. 22-105 (Mar. 21, 2023). The Court in 2017 opined that "class certification often leads to a hefty settlement." *Baker*, 582 U.S. at 24, citing *Coopers & Lybrand v. Livesay*, an earlier decision acknowledging "criticism of the class action as a vexatious kind of litigation" and noting that "[c]ertification of a large class may so increase the defendant's potential damages liability and litigation costs that he may find it economically prudent to *settle* and to abandon a meritorious defense." 437 U.S. 463, 470, 476 (1978); *see also Amgen*, 568 U.S. at 485 (Scalia, J., dissenting) (stating that class certification "is often, if not usually, the prelude to a substantial settlement by the defendant because the costs and risks of litigating further are so high"); *AT&T Mobility LLC v. Concepcion*, 563 U.S. 333, 350 (2011) (explaining that, "when damages allegedly owed to tens of thousands of potential claimants are aggregated and decided at once, the risk of an error will often become unacceptable. Faced with even a small chance of a devastating loss, defendants will be pressured into settling questionable claims"); *Halliburton Co. v. Erica P. John Fund, Inc.*, 573 U.S. 258, 296 n.7 (2014) (*Halliburton II*) (Thomas, J., concurring in the judgment) (referring to "the substantial *in terrorem* settlement pressures brought to bear by certification.")[17]

Justices across the bench have expressed similar concerns about pressure and costs from high-stakes litigation. During oral arguments Justice Kagan alluded to how the Court "has sometimes indicated real concern with abuse of private suits and particularly with the opportunity for strike litigation." Transcript of Oral Argument at 70, *Emulex Corp. v. Varjabedian*, No. 18-459, 2019 WL 1598075 (Apr. 15, 2019). Justice Ginsburg's dissent in *Shady Grove* notes that "[w]hen representative plaintiffs seek statutory damages, pressure to settle may be heightened because a class action poses the risk of massive liability unmoored to actual injury." 559 U.S. at 445 n.3 (Ginsburg, J., dissenting) (citations omitted). And Justice Sotomayor, while on the Second Circuit, wrote that "[t]he effect of certification on parties' leverage in settlement negotiations is a fact of life for class action litigants." *In re Visa Check/MasterMoney Antitrust Litig.*, 280 F.3d 124, 145 (2d Cir. 2001), *cert. denied*, 536 U.S. 917 (2002), *superseded by statute on other grounds as stated in Attenborough v. Constr. & Gen. Bldg. Laborers' Local 79*, 238 F.R.D. 82, 100 (S.D.N.Y. 2006).

In 1998, the Supreme Court adopted the discretionary appeal provision of Rule 23(f), essentially as a safety valve for parties faced with erroneous class certification decisions. *See Baker*, 582 U.S. at 30–33. The advisory committee observed that, just as an order denying certification may preclude appellate review for a plaintiff who chooses not to proceed to judgment individually, so may an order granting certification "force a defendant to settle rather than incur the costs of defending a class action and run the risk of potentially ruinous liability." Fed. R. Civ. P. 23(f) advisory committee's note (1998). Rule 23 makes no mention of settlement pressure, however, and certification of a class does not technically change a defendant's aggregate liability. *See Shady Grove*, 559 U.S. at 408 (plurality opinion). Thus, it has been held in the lower courts that "[m]ere pressure to settle is not a sufficient reason . . . to avoid certifying an otherwise meritorious class action suit." *Klay v. Humana, Inc.*, 382 F.3d 1241, 1275 (11th Cir. 2004), *cert. denied*, 543 U.S. 1081 (2005), *abrogated in part on other grounds by Bridge v. Phoenix Bond & Indem. Co.*, 553 U.S. 639 (2008).[18]

c. Attorney vs. Client

Closely related to the policy of small-claims aggregation is the contingency litigation incentive. That class counsel in a successful case usually make out better than their clients has not been lost on the Supreme Court—a class action's "benefits to class members are often nominal and symbolic, with persons other than class members becoming the chief beneficiaries." *Roper*, 445 U.S. at 339; *see, e.g.*, *Falcon*, 457 U.S. at 153 n.7 (noting that the plaintiff's recovery was $1,040.33 and "[a] large share of the class award, $28,827.50, represented attorney's fees."). Special concern arises from "the possibility of a tradeoff between merits relief and attorney's fees" in negotiation of a class settlement. *Evans v. Jeff D.*, 475 U.S. 717, 733 (1986); *see Thorogood v. Sears, Roebuck & Co.*, 547 F.3d 742, 744–45 (7th Cir. 2008) (describing diverging incentives of class counsel and class members). Though not without pitfalls, the contingency incentive serves to "vindicat[e] the rights of individuals who otherwise might not consider it worth the candle to embark on litigation in which the optimum result might be more than consumed by the cost." *Roper*, 445 U.S. at 338.[19]

---

[17] Stockholder derivative actions, too, "sometimes were brought not to redress real wrongs, but to realize upon their nuisance value. They were bought off by secret settlements in which any wrongs to the general body of share owners were compounded by the suing stockholder, who was mollified by payments from corporate assets." Cohen v. Beneficial Indus. Loan Corp., 337 U.S. 541, 548 (1949).

[18] *Accord Visa Check/MasterMoney*, 280 F.3d at 145; Bateman v. American Multi-Cinema, Inc., 623 F.3d 708, 722 (9th Cir. 2010).

[19] *See Evans*, 475 U.S. at 741 (concluding that the fee-shifting statute for civil rights claims, 42 U.S.C. § 1988, "has given the victims of civil rights violations a powerful weapon that improves their ability to employ counsel, to obtain access to the courts, and thereafter to vindicate their rights by means of settlement or trial"); Lewis v. Casey, 518 U.S.

In awarding prevailing class counsel a reasonable fee, courts use one or both of two methods: percentage and lodestar.[20] First, attorneys' fees under the "common fund doctrine" may be based "on a percentage of the fund bestowed on the class." *Blum v. Stenson*, 465 U.S. 886, 900 n.16 (1984). A court's authority to award attorneys' fees as a percentage of a common fund derives from the equitable power to prevent unjust enrichment. Public policy disfavors allowing parties to free-ride off others' work, so "a litigant or a lawyer who recovers a common fund for the benefit of persons other than himself or his client is entitled to a reasonable attorney's fee from the fund as a whole." *Boeing Co. v. Van Gemert*, 444 U.S. 472, 478 (1980) (citing *Internal Imp. Fund Trustees v. Greenough*, 105 U.S. 527 (1881); *Central R.R. & Banking Co. v. Pettus*, 113 U.S. 116 (1885); *Sprague v. Ticonic Nat'l Bank*, 307 U.S. 161 (1939); *Mills v. Electric Auto-Lite Co.*, 396 U.S. 375 (1970)). Courts determine what percentage is reasonable by considering case-specific factors, particularly the benefits for the class as compared to the expected value of the claims and the risks of litigation. *See* Federal Judicial Center, *Manual for Complex Litigation* § 14.121 (4th ed. 2004); Fed. R. Civ. P. 23(e)(2) advisory committee's note (2018).

Second, courts typically apply the "lodestar" method in statutory fee-shifting cases or when it is difficult to assign a monetary value to classwide relief. In those circumstances, the lodestar—"the number of hours reasonably expended on the litigation multiplied by a reasonable hourly rate"—is presumptively reasonable. *Hensley v. Eckerhart*, 461 U.S. 424, 433 (1983); *Blum*, 465 U.S. at 897. The lodestar calculation looks to the rates "prevailing in the community for similar services by lawyers of reasonably comparable skill, experience and reputation." *Blum*, 465 U.S. at 895 n.11. "Ideally, of course, litigants will settle the amount of a fee." *Hensley*, 461 U.S. at 437; *see Evans*, 475 U.S. at 735 (in civil rights cases, "potential liability for attorney's fees may overshadow the potential cost of relief on the merits and darken prospects for settlement if fees cannot be negotiated."). If the fee is not settled, class counsel "bears the burden of establishing entitlement to an award and documenting the appropriate hours expended and hourly rates." *Hensley*, 461 U.S. at 437. In "rare" cases of "exceptional success," the court has discretion to enhance a lodestar-based award. *Id.* at 434–37; *Perdue v. Kenny A. ex rel. Winn*, 559 U.S. 542, 551–56 (2010). "But trial courts need not, and indeed should not, become green-eyeshade accountants." *Fox v. Vice*, 563 U.S. 826, 838 (2011); *see also Hensley*, 461 U.S. at 437 n.12.

The monetary incentives of plaintiffs' counsel largely account for "the possibility of abuses in class-action litigation." *Gulf Oil*, 452 U.S. at 104; *see Thorogood v. Sears, Roebuck & Co.*, 627 F.3d 289, 293–95 (7th Cir. 2010). Settlement negotiations present the risk of counsel unfairly trading off the interests of class members to secure a fee: "In a strictly rational world, plaintiffs' counsel would always press for the limit of what the defense would pay. But with an already enormous fee within counsel's grasp, zeal for the client may relax sooner than it would in a case brought on behalf of one claimant." *Ortiz*, 527 U.S. at 852 n.30.[21] A court may also face "canned objections filed by professional objectors who seek out class actions to simply extract a fee by lodging generic, unhelpful protests." *Devlin v. Scardelletti*, 536 U.S. 1, 22 n.5 (2002) (Scalia, J., dissenting) (internal quotation marks and citation omitted); *see* Fed. R. Civ. P. 23(e)(5), (h)(2) (authorizing class member objections to attorney fee requests and proposed settlements). A "reverse auction" can result in

---

343, 374 n.4 (1996) (Thomas, J., concurring) (noting that "[f]ederal fee-shifting statutes and the promise of a contingency fee" create an "incentive for counsel to take meritorious cases").

[20] *See* Fed. R. Civ. P. 23(h); John C. Coffee, *Understanding the Plaintiff's Attorney: The Implications of Economic Theory for Private Enforcement of Law Through Class and Derivative Actions*, 86 Colum. L. Rev. 669, 670 (1986) (arguing that, "[i]nevitably, these rules [for awarding attorneys' fees] create an incentive structure that either encourages or chills private enforcement of law").

[21] *See also, e.g.*, International Precious Metals Corp. v. Waters, 530 U.S. 1223 (2000) (statement of O'Connor, J., respecting denial of certiorari); Marek v. Lane, 571 U.S. 1003 (2013) (statement of Roberts, C.J., respecting denial of certiorari).

the defendant settling with the plaintiff attorney "willing to accept the lowest bid on behalf of the class. This gamesmanship is not in class members' interest, nor in the interest of justice." *China Agritech*, 584 U.S. at 754 (Sotomayor, J., concurring in the judgment) (internal quotation marks and citation omitted). To counteract these dangers and concentrate case leadership, an order certifying a class must appoint class counsel. *See* Fed. R. Civ. P. 23(c)(1)(B), (g).

d. Plaintiff vs. Absent Class Members

One of the more vexing areas of class action law concerns the status of unnamed class members—whom Justice Story termed "quasi parties." *West*, 29 F. Cas. at 723. There are "few odder parties" in American law "than the absent class member in a class action lawsuit." 3 William B. Rubenstein, *Newberg on Class Actions* § 9:1 (5th ed. 2013).

A certification order gives the class an "independent status" such that its members may be bound by the judgment. *Campbell–Ewald Co. v. Gomez*, 577 U.S. 153, 165 (2016); Fed. R. Civ. P. 23(c)(2)(B)(vii), (c)(3); *see also Molock v. Whole Foods Mkt. Grp., Inc.*, 952 F.3d 293, 298 (D.C. Cir. 2020) (citing *In re Bayshore Ford Trucks Sales, Inc.*, 471 F.3d 1233, 1245 (11th Cir. 2006)). So too, "if a class has been properly certified, the case does not become moot simply because the class representative's individual interest in the merits of the litigation has expired." *Roper*, 445 U.S. at 342 n.1 (Stevens, J., concurring); *see Sosna v. Iowa*, 419 U.S. 393, 402 (1975); *Franks v. Bowman Transp. Co.*, 424 U.S. 747, 755–56 (1976). But whether, at any point in the litigation, courts treat absent class members as parties depends on the procedural context at hand. *Devlin*, 536 U.S. at 9–10.

Only if joinder of all class members is impracticable may a class be certified. Fed. R. Civ. P. 23(a)(1); *see Eisen*, 417 U.S. at 183 (Douglas, J., dissenting in part) (listing numerosity factors: "[s]ize, modesty of monetary interest, inability to locate members and difficulty of obtaining jurisdiction") (citation omitted). By definition, absent class members are not "present" or joined in the action but are instead represented. *See* Fed. R. Civ. P. 23(d)(1)(B)(iii) (the court may allow individual class members to intervene or "otherwise come into the action"). As such, they are not treated as party plaintiffs for most purposes.

Absent class members are not parties, in non-CAFA-based diversity suits,[22] for purposes of calculating the amount in controversy or determining whether complete diversity of citizenship exists. *Snyder*, 394 U.S. at 338; *Devlin*, 536 U.S. at 10. Class members, furthermore, need not appear and "are almost never subject to counterclaims or cross-claims, or liability for fees or costs." *Shutts*, 472 U.S. at 810. Nor are they usually subject to discovery. *See id.* at 810 n.2. And, unless a class is certified, the judgment neither binds them as parties nor precludes them from seeking certification in a follow-on case. *Smith v. Bayer Corp.*, 564 U.S. 299, 313–17 (2011); *Standard Fire*, 568 U.S. at 593.

A named plaintiff must be part of the class and have the same interest and alleged injury as its other members. *East Texas*, 431 U.S. at 403. Hence, the safeguards of Rule 23(a)(2), (a)(3), and (a)(4) "effectively limit the class claims to those fairly encompassed by the named plaintiff's claims." *Falcon*, 457 U.S. at 156 (internal quotation marks and citation omitted). The Supreme Court has sometimes applied Article III standing constraints to the same end. *See, e.g.*, *Blum v. Yaretsky*, 457 U.S. 991, 1001–02 (1982) (holding that Medicaid-assisted nursing home patients who were transferred to lower levels of care, allegedly without sufficient notice and an opportunity to challenge the transfers, lacked standing to maintain claims on behalf of patients transferred to more intensive care). The Court's case

[22] The Court's latest decision related to the Class Action Fairness Act of 2005 (CAFA), *Home Depot*, 587 U.S. 435, holds that CAFA does not permit a third-party counterclaim defendant to remove the claim filed against it to federal court. Earlier CAFA decisions concern how the statute's $5 million amount-in-controversy requirement may be satisfied or disproved. *See* Dart Cherokee Basin Op. Co., LLC v. Owens, 574 U.S. 81 (2014); Standard Fire Ins. Co. v. Knowles, 568 U.S. 588 (2013).

law thus includes a "tension" between applying Rule 23(a) or standing doctrine with respect to factual differences between the claims of named plaintiffs and unnamed potential class members. *Gratz v. Bollinger*, 539 U.S. 244, 263 & n.15 (2003).

In *Lewis v. Casey*, the Court held that standing is evaluated at least initially by reference to the named plaintiffs, not unnamed members of a putative class: "That a suit may be a class action adds nothing to the question of standing, for even named plaintiffs who represent a class must allege and show that they personally have been injured, not that injury has been suffered by other, unidentified members of the class to which they belong and which they purport to represent." 518 U.S. at 357 (internal quotation marks and alteration omitted) (quoting *Simon v. Eastern Ky. Welfare Rights Org.*, 426 U.S. 26, 40 n.20 (1976) (quoting *Warth v. Seldin*, 422 U.S. 490, 502 (1975)). A separate opinion joined by three Justices adds that "[u]nnamed plaintiffs need not make any individual showing of standing in order to obtain relief, because the standing issue focuses on whether the plaintiff is properly before the court, not whether represented parties or absent class members are properly before the court." *Lewis*, 518 U.S. at 395–96 (Souter, J., concurring in part, dissenting in part, and concurring in the judgment) (citation and alterations omitted). The opinion of the Court reminds lower courts to assess a plaintiff's standing based upon the pleading or proof requirements that apply to the particular stage of litigation. *Id.* at 357–58; *TransUnion*, 594 U.S. at 431. The separate opinion, along similar lines, points out that a judgment for the defendant equates to a decision that the plaintiff lacks standing. *Lewis*, 518 U.S. at 395 (Souter, J., concurring in part, dissenting in part, and concurring in the judgment).

The Court's 2021 *TransUnion v. Ramirez* decision advances its class action standing jurisprudence, squarely holding that "[e]very class member must have Article III standing in order to recover individual damages." 594 U.S. at 431. As *TransUnion* concerns the post-trial setting, however, the Court left unaddressed "the distinct question whether every class member must demonstrate standing before a court certifies a class." *Id.* at 431 n.4. Practitioners facing this question of procedure may take guidance from footnote 4's citation to *Cordoba v. DIRECTV, LLC*, 942 F.3d 1259, 1277 (11th Cir. 2019).

Although class members in most contexts are not treated as parties, they effectively acquire party status for purposes of (1) benefiting from tolling of the statute of limitations to pursue individual claims after a denial of certification, and (2) appealing the approval of a class settlement.

In *American Pipe*, the Court fashioned a prudential tolling rule: "[T]he commencement of a class action suspends the applicable statute of limitations as to all asserted members of the class who would have been parties had the suit been permitted to continue as a class action." 414 U.S. at 554. Absent such tolling, putative class members concerned about preserving their rights would need to intervene (or file separate cases), lest their claims be time-barred upon denial of certification. *Id.* at 550–56. Such "duplication" would "needless[ly]" contravene Rule 23's "purposes of litigative efficiency and economy" where the class complaint put the defendant on notice of its alleged violations. *Id.* at 553–56.

The Supreme Court has since clarified that *American Pipe* tolling applies to individual actions filed after a certification denial, *Crown, Cork & Seal Co. v. Parker*, 462 U.S. 345 (1983), but not to successive class actions. *China Agritech*, 584 U.S. 732. The Court also held, in a 5–4 decision, that *American Pipe* tolling does not apply to statutes of repose under the federal securities laws. *California Pub. Emps.' Ret. Sys. v. ANZ Sec., Inc.*, 582 U.S. 497 (2017). The Court reasoned that statutes of repose, in contrast to statutes of limitations, grant "unqualified" immunity to a defendant at a "fixed" time after its last alleged unlawful act or omission. *Id.* at 508.

In *Devlin*, another divided Court held that absent class members may appeal an order approving a settlement without intervening. 536 U.S. at 14. Justice O'Connor's opinion for the Court deems it illogical to deny class members the appeal rights of a party when the judgment would finally adjudicate their rights and, as permitted by Rule 23(e), they objected to settlement approval in the district court. *See id.* at 8–11. Justice Scalia's hard-hitting dissent, joined by Justices Kennedy and Thomas, contends that the only persons entitled to appeal are those named in the operative complaint or made a party by operation of a counterclaim, third-party claim, or complaint in intervention, or whose rights were adjudicated in a collateral order incorporated into the final judgment—like an order denying a motion to intervene under Rule 24. *Id.* at 15–22 (Scalia, J., dissenting) (citing, *inter alia*, *Marino v. Ortiz*, 484 U.S. 301, 304 (1988)). A 2022 concurrence by Justice Thomas revives this critique of *Devlin*'s "vague, functionalist inquiry" into party status and calls for the decision to be overruled. *See Cameron v. EMW Women's Surgical Ctr., P.S.C.*, 595 U.S. 267, 286–87 (2022) (Thomas, J., concurring).

e. Derivative vs. Direct

Class actions involve claims that are "direct" in that they assert breaches of duties owed to (or by)[23] numerous class members. Derivative actions involve alleged breaches of duties owed to a single entity—typically, a corporation owned by stockholders.[24] Notwithstanding this distinction, "derivative suits are a form of representative action. Indeed, they should be seen for what they are, a form of class action." *Parfi Holding AB v. Mirror Image Internet*, 954 A.2d 911, 940 (Del. Ch. 2008); *see also Ross v. Bernhard*, 396 U.S. 531, 541 (1970) (the Supreme Court was "inclined to agree with the description" of the shareholder derivative suit as a form of "true" class action); Benjamin Kaplan, *Continuing Work of the Civil Committee: 1966 Amendments of the Federal Rules of Civil Procedure (I)*, 81 Harv. L. Rev. 356, 387 n.118 (1967) (noting differences and similarities between class actions and certain derivative actions). By pursuing the corporation's claim against its allegedly malfeasant managers, the shareholder plaintiff seeks a recovery for the corporation and, hence, for all of its constituent owners. *See Cohen*, 337 U.S. at 549 (a derivative plaintiff "sues, not for himself alone, but as representative of a class comprising all who are similarly situated."); *Ross*, 396 U.S. at 538 ("The proceeds of the action belong to the corporation and it is bound by the result of the suit.").

Rule 23.1, which was split off from Rule 23 as part of the 1966 amendments, governs derivative actions and codifies requirements laid down by the Supreme Court in 1881. *Hawes v. City of Oakland*, 104 U.S. 450, 460–61 (1881); *see Ross*, 396 U.S. at 534 n.4. Rule 23.1 "does not disturb the procedural balance previously established in this kind of litigation." Kaplan, *Continuing Work of the Civil Committee*, 81 Harv. L. Rev. at 387 n.118. Subdivision (a) defines a derivative action as one to enforce an enforceable, yet unasserted, corporate right and mandates that plaintiff fairly and adequately represent the interests of similarly situated stockholders. Subdivision (b) sets out pleading requirements, most consequentially that the plaintiff state with particularity any efforts to obtain the desired result from directors, or why no efforts were made or the result was not obtained. In addition, "[t]o prevent collusive settlements and abuses, the Court must approve dismissal or compromise" of a derivative suit. *Koster*, 330 U.S. at 525; *see Cohen*, 337 U.S. at 549–50. Rule 23.1(c) thus requires court approval, along with notice to the stockholders, of a proposed settlement or voluntary dismissal.

Derivative suits usually pit state law claims for breach of fiduciary duty against a busi-

[23] *See* Fed. R. Civ. P. 23(a) (providing that one or more members of a class "may sue *or be sued*" on behalf of all members) (emphasis added). For a good discussion of issues relating to defendant classes, which are "rare birds," CIGNA HealthCare of St. Louis, Inc. v. Kaiser, 294 F.3d 849, 853 (7th Cir. 2002), *see* Thillens, Inc. v. Community Currency Exch. Ass'n of Ill., Inc., 97 F.R.D. 668, 673–76 (N.D. Ill. 1983).

[24] *See, e.g.*, Koster v. (Am.) Lumbermens Mut. Cas. Co., 330 U.S. 518, 522 (1947) (explaining that "[t]he cause of action which such a plaintiff brings before the court is not his own but the corporation's"); Pepper v. Litton, 308 U.S. 295, 307 & n.15 (1939) (contrasting derivative actions with "direct actions by stockholders in their own right"); *Cohen*, 337 U.S. at 548 (equity may allow a derivative plaintiff "to step into the corporation's shoes and to seek in its right the restitution he could not demand in his own").

ness judgment defense. The action itself, too, has a "dual nature": first, the plaintiff must show an entitlement to maintain suit on the corporation's behalf, and only then may the merits of the corporate claim be litigated. *Ross*, 396 U.S. at 534–35; *see Hawes*, 104 U.S. at 460 (summarizing traditional categories of violations that may give rise to director liability: fraud, self-dealing, *ultra vires* conduct, or oppression of minority stockholders). The battle among litigants is joined at the first stage focusing on the question of "demand futility" or, less often, "wrongful refusal" of a demand. The stockholder demand requirement "affords the directors an opportunity to exercise their reasonable business judgment and waive a legal right vested in the corporation in the belief that its best interests will be promoted by not insisting on such right." *Daily Income Fund, Inc. v. Fox*, 464 U.S. 523, 533 (1984) (internal quotation marks and citation omitted). At the same time, their position of control may allow accused directors to "obstruct any remedy" and abet "stockholder helplessness" by rebuffing a demand. *Cohen*, 337 U.S. at 548; *Koster*, 330 U.S. at 522. In recognition of this potential conflict, and the general policy of non-interference by courts in corporate affairs,[25] equity strikes a balance. To seize authority to pursue the claim, a derivative plaintiff must at a minimum "show[] that the corporation on proper demand has refused to pursue a remedy, or show facts that demonstrate the futility of such a request." *Koster*, 330 U.S. at 522; *Hawes*, 104 U.S. at 460–61. Though embodied in Rule 23.1, this standard arises from substantive equity jurisprudence.[26]

4. LEADING CASES: *HANSBERRY, SHUTTS, AMCHEM*

During the class action's formative years in the mid-to-late twentieth century, the Supreme Court handed down a trio of decisions—*Hansberry v. Lee*, 311 U.S. 32 (1940), *Phillips Petroleum Co. v. Shutts*, 472 U.S. 797 (1985), and *Amchem Products, Inc. v. Windsor*, 521 U.S. 591 (1997)—that stand for pivotal class action concepts and doctrines. While these are by no means the only leading class action cases, studying them sheds light on such advanced topics as preclusion, choice of law, and the procedural rights and status of absent class members, including in connection with proposed settlements. *Hansberry* firmed up adequate representation as the central justification for giving preclusive effect to a classwide judgment. *Shutts* held that any court of competent jurisdiction may bind a properly notified class vested with opt-out rights, consistent with due process. And the holdings of *Amchem*—the Court's first opinion to focus on class settlements—continue to reverberate in courtrooms and law offices across the country. Together these three decisions jut out in the landscape of class action law and merit close study by practitioners in the field.

a. *Hansberry v. Lee*

A cardinal principle of Anglo-American law, grounded in individualism and notions of basic fairness, is that all interested parties deserve their day in court. *See Richards v. Jefferson Cty., Ala.*, 517 U.S. 793, 798 (1996). It follows that a judgment cannot determine the rights or duties of parties not joined in the suit—"strangers"—except if the court has specific assurance that their interests are protected. *Martin v. Wilks*, 490 U.S. 755, 762 (1989). In *Taylor v. Sturgell*, the Supreme Court described six general situations in which a judgment may preclude nonparties without violating their due process rights. 553 U.S. 880, 893–85 (2008). One of these situations is when a party adequately represents a class. *Id.* at 894–95; *see Sosna*, 419 U.S. at 403 ("Since it is contemplated that all members of the class will be bound by the ultimate ruling on the merits . . . the district court must assure itself that the named representative will adequately protect the interests of the class.") (internal citation omitted). The

[25] *See In re* Caremark Int'l Inc. Deriv. Litig., 698 A.2d 959, 968 (Del. Ch. 1996) (citing Barnes v. Andrews, 298 F. 614, 618 (S.D.N.Y. 1924) (Hand, J.)).

[26] Kamen v. Kemper Fin. Servs., Inc., 500 U.S. 90, 96 (1991); *see, e.g.*, Rales v. Blasband, 634 A.2d 927 (Del. 1993).

Court's 1940 decision in *Hansberry* contains the definitive exposition of this principle.

Hansberry concerned civil rights. A racially restrictive covenant in the South Side of Chicago that barred African Americans from buying or leasing land had been upheld in a prior class action, *Burke v. Kleiman*, 277 Ill. App. 519 (1934), brought by local white property owners. When Carl Hansberry, a black man, managed to purchase a house covered by the restrictive covenant, white property owners sued again to exclude Hansberry under the covenant, arguing that the judgment in *Burke* controlled. But to be effective, the covenant required signatures from owners of 95 percent of the neighborhood properties, and evidence showed that owners of only about half of the properties had signed. The trial court found that the earlier judgment depended on a false stipulation that owners of 95 percent of the properties had signed the covenant. The court nevertheless deferred to the judgment, and the Illinois Supreme Court affirmed on the basis that the judgment bound the class unless it was set aside on direct attack. *See* 311 U.S. at 37–40.

The U.S. Supreme Court reversed. It first explained that the Due Process Clause of the Fourteenth Amendment limits state courts' otherwise unfettered authority to describe, and dispose of, litigations as they see fit under state law. *Id.* at 40. The Court then held that, despite the rule against nonparty preclusion—"a principle of general application in Anglo-American jurisprudence"—"members of a class not present as parties to the litigation may be bound by the judgment where they are in fact adequately represented by parties who are present." *Id.* at 42–43.

Applying these principles, the Court concluded that the plaintiffs in the prior Illinois case did not adequately represent the group of signatories to the Chicago covenant, so *res judicata* did not apply. Any given signatory was free to either defend or challenge the covenant's validity, and the covenant lacked signatories for nearly half of the properties at issue. *Id.* at 45–46. The "dual and potentially conflicting interests" between the earlier plaintiffs and the absent landowners meant that "some" could not "be permitted to stand in judgment for all." *Id.* at 44.

That all signatories were similarly situated in relation to the covenant was not enough to ensure the fair and adequate representation of all by some. Rather, "a selection of representatives for purposes of litigation, whose *substantial interests* are not necessarily or even probably the same as those whom they are deemed to represent, does not afford that protection to absent parties which due process requires." *Id.* at 45 (emphasis added). The Court's reference to "substantial interests" demonstrates that the relevant interests of all class members need not be absolutely congruent.

The Court's intervening precedents teach that the adequacy inquiry is fact-dependent and "serves to uncover conflicts of interest between named parties and the class they seek to represent." *Amchem*, 521 U.S. at 625 (citing *Falcon*, 457 U.S. at 157–58 n.13); *see* 7A Charles Alan Wright, Arthur R. Miller & Mary Kay Kane, *Federal Practice & Procedure* § 1768 (3d ed. 2005). "In order to defeat a motion for certification, however, the conflict 'must be fundamental'" and subclassing may cure it. *In re Flag Telecom Holdings, Ltd. Sec. Litig.*, 574 F.3d 29, 35–37 (2d Cir. 2009) (quoting *Visa Check/MasterMoney*, 280 F.3d at 145); *see Dewey v. Volkswagen Aktiengesellschaft*, 681 F.3d 170, 184 (3d Cir. 2012) (stating that an "unduly speculative" conflict "is generally not fundamental" but that a fundamental conflict exists if the same conduct alleged to have harmed some class members benefited others); *Ortiz*, 527 U.S. at 856 (explaining conflicts could be eliminated by dividing "holders of present and future claims" into separately represented subclasses); Fed. R. Civ. P. 23(c)(5) (authorizing the court to designate subclasses).

Of additional note, *Hansberry* scrutinizes a prior judgment, and representation must have been "grossly deficient" for an adverse judgment to be set aside on inadequacy grounds. Restatement (Second) of Judgments § 42 cmt. f (1982). That heightened standard for a collateral attack is inapplicable to a court's assessment of the adequacy of representation during a class action, when the finality interest is not yet implicated. *See Tyson Foods*, 577 U.S. at 467 (Thomas, J., dissenting) (Rule 23 must remain satisfied throughout the case); *Amgen*, 568 U.S. at 479 n.9 ("[C]ertifications are not frozen once made.") (citing Fed. R. Civ. P. 23(c)(1)(C)).

b. *Phillips Petroleum Co. v. Shutts*

While *Hansberry* cemented the due process foundations of the adequacy of representation requirement, *Shutts* confirmed that the best notice practicable and an opt-out right are universally required to release class claims for damages. Decided at a time of accelerating civil litigation activity, *Shutts* broadly addresses how any court, state or federal, may apply the class mechanism to resolve national disputes involving alleged past harm.

Before *Schutts*, the Supreme Court had upheld certification of a nationwide injunctive-relief class in federal court. *See Califano*, 442 U.S. at 702 (holding that "the scope of injunctive relief is dictated by the extent of the violation established, not by the geographical extent of the plaintiff class" but that "a federal court when asked to certify a nationwide class" should consider whether certification would "improperly interfere with the litigation of similar issues in other judicial districts"). *Shutts*, however, concerned damages claims in state court. A Kansas judge, asserting jurisdiction even though only one-quarter of 1 percent of the relevant leases were in Kansas, certified a class of some 33,000 owners of gas-royalty interests around the country on claims of overdue interest. Class members received a notice via first-class mail describing the action and disclosing that they would be represented by the named plaintiffs and bound by the judgment unless they "opted out" by returning an enclosed "request for exclusion." 472 U.S. at 801. The plaintiffs prevailed at trial and the verdict was affirmed. *Id.* at 801–03.

Phillips Petroleum contended on appeal that the Kansas courts lacked personal jurisdiction over the non-Kansas class members because they lacked the "minimum contacts" with the forum required of a defendant in civil litigation. It further argued that Kansas law could not apply to their claims. *Id.* at 802–03. The Supreme Court rejected the jurisdictional argument but accepted the choice-of-law argument.

First, the Due Process Clause of the Fourteenth Amendment affords less protection to absent class members than to defendants in civil suits. Whereas a defendant must appear and answer under threat of a default judgment, and fend for itself in the litigation, "an absent class member is not required to do anything." *Id.* at 809–11. "The court and named plaintiffs protect his interests"—a responsibility codified, for instance, in the rule that the court must approve the dismissal or compromise of a class suit. *Id.* at 809; *see In re General Motors Corp. Pick-Up Truck Fuel Tank Prods. Liab. Litig.*, 55 F.3d at 784 (the court "plays the important role of protector of the absentees' interests, in a sort of fiduciary capacity").[27] And, with absent class members along for the ride, to resolve their damage claims the court need only afford them "minimal procedural due process protection," instead of requiring that they have minimum contacts with the forum. *Shutts*, 472 U.S. at 811–12 & n.3.

Together with adequate representation, the constitutionally mandated protections for

---

[27] *See also Roper*, 445 U.S. at 331 (the court has the responsibility "to protect both the absent class and the integrity of the judicial process by monitoring the actions of the parties before it"); *Amchem*, 521 U.S. at 629 (the court when applying Rule 23 should keep "the interests of absent class members in close view").

class members in damages actions[28] consist of the best notice practicable,[29] the opportunity to participate in the litigation,[30] and the opportunity to withdraw from the class to avoid being bound by the judgment.[31] *Shutts*, 472 U.S. at 811–12 & n.3. Since the non-Kansan class members received these protections in *Shutts*, the Kansas courts properly exercised jurisdiction over their claims. *Id.* at 812–14.

Second, the Kansas courts erred in applying Kansas law to hold Phillips Petroleum liable for interest on the suspended royalties. There were material conflicts between the pertinent laws of Kansas and of other states where leases existed, and there was no *res* in Kansas to otherwise support classwide application of Kansas law. *Id.* at 816–22. Although a state may exercise "jurisdiction over the claims of plaintiffs whose principal contacts are with other States, it may not use this assumption of jurisdiction as an added weight in the scale when considering the permissible constitutional limits on choice of substantive law." *Id.* at 821. Accordingly, the Supreme Court reversed the choice-of-law determination. *Id.* at 823.

Shutts paved the way for more proposed nationwide class actions, which, when settled, have generated the notices many associate with class actions. Moreover, after *Shutts*, choice of law "became the fault line in the battles over class certification." Samuel Issacharoff, *Settled Expectations in A World of Unsettled Law: Choice of Law After the Class Action Fairness Act*, 106 Colum. L. Rev. 1839, 1859–61 (2006). In cases where Rule 23 is satisfied but there is no unifying cause of action, organizational options available to the court include subclassing based on materially identical state-law claims, *see Klay*, 382 F.3d at 1262, and sequencing of state-by-state bellwethers. *See* Eldon E. Fallon et al., *Bellwether Trials in Multidistrict Litigation*, 82 Tul. L. Rev. 2323, 2325 (2008). Or, as recognized in *Shutts*, the law of a single state may apply "if it is not in conflict with that of any other jurisdiction connected to th[e] suit." 472 U.S. at 816.

Shutts also underpinned the decision in *Matsushita Electric Industrial Co. v. Epstein* granting preclusive effect to a state court judgment extinguishing claims that only federal courts could have adjudicated. 516 U.S. 367 (1996). Resolving this "important" procedural issue, the Court held that preclusion comported with due process and Delaware law because the *Shutts* protections had been furnished and the settled claims arose from the same facts. *Id.* at 373, 376–79; *see also* 2 Joseph M. McLaughlin, *McLaughlin on Class Actions* § 6:29 (21st ed. 2024) (citing cases applying the "identical factual predicate" preclusion doctrine to class judgments). Further, because an order approving a settlement agreement does not enter judgment on the merits, the state court did not transgress the bounds of its jurisdiction by releasing exclusively federal claims. *Matsushita*, 516 U.S. at 382. Justice Ginsburg's separate opinion anticipated her opinion for the Court the following term in *Amchem*, "stress[ing] . . . the centrality of the procedural due process protection of adequate representation in class action lawsuits, emphatically including those resolved by settlement." *Matsushita*, 516 U.S. at 399 (Ginsburg, J., concurring in part and dissenting in part).

---

[28] *Cf. Wal-Mart*, 564 U.S. at 363 (unanimous Section III.A) (recognizing, in dicta, "the serious possibility" that class members have notice and opt-out rights even "where the monetary claims do not predominate") (referencing *Shutts*, 472 U.S. 797); Ticor Title Ins. Co. v. Brown, 511 U.S. 117, 121 (1994) (per curiam) (dismissing writ of certiorari as improvidently granted but acknowledging, in dicta, "at least a substantial possibility" that actions seeking monetary damages may be certified only under Rule 23(b)(3)).

[29] *See* Fed. R. Civ. P. 23(c)(2)(B), (d)(1)(B), (e)(1); *Eisen*, 417 U.S. at 173–77 ("Individual notice must be sent to all class members whose names and addresses may be ascertained through reasonable effort.") (citing Mullane v. Central Hanover Bank & Trust Co., 339 U.S. 306, 314–18 (1950)); Fed. R. Civ. P. 23(c)(2) advisory committee's note (2018) (directing "courts and counsel to focus on the means or combination of means most likely to be effective in the case before the court").

[30] *See* Fed. R. Civ. P. 23(c)(2)(B)(iv), (d)(1)(B)(iii).

[31] *See* Fed. R. Civ. P. 23(c)(2)(B)(v), (c)(2)(B)(vi), (c)(3)(B), (e)(4).

c. *Amchem Products, Inc. v. Windsor*

The approach of the twenty-first century brought increasingly complex agreements to settle controversies in the mass economy. The Supreme Court in *Amchem* held one of these arrangements—a global resolution of claims for personal injuries caused by asbestos inhalation—too unwieldy and unfair to stand. In doing so, the Court provided indispensable guidance on how proposed settlement classes should be structured and analyzed.

The high volume of asbestos lawsuits prompted a settlement that would have created an administrative structure to compensate class members for certain asbestos-related diseases. 521 U.S. at 597–605. But the group whose claims were proposed to be released included people with different asbestos-related injuries and people who, though exposed to asbestos, had not yet manifested a disease. The Supreme Court held class certification inappropriate where all segments of this disparate group were represented by the same class counsel and class representatives. For there was "no structural assurance of fair and adequate representation for the diverse groups and individuals affected." *Id.* at 627. Those currently sick had an interest in maximizing immediate payments, but those not yet sick had an interest in an "ample, inflation-protected fund." So the claims could not all be settled together, at least not without subclassing. *Id.* at 626–27. Similarly, in *Ortiz*, the Court rejected a limited-fund asbestos settlement plagued by disparities even in eligibility for coverage under the insurance policies that would have provided the bulk of the financing. 527 U.S. at 852–58.

Public policy encourages settlements[32] yet class certification is not necessarily appropriate even if a settlement is fair and adequate. *Amchem*, 521 U.S. at 619–23. In deciding whether to certify a class under Rule 23(b)(3) for litigation purposes, the court considers issues of case management, such as how the case would be tried and whether common proof can resolve key questions of fact or law. *See Eisen*, 417 U.S. at 164 (manageability criteria of Rule 23(b)(3)(D) "encompass[] the whole range of practical problems that may render the class action format inappropriate for a particular suit"). By contrast, when parties wish to settle, the manageability of litigation is irrelevant—"for the proposal is that there be no trial." *Amchem*, 521 U.S. at 620. Meanwhile questions of fair representation and "preexist[ing]" class cohesion become *more* important given the risks of conflicts and unfair allocation of funds. *See, e.g., id.* at 620–27 (identifying the need "to protect absentees by blocking unwarranted or overbroad class definitions"); *Sullivan v. DB Invs., Inc.*, 667 F.3d 273, 336 (3d Cir. 2011) (en banc) (Scirica, J., concurring) ("If the class presented a grab-bag of unrelated claims, a trial court would be unable to ensure that absent class members' interests were protected.").

Amchem, therefore, "call[s] for caution" in certifying a class "when individual stakes are high and disparities among class members great." 521 U.S. at 625. The chart below extends on this principle.

[32] Marek v. Chesny, 473 U.S. 1, 10 (1985); FTC v. Actavis, Inc., 570 U.S. 136, 153 (2013).

	Low Variance Between Individual Claims	High Variance Between Individual Claims
Low Value of Individual Claims	Class actions indispensable for private prosecution	Private enforcement difficult because of manageability concerns
High Value of Individual Claims	Class actions necessary but greater concern for individual opt-out and other right of control	Aggregate treatment not essential and class actions held suspect

Principles of the Law of Aggregate Litigation § 2.02 cmt. b, reporters' note.

5. CLASS ACTIONS IN THE TWENTY-FIRST CENTURY

In the twenty-first century, the confirmation process for Justices grew ever more politicized and their opinions took on a sharper overall tone. The Court reversed some class certifications (*Wal–Mart*, *Comcast*) and upheld others (*Amgen*, *Tyson Foods*), while building impactful lines of authority regarding arbitration and issues of jurisdiction[33] and Article III standing. These cases reflect disagreement over the utility and proper role of class actions in regulating business conduct, and they arrived at a time that saw increased class litigation activity in the federal courts due to CAFA, with major controversies increasingly being resolved in a single multidistrict or other federal litigation.

a. Back to *Basic*: Recent Securities Class Action Precedents

Securities litigation, a mainstay of class action practice,[34] and the subject of congressional reform legislation in the 1990s,[35] garnered attention in a series of Supreme Court decisions concerning the "fraud-on-the-market" presumption of investor reliance. The presumption, recognized in *Basic Inc. v. Levinson*, accepts that the market price of a publicly traded security reflects all publicly available information and that investors attribute value to the stock based on its pricing. It follows that investors rely on all public information connected with the stock, including any material misrepresentations, when they buy or sell shares. 485 U.S. 224, 245–47 (1988). For the presumption to arise, a plaintiff alleging securities fraud must

[33] Jurisdictional issues arising in mass tort litigation may also arise in class actions. *See, e.g.*, Ford Motor Co. v. Montana Eighth Jud. Dist. Ct., 592 U.S. 351, 359–62 (2021) (discussing in-state contacts needed for specific personal jurisdiction) (citing Bristol-Myers Squibb Co. v. Superior Ct. of Cal. S.F. County, 582 U.S. 255 (2017)).

[34] *See, e.g.*, *Amchem*, 521 U.S. at 625 (stating that "[p]redominance is a test readily met in certain cases alleging consumer or securities fraud or violations of the antitrust laws"); Robert H. Klonoff, *Class Actions in the Year 2026: A Prognosis*, 65 Emory L.J. 1569, 1589 (2016) (arguing that securities fraud cases tend to be well suited for class certification because the *Basic* presumption minimizes individual issues, common evidence determines liability, and stock ownership records permit calculation of individual awards).

[35] Congress enacted, in 1995, the Private Securities Litigation Reform Act, 109 Stat. 737, and in 1998 the Securities Litigation Uniform Standards Act, 112 Stat. 3227.

show that the alleged misrepresentations were public and material[36] and that the security in question traded in an efficient market. *Id.* at 248 n.27. The defendant may rebut the presumption by showing, for example, that the alleged misrepresentations did not affect the share price or the plaintiff's relevant trading decisions. *Id.* at 248–49. *Basic* is pivotal to class certification of claims under the Securities Exchange Act of 1934 given that, without a presumption of investor reliance, the question whether individual investors did or did not rely on the alleged fraud would make it impossible to decide their claims in a single proceeding. *See Amgen*, 568 U.S. at 462–63.

Amgen holds that, for two reasons, a securities fraud plaintiff need not prove materiality to obtain certification. First, materiality presents a common question, assessed using an objective standard, the answer to which will not vary from class member to class member. *Id.* at 467. Second, given that materiality is an element not merely of the *Basic* presumption but also of the cause of action, a failure of proof as to materiality would not produce individual questions but would, instead, be a "fatal similarity" that ends the case for the class. *Id.* at 459–60, 468–70 & n.5 (quoting Nagareda, *Class Certification in the Age of Aggregate Proof*, 84 N.Y.U. L. Rev. at 107). Justices Scalia and Thomas filed separate dissents. *See Amgen*, 568 U.S. at 483–86 (Scalia, J., dissenting) (terming the Court's holding "unquestionably disastrous"); *id.* at 486–502 (Thomas, J., dissenting) (arguing that "only by establishing all of the elements of the fraud-on-the-market presumption" can classwide reliance be proved, and "[t]herefore, if a plaintiff wishes to use *Basic*'s presumption to prove that reliance is a common question, he must establish the entire presumption, including materiality, at the class certification stage").

A year after addressing the materiality element in *Amgen*, the Supreme Court upheld the *Basic* presumption as a whole. *See Halliburton II*, 573 U.S. 258. *Halliburton* returned to the Court after it previously took the case to clarify that neither the *Basic* presumption, nor a decision to certify an investor class, requires proof of loss causation. *See Halliburton I*, 563 U.S. at 813. *Halliburton II* rejects empirical challenges to the efficient markets hypothesis used to justify the presumption, as well as contentions that investors try to "beat the market" instead of relying on the accuracy of prevailing pricing. 573 U.S. at 270–74. Unlike materiality, however, the presumption's unique, core "price impact" elements of publicity and market efficiency must be established, over the defendant's rebuttal evidence, at the class certification stage because otherwise the presumption "completely collapses." *Id.* at 282–84. In short, the defendant may rebut the *Basic* presumption at class certification by showing that "an alleged misrepresentation did not actually affect the market price of the stock." *Id.* at 284. To reconcile this holding with *Amgen*, the Court explained that "the common issue of materiality can be left to the merits stage without risking the certification of classes in which individual issues will end up overwhelming common ones." *Halliburton II*, 573 U.S. at 282. Justice Thomas, joined by Justices Scalia and Alito, filed a separate opinion assailing *Basic*. *See Halliburton II*, 573 U.S. at 284–301 (Thomas, J., concurring in the judgment).

The Court's securities class action decision in *Goldman Sachs Group v. Arkansas Teacher Retirement System*, 594 U.S. 113 (2021), offers little guidance to lower courts navigating between (1) *Amgen*'s holding that certification does not depend on the materiality of alleged misstatements, and (2) *Halliburton*'s leeway for defendants to contest their price impact—a distinction that may require "split[ting] some very fine hairs." *In re Allstate Corp. Sec. Litig.*, 966 F.3d 595, 600 (7th Cir. 2020). In *Goldman*, the Court held that the "generic" or generalized nature of alleged misrepresentations may be relevant to determining whether the *Basic* presumption crumbles upon a failure to establish price impact. As Justice Barrett's opinion for the Court explains, "when the earlier misrepresentation is generic (*e.g.*, 'we have faith in our business model') and the later corrective disclosure is specific (*e.g.*, 'our fourth quarter earnings did not meet expectations')," this "mismatch" in informa-

[36] *See, e.g.*, TSC Indus., Inc. v. Northway, Inc., 426 U.S. 438, 449 (1976) (defining materiality for purposes of securities claims based on alleged omissions).

tional content makes it "less likely that the specific disclosure actually corrected the generic misrepresentation, which means that there is less reason to infer front-end price inflation—that is, price impact—from the back-end price drop." *Goldman*, 594 U.S. at 123. Justice Gorsuch, joined by Justices Thomas and Alito, disagreed with the Court's holding that the defendant bears the burden of persuasion to show prices were not affected. *See id.* at 130–38 (Gorsuch, J., concurring in part and dissenting in part).

In another decision, the Court unanimously confirmed state courts' jurisdiction to adjudicate claims for violations of the Securities Act of 1933. *Cyan, Inc. v. Beaver Cty. Emps. Ret. Fund*, 583 U.S. 416 (2018). Many companies responded by amending their bylaws or charter to select Delaware Court of Chancery as the forum for securities disputes; the enforceability of these provisions is unsettled. *Compare Lee v. Fisher*, 70 F.4th 1129 (9th Cir. 2023) (en banc) (6–5 majority enforcing exclusive forum bylaw), *with Seafarers Pension Plan on behalf of Boeing Co. v. Bradway*, 23 F.4th 714 (7th Cir. 2022) (holding similar bylaw unenforceable).

b. *Wal-Mart Stores, Inc. v. Dukes*

The Roberts Court's signature class action decision, *Wal-Mart*, overturned certification of a nationwide class of around 1.5 million current and former female employees of Wal-Mart. The plaintiffs sued for injunctive and declaratory relief and backpay, alleging Wal-Mart engaged in a pattern and practice of discriminating against women in violation of Title VII of the Civil Rights Act of 1964. *See* 564 U.S. at 343–45. In support of class certification, the plaintiffs offered statistical evidence of gender disparities in pay and promotion decisions, anecdotes of discrimination from about 120 class members, and expert testimony from a sociologist. *Id.* at 346.

The Supreme Court held that the plaintiffs had failed to demonstrate common questions of law or fact under Rule 23(a)(2). 564 U.S. at 349–60. Local Wal-Mart managers in the companies' 3,400 stores exercised their own discretion to make pay and promotion decisions, making the sprawling class alleging disparate treatment too disparate to be certified. *Id.* at 342–43. The women "wish to sue about literally millions of employment decisions at once," the Court noted; yet, "[w]ithout some glue holding the alleged *reasons* for all those decisions together, it will be impossible to say that examination of all the class members' claims for relief will produce a common answer to the crucial question *why was I disfavored*." *Id.* at 352. In other words, to prevail under Title VII, "[m]erely showing that Wal-Mart's policy of discretion has produced an overall sex-based disparity does not suffice." *Id.* at 357. Commonality was thus lacking because the record disclosed neither a general policy of discrimination nor a "common mode of exercising discretion that pervades the entire company." *Id.* at 353–58. A class trial on backpay damages, moreover, would have abridged the defendant's substantive rights by preventing it from raising affirmative defenses regarding individual employment decisions. *Id.* at 366–67 (citing 28 U.S.C. § 2072(b)).

Four Justices dissented in part but joined the unanimous Section III, which examines Rule 23(b)(2). *See Wal-Mart*, 564 U.S. at 360–67. That subdivision "applies only when a single injunction or declaratory judgment would provide relief to each member of the class. It does not authorize class certification when each individual class member would be entitled to a *different* injunction or declaratory judgment against the defendant." *Id.* at 360. Rule 23(b)(2) therefore requires that the equitable relief requested be "indivisible," *id.* (citation omitted), and such relief may "have widespread effect." *Labrador v. Poe by and through Poe*, 144 S. Ct. 921, 932 (2024) (Kavanaugh, J., concurring in grant of stay).

c. *Comcast Corp. v. Behrend*

Antitrust, like securities, claims have long been certified for class treatment,[37] despite a

[37] *See* 1 Joseph M. McLaughlin, McLaughlin on Class Actions §§ 5:31, 5:74 (21st ed. 2024) ("In practice, courts have

reputation for raking accused companies over the "hot coals" of costly discovery.[38] To prevail on an antitrust claim and recover treble damages, a plaintiff must prove (1) violation (e.g., lawful monopoly acquisition or maintenance, or an anticompetitive agreement), (2) antitrust injury (or "impact"), and (3) damages.[39] Around the turn of the twenty-first century, courts generally agreed that whether an unlawful monopoly or anticompetitive conspiracy existed "is a common question that is thought to predominate." 7AA Charles Alan Wright, Arthur R. Miller & Mary Kay Kane, *Federal Practice & Procedure* § 1781 (3d ed. 2005).[40] In *Comcast Corporation v. Behrand*, 569 U.S. 27 (2013), the Supreme Court focused not on the first element of violation but on the "fit" between evidence offered to satisfy the second and third elements on a classwide basis.

Comcast rejects certification based on failure to align common proof of classwide injury with common proof of classwide damages. The case arose from an alleged scheme to monopolize cable television service in the greater Philadelphia area. *See id.* at 29–30. Although the plaintiffs presented four theories of antitrust impact, the district court accepted only one: that Comcast's dealings with other cable providers reduced competition from "overbuilder" firms with a history of building competing networks challenging incumbent cable companies. *Id.* at 31. The plaintiffs' damages model used regression analysis to compare actual cable prices to the prices that would have prevailed but for Comcast's alleged scheme. *Id.* at 32. But the classwide damages that the model calculated were not limited to damages associated with the overbuilder theory. *Id.* And for that reason, it was improper to certify a class of Comcast subscribers. *Id.* at 35. *Comcast* holds, therefore, that a damages model supporting class certification "must be consistent with"—and cannot sweep beyond—the plaintiffs' certified theory of harm. *Id.* (citation omitted). A dissent joined by four Justices states that the Court's opinion "breaks no new ground" and that aggregate proof of damages is not required to certify a class under Rule 23(b)(3). *Id.* at 41–43 (Ginsburg and Breyer, JJ., dissenting).

d. *Tyson Foods*: Issue Classes and the Comparison to Individual Suits

Tyson Foods recognizes that a class may be certified with respect to certain issues, as opposed to entire claims: "When one or more of the central issues in the action are common to the class and can be said to predominate, the action may be considered proper under Rule 23(b)(3) even though other important matters will have to be tried separately, such as damages or some affirmative defenses peculiar to some individual class members." 577 U.S. at 453–54 (internal quotation marks and citation omitted); *but see id.* at 473 (Thomas, J. dissenting) (criticizing this holding as inconsistent with *Comcast*). Where, for example, common issues predominate as to liability but damages are highly individualized, the court may bifurcate the case under Rule 23(c)(4), certifying liability issues for determination in a single trial and leaving connected damages issues for later, individual proceedings. *See* Fed. R. Civ. P. 23(c)(4) advisory committee's note (1966) ("[T]he action may retain its 'class' character only through the adjudication of liability to the class; the members of the class may thereafter be required to come in individually and prove the amounts of their respective

---

frequently certified classes alleging violations of the antitrust laws under Rule 23(b)(3)" and "have been willing to certify such classes to promote private enforcement as a supplement to government suits, especially in cases where individual claims are too small to justify individual action."); *Amchem*, 521 U.S. at 625.

[38] Asahi Glass Co. v. Pentech Pharms., Inc., 289 F. Supp. 2d 986, 992 (N.D. Ill. 2003) (Posner, J., sitting by designation); *see* Bell Atl. Corp. v. Twombly, 550 U.S. 544, 558–60 & n.6 (2007).

[39] *See* United States v. Grinnell Corp., 384 U.S. 563, 570–71 (1966) (setting forth monopolization standards); Atlantic Richfield Co. v. USA Petroleum Co., 495 U.S. 328, 334 (1990) (defining antitrust injury).

[40] *See, e.g.*, In re Vitamins Antitrust Litig., 209 F.R.D. 251 (D.D.C. 2002); In re Carbon Black Antitrust Litig., No. 03-10191, 2005 WL 102966 (D. Mass. Jan. 18, 2005); Gold Strike Stamp Co. v. Christensen, 436 F.2d 791, 795 (10th Cir. 1970).

claims."). In deciding whether to grant class certification as to a particular issue, the court considers whether its adjudication would "materially advance[] the disposition of the litigation as a whole." 2 William B. Rubenstein, *Newberg on Class Actions* § 4:90 (5th ed. 2012) (quoting Federal Judicial Center, *Manual for Complex Litigation* § 21.24 (4th ed. 2004)). Beyond this superiority-like inquiry, it remains unclear whether issue class certification requires that common questions predominate for the entire claim. *See Harris v. Med. Transp. Mgmt., Inc.*, 77 F.4th 746, 756 (D.C. Cir. 2023) (citing competing and overlapping interpretations of Rule 23(c)(4)).

In *Tyson Foods*, the Court approved reliance on statistical sampling to prove class claims for overtime pay "to fill an evidentiary gap created by the employer's failure to keep adequate records" of how much time workers spent donning and doffing protective clothing. 577 U.S. at 455–57. A significant holding was that evidence a party can permissibly introduce in an individual action should be equally available for use in a corresponding class action. *Id.* at 455–59 (citing 28 U.S.C. § 2072(b) and distinguishing *Wal-Mart*, 564 U.S. at 367).

e. The Arbitration Trend

The Court's recent arbitration jurisprudence upended most class actions arising from form contracts, placing tort and statutory claims front and center in the class action arena. This line of cases, involving agreements that waive representative litigation, mandates that arbitration clauses be enforced as written, and "[p]ropelled by the Court's decisions, mandatory arbitration clauses in employment and consumer contracts have proliferated." *Lamps Plus, Inc. v. Varela*, 587 U.S. 176, 192 (2019) (Ginsburg, J., dissenting).

Form arbitration provisions previously had been invalidated as unconscionable in violation of public policy. But in *Concepcion*, the Supreme Court made clear that these clauses normally must be enforced, as "the times in which consumer contracts were anything other than adhesive are long past." 563 U.S. at 346–47. Since arbitration is a matter of contract, courts must "'rigorously enforce' arbitration agreements according to their terms." *Italian Colors*, 570 U.S. at 233 (citation omitted). Furthermore, the FAA's policy favoring arbitration demands that agreements to arbitrate be treated like any other contract—they may not be nullified by rules that burden arbitration, whether overtly or covertly. *Concepcion*, 563 U.S. at 339; *Epic Systems*, 584 U.S. at 507–08; *Kindred Nursing Centers Ltd. P'ship v. Clark*, 581 U.S. 246 (2017). Nor may a class arbitration proceed unless the relevant agreement expressly permits it. *Stolt-Nielsen S.A. v. AnimalFeeds Int'l Corp.*, 559 U.S. 662 (2010); *Lamps Plus*, 587 U.S. 176. Praising arbitration for its speed, affordability, and informality, the Court held that only generally applicable contract defenses, such as lack of formation, may justify declining to enforce an arbitration agreement under the FAA's saving clause, 9 U.S.C. § 2. *See Epic Systems*, 584 U.S. at 505–08; *Concepcion*, 563 U.S. at 343–45; *id.* at 355 n.* (Thomas, J., concurring) (reporting that "every specific contract defense that the Court has acknowledged is applicable under § 2 relates to contract formation"). And in 2023 a divided Court further held that, when a defendant that lost a motion to compel arbitration appeals as of right under 9 U.S.C. § 16(a), the district court must stay the federal case pending the interlocutory appeal. *Coinbase, Inc. v. Bielski*, 599 U.S. 736 (2023).

As this arbitration case law developed, dissenting Justices argued that enforcement of take-it-or-leave-it arbitration clauses impedes access to the courts, enabling corporations to avoid accountability in class actions. *See, e.g.*, *Italian Colors*, 570 U.S. at 241 (Kagan, J., dissenting) (faulting the majority opinion for allowing an alleged antitrust violator to effectively "use its monopoly power to protect its monopoly power"); *Lamps Plus*, 587 U.S. at 205 (Sotomayor, J., dissenting) (remarking that "the new federal common law of arbitration contracts" is "ill advised"); *Concepcion*, 563 U.S. at 365 (Breyer, J., dissenting).

6. CONCLUSION

Rule 23 is but one of many rules that govern the conduct of class actions, so it is unsurprising that some of the Supreme Court decisions that have had the greatest influence on class action practice do not address Rule 23 at all. In *Twombly*, 550 U.S. 544, and *Ashcroft v. Iqbal*, 556 U.S. 662 (2009), the Court established a "plausibility" standard for stating a claim; in response, complaints grew much longer and litigation on a motion to dismiss became standard practice in class actions. In *Daubert v. Merrell Dow Pharmaceuticals, Inc.*, 509 U.S. 579 (1993), the Court expounded on the standard for analyzing admissibility of expert testimony under Federal Rule of Evidence 702, with lasting ramifications for the expert work that often dominates complex cases. And in *Spokeo*, 578 U.S. 330, and *TransUnion*, 594 U.S. 413, the Court outlined a framework for deciding standing questions in privacy and other disputes in the era of big data.

Depending on how it is interpreted, the Court's personal jurisdiction decision in *Bristol-Myers Squibb Co. v. Superior Court of California, San Francisco County* may affect class action practice as well. 582 U.S. 255 (2017). In *BMS* the Court held that claims of non-Californians were improperly joined in mass tort proceedings in California state court. General jurisdiction over the defendant did not exist, nor, absent a meaningful link between California and the non-resident plaintiffs' claims, was the defendant subject to specific jurisdiction. *Id.* at 1779–82; *see Burger King Corp. v. Rudzewicz*, 471 U.S. 462, 472–78 (1985). Justice Sotomayor, dissenting, observed that the Court did "not confront the question whether its opinion . . . would also apply to a class action in which a plaintiff injured in the forum State seeks to represent a nationwide class of plaintiffs, not all of whom were injured there." *BMS*, 582 U.S. at 278 n.4 (Sotomayor, J., dissenting). Lower courts deciding the first wave of post-*BMS* cases declined to extend its reasoning to foreclose representative claims on personal jurisdiction grounds.[41]

The Supreme Court has also left unaddressed other substantial questions bound up with the application of Rule 23, including:

- May a class that includes uninjured members be certified? *See TransUnion*, 594 U.S. at 431 & n.4; *Tyson Foods*, 577 U.S. at 460.
- Must evidence be admissible to be considered at class certification? *See Wal–Mart*, 564 U.S. at 354; *Comcast*, 569 U.S. at 39 (Ginsburg and Breyer, JJ., dissenting).
- Must common questions predominate across the entire claim for issue class certification to be appropriate? *See Harris*, 77 F.4th at 756.
- May a defendant moot a class case by depositing the full amount of the individual claim in an account payable to the plaintiff? *See Campbell–Ewald*, 577 U.S. at 166.
- Under what circumstances may settlement proceeds be distributed other than to class members, and what principles govern *cy pres* distributions? *See Frank v. Gaos*, 586 U.S. 485, 495 (2019) (Thomas, J., dissenting).

Beyond these questions, there is a relative dearth of Supreme Court precedent on issues relating to class definitions and settlements. The Court's decisions on the books demonstrate that it will continue shaping the development of class action law by reference to constitutional mandates and the text of Rule 23.

---

[41] Lyngaas v. Curaden AG, 992 F.3d 412 (6th Cir. 2021); Mussat v. IQVIA, Inc., 953 F.3d 441 (7th Cir. 2020); Molock v. Whole Foods Mkt. Grp., Inc., 952 F.3d 293 (D.C. Cir. 2020); *see also* Cruson v. Jackson Nat'l Life Ins. Co., 954 F.3d 240 (5th Cir. 2020).

DISTRICT OF COLUMBIA CIRCUIT

By Mark A. Miller and Erin C. Nebbia
Hollingsworth LLP

1. INTRODUCTION

The D.C. Circuit sits in the nation's capital and hears appeals from the U.S. District Court for the District of Columbia.[1] There are no states within its geographic territory. As can be expected given its location, the Court hears numerous appeals involving the Federal Government and its agencies, including employment class actions.

The D.C. Circuit and the District Court have given weight to the Supreme Court's rulings in *Wal-Mart v. Dukes* (2011) and *Comcast v. Behrend* (2013), which addressed the commonality and predominance prerequisites, respectively. The D.C. Circuit observed, for example, that "[b]efore *Behrend*, the case law was far more accommodating to class certification under Rule 23(b)(3)." *In re Rail Freight Fuel Surcharge Antitrust Litig. MDL* No. 1869, 725 F.3d 244, 255 (D.C. Cir. 2013). To the extent a generalization may be made, the Courts in this Circuit tend to take a close and pragmatic look at certification issues.

Recently, in a high-profile class action seeking injunctive relief against a government policy that effectively denied pregnant, unaccompanied alien minors in federal custody access to abortions in all cases, the D.C. Circuit held that the inherently transitory exception to the mootness doctrine applied to the class and affirmed certification of the core (b)(2) class. *J.D. v. Azar*, 925 F.3d 1291 (D.C. Cir. 2019). In so doing, the D.C. Circuit ruled that the class representatives could adequately represent the class even though many absent class members choose to carry their pregnancies to term and some are ideologically opposed to abortion. *Id.* at 1313-20.

2. JURISDICTIONAL PREREQUISITES

a. Class Action Fairness Act (CAFA) Requirements

CAFA amended 28 U.S.C. § 1332 to provide federal district courts with original jurisdiction over class actions where (1) the number of members of all proposed plaintiff classes is 100 or more; (2) minimum diversity exists (i.e., any one member of the proposed or certified plaintiff class (named or unnamed) and any one defendant is diverse); and (3) the amount in controversy, in the aggregate, exceeds $5 million. 28 U.S.C. § 1332(d). Because Congress enacted CAFA to facilitate adjudication of interstate class actions in federal court, no anti-removal presumption applies in assessing the court's CAFA jurisdiction. *Dart Cherokee Basin Operating Co. v. Owens*, 135 S. Ct. 547 (2014); *Bradford v. George Wash. Univ.*, 249 F. Supp. 3d 325, 331 (D.D.C. 2017). The proponent of removal bears the burden of establishing the court's jurisdiction. *McMullen v. Synchrony Bank*, 82 F. Supp. 3d 133, 138 (D.D.C.

[1] Washington, D.C., is the only city to host two federal circuit courts—the U.S. Court of Appeals for the D.C. Circuit and the U.S. Court of Appeals for the Federal Circuit—in separate federal courthouses approximately 1.5 miles apart. The D.C. Circuit is located at 333 Constitution Avenue, N.W., Washington, D.C. 20001, and the Federal Circuit is at 717 Madison Place, N.W., Washington, D.C. 20439. This chapter focuses on case law from the D.C. Circuit and the U.S. District Court for the District of Columbia.

2015). A preponderance of evidence standard applies to satisfaction of the jurisdictional elements. *See Bradford*, 249 F. Supp. 3d at 334.

Regarding the aggregate size of the class, mere reliance on the plaintiffs' estimate of the class size is insufficient. *Wexler v. United Air Lines, Inc.*, 496 F. Supp. 2d 150, 155 (D.D.C. 2007). Courts, however, have accepted declarations based on a review of the defendant's business records to find this element satisfied. *Bradford*, 249 F. Supp. 3d at 333; *McMullen*, 82 F. Supp. 3d at 138.

As for citizenship, the statute provides that an unincorporated association or limited liability company is treated as a citizen of the state "where it has its principal place of business and . . . under whose laws it is organized." 28 U.S.C. § 1332(d)(10); *McMullen*, 82 F. Supp. 3d at 142.

The amount in controversy is perhaps the element that is most frequently litigated. The Supreme Court thoroughly explored the standards and procedures for determining the amount in controversy in *Dart Cherokee Basin Operating Co.*, 135 S. Ct. at 553–54. Where plaintiffs' complaint does not set forth the amount in controversy, the defendant's removal notice generally need only advance a plausible, "short and plain" statement that the amount-in-controversy requirement is met and evidentiary proofs are not required. *Id.* at 553; *see McMullen*, 82 F. Supp. 3d at 139 (amount alleged by defendant is accepted unless controverted or questioned by the court). If the amount is controverted, both sides can submit proof, and the amount is determined under the preponderance of evidence standard. *Dart Cherokee Basin Operating Co.*, 135 S. Ct. at 554. Requests for punitive damages, statutory treble damages, and statutory attorney's fees are considered in determining the amount in controversy. *Bradford*, 249 F. Supp. 3d at 331.

Exceptions: CAFA contains a number of abstention exceptions to its grant of federal jurisdiction for class actions that are significantly local in character. 28 U.S.C. § 1332(d)(3) (permissive "interest of justice" exception), (d)(4)(A) (mandatory "local controversy" exception), and (d)(4)(B) (mandatory "home state controversy" exception). Perhaps in part because the District of Columbia encompasses a small geographic area, the number of cases addressing these exceptions is relatively modest.

In *McMullen*, the District Court applied the local controversy exception set forth in 28 U.S.C. § 1332(d)(4)(A). This exception requires that greater than two-thirds of the members of all proposed classes in the aggregate are citizens of the state of filing; at least one defendant is a citizen of the State where the action was filed; significant relief is sought from that citizen defendant; the citizen defendant's conduct forms a significant basis for the claims asserted by the proposed class; the principal injuries resulting from the alleged conduct or related conduct of each defendant were incurred in the state of filing, and no class action was filed in the prior three years against any of the defendants asserting the same or similar factual allegations. 28 U.S.C. § 1332(d)(4)(A).

In seeking remand under § 1332(d)(4)(A), the proponent of the exception bears the burden of proof and doubts are resolved in favor of exercising jurisdiction. *McMullen*, 82 F. Supp. 3d at 140 (citations omitted). The citizenship of an unincorporated, limited liability company is controlled by § 1332(d)(10); therefore, it is a citizen of the states of its organization and where it has its principal place of business. *Id.* at 142. Significance is assessed based on the allegations and relief sought in the complaint. *Id.* at 142–43. The significant basis requirement must include a comparison of the alleged conduct of all defendants in multi-defendant cases. *Id.* at 143. In assessing the significance of the relief sought, the likelihood of recovery is not relevant. *Id.* at 143–44.

The interest of justice exception "permits federal courts to decline jurisdiction over predominantly local disputes if between one-third and two-thirds of the proposed class members are citizens of the state forum." *Doe v. Georgetown Synagogue-Kesher Israel Congregation*, 118 F. Supp. 3d 88, 90 (D.D.C. 2015). In exercising its discretion, the court must consider the factors set forth in § 1332(d)(3). *Id.* at 93. There must be some facts in evidence upon which the citizenship findings can be made, but citizenship need not be proved with "mathematical certainty." *Id.* at 95.

b. Standing

A named plaintiff must have Article III standing, which requires demonstrating injury-in-fact, causation, and redressability. *See Welborn v. IRS*, 218 F. Supp. 3d 64, 76 (D.D.C. 2016), *appeal dismissed*, No. 16-5365, 2017 WL 2373044 (D.C. Cir. Apr. 18, 2017). The causation and redressability requirements of standing are closely related such that, if a plaintiff challenges conduct is at most an indirect or contributing cause of the plaintiff's injury, the plaintiff "faces an uphill climb in pleading and proving redressability." *Johnson v. Becerra*, 111 F.4th 1237 (D.C. Cir. 2024) (quoting *West v. Lynch*, 845 F.3d 1228, 1235–36 (D.C. Cir. 2017)). Standing is jurisdictional. *See In re Lorazepam & Clorazepate Antitrust Litig.*, 289 F.3d 98, 108 (D.C. Cir. 2002). "The burden to make all of these showings always remains with the plaintiff, but the burden grows as the litigation progresses." *Attias v. Carefirst, Inc.*, 865 F.3d 620, 625 (D.C. Cir. 2017) (citation omitted). The D.C. Circuit has recently held that a plaintiff's desire to serve as a class representative and to claim the interests of others does not meet the necessary requirements of Article III injury without the presence of some personal stake. *Lewis v. Becerra*, 111 F.4th 65, 72 (D.C. Cir. 2024).

In cases involving a direct pecuniary injury to the class, standing issues are usually straightforward. *See Shaw v. Marriott Int'l, Inc.*, 605 F.3d 1039, 1042 (D.C. Cir. 2010) (pecuniary injury conferred standing in hotel overcharge case). Mere statutory violations without pecuniary or other concrete harm, however, are generally insufficient to confer standing. *See Hancock v. Urban Outfitters, Inc.*, 830 F.3d 511, 514 (D.C. Cir. 2016) (mandating dismissal of a complaint that alleged that a retailer's collection of zip codes violated D.C. consumer protection laws because plaintiffs pled only a statutory violation and not a concrete harm to them).

Putative data breach class actions, where the class does not experience actual identify theft, present more complex standing issues. In a recent appeal of a dismissal of a data breach class action complaint against a health insurer, the D.C. Circuit reversed the dismissal because the plaintiffs had adequately alleged facts—including a deliberate breach and theft of Social Security numbers, credit card numbers, and other personal identification information—that showed the plaintiffs to be at a "substantial risk of identity theft[.]" *See Attias*, 865 F.3d at 627. Thus, plaintiffs met the injury-in-fact requirement. The Court also noted that allegations of risk mitigation measures taken by the plaintiffs supported the redressability element but noted that "self-imposed risk mitigation costs" that were incurred in response to a speculative threat would not satisfy the injury-in-fact element. *Id.* at 629. More recently, the district court held, as a matter of first impression, that a breach of contract claim related to a data breach, by itself, supplied the putative class members with a concrete injury satisfying Article III standing. *Attias v. CareFirst, Inc.*, 346 F.R.D. 1 (D.D.C. 2014), *motion to certify appeal denied*, 15-CV-882 (CRC), 2024 WL 3886643 at *7 (D.D.C. Aug. 20, 2024).

In re Science Applications International Corp. (SAIC) Backup Tape Data Theft Litigation, 45 F. Supp. 3d 14 (D.D.C. 2014), presents an interesting juxtaposition to *Attias*. There, plaintiffs alleged that they were at an increased risk of suffering identity theft from a data breach that implicated the personal information, including Social Security numbers and medical records of 4.7 million members of the military and their families. In that case, a thief stole backup tapes from the car of a government contractor that contained this data, along with a GPS and a stereo. The court dismissed the plaintiffs' claims where no actual identity theft was alleged because a mere increased future risk of harm from the breach was insufficient to confer standing. The case did not involve a deliberate cyber-attack, and the chain of events from the thief stealing the tapes from the car, to the possibility of someone actually accessing the data on the tapes, to the misuse of that data, was too attenuated. *Id.* at 25–26.

3. PERSONAL JURISDICTION OVER NONRESIDENT PUTATIVE CLASS MEMBERS

In *Molock v. Whole Foods Market, Inc.*, 297 F. Supp. 3d 114 (D.D.C. 2018), *motion to certify appeal granted sub nom. Molock v. Whole Foods Mkt. Grp., Inc.*, 317 F. Supp. 3d 1 (D.D.C. 2018), the defendants argued that, under the Supreme Court's personal jurisdiction precedent as announced in *Bristol-Myers Squibb C. v. Sup. Ct. of Cal.*, 137 S. Ct. 1773 (2017) (*BMS*), the court should dismiss the claims of any nonresident putative class members, because such members' claims do not arise out of the case-specific contacts with the forum. The U.S. District Court for the District of Columbia rejected the argument, finding key differences between the types of mass actions at issue in *BMS* and class actions. "[I]n a mass tort action, each plaintiff is a real party in interest to the complaints; by contrast, in a putative class action, one or more plaintiffs seek to represent the rest of the similarly situated plaintiffs, and the 'named plaintiffs' are the only plaintiffs actually named in the complaint." *Molock*, 297 F. Supp. 3d at 126. Additionally, unlike a mass tort action, for a case to qualify for class action treatment, it needs to meet the additional due process standards for class certification under Rule 23—numerosity, commonality, typicality, adequacy of representation, predominance and superiority." *Id.* (quotations omitted). The court thus found that the claims of nonresident putative class members were properly before the court. It did, however, dismiss the claims of two named plaintiffs who could not meet the *BMS* standards. *Id.*

On appeal to the District of Columbia Circuit, the Court of Appeals affirmed the district court's denial of dismissal, but on different grounds. *Molock v. Whole Foods Market Group, Inc.*, 952 F.3d 293, 295 (D.C. Cir. 2020). The appellant/defendants argued that the district court lacked both personal and subject matter jurisdiction based largely on the reasoning detailed above. *Id.* at 296. The appellee/plaintiffs argued that class actions present an exception to the general rule that a federal court sitting in diversity typically exercises personal jurisdiction conterminously with that of the state in which it sits. *Id.* Appellees argued that "Federal Rule of Civil Procedure 23 permits a federal court in diversity to exercise personal jurisdiction over unnamed, non-resident, class members' claims, even if a state court could not." *Id.* Alternatively, appellees argued that the motion to dismiss was premature because, prior to class certification, putative class members are not parties to the action. The Court of Appeals agreed with Appellees' latter argument, namely that "putative class members become parties to an action—and thus subject to dismissal—only after class certification" *Id.* at 298.

4. MOOTNESS DOCTRINE

A case becomes moot if "it is impossible for a court to grant any effectual relief whatever to the prevailing party." *Campbell-Ewald Co. v. Gomez*, 136 S. Ct. 663, 669 (2016) (quotation omitted). A named representative can have standing to appeal denial of class certification despite settling his individual claim because of his interest in spreading litigation costs among the members of the class. *Stephens v. Pension Benefit Guar. Corp.*, 755 F.3d 959, 964 (D.C. Cir. 2014); *see also Richards v. Delta Air Lines, Inc.*, 453 F.3d 525, 528–29 (D.C. Cir. 2006).

Intervening circumstances can render a case moot at any stage in the litigation. *See Campbell-Ewald Co.*, 136 S. Ct. at 669. A proposed class representative must keep his or her individual dispute alive until certification, or else the class action based on the claim generally becomes moot. *Givens v. Bowser*, 111 F.4th 117, 121 (D.C. Cir. 2024) (quoting *J.D. v. Azar*, 925 F.3d 1291, 1307 (D.C. Cir. 2019)). In *DL v. District of Columbia*, the D.C. Circuit addressed mootness in the context of a long-running dispute between parents of certain school age children and the District over the District's systemic failures to timely provide children special education services as required by law. 860 F.3d 713, 724 (D.C. Cir. 2017). The original class certification order had been vacated as erroneous on appellate review, and by the time the District Court's second class certification decision reached the Court of Appeals, the children had grown and the case was moot. The Court held that the "relation back exception" to the mootness doctrine applied:

> In this case, the mootness issue stems neither from the lack of real dispute nor from any deficiency in the parents' advocacy, but rather from judicial error. The separation of powers concerns that animate justiciability jurisprudence are absent in this context. In *Geraghty*, the [Supreme] Court emphasized that the two elements of a justiciable controversy—"sharply presented issues in a concrete factual setting and self-interested parties vigorously advocating opposing positions"—can "exist with respect to . . . class certification . . . notwithstanding the fact that the named plaintiff's claim on the merits has expired." Both elements remain present here.

DL, 860 F.3d at 721–22 (quoting *U.S. Parole Comm'n v. Geraghty*, 445 U.S. 388, 403 (1980)). Because the case was live when the parents first sought certification in the district court, the case remained justiciable. *Id.* at 721.

In *J.D. v. Azar*, the D.C. Circuit elaborated on and applied the "inherently transitory" exception to the mootness doctrine in a (b)(2) class action brought by pregnant, unaccompanied alien minors that were in federal custody and denied access to abortions by a shift in government policy. 925 F.3d 1291. These minors have no lawful immigration status and no parent or guardian in the United States. *Id.* at 1299. They are under the care of the Office of Refugee Resettlement (ORR), a program of the Department of Health and Human Services (DHS), and a child can remain there for a variable period of time until an event occurs such as (1) a sponsor for the child is found; (2) the child turns 18 and is transferred to DHS's custody; (3) the child obtains lawful immigration status; or (4) the child voluntarily departs or is removed from the country. *Id.* at 1301. Each year, ORR has custody of several hundred pregnant unaccompanied minors, some of whom seek abortions. *Id.* at 1302–03. While DHS permits alien adults in its custody to obtain abortions, in 2017 ORR implemented a policy that functionally operated as a blanket ban on any unaccompanied alien minor obtaining an abortion, even in cases of rape. *Id.* at 1303. In the class action litigation, the two class representatives challenged ORR's policy as an infringement of their constitutional rights, obtained class certification, and a preliminary injunction on the merits. *Id.* at 1305–06. However, their claims had become moot because one representative had an abortion after obtaining a temporary restraining order and the other was transferred from ORR's to DHS's custody. *Id.* at 1307.

Elaborating on the inherently transitory exception to the mootness doctrine, the panel majority ruled that class certification would relate back to the time of the pleadings if: (1) an individual's claim might end before the district court has a reasonable amount of time to decide certification; and (2) some class members will have a live claim at every stage of the litigation. *Id.* at 1311. The majority held that the first element was satisfied because, *inter alia*, the minors could be in ORR's custody for a short period of time, they could leave ORR's custody for various reasons, and there is limited time to have a pre-viability abortion after discovery of the pregnancy. *Id.* at 1311. The fact that the district court had enough time to grant emergency, temporary relief was immaterial because such relief can be issued in virtually every case and in short order, in contrast to a certification decision. *Id.* As for the second element, the government did not dispute its applicability and, indeed, ORR continued to have pregnant, unaccompanied minors in its custody. *Id.* at 1311–12.

Recently, the D.C. District Court issued an opinion that affirmed *J.D. v. Azar* and further elaborated on the inherently transitory exception. In *Hinton v. District of Columbia*, a transgender inmate detained in the men's unit of the D.C. Jail brought action for a preliminary injunction on behalf of herself and a putative class of transgender individuals to challenge the Department of Correction's (DOC) housing policy that placed inmates based on their anatomical gender. No. 21-cv-1295, 2021 WL 4476775, at *1 (D.D.C. Sept. 30, 2021). After the named plaintiff's detainment, DOC changed this aspect of the housing policy. *Id.* Additionally, Hinton was released from custody after she filed the lawsuit challenging the DOC's policy. *Id.* at *2. The plaintiff argued that her claims could go forward because the as-amended policy allegedly still unlawfully discriminated against transgender individuals and, notwithstanding her release, the class claims are not moot because of their inherently transitory nature. *Id.* at *1. The court denied Hinton's motion for class certification based on numerosity. *Id.* at *15–17. Without a certifiable class, the court held that Hinton could not rely on the inherently transitory exception to mootness as the exception "does not apply outside the class context." *Id.* at *9.

5. PLEADING REQUIREMENTS

Counsel should consult the Local Rules for the District Court for the District of Columbia for specific class action pleading requirements. L.R. 23.1(a). "Local Rule of Civil Procedure 23.1(b) requires a plaintiff to move for certification under Fed. R. Civ. P. 23(c)(1) within 90 days of filing the first complaint bringing a class-wide claim." *Harriott v. Washington Metro. Area Transit Auth.*, No. CV 19-1656 (TJK), 2019 WL 7066631, at *1 (D.D.C. Dec. 23, 2019). "Local Rule 23.1(b) and its predecessors have been strictly applied in this Circuit." *Id.* (quoting *Howard v. Gutierrez*, 474 F. Supp. 2d 41, 53 (D.D.C. 2007)).

6. PREREQUISITES TO CLASS CERTIFICATION

"The class action is an exception to the usual rule that litigation is conducted by and on behalf of the individual named parties only." *Comcast Corp. v. Behrend*, 133 S. Ct. 1426, 1432 (2013) (citation omitted); *Hoyte v. Dist. of Columbia*, 325 F.R.D. 485, 489 (D.D.C. 2017). Rule 23 authorizes certification of a class if the plaintiffs satisfy the burdens set forth in Rule 23(a) and (b). *In re Rail Freight Fuel Surcharge Antitrust Litig., MDL No. 1869*, 725 F.3d 244, 249 (D.C. Cir. 2013). "First, the proposed class must satisfy all four prerequisites to certification: numerosity, commonality, typicality, and adequate representation. . . . Second, the proposed class must fit one of three categories defined by Rule 23(b)[.]" *Id.* (citations omitted).

A party seeking certification must be prepared to prove that "*in fact*" the requirements of Rule 23 are satisfied. *Wal-Mart Stores, Inc. v. Dukes*, 564 U.S. 338, 350–51 (2011). "The party seeking certification bears the burden of persuasion, and must show that the putative class[ ] meet[s] the requirements of Rule 23 by a preponderance of the evidence. To carry that burden, Plaintiffs must affirmatively demonstrate . . . compliance with the Rule." *C.G.B. v. Wolf*, No. 20-CV-1072 (CRC), 2020 WL 2935111, at *15 (D.D.C. June 2, 2020) (quotations & citations omitted; alteration in original). "Oftentimes, this inquiry resembles an appraisal of the merits." *In re Rail Freight Fuel Surcharge*, 725 F.3d at 249. *But see Afghan & Iraqi Allies Under Serious Threat Because of Their Faithful Serv. to the United States v. Pompeo*, 334 F.R.D. 449, 458 (D.D.C. 2020) ("in determining whether to certify a class, a court may not examine whether plaintiffs have stated a cause of action or will prevail on the merits") (quotations omitted). A preponderance of the evidence standard is normally applied. *Hoyte*, 325 F.R.D. at 491. A "district court's order . . . granting class status is inherently tentative." *Borum v. Brentwood Vill., LLC*, No. CV 16-1723 (RC), 2019 WL 2437686, at *12 (D.D.C. June 11, 2019) (quotations omitted). "Because class certification problems are constantly subject to reconsideration as the facts develop, Rule 23 expressly grants courts the discretion to revisit the propriety of continued class certification in later stages of litigation." *Id.* (quotations & citations omitted); *see also* Fed. R. Civ. P. 23(c)(1)(C)) ("An order that grants or denies class certification may be altered or amended before final judgment.").

a. Rule 23(a) Requirements

Numerosity

Under Rule 23, the class must be "so numerous that joinder of all members is impracticable." Fed. R. Civ. P. 23(a)(1). While some Circuits have applied a presumption that 40 class members is sufficiently numerous, the D.C. Circuit has not addressed this issue. *See Hoyte*, 325 F.R.D. at 490. The district court, however, has found this requirement satisfied when the proposed class has 40 or more members. *See Richardson v. L'Oreal USA, Inc.*, 991 F. Supp. 2d 181, 195 (D.D.C. 2013); *cf. also Lewis v. D.C.*, No. CV 15-352 (RBW), 2020 WL 5254976, at *4 (D.D.C. Sept. 3, 2020) (12 to 20 "class members is too low to satisfy the numerosity requirement") (quotations omitted); *see also Coleman v. Dist. of Columbia,* 306 F.R.D. 68, 76 (D.D.C. 2015) ("[a]t the lower end, 'a class that encompasses fewer than [twenty] members will likely not be certified[.]'"). "It is also important to note that numerosity is about much more than just the total number of class members. In many cases, it is difficult to ascertain how many class members there will be, and the question simply becomes whether the existence of unknown and unnamed future class members would make joinder difficult." *N.S. v. Hughes*, No. 1:20-CV-101-RCL, 2020 WL 2219441, at *11 (D.D.C. May 7, 2020), *reconsideration denied*, No. 1:20-CV-101-RCL, 2020 WL 4260739 (D.D.C. July 24, 2020). Classes that include "future claimants generally meet the numerosity requirement due to the impracticality of counting such class members, much less joining them." *J.D. v. Azar*, 925 F.3d 1291, 1322 (D.C. Cir. 2019) (quotations omitted).

A plaintiff need not prove the exact class size. *Feinman v. FBI*, 269 F.R.D. 44, 50 (D.D.C. 2010). Rather, the district court looks to whether there is at least a reasonable basis for the estimate of class size. *E.g., Hoyte*, 425 F.R.D. at 490; *Smith v. Ergo Solutions, LLC*, 306 F.R.D. 57, 67 (D.C. 2015). Estimates of class size that are not supported by record evidence can readily fail to carry the proponent's burden of showing that the class in fact is sufficiently numerous. *See id.* "Mere conjecture, without more, is insufficient to establish numerosity." *Proctor v. D.C.*, 310 F. Supp. 3d 107, 117 (D.D.C. 2018) (quotations omitted) (proposed class of homeless individuals subject to D.C. protocols for disposing of property found at homeless encampments failed numerosity requirements, because plaintiffs relied only on general census data concerning "unsheltered" individuals residing in D.C rather than information pertaining to individuals potentially subject to property protocols at encampments).

To substantiate a plaintiff's assertion regarding sufficiency of numerosity, the district courts may also consider non-numerical factors affecting the impracticability of joinder, which would militate in favor of class certification. *Lewis v. Becerra*, No. 18-2929 (RBW), 2022 WL 1262122, at *12 (D.D.C. April 28, 2022) quoting *Hinton v. Dist. of Columbia*, 567 F. Supp. 3d 30, 43 (D.D.C. 2021) (acknowledging that DOC population custody is fluid and unpredictable, a factor that might make joinder impractical).

Commonality

The D.C. Circuit adheres to the Supreme Court's instruction in *Wal-Mart* that the "plaintiffs' claims must depend upon a common contention that is of such a nature that it is capable of classwide resolution—which means that determination of its truth or falsity will resolve an issue that is central to the validity of each one of the claims in one stroke." *DL v. Dist. of Columbia*, 713 F.3d 120, 125 (D.C. Cir. 2013) (quoting *Wal-Mart*, 564 U.S. at 350–51) (quotations omitted); *see also Brown v. D.C.*, 928 F.3d 1070, 1082 (D.C. Cir. 2019) ("There is no commonality problem here because common *proof* will lead to common *answers* to each of the five *questions* on which *resolution of Plaintiffs' claims* turns.") (emphasis in original). A single question common to all the class member claims can be enough. *In re Dist. of Columbia*, 792 F.3d 96, 100 (D.C. Cir. 2015). For commonality to exist, class members must "have suffered the same injury" and not merely a violation of the same provision of law. *L'Oreal USA, Inc.*, 991 F. Supp. 2d at 196 (citing *Wal-Mart*).

The definition of the class can materially impact the commonality determination. In

DL, the D.C. Circuit vacated the District Court's initial order certifying a class of 3- to 5-year-old children potentially eligible for special services who did not receive a free and appropriate education as required by law because the proposed class implicated different policies and practices at different stages of the District's processes, without a single or uniform policy practice that bridged all the claims. *DL*, 713 F.3d at 127. The matter was remanded for further considerations as to whether a class, classes, or subclasses that were designed around a policy or practice that linked the class as a whole could be certified. *Id.*; *see also C.G.B. v. Wolf*, No. 20-CV-1072 (CRC), 2020 WL 2935111, at *16 (D.D.C. June 2, 2020) (commonality not present where "[a]ssessing the sufficiency of [the defendant's] operations requires the Court to evaluate thousands of individual, discretionary . . . decisions by various ICE officials, employees, and contractors across the country") (quotations omitted).

The case returned to the D.C Circuit after the District Court certified four separate subclasses, which corresponded to deficiencies in different, specific administrative functions in the District's free education process: (1) identification of the child, (2) evaluation within 120 days for referral, (3) eligibility determination within 120 days of referral, and (4) smooth transitions from early intervention to preschool. *DL v. Dist. of Columbia*, 860 F.3d 713, 724 (D.C. Cir. 2017) (*DL II*). The Court found sufficient commonality in the four subclasses because they were "cast around common harms, susceptible to common proof, and curable by a single injunction" requiring annual improvement. *Id.* at 724–25 (quotation & citation omitted). The Court distinguished *Wal-Mart* because the "crux" of a Title VII claim is the reason for a particular employment decision and Wal-Mart supervisors might have had different reasons for millions of such decisions, whereas the statute here "requires the District to find and serve all children with disabilities as a condition of funding." *Id.* at 725.

Where class certification depends on a defendant's alleged custom, policy, and practice causing classwide injury, the district court applies a heightened, "significant proof" standard to show that the alleged custom, policy, or practice exists. *Parker v. Bank of Am., N.A.*, 99 F. Supp. 3d 69, 81 (D.D.C. 2015) (citation omitted); *see Hoyte*, 425 F.R.D. at 492 (*Wal-Mart* "ostensibly heightened the standard"); *Ross v. Lockheed Martin Corp.*, 267 F. Supp. 3d 174, 198 (D.D.C. 2017) (finding no significant proof that the defendant operated under a general policy of discrimination). These courts have joined others that have determined that the "significant proof" standard is not confined to employment cases alleging systemic discrimination, but rather where class certification turns on a policy or practice alleged to cause classwide injury. *See Parker*, 99 F. Supp. 3d at 81; *Hoyte*, 425 F.R.D. at 492.

In employment discrimination cases, the proponent of the class must "identify a company-wide 'common contention' regarding the *reasons* that each member of the class has suffered an injury." *Lockheed Martin Corp.*, 267 F. Supp. 3d at 197 (emphasis in original). Plaintiffs can establish the requisite common contention by (1) identification of a "testing procedure or other companywide evaluation procedure that can be charged with bias," or (2) "significant proof" that an employer "operated under a general policy of discrimination." *Id.* at 196 (quotations & emphasis omitted); *see Moore v. Napolitano*, 926 F. Supp. 2d 8, 29 (D.D.C. 2013). Flaws in a statistical analysis offered to support commonality can defeat certification. *E.g.*, *Garcia v. Johanns*, 444 F.3d 625, 63 (D.C. Cir. 2006) (plaintiffs "statistical analyses were analytically flawed because they did not incorporate key relevant variables connecting disparate impact to loan decisionmaking criteria").

Typicality

Rule 23(a)(3) requires that the "claims or defenses of the representative parties are typical of the claims or defenses of the class." Fed. R. Civ. P. 23(a)(3). "The typicality requirement 'aims at ensuring that the class representatives have suffered injuries in the same general fashion as absent class members.'" *Hoyte*, 425 F.R.D. at 490 (quoting *Hardy v. Dist. of Columbia*, 283 F.R.D. 20, 26 (D.D.C. 2012)). Generally, typicality requires that a representative plaintiff's claim arises from the same course of events as each class member's claims and the claims are based on the same legal arguments to prove liability. *In re Navy Chap-*

laincy, 306 F.R.D. 33, 53 (D.D.C. 2014); *Hardy*, 283 F.R.D. at 25; *Pigford v. Glickman*, 182 F.R.D. 341, 349 (D.D.C. 1998).

Evidentiary challenges may be raised as to whether the putative class representatives, in fact, possess the factual predicate to assert the claim typical of the class. *See Hoyte*, 425 F.R.D. at 496–97 (assessing competing evidence as to whether representatives received statutorily required notice of property forfeiture). At least one of the representatives must be able to assert a particular class claim. *Id.*

Adequacy

Rule 23(a) further requires that the "the representative parties will fairly and adequately protect the interests of the class." Fed. R. Civ. P. 23(a)(4). "Two criteria for determining the adequacy of representation are generally recognized: (1) the named representative must not have antagonistic or conflicting interests with the unnamed members of the class, and (2) the representative must appear able to vigorously prosecute the interests of the class through qualified counsel." *Twelve John Does v. Dist. of Columbia*, 117 F.3d 571, 575 (D.C. Cir. 1997) (citation omitted); *see also, e.g., Stephens v. Farmers Rest. Grp.*, No. CV 17-1087 (TJK), 2019 WL 2550674, at *4 (D.D.C. June 20, 2019) (same); *Hardy*, 283 F.R.D. at 25 (same). A *pro se* plaintiff who is not trained as a lawyer is not an adequate class representative. *DeBrew v. Atwood*, 792 F.3d 118, 132 (D.C. Cir. 2015).

Potential conflict was fatal in a proposed class action alleging that the Navy discriminated against non-liturgical Protestant chaplains on the basis of religion. *In re Navy Chaplaincy*, 306 F.R.D. 33 (D.D.C. 2014). The court cited a number of considerations, including the facts the plaintiffs had not brought suit in the Court of Claims, that jeopardized monetary relief to absent class members, had pursued a campaign of institutional reform over prompt adjudication, and had drawn divisions within the proposed class. *Id.* at 54–56.

Although mootness of the proposed class representatives' claims raises potential adequacy of representation concerns, they are separate issues. *DL v. Dist. of Columbia*, 860 F.3d 713, 726 (D.C. Cir. 2017). Here, the D.C. Circuit credited the district court's then eight-year experience with the adequacy of the plaintiffs' and lawyers' representation over a challenge to adequacy grounded in mootness. *Id. See also J.D. v. Azar*, 925 F.3d 1391, 1313 (D.C. Cir. 2019) (ruling that mootness of the representatives' claims does not establish inadequacy).

In *J.D. v. Azar*, one of the government's primary arguments against certification of the (b)(2) class of pregnant, unaccompanied alien minors in federal custody was that most class members will choose to carry their pregnancies to term. *Id.* at 1313–14. This, the government argued, defeated adequacy because the class representatives' interests were in conflict with most of the unnamed class members. In a 2–1 decision, the majority perceived no conflict because the class was asserting the constitutional right to make a choice whether or not to terminate a pregnancy before viability. *Id.* at 1314. "The class members all assert a common entitlement to make that choice on their own, free from any veto power retained [by the government]." *Id.* The majority also was unpersuaded that a conflict existed because some absent class members would be religiously or ideologically opposed to abortion. The majority reasoned, *inter alia*, that a (b)(2) class is intended to remedy classwide deprivations of civil rights, the Rule does not mandate an opt out right for class members, and nothing is required from absent (b)(2) class members. *Id.* at 1314–19.

The crux of the dissent's objection to certification was that the class was overbroad and should not include pregnant minors who did not wish to have an abortion or were religiously opposed. *See id.* at 1340 (J. Silberman, dissenting). Put another way, the class should all be claiming the same injury. *Id.* at 1346. The majority was disinclined to address the dissent's objections definitionally: "as long as the relief sought in a (b)(2) action is uniform and indivisible and the members of the class are otherwise similarly situated, a district court need not append to the class definition a carve-out for members who subjectively oppose the action." *Id.* at 1320.

Proposed settlement classes can raise adequacy of representation issues. A class settlement is not like an ordinary settlement in that class settlements resolve matters even for those who may have been unaware of the settlement. Therefore, unlike other settlements that are typically left to the parties' discretion, the courts recognize a duty to protect absent class members in assessing the proposed settlement agreement. *See Gur-Ravantab v. Georgetown Univ.*, 1:22-CV-01038 (TNM), 2024 WL 3443481 at *2 (D.D.C. July 16, 2024). When settlement classes are at issue and "[w]hen parties seek a global compromise settling multiple types of claims, . . . the reviewing court must look for 'structural assurance[s] of fair and adequate representation for the diverse groups and individuals affected.' Indeed, when tensions exist among subgroups of a settlement class, 'members of each subgroup cannot be bound to [the] settlement except by consents given by those who understand that their role is to represent solely the members of their respective subgroups.'" *Stephens*, 2019 WL 2550674, at *4 (quoting *Amchem*, 521 U.S. at 627). Such assurances can be found, for example, when the damages for the various class members are negotiated based on similar theories. *Id.*

Definiteness: Adequately Defined and Clearly Ascertainable

Other courts have applied an implicit requirement that a class must be sufficiently definite and ascertainable to be certified. The D.C. Circuit has not ruled on the requirement, but district court in the D.C. Circuit has applied a definiteness standard when evaluating class certification under Rule 23(a). *See O.A. v. Trump*, 404 F. Supp. 3d 109, 159 (D.D.C. 2019) (the D.C. Circuit has not opined on the ascertainability requirement); *Hoyte v. Dist. of Columbia*, 325 F.R.D. at 489 & n.3 (recognizing that "the D.C. Circuit has not opined on the [definiteness] requirement" and applying the requirement "out of an abundance of caution"); *Covelo Indian Cmty. v. Watt*, 551 F. Supp. 366, 376 n.4 (D.D.C. 1982) ("definiteness is not explicitly required under Rule 23" but it has "been implied by many courts as a common sense adjunct to the other elements of Rule 23(a)"); *Thorpe v. Dist. of Columbia*, 303 F.R.D. 120, 139 (D.D.C. 2014) (applying a definiteness standard).

Under the definiteness requirement, a class must be (1) adequately defined and (2) clearly ascertainable. *See DL v. Dist. of Columbia*, 302 F.R.D. 1, 16 (D.D.C. 2013); *Parker v. Bank of Am., N.A.*, 99 F. Supp. 3d 69, 78 (D.D.C. 2015). "The requirement that a class be clearly defined is designed primarily to help the trial court manage the class. . . . It is not designed to be a particularly stringent test, but plaintiffs must at least be able to establish that the general outlines of the membership of the class are determinable at the outset of the litigation." *Pigford v. Glickman*, 182 F.R.D. 341, 346 (D.D.C. 1998) (quotation & citation omitted). Based on the class definition, an individual should be able to determine whether he is a member of the class. *See id.* at 346 (a person could easily ascertain class membership based on the class definition); *Artis v. Yellen*, 307 F.R.D. 13, 24 (D.D.C. 2014) (the "convoluted definition" for the proposed class "would render it difficult for a potential class member to decide" whether he is a member of the class).

Recently, the D.C. District Court adopted the "fail-safe" class rule to bar class certification on the grounds that fail-safe classes are not clearly ascertainable, acknowledging district and circuit splits on the rule's applicability. *White v. Hilton Ret. Plan*, No. 16-856 (CKK), 2022 U.S. Dist. LEXIS 51151, at *1 (D.D.C. Mar. 22, 2022). A fail-safe class exists where the class definition depends upon the merits of the underlying claim, rendering it impossible to determine who is in the class until the case concludes. *Id.* at *5 (quoting *Messner v. NorthShore Univ. HealthSystem*, 669 F.3d 802, 825 (7th Cir. 2012)). The court explained that, while the D.C. Circuit has not opined on the applicability of the fail-safe rule in barring class certification, the absence of a clear derivative leaves open the question of the rule's applicability and does not negate the rule itself. *White*, at *7. Further, at least one court in the circuit has adopted the rule, *see Campbell v. Nat'l R.R. Passenger Corp.*, 311 F. Supp. 3d 281, 313–15 (D.D.C. 2018), and eight circuit courts have adopted the rule or implied it to be a "common-sense" rule, in light of "compelling principles of fairness." *White,* at *8. This suggests that the "fail-safe" rule will continue to be highly persuasive in the D.C. Circuit when resolving class certification disputes. *Id.* at *9.

Courts have called for a "high level of precision" in the class definition for a Rule 23(b)(3) class because the class members must be identified to provide all class members notice and the opportunity to opt out and to distribute any monetary relief. *Thorpe*, 303 F.R.D. at 139 (quoting *Kenneth R. v. Hassan*, 293 F.R.D. 254, 263–64 (D.N.H. 2013)). Conversely, definiteness is relaxed or not applied in the (b)(2) injunctive class context because individualized notice, opt outs, and individualized damage determinations are generally not implicated. *Id.* at 140.

b. Rule 23(b) Requirement

Rule 23(b)(1)(A) and (B) Classes

Rule 23(b)(1)(A) provides for class treatment if individual actions create a risk of "inconsistent or varying adjudications with respect to individual class members that would establish incompatible standard of conduct" for the defendant, Fed. R. Civ. P. 23(b)(1)(A), or if adjudications that "as a practical matter, would be dispositive of the interests of the other class members not parties to the individual adjudications or would substantially impair or impede their ability to protect their interests," Fed. R. Civ. P. 23(b)(1)(B).

These provisions are intended to address circumstances in which "individual adjudications would be impossible or unworkable." *Wal-Mart Stores, Inc. v. Dukes*, 564 U.S. 338, 361–62 (2011). Once certified, these are mandatory classes. The Rule provides no opportunity to "opt out," and notice of the action to absent class members is not required. Fed. R. Civ. P. 23(b)(1); *Wal-Mart*, 564 U.S. at 361–62.

Claims that implicate individualized circumstances or determinations are not suited for (b)(1)(A) certification. *See Daskalea v. Wash. Humane Soc'y*, 275 F.R.D. 346, 378 (D.D.C. 2011). Classes under (b)(1)(B) have been used when the "shared character of rights claim or relief awarded" necessarily effects the absent putative class members, such as actions by shareholders to declare a dividend or where property requires distribution or management. *Ortiz v. Fibreboard Corp.*, 527 U.S. 815, 834 (1999). A stare decisis effect is not enough. *Daskalea*, 275 F.R.D. at 379.

Rule 23(b)(2) Classes

Rule 23(b)(2) authorizes certification of an injunctive relief class if "the party opposing the class has acted or refused to act on grounds that apply generally to the class, so that final injunctive relief or corresponding declaratory relief is appropriate respecting the class as a whole." Fed. R. Civ. P. 23(b)(2). "To certify a class under this provision, a single injunction must be able to provide relief to each member of the class." *DL*, 860 F.3d at 726 (quotation omitted); *see also Samma v. United States Dep't of Def.*, No. 20-CV-1104 (ESH), 2020 WL 4501000, at *9 (D.D.C. Aug. 4, 2020) (Rule 23(b)(2) satisfied where "a single injunction or declaratory judgment vacating the applicable [policy] would provide relief to each member of the class.") (quotations omitted). The Rule "does not authorize class certification when each individual class member would be entitled to a different injunction or declaratory judgment against the defendant." *Wal-Mart*, 564 U.S. at 360–61; *Brown*, 2019 WL 2895992, at *9 ("a Rule 23(b)(2) class action is appropriate only 'when a single injunction or declaratory judgment would provide relief to each member of the class,' not 'when each individual class member would be entitled to a different injunction or declaratory judgment against the defendant.'") (quoting *Wal-Mart*, 564 U.S. at 360). "Rule 23(b)(2) was intended for civil rights cases." *In re Dist. of Columbia*, 792 F.3d 96, 102 (D.C. Cir. 2015).

The D.C. Circuit affirmed certification of several (b)(2) classes that each challenged different, specific, classwide failures by the District of Columbia to meet its legal obligations to provide a free and appropriate public education to children with disabilities. *DL*, 860 F.3d at 726. The district court noted that the district court's comprehensive order, which set an improvement plan and time frames for the District to improve in each defective function, provided relief to each member of the different subclasses. *Id.*; *see also Thorpe*, 303 F.R.D. at 151 (District's alleged failure to implement an effective transition assistance could be declared unlawful as to all class members or none of them) (citing *Wal-Mart*, 131 S. Ct. at 2557).

The Supreme Court's *Wal-Mart* decision raises some doubt as to whether proposed (b)(2) classes seeking even incidental monetary relief can be certified exclusively under this section of the Rule. 564 U.S. at 360. "[A]t a minimum, claims for *individualized* relief (like the backpay at issue here) do not satisfy the Rule." *Id.* (emphasis in original). The D.C. Circuit has authorized use of hybrid classes, where the court may exercise its discretion to certify the injunctive relief claims under (b)(2) and the monetary claims under (b)(3). *See Eubanks v. Billington*, 110 F.3d 87, 96 (D.C. Cir. 1997).

Rule 23(b)(3) Classes

If the Rule 23(a) requirements are satisfied, Rule 23(b)(3) authorizes certification of a class action upon a finding that "questions of law or fact common to class members predominate over any questions affecting only individual members, and that a class action is superior to other available methods for fairly and efficiently adjudicating the controversy." Fed. R. Civ. P. 23(b)(3). These elements are commonly referred to as predominance and superiority. Rule 23(b)(3) further sets forth four nonexclusive factors relevant to the superiority analysis. *See id.*

c. Predominance of Common Questions

The predominance element "tests whether proposed classes are sufficiently cohesive to warrant adjudication by representation." *Amchem Prods., Inc. v. Windsor*, 521 U.S. 591, 623 (1997). Generally, this involves an assessment of what issues are common versus individualized proof and a qualitative assessment of whether the common or individual question predominates. *See Coleman v. Dist. of Columbia*, 306 F.R.D. 68, 85 (D.D.C. 2015).

After the Supreme Court's decision in *Comcast Corp. v. Behrend*, 133 S. Ct. 1426 (2013), the D.C. Circuit issued a significant predominance opinion in a putative class action involving allegations that rail carriers engaged in a price-fixing conspiracy that resulted in supra-competitive fuel surcharges to shippers. *See In re Rail Freight Fuel Surcharge Antitrust Litig.-MDL No. 1869*, 725 F.3d 244, 252 (D.C. Cir. 2013). There, upon taking a Rule 26(f) appeal, the Court focused on the plaintiffs' expert's damages report, which purported to show injury-in-fact and damages for all class members, but generated a false positive as to legacy shippers who could not have been injured by the alleged conspiracy. The D.C. Circuit observed that predominance required more than common evidence of collusion, "[t]he plaintiffs must also show that they can prove, through common evidence, that all class members were in fact injured by the alleged conspiracy." *Id.* at 252. The Court reiterated that "we do expect the common evidence to show all class members suffered *some* injury." *Id.* (emphasis in original).

With these principles in view, the D.C. Circuit vacated the certification order and remanded the case. The court reasoned that *Behrend* "sharpens the defendants' critique of the damages model as prone to false positives. It is now indisputably the role of the district court to scrutinize the evidence before granting certification, even when doing so 'requires inquiry into the merits of the claim.' If the damages model cannot withstand this scrutiny then, that is not just a merits issue. . . . No damages model, no predominance, no class certification." *Id.* at 253 (quoting *Behrend*, 133 S. Ct. at 1433). Proof of classwide injury from the challenged action is defective or absent, as such, this raises a serious if not fatal challenge for showing predominance.

In pattern and practice discrimination cases, courts sometimes certify the threshold liability issue while reserving separate hearings to adjudicate individual defenses or justifications for the employment decision. *See In re Johnson*, 760 F.3d 66, 75 (D.C. Cir. 2014) (district court's certification of class to resolve discrimination issue only was not manifestly erroneous); *see also Taylor v. Dist. of Columbia Water & Sewer Auth.*, 241 F.R.D. 33, 48 (D.D.C. 2007) (certifying a (b)(2) class for purposes of determining liability and deferring decision on a (b)(3) class or other proceedings). Still, the need for individualized determinations may counsel against (b)(3) certification. *See Little v. Wash. Metro. Area Transit Auth.*, 249 F. Supp. 3d 394, 425 (D.D.C. 2017) (certifying a (b)(2) class in a disparate impact case challenging a specific employment policy, but declining to find predominance for a (b)(3) class because the "trier of fact must also determine, for each individual class member, whether the class member was not hired or fired due to the [challenged policy] or for some other reason[,]" such as lying on an application); *see also Lewis v. D.C.*, No. CV 15-352 (RBW), 2020 WL 5254976, at *5 (D.D.C. Sept. 3, 2020) (The "Court cannot . . . resolve in 'one stroke' the question of whether the strip[ ]search of each putative class member violated the Fourth Amendment, and instead must conduct individualized liability determinations on a case-by-case basis to ascertain whether each putative class member was subjected to a strip search pursuant to an alleged blanket strip search policy or pursuant to a reasonable suspicion that the individual in question was concealing a weapon or other contraband. And, the need for such individualized determinations defeat the predominance requirement of Rule 23(b)(3).") (quotations & citations omitted); *In re Brewer*, 863 F.3d 861, 875–76 (D.C. 2017) (ruling that district court did not manifestly err by declining to utilize discretionary case management tools such as bifurcation or certifying a liability issue class).

In this Circuit, the "mere fact that damage awards will ultimately require individualized fact determinations is insufficient by itself to preclude class certification." *McCarthy v. Kleindienst*, 741 F.2d 1406, 1415 (D.C. Cir. 1984) (noting bifurcation as an option). The more complex and individualized the damages determinations are, however, the greater the potential impact on the determination of predominance and superiority. *E.g.*, *Daskalea v. Wash. Humane Soc'y*, 275 F.R.D. 346, 380–82 (D.D.C. 2011).

d. Superiority of Class Adjudication

Certification under Rule 23(b)(3) requires a finding that a "class action is superior to other available methods for fairly and efficiently adjudicating the controversy." Fed. R. Civ. P. 23(b)(3). This requirement explores whether certification of the class would "achieve economies of time, effort, and expense, and promote . . . uniformity of decision as to persons similarly situated, without sacrificing procedural fairness or bringing about other undesirable results." *Amchem*, 521 U.S. at 615 (1997) (quoting Fed. R. Civ. P. 23(b)(3) Adv. Comm. Notes to 1966 Amendment).

"Courts have recognized that as the number of individual issues rises, the class action device becomes a less superior method for adjudication." *Daskalea*, 275 F.R.D. at 381. Conversely, if "common issues predominate strongly," a class action is more likely to be found to advance efficiency and support superiority. *Coleman v. Dist. of Columbia*, 306 F.R.D. 68, 87 (D.D.C. 2015). Whether damages can be determined on a classwide basis or require individualized determinations is pertinent to superiority. *See Hoyte*, 325 F.R.D. at 497 (certifying class where court was satisfied that "individualized damages can be calculated for [the class] without resorting to separate mini-trials"). A determination that certification would "enable individuals to pursue small claims[]" lends support to a finding of superiority. *Nat'l Veterans Legal Servs. Program v. United States*, 235 F. Supp. 3d 32, 44 (D.D.C. 2017); *Hardy v. Dist. of Columbia*, 283 F.R.D. 20, 29 (D.D.C. 2012).

7. CASE MANAGEMENT

a. Appointing Counsel

When a court certifies a class action, it must appoint class counsel under Rule 23(g). *See* Fed. R. Civ. P. 23 (c)(1)(B). Rule 23(g) sets out specific factors that the court must and may consider. *See Radosti v. Envision EMI, LLC*, 717 F. Supp. 2d 37, 54 (D.D.C. 2010). Where class counsel is uncontested, the court typically appoints plaintiff's counsel upon a finding that counsel has satisfied the requirements of Rule 23(g). *See Bynum v. D.C.*, 412 F. Supp.

2d 73, 78 (D.D.C. 2006); *Greenberg v. Colvin*, 63 F. Supp. 3d 37, 47 (D.D.C. 2014); *Little v. Wash. Metro. Area Transit Auth.*, 249 F. Supp. 3d 394, 426 (D.D.C. 2017). Where multiple counsel with similar qualifications apply to be class counsel, the court may consider the proposal of a team of attorneys from different law firms, not merely the qualifications of the person or firm designated lead counsel. *See Steele v. United States*, No. 14-cv-1523, 2015 WL 4121607, at *3 (D.D.C. June 30, 2015).

b. Timing of Class Certification

Rule 23(c) requires the district court to determine whether to certify a class "at an early practicable time." Under the district court local rules (hereinafter, L.R.), plaintiffs must move for class certification within 90 days after filing the complaint, unless the court exercises discretion to extend that period. *See* L.R. 23.1(b). The 90-day period commences with the filing of the first complaint alleging a class action, not any subsequent filing of an amended complaint. *See Black Panther Party v. Smith*, 661 F.2d 1243, 1279 (D.C. Cir. 1981), *vacated on other grounds*, 458 U.S. 1118 (1982) (refusing to grant a motion for extension of time to file for class certification where the request was filed 11 days after the 90-day period expired); *Howard v. Gutierrez*, 474 F. Supp. 2d 41, 54-55 (D.D.C. 2007).

Generally, unless extended, the 90-day rule is strictly enforced. *See Howard*, 474 F. Supp. 2d at 57 n.11; *Little v. Wash. Metro. Area Transit Auth.*, 100 F. Supp. 3d 1 (D.D.C. 2015). "The law is clear and the Rule has serious consequences." *Id.* at 6. Even where a court stays discovery or a motion to dismiss is pending, the 90-day rule for class certification still applies. *Id.* The local rules specifically provide the district court discretion to extend the period. *See id.* In addition, "[a] district court may forgive a party's failure to file a timely certification motion if that party makes a showing of excusable neglect." *Id.*; *see Howard*, 474 F. Supp. 2d at 55. To determine whether plaintiff's delay is excusable, the court weighs the equities and considers "the danger of prejudice to the other party, the length of delay and its potential impact on judicial proceedings, the reason for delay, including whether it was within the reasonable control of the movant, and whether the movant acted in good faith." *Id.* at 56 (quotations omitted); *see also Smith v. Ergo Solutions, LLC*, 306 F.R.D. 57, 66 (D.D.C. 2015).

Upon plaintiff's motion to certify a class, the court may allow the class action to proceed, deny the motion, or postpone a ruling pending "discovery or other appropriate preliminary proceedings." L.R. 23.1(b). Note, however, that "a class-action pleading must present *plausible* classwide claims before plaintiffs can proceed with class discovery." *Ross v. Lockheed Martin Corp.*, No. 16-CV-2508 (KBJ), 2020 WL 4192566, at *2 (D.D.C. July 21, 2020) (emphasis in original). "[T]o determine whether pre-certification discovery is warranted, courts must refrain from going beyond a consideration of a prima facie showing and into a consideration of Plaintiff's likelihood of success at the class certification stage." *Id.* at *3. The language in Rule 23(c) and "the word practicable allow[ ] for wiggle room," leaving the trial court discretion to decide the order of disposition of summary judgment motions and class certification. *Curtin v. United Airlines, Inc.*, 275 F.3d 88, 92 (D.C. Cir. 2001) (quotation omitted).

8. CLASS NOTICE

The Federal Rules require that absent class members in a (b)(3) class be given both notice of the existence of a class action lawsuit and notice of settlement. The court has discretion to require notice to class members at other points in the litigation. For Rule 23(b)(1) and (b)(2) classes, the court "may direct appropriate notice to the class." Fed. R. Civ. P. 23(c)(2)(A).

a. Notice of (b)(3) Class Action

For (b)(3) classes, the court must "direct to class members the best notice that is practicable under the circumstances." Fed. R. Civ. P. 23(c)(2)(B). The notice of class action must "clearly and concisely state in plain, easily understood language" details about the class action, definition of class members, claims and defenses, the options to appear through an attorney or be excluded from the class, and the binding impact of class judgment. *Id.*

The Local Rules require plaintiffs to submit a notice plan. *See* L.R. 23.1(c). In a motion for certification, plaintiff must include a proposal for "(1) how, when, by whom, and to whom the notice required by Fed. R. Civ. P. 23(c)(2) shall be given, (2) how and by whom payment therefore is to be made, and (3) by whom the response to the notice is to be received." *Id.* Alternatively, the plaintiff can explain why it cannot determine these details and propose when a determination should be made. When the court certifies a class under (b)(3), the court can either include the provisions for notice in the order or postpone determination.

Notice must be reasonably calculated to inform interested parties of the action and provide an opportunity to object. *See Brown v. Wells Fargo Bank, N.A.*, 869 F. Supp. 2d 51, 64 (D.D.C. 2012). "Individual notice must be sent to all class members whose names and addresses may be ascertained through reasonable effort." *Eisen v. Carlisle & Jacquelin*, 417 U.S. 156, 173 (1974); *see Pigford v. Veneman*, 355 F. Supp. 2d 148, 162 (D.D.C. 2005). Notice by first-class mail is typically sufficient, whether or not the class member actually receives the notice. *See Peters v. Nat'l R.R. Passenger Corp.*, 966 F.2d 1483, 1486 (D.C. Cir. 1992). Notice by email and on the internet, often in conjunction with traditional means, has become commonplace, particularly when email addresses are accessible. *See Nat'l Veterans Legal Servs. Program v. United States*, 235 F. Supp. 3d 32, 45 (D.D.C. 2017) (approving a "class-notice plan involving email notice . . . to each class member using the contact information maintained by the government for PACER users") (quotations omitted); *In re APA Assessment Fee Litig.*, 311 F.R.D. 8, 13 (D.D.C. 2015) (detailing notice procedures for roughly 75,000 class members, 51,000 of whom received email notice while the rest received mailed postcards). *In re Fed. Nat'l Mortg. Ass'n Sec., Derivative, & "ERISA" Litig.*, 4 F. Supp. 3d 94, 101 (D.D.C. 2013) (notice adequate where counsel hired a processing firm to mail copies of the notice and proof of claim to potential class members and their nominees, publish notice in two major newspapers, and set up a dedicated website, email address, and telephone hotline). *But see Galloway v. Chugach Gov't Servs., Inc.*, 263 F. Supp. 3d 151, 159-60 (D.D.C. 2017) (ordering notice by mail where furnishing email addresses would reveal inherently private information).

b. Notice of Settlement

For settlement classes, Rule 23(e) requires that a court direct notice "in a reasonable manner" to all class members potentially bound by the proposal before approving a settlement. Fed. R. Civ. P. 23(e)(1); *see Pigford v. Veneman*, 355 F. Supp. 2d 148, 161 (D.D.C. 2005). Because class members who do not opt out of a settlement will be bound by its terms—a "serious consequence[] of class action litigation"—the standard for providing notice is generally high. *Id.*; *see In re LivingSocial. Mktg. & Sales Practice Litig.*, 298 F.R.D. 1, 10 (D.D.C. 2013) (applying class notice rules under Rule 23(c)(2)(B) to a settlement class notice); *Trombley v. Nat'l City Bank*, 826 F. Supp. 2d 179, 185, 201 (D.D.C. 2011) (individualized and publication notice); *Cohen v. Chilcott*, 522 F. Supp. 2d 105, 112 (D.D.C. 2007) (approving notice by publication in the weekend edition of a major newspaper and an internet notice campaign without individualized notice).

As the district court explained:

> The bottom line is this: a putative class member needs to be able to make an informed determination regarding whether or not to opt out of a class settlement, and this is especially so when the proposed agreement requires him or her to give up potentially viable legal claims in exchange for the promise of a monetary recovery. Ordinarily, and ideally, when faced with such a choice, the class member would

> want to know how much the claims he is releasing are likely to be worth, so that this figure can be compared to the amount being offered in settlement of those claims.

Ross v. Lockheed Martin Corp., 267 F. Supp. 3d 174, 203–04 (D.D.C. 2017).

c. Other Forms of Notice

Under Rule 23(d)(1)(B), the court may require appropriate notice to some or all class members of any step in the action, the proposed extent of the judgment, or "members' opportunity to signify whether they consider the representation fair and adequate, to intervene and present claims or defenses, or to otherwise come into the action. . . ." Rule 23(d)(1)(B)(iii). This provision has been used to require parties to notice class members of a modification to a settlement agreement that did not materially impact class members' rights. *Keepseagle v. Vilsack*, 102 F. Supp. 3d 306, 316 (D.D.C. 2015).

9. OPT-OUTS

Rule 23(b)(3) class members must be afforded the opportunity to be excluded from a class action, Fed. R. Civ. P. 23(c)(2)(B)(v). In contrast, no such right is expressly provided in the Rule for (b)(1) and (b)(2) classes. Given the cohesiveness underlying (b)(1) and (b)(2) classes, the opportunity to opt out is not commonly afforded but may be permitted in limited circumstances, such as where a member filed her own action before the putative class action. *See Thomas v. Albright*, 139 F.3d 227, 235 (D.C. Cir. 1998) (discussing circumstances where court may allow (b)(2) opt outs but finding abuse of discretion on the record); *Eubanks v. Billington*, 110 F.3d 87, 94 (D.C. Cir. 1997) (finding authority for such opt outs under (d)(5)); *Pate v. United States*, 328 F. Supp. 2d 62, 70 (D.D.C. 2004) (holding that due process for absent class members of a (b)(2) class requires only adequate representation, not notice or an opportunity to opt out). *Compare Keepseagle v. Johanns*, 236 F.R.D. 1, 5–6 (D.D.C. 2006) (allowing class members to opt out where the members "always contended that they [were] 'trapped'" in the action, filed administrative claims predating the class action that advanced different legal theories, and maintained separate counsel), *with In re Black Farmers Discrimination Litig.*, 856 F. Supp. 2d 1, 32 (D.D.C. 2011) (permitting opt outs would destroy the fairness of the proposed settlement).

Members of a (b)(3) class must be provided an opportunity to be excluded from the class action. *See* Fed. R. Civ. P. 23(c)(2)(B)(v). Procedures for opting out of a (b)(3) class must be identified in the notice of class action. Fed. R. Civ. P. 23(c)(2)(B). Class members who opt out have no standing to object to a subsequent class settlement. *See In re Vitamins Antitrust Class Actions*, 215 F.3d 26, 28–29 (D.C. Cir. 2000). Members must affirmatively opt out to be excluded from a class action. *See Cryer v. InterSolutions, Inc.*, No. 06-2032, 2007 WL 1191928, at *2 (D.D.C. Apr. 20, 2007).

Persons who fail to opt out of a class are bound by the disposition of the action and cannot subsequently seek relief for alleged injuries that may have been redressed by the class litigation. *See White v. Vilsack*, 80 F. Supp. 3d 123, 125–26 (D.D.C. 2015), *aff'd*, No. 15-5108, 2015 WL 5210421 (D.C. Cir. Aug. 6, 2015); *Pigford v. Veneman*, 355 F. Supp. 2d 148, 161 (D.D.C. 2005) (class members who did not timely opt out of a prior class settlement were bound by the terms of that prior settlement); *Razmyar v. Bombay Club, Inc.*, No.15-cv-807, 2016 WL 4249757, at *2 (D.D.C. Feb. 26, 2016) (persons who do not timely opt out will be considered members of the settlement class). Courts have forgiven failures to follow "fixed deadlines and procedures for opting-out of class action suits" if "such requirements would produce an unfair result." *Butler v. Fairbanks Capital*, No. 04-cv-367, 2005 WL 5108537, at *5–6 (D.D.C. Jan. 3, 2005) (a potential class member "reasonably indicated her intent to be excluded" where she filed independent litigation addressing the issues in the class action prior to the deadline for opting out); *Augst-Johnson v. Morgan Stan-*

ley & Co., 247 F.R.D. 25, 26 (D.D.C. 2008) (allowing a class member to opt out where the notice of proposed settlement was not mailed to the member's correct address).

10. ABSENT CLASS MEMBER ISSUES

a. Communications with Absent Class Members

The district court may limit communications between litigants and putative class members prior to certifying a class. *See Keystone Tobacco Co. v. U.S. Tobacco Co.*, 238 F. Supp. 2d 151, 154 (D.D.C. 2002) (citing *Gulf Oil Co. v. Bernard*, 452 U.S. 89, 100 (1981)). "Because of the potential for abuse [of the class action process], a district court has both the duty and the broad authority to exercise control over a class action and to enter appropriate orders governing the conduct of counsel and parties." *Id.* at 155 (citing *Gulf Oil*, 452 U.S. at 100); *see Cobell v. Norton*, 225 F.R.D. 41, 51 (D.D.C. 2004). To avoid conflict with the First Amendment, orders limiting communications must be based on a "clear record and specific findings that reflect the weighing of a need for a limitation and the potential interference with the rights of the parties." *Keystone Tobacco Co.*, 238 F. Supp. 2d at 155 (citing *Gulf Oil*, 452 U.S. at 101). A defendant may continue regular business communications with class members. *See Cobell v. Norton*, 212 F.R.D. 14, 20 (D.D.C. 2002).

b. Discovery from Absent Class Members

Discovery of or from absent class members is available at the Court's discretion. *See Dellums v. Powell*, 566 F.2d 167, 187 (D.D.C. 1977). Courts have considered whether "the information requested is relevant to the decision of common questions, when the interrogatories or document requests are tendered in good faith and are not unduly burdensome, and when the information is not available from the representative parties." *Id.*; *Barham v. Ramsey*, 246 F.R.D. 60, 62–63 (D.D.C. 2007) ("[T]he Court has the power . . . to permit reasonable discovery when the circumstances of the case justify it."). Courts may allow questionnaires for discovery from absent class members, as well as document discovery and depositions. *Disability Rights Council of Greater Wash. v. Wash. Metro. Area Transit Auth.*, Civ. A. No. 04-498, 2006 WL 2588710, at *1 (D.D.C. Sept. 7, 2006); *Barham*, 246 F.R.D. at 62.

11. DAMAGES

a. Proof

Class damages issues are frequently explored in the predominance analysis, *e.g.*, *In re Rail Freight Fuel Surcharge Antitrust Litig.*, 725 F.3d 244, 252 (D.C. Cir. 2013), which is discussed *supra*. For damages to be determined on a classwide basis, courts look for a formulaic method. *See Little v. Wash. Metro. Area Transit Auth.*, 249 F. Supp. 3d 394, 425 (D.D.C. 2017) (rejecting certification of (b)(3) class because, inter alia, expert's damages model "does not provide a formulaic approach for determining class-wide damages or provide a universal system of damages"); *Hoyte*, 325 F.R.D. at 494 ("A formulaic approach to determining individualized damages is indeed consistent with Rule 23, and has been used in others cases.").

b. Distribution

In determining whether an allocation plan is appropriate, the district court uses the same metrics for whether a class action settlement is "fair, reasonable, and adequate." *In re Fed. Nat'l Mortg. Ass'n Sec., Derivative, & "ERISA" Litig.*, 4 F. Supp. 3d 94, 107 (D.D.C. 2013) (quotation omitted). To do this, the courts may evaluate the strengths and weaknesses of a class member's claim, which can result in different amounts owing to different class members. *See, e.g.*, *Trombley v. Nat'l City Bank*, 826 F. Supp. 2d 179, 202 (D.D.C. 2011). A plan will not be deemed inadequate if distribution of settlement funds is deferred, such as pending final case resolution. *See In re Domestic Airline Travel Antitrust Litig.*, 378 F. Supp. 3d 10 (D.D.C. 2019).

The allocation plan "need not be perfect," but rather Courts looks to whether the "plan has a reasonable, rational basis, particularly if recommended by experienced and competent class counsel." *In re Fed. Nat'l Mortg. Ass'n Sec., Derivative, & "ERISA" Litig.*, 4 F. Supp. 3d at 108–09 (quotations & citation omitted). One method for allocating approved settlement funds is a pro rata distribution, where funds are divided between the class members on some proportional basis, even if a class member does not receive the full amount of his actual damages. *See, e.g., In re Sea Containers Ltd. Class Action Sec. Litig.*, No. 89-0930, 1990 WL 99307, at *10 (D.D.C. July 6, 1990) ("Due to a number of factors described below, it is possible that Eligible Claimants may not receive the full amount of an otherwise allowed claim, but only a *pro rata* amount thereof, which could be a significant reduction."). Allocation can be determined based on losses incurred during a specific period of time if such an allocation fits the facts of the case. *See Trombley v. Nat'l City Bank*, 759 F. Supp. 2d 20, 27 (D.D.C. 2011) (limiting the recovery period to two months of incurring overdraft fees "with the remaining funds then distributed among Class Members on a pro rata basis"). Courts have used a claims process, whereby class members submit some proof of their claim and damages, to aid the distribution process. *See, e.g., Trombley*, 826 F. Supp. 2d at 201 ("a claims process is often used to ensure that money is fairly distributed for valid claims").

12. SETTLEMENTS

Class action settlements are generally favored within the D.C. Circuit. *See, e.g., Kinard v. E. Capitol Family Rental, L.P.*, No. CV 15-1935 (TJK), 2019 WL 2289490, at *3 (D.D.C. May 28, 2019) ("there is a 'long-standing judicial attitude favoring class action settlements'") (quoting *In re Vitamins Antitrust Litig.*, 305 F. Supp. 2d 100, 103 (D.D.C. 2004)).

a. Drafting Considerations

The D.C. Circuit permits class settlement agreements to include payment for certain amounts of attorney's fees if those fees are reasonable. *See Moore v. Nat'l Ass'n of Sec. Dealers, Inc.*, 762 F.2d 1093, 1099 (D.C. Cir. 1985) ("simultaneous negotiations of merits, fees, and costs [in a class action settlement] should not be prohibited completely"); *Prince*, 257 F. Supp. 3d at 26 ("Courts have a duty to ensure that claims for attorneys' fees are reasonable, and the fact that the attorney's fees are structured into the settlement agreement does not excuse the Court from examining whether the attorney's fees agreed upon as a part of the settlement are fair, reasonable, and adequate.") (quotations and citations omitted).

b. Preliminary Approval

Preliminary approval will generally be granted if the proposed settlement falls "within the range of possible approval" and "does not disclose grounds to doubt its fairness or other obvious deficiencies, such as unduly preferential treatment of class representatives or of segments of the class, or excessive compensation for attorneys." *Trombley*, 759 F. Supp. 2d at 23 (D.D.C. 2011) (quotations omitted); *see id.* at 24–25 (finding a settlement allegedly representing 17 to 24 percent of the potential recovery at trial to be within the "range of possible approval" and citing cases where settlements ranging from 6 to 54 percent of the potential trial recovery were also approved). At the preliminary approval stage, "the Court's primary role is to evaluate the relief provided in the settlement against the relative strength of plaintiffs' case, including their ability to obtain recovery at trial. The Court may refuse to approve a settlement where the plaintiffs' basis for estimating the potential value of the settlement is not clear." *Id.* at 24 (citations omitted). To make this determination, the courts will typically consider:

- whether the proposed settlement appears to be the product of serious, informed, non-collusive negotiations;
- whether it falls within the range of possible judicial approval; and
- whether it has any obvious deficiencies, such as granting unduly preferential treatment.

Richardson v. L'Oreal, Inc., 951 F. Supp. 2d 104,106-07 (D.D.C. 2013). Preliminary approval "lies within the sound discretion of the court." *See In re Vitamins Antitrust Litig.*, No. 99-cv-197, 1999 WL 1335318, at *5 (D.D.C. Nov. 23, 1999). But "[w]hen a settlement is negotiated prior to class certification . . . it is subject to a higher degree of scrutiny in assessing its fairness." *Richardson*, 951 F. Supp. 2d 104,107 (quoting *D'Amato v. Deutsche Bank*, 236 F.3d 78, 85 (2d Cir. 2001)); *see Ross v. Lockheed Martin Corp.*, 267 F. Supp. 3d at 201-04 (denying preliminary approval because of concerns with broad waivers of all racial discrimination claims and strict opt out procedures, among other issues).

c. Objections by Class Members

The Federal Rules of Civil Procedure provide that "[a]ny class member may object to the [settlement] proposal if it requires court approval. . . ." Fed. R. Civ. P. 23(e)(5). This language provides standing only for class members to object to a proposed settlement. Individuals who are outside the class entirely, or who have opted out of the class, have no standing to object. *See In re Vitamins Antitrust Class Actions*, 215 F.3d 26, 28–29 (D.C. Cir. 2000) ("class members who have opted out of a 23(b)(3) class action have no standing to object to a subsequent class settlement"); *In re Black Farmers Discrimination Litig.*, 953 F. Supp. 2d 82, 91 (D.D.C. 2013) (objections will not be considered if "submitted by individuals who were not class members and therefore had no right to object to either the Settlement Agreement or class counsel's motion for a fee award"). An exception exists, however, for those non-class members who "demonstrate 'prejudice' from the settlement." *Mayfield v. Barr*, 985 F.2d 1090, 1093 (D.C. Cir. 1993). The D.C. Circuit has held that "'prejudice' in this context means 'plain legal prejudice,' as when 'the settlement strips the party of a legal claim or cause of action.'" *Id.* (quoting *Agretti v. ANR Freight Sys., Inc.*, 982 F.2d 242, 247 (7th Cir. 1992)).

In determining whether a proposed settlement is fair and reasonable, the court may also take into account the absence of any objections, if there is sufficient indicia that potential objectors had incentive to make their views known. *See Stephens*, 2019 WL 2550674, at *8 ("[T]he absence of *any* objector is critical. Despite clear notice of the settlement terms and a chance to object, not one individual of the over 800 notified filed an objection or sought to opt out, and over one-quarter of those individuals affirmatively sought to partake by filing claims—a high participation rate." (emphasis in original)).

d. Final Approval

Before a district court can grant final approval of a class settlement, it "must find that the settlement is fair, adequate and reasonable and is not the product of collusion between the parties." *Thomas v. Albright*, 139 F.3d 227, 231 (D.C. Cir. 1998) (citation omitted). The appellate court will not disturb a district court decision approving settlement unless the appellant can make a "clear showing that an abuse of discretion has occurred." *Keepseagle v. Perdue*, 856 F.3d 1039, 1048–49 (D.C. Cir. 2017), *petition for cert. filed*, No. 17-897, U.S. Sup. Ct. (Dec. 19, 2017).

Factors the courts have examined include:

- whether the settlement is the result of arm's-length negotiations;
- the terms of the settlement in relation to the strength of the case;
- the stage of the litigation proceedings at the time of settlement;
- the reaction of the class; and

- the opinion of experienced counsel.

Trombley v. Nat'l City Bank, 826 F. Supp. 2d 179, 194 (D.D.C. 2011); *see also Abraha v. Colonial Parking, Inc.*, No. CV 16-680 (CKK), 2020 WL 4432250, at *7 (D.D.C. July 31, 2020) (articulating the same standards); *Prince*, 257 F. Supp. 3d at, 24–25 (same); *In re Fed. Nat'l Mortg. Ass'n Sec., Derivative, & "ERISA" Litig.*, 4 F. Supp. 3d 94, 102 (D.D.C. 2013) (same); *In re Lorazepam & Clorazepate Antitrust Litig.*, 205 F.R.D. 369, 375 (D.D.C. 2002) (collecting cases).

e. *Cy Pres*

According to the American Law Institute, *cy pres* awards are appropriate "only when direct distributions to class members are not feasible—either because class members cannot be reasonably identified or because distribution would involve such small amounts that, because of the administrative costs involved, such distribution would not be economically viable." *Principles of the Law of Aggregate Litigation* § 3.07 cmt. b (Am. Law Inst. 2010).

The D.C. Circuit has noted *in dicta* that "[i]n class actions, some courts have applied the equitable doctrine of *cy pres* to undistributed damage or settlement funds." *Democratic Cent. Comm. of the Dist. of Columbia v. Wash. Metro. Area Transit Comm'n*, 84 F.3d 451, 455 (D.C. Cir. 1996); *cf. also Keepseagle*, 856 F.3d at 1043 (refusing to consider the merits of a challenge to a *cy pres* award because the appellant had waived his right to challenge the award in the district court). As the D.C. Circuit noted from its review of *cy pres* cases in other jurisdictions, the doctrine allows unclaimed settlement funds to be allocated to the "next best" use for the indirect benefit of the class. *Dem. Cent. Comm. of the Dist. of Columbia*, 84 F.3d at 455. "The object of applying the funds to the 'next best' class is to parallel the intended use of the funds as nearly as possible by maximizing the number of plaintiffs compensated." *Id.*

The district court has permitted *cy pres* distributions in class settlements. *See, e.g.*, *Keepseagle v. Vilsack*, 307 F.R.D. 233, 237 (D.D.C. 2014); *Radosti v. Envision EMI, LLC*, 760 F. Supp. 2d 73, 76 (D.D.C. 2011); *In re Dep't of Veterans Affairs Data Theft Litig.*, 653 F. Supp. 2d 58, 59 (D.D.C. 2009). Relying on precedent from other jurisdictions, one court has applied the following factors to determine whether a *cy pres* award was appropriate:

- the objectives of the underlying statute(s);
- the nature of the underlying suit;
- the interests of the class members; and
- the geographic scope of the case.

Diamond Chem. Co. v. Akzo Nobel Chems. B.V., 517 F. Supp. 2d 212, 220 (D.D.C. 2007) (quoting *Schwartz v. Dallas Cowboys Football Club, Ltd.*, 362 F. Supp. 2d 574, 576 (E.D. Pa. 2005)).

13. ATTORNEYS' FEES AND COSTS

"In a certified class action, the court may award reasonable attorney's fees and nontaxable costs that are authorized by law or by the parties' agreement. . . . However, [a]n award of attorneys' fees must be reasonable in light of the results obtained." *In re LivingSocial Mktg. & Sales Practice Litig.*, 298 F.R.D. 1, 15 (D.D.C. 2013) (quotations omitted; alteration in original; citing Fed. R. Civ. P. 23(h)); *In re Dep't of Veterans Affairs Data Theft Litig.*, 653 F. Supp. 2d 58, 60 (D.D.C. 2009).

The D.C. Circuit has held that different forms of attorney fee calculations may be appropriate. For example, where a common fund is at issue, the D.C. Circuit has endorsed the use of a percentage of that fund as a proper method for calculating an attorney's fee award. *See Swedish Hosp. Corp. v. Skalala*, 1 F.3d 1261, 1271 (D.C. Cir. 1993). In determining the percentage, courts have considered:

- the size of the fund created and the number of persons benefitted;
- the presence or absence of substantial objections by members of the class to the settlement terms and/or fees requested by counsel;
- the skill and efficiency of the attorneys involved;
- the complexity and duration of the litigation;
- the risk of nonpayment;
- the amount of time devoted to the case by plaintiffs' counsel; and
- the awards in similar cases.

Ceccone v. Equifax Info. Servs. LLC, No. 13-cv-1314, 2016 WL 5107202, at *11 (D.D.C. Aug. 29, 2016). Fee awards in common fund cases typically range from 15 to 45 percent of the common fund. *See Rogers v. Lumina Solar, Inc.*, No. 18-CV-2128 (KBJ), 2020 WL 3402360, at *11 (D.D.C. June 19, 2020); *In re Lorazepam & Clorazepate Antitrust Litig.*, No. MDL 1290, 2003 WL 22037741, at *7 (D.D.C. June 16, 2003).

The D.C. Circuit has endorsed the use of a lodestar calculation to cross-check the reasonableness of a percentage fee award. *See, e.g., In re Fed. Nat'l Mortg. Ass'n Sec., Derivative, & "ERISA" Litig.*, 4 F. Supp. 3d at 113 ("While our Circuit does not require such a lodestar cross-check, performing one in this case confirms the reasonableness of a 22% award.") (citation omitted); *In re LivingSocial Mktg. & Sales Practice Litig.*, 298 F.R.D. at 15 (same). When a cross check is performed, the "lodestar" is "calculated by multiplying the hours reasonably expended in the litigation by a reasonable hourly fee." *In re Fed. Nat'l Mortg. Ass'n Sec., Derivative, & "ERISA" Litig.*, 4 F. Supp. 3d at 113. An attorney's "usual billing rate is presumptively the reasonable rate, provided that the rate is 'in line with those prevailing in the community for similar services by lawyers of reasonably comparable skill, experience and reputation.'" *In re LivingSocial Mktg. & Sales Practice Litig.*, 298 F.R.D. at 18 (quoting *Kattan ex rel. Thomas v. Dist. of Columbia*, 995 F.2d 274, 278 (D.C. Cir. 1993)). The fees may be reduced, however, if counsel fails to submit proper supporting documentation or the fee would otherwise be disproportionate to the complexity of the case. *Id.* (citing *Miller v. Holzmann*, 575 F. Supp. 2d 2, 45 (D.D.C. 2008), *amended in part, vacated in part, U.S. ex rel. Miller v. Bill Harbert Int'l Constr. Inc.*, 786 F. Supp. 2d 110 (D.D.C. 2011).

Although not common, there is precedent for the district court awarding attorney's fees from the common fund based on the number of hours the attorneys worked, minus a discount for what the court perceived as inefficiencies, multiplied by an hourly rate. *Larionoff v. United States*, 365 F. Supp. 140, 146–47 (D.D.C. 1973), *aff'd*, 533 F.2d 1167, 1187 (D.C. Cir. 1976); *see also Kiser v. Huge*, 517 F.2d 1237 (D.C. Cir. 1974) (affirming fee award based on the same method as *Larionoff*).

14. APPELLATE ISSUES

a. Standing to Appeal

Class members, whether named or absent, who object to a settlement at the district court fairness hearing may appeal an order entering the settlement agreement. *See Devlin v. Scardelletti*, 536 U.S. 1, 7, 14 (2002); *Latham v. Vilsack*, No. 11-5326, 2012 WL 10236550, at *1 (D.C. Cir. July 25, 2012) (citing *Devlin*, 536 U.S. at 11).

In *In re Brewer*, 863 F.3d 861 (D.C. Cir. 2017), the Court held that when a named plaintiff settles claims with defendant without appealing an adverse class certification decision, an absent class member may intervene to appeal the decision. Thus, the D.C. Circuit found that it had "jurisdiction under Rule 23(f) to hear the motion to intervene in the interlocutory petition for review of the denial of class certification, notwithstanding the stipulated dismissal of the named plaintiff's claims." *Id.*

b. Interlocutory Appeal of Class Certification

Rule 23(f) provides that a "court of appeals may permit an appeal from an order granting or denying class-action certification under this rule if a petition for permission to appeal is filed with the circuit clerk within 14 days after the order is entered." Fed. R. Civ. P. 23(f). With respect to a prior version of Rule 23(f) that allotted only ten days from the certification order, the D.C. Circuit stated that the time to appeal is "strict and mandatory." *In re DC Water & Sewer Auth.*, 561 F.3d 494, 495 (D.C. Cir. 2009) (denying review when the appeal was filed ten days after a ruling on a motion to clarify the certification order rather than the original certification order). Review is at the sole discretion of the court of appeals. *See* Fed. R. Civ. P. 23(f), Advisory Comm. Notes (1998).

Review is restricted to issues of class certification. The Court of Appeals may consider the merits of a case "only insofar as they bear upon the propriety of class certification[.]" *In re Lorazepam & Clorazepate Antitrust Litig.*, 289 F.3d 98, 105, 107 (D.C. Cir. 2002).

The D.C. Circuit has identified three primary instances when it may grant interlocutory review:

- when there is a death-knell situation for either the plaintiff or defendant that is independent of the merits of the underlying claims, coupled with a class certification decision by the district court that is questionable, taking into account the district court's discretion over class certification;
- when the certification decision presents an unsettled and fundamental issue of law relating to class actions, important both to the specific litigation and generally that is likely to evade end-of-the-case review; and
- when the district court's class certification decision is manifestly erroneous.

In re Brewer, 863 F.3d 861, 873–74 (D.C. Cir. 2017) (citing *In re Lorazepam & Clorazepate Antitrust Litig.*, 289 F.3d at 99–100). The D.C. Circuit has also recognized that there may be other "special circumstances" supporting interlocutory review but, in any event, "interlocutory appeals are generally disfavored as disruptive, time-consuming, and expensive for both the parties and the courts." *Id.* at 876 (quotations omitted).

A "death-knell" situation exists only in "rare instances" when "the grant of class status raises the cost and stakes of the litigation so substantially that a rational defendant would feel irresistible pressure to settle." *In re Rail Freight Fuel Surcharge Antitrust Litig.-MDL No. 1869*, 725 F.3d 244, 251 (D.C. Cir. 2013) (quoting *Prado-Steiman ex rel. Prado v. Bush*, 221 F.3d 1266, 1274 (11th Cir. 2000)). The party claiming a "death knell" must offer specific facts proving the financially ruinous conditions that would result if review is not granted. *See, e.g.*, *id.* at 252. In *In re Rail Freight Fuel Surcharge*, the Court found that the proof of death knell fell short but the magnitude of the relief sought combined with other considerations warranted granting the petition. *Id.* at 254; *see In re Visa Inc., et al.*, No. 21-8005 (D.C. Cir. Oct 2, 2021) (granting permission to appeal where plaintiff's had shown "that the district court's class certification decision was at least, 'questionable' and is accompanied by a potential 'death knell'").

A "fundamental issue of law relating to class actions" exists when the certification decision presents an "[1] unsettled and fundamental issue of law relating to class actions, [2] important both to the specific litigation and generally, [3] that is likely to evade end-of-the-case review." *In re Brewer*, 863 F.3d at 874–75 (quoting *In re Lorazepam*, 289 F.3d at 99–100). Meeting this standard requires specific identification of the novel and fundamental issues presented by the order, which must be more than a mere disagreement with how the district court interpreted the facts under existing law. *See, id.* If any element is missing, the Court may deny review. *See, e.g.*, *In re Veneman*, 309 F.3d 789, 795 (D.C. Cir. 2002) (finding the existence of a fundamental issue of class action law that no other circuit had addressed, but denying interlocutory review because the issue would not evade end-of-the-case review).

"Manifest error" requires "a showing that the District Court failed to apply the correct legal standard, reached a decision squarely foreclose[d] by precedent, or otherwise committed an error that is plain and indisputable, and that amounts to a complete disregard of the controlling law or the credible evidence in the record." *In re Dist. of Columbia*, 792 F.3d 96, 97–98 (D.C. Cir. 2015) (quotations & citations omitted). Manifest error is a high standard: "[c]lass certification decisions rarely will involve legal errors . . . simply because class actions typically involve complex facts that are unlikely to be on all fours with existing precedent." *In re Johnson*, 760 F.3d 66, 72 (D.C. Cir. 2014); *see In re Brewer*, 863 F. 3d at 875 (noting that the D.C. Circuit has not yet found a certification decision manifestly erroneous).

FIRST CIRCUIT

Districts of Maine, Massachusetts, New Hampshire, Puerto Rico, and Rhode Island

John Joseph Moakley U.S. Courthouse
1 Courthouse Way
Boston, MA 02210

By Joshua D. Dunlap and Lucas A. Ritchie[1]
Pierce Atwood LLP

1. INTRODUCTION

The First Circuit comprises the Districts of Maine, Massachusetts, New Hampshire, Puerto Rico, and Rhode Island, and the appellate bench includes judges from each of them. There are six active judges and four senior judges, making it the smallest of the regional circuit courts.

The small number of judges on the First Circuit has several practical consequences, two of which will be mentioned here. First, the court frequently turns to visiting judges to round out its three-judge panels. Second, because en banc review requires the vote of a majority of First Circuit judges who are in regular active service[2] and there are only six of them, when a panel of three such judges renders a unanimous opinion, en banc review generally becomes unattainable. Contrast this structure with that of the Ninth Circuit, which has far more active judges able to vote on petitions for rehearings en banc and frequently decides important issues, including class action issues, through en banc review.

The following discussion describes key principles practitioners can glean from class action decisions of the First Circuit and its district courts.

2. JURISDICTIONAL PREREQUISITES

a. CAFA Requirements

The First Circuit has observed that Congress enacted the Class Action Fairness Act (CAFA) with the stated purpose of expanding the number of class actions that could be heard in federal court. *Amoche v. Guarantee Trust Life Ins. Co.*, 556 F.3d 41, 47, 49 (1st Cir. 2009). Congress effectuated that purpose "by imposing only a minimal diversity requirement, eliminating the statutory one-year time limit for removal, and providing for interlocutory appeal of a federal district court's remand order." *Id.* at 47–48 (citing 28 U.S.C. §§ 1332(d)(2), 1453(b), (c)). CAFA limited this expansion of federal court jurisdiction over class actions, however, by imposing a $5 million amount-in-controversy requirement. *Pazol v. Tough Mudder Inc.*, 819 F.3d 548, 552 (1st Cir. 2016).

[1] The authors thank Donald R. Frederico for his previous contributions to this chapter.

[2] Local Rule 35(a).

Burden of proof. The defendant seeking to remove a lawsuit to federal district court under CAFA bears the burden to demonstrate jurisdiction.[3] *Amoche*, 556 F.3d at 48. In carrying its burden of proof, the removing defendant must demonstrate to a "reasonable probability" that the jurisdictional prerequisites of CAFA have been satisfied. *Id.* at 48–49. This standard is identical to the "preponderance of the evidence" standard. *Romulus v. CVS Pharmacy, Inc.*, 770 F.3d 67, 80 n.13 (1st Cir. 2014). Accordingly, the removing defendant must show a reasonable probability that more than $5 million is at stake if the case were certified, *Amoche*, 556 F.3d at 50, and, in doing so, should consider the availability of attorneys' fees and damage multipliers, *Pazol*, 819 F.3d at 553. In deciding whether the removing defendant has shown a reasonable probability that the amount-in-controversy requirement has been met, the First Circuit has said that district courts can and should analyze what both parties have shown. That is, a court should not reject a defendant's proof as to the amount in controversy without concluding that the proof has been discredited. *Amoche*, 556 F.3d at 50–51. In conducting this inquiry, the court should bear in mind which party has the best access to relevant information. *Pazol*, 819 F.3d at 552. The First Circuit has also said that the amount in controversy should be determined as of the time of removal; later events that reduce the amount in controversy cannot divest the court of jurisdiction. *Amoche*, 556 F.3d at 51. Finally, the First Circuit has determined that courts should not consider the plaintiffs' likelihood of success in determining the amount in controversy because "the pertinent question is what is *in controversy* in the case, not how much the plaintiffs are ultimately likely to recover." *Id.* (emphasis in original). If a motion for remand is filed by the plaintiff, the plaintiff bears the burden of proving a valid basis for remand. *In re Hannaford Bros. Co. Customer Data Sec. Breach Litig.*, 564 F.3d 75, 78 (1st Cir. 2009); *Saunders v. Sappi N. Am., Inc.*, 2021 WL 5984996, at *3 (D. Me. Dec. 16, 2021). Courts have discussed this standard both in terms of a "preponderance of the evidence" and a "reasonable probability." *Dee v. Chelsea Jewish N. Shore Assisted Living, Inc.*, 585 F. Supp. 3d 119, 122 (D. Mass. 2022).

Minimal Diversity. Unlike diversity jurisdiction in most other contexts, CAFA allows minimal diversity of the parties—as long as one class plaintiff maintains citizenship in a state different from one defendant's citizenship, diversity is satisfied. This requirement is not met if all named plaintiffs share the same citizenship as the defendant, even if there are members of the putative class who are citizens of other states. *Kelledy v. Dunkin' Brands, Inc.*, 2023 WL 4053011, at *1–2 (D. Mass. June 16, 2023) (citing *Jalbert v. U.S. Sec. & Exch. Comm'n*, 945 F.3d 587, 594 (1st Cir. 2019) ("When a class action is filed, it 'includes only the claims of the named plaintiff or plaintiffs. The claims of unnamed class members are added to the action later, when the action is certified as a class under [Federal Rule of Civil Procedure] 23.'")).

Timing of Removal. The First Circuit has held that Section 1446(b)'s 30-day clocks are triggered only when the complaint or the plaintiff's "other paper" provides the defendant with sufficient information to easily determine that the matter is removable. *Romulus*, 770 F.3d at 72, 74. In *Romulus*, the court also held that the defendant has no duty to investigate or supply facts outside those provided by the plaintiff. *Id.* at 75. A document does not have to be a court filing to constitute an "other paper" that triggers the removal clock. *Id.* at 78. Successive attempts at removal are permissible where the grounds for removal become apparent only later in the litigation. *Amoche*, 556 F.3d at 553. Motions to remand must generally be filed within 30 days of removal. 28 U.S.C. § 1447(c). Motions to remand under the local controversy exception are subject to this general rule, because that exception is not jurisdictional but is instead a form of statutorily-mandated abstention. *Nightingale v. Nat'l Grid USA Serv. Co.*, 578 F. Supp. 3d 190, 192 (D. Mass 2022).

[3] While the burden is on the defendant to prove that CAFA's jurisdictional requirements have been met, the burden is on the plaintiff to show that an exception to CAFA's jurisdiction applies. In re Hannaford Bros. Co. Customer Data Sec. Breach Litig., 564 F.3d 75, 78 (1st Cir. 2009).

Defined Class Requirement. To satisfy CAFA's definition of a class action, a case need only be filed under either Fed. R. Civ. P. 23 or some state law analogue to that rule. Accordingly, invocation of a state's class action rules, allegations of harm to members of a class, and claims for class-wide relief are sufficient to satisfy CAFA's class requirement. *Coll. of Dental Surgeons v. Conn. Gen. Life Ins. Co*., 585 F.3d 33, 40 (1st Cir. 2009). While one district court has observed that CAFA does not clearly establish when a state statute is "similar" to Rule 23, it also noted that courts generally require that the state analogue must "at a minimum, provide a procedure by which a member of a class whose claim is typical of all members of the class can bring an action not only on his own behalf but also on behalf of all others in the class." *Massachusetts v. Exxon Mobil Corp*., 462 F. Supp. 3d 31, 48 (D. Mass. 2020) (quoting *Purdue Pharma L.P. v. Kentucky*, 704 F.3d 208, 217 (2d Cir. 2013)). Generally, *parens patriae* actions do not satisfy this standard. *Id*. (finding that CAFA jurisdiction was lacking over claims brought by the Massachusetts Attorney General under Mass. Gen Laws ch. 93A, § 4).

Appeal. CAFA allows a court of appeals to accept, in its discretion, an appeal from an order of a district court granting or denying a motion to remand a class action to state court. *Coll. of Dental Surgeons*, 585 F.3d at 38. The First Circuit has enumerated various factors that it considers in determining whether to permit appeal from a remand decision. The court will consider (1) "the presence of an important CAFA-related question," (2) the "uncertainty" surrounding this question, (3) the likelihood that the district court decided the question correctly, (4) the extent to which the "question is consequential to the resolution of the particular case," (5) "whether the question is likely to evade effective review if left for consideration only after final judgment," (6) "whether the application arises from a decision or order that is sufficiently final to position the case for intelligent review," and (7) "a balance of relevant harms" from granting an appeal. *Id*. at 38–39. These criteria, however, "are merely guides," and the Court retains its discretion as to whether to entertain an appeal. *Id*. at 39.

b. Personal Jurisdiction

In 2017, the Supreme Court held that personal jurisdiction did not attach to the claims of non-resident mass tort plaintiffs against a defendant that was not subject to general jurisdiction in the forum state and where the non-resident plaintiffs' claims did not arise from the defendant's conduct in the forum state. *Bristol-Myers Squibb Co. v. Superior Court*, 582 U.S. 255 (2017). To date, neither the First Circuit nor the Supreme Court has ruled on whether *Bristol-Myers Squibb* applies to multi-state class actions. At least one judge in the District of Massachusetts and one in the District of New Hampshire have held that the decision whether to exert jurisdiction over out-of-state class members should be made at the time of the class certification motion and not on a motion to dismiss. *Daschbach v. Adv. Mktg. & Processing, Inc*., 2021 WL 1163010 (D.N.H. Mar. 26, 2021); *Rain v. Conn. Gen. Corp*., 2019 WL 7604856 (D. Mass. Aug. 6, 2019). Also, in two decisions, a judge in the District of Massachusetts has concluded that *Bristol-Meyers Squibb* does not apply to class actions because: (1) unlike plaintiffs in a mass tort case, absent class members are not considered full parties in a class action, but are represented by the named plaintiffs; and (2) additional due process safeguards apply in a class action that do not apply in a mass tort case. *Rosenberg v. LoanDepot.com LLC*, 435 F. Supp. 3d 308, 326 (D. Mass. Jan. 24, 2020); *see Munsell v. Colgate-Palmolive Co.*, 463 F. Supp. 3d 43, 54–56 (D. Mass. 2020).

c. Standing

Who May Bring a Class Action

Article III standing is an "indispensable part" of any case and must be present at every stage of the case. *In re Nexium Antitrust Litig.*, 777 F.3d 9, 31–32 (1st Cir. 2015). A named plaintiff who fails to establish a continuing controversy normally may not invoke the power of the federal courts to seek relief on its own behalf or that of other members of a putative class. *In re New Motor Vehicles Canadian Exp. Antitrust Litig.*, 522 F.3d 6, 13–14 (1st Cir.

2008).

The First Circuit has concluded that "traditional standing rules" apply in the class action context, such that a defendant generally may not be sued unless a named plaintiff (not just a class member) has a claim against that defendant. *Plumbers' Union Local No. 12 Pension Fund v. Nomura Asset Acceptance Corp.*, 632 F.3d 762, 769–70 (1st Cir. 2011); *see Yan v. ReWalk Robotics, Ltd.*, 973 F.3d 22, 35 (1st Cir. 2020) ("Persons who wish to represent a class 'must allege and show that they personally have been injured, not that injury has been suffered by other unidentified members of the class to which they belong and which they purport to represent.'"); *Maldonado v. Cultural Care, Inc.*, 2021 WL 3190890, *4–5 (D. Mass. July 28, 2021) (named plaintiffs who could not show that they were paid below minimum wage lacked standing to represent a class of underpaid employees). As a general matter, therefore, to establish standing, one looks only to the named plaintiffs and their claims. In most respects, the class members other than the named plaintiffs are merely potential parties until a class has been certified. *Pruell v. Caritas Christi*, 645 F.3d 81, 83–84 (1st Cir. 2011).

Injury is a prerequisite to standing, and named plaintiffs need to satisfy this standing requirement throughout the stages of the litigation. *In re Nexium Antitrust Litig.*, 777 F.3d at 31–32. The plaintiff must allege personal harm caused by the defendant, and "that such conduct implicates the same set of concerns as the conduct alleged to have caused injury to other members of the putative class by the same defendants." *In re Biogen, Inc. ERISA Litig.*, 2021 WL 3116331, at *3–4 (D. Mass. July 22, 2021) (ERISA plan participants have standing to sue plan administrators for breach of fiduciary duty on behalf of other plan participants even though the named plaintiffs did not invest in every fund cited in the complaint). Injunctive relief is available when a plaintiff faces a threat of injury that is both "real and immediate, not conjectural or hypothetical." *In re New Motor Vehicles Canadian Exp. Antitrust Litig.*, 522 F.3d at 14. Mere "past exposure to illegal conduct" does not show a present case or controversy regarding injunctive relief. *Id.*; *see Waldner v. Natixis Inv. Managers, L.P.*, 2023 WL 3466272, at *14–15 (D. Mass. Mar. 24, 2023) (plaintiff who was no longer a plan participant lacked standing to pursue claims for prospective relief).

The First Circuit has held that, if a sole named plaintiff lacks standing, the complaint must be dismissed, but the trial court may allow the plaintiff's motion to amend the complaint to add or substitute a new plaintiff who has standing, at least when the original plaintiff's dismissal is based on a lack of statutory standing and not on a lack of Article III standing. *Yan*, 973 F.3d at 36–39 & n.6; *see also Sheet Metal Workers Local No. 20 Welfare & Benefit Fund v. CVS Pharmacy, Inc.*, 540 F. Supp. 3d 182, 200 (D.R.I. 2021) (if court determines that named plaintiffs lack capacity to sue as trusts, "First Circuit authority favors directing plaintiff-trusts to substitute their trustees as plaintiffs, not dismissal of the claims").

Absent Class Member Standing

Named plaintiffs have Article III standing "to litigate as class representatives materially identical claims by other persons under the same laws under which the named plaintiffs' claims arise." *In re Asacol Antitrust Litig.*, 907 F.3d 42, 47 (1st Cir. 2018). The claims of the named plaintiffs and the claims of the class members need not be identical in all respects. In such cases, Article III standing exists so long as the differences that exist do not "leave the class representative with an insufficient personal stake in the adjudication of the class members' claims." *Id.* at 49.

Thus, the First Circuit has held that a named plaintiff whose claim is based on one state's law may represent class members whose claims are based on other states' laws where the laws are sufficiently similar that success on the named plaintiff's claim "will more or less dictate success" on the class members' claims. *Id.* The court expressly has not decided "how to apply Article III standing principles to a case in which a putative class representative has a personal stake in proving most but not all of the elements of a class member's claim." *Id.* at 50.

d. Mootness Doctrine

When a case is moot—that is, when the issues presented are no longer live or when the parties lack a legally cognizable interest in the outcome—a case or controversy ceases to exist, and dismissal of the action is compulsory. *Cruz v. Farquharson*, 252 F.3d 530, 533 (1st Cir. 2001). Accordingly, even if a case is brought as a putative class action, it ordinarily must be dismissed as moot if no decision on class certification has occurred by the time the individual claims of all named plaintiffs have been fully resolved. *Id.* at 533–34. Only after a class has been certified does the class acquire a legal status independent of the interest asserted by the named plaintiffs, permitting the class action to survive the mooting of the named plaintiff's individual claim. *Id.* There is a narrow exception for issues that are capable of repetition yet evading review. A claim may escape mootness under this exception, however, only if there is a demonstrated probability that the same controversy involving the same parties will reoccur. *Id.*

Before the Supreme Court's decision in *Campbell-Ewald Co. v. Gomez*, 577 U.S. 153 (2016), the First Circuit had held that an unaccepted Rule 68 offer cannot, by itself, moot a plaintiff's claim. *Bais Yaakov of Spring Valley v. ACT, Inc.*, 798 F.3d 46, 52 (1st Cir. 2015). After that ruling and the decision in *Campbell-Ewald*, the District of Massachusetts held that even an unconditional tender of full and complete relief to a proposed class representative does not moot the class representative's individual claims and preclude certification of a proposed class action under Rule 23, because allowing a defendant to moot a class representative's claim by tendering full payment would mean that the class issues would likely evade review. *See Bais Yaakov of Spring Valley v. ACT, Inc.*, 221 F. Supp. 3d 183, 188 (D. Mass. 2016). On a second appeal, the First Circuit rejected defendant's argument that defendant's tendering of a check in the maximum amount of the named plaintiff's potential recovery mooted the plaintiff's claim. *Bais Yaakov of Spring Valley v. ACT, Inc.*, 12 F. 4th 81, 94–95 (1st Cir. 2021) ("[T]he transmittal of an ordinary check does not differ for present purposes from an offer to pay: The recipient has a promise, but no funds. . . . Indeed, the Rule 68 offer at least conveys the ability to obtain a judgment, while the check conveys only a hope that the bank account will have the promised funds.").

3. PLEADING CONSIDERATIONS

The First Circuit has recognized that district courts may grant motions to strike class allegations under Fed. R. Civ. P. 12(f) when "it is obvious from the pleadings that the proceeding cannot possibly move forward on a classwide basis." *Manning v. Bos. Med. Ctr. Corp.*, 725 F.3d 34, 59 (1st Cir. 2013). In *Manning*, the court also admonished that "courts should exercise caution when striking class action allegations based solely on the pleadings." *Id.* It explained that striking a portion of a pleading is a drastic, disfavored remedy and that striking class allegations is even more disfavored because it preemptively terminates class aspects of litigation and deprives plaintiffs an opportunity to complete the discovery they may need to support class certification. *Id.* (quoting *Mazzola v. Roomster Corp.*, 849 F. Supp. 2d 395, 410 (S.D.N.Y. 2012)). "Accordingly," the First Circuit held, "a court should typically await the development of a factual record before determining whether the case should move forward on a representative basis." 725 F.3d at 59; *see Savage v. City of Springfield*, 2021 WL 858409, at *8 (D. Mass. Mar. 8, 2021); *Ortiz v. Sig Sauer, Inc.*, 448 F. Supp. 3d 89, 99 (D.N.H. 2020) (declining to strike class definition because it was not "obvious from the pleadings" that the class definition was "so overbroad and beyond tailoring as to preclude . . . moving forward on a classwide basis"). Nevertheless, "a court may strike class allegations that plainly encompass individuals whose claims are barred by jurisdictional or time limitations." *Monteferrante v. Williams-Sonoma, Inc.*, 241 F. Supp. 3d 264, 269 (D. Mass. 2017) (striking class allegations without prejudice to a motion to amend the complaint with a new class definition). Similarly, a court may strike class allegations where it is clear that plaintiffs will be unable to establish that all applicable requirements for class certification have been met. *Rovinelli v. Trans World Entm't Corp.*, 2021 WL 752822, at *13 (D. Mass. Feb. 2, 2021) (striking class allegations of consumer claims because plaintiffs' reliance on unscripted oral solicitations precludes possibility of establishing predominance under Rule 23(b)(3)).

The class definition proposed in the operative complaint is critical. At least one court in the First Circuit has observed that, while a plaintiff may propose a new class definition when it moves for certification, the class definition may only be narrowed—not expanded. *Douglas v. EF Institute for Cultural Exchange, Inc.*, 2024 WL 3070251, at *4–5 (D. Mass. June 20, 2024). Enlarging the class may be prejudicial to the defendant. *Id. See also Turner v. Liberty Mut. Ret. Benefit Plan*, 2024 WL 3416070, at *5 (D. Mass. July 15, 2024) (denying certification of a class based on a claim not plead in complaint where complaint did not provide adequate notice of legal theory underlying proposed class definition).

4. PREREQUISITES

A district court must conduct a rigorous analysis of Rule 23's prerequisites. *In re New Motor Vehicles Canadian Exp. Antitrust Litig.*, 522 F.3d 6, 25 (1st Cir. 2008); *see Smilow v. Sw. Bell Mobile Sys., Inc.*, 323 F.3d 32, 38 (1st Cir. 2003). As part of its rigorous analysis, a district court must formulate some prediction as to how specific issues will play out. *In re New Motor Vehicles*, 522 F.3d at 25; *see Waste Mgmt. Holdings, Inc. v. Mowbray*, 208 F.3d 288, 298 (1st Cir. 2000). This is true of both the named plaintiff's case-in-chief and the defendant's affirmative defenses. *Smilow*, 323 F.3d at 39; *see Mowbray*, 208 F.3d at 295. Accordingly, when legal and factual premises are disputed, the court may probe behind the pleadings for purposes of determining whether class certification is appropriate under Rule 23. *In re New Motor Vehicles*, 522 F.3d at 17; *see In re PolyMedica Corp. Sec. Litig.*, 432 F.3d 1, 17 (1st Cir. 2005) (a district court considering a class certification motion "must evaluate the plaintiff's evidence . . . critically without allowing the defendant to turn the class-certification proceeding into an unwieldy trial on the merits"). In short, a court has the power to test disputed premises at the certification stage if and when the class action would be proper on one premise but not another. *Tardiff v. Knox Cty.*, 365 F.3d 1, 4–5 (1st Cir. 2004); *see In re PolyMedica Corp. Sec. Litig.*, 432 F.3d at 6.

a. Rule 23(a) Requirements

Numerosity

The facts and circumstances of each case are to be taken into account to determine numerosity under Rule 23(a)(1). *Andrews v. Bechtel Power Corp.*, 780 F.2d 124, 131 (1st Cir. 1985). The First Circuit has noted that there is no minimum number of plaintiffs required to maintain a suit as a class action, but has also cited approvingly the general rule that if the potential number of class members exceeds 40, the first prong of Rule 23(a) has been met. *Garcia-Rubiera v. Calderon*, 570 F.3d 443, 460 (1st Cir. 2009). Despite this rule of thumb, some district judges within the Circuit have certified classes consisting of fewer than 40 members, sometimes focusing on non-numeric factors relevant to whether joinder of all class members is practicable. *See, e.g.*, *In re Ranbaxy Generic Drug Applic. Antitrust Litig.*, 338 F.R.D. 294, 301 (D. Mass. 2021) (certifying class containing 39 members, of which five suffered no injury, where "class members are geographically dispersed and judicial economy favors proceeding as a class action"); *In re Nexium Antitrust Litig.*, 296 F.R.D. 47, 51–53 (D. Mass. 2013), *aff'd*, 777 F. 3d 9 (1st Cir. 2015) (finding numerosity satisfied where there were fewer than 30 class members); *Ruiz v. NEI Gen. Contracting, Inc.*, 2024 WL 869445, at *7, *9 (D. Mass. Feb. 29, 2024) (finding numerosity for class of 35 members but also finding numerosity lacking for second proposed class with 11 putative members). Numbers alone are not always determinative; a small class may not meet the numerosity requirement because joinder of all members is practicable. Joinder is often considered practicable when all members of the class are from the same geographic area and can easily be identified. *Andrews*, 780 F.2d at 131–32.

Plaintiff bears the burden of satisfying the numerosity requirement (and other Rule 23(a) requirements). *Makuc v. Am. Honda Motor Co.*, 835 F.2d 389, 394 (1st Cir. 1987). In one recent case, the court found numerosity lacking because plaintiff's evidence did not support his estimated total of more than 150,000 class members. *Rowan v. Pierce*, 2024 WL 1693859, at *5 (D.P.R. Apr. 19, 2024) (discussing problems with plaintiff's expert's estimate of potential class members and finding that mere assertion of large numbers of class members did not satisfy numerosity requirement).

Commonality

The First Circuit has applied the commonality standard set out in *Wal-Mart Stores, Inc. v. Dukes*, 564 U.S. 338 (2011) to affirm a district court decision that had denied a motion for class certification. In *Parent/Professional Advocacy League v. City of Springfield*, 934 F.3d 13 (1st Cir. 2019), plaintiffs alleged that the city's public school system violated Title II of the Americans with Disabilities Act, 42 U.S.C. §§ 12131–12134, and the Individuals with Disabilities Education Act, 20 U.S.C. §§ 1400 *et seq.*, by failing to provide class members special educational services they needed in the least restrictive environment. The court held that commonality was not satisfied because plaintiffs had failed to show that the harms they alleged were caused by a uniform policy or practice affecting all class members, or that individual placement teams exercised discretion in a common manner (analogizing the facts to the exercise of discretion by store managers in *Dukes*). Because each class member's claim would depend on his or her unique disabilities and educational needs, the court held that *Dukes* precluded a finding of commonality.

District courts in the First Circuit have also applied *Dukes*' holding that, in determining whether the commonality standard has been satisfied, "a court should not consider 'common questions' but rather 'the capacity of a classwide proceeding to generate common *answers* apt to drive the resolution of the litigation.'" *Raposo v. Garelick Farms, LLC*, 293 F.R.D. 52, 55 (D. Mass. 2013) (quoting *Dukes*, 564 U.S. at 350). As a result, under Rule 23(a)(2), a plaintiff must show that the claims asserted rest on a "common contention," which must be of such a nature that "determination of its truth or falsity will resolve an issue that is central to the validity of each one of the claims in one stroke." *Id.* (quoting *Dukes*, 564 U.S. at 350); *Plastic Surgery Assocs., S.C. v. Cynosure, Inc.*, 407 F. Supp. 3d 59, 74 (D. Mass. 2019) (same, and holding that commonality was not met for claims under the Massachusetts Consumer Protection Act based on oral representations and individualized issues of injury and causation). "In other words, the commonality requirement is met where the 'questions that go to the heart of the elements of the cause of action' will 'each be answered either "yes" or "no" for the entire class' and 'the answers will not vary by individual class member.'" *Id.* (quoting *Donovan v. Philip Morris USA, Inc.*, 2012 WL 957633, at *21 (D. Mass. Mar. 21, 2012)); *see Fitzmorris v. Weaver*, 2023 WL 2974245, at *6 (D.N.H. Apr. 17, 2023) (plaintiffs' claims did not turn on a common contention because they identified no common policy or practice); *Kress Stores of P.R., Inc. v. Wal-Mart P.R., Inc.*, 573 F. Supp. 3d 604, 609–10 (D. Mass. 2021) (denying class certification because individual issues of causation and injury precluded a showing of commonality under Rule 23(a)(2)); *Pagliaroni v. Mastic Home Exteriors, Inc.*, 2015 WL 5568624, at *10–12 (D. Mass. Sept. 22, 2015) (denying class certification in building products case, in part because individual issues of causation and injury defeated showing of Rule 23(a)(2) commonality); *Loef v. First Am. Title Ins. Co.*, 2012 WL 6113844, at *6 (D. Me. Dec. 10, 2012).

District courts have noted that this commonality standard is "stricter" than the pre-*Dukes* commonality standard. *P.R. Coll. of Dental Surgeons v. Triple S Mgmt. Inc.*, 290 F.R.D. 19, 26 (D.P.R. 2013). Accordingly, a plaintiff must allege sufficient facts for the district court to be able to determine a common legal or factual basis for their claims. *Id.* at 26–

29. Further, plaintiffs seeking to satisfy the commonality standard must,

> among other things, (1) avoid framing common questions so generally that they encompass myriad, distinct claims; (2) provide significant proof that there exists a common policy or practice . . . that is the alleged source of the harm to [the] class members, . . . (3) identify common questions of fact or law that can be answered either "yes" or "no" for the entire class, that is, identify central questions whose answers will not vary by individual class members, . . . and (4) show that dissimilarities in the proposed class do not impede the generation of common answers.

Kenneth R. ex rel. Tri-Cty. CAP, Inc./GS v. Hassan, 293 F.R.D. 254, 266–67 (D.N.H. 2013) (citations and quotation marks omitted). However, a plaintiff need not demonstrate that every issue is common. *Mantha v. QuoteWizard.com*, 2024 WL 3912459, at *12 (D. Mass. Aug. 16, 2024).

Typicality

"The representative plaintiff satisfies the typicality requirement [under Rule 23(a)(3)] when its injuries arise from the same events or course of conduct as do the injuries of the class and when plaintiff's claims and those of the class are based on the same legal theory." *In re Credit Suisse–AOL Sec. Litig.*, 253 F.R.D. 17, 23 (D. Mass. 2008); *see Garcia-Rubiera v. Calderon*, 570 F.3d 443, 460 (1st Cir. 2009); *Pagliaroni v. Mastic Home Exteriors, Inc.*, 2015 WL 5568624, at *13–14 (D. Mass. Sept. 22, 2015) (finding no typicality in building products case). The typicality inquiry "is designed to align the interests of the class and the class representatives so that the latter will work to benefit the entire class through the pursuit of their own goals." *Hochstadt v. Bos. Sci. Corp.*, 708 F. Supp. 2d 95, 103 (D. Mass. 2010) (quotation marks omitted). "Rule 23(a)(3), however, does not require that the representative plaintiff's claims be identical to those of absent class members." *In re Credit Suisse*, 253 F.R.D. at 23.

"The primary focus of the typicality analysis is the functional question of whether the putative class representative can fairly and adequately pursue the interests of the absent class members without being sidetracked by her own particular concerns." *In re Credit Suisse-AOL Sec. Litig.*, 253 F.R.D. at 23 (quotation marks omitted). An examination of potential unique defenses is necessary as part of the typicality analysis because "where a named plaintiff may be subject to unique defenses that would divert attention from the common claims of the class, that plaintiff cannot be considered typical of the class." *In re Bank of Bos.*, 762 F. Supp. 1525, 1532 (D. Mass. 1991); *see Swack v. Credit Suisse First Bos.*, 230 F.R.D. 250, 260 (D. Mass. 2005). Typicality "may also be defeated where class members have additional claims or remedies that are unavailable to the class representative." *Garcia v. E.J. Amusements of N.H., Inc.*, 98 F. Supp. 3d 277, 288 (D. Mass. 2015).

Adequacy

The adequacy requirement of Rule 23(a)(4) has two components. First, the plaintiff must establish "that the interests of the representative party will not conflict with the interests of any of the class members." *Andrews v. Bechtel Power Corp.*, 780 F.2d 124, 130 (1st Cir. 1985). Although a named plaintiff must have some knowledge about the claims advanced on behalf of the class, it is a low bar, and it is sufficient for the plaintiff to have a "minimal degree of knowledge" and to rely on the expertise of counsel. *Sheet Metal Workers Local No. 20 Welfare & Benefit Fund v. CVS Pharmacy, Inc.*, 540 F. Supp. 3d 182, 201 (D.R.I. 2021). Second, the plaintiff must show "that counsel chosen by the representative party is qualified, experienced and able to vigorously conduct the proposed litigation." *Andrews*, 780 F.2d at 130. The First Circuit has noted that this element "is particularly important because of the *res judicata* implications of a class judgment." *Id.; see Bezdek v. Vibram USA Inc.*, 79 F. Supp. 3d 324, 339 (D. Mass. 2015); *DeRosa v. Mass. Bay Commuter Rail Co.*, 694 F. Supp. 2d 87, 100 (D. Mass. 2010).

"To defeat the adequacy requirement of Rule 23, a conflict must be more than merely speculative or hypothetical." *In re Light Cigarettes Mktg. Sales Practices Litig.*, 271 F.R.D. 402, 415 (D. Me. 2010). Moreover, "perfect symmetry of interest is not required and not every discrepancy among the interests of class members renders a putative class action untenable." *Matamoros v. Starbucks Corp.*, 699 F.3d 129, 138 (1st Cir. 2012). Rather, "to forestall class certification the intra-class conflict must be so substantial as to overbalance the common interests of the class members as a whole." *Id.; see, e.g., Karth v. Keryx Biopharmaceuticals, Inc.*, 334 F.R.D. 7, 18 (D. Mass. 2019) (no adequacy where named plaintiff purchased securities "in a markedly different disclosure environment than other proposed class members"). The conflict therefore must be "fundamental to the suit" and "go to the heart of the litigation" to breach the adequacy standard. *Matamoros*, 699 F.3d at 138; *see Murray v. Grocery Delivery E-Servs. USA, Inc.*, 55 F.4th 340, 345–46 (1st Cir. 2022). A showing of an alignment of incentives between the representatives and the class can overcome a challenge on conflict-of-interest grounds. *In re Nexium (Esomeprazole) Antitrust Litig.*, 297 F.R.D. 168, 172 (D. Mass. 2013).

b. Rule 23(b) Requirements

Rule 23(b)(1) Classes

Courts in the First Circuit have recently expressed doubt "that Rule 23(b)(1) certification is available in actions that seek monetary relief." *Glynn v. Martin Sports & Entm't, LLC*, 2023 WL 2601609, at *7 (D. Mass. Mar. 22, 2023) (quoting *Pimentel v. City of Methuen*, 2019 WL 6699667, at *7 (D. Mass. Dec. 9, 2019)). This limitation is based on due process concerns, and the observation in *Wal-Mart Stores, Inc. v. Dukes* that individualized monetary claims belong in Rule 23(b)(3) because of the procedural protections for Rule 23(b)(3) certification. *Id.* Thus, where a party does not seek injunctive or declaratory relief, but rather individualized monetary relief, certification under Rule 23(b)(1) is inappropriate. *Id.*

Rule 23(b)(1)(A). Rule 23(b)(1)(A) provides for certification of a mandatory class when "inconsistent or varying adjudications with respect to individual members of the class . . . would establish incompatible standards of conduct for the party opposing the class." Fed. R. Civ. P. 23(b)(1)(A). The First Circuit "has yet to develop a definitive framework within which to decide whether to certify a class under 23(b)(1)(A)." *Kent v. SunAmerica Life Ins. Co.*, 190 F.R.D. 271, 280 (D. Mass. 2000). District courts in the First Circuit have, however, observed that "[c]ourts have certified classes under 23(b)(1)(A) in cases in which a defendant might be forced to violate a judgment made in one court in order to satisfy a judgment imposed by another court." *Id.* Accordingly, to certify a class, plaintiffs "must show some likelihood that a particular controversy will . . . generate separate adjudications that will require the defendant to take inconsistent actions." *Id.*; *see In re New England Mut. Life Ins. Co.*, 183 F.R.D. 33, 41 (D. Mass. 1998). District courts have observed that certification under 23(b)(1)(A) is generally inappropriate where the plaintiff seeks primarily monetary damages as opposed to equitable relief. *See Hochstadt v. Bos. Scientific Corp.*, 708 F. Supp. 2d 95, 104 n.11 (D. Mass. 2010); *Campbell v. First Am. Title Ins. Co.*, 269 F.R.D. 68, 76 (D. Me. 2010).

Rule 23(b)(1)(B). Rule 23(b)(1)(B) provides for certification of a mandatory class if separate actions would create a risk of "adjudications with respect to individual class members that, as a practical matter, would be dispositive of the interests of the other members not parties to the individual adjudications or would substantially impair or impede their ability to protect their interests." Fed. R. Civ. P. 23(b)(1)(B). The most common kinds of cases in which subsection (b)(1)(B) applies are those "in which class members are seeking to recover against a common fund with insufficient assets to satisfy all possible claimants" or where "disposition of an individual action by one class member could substantially impair the ability of absent class members to recover on their claims." *In re Tyco Int'l, Ltd.*, 2006 WL 2349338, at *7 (D.N.H. Aug. 15, 2006). District courts have found that this provision is "applicable not only to adjudications that legally would be *dispositive* of the interests of other members but also that would, in practice, have a *significant adverse impact* on interests of other members." *In re New England Mut. Life Ins. Co. Sales Practices Litig.*, 183 F.R.D. 33, 42 (D. Mass. 1998) (emphasis in original). The First Circuit has held that "the anticipated effect of stare decisis on subsequent cases brought by absent class members, without more, is an insufficient justification for class certification under Rule 23(b)(1)(B)." *Tilley v. TJX Cos.*, 345 F.3d 34, 41 (1st Cir. 2003). On the other hand, a "realistic prospect" of issue preclusion "may afford a cognizable basis for a finding of substantial impairment" under Rule 23(b)(1)(B). *Id.* at 43 n.7.

Rule 23(b)(2) Classes

A mandatory class may be certified under Rule 23(b)(2) when "the party opposing the class has acted or refused to act on grounds that apply generally to the class, so that final injunctive relief or corresponding declaratory relief is appropriate respecting the class as a whole." Fed. R. Civ. P. 23(b)(2). A (b)(2) class must primarily seek injunctive relief. *DeRosa v. Mass. Bay Commuter Rail Co.*, 694 F. Supp. 2d 87, 94 (D. Mass. 2010). Certification under Rule 23(b)(2) is inappropriate if the requested injunctive relief is merely "incidental to seeking monetary damages." *In re Nexium Antitrust Litig.*, 297 F.R.D. 168, 174 (D. Mass. 2013). Also, "defendant classes generally lie outside the contemplation of Rule 23(b)(2)." *Tilley v. TJX Cos.*, 345 F.3d 34, 39 (1st Cir. 2003).

District courts have observed that plaintiffs must prove each element of a three-step inquiry to certify a (b)(2) class: (1) that the defendant acted on grounds that apply generally to the whole class, (2) that final injunctive relief is appropriate, and (3) that relief is appropriate for the whole class. *Donovan v. Philip Morris USA, Inc.*, 268 F.R.D. 1, 11 (D. Mass. 2010). The first prong, acting on grounds generally applicable to the class, requires that the case will not depend on adjudication of facts particular to any subset of the class. *Id.* The second, whether injunctive relief is appropriate, depends on the factors of irreparable harm, inadequate remedy at law, and balance of the equities. *Id.* The third requires that group relief must operate across the board and address generalized needs, not particular injuries. *Id.* If the same relief can be obtained without class certification, a district court may be justified in denying class certification under Rule 23(b)(2). *See Dionne v. Bouley*, 757 F.2d 1344, 1356 (1st Cir. 1985); *Van Meter v. Harvey*, 272 F.R.D. 274, 283 (D. Me. 2011). On the other hand, where "non-individualized declaratory or injunctive remedies could provide relief to all class members, class certification under Rule 23(b)(2) is appropriate." *Gomes v. Acting Secretary, U.S. Dept. of Homeland Sec.*, 561 F. Supp. 3d 93, 104 (D.N.H. 2021).

Under the "inherently transitory" exception, a class action seeking injunctive relief may be certified even if the claims of the named plaintiffs have become moot. That is, a court may certify such a class where "it is certain that other persons similarly situated will continue to be subject to the challenged conduct and the claims raised are so inherently transitory that the trial court will not have even enough time to rule on a motion for class certification before the proposed representative's individual interest expires." *Brito v. Barr*, 395 F. Supp. 3d 135, 146 (D. Mass. 2019) (quoting *Genesis Healthcare Corp. v. Symczyk*, 569 U.S. 66, 76 (2013) (quotation marks omitted)).

Rule 23(b)(3) Classes

The First Circuit has observed that "Rule 23(b)(3) is intended to be a less stringent requirement than Rule 23(b)(1) or (b)(2)." *Smilow v. Sw. Bell Mobile Sys., Inc.*, 323 F.3d 32, 41 (1st Cir. 2003). According to the court, "[t]he core purpose of Rule 23(b)(3) is to vindicate the claims of consumers and other groups of people whose individual claims would be too small to warrant litigation." *Id.*; *see Gintis v. Bouchard Transp. Co.*, 596 F.3d 64, 68 (1st Cir. 2010).

Predominance. The predominance inquiry requires courts to carefully scrutinize the relation between common and individual questions in a case. *Ortiz v. Sig Sauer, Inc.*, 2023 WL 1928094, at *8 (D.N.H. Feb. 10, 2023) (citing *Tyson Foods v. Bouaphakeo*, 577 U.S.

442, 453 (2016)). Individual questions are those where putative class members "will need to present evidence that varies from member to member," while a common question "is one where the same evidence will suffice for each member to make a prima facie showing or the issue is susceptible to generalized, class-wide proof." *Id.* (quoting *Tyson Foods*, 577 U.S. at 453). Rule 23(b)(3) requires "that common issues predominate, not that all issues be common to the class." *Smilow*, 323 F.3d at 39. That is, there must be a "sufficient constellation" of common issues to bind the class together. *Waste Mgmt. Holdings, Inc. v. Mowbray*, 208 F.3d 288, 296 (1st Cir. 2000). Accordingly, "[t]he aim of the predominance inquiry is to test whether any dissimilarity among the claims of class members can be dealt with in a manner that is not 'inefficient or unfair.'" *In re Asacol Antitrust Litig.*, 907 F.3d 42, 51 (1st Cir. 2018). "[A] class may be certified notwithstanding the need to adjudicate individual issues so long as the proposed adjudication will be both 'administratively feasible' and 'protective of defendants' Seventh Amendment and due process rights.'" *Id.* at 52 (quoting *In re Nexium Antitrust Litig.*, 777 F. 3d 9, 19 (1st Cir. 2015)).

To establish predominance under Rule 23(b)(3), therefore, plaintiffs must demonstrate that the proposed class is "sufficiently cohesive to warrant adjudication by representation." *In re Light Cigarettes Mktg. Sales Practices Litig.*, 271 F.R.D. 402, 416 (D. Me. 2010). Thus, the predominance inquiry "involves an individualized, pragmatic evaluation of the relationship between and the relative significance of the common and individual issues." *P.R. Coll. of Dental Surgeons v. Triple S Mgmt. Inc.*, 290 F.R.D. 19, 29 (D.P.R. 2013). Mere speculation regarding individual issues is not enough; rather, it must rest on an assessment of how the litigation will play out. *Bais Yaakov of Spring Valley v. ACT, Inc.*, 12 F.4th 81, 89 (1st Cir. 2021). The predominance analysis thus begins with the elements of the underlying cause of action. *Ortiz*, 2023 WL 1928094, at *9 (citing *Erica P. John Fund, Inc. v. Halliburton Co.*, 563 U.S. 804, 809 (2011)). A defendant's affirmative defenses should also be considered for purposes of determining whether common issues predominate. *Smilow*, 323 F.3d at 39; *see Marti v. Schreiber/Cohen, LLC*, 2020 WL 30421, at *2–3 (D. Mass. Jan. 2, 2020) (defenses based on arbitration provisions in hundreds of third-party contracts precluded certification). The First Circuit has also observed, however, that "where common issues otherwise predominated, courts have usually certified classes even though individual issues were present in one or more affirmative defenses." *Smilow*, 323 F.3d at 39.

As these cases establish, the predominance inquiry is heavily shaped by the particular claims and defenses at issue. *See, e.g.*, *Brown v. Saint-Gobain Performance Plastics*, 2023 WL 9023158, at *15–19 (D.N.H. Dec. 29, 2023) (analyzing predominance claim-by-claim). Variations in state law with respect to the claims and defenses at issue can defeat predominance. *See Ortiz*, 2023 WL 1928094, at *12. Further, the predominance requirement is not met when claims are based on non-uniform facts, such as varied written or oral representations, or when reliance or fairness is an issue. *Id.* at *15–19 (no predominance where unjust enrichment claim would require individual assessments of equity and where fraudulent concealment claim would require individual reliance assessments); *Rovinelli v. Trans World Entm't Corp.*, 2021 WL 752822, at *10–11 (D. Mass. Feb. 2, 2021) (no predominance where claims depended on unscripted oral solicitations made by store's sales representative at checkout); *Rothwell v. Chubb Life Ins. Co. of Am.*, 191 F.R.D. 25, 30–31 (D.N.H. 1998); *see Pimentel v. City of Methuen*, 2019 WL 6699667, at *5 (D. Mass. Dec. 9, 2019) (reliance raises "factual questions that cannot be resolved on a class-wide basis"). By contrast, "[c]ommon issues predominate where individual factual determinations can be accomplished using computer records, clerical assistance, and objective criteria—thus rendering unnecessary an evidentiary hearing on each claim." *Smilow*, 323 F.3d at 40.

Superiority. The superiority requirement is intended to ensure that certification of a class "would achieve economies of time, effort, and expense" while not sacrificing procedural fairness or bringing about other undesirable results. *Van West v. Midland Nat'l Life Ins. Co.*, 199 F.R.D. 448, 454 (D.R.I. 2001). The superiority element of Rule 23(b)(3) may be satisfied if most claims would not be brought except for the class action mechanism. *Tardiff v. Knox Cty.*, 365 F.3d 1, 4 (1st Cir. 2004). Courts consider the size of the proposed class and the amount of damages at stake in determining whether a class action is superior to other available methods for adjudicating the controversy. *In re Bos. Sci. Corp. Secs. Litig.*, 604 F. Supp. 2d 275, 287–88 (D. Mass. 2009). Courts also consider plaintiffs' interest in individually prosecuting separate actions, the existence of pending litigation involving the same factual circumstances in other courts, the propriety of concentrating the litigation in the forum, manageability, and other factors. *Grogan v. All My Sons Moving & Storage Bus. Dev. LLC*, 2021 WL 2627972, at *5 (D. Mass. Mar. 31, 2021) (superiority met where named plaintiffs in wage case alleged that defendants had retaliated against them, "giving the Court some reason to believe that other plaintiffs may hesitate to litigate their claims on an individual basis for fear of reprisal"); *Plastic Surgery Assocs., S.C. v. Cynosure, Inc.*, 407 F. Supp. 3d 59, 77 (D. Mass. 2019) (no superiority where alleged injury for each plaintiff exceeded $150,000 and individual class members brought separate lawsuits in related cases); *Otte v. Life Ins. Co. of N. Am.*, 275 F.R.D. 50, 58 (D. Mass. 2011); *Coffin v. Bowater Inc.*, 228 F.R.D. 397, 406 (D. Me. 2005); *In re Relafen Antitrust Litig.*, 218 F.R.D. 337, 346–47 (D. Mass. 2003).

Injury-in-Fact. The First Circuit has clarified its position on whether a class that includes uninjured class members may be certified. In *In re Nexium Antitrust Litig.*, 777 F.3d 9 (1st Cir. 2015), plaintiffs claimed that defendant drug companies had conspired to delay the entry of certain generic drug products into the market, thus inflating the prices they had to pay for the drug. In opposing class certification, defendants argued that predominance was not satisfied because some putative class members would have purchased the higher priced branded product even after the generic products came onto the market, and such uninjured class members could be identified only through individualized proof. The district court granted class certification over this objection, and a divided panel of the First Circuit affirmed, holding "that a certified class may include a de minimis number of potentially uninjured parties." *Id.* at 25. Over a strong dissent, the majority concluded that the number of uninjured class members was de minimis, and that a mechanism could be identified to sort out the injured from the uninjured parties later in the litigation, in the form of unrebutted testimony of each class member, by affidavit or declaration, that, if given the choice, he or she would have purchased the lower priced generic product. *Id.* at 20–21. District courts have relied upon *In re Nexium* to certify classes involving uninjured class members where it is possible to subsequently identify such individuals through ministerial calculations. *See Waldner v. Natixis Inv. Managers, L.P.*, 2023 WL 3466272, at *9–10 (D. Mass. Mar. 24, 2023).

Three years after *Nexium*, in *In re Asacol Antitrust Litigation*, 907 F.3d 42 (1st Cir. 2018), a unanimous panel of the First Circuit, in an opinion authored by the dissenting judge from *Nexium*, reversed certification of a class in a similar case. It held that, where a defendant intends to challenge the testimony of putative class members who claim injury, the rules of evidence, the Seventh Amendment, and the Rules Enabling Act, 28 U.S.C. § 2072(b), preclude reliance on affidavits to prove such injury. *In re Asacol*, 907 F.3d at 53. The court distinguished *Nexium* on the ground that *Nexium* had held only that unrebutted affidavits could be used to establish injury; the court never "learned whether the defendants would in fact rebut any affidavits." *Id.* at 52. In *Asacol*, by contrast "defendants . . . expressly stated their intention to challenge any affidavits," and there was no basis to conclude that those challenges would be implausible. *Id.* at 52–53. The *Asacol* court concluded that, "to determine whether a class certified for litigation will be manageable, the district court must at the time of certification offer a reasonable and workable plan for how [the opportunity to challenge allegations of injury-in-fact] will be provided in a manner that is protective of the defendant's constitutional rights and does not cause individual inquiries to overwhelm common issues." *Id.* at 58. The First Circuit reached a similar result three years later in *Bais Yaakov of Spring Valley v. ACT, Inc.*, 12 F.4th 81 (1st Cir. 2021) (affirming denial of class certification in Telephone Consumer Protection Act (TCPA) case, where defendant had produced declarations from representatives of 78 putative class members stating that they gave defendant permission to send the type of information at issue by fax). District courts also have applied *Asacol* to similar cases. *See In re Loestrin 24 FE Antitrust Litig.*, 410 F. Supp. 3d 352, 367 (D.R.I. 2019) (holding that *Asacol* precluded certification of consumer class in pay-for-delay antitrust case). *Compare In re Intuniv Antitrust Litig.*, 2019 WL 3947262 (D. Mass. Aug. 21, 2019) (predominance not satisfied in pay-for-delay case where significant percentage of indirect purchaser class suffered no antitrust injury and individualized inquiry would be required to determine which class members those were) *with In re Intuniv Antitrust Litig.*, 2019 WL 4645502 (D. Mass. Sept. 24, 2019) (predominance satisfied where expert credibly opined that all or nearly all members of direct purchaser class were injured). *See also Loughlin v. Vi-Jon, LLC*, 2024 WL 1347092, at *8–13 (D. Mass. Mar. 29, 2024) (state unfair trade practices claim failed predominance test where the defendant expressed intent to challenge affidavits); *Sandoe v. Bos. Sci. Corp.*, 333 F.R.D. 4, 9 (D. Mass. 2019) (in case brought under the TCPA, predominance not established where defendant expressed intent to challenge affidavits).

c. Ascertainability

Although ascertainability is not explicitly mentioned in Rule 23, the First Circuit has recognized it as an implied requirement for class certification. *In re Nexium Antitrust Litig.*, 777 F.3d 9, 19 (1st Cir. 2015). "To meet their burden on a motion for class certification, named Plaintiffs must demonstrate, 'by a preponderance of the evidence, that the class is currently and readily ascertainable based on objective criteria.'" *Sheet Metal Workers Local No. 20 Welfare & Benefit Fund v. CVS Pharmacy, Inc.*, 540 F. Supp. 3d 182, 202 (D.R.I. 2021) (internal quotation marks omitted); *Donovan v. Philip Morris USA, Inc.*, 268 F.R.D. 1, 9 (D. Mass. 2010) ("[A]n implicit prerequisite to class certification is that a 'class' exists—in other words, it must be 'administratively feasible for the court to determine whether a particular individual is a member.'" (quoting *Kent v. SunAmerica Life Ins. Co.*, 190 F.R.D. 271, 278 (D. Mass. 2000)). At least one court in the First Circuit has concluded, however, that the ascertainability requirement applies only Rule 23(b)(3) classes, and not Rule 23(b)(2) classes. *Fitzmorris v. N.H. Dep't of Health & Human Servs.*, 2023 WL 8188770, at *6–8 (D.N.H. Nov. 27, 2023.

"To be ascertainable, all class members need not be identified at the outset; the class need only be determinable by 'stable and objective factors.'" *Id.* (quoting *Kent*, 190 F.R.D. at 278). That is, the court must be able to determine "whether class members are included or excluded from the class by reference to objective criteria." *Matamoros v. Starbucks Corp.*, 699 F.3d 129, 139 (1st Cir. 2012). "At the certification stage, it is unnecessary to identify every class member but the class must be 'sufficiently ascertainable to permit a court to decide and declare who will receive notice, who will share in any recovery, and who will be bound by the judgment." *In re Ranbaxy Generic Drug Applic. Antitrust Litig.*, 338 F.R.D. 294, 307 (D. Mass. 2021) (quoting *Schonton v. MPA Granada Highlands LLC*, 2019 WL 1455197, at *3 (D. Mass. Apr. 2, 2019)). The availability of unrebutted affidavits may suffice to satisfy this standard. *Ortiz v. Sig Sauer, Inc.*, 2023 WL 1928094, at *7 (D.N.H. Feb. 10, 2023). Where it is "impossible to identify" class members "prior to individualized factfinding and litigation, the class fails" this "basic requirement[] for a class action under Rule 23." *Crosby v. Soc. Sec. Admin. of U.S.*, 796 F.2d 576, 580 (1st Cir. 1986).

The objective terms used to ascertain the class must not rely upon the merits of the claim itself, lest it be a "fail-safe" class. *Mantha v. QuoteWizard.com*, 2024 WL 3912459, at *11 (D. Mass. Aug. 16, 2024) (citing *Ruiz v. NEI Gen. Contracting, Inc.*, 2024 WL 869445, at *4 (D. Mass. Feb. 29, 2024). A putative class is an impermissible fail-safe class if it is defined "based on terms which depend on the outcome of the litigation, *i.e.*, 'a class defined in terms of the legal injury.'" *Ruiz*, 2024 WL 869445, at *4 (quoting *In re Nexium*, 777 F.3d at 22); *see Mantha*, 2024 WL 3912459, at *11. Courts, however, may resolve issues relating to fail-safe classes by refining the class definition. *Mantha*, 2024 WL 3912459, at *11.

5. CASE MANAGEMENT

a. Appointing Counsel

Pursuant to Rule 23(c)(1)(B), an order that certifies a class action must also appoint class counsel under Rule 23(g). Although Rule 23(g)(1) identifies several considerations in appointing class counsel, in cases in which several counsel are not competing for the class counsel role, district courts that find that plaintiffs' attorneys satisfy the adequacy requirement of Rule 23(a)(4) typically will appoint such counsel to represent the class. An order appointing class counsel often specifies the duties attendant with that role, which may include, for example, making work assignments on behalf of the plaintiffs and the certified classes to promote the orderly and efficient conduct of the litigation; determining and presenting the positions of the plaintiffs and the certified classes; seeking relief on behalf of the plaintiffs and certified classes; acting as spokespersons for the plaintiffs and certified classes at court conferences; conducting and coordinating discovery; conducting all proceedings on behalf of the plaintiffs and the certified classes; retaining experts; conducting settlement negotiations; and recommending apportionment and allocation of fees and expenses. *See, e.g.*, *In re TRS Recovery Serv., Inc. and TeleCheck Serv., Inc., Fair Debt Collection Practices Act (FDCPA) Litig.*, C.A. No. 2:13-MD-2426-DBH, Doc. No. 17 (D. Me. June 4, 2013).

b. Discovery Issues

Courts within the First Circuit have recognized "that pre-certification discovery is often necessary to determine if a class is maintainable and to define the scope of the class." *Fiorentine v. Sarton P.R., LLC*, 2021 WL 2070535, at *2 (D.P.R. May 20, 2021) (granting motion to compel discovery of call log in TCPA case and citing *Rodriguez v. Banco Central,* 102 F.R.D. 897 (D.P.R. 1984)). "Ultimately, whether class certification discovery will be permitted lies within the sound discretion of the court." *Id.*, at *3. On the other hand, where merits discovery may establish that named plaintiffs lack viable claims, courts may bifurcate discovery, staying class discovery pending the completion of such merits discovery and determination of dispositive motions relating to the named plaintiffs' claims. *Katz v. Liberty Power Corp., LLC*, 2019 WL 957129, at *1–2 (D. Mass. Feb. 27, 2019).

After a class is certified, discovery as to absent class members is generally inappropriate. *In re Intuniv Antitrust Litig.*, 2024 WL 3548241, at *11 (D. Mass. Jan. 22, 2024). However, post-certification discovery may be allowed if the defendant has a good faith purpose and the request is not unduly burdensome. *Id.* (citing *In re Porsche Automobil Holding SE*, 985 F.3d 115, 121 (1st Cir. 2021)). In applying this analysis, courts in the First Circuit have considered whether the discovery (1) is needed for the purposes of the trial or issues common to the class, (2) is narrowly tailored, (3) will impose undue burden on the absent class members, and (4) is not available from representative plaintiffs. *Id.* (citing *Briggs v. Mass. Dep't of Corr.*, 2022 WL 16702402, at *1 (D. Mass. Oct. 20, 2022)).

c. Timing of Class Certification

Rule 23(c)(1)(A) directs courts to address class certification at "an early practicable time." The First Circuit has commented that the rule "permits a district court, in appropriate circumstances, to defer the issue of class certification until after disposing of summary judgment motions." *Danny B. ex rel. Elliott v. Raimondo*, 784 F.3d 825, 837–38 (1st Cir. 2015). However, it has frowned on the practice of deferring a ruling on class certification until after trial on the merits. *Id.* at 838. As the court observed, "at best, trying the individual claims first may prove inefficient; at worst, doing so may create substantial prejudice." *Id.* The court has also held that it was not abuse of discretion for a district court to decide that a class certification motion made by a successful plaintiff after judgment on the merits was untimely. "Such a delay in adding class allegations deprives a defendant of fair warning as to the true stakes and, by eliminating mutuality, leaves the defendant liable on class claims (if he loses the summary judgment motion) without protecting him (if he wins)." *Kerkhof v. MCI WorldCom, Inc.*, 282 F.3d 44, 55 (1st Cir. 2002).[4]

Although courts are authorized to decertify a class at any time before final judgment, courts in the First Circuit have observed that a decision to decertify a class is "not taken lightly" and should be done only if defendants "have met their heavy burden of proving the necessity" of decertification. *Donovan v. Philip Morris USA, Inc.*, 2012 WL 957633, at *4 (D. Mass. Mar. 21, 2012); *see Gonzalez v. RXO Last Mile, Inc.*, 2024 WL 3697543, at *2 (D. Mass. Aug. 7, 2024). Decertification must generally be justified by discovery of new facts, changes in the parties, or changes in the law. *Donovan*, 2012 WL 957633, at *4.

6. CLASS NOTICE

Rule 23(c)(2)(A) provides that, "[f]or any class certified under Rule 23(b)(1) or (b)(2), the court may direct appropriate notice to the class." Rule 23(c)(2)(B) provides that, "[f]or any class certified under Rule 23(b)(3), the court must direct to class members the best notice that is practicable under the circumstances, including individual notice to all members who can be identified through reasonable effort." The rule goes on to describe the required contents of the notice, which must be stated "clearly and concisely" in "plain, easily understood language."

The First Circuit has explained that notice to members of a damages class

> must include, as stated in the rule, the right of the class member to seek to appear by his or her own attorney or to opt out of the class and—if he or she fails to opt out—a warning that he or she will be bound by the judgment.

Brown v. Colegio de Abogados de Puerto Rico, 613 F.3d 44, 51 (1st Cir. 2010). Further, "[a]lthough the rule does not say when notice must be given, '[t]he purpose of Rule 23(c)(2) is to ensure that the plaintiff class receives notice of the action well before the merits of the case are adjudicated.'" *Id.* (citations omitted).

Consistent with the Rule's language, the First Circuit has held that

> [a]lthough it is a fundamental requirement of due process that interested parties be apprised of the pendency of actions in which they have an interest, and be afforded an opportunity to present their allegations, such requirements can be met in appropriate cases by methods of notification other than actual personal notice.

Reppert v. Marvin Lumber & Cedar Co., 359 F.3d 53, 56 (1st Cir. 2004). In one case, the District of Massachusetts approved a notice program that included mailed notice to class members whose names and addresses were found, as well as print publication and geo-targeted internet publication for the benefit of class members whose names and addresses remained unknown. *Gulbankian v. MW Mfrs., Inc.*, C.A. No. 10-10392-RWZ, Doc. No. 209 (D. Mass. Dec. 29, 2014).

[4] *Kerkhof* was decided before the 2003 Amendments to Rule 23 replaced the requirement that the court determine class certification "as soon as practicable after commencement of an action" with the requirement that the court make the determination "at an early practicable time." The amended language likely would not have affected the outcome of the case.

7. DAMAGES

Damages issues are closely tied to the predominance inquiry under Rule 23(b)(3). The First Circuit has observed that "[t]he mere fact that there are differences among members of a class regarding individual amounts of damages does not preclude class certification" under Rule 23(b)(3), at least where these damages issues can be resolved "according to a universal mathematical or formulaic calculation, obviating the need for evidentiary hearings on individual claims." *In re New Motor Vehicles Canadian Exp. Antitrust Litig.*, 522 F.3d 6, 23 (1st Cir. 2008); *see Tardiff v. Knox Cty.*, 365 F.3d 1, 6–7 (1st Cir. 2004); *Smilow v. Sw. Bell Mobile Sys., Inc.*, 323 F.3d 32, 40 (1st Cir. 2003). Moreover, the First Circuit has approved the use of aggregate damages calculations. *In re Pharm. Indus. Average Wholesale Price Litig.*, 582 F.3d 156, 197 (1st Cir. 2009). Plaintiffs must demonstrate at the class certification stage that their damages theory is tied to their theory of liability and is subject to calculation by a common methodology applicable to the class as a whole. *In re Dial Complete Mktg. & Sales Practices Litig.*, 312 F.R.D. 36, 77 (D.N.H. 2015); *see Omori v. Brandeis Univ.*, 673 F. Supp. 3d 21 (D. Mass. 2023).

The First Circuit has held that plaintiffs must propose "some means of determining that each member of the class was in fact injured, even if the amount of each individual injury could be determined at a separate proceeding." *In re New Motor Vehicles*, 522 F.3d at 28. The ability to calculate "the aggregate amount of damages," however, "does not absolve plaintiffs from the duty to prove each class member was harmed by the defendants' practice." *Id.*; *see In re Asacol Antitrust Litig.*, 907 F.3d 43, 55 (1st Cir. 2018) (where "the aggregate damage amount is the sum of damages suffered by a number of individuals," and where the determination "whether any given individual was injured (and therefore has a claim) turns on an assessment of the individual facts concerning that person," then "the defendant must be offered the opportunity to challenge each class member's proof that the defendant is liable to that class member").

Where individualized damage issues would "swamp" the litigation with individualized, fact-intensive hearings, certification is not appropriate. *Fleming v. Select Portfolio Servicing*, 342 F.R.D. 361, 367 (D. Mass. 2022). However, if core liability issues are subject to classwide proof, courts may bifurcate liability and damages issues to address individualized damages issues separately. *Brown v. Saint-Gobain Performance Plastics*, 2023 WL 9023158, at *20–22 (D.N.H. Dec. 29, 2023).

8. SETTLEMENTS

The First Circuit follows a pragmatic approach in reviewing class action settlements. It recognizes that a district court's decision whether to approve a class settlement comes down to "balancing the advantages and disadvantages of the proposed settlement as against the consequences of going to trial or other possible but perhaps unattainable variations on the proffered settlement." *Bezdek v. Vibram USA, Inc.*, 809 F.3d 78, 82 (1st Cir. 2015) (quoting *Nat'l Ass'n of Chain Drug Stores v. New England Carpenters*, 582 F.3d 30, 44 (1st Cir. 2009)).

Rule 23(e)(1) provides that a court's decision whether to direct notice of a proposed settlement to class members depends on a finding "that the court will likely be able to: (i) approve the proposal under Rule 23(e)(2); and (ii) certify the class for purposes of judgment on the proposal." The process and standards courts within the First Circuit apply to motions to approve class settlements are no different from those applied by judges in other federal courts. One judge applied the following factors in assessing the fairness of a class settlement: (1) comparison of the proposed settlement with the likely result of litigation; (2) stage of the litigation and the amount of discovery completed; (3) reaction of the class to the settlement; (4) quality of counsel; (5) conduct of the negotiations; and (6) prospects of the case, including risk, complexity, expense, and duration. *In re TRS Recovery Serv., Inc. and*

TeleCheck Serv., Inc., Fair Debt Collection Practices Act (FDCPA) Litig., 2016 WL 543137, at *5 (D. Me. Feb. 10, 2016).

More recently, Rule 23(e)(2) was amended to include a different, although overlapping, list of considerations. When considering certification of a settlement class, a court will consider the requirements of Rule 23(a) and (b), but will "apply the criteria differently." *Rapuano v. Trs. of Dartmouth Coll.*, 334 F.R.D. 637, 643 (D.N.H. 2020). For instance, a court will not consider whether management problems would preclude certification, while "other aspects of Rule 23—for example, those preventing overbroad class definitions—deserve 'undiluted, even heightened attention' in the settlement context." *Id.* at 644 (quoting *Amchem Prods., Inc. v. Windsor*, 521 U.S. 591, 620 (1997)). Thus, courts apply Rule 23 requirements "in some ways more leniently, in other ways more vigorously" in "certifying a class for the purposes of settlement only." *Id.*

Similarly, in evaluating the "adequacy of representation" requirement of Rule 23(e)(2)(A), the First Circuit has noted that "much, if not all, of [the court's] analysis would apply to Rule 23(a)'s adequate representation requirement in the context of class certification for settlement." *Murray v. Grocery Delivery E-Services USA Inc., d/b/a/ HelloFresh*, 55 F.4th 340 (1st Cir. 2022) (*HelloFresh*). In *HelloFresh*, the court reversed and remanded for further proceedings a district court's order approving a common fund settlement where members of a single class advanced three different types of claims under the Telephone Consumer Protection Act (TCPA). The court held that the differences in proof required to establish each type of claim, as well as differences in the defenses available for each, required the district court to consider whether each group seeking recovery from the fund should be separately represented. In a thorough and informative analysis of Rule 23(e)'s adequacy-of-representation requirement, the court explained that the "structural assurance that a negotiated agreement accounts for any differences between the claims . . . is absent when a single lawyer represents groups with significantly different claims in the context of allocating a lump-sum settlement." *Id.* at 346; *see also Purinton v. Moody's Co-Worker Owned, Inc.*, 2023 WL 167560, at *3–4 (D. Me. Jan. 12, 2023) (finding that *HelloFresh* did not limit Court's ability to approve class action settlement involving multiple subclasses and claims where interests of groups of class members overlapped and class counsel articulated a "clear cut" explanation for the relative value of the different claims).

One district court has observed that the amended rule has clarified the "standard the court should apply at the preliminary approval stage." *Rapuano*, 334 F.R.D. at 642. Because Rule 23(e)(1)(B) "provides that, in order to preliminarily approve the settlement, the court must find that it 'will likely be able to' certify the class for the purposes of settlement," a court must then conduct a "searching—not a relaxed—inquiry." *Id.* at 643 (quoting Fed. R. Civ. P. 23(e)(1)(B)). Accordingly, courts will "conduct a careful review at this preliminary stage to ensure that it will likely be able to approve the settlement and certify the class after final hearing." *Id.*

Where the requirements for the application of res judicata exist, a class action settlement will bar future claims by disgruntled class members. *Budrow v. Nat'l City Mortg. Co.*, 2022 WL 14829551, at *8–9 (D. Mass. Oct. 26, 2022); *Efreom v. McKee*, 2021 WL 1424974, at *4–7 (D.R.I. Apr. 15, 2021) (dismissing complaint of 49 members of state employees' retirement system because of prior class action settlement); *Wellness Med. Ctr. LLC v. Liberty Mut. Ins. Co.*, 703 F. Supp. 3d 289, 295–96 (D. Mass. 2023) (ruling that settlement class member was barred from bringing new individual action for claims released in class settlement absent a showing that class judgment deprived class member of due process).

a. *Cy Pres*

The First Circuit first addressed the issue of *cy pres* distributions in *In re Pharm. Indus. Average Wholesale Price Litig.*, 588 F.3d 24 (1st Cir. 2009) (the AWP case). There, the court affirmed a district court's approval of a *cy pres* distribution as part of a class action settlement that provided for payment of all class members' damages, trebled, before any *cy pres* money was to be paid to charity. Although the court recognized that not all class members would file claims under the settlement, it rejected the argument that the class members were entitled to receive all of the settlement funds, especially where those who did submit claims would be more than fully compensated.

The issue in the AWP case was whether *cy pres* distributions are permissible, but not where the funds may be directed. The First Circuit took up that issue in *In re Lupron Mktg. and Sales Practices Litig.*, 677 F.3d 21 (2012). In that case, the court adopted the "reasonable approximation" test set forth in the American Law Institute's Principles of the Law of Aggregate Litigation (ALI Principles). *Id.* at 32–33. The purpose of the test is to determine whether the proposed distributions reasonably approximate the interests of the class members. In making that determination, the First Circuit will apply the following factors:

- The purposes of the underlying statutes claimed to have been violated;
- The nature of the injury to the class members;
- The characteristics and interests of the class members;
- The geographical scope of the class;
- The reasons the settlement funds have gone unclaimed; and
- The closeness of the fit between the class and the *cy pres* recipient.

Id. at 33. As the court also explained, "[f]ailure to meet the reasonable approximation test can lead to reversal." *Id.* Although the court approved the *cy pres* provision in *Lupron*, it cautioned that the settling parties should not leave the selection of a *cy pres* recipient to the discretion of the district judge, but should choose a recipient in the first instance, to be tested by the district court against the principles that the First Circuit has articulated. *Id.* at 38.

9. FEES AND COSTS

"Attorneys in a certified class action may be awarded reasonable fees and costs, subject to the wide discretion of the trial judge." *Bezdek v. Vibram USA Inc.*, 79 F. Supp. 3d 324, 349 (D. Mass. 2015); *see* Fed. R. Civ. P. 23(h). "Under the 'common fund doctrine,' an attorney who succeeds in creating a fund for the benefit of the class is entitled to a reasonable attorney's fee from the fund as a whole." *In re Relafen Antitrust Litig.*, 231 F.R.D. 52, 77 (D. Mass. 2005); *see In re Thirteen Appeals Arising Out of the San Juan Dupont Plaza Hotel Fire Litig.*, 56 F.3d 295, 305 n.6 (1st Cir. 1995). In awarding fees and costs, the court's "wide latitude in shaping the contours" of an award is tempered by the court's "quasi-fiduciary" duty to class members to protect the corpus of the fund for the benefit of the plaintiff class. *In re Fidelity/Micron Secs. Litig.*, 167 F.3d 735, 737 (1st Cir. 1999); *see Noll v. Flowers Foods Inc.*, 2022 WL 1438606, at *8 (D. Me. May 3, 2022) ("district judges are expected to give careful scrutiny to the terms of the proposed settlements in order to make sure that class counsel are behaving as honest fiduciaries for the class as a whole" (quoting *In re Pharm. Indus. Average Wholesale Price Litig.*, 588 F.3d 24, 36 (1st Cir. 2009) (citations omitted))).

The First Circuit recognizes two methods for calculating attorneys' fees in the "common fund" context. *In re Relafen Antitrust Litig.*, 231 F.R.D. at 77; *see In re Thirteen Appeals*, 56 F.3d at 307. "Under the 'percentage of the fund' ('POF') method, counsel may be awarded a reasonable percentage of the common fund." *Bezdek*, 79 F. Supp. 3d at 349. Generally, courts in the First Circuit award fees "in the range of 20–30%, with 25% as the benchmark." *Latorraca v. Centennial Techs., Inc.*, 834 F. Supp. 2d 25, 27–28 (D. Mass. 2011) (collecting cases). The POF method is "generally favored in the class action context." *Bezdek*, 79 F. Supp. 3d at 350; *see Wright v. S. N.H. Univ.*, 561 F. Supp. 3d 211, 214 (D.N.H. 2021); *Walsh v. Popular, Inc.*, 839 F. Supp. 2d 476, 483 (D.P.R. 2012); *In re Cabletron Sys., Inc. Secs. Litig.*, 239 F.R.D. 30, 37–38 (D.N.H. 2006). The First Circuit also recognizes the "lodestar" method, pursuant to which the "court determines the number of hours reasonably expended multiplied by a reasonable hourly rate for attorneys of similar skill within that geographic area." *Bezdek*, 79 F. Supp. 3d at 350. "This calculation is subject to a multiplier or discount for special circumstances, plus reasonable disbursements." *Id.* "Although the lodestar serves as a base figure, the court may modify it by subtracting hours that are excessive in light of the legal task, not recorded with sufficient specificity as to the tasks performed, or redundant to hours of another lawyer without justification for the need for duplicity." *Id.* The lodestar method may be used alone or as a check on a POF calculation. *Id.*

"Regardless of the calculation method employed, the touchstone of the inquiry is reasonableness." *Id.* at 350. Although the First Circuit has not endorsed a specific set of factors to be used in determining whether a fee request is reasonable, district courts have considered factors such as the size of the fund and number of persons benefited, the presence or absence of substantial objections by members of the class to the fees requested, the skill and efficiency of the attorneys, the complexity and duration of the litigation, the risk of nonpayment, the amount of time devoted to the case, and awards in similar cases. *In re Relafen*, 231 F.R.D. at 79; *see Walsh*, 839 F. Supp. 2d at 483.[5] Courts also may examine costs incurred to ensure that the costs are neither excessive nor unnecessary. *Walsh*, 839 F. Supp. 2d at 487.

In *Murray v. Grocery Delivery E-Services USA Inc., d/b/a/ HelloFresh*, 55 F.4th 340 (1st Cir. 2022), the First Circuit rejected the Eleventh Circuit's conclusion that incentive awards in class action settlements are prohibited by two Supreme Court decisions from the 1880s that arose in different contexts. *Id.* at 353 ("we choose to follow the collective wisdom of courts over the past several decades that have permitted these sorts of incentive payments, rather than create a categorical rule that refuses to consider the facts of each case"); *see Noll*, 2022 WL 1438606, at *9 ("Incentive awards serve the important purpose of compensating plaintiffs for the time and effort expended in assisting the prosecution of the litigation, the risks incurred by becoming and continuing as a litigant, the public nature of a collective action filing, and any other burdens they sustain." (quoting *Lauture v. A.C. Moore Arts & Crafts, Inc.*, 2017 WL 6460244, at *2 (D. Mass. June 8, 2017))).

10. APPELLATE ISSUES

a. Standing to Appeal

As a general matter, an individual has standing to appeal a class certification order only if that individual is directly affected by the order. The fact that a class certification order has "an indirect or incidental effect" on an individual does not give that person standing to appeal. *Tilley v. TJX Cos.*, 345 F.3d 34, 36 (1st Cir. 2003). The First Circuit has held, however, that only one petitioner must have standing in order for the appeal to go forward. If one petitioner has standing, "the proceeding may go forward without any consideration of the standing of co-petitioners." *Id.*

Specific standing issues can arise in the context of class settlements. The Supreme Court has held that unnamed members of a mandatory class who object in a timely manner to approval of a settlement at the fairness hearing have the power to bring an appeal without first intervening. *Devlin v. Scardelletti*, 536 U.S. 1, 10 (2002). The First Circuit has extended *Devlin* to apply to opt out classes. *Nat'l Ass'n of Chain Drug Stores v. New England Carpenters Health Benefits Fund*, 582 F.3d 30, 39–40 (1st Cir. 2009).

[5] The multi-factor approach has been criticized and rejected by some judges within the First Circuit in favor of a "market mimicking approach" that is designed to award a fee that is the "market price for legal services, in light of the risk of nonpayment and the normal rate of compensation in the market at the outset of the case." In re Cabletron Sys., Inc. Secs. Litig., 239 F.R.D. at 39–40; *see* Nilsen v. York Cty., 400 F. Supp. 2d 266, 276–79 (D. Me. 2005).

b. Interlocutory Review

Rule 23(f) provides the court with discretion to hear an interlocutory appeal of a district court order certifying or decertifying a class. *Smilow v. Sw. Bell Mobile Sys., Inc.*, 323 F.3d 32, 37 n.4 (1st Cir. 2003). The First Circuit has described three categories of cases that would warrant the exercise of discretionary appellate jurisdiction. "First, an appeal ordinarily should be permitted when a denial of class status effectively ends the case (because, say, the named plaintiff's claim is not of a sufficient magnitude to warrant the costs of stand-alone litigation)." *Waste Mgmt. Holdings, Inc. v. Mowbray*, 208 F.3d 288, 293 (1st Cir. 2000). "Second, an appeal ordinarily should be permitted when the grant of class status raises the stakes of the litigation so substantially that the defendant likely will feel irresistible pressure to settle." *Id.* An applicant who invokes either of these two classifications also must demonstrate that the district court's ruling is "questionable." *Id.* "Third, an appeal ordinarily should be permitted when it will lead to clarification of a fundamental issue of law"; that is, the appeal would "permit the resolution of an unsettled legal issue that is important to the particular litigation as well as important in itself and likely to escape effective review if left hanging until the end of the case." *Id.* at 293–94.

While these three criteria serve as guides, the court has noted that it retains its discretion and that therefore "special circumstances may lead [the court] either to deny leave to appeal in cases that seem superficially to fit into one of these three pigeonholes, or conversely, to grant leave to appeal in cases that do not match any of the three described categories." *Id.* at 294. The court also has reiterated that it generally exercises its "discretion judiciously" because interlocutory appeals are "disruptive, time-consuming, and expensive"—considerations that "counsel in favor of some restraint" in granting an appeal. *Id.*[6]

The First Circuit has provided additional guidance regarding the types of cases in which interlocutory appeal is appropriate or inappropriate.

> Interlocutory appeals from class certification under Rule 23(f) are especially appropriate where the plaintiffs' theory is novel or where a doubtful class certification results in financial exposure to defendants so great as to provide substantial incentives for defendants to settle non-meritorious cases in an effort to avoid both risk of liability and litigation expense.

In re New Motor Vehicles Canadian Exp. Antitrust Litig., 522 F.3d 6, 8 (1st Cir. 2008). "By the same token, an erroneous failure to certify a class where individual claims are small may deprive plaintiffs of the only realistic mechanism to vindicate meritorious claims." *Id.* Also, the court will "normally grant Rule 23(f) review when a class decertification ruling, apparently premised on an abuse of discretion by the district court, would have the practical effect of compelling a party to abandon a potentially meritorious claim." *Smilow*, 323 F.3d at 37 n.4.

An appeal under Rule 23(f) "does not stay proceedings in the district court unless the district judge or the court of appeals so orders." Fed. R. Civ. P. 23(f). In determining whether to grant a stay, a district court will consider four factors: "(1) whether the stay applicant has made a strong showing that he is likely to succeed on the merits; (2) whether

[6] The First Circuit has noted that the first and third categories of cases are equally applicable to plaintiff and defendant classes, but that the second category of cases generally would not apply to actions involving defendant classes. In *Tilley v. TJX Cos.*, 345 F.3d 34, 37–38 (1st Cir. 2003), the court summarized the application of Rule 23(f) to cases involving defendant classes as follows: interlocutory appeal is appropriate "when one of three circumstances exists: (i) denial of certification effectively disposes of the litigation because the plaintiff's claim would only be worth pursuing as against a full class of defendants; or (ii) an interlocutory appeal would clarify an important and unsettled legal issue that would likely escape effective end-of-case review; or (iii) an interlocutory appeal is a desirable vehicle either for addressing special circumstances or for avoiding manifest injustice." *Id.* at 39.

the applicant will be irreparably injured absent a stay; (3) whether issuance of the stay will substantially injure the other parties interested in the proceeding; and (4) where the public interest lies." *Picone v. Shire, LLC*, 2020 WL 3051871, at *2 (D. Mass. June 8, 2020) (internal quotation marks omitted).

c. Standard of Review

The First Circuit reviews orders granting or denying class certification for abuse of discretion. *See McKenna v. First Horizon Home Loan Corp.*, 475 F.3d 418, 422 (1st Cir. 2007); *Tilley v. TJX Cos.*, 345 F.3d 34, 39 (1st Cir. 2003). "A district court abuses its discretion when a relevant factor deserving of significant weight is overlooked, or when an improper factor is accorded significant weight, or when the court considers the appropriate mix of factors, but commits a palpable error of judgment in calibrating the decisional scales." *Id.* While class certification is generally left to the district court's discretion, legal conclusions are reviewed de novo. *See McKenna*, 475 F.3d at 422; *Tardiff v. Knox Cty.*, 365 F.3d 1, 4 (1st Cir. 2004).

11. TOLLING STATUTE OF LIMITATIONS

Prior to the Supreme Court's decision in *China Agritech, Inc. v. Resh*, 138 S. Ct. 1800 (2018), the First Circuit had observed that, although the "commencement of a class action suspends the applicable statute of limitations as to all asserted members of the class who would have been parties had the suit been permitted to continue as a class action," plaintiffs may not "stretch out limitations periods by bringing successive class actions." *Basch v. Ground Round, Inc.*, 139 F.3d 6, 10–11 (1st Cir. 1998) (discussing *Am. Pipe & Const. Co. v. Utah*, 414 U.S. 538 (1974), and *Crown, Cork & Seal Co. v. Parker*, 462 U.S. 345 (1983)). In *Basch*, the First Circuit held that plaintiffs "may not stack one class action on top of another and continue to toll the statute of limitations indefinitely." *Id.* at 11. Pursuant to *Basch*, class actions toll statutes of limitations only for subsequent individual actions, not for subsequent class actions alleging similar classes and similar claims. *Id.* at 11–12. In *China Agritech*, the Supreme Court adopted the same approach. 138 S. Ct. at 1804.

The First Circuit has declined to apply *China Agritech* narrowly. In *In re Celexa and Lexapro Mktg. & Sales Practices Litig.*, 915 F.3d 1 (1st Cir. 2019), the First Circuit observed that "*China Agritech* clarified that [*American Pipe*] tolling has limits: While a putative class member may join an existing suit or file an individual action upon denial of class certification, a putative class member may not commence a class action anew beyond the time allowed by the untolled statute of limitations." *Id.* at 16. The court refused to limit *China Agritech*'s application to situations in which class certification was denied in the earlier-filed class action. Instead, the First Circuit held that *China Agritech* stands for the broad proposition that the "tolling effect of a motion to certify a class applies only to individual claims, no matter how the motion is ultimately resolved. To hold otherwise would be to allow a chain of withdrawn class-action suits to extend the limitations period forever." *Id.* at 17. In the First Circuit, therefore, it is clear that a class action—however resolved—does not toll the statute of limitations for subsequent class actions. *See Concepcion v. Office of Comm'r of Baseball*, 2023 WL 4110155, at *9–10 (D.P.R. May 31, 2023).

Subsequent to *In re Celexa*, a district court concluded that *American Pipe* tolling continues "'only as far as is justified by the objectively reasonable reliance interests of the absent class members.'" *Desmesmin v. City of Bos.*, 2020 WL 2079389, at *2 (D. Mass. Apr. 30, 2020) (quoting *Bridges v. Dep't of Md. State Police*, 441 F.3d 197, 211 (4th Cir. 2006) (alterations omitted)). Thus, even dismissal without prejudice of a class certification motion may end tolling and place upon any latecomers an obligation to diligently pursue their claims. *Id.* at *4 (finding claims time-barred where class certification was denied without prejudice and the motion was not renewed until after a full trial on the merits).

12. ARBITRATION ISSUES

Under the Federal Arbitration Act (FAA), "[a] written provision in . . . a contract . . . to settle by arbitration a controversy thereafter arising out of such contract . . . shall be valid, irrevocable, and enforceable." 9 U.S.C. § 2. The FAA "reflects 'a liberal policy favoring arbitration agreements,'" *Cullinane v. Uber Techs., Inc.*, 893 F.3d 53, 60 (1st Cir. 2018) (quoting *AT&T Mobility LLC v. Concepcion*, 563 U.S. 333, 346 (2011)), as well as "Congress' intention to 'place arbitration agreements upon the same footing as other contracts,'" *id.* (quoting *Scherk v. Alberto-Culver Co.*, 417 U.S. 506, 511 (1974)). Class action waivers included in arbitration provisions are generally enforceable. *See Christensen v. Barclays Bank Del.*, 2019 WL 1921710, at *6 (D. Mass. Apr. 30, 2019) (citing *Am. Express v. Italian Colors Rest.*, 570 U.S. 228, 235–36 (2013), and *AT&T Mobility LLC*, 563 U.S. at 344).

"Arbitration is a matter of contract and a party cannot be required to submit to arbitration any dispute which it has not agreed to so submit." *Hogan v. SPAR Grp., Inc.*, 914 F.3d 34, 38 (1st Cir. 2019). Accordingly, in the First Circuit, a party seeking to compel arbitration "must show (1) that a valid agreement to arbitrate exists, (2) that the movant is entitled to invoke the arbitration clause, (3) that the other party is bound by that clause, and (4) that the claim asserted comes within the clause's scope. *Id.* (quoting *Ouadani v. TF Final Mile LLC*, 876 F.3d 31, 36 (1st Cir. 2017)). Because "arbitration is a matter of contract," principles of state contract law generally govern. *Cullinane*, 893 F.3d at 61. The First Circuit has applied state law contract principles to invalidate an online arbitration agreement where the link to the agreement was not sufficiently conspicuous and customers were not required to click to view the agreement. *Id.*

The First Circuit's recent class action arbitration decisions have reflected developing case law in the Supreme Court. In *Stolt-Nielsen S.A. v. AnimalFeeds Int'l Corp*, the Supreme Court held that a court may not compel arbitration on a classwide basis when an agreement is silent on the availability of such arbitration. 559 U.S. 662, 684–87 (2010). In *Lamps Plus, Inc. v. Varela*, the Supreme Court held that, "[l]ike silence, ambiguity does not provide a sufficient basis to conclude that parties to an arbitration agreement agreed to sacrifice the principal advantage of arbitration." 139 S. Ct. at 1407, 1416 (2019). Although the First Circuit had previously adopted a more flexible standard, it has held since *Lamps Plus* that courts may not permit class arbitration where an agreement is either silent or ambiguous about whether the parties agreed to arbitrate on a classwide basis. *Am. Inst. for Foreign Study, Inc. v. Fernandez-Jimenez*, 6 F.4th 120, 123 (1st Cir. 2021); *cf. Fantastic Sams Franchise Corp. v. FSRO Ass'n*, 683 F.3d 18, 22 (1st Cir. 2012).

The First Circuit has held that the class claims of delivery workers who contracted with Amazon to transport goods locally on the last legs of interstate journeys are not covered by the Federal Arbitration Act because they fall within the exemption for interstate transportation workers set forth in Section 1 of the Act. Their claims, the court held, were thus not barred by the Supreme Court's decision in *Concepcion. Waithaka v. Amazon.com, Inc.*, 966 F.3d 10 (1st Cir. 2020). More recently, the First Circuit held that Lyft drivers are not subject to the FAA's interstate transport worker exemption because, unlike the Amazon drivers in *Waithaka*, they have no agreements with companies engaged in interstate transport to drive "the last mile," but instead work for a company that is "primarily in the business of facilitating local, intrastate trips." *Cunningham v. Lyft, Inc.,* 17 F.4th 244, 253 (2021) (footnote omitted).

Beyond the interstate transportation exemption, in cases involving contract formation through hyperlinks, district courts within the First Circuit have reached different outcomes depending on fact-specific inquiries regarding whether the plaintiff had reasonable notice of the arbitration agreement and expressed acceptance of its terms. *See, e.g., Eubanks v. GasBuddy, LLC*, 2022 WL 16963807 (D. Mass. Nov. 16, 2022) (granting motion to compel arbitration where defendant presented detailed evidence that plaintiff was required to click button agreeing to terms and conditions and plaintiff failed to provide specific evidence to the contrary); *Murray v. Grocery Delivery E-Services USA Inc.*, 460 F. Supp. 3d 93 (D. Mass. 2020); *In re Daily Fantasy Sports Litig.*, 2019 WL 6337762 (D. Mass. Nov. 27, 2019). At least one district court within the First Circuit has held "that whether the parties agreed to proceed to arbitration on a class or individual basis is a foundational question of arbitrability for the Court to decide absent a clear and unambiguous delegation of such authority to the arbitrator." *Am. Inst. for Foreign Study, Inc. v. Fernandez-Jimenez*, 468 F. Supp. 3d 414, 421 (D. Mass. 2020). On the other hand, where an arbitration agreement delegates the issue of arbitrability to the arbitrator, the arbitrator, and not the court, is to determine whether a non-signatory to the arbitration agreement can compel a party to the agreement to arbitrate its claims. *Fairfield v. DCD Auto. Holdings, Inc.*, 2023 WL 4186191, at *3–4 (D. Mass. June 26, 2023); *In re Intuniv Antitrust Litig.*, 2021 WL 517386, at *12 (D. Mass. Feb. 11, 2021).

SECOND CIRCUIT

Districts of Connecticut, New York, and Vermont

Thurgood Marshall United States Courthouse
40 Foley Square
New York, NY 10007

By Amy Miller
Cohen Milstein Sellers & Toll PLLC

1. INTRODUCTION

This chapter provides an overview of the law related to issues concerning class actions in the Second Circuit. The court hears appeals from the six federal district courts in the states of Connecticut, New York, and Vermont. The Second Circuit has thirteen active judges and fourteen senior judges, and the Honorable Debra Ann Livingston serves as the Chief Judge.

Recently, in *Salazar v. National Basketball Association*, the Second Circuit reversed a district court's dismissal of a putative class action under the Video Privacy Protection Act (VPPA), relying on a different interpretation of the VPPA's definition of "consumer" than the majority of the courts. Specifically, the Second Circuit found that the phrase "goods or services" in the definition of "consumer" was not limited to audiovisual goods or services as long as audiovisual content was part of the "provider's book of business," and therefore, an online newsletter could qualify as a "good or service." 118 F.4th 533, 537 (2d Cir. 2024). In *Salazar*, the plaintiff signed up for a digital NBA newsletter to watch videos on NBA.com and allegedly provided his personal information as part of that exchange, which the Second Circuit determined was sufficient to allege he was a "subscriber" for the purposes of the VPPA's "consumer" definition. This decision may lead to a new wave of VPPA lawsuits involving consumer newsletter subscriptions in the Second Circuit because other courts across the nation have previously dismissed claims filed by free-newsletter subscribers due to findings that they were not "consumers."

In *Moses v. New York Times Co.*, the Second Circuit vacated and remanded the approval of a class action settlement where the district court applied the wrong legal standard under Rule 23(e). The Second Circuit explained that:

> Courts evaluating the fairness, reasonableness, and adequacy of a proposed settlement must consider the four factors outlined in Rule 23(e)(2) holistically, taking into account—among other substantive considerations stated in the rule—the proposed attorneys' fees and incentive awards. As discussed below, the revised Rule 23(e)(2) does not displace our traditional *Grinnell* factors, which remain a useful framework for considering the substantive fairness of a settlement. But the rule now mandates courts to evaluate factors that may not have been highlighted in our prior case law, and its terms prevail over any prior analysis that are inconsistent with its requirements.

79 F.4th 235, 243 (2d Cir. 2023).

In *Moses*, the Second Circuit affirmed that district courts may grant incentive awards in class action settlements, rejecting an argument to follow the Eleventh Circuit's ruling that bars such awards.

In a number of other recent opinions, the Second Circuit has clarified and added to its holdings on important class action issues:

- In *Krasner v. Cedar Realty Trust, Inc., et al.*, the court affirmed the dismissal of a class action finding that the Class Action Fairness Act exception applied, and therefore, the case was properly remanded to state court. 86 F.4th 522 (2d Cir. 2023).

- In *Edmundson v. Klarna*, the court reversed the denial of a motion to compel arbitration in a putative class action by finding that plaintiff was provided with "reasonably conspicuous notice" of the company's mandatory arbitration agreement clause in its widget. 85 F.4th 695, 707 (2d Cir. 2023). The court further confirmed that "no particular features must be present to satisfy the reasonably conspicuous standard," but under the circumstances of this case, reasonable internet users would understand that selecting "Confirm and continue" on Klarna's widget would constitute their confirmation that they "agree on the payment terms" including the arbitration agreement provision. *Id.*

- In *Cedeno v. Sasson et al.*, the court affirmed the denial of a motion to compel arbitration of a putative class action seeking equitable remedies under ERISA for alleged mismanagement of an employee stock ownership plan. Specifically, in a 2–1 decision, the court affirmed the district court's finding that an arbitration provision was unenforceable because it acted as a "prospective waiver[] of [a] statutory right." 100 F.4th 386, 393 (2d Cir. 2024).

- In *Oberlander v. Coinbase Glob., Inc.*, the court reversed the district court's determination in a putative class action that a crypto exchange was not a "statutory seller;" concluding instead that Coinbase operates as an online trading platform where users can buy and sell digital assets, and therefore, is subject to plausibly alleged claims under Section 12(a) of the Securities Act. 2024 WL 1478773, at *2 (2d Cir. Apr. 5, 2024).

- In *Maso Capital Investments Ltd. et al. v. E-House (China) Holdings Ltd. et al.*, the court affirmed the dismissal of a securities class action relying on the United States Supreme Court's holding in *Macquarie Infrastructure Corp. v. Moab Partners, L.P.*, 601 U.S. 257 (2024), rejecting plaintiffs' argument that defendants "had an independent duty" to disclose certain omitted information from proxy materials. The court explained that "[t]he investors' pure-omission arguments . . .fail because '[p]ure omissions' are no longer 'actionable under Rule 10b-5.'" 2024 WL 2890968 at *4 (2d Cir. June 10, 2024).

- In *Elisa W. v. City of New York*, the court reversed the denial of class certification, finding the district court erred in its analysis of commonality and typicality under Rule 23 because it "did not determine whether commonality and typicality exist with respect to each of plaintiffs' claims." 82 F.4th 115, 123 (2d Cir. 2023).

- In *Bohnak v. Marsh & McLennan Cos., Inc.*, the court reversed a decision where the district court found that plaintiffs did not suffer a concrete harm to establish Article III standing. In this regard, the court relied on *TransUnion LLC v. Ramirez*, where the Supreme Court specifically recognized that "disclosure of private information" was an intangible harm "traditionally recognized as providing a basis for lawsuits in American courts." 141 S. Ct. at 2204 (citing *Davis v. Fed. Election*

Comm'n, 554 U.S. 724, 733, 128 S. Ct. 2759, 171 L. Ed. 2d 737 (2008)). 79 F.4th 276, 286 (2d Cir. 2023).

- In *Bruce v. Citigroup Inc.*, the court reversed a bankruptcy court's decision while stating its disagreement "that a bankruptcy court has the authority to hear and adjudicate a class-wide contempt proceeding." 75 F.4th 297, 299 (2d Cir. 2023).
- In *Hyland v. Navient Corp.*, the court affirmed the district court's certification of a Rule 23(b)(2) injunctive relief settlement class and held that class standing was satisfied even though some class members no longer had any relationship with the defendant. In this regard, the court explained that "[s]tanding is satisfied so long as at least one named plaintiff can demonstrate the requisite injury." 48 F.4th 110, 117–18 (2d Cir. 2022).

2. JURISDICTIONAL PREREQUISITES

a. Requirements of the Class Action Fairness Act (CAFA)

Class action jurisdiction is governed by 28 U.S.C. § 1332, which was amended by the Class Action Fairness Act of 2005 (CAFA) to "expand[] the availability of diversity jurisdiction for class action lawsuits." *Blockbuster, Inc. v. Galeno*, 472 F.3d 53, 56 (2d Cir. 2006); *see* 28 U.S.C. § 1332(d). CAFA does not disturb the rule that "the party asserting federal jurisdiction [bears] the burden of proving that the case [is] properly in federal court." *Hart v. Rick's NY Cabaret Int'l, Inc.*, 967 F. Supp. 2d 955, 959–60 (S.D.N.Y. 2014) (quoting *DiTolla v. Doral Dental IPA of New York, LLC*, 469 F.3d 271, 275 (2d Cir. 2006)).

Under 28 U.S.C. § 1332, federal district courts exercise original jurisdiction over "any class action involving (1) 100 or more class members, (2) an aggregate amount in controversy of at least $5,000,000, exclusive of interest and costs, and (3) minimal diversity, i.e., where at least one plaintiff and one defendant are citizens of different states." *Blockbuster*, 472 F.3d at 56 (citing 28 U.S.C. § 1332(d)(2), (5)(b), (6)).[1] Thus, the party seeking to establish federal subject matter jurisdiction must demonstrate "that it appears to a 'reasonable probability' that the aggregate claims of the plaintiff class are in excess of $5 million." *Blockbuster*, 472 F.3d at 58 (citation omitted).

While CAFA introduced the concept of minimal diversity (as opposed to the "complete diversity" that governs outside the class context), it provided for three exceptions (among other exceptions) that may apply to particular securities-related class actions so as "to keep purely local matters and issues of particular state concern in the state courts[.]" *Estate of Pew v. Cardarelli*, 527 F.3d 25, 30 (2d Cir. 2008) (quoting *Lowery v. Alabama Power Co.*, 483 F.3d 1184, 1194 (11th Cir. 2007)). Section 1332(d)(9) provides that the $5 million amount in controversy and minimal diversity requirements do not apply to class actions that solely involve claims: (A) for covered securities already subject to federal jurisdiction under SLUSA; (B) that "relate[] to the internal affairs or governance of a corporation or other form of business enterprise and that arises under or by virtue of the laws of the State in which such corporation or business enterprise is incorporated or organized"; or (C) "that relate[] to the rights, duties (including fiduciary duties), and obligations relating to or created by or pursuant to any security (as defined under section 2(a)(1) of the Securities Act of 1933 (15 U.S.C. 77b(a)(1)) and the regulations issued thereunder)." 28 U.S.C. § 1332(d)(9). Congress reasoned that matters involving a state's corporate creatures are of traditional concern to that state and "chiefly local import[.]" *Pew*, 527 F.3d at 26.

---

[1] The $5 million aggregate threshold represents a significant shift from the standard that governed prior to 2005, which required that at least one class member assert a claim of at least $75,000, exclusive of interest and costs. *See* Exxon Mobil Corp. v. Allapattah Servs., Inc., 545 U.S. 546, 566 (2005); *Blockbuster*, 472 F.3d at 59.

In addition to amending § 1332, CAFA also amended rules and procedures for removing class actions originally filed in state court to federal court. In particular, 28 U.S.C. § 1453 provides defendants the right to "remove a class action even if a co-defendant is a citizen of the state in which the action was originally brought and without the consent of the other defendants in the action." *Blockbuster*, 472 F.3d at 56 (citing 28 U.S.C. § 1453(b)). Furthermore, the one-year statute of limitation for removing non-class actions under § 1446 does not apply in the class context. 28 U.S.C. § 1453(b).

b. Standing

In class actions, as in individual actions, "[s]tanding is 'the threshold question in every federal case, determining the power of the court to entertain the suit.'" *Nnebe v. Daus*, 644 F.3d 147, 156 (2d Cir. 2011) (quoting *Denney v. Deutsche Bank AG*, 443 F.3d 253, 263 (2d Cir. 2006)). "To establish Article III standing, 'a plaintiff must have suffered an 'injury in fact' that is 'distinct and palpable'; the injury must be fairly traceable to the challenged action; and the injury must be likely redressable by a favorable decision.'" *Id.* (quoting *Lujan v. Defenders of Wildlife*, 504 U.S. 555, 560–61 (1992)).

In May 2016, the Supreme Court issued *Spokeo, Inc. v. Robins*, in which it held that an appellate court had performed an "incomplete" analysis of whether the plaintiff had suffered an injury-in-fact. *See Spokeo, Inc. v. Robins*, 136 S. Ct. 1540, 1545 (2016). The Supreme Court remanded the action to the appellate court for the court to determine not only whether the plaintiff's injury was particularized—i.e., it "affect[ed] the plaintiff in a personal and individual way"—but also "whether the particular procedural violations alleged in [the] case entail a degree of risk sufficient to meet the concreteness requirement." *Id.* at 1548, 1550. The Supreme Court further explained that "an intangible harm constitutes injury in fact" for purposes of the concreteness inquiry when it "actually exist[s]" and is "not 'abstract.'" *Id.* at 1548, 1549. A "bare procedural violation" of a statute will not satisfy the requirements of Article III. *Id.* at 1550.

In *Strubel*, the Second Circuit discussed *Spokeo*'s implications:

> [W]e understand Spokeo, and the cases cited therein, to instruct that an alleged procedural violation can by itself manifest concrete injury where Congress conferred the procedural right to protect a plaintiff's concrete interests and where the procedural violation presents a "risk of real harm" to that concrete interest. But even where Congress has accorded procedural rights to protect a concrete interest, a plaintiff may fail to demonstrate concrete injury where violation of the procedure at issue presents no material risk of harm to that underlying interest.

Strubel v. Comenity Bank, 842 F.3d 181, 190 (2d Cir. 2016) (citations omitted). The Second Circuit cautioned, however, that "even where Congress has accorded procedural rights to protect a concrete interest, a plaintiff may fail to demonstrate concrete injury where violation of the procedure at issue presents no material risk of harm to that underlying interest." *Id.*

The Second Circuit has applied *Spokeo* to dismiss several class actions. *See Schwartz v. HSBC Bank USA, N.A.*, 750 F. App'x 34, 36 (2d Cir. 2018) (finding no standing for Article III purposes, where court found no allegation of "a particularized or concrete 'risk of real harm'" based on a bank's failure to inform plaintiff, a credit card holder, that late payments would result in a penalty and plaintiff was never assessed such a penalty); *Crupar-Weinmann v. Paris Baguette Am., Inc.*, 861 F.3d 76, 82 (2d Cir. 2017) ("holding that the printing of an expiration date on an otherwise properly redacted receipt does not constitute an injury in fact sufficient to establish Article III standing to bring a claim alleging a bare procedural violation of [the Fair and Accurate Credit Transactions Act]"); *Katz v. Donna Karan Co. Store, L.L.C.*, 872 F.3d 114, 121 (2d Cir. 2017) (printing of entire credit card number was not in itself a "concrete" harm actionable under FACTA); *Bank v. All. Health Networks, LLC*, 669 F. App'x 584, 585 (2d Cir. 2016) (offer of judgment rendered Telephone Consumer Protection Act and state law claim moot such that no concrete harm could any longer be remedied); *Ross v. AXA Equitable Life Ins. Co.*, 680 F. App'x 41, 45 (2d Cir. 2017) (alleged misrepresentations violating state insurance law did not confer standing where harm was merely speculative); *Zirogiannis v. Seterus, Inc.*, 707 Fed. App'x 724, 728 (2d Cir. 2017) (alleged Fair Debt Collection Practices Act violations "flatly contradicted by the document itself" did not constitute a concrete harm).

In contrast, the Second Circuit has affirmed class certification where there were "concrete" injuries. *See Melito v. Experian Mktg. Sols., Inc.*, 923 F.3d 85, 93 (2d Cir. 2019) (holding that spam text messages constituted a concrete injury of "nuisance and privacy invasion" identified by Congress in the Telephone Consumer Protection Act, and was sufficient to demonstrate Article III standing); *John v. Whole Foods Mkt. Grp., Inc.*, 858 F.3d 732, 734 (2d Cir. 2017) (allegations that a grocer "systematically overstated the weights of pre-packaged food products and overcharged customers as a result" gave rise to standing); *Strubel*, 842 F.3d at 185 (two of four "billing-rights" disclosures in a credit card agreement created risk of concrete injury under the Truth in Lending Act).

Who May Bring a Class Action

The pleading requirements for Article III standing are unchanged in the class context. Thus, "in a putative class action, a plaintiff has class standing if he plausibly alleges (1) that he 'personally has suffered some actual . . . injury as a result of the putatively illegal conduct of the defendant,' [. . .] and (2) that such conduct implicates 'the same set of concerns' as the conduct alleged to have caused injury to other members of the putative class by the same defendants[.]" *NECA-IBEW Health & Welfare Fund v. Goldman Sachs & Co.*, 693 F.3d 145, 162 (2d Cir. 2012) (citations and quotations omitted).

Furthermore, "for every named defendant there must be at least one named plaintiff who can assert a claim directly against that defendant, and at that point standing is satisfied and only then will the inquiry shift to a class action analysis." *Id.* at 159 (quoting *Cent. States Se. & Sw. Areas Health & Welfare Fund v. Merck-Medco Managed Care, LLC*, 504 F.3d 229, 241 (2d Cir. 2007)).

In *NECA-IBEW*, the Second Circuit addressed the standing requirements to bring a class action under §§ 11, 12(a)(2) and 15 of the Securities Act. A holder of mortgage-backed securities sought to bring a class action for seventeen offerings sold under the same Form S-3 shelf registration statements, but each had unique prospectus supplements. *Id.* at 151. The offerings were backed by mortgages from at least six different loan originators; however, the plaintiff did not purchase securities backed by mortgages originated by all six lenders. *Id.* at 152. The Second Circuit held that the "plaintiff has class standing to assert the claims of purchasers of certificates backed by mortgages originated by the same lenders that originated the mortgages backing plaintiff's certificates, because such claims implicate 'the same set of concerns' as plaintiff's claims." *Id.* at 148–49 (quoting *Gratz v. Bollinger*, 539 U.S. 244, 267 (2003)). The court stated that "in the context of claims alleging injury based on misrepresentations, the misconduct alleged will almost always be the same: the making of a false or misleading statement." *Id.* at 162. "Whether that conduct implicates the same set of concerns for distinct sets of plaintiffs, however, will depend on the nature and content of the specific misrepresentation alleged." *Id.*

In *Reynolds v. Mercy Inv. Services, Inc.*, a district court dismissed a class action based on "longstanding" Second Circuit precedent that prohibits a plaintiff from proceeding *pro se* as both class counsel and class representative because that would create "too close a relationship between the class representative and class counsel," which is a "disqualifying conflict of interest." In this regard, "an attorney should not have a personal interest in the outcome of the litigation while a class representative must be personally invested in its outcome." Those "dual priorities cannot be reconciled in the same person." 2024 WL 1740870, at *5 (E.D.N.Y. Apr. 23, 2024).

In *Burrell v. DOCCS*, a district court denied class certification, recognizing that "it is well settled that a class action cannot be maintained by a pro se litigant because non-attorneys may not represent anyone other than themselves." No. 9:22-CV-0702, 2023 WL 1861566, at *15 (N.D.N.Y. Feb. 9, 2023) (citing *Miller v. Zerillo*, No. 07-CV-1719, 2007 WL 4898361, at *1 (E.D.N.Y. Nov. 2, 2007) (citing cases and recommending denial of class certification without prejudice until an attorney makes an appearance)); *see also Iannaccone v. Law*, 142 F.3d 553, 558 (2d Cir. 1998); 28 U.S.C. § 1654.

In *Maddox v. Bank of N.Y. Mellon Tr. Co., N.A.*, on rehearing, the Second Circuit found that plaintiffs did not suffer a concrete harm, and thus they lacked Article III standing to pursue claims statutory penalties in federal court. Specifically, the court explained that the U.S. Supreme Court's recent holding in *TransUnion* "established that in suits for damages[,] plaintiffs cannot establish Article III standing by relying entirely on a statutory violation or risk of future harm[.]" 19 F.4th 58 (2d Cir. 2021) (citing *TransUnion LLC v. Ramirez*, 141 S. Ct. 2190, 2214 (2021)).

In *Fund Liquidation Holdings LLC v. Bank of Am. Corp.*, the Second Circuit remanded a class action for further proceedings after determining that Article III was satisfied by the plaintiff's "standing to bring suit and willingness to join the action under Rule 17." 991 F.3d 370, 392 (2d Cir. 2021).

Absent Class Member Standing

In the class action context, Article III does not require that each member of a certified class be able to demonstrate his or her own standing to sue. *Denney*, 443 F.3d at 263–64 (citing Herbert B. Newberg & Alba Conte, 1 *Newberg on Class Actions* § 2.7 (4th ed. 2002) ("[P]assive members need not make any individual showing of standing, because the standing issue focuses on whether the plaintiff is properly before the court, not whether represented parties or absent class members are properly before the court.")). At the same time, the class must be defined "in such a way that anyone within it would have standing." *Id.* at 264.

While the Second Circuit has not yet had occasion to clarify the relationship between these two holdings in *Denney*, the most plausible reading—consistent with the law in several other circuits—is that a class must be defined so that every member in the class *could* have suffered injury, even though it is "almost inevitable" that some absent class members did not. *Kohen v. Pac. Inv. Mgt. Co.*, 571 F.3d 672, 677 (7th Cir. 2009) (Posner); *see also In re Nexium Antitrust Litig.*, 777 F.3d 9, 23–25 (1st Cir. 2015) (class properly certified despite including a *de minimis* number of uninjured purchasers); *see, e.g., Tomassini v. FCA US LLC*, 326 F.R.D. 375, 386 (N.D.N.Y. 2018) (court denied class certification, where class involved purchasers of a model of a car with a faulty part because there were "inevitably" purchasers included in the class definition who purchased that model with the faulty part replaced, and thus could not have suffered injury).

In other words, all class members must have been exposed to the wrongful conduct, but it is not necessary that all class members actually be able to recover for it. *See, e.g.*, *Dover v. British Airways, PLC (UK)*, 321 F.R.D. 49 (E.D.N.Y. 2017) (certifying a class in which all members were exposed to an allegedly wrongful fuel surcharge, even though a small portion of the class may not have actually paid a higher charge than they would otherwise have paid), *leave to appeal denied*, No. 17-1121, 2017 WL 2590319 (2d Cir. June 14, 2017).

In *Denney*, plaintiffs sued their tax advisors for improper and fraudulent tax counseling. 443 F.3d at 259. The U.S. District Court for the Southern District of New York (Scheindlin, J.) certified a proposed class under Fed. R. Civ. P. 23(b)(3) and approved a class settlement. Two class members objected to the settlement, contending that the class contained members for whom tax penalties had not yet been assessed and who therefore lacked standing. On appeal, the Second Circuit held that all members of the class, as defined, had "suffered injuries-in-fact, irrespective of whether" those injuries were "sufficient to sustain any cause of action." *Denney*, 443 F.3d at 265.

c. The Mootness Doctrine

Federal courts have limited jurisdiction and may only hear "cases" or "controversies." U.S. Const. art. III, § 2, cl. 1. As such, federal courts may only exercise subject matter jurisdiction over a case if "the dispute before the court [is] real and live, not feigned, academic, or conjectural." *Russman v. Bd. of Educ. of Enlarged City Sch. Dist. of City of Watervliet*, 260 F.3d 114, 118 (2d Cir. 2001). Moreover, a "real and live" controversy must continue throughout the pendency of the action. *Id.* at 118–19 (citation omitted). Should the dispute "dissolve at any time due to a change in circumstances, the case becomes moot." *Id.* at 118. The "mootness doctrine" demands that "[w]henever mootness occurs, the court—whether trial, appellate, or Supreme—loses jurisdiction over the suit, which therefore must be dismissed." *Id.* (citing *Fox v. Bd. of Trs. of the State Univ. of N.Y.*, 42 F.3d 135, 140 (2d Cir. 1994)).

Inherently Transitory Claims

There is an exception to the mootness doctrine in class action litigation that applies to "inherently transitory" claims brought by a named plaintiff. *Salazar v. King*, 822 F.3d 61, 74 (2d Cir. 2016) (challenging the U.S. Department of Education's collection of student loan debt); *see also, e.g.*, *Amador v. Andrews*, 655 F.3d 89 (2d Cir. 2011) (current and former inmates brought a class action suit against officers and supervisors employed at state prisons for sexual harassment); *Jones-Bartley v. McCabe, Weisberg & Conway, P.C.*, 59 F. Supp. 3d 617 (S.D.N.Y. 2014) (challenging debt collection practices). In such cases, the claims shall "'relate back' to the time of the filing of the complaint with class allegations." *Salazar*, 822 F.3d at 73 (citing *Comer v. Cisneros*, 37 F.3d 775, 799 (2d Cir. 1994)). A named plaintiff will maintain standing to bring a claim under this exception if "(1) it is uncertain that a claim will remain live for any individual who could be named as a plaintiff long enough for a court to certify the class; and (2) there will be a constant class of persons suffering the deprivation complained of in the complaint." *Id.* (citations and quotations omitted). "Whether claims are inherently transitory is an inquiry that must be made with reference to the claims of the class as a whole as opposed to any one individual claim for relief." *Amador*, 655 F.3d at 100 (citation omitted).

For example, in *Salazar*, former students of for-profit beauty schools challenged the failure of the U.S. Department of Education (DOE) to temporarily suspend loan collections and notify borrowers of their discharge rights due to the schools' fraudulent certification of borrowing eligibility. Before the class was certified, however, the named plaintiffs' loans were discharged. The Second Circuit held that the inherently transitory exception applied: it was "uncertain that a claim [would] remain live for any individual who could be named as a plaintiff long enough for a court to address a class certification motion because the DOE [processed] discharge applications from [the beauty schools] borrowers relatively quickly." 822 F.3d at 74. There were, moreover, at least 61,300 loans that could potentially be eligible for discharge, and as a result, "there [would] be a constant class of persons suffering the deprivation complained of in the complaint." *Id.* "The inherently transitory exception, which is properly focused on the time it will take for a court to review a claim a plaintiff has standing to pursue, does not require a plaintiff to forgo remedies to which she is entitled in order to seek broader remedies" in federal court. *Id.* at 75. "The critical question for the 'inherently transitory' exception to mootness is whether the court will have time to rule on a motion for class certification brought by a plaintiff who has standing to bring a particular claim before the claim will become moot; the inquiry is not *why* the claim will become moot." *Id.* at 74.

Likewise, in *Bellin v. Zucker M.D., J.D.*, the Second Circuit also held that inherently transitory exception applied where a Medicaid beneficiary filed a class action alleging that the class's due process rights were violated because they were only allowed the right to appeal initial determinations related to personal care hours that a managed long-term care plans make if they chose to enroll in them. 6 F.4th 463, 474 (2d Cir. 2001). The Second Circuit rejected the State's argument that the case was moot because the plaintiff was now receiving her requested 24-hour, live-in care. Instead, the Second Circuit explained how there is a "significant possibility" that any plaintiff who brings the claims Bellin asserted would have her request for additional care resolved before a decision on class certification could be made, and therefore, the inherently transitory exception to the mootness doctrine applied. *Id.*

Mootness and Rules 67 and 68

Applying *Campbell-Ewald Co. v. Gomez*, 136 S. Ct. 663 (2016), the Second Circuit treats an unaccepted Rule 68 offer of compromise[2] as a legal nullity that does not result in dismissal. *See, e.g.*, *Lary v. Rexall Sundown, Inc.*, 686 F. App'x 63, 65 (2d Cir. 2017) (citing *Radha Geismann, M.D., P.C. v. Zocdoc, Inc.*, 850 F.3d 507, 512 (2d Cir. 2017) (*Geismann II*) ("In light of *Campbell-Ewald*, the district court's conclusion that Geismann's claim was 'mooted by the amount and content of the Rule 68 offer made by Zocdoc,' *Geismann*, 60 F. Supp. 3d at 407, is incorrect." The Second Circuit, like the Supreme Court, has not had occasion to decide whether a class action would be mooted if the defendant actually "deposit[ed] the full amount of the plaintiff's individual claim in an account payable to the plaintiff, and the court *then* enter[ed] judgment for the plaintiff in that amount." *Geismann II*, 850 F.3d at 514 (citing *Campbell-Ewald*, 136 S. Ct. at 672) (emphasis added).

In October 2018, the Second Circuit once again faced mootness issues but this time under Rule 67, in a further appeal of the *Geismann II* case. *Geismann v. ZocDoc, Inc.*, 909 F.3d 534 (2d Cir. 2018) (*Geismann III*). After *Geismann II* was remanded back to the U.S. District Court for the Southern District of New York, the putative class action was once again dismissed, and Geismann appealed the judgment. *Id.* This time, defendants Zocdoc deposited additional funds in the district court's registry pursuant to Rule 67, and moved for summary judgment in favor of Geismann, and for the claims to be mooted. *Id.* at 537. The Second Circuit sided with the Seventh Circuit when it deemed "no material difference between a plaintiff rejecting a tender of payment (pursuant to Rule 67) and an offer of payment (pursuant to Rule 68)." *Id.* at 541. The Second Circuit further ruled that entering judgment and declaring an action moot based solely on individual relief to a plaintiff allows the defendant to use "tactical procedural maneuvers to thwart class litigation at will," and therefore, pending motions for class certification must be resolved before judgment in that circumstance. *Id.* at 543 (citation omitted).

3. PREREQUISITES

a. Ascertainability

While the Second Circuit recognizes the existence of an ascertainability prerequisite to class certification, it has rejected the existence of an administrative feasibility component to that requirement. *In re Petrobras Securities*, 862 F.3d 250, 265 (2d Cir. 2017). The Second Circuit instead requires that classes be defined by reference to "objective criteria that establish a membership with definite boundaries. This modest threshold requirement will only preclude certification if a proposed class definition is indeterminate in some fundamental way." *Id.* at 269.[3]

---

[2] *See* Fed. R. Civ. P. 68(a) ("At least 14 days before the date set for trial, a party defending against a claim may serve on an opposing party an offer to allow judgment on specified terms, with the costs then accrued. If, within 14 days after being served, the opposing party serves written notice accepting the offer, either party may then file the offer and notice of acceptance, plus proof of service. The clerk must then enter judgment.").

[3] *See, e.g.*, Ciaramella v. Zucker, No. 18-CV-6945, 2019 WL 4805553, at *14 (S.D.N.Y. Sept. 30, 2019) (court noted that where plaintiffs seek to certify "a putative Rule 23(b)(2) class seeking only declaratory and injunctive relief, the Court does not need to undertake" an analysis of whether the class definition has "precise ascertainability") (citing Marisol A. v. Giuliani, 126 F.3d 372 (2d Cir. 1997)).

b. Rule 23(a) Requirements

To obtain class certification, the plaintiff has the burden to prove that he or she meets the four prerequisites of Rule 23(a) of the Federal Rules of Civil Procedure: numerosity, commonality, typicality, and adequacy. *See, e.g.*, *Amgen Inc. v. Conn. Ret. Plans & Tr. Funds*, 568 U.S. 455, 459 (2013); *Roach v. T.L. Cannon Corp.*, 778 F.3d 401, 405 (2d Cir. 2015); *Sykes v. Mel S. Harris & Assocs. LLC*, 780 F.3d 70, 80 (2d Cir. 2015).

Numerosity

To establish numerosity, the plaintiff must show that "the class is so numerous that joinder of all members is impracticable." Fed. R. Civ. P. 23(a)(1). Numerosity is presumed if a class is totaling in forty or more members. *Marisol A. v. Giuliani*, 126 F.3d 372 (2d Cir. 1997); *see also, e.g.*, *Dover*, 321 F.R.D. at 53–54.

Commonality

Commonality requires that there be a question of fact or law common to the class. Fed. R. Civ. P. 23(a)(2). In particular, plaintiffs must show that there is at least one common question such that "a class-wide proceeding [can] generate common *answers* apt to drive the resolution of the litigation." *Wal-Mart Stores v. Dukes*, 564 U.S. 338, 350 (2011) (citation omitted); *see also id.* at 359 ("[E]ven a single [common] question will do.") (citation omitted). In many cases, this is not a particularly high bar. For example, commonality is readily met in cases where plaintiffs allege breach of a materially identical contract because the question of contract interpretation is common to all class members, and the common answer as to how that contract is interpreted will drive the resolution of the case. *In re U.S. Foodservice Inc. Pricing Litig.*, 729 F.3d 108, 124 (2d Cir. 2013), *cert. denied*, 572 U.S. 1087 (2014); *see also Abbananto v. Cnty. of Nassau*, No. 19-CV-01102, 2022 WL 326982 (E.D.N.Y. Feb. 3, 2022) (certifying class, where court found commonality requirement can be satisfied in employment litigation even if the proposed class contains both sexes and sex discrimination is alleged). At the opposite extreme, commonality is lacking when the vast majority of the proposed class is not exposed to the same type of challenged conduct. *See, e.g., Pagan v. Abbott Labs., Inc.*, 287 F.R.D. 139, 148 (E.D.N.Y. 2012) (no commonality when only 0.16 percent of the proposed class purchased the allegedly defective product). It bears emphasis that while commonality requires at least one common answer that is applicable to the class, that common answer may well impact different class members differently. *See, e.g., Pub. Emps.' Ret. Sys. of Mississippi v. Merrill Lynch & Co.*, 277 F.R.D. 97, 116 (S.D.N.Y. 2011) (statute of limitations does not bar class certification because all claims under any statute of limitations period are subject to generalized proof that impacts members of the class uniformly, even if that uniform decision means that certain class members' claims are time-barred, while other class members' claims are not); *see also U.S. Foodservice*, 729 F.3d at 127 n.10 (referencing the district court's unchallenged finding that statute of limitations issues did not bar class certification).

Typicality

Plaintiffs must show that the representative plaintiffs' claims are typical. *See* Fed. R. Civ. P. 23(a)(3). Typicality is satisfied "when each class member's claim arises from the same course of events and each class member makes similar legal arguments to prove the defendant's liability." *Shahriar v. Smith & Wollensky Rest. Grp., Inc.*, 659 F.3d 234, 252 (2d Cir. 2011) (quoting *Robidoux v. Celani*, 987 F.2d 931, 936 (2d Cir. 1993)); *cf. Sykes*, 780 F.3d at 80 (explaining that in some cases, the "commonality and typicality requirements of Rule 23(a) tend to merge"). In other words, the named plaintiffs must bring claims "for the same type of injury under the same legal theory as the rest of the class." *Marshall v. Deutsche Post DHL*, No. 13-CV-1471, 2015 WL 5560541, at *3 (E.D.N.Y. Sept. 21, 2015).

Adequacy

Plaintiffs must show that they will "fairly and adequately protect the interests of the class."

Fed. R. Civ. P. 23(a)(4). *See also Amchem Prods., Inc. v. Windsor*, 521 U.S. 591, 625 (1997). The adequacy inquiry asks (1) whether "the named plaintiffs and their counsel have any conflicts of interest with other class members" and (2) whether "the named plaintiffs and their counsel [will] prosecute the action vigorously on behalf of the class[.]" *Ellis v. Costco Wholesale Corp.*, 657 F.3d 970, 985 (9th Cir. 2011) (citation omitted); *Robinson v. Metro-North Commuter R.R. Co.*, 267 F.3d 147, 170 (2d Cir. 2001) (same).[4] Put another way, while class representatives should not have conflicts of interests with the class they seek to represent, only a fundamental conflict can defeat a motion for class certification. *MacNamara v. City of N.Y.*, 275 F.R.D. 125, 144 (S.D.N.Y. 2011) (citing *In re Flag Telecom Holdings, Ltd. Sec. Litig.*, 574 F.3d 29, 35 (2d Cir. 2009)).

In *Jin v. Shanghai Original, Inc.*, the Second Circuit affirmed the *sua sponte* decision to decertify a class prior to a bench trial, where a judgment was entered in the plaintiff's favor. Specifically, the Second Circuit explained that "[t]he district court acted within its discretion in decertifying the class on the ground that class counsel was no longer adequately representing the class. Competent representation by class counsel is crucial to the prosecution of a class action." 990 F.3d 251, 262 (2d Cir. 2021) (citation omitted).

c. Rule 23(b) Requirements

Rule 23(b)(1)(A) Classes

Rule 23(b)(1)(A) "covers cases in which multiple suits would create a risk of inconsistent adjudications or would possibly establish incompatible standards of conduct for the party opposing the class[.]" *Richards v. Fleetboston Fin. Corp.*, 238 F.R.D. 345, 353 (D. Conn. 2006). Although the language in Rule 23(b)(1)(A) can be broad enough to encompass all class actions, courts have not applied it in this manner. *See Cashman v. Dolce Int'l/Hartford, Inc.*, 225 F.R.D. 73, 93 (D. Conn. 2004); *Petrolito v. Arrow Fin. Servs., LLC*, 221 F.R.D. 303, 313 (D. Conn. 2004). Instead, this rule applies to cases so that "multiple grievances stemming from a single action by the defendant (such as a decision by a municipality or a public nuisance created by a factory) do not result in multiple courts imposing incompatible standards of conduct upon the defendant." *Cashman*, 225 F.R.D. at 93. Many courts have also held that Rule 23(b)(1)(A) does not apply to actions seeking compensatory damages, but rather only to actions for declaratory or injunctive relief. *Petrolito*, 221 F.R.D. at 313.

Rule 23(b)(1)(B) Requirements

Rule 23(b)(1)(B) allows for certification when "adjudications with respect to individual members of the class . . . would as a practical matter . . . substantially impair or impede their ability to protect their interests." *Cty. of Suffolk v. Long Island Lighting Co.*, 710 F. Supp. 1407, 1417 (E.D.N.Y. 1989) (citing Fed. R. Civ. P. 23(b)(1)(B)). Classes are certified under Rule 23(b)(1)(B) to ensure that certain class members do not undermine other class members by pursuing their own litigation on a separate track. *See generally In re Joint E. & S. Dist. Asbestos Litig.*, 78 F.3d 764, 778 (2d Cir. 1996); *In re Drexel Burnham Lambert Grp.*, 960 F.2d 285, 292–93 (2d Cir. 1992); *In re AOL Time Warner ERISA Litig.*, 2006 WL 2789862, at *3 (S.D.N.Y. Sept. 27, 2006). Typically, Rule 23(b)(1)(B) classes are "limited fund" class actions where each claim must be satisfied by a limited fund of assets with the claims satisfied on a "first come, first served" basis. *See Drexel Burnham Lambert Grp.*, 960 F.2d at 292 (citing 7A Charles A. Wright et al., *Federal Practice & Procedure* § 1774 at 441–43 (1986)). The Second Circuit has, however, held that mandatory class actions may be appropriate even if assets of the limited fund cannot be distributed on a "first come, first served" basis, as in certain bankruptcy cases. *Id.* (certifying mandatory non-opt out class

[4] Incorporated into the second factor is the requirement that class counsel be "qualified, experienced and able to conduct the litigation." Baffa v. Donaldson, 222 F.3d 52, 60 (2d Cir. 2000) (citing In re Drexel Burnham Lambert Grp., Inc., 960 F.2d 285, 291 (2d Cir. 1992)).

where defendant was in bankruptcy).

Rule 23(b)(2)
Rule 23(b)(2) authorizes a class action if "the party opposing the class has acted or refused to act on grounds that apply generally to the class, so that final injunctive relief or corresponding declaratory relief is appropriate respecting the class as a whole[.]" Fed. R. Civ. P. 23(b)(2). "Certification is appropriate under Rule 23(b)(2) where declaratory or injunctive relief is an important aspect of the overall relief sought." *In re NASDAQ Market-Makers Antitrust Litig.*, 169 F.R.D. 493, 516 (S.D.N.Y. 1996) (citing *Gelb v. American Telephone & Telegraph Co.*, 150 F.R.D. 76, 78 (S.D.N.Y. 1993)). Whether the relief is primarily declaratory or injunctive, or monetary, requires careful analysis. *See Parker v. Time Warner Entm't Co., L.P.*, 331 F.3d 13, 20 (2d Cir. 2003) ("[A] district court must 'consider[] the evidence presented at a class certification hearing and the arguments of counsel,' and then assess whether (b)(2) certification is appropriate in light of 'the relative importance of the remedies sought, given all of the facts and circumstances of the case'" (citing *Robinson v. Metro-North Commuter R.R.*, 267 F.3d 147 (2d Cir. 2001) (quoting *Hoffman v. Honda of Am. Mfg., Inc.*, 191 F.R.D. 530, 536 (S.D. Ohio 1999)).

In *Wal-Mart Stores, Inc. v. Dukes*, the Supreme Court considered "one of the most expansive class actions ever[,]" comprising a class of approximately 1.5 million current and former female employees of *Wal-Mart Stores*, the nation's largest private employer. *Dukes*, 564 U.S. at 342. The plaintiffs in *Dukes* succeeded before the trial and appellate courts in certifying a (b)(2) (i.e., injunctive/declaratory) class and (b)(3) (i.e., opt-out, monetary) class alleging sex discrimination based on statistical evidence of disparities between men and women at Wal-Mart, anecdotal reports of discrimination, and a sociological analysis of Wal-Mart's culture concluding that the company was vulnerable to discrimination. *Id.* at 346. The Supreme Court vacated class certification of both the (b)(2) and (b)(3) classes, because monetary relief did not predominate over injunctive relief and there was no class-wide common issue, respectively. *Id.* at 359–63.

Prior to *Dukes*, the Second Circuit had employed a more permissive standard:

> [We] decline to adopt the incidental damages approach set out by the Fifth Circuit in *Allison* and followed by the district court below. Rather, we hold that when presented with a motion for (b)(2) class certification of a claim seeking both injunctive relief and non-incidental monetary damages, a district court must "consider[] the evidence presented at a class certification hearing and the arguments of counsel," and then assess whether (b)(2) certification is appropriate in light of "the relative importance of the remedies sought, given all of the facts and circumstances of the case." *Hoffman v. Honda of Am. Mfg., Inc.*, 191 F.R.D 530, 536 (S.D. Ohio 1999). The district court may allow (b)(2) certification if it finds in its "informed, sound judicial discretion" that (1) "the positive weight or value [to the plaintiffs] of the injunctive or declaratory relief sought is predominant even though compensatory or punitive damages are also claimed," *Allison v. Citgo Petroleum Corp.*, 151 F.3d 402, 430 (5th Cir. 1998) (Dennis, J., dissenting), and (2) class treatment would be efficient and manageable, thereby achieving an appreciable measure of judicial economy.

Robinson v. Metro-North Commuter R.R., 267 F.3d 147, 164 (2d Cir. 2001). However, in *Dukes*, the Supreme Court cited favorably the "incidental" approach applied by the Fifth Circuit in *Allison* and left open the question as to whether even incidental monetary relief can be awarded. 564 U.S. at 365–67 (citing *Allison*, 151 F.3d at 415). The Second Circuit has acknowledged that *Robinson* has been abrogated and is no longer good law as a test for (b)(2) certification. *Hecht v. United Collection Bureau, Inc.*, 691 F.3d 218, 223 (2d Cir. 2012).

Subsequent to *Dukes*, the Second Circuit has, for example, refused certification of a (b)(2) class where monetary relief was more than "incidental." *See Nationwide Life Ins. Co. v. Haddock*, 460 F. App'x 26, 28–29 (2d Cir. 2012) (disgorgement of payments to fund predominated over prospective declaratory and injunctive relief). However, incidental monetary benefits may still be available where they are the effect of an adjudication that establishes a corrected manner of determining benefits running to the class. *See, e.g.*, *Caufield v. Colgate-Palmolive Co.*, No. 16 Civ. 4170, 2017 WL 3206339, at *6 (S.D.N.Y. July 27, 2017) ("the objective of this action is to determine the correct method for calculating the RAA, which could have the incidental effect of causing the Plan to distribute monetary benefits to class members. Plaintiffs have cited many similar cases that were certified under Rule 23(b)(1)" (citing cases)).

In addition, in *Berni v. Barilla S.p.A.*, 964 F.3d 141 (2d Cir. 2020), the Second Circuit decertified a class action under Rule 23(b)(2) where it found that injunctive relief under the proposed settlement agreement did not remedy all class members' injuries. Specifically, the court explained that the alleged injury was a "past harm" and stated that "courts cannot permit injunctive relief through class settlement when plaintiffs would otherwise lack standing to seek such relief under Article III." *Id.* at 148–49. The court then held that "[w]here there is no likelihood of future harm, there is no standing to seek an injunction, and so no possibility of being certified as a Rule 23(b)(2) class." *Id.* at 149.

Rule 23(b)(3)

Rule 23(b)(3) requires that a plaintiff show that common questions of law or fact predominate over individual ones. Predominance is present "if resolution of some of the legal or factual questions that qualify each class member's case as a genuine controversy can be achieved through generalized proof, and if these particular issues are more substantial than the issues subject only to individualized proof." *In re Foodservice Inc. Pricing Litig.*, 729 F.3d 108, 118 (2d Cir. 2013) (citing *UFCW Local 1776 v. Eli Lilly & Co.*, 620 F.3d 121, 131 (2d Cir. 2010)). Although this is a "more demanding" inquiry than commonality, "Rule 23(b)(3) 'does not require a plaintiff seeking class certification to prove that each elemen[t] of [her] claim [is] susceptible to classwide proof.'" *Sykes,* 780 F.3d at 81 (quoting *Amgen Inc. v. Conn. Ret. Plans and Tr. Funds*, 568 U.S. 455, 469 (2013)). Rather, the predominance inquiry asks "whether the common, aggregation-enabling, issues in the case are *more prevalent or important* than the non-common, aggregation-defeating, individual issues." *In re Petrobras Securities*, 862 F.3d at 270 (quoting *Tyson Foods, Inc. v. Bouaphakeo*, 577 U.S. 442, 453 (2016)). "This analysis is 'more [] qualitative than quantitative,' . . . and must account for the nature and significance of the material common and individual issues in the case[.]" *Id.* at 271 (citations omitted). However, when determining class certification under Rule 23(b)(3), "district court[s] [have] a 'duty' . . . to 'take a close look' at whether the common legal questions predominate over individual ones [*Comcast Corp. v. Behrend*, 569 U.S. 27, 34 (2013)] . . . [and] must do more than take the plaintiff's word that no material differences exist." *Langan v. Johnson & Johnson Consumer Cos.*, 897 F.3d 88, 97 (2d Cir. 2018) (citing *Walsh v. Ford Motor Co.*, 807 F.2d 1000, 1016 (D.C. Cir. 1986)).

Frequently, a defendant will state that it intends to offer affirmative defenses that could vary based on the individual class member. To that end, and while plaintiffs at all times bear the burden of establishing the propriety of class certification, it is important to note that a defendant must do more than simply raise the possibility of individual affirmative defenses: it must show that such defenses are "meritorious" and "detract significant attention from the common issues in [the] litigation." *Vincent v. Money Store*, 304 F.R.D. 446, 462 (S.D.N.Y. 2015) (citing *In re Nassau Cnty. Strip Search Cases*, 461 F.3d 219, 225 (2d Cir. 2006)); *cf. Sykes*, 780 F.3d at 81 ("Individual questions need not be absent. The text of Rule 23(b)(3) itself contemplates that such individual questions will be present." (citing *Messner v. Northshore Univ. HealthSystem*, 669 F.3d 802, 815 (7th Cir. 2012))).

Rule 23 also requires plaintiff to show that "a class action is superior to other available methods for fairly and efficiently adjudicating the controversy." Fed. R. Civ. P. 23(b)(3). In making this determination, a court considers (i) "the class members' interests in individually controlling the prosecution or defense of separate actions;" (ii) "the extent and nature of any litigation concerning the controversy already begun by or against class members;" (iii) "the desirability or undesirability of concentrating the litigation of the claims in the particular forum;" and (iv) "the likely difficulties in managing a class action." *Id.*

In *Johnson & Johnson*, the Second Circuit clarified its holding in *In re Foodservice Inc. Pricing Litig.*, as the decision had caused a split among district courts with respect to the required standing when bringing a class action that represents out-of-state, nonparty class members, with claims subject to different state laws. *Johnson & Johnson*, 897 F.3d at 93. In clarifying *In re Foodservice*, the Second Circuit held that the issue was actually an issue of predominance and not standing. *Id.*

In *Waggoner v. Barclays PLC,* 875 F.3d 79 (2d Cir. 2017), the Second Circuit addressed Rule 23(b)(3), where plaintiffs invoke the rebuttable presumption of reliance deriving from the fraud-on-the-market theory.[5] The Second Circuit held that defendants opposing class certification bear the burden of persuasion, rather than a burden of production, by a preponderance of the evidence. *Id.* at 99. Specifically, defendants wishing to rebut the presumption are required "to do more than merely produce evidence that might result in a favorable outcome[.]" *Id.* at 101.

In *Scott v. Chipotle Mexican Grill, Inc.*, 954 F.3d 502 (2d Cir. 2020), *petition for cert. filed*, No. 20-257 (Aug. 28, 2020), the Second Circuit focused on the "predominance" requirement of Rule 23(b)(3) to uphold the denial of class certification under the Fair Labor Standards Act (FLSA), 29 U.S.C. § 216(b). Notably, the court explained that "the *primary duty* performed by class plaintiffs—the dispositive question of the exemption inquiry—was not adequately similar." *Id.* at 513. In addition, the court further explained how Rule 23 and the FLSA's § 216 "serve fundamentally different purposes," and no right to proceed as a "collective" exists under Rule 23. *Id.* at 519 (citing cases).

4. TYPES OF CLASSES

a. Plaintiff Classes

Class Identification

District courts in the Second Circuit have broad discretion to approve or reject class definitions, but, where appropriate, they must reassess such rulings as the case develops. *Boucher v. Syracuse Univ.*, 164 F.3d 113, 118 (2d Cir. 1999) ("[U]nder Rule 23(c)(1), courts are 'required to reassess their class rulings as the case develops.'") (quoting *Barnes v. The American Tobacco Co.*, 161 F.3d 127, 140 (3d Cir. 1998) (citing *Kuehner v. Heckler*, 778 F.2d 152, 163 (3d Cir. 1985))); *see also Marisol A.*, 126 F.3d at 378–79 (affirming class certification but ordering a district court to divide the certified class into subclasses); *Richardson v. Byrd*, 709 F.2d 1016, 1019 (5th Cir. 1983). While courts in the Second Circuit have the authority to decertify a class following trial, they "must defer to any factual findings the jury necessarily made unless those findings were 'seriously erroneous,' a 'miscarriage of justice,' or 'egregious.'" *Mazzei v. Money Store*, 829 F.3d 260, 269 (2d Cir. 2016) (affirming the ability of a district court to decertify a class, even after trial, but clarifying that the district court in so doing is ordinarily bound by the jury's factual findings under the Seventh Amendment).

Relatedly, the district court has discretion to modify the class definition at any time before final judgment. *Spread Enters., Inc. v. First Data Merch. Servs. Corp.*, 298 F.R.D. 54, 69 (E.D.N.Y. 2014); *see also Brooklyn Ctr. for Indep. of the Disabled v. Bloomberg*, 287

[5] *See* Basic Inc. v. Levinson, 485 U.S. 224 (1988).

F.R.D. 240, 250 (S.D.N.Y. 2012) ("Under Rule 23, district courts have the power to amend class definitions or decertify classes as necessary. . . . 'In fact, the court has a duty to ensure that the class is properly constituted and has broad discretion to modify the class definition as appropriate to provide the necessary precision.'") (quoting *Morangelli v. Chemed Corp.*, 275 F.R.D. 99, 114 (E.D.N.Y. 2011)).

Subclasses

If conflicts exist between members of a particular class, the court may divide it into subclasses. *Mazzei*, 829 F.3d at 273. "Ordinarily, if a court discerns a conflict . . . the proper solution is to create subclasses of persons whose interests are in accord." *Boucher*, 164 F.3d at 118–19 (quoting *Payne v. Travenol Labs, Inc.*, 673 F.2d 798, 812 (5th Cir. 1982)). Thus, even "[w]here a fundamental conflict exists that goes 'to the very heart of the litigation,'" *Charron v. Wiener*, 731 F.3d 241, 250 (2d Cir. 2013) (quoting *Cent. States Se. & Sw. Areas Health & Welfare Fund v. Merck-Medco Managed Care, LLC*, 504 F.3d 229, 246 (2d Cir. 2007)), it may be possible to "cure[]" the conflict "by dividing the class 'into homogeneous subclasses . . . with separate representation to eliminate conflicting interests of counsel.'" *Charron*, 731 F.3d at 250 (quoting *Ortiz v. Fibreboard Corp.*, 527 U.S. 815, 856 (1999)). Indeed, "[s]uch subclassing may provide a key 'structural assurance of fair and adequate representation for the diverse groups and individuals affected,'" *Id.* (quoting *Amchem*, 521 U.S. at 627), "and 'serve[s] to inhibit appraisals of the chancellor's foot kind—class certifications dependent upon the court's gestalt judgment or overarching impression of the settlement's fairness[.]'" *Id.* (quoting *Amchem*, 521 U.S. at 621).

District courts, however, are not obligated to do the plaintiff's work by carving out an appropriate class or subclass. *Lundquist v. Sec. Pac. Auto. Fin. Servs. Corp.*, 993 F.2d 11, 14–15 (2d Cir. 1993). The plaintiff bears the burden to show that subclassing would be appropriate given the facts. *Id.* ("We are aware that the district court 'is not bound by the class definition proposed in the complaint and should not dismiss the action simply because the complaint seeks to define the class too broadly.'") (quoting *Robidoux*, 987 F.2d at 937) (citing 7B Charles A. Wright, Arthur R. Miller, & Mary K. Kane, *Federal Practice and Procedure* § 1790, at 270–71 (1986))).

5. CASE MANAGEMENT

a. Appointment of Counsel

Rule 23(c)(1)(B) requires an order certifying a class action to appoint class counsel under Rule 23(g). In appointing class counsel the court must consider:

(i) the work counsel has done in identifying or investigating potential claims in the action;
(ii) counsel's experience in handling class actions, other complex litigation, and the types of claims asserted in the action;
(iii) counsel's knowledge of the applicable law; and
(iv) the resources that counsel will commit to representing the class.

Fed. R. Civ. P. 23(g)(1)(A). In addition, Rule 23(g)(1)(B) allows a court to "consider any other matter pertinent to counsel's ability to fairly and adequately represent the interests of the class." For example, courts have considered such factors as (1) the cooperation among counsel before their lead counsel applications and (2) whether the law firms previously prosecuted similar class actions together. *See Deangelis v. Corzine*, 286 F.R.D. 220, 225 (S.D.N.Y. 2012) ("[T]he Court gives significant weight to [one plaintiff counsel group's] willingness to cooperatively develop a leadership structure among ten of the twelve plaintiffs whose cases have been consolidated"); *In re Bear Stearns Cos., Inc. Sec. Derivative, and ERISA Litig.*, No. 08 M.D.L. 1963, 2009 WL 50132, at *10 (S.D.N.Y. Jan. 5, 2009) (finding it significant that the two law firms had previously worked as co-lead counsel prosecuting class actions involving similar claims).

District courts in the Second Circuit use the same criteria when evaluating appointment of interim lead counsel for class actions. *See In re Interest Rate Swaps Antitrust Litig.*, No. 16-MD-2704, 2016 WL 4131846, at *2 (S.D.N.Y. Aug. 3, 2016) ("When appointing interim class counsel, courts generally look to the same factors used in determining the adequacy of class counsel under Rule 23(g)(1)(A)") (quoting *In re Mun. Derivatives Antitrust Litig.*, 252 F.R.D. 184, 186 (S.D.N.Y. 2008)); *Deangelis*, 286 F.R.D. at 223 ("Candidates for interim class counsel are evaluated under the same rubric as potential counsel for certified classes.") (citing cases).

b. Discovery

Discovery is proper before certification of a class. Among other things, discovery should inform the court's certification decision under Rule 23. *Sirota v. Solitron Devices, Inc.*, 673 F.2d 566, 571 (2d Cir. 1982); *see also Parker*, 331 F.3d at 21 ("[I]t is likely that at least minimal class discovery must be conducted in order to provide the court with the factual information necessary to decide whether or not to certify a Rule 23(b)(2) class."). However, such discovery is not unlimited. *See Philip Morris Inc. v. Nat'l Asbestos Workers Med. Fund*, 214 F.3d 132, 135 (2d Cir. 2000) ("[I]n making a certification decision, a judge must look somewhere between the pleading[s] and the fruits of discovery. . . . [E]nough must be laid bare to let the judge survey the factual scene on a kind of sketchy relief map, leaving for later view the myriad of details that cover the terrain." (quoting *Sirota*, 673 F.2d at 571–72)).

c. Timing of Class Certification

Rule 23(c)(1)(A) instructs courts to address class certification at "an early practicable time[.]" This language, adopted in 2003, relaxes the prior requirement that certification be decided "[a]s soon as practicable after the commencement of an action" brought as a class action." Fed. R. Civ. P. 23(c)(1)(A), 2003 committee notes. The rule was relaxed because the older "as soon as practicable" language "neither reflects prevailing practice nor captures the many valid reasons that may justify deferring the initial certification decision." *Id.* (citation omitted). That certification decisions should come only after the record is sufficiently developed is consistent with the Supreme Court's holdings that "certification is only proper if the trial court is satisfied, after a rigorous analysis, that the prerequisites of Rule 23(a) have been satisfied" and "[f]requently that 'rigorous analysis' will entail some overlap with the merits of the plaintiff's underlying claim." *Dukes*, 564 U.S. at 351 (citation omitted).

6. CLASS NOTICE

Rule 23(c)(2)(A) states that "[f]or any class certified under Rule 23(b)(1) or (b)(2), the court may direct appropriate notice to the class." In *Hecht*, the parties' settlement agreement provided that the putative class would be notified solely by the one-time publication of a notice in *USA Today*. 691 F.3d 218 (2d Cir. 2012). The district court ruled that such notice was sufficient. The Second Circuit reversed, holding that a one-time newspaper notice was constitutionally inadequate under the circumstances of the case. *Id.* at 224–26 (observing that "when courts have approved notice by publication, they have tended to do so where the notices either ran more than once or appeared in more than one publication").

7. OPT-OUTS

"[A] class member seeking permission to opt out late must first demonstrate 'excusable neglect' for his or her failure to comply with a fixed deadline." *In re Painewebber Ltd. P'ships Litig.*, 147 F.3d 132, 135 (2d Cir. 1998) (citing *Pioneer Inv. Servs. Co. v. Brunswick Assocs.*

Ltd. P'ship, 507 U.S. 380, 391 (1993)). "When 'excusable neglect' is established, it is within the Court's discretionary power to accept or reject an untimely Notice of Exclusion in a class action." *Morris v. Affinity Health Plan*, 928 F. Supp. 2d 805, 809 (S.D.N.Y 2013) (citation omitted). The Second Circuit uses several factors to determine whether there is excusable neglect: (i) danger of prejudice; (ii) length of the delay and its potential impact on judicial proceedings; (iii) reason for the delay, including whether it was within the reasonable control of the movant; and (iv) whether the movant acted in good faith. *Shumsker v. Citigroup Glob. Mkts. Inc.*, 569 F. App'x 16, 18 (2d Cir. 2014) (citing *Pioneer*, 507 U.S. at 395).

8. DAMAGES

a. Proof

"'[T]he fact that damages may have to be ascertained on an individual basis is not sufficient to defeat class certification' under Rule 23(b)(3)." *Roach*, 778 F.3d at 405 (quoting *Seijas v. Republic of Arg.*, 606 F.3d 53, 58 (2d Cir. 2010)). In *Roach*, the Second Circuit concluded that *Comcast Corp. v. Behrend*, 133 S. Ct. 1426 (2013), did:

> not hold that a class cannot be certified under Rule 23(b)(3) simply because damages cannot be measured on a classwide basis. . . . *Comcast*'s holding was narrower. *Comcast* held that a model for determining classwide damages relied upon to certify a class under Rule 23(b)(3) must actually measure damages that result from the class's asserted theory of injury; but the Court did not hold that proponents of class certification must rely upon a classwide damages model to demonstrate predominance.

Id. at 407 (citations omitted).

The Second Circuit also has reaffirmed that "[c]ommon issues may predominate when liability can be determined on a class-wide basis, even when there are some individualized damage issues." *Sykes*, 780 F.3d at 81 (quoting *In re Visa Check/MasterMoney*, 280 F.3d at 139). In *Sykes*, the court recognized that under *Comcast*, a plaintiff seeking certification of a class may only identify damages that are the result of the wrong—i.e., damages that arose from the conduct allegedly giving rise to liability. *Id.* at 82.

b. Distribution

Cy Pres

Cy pres ("as near as possible") is an approach to distributing settlement funds "where class members are difficult to identify, or where they change constantly, or where there are unclaimed funds." *Masters v.* Wilhelmina *Model Agency, Inc.*, 473 F.3d 423, 436 (2d Cir. 2007) (citing 2 Herbert B. Newberg & Alba Conte, *Newberg on Class Actions* § 10:16 n.1 (4th ed. 2002)). The purpose of a *cy pres* distribution is to "put[] the unclaimed fund to its *next best* compensation use, e.g., for the aggregate, indirect, prospective benefit of the class." *Id.* In addition, "[a] proposed *cy pres* designee is appropriate if its interests 'reasonably approximate the interests of the class.'" *Xiao Ling Chen v. XpresSpa at Terminal 4 JFK LLC*, No. 15 CV 1347, 2018 WL 1633027, at *4 (E.D.N.Y. Mar. 30, 2018) (quoting *In re Citigroup Secs. Litig.*, 199 F. Supp. 3d 845, 852 (S.D.N.Y. 2016)).

There are two standards that have been used by courts to determine a *cy pres* designee, *i.e.*, the "reasonable approximation" standard and "next best" standard. *Capsolas v. Pasta Res. Inc.*, 505 F. Supp. 3d 255, 259 (S.D.N.Y. 2020) (citing *In re Citigroup*, 199 F. Supp. 3d at 848). The Second Circuit has yet to hold definitively which of these standards applies. *See id.*

Fluid Recovery

The Second Circuit has expressly rejected so-called fluid recovery procedures to distribute damages—i.e., requiring a court to create a fund consisting of the estimated aggregate damages of an entire class, then distribute funds to people who file claims, and then distribute the balance *cy pres*. *McLaughlin v. Am. Tobacco Co.*, 522 F.3d 215, 231 (2d Cir. 2008) (citing *Eisen v. Carlisle & Jacquelin*, 479 F.2d 1005, 1008 (2d Cir. 1973)). The Second Circuit reasoned that "[r]oughly estimating the gross damages to the class as a whole and only subsequently allowing for the processing of individual claims would inevitably alter defendants' substantive right to pay damages reflective of their actual liability." *Id.* (citating cases). Rather, because "actual injury cannot be presumed," distribution methods will only be approved where they do not "mask the prevalence of individual issues[.]" *Id.* at 232; *see, e.g.*, *In re NYSE Specialists Sec. Litig.*, 260 F.R.D. 55 (S.D.N.Y. June 5, 2009) (certifying a class where plaintiff demonstrated efficacy of analysis capable of ascertaining damages on a classwide basis).

9. SETTLEMENTS

a. Drafting Considerations

It is "well established" in the Second Circuit that settlement agreements must be drafted such that no claims are waived that could not have been pled based on the integral facts alleged in the operative complaint, but "may include claims not presented and even those which could not have been presented as long as the released conduct arises out of the 'identical factual predicate' as the settled conduct." *Oladapo v. Smart One Energy, LLC*, No. 14-CV-7117, 2017 WL 5956907, at *15 (S.D.N.Y. Nov. 9, 2017) (quoting *Wal-Mart Stores, Inc. v. Visa U.S.A. Inc.*, 396 F.3d 96, 106–07 (2d Cir. 2005)). Releases thus are limited by the "identical factual predicate" and "adequacy of representation" doctrines *Mayhew v. KAS Direct, LLC*, No. 16 CV 6981, 2018 WL 3122059, at *8 (S.D.N.Y. June 26, 2018). Overly broad releases will not pass muster because "[c]lass action settlements simply will not occur if the parties cannot set definitive limits on defendants' liability." *Stephenson v. Dow Chem. Co.*, 273 F.3d 249, 254 (2d Cir. 2001) (citation omitted). For example, in *In re Payment Card Interchange Fee and Merchant Discount Antitrust Litigation*, the court held that due process principles precluded approval of a settlement involving a $7.25 billion damages class and an injunctive relief class. 827 F.3d 223 (2d Cir. 2016).[6] The *Payment Card* settlement contained a broad release of future claims and included potential class members who obtained no benefit from the injunction but were bound by the release and prevented from opting out. Because of the broad release, the Second Circuit held that the settlement violated class members' due process rights, demonstrating the court's continued commitment to protecting class members' due process rights over the "benefits of litigation peace[.]" *Id.* at 240. The Supreme Court denied certiorari. *Photos Etc. Corp. v. Home Depot U.S.A., Inc.*, 580 U.S. 1224 (2017).

b. Preliminary Approval

"Preliminary approval is the first step in the settlement of a class action whereby the court 'must preliminarily determine whether notice of the proposed settlement . . . should be given to class members in such a manner as the court directs, and an evidentiary hearing scheduled to determine the fairness and adequacy of settlement.'" *Surdu v. Madison Glob., LLC*, No. 15 Civ. 6567, 2017 WL 3842859, at *9 (S.D.N.Y. Sep. 1, 2017) (quoting *Manley v. Midan Rest. Inc.*, No. 14 Civ. 1693, 2016 WL 1274577, at *8 (S.D.N.Y. Mar. 30, 2016)). "Before approving a class settlement agreement, a district court must first determine whether the requirements for class certification in Rule 23(a) and (b) have been satisfied." *In re Am. Int'l*

[6] *See also, e.g.*, Brecher v. Republic of Arg., 806 F.3d 22 (2d Cir. 2015); *Sykes*, 780 F.3d 70; *Roach*, 778 F.3d 401.

Grp., Inc. Sec. Litig., 689 F.3d 229, 238 (2d Cir. 2012) (citation omitted). A court conducting a preliminary review must ensure that a settlement meets the requirements of Rules 23(a) and (b) and is "fair, reasonable, and adequate" under Rule 23(e). *Id.* The settlement cannot be the product of collusion, contain an ambiguous release, or provide for an inadequate notice. *McReynolds*, 588 F.3d at 798. A class settlement can only be approved following notice in the manner directed by the court and by judicial approval. Fed. R. Civ. P. 23(e). A higher degree of scrutiny in assessing a settlement's fairness is also appropriate during the preliminary approval stage if the settlement was negotiated before asking the court to certify a class. *Etienne v. Reliant Cap. Sols., LLC*, No. 16-CV-2359, 2018 WL 6335560, at *3 (E.D.N.Y. Sep. 25, 2018) (citing *Cnty. of Suffolk*, 907 F.2d at 1323).

Preliminary approval of a proposed settlement is considered the "first in a two-step process required before a class action may be settled." *In re NASDAQ Market-Makers Antitrust Litig.*, 176 F.R.D. 99, 102 (S.D.N.Y. 1997) (citing *Manual for Complex Litigation, Third*, § 30.41 (1995)). "Where the proposed settlement appears to be the product of serious, informed, non-collusive negotiations, has no obvious deficiencies, does not improperly grant preferential treatment to class representatives or segments of the class and falls within the range of possible approval, preliminary approval is granted." *Id.*

c. Objectors

Any class member may object to preliminary approval of a class settlement. Fed. R. Civ. P. 23(e). Objectors also may obtain reversal of an approved settlement upon showing that the district court abused its discretion in approving the settlement. *City of Detroit v. Grinnell Corp.*, 495 F.2d 448, 455 (2d Cir. 1974) (citing, *inter alia*, *Newman v. Stein*, 464 F.2d 689 (2d Cir. 1972)). Approval will also be set aside if the court acted "'without (knowledge of) sufficient facts concerning the claim' or if it 'failed to allow objectors to develop on the record facts going to the propriety of the settlement.'" *Id.* at 462 (citing *Newman*, 464 F.2d at 692).

d. Final Approval

A court considering final approval of a settlement evaluates "substantive fairness" under the nine "*Grinnell* factors":

> (1) the complexity, expense and likely duration of the litigation; (2) the reaction of the class to the settlement; (3) the stage of the proceedings and the amount of discovery completed; (4) the risks of establishing liability; (5) the risks of establishing damages; (6) the risks of maintaining the class action through the trial; (7) the ability of the defendants to withstand a greater judgment; (8) the range of reasonableness of the settlement fund in light of the best possible recovery; [and] (9) the range of reasonableness of the settlement fund to a possible recovery in light of all the attendant risks of litigation.

Charron, 731 F.3d at 247 (quoting *Detroit*, 495 F.2d at 463). If the balance of factors weighs in favor of settlement, a court will enter final approval. *Id.*, accord *In re LIBOR-Based Fin. Instruments Antitrust Litig.*, 327 F.R.D. 483, 495–96 (S.D.N.Y. 2018).

A district court's factual findings relating to a settlement agreement in a class action are reviewed under the clearly erroneous standard of review. *Omega Eng'g, Inc. v. Omega, S.A.*, 432 F.3d 437, 443 (2d Cir. 2005)). The Second Circuit "'will disturb a judicially-approved [class action] settlement' only when there is a clear showing that the District Court abused its discretion." *McReynolds*, 588 F.3d at 803 (quoting *D'Amato v. Deutsche Bank*, 236 F.3d 78, 85 (2d Cir. 2001)).

10. FEES AND COSTS

Attorneys' fees can be determined in several ways in the Second Circuit. For cases in which a common fund has been created, both the percentage of the fund and lodestar methods are appropriate to determine attorneys' fees. *Goldberger v. Integrated Res., Inc.*, 209 F.3d 43, 50 (2d Cir. 2000). The lodestar method calls for multiplication of a reasonable hourly rate and the number of hours worked by counsel, and courts in their discretion may apply a multiplier based on, for example, the risks of the litigation, the results obtained, and the overall performance of counsel. *Visa U.S.A., Inc.*, 396 F.3d at 121.

Courts in the Second Circuit generally prefer the percentage of the fund method in common fund cases. *In re Visa Check/Mastermoney Antitrust Litig.*, 297 F. Supp. 2d 503, 520 (E.D.N.Y. 2003); *see Elkind v. Revlon Consumer Prods. Corp.*, No. CV 14-2484, 2017 U.S. Dist. LEXIS 24512, at *52 (E.D.N.Y. Feb. 17, 2017). This method "directly aligns the interests of the class and its counsel and provides a powerful incentive for the efficient prosecution and early resolution of litigation[.]" *In re Lloyd's Am. Tr. Fund Litig.*, No. 96 Civ. 1262, 2002 WL 31663577, at *25 (S.D.N.Y. Nov. 26, 2002). "In contrast, the 'lodestar create[s] an unanticipated disincentive to early settlements, tempt[s] lawyers to run up their hours, and compel[s] district courts to engage in a gimlet-eyed review of line-item fee audits.'" *Visa U.S.A., Inc*, 396 F.3d at 121 (quoting *Baffa v. Donaldson Lufkin & Jenrette Sec. Corp.*, No. 96 Civ. 0583, 2002 WL 1315603 (S.D.N.Y. June 17, 2002)). Courts applying the percentage of fund method can also apply the lodestar method as a "cross check" to ensure that the award of fees is reasonable. *Masters*, 473 F.3d at 436 (citing *Goldberger*, 209 F.3d at 49–50).

In 2017, the United States District Court for the Western District of New York distinguished the method for calculating attorneys' fees used in *Masters* from fees requested in cases where the settlement agreement did not include a *cy pres* provision, but instead included reversion clauses and a clear sailing provision. *Cunningham v. Suds Pizza, Inc.*, 290 F. Supp. 3d 214, 224 (W.D.N.Y. 2017). Specifically, the Court ruled that attorney fee requests in these types of cases could not be calculated based on the entire value of the negotiated settlement, but rather the true value of the settlement based on claims filed. *Id.* at 225.

Regardless of the method used, "the reasonableness of a common fund fee award is governed by the so-called *Goldberger* factors: (1) counsel's time and labor; (2) the litigation's complexities and magnitude; (3) the litigation risks; (4) quality of representation; (5) the relationship of the requested fee to the settlement; and (6) considerations of public policy." *Masters*, 473 F.3d at 436 (citing *Visa U.S.A., Inc.*, 396 F.3d at 121).

In addition, in *Fresno Cty. Emps.' Ret. Ass'n v. Isaacson/Weaver Fam. Tr.*, 925 F.3d 63, 66 (2d Cir. 2019), *cert. denied*, 140 S. Ct. 385 (2019), the court agreed with the Seventh and Ninth Circuits by holding that "regardless of whether a case is brought pursuant to a statute with a fee-shifting provision, if the parties settle the case by creating a common fund, common-fund principles control class counsel's fee recovery." *Id.* at 67. The court then affirmed the district court's fee award to class counsel. *Id.* at 72.

11. APPELLATE ISSUES

a. Standing to Appeal

As a general rule, only parties to a lawsuit may appeal an adverse judgment. *Rothstein v. Am. Int'l Grp., Inc.*, 837 F.3d 195, 204 (2d Cir. 2016) (citing *Marino v. Ortiz*, 484 U.S. 301, 304 (1988)). There are two exceptions to this rule: (1) "a nonparty may appeal a judgment by which it is bound" and (2) "a nonparty may appeal if it has an interest affected by the judgment." *Id.* (quoting *Official Comm. of Unsecured Creditors of WorldCom, Inc. v. SEC*, 467 F.3d 73, 78 (2d Cir. 2006)).

The first exception includes nonnamed members of a class where a settlement would dispose of their claims. *Devlin v. Scardelletti*, 536 U.S. 1, 10 (2002). Under the second exception, a nonparty must state a "plausible affected interest" relating to the judgment. *Rothstein*, 837 F.3d at 204 (quoting *WorldCom*, 467 F.3d at 78); *see also SEC v. Certain Unknown Purchasers of the Common Stock of and Call Options for the Common Stock of Santa Fe Int'l Corp.*, 817 F.2d 1018, 1021 n.1 (2d Cir. 1987).

The Second Circuit has found a variety of interests to be sufficiently affected to permit a nonparty to appeal. *See Rothstein*, 837 F.3d at 204 (holding that nonparties had identified an "affected interest" where they had (i) *bona fide* beliefs that they were members of the class; (ii) reasonably relied on submission of claims to the claims administrator, who gave them no indication they might have been ineligible; and (iii) "most important," their exclusion from the class would deprive of millions in recognized losses); *Kaplan v. Rand*, 192 F.3d 60, 68–69 (2d Cir. 1999) (holding that shareholder had standing to appeal award of attorneys' fees that was part of settlement of shareholder derivative suit because, while fees would be paid by insurance, corporation's insurance premiums could plausibly increase as a result of the payment); *Santa Fe*, 817 F.2d at 1021 n.1 (allowing nonparty to appeal because "the district court judgment may affect the ability of [the nonparty] to pursue his Rule 10b-5 claims against defendants"); *but see Hisp. Soc'y of N.Y.C. Police Dep't, Inc. v. N.Y.C Police Dep't*, 806 F.2d 1147 (2d Cir. 1986) (rejecting appeal by nonparty who objected to settlement of employment discrimination suit by claiming it diminished his shot at promotion).

In addition, in *Jin*, the Second Circuit found a plaintiff, who won a bench trial, had Article III standing to appeal the judge's decision to decertify a class due to inadequate representation by class counsel. 990 F.3d at 261. Specifically, the Second Circuit found that under the specific factual circumstances alleged the plaintiff's "private attorney general interest suffices to establish his personal stake in this appeal" for jurisdiction. *Id.* at 260.

b. Interlocutory Review

As a general rule, only final judgments are appealable. 28 U.S.C. § 1291. There are certain non-final orders that are immediately reviewable, but the number of such orders is limited. *See, e.g.*, 9 U.S.C. § 16(a) (order denying arbitration); 28 U.S.C. § 1292(a) (orders granting, modifying, or denying a preliminary injunction).

A class certification order, while not final within the meaning of 28 U.S.C. § 1291, is subject to a discretionary appeal under Fed. R. of Civ. P. 23(f): "A court of appeals may permit an appeal from an order granting or denying class-action certification under this rule" if a petition for permission to appeal is filed with the circuit clerk within 14 days after the order is entered. A Rule 23(f) appeal "does not stay proceedings in the district court unless the district judge or the court of appeals so orders." *Id.* "In applying Rule 23(f), courts of appeals enjoy 'unfettered discretion' to grant or deny permission to appeal based on 'any consideration that the court of appeals finds persuasive.'" *Hevesi v. Citigroup Inc.*, 366 F.3d 70, 76 (2d Cir. 2004) (quoting Fed. R. Civ. P. 23(f), advisory committee's notes)). "The Court of Appeals has emphasized that 'the standards of Rule 23(f) will rarely be met.'" *Roseman v. Bloomberg L.P.*, No. 14cv2657, 2017 WL 5176379, at *2 (S.D.N.Y. Nov. 7, 2017) (quoting *Sumitomo Copper Litig. v. Credit Lyonnais Rouse, Ltd.*, 262 F.3d 134, 140 (2d Cir. 2001)).

In the Second Circuit, interlocutory review under Rule 23(f) requires a petitioner to "demonstrate either (1) that the certification order will effectively terminate the litigation and there has been a substantial showing that the district court's decision is questionable, or (2) that the certification order implicates a legal question about which there is a compelling need for immediate resolution." *Sumitomo Copper*, 262 F.3d at 139; *see also Hevesi*, 366 F.3d at 76. However, the Second Circuit has cautioned that this two-prong test "should not be reduced to any bright-line rules." *Hevesi*, 366 F.3d at 76 n.4. With respect to the second prong, "a novel legal question will not compel immediate review unless it is of fundamental importance to the development of the law of class actions and it is likely to escape effective review after entry of final judgment." *Sumitomo*, 262 F.3d at 140 (citing cases).

In *Hevesi*, the Second Circuit granted interlocutory review of the district court's certification of a class based on the fraud-on-the-market doctrine of *Basic Inc. v. Levinson*, 485 U.S. 224. The court explained that the "decision to apply the *Basic* presumption at the certification stage is 'likely to escape effective review after entry of final judgment.'" *Hevesi*, 366 F.3d at 80 (quoting *Sumitomo*, 262 F.3d at 140). The court explained that "'very few securities class actions are litigated to conclusion, so review of [a] novel and important legal issue [concerning the scope of the *Basic* presumption] may be possible only through the Rule 23(f) device.'" *Id.* (quoting *West v. Prudential Sec., Inc.*, 282 F.3d 935, 937 (7th Cir. 2002).

In addition to the express exceptions to the final judgment rule, non-final orders can be appealed pursuant to 28 U.S.C. § 1292(b), the collateral order doctrine, and by pursuing a writ of mandamus. *U.S. v. Prevezon Holdings Ltd.*, 839 F.3d 227, 235 (2d Cir. 2016).

- Section 1292(b) allows for an interlocutory appeal where the non-final order: (i) "involves a controlling question of law," (ii) "as to which there is substantial ground for difference of opinion," and (iii) "an immediate appeal from the order may materially advance the ultimate termination of the litigation[.]" 28 U.S.C. § 1292(b). Section 1292(b) also requires certification from both the district court and the Second Circuit. *Id.* "[U]se of this certification procedure should be strictly limited because only exceptional circumstances will justify a departure from the basic policy of postponing appellate review until after the entry of a final judgment." *Flor v. BOT Fin. Corp. (In re Flor)*, 79 F.3d 281, 284 (2d Cir. 1996) (citations omitted) (internal quotation marks omitted).
- "Orders that fall into the collateral order doctrine are immediately appealable." *In re Eljamal*, No. 17-cv-00609, 2018 WL 3207120, at *2 (S.D.N.Y. June 29, 2018). The collateral order doctrine covers some 'collateral' rulings that create sufficiently 'final' rulings but do not terminate the litigation in the court below. Unlike interlocutory review under Rule 23(f), under the collateral order doctrine, the order sought to be appealed must: (1) conclusively determine the disputed question, (2) resolve an important issue completely separate from the merits of the action, and (3) be effectively unreviewable on appeal from a final judgment. *See Schwartz v. City of New York*, 57 F.3d 236, 237 (2d Cir. 1995); *Prevezon Holdings Ltd.*, 839 F.3d at 235.
- Under the All Writs Act, the Second Circuit can "issue a writ of mandamus directing a district court to correct an erroneous order." *Prevezon Holdings Ltd.*, 839 F.3d at 237; *see* 28 U.S.C § 1651(a) ("[A]ll courts established by Act of Congress may issue all writs necessary or appropriate in aid of their respective jurisdictions and agreeable to the usages and principles of law."). "[O]nly exceptional circumstances amounting to a judicial usurpation of power, or a clear abuse of discretion, will justify the invocation of this extraordinary remedy." *Prevezon Holdings Ltd.*, 839 F.3d at 237 (quoting *Cheney v. U.S. Dist. Ct. for D.C*, 542 U.S. 367, 380 (2004)). For a party to obtain a writ of mandamus, "(1) 'the party seeking issuance of the writ must have no other adequate means to attain the relief [it] desires'; (2) 'the issuing court, in the exercise of its discretion, must be satisfied that the writ is appropriate under the circumstances'; and (3) the petitioner must demonstrate that the 'right to issuance of the writ is clear and indisputable.'" *In re City of New York*, 607 F.3d 923, 932–33 (2d Cir. 2010) (quoting *Cheney*, 542 U.S. at 380–81)); *accord In re Nielsen*, No. 17-3345, 2017 U.S. App. LEXIS 27681, at *7 (2d Cir. Dec. 27, 2017).

12. TOLLING THE STATUTE OF LIMITATIONS

Tolling pauses or suspends the running of the time period set forth by a statute of limitations.

In *American Pipe & Construction Co. v. Utah*, the Supreme Court held that the statute of limitations is tolled for the period between the filing of a class action complaint and the denial of a motion to certify the class "for all purported members of the class who make timely motions to intervene after the court has found the suit inappropriate for class action status." 414 U.S. at 553 (1974). The Supreme Court clarified that this rule "applies not only to putative class members who seek to intervene in an action, but also to would-be class members who later file their own independent actions." *Police & Fire Ret. Sys. of City of Detroit v. IndyMac MBS, Inc.*, 721 F.3d 95, 105 (2d Cir. 2013) (citing *Crown, Cork & Seal Co., Inc. v. Parker*, 462 U.S. 345, 353–54 (1983)). The tolling doctrine adopted in *American Pipe* does not "permit putative class members to file a subsequent class action." *Korwek v. Hunt*, 827 F.2d 874, 878 (2d Cir. 1987). *See also Chavez v. Occidental Chem. Corp.*, 8 F.4th 91 (2d Cir. 2021) (ordering dismissal of plaintiffs' class action claims as time barred, where a prior district court's "final judgment" ended the tolling of those claims, which were found untimely under New York's three-year statute of limitations for personal injury actions, which the parties agreed applied). Where jurisdiction rests on diversity, "state rather than federal law applies to tolling issues[.]" *Casey v. Merck & Co., Inc.*, 653 F.3d 95, 100 (2d Cir. 2011).

13. ARBITRATION ISSUES

The Federal Arbitration Act requires the federal courts to enforce valid and binding arbitration agreements, "reflecting Congress' recognition that arbitration is to be encouraged as a means of reducing the costs and delays associated with litigation." *Vera v. Saks & Co.*, 335 F.3d 109, 116 (2d Cir. 2003) (per curiam) (quoting *Deloitte Noraudit v. Deloitte Haskins & Sells, U.S.*, 9 F.3d 1060, 1063 (2d Cir. 1993). In deciding whether a dispute is arbitrable, the Second Circuit looks at two questions: "(1) whether the parties agreed to arbitrate, and, if so, (2) whether the scope of that agreement encompasses the claims at issue." *Virk v. Maple-Gate Anesthesiologists, P.C.*, 657 F. App'x 19, at *21 (2d Cir. 2016) (quoting *Holick v. Cellular Sales of N.Y., LLC*, 802 F.3d 391, 394 (2d Cir. 2015)).

In the Second Circuit, a class action waiver provision in an arbitration agreement is generally enforceable in employment contracts. *See Sutherland v. Ernst & Young LLP*, 726 F.3d 290 (2d Cir. 2013). Recently, the Second Circuit held that absent class members who have "[']obligated [themselves], by contract, to submit to arbitration' . . . may be bound by the arbitrator's class arbitrability determination" if the arbitrator is authorized to decide such issue. *See Jock v. Sterling Jewelers Inc.*, 942 F.3d 617, 626 (2d Cir. 2019) (quoting *Porzig v. Dresdner, Kleinwort, Benson, North America LLC*, 497 F.3d 133, 140 (2d Cir. 2007)).

Arbitration agreements within consumer contracts are also generally enforceable. *See AT&T Mobility LLC v. Concepcion*, 563 U.S. 333 (2011). In *Meyer v. Uber Technologies, Inc.*, 868 F.3d 66 (2d Cir. 2017), the court held Uber's clickwrap arbitration agreement enforceable. Conversely, a party cannot be required to submit to arbitration any dispute that he has not agreed to so submit. *United Steelworkers of Am. v. Warrior & Gulf Navigation Co.*, 363 U.S. 574, 582 (1960); *see, e.g.*, *Necchi S.p.A. v. Necchi Sewing Mach. Sales Corp.*, 348 F.2d 693 (2d Cir. 1965) (reversing in part and holding that the district court too broadly construed the scope of an arbitration provision). Recently, the Second Circuit distinguished *Meyer's* clickwrap arbitration agreement from the notice of arbitration provided in *Starke v. Squaretrade, Inc.*, 913 F.3d 279, 292-94 (2d Cir. 2019). In *Squaretrade*, the court found that reasonable notice of the arbitration provision was not provided in a clear and conspicuous way due to "none of the language in the cluttered email directed [the Plaintiff's] attention to the hyperlink containing the [terms and conditions][,]" "various communications [did not] put [the Plaintiff] on notice that his 'Service Contract' would come in the form of a hyperlink," there was no language advising that the Terms and Conditions should be clicked, and there was not a "clear prompt directing [the Plaintiff] to read the Terms and Conditions." *Id.* at 292–93 (citations omitted).

Under generally applicable contract law principles, whether a consumer can fairly be deemed to have assented to a term is a pragmatic inquiry, which "depends on various factors including, but not limited to, the conspicuousness of the term, the course of dealing between the parties, and industry practices." *Schnabel v. Trilegiant Corp.*, 697 F.3d 110, 124 (2d Cir. 2012). "[T]he touchstone of the analysis is whether reasonable people in the position of the parties would have known about the terms and the conduct that would be required to assent to them." *Id.* Furthermore, "cases applying the 'duty to read' principle to terms delivered after a contracting relationship has been initiated do not nullify the requirement that a consumer be on notice of the existence of a term before he or she can be legally held to have assented to it." *Id.*

14. ETHICAL CONSIDERATIONS

a. Settlement Issues

Settlement of class actions can present potential ethical concerns—involving, for example, the interplay between the interests of the class and class counsel in receiving compensation. *Cf. Plummer v. Chem. Bank*, 668 F.2d 654, 658 (2d Cir. 1982) ("Because of the limited control exercisable by class members, class settlements are susceptible to abuse." (citing *Pettway v. Am. Pipe Co.*, 576 F.2d 1157, 1169 (5th Cir. 1978))). "The ultimate responsibility to ensure that the interests of class members are not subordinated to the interests of either the class representatives or class counsel rests with the district court." *Maywalt v. Parkert & Parsley Petroleum Co.*, 67 F.3d 1072, 1078 (2d Cir. 1995). *See also* Fed. R. Civ. P. 23(e); *D'Amato*, 236 F.3d at 85 ("The District Court determines a settlement's fairness by examining the negotiating process leading up to the settlement as well as the settlement's substantive terms.") (citing *Malchman v. Davis*, 706 F.2d 426, 433 (2d Cir. 1983)). At the same time, "a district court may not 'dictate the terms of a class settlement; he should approve or disapprove a proposed agreement as it is placed before him and should not take it upon himself to modify its terms.'" *Deangelis*, 151 F. Supp. 3d at 361–62 (quoting *In re Warner Commc'ns Sec. Litig.*, 798 F.2d 35, 37 (2d Cir. 1986)). In submitting proposed settlements for court approval, practitioners are cautioned not to compromise the interests of the class for the sake of higher remuneration. *See, e.g.*, *In re Am. Express Anti Steering Rules Antitrust Litig.*, No. 11-MD-2211, 2015 WL 4645240, at *20 (E.D.N.Y. Aug. 4, 2015) (refusing to approve a settlement that would have provided for injunctive relief while also allowing class counsel to gain $75 million in attorneys' fees: "The court is concerned that *none* of the Co-Lead Class Counsel were, or are, acting in the class's best interests, as opposed to their own interests in effectuating this settlement agreement and collecting a fee.").

b. Absent Class Members Communications

In general, counsel may not communicate about the subject of a representation with a party the lawyer knows to be represented by another lawyer. *See, e.g.*, N.Y. Comp. Codes R. & Regs. tit. 22, § 1200.0 ("[A] lawyer shall not communicate or cause another to communicate about the subject of the representation with a party the lawyer knows to be represented by another lawyer in the matter, unless the lawyer has the consent of the other lawyer or is authorized to do so by law."); CT R RPC Rule 4.2. District courts have held that rules proscribing such contacts "appl[y] to members of a class after class certification." *Cazares v. AVA Rest. Corp*, No. 15-CV-0477, 2017 WL 1229727, at *10 (E.D.N.Y. Mar. 31, 2017) (citing *Jackson v. Bloomberg, L.P.*, No. 13-CV-2001, 2015 WL 1822695, at *2 (S.D.N.Y. Apr. 22, 2015)); *see also Brown v. Mustang Sally's Spirits & Grill, Inc.*, No. 12-CV-529S, 2012 WL 4764585, at *5 (W.D.N.Y. Oct. 5, 2012); *Gortat v. Capala Bros., Inc.*, No. 07-CV-3629, 2010 WL 1879922, at *4 (E.D.N.Y. May 10, 2010), *objections overruled*, 2010 WL 3417847 (E.D.N.Y. Aug. 27, 2010).

Both before and after class certification, the court has authority to regulate defense counsel's ability to communicate with potential class members. *See* Fed. R. Civ. P. 23(d) (court has general authority to impose conditions on parties and counsel in a class action); *see also Manual for Complex Litigation, Fourth* § 21.12. Courts in the Second Circuit have exercised their authority under Rule 23(d) "to limit communications to protect class members from 'misleading communications from the parties or their counsel[.]'" *Dodona I, LLC v. Goldman, Sachs & Co.*, 300 F.R.D. 182, 184 (S.D.N.Y. 2014) (citation omitted).

THIRD CIRCUIT

Districts of Delaware, New Jersey, Pennsylvania, and the United States Virgin Islands

James A. Byrne United States Courthouse
601 Market Street
Philadelphia, PA 19106

By Angelo A. Stio III and Nicole E. Crossey
Troutman Pepper Hamilton Sanders LLP

1. INTRODUCTION

Despite the Third Circuit's relatively active role in shaping class action law, defining the court's class-related ideology is a tall order. For one, the court issues a remarkably small number of *en banc* opinions. Moreover, the court, like many circuit courts, is home to judges with substantially differing views on the role class actions can and should play in resolving disputes. These characteristics make it difficult to define the Third Circuit as either being friendly or hostile to class actions.

If forced to make a relative assessment of the court's jurisprudence, no one would label the court as being as friendly to class actions as the Ninth Circuit. But a review of the case law demonstrates that defining the Third Circuit as hostile to class actions would be equally inapt. By way of example, the Third Circuit held that the plaintiffs in *Comcast Corp. v. Behrend*, 569 U.S. 27 (2013), had satisfied Rule 23(b)(3)'s predominance requirement before the Supreme Court reversed that decision.

While a review of Third Circuit case law does not yield a clear answer about the court's attitude toward class actions, it does suggest three trends that practitioners should note when litigating in this circuit. ***First***, the court is not reluctant to interpret Rule 23's requirements in ways that break new ground. For example, in *Carrera v. Bayer Corp.*, 727 F.3d 300 (3d Cir. 2013), and *In re Modafinil Antitrust Litigation*, 837 F.3d 238 (3d Cir. 2016), the Third Circuit charted new territory regarding ascertainability and numerosity, respectively. *Carrera* has, in fact, given rise to a circuit split[1] with respect to how class action plaintiffs must demonstrate

[1] The Sixth, Seventh, Eighth, Ninth, and Eleventh Circuits have rejected *Carrera*'s ascertainability requirement as overly burdensome and untethered to the text of Rule 23. Rikos v. Procter & Gamble Co., 799 F.3d 497, 525 (6th Cir. 2015); Mullins v. Direct Digital, LLC, 795 F.3d 654, 662 (7th Cir. 2015); Sandusky Wellness Ctr., 821 F.3d at 996; Briseno v. ConAgra Foods, Inc., 844 F.3d 1121, 1123 (9th Cir. 2017); Cherry v. Dometic Corp., 986 F.3d 1296, 1304 (11th Cir. 2021). The Third Circuit in *In re Niaspan Antitrust Litig.*, 67 F.4th 118, 133–34 (3d Cir. 2023), recently explained that although these courts have eschewed the approach in *Carrera*, "some version of an administrative feasibility test is applied, albeit under a different name." For instance, the court noted, the Eleventh Circuit recognized that "administrative feasibility has relevance for Rule 23(b)(3), in the light of the manageability criterion of Rule 23(b)(3)(D)." *Id.* at 134

ascertainability that the Supreme Court seems disinclined to address in the near future.

Second, in breaking new ground, the Third Circuit has focused on how the presence of potentially uninjured class members should impact class certification decisions. In *Carrera*, for example, the court reaffirmed its previous subtle creation of a "heightened" ascertainability standard, which requires that (1) the class is defined with reference to "objective criteria" and (2) there is a "reliable and administratively feasible" mechanism for determining whether putative class members fall within the class definition. 727 F.3d at 306–08 (internal quotation marks omitted). The *Carrera* court held that affidavits attesting to class membership are not sufficiently reliable to delineate a class without additional evidence, implicitly suggesting that individuals not actually harmed by the defendant's conduct would recover if it reached a contrary holding. *Id.* at 309–12. This heightened ascertainability standard was most recently confirmed by the Court in *In re Niaspan Antitrust Litig.*, 67 F.4th 118, 132 (3d Cir. 2023), where the Third Circuit reiterated that the requirement of ascertainability is "true to the text, structure and purpose of Rule 23." *See also id.* at 133 (observing that "[s]everal of our sister circuits have followed our lead and apply our ascertainability standard, or a standard that is substantively the same").

This heightened ascertainabiltiy standard also was discussed in *In re Modafinil Antitrust Litig.*, 837 F.3d 238 (3d Cir. 2016). There, the Third Circuit decertified a district court's decision to certify a 22-member class, the majority appears to wonder aloud why the three absent class members with claims of allegedly over $3 billion that represented 97 percent of the putative class's damages had not pursued individual claims against the defendants. 837 F.3d at 258. The court's growing concern with the impact of uninjured class members on class certification also was addressed in *In re Lamictal Direct Purchaser Antitrust Litig.*, 957 F.3d 184 (3d Cir. Apr. 22, 2020). There, the Third Circuit confirmed that the decision to certify a class requires a "rigorous analysis" of evidence, and the party seeking certification must show by a preponderance of the evidence that each element of the legal claim is capable of proof with evidence that is common to the putative class. *Id.* at 190–91 (quoting *In re Hydrogen Peroxide Antitrust Litig.*, 552 F.3d 305, 309 (3d Cir. 2008), *as amended* (Jan. 16, 2009)). In so holding, the Third Circuit rejected the contention that *Tyson v. Bouaphakeo*, 136 S. Ct. 1036, 1049 (2016) relaxed the predominance standard under Rule 23(b)(3), which plaintiffs argued could now be met if their "evidence of class-wide antitrust injury *could* sustain a jury finding." *Id.* at 191 (emphasis added) (limiting *Tyson* to the specific context of the Fair Labor Standards Act). Instead, the Third Circuit reiterated that "plaintiffs must prove their claim is capable of common proof by a preponderance of the evidence" at the class certification stage. *In re Lamictal*, 957 F.3d at 192.

Third, the Third Circuit's interest in preventing potentially uninjured class members from obtaining class relief has not, to date, impacted the court's evaluation of predicate questions like whether the dispute meets Article III's case and controversy requirement. In *Neale v. Volvo Cars of N. Am., LLC*, 794 F.3d 353 (3d Cir. 2015), for example, the court concluded that absent class members need not have standing for a named class representative to pursue their claims. *Id.* at 362. Indeed, while the court seems hesitant to permit certification of classes with uninjured members, it has had no qualms about allowing plaintiffs to pursue class claims up through the class certification stage. In *Wallach v. Eaton Corp.*, 837 F.3d 356 (3d Cir. 2016), the court held that the assignment of a claim by an entity that fit within the class definition to an entity that did not was valid because the assignment was express and in writing, even if no consideration changed hands as part of the assignment transaction. *Id.* at 371.

The following discussion describes key principles, providing practitioners with a solid foundation in Third Circuit class action law and giving a head start to others on potential fu-

---

(citing *Cherry*, 986 F.3d at 1303). Similarly, the Sixth, Seventh, Eighth, and Ninth Circuits "have all adopted a similar approach. Instead of having a separate administrative feasibility requirement, those courts often address administrative concerns through a rigorous analysis of Rule 23's 'superiority' requirement.'" *Id.* (citing cases).

ture jurisprudential trends.

2. JURISDICTIONAL PREREQUISITES

a. CAFA Requirements

Before Congress enacted the Class Action Fairness Act (CAFA) in 2005, "many class actions were excluded from federal courts even if those actions implicated matters of national importance affecting millions of parties from many different states." *Kaufman v. Allstate N.J. Ins. Co.*, 561 F.3d 144, 148 (3d Cir. 2009). That is because unless a class action raised a federal question under 28 U.S.C. § 1331, federal courts demanded complete diversity, requiring that no plaintiff be a citizen of the same state as any defendant, and disallowed the aggregation of claims, meaning that each plaintiff must have sought at least the jurisdictional threshold amount in controversy. *Id.* at 148–49. CAFA fundamentally altered the landscape of class action litigation across the country by providing that, with a few specific exceptions—such as cases in which the primary defendants are government actors, 28 U.S.C. § 1332(d)(5)(B), or the case is governed by the corporate internal affairs doctrine, 28 U.S.C. § 1332(d)(9)(b)—"federal courts have jurisdiction over class actions [advancing state-law claims] in which the amount in controversy exceeds $5,000,000 in the aggregate, any class member and any defendant are citizens of different states, and there are at least 100 members in the putative class." *Kaufman*, 561 F.3d at 149 (citations omitted). CAFA's general requirements and exceptions also apply to covered mass actions. *Abraham v. St. Croix Renaissance Grp., LLP*, 719 F.3d 270, 275 (3d Cir. 2013); *see also* 28 U.S.C. § 1332(d)(11)(B) (providing criteria for covered mass actions); *Robert D. Mabe, Inc. v. OptumRX*, 43 F.4th 307 (3d Cir. Aug. 4, 2022) (holding that district courts have jurisdiction over mass actions if they otherwise meet CAFA's requirements).

In determining whether federal jurisdiction exists under CAFA, the Third Circuit has placed limits on a district court's ability to look beyond the four corners of the complaint to determine whether CAFA requirements were met. For example, in *Erie Ins. Exch. v. Erie Indem. Co.*, 68 F.4th 815, 817–18 (3d Cir. 2023), the plaintiffs initially filed a putative class action under Pennsylvania's version of Fed. R. Civ. P. 23 (i.e., Pa. R. Civ. P. 2152), which was removed to federal court and ultimately voluntarily dismissed. Soon thereafter, the plaintiffs filed a nearly identical case in state court under a different state rule (i.e., Pa. R. Civ. P. 2177) that allowed suits by an association in the name of its members as trustees *ad litem*. Although the second action was not formally a class action, the defendant once again removed to federal court because it argued that the case was a class action "in substance." *Id.* at 818. In affirming the district court's holding that there was no basis for exercising federal jurisdiction, the Third Circuit held the newly-filed case was neither "a class action as that term is defined in CAFA"—a civil action filed under Fed. R. Civ. P. 23 or a "similar State statute or rule of judicial procedure authorizing an action to be brought by 1 or more representative persons as a class action"—nor a continuation of the voluntarily dismissed class action. *Id.* at 819, 824. The Third Circuit rejected the defendant's "invitation" to look outside the four corners of the plaintiff's complaint because it reasoned that doing so was only proper to assess "factual predicates, not legal requirements." *Id.* at 820. The Third Circuit concluded "no facts beyond the Complaint that could alter our conclusion that the relevant state rules are dissimilar to Rule 23 and that this case therefore falls beyond the scope of CAFA jurisdiction." *Id.* at 820.

Although CAFA's jurisdictional threshold orbits around the monetary value of the claim at issue, the requirements apply even when the putative class seeks nonmonetary relief. When the claims seek only injunctive or declaratory relief, courts must still "put a value on the relief sought when deciding whether the $5 million jurisdictional threshold is met." *See, e.g.*, *Excel Pharmacy Servs., LLC v. Liberty Mut. Ins. Co.*, 825 F. App'x 65 (3d Cir. 2020). There, the court addressed whether the value of an injunction or declaration exceeds the $5 million jurisdictional threshold and found that "the court may look not only at past losses but also potential harm" in the future that could be remedied in the action to determine if CAFA's requirements were met. *Id.* (citing *A.F.A. Tours, Inc. v. Whitchurch*, 937 F.2d 82, 88 (2d Cir. 1991)).

Exceptions to Federal Court Jurisdiction under CAFA. To protect against the use of federal courts to adjudicate local matters, CAFA contains two mandatory exceptions from federal jurisdiction: (i) the "local controversy" exception, and (ii) the "home-state" exception.

The "local controversy" exception "seeks to identify a truly local controversy—a controversy that uniquely affects a particular locality to the exclusion of all others and enables State courts to adjudicate truly local disputes involving principal injuries concentrated within the forum State." *Vodenichar v. Halcon Energy Props.*, 733 F.3d 497, 508 n.11 (3d Cir. 2013) (quotation marks and citation omitted). The local controversy exception applies when

> (1) greater than two-thirds of the putative class are citizens of the state in which the action was originally filed; (2) at least one defendant is a citizen of the state in which the action was originally filed (the 'local defendant'); (3) the local defendant's conduct forms a significant basis for the claims asserted; (4) plaintiffs are seeking significant relief from the local defendant; (5) the principal injuries occurred in the state in which the action was originally filed; and (6) no other class action asserting the same or similar allegations against any of the defendants had been filed in the preceding three years.

Id. at 506–07.

Although the Third Circuit seldom reviews remand orders, a few decisions shed additional light on the local controversy exception requirements. For example, in *Walsh v. Defs., Inc.*, 894 F.3d 583 (3d Cir. 2018), the Third Circuit affirmed a district court's decision to remand after evaluating whether a named defendant was a real party in interest, such that the party could qualify as the local defendant. *Id.* at 589–91. The *Walsh* court rejected the argument that an assignment of liability related to the contracts at issue from one corporation to another stripped the plaintiff of a basis to pursue claims against the assignor: the plaintiff had not consented to the assignment, the assignor did not dissolve itself or transfer all of its liability to the assignee, and the assignor "is subject to liability in this case, depending on its outcome, and can defend the claims against it." *Id.* at 591. The *Walsh* court has also reviewed whether the local defendant's conduct forms a "significant basis" for the plaintiff's claims, clarifying that this requirement necessarily triggers "a substantive analysis comparing the local defendant's alleged conduct to the alleged conduct of all the Defendants," and "[i]f the local defendant's alleged conduct is a significant part of the alleged conduct of all the Defendants, then the significant basis provision is satisfied." *Kaufman*, 561 F.3d at 156; *see also id.* at 157 (defining "significant" as "important, notable" but declining to put a finer point on it). When evaluating whether a plaintiff seeks "significant relief" from a particular defendant, the Third Circuit has instructed lower courts to look "to the complaint rather than extrinsic materials . . . as the complaint is the best evidence of the relief that the plaintiffs seek." *Walsh*, 894 F.3d at 591–92. The court has also concluded that a class action filed earlier by the same plaintiffs against at least some of the same defendants that brought the same claims and was voluntarily dismissed for procedural reasons did not qualify as an "other class action" for the purposes of the sixth requirement because to hold otherwise would have violated the spirit of the local controversy exception. *Vodenichar*, 733 F.3d at 509–10.

The "home-state" exception requires a federal court to decline to exercise subject matter jurisdiction over claims that otherwise meet CAFA's requirements when "two-thirds or more of the members of the putative class are citizens of the same state as the primary defendants." *Id.* at 503–04. The question that arises most frequently in the context of the home state exception is which defendants qualify as "primary." When conducting that inquiry, the Third Circuit has directed courts to "assume liability will be found and determine whether the defendant is the 'real target' of the plaintiffs' accusations," whether "the plaintiffs seek to hold the defendant responsible for its own actions, as opposed to seeking to have it pay for the actions of others" and "whether, given the claims asserted against the defendant, it has potential exposure to a significant portion of the class and would sustain a substantial loss as compared to other defendants if found liable." *Id.* at 505–06.

In addition to the two mandatory jurisdictional exceptions, CAFA also recognizes a jurisdictional exception that grants district courts discretion "in the interests of justice and looking at the totality of the circumstances" to decline to exercise jurisdiction if more than one-third but less than two-thirds of the proposed class and the primary defendants are citizens of the state in which the action was originally filed, and lists factors for courts to consider when exercising their discretion. 28 U.S.C. § 1332(d)(3). *Vodenichar*'s "primary defendant" guidance applies equally to this discretionary exception. *Alegre v. Atl. Cent. Logistics*, No. 15-2342, 2015 U.S. Dist. LEXIS 100214, at *24–25, 2015 WL 4607196, at *9–10 (D.N.J. July 31, 2015). The Third Circuit has not otherwise provided guidance to lower courts regarding § 1332(d)(3). *See Hirschbach v. NVE Bank*, 496 F. Supp. 2d 451, 461 n.4 (D.N.J. 2007) (noting lack of precedent regarding factors, in particular).

Burden of Proof. "CAFA itself is silent regarding which party should bear the burden of proof with respect to the establishment of federal jurisdiction." *Anthony v. Small Tube Mfg. Corp.*, 535 F. Supp. 2d 506, 512 (E.D. Pa. 2007). In the face of this silence, the Third Circuit has held that the burden of establishing CAFA jurisdiction rests with the party asserting jurisdiction, which frequently falls to defendants attempting to remove a class action to federal court. *Morgan v. Gay*, 471 F.3d 469, 472–73 (3d Cir. 2006) (recognizing agreement with the Seventh, Ninth, and Eleventh Circuits). Once CAFA jurisdiction is established, a party seeking to invoke an exception requiring a court to decline that jurisdiction "bears the burden of proving by a preponderance of the evidence that the exception applies." *Ellis v. Montgomery Cty.*, 267 F. Supp. 3d 510, 514 (E.D. Pa. 2017) (quoting *Vodenichar*, 733 F.3d at 504).

Timing of Removal. 28 U.S.C. § 1446(b)'s 30-day time limit for removal applies equally to CAFA cases and starts to run "as soon as [the defendant] can 'ascertain' a basis for federal jurisdiction from the pleadings, motion documents, orders, or 'other paper.'" *Fenza's Auto, Inc. v. Montagnaro's, Inc.*, No. 10-3336, 2011 U.S. Dist. LEXIS 29696, at *33–34, 2011 WL 1098993, at *11 (D.N.J. Mar. 21, 2011) (quoting *Sikirica v. Nationwide Ins. Co.*, 416 F.3d 214, 223 (3d Cir. 2005)). To conduct a jurisdictional inquiry, a defendant must look beyond the face of the complaint. *See LaCaffinie v. Std. Fire Ins. Co.*, No. 10-207, 2010 U.S. Dist. LEXIS 53151, at *10–11, 2010 WL 2207986, at *4 (W.D. Pa. May 28, 2010). "Thus, the time to remove under § 1446(b) begins to run when the circumstances described in the complaint combined with relevant information available to the defendant would demonstrate the basis for federal jurisdiction." *Fenza's Auto, Inc.*, 2011 U.S. Dist. LEXIS 29696, at *34, 2011 WL 1098993, at *11.

As the Third Circuit has noted "28 U.S.C. § 1453 provides that the 1-year limitation for removal under § 1446(c)(1) does not apply to removal under CAFA." *Judon v. Travelers Prop. Cas. Co. of Am.*, 773 F.3d 495, 508–09 (3d Cir. 2014). Instead, "a defendant may be able to remove an action under CAFA well into the course of the litigation once facts are discovered supporting removal." *Id.* (citing Georgene M. Vairo, *Moore's Federal Practice: The Complete CAFA: Analysis and Developments Under the Class Action Fairness Act of 2005*, p. 167 (Matthew Bender 2011); and *Farina v. Nokia Inc.*, 625 F.3d 97, 101, 113 n.17 (3d Cir. 2010), for the proposition that "'CAFA operates as an expansion of diversity jurisdiction' and that although an action may not be initially removable, it is removable upon receipt of appropriate facts pursuant to 28 U.S.C. § 1446(c)").

Parties Who May Remove. While the original defendant in a class case possesses substantial authority to remove whenever he discovers the basis for CAFA jurisdiction, third parties do not enjoy that flexibility, or, indeed, the right to remove the class claims against them to federal court under CAFA or otherwise. In a decision that purported to follow statutory text and leave practical implications to Congress, the Supreme Court held in *Home Depot U.S.A., Inc. v. Jackson*, 139 S. Ct. 1743 (2019), that neither the general removal provision, 28 U.S.C. § 1441(a), nor the CAFA removal provision, § 1453(b), permit a third-party counterclaim defendant to remove a class claim from state to federal court. *Id.* at 1746.

Duration of CAFA-Based Jurisdiction. Once a party establishes entitlement to CAFA jurisdiction, the federal court retains jurisdiction throughout the duration of the case. The named class plaintiffs in *Coba v. Ford Motor Co.*, No. 17-2933, 932 F.3d 114 (3d Cir. 2019), lost their bid for class certification, proceeded with individual claims only, and ultimately failed to defeat Ford's motion for summary judgment, resulting in dismissal of their individual claims. On appeal, the plaintiffs argued that the district court did not have jurisdiction over their individual claims post-certification decision, and thus could not have dismissed them, because CAFA (and no other jurisdictional rule) had provided the basis for federal jurisdiction when the case was filed as a class action. Had the plaintiffs pursued individual claims only from the outset, a federal court could not have exercised jurisdiction over the individual claims. The Third Circuit rejected the plaintiffs' argument that a class certification decision could strip a federal court of jurisdiction, relying on CAFA's text and general jurisdictional principles to hold that "[i]f a federal court properly exercises jurisdiction pursuant to § 1332(d) at the time a claim is filed or removed, . . . a subsequent denial of class certification" does not "divest the court of subject-matter jurisdiction." *Id.* at 119.

b. Standing

Named Plaintiff Standing

"It makes no difference to the question of Article III standing that a suit is a class action"—named plaintiffs, like all non-class plaintiffs, "must allege that they personally have been injured, not that injury has been suffered by other, unidentified members of the class to which they belong and which they purport to represent." *Federman v. Bank of Am.*, N.A., No. 14-0441, 2014 U.S. Dist. LEXIS 175565, at *28, 2014 WL 12774688, at *8 (D.N.J. Dec. 16, 2014) (quoting *Lewis v. Casey*, 518 U.S. 343, 357 (1996)); *see also In re Magnesium Oxide Antitrust Litig.*, No. 10-5943, 2011 U.S. Dist. LEXIS 121373, at *24–25, 2011 WL 5008090, at *7 (D.N.J. Oct. 20, 2011) ("It is well-settled that a named plaintiff in a class action lawsuit is required to establish Article III standing."); *Thole v. U.S. Bank N.A.*, 140 S. Ct. 1615, 1622 (2020) (remarking in an ERISA class action that "[c]ourts sometimes make standing law more complicated than it needs to be," and holding that where named plaintiffs "have received all of their vested pension benefits so far" and their entitlement to them would not be changed by the disposition of the case, standing was lacking). A plaintiff's allegations, rather than the merits of her claim, control the standing analysis. *Cottrell v. Alcon Labs*., 874 F.3d 154, 164 (3d Cir. 2017) ("[W]hether a plaintiff has alleged an invasion of a 'legally protected interest' does not hinge on whether the conduct alleged to violate a statute does, as a matter of law, violate the statute. Were we to conclude otherwise, we would effectively collapse our evaluation under Federal Rule of Civil Procedure 12(b)(6) for failure to state a claim into an Article III standing evaluation.").

It bears noting that the Third Circuit initially adopted a narrow reading of *Spokeo, Inc. v. Robins*, 136 S. Ct. 1540 (2016), explaining that "[a]lthough it is possible to read the Supreme Court's decision in *Spokeo* as creating a requirement that a plaintiff show a statutory violation has caused a 'material risk of harm' before he can bring suit, we do not believe that the Court so intended to change the traditional standard for the establishment of standing." *In re Horizon Healthcare Servs. Data Breach Litig.*, 846 F.3d 625, 637 (3d Cir. 2017). "The contours of the injury-in-fact requirement, while not precisely defined, are very generous, requiring only that claimant allege[] some specific, identifiable trifle of injury." *Id.* at 633. Accordingly, in the years immediately following *Spokeo*, a plaintiff in the Third Circuit could establish standing by alleging either an injury closely related to one traditionally recognized by English or American courts, or an injury that Congress, through a statute, made redressable. *Id.* at 637; *see also id.* at 629 ("[T]he *Spokeo* Court meant to reiterate traditional notions of standing, rather than erect any new barriers that might prevent Congress from identifying new causes of action though they may be based on intangible harms."); *Taha v. Cty. of Bucks*, 862 F.3d 292, 301–02 (3d Cir. 2017) (reiterating that "plaintiffs—who had alleged a 'perhaps intangible' harm when their legally protected information was unlawfully disclosed on the internet—had pled facts sufficient to establish Article III standing" and that "focusing on 'economic loss' in determining whether a plaintiff has Article III standing is 'misplaced'" (quoting *In re Nickelodeon Consumer Privacy Litig.*, 827 F.3d 262, 272– 73 (3d Cir. 2016)); *O'Dell v. Nat'l Recovery Agency*, 291 F. Supp. 3d 687, 695–96 (E.D. Pa. 2018) (holding that plaintiffs had standing under *Horizon* standard because, by including a technical requirement in the Fair Debt Collection Practices Act, Congress evidenced an intent to make breach of technical requirement redressable; noting tension between *Horizon* and *Spokeo*); *Weichsel v. JP Morgan Chase Bank, N.A.*, 65 F.4th 105, 112 (3d Cir. 2023) (reasoning that "while a statutory violation gives [the plaintiff] his cause of action," the plaintiff "need not allege any additional injury with a connection to the statute's purpose" where "that statutory cause of action is distinct from his Article III injury").

Nevertheless, the Third Circuit's rulings on standing have provided some insight into its application of the *Spokeo* standard and standing under the Supreme Court's decision in *TransUnion LLC v. Ramirez*, 141 S. Ct. 2190, 2214 (2021), which confirms that all class members must have standing to recover damages. For example, in *Huber v. Simon's Agency, Inc.*, 84 F.4th 132 (3d Cir. 2023), the Third Circuit addressed whether "informational injury" was sufficient to establish standing under *Ramirez*, 141 S. Ct. at 2213–14. In *Huber*, a divided Third Circuit affirmed a district court's determination that a collection agency violated the Fair Debt Collection Practices Act by sending misleading and deceptive collection notices to a class of consumers, but the majority disagreed with the district court's standing analysis and class certification determination. The majority found the district court erred in finding the named plaintiff suffered a cognizable harm under the "informational injury" doctrine. It reasoned that the decisions in *Kelly v. Realpage Inc.*, 47 F.4th 202, 212–13 (3d Cir. 2022), and *Ramirez*, 141 S. Ct. at 2213–14, made the doctrine applicable only when a plaintiff is denied information to which she is legally entitled. *Id.* at 145–46. The plaintiff attempted to expand the informational injury doctrine to encompass a failure to disclose information "clearly and effectively," but the Third Circuit rejected this argument. *Id.* at 146. In rejecting this argument, the Third Circuit explained that unclear disclosures do not equate to outright omissions and that "[o]pening the courthouse doors whenever required disclosures could arguably be clearer would vitiate the concrete injury requirement in almost any case involving information." *Id.* The Third Circuit concluded that plaintiff had not alleged that defendant omitted information to which she was entitled, and therefore, she did not suffer an informational injury. *Id.*

Following *Huber* and *Kelly*, the Third Circuit revisited the informational injury doctrine in *George v. Rushmore Serv. Ctr., LLC*, 114 F.4th 226, 234 (3d Cir. 2024). There, the Third Circuit addressed whether a letter from a debt collector that causes confusion as to whether a legitimate debt exists was sufficient to satisfy the Article III standing requirement. The Third Circuit held that it does not. Noting *Huber* distinguished *Kelly* in clarifying that the informational injury doctrine does not extend to the failure to disclose clearly and effectively, the court found plaintiff had not established she suffered any informational injury because she did not allege specific, adverse effects stemming from defendant's omission of the creditor to whom the debt was owed—she had only claimed the omission would have left the "least sophisticated consumer" in doubt about who was owed the debt and whether it was legitimate. *Id.* at 235–36. "Nothing in the complaint indicates that George could not pay her debt as a result of the letter, that the omission caused downstream financial consequences, or that George suffered distress," the court wrote, noting that George did not even allege she was confused by the letter. *Id.* George had also failed to show any traditional harm under *Ramirez* and *Huber*, reasoning that the mere receipt of a misleading statement, or even confusion, without any further consequence was insufficient for standing purposes. *Id.* at

237–38. Accordingly, the Third Circuit vacated the district court's orders compelling arbitration and denying vacatur of the arbitration award with instructions to dismiss the case for lack of standing. *Id.* at 240.

In *Clemens v. ExecuPharm Inc.,* 48 F.4th 146, 152 (3d Cir. 2022) (*Clemens*), the Third Circuit also addressed standing based on an alleged increased risk of future harm that a plaintiff claimed existed from the known misuse of her personal information following a data breach. In addressing the injury-in-fact requirement for standing, the *Clemens* Court refined its decision in *Reilly v. Ceridian Corp.*, 664 F.3d 38 (3d Cir. 2011) (*Reilly*) and declared that did not "create a bright line rule precluding standing based on the alleged risk of identity theft or fraud." 48 F.4th at 153. Instead, the *Clemens* Court stated that *Reilly* required "consideration of whether an injury is present versus future, and imminent versus hypothetical." *Id.* In this regard, the *Clemens* Court noted that allegations of future injury will suffice for purpose of standing only if there is "a realistic danger of sustaining a direct injury in the future." *Id.* (quoting *Pennell v. City of San Jose,* 485 U.S. 1, 8 (1988)). In other words, the *Clemens* Court recognized that the possibility of a future injury, even if reasonably likely to occur, will not suffice. *Id.*

With regard to the imminence of a future injury, the *Clemens* Court identified three factors courts consider when determining if an injury-in-fact is imminent: (1) whether the data breach was intentional; (2) whether the data was misused; and (3) whether the nature of the information accessed through the data breach could subject a plaintiff to a risk of identity theft. *Id.* at 153–54.

In addition to an injury-in-fact being imminent, the *Clemens* Court reiterated that the injury-in-fact must be concrete. In other words, it must be "real, and not abstract." *Id.* at 154 (quoting *Spokeo, Inc. v. Robins*, 578 U.S. 330, 340 (2016)). And, while the *Clemens* Court acknowledged that allegations of intangible harms arising from a data breach can be concrete, including an increased risk of future identity theft or fraud under certain circumstances, it also made clear that when the allegations are a risk of future injury, a court also must consider the type of relief being sought. *Id.* (citing *TransUnion LLC v. Ramirez*, 141 S. Ct. 2190, 2200 (2021)). For example, if the relief being sought is injunctive relief, a risk of future harm alone will qualify as concrete when it "is sufficiently imminent and substantial." *Id.* at 155 (quoting *Ramirez,* 141 S. Ct. at 2210). However, if the relief being sought is monetary, the *Clemens* Court noted that something more is required in the form of evidence that the future risk of harm caused a plaintiff to suffer a separate concrete harm, such as emotional distress, or out-of-pocket mitigation expenses, such as credit monitoring. *Id.* at 156.

Relying on *Clemens*, courts have delved deeper into standing for injunctive and equitable relief. In *Kimball v. Volkswagen Grp. of Am., Inc.*, 2024 U.S. Dist. LEXIS 158485, 2024 WL 4038171 (D.N.J. Sept. 3, 2024), the plaintiff brought a putative class action for violations of the California Consumers Legal Remedies Act and unfair competition law arising from an alleged engine defect present in certain Audi and Volkswagen vehicles. The court granted defendant's motion to dismiss plaintiff's claims for injunctive and equitable relief for lack of standing. As to the injunctive relief claim, the court found that plaintiff was not at risk of future harm of purchasing new class vehicles from defendant in light of the "lengths at which she has alleged [d]efendant's fraudulent and deceptive practices. . . . "[S]uch a request for injunctive relief therefore amounts to a 'stop me before I buy again claim' that precludes Article III standing." 2024 U.S. Dist. LEXIS 158485 at *7, 2024 WL 4038171 at *3 (citation omitted). The equitable relief claim for alleged past harm was similarly rejected by the court because plaintiff failed to allege and establish that there was no adequate alternative remedy at law. 2024 U.S. Dist. LEXIS 158485 at *8–9, 2024 WL 4038171 at *4.

As to monetary relief, the Third Circuit recently analyzed what constitutes a concrete financial injury-in-fact in the wake of *Ramirez*. In *Lewis v. GEICO*, 98 F.4th 452, 460–61 (3d Cir. 2024), the Third Circuit held that plaintiffs did not have standing to sue GEICO, on grounds that they were financially harmed by the insurer's application of a downward condition adjustment in the valuation of their car, because the company ultimately paid them more than the value of that alleged harm. The vendor GEICO retained to evaluate the value of the totalled car initially applied a downward condition adjustment of $1,006, the harm that the plaintiffs alleged. *Id.* at 460. However, the vendor also applied an upward adjustment of $886 because of the car's above-average condition, and the plaintiffs ultimately negotiated a $1,200 upward settlement adjustment with GEICO. *Id.* The plaintiffs alleged that they sustained a "quintessential financial injury" when GEICO paid them less than their car was worth as a result of the condition adjustment and might have paid them even more if the condition adjustment was not applied. *Id.* Vacating the district court's order and remanding with instructions to dismiss, the Third Circuit found that the named plaintiffs "stake[d] their claim on an isolated intermediate step within GEICO's valuation process, but they ultimately avoided any financial injury." *Id.* at 460. Even if the downward adjustment the plaintiffs challenged were illegal, the plaintiffs could not rely on such a "'bare procedural violation[], divorced from any concrete harm.'" *Id.* at 461. Additionally, "conjecture about how a negotiation might have played out" had it not been for that adjustment was "too speculative to confer standing." *Id.*

As a foil to *Lewis*, a district court recently analyzed the confines of a sufficient particularized monetary injury to confer Article III standing. In *Budet v. Rutgers Business School*, 2024 U.S. Dist. LEXIS 121782, 2024 WL 3371408 (D.N.J. July 11, 2024), *appeal filed* (No. 24-2316), a graduate of Rutgers' part-time MBA program filed a putative class action lawsuit against Rutgers Business School alleging Rutgers manipulated employment data of its full-time MBA program to boost the program's rankings and increase enrollment in all programs. Plaintiff claimed that he was entitled to a refund of the difference between what he paid Rutgers and what he would have paid if he enrolled in other unranked or lower ranked programs because but for the "tainted rankings," he would have selected a different program and he would not have agreed to pay Rutgers' premium tuition. 2024 U.S. Dist. LEXIS 121782 at *11–12, 2024 WL 3371408 at *4. In granting defendant's motion to dismiss, the court held that plaintiff lacked standing because Budet could not allege he suffered a concrete and particularized injury traceable to Rutgers' reporting since his alleged injuries were tied solely to Rutgers' rankings—which had remained unchanged despite the allegedly false reporting—and no "demonstrable diminution in the true value of Budet's education or degree" had been shown. 2024 U.S. Dist. LEXIS 121782 at *14–15, 2024 WL 3371408 at *5. According to the court, all that had changed since learning of Rutgers' reporting was Budet's subjective value of his degree. 2024 U.S. Dist. LEXIS 121782 at *15, 2024 WL 3371408 at *5. "Without showing how he was injured, Budet cannot establish an ascertainable loss, even where the benefit that catalyzed his bargain with Rutgers was tainted." 2024 U.S. Dist. LEXIS 121782 at *18, 2024 WL 3371408 at *8.

Two additional Third Circuit cases provide further guidance on standing. In *Long v. SEPTA*, 903 F.3d 312 (3d Cir. 2018), the court examined whether the plaintiff had standing to pursue class claims related to the defendant's alleged violation of the Fair Credit Reporting Act's requirements that a potential employer provide the plaintiff with (1) a copy of any consumer report that caused an adverse employment decision and (2) a description of the employee's rights under the FCRA. The court held that the plaintiff had standing to pursue the FCRA claim based on his failure to receive a copy of the relevant consumer report for two reasons. First, Congress clearly expressed an intent to make the injury associated with failure to receive a consumer report redressable, providing a right to receive the report before adverse action is taken and for statutory damages for non-compliance. *Id.* at 323. In addition, failure to provide the report was "analogous" to "three types of privacy torts" recognized at common law related to "interference with an individual's ability to control his personal information." *Id.* at 324. By contrast, because the plaintiff could not demonstrate any actual injury associated with the potential employer's failure to provide the required FCRA notice—after all, the plaintiff pursued his right by filing the class action complaint—the court concluded that the potential employer's technical statutory violation did not give rise to standing for the notice-related claim. *Id.* at 325. The court explained its seeming departure from *Horizon*'s holding that standing could rest on an injury that Congress made redressable by noting that *Horizon* and the court's early efforts to apply *Spokeo* all involved privacy statutes with historical common law analogs. *Id.* at 322.

In *Kamal v. J. Crew Group, Inc.*, 918 F.3d 102 (3d Cir. 2019), the court more explicitly walked back its earlier pronouncements that a harm sufficient to create standing could be created *either* by analogy to a common law tort *or* by Congressional intent, no matter the historical analog. Specifically, the court held that "in *Horizon*, it was the alleged [statutory] injury's close relationship to a traditional harm that showed it was sufficiently concrete to create standing." *Id.* at 115. The plaintiff in *Kamal* argued that he had standing to pursue claims against the defendant for printing too many digits of his credit card number on a receipt, which violated the Fair and Accurate Credit Transactions Act of 2003 (FACTA). The Third Circuit rejected the argument because the connection between a credit card receipt with a few too many digits and the traditional harm associated with loss of privacy was too speculative, notwithstanding that a technical violation of FACTA had occurred. *Id.* at 116. Whereas a named plaintiff must generally have standing to bring suit, it is less settled "whether, pre-class certification, named plaintiffs are required to establish standing for each and every claim set forth in a class action complaint, or whether it is sufficient to establish standing for a single claim." *Magnesium Oxide*, 2011 U.S. Dist. LEXIS 121373, at *25–26, 2011 WL 5008090, at *8 (D.N.J. Oct. 20, 2011). The Third Circuit has not resolved the question, and district courts within the circuit have reached opposite conclusions. For example, in *In re Ductile Iron Pipe Fittings Indirect Purchaser Antitrust Litigation*, the court held that "at least one plaintiff [must] demonstrate standing for each claim asserted in the complaint prior to class certification." No. 12-169, 2013 U.S. Dist. LEXIS 142466, at *34–35, 2013 WL 5503308, at *11 (D.N.J. Oct. 2, 2013). By contrast, in *In re Hypodermic Prods. Antitrust Litigation*, the court concluded that whether the named plaintiff has standing to allege violations of state laws in states other than those in which the named plaintiff was injured arises only if class certification is granted. No. 05-1602, 2007 U.S. Dist. LEXIS 47438, at *57, 2007 WL 1959225, at *15 (D.N.J. June 29, 2007); *see also In re Generic Pharm. Pricing Antitrust Litig.*, 368 F. Supp. 3d 814, 831 (E.D. Pa. 2019) (reviewing decisions of district courts within the Third Circuit and other circuit courts and concluding that "[b]ecause the state law claims of the named [plaintiffs] largely parallel those of the putative class members, it is both proper and more efficient to consider whether they may pursue their claims on behalf of the unnamed class members in the context of the class certification analysis"). The Third Circuit has hinted in *dicta* that it may prefer the former approach. *See Neale*, 794 F.3d at 359 ("Standing requires that the party seeking to invoke federal jurisdiction 'demonstrate standing for each claim he seeks to press.'" (quoting *DaimlerChrysler Corp. v. Cuno*, 547 U.S. 332, 352 (2006)).

While a party must generally experience a harm to have standing, assignment of a claim alters that analysis. In *Wallach v. Eaton Corp.*, 837 F.3d 356 (3d Cir. 2016), the Third Circuit resolved whether a class member's assignment of its federal antitrust claims to an entity that was not within the class definition conveyed standing to the non-member entity despite the fact that the assignment was not supported by consideration. Applying federal common law, the court held that an assignment is valid as long as it is written and express, "with or without consideration." *Id.* at 371.

Absent Class Member Standing

The Third Circuit held in 2015 that absent class members need not have standing for the case to proceed: "We now squarely hold that unnamed, putative class members need not establish Article III standing" and that "the 'cases or controversies' requirement is satisfied so long as a class representative has standing, whether in the context of a settlement or litigation class." *Neale*, 794 F.3d at 362. The court further explained in *Mielo v. Steak 'N Shake Operations, Inc.*, 897 F.3d 467 (3d Cir. 2018), that "the standing inquiry must be limited to a consideration of the class representatives themselves" and whether the class representatives had standing to pursue their individual claims. *Id.* at 480 (rejecting defendant's argument that named plaintiffs lacked standing to pursue claims under Americans with Disabilities Act associated with facilities not visited by named plaintiffs because such a challenge should be addressed in the context of Rule 23, not Article III).

More recently, *Huber v. Simon's Agency, Inc.*, 84 F.4th 132, 154 (3d Cir. 2023), declined the defendant's invitation to depart from *Neale* and *Mielo* based on *Ramirez*'s purported requirement that each unnamed class member have standing for a class action to present a justiciable case or controversy. The court reasoned that *Ramirez*, 141 S. Ct. at 2208, "suggests that the need for unnamed class members to demonstrate Article III standing depends on the stage of litigation. At the remedial phase, each class member must establish standing to recover individual damages. By contrast, at the class certification stage, the standing of individual class members may inform whether a proposed class satisfies the requirements of Federal Rule of Civil Procedure 23, but it is not necessary for each member to prove his or her standing for the class action to be justiciable." *Id.* at 155 (internal citations omitted). Therefore, the Third Circuit opted to abide by *Neale*'s precept that a class action presents a justiciable case or controversy as long as a named class representative has standing, noting that "[o]ur cases since *TransUnion* have similarly hewed to *Neale* and *Mielo*, albeit without explicitly grappling with the Supreme Court's remarks on standing in class actions." *Id.* (citing *Boley v. Universal Health Servs., Inc.*, 36 F.4th 124, 133 (3d Cir. 2022); *Duncan v. Governor of V.I.*, 48 F.4th 195, 203 (3d Cir. 2022); *Clemens v. ExecuPharm Inc.*, 48 F.4th 146, 153 n.4 (3d Cir. 2022)).[2]

c. Mootness Doctrine

"[S]pecial mootness rules apply in the class action context, where the named plaintiff purports to represent an interest that extends beyond his own." *Lusardi v. Xerox Corp.*, 975 F.2d 964, 974 (3d Cir. 1992). If a class has been certified, mooting the named plaintiff's claim does not moot all class claims because the class "acquire[s] a legal status separate from the interest asserted by [the named plaintiff]." *Weiss v. Regal Collections*, 385 F.3d 337, 342 (3d Cir. 2004) (quoting *Sosna v. Iowa*, 419 U.S. 393, 399 (1975)). Ordinarily, before certification, when the named plaintiff's claims become moot, a court must dismiss the action. *Lusardi*, 975 F.2d at 974–75 (citing cases). This does not mean that a defendant can pick off a class representative early in the case by settling for a small amount. In *Whitefield v. Nationstar Mortgage*, the Court applied the "picking off exception" to mootness and found that at the pre-certification stage class claims are not mooted by a class representative's settlement of the individual claim. 434 F. Supp. 238, 242–43 (E.D. Pa. 2020) (holding that pre-certification class claims were not mooted even though the named plaintiff's claims were settled and recognizing that the "picking off exception" to mootness prevents a defendant repeatedly buying off the small individual claims of the named plaintiffs to prevent certification from occurring).

Nor does the mooting of a named plaintiff's case after certification is sought (but before it is decided) dispose of the putative class's claims. "[I]n certain circumstances, 'class claims can breathe life into an otherwise moot case' and permit an individual plaintiff to continue seeking class certification." *LaSpina v. SEIU Penn. State Council*, 985 F.3d 278, 290 (3d Cir. Jan. 5, 2021). As the Third Circuit explained in *LaSpina*, "when a plaintiff files a motion to certify a class when his individual claim is still live, the mooting of that claim while the motion is pending permits the court to decide the certification motion. In that case, the plaintiff remains able to vigorously press the class's claim." *Id.* However, where a plain-

[2] An example of the application of standing under *Neale* and *Mielo* occurred in *Back2Health Chiropractic Ctr., LLC v. Sentinel Ins. Co., Ltd.*, No. 20-6717 (JMV-MF), 2021 U.S. Dist. LEXIS 47791, at *16–19, 2021 WL 960875, at *6–7 (D.N.J. Mar. 15, 2021). There, the District of New Jersey applied the holdings from *Neale* and *Mielo* directly to named class members and held that "as long as the named plaintiff has standing, it can bring claims on behalf of a nationwide class." *Id.* at 2021 U.S. Dist. LEXIS 47791, at *16–19, 2021 WL 960875, at *6–7.

tiff has not yet moved for class certification and his claim is mooted, the lack of a personal stake in the outcome can render the named plaintiff "a particularly inappropriate class representative." *Id.* ("Because LaSpina's individual claim is moot and she has not filed for class certification, the class claims do not survive either.").

3. PLEADING CONSIDERATIONS

In a putative class action, courts within the Third Circuit generally permit a plaintiff to conduct discovery relevant to Rule 23 class certification requirements rather than dismiss class allegations at the pleading stage. To dismiss class claims before discovery, a court must conclude that the "complaint itself demonstrates that the requirements for maintaining a class action cannot be met." *See Landsman & Funk PC v. Skinder-Strauss Assocs.*, 640 F.3d 72, 93 n.30 (3d Cir. 2011), *opinion vacated in part on other grounds*, No. 09-3105, 2012 U.S. App. LEXIS 11946, 2012 WL 2052685 (3d Cir. Apr. 17, 2012). District courts have interpreted this language to mean that a motion to strike class allegations should be granted only when "no amount of discovery or time will allow for plaintiffs to resolve deficiencies in class definitions under Rule 23." *McPeak v. S-L Distrib. Co., Inc.*, No. 12-348, 2014 U.S. Dist. LEXIS 123728, at *9, 10, 2014 WL 4388562, at *4 (D.N.J. Sept. 5, 2014) ("If the viability of a class depends on factual matters that must be developed through discovery, a motion to strike will be denied pending the full-blown certification motion." (quotation marks omitted)); *accord Zarichny v. Complete Payment Recovery Servs.*, 80 F. Supp. 3d 610, 615–16 (E.D. Pa. 2015). This was the case in *Mladenov v. Wegmans Food Mkts., Inc.,* 124 F. Supp. 3d 360, 369–70 (D.N.J. 2015), where the court struck class allegations at the motion to dismiss stage because the Complaint revealed Plaintiffs could not satisfy the requirements under Fed. R. Civ. P. 23(b)(2) on the grounds that the complaint primarily sought monetary damages, and could not satisfy the requirements under Fed. R. Civ. P. 23(b)(3) as there was no way to ascertain class members.

Concluding that most motions to strike class allegations are premature makes sense in light of other Third Circuit precedent. The Third Circuit's 2008 decision in *In re Hydrogen Peroxide Antitrust Litigation*, 552 F.3d 305 (3d Cir. 2008), requires that a lower court conduct a "rigorous analysis" to determine whether the requirements of Rule 23 have been satisfied. *Id.* at 309. Although it did not expressly require discovery to evaluate all class allegations, the Third Circuit reiterated that a "court may 'delve beyond the pleadings to determine whether the requirements for class certification are satisfied.'" *Id.* at 316 (quoting *Newton v. Merrill Lynch, Pierce, Fenner & Smith, Inc.*, 259 F.3d 154, 167 (3d Cir. 2001)). In the Third Circuit, except in rare circumstances, district courts will hold that it is "appropriate . . . that the class action process should be able to 'play out' according to the directives of Rule 23 and should permit due deliberation by the parties and the court on the class certification issues" following class-related discovery. *Weiss*, 385 F.3d at 347–48.

4. PREREQUISITES

Much of the Third Circuit precedent regarding the appropriateness of class certification follows the oft-cited refrain that "[t]he class action is an exception to the usual rule that litigation is conducted by and on behalf of the individual named parties only." *Modafinil*, 837 F.3d at 248 (quoting *Wal-Mart Stores, Inc. v. Dukes*, 564 U.S. 338, 348 (2011)). To warrant certification, a "class action must satisfy the four requirements of Rule 23(a) and the requirements of either Rule 23(b)(1), (2), or (3)." *Marcus v. BMW of N. Am., LLC*, 687 F.3d 583, 590 (3d Cir. 2012). A case merits class treatment only when a plaintiff establishes the required elements of Rule 23 by a preponderance of the evidence, "not merely a 'threshold showing' by a party." *In re Insulin Pricing Litig.*, 2024 U.S. Dist. LEXIS 19894 at *51, 2024 WL 416500 at *14 (D.N.J. Jan. 25, 2024), *appeal filed* (No. 24-8002) (citation omitted). *See Hydrogen Peroxide*, 552 F.3d at 320 ("[T]o certify a class the district court must find that the evidence more likely than not establishes each fact necessary to meet the requirements of Rule 23." (citation omitted)); *see also Mielo*, 897 F.3d at 483–84 ("We repeat (hopefully for the last time) the 'relaxed' Rule 23 standard suggested in *Eisenberg* [*v. Gagnon*, 766 F.2d 770, 785 (3d Cir. 1985)] is no longer the law of this circuit" and that Rule 23 "calls for a rigorous analysis in which '[f]actual determinations supporting Rule 23 findings must be made by a preponderance of the evidence.'" (quoting *Hydrogen Peroxide*, 552 F.3d at 307)); *Reyes v. Netdeposit, LLC*, 802 F.3d 469, 485 (3d Cir. 2015) (in case where district court required excessive proof, stressing "that the preponderance of the evidence standard governs. The perfection of proof that the District Court demanded here is simply not required").

The Third Circuit's rigorous analysis requirement mandates that lower courts thoroughly examine "the factual and legal allegations," which may "include a preliminary inquiry into the merits." *Hydrogen Peroxide*, 552 F.3d at 317 (quoting *Newton*, 259 F.3d at 166, 168). The analysis may "involve[] judging credibility, weighing evidence, or deciding issues that overlap with the merits of a plaintiff's claims." *In re Insulin*, 2024 U.S. Dist. LEXIS 19894 at *52, 2024 WL 416500 at *14. This standard invites courts to reach conclusions regarding the merits at the class certification stage when necessary. *Id.* at 316. "An overlap between a class certification requirement and the merits of a claim is no reason to decline to resolve relevant disputes when necessary to determine whether a class certification requirement is met." *Id.* at 316–17; *see, e.g.*, *In re Citizens Bank, N.A.*, 15 F.4th 607, 616 (3d Cir. 2021) (rejecting "trial-before-certification" approach in hybrid FLSA opt-in collective action and state-law Rule 23 opt-out class action because "[s]uch a procedural sequence would be ignoring Rule 23's text and history, flouting Supreme Court precedent, and departing from the case law of seven circuits while undercutting four others"). A court must not only perform a rigorous analysis, but it must also show its work: "Although a motion for class certification presents a discretionary question for a district court, the court 'must clearly articulate its reasons, in part, so [the Third Circuit] can adequately review the certification decision on appeal under Rule 23(f).'" *Neale v. Volvo Cars of N. Am., LLC*, 794 F.3d 353, 369 (3d Cir. 2015) (quoting *Beck v. Maximus, Inc.*, 457 F.3d 291, 297 (3d Cir. 2006)).

Lower courts also must examine expert testimony carefully and may reach conclusions regarding whether to rely on such testimony. Analysis of expert testimony is "not only permissible; it may be integral to the rigorous analysis Rule 23 demands." *Id.* To the extent a defendant challenges the admissibility of the plaintiff's expert report as part of its general opposition to a motion for class certification, the court's "rigorous analysis" must include an evaluation of the expert testimony under *Daubert*. *In re Blood Reagents Antitrust Litig.*, 783 F.3d 183, 187 (3d Cir. 2015) ("[A] plaintiff cannot rely on challenged expert testimony, when critical to class certification, to demonstrate conformity with Rule 23 unless the plaintiff also demonstrates, and the trial court finds, that the expert testimony satisfies the standard set out in *Daubert*."); *see also Cole's Wexford Hotel v. Highmark Inc.*, No. 10-1609, 2019 U.S. Dist. LEXIS 32573, at *19–21, 2019 WL 988655, at *2 (W.D. Pa. Mar. 1, 2019) (finding motion for class certification "premature" when defendant's opposition centered on challenge to plaintiff's expert's reliability, but defendant did not move to exclude opinion under *Daubert*). Importantly, however, a defendant need not explicitly raise a *Daubert* challenge to trigger a lower court's obligation to weigh "conflicting expert testimony at the certification stage," which is "integral to the rigorous analysis Rule 23 demands." *Hydrogen Peroxide*, 552 F.3d at 323. Rather, "opinion testimony should not be uncritically accepted as establishing a Rule 23 requirement merely because the court holds the testimony should not be excluded, under *Daubert* or for any other reason." *Id.*; *see also Comcast*, 569 U.S. at 32 n.4 (holding that *Daubert* goes to admissibility, not to whether injury is susceptible to classwide proof).

Recently, courts have outlined the two-step analysis to admitting expert opinion—whether offered by a party seeking class certification or by a party opposing it—where the reliability the opinion is challenged on class certification before analyzing whether Federal Rule of Civil Procedure requirements have been met: (1) whether the party's challenges bear upon "those aspects of [the] expert testimony offered to satisfy Rule 23" and (2) if so, whether the opinion is admissible as to those aspects under Federal Rule of Evidence 702 and *Daubert*." *Johnson v. Comodo Grp., Inc.*, 2024 U.S. Dist. LEXIS 103430 at *8–9, 2024 WL 2933195 at *4 (D.N.J. June 10, 2024) (citation omitted). The Federal Rules of Evidence embrace a liberal policy of admissibility, including with respect to expert testimony, and districts act as gatekeepers responsible for "ensuring that an expert's testimony both rests on a reliable foundation and is relevant to the task at hand." 2024 U.S. Dist. LEXIS 103430 at *9, 2024 WL 2933195 at *4 (citations omitted). The test of the admissibility of expert testimony is not whether a particular scientific opinion has the best foundation, or even whether the opinion is supported by the best methodology or unassailable research; instead, the court looks to whether the expert's testimony is supported by good grounds, i.e. it is "based on valid reasoning and reliable methodology." *In re Insulin Pricing Litig.*, 2024 U.S. Dist. LEXIS 19894 at *34, 2024 WL 416500 at *9 (D.N.J. Jan. 25, 2024) (citations and quotation marks omitted). "The court must consider whether: (1) the expert is qualified; (2) the expert's testimony is reliable; and (3) the expert's testimony is helpful to the trier of fact, i.e., it must 'fit' the facts of the case." 2024 U.S. Dist. LEXIS 103430 at *9–10, 2024 WL 2933195 at *4 (citations omitted). "The proponent of the expert testimony must prove these requirements by a preponderance of the evidence." *Id.* While the standard for reliability is "not that high," an expert's opinion must be based on the methods and procedures of science rather than on subjective belief or unsupported speculation to be considered reliable under FRE 702; the expert must have good grounds for his or her belief." 2024 U.S. Dist. LEXIS 19894 at *35, 2024 WL 416500 at *10. In deciding whether the proposed expert testimony is reliable, the court should examine:

> (1) whether a method consists of a testable hypothesis; (2) whether the method has been subject to peer review; (3) the known or potential rate of error; (4) the existence and maintenance of standards controlling the technique's operation; (5) whether the method is generally accepted; (6) the relationship of the technique to methods which have been established to be reliable; (7) the qualifications of the expert witness testifying based on the methodology; and (8) the non-judicial uses to which the method has been put.

2024 U.S. Dist. LEXIS 19894 at *35–36, 2024 WL 416500 at *10 (quoting *In re Paoli R.R. Yard PCB Litig.*, 35 F.3d 717, 742 n.8 (3d Cir. 1994)). "[T]he reliability analysis applies to all aspects of an expert's testimony: the methodology, the facts underlying the expert's opinion, and the link between the facts and the conclusion, *et alia*." *Id.* (citation omitted). *See, e.g., id.*, 2024 U.S. Dist. LEXIS 19894 at *36–44, 2024 WL 416500 at *10–12 (partially granting and denying motion to exclude expert testimony where expert's methodology was reliable for identifying significant trend changes but not for determining the causation or legality of defendants' actions).

Expert opinions may also be excluded pursuant to Federal Rule of Civil Procedure 26. In *Johnson v. Comodo Grp., Inc.*, the defendant argued that an expert report should be excluded because it significantly changed her prior opinions and attempted to rectify her deposition testimony. 2024 U.S. Dist. LEXIS 103430 at *19, 2024 WL 2933195 at *8. Plaintiff countered that the declaration corrected an error in the class notice list, reducing the number of names and addresses from 15,476 to 12,757, and was consistent with the expert's original methods for identifying class members. *Id.* The court noted that under Federal Rule of Civil Procedure 26(a)(2)(B), expert reports must fully disclose all opinions and their bases, and any supplementation must follow Rule 26(e) if the information is found to be incomplete or incorrect. 2024 U.S. Dist. LEXIS 103430 at *19–20, 2024 WL 2933195 at *8. Although recognizing that courts generally reject attempts to introduce new opinions or information contradictory to that set forth in the expert report under the guise of supplementation, the court held that the expert's declaration was an elaboration of, and consistent with, her previous opinions. 2024 U.S. Dist. LEXIS 103430 at *20–24, 2024 WL 2933195 at *9–10. Accordingly, the court ruled that the declaration was permissible under Rule 26(e) and denied defendant's motion to exclude.

a. Rule 23(a) Requirements

Numerosity

In the Third Circuit, a plaintiff presumptively establishes that "the class is so numerous that joinder of all members is impracticable," thus satisfying Rule 23(a)(1), if "the potential number of plaintiffs exceeds 40." *Stewart v. Abraham*, 275 F.3d 220, 226–27 (3d Cir. 2001). Although the appellate court has not yet "specif[ied] a 'floor' at which a putative class will fail to satisfy the numerosity requirement," it cited leading treatises that "recognize[] the general rule that a class of 20 or fewer is usually insufficiently numerous." *In re Modafinil*, 837 F.3d at 250; *but see Grant v. Sullivan*, 131 F.R.D. 436 (M.D. Pa. 1990) (certifying a class of 14 members seeking injunctive and declaratory relief related to a government benefits program).

In recent years, the Third Circuit has embraced more stringent evidentiary requirements for establishing the number of class members, a change that some courts suggest stems from the Supreme Court's insistence on rigor in the Rule 23 analysis in *Dukes*. *See, e.g.*, *In re Insulin*, 2024 U.S. Dist. LEXIS 19894 at *67, 2024 WL 416500 at *18 ("[A] plaintiff must present evidence for the court to make a factual determination on whether the numerosity requirement is met.") (citation omitted); *Frompovicz v. Niagara Bottling, LLC*, 420 F. Supp. 3d 361, 369 (E.D. Pa. 2019) (holding that plaintiff failed to adduce sufficient evidence to meet numerosity requirement); *Wilson v. Consol. Rail Corp. (In re Paulsboro Derailment Cases)*, No. 13-784, 2014 U.S. Dist. LEXIS 115542, at *34, 2014 WL 4162790, at *9 (D.N.J. Aug. 20, 2014). Under these more stringent requirements, "[m]ere speculation as to the number of class members—even if such speculation is a bet worth making—cannot support a finding of numerosity." *Hayes v. Wal-Mart Stores, Inc.*, 725 F.3d 349, 357 (3d Cir. 2013) (quotation marks omitted); *see also Mielo*, 897 F.3d at 486 (in case brought on behalf of disabled individuals with accessibility claims against restaurant chain, rejecting numerosity argument premised on total number of disabled people in United States, speculation by restaurant chain executive that "thousands of people with disabilities" used facilities each year, and common sense); *Allen v. Ollie's Bargain Outlet, Inc.*, 37 F.4th 890, 897 (3d Cir. 2022) (in case brought on behalf of disabled individuals with accessibility claims against large retailer, rejecting numerosity argument based on statistical census data, extrapolation that thousands of individuals with mobility impairments resided in the zip codes of two Ollie's stores left "no basis to determine what portion" were Ollie's customers, "let alone what portion have suffered a common ADA injury"). Generally, estimates are acceptable only when bolstered by "sufficient circumstantial evidence specific to the products, problems, parties, and geographic areas actually covered by the class definition to allow a district court to make a factual finding." *Marcus*, 687 F.3d at 593 ("Only then may the court rely on 'common sense' to forgo precise calculations and exact numbers.").

While the number of class members may give rise to certain presumptions in the numerosity context, all classes, no matter their size, must satisfy Rule 23(a)(1)'s requirement that joinder of all members be impracticable. In 2016, the Third Circuit set forth a non-exhaustive list of factors relevant to that determination: "judicial economy, the claimants' ability and motivation to litigate as joined plaintiffs, the financial resources of class members, the geographic dispersion of class members, the ability to identify future claimants, and whether the claims are for injunctive relief or for damages." *In re Modafinil*, 837 F.3d at 253. The appellate court stressed that "judicial economy and the ability to litigate as joined parties are of primary importance" and chastised the district court for (1) considering the time already spent litigating the case as a class action as a reason to certify the class under the judicial economy rubric and (2) not considering the ability of individual class members to pursue their claims through joinder, rather than through individual actions. *Id.* at 253–54, 258. Although the court recognized that numerosity "calls for an inherently fact-based analysis that requires a district court judge to 'take into account the context of the particular case,' thereby providing district courts considerable discretion in making numerosity determinations," a lower court abuses its discretion when it considers issues that "have no place in the numerosity requirement." *Id.* at 249–50; *see also King Drug Co. of Florence v. Cephalon, Inc.*, No. 2:06-cv-1797, 2017 U.S. Dist. LEXIS 137601, at *11, 2017 WL 3705715, at *1 (E.D. Pa. Aug. 28, 2017) (on remand from *Modafinil*, applying factors and denying class certification).

Commonality

"There is a low threshold for satisfying Rule 23(a)'s commonality requirement." *In re Insulin Pricing Litig.*, 2024 U.S. Dist. LEXIS 19894 at *69, 2024 WL 416500 at *19 (citation omitted). Commonality does not require all putative class members to have identical claims. 2024 U.S. Dist. LEXIS 19894 at *70–71, 2024 WL 416500 at *20 (citation omitted). In *Dukes*, the Supreme Court clarified the commonality analysis required by Rule 23(a)(2) in at least two important ways. First, it held that commonality means plaintiffs must "demonstrate that the class members have suffered the same injury," which requires more than a determination that class members "have all suffered a violation of the same provision of the law." *Id.* at 349–50 (quotation marks omitted). When a statute can be violated in multiple ways, for example, class members share a common injury only where the statute was violated in the same way as to each member. *Id. Dukes* also clarified that a court should not consider "common questions but rather the capacity of a classwide proceeding to generate common *answers* apt to drive the resolution of the litigation." 564 U.S. at 350 (quotation marks omitted).

The Third Circuit easily applied the first *Dukes* principle in *Mielo*, concluding that a proposed class of "[a]ll persons with qualified mobility disabilities who were or will be denied the full and equal enjoyment of the goods, services, facilities, privileges, advantages or accommodations of any Steak 'n Shake restaurant location in the United States on the basis of a disability because such persons encountered accessibility barriers at any Steak 'n Shake restaurant" was too broad to permit a commonality finding. 897 F.3d at 487–88. "One person, for example, might allege that Steak 'n Shake violated the ADA by failing to correct a steep slope in a parking facility, while other class members might allege that Steak 'n Shake violated the ADA by failing to replace inaccessible door hardware, by failing to widen bathroom doors, or by failing to replace inaccessible water fountains." *Id.* at 490. These claims would be "so widely divergent that they would be better pursued on either an individual basis or by a sufficiently numerous class of similarly-aggrieved patrons." *Id.*; *see also S.R. v. Pa. Dep't of Human Servs.*, 325 F.R.D. 103, 110 (M.D. Pa. 2018) (applying same principle but concluding that plaintiffs met the commonality prong with allegations of "systemic deficiencies in the availability of placements and services" that caused "each violation of Title XIX [and] discrimination under the ADA and Section 504," which amounted to "exactly the type of 'common mode' or practice predicating each alleged violation that was noticeably absent from *Dukes*").

Similar to *Mielo*, in *Allen v. Ollie's Bargain Outlet, Inc.*, the Third Circuit held that a proposed class of "disabled individual[s] who shop[] at any Ollie's store in the United States and has or will encounter interior access barriers" did not satisfy the commonality requirement because it was geographically overbroad. 37 F.4th 890, 900 (3d Cir. 2022). In that case, the plaintiffs claimed that the retailer had nationwide store layout policies which created "inaccessible interior aisles" for disabled individuals needing wheelchairs. *Id.* at 901. The district court granted certification, concluding that "[i]f Ollie's policies and procedures do, in fact, cause access barriers to unlawfully restrict individuals with disabilities from obtaining their desired goods, then proposed members who endured violations have suffered the same injury." *Id.* However, the Third Circuit ruled "stitching together a corporate-wide class requires more" than showing "that [the defendant] has corporate policies and that some or all stores in Pennsylvania pay inadequate attention to aisle accessibility." *Id.* Since the plaintiffs' evidence of inaccessible aisles was limited to Pennsylvania, it could not be determined whether the store's visual standards caused discrimination "in some regions" but not others. *Id.* at 902. Evidence from one state was not sufficient to support "[p]roceeding on a corporate-wide basis against a corporation with over four hundred stores in twenty-nine states." *Id.*

Until more recently, *Dukes*' "common answer" principle has been less reliably adopted, with both the Third Circuit and its district courts continuing to cite pre-*Dukes* cases for the proposition that commonality requires a common question. *E.g.*, *Rodriguez v. Nat'l City Bank*, 726 F.3d 372, 382 (3d Cir. 2013) ("A putative class satisfies Rule 23(a)'s commonality requirement if 'the named plaintiffs share at least one question of fact or law with the grievances of the prospective class.'") (citing *Baby Neal v. Casey*, 43 F.3d 48, 56 (3d Cir. 1994)). But that post-*Dukes* focus on common questions instead of common answers has abated. In *Ferreras v. American Airlines, Inc.*, 946 F.3d 178, 185 (3d Cir. Dec. 24, 2019), the Third Circuit explicitly applied the *Dukes*' "common answer" analysis in holding that whether employees were being compensated for all hours worked and whether the defendant was in violation of New Jersey law were not questions that can "generate common *answers* apt to drive the resolution of the litigation." *Id.* at 185 (quoting *Dukes*, 564 U.S. at 350).

Moreover, even before *Ferreras* was decided, the Third Circuit's post-*Dukes* focus on "common questions" did not appear to be a meaningful break with *Dukes*. Rather, the Third Circuit seems to be endorsing the idea that questions are common when the defendant's conduct is common to all class members, necessarily yielding common evidence. Thus, in *Rodriguez*, the court likened the case before it to *Dukes*, explaining that "the exercise of broad discretion by an untold number of unique decision-makers in the making of thousands upon thousands of individual decisions undermines the class claim." 726 F.3d at 386. The court has also twice affirmed certification by distinguishing *Dukes*. In *In re Community Bank of N. Va. Mortgage Lending Practices Litigation, PNC Bank NA* (*Cmty. Bank II*), 795 F.3d 380 (3d Cir. 2015), the court drew a distinction between allegations in *Dukes* about the application of a discretionary policy, which made certification impossible, and allegations that "the class was subjected to the same kind of illegal conduct by the same entities, and that class members were harmed in the same way, albeit to potentially different extents," which in its view satisfied the commonality requirement. *Id.* at 399. Similarly, in *In re NFL Players Concussion Injury Litigation*, 821 F.3d 410 (3d Cir. 2016), the court concluded that "[t]he concerns in *Wal-Mart* do not apply here because the NFL Parties allegedly injured retired players through the same course of conduct," for "[e]ven if players' particular injuries are unique, their negligence and fraud claims still depend on the same common questions regarding the NFL's conduct." *Id.* at 427.

As the Third Circuit has attempted to incorporate *Dukes*' commonality principles, it has struggled with whether the common proof requirement allows individuals without valid claims to be part of the class. In *Sullivan*, for example, Judge Jordan dissented because the majority had affirmed certification of a settlement class that included "members who lack any claim at all." 667 F.3d at 340 (Jordan, J., dissenting). In Judge Jordan's view, "common questions" as defined by *Dukes* "are those that, because they have answers that will affect the validity of all class members' claims, can be said to be legally relevant," from which it follows that "for there to be any common questions, all class members must have at least some colorable legal claim." *Id.* at 344. The *Sullivan* majority did not go so far, but rather required only an analysis of "whether the elements of asserted claims are *capable* of proof through common evidence," not whether the claims rest on legally valid and sound conclusions. *Id.* at 305.[3]

Typicality

The typicality inquiry is intended to assess whether the action can be efficiently maintained as a class and whether the named plaintiffs have incentives that align with those of absent class members so as to ensure that the absentees' interests will be fairly represented. *Baby Neal for and by Kanter v. Casey*, 43 F.3d 48, 57 (3d Cir. 1994). Thus, to satisfy Rule 23(a)(3)'s typicality requirement in the Third Circuit, a plaintiff must show that neither his individual circumstances nor his legal claims are markedly different from the facts and laws upon which the claims of other class members will rest. *Id.* at 57–58 (citing *Hassine v. Jeffes*, 846 F.2d 169 (3d Cir. 1988)).

Although courts hold that typicality is a "low threshold" to satisfy (*In re Insulin*, 2024 U.S. Dist. LEXIS 19894, at *78, 2024 WL 416500 at *22), meeting the typicality requirement proves a surmountable hurdle for nearly all named plaintiffs within the Third Circuit. "Factual differences [between claims] will not render a claim atypical if the claim arises from the same event or practice or course of conduct that gives rise to the claims of the class members, and if it is based on the same legal theory." *Hoxworth v. Blinder, Robinson & Co., Inc.*, 980 F. 2d 912, 923 (3d Cir. 1992); *accord Boley v. Universal Health Servs., Inc.*, 36 F.4th 124, 134 (3d Cir. 2022). Thus, in *Stewart*, when an arrestee brought class claims to challenge that a city policy violated the Fourth Amendment rights of all arrestees subject to the policy, the differences in circumstances that led to the class members' arrests did not render the named plaintiff's claim atypical. 275 F.3d at 227–28.

Different potential damages are also unlikely to prevent a finding of typicality. In *Safran v. United Steelworkers of America, AFL-CIO*, 132 F.R.D. 397 (W.D. Pa. 1989), seniority differences among class members that would result in different amounts of damages did not make the named plaintiff's claims atypical where all class members had suffered at least some degree of injury from a particular contracting practice. Nor does the named plaintiff need to share all claims of the class, so long as all of the class members' claims stem from a single course of conduct. *Grasty v. Amalgamated Clothing and Textile Workers Union, AFL-CIO, CLC*, 828 F.2d 123 (3d Cir. 1987) (overruled on other grounds recognized by *Collier v. Montgomery Cty. Housing Auth.*, 192 F.R.D. 176 (E.D. Pa. 2000) and overruled on other grounds as recognized by *Fry v. Hayt, Hayt & Landau*, 198 F.R.D. 461 (E.D. Pa. 2000)). Nevertheless, variations among putative class members' *damages* or *claims*, which often do not prevent certification, should not be confused with individualized variations as to whether putative class members were *injured*, which ordinarily do prevent certification. *See In re Lamictal*, 957 F.3d at 194–95; *see also In re Suboxone (Buprenorphine Hydrochlorine & Naloxone) Antitrust Litig.*, 967 F.3d 264, 269 (3d Cir. 2020) (holding that the individualized nature of the damages inquiry did not prevent certification under Rule 23(b)(3) where injury could be shown by classwide evidence).

Despite the permitted variation in class members' claims, unique defenses may bear on the typicality of a class representative. The Third Circuit has agreed with several of its sister circuits in recognizing that "the challenge presented by a defense unique to a class representative [is that] the representative's interests might not be aligned with those of the class, and the representative might devote time and effort to the defense at the expense of issues that are common and controlling for the class." *Beck v. Maximus, Inc.*, 457 F.3d 291, 297 (3d Cir. 2006). Thus, for example, in a securities class action, the district court concluded that one named plaintiff was atypical and could not serve as the class representative because

[3] The same issues tend not to arise in the context of injunctive relief classes. *See, e.g.*, Anderson v. Penn. Dep't of Public Welfare, 1 F. Supp. 2d 456 (E.D. Pa. 1998) (certifying a class of all medical assistance recipients participating in the state's managed care program, despite the fact that the class members did not establish a common method of proving actual injury, because injunctive relief made the individual injury determinations unnecessary).

he both purchased and sold all of his shares before either of the purported misstatements. *Weikel v. Tower Semiconductor, Ltd.*, 183 F.R.D. 377, 391 (D.N.J. 1998); *see also Frompovicz v. Niagara Bottling*, 420 F. Supp. 3d 361, 371 (E.D. Pa. 2019) (holding plaintiff's susceptibility to statute of limitations defense rendered claims atypical); *Minersville Coal Co. v. Anthracite Export Ass'n*, 55 F.R.D. 426 (M.D. Pa. 1971) (named plaintiff who had signed release in defendant's favor had a conflict of interests with class members and thus was not typical); *but see Li v. Aeterna Zentaris, Inc.*, 324 F.R.D. 331, 340 (D.N.J. 2018) (rejecting defendant's attempt to defeat typicality where "unique defenses" were unlikely to "become a major focus of the litigation" given their lack of merit (quoting *Beck*, 457 F.3d at 301)).

Adequacy

"Rule 23(a)'s adequacy of representation requirement 'serves to uncover conflicts of interest between named parties and the class they seek to represent.'" *In re Insulin*, 2024 U.S. Dist. LEXIS 19894 at *85–86, 2024 WL 416500 at *24 (citation omitted). It also ensures that counsel has adequate experience, will vigorously prosecute the action, and will act at arm's length from the defendant. *Id.* (citation omitted). "Adequacy functions as a 'catch-all requirement' that tends to merge with the commonality and typicality criteria of Rule 23(a)." *Id.* (citation omitted). Mirroring the requirements in several other circuits, a plaintiff must establish both (1) that his attorney is "qualified, experienced, and generally able to conduct the proposed litigation" and (2) that he does not have "interests antagonistic to those of the class" in order to meet Rule 23(a)(4)'s adequacy requirement. *Hoxworth v. Blinder, Robinson & Co.*, 980 F.2d 912, 923 (3d Cir. 1992).

As to the first prong, "[a]lthough questions concerning the adequacy of class counsel were traditionally analyzed under the aegis of the adequate representation requirement of Rule 23(a)(4), . . . those questions have, since 2003, been governed by Rule 23(g)." *Sheinberg v. Sorensen*, 606 F.3d 130, 132 (3d Cir. 2010). That subsection lists several nonexclusive factors that a district court must consider in determining counsel's ability to represent the interests of the class, including (1) "the work counsel has done in identifying or investigating potential claims in the action"; (2) "counsel's experience in handling class actions, other complex litigation, and the types of claims asserted in the action"; (3) "counsel's knowledge of the applicable law"; and (4) "the resources that counsel will commit to representing the class." Fed. R. Civ. P. 23(g)(1)(A).

Even with this seemingly more rigorous list of requirements for class counsel, "the presumption fairly arises that all members of the bar in good standing are competent." *Zeno v. Ford Motor Co., Inc.*, 238 F.R.D. 173, 188 (W.D. Pa. 2006). Indeed, even past ethical issues serious enough to trigger disbarment have not prevented courts within this circuit from finding that class counsel would adequately serve absent class member interests as long as his license had been reinstated. *Hall v. Midland Grp.*, No. 99-3108, 2000 U.S. Dist. LEXIS 16751, at *13, 2000 WL 1725238, at *4 (E.D. Pa. Nov. 17, 2000); *but see Walter v. Palisades Collection, LLC*, No. 06-378, 2010 U.S. Dist. LEXIS 7374, at *30, 2010 WL 308978, at *9 (E.D. Pa. Jan. 26, 2010) (preventing the same attorney from serving as class counsel where he proposed to serve as co-counsel with his daughter and had engaged in the unlicensed practice of law while disbarred). Despite the strong presumptions that protect class counsel, membership by counsel and membership of counsel's law firm partner in the class have led to findings that counsel was inadequate under Rule 23(a)(4). *Fechter v. HMW Indus.*, 117 F.R.D. 362 (E.D. Pa. 1987); *Kramer v. Scientific Control Corp.*, 534 F.2d 1085 (3d Cir. 1976).

Because of the presumptions that apply to the competence of class counsel, adequacy analyses in the Third Circuit more frequently turn on "conflicts of interest between named parties and the class they seek to represent." *Drennan v. PNC Bank, NA*, 622 F.3d 275, 303 (3d Cir. 2010) (quoting *Amchem Prods. v. Windsor*, 521 U.S. 591, 625 (1997)). But not every intra-class conflict is consequential. Rather, "[a] conflict is fundamental," and therefore problematic for adequacy, "where it touches the specific issues in controversy." *Dewey v. Volkswagen Aktiengesellschaft*, 681 F.3d 170, 184 (3d Cir. 2012) (quotation marks omitted). Thus, a named plaintiff will only need "a minimal degree of knowledge" to meet the adequacy standard. *New Directions Treatment Servs. v. City of Reading*, 490 F.3d 293, 313 (3d Cir. 2007); *Duncan v. Governor of the Virgin Islands*, 48 F.4th 195, 211–12 (3d Cir. 2022) (holding that a plaintiff "need not present the type of evidence one might expect on summary judgment" because the class definition, the factual allegations in the complaint, and the relief sought are "highly indicative" of whether the putative class representative is adequate). Similarly, neither minimal financial resources nor unique motives are typically independently sufficient to render a class representative inadequate. *Wilmington Firefighters Local 1590 v. City of Wilmington*, 109 F.R.D. 89 (D. Del. 1985) ("Denial of certification [on financial resource grounds] alone is rarely appropriate"); *Dorfman v. First Boston Corp.*, 62 F.R.D. 466, 473 (E.D. Pa. 1973) ("[N]either the personality nor the motives of the plaintiffs is determinative of whether they will provide vigorous advocacy for members of the class."); *but see Frompovicz v. Niagara Bottling*, 420 F. Supp. 3d 361, 372 (E.D. Pa. 2019) ("Plaintiff's longstanding grudge against [a defendant] renders him an inadequate class representative."). By contrast, familial relationships between the class representative and class counsel have led courts to decline to certify for adequacy reasons. *E.g.*, *McDonough v. Toys R. Us, Inc.*, 638 F. Supp. 2d 461, 478 (E.D. Pa. 2009) (finding class representative inadequate because she was the sister of class counsel).

b. Rule 23(b) Requirements

Rule 23(b)(1)(A) Classes

The Third Circuit has described Rule 23(b)(1) generally as authorizing "the use of class actions when necessary to prevent potentially adverse effects of separate actions." *Beck*, 457 F.3d at 301. Subsection (b)(1)(A) specifically addresses the "possible prejudice to the party opposing the class and is intended to eliminate the possibility of separate actions imposing inconsistent courses of conduct on the defendant." *Id.* Courts frequently cite the difficulty of complying with the conflicting prospective declaratory and injunctive relief sought by different plaintiffs as a reason that certification of a mandatory class is appropriate under Rule 23(b)(1)(A). *E.g.*, *Thomas v. SmithKline Beecham Corp.*, 201 F.R.D. 386, 397 (E.D. Pa. 2001). Defendants may not defeat a motion for class certification "by declaring that they are willing to assume the risk of inconsistent adjudications." *In re Merck & Co., Inc. Sec., Derivative & ERISA Litig.*, Nos. 1658, 05-1151, 05-2369, 2009 U.S. Dist. LEXIS 10243, at *34, 2009 WL 331426, at *2 (D.N.J. Feb. 10, 2009) (certifying under Rule 23(b)(1)(A) an ERISA action seeking damages and equitable relief to ensure that two equitable judgments did not give rise to incompatible standards of conduct).

Rule 23(b)(1)(A) "requires more than a risk that separate judgments would oblige the opposing party to pay damages to some class members but not to others or to pay them different amounts." *Rowe v. E.I. DuPont de Nemours & Co.*, Nos. 06-1810, 06-3080, 2008 U.S. Dist. LEXIS 103528, at *28, 2008 WL 5412912, at *10 (D.N.J. Dec. 23, 2008). A plaintiff's decision to seek monetary relief, however, does not necessarily preclude certification under Rule 23(b)(1)(A). *See also In re Merck*, 2009 U.S. Dist. LEXIS 10243, 2009 WL 331426 (D.N.J. Feb. 10, 2009) (certifying under Rule 23(b)(1)(A) an ERISA action seeking damages and equitable relief to ensure that two equitable judgments did not give rise to incompatible standards of conduct). Generally, courts will consider certifying a Rule 23(b)(1)(A) class in a mixed remedy case so long as the claim for money damages does not predominate. *Allen v. Holiday Universal*, 249 F.R.D. 166, 189–90 (E.D. Pa. 2008). In the context of ERISA claims for monetary damages brought by a named plaintiff on behalf of all members of an employee savings plan, however, courts will certify a class under Rule 23(b)(1)(A) class on the theory that "if a court entertaining an individual account claim were to reach a different conclusion from a court entertaining a plan-wide claim, the fiduciaries would be left with incompatible orders concerning the same account." *See Stanford v.*

Foamex L.P., 263 F.R.D. 156, 173 (E.D. Pa. 2009) (citing cases).

Rule 23(b)(1)(B) Classes

Whereas the certification inquiry under Rule 23(b)(1)(A) examines how individual suits may prejudice defendants, Rule 23(b)(1)(B) focuses on the impact of individual actions on potential class members' rights. Thus, Rule 23(b)(1)(B) provides that

> a class should be certified under Rule 23(b)(1)(B) when "prosecuting separate actions by or against individual class members would create a risk of . . . adjudications with respect to individual class members that, as a practical matter, would be dispositive of the interests of the other members not parties to the individual adjudications or would substantially impair or impede their ability to protect their interests."

In re Schering Plough Corp. ERISA Litig., 589 F.3d 585, 604 (3d Cir. 2009) (quoting Fed. R. Civ. P. 23(b)(1)(B)).

Despite the relatively broad language of the Rule, "[t]he principles of stare decisis do not create authorization for a Rule 23 (b)(1)(B) certification." *Bogosian v. Gulf Oil Corp.*, 62 F.R.D. 124, 132 (E.D. Pa. 1973). Rather, "precedent plus some other factor" is required. *Resolution Trust Corp. v. KMPG Peat Marwick*, No. 92-1373, 1992 U.S. Dist. LEXIS 16670, at *10, 1992 WL 245705, at *3 (E.D. Pa. Sept. 23, 1992). Thus, in *In re Phar-Mor, Inc. Securities Litig.*, 875 F. Supp. 277 (W.D. Pa. 1994), the district court certified a Rule 23(b)(1)(B) class where, in addition to precedential effect, a partner's statements in the first case would be admissible against other partners in subsequent litigation. *Id.* at 280.

The most common type of Rule 23(b)(1)(B) class is a limited fund class in which a large number of individuals is expected to make claims against a fund insufficient to satisfy all claims. A limited fund class will only be certified under Rule 23(b)(1)(B), however, where a plaintiff presents "substantive evidence" that the defendant's assets would not cover class member claims. *See In re Sch. Asbestos Litig.*, 789 F.2d 996, 999 (3d Cir. 1986); *Fanning v. AcroMed Corp. (In re Orthopedic Bone Screw Prods. Liab. Litig.)*, 176 F.R.D. 158, 176–77 (E.D. Pa. 1997); *see also In re Amtrak Train Derailment in Phila.*, No. 2654, 2016 U.S. Dist. LEXIS 46552, at *21–25, 2016 WL 1359725, at *5–7 (E.D. Pa. Apr. 6, 2016) (declining to certify a settlement class under Rule 23(b)(1)(B) without "evidence, outside of the basic facts of this case, to support their contention that the damages here will exceed the $295 million [statutory damages] limit").[4] In evaluating the plaintiffs' evidence, a court "must keep focused on its duty to test all of the factors that may point to an equitable determination to see if a limited fund exists" and determine "whether, without a limited fund designation, [the relevant assets] would be depleted by defense costs, or other unavoidable uses before the majority of claimants had an opportunity to advance a worthy claim to the point of a recovery." *Fanning*, 176 F.R.D. at 176–77 (citing *In re Agent Orange Prod. Liab. Litig.*, 100 F.R.D. 718 (E.D.N.Y. 1983)).

Finally, although certification under Rule 23(b)(1)(B) creates a mandatory class and the Rule itself does not require that absent class members be notified (there is no ability to opt out, after all), the Third Circuit has strongly suggested that notice must be provided to a Rule 23(b)(1)(B) class to the same extent as a Rule 23(b)(3) class. In *In re Orthopedic Bone Screw Products Liability Litigation*, 246 F.3d 315 (3d Cir. 2001), the Third Circuit noted that "the [Supreme] Court expressed skepticism that Rule 23(b)(1)(B) limited fund class ac-

---

[4] The court ultimately approved a settlement in *In re Amtrak Train Derailment in Phila.*, 268 F. Supp. 3d 739 (E.D. Pa. 2017). It did so without certifying a settlement class under Rule 23(b)(1)(B). Instead, it implemented a Settlement Program that involved a negotiated claims process administered by Special Masters. Despite the fact that the settlement was not technically a class settlement, the court approved it only after analyzing the factors typically applied to class settlements as required by *Girsh v. Jepson*, 521 F.2d 153 (3d Cir. 1975).

tions are valid at all under Rule 23, and stated that, if these class actions were to be valid, they would have to conform closely to the contours of traditional limited fund cases that predated Rule 23." *Id.* at 327 n.11 (citing *Ortiz v. Fibreboard Corp.*, 527 U.S. 815 (1999)). Thus, "*Ortiz* seems to imply (although it specifically declined to rule) that the level of notice required for a [Rule 23(b)(1)(B) settlement] is the same as is required in a Rule 23(b)(3) action: the best notice practicable, 'including individual notice to all members who can be identified through reasonable effort.'" *Id.* (quoting Fed R. Civ. P. 23(c)(2)).

Rule 23(b)(2) Classes

"Rule 23(b)(2) authorizes class actions seeking injunctive relief in instances where the defendant 'has acted or refused to act on grounds that apply generally to the class, so that final injunctive relief . . . is appropriate respecting the class as a whole.'" *Sullivan*, 667 F.3d at 296 (quoting Fed. R. Civ. P. 23(b)(2)). The Supreme Court has held that certifying a Rule 23(b)(2) class "applies only when a single injunction or declaratory judgment would provide relief to each member of the class." *In re Insulin*, 2024 U.S. Dist. LEXIS 19894 at *91, 2024 WL 416500 at *25 (citing *Dukes*, 564 U.S. at 360). Therefore, "[c]laims for individualized relief may not be certified under 23(b)(2), nor may claims for monetary relief that are 'not incidental to the injunctive or declaratory relief. Plaintiffs' sought injunction must be more specific than merely requiring that Defendants follow the law." *Id.* (citations and quotation marks omitted). The Third Circuit has noted that the requirements of Rule 23(b)(2) are "almost automatically satisfied in actions primarily seeking injunctive relief." *Baby Neal*, 43 F.3d at 58 (citing *Weiss v. York Hosp.*, 745 F.2d 786, 811 (3d Cir. 1984)). "It is the (b)(2) class which serves most frequently as the vehicle for civil rights actions and other institutional reform cases that receive class action treatment." *Id.* at 58–59.

In *Dukes*, the Supreme Court held that "Rule 23(b)(2) applies only when a single injunction or declaratory judgment would provide relief to each member of the class" but left open the question "whether there are any forms of 'incidental' monetary relief that are consistent with . . . Rule 23(b)(2) and that comply with the Due Process Clause." 564 U.S. at 360, 366. Courts within the Third Circuit have interpreted *Dukes* to permit certification under Rule 23(b)(2) so long as "the primary relief which Plaintiffs seek . . . is indeed the issuance of one and/or declaration applicable to all of the members of the class (now known or unknown), and that any monetary compensation which may flow therefrom would be merely incidental." *Augustin v. City of Phila.*, 318 F.R.D. 292, 301 (E.D. Pa. 2016). The Third Circuit has "not yet spoken on how the predominance of monetary relief in the Rule 23(b)(2) context should be measured," noting only that other circuits

> are split on that question, with some adopting the 'incidental damages' standard set forth by the Court of Appeals for the Fifth Circuit in *Allison v. Citgo Petroleum Corp.*, 151 F.3d 402 (5th Cir. 1998), and others opting for a more discretionary, 'ad hoc balancing' approach such as that used by the Court of Appeals for the Second Circuit in *Robinson v. Metro-North Commuter R.R. Co.*, 267 F.3d 147 (2d Cir. 2001).

Hohider v. UPS, 574 F.3d 169, 198 (3d Cir. 2009).[5]

---

[5] A particular cause of action under Pennsylvania law that "allows those exposed to toxic substances to recover the costs of periodic medical appointments and the costs of tests to detect the early signs of diseases associated with exposure" has generated substantial debate about the type of relief that a plaintiff may seek under Rule 23(b)(2). Gates v. Rohm & Haas Co., 655 F.3d 255, 262 (3d Cir. 2011). In light of *Dukes*, the Third Circuit has "question[ed] whether [medical monitoring claims] can be certified under Rule 23(b)(2)" but has not yet resolved the issue, relying instead on the extent to which "class members' regimes of medical screenings and the corresponding cost will vary individual by individual" to affirm a decision that certification of the most recently considered medical monitoring class claim was inappropriate under Rule 23(b)(2). *Id.* at 263.

Because Rule 23(b)(2) focuses "on the nature of the remedy sought, and because a remedy obtained by one member will naturally affect the others, the identities of individual class members are less critical in a (b)(2) action." *Augustin*, 318 F.R.D. at 300 (citing *Shelton v. Bledsoe*, 775 F.3d 554, 561 (3d Cir. 2015)). That said, although "23(b)(2) class actions have no predominance or superiority requirements, it is well established that the class claims must be cohesive." *Barnes v. Am. Tobacco Co.*, 161 F.3d 127, 143 (3d Cir. 1998). District courts have "discretion to deny certification in Rule 23(b)(2) cases in the presence of disparate factual circumstances." *Id.* at 143; *see Henry v. St. Croix Alumina, LLC*, No. 99-0036, 2008 U.S. Dist. LEXIS 43755, *29, 2008 WL 2329223, at *9 (D.V.I. June 3, 2008). "For a court to find a class cohesive, it must find that the 'class's claims are common ones and that adjudication of the case will not devolve into consideration of myriad individual issues.'" *In re Insulin,* 2024 U.S. Dist. LEXIS 19894 at *91, 2024 WL 416500 at *26. Not only do "individual issues that defeat the predominance requirement of Rule 23(b)(3) also defeat the cohesion requirement of Rule 23(b)(2)," *Gates v. Rohm & Haas Co.*, 265 F.R.D. 208, 231 (E.D. Pa. 2010), but "a (b)(2) class may require more cohesiveness than a (b)(3) class . . . because in a (b)(2) action, unnamed members are bound by the action without the opportunity to opt out." *Barnes*, 161 F.3d at 142–43. "Injuries remedied through (b)(2) actions are really group, as opposed to individual injuries," and "[t]he members of a (b)(2) class are generally bound together through preexisting or continuing legal relationships or by some significant common trait such as race or gender." *Id.* at 143 n.18 (quotation marks omitted). "Rule 23(b)(2) is not appropriate where 'significant individual liability or defense issues . . . would require separate hearings for each class member in order to establish defendants' liability.'" *In re Insulin Pricing Litig.*, 2024 U.S. Dist. LEXIS 19894 at *49, 2024 WL 416500 at *13 (D.N.J. Jan. 25, 2024), *appeal filed* (No. 24-8002) (citation omitted).

Despite the focus on group injury, Rule 23(b)(2) "does not require that all members of the class be already injured for the class action to proceed." *Colon v. Passaic County*, No. 08-CV-4439, 2009 U.S. Dist. LEXIS 45151, at *16, 2009 WL 1560156, at *5 (D.N.J. May 27, 2009). In *Dittimus-Bey v. Taylor*, 244 F.R.D. 284 (D.N.J. 2007), for example, which the court called a "paradigm of the type of class suitable for certification under Rule 23(b)(2)," the plaintiffs alleged that they had "suffered injury due to the unconstitutional overcrowding of the [prison] and that Defendants' actions threaten similar injury to all members of the class." *Id.* at 293. Similarly, in *Neale*, the Third Circuit explained that "certification is appropriate [under Rule 23(b)(2)] even if the defendant's action or inaction has taken effect or is threatened only as to one or a few members of the class, provided it is based on grounds which have general application to the class." 794 F.3d at 367–68 (quotation marks omitted). However, standing for injunctive relief to prevent future harm is viewed with some skepticism where the plaintiffs have an opportunity to avoid the future harm. This was the case in the Third Circuit's decision in *Thorne v. Pep Boys Manny Moe & Jack Inc.*, 980 F.3d 879, 896 (3d Cir. Nov. 20, 2020), where the Court noted that a plaintiff must be afforded the "dignity of assuming [they] act[] rationally, and that [they] will not act in such a way that [they] will again suffer the same alleged 'injur[ies].'" In agreeing that the plaintiff lacked Article III standing, the *Thorne* court recognized that the plaintiff's "allegations reveal that she knows of Pep Boys's practices, Thorne's request for injunctive relief amounts to a 'stop me before I buy again' claim that precludes Article III standing." *Id.* (internal quotation marks omitted) (quoting *In re Johnson & Johnson*, 903 F.3d 278, 292–93 (3d Cir. 2018)).

Finally, although the vast majority of Rule 23(b)(2) classes are plaintiff classes, there is tepid support in the Third Circuit for the prospect of certifying a class of defendants against whom injunctive relief would apply. Reviewing the marked circuit split on the issue, Judge Kugler evaluated the four cases in which district courts within the Third Circuit had certified defendant classes under Rule 23(b)(2) as of 2003 and concluded that such class claims had "met success, if at all, only in cases where the individual defendants of the class are alleged to be acting in conformity with an illegal state statute, rule, or regulation." *Clark v. McDonald's Corp.*, 213 F.R.D. 198, 220 (D.N.J. 2003).

Rule 23(b)(3) Classes

Predominance. For certification to be appropriate under Rule 23(b)(3), the proposed class must be "sufficiently cohesive to warrant adjudication by representation." *Hydrogen Peroxide*, 552 F.3d at 310–11 (quotation marks omitted). The predominance inquiry thus asks whether "the questions of law or fact common to class members predominate over any questions affecting only individual members." Fed. R. Civ. P. 23(b)(3). "An individual question is one where members of a proposed class will need to present evidence that varies from member to member, while a common question is one where the same evidence will suffice for each member to make a *prima facie* showing [or] the issue is susceptible to generalized, class-wide proof." *In re Insulin*, 2024 U.S. Dist. LEXIS 19894 at *100, 2024 WL 416500 at *28 (citing *Tyson Foods*, 577 U.S. at 453) (internal citations and quotation marks omitted). Although predominance is related to commonality, predominance is "far more demanding," *Amchem*, 521 U.S. at 623–24, and requires "more than a common claim," *Newton*, 259 F.3d at 187.[6] The Third Circuit has explained that "the question of predominance imposes a . . . stringent obligation on the reviewing court to ensure that issues common to the class truly overshadow those pertinent to individuals or to subgroups of class members." *Sullivan*, 613 F.3d at 144.

Because the "nature of the evidence that will suffice to resolve a question determines whether the question is common or individual," lower courts "must formulate some prediction as to how specific issues will play out in order to determine whether common or individual issues predominate in a given case." *Hydrogen Peroxide*, 552 F.3d at 311 (quotation marks omitted). In *Hydrogen Peroxide*, the Third Circuit emphasized that "class certification is unsuitable" in cases where "proof of the essential elements of the cause of action requires individual treatment." *Id.*; *see also Winoff Indus. v. Stone Container Corp. (In re Linerboard Antitrust Litig.)*, 305 F.3d 145, 156 (3d Cir. 2002) ("Clearly, if proof of the essential elements of the cause of action require individual treatment, then there cannot be a predominance of questions of law and fact common to the members of the class." (quotation marks omitted)); *In re Insulin*, 2024 U.S. Dist. LEXIS 19894 at *102, 2024 WL 416500 at *29 ("Practically, this means a district court must look first to the elements of the plaintiffs' underlying claims and then, through the prism of Rule 23, undertake a rigorous assessment of the available evidence and the method or methods by which [the] plaintiffs propose to use the evidence to prove those elements.") (citation omitted).

Although the case-specific nature of the predominance inquiry makes providing overarching guiding principles difficult, examining several recurring issues sheds some light on how courts may react to particular arguments. For example, courts within the Third Circuit generally hold that certification is appropriate under Rule 23(b)(3) if all claims depend on establishing that the defendant engaged in a particular course of conduct and the case does not raise substantial questions about whether each class member felt the impact of that conduct.[7] Thus, in *Linerboard Antitrust Litigation*, the Third Circuit found that common issues predominated because all plaintiff claims depended in part on establishing the defendants had conspired to restrict the supply of containerboard. 305 F.3d 145, 163 (3d Cir. 2002); *see*

[6] In Rule 23(b)(3) cases, courts examine commonality separately only infrequently; instead, they incorporate the commonality requirement "into the more stringent Rule 23(b)(3) predominance requirement, and therefore deem it appropriate to analyze the two factors together, with particular focus on the predominance requirement." In re Ins. Brokerage Antitrust Litig., 579 F.3d at 266 (quotation marks omitted); *see also* Adams Pointe I, L.P. v. Tru-Flex Metal Hose Corp., No. 20-3528, 2021 U.S. App. LEXIS 24315, at *8, 2021 WL 361255, at *3 (3d Cir. 2021) ("It is often appropriate to discuss commonality and predominance together because the commonality inquiry is subsumed into the predominance inquiry." (quoting Reyes v. Netdeposit, LLC, 802 F.3d 469, 486 (3d Cir. 2015)).

[7] Notably, in *Neale*, the Third Circuit clarified that even when the defendant's conduct was common to all class members, a court cannot certify the class under Rule 23(b)(3) without analyzing how that conduct relates to the class members' claims. 794 F.3d 353. The court reversed the decision certifying the class because "the District Court made no distinction between the six statewide classes or the relevant claims brought by those putative classes." *Id.* at 371.

also Reyes, 802 F.3d at 492 ("The 'complete sham' theory, if supported by an appropriate record, can satisfy the predominance prong of Rule 23(b)(3) by focusing on the overarching material and defining aspects of a defendant's conduct."). By contrast, in *Monahan v. City of Wilmington*, 49 F. Appx 383 (3d Cir. 2002), the court determined that certification was not appropriate because even though the plaintiffs could not prevail without establishing that the defendant police department engaged in a pattern and practice of discrimination, "questions as to whether an individual plaintiff suffered discrimination by the Police Department and, if so, whether the discrimination against that plaintiff encompassed promotions and overtime, patrol, and detective unit assignments, raise issues pertaining only to individuals." *Id.* at 384. The same analysis led the Third Circuit to affirm the denial of certification in *Newton*, where the plaintiffs sought certification of a class that contained tens of thousands of investors allegedly defrauded by stockbrokers. 259 F.3d at 162. The court concluded that common questions did not predominate because determining which class members were economically harmed would require resolving "overpowering" individual inquiries. *Id.* at 189. Similarly, in *Gonzalez v. Owens Corning*, 885 F.3d 186 (3d Cir. 2018), the court rejected the plaintiffs' argument that common issues predominated where the purported class members had entered a "shingle lottery" by purchasing homes with roofs covered by the defendants' shingles. *Id.* at 197. Whereas certification might be appropriate in "product-defect cases . . . despite an alleged defect not manifesting itself in each product," the plaintiffs in *Owens Corning* could not establish that all shingles were defective, and thus could not satisfy predominance. *Id.* (contrasting case with *In re Whirlpool Corp. Front-Loading Washer Prods. Liab. Litig.*, 722 F.3d 838 (6th Cir. 2013), in which all washing machines were allegedly defective, even if some defects remained latent).

Some of the Third Circuit's recent evaluations of claimed class-wide injury involve examining and applying the Supreme Court's 2016 decision in *Tyson Foods, Inc. v. Bouaphakeo*, 136 S. Ct. 1036 (2016). There, the Court held that a class plaintiff can satisfy predominance by relying on representative and statistical evidence if "each class member could have relied on that sample to establish liability if he or she had brought an individual action." *Id.* at 1046, 1049 (allowing statistical evidence in FLSA action because "inferring the hours an employee has worked from a study [of statistical evidence] has been permitted by the Court so long as the study is otherwise admissible"). In *Reinig v. RBS Citizens, N.A.*, 912 F.3d 115 (3d Cir. 2018), the Third Circuit explained that it had "serious doubts" that the evidence of a company-wide policy urging employees to underreport overtime hours was "sufficiently representative of the class as a whole such that each individual plaintiff could have relied on the sample" to establish individual injury, potentially distinguishing the case from *Tyson Foods*. *Id.* at 130 (quotation marks omitted) (remanding with "instructions that the District Court conduct a 'rigorous' examination").

The "serious doubts" identified in *Reinig* were revisited and vindicated in the court's recent decision in *In re Lamictdal Direct Purchaser Antitrust Litigation*, 957 F.3d 184 (3d Cir. Apr. 22, 2020). In that case, the court rejected the district court's use of average pharmaceutical prices as an acceptable means to demonstrate common proof of injury in an antitrust action for direct purchasers of generics. On appeal, the direct purchasers argued that the district court's decision was proper because *Tyson Foods* could be read to "suggest[] an even lower standard for predominance whereby [injury predominates] unless no reasonable juror could believe the common proof at trial." *Id.* at 191. The court ruled that *Tyson Foods* was inapplicable for multiple reasons. First, it was decided in the idiosyncratic context of an FLSA claim. *Id.* (referring to the FLSA as "a unique labor situation in which, often due to inadequate record keeping, a representative sample [of employees] may be the only feasible way to establish liability." (quoting *Tyson Foods*, 136 S. Ct. at 1040)). Second, the posture of *Tyson Foods* was different because it concerned decertification of a class after a jury verdict in favor of the plaintiff class. *Id.* at 192. Having rejected the contention that *Tyson Foods* lowers the predominance standard for demonstrating injury, the court reiterated that under *In re Hydrogen Peroxide*, district courts are required "to resolve factual determinations . . . at the class certification stage" and, to certify a class, the "plaintiffs must prove their claim is capable of common proof by a preponderance of the evidence." *Id.* at 192; *see also In re Niaspan Antitrust Litig.*, 42 F. Supp. 3d 735 (E.D. Pa. 2014) (holding predominance could not be met where plaintiffs did not satisfy the court that they "have a non-individualized means of identifying . . . uninjured class members in a way that protects defendants' constitutional rights").

Whereas questions about whether class members are injured at all raise serious doubts about predominance, individualized damages calculations generally do not defeat certification. *See Harnish v. Widener Univ. Sch. of Law*, 833 F.3d 298, 306 (3d Cir. 2016) (affirming denial of class certification where "the District Court was concerned not merely with the plaintiffs' ability to calculate the precise measure of damages, but rather with their ability to demonstrate the fact of damage—'ascertainable loss' and a 'causal relationship'—class-wide"); *see also In re Suboxone (Buprenorphine Hydrochlorine & Naloxone) Antitrust Litig.*, 967 F.3d 264, 269 (3d Cir. 2020) (holding that the individualized nature of the damages inquiry did not prevent certification under Rule 23(b)(3)). The Third Circuit explained in *Chiang v. Veneman*, 385 F.3d 256 (3d Cir. 2004), "that the necessity for calculation of damages on an individual basis" does not typically render certification under Rule 23(b)(3) inappropriate "when common issues which determine liability predominate." *Id.* at 273 (quotation marks omitted); *see also Taha v. Cty. of Bucks*, 862 F.3d 292, 309 (3d Cir. 2017) (certifying class for trial when only issue that remained following summary judgment was whether defendants wilfully violated statute, which would trigger punitive damages of varying amounts; trier of fact could determine wilfulness—"the only remaining factual issue"—by considering common evidence). Although *Comcast* cast doubt on that principle, the Third Circuit has limited *Comcast*, noting that a "close reading" of the case "makes it clear that the predominance analysis was specific to the antitrust claim at issue." *Neale*, 794 F.3d at 374; *see also Sterling Heights Gen. Employees' Ret Sys. v. Prudential Fin. Inc.*, No. 12-5275, 2015 U.S. Dist. LEXIS 115287, at *35, 2015 WL 5097883, at *13 (D.N.J. Aug. 31, 2015) ("Class certification will not necessarily be defeated where there are individual issues with respect to the calculation of damages. Indeed, in securities cases such as this one where all other issues are provable by common evidence, denial of class certification solely on the basis of individual damages calculations would be an abuse of discretion." (quotation marks omitted)); *Forsythe v. Teva Pharm. Indus. Ltd*, 102 F.4th 152, 158 (3d Cir. 2024) (in securities case, finding proposed damages model in *Comcast* was unrelated to class's theory of liability).

There remain, however, at least three exceptions to the general rule that individualized damages do not defeat predominance. First, courts have declined to certify classes under Rule 23(b)(3) where "individual damage calculations [would] inevitably overwhelm questions common to the class." *Royal Mile Co., Inc. v. UPMC*, 40 F. Supp. 3d 552, 585 (W.D. Pa. 2014); *see also Verma v. 3001 Castor, Inc.*, No. 13-3034, 2014 U.S. Dist. LEXIS 88459, at *49, 2014 WL 2957453, at *15 (E.D. Pa. June 30, 2014) ("[T]he rigorous analysis standard requires additional evidence to demonstrate that damages calculations will not inevitably overwhelm questions common to the class." (quotation marks omitted)). Second, courts have relied on *Comcast* to reject certification where the plaintiffs failed to show a connection between their liability theory and their damages methodology. *E.g.*, *Brady Enters. v. Medco Health Sols., Inc. (In re Pharm. Benefit Managers Antitrust Litig.)*, No. 06-1782, 2017 U.S. Dist. LEXIS 6987, at *68, 2017 WL 275398, at *19 (E.D. Pa. Jan. 18, 2017) (denying certification where complaint asserted two distinct conspiracy theories but damages model was not capable of distinguishing damages attributable to each conspiracy theory). Third, to the extent a cause of action requires finding injury at the liability phase rather than the damages phase, individualized injury inquiries may defeat predominance. *E.g.*, *Hydrogen Peroxide*, 552 F.3d at 311 ("In antitrust cases, impact often is critically important for the purpose of evaluating Rule 23(b)(3)'s predominance requirement because it is an element of the claim that may call for individual, as opposed to common, proof.").

Generally, individualized questions that relate to affirmative defenses do not render certification inappropriate under Rule 23(b)(3). *See Demmick v. Cellco P'ship*, No. 06-2163, 2010 U.S. Dist. LEXIS 94041, at *36, 2010 WL 3636216, at *12 (D.N.J. Sept. 8, 2010) ("[C]ourts traditionally have been reluctant to deny class action status under Rule 23(b)(3) simply because affirmative defenses may be available against individual members." (quotation marks omitted)). Thus, for example, the Third Circuit concluded in *Hoxworth* that "individualized determinations" regarding whether "a subset of the class members' claims are time-barred" did not defeat predominance. 980 F.2d at 924. A decade later in *Linerboard Antitrust Litigation*, the appellate court expressly adopted the First Circuit's approach to statute of limitations determinations, rejecting a "per se rule that treats the presence of such issues as an automatic disqualifier." 305 F.3d at 162–63 (quoting *Waste Mgmt. Holdings, Inc. v. Mowbray*, 208 F.3d 288, 296 (1st Cir. 2000)). To the extent individualized fraudulent concealment issues threatened predominance, the court held that such determinations "may be adjudicated in the same fashion and at the same time as individual damages issues." *Id.* at 163.

The Third Circuit's jurisprudence regarding the extent to which reliance issues defeat predominance has been much less consistent. For example, in *In re Prudential Insurance Co. American Sales Practice Litigation Agent Actions*, 148 F.3d 283 (3d Cir. 1998), the plaintiffs alleged that the defendant had engaged in fraudulent sales practices. *Id.* at 289. The court held that the common questions related to the sales practices made certification appropriate despite the fact that individual reliance issues remained. *Id.* at 310. By contrast, in *Malak v. BDO Seidman LLP*, 617 F.3d 743 (3d Cir. 2010), the Third Circuit affirmed the denial of certification because individual issues of reliance predominated in a securities fraud class action where no presumption of reliance applied. *Id.* at 756. Despite the confusion, courts are more likely to find certification palatable despite individualized reliance issues where the underlying misrepresentations were written and uniform. *Prudential*, 148 F.3d at 319. If an action is "based substantially on oral rather than written communications," reliance determinations become more difficult and individualized inquiries make certification under Rule 23(b)(3) less likely. *Johnson v. HBO Film Mgmt., Inc.*, 265 F.3d 178, 186 (3d Cir. 2001) ("[B]ecause the plaintiffs claimed affirmative oral misrepresentations, as opposed to omissions, determining reliance necessarily required individual assessment.").

Finally, as a general rule, the application of different state laws to different plaintiffs' claims gives rise to predominance issues that may defeat certification. In *Powers v. Lycoming Engines*, 328 F. App'x 121, 128 (3d. Cir. 2009), the Third Circuit observed that "nationwide class action movants must credibly demonstrate, through an 'extensive analysis' of state law variances, 'that class certification does not present insuperable obstacles.'" *Id.* at 124 (quoting *In re Sch. Asbestos Litig.*, 789 F.2d at 1010); *see also Adams Pointe I, L.P.*, 2021 U.S. App. LEXIS 24315, at *12–13, 2021 WL 3612155, at *4 (affirming denial of class certification where Plaintiffs did not show how the court could navigate variations within state law). Because "the District Court's choice of law exploration was insufficient and, consequently, the inquiry into Rule 23's predominance and superiority requirements rested on questionable premises," the court vacated the certification order and remanded for an additional choice of law analysis. *Id.* at 128; *see also In re LifeUSA Holding Inc.*, 242 F.3d 136, 147 (3d Cir. 2001) (finding error where the "District Court failed to consider how individualized choice of law analysis of the forty-eight different jurisdictions would impact on Rule 23's predominance requirement. . . ."); *Georgine v. Amchem Prods., Inc.*, 83 F.3d 610, 627 (3d Cir. 1996) ("[B]ecause we must apply an individualized choice of law analysis to each plaintiff's claims . . . the proliferation of disparate factual and legal issues is compounded exponentially." (internal citation omitted)); *Valli v. Avis Budget Rental Car Grp., LLC*, 2023 U.S. Dist. LEXIS 181799, at *17, 2023 WL 6579150 at *6 (D.N.J. Oct. 10, 2023) (denying certification of nationwide class of rental car customers holding that because the laws of all fifty states could govern class members' claims, the court could not properly instruct a jury on the applicable law, therefore common questions did not predominate within the class). By contrast, where "relatively minor differences in state law could be overcome at trial by grouping similar state laws together and applying them as a unit," certification may be appropriate despite choice of law issues. *See Prudential*, 148 F.3d at 315; *see also Adams Point I, L.P.*, 2021 U.S. App. LEXIS 24315, at *13, 2021 WL 3612155, at *4 (affirming denial of class certification where plaintiffs' comparison of various states' laws "provides no analysis of how the elements of the various causes of action in the different jurisdictions compare to each other or could be grouped so as to be manageable at trial").

Superiority. The superiority prong of Rule 23(b)(3) requires courts "to balance, in terms of fairness and efficiency, the merits of a class action against those of alternative available methods of adjudication." *Georgine*, 83 F.3d at 632 (quotation marks omitted). Superiority will generally be satisfied when "there are a potentially large number of class members. . . . [and] each [potential class member] has a very small claim in relation to the cost of prosecuting a lawsuit." *In re Warfarin Sodium Antitrust Litig.*, 391 F.3d 516, 533–34 (3d Cir. 2004) ("[A] class action [that] facilitates spreading of the litigation costs among the numerous injured parties and encourages private enforcement of the statutes" will generally meet the superiority requirement); *but see Georgine*, 83 F.3d at 633 (denying certification under superiority because "this action involves claims for personal injury and death—claims that have a significant impact on the lives of the plaintiffs and that frequently receive huge awards in the tort system"). In the context of securities litigation, the court recognized that a class action is often the only recourse for a defrauded investor. *Roofer's Pension Fund v. Papa*, 33 F.R.D. 66, 78 (D.N.J. Nov. 14, 2019) ("Generally, '[a]s a practical matter, investors defrauded by securities law violations have no recourse other than class relief.'" (quoting *Shapiro v. Alliance MMA, Inc.*, No. 17-2583, 2018 U.S. Dist. LEXIS 108132, at *16, 2018 WL 3158812, at *6 (D.N.J. June 28, 2018))).

In addition to "the relatively modest size of individual claims and the sheer volume of those claims in the aggregate," courts engaging in a superiority analysis will also examine whether class members have "a compelling interest to control the prosecution of their own claims," the extent to which individual suits would "represent[] a potentially great strain on judicial resources," whether there is a reason that all claims should be litigated in the same venue, and whether trying the case would "present insurmountable case management problems." *Prudential*, 148 F.3d at 316; *see also Newton*, 259 F.3d at 192 (denying certification on superiority grounds where issues were too complex to try the case on a class basis).

c. Ascertainability

Beginning in 2012, the Third Circuit recognized that beyond the requirement that a class be clearly defined by a court pursuant to Rule 23(c)(1)(B) (discussed below), Rule 23 implicitly requires that the class's members be identifiable. *Marcus*, 687 F.3d at 593 ("If class members are impossible to identify without extensive and individualized fact-finding or 'mini-trials,' then a class action is inappropriate."). In *Carrera*—a case that has become a guidepost in the brewing ascertainability circuit split—the Third Circuit recognized the import of its holding in *Marcus* and clarified that a class must be both (1) "currently and readily ascertainable based on objective criteria" and (2) capable of identification "without extensive and individualized fact-finding or mini-trials." 727 F.3d at 305 (quoting *Marcus*, 687 F.3d at 592–93). And confronted with a challenge to the very requirement of ascertainability, in 2023 the Third Circuit reiterated that the requirement of ascertainability is "true to the text, structure and purpose of Rule 23." *In re Niaspan*, 67 F.4th at 132; *see also id.* at 133 (observing that "[s]everal of our sister circuits have followed our lead and apply our ascertainability standard, or a standard that is substantively the same").

Three additional developments related to ascertainability bear noting. First, the Third Circuit has taken pains to clarify that the ascertainability requirement does not require a plaintiff to come forward with evidence of class membership at the certification stage. Rather, "*Carrera* stands for the proposition that a party cannot merely provide assurances to the district court that it will later meet Rule 23's requirements" or "propose a method of ascertaining a class without any evidentiary support that the method will be successful." *Byrd v. Aaron's Inc.*, 784 F.3d 154, 164 (3d Cir. 2015) (quotation marks omitted); *see also Gibbons v. Weltman, Weinberg & Reis Co., LPA*, No. 17-1851, 2018 U.S. Dist. LEXIS 187146, at *31, 2018 WL 5720749, at *11 (E.D. Pa. Oct. 31, 2018) ("At this stage, even though Plaintiff has not already identified all members of her proposed class, she has met her burden of demonstrating that class members *can* be identified." (emphasis in original)); *see also Hargrove v. Sleepy's LLC*, 974 F.3d 467, 479 (3d Cir. Sept. 9, 2020) (reversing a finding of lack of ascertainability where the district court "essentially demanded that Appellants identify the class members at the certification stage"). The Third Circuit reemphasized the distinction, reversing a district court's class certification denial on ascertainability grounds where the plaintiff had provided voluminous evidence that the class could be ascertained, but the evidence was admittedly incomplete, largely as a result of the defendant's poor record keeping. *See id.* at 479–80.[8] The court explained that the plaintiffs had met the requirement of showing there was a reliable and administratively feasible mechanism of determining class membership, which was the operative inquiry. *Id.* ("[Plaintiffs] do not have to prove at this stage that each proposed class member was indeed a full-time driver, but only that the members can be identified.").

On the other hand, the Third Circuit also has held that class certification should not be denied on a lack of ascertainability based solely on the volume of records to be reviewed to determine class membership. In *Kelly v. Realpage Inc.*, 47 F.4th 202, 224 (3d Cir. 2022), the Third Circuit reasoned that "a straightforward 'yes-or-no' review of existing records to identify class members is administratively feasible even if it requires review of individual records with cross-referencing of voluminous data from multiple sources." The "number of records that must be individually reviewed," the court continued, was not a valid objection to ascertainability because "[t]o hold otherwise would be to categorically preclude class actions where defendants purportedly harmed too many people." *Id.* at 224–25.

Second, the Third Circuit has expressed some skepticism that a plaintiff can meet the ascertainability requirement by reference to individual class member affidavits, noting that whatever method is employed must amount to "more than ascertaining by potential class members' say so." *Carrera*, 727 F.3d at 306 (quoting *Marcus*, 687 F.3d at 594). That said, a recent ascertainability pronouncement from the court clarifies that affidavits may be appropriate in some circumstances. Specifically, the court held that affidavits could render a class ascertainable if paired with an overinclusive list of all potential class members, depending on the extent of the list's overinclusiveness. *City Select Auto Sales, Inc. v. BMW Bank of N. Am. Inc.*, 867 F.3d 434, 441–42 (3d Cir. Aug. 16, 2017); *see also Hargrove*, 974 F.3d at 481 ("[Defendant] failed to explain why, in light of our precedents, [its business] records as a whole, *together with the affidavits*, did not provide a reliable and feasible mechanism to ascertain class members." (emphasis added)). *Cf. Dukich v. IKEA US Retail LLC*, 343 F.R.D. 296, 306 (E.D. Pa. 2022) (continuing the Third Circuit's stringent application of the ascertainability requirement and highlighting the limitations of self-identification affidavits by rejecting a putative class defined as purchasers who had no notice of recall using class member affidavits and the defendants' customer email lists).

---

[8] The *Hargrove* court expressed concern over a plaintiff's obligation to show an ascertainable class in the face of a defendant's poor record keeping. In reversing the district court, the Third Circuit remarked that the lower court's focus on "the gaps in the record is especially troubling given that Appellants are only able to rely on the records that Sleepy's kept and produced . . . . [W]e also clarify that where an employer's lack of records makes it more difficult to ascertain members of an otherwise objectively verifiable class, the employees who make up that class will not be made to bear the cost of the employer's faulty record keeping." *Id.* at 482. The Court held that "where an employer has failed to keep records it was required to keep by law, employees can prove ascertainability (it remains their burden) by producing 'sufficient evidence' to define their proposed class as 'a matter of just and reasonable inference.'" *Id.* (quoting Anderson v. Mt. Clemens, 328 U.S. 680, 687 (1946)).

Third, in *Shelton v. Bledsoe*, the Third Circuit refused to extend the ascertainability requirement to injunctive/declaratory relief class actions arising under Rule 23(b)(2) and opined that "it does not follow from our holding in *Marcus* that ascertainability is always a prerequisite to class certification." 775 F.3d at 562 ("The ascertainability requirement ensures that the procedural safeguards necessary for litigation as a (b)(3) class are met, but it need not (and should not) perform the same function in Rule 23(b)(2) litigation.").

d. Rule 23(c)(4)

The Third Circuit's jurisprudence on a final category of class warrants discussion—the Rule 23(c)(4) issues class. Rule 23(c)(4) states that "[w]hen appropriate, an action may be brought or maintained as a class action *with respect to particular issues.*" (emphasis added). The Third Circuit has observed, however, that "with that permission comes restrictions." *Russell v. Educ. Comm. for Foreign Medical Grads.*, No. 20-2128, 15 F.4th 259, 266 (3d Cir. 2021). To certify a class on only particular issues, a party must satisfy all of Rule 23's other strictures, including Rule 23(a)'s prerequisites and a showing that a class is maintainable under Rule 23(b)(1), (2), or (3). *Id.* at 267 (citing *Amchem Prods., Inc. v. Windsor*, 521 U.S. 591, 614 (1997)). Once those hurdles are overcome, an additional threshold question remains: Under the text of Rule 23(c)(4), which kind of issues are "appropriate" for issue-only certification?

The Third Circuit's cases applying Rule 23(c)(4) reveal how challenging that question has been to answer. *See generally Hohider v. United Parcel Service, Inc.*, 574 F.3d 169, 200 (3d Cir. 2009) ("The interaction between the requirements for class certification under Rule 23(a) and (b) and the authorization of issue classes under Rule 23(c)(4) is a difficult matter that has generated divergent interpretations among the courts."). Prior to *Russell*, the Circuit's leading authority on Rule 23(c)(4) classes was *Gates v. Rohm and Haas Co.*, 655 F.3d 255 (3d Cir. 2011). In *Gates*, the Court identified nine non-exclusive factors that could guide courts faced with a request to certify a Rule 23(c)(4) issue. 655 F.3d at 273. These factors focus on the nature of the claims and litigation, the potential administrative and preclusive effects of issue certification, and the kind of evidence at issue. *Russell*, 15 F.4th at 268 (citing *Gates*, 655 F.3d at 273). But as the Court acknowledged in *Russell*, the *Gates* factors did not address one central issue—whether a party seeking issue certification under Rule 23(c)(4) must show that the issue is also dispositive of the defendant's liability. *Id.* at 269.

Russell resolves this issue. After reviewing the authority on Rule 23(c)(4), the Court noted that out-of-circuit authority and the text of Rule 23(c)(4) both allowed certification regardless of whether resolution of the issue also resolved the defendant's ultimate liability. *Id.* at 270 ("The Rule permits an action to be brought or maintained as a class action 'with respect to particular issues,' not just those that decide liability."). The post-*Russell* test for issue certification is accordingly a three part inquiry: (1) "[D]oes the proposed issue class satisfy Rule 23(a)'s requirements?"; (2) "[D]oes the proposed issue class fit within one of Rule 23(b)'s categories?"; and (3) "If the proposed issue class does both those things, is it 'appropriate' to certify these issues as a class?" *Id.* The Court noted that the first two steps of the inquiry will be resolved by general class-action doctrine, while the third will continue to be informed by *Gates*' nine-factor analysis. *Id.*

5. CASE MANAGEMENT

a. Timing of Class Certification

In 2003, the Federal Rules were amended to call for a decision on class certification "[a]t an early practicable time after a person sues or is sued as a class representative," while the prior version had required that a certification decision be made "as soon as practicable after commencement of an action." In *Weiss*, the Third Circuit recognized that this relatively small linguistic shift reflects the need for a careful analysis of the Rule 23 factors and that the new rule does not "require or encourage premature certification determinations." 385 F.3d at 347.

Neither plaintiffs nor defendants have any incentive to seek summary judgment before class certification issues are resolved. As the district court explained decades ago, when defendants move for summary judgment "prior to the sending out of class notice," they "assume the risk that a judgment in their favor will not protect them from subsequent suits by other potential class members, for only the slender reed of stare decisis stands between them and the prospective onrush of litigants." *Haas v. Pittsburgh Nat'l Bank*, 381 F. Supp. 801, 806 (W.D. Pa.1974). Plaintiffs have no more ability to bind would-be class members than do defendants prior to class certification. *See McNulty v. Fed. Hous. Fin. Agency*, 954 F. Supp. 2d 294, 298 n.2 (M.D. Pa. 2013) (holding "any ruling by the court prior to class certification would bind only the named parties"). Litigants therefore frequently request that class certification motions be due far in advance of motions for summary judgment, and judges frequently grant such requests. Even so, the speed with which complex motions for class certifications are resolved means that litigants nearly as frequently brief summary judgment issues before receiving decisions on their motions for class certification.

No matter the timing of the initial certification decision, "[u]nder Rule 23, a district court may decertify or modify a class at any time during the litigation if it proves to be unmanageable." *Prudential*, 148 F.3d at 321.

b. Certification Order

Rule 23(c)(1) requires that a certification order "define the class and the class claims, issues, or defenses." In the Third Circuit, that means that the order must include "(1) a readily discernible, clear, and precise statement of the parameters defining the class or classes to be certified, and (2) a readily discernible, clear, and complete list of claims, issues or defense to be treated on a class basis." *Wachtel v. Guardian Life Ins. Co.*, 453 F.3d 179, 187–88 (3d Cir. 2006). A statement that a particular class has been certified coupled with a cross-reference to a docket entry or other documents does not suffice. *Marcus*, 687 F.3d at 592. The Third Circuit reaffirmed that "[a]lthough [it has] declined to impose a strict format necessary to meet Rule 23(c)(1)(B)'s requirements, [it has] explicitly rejected orders that force [it] to 'cobble together . . . various statements' and 'comb the entirety of its text' in search of 'isolated statements that may add up to a partial list of class claims, issues, or defenses.'" *Reinig*, 912 F.3d at 127 (quoting *Wachtel*, 453 F.3d at 188 n.10, 189).

c. Appointing Counsel

When a district court certifies a class, it must also appoint class counsel. *See In re CertainTeed Corp. Roofing Shingle Prods. Liab. Litig.*, 269 F.R.D. 468, 480 n.9 (E.D. Pa. 2010) ("Under the plain language of Fed. R. Civ. P. 23(g)(1), a district court's decision to certify a class must precede the appointment of class counsel."); *In re Pressure Sensitive Labelstock Antitrust Litig.*, MDL Docket No. 1556, 2007 U.S. Dist. LEXIS 85466, at *71–72, 2007 WL 4150666, at *22 (M.D. Pa. Nov. 19, 2007) ("The Court is required to appoint class counsel when it certifies a class."). The court must evaluate whether class counsel will "fairly and adequately represent the interests of the class." Fed. R. Civ. P. 23(g)(1)(B). It does so by considering four criteria: (1) "the work counsel has done in identifying or investigating potential claims in the action," (2) counsel's experience litigating class actions in general and antitrust claims in particular, (3) "counsel's knowledge of the applicable law," and (4) "the resources counsel will commit to representing the class." Fed. R. Civ. P. 23(g)(1)(A)(i–iv). Because Rule 23(a)(4)'s adequacy requirements track Rule 23(g)(1)'s requirements for class counsel and because the analyses are typically conducted at the same time, adequacy and of the choice of class counsel are rarely, if ever, evaluated separately. *See Sheinberg*, 606 F.3d at 132.

6. CLASS NOTICE

Rule 23(c)(2) requires notice of class certification for non-mandatory classes certified under Rule 23(b)(3). The "unambiguous requirement" mandates that "individual notice must be provided to those class members who are identified through reasonable effort." *Eisen v. Carlisle & Jacquelin*, 417 U.S. 156, 175 (1974); *Beck*, 457 F.3d at 301 n.7 (requiring that individual notice be providing to all class members who can be identified through reasonable effort). "The requirements of Rule 23(c)(2) are . . . arguably stricter than the due process clause," *Carlough v. Amchem Products, Inc.*, 158 F.R.D. 314, 324–25 (E.D. Pa. 1993), which stems in part from "the fact that personal jurisdiction over absent class members only attaches upon the satisfaction of Rule 23(c)(2)'s notice requirements," *Alberton v. Commonwealth Land Title Ins. Co.*, No. 06-3755, 2010 U.S. Dist. LEXIS 25476, at *7, 2010 WL 1049581, *2 (E.D. Pa. Mar. 17, 2010). As the Third Circuit explained in *Prudential*, "[i]n the class action context, the district court obtains personal jurisdiction over the absentee class members by providing proper notice of the impending class action and providing the absentees with the opportunity to be heard or the opportunity to exclude themselves from the class." 148 F.3d at 306; *see also Georgine v. Amchem Prods., Inc.*, 160 F.R.D. 478, 490 (E.D. Pa. 1995) ("Because many of the advantages of a class action come at the cost of binding individual class members through the res judicata effects of litigation over which many lack control, Rule 23 offers eligible members of a class the right of exclusion from a class.").

Content. Class notice "is designed to summarize the litigation and the settlement [where relevant] and to apprise class members of the right and opportunity to inspect the complete settlement documents, papers, and pleadings filed in the litigation." *Prudential*, 148 F.3d at 327 (internal quotation marks omitted). "Generally speaking, the notice should contain sufficient information to enable class members to make informed decisions on whether they should take steps to protect their rights, including objecting to the settlement or, when relevant, opting out of the class." *In re Baby Prods. Antitrust Litig.*, 708 F.3d 163, 180 (3d Cir. 2013); *see also Rodgers v. U.S. Steel Corp.*, 70 F.R.D. 639, 647 (W.D. Pa. 1976) (holding that notice is adequate when it "enable[s] reasonable and competent individuals to make an informed choice" and that there is "no reason to believe . . . that the language of the tender notice and release forms must be reduced to a pablum in order for [class members] to digest its import").

Distribution. Although Rule 23(c)(2) requires "individual notice to all members who can be identified through reasonable effort," individual notice to all class members is far from the norm. *Prudential*, 148 F.3d at 306 (3d Cir. 1998) ("[T]he provision of individual notice to each class member is by no means typical of the notice provided in most class actions, and certainly qualifies as unprecedented."); *see also Tenuto v. Transworld Sys.*, No. 99-4228, 2000 U.S. Dist. LEXIS 14344, at *14, 2000 WL 1470213, at *5 (E.D. Pa. Sept. 29, 2000) (explaining that "the best notice practicable under the circumstances must be provided to class members of the existence and nature of the action, their right to opt out and the consequences of not doing so," but concurrently noting that the court was unable to determine "whether records exist from which personal notice could be effectuated").

Where individual notice to all class members is not practicable, "[i]t is well settled that in the usual situation first-class mail [to identifiable class members] and publication fully satisfy the notice requirements of both Fed. R. Civ. P. 23 and the due process clause." *Zimmer Paper Prods., Inc. v. Berger & Montague, P.C.*, 758 F.2d 86, 90 (3d Cir. 1985); *see also Bradburn Parent Teacher Store, Inc. v. 3M*, 513 F. Supp. 2d 322, 328–29 (E.D. Pa. 2007) (finding due process requirements satisfied where class action administrator mailed notice to class members via first-class mail and re-mailed undeliverable notices to class members after conducting search for updated addresses); *Wilson v. United Intern. Investigative Servs. 401(k) Sav. Plan*, No. 01-6126, 2002 U.S. Dist. LEXIS 7235, at *21, 2002 WL 734339, at *7 (D.N.J. Apr. 23, 2002) (due process requirements satisfied when "[d]efendants . . .

mail[ed] . . . notice to the last known address of the members as contained in the records."); *In re CertainTeed Corp.*, 269 F.R.D. at 481–82 (approving a class action settlement with a notice program including ads placed on four national cable networks); *In re Aetna Inc. Sec. Litig.*, MDL No. 1219, 2001 U.S. Dist. LEXIS 68, at *17–18, 2001 WL 20928, at *5 (E.D. Pa. Jan. 4, 2001) (approving notice program that included first-class mail and publication notice in the *Wall Street Journal*). Finally, district courts within the Third Circuit have praised the use of a professional firm experienced in providing class action notice as a way of improving the prospect that class members will receive such notice. *E.g.*, *Nichols v. SmithKline Beecham Corp.*, No. 00-6222, 2005 U.S. Dist. LEXIS 7061, at *31–34, 2005 WL 950616, at *9–10 (E.D. Pa. Apr. 22, 2005).

7. SUBCLASSES

Rule 23(c)(5) provides that a class may be divided into subclasses, after which point each subclass is treated as a separate class under Rule 23. *See Josephat v. St. Croix Alumina, LLC*, No. 1999-0036, 2000 U.S. Dist. LEXIS 13102, at *8, 2000 WL 1679502, at *1 (D.V.I. Aug. 7, 2000) ("[T]o to obtain class certification, plaintiffs must prove numerosity, commonality, typicality, adequate representation, predominance and superiority with respect to the four subclasses sought to be certified."). When the adequacy inquiry under Rule 23(a)(4) uncovers conflicts of interest between named plaintiffs and class members, the creation of subclasses to minimize intra-class conflict may be appropriate. *See Dewey*, 681 F.3d at 182 (citing *Amchem*, 521 U.S. at 610–11). In some instances, when class members have substantially divergent interest or when certain class representatives only represent one group within the proposed class, subclasses may be required. *Wetzel v. Liberty Mut. Ins. Co.*, 508 F.2d 239, 253 (3d Cir. 1975); *see also Cmty. Bank II*, 795 F.3d at 394–95 (noting that "it may well be necessary to appoint separate counsel to represent newly divergent interests" within a class).

Just as the proponent of class certification bears the burden of establishing that class treatment is appropriate under Rule 23 and the case law interpreting it, so too does a proponent of subclasses bear the burden of submitting proposals to the court. *Reyes*, 802 F.3d at 494. But a request for subclasses need not necessarily precede their creation. Rather, "there is no question that a district court may properly act *sua sponte*" to create subclasses, despite the fact that it has no obligation to do so. *See In re Plastics Additives Antitrust Litig.*, No. 03-2038, 2006 U.S. Dist. LEXIS 98277, at*11–12, 2006 WL 6172033, at *2 (E.D. Pa. Dec. 20, 2006).

8. ABSENT CLASS MEMBERS

Whereas named plaintiffs occupy roughly the same position as parties to a non-class case, the rights and obligations borne by absent class members differ substantially from those associated with named plaintiffs. For example, while an attorney-client relationship between a typical party and its counsel prevents opposing counsel from contacting the party directly, various applicable state laws provide conflicting guidance about when an attorney-client relationship forms between an absent class member and class counsel. Under Pennsylvania law, for example, putative class members "are more properly characterized as parties to the action," *Bell v. Beneficial Consumer Discount Co.*, 348 A.2d 734, 736 (Pa. 1975). Consequently, several district courts within the state have held that absent class members cannot be contacted by opposing counsel. *Dondore v. NGK Metals Corp.*, 152 F. Supp. 2d 662, 666 (E.D. Pa. 2001); *Gates v. Rohm & Haas Co.*, No. 06-1743, 2006 U.S. Dist. LEXIS 85562, at *7 n.2, 2006 WL 3420591, at *2 (E.D. Pa. Nov. 22, 2006).

On the other hand, at certain times during the course of a class action, courts have hesitated to allow *class counsel* to contact absent class members. For example, in *Walney v.*

SWEPI LP, the court explained that "[d]uring the time between the institution of a class action and the close of the opt-out period, the status of plaintiffs' counsel in relation to the class members cannot be stated with precision." No. 13-102, 2017 U.S. Dist. LEXIS 8679, at *37–39, 2017 WL 319801, at *14 (W.D. Pa. Jan. 23, 2017) (quoting *Impervious Paint Indus., Inc. v. Ashland Oil*, 508 F. Supp. 720, 722 (W.D. Ky. 1981)); *see also In Cmty. Bank of N. Va. & Guar. Nat'l Bank of Tallahassee Second Mortg. Loan Litig.* (*Cmty. Bank I*), 418 F.3d 277, 313 (3d Cir. 2005) (intimating that something less than a traditional "attorney-client relationship" exists between class counsel and absent class members during the opt out phase of class litigation). After making relevant evidentiary findings, a district court may limit contact between class counsel and absent class members during that phase if it finds, for example, that class counsel intends to discourage opt outs. *Walney*, 2017 U.S. Dist. LEXIS 8679, at *30–31, 2017 WL 319801, at *10–11. This power stems from Rule 23(d), which provides that "a district court has a duty to 'safeguard class members from unauthorized [and] misleading communications from the parties and their counsel.'" *Bayshore Ford Truck Sales, Inc. v. Ford Motor Co.*, 541 F. App'x 181, 186 (3d Cir. 2013) (quoting *Cmty. Bank I*, 418 F.3d at 310) (alteration in original).

Absent class member issues also occasionally arise when opposing counsel solicits discovery from an absent class member. The Third Circuit has not addressed this issue directly, but district courts within the circuit have permitted written discovery from absent class members "(1) where the information requested is relevant to the decision of common questions, (2) when the discovery requests are tendered in good faith and are not unduly burdensome[,] and (3) when the information is not available from the class representative parties." *Gunter v. Ridgewood Energy Corp.*, No. 95-438, 1996 U.S. Dist. LEXIS 22298, at *7–8 (D.N.J. Oct. 15, 1996); *Kline v. First W. Gov't Secs.*, No. 83-1076, 1996 U.S. Dist. LEXIS 3329, at *8–9, 1996 WL 122717, at *3 (E.D. Pa. Mar. 11, 1996). Substantially less authority discusses the availability of depositions of absent class members, although in *dicta*, the Third Circuit cited with approval a Seventh Circuit case that held "[t]he taking of depositions of absent class members is—as is true of written interrogatories—appropriate in special circumstances." *Modafinil*, 837 F.3d at 256 n.17 (quoting *Clark v. Universal Builders, Inc.*, 501 F.2d 324, 341 (7th Cir. 1974)).

9. SETTLEMENTS

a. Approval Process

Prerequisites to Class Settlement

In *Sullivan v. DB Investments, Inc.*, 667 F.3d 273 (3d Cir. 2011) (en banc), and *Ehrheart v. Verizon Wireless*, 609 F.3d 590 (3d Cir. 2010), among other cases, the Third Circuit has articulated a strong preference for voluntary settlement in class actions. Even so, it has consistently observed that before approving a class settlement agreement, "a district court first must determine that the requirements for class certification under Rule 23(a) and (b) are met." *In re Pet Food Prods. Liab. Litig.*, 629 F.3d 333, 341 (3d Cir. 2010). Put differently, "parties cannot choose to avoid the judicial scrutiny demanded by Rule 23" through a voluntary settlement. *Rodriguez*, 726 F.3d at 382; *see also Amchem*, 521 U.S. at 620 (Class certification "demand[s] undiluted, even heightened, attention in the settlement context."); *Turner v. NFL (In re NFL Players' Concussion Injury Litig.)*, 307 F.R.D. 351, 370 (E.D. Pa. 2015) ("For a class action to have preclusive effect and bind absent class members, a class must first be certified."); *Home Depot USA, Inc. v. Lafarge N. Am., Inc.*, 59 F.4th 55, 63–64 (3d Cir. 2023) (holding that pre-certification decisions can only bind the parties at the time and not absent class members who later become part of the certified class). *Cf. Madlinger v. LexisNexis Risk Sols. Inc.*, 2024 U.S. Dist. LEXIS 114221 at *7–10, 2024 WL 3219495 at *3–4 (D.N.J. June 28, 2024) (dismissing putative Rule 23(b)(2) class action because of release under prior class action settlement).

That said, the settlement context means that "certain Rule 23 considerations . . . are not applicable." *Rodriguez*, 726 F.3d at 378. Most importantly, because a settlement obviates the need for trial, concerns regarding the manageability of a Rule 23(b)(3) class do not apply. *See Amchem*, 521 U.S. at 620; *see also Sullivan*, 667 F.3d at 297 (noting that "concerns regarding variations in state law largely dissipate when a court is considering the certification of a settlement class"); *Warfarin*, 391 F.3d at 529 ("[C]oncerns with regards to case manageability that arise with litigation classes are not present with settlement classes, and thus those variations are irrelevant. . . ." (citing *Amchem*, 521 U.S. at 620)).

Preliminary Approval

"Rule 23(e) imposes on the trial judge the duty of protecting absentees, which is executed by the court's assuring that the settlement represents adequate compensation for the release of the class claims." *In re Concussion Injury Litig.*, 961 F. Supp. 2d 708, 713 (E.D. Pa. 2014) (quoting Alba Conte & Herbert Newberg, *Newberg on Class Actions* § 11:46 (4th ed. 2002)). Rule 23 therefore appropriately requires court approval for class settlement, which may issue only "on finding that [the settlement] is fair, reasonable, and adequate." Fed. R. Civ. P. 23(e)(2). At the preliminary approval stage, the court is required to determine whether "the proposed settlement discloses grounds to doubt its fairness or other obvious deficiencies such as unduly preferential treatment of class representatives or segments of the class, or excessive compensation of attorneys, and whether it appears to fall within the range of possible approval." *Thomas v. NCO Fin. Sys.*, No. 00-5118, 2002 U.S. Dist. LEXIS 14157, at *14, 2002 WL 1773035, at *5 (E.D. Pa. July 31, 2002) (citation omitted).

"To determine whether a settlement falls within the range of possible approval, a court must consider plaintiffs' expected recovery balanced against the value of the settlement offer." *In re NFL Players' Concussion Injury Litig.*, 961 F. Supp. 2d at 714 (internal quotations and citations omitted). In *In re GMC Pick-Up Truck Fuel Tank Prods. Liab. Litig.* (*General Motors*), 55 F.3d 768 (3d Cir. 1995), the Third Circuit explained that a lower court's preliminary approval of a settlement creates a presumption of fairness when it concludes that "(1) the negotiations occurred at arm's length; (2) there was sufficient discovery; (3) the proponents of the settlement are experienced in similar litigation; and (4) only a small fraction of the class objected." *Id.* at 785–86. Despite the seeming leniency of this test, two caveats bear noting. First, where settlement negotiations precede class certification and approval for settlement and certification are sought simultaneously, the Third Circuit requires "district courts to be even 'more scrupulous than usual' when examining the fairness of the proposed settlement." *Warfarin*, 391 F.3d 516, 534 (3d Cir. 2004) (citing *General Motors*, 55 F.3d at 805). Second, "there is no bar to conducting a more thorough analysis [than the analysis suggested by *General Motors*] at the preliminary approval stage," and indeed, "[i]f a proposed settlement appears obviously deficient, the ruling should be issued before rather than after the parties incur the administrative expense to publish notice to the class and handle any objections." *Zimmerman v. Zwicker & Assocs., P.C.*, No. 09-3905, 2011 U.S. Dist. LEXIS 2161, at *10 n.5, 2011 WL 65912, at *3 (D.N.J. Jan. 10, 2011).

Notice and Objections

Under Rule 23(3), notice of a class settlement must be reasonably calculated to alert potential class members to the existence of the settlement and make it known that they will have an opportunity to present objections. *Varacallo v. Mass. Mut. Life Ins. Co.*, 226 F.R.D. 207, 225 (D.N.J. 2005). More specifically, notice of a proposed settlement must provide information about (1) "the nature of the pending litigation" and (2) "the settlement's general terms" and must explain that (3) "complete information is available from the court files" and (4) "that any class member may appear and be heard at the Fairness Hearing." *In re Prudential Ins. Co. of Am. Sales Practices Litig.*, 962 F. Supp. 450, 527 (D.N.J. 1997). District courts possess broad discretion when evaluating whether a settlement notice meets Rule 23(e)'s requirements. *Zimmer Paper Prods.*, 758 F.2d at 90 (observing that Rule 23(e) commits the form of the notice to the court's discretion); *Walsh v. Great Atl. & Pac. Tea Co.*, 96 F.R.D. 632, 642–43 (D.N.J.) (same), *aff'd*, 726 F.2d 956, 962 (3d Cir. 1983) (same).

"Any class member may object" in response to the notice of settlement. Fed. R. Civ. P. 23(e)(5). Although there are procedural requirements that apply to objections, "[t]o ignore the vigorous protests of class members because of minor technicalities would be to exalt form over substance and abdicate this Court's responsibilities as a fiduciary for the absent class members." *O'Brien v. Brain Research Labs, LLC*, No. 12-204, 2012 U.S. Dist. LEXIS 113809, at *43, 2012 WL 3242365, at *14 (D.N.J. Aug. 8, 2012) (citing *Ehrheart*, 609 F.3d at 593).

While sufficient notice coupled with failure to opt out typically binds a class member to the settlement's terms, the Third Circuit created an exception to that general rule in one of its last decisions of 2017. There, the court held that a sovereign state that is member of a settlement class need not object to avoid the settlement's binding effect. The district court's settlement approval order in that case enjoined all members of the settlement class from bringing released claims. *In re Flonase Antitrust Litig.*, 879 F.3d 61, 64 (3d Cir. 2017). The appellate court held, however, that the settlement court lacked jurisdiction to issue such an equitable remedy against the state because the state had not waived its Eleventh Amendment sovereign immunity, rejecting the argument that receiving notice and declining to opt out amounted to a waiver. *Id.* at 69.

Courts have recently shown a resistance to bending explicit instructions for opting out of a complex class action to allow plaintiffs to opt out. In *Roofer's Pension Fund v. Papa*, 2024 U.S. Dist. LEXIS 164194 at *17–26, 2024 WL 4205638 at *6–8 (D.N.J. Sept. 12, 2024), *appeal filed* (No. 24-2861), the Chief Judge of the District of New Jersey refused to allow a plaintiff to opt out of a $97 million federal securities class action settlement, dismissing the argument that maintaining its own lawsuit separate from the class action was a "reasonable indication" that it was opting out. In so holding, the court reasoned that the reasonable indication approach was outdated, "ignores the complexities of class actions that courts face today," and could "frustrate efficient administration and complicate settlement efforts." 2024 U.S. Dist. LEXIS 164194 at *18, 25, 2024 WL 4205638 at *6, 8 (noting a circuit split among the Second, Fifth, Seventh and Tenth Circuits and relying on recent cases from the Fifth and Seventh Circuits declining to apply the reasonable indication approach). Finding that "[m]echanical rules on opt outs help courts to decide whether a proposed settlement is fair and adequate by telling the court who's in and who's out," plaintiff failed to follow the opt-out instructions and failed to take any action to verify its opt-out status despite the opt-out list being published three-and-a half years prior. 2024 U.S. Dist. LEXIS 164194 at *25, 2024 WL 4205638 at *8.

Final Approval

Two Third Circuit cases, decided decades apart, set forth relevant factors for district courts to consider when determining whether a proposed settlement is fair. In *Girsh v. Jepson*, 521 F.2d 153 (3d Cir. 1975), the court noted nine mandatory factors to be considered when determining the fairness of a proposed settlement:

> (1) the complexity, expense and likely duration of the litigation; (2) the reaction of the class to the settlement; (3) the stage of the proceedings and the amount of discovery completed; (4) the risks of establishing liability; (5) the risks of establishing damages; (6) the risks of maintaining the class action through the trial; (7) the ability of the defendants to withstand a greater judgment; (8) the range of reasonableness of the settlement fund in light of the best possible recovery; and (9) the range of reasonableness of the settlement fund to a possible recovery in light of all the attendant risks of litigation.

Id. at 157 (internal quotation marks and ellipses omitted). "The settling parties bear the burden of proving that the *Girsh* factors weigh in favor of approval of the settlement." *Pet Food Prods.*, 629 F.3d at 350. A lower court's findings regarding the *Girsh* factors are factual and upheld unless clearly erroneous. *Id.*

Later, in *Prudential*, the court held that because of a "sea-change in the nature of class actions," additional non-mandatory factors could be considered, including:

> [(1)] the maturity of the underlying substantive issues, as measured by experience in adjudicating individual actions, the development of scientific knowledge, the extent of discovery on the merits, and other factors that bear on the ability to assess the probable outcome of a trial on the merits of liability and individual damages; [(2)] the existence and probable outcome of claims by other classes and subclasses; [(3)] the comparison between the results achieved by the settlement for individual class or subclass members and the results achieved—or likely to be achieved—for other claimants; [(4)] whether class or subclass members are accorded the right to opt out of the settlement; [(5)] whether any provisions for attorneys' fees are reasonable; and [(6)] whether the procedure for processing individual claims under the settlement is fair and reasonable.

148 F.3d at 323; *see also Baby Prods.*, 708 F.3d at 174 ("Unlike the *Girsh* factors, each of which the district court must consider before approving a class settlement, the *Prudential* considerations are just that, prudential.").

The timing of a settlement certainly bears on the settling parties' ability to present the court with complete information regarding many of the mandatory *Grish* and non-mandatory *Prudential* factors. A deficit in the record as to even mandatory elements, however, need not prevent early settlement. As the Third Circuit held in *Halley v. Honeywell Int'l, Inc.*, 861 F.3d 481 (3d Cir. 2017), "[d]istrict courts may approve settlements in which calculating the best possible recovery for the class in the aggregate would be exceedingly speculative if the reasonableness of the settlement nevertheless can be fairly judged." *Id.* at 493 (quotation marks and citations omitted). "To conclude otherwise might risk requiring parties to continue to litigate cases unnecessarily after a fair settlement has been reached." *Id.*; *see also id.* at 492 (distinguishing *Halley* from *Pet Food Prods.*, 629 F.3d 333, in which parties did not tell the district court whether evidence existed to calculate a best possible recovery for a particular subclass, leading the Third Circuit to remanded with instructions for the lower court to consider whether a best possible recovery calculation was possible).

In addition, a district court's obligations to evaluate the fairness of the settlement necessarily encompasses addressing "the non-frivolous arguments and objections that are put to them." *Sullivan*, 667 F.3d at 346 n.11. Courts may discount the value of an objection if it was put forth by a professional objector. *O'Keefe v. Mercedes-Benz United States, LLC*, 214 F.R.D. 266, 296 (E.D. Pa. 2003) (noting that court was "suspect" of objections because "one of [the objector's] attorneys is a professional objector").

b. *Cy Pres*

The Third Circuit joined "other courts of appeals in holding that a district court does not abuse its discretion by approving a class action settlement agreement that includes a *cy pres* component directing the distribution of excess settlement funds to a third party to be used for a purpose related to the class injury." *Baby Prods.*, 708 F.3d at 172. A *cy pres* provision, like any other term of a class settlement agreement, must be evaluated to determine whether the allocation of the *cy pres* funds is "fair, reasonable, and adequate when considered from the perspective of the class as a whole." *Id.* at 174.

In addition to the mandatory *Girsh* factors and nonmandatory *Prudential* factors, the Third Circuit has held that a "thorough analysis" of a settlement with a *cy pres* term will include evaluation of "the degree of direct benefit provided to the class," including "among other things, the number of individual awards compared to both the number of claims and the estimated number of class members, the size of the individual awards compared to claimants' estimated damages, and the claims process used to determine individual awards." *Baby Prods.*, 708 F.3d at 174. "Barring sufficient justification," the court explained, "*cy pres* awards should generally represent a small percentage of total settlement funds." *Id.* (reversing final approval of *cy pres* settlement where lower court did not calculate what portion of the settlement funds would go to class members and what portion would go to *cy pres* fund). Practitioners expected additional guidance from the Supreme Court in *Frank v. Gaos*, 139 S. Ct. 1041 (2019), following the Court's grant of certiorari in 2018 to review whether a settlement that would require the defendant to make certain disclosures, and would distribute "more than $5 million to *cy pres* recipients, more than $2 million to class counsel, and no money to absent class members" satisfied "the requirement that class settlements be "fair, reasonable, and adequate." *Id.* at 1043. Instead, in a per curiam opinion the Court remanded for consideration of standing in light of *Spokeo*. *Id.* at 1046. Justice Thomas dissented and questioned "whether a class action is 'superior to other available methods for fairly and efficiently adjudicating the controversy' when it serves only as a vehicle through which to extinguish the absent class members' claims without providing them any relief." *Id.* at 1047 (Thomas, J., dissenting).

10. FEES AND COSTS

Rule 23(h) provides that "[i]n a certified class action, the court may award reasonable attorney's fees and nontaxable costs that are authorized by law or by the parties' agreement." Courts typically make such awards in the context of a class action settlement in which the parties have agreed to the amount or percent of settlement proceeds that will cover class counsel's fees and costs. To make an award under Rule 23(h), a court must conduct "[a] thorough judicial review of fee applications" submitted by class counsel. *Prudential*, 148 F.3d at 333 (quoting *General Motors*, 55 F.3d at 819); *see also Baby Prods.*, 708 F.3d at 178–80. The Third Circuit has explained that "the danger inherent in the relationship among the class, class counsel, and defendants 'generates an especially acute need for close judicial scrutiny of fee arrangements'" in class actions. *Welch & Forbes, Inc. v. Cendant Corp. (In re Cendant Corp. Prides Litig.)*, 243 F.3d 722, 730 (3d Cir. 2001) (quoting *General Motors*, 55 F.3d at 820). A court's "oversight function serves not only to detect instances of 'the actual abuse [that potential attorney-class conflicts] may cause, but also [the] potential public misunderstandings they may cultivate in regard to the interests of class counsel.'" *General Motors*, 55 F.3d at 820 (alteration in original) (quoting *In re Agent Orange Prod. Liab. Litig.*, 818 F.2d 216, 224, 225 (2d Cir. 1987)).

Courts within the Third Circuit generally use either the lodestar method or the percentage-of-recovery method for assessing attorneys' fee requests. Even after choosing one method, however, the other may remain relevant, for the appellate court has suggested that "it is sensible for a court to use a second method of fee approval to cross-check its initial fee calculation." *In re Rite Aid Corp. Sec. Litig.*, 396 F.3d 294, 300 (3d Cir. 2005).

Statutory fee-shifting cases lend themselves to the lodestar method. *Prudential*, 148 F.3d at 333. "Because the lodestar award is de-coupled from the class recovery, the lodestar assures counsel undertaking socially beneficial litigation (as legislatively identified by the statutory fee shifting provision) an adequate fee irrespective of the monetary value of the final relief achieved for the class." *General Motors*, 55 F.3d at 821. While the de-coupling removes the disincentive to pursue less lucrative cases and "has the added benefit of resembling modes of fee determination in conventional bipolar litigation," it "has been criticized as giving class counsel the incentive to delay settlement in order to run up fees while still failing to align the interests of the class and its counsel. . . ." *Id.*

The percentage-of-recovery method is generally favored in cases involving a common fund, although it is typically accompanied by a lodestar cross-check. *Id.*; *Halley v. Honeywell Int'l, Inc.*, 861 F.3d 481, 496 (3d Cir. 2017). The percentage-of-recovery doctrine "provides that a private plaintiff, or plaintiff's attorney, whose efforts create, discover, increase, or preserve a fund to which others also have a claim, is entitled to recover from the fund the costs of his litigation, including attorneys' fees." *General Motors*, 55 F.3d at 820 n.39. Ten factors govern what constitutes a reasonable percentage fee award:

> (1) the size of the fund created and the number of beneficiaries, (2) the presence or absence of substantial objections by members of the class to the settlement terms and/or fees requested by counsel, (3) the skill and efficiency of the attorneys involved, (4) the complexity and duration of the litigation, (5) the risk of nonpayment, (6) the amount of time devoted to the case by plaintiffs' counsel, (7) the awards in similar cases, (8) the value of benefits attributable to the efforts of class counsel relative to the efforts of other groups, such as government agencies conducting investigations, (9) the percentage fee that would have been negotiated had the case been subject to a private contingent fee arrangement at the time counsel was retained, and (10) any innovative terms of settlement.

In re Diet Drugs Prod. Liab. Litig., 582 F.3d 524, 541 (3d Cir. 2009) (citing *Gunter v. Ridgewood Energy Corp*., 223 F.3d 190, 195 n.1 (3d Cir. 2000); *Prudential*, 148 F.3d at 336–40). Thus, for example, the Third Circuit has criticized lower courts for "not attempting to distinguish between those benefits created by the [state's attorneys] and those created by class counsel" in rejecting a fee award where state government lawyers performed a substantial portion of the investigation and negotiation. *Prudential*, 148 F.3d at 338. When a settlement compensates multiple counsel representing a single class member, courts evaluate the ratio of a class member's settlement allocated to counsel fees. In *In re NFL Players' Concussion Injury Litigation*, the district court capped fees for individual counsel at 22 percent of a class member's total recovery and class counsels' fees at 11 percent of the total recovery to ensure that no individual class member paid more than 33 percent of his or her total recovery toward counsel fees. No. 2:12-md-02323-AB, 2018 U.S. Dist. LEXIS 57798, at *18, 2018 WL 1635648, at *7 (E.D. Pa. Apr. 5, 2018).

Where a court employs the percentage-of-recovery method, the Third Circuit has noted that "awarding attorneys' fees based on the entire settlement amount [including *cy pres*] rather than individual distributions creates a potential conflict of interest between absent class members and their counsel." *Baby Prods.*, 708 F.3d at 178. "Class members are not indifferent to whether funds are distributed to them or to *cy pres* recipients, and class counsel should not be either." *Id.* Thus, the court explained, "where a district court has reason to believe that counsel has not met its responsibility to seek an award that adequately prioritizes direct benefit to the class," it is "appropriate for the court to decrease the fee award." *Id.* (citations omitted).

Although the auction method of fee calculation has been endorsed by some courts, the Third Circuit "has been wary" of that approach. *In re Cendant Corp. Sec. Litig.*, 404 F.3d 173, 188 n.9 (3d Cir. 2005). A circuit-specific Task Force on the Selection of Class Counsel concluded that "auctions generally fail in their basic stated purpose of replicating the private market for legal services" and therefore recommended that auctions be used only "in certain limited situations." Stephen A. Saltzburg et al., *Third Circuit Task Force Report on Selection of Class Counsel*, 74 Temp. L. Rev. 689, 737, 741 (2001). Prominent among those limited situations is the absence of a sophisticated lead plaintiff. As the Task Force explained, "[t]here is no need for a court to be heavily involved in creating a market through an artificial structure if an experienced plaintiff with substantial resources is capable and willing to enter into a competitive search for, and fee negotiation with, qualified counsel." *Id.* at 744.

While nearly all fee and costs issues in class cases arise in the context of a class settlement that needs court approval, prevailing parties are also generally entitled to costs in civil actions under Rule 54(d) and 28 U.S.C. § 1920. In a class case that generated significant discovery-related costs before the lower court granted a motion to dismiss the named plaintiffs' claims with prejudice, the Third Circuit held in a non-precedential opinion that the defendants were entitled to more than $300,000 in costs associated with converting electronic files to TIFF format. *Camesi v. Univ. of Pittsburgh Med. Ctr.*, 753 F. App'x 135, 139–41 (3d Cir. 2019). The court's earlier decision in *Race Tires America, Inc. v. Hoosier Racing Tire Corp.*, 674 F.3d 158 (3d Cir. 2012), provided grounds to hold that "scanning and file format conversion can be considered to be 'making copies.'" *Id.* at 160. In addition, the court rejected the argument that the defendants did not qualify as prevailing parties because the claims by unnamed plaintiffs had been dismissed without prejudice. *Camesi*, 753 F. App'x at 139–41 (holding that "a defendant can still be the 'prevailing party' where a plaintiff's claims are dismissed without prejudice (citing *In re Paoli R.R. Yard PCB Litig.*, 221 F.3d 449, 471 n.10 (3d Cir. 2000)), and that the "vast majority" of the "very few other courts" to address the issue "have concluded that a defendant can be a prevailing party against unnamed plaintiffs who have voluntarily dismissed their claims" (citing, inter alia, *Frye v. Baptist Mem'l Hosp.*, Inc., 507 F. App'x 506, 508 (6th Cir. 2012)).

Finally, the Third Circuit took the opportunity to address and clarify its precedent concerning fee awards for class action and derivative settlement *objectors'* counsel. *See In re S.S. Body Armor I Inc.*, 961 F.3d 216, 226 (3d Cir. 2020). After remarking that it had "not had much occasion to consider fee awards to settlement objectors," the court held that "in both class and derivative actions, trial courts may, in their discretion, consider nonmonetary factors in determining whether an objector's participation improved a settlement. *Id.* at 227. In that case, although the objector's presence had not directly contributed to the recovery fund, it resulted in removing a $186 million indemnification obligation and thereby "helped to preserve the money which later funded (in part) the 2015 settlement[.]" *Id.* at 230. The objector's counsel had originally sought fees valued at $1.86 million, and the Third Circuit remanded for consideration of appropriate fees for objectors' counsel. *Id.* at 223.

11. APPELLATE ISSUES

a. Standing to Appeal

The Third Circuit has long held that "aggrieved class members may appeal any final order of a district court in proceedings held pursuant to Rule 23." *Ace Heating & Plumbing Co. v. Crane Co.*, 453 F.2d 30, 32 (3d Cir. 1971). While named class-member appeals follow typical appellate rules (with a specific rule dedicated to interlocutory review of class decisions, as noted below), appeals by unnamed class members must meet additional criteria.

To appeal a court-approved settlement or fee award, an unnamed class member must have objected to the proposed settlement or fee award in the district court, but need not have intervened. *Bell Atl. Corp. v. Bolger*, 2 F.3d 1304, 1309–10 (3d Cir. 1993); *see also In re Rite Aid Corp. Sec. Litig.*, 396 F.3d 294, 299 (3d Cir. 2005); *Fanning v. AcroMed Corp. (In re Orthopedic Bone Screw Prods. Liab. Litig.)*, 350 F.3d 360, 363 n.3 (3d Cir. 2003).

When an unnamed class member wishes to appeal the denial of class certification, he or she must intervene in the district court proceeding to have standing to appeal. *See United Airlines, Inc. v. McDonald*, 432 U.S. 385, 387 (1977). "[W]here the purpose of a motion to intervene is to obtain appellate review of a district court order determining the status of a class, the motion may be considered timely if filed within the time limit for filing a notice of appeal. . . ." *Halderman v. Pennhurst State Sch. & Hosp.*, 612 F.2d 131, 134 (3d Cir. 1979). Although the Third Circuit does not appear to have addressed the question directly, other circuit courts have held that the same intervention requirement applies for appeals of dispositive motions. *E.g.*, *In re Brand Name Prescription Drugs Antitrust Litig.*, 115 F.3d 456, 457 (7th Cir. 1997) (holding that unnamed class members in a plaintiff class action may not appeal entry of summary judgment for defendants). The Third Circuit, for its part, has recognized a presumption of timeliness for intervention motions filed by purported class members both before and after a class certification decision. *Cmty. Bank I*, 418 F.3d at 314 (motion to intervene presumed timely when made within the opt out period after class certified); *Wal-*

lach, 837 F.3d at 373 (timeliness presumption applies precertification).

b. Appeals as of Right: Final Judgment Rule

The final judgment rule, codified in 28 U.S.C. § 1291, generally prevents piecemeal appeals by requiring a final decision from a district court to trigger the jurisdiction of an appellate court. A dismissal with prejudice constitutes an appealable final order under § 1291. *See, e.g.*, *In re Merck & Co. Sec., Derivative & ERISA Litig.*, 493 F.3d 393, 399 (3d Cir. 2007). In addition, "[u]nder the 'merger rule,' prior interlocutory orders [such as class-certification decisions] merge with the final judgment in a case, and the interlocutory orders (to the extent that they affect the final judgment) may be reviewed on appeal from the final order." *In re Westinghouse Sec. Litig.*, 90 F.3d 696, 706 (3d Cir. 1996).

"[A] class certification decision, per se, is not an appealable final order. . . ." *Sullivan v. Pac. Indem. Co.*, 566 F.2d 444, 445 (3d Cir. 1977). Neither dismissal for failure to prosecute individual claims following the denial of a class certification order, nor voluntary dismissal under Rule 41(a) qualify as final appealable orders that trigger mandatory appellate review. *Id.*; *Camesi v. Univ. of Pittsburgh Med. Ctr.*, 729 F.3d 239, 244–45 (3d Cir. 2013). The Supreme Court adopted this approach in 2017 in *Microsoft Corp. v. Baker*, 137 S. Ct. 1702 (2017). Quoting *Camesi*, the Court bolstered its analysis by noting that the plaintiffs "after all, '[sought] review of only the [inherently interlocutory] orde[r]' striking their class allegations; they 'd[id] not complain of the 'final' orde[r] that dismissed their cas[e].'" *Id.* at 1715 (quoting *Camesi*, 729 F. 3d at 244).

c. Interlocutory Review

Litigants in federal class actions may pursue the typical, though rarely used, mechanisms for interlocutory review available to all federal civil litigants, including a request that the district court to certify its interlocutory order denying class certification for appeal under 28 U.S.C. § 1292(b) and a petition for a writ of mandamus. Rule 23(f) also provides a specific mechanism for potential interlocutory review of an order granting or denying a motion for class certification.

Rule 23(f) Standard. The Third Circuit perceives that it has "very broad discretion in deciding whether to grant permission to pursue" an appeal of an order granting or denying certification pursuant to Rule 23(f). *Gutierrez v. Johnson & Johnson*, 523 F.3d 187, 192 (3d Cir. 2008). In *Newton*, the court identified several circumstances in which appellate review is appropriate, including (1) "when denial of certification effectively terminates the litigation because the value of each plaintiff's claim is outweighed by the costs of stand-alone litigation; (2) when class certification risks placing inordinate . . . pressure on defendants to settle"; "(3) when an appeal implicates novel or unsettled questions of law"; (4) when the district court committed error in resolving a motion for class certification; and (5) when the appeal may "facilitate development of the law on class certification." 259 F.3d at 164–65 (internal quotation marks omitted). "By contrast, [interlocutory] review is discouraged when the natural course of litigation will provide the moving party with an adequate remedy, or when the certification decision was routine and easily resolved." *Rodriguez*, 726 F.3d at 377.

Timing. Rule 23(f) provides that "[a] party must file a petition for permission to appeal with the circuit clerk within 14 days after the order [regarding class certification] is entered," with very limited and specific exceptions. *See, e.g.*, *Wolff v. Aetna Life Ins. Co.*, 77 F.4th 164, 167 (3d Cir. 2023) (ruling that "a modified class certification order triggers a new 23(f) petition period only when the modified order materially alters the original order granting (or denying) class certification"). That deadline applies no matter whether the losing party moves for reconsideration. As the Supreme Court held in *Nutraceutical Corp. v. Lambert*, 139 S. Ct. 710 (2019), Rule 23(f)'s 14-day deadline is not subject to equitable tolling. *Id.* at 713.

Pendant Jurisdiction. In *Reinig*, 912 F.3d 115, the Third Circuit joined the Second Circuit (and rejected the reasoning of the Seventh, Tenth, and Eleventh Circuits) in concluding that although it had granted a Rule 23(f) petition for interlocutory review, it did not have pendant jurisdiction over a decision to certify a collective action under the Fair Labor Standards Act. *Id.* at 131. The court found persuasive the Second Circuit's conclusion that the FLSA and Rule 23 questions were not "inextricably intertwined" because a court "[could] easily[] determine[] that the higher predominance standard [of Rule 23] ha[d] not been met without addressing whether the same evidence plaintiffs have put forward in support of Rule 23 class certification could satisfy the lower [FLSA] standard." *Id.* (quoting *Myers v. Hertz Corp.*, 624 F.3d 537, 556 (2d Cir. 2010)).

d. Standard of Review

The Third Circuit reviews a decision to certify, or to deny certification of, a class action for abuse of discretion. *See Prudential*, 148 F.3d at 299 (citing *General Motors*, 55 F.3d, at 782). The appellate court is likely to find an abuse of discretion "where the district court's decision rests upon a clearly erroneous finding of fact, an errant conclusion of law or an improper application of law to fact." *Holmes v. Pension Plan of Bethlehem Steel Corp.*, 213 F.3d 124, 136 (3d Cir. 2000) (internal quotation marks omitted).

12. TOLLING STATUTE OF LIMITATIONS

Under the doctrine articulated by the Supreme Court in *American Pipe & Construction Co. v. Utah*, 414 U.S. 538 (1974), "the filing of a class action complaint tolls the statute of limitations for all members of the putative class who, following the denial of certification, intervene or file an independent action." *McKowan Lowe & Co. v. Jasmine, Ltd.*, 295 F.3d 380, 382 (3d Cir. 2002). Prior to the Supreme Court's 2018 decision in *China Agritech v.* Resh, 138 S. Ct. 1800 (2018), circuit courts across the country were split regarding whether the *American Pipe* rule tolled successive class actions. The Third Circuit had adopted a nuanced approach, holding that "class claims of intervening class members are tolled" only "if a district court declines to certify a class for reasons unrelated to the appropriateness of the substantive claims for certification," relying instead on issues specific to the class representative. *McKowan Lowe & Co.*, 295 F.3d at 389.

The Supreme Court upended that precedent in *China Agritech*, holding that the *American Pipe* rule permits only later-filed individual actions, not class actions, no matter the reason the class allegations may have failed. 138 S. Ct. at 1806 ("The efficiency and economy of litigation that support tolling of individual claims do not support maintenance of untimely successive class actions; any additional class filings should be made early on, soon after the commencement of the first action seeking class certification." (quotation marks and citation omitted)); *see also Weitzner v. Sanofi Pasteur Inc.*, 909 F.3d 604, 610 (3d Cir. 2018) (recognizing abrogation of Third Circuit precedent and confirming that "American Pipe tolling thus permits putative class members to file only *individual* claims after a denial of class certification." (emphasis in original)). Unsurprisingly given *China Agritech*'s clear-cut holding, the Third Circuit rejected two plaintiffs' attempts to distinguish it on the ground that they had filed suit not after the original class action had fully ended, but while the original class action was pending on appeal. *Blake v. JP Morgan Chase Bank N.A.*, No. 18-2368, 927 F.3d 701, 709 (3d Cir. 2019) (calling *China Agritech* "clear and unequivocal").

China Agritech did not, however, evaluate whether a pending putative class action tolls a *named* class plaintiff's individual claims. In *Weitzner*, the Third Circuit acknowledged "*American Pipe*'s broad language" that appeared allow tolling for all class members, including named plaintiffs. 909 F.3d at 611. It nonetheless determined that the "two primary purposes underlying the Supreme Court's holding in *American Pipe*"—efficiency and economy of litigation, and treating unnamed plaintiffs as though they were named plaintiffs during the pendency of the class action—would not be served by allowing a named plaintiff's class action in one jurisdiction to toll the statute of limitation on an individual action filed later in time in a second jurisdiction by the same plaintiff. *Id.* at 610–12. The court went even further, holding that a corporation's individual claims similarly had not been tolled by the first-class suit because that corporation's sole shareholder was the first suit's named plaintiff, meaning that the corporation was not the type of unaware, absent class member that *American Pipe* tolling was designed to protect. *Id.* at 612–13.

China Agritech, however, did not resolve all open questions concerning the application of *American Pipe* tolling. Joining the majority approach of the Second, Ninth and Tenth Circuits, the Third Circuit held in *Aly v. Valeant Pharmaceuticals International Inc.*, 1 F.4th 168 (3d Cir. June 16, 2021), that *American Pipe* tolling also applies to individual actions filed *after* a class action is filed, but *before* the denial of class certification.[9] In other words, while the filing of a class action commences the *American Pipe* tolling period and the denial of certification ends it, a plaintiff need not wait until the denial to file an individual action. "*American Pipe* makes clear that the filing of a class action is the operative event that tolls the limitations period, and that once the period is tolled, it remains tolled for all putative members until they are no longer part of the class." *Id.* at 175.

Recently, the Third Circuit in *Williams v. Tech. Mahindra (Ams.) Inc.*, 70 F.4th 646, 650–51 (3d Cir. 2023), ruled that the rationales of *China Agritech* for precluding the application of *American Pipe* tolling to successive class actions did not extend to wrong-forum tolling. The *Williams* court explained that while a successive class action would not be permitted under equitable tolling if a plaintiff made "no effort" to seek "lead-plaintiff status or [bring their] own claim" during the limitations period, the unavailability of *American Pipe* tolling does not necessarily preclude the application of other forms of equitable tolling, such as deception tolling, extraordinary-circumstances tolling, and wrong-forum tolling. *Id.*

13. ARBITRATION ISSUES

As is true across the federal courts, potential litigants are free to enter into arbitration agreements that require class arbitration. If the parties entered into an agreement that contains an "arbitration clause, it is reasonable that the arbitrator initially determine whether there is any consent or agreement to include class arbitration within the arbitration clause." *Chassen v. Fid. Nat'l Fin., Inc.*, No. 09-00291, 2012 U.S. Dist. LEXIS 133102, at *14, 2012 WL 4120902, at *5 (D.N.J. Sept. 18, 2012). In making that determination, the arbitrator may not infer "[a]n implicit agreement to authorize class-action arbitration . . . solely from the fact of the parties' agreement to arbitrate." *Sutter v. Oxford Health Plans, LLC*, 675 F.3d 215, 221 (3d Cir. 2012). In *Lamps Plus, Inc. v. Varela*, 139 S. Ct. 1407 (2019), the Supreme Court agreed, holding that ambiguity in an arbitration clause does not provide the necessary contractual basis for compelling class arbitration. *Id.* at 1419. In other words, "[t]here must be an 'affirmative contractual basis' for finding that the parties consented specifically to class arbitration." *Marbaker v. Statoil USA Onshore Props., Inc.*, 801 F. App'x 56, 60 (3d Cir. 2020) (quoting *Lamps Plus*, 129 S. Ct. at 1416) (holding that leases that "do not even mention class arbitration" fell "well short" of the *Lamps Plus* standard).

By contractually limiting the issues subject to arbitration, parties to an arbitration agreement may place limits upon the arbitrator's powers that are enforceable by the courts. *See Puleo v. Chase Bank USA, N.A.*, 605 F.3d 172, 181 (3d Cir. 2010) (en banc). An arbitrator oversteps those limits and subjects the arbitration award to vacatur in the courts if the ar-

[9] The lone Circuit Court to hold otherwise, the Sixth Circuit, held that plaintiffs forfeit the benefit of *American Pipe* tolling by filing individual claims before class certification has been resolved. Wyser-Pratte Mgmt. Co. v. Telxon Corp., 413 F.3d 553, 569 (6th Cir. 2005). Nevertheless, since ruling in *Wyser-Preatte*, the Sixth Circuit has acknowledged that it "may have doubts about its holding." Stein v. Regions Morgan Keegan Select High Income Fund, Inc., 821 F.3d 780, 789 (6th Cir. 2016).

bitrator does more than interpret and enforce a contract. Put differently, when the arbitrator "strays from interpretation and application of the agreement and effectively 'dispense[s] his own brand of industrial justice,'" he exceeds his powers and his award will be unenforceable. *Stolt-Nielsen S.A. v. AnimalFeeds Int'l Corp.*, 559 U.S. 662, 671 (2010) (quoting *Major League Baseball Players Ass'n v. Garvey*, 532 U.S. 504, 509, (2001) (per curiam)).

It follows that in the class context "[a]n arbitrator may exceed his powers by ordering class arbitration without authorization." *Sutter*, 675 F.3d at 220. *Cf. Coinbase, Inc. v. Suski*, 602 U.S. 143, 152 (2024) (issue of whether parties' prior agreement was superseded by subsequent agreement was for court, not arbitrator). "Even if [a party] cannot effectively prosecute his claim in an individual arbitration," individual arbitration "is his only remedy, illusory or not," if the arbitration agreement does not require class arbitration. *Homa v. Am. Express Co.*, 494 F. App'x 191, 196 (3d Cir. 2012). The Supreme Court enforced a contractual term that precluded class arbitration, notwithstanding a state law suggesting that such a term was unconscionable, *AT&T Mobility LLC v. Concepcion*, 563 U.S. 333, 343 (2011), and precluded class arbitration on the basis of a mandatory arbitration clause that permitted only individualized proceedings, notwithstanding a claim by the National Labor Relations Board that the NLRA effectively nullified the Federal Arbitration Act by virtue of its "collective action" language, *Epic Sys. Corp. v. Lewis*, 138 S. Ct. 1612, 1619 (2018). Relatedly, the Supreme Court recently determined that an exemption to the Federal Arbitration Act excluding workers engaged in foreign or interstate commerce from coverage under the Act included a transportation worker employed by a company outside of the transportation industry. *Bissonnette v. LePage Bakeries Park St., LLC*, 601 U.S. 246, 252 (2024).

FOURTH CIRCUIT

Districts of Maryland, North Carolina, South Carolina, Virginia, and West Virginia

Lewis F. Powell Jr. Courthouse & Annex
1100 East Main Street, Suite 501
Richmond, VA 23219

By Nina Fields Britt and Caleb M. Hodge
Rogers, Patrick, Westbrook & Brickman, LLC

1. INTRODUCTION

The Fourth Circuit Court of Appeals and federal judges in the Mid-Atlantic and South regions have played a significant role in defining national power in the United States. The Fourth Circuit's judicial authority was conferred through the provisions of the Judiciary Act of 1789, adopted on September 24, 1789, in the first session of the First United States Congress, which established the United States federal judiciary. The Fourth Circuit subsequently operated under the Judiciary Act of 1801 (the so-called Midnight Judges Act), which was enacted in the last days of President John Adams's administration and reorganized the federal judiciary. The incoming president, Thomas Jefferson, criticized the Midnight Judges Act as a last-minute attempt by the Adams administration to retain party control of the judiciary. The Midnight Judges Act was repealed by the Judiciary Act of 1802, which again reorganized the federal court system.

In 1866, one year after the Civil War ended, the federal circuits were realigned, resulting in the Fourth Circuit as it is today, with jurisdiction over appeals from federal district courts in Maryland, Virginia, West Virginia, North Carolina, and South Carolina. The Lewis F. Powell, Jr., U.S. Courthouse, where the Fourth Circuit sits in Richmond, Virginia, was completed in 1858. Remarkably, the courthouse was one of only two buildings that survived the disastrous 1865 fire that marked the Confederate Army's evacuation during the Civil War's final stages.

One of the Fourth Circuit's most notable cases was the trial of Aaron Burr, who served as vice president under Thomas Jefferson in his first term. Burr was tried for treason for planning to annex Spanish territory in Louisiana and Mexico for the establishment of an independent republic. More recently, notable litigation in the Fourth Circuit has included lawsuits relating to government contractor's interrogation practices after the 2003 invasion of Iraq. *See Al Shimari v. CACI Intern., Inc.*, 679 F.3d 205 (4th Cir. 2012).

In the class action context, some of the Fourth Circuit's more notable decisions include finding a putative class of embryos lacked Article III standing to sue, *see Doe v. Obama*, 631 F.3d 157 (4th Cir. 2011), and finding the Telephone Consumer Protection Act creates a private right of action for individuals that satisfies Article III's standing requirement, *see Krakauer v. Dish Network, L.L.C.*, 925 F.3d 643 (4th Cir. 2019).

Today, the Fourth Circuit is comprised of 15 active circuit judges and four senior judges, with Judge Albert Diaz serving as Chief Judge. According to the most current data, around 3,400 appeals are filed annually. The court's current median disposition time for cases decided on the merits is about nine months from notice of appeal to entry of judgment.

2. JURISDICTIONAL PREREQUISITES

a. The Class Action Fairness Act's Requirements

The Fourth Circuit generally takes a conservative approach to construing the requirements of the Class Action Fairness Act of 2005 (CAFA). Nevertheless, a party invoking jurisdiction under CAFA must still plausibly allege—and if challenged, demonstrate—that jurisdiction exists. *See Monaco v. WV Parkways Auth.*, 57 F.4th 185, 189 (4th Cir. 2023). Thus, in the Fourth Circuit, a party seeking removal under CAFA must establish federal jurisdiction over a class action whereas a party seeking remand must prove one of CAFA's three exceptions to removal applies. *Dominion Energy, Inc. v. City of Warren Police & Fire Ret. Sys.*, 928 F.3d 325, 335–36 (4th Cir. 2019).

Minimal Diversity Under CAFA

CAFA "expanded diversity jurisdiction over certain interstate class actions" by providing that "district courts shall have original jurisdiction of any civil action in which the matter in controversy exceeds the sum or value of $5,000,000, exclusive of interest and costs, and is a class action in which . . . any member of a class of plaintiffs is a citizen of a State different from any defendant." *Monaco v. WV Parkways Auth.*, 57 F.4th 185, 188 (4th Cir. 2023) (quoting 28 U.S.C. § 1332(d)(2)(A)).

In the Fourth Circuit, plaintiffs may defeat minimal diversity under CAFA by limiting their class definition to citizens of a particular state of which a corporate defendant is also a citizen. *See Johnson v. Advance America*, 549 F.3d 932 (4th Cir. 2008). This is because in determining diversity jurisdiction, "a corporation shall be deemed to be a citizen of any State by which it has been incorporated and of the State where it has its principal place of business." 28 U.S.C. § 1332(c)(1). For instance, in *Johnson v. Advance America*, the defendant corporation was a citizen of South Carolina and Delaware and the putative classes were defined to only include South Carolina residents. 549 F.3d at 934–36. There, the Fourth Circuit rejected the defendant's argument that minimal diversity was met because of its Delaware citizenship. *Id.* at 936. Instead, the court recognized that plaintiffs, "as masters of their complaint," can limit their class definition and restrict their allegations "so as to avoid federal jurisdiction under CAFA." *Id.* at 937.

The Fourth Circuit has also held that in determining diversity under CAFA, a limited liability company is considered an "unincorporated association," as that term is used in 28 U.S.C. § 1332(d)(10). *See Ferrell v. Express Check Advance of S.C. LLC*, 591 F.3d 698, 704 (4th Cir. 2010). Therefore, for purposes of minimal diversity under CAFA, a limited liability company is a citizen of the state under whose laws it is organized and the state where it has its principal place of business. *See id.*

Aggregation of Damages Under CAFA's Amount-in-Controversy Requirement

Under CAFA, whether the plaintiffs have satisfied the $5 million jurisdictional threshold is determined based on the amount in controversy, not the damages the plaintiffs will ultimately recover. *See Lanier v. Norfolk S. Corp.*, 256 F. App'x 629, 631 (4th Cir. 2007). Most often, the damages specified in good faith in the complaint will establish whether CAFA's jurisdictional threshold is met. *See Ministry of Defence of State of Kuwait v. Naffa*, 105 F.4th 154, 159 (4th Cir. 2024) (citing *JTH Tax, Inc. v. Frashier*, 624 F.3d 635, 638 (4th Cir. 2010)). In determining whether CAFA's jurisdictional threshold is met, courts look to the aggregated value of class members' claims. *Bartnikowski v. NVR, Inc.*, 307 F. App'x 730, 734 (4th Cir. 2009) (citing 28 U.S.C. § 1332(d)(6)). Statutory damages and statutory substantive rights, such as entitlement to attorneys' fees, may be properly considered in calculating the amount in controversy. *See id.* at 735; *id.* at 736 n.12.

However, when plaintiffs leave damages unspecified in their complaint, the defendant must establish that the amount in controversy satisfies the jurisdictional requirements for removal under CAFA. *See id.* This requires removing defendants to support their position on the amount in controversy with non-speculative evidence. *See id.* at 735–37. Given the difficulty CAFA defendants face in trying to establish the amount in controversy when plaintiffs leave damages unspecified in their complaint, the Fourth Circuit has recognized that plaintiffs may "use their pleadings in state court tactically, leaving damages unspecified to block removal without foreclosing an ultimate recovery of more than the federal jurisdictional minimum." *Id.* at 739. Nevertheless, the Fourth Circuit has also noted that "a CAFA defendant who cannot meet his burden for removal at the early stages of litigation may still have recourse to the federal courts later, as Congress has eliminated the one-year time limit on CAFA removal actions." *Id.*

The Local Controversy Exception to CAFA

The Fourth Circuit has recognized that although CAFA was intended to expand federal jurisdiction over class actions, it was not intended to deprive state courts of jurisdiction over class actions. *See Quicken Loans Inc. v. Alig*, 737 F.3d 960, 965 (4th Cir. 2013). Instead, under the "local controversy exception," state courts retain jurisdiction over primarily local disputes. *See id.* at 965–66. The local controversy exception applies when:

> (1) more than two-thirds of the members of the proposed plaintiff class are citizens of the state where the suit was filed originally; (2) at least one defendant (a) is a defendant from whom members of the plaintiff class are seeking "significant relief," (b) is a defendant whose conduct "forms a significant basis" for the proposed plaintiff class's claims, and (c) is a citizen of the state in which the action originally was filed; (3) the principal injuries stemming from the conduct alleged in the complaint occurred in the state where the action was filed originally; and (4) in the three years before the filing of the class action complaint, no other similar class action was filed against any of the defendants on behalf of the same or other class.

Id. at 964 (quoting 28 U.S.C. § 1332(d)(4)(A)). If the local controversy exception applies, the district court must decline to exercise jurisdiction over the action and remand the case to state court. *See id.* The "purpose of the local controversy exception is to permit class actions with a truly local focus to remain in state court." *Id.* at 965 (citing legislative history).

In *Quicken Loans Inc. v. Alig*, the Fourth Circuit found that in examining whether the local controversy exception applies, district courts may aggregate the named defendants in a putative defendant class and consider them as a group to determine whether the "at least one defendant" standard is met. 737 F.3d 960, 966 (4th Cir. 2013). However, it also held district courts cannot consider unnamed parties in evaluating whether the exception applies. *Id.*

The "Covered Security," "Internal Affairs," and "Securities-Related" Exceptions to CAFA

Under what are known as the "covered security" exception, the "internal affairs" exception, and the "securities-related exception," Congress excluded three types of class actions from federal court jurisdiction and removal to federal court, even if they otherwise satisfy CAFA's jurisdictional criteria. *Dominion Energy, Inc. v. City of Warren Police & Fire Ret. Sys.*, 928 F.3d 325, 330–31 (4th Cir. 2019). Specifically, 28 U.S.C. § 1332(d)(9) states CAFA jurisdiction does not apply to any class action involving *solely*:

(1) a claim concerning a covered security as defined under section 16(f)(3) of the Securities Act of 1933 and section 28(f)(5)(E) of the Securities Exchange Act of 1934;
(2) a claim that relates to the internal affairs or governance of a corporation or other

form of business enterprise and arises under or by virtue of the laws of the State in which such corporation or business enterprise is incorporated or organized; or

(3) a claim that relates to the rights, duties (including fiduciary duties), and obligations relating to or created by or pursuant to any security (as defined under section 2(a)(1) of the Securities Act of 1933 and the regulations issued thereunder).

(internal footnote and citations omitted); *see also* 28 U.S.C.§ 1453(d) (listing same exceptions for removal). Importantly, the Fourth Circuit has held these exceptions only apply to class actions exclusively involving the excepted claims. *Dominion Energy, Inc.*, 928 F.3d at 331. Thus, if a class action includes one of the excepted claims listed above and another, permissible claim, then the class action can be removed under CAFA. *See id.*

The Fourth Circuit examined these exceptions in *Dominion Energy, Inc. v. City of Warren Police & Fire Retirement System*, 928 F.3d 325 (4th Cir. 2019). There, the plaintiff stockholders brought breach of fiduciary duty claims and claims for aiding and abetting the breach of a fiduciary duty stemming from a contested merger. *Id.* at 331. The parties agreed the breach of fiduciary duty claims were excepted from removal under CAFA, but they disagreed about whether the aiding and abetting claim also fell within an exception. *Id.* at 336. Ultimately, the Fourth Circuit found the aiding and abetting claims were not excepted under CAFA because they were based on relationships other than those between the company at issue and its directors and shareholders. *See id.* at 337. Thus, they did not fall within the "internal affairs" exception, which the court found to apply only to "matters peculiar to the relationships among or between the corporation and its current officers, directors, and shareholders." *See id.* (quoting *LaPlant v. Nw. Mut. Life Ins. Co.*, 701 F.3d 1137, 1140 (7th Cir. 2012)). The court also found the aiding and abetting claims did not meet the "securities-related exception," holding the claims against corporate outsiders did not relate to the rights and duties created by a security. *See id.* at 341–43; *see also Kim v. Cedar Realty Tr., Inc.*, No. 23-1905, 2024 WL 4031409, at *5 (4th Cir. Sept. 4, 2024) (recognizing this holding). Thus, the court found that because none of the exceptions under 28 U.S.C. § 1453(d) applied and because all claims must be excepted to prevent removal under CAFA, the plaintiffs' class actions were properly removed to federal court. *See Dominion Energy, Inc.*, 928 F.3d at 343.

b. Standing

A plaintiff must have standing, i.e., a "personal stake" in the case, for federal courts to have jurisdiction under Article III of the Constitution. *See Penegar v. Liberty Mut. Ins. Co.*, 115 F.4th 294, 299 (4th Cir. 2024) (quoting *TransUnion LLC v. Ramirez*, 594 U.S. 413, 423 (2021)). Standing is required for each claim and for each form of relief sought. *Carolina Youth Action Project; D.S. by & through Ford v. Wilson*, 60 F.4th 770, 778 (4th Cir. 2023). Standing exists where a plaintiff shows: (1) she "suffered an injury in fact that is concrete, particularized, and actual or imminent;" (2) the injury "was likely caused by the defendant;" and (3) "the injury would likely be redressed by judicial relief." *Penegar*, 115 F.4th at 299 (quoting *TransUnion*, 594 U.S. at 423). The Fourth Circuit has stated that while standing's requirements are "pesky," they ensure judges "do not exceed the authority to decide cases and controversies conferred on [them] by the Constitution." *Id.* at 304.

To have standing, the plaintiff's injury must be real and impact the plaintiff in a personal and individual way. *See id.* at 209–300. The injury can be a tangible one, "such as physical or monetary injury," or it can be an intangible one, "such as emotional harm or a violation of one's constitutional rights." *See id.* (citing *TransUnion*, 594 U.S. at 425). But for intangible injuries to be concrete, they must be closely related to those harms "traditionally recognized as providing a basis for lawsuits in American courts." *Id.* (quoting *TransUnion*, 594 U.S. at 425). The plaintiff bears the burden of establishing standing. *See id.* at 300. A plaintiff's alleged injury must exist when the case is filed. *Id.* at 304. Notably, while a risk of future harm may be a sufficient injury to seek injunctive relief, the risk of future harm alone does not provide standing to seek damages. *See id.* at 302 (citing *TransUnion*, 594 U.S. at 436).

Recently, the Fourth Circuit clarified that a statutory violation alone does not establish standing; the plaintiff must have suffered a concrete and particularized injury from the violation to have standing. *Penegar*, 115 F.4th at 300 ("No matter what right or cause of action a statute may grant a plaintiff, she must still have an injury in fact to sue in federal court."); *Garey v. James S. Farrin, P.C.*, 35 F.4th 917, 921 (4th Cir. 2022) ("[P]laintiffs cannot establish a cognizable injury simply by pleading a statutory violation."). Plaintiffs proceeding based on a statutory violation can establish a sufficient injury to confer standing by identifying "a close historical or common-law analogue for their asserted injury for which courts have traditionally provided a remedy." *Garey*, 35 F.4th at 921 (internal quotations omitted) (quoting *TransUnion*, 594 U.S. at 425). "A plaintiff who does so has standing even if the precise injury would not, absent the statute, be sufficient for Article III standing purposes." *Id.*

Standing for Named Plaintiffs in Class Action Litigation

"The strictures of Article III standing apply with no less force in the context of class actions." *Fernandez v. RentGrow, Inc.*, 116 F.4th 288, 295 (4th Cir. 2024). Although each class member must have standing to recover individual damages, in the early stages of class action litigation, standing is typically analyzed based on the named plaintiffs' allegations. *See id.*; *Beck*, 848 F.3d at 269–70 (citations omitted). The Fourth Circuit has clarified that once a class representative makes a threshold showing of his or her individual standing, "there is no further, separate class action standing requirement." *See Wilson*, 60 F.4th at 779 (quotations omitted) (citing 1 *Newberg and Rubenstein on Class Actions* § 2:1 (6th ed. 2022)). Thus, if a class representative has standing to seek the particular relief sought, then "the case is justiciable and the proponent of the class suit need not demonstrate that each class member has standing to obtain class certification." *See id.* (quotation omitted).

A named plaintiff must not only have a personal stake in the substantive claim asserted but must also have "a distinct procedural right to represent the interests of similarly situated individuals." *Rhodes*, 636 F.3d at 99 (internal quotation marks and citation omitted). "This second, representative interest sometimes gives a putative class representative a sufficient 'stake' in the class certification question to appeal an adverse certification ruling even after the putative class representative's claim is mooted by intervening events." *Id.* In *Doe v. Obama*, for example, a putative class of human embryos (among other plaintiffs) challenged the federal funding research involving embryonic stem cells that was permitted by Executive Order 13505, Removing Barriers to Responsible Scientific Research Involving Human Stem Cells, signed by President Barack Obama on March 9, 2009. *See* 631 F.3d at 160. There, the Fourth Circuit declined to find standing because the complaint failed to allege and show that the putative class members suffered an injury as mandated by and articulated in *Friends of the Earth, Inc. v. Laidlaw Envtl. Servs. (TOC), Inc.*, 528 U.S. 167, 180–81 (2000):

> Instead, it leaves us only with questions such as whether the embryo will ever be used for research and whether that research will be funded by the NIH. We have no idea under what terms the named plaintiff embryo was donated or stored or what its status even is. In the absence of answers, the chosen appellation of Mary Scott Doe could equally designate any member of an amorphous frozen embryo class. . . . Because the class of frozen embryos includes several subsets, we have no way of knowing whether "the claims or defenses of the representative part[y] are typical of the claims or defenses of the classes [] which is to say whether the named plaintiff is threatened with the harm plaintiffs impute to the class as a

whole."

Id. at 160–61. Holding that the putative class thus did not have standing, the court added that the alleged injury could neither be "fairly traced" to Executive Order 13505 nor to the NIH Guidelines. *Id.* at 161.

The Fourth Circuit has established an approach for evaluating the standing of class plaintiffs who cannot "satisfy the statutory requirements of the laws of the States they are invoking" at the motion to dismiss stage. *Mayor of Baltimore v. Actelion Pharms. Ltd.*, 995 F.3d 123, 133–34 (4th Cir. 2021). In *Mayor of Baltimore v. Actelion Pharmaceuticals Ltd.*, the plaintiffs brought class claims under numerous states' statutes, even though the plaintiffs only alleged they were injured in three states. *Id.* Finding that the plaintiffs must show both Article III and "statutory" standing, the Fourth Circuit held that the plaintiffs could only seek relief for their own injuries under the statutes of states where they were injured. *Id.* at 134. Nevertheless, the Fourth Circuit let the plaintiffs bring class claims on behalf of people injured in other states, stating that if the requirements for class certification were met "the plaintiffs could then represent the class members who sustained damages under those laws." *Id.*

To meet Article III's traceability requirement, "there must be a causal connection between the injury and the conduct complained of—the injury has to be 'fairly . . . trace[able] to the challenged action of the defendant, and not . . . the[e] result [of] the independent action of some third party not before the court.'" *Lujan v. Defenders of Wildlife*, 504 U.S. 555, 560 (1992) (citations omitted). The Fourth Circuit has made clear, however, that the "fairly traceable standard is not equivalent to a requirement of tort causation." *Hutton v. Nat'l Board of Examiners in Optometry, Inc.*, 892 F.3d 613, 623 (4th Cir. 2019) (citations omitted). In *Hutton*, a putative class of optometrists brought suit after personal information maintained by the National Board of Examiners in Optometry (NBEO) allegedly was stolen in a data breach. *Id.* at 616. The district court found that the plaintiffs sufficiently alleged neither "injury-in-fact" nor "traceability" to satisfy Article III standing, and plaintiffs appealed. Addressing "traceability," the Fourth Circuit found that the plaintiffs' allegations that optometrists around the country began noticing that fraudulent credit cards had been opened in their names and that, during the relevant time periods, the NBEO was the only common source that collected and continued to store social security numbers, among other data, needed to open credit card accounts were sufficient factual allegations that NBEO was the "plausible source" of the plaintiffs' information for purposes of traceability. *Id.* at 623–34.

Standing in Privacy Litigation

The Fourth Circuit has issued several opinions about standing in privacy cases. In the privacy context, plaintiffs can establish standing by analogizing their alleged harms to the invasion of privacy, which has historically provided a basis for bringing claims under the common law. *See Garey v. James S. Farrin, P.C.*, 35 F.4th 917, 921 (4th Cir. 2022).

The Fourth Circuit has determined that privacy violations constitute a legally cognizable injury for purposes of standing. In *Garey v. James S. Farrin, P.C.*, the court found that a class of plaintiffs alleging North Carolina personal injury lawyers violated the Driver's Privacy Protection Act by obtaining their accident reports from state agencies and private data brokers had standing to seek monetary damages because their claims were closely related to the invasion of privacy. 35 F.4th 917, 921 (4th Cir. 2022). However, the court found that the plaintiffs lacked the requisite standing to seek injunctive relief because they could not show that future violations of their privacy were imminent. *See id.* at 923–24.

In the privacy context, the Fourth Circuit has also stated that "Article III excludes plaintiffs who rely on an abstract statutory privacy injury unless it came with a nonspeculative increased risk of identity theft." *See O'Leary*, 60 F.4th at 244. In fact, in recent data breach cases, the Fourth Circuit has held "that being subjected to a data breach isn't in and of itself sufficient to establish Article III standing without a nonspeculative, increased risk of identity theft." *See id.* For example, in *Beck v. McDonald*, the Fourth Circuit held that plaintiffs whose personal information was compromised in a data breach had not demonstrated an Article III injury based on an alleged "increased risk of future identity theft and the cost of measures to protect against it" where the plaintiffs' alleged increased risk was only speculative. *See* 848 F.3d 262, 267 (4th Cir. 2017). There, even though the plaintiffs alleged that a laptop and reports with their personal information had been stolen, the Fourth Circuit found that "the mere theft of these items, without more, cannot confer Article III standing." *Id.* at 275. By contrast, in *Hutton v. National Board of Examiners in Optometry, Inc.*, the Fourth Circuit found the plaintiffs had standing where they actually suffered identity theft and credit card fraud traceable to the defendant's data breach, and thus there was "no need to speculate on whether substantial harm will befall" them. *See* 892 F.3d 613, 621–22 (4th Cir. 2018). Thus, in privacy cases, plaintiffs must sufficiently allege a nonspeculative, increased risk of identity theft to satisfy the standing requirement. *See O'Leary*, 60 F.4th at 244–45. Alternatively, plaintiffs alleging privacy violations must sufficiently allege "an injury with a close relationship to a traditional or common-law analog," such as "intrusion upon seclusion" or the "disclosure of private information." *See id.* at 245–46 (quotations omitted).[1]

Standing in Other Contexts

To have Article III standing, a plaintiff must have a "personal stake" in the litigation. *Rhodes v. E.I. du Pont de Nemours and Co.*, 636 F.3d 88, 99 (4th Cir. 2011); *see also Krakauer v. Dish Network, L.L.C.*, 925 F.3d 643, 653 (4th Cir. 2019) (class representative had standing under the TCPA to sue on behalf of others similarly situated because the TCPA created a cause of action that protects individuals' "particular and concrete privacy interests. . . ."); *Curtis v. Propel Property Tax Funding*, LLC, 915 F.3d 234, 240–42 (4th Cir. 2019) (plaintiff alleging violations of the Electronic Funds Transfer Act (EFTA) had standing because he alleged a substantive statutory violation that subjected him to the exact risks the EFTA was designed to protect against, and the risks were particularized, real and not abstract, sufficiently concrete, and actual or imminent, not conjectural or hypothetical). In *Krakauer*, the court rejected defendant-appellant's interpretation of the Supreme Court's opinion in *Spokeo* as requiring that the plaintiff's alleged harm rise to the level that would support a common law cause of action. 925 F.3d at 653–54 (citing *Spokeo, Inc. v. Robins*, 578 U.S 330 (2016)).

In *Baehr v. Creig Northrop Team*, the Fourth Circuit addressed the requirement that, to show an injury-in-fact, a plaintiff must show "'an invasion of a legally protected interest'—i.e., an injury—that is 'concrete and particularized.'" 953 F.3d 244, 252 (4th Cir. 2020). The court explained that "concrete and particularized" are distinct requirements. "An injury is

[1] A district court in the Fourth Circuit analyzed the "traceability" requirement of Article III standing in the context of a consumer data breach class action. *See* In re Blackbaud, Inc., Customer Data Breach Litig., No. 3:20-mn-02972-JMC, 2021 WL 2718439 (D.S.C. July 1, 2021) (Childs, J.). In *In re Blackbaud*, a putative class of individuals whose personally identifiable and protected health information "was provided to Blackbaud's customers and managed by Blackbaud" brought suit after a ransomware attack comprised the putative class's data. *See id.* at *1. In a motion to dismiss, Blackbaud maintained that the injuries alleged did not satisfy Article III's traceability requirements. Considering Blackbaud's facial challenge to traceability, Judge Childs stated that "plaintiffs in a data breach case must sufficiently allege that the defendant was a plausible source of their personal information," before recognizing that the burden "is relatively modest." *Id.* at *8 (quotations omitted and alterations adopted). Denying Blackbaud's motion, the court observed that the plaintiffs had "pled a plausible connection between the types of data allegedly compromised . . . and their subsequent injuries." *Id.* at *9. The court also found that plaintiffs' assertions that "Blackbaud was a common repository of Plaintiffs' personal Information, potentially all of Plaintiffs' personal information maintained by Blackbaud was compromised . . . and Plaintiffs suffered injuries [in the form of, among other things, actual identity theft, increased risk of identity theft, and time and/or money to mitigate the risk of identity theft] shortly after the data breach" were "more than an 'ingenious academic exercise in the conceivable.'" *Id.* (citations omitted).

particularized if it 'affect[s] the plaintiff in a personal and individual way.' And an injury is concrete if it is '*de facto*'—that is, if it 'actually exist[s].'" *Id.* Injury-in-fact may be predicated on intangible harm, but "a statutory violation is not necessarily synonymous with an intangible harm that constitutes injury-in-fact." Therefore, when suing to vindicate a statutory right, a plaintiff "still must establish that she suffered a concrete injury from the violation of that right" and "cannot merely allege a 'bare procedural violation, divorced from any concrete harm' to satisfy the injury-in-fact requirement." *Id.* (citing *Spokeo, Inc. v. Robins*, 578 U.S. 330, (2016)). For statutory violations, a plaintiff meets the "concrete injury" requirement when the plaintiff "shows the harm stemming from the 'defendant's statutory violation is the type of harm Congress sought to prevent when it enacted the statute.'" *Id.* (citing *Curtis v. Propel Prop. Tax Funding*, 915 F.3d 234, 240–41 (4th Cir. 2019)).

The *Baehr* court found that plaintiffs' claim of injury under the Real Estate Settlement Procedures Act (RESPA)— that defendants allegedly engaged in illegal business referrals, which deprived plaintiffs and putative class member of "'impartial and fair competition between settlement service[s] providers,' in contravention of [RESPA]"—was not an injury-in-fact and therefore plaintiffs had no standing. *Id.* at 247. Further, the homeowners suing under RESPA based on a purported kickback scheme between defendant real estate agents and defendant title company failed to show concrete injury, or that they suffered any real-world harm at all, based on the deprivation of impartial and fair competition between real estate settlement providers. *Baehr*, 953 F.3d at 256. The named plaintiffs did not claim they were harmed by being overcharged for settlement services. *Id.* at 254. And the named plaintiffs could not show concrete injury based on an unjust enrichment theory because they failed to show that the kickback benefit gained by the real estate agent defendants caused any harm other than the statutory violation under RESPA, and the named plaintiffs' "bald allegation of unjust enrichment" was insufficient to establish concrete injury. *Id.* at 257–58.

The Fourth Circuit analyzed statutory standing in a case brought by former employees who asserted claims against fiduciaries of their former employers' defined contribution retirement plans brought suit under ERISA. *In re Mutual Funds Inv. Litig.*, 529 F3d 207 (4th Cir. 2008). Plaintiffs and the putative class took full distribution of vested benefits upon leaving their employment and sought additional benefits that purportedly would have been in their accounts absent the alleged breaches. Because the plaintiffs and putative class members sought *additional benefits* rather than *damages*, they had standing to sue under ERISA. *Id.* at 219 (finding that plaintiffs had statutory standing and constitutional standing).

In another ERISA case, the Fourth Circuit held that a named plaintiff seeking declaratory, injunctive, and other equitable relief under ERISA does not need to show financial injury to have Article III standing. *See Peters v. Aetna Inc.*, 2 F.4th 199, 219–21 (4th Cir. 2021) (finding no personal financial injury needed to have standing for claims of surcharge, disgorgement, and declaratory and injunctive relief based on allegations of breach of fiduciary duty). Rather, a plaintiff must only allege the violation of the fiduciary duty owed to them as a participant and beneficiary of their ERISA plan. *Id.* Further, the Fourth Circuit determined that although a showing of financial injury is required to bring a claim for restitution, the standing analysis of injury differs from the merits analysis. *See id.* at 217–18. For purposes of standing, it is sufficient to show the named plaintiff was harmed by some aspect of the defendant's conduct, even if the plaintiff ultimately benefitted from other parts of the defendant's conduct. *See id.* at 218–19; *see also Alig v. Quicken Loans Inc.*, 990 F.3d 782, 792 (4th Cir. 2021) ("[O]nce injury is shown, no attempt is made to ask whether the injury is outweighed by benefits the plaintiff has enjoyed from the relationship with the defendant." (quotation omitted)).

In the antitrust context, the named plaintiff and putative class must establish both Article III standing and antitrust standing. *In re Zetia (Ezetimibe) Antitrust Litig.*, 7 F.4th 227, 238 (4th Cir. 2021). The Fourth Circuit has found that industry and class-wide averages may be used to prove injury for both Article III and antitrust standing. *Id.*

c. The Mootness Doctrine

Article III of the Constitution limits the jurisdiction of the federal courts to the consideration of "cases" and "controversies." U.S. Const. art. III, § 2. As discussed above, a plaintiff must have a personal interest—or personal stake—in the outcome of the case; otherwise, the case is neither a "case" nor "controversy" as required by Article III. Rhodes *v. E.I. du Pont de Nemours and Co.*, 636 F.3d 88, 99 (4th Cir. 2011) (citing *United States v. Hardy*, 545 F.3d 280, 283 (4th Cir. 2008)). "Standing is determined at the commencement of a lawsuit. However, even if a plaintiff has standing when he or she files a complaint, subsequent events can moot the claim." *Pashby v. Delia*, 709 F.3d 307, 316 (4th Cir. 2013) (citations omitted). "[T]he doctrine of mootness constitutes a part of the constitutional limits of federal court jurisdiction .... [A] case is moot when the issues presented are no longer 'live' or the parties lack a legally cognizable interest in the outcome." *Simmons v. United Mortg. and Loan Inv., LLC*, 634 F.3d 754, 763 (4th Cir. 2011) (citing *United States v. Hardy*, 545 F.3d 280, 283 (4th Cir. 2008) (internal quotation marks and citations omitted)). Intervening changes to factual circumstances or a change in the law can cause a case to become moot, as can the circumstance when a claimant receives the relief he or she sought. *Id.*

In class actions, the named class representatives "'must allege and show that they personally have been injured, not that injury has been suffered by other, unidentified members of the class to which they belong.'" *Pashby*, 709 F.3d at 316 (citing *Blujm v. Yaretsky*, 457 U.S. 991, 1001 n.13 (1983)). Importantly, however, in the context of class actions, the Fourth Circuit has held that "[i]f the named plaintiff's claim is a live controversy at the time of class certification, the case will *not* become moot even if the named plaintiff's personal claim later expires." *Id.* at 316 (citing *U.S. Parole Comm'n v. Geraghty*, 445 U.S. 388, 398–99 (1980)). That is because the class members themselves are parties to the lawsuit after a grant of class certification. And even if the named plaintiff's individual claim becomes moot before a class is certified, the Fourth Circuit has determined that class "certification may relate back to the filing of the complaint if other class members will continue to be subject to the challenged conduct and the claims raised are inherently transitory." *Jonathan R. by Dixon v. Justice*, 41 F.4th 316, 325 (4th Cir. 2022) (quotation omitted and alteration adopted). This exception applies in situations where there is uncertainty about whether a named plaintiff's claim will remain alive, where defendants create a significant possibility that any named plaintiff would be dismissed prior to certification, and where the court may safely assume that counsel has other clients with a continuing live interest in the case. *See id.* at 326.

3. PLEADING CONSIDERATIONS

The Fourth Circuit examined the *Iqbal/Twombly* pleading requirement in a putative class action in which the plaintiff alleged police officers in Charlottesville, Virginia, violated the Equal Protection Clause and Fourth Amendment by approaching black men and asking for DNA samples as part of a long-term investigation of a serial rapist. *See Monroe v. City of Charlottesville, Va.*, 579 F.3d 380, 384 (4th Cir. 2009) (citation omitted). The Fourth Circuit affirmed the district court's dismissal of plaintiff's Fourth Amendment seizure claim following the *Twombly* precedent that a "complaint must be dismissed if it does not allege 'enough facts to state a claim to relief that is plausible on its face.'" *Id.* at 385. (citations omitted). To elevate an encounter to the level of a seizure is an objective analysis based on a reasonable person standard. Because the plaintiff did not plead sufficient facts showing that a reasonable person would not have felt free to terminate the encounter, his Fourth Amendment claim was properly dismissed on a Rule 12(b)(6) motion. *Id.* at 386–87. For similar reasons, the Fourth Circuit concluded that district court also properly dismissed plaintiff's equal protection claim because the complaint failed to show that the city classified him based on his race but, rather, that officers approached him because he fit the description of a suspect. *Id.* at 388.

In the securities fraud class action context, the Fourth Circuit applies the exacting pleading requirements for, among other things, loss causation under the Private Securities Litigation Reform Act of 1995 (PSLRA). *See Katyle v. Penn Nat. Gaming, Inc.*, 637 F.3d 462, 466 (4th Cir. 2011); *Teachers' Ret. Sys. v. Hunter*, 477 F.3d 162, 186 (4th Cir. 2007). The Fourth Circuit reviews loss-causation allegations for "'sufficient specificity,' a standard largely consonant with Fed. R. Civ. P. 9(b)'s requirement that averments of fraud be pled with particularity." *Katyle*, 637 F.3d at 471 (citation omitted). "Of course in this Circuit, pleading practice requires that a plaintiff, as a precursor to proof, allege loss causation in the complaint 'with sufficient specificity to enable the court to evaluate whether the necessary causal link exists.'" *Id.* at 466–67 (citing *Hunter*, 477 F.3d at 186). The Fourth Circuit requires that the allegations show the misrepresentation or omission was "'one substantial cause of the investment's decline in value.'" *Katyle*, 637 F.3d at 472 (quoting *In re Mutual Funds Inv. Litig.*, 566 F.3d 111, 128 (4th Cir. 2009)).

> [T]he complaint must allege a sufficiently direct relationship between the plaintiff's economic loss and the defendant's fraudulent conduct .... "[I]f the connection is attenuated ... a fraud claim will not lie. That is because the loss causation requirement—as with the foreseeability limitation in tort—is intended to fix a legal limit on a person's responsibility, even for wrongful acts."

Katyle, 637 F.3d at 472; *see also Lentell v. Merrill Lynch & Co., Inc.*, 396 F.3d 161, 171 (4th Cir. 2005) (affirming dismissal of securities fraud claims because plaintiffs failed to meet the heightened pleading requirement of the PSLRA for loss causation).

In 2023, however, the Fourth Circuit relaxed Fed. R. Civ. P. 9(b)'s standard for allegations of fraud by omission or concealment. The Fourth Circuit joined several other jurisdictions in holding that "[w]hen alleging fraud by omission or concealment, plaintiffs may partly rely on information and belief without running afoul of Rule 9(b)" as long as they "state the factual allegations that make their belief plausible." *See Corder v. Antero Res. Corp.*, 57 F.4th 384, 402 (4th Cir. 2023). Nevertheless, the Fourth Circuit emphasized that this relaxed Rule 9(b) standard for allegations of fraud by omission or concealment does not eliminate the particularity requirement. *See id.*

4. PREREQUISITES

a. Ascertainability

The Fourth Circuit considers ascertainability to be an implicit threshold requirement of Rule 23. *EQT Production Co. v. Adair*, 764 F.3d 347, 358 (4th Cir. 2014). The ascertainability requirement applies to Rule 23(b)(1) and Rule 23(b)(3) cases. *See Kadel v. Folwell*, 100 F.4th 122, 160 (4th Cir. 2024). But there is no ascertainability requirement for Rule 23(b)(2) cases seeking only injunctive relief. *See id.* at 161 ("There is no threshold ascertainability requirement in this Rule 23(b)(2) case, which seeks only declaratory and injunctive relief from a discriminatory policy."). Ascertainability requires that "members of a proposed class be readily identifiable." *EQT*, 764 F.3d at 358. To be certified as a class, the class members must be readily identifiable through objective criteria. *Id.* "The plaintiffs need not be able to identify every class member at the time of certification. But if class members are impossible to identify without extensive and individualized fact-finding or mini-trials, then a class action is inappropriate." *See id.* (internal quotation marks and citation omitted). A class definition written with strict adherence to a statutory cause of action pertaining to who may sue thereunder provides clear guidance for crafting an identifiable class. *Krakauer v. Dish Network, L.L.C.*, 925 F.3d 643, 656 (4th Cir. 2019). Furthermore, the Fourth Circuit has indicated ascertainability may be satisfied where class members can be objectively identified through the defendant's own data. *See Peters v. Aetna Inc.*, 2 F.4th 199, 242 (4th Cir. 2021) ("the proposed class members appeared to be objectively identifiable based on Appellees' own data").

b. Rule 23(a) Requirements

Numerosity

Rule 23 provides that certification is proper only if "the class is so numerous that joinder of all members is impracticable." Fed. R. Civ. P. 23(a)(1). "Though no specified number is needed to maintain a class action, as a general guideline, a class that encompasses fewer than 20 members will likely not be certified while a class of 40 or more members raises a presumption of impracticability of joinder based on numbers alone." *In re Zetia (Ezetimibe) Antitrust Litig.*, 7 F.4th 227, 234 (4th Cir. 2021) (internal citations and quotations omitted and alterations adopted). "For the gray area cases between twenty and forty members, all the circumstances of the case should be taken into consideration in evaluating the impracticability of joinder." *Id.* (internal citations and quotations omitted). The Fourth Circuit has indicated that some factors to be considered in the numerosity analysis are "'judicial economy, the claimants' ability and motivation to litigate as joined plaintiffs, the financial resources of class members, and the geographic dispersion of class members.'" *Id.* (alteration adopted) (quoting *In re Modafinil Antitrust Litig.*, 837 F.3d 238, 253 (3d Cir. 2016)). However, for purposes of numerosity, the critical question is not whether individual suits would be uneconomical but whether joinder itself would be impracticable. *Id.* at 234–36 (finding the district court erred by focusing on the impracticability of individual suits rather than the impracticability of joinder).

Commonality

Rule 23(a)(2) requires a plaintiff to show that "there are questions of law or fact common to the class." Fed. R. Civ. P. 23(a)(2). "Although the rule speaks in terms of common questions, 'what matters to class certification is the capacity of a classwide proceeding to generate common *answers* apt to drive the resolution of the litigation.'" *EQT Production Co. v. Adair*, 764 F.3d 347, 360 (4th Cir. 2014) (quoting *Wal-Mart Stores, Inc. v. Dukes*, 564 U.S. 338 (2011)). "A single common question will suffice, but it must be of such a nature that its determination 'will resolve an issue that is central to the validity of each one of the claims in one stroke.'" *Id.* Not just any common question will suffice. Rather, "[c]ommonality requires the plaintiff to demonstrate that the class members have suffered the same injury[,] . . . a shared injury that also springs forth from the same 'common contention.'" *Ealy v. Pinkerton Gov't Serv., Inc.*, 514 F. App'x 299, 304 (4th Cir. 2013) (quoting *Wal-Mart*, 564 U.S. at 349–50). "It is not enough that the class members 'have all suffered a violation of the same provision of law.' Rather, all class members' 'claims must depend upon a common contention' that is capable of classwide resolution. 'Dissimilarities within the proposed class' have 'the potential to impede the generation of common answers.'" *G.T. v. Bd. of Educ. of Cnty. of Kanawha*, No. 21-2286, 2024 WL 4049222, at *5 (4th Cir. Sept. 5, 2024) (internal citations omitted) (quoting *Wal-Mart*, 564 U.S. at 349–50).

The Fourth Circuit has emphasized the rigorous analysis required by Rule 23, referencing the *Wal-Mart* decision. *See Ealy*, 514 F. App'x at 306. Finding the district court's requisite rigorous analysis exemplary, in *Krakauer v. Dish Network, L.L.C.*, the court wrote:

> Class adjudication is complicated, and getting it right requires a careful parsing of the claims and the evidence from the start. It also requires striking a balance between efficient administration and fairness to all those affected, whether they be the class members, the defendants, or absent parties who are nonetheless bound by the judgment. The proceedings below reflected just the measured and thorough approach that we might hope for in such demanding situations.

925 F.3d 643, 663 (4th Cir. 2019).

Based chiefly on this principle, the Fourth Circuit held that the *Ealy* district court's "oral ruling and brief written order" did not adequately analyze common questions of fact, did not address the typicality requirement "in any meaningful way," and did not conduct the separate inquiry as to whether common questions of law or fact predominate over individual ones. *Ealy*, 514 F. App'x at 306.

In *EQT Production*, the Fourth Circuit vacated the district court's decision to certify five related class action lawsuits, in part, for failing to conduct a merits analysis critical to a finding of commonality. 764 F.3d at 359–60, 361. The *EQT* plaintiffs alleged that defendants unlawfully deprived class members of royalty payments from the production of coalbed methane gas (CBM) in Virginia. While originally considered a dangerous waste by-product of coal mining, CBM was recognized as a material that could be used as an energy resource by the 1970s and since then has been recognized in Virginia as a "distinct mineral estate." *Id.* at 353. Being a distinct mineral estate means ownership rights to it may be severed from the land. *Id.*

Gas estate and coal estate ownership rights have "long plagued" CBM's commercial development in Virginia. *Id.* at 353. In a pivotal case, *Harrison-Wyatt, LLC v. Ratliff*, 267 Va. 549, 593 S.E.2d 234, 248 (2004), the Supreme Court of Virginia considered a nineteenth-century severance deed and held that the conveyance of coal did not transfer title to the CBM estate. *Id.* at 360. And the Virginia legislature subsequently codified the *Harrison-Wyatt* holding in Va. Code Ann. 45.1-361.21:1. *Id.* Commonality, therefore, turned on the proper interpretation of *Harrison-Wyatt*—whether its holding means that a severance deed conveying coal never transfers title to CBM (as plaintiffs argued) or whether deed language varies such that the ownership can be determined only on a deed-by-deed basis (as defendants argued). *Id.* at 361.

The Fourth Circuit concluded the district court erred by not resolving this central, merits issue. If plaintiffs do not prevail on their argument that a severance deed never transfers title to the CBM estate and they have no other argument as to how CBM ownership can be resolved on a classwide basis, "they will have failed to carry their burden of establishing even a single common question." *Id.*

Further, the Fourth Circuit addressed the predominance factor and concluded that the district court's certification of classes asserting claims of royalty underpayment also was error because the district court did not identify how defendants' uniform conduct was significant to the "broader litigation." *Id.* at 365.

> [T]he mere fact that the defendants engaged in uniform conduct is not, by itself, sufficient to satisfy Rule 23(b)(3)'s more demanding predominance requirement. The predominance inquiry focuses not only on the existence of common questions, but also on how those questions relate to the controversy at the heart of the litigation. Even a plethora of identical practices will not satisfy the predominance requirement if the defendants' common conduct has little bearing on the central issue in the litigation—in this case, whether the defendants underpaid royalties. Absent such a relationship, there is no basis for concluding that individual issues will not predominate.

Id. at 366 (internal citation omitted).

The court concluded that the district court placed an "inordinate emphasis on the sheer number" of common practices without concluding whether they were relevant to defendants' ultimate liability. *Id.* The court—holding that the district court's analysis "lacked the requisite rigor" to ensure Rule 23's requirements were satisfied—vacated the decision granting class certification and remanded for further consideration consistent with its opinion. *Id.* at 371 ("We are not unsympathetic to [the] plight of [CBM owners 'who haven't received a penny of CBM royalties . . .']. But sympathy alone cannot justify certification under Rule 23.").

Echoing this approach, but upholding class certification, the court in *Krakauer* readily concluded that the trial court thoroughly documented that "all of the major issues [in this TCPA litigation] could be shown through aggregate records," and as such, the case met the predominance requirement. 925 F.3d at 658.

Reversing the denial of class certification in a race discrimination class action, the Fourth Circuit held, in part, that plaintiffs' direct anecdotal evidence of discrimination was "worthy of class certification." *See Brown v. Nucor Corp.*, 576 F.3d 149, 150 (4th Cir. 2009). Further, the Fourth Circuit concluded that the district court erred by excluding plaintiff's statistical evidence because the relevant question was not whether the statistical data proves discrimination but rather whether it was sufficient to support class certification. *Id.* at 156. The court therefore remanded the case to the district court.

Six years later, the Fourth Circuit again vacated the district court's decertification of a promotion class in *Brown v. Nucor Corp.*, 785 F.3d 895, 898 (4th Cir. 2015) (*Nucor II*). Reviewing the decertification order, the Fourth Circuit stated that the district court "fundamentally misapprehended the reach of *Wal-Mart*. . . ." *Id.* In *Nucor II*, the court distinguished *Wal-Mart* on the basis that the case before it concerned approximately 100 class members in a single steel plant. The class members shared common spaces, had regular interaction with departments other than their own, and were free to apply for promotions in other departments. In contrast, *Wal-Mart* involved approximately 1.5 million employees working at 3,400 stores, and the *Wal-Mart* "plaintiffs could not establish that a store greeter in Northern California, for instance, was subject to the same discrimination as a cashier in New Hampshire." *Id.* at 909 (noting also that the *Nucor* plaintiffs had substantial anecdotal evidence that supported plaintiffs' allegation that Nucor had a pattern and practice of tolerating discriminatory conduct).

Notably, in 2022, the Fourth Circuit held that in a Rule 23(b)(3) class action, "the commonality requirement of Rule 23(a)(2) is subsumed under, or superseded by, the more stringent Rule 23(b)(3) requirement that questions common to the class predominate over other questions." *1988 Tr. for Allen Child. Dated 8/8/88 v. Banner Life Ins. Co.*, 28 F.4th 513, 522 (4th Cir. 2022) (quotations omitted).

The Fourth Circuit has also clarified that at the class certification stage, courts may only consider merits questions "to the extent necessary to verify that Rule 23 has been satisfied." *Williams v. Martorello*, 59 F.4th 68, 91 (4th Cir. 2023) (quotation omitted). Thus, it is improper for a district court to deny class certification simply because it finds the plaintiffs' evidence unpersuasive or because it believes the plaintiffs are unlikely to succeed on the merits. *See id.* at 92.

In 2024, the Fourth Circuit dismissed a class action brought under the Individuals with Disabilities Education Act (IDEA), agreeing with other circuits that "to meet the commonality prerequisite for class certification, plaintiffs in an IDEA case . . . must identify a uniformly applied, official policy of the school district, or an unofficial yet well-defined practice, that drives the alleged violation." *G.T. v. Bd. of Educ. of Cnty. of Kanawha*, No. 21-2286, 2024 WL 4049222, at *7 (4th Cir. Sept. 5, 2024). In that case, the court found commonality was not satisfied because the plaintiffs could not identify "a common contention central to the validity of all class members' claims." *Id.*

Typicality

"The commonality and typicality requirements of Rule 23(a) tend to merge." *1988 Tr. for Allen Child. Dated 8/8/88 v. Banner Life Ins. Co.*, 28 F.4th 513, 523 (4th Cir. 2022) (quotation omitted). Typicality under Rule 23(a)(2) examines whether the named plaintiff—or class representative—can sufficiently represent the interests of the class as a whole. *Ealy v. Pinkerton Gov't Serv., Inc.*, 514 F. App'x 299, 304–05 (4th Cir. 2013) (citing *Deiter v. Microsoft Corp.*, 436 F.3d 461, 466 (4th Cir. 2006)). Meeting the typicality requirement does not, of course, mean that the interest of the class representative must be identical to the interests of the class members; rather typicality requires that "the representative's pursuit of his own interests must simultaneously tend to advance the interests of the absent class members." *Id.* at 305.

> In order to conduct a typicality analysis a court must compare the plaintiffs' claims or defenses with those of the absent class members. That analysis will necessarily entail [1] a review of the elements of plaintiffs' *prima facie* case; [2] the facts on which the plaintiffs would necessarily rely to prove those elements; and [3] a determination of to what extent those facts would also prove the claims of the absent class members.

Id. at 304–05 (internal citation and quotation marks omitted). The Fourth Circuit has stated that "the essence of the typicality requirement is captured by the notion that as goes the claim of the named plaintiff, so go the claims of the class." *Soutter v. Equifax Information Serv., LLC*, 498 F. App'x 260, 264 (4th Cir. 2012) (internal quotation marks and citation omitted). Additionally, the Fourth Circuit has stated that "contesting a class representative's injury does not defeat typicality" if the representative "will rely on the same common evidence as the class to prove its injury at trial." *In re Zetia (Ezetimibe) Antitrust Litig.*, 7 F.4th 227, 237 (4th Cir. 2021).

Reversing the district court in *Ealy*, the Fourth Circuit demonstrated that typicality must be given the rigorous analysis required by *Wal-Mart*. *See* 514 F. App'x at 305–06 (holding that the district court did not compare the claims of the representative parties with the class as a whole and referencing the *Wal-Mart* decision). And in *Soutter*, the Fourth Circuit found that the district court wrongly certified a class where the evidence needed to prove the class representative's claims was not the same evidence that would prove the claims of the class members because the defendant consumer reporting agency engaged in multiple practices when retrieving and reporting judgments entered against individual consumers. 498 F. App'x at 265. Similarly, the court affirmed a decertification order in *Hart v. Louisiana-Pacific Corp.*, because, in large part, the defendant provided substantially different remedy provisions in its product warranties before and after 2005, which undermined typicality. 641 F. App'x 222 (4th Cir. 2016).

Adequacy

Under Rule 23(a)(4), a district court may certify a class only if the class representative "will fairly and adequately protect the interests of the class." *Ward v. Dixie Nat. Life Ins. Co.*, 595 F.3d 164, 179 (4th Cir. 2010). To satisfy adequacy, a class representative must "be of a character to vigorously pursue the case." *Monroe*, 579 F.3d at 385. A class representative must have "sufficient interest, credibility, or either knowledge or an understanding of the case—although a knowledge or understanding of all the intricacies of the litigation is not required. . . ." *Id.* The adequacy requirement is intended to ensure that representative parties are not "simply lending their names to a suit controlled entirely by the class attorney." *Id.*

The adequacy requirement also ensures class counsel is competent and protects against fundamental conflicts of interest between the named parties and the class they seek to represent. *1988 Tr. for Allen Child. Dated 8/8/88 v. Banner Life Ins. Co.*, 28 F.4th 513, 524 (4th Cir. 2022). Notably, a conflict of interest will not defeat the adequacy requirement for class certification where the conflict is merely speculative or hypothetical. *Id.* As the Fourth Circuit has explained, a "conflict is not fundamental when [] all class members share common objectives and the same factual and legal positions and have the same interest in establishing the liability of defendants." *Ward*, 595 F.3d at 180. In *Ward*, the Fourth Circuit held that the "uncertain prediction" the lawsuit will cause insurance premiums to increase, adversely impacting certain class members, did not create a fundamental conflict of interest because that prediction was merely speculative. *Id.* The Fourth Circuit has also recognized that adequacy is not defeated where a class representative is "*more* highly motivated than unnamed class members to advance their shared interests." *Carolina Youth Action Project; D.S. by & through Ford v. Wilson*, 60 F.4th 770, 781 (4th Cir. 2023).

c. Rule 23(b) Requirements

Rule 23(b)(2) Classes

A "(b)(2) class," as it is commonly called, is a class that seeks injunctive relief—relief requiring a defendant to either do something or refrain from doing something. To obtain class treatment as a (b)(2) class, the plaintiff must show that "the party opposing the class has acted or refused to act on grounds that apply generally to the class, so that final injunctive relief or corresponding declaratory relief is appropriate respecting the class as a whole." *EQT Production Co. v. Adair*, 764 F.3d 347, 357 (4th Cir. 2014). The Fourth Circuit has stated that the "key" to a (b)(2) case is the "'indivisible nature of the . . . remedy warranted.'" *Id.* (quoting Wal-Mart *Stores, Inc.* v. Dukes, 564 U.S. 338 (2011)). "Certification under this provision is appropriate only where a single injunction or declaratory judgment would provide relief to each member of the class." *EQT Production*, 764 F.3d at 357.

Federal circuits, including the Fourth Circuit, have held that (b)(2) classes may be certified in some circumstances even where monetary relief also is at issue for the class members. The test is which relief predominates. Where monetary relief is more predominate than the injunctive relief sought by the (b)(2) class members, certification of a (b)(2) class is not appropriate. However, where "monetary relief is 'incidental' to the injunctive or declaratory relief, (b)(2) class certification is permissible." *Berry v. Schulman*, 807 F.3d 600, 609 (4th Cir. 2015).

In *Berry*, plaintiffs alleged that defendant Lexis failed to provide the protections of the Fair Credit Reporting Act (FCRA) in the sale of consumers' personal data reports to debt collectors. *Id.* at 604. After years of litigation and negotiations, the parties reached a settlement whereby Lexis agreed to make sweeping changes to its processes. In exchange, the (b)(2) class members agreed to release their claims to statutory damages under the FCRA, although the class members retained their rights to pursue any actual damages. *Id.* A (b)(3) class also sought class certification as a settlement class and released all claims against Lexis in exchange for approximately $300 per person. *Id.* at 606. Not everyone liked this deal and "a group of class members claiming the right to opt out of the settlement class and pursue statutory damages individually" (the objectors) sought to undo it. *Id.* The objectors challenged only the (b)(2) class settlement.

The objectors argued that the statutory damages that were waived by the (b)(2) class predominated over and were not incidental to the injunctive relief obtained. *Id.* at 609. The Fourth Circuit disagreed, affirming the district court's decision and endorsing its reasoning that the lawsuit presented a "paradigmatic Rule 23(b)(2) case," whereby Lexis provided "meaningful, valuable injunctive relief" that was indivisible to the class members and benefited them all at once. *Id.* Because the statutory damages released under the agreement flowed "'directly from liability to the class as a whole on the same set of claims,'" they were not individualized, they were merely incidental, and certification of the (b)(2) class was proper. *Id.* at 610 (internal citation omitted).

Rule 23(b)(3) Classes

Rule 23(b)(3) permits certification where "questions of law or fact common to the members of the class *predominate* over any questions affecting only individual members, and that a class action is *superior* to other available methods for the fair and efficient adjudication of the controversy." Fed. R. Civ. P. 23(b)(3) (emphasis added). The plaintiff bears the burden of proving the elements of Rule 23 are met, and in a (b)(3) class certification context, the focus of proof is predominance and superiority. The Fourth Circuit has explained that predominance is a more exacting standard than Rule 23(a)(2)'s commonality requirement. "[T]he commonality requirement of Rule 23(a)(2) is subsumed under, or superseded by, the more stringent Rule 23(b)(3) requirement that questions common to the class predominate over other questions." *Gray v. Hearst Communications, Inc.*, 444 F. App'x 698, 700 (4th Cir. 2011) (internal quotation marks and citation omitted). "The Rule 23(b)(3) predominance requirement is 'far more demanding' than Rule 23(a)(2)'s commonality requirement, and the 'predominance inquiry tests whether proposed classes are sufficiently cohesive to warrant adjudication by representation.'" *Id.* at 701 (quoting *Amchem Prods. Inc. v. Windsor*, 521 U.S. 591 (1997)). "[T]o satisfy Rule 23(b)(3), '[c]ommon questions must predominate over any questions affecting only individual members; . . . [such that] a class action would achieve economies of time, effort, and expense, and promote . . . uniformity of decision as to persons similarly situated.'" *Id.* (quoting *Amchem*, 521 U.S. at 615 (internal quotation marks omitted)).

Importantly, in a Rule 23(b)(3) case, "the predominance inquiry focuses not only on the existence of common questions, but also on how those questions relate to the controversy at the heart of the litigation."*1988 Tr. for Allen Child. Dated 8/8/88 v. Banner Life Ins. Co.*, 28 F.4th 513, 522 (4th Cir. 2022) (internal quotations and citations omitted). Thus, in evaluating whether predominance has been met, courts must "give careful scrutiny to the relation between common and individual questions" because "even a plethora of identical practices will not satisfy the predominance requirement if the defendants' common conduct has little bearing on the central issue in the litigation." *Williams v. Martorello*, 59 F.4th 68, 86 (4th Cir. 2023) (quotations omitted and alteration adopted).

In *Krakauer v. Dish Network, L.L.C.*, the court observed that "[e]fficient and manageable classes require common proof," such that Rule 23 applicability often turns on the cause of action itself. 925 F.3d 643, 655 (4th Cir. 2019). Under the TCPA, proof is made simple. A plaintiff must show: a telephone number on the Do-Not-Call registry, two calls made to that number in a year, and damages may be set up to $500 with no proof of actual loss. *Id.* "The problems that so often plague class actions under Rule 23(b)(3) are wholly absent from this [statutory] scheme." *Id.* "The liability determinations [under the TCPA] involve no questions of individual reliance . . . no complicated contractual obligations . . . and no theories of probabilistic injury. . . ." *Id.* at 655–56 (citations omitted). Importantly, the Fourth Circuit also observed that "[t]he entire notion of predominance implies that the plaintiffs' claims need not be identical, and, as the Supreme Court has noted, a class can meet this requirement 'even though other important matters will be tried separately.'" *Id.* at 658 (quoting *Tyson Foods, Inc. v. Bouaphakeo*, 577 U.S. 442, 453 (2016)). Finding that "issues common to the plaintiffs clearly predominated over individual issues" in that case, the Fourth Circuit noted that "all of the major issues in the case could be shown through aggregate records[,] ... [t]he facts that were relevant to [the defendant's] liability were also common to the class[,] ... [and] the plaintiffs sought a statutory damages award, preventing the need to measure individual compensatory damages." *Id.* (citations omitted).

To determine whether the superiority requirement is met, the "court initially must consider what other procedures, if any, exist for disposing of the dispute before it." *Stillmock v. Weis Markets, Inc.*, 385 F. App'x 267, 274 (4th Cir. 2010). "The court must compare the possible alternatives to determine whether Rule 23 is sufficiently effective to justify the expenditure of the judicial time and energy that is necessary to adjudicate a class action and to assume the risk of prejudice to the rights of those who are not directly before the court." *Id.* (internal citation omitted).

Recently, the Fourth Circuit addressed the importance of considering superiority in the context of issue certification. Rule 23(c)(4) of the Federal Rules of Civil Procedure provides that "[w]hen appropriate, an action may be brought or maintained as a class action with respect to particular issues." The Fourth Circuit has determined that this rule allows class actions to be certified with respect to particular causes of action, even where the lawsuit as a whole would not meet Rule 23(b)'s predominance requirement. *See In re Marriott Int'l, Inc.*, 78 F.4th 677, 688 (4th Cir. 2023) (citing *Gunnells v. Healthplan Services, Inc.*, 348 F.3d 417 (4th Cir. 2003)). However, the Fourth Circuit has not yet ruled whether common questions need only predominate over individual questions relating to the specific issues that are certified or over those relating to the entire cause of action. *See id.* at 689. Nevertheless, in *In re Marriott Int'l, Inc.*, the Fourth Circuit stated that "if courts certify classes on individual elements of a cause of action, Rule 23(b)(3)'s superiority requirement takes on special importance." *See id.* at 689. In so doing, the court stated that "the superiority component of Rule 23(b)(3) frequently comes into play to defeat issue certification." *See id.* This is because the efficiency of a class action proceeding with respect to certain issues can sometimes be outweighed by the time and resources needed to address the remaining individualized issues. *See id.* at 689–90. Accordingly, the Fourth Circuit clarified that "[i]n the Rule 23(c)(4) issue-class context . . . the superiority of class proceedings simply cannot be taken for granted, even when common questions predominate as to the certified issues. Instead, courts must evaluate this question of efficiency carefully." *See id.* at 690 (quotation omitted).

5. DEFENDANT CLASS ACTIONS

Referring to them as "unicorns," the Fourth Circuit examined an order certifying a class action in "one of the rarest types of complex litigation, the defendant class action." *Bell v. Brockett*, 922 F.3d 502, 504 (4th Cir. 2019) (citation omitted). In *Bell*, the court considered whether the district court erred in certifying a class without simultaneously appointing class counsel and by not analyzing the adequacy of class counsel. Additionally, the Fourth Circuit determined that the district court did, in fact, err by failing to properly follow Rule 23 class certification procedure but decided that the errors did not require reversal "due to the unique circumstances of [the] case." *Id.*

Bell involved an alleged Ponzi scheme related to revenues ostensibly generated from an online auction business. Revenues, however, were actually generated from "Affiliates" who purchased VIP bids entitling them to share in profits of the online auction. *Id.* After the SEC filed an enforcement action that shuttered the operation, Kenneth Bell was appointed as the receiver. Bell filed an action to recover proceeds paid to the "Net Winners" to be returned to the "Net Losers" and sought certification of a defendant class under Rules 23(a), 23(b)(1)(A) and 23(b)(1)(B).

In moving to certify the defendant class, Bell argued that the proposed class representatives and their counsel would provide "fair and adequate representation of the defendant class's interest under Rule 23(a)(4)." *Id.* at 505. Bell further argued that "'[c]ounsel retained by the proposed Class Representatives are experienced and qualified attorneys, fully capable of protecting the interests of their clients and consequently the class.'" *Id.* Bell also contended that "'by virtue of defending themselves, the named Defendants will inevitably and fully litigate the merits of the claims against the other class members.'" *Id.* at 505–06.

In opposing class certification, some of the named defendants argued against adequacy on cost grounds, detailing the extensive costs that would be imposed on the proposed class representatives and class counsel. Notably, however, they did not address the due process concerns related to whether the court had personal jurisdiction of the absent class members or whether the absent class members should have notice or opt-out rights. *Id.* at 506.

In certifying the class, and although not required under Rule 23, the district court approved a notice of class certification that informed class members of their membership in the defendant class. The notice further informed class members that any ruling on the merits would be legally binding on them, stating in part:

> You will, however, have an opportunity to participate in the process if the Net Winner Class is found to be required to repay their net winnings. If liability is found, the Receiver intends to seek a court Judgment against each class member in the amount of their individualized net winnings plus interest. . . . While the specifics of the process for determining those amounts has not yet been decided, the Receiver intends to seek a process that will notify you of the amount of your net winnings according to [a defendant's] records, allow you a reasonable opportunity to provide a response . . . and then either reach an agreement on the amount or have

> the amount determined by a judicial process.

Id. at 506.

Fact and expert discovery proceeded, liability was determined on summary judgment in favor of Bell against the defendant class, and the damages phase proceeded with ultimate notice to the defendant class of the amount of their individual liability. *Id.* at 507–08. Over two years after the district court's certification order and notice to the defendant class, and almost two years after the appointment of class counsel, the first objection was raised by an absent class member that challenged the adequacy of class counsel. *Id.* at 509. Without ruling on the objection, the district court entered final judgment against the class. About one month later, additional absent class members moved to intervene, decertify, and alternatively, alter or vacate the final judgment on the grounds that due process was violated because class counsel failed to adequately and vigorously represent the class. At this point in the litigation, other class members had reached over 2,500 settlements in reliance on the class-action proceedings. *Id.* at 509. In denying decertification, the district court dismissed the absent class members' arguments as "'nothing less than an attempt to second guess the strategic choices made by counsel as to the best arguments to make or investigation to pursue.'" *Id.*

The Fourth Circuit affirmed, highlighting the fact that due process concerns are "especially important for a defendant class where due process risks are magnified." *Id.* at 511.

> In defendant class actions, an unnamed class member can be brought into a case, required to engage in discovery and even be subjected to a judgment compelling the payment of money or other relief without ever being individually served with a lawsuit.

Id. On this reasoning, the court noted that compliance with Rule 23 is necessary to protect against the heightened due process concerns. *Id.*

The Fourth Circuit found that the district court did not properly follow Rule 23 by failing to appoint class counsel at the time of certification and appointing class counsel seven months thereafter. *Id.* at 512. The court further concluded that the district court did not comply with Rule 23(g), which sets forth the factors that must be considered in determining the adequacy of class counsel. *Id.*

While the court acknowledged that failure to comply with Rule 23 in the "vast majority of cases" renders class certification "fatally defective," the court nevertheless found the unique circumstances of this case compelled affirmance. *Id.* Although the absent class members argued that their objections were raised below, the Fourth Circuit determined that they were not. Concluding that appellants may not raise arguments on appeal that were not raised before the district court, the Fourth Circuit ultimately affirmed. *Id.* at 513. In addition, the court noted that, given the posture of the litigation, it would be difficult—if not impossible—to remedy the errors now raised by the absent class members, including the fact that over 2,500 class members settled the claims against them.

6. CLASS NOTICE

Rule 23(d)(1)(B) permits the court to issue orders that "require—to protect class members and fairly conduct the action—giving appropriate notice to some or all class members of (i) any step in the action; (ii) the proposed extent of the judgment; or (iii) the members' opportunity to signify whether they consider the representation fair and adequate, to intervene and present claims or defenses, or to otherwise come into the action."

"Rule 23(b)(3) requires notice to class members, who are afforded an opportunity to opt-out of the class at the certification stage . . . . The rule is 'designed to secure judgments binding all class members save those who affirmatively elected to be excluded.'" *Krakauer v. Dish Network, L.L.C.*, 925 F.3d 643, 655 (4th Cir. 2019).

For a class action settlement to bind absent class members, class notice must be "reasonably calculated, under all the circumstances, to apprise absent class members of the pendency of the action and afford them an opportunity to present their objections." *McAdams v. Robinson*, 26 F.4th 149, 157–58 (4th Cir. 2022) (quotations omitted and alteration adopted). The class notice must describe the terms of the settlement in sufficient detail to "alert those with adverse viewpoints to investigate and to come forward and be heard." *Id.* at 158 (quotation omitted). There is no requirement that class notice estimate class members' recovery. *See id.* Instead, class notice is adequate when class members are given access to information about the total settlement, attorneys' fees, and distribution method, and the notice provides class members with the means to find more information if they want it. *See id.* at 159. Importantly, class notice must only "fairly apprise" class members, and "it need not give them every detail." *Id.* at 158 n.7 (quotation omitted).

Prior to class certification, however, a district court need not order notice to putative class members regarding named plaintiffs' agreement to settle their claims. *See Gardner v. GMAC, Inc.*, 796 F.3d 390, 398 (4th Cir. 2015). This is because "unlike the situation in a certificated class action, a 'pre-certification dismissal does not legally bind absent class members,' and, before certification, the absent putative class member has at best a mere 'reliance interest,' the strength of which will vary with the facts of the particular case." *Id.* (citing *Shelton v. Pargo, Inc.*, 582 F.2d 1298, 1314–15 (4th Cir. 1978)).

7. OPT-OUTS

While class members have the right to opt out of a class certified under Rule 23(b)(3), that same right does not exist for Rule (b)(2) class members seeking injunctive relief. Because of "the group nature of the harm alleged and the broad character of the relief sought, the (b)(2) class is, by its very nature, assumed to be a homogenous and cohesive group with few conflicting interests among its members." *Berry*, 807 F.3d at 614–15. As a result, "Rule 23(b)(2) classes are 'mandatory,' in that 'opt-out rights' for class members are deemed unnecessary and are not provided under the rule." *Id.* at 609.

When a member of a class action has the right to opt out of a settlement, the member must send the opt-out form before the deadline provided in the notice and thereafter must not participate in the settlement and receive payments; otherwise, the member will have waived its settlement opt-out right. *See McKenzie v. Norfolk Southern Ry. Co.*, 497 F. App'x 305, 311 (4th Cir. 2012) ("The record demonstrates that [the member] submitted an optout form but later participated in the settlement and received payments. [Another member] produced a copy of an opt-out form without a barcode and date-stamp to prove receipt ..., and the affidavit submitted ... claiming that the opt-out form was timely submitted fails to indicate who mailed the form or that the form was sent before the deadline. Thus, the district court did not abuse its discretion in denying the motion for reconsideration filed by [the members].").

8. ABSENT CLASS MEMBERS

"An 'absent class member' is one who isn't named in the complaint." *McAdams v. Robinson*, 26 F.4th 149, 154, n.2 (4th Cir. 2022) (citations omitted). Absent class members, sometimes referred to as, "[n]onnamed class members . . . may be parties for some purposes and not for others . . . Nonnamed class members are, for instance, parties in the sense that the filing of an action on behalf of a class tolls a statute of limitations against them . . . Otherwise, all class members would be forced to intervene to preserve their claims, and one of the major goals of class action litigation—to simplify litigation involving a large number of class members with similar claims—would be defeated." *Devlin v. Scardelletti*, 546 U.S. 1, 9–10

(2002) (citations omitted).

The claims of absent class members can impact whether class certification is appropriate. Under Rule 23(a)(2), class certification requires "questions of law or fact common to the class." Absent class members of a proposed multistate class may pose class-certification barriers because of the increased risk that citizenship in multiple states might destroy commonality. "In a class action potentially governed by the laws of multiple states, identifying the applicable body or bodies of state law is critical because variations in state law may swamp any common issues and defeat predominance." *Ward v. Dixie Nat. Life Ins. Co.*, 257 F. App'x 620, 628–29 (4th Cir. 2007) (quoting *Castano v. Am. Tobacco Co.*, 84 F.3d 734, 741 (5th Cir. 1996) (internal quotation marks omitted)).

In *Ward*, the plaintiff seeking class certification "never identified what state law would apply to the claims of absent class members who are not residents of South Carolina and whose claims have no connection to that state." *Id.* at 628. "In light of [the plaintiff's] failure to show that common issues of law would be predominant in a multistate class, [the court] affirm[ed] the decision of the district court to limit class membership to South Carolina residents ...." *Id.* at 628–29.

Moreover, the Fourth Circuit has held that absent class members are not parties under 28 U.S.C. § 636(c), which allows a magistrate judge to approve a class action settlement and enter judgement only by the consent of the parties. *McAdams*, 26 F.4th at 155. Absent class members are not named parties, and they cannot control proceedings. *Id.* at 156.

9. DAMAGES

a. Damages Considerations in Class Certification

Rule 23(b)(3)'s predominance requirement states, in part, that "questions of law or fact common to class members predominate over any questions affecting individual members ...." Fed. R. Civ. P. 23(b)(3). Notably, "individualized damage determinations cut against class certification under Rule 23(b)." *Ward v. Dixie Nat. Life Ins. Co.*, 595 F.3d 164, 180 (4th Cir. 2010); *see also Stillmock v. Weis Markets, Inc.*, 385 F. App'x 267, 273 (4th Cir. 2010) ("[C]ourts have properly denied class certification where individual damage issues are especially complex or burdensome."). However, the predominance requirement is "qualitative rather than quantitative" and "where ... the qualitatively overarching issue by far is the liability issue of the defendant's willfulness, and the purported class members were exposed to the same risk of harm every time the defendant violated the statute in the identical manner, the individual ... damages issues are insufficient to defeat class certification under Rule 23(b)(3)." *Stillmock*, 385 F. App'x at 273. Further, individualized damages will not defeat class certification when the formula for calculating individualized damages is common to all class members. *See id.* ("[T]he district court did not abuse its discretion in determining that the damage calculation in this case was, at least in one important respect, not individualized .... [T]he formula for damages was identical for all class members ...."). And although individualized damage calculations may sometimes defeat predominance, damages do not have to be susceptible to class-wide measurement to satisfy the requirements of Rule 23(b)(3). *See In re Zetia (Ezetimibe) Antitrust Litig.*, 7 F.4th 227, 237 (4th Cir. 2021); *see also Gunnells v. Healthplan Servs., Inc.*, 348 F.3d 417, 4299 (4th Cir. 2003) ("[T]he need for individualized proof of damages alone will not defeat class certification."). In certain types of class action suits, the district court generally may first determine liability and then address the class members' individualized proof of damages. *Brown v. Nucor Corp.*, 576 F.3d 149, 159 (4th Cir. 2009) ("The district court can address plaintiffs' claims for .... relief after liability and other common issues are determined.").

b. Distribution of Damages

In *Gentry v. Siegel*, the named claimants in a bankruptcy proceeding filed "class proofs of claim" in consolidated bankruptcy proceedings in which Circuit City Stores and others were the debtors. 668 F.3d 83 (4th Cir. 2012). The four named claimants sought to represent four classes of several hundred similarly situated former Circuit City employees alleging claims for overtime wages against the bankruptcy estate. *Id.* at 89. The proofs of claim asserted that each was filed on behalf of the named claimant individually and on behalf of a class of other former employees similarly situated. The bankruptcy court ruled that the named claimants were not authorized to file class proofs of claim. *Id.* at 83.

The Fourth Circuit observed that the bankruptcy rules addressing proofs of claim are silent about whether creditors—who may file proofs of claim under the bankruptcy rules—may file such proofs of claims on behalf of a class of similarly situated and unnamed claimants proceeding as a class action. *Id.* at 88–89. The court stated that a strict construction of the bankruptcy rules, which do not authorize class proofs of claim, could mean the claimants may never be able to pursue a class action. *Id.* at 89. The court stated that this construction of the bankruptcy rules was "unduly cramped ...." *Id.*

Applying Rule 23 principles, the Fourth Circuit held that prior to a class certification order, the named claimants were putative agents of the similarly situated unnamed claimants. Because the bankruptcy rules "accept the notion" that class action rules may apply, the court concluded that the bankruptcy rules "therefore necessarily embrace the notion that the proposal to represent a class is tentative pending approving. [] Thus, we conclude that [the bankruptcy rules] should be construed to allow class proofs of claim, at least on a tentative basis, until the court rejects the class-action process." *Id.* at 90.

10. OFFERS OF JUDGMENT

Under the Federal Rules of Civil Procedure, a party defending a claim may make an offer of judgment to the opposing party in advance of trial to settle the claims. Fed. R. Civ. P. 68. In a Fair Labor Standards Act (FLSA) case, the Fourth Circuit addressed whether an offer of judgment mooted class claims. In *Simmons,* defendants served a Rule 68 offer of judgment on the named plaintiffs, later clarifying that the offer of judgment also pertained to the opt-in plaintiffs and included liquidated damages as allowed under FLSA. *Simmons v. United Mortg. and Loan Inv., LLC*, 634 F.3d 754, 763 (4th Cir. 2011) (quoting *U.S. v. Hardy*, 545 F.3d 280, 283 (4th Cir. 2008)). Finding first that the offer of judgment did not comply with the requirements of Rule 68, the court then analyzed whether the offer of judgment otherwise rendered plaintiffs' and opt-in plaintiffs' claims moot. The defendants argued their settlement offer rendered the plaintiffs' FLSA class action claims moot because "a live case or controversy no longer existed with respect to such claims ...." *Id.* at 762. However, the Fourth Circuit held that an "offer to settle the Plaintiffs' FLSA claims ... did not offer for judgment to be entered against the Defendants, was ambiguous as to the amounts of actual and liquidated damages to be recovered, and was conditioned upon an agreement by the Plaintiffs to keep the settlement confidential, which prevented the mooting of the Plaintiffs' FLSA claims." *Id.* at 767.

11. SETTLEMENTS

a. Objectors

Rule 23 (e)(5) permits "[a]ny class member [to] object" to a proposed class settlement that requires court approval. Fed. R. Civ. P. 23(e)(5).

The Fourth Circuit recently addressed the burden of proof for Rule 23(e)(5) objections in *1988 Trust for Allen Child. Dated 8/8/88 v. Banner Life Insurance Company*, 28 F.4th 513 (4th Cir. 2022). There, the court held that class settlement objectors must state the basis for their objection with enough specificity to allow the parties to respond and the court to evaluate the issues at hand. *Id.* at 521. Thereafter, in addition to showing that the class meets the requirements for certification, the parties seeking approval of the settlement have the burden to demonstrate that the settlement is fair, reasonable, and adequate, and that the objection does not show that the settlement fails to meet one of those requirements. *Id.* Additionally, at all times, the district court remains a fiduciary of the class and must protect the class's interests from frivolous objectors on one hand and parties overeager to settle on the other hand. *Id.* To that end, the court may, in its discretion, grant additional discovery to assist the court in determining the merits of an objection. *Id.* The necessary showing to prevent an objection from derailing a settlement varies with the strength of the objection, and "frivolous objections may need very little to overcome them, while weightier objections will require more." *Id.*

In *Berry v. Schulman*, a group of objectors sought to undo a settlement that was the culmination of years of litigation and negotiations. 807 F.3d 600, 604 (4th Cir. 2015) (internal quotation marks and citation omitted). The objectors challenged only the (b)(2) settlement class and the terms of the (b)(2) settlement agreement, arguing that its terms were unfair and inadequate. *Id.* at 614. Because the Fourth Circuit reverses a district court's decision to approve a class settlement only "'upon a clear showing that the district court abused its discretion in approving the settlement,'" the court gave the district court's order substantial deference and affirmed its order. *Id.* (internal citation omitted). The court stated that the district court properly considered the factors the Fourth Circuit had identified as bearing on the inquiry and properly examined whether releasing statutory rights to damages was fair and reasonable in light of the fact that the (b)(2) class received only injunctive relief. *Id.* at 614–15. The court further held that it would not disturb the attorney fee award of $5.3 million given that the district court's approval was based on substantial evidence supporting the amount of time expended, the rates applied, and the degree of success achieved by the injunctive relief. *Id.* at 618–19.

b. Professional Responsibilities of Class Counsel, Conflicts of Interest, Intra-Class Conflicts, and "Group Opt-Outs"

The Fourth Circuit examined a particularly complex class action settlement in *Sharp Farms v. Speaks*, 917 F.3d 276 (4th Cir. 2019). There, the court evaluated long-standing litigation and complex settlement issues in two parallel class actions that involved, among other issues, claims of counsel collusion and violations of applicable rules of professional responsibility. The opinion also addressed conflicts of interest between class representatives on one hand, and settlement class members on the other; intra-class conflicts; and contradictory court opinions issued by state and federal courts in related class actions.

Speaks involved two class actions: one initiated in North Carolina state court, *Fisher v. Flue-Cured Tobacco Coop. Stabilization Corp.*, 794 S.E.2d 699 (N.C. 2016) (*Fisher-Lewis*) (filed in January 2005) and another initiated in federal court in the Eastern District of North Carolina, *see Sharp Farms*, 917 F.3d at 276. The two cases arose from a controversy between the U.S. Tobacco Cooperative, Inc.—an agricultural cooperative comprised of flue-cured tobacco growers in North Carolina—and its members. The *Fisher-Lewis* and *Speaks* putative class members were cooperative members, and the *Fisher-Lewis* putative class formed a subset of the *Speaks* putative class. *Id.* at 280.

In 2006, well before the *Speaks* action was filed, the state court in *Fisher-Lewis* reviewed a proposed settlement and concluded that $76.8 million in relief was "not even in the 'ball park' of being fair, reasonable, and adequate for class members." *Id.* As a consequence, the *Fisher-Lewis* parties continued hard-fought litigation, eventually resulting in the denial of motions to dismiss and the issuance of an order certifying the *Fisher-Lewis* class.

While the *Fisher-Lewis* litigation proceeded in state court, the *Speaks* parties reached a tentative settlement for $24 million, which included payments to the *Fisher-Lewis* certified class and extinguished its claims. *Id.* at 280–81. Certain *Fisher-Lewis* class members objected to the *Speaks* settlement, claiming "they got a raw deal." *Id.* at 281. They argued, in part, that the district court abused its discretion in certifying the *Speaks* settlement class under

Rule 23(a) because the *Speaks* class counsel and class representatives did not adequately protect their interests; the $24 million settlement was not fair, reasonable and adequate under Rule 23(e); and the district court erred in denying certain *Fisher-Lewis* class members the right to opt out the entire *Fisher-Lewis* certified class from *Speaks*. *Id.*

The Fourth Circuit, after reviewing the 5,000-page record that spanned 15 years, agreed with the district court's denial of the attempted "group out-out" but reversed the court's settlement approval order for, among other reasons, that the district court in *Speaks* erroneously rejected the *Fisher-Lewis* class's arguments regarding possible collusion and violations of ethical rules in connection with the settlement agreement. *Id.*

In particular, after the North Carolina Supreme Court affirmed class certification of the *Fisher-Lewis* class in December 2016, the Cooperative's counsel contacted *Speaks* counsel to discuss next steps given the class-certification ruling in *Fisher-Lewis. Id.* at 286. Those discussions led to an agreement that the parties would mediate *Speaks*. Thereafter, counsel for the *Fisher-Lewis* plaintiffs wrote to one of the attorneys for the *Speaks* plaintiffs expressing concern that he had a conflict of interest stemming from prior representation and that the *Fisher-Lewis* plaintiffs did not consent to his representation of the *Speaks* plaintiffs because such representation could be materially adverse to the interests of the *Fisher-Lewis* class. *Id.* at 286.

The *Speaks* mediation nevertheless proceeded and resulted in a settlement of $24 million. The district court granted preliminary approval of the settlement and scheduled a final fairness hearing. *Id.* The district court rejected the *Fisher-Lewis* plaintiffs' argument that counsel's actions in mediating *Speaks* violated North Carolina Rules of Professional Conduct. *Id.* at 287. Meanwhile, two days before the *Speaks* final approval hearing, the *Fisher-Lewis* court granted plaintiffs' motion for an order finding that "'the settlement reached in *Speaks*, insofar as it attempts to bind and preclude this certified [] class, is not approved,' and finding that the settlement 'was reached in a collusive manner to avoid the jurisdiction of th[e] court to promote an inadequate settlement.'" *Id.* at 288. The state court held that the *Speaks* settlement was not fair, reasonable, and adequate and that counsel for both parties in *Speaks* violated Rules 4.1 and 4.2 of the North Carolina Rules of Professional Conduct, finding "'ample evidence of collusion between the parties'" in relation to excluding the *Fisher-Lewis* plaintiffs from participation in the settlement discussions and misleading members of the *Fisher-Lewis* class. *Id.*

However, the *Speaks* district court certified the *Speaks* settlement class and granted final approval of the class-action settlement, finding it fair, reasonable, and adequate. *Id.* Objectors/Appellants (some members of the *Fisher-Lewis* class) appealed to the Fourth Circuit, contending that *Speaks* class counsel did not adequately and fairly represent the *Fisher-Lewis* class members when they became members of the *Speaks* settlement class and that the district court erred in denying some of the *Fisher-Lewis* class representatives' attempt to opt out the entire *Fisher-Lewis* certified class from the *Speaks* settlement. *Id.* at 290.

The Fourth Circuit agreed with Objectors/Appellants that the district court erred by rejecting the possibility of collusion and insufficiently "grappling" with the state court's order setting forth the allegedly collusive conduct. *Id.* at 292 (observing that the mediator did not yet have the benefit of the state court's order at the time of mediation and did not have all relevant information about collusion during the mediation). The Fourth Circuit concluded that by failing to sufficiently evaluate the merits of the state court's findings, the district court did "not act as a fiduciary of the class" and abused its discretion in certifying the *Speaks* settlement class. *Id.* at 293–94 (citing *Kaufman v. Am. Express Travel Related Servs. Co.*, 877 F.3d 267, 283 (7th Cir. 2017) (district courts "should act as the fiduciary of the class, subject to the high duty of care that the law requires of fiduciaries")). The Fourth Circuit also found that certain conflicts of interest existed between the *Speaks* class representatives and the *Fisher-Lewis* class members. *Id.* at 295–98.

The court, however, affirmed the district court's refusal to permit certain of the *Fisher-Lewis* class members to opt out the entire *Fisher-Lewis* class from the *Speaks* settlement. *Id.*

at 299. The court stated that the "Due Process Clause reposes only in '*individual class members* ... the right to intelligently and individually choose whether to continue in a suit as class members,'" and that even though the *Fisher-Lewis* class is certified, "the policy concerns that militate against permitting group opt-outs in the putative class context are present here as well—allowing representatives to opt out a group of class members would deprive those members of their due-process right to make that choice for themselves ...." *Id.* at 298–99 (citations omitted).

Finally, the court reversed the class-settlement approval order under Rule 23(e). The Objectors/Appellants stressed that the settlement amount, while arguably reasonable for the *Speaks* class, was unreasonable for the *Fisher-Lewis* class. *Id.* at 300. Providing a detailed review of the legal claims, theories, and strengths and weaknesses of both cases, the Fourth Circuit concluded that the "strength of the *Fisher-Lewis* case drove the *Speaks* settlement negotiations," and the district court "erroneously relied on the weaknesses of the *Speaks* claims to justify the $24 million settlement as reasonable for the class "when that amount is plainly inadequate for the *Fisher-Lewis* class members." *Id.* at 301. The case was remanded for further proceedings consistent with the opinion.

In a thoughtful concurrence, Judge Quattlebaum observed that class actions are "an important innovation in our legal system," but come with risks—chiefly, the risk of due process violations. *Id.* at 305. Reaching the same conclusions as the majority, but for different reasons, the concurrence concluded that the adequacy requirement was not met because of complex intra-class conflicts, and the concurrence provided a detailed analysis of Fourth Circuit and Supreme Court precedence on the issue of intra-class conflicts. *Id.* at 306–07 (discussing *Amchem Prod., Inc. v. Windsor*, 521 U.S. 591, 625 (1997) and *Ortiz v. Fibreboard*, 527 U.S. 815, 856–58 (1999)).

Agreeing with the majority that class counsel was inadequate, in his concurrence, Judge Quattlebaum wrote that class counsel was inadequate because the settlement class should not have been certified in the presence of the intra-class conflicts. *Id.* at 307 (concluding differently than the majority opinion that the district court did, in fact, adequately "grapple" with the state court's findings of collusion). The concurrence disagreed, however, with the majority's reasoning, finding that the Fourth Circuit did not afford substantial deference to the district court conclusion that the $24 million settlement was reasonable, and that the court, rather, inappropriately substituted its own judgment for that of the district court's on the reasonableness of the settlement. *Id.*

c. Scope of Released Claims

Along with several other circuits, the Fourth Circuit recognizes the "identical factual predicate" doctrine. *In re Lumber Liquidators Chinese-Manufactured Flooring Prod. Mktg., Sales Pracs. & Prod. Liab. Litig.*, 91 F.4th 174, 183 (4th Cir. 2024). This means that class action settlements can only release those claims that the putative class could have asserted based upon the same, identical set of facts underlying the class action. *See id.* The doctrine is applied by the court enforcing the settlement release. *See id.* at 184.

d. Final Approval

Rule 23(e) provides that a class action may only be settled upon approval by the court. In reviewing a proposed class-action settlement, a district court acts as a fiduciary for the class and must conclude that the proposed settlement is fair, reasonable, and adequate. *1988 Tr. for Allen Child. Dated 8/8/88 v. Banner Life Ins. Co.*, 28 F.4th 513, 525 (4th Cir. 2022).

Rule 23(e)'s primary concern is "the protection of class members whose rights may not have been given adequate consideration during the settlement negotiations." *In re Jiffy Lube Sec. Litig.*, 927 F.2d 155, 158 (4th Cir. 1991). Due process requires each individual class member's interest be adequately represented when the settlement of a class action will preclude further litigation by the entire class. *Id. See Berry*, 807 F.3d at 612. "Rule 23(e)'s settlement approval process provides additional protection, ensuring that Rule 23(b)(2) class members receive notice of a proposed settlement and an opportunity to object and that a settlement will not take effect unless the trial judge—after analyzing the facts and law of the case and considering all objections to the proposed settlement—determines it to be fair, adequate, and reasonable." *Id.* (quoting *Kincade v. Gen. Tire and Rubber Co.*, 635 F.2d 501, 507–08 (5th Cir. 1981)).

Rule 23(e)(2)'s "fairness" analysis is intended primarily to ensure that a "settlement is reached as a result of good-faith bargaining at arm's length, without collusion." *1988 Tr. for Allen Child.*, 28 F.4th at 525 (quotation omitted). The Fourth Circuit applies for four factors for determining a settlement's fairness, which are: "(1) the posture of the case at the time settlement was proposed; (2) the extent of discovery that had been conducted; (3) the circumstances surrounding the negotiations; and (4) the experience of counsel in the area of the class action litigation." *Id.* (quotation omitted).

Factors pertinent to determining a settlement's "adequacy" include (1) the relative strength of the plaintiffs' case on the merits, (2) the existence of any difficulties of proof or strong defenses the plaintiffs are likely to encounter if the case goes to trial, (3) the anticipated duration and expense of additional litigation, (4) the solvency of the defendants and the likelihood of recovery on a litigated judgment, and (5) the degree of opposition to the settlement. *Jiffy Lube*, 927 F2d at 159 (citing *In re Montgomery Cty. Real Estate Antitrust Litig.*, 83 F.R.D. at 305 (D. Md. 1979)). Importantly, the "adequacy" analysis for Rule 23(e)(2) settlement approval purposes is not identical to the "adequacy" analysis in the Rule 23(a)(4) class certification context, although the two can overlap. *1988 Tr. for Allen Child.*, 28 F.4th at 526 n.7. "The former addresses whether a settlement is good enough to justify extinguishing the claims of absent individual class members; the latter addresses whether the class representatives will do a good enough job to justify allowing the plaintiffs to proceed as a class at all." *Id.* Moreover, "[a] settlement agreement may be inadequate if it forces class members to release valuable claims for nothing in return." *Id.* at 526–27.

The Fourth Circuit has suggested that assessing whether a class settlement is "reasonable" involves examining the amount of the settlement. *See id.* at 527. At a minimum, the reasonableness analysis, "ensures that the amount on offer is commensurate with the scale of the litigation and the plaintiffs' chances of success at trial." *Id.* However, in considering whether to approve a class settlement, the court is not required to estimate what class members would have received had they prevailed at trial. *McAdams v. Robinson*, 26 F.4th 149, 160 (4th Cir. 2022). And with regard to settlement releases, district courts can approve class releases that share an "identical factual predicate" with the claims alleged in a case, meaning that the claims depend upon the same set of facts. *See id.* (quotation omitted).

In *Herrera v. Charlotte School of Law,* former students sued their law school and related parties for unfair or deceptive trade practices, fraud and fraudulent misrepresentation, and negligent misrepresentation based on the law school's loss of its ABA accreditation and actions relating thereto. 818 F. App'x 165, 170 (4th Cir. 2020). After a hearing in which the law school's CFO and experts advised that the settlement fund represented all that the defendants could pay, the district court found that the defendants' liabilities far exceeded their assets and approved a limited fund, non-opt-out settlement pursuant to Rule 23(b)(1)(B). *Id.* at 171. Some plaintiffs objected to the settlement and appealed the district court's approval of the settlement, arguing that the district court erred in approving the settlement as fair, reasonable, and adequate under Rule 23(e). *Id.* at 171–72. The Fourth Circuit held, however, that the district court did not abuse its discretion in approving the limited fund settlement. *Id.* at 175.

In its opinion, the Fourth Circuit recited the conditions necessary to bind absent members under Federal Rule of Civil Procedure 23(b)(1)(B), as set out by the Supreme Court in *Ortiz v. Fibreboard Corp.*:

(1) The totals of the aggregated liquidated claims and the fund available for satisfying them, set definitely at their maximums, demonstrate the inadequacy of the fund to

pay all the claims;

(2) The whole of the inadequate fund was to be devoted to the overwhelming claims; and

(3) The claimants identified by a common theory of recovery were treated equitably among themselves.

Herrera, 818 F. App'x at 173 (citing *Ortiz v. Fibreboard Corp.*, 527 U.S. 815 (1999)). Under this framework, the Fourth Circuit held the district court did not err in finding these three conditions were present. First, the district court (unlike the trial court in *Ortiz*), "copiously and carefully sifted through evidence presented and made detailed findings" with respect to the limited settlement agreement figures and "established the inadequacy for the fund when it observed that the damages claims exceeded the limited fund ... by 'roughly 40 times.'" *Id.* at 175. Second, the district court properly found that the entire limited fund would be devoted to payment of the claims and that "if additional litigation were to commence, there would be no funds left for the remaining Plaintiffs." *Id.* Third, the district court found that the mechanism by which the settlement funds would be proportionally distributed according to tiers of plaintiffs based on the strength of each claim and the amount of alleged damages was fair and had a "reasonable, rational basis." *Id.* at 176. The Fourth Circuit agreed since the "mechanism developed for distributing the fund is proportionate to what each member of the class suffered, awarding those who suffered more . . . a greater share." *Id.*

Finally, the *Herrera* court held that the district court did not abuse its discretion in approving the settlement as fair, reasonable, and adequate for multiple reasons, including: (1) the settlement was approved after extensive litigation "involving significant motions practice and discovery" that allowed the parties to develop their negotiation positions; (2) the settlement was negotiated at arm's length after a two-day mediation led by an experienced class action mediator; (3) class counsel was experienced in class action litigation and school closures; (4) the limited settlement fund and potential recovery would be quickly reduced by further litigation; (5) the defendants' liabilities were far greater than their assets; (6) the vast majority of the class approved the settlement (the objectors made up only about 4 percent of the class); and (7) the plaintiffs' theory of liability was complex and the defendants' arguments could potentially reduce or preclude recovery. *Id.* at 177–79.

12. FEES AND COSTS

Rule 23(h) provides that "in a certified class action, the court may award reasonable attorney's fees and nontaxable costs that are authorized by law or by the parties' agreement." And in the Fourth Circuit, district courts may use either the lodestar or the percentage-of-recovery method to calculate the reasonableness of attorneys' fees. *McAdams v. Robinson*, 26 F.4th 149, 162 (4th Cir. 2022). Indeed, "[t]he Fourth Circuit has neither announced a preferred method for determining the reasonableness of attorneys' fees in common fund class actions nor identified factors for district courts to apply when using the percentage method." *See id.* (quoting *Jones v. Dominion Res. Servs., Inc.*, 601 F. Supp. 2d 756, 760 (S.D. W. Va. 2009)). Therefore, the Fourth Circuit does not expressly require district courts that choose to use the percentage-of-recovery method to perform a lodestar cross-check. *See id.*; *see also In re Peanut Farmers Antitrust Litig.*, No. 2:19-CV-00463, 2021 WL 9494033, at *6 (E.D. Va. Aug. 10, 2021) (noting that a lodestar cross-check is not required).

"The percentage-of-recovery method considers the portion of the total settlement fund that will go to attorneys' fees." *McAdams,* 26 F.4th at 162. Under the percentage-of-recovery method, an attorneys' fee award of 43 percent of the common fund "approaches the upper limit of a permissible recovery" in the Fourth Circuit. *See id.* ("Courts have allowed attorney compensation ranging from 19 to 45% of the settlement fund created." (quotation omitted)).

By contrast, "[t]he lodestar method calculates reasonable fees by multiplying the number of reasonable hours expended times a reasonable rate," and there is a "strong presumption" that the lodestar figure is reasonable. *See id.* (internal quotations omitted). The Fourth Circuit has endorsed a three-part standard for use in calculating attorney's fees under the lodestar approach: (1) First, courts must determine the lodestar figure by multiplying the number of reasonable hours expended times a reasonable rate, using the factors set forth in *Johnson v. Georgia Highway Express Inc.*, 488 F.2d 714, 717–19 (5th Cir. 1974), to determine what is reasonable in terms of hours expended and the rate charged; (2) next, courts must subtract fees for hours spent on unsuccessful claims unrelated to successful ones; and (3) finally, courts should award some percentage of the remaining amount, depending on the degree of success enjoyed by the plaintiff. *In re Lumber Liquidators Chinese-Manufactured Flooring Prod. Mktg., Sales Pracs. & Prod. Liab. Litig.*, 27 F.4th 291, 303 (4th Cir. 2022) (citing *McAfee v. Boczar*, 738 F.3d 81, 88 (4th Cir. 2013)). "Once a district court has calculated an initial lodestar figure, the court may increase or decrease that figure by using a 'multiplier,' which may be derived from a number of factors, such as the benefit achieved for the class and the complexity of the case.'" *Id.* at 300 n.6 (4th Cir. 2022) (quoting *Berry v. Schulman*, 807 F.3d 600, 617 n.9 (4th Cir. 2015)). Under the lodestar method, the degree of success obtained is "the most critical factor" in determining whether a certain fee is reasonable. *Id.* at 303 (quotation omitted). That analysis examines whether the level of success obtained "makes the hours reasonably expended a satisfactory basis for making the fee award." *Id.* (quotation omitted). Importantly, district courts that employ the lodestar method for determining fee awards are not required to use the percentage-of-recovery method to "cross-check" the reasonableness of the lodestar award. *Id.* at 307.

District courts have a "ringside view" of the quality of class action lawyers' work, and, therefore, they have substantial discretion in formulating appropriate fee awards. *See In re Lumber Liquidators*, 27 F.4th at 301 (quotation omitted). However, in reviewing a class action fee award, the district court must engage in a full and meaningful review. *See Blankenship v. Schweiker*, 676 F.2d 116, 118 (4th Cir. 1982) (vacating fee award because district court's review was not sufficiently thorough).

In *Berry*, the court evaluated the $5.3 million fee award to counsel for securing injunctive relief for the (b)(2) class. *Berry*, 807 F.3d at 617. The district court, applying the lodestar method, found that the lodestar of $3,349,379.99 and a multiplier of 1.99 was reasonable considering that class counsel allocated approximately 80 percent of their time to achieving the injunctive relief for the (b)(2) class. *Id.* (the district court also writing that the relief provided "'substantial benefits'" for over 200 million consumers) (citing *Berry v. LexisNexis Risk & Info. Analytics Grp., Inc.*, No. 3:11-cv-754, 2014 WL 4403524, at *15 (E.D. Va. Sept. 5, 2014)). Although the district court's discussion was brief, its conclusions concerning the time expended and rates applied were supported by substantial evidence. *Id.* at 617–18.

In *Brundle on behalf of Constellis Employee Stock Ownership Plan v. Wilmington Trust, N.A.*, the court affirmed the district court's award of $1.5 million (in addition to statutory fees) as a partial common fund award in a class action brought under ERISA. 919 F.3d 763, 784 (4th Cir. 2019). The court found that the common fund doctrine permits a court to award "'a reasonable attorney's fee' to 'a litigant or a lawyer who recovers a common fund for the benefit of persons other than himself or his client . . . from the fund as a whole'" *Id.* (citations omitted). The court concluded that statutory fee-shifting provisions, such as that of ERISA, do not "necessarily displace the [common fund] doctrine or render it superfluous." *Id.* at 786. The court concluded that "although both the common fund doctrine and fee-shifting statutes facilitate suit by plaintiffs who may otherwise lack the means to hire counsel, they operate in distinct ways and serve distinct purposes." *Id.* The *Brundle* court held further, over plaintiff's argument to the contrary, that the district court properly weighed appropriate factors in setting the amount of the common fund award, including the contingency risk. *Id.* at 788.

a. Clear Sailing Provisions

"Clear sailing agreements" are agreements whereby the defendant agrees not to contest class counsel's fee petition if it does not exceed a specified amount. *Newberg on Class Actions* § 13:9 (5th ed.). Although clear sailing agreements are "troubling because they demonstrate that class counsel negotiated some aspect of their fee arrangement with the defendant, when counsel's ethical obligation is to the class," they are not "per se unreasonable." *McAdams v. Robinson*, 26 F.4th 149, 162 (4th Cir. 2022) (quotations omitted). "Rather, courts are directed to give extra scrutiny to such agreements." *Id.* at 162–63 (quotation omitted). Notably, settlements with clear sailing agreements have been approved where they were negotiated at arms-length and class counsel supported their fee request with billing records and other competent evidence. *See id.* at 163.

b. Quick Pay Fees and Value of Coupons Factored into Fee Determination

The Fourth Circuit's decision in *In re Lumber Liquidators Chinese-Manufactured Flooring Product Marketing, Sales Practices & Product Liability Litigation* addresses "quick pay" settlement agreement provisions providing for the upfront payment of attorneys' fees and CAFA's rules on "coupon settlements." 952 F.3d 471, 487 (4th Cir. 2020). In that case, a flooring manufacturer was sued by classes of customers seeking damages resulting from allegedly defective flooring materials. *Id.* at 476–77. The district court approved a settlement agreement that was funded by $22 million in cash and $14 million in store vouchers. *Id.* at 481. The settlement agreement provided for the upfront payment of attorneys' fees. In approving the attorneys' fees, the lower court attributed a $14 million value to the vouchers, despite the objectors' argument that the vouchers were "coupons" under CAFA. *Id.* at 482, 487. On appeal, the Fourth Circuit rejected the objectors' argument that the upfront payment of fees to class counsel out of the cash settlement left the class "at the mercy of [Lumber Liquidators'] financial volatility" since there was "no established danger that the nonmonetary relief [the vouchers] awarded to the class will actually be rendered worthless," and thus, it mattered little when the attorneys got paid. *Id.* at 487. The Fourth Circuit noted that such quick pay provisions had generally been approved by other federal courts and that it saw "no reason to buck that trend in these proceedings." *Id.*

However, the *Lumber Liquidators* court did find that the district court failed to apply CAFA's coupon settlement provisions when calculating the attorneys' fee award. *Id.* at 489. Notably, the court found that the vouchers were "coupons" based on the legislative history of CAFA, the plain meaning of "coupon," and decisions from other circuits. *Id.* at 489.

One of the reasons Congress enacted CAFA was to address abuses of class actions, including "coupon settlement[s]" by which class members receive coupons while the class counsel receive cash. *Id.* at 488. CAFA requires that courts use certain rules for calculating attorneys' fees for such settlements. This requirement is motivated by the concern that fee awards could be inflated based on courts' unreasonable acceptance of the face value of nonmonetary relief, thus leaving attorneys with a disproportionate share of the settlement benefits compared to the class members (who receive coupons, rather than cash). *Id.*

The court observed that the Ninth Circuit used the following factors to determine whether a settlement award is "coupon" relief warranting application of CAFA's attorney fee provisions: "(1) whether class members have to hand over more of their own money before they can take advantage of a credit, (2) whether the credit is valid only for select products or services, and (3) how much flexibility the credit provides, including whether it expires or is freely transferrable." *Id.* at 489 (quoting *In re Easysaver Rewards Litig.*, 906 F.3d 747, 755 (9th Cir. 2018)). The court used these factors to find that the *Lumber Liquidators* fee award was a coupon settlement because: (1) the voucher holders would likely have to pay more money before they can take advantage of the voucher, as the voucher would be insufficient to replace the entirety of a class member's defective flooring; (2) the vouchers could only be used to purchase flooring and flooring tools, a limited category; and (3) the vouchers had somewhat limited flexibility (the court found, at best, this factor was a wash because the vouchers were only transferrable for a limited period to family members or charities and expired after three years). *Id.* at 490–91.

The court also considered that forcing the voucher holders to do further business with Lumber Liquidators was within the scope of concerns Congress was seeking to address in passing CAFA. *Id.* at 489–90. The vouchers in question also "fit comfortably within the contemporary dictionary definitions of 'coupon.'" *Id.* at 490. Finally, the court rejected the class counsel's argument that because the settlement included an option of cash or the vouchers, the "coupon settlement" provisions of CAFA did not apply. *Id.* at 491. The court followed the Seventh and Ninth Circuits in finding CAFA's coupon settlement provisions apply even when only part of the settlement constitutes coupons (and the other part is cash). *Id.*

After the court sent the case back to the lower court, the objectors filed a second appeal with the Fourth Circuit, this time arguing that the lower court erred in applying CAFA's settlement provisions and in using the lodestar method in calculating attorney's fees. *See In re Lumber Liquidators Chinese-Manufactured Flooring Prod. Mktg., Sales Pracs. & Prod. Liab. Litig.*, 27 F.4th 291, 294 (4th Cir. 2022). The Fourth Circuit rejected the objectors' arguments, holding that CAFA authorizes the use of the lodestar method to calculate attorneys' fees where "coupon" relief makes up part of a class action settlement. *See id.* at 302. The court also held that when they are performing the lodestar analysis for "coupon" settlements, district courts are not bound to consider the redemption rates of any "coupons." *Id.* at 305. "Rather, a district court applying the lodestar approach must carefully contemplate the makeup of the settlement at hand in deciding whether the calculated lodestar award is reasonable, and that judgment is committed to the court's discretion." *Id.*

13. APPELLATE ISSUES

a. Standing to Appeal

To bring a lawsuit, a party must have standing to sue, which requires that the party have a personal stake in the litigation. *Rhodes v. E.I. du Pont de Nemours and Co.*, 636 F.3d 88, 99 (4th Cir. 2011). The party must maintain the personal stake throughout the litigation, even on appeal. *Id.* In the class action context, a class representative generally has both a personal stake in his or her substantive claim and "a distinct procedural right to represent the interests of similarly situated individuals." *Id.* (citing *U.S. Parole Comm'n v. Geraghty*, 445 U.S. 388, 402 (1980)).

In *Rhodes*, the representative plaintiffs voluntarily dismissed their individual medical monitoring claims, the district court denied certification of the medical monitoring claims, and the representative plaintiffs appealed the certification denial. The question before the *Rhodes* court was whether a plaintiff who voluntarily settles his or her individual claims (or those individual claims are otherwise dismissed) may still appeal a certification denial of those same claims. *Id.* at 100. The Fourth Circuit observed that (as of 2011, the date of the decision) federal circuit courts were split over this issue. *Rhodes*, 636 F.3d at 100 (the Circuit Court of Appeals for the District of Columbia and the Fifth Circuit have held that an express reservation of right may be sufficient to give putative class representative appellate standing; the Ninth Circuit and Seventh Circuit have held to the contrary). The Fourth Circuit held that when a named plaintiff voluntarily dismisses his or her claim, "there is no longer a 'self-interested party advocating' for class treatment in the manner necessary to satisfy Article III standing requirements." *Id.*

b. Standard of Review on Appeal

The Fourth Circuit reviews decisions to certify a class action for abuse of discretion. *Carolina Youth Action Project; D.S. by & through Ford v. Wilson*, 60 F.4th 770, 777 (4th Cir.

2023). An abuse of discretion occurs when the district court "materially misapplies the requirements of Rule 23" or "clearly errs in its factual findings." *Williams v. Martorello*, 59 F.4th 68, 85–86 (4th Cir. 2023) (internal quotations and citations omitted).

c. Interlocutory Review

Generally, only final district court decisions are afforded federal appellate jurisdiction under 28 U.S.C. § 1291. *Al Shimari v. CACI Intern., Inc.*, 679 F.3d 205, 212 (4th Cir. 2012). However, Rule 23(f) provides an exception to this general rule; it affords a party the opportunity to seek an interlocutory appeal from a court order granting or denying class certification. *See Pashby*, 709 F.3d at 318.

Pursuant to Rule 23(f), the appellant must file its petition to appeal within 14 days of the district court's order regarding class certification, and pursuant to Fed. R. App. P. 5(b), the petition must include (1) the question presented, (2) the facts necessary to understand the question presented, (3) the relief sought, (4) the rule or statute that authorizes the appeal and the reasons the Court should allow it, and (5) a copy of the order. *Id.* "Appellate jurisdiction pursuant to Rule 23(f)'s interlocutory provision lies only where the subject matter of the appeal is the grant or denial of class certification." *Scott v. Family Dollar Stores, Inc.*, 733 F.3d 105, 111 (4th Cir. 2013); *see also Dell Webb Communities, Inc. v. Carlson*, 817 F.3d 867, 875 (4th Cir. 2016) ("[C]ertification decisions may be appealed on both an interlocutory basis and after a final judgment ….").

The Fourth Circuit uses a five-factor test to determine whether to hear a class certification appeal: "(1) whether the certification ruling is likely dispositive of the litigation; (2) whether the district court's certification decision contains a substantial weakness; (3) whether the appeal will permit the resolution of an unsettled legal question of general importance; (4) the nature and status of the litigation before the district court (such as the presence of outstanding dispositive motions and the status of discovery); and (5) the likelihood that future events will make appellate review more or less appropriate." *Ward*, 257 F. App'x at 629–30 (citing *Lienhart v. Dryvit Sys.*, 255 F.3d 138, 145 (4th Cir. 2001)). The court considers these factors holistically but should grant the petition notwithstanding the other factors "[w]here a district court's certification decision is manifestly erroneous and virtually certain to be reversed on appeal." *EQT*, 764 F.3d at 357 (citing *Lienhart*, 255 F.3d at 145).

Further, Section 1453(c)(1) of Title 28, which derives from CAFA, authorizes an appeal "from an order of a district court granting or denying a motion to remand a class action to the State court from which it was removed." Although the Fourth Circuit has accepted appeals under Section 1453(c)(1), in a case of first impression, *Dominion Energy, Inc. v. City of Warren Police and Fire Retirement System*, 928 F.3d 325, 333–34 (4th Cir. 2019), the court enunciated the legal standards applicable to such consideration. Relying on "useful guidance" from its sister circuits, the Fourth Circuit adopted the following factors:

(1) Whether the petition presents an important CAFA-related question;
(2) Whether the question presented by the CAFA appeal petition is unsettled;
(3) Whether the district court's jurisdictional decision under CAFA is incorrect, or at least fairly debatable;
(4) Whether the CAFA-related question is consequential to the resolution of the particular class action;
(5) Whether that question is likely to evade effective review if left for consideration only after final judgment;
(6) Whether the CAFA-related question is likely to recur;
(7) Whether the petition arises from a decision that is sufficiently final to position the class action for intelligent review; and
(8) Whether the probable harm to the petitioners if an immediate appeal is denied outweighs the probable harm to the other parties should an immediate appeal be entertained.

Id. at 334 (relying on and citing decisions from the Second, Seventh, Tenth, and Eleventh Circuits). The court noted, however, that these factors are nonexhaustive. *Id.* (permitting interlocutory appeal because the petitions for review presented "the important and unsettled question of whether a claim for aiding and abetting the breach of a fiduciary duty falls within one or more of CAFA's removal exceptions," no additional factual development was necessary, and the balance of harms favored petitioners, who "will lose almost any chance of litigating th[eir] case[s] in a federal forum" if not permitted to appeal now) (citations omitted)).

An additional exception to the final judgment rule that may impact class actions lies in the Federal Arbitration Act (FAA). 9 U.S.C. §§ 1–14. The FAA permits appeals of orders denying a motion to compel arbitration or refusing to stay any action pending arbitration. *See Rota-McLarty v. Santander Consumer USA, Inc.*, 700 F.3d 690, 696 (4th Cir. 2012). Congress created appellate jurisdiction for these orders to "effectuate the strong policy favoring arbitration," even if the order was "interlocutory in nature." *See id.* (citing *Stedor Enters., Ltd. v. Armtex, Inc.*, 947 F.2d 727, 730 (4th Cir. 1991)). This public policy is honored in the class action context as well.

In addition, the court of appeals has discretion to review issues that are not otherwise immediately appealable under the pendent appellate jurisdiction doctrine. *EQT Production Co. v. Adair*, 764 F.3d 347, 364 (4th Cir. 2014). Under pendant jurisdiction, the Fourth Circuit reviews issues that are not otherwise subject to immediate appeal "when such issues are so interconnected with immediately appealable issues that they warrant concurrent review." *Id.* (internal quotation marks and citation omitted). This doctrine requires a showing that the issue is "inextricably intertwined with a question that is the proper subject of an immediate appeal or [] review of a jurisdictionally insufficient issue is necessary to ensure meaningful review of an immediately appealable issue." *Id.* (quoting *Rux v. Republic of Sudan*, 461 F.3d 461, 475 (4th Cir. 2006)) (internal quotation marks omitted).

14. TOLLING THE STATUTE OF LIMITATIONS

Commencing a class action tolls the statute of limitations for any individual's claim that would be covered by the proposed class from the time of filing until the court denies the class certification. *Am. Pipe & Constr. Co. v. Utah*, 414 U.S. 538, 553 (1974); *see also Devlin v. Scardelletti*, 546 U.S. 1, 9–10 (2002) ("Nonnamed class members are, for instance, parties in the sense that the filing of an action on behalf of a class tolls a statute of limitations against them." (citations omitted)). However, the filing of a motion for leave to file an amended complaint does not toll the statute of limitations period. *Angles v. Dollar Tree Stores, Inc.*, 494 F. App'x 326, 329 (4th Cir. 2012). Until the court grants leave for the amendment, the amended complaint is not actually filed. *Id.* Without being filed, the amended complaint has no legal effect and cannot toll the statute of limitations period. *Id.*

The doctrine of fraudulent concealment can be used to estop a party from asserting a statute-of-limitations defense. *EQT Production Co. v. Adair*, 764 F.3d 347, 370 (4th Cir. 2014). The party invoking fraudulent concealment must prove that "(1) the party pleading the statute of limitations fraudulently concealed facts that are the basis of plaintiff's claim, and (2) the plaintiff failed to discover those facts within the statutory period, despite (3) the exercise of due diligence." *Id.* at 370 (quoting *Detrick v. Panalpina, Inc.*, 108 F.3d 529, 541 (4th Cir. 1997)). If a party effectively proves fraudulent concealment, the statute of limitations period does not begin to run until that party discovers the fraud. *In re Cotton Yarn Antitrust Litig.*, 505 F.3d 274, 291 (4th Cir. 2007).

15. ARBITRATION ISSUES

The Federal Arbitration Act (FAA) "is a congressional declaration of a liberal federal policy favoring arbitration agreements." *Noohi v. Toll Bros., Inc.*, 708 F.3d 599, 606 (4th Cir. 2013) (quoting *Moses H. Cone v. Mem'l Mercury Constr. Corp.*, 460 U.S. 1, 24 (1983)). Claims brought under federal statutes can generally be arbitrated if: (1) Congress has not indicated an intent to forbid the arbitration of the claim and (2) the arbitration agreement's language is broad enough to cover such claim. *In re Cotton Yarn Antitrust Litig.*, 505 F.3d at 282.

"Arbitration is a matter of contract." *Hengle v. Treppa*, 19 F.4th 324, 334 (4th Cir. 2021) (alteration adopted and quotation omitted). Therefore, courts in the Fourth Circuit "must enforce arbitration agreements on an equal footing with other contracts, and may invalidate an arbitration agreement based on generally applicable contract defenses." *Id.* (internal quotations and citations omitted). Furthermore, courts must read an arbitration provision in a way that gives effect to all its terms and renders them consistent with each other. *Id.* at 341. And "the existence of a severability clause cannot save an arbitration provision if the invalid terms are integral to the agreement." *Id.* at 344. Ordinary state law principles govern the formation and interpretation of arbitration agreements. *Lyons v. PNC Bank, Nat'l Ass'n*, 26 F.4th 180, 189 (4th Cir. 2022).

The specific language of the arbitration agreement is important because of "the contractual nature of arbitration agreements." *Dell Webb Communities, Inc. v. Carlson*, 817 F.3d 867, 873 (4th Cir. 2016). Courts should therefore be "careful to avoid forcing parties to resolve their disputes through means not intended at the time of contract formation." *Id.* This includes not compelling class arbitration when the parties agreed instead to arbitrate with an individual and not a class. *See Noohi*, 708 F.3d at 606; *see also Dell Webb Communities, Inc.*, 817 F.3d at 876 ("[P]arties cannot be forced to arbitrate on class-wide basis absent contractual basis for concluding that party agreed to do so."). The Fourth Circuit has held that the inability to bring a class action because of an arbitration clause does not in and of itself render an arbitration agreement unenforceable. *Adkins v. Labor Ready, Inc.*, 303 F.3d 496, 503 (4th Cir. 2002). But the Fourth Circuit also has acknowledged that if "a party could demonstrate that the prohibition on class actions likely would make arbitration prohibitively expensive, such a showing could invalidate an agreement." *Id.* at 502–03.

Parties may agree to have an arbitrator decide gateway questions of arbitrability through what is known as a "delegation clause." *Hengle*, 19 F.4th at 335. Delegation clauses are treated like any other arbitration agreement under the FAA, and a party may directly challenge the validity of the delegation clause with the same arguments it employs to contest the enforceability of the overall arbitration agreement. *Id.* at 335. "As with any other agreement to arbitrate, when a party challenges a delegation clause specifically, the court must evaluate the validity of the delegation [clause] before ordering compliance with the clause." *Id.* (quotation omitted).

Pursuant to the prospective waiver doctrine, courts will not enforce an arbitration agreement where the agreement prevents a litigant from vindicating his or her federal substantive statutory rights by waiving the right to pursue statutory remedies. *Id.* at 334–35. Even if Congress has not forbidden the arbitration and the scope of the agreement covers the claim, the court still will not compel arbitration of a claim if the litigant "cannot effectively vindicate his statutory rights in the arbitral form." *In re Cotton Yarn Antitrust Litig.*, 505 F.3d 274, 282 (4th Cir. 2007). Notably, "[t]he possibility that a party to an arbitration clause will be inconvenienced and will incur some extra expense, however, does not necessarily mean that the party cannot effectively vindicate its statutory rights through arbitration." *Id.* at 285.

In *CarMax Auto Superstores, Inc. v. Sibley*, the Fourth Circuit held that the district court abused its discretion in awarding sanctions, in part, based on plaintiff's claims that the class-action waiver in the arbitration agreement violated the National Labor Relations Act. 767 F. App'x 462, 464–65. First, the Fourth Circuit stated that the district court's grant of sanctions predated the Supreme Court's ruling in *Epic Sys. Corp. v. Lewis*, 138 S. Ct. 1612, 1619 (2018), which held that class action waivers in arbitration agreements do not violate the NLRA. *Carmax*, 767 F. App'x at 464–65. Second, the Fourth Circuit found that sanctions are not appropriate "'[w]here neither the Supreme Court nor any courts within this circuit have ruled on the issue and the statute itself does not offer a clear answer.'" *Id.* at 465 (citations omitted).

In *Hill v. Employee Resources Group*, a class of employees sued their employer for failing to pay minimum wage in violation of the Fair Labor Standards Act. 816 F. App'x 804, 805 (4th Cir. 2020), as amended (June 12, 2020). The employer moved to compel arbitration, but the district court granted the motion only as to potential class members for whom signed agreements were produced. *Id.* at 806. The employer appealed, arguing that the district court erred in not compelling arbitration for the named plaintiff and 71 other FLSA opt-in plaintiffs for whom no arbitration agreements were produced. *Id.* at 807. The Fourth Circuit affirmed the district court and held that the employer failed to establish the existence of the arbitration agreements in question. *Id.* at 809. The affidavit of the employer's human resource director attesting that all employees were required to sign arbitration agreements and the employer's production of 780 arbitration agreements with other employees did not meet the heightened standard of proof—taken from the state law principles of the states in which the class members worked—for proving the existence of lost agreements through parole evidence. *Id.* at 808–09.

A party also may lose its right to stay court proceedings in favor of arbitration if it delays invoking its right to arbitrate. *Wheeling Hosp., Inc. v. Health Plan of the Upper Ohio Valley, Inc.*, 683 F.3d 577, 586 (4th Cir. 2012); 9 U.S.C. § 3. A party can lose "its right to arbitration if it so substantially utilize[s] the litigation machinery that to subsequently permit arbitration would prejudice the party opposing the stay." *Id.* (quoting *Forrester v. Penn Lyon Homes, Inc.*, 553 F.3d 340, 343 (4th Cir. 2009)). Under the FAA, a party will lose its right to arbitrate if it is in default of the arbitration clause, which is akin to waiver. *Rota-McLarty v. Santander Consumer USA, Inc.*, 700 F.3d 690, 702 (4th Cir. 2012). The burden of proving default is on the party that opposes the arbitration. *Id.* However, because of the federal policy favoring arbitration, "the party opposing arbitration bears a heavy burden." *Id.*

In addition, the contractual nature of arbitration agreements requires specific arbitration provisions be supported by mutual consideration independent of the underlying contract. *Noohi v. Toll Bros., Inc.*, 708 F.3d 599, 609 (4th Cir. 2013) (applying Maryland law). In *Noohi*, the named plaintiffs (husband and wife) sued a real estate development company and several of its subsidiaries, claiming they refused to return deposits when prospective buyers could not obtain mortgage financing. *Noohi*, 708 F.3d at 599. When the named plaintiffs were unable to secure a mortgage for a luxury home in Maryland, the defendant Toll Bros., Inc., refused to return plaintiffs' deposit of approximately $77,000. *Id.* Plaintiffs sued on behalf of themselves and home buyers around the country who lost their deposits in a similar manner. *Id.* at 603. Defendants moved to stay or dismiss the suit pending arbitration pursuant to the arbitration clause in its Agreement of Sale. *Id.* at 599. The district court denied the motion, finding the arbitration clause unenforceable on the grounds that it lacked mutuality of consideration under Maryland law because it required only the buyer—and not the seller—to submit disputes to arbitration. The Fourth Circuit affirmed. *Id.*

Section 2 of the FAA permits arbitration agreements to be invalidated "'upon such grounds as exist at law or in equity for the revocation of any contract.'" *Id.* at 606, citing 9 U.S.C. § 2. "'This saving clause permits agreements to arbitrate to be invalidated by generally applicable contract defenses, such as fraud, duress, or unconscionability, but not by defenses that apply only to arbitration or that derive their meaning from the fact that an agreement to arbitrate is at issue.'" *Id.* (citing *AT&T Mobility LLC v. Concepcion*, 563 U.S. 333, 131 S. Ct. 1740, 1746, 179 L. Ed. 2d 742 (2011) (internal quotation marks omitted)). Because the agreement bound only plaintiffs to arbitration, the Fourth Circuit found that it lacked mutuality of consideration and, therefore, was invalid and unenforceable. *Id.* at 610.

In *Mey v. DIRECTV,* the Fourth Circuit upheld an agreement signed by AT&T customers in which the customers agreed to arbitrate "all disputes and claims" between the customer and AT&T or any of AT&T's subsidiaries and affiliates. 971 F.3d 284, 286 (4th Cir. 2020). The agreement prohibited class action proceedings and specifically included "claims that are currently the subject of purported class action litigation in which you are not a member of a certified class." *Id.* Mey filed a class action against DIRECTV for alleged unlawful telemarketing calls, but DIRECTV moved to compel arbitration on the grounds that Mey entered into AT&T's arbitration agreement. *Id.* Mey argued that since DIRECTV only became an affiliate of AT&T after she entered into the arbitration agreement, the agreement should not apply to disputes with AT&T. The Fourth Circuit disagreed, holding that "the ordinary meaning of 'affiliates' and the contractual context convinces us that the term includes affiliates acquired after the agreement was signed" and overturned the district court's order denying the motion to compel arbitration. *Id.*

Notably, the Fourth Circuit has held that it may exercise pendent appellate jurisdiction over orders compelling arbitration even though such orders are not typically appealable. *Lyons*, 26 F.4th at 189–90. Pendant appellate jurisdiction is appropriate "only (1) when an issue is inextricably intertwined with a question that is the proper subject of an immediate appeal; or (2) when review of a jurisdictionally insufficient issue is necessary to ensure meaningful review of an immediately appealable issue." *Id.* at 190 (internal quotations omitted).

16. CLASS ACTION WAIVERS

The Fourth Circuit recently became the first court to hold that "the time to address a contractual class waiver is before, not after, a class is certified." *In re Marriott Int'l, Inc.*, 78 F.4th 677, 686 (4th Cir. 2023). Noting that a class waiver defense differs from a typical merits defense because it is a defense to "being required to litigate a class action at all," the court found that refusing to address a class action waiver before litigating a class action to the merits would effectively result in losing the defense, thereby denying the defendant of the benefit of its contractual bargain. *See id.* at 687. The court also noted that even if a class action waiver defense is considered a merits question, there would be "nothing unusual or counter-intuitive" in "requiring courts to consider aspects of the merits in connection with class certification." *See id.*

The Fourth Circuit also recently found that principles of estoppel do not prevent a nonsignatory to a contract from challenging a class action waiver on the grounds that their claims do not fall within the scope of the class action waiver clause. *See Williams v. Martorello*, 59 F.4th 68, 79 (4th Cir. 2023). In addition, the Fourth Circuit found that the prospective waiver doctrine may sometimes apply to class action waivers. *See id.* at 80–81. The prospective waiver doctrine invalidates certain agreements as unenforceable as a matter of public policy if they prospectively waive a party's right to pursue statutory remedies in certain circumstances. *See id.* at 80.

FIFTH CIRCUIT

Districts of Louisiana, Mississippi, and Texas

600 S. Maestri Place
Suite 115
New Orleans, LA 70130

By Margaret Lyle, Jones Day,
and Tyler Harris, Suntex Marinas[1]

1. INTRODUCTION

A leader in the judicial management and resolution of mass tort claims and renowned for its landmark decisions in the civil rights era, the Fifth Circuit hears appeals from federal district courts in Louisiana, Mississippi, and Texas. Led by Chief Judge Jennifer Walker Elrod, 25 active and senior judges resolve more than 5,500 civil and criminal appeals per year, with an overall reversal rate of 8.2 percent and 18.9 percent in cases where the court hears argument. According to the most recent court statistics, the Fifth Circuit grants oral argument in about 33 percent of cases. The court's website offers a variety of resources, including the Fifth Circuit's local rules and operating procedures, sample briefs, a practitioner's guide, and recordings of oral arguments. The court also has its own YouTube channel for audio recordings of arguments. The court's electronic filing document system offers an Attorney Toolbox Utility with templates for briefs and other assistance with document preparation.

The Fifth Circuit achieved its place in history with a series of groundbreaking civil rights decisions that desegregated schools and vindicated the voting rights of African Americans in the 1950s and 1960s. These decisions were foundational to the 1966 revision of Federal Rule of Civil Procedure 23, which framed Rule 23(b)(2) class actions for injunctive relief with civil rights cases in mind. Indeed, when the Federal Rules Advisory Committee first described the Rule 23(b)(2) class, it cited four of these important Fifth Circuit cases, explaining that "[i]llustrative are various actions in the civil-rights field where a party is charged with discriminating unlawfully against a class." *See* Fed. R. Civ. P. 23 advisory committee's note to 1966 amendment. The Fifth Circuit's courthouse, the John Minor Wisdom U.S. Court of Appeals Building, has been designated as a National Historic Landmark for the court's historic role in deciding these Civil Rights Movement era cases.

In the decades that followed, the Fifth Circuit took on a new leading role, this time in the management and resolution of mass tort litigation. In response to the asbestos-litigation crisis of the 1980s and 1990s, a trio of Fifth Circuit trial plan decisions—*Jenkins v. Raymark Industries, Inc.* (1986), *In re Fibreboard Corp.* (1990), and *Cimino v. Raymark Industries, Inc.* (1998)—grappled with how a massive number of individual tort claims, each requiring proof of causation, could be managed within the framework of the jury trial and the Constitutional guarantee of due process. In 1996, the Fifth Circuit's landmark decision in *Castano*

[1] The authors wish to thank Elijah Stone, Nicole Bronnimann, Clayton Cromer, Rebecca Duncan, Michael Murtha, and Jonathan Pevey for their assistance. The views and opinions set forth are the personal views or opinions of the authors and do not necessarily reflect views or opinions of the law firm or organization with which they are associated.

v. American Tobacco Co. reversed certification of a nationwide tobacco class action, demanding a "rigorous analysis" of Rule 23's class certification requirements and anticipating the U.S. Supreme Court's later decision in *Amchem Products, Inc. v. Windsor*. In 2010, the Fifth Circuit established the ground rules for Rule 23(b)(1)(B) "limited fund" class settlements in the *Katrina Canal Breaches* mass tort litigation. And in its recent *Deepwater Horizon* opinions, the Fifth Circuit continues to answer questions about standing, proof of causation, and the proper role of the courts in approving a class settlement and implementing a court-supervised settlement program.

The Supreme Court's holdings in *Wal-Mart* (2011), *Comcast* (2013), *Amgen* (2013), *Halliburton* (2014), *Spokeo* (2016), and *TransUnion* (2021) have given the Fifth Circuit reason to speak anew about key aspects of Rule 23 in mass tort settlements and other proposed class actions: the commonality requirement; the proper roles for damages theories and models in the class certification decision; the expert evidentiary standard for class certification; how a class must establish standing at successive stages of the litigation; and which matters must be decided at the class certification stage, even though they may overlap with the merits. The Supreme Court's arbitration jurisprudence in such cases as *EPIC Systems* (2018), *Henry Schein* (2019), and *Lamps Plus* (2019) will likewise shape the Fifth Circuit's application of arbitration clauses in proposed class actions. We can expect further word on these developing issues in the future.

2. JURISDICTIONAL PREREQUISITES

a. CAFA Requirements

The Class Action Fairness Act of 2005 (CAFA) expanded federal diversity jurisdiction to include certain class actions where "the class has more than 100 members, the parties are minimally diverse, and the amount in controversy exceeds $5 million." *Dart Cherokee Basin Operating Co. v. Owens*, 574 U.S. 81, 84–85, 135 S. Ct. 547, 552 (2014) (citing 28 U.S.C. § 1332 (d)(2), (5)(B)); *see also Butler v. Denka Performance Elastomer, L.L.C.*, 16 F.4th 427, 435 (5th Cir. 2021); *Madison v. ADT, L.L.C.*, 11 F.4th 325, 327 (5th Cir. 2021) (citing *Home Depot U.S.A., Inc. v. Jackson*, 587 U.S. 435, 438 (2019)); *Watson v. City of Allen, Texas*, 821 F.3d 634, 637–38 (5th Cir. 2016); *City of Walker v. Louisiana*, 877 F.3d 563, 567 (5th Cir. 2017).

CAFA Removal

A defendant removing a class action to federal court under CAFA bears the burden of establishing federal jurisdiction. *See Robertson v. Exxon Mobil Corp.*, 814 F.3d 236, 239 (5th Cir. 2015). "No anti-removal presumption attends cases invoking CAFA," however, because Congress intended CAFA to facilitate adjudication of class actions in federal court. *See Dart*, 574 U.S. at 89, 135 S. Ct. at 554. "CAFA eliminated the requirement of unanimity of consent to removal." *Frazier v. Pioneer Americas LLC*, 455 F.3d 542, 546–47 (5th Cir. 2006) (citing 28 U.S.C. § 1453(b)).

"[T]he pleadings at the time the class action is removed," and not any later amendments, determine CAFA jurisdiction. *See Cedar Lodge Plantation, L.L.C. v. CSHV Fairway View I, L.L.C.*, 768 F.3d 425, 427 (5th Cir. 2014). Under this "time-of-removal rule," post-removal actions do not "destroy[] jurisdiction that attached in a federal court under CAFA" at the time of removal. *See id.*; *see also Arbuckle Mountain Ranch of Texas, Inc. v. Chesapeake Energy Corp.*, 810 F.3d 335, 339, 343 (5th Cir. 2016) (limiting review to plaintiff's pleadings at the time of removal when determining whether an exception to CAFA jurisdiction applied). In keeping with the rule that the pleadings at the time of removal determine jurisdiction, the Fifth Circuit will not second guess procedural rulings made by the State court before CAFA removal. *See Turner v. GoAuto Ins. Co.*, 33 F.4th 214, 216–17 (5th Cir. 2022) (per curiam) (refusing to look behind pre-removal amendment to proposed class definition that defeated minimal diversity).

A defendant's notice of removal under CAFA should contain "a plausible allegation that the amount in controversy exceeds the jurisdictional threshold," but no evidentiary submission is required. *See Dart*, 574 U.S. at 89, 135 S. Ct. at 551, 554. Evidence establishing the amount in controversy is needed only if "the plaintiff contests, or the court questions, the defendant's allegation." *Id.* In that case, "both sides submit proof and the court decides, by a preponderance of the evidence, whether the amount-in-controversy requirement has been satisfied." *Id.* (citing 28 U.S.C. § 1446(c)(2)(B)).

A defendant removing under CAFA can meet its evidentiary burden to establish a contested amount in controversy either by showing that the amount "is 'facially apparent' from the plaintiffs' pleadings alone, or by submitting summary-judgment-type evidence." *See Robertson*, 814 F.3d at 240 (internal citations omitted). To determine the amount in controversy, the court can make "common-sense inferences" from "the injuries the plaintiffs claim." *See id.*; *see also Frazier v. Pioneer Americas LLC*, 455 F.3d. 542, 545 (5th Cir. 2006) (holding that a "petition, seeking damages for severe injuries suffered by at least 500 people and attorneys' fees, makes it 'facially apparent' that at least $5 million is in controversy" (footnotes omitted)). *Cf. Henry v. Howard L. Nations, A.P.C.*, No. 23-30467, 2024 WL 3673539, at *3 (5th Cir. Aug. 6, 2024) (unpublished) (CAFA amount-in-controversy requirement satisfied when class plaintiffs who brought original action in federal court alleged in good faith a minimum amount of $38 million; their expert detailed why total amount would exceed $5 million based on available information; amount was facially apparent from complaint; and it did not appear to a legal certainty that claim was really for less than the jurisdictional amount).

"The required demonstration concerns what the plaintiff is claiming" and "not whether the plaintiff is likely to win or be awarded everything he seeks." *Robertson*, 814 F.3d at 240 (internal citations and quotations omitted). A class action plaintiff's stipulation, prior to class certification, that he and his proposed class will not seek damages over $5 million does not destroy CAFA jurisdiction because such precertification stipulations cannot bind members of the proposed class. *See Standard Fire Ins. Co. v. Knowles*, 568 U.S. 558, 133 S. Ct. 1345, 1348–49 (2013).

"Unlike normal diversity jurisdiction where every defendant must be diverse from every plaintiff," CAFA requires only "minimal diversity for jurisdiction over class actions." *Turner*, 33 F.4th at 216 (citing 28 U.S.C. § 1332(d)(2)). "This is achieved when 'at least one class member is a citizen of a State different from the defendant.'" *Id.* (citing *Madison*, 11 F.4th at 327). Thus, when "every class member is from the same state as the defendant," there is no minimal diversity. *Turner*, 33 F.4th at 217 (citing *Madison*, 11 F.4th at 327)

Under CAFA, a state is not a citizen for diversity purposes, and a "a state's presence does not affect CAFA's minimal—rather than complete—diversity requirement." *Butler*, 16 F.4th at 435–36. Defendants may "remove a case to federal court without first obtaining consent—and therefore waiver of sovereign immunity—from any joined state defendants," and the nonconsenting State can still assert immunity after removal if it has taken no affirmative act to waive it. *Id.* at 436 (State agencies waiving immunity only after removal).

CAFA "excludes federal subject-matter jurisdiction over a class action where 'the number of members of all proposed plaintiff classes in the aggregate is less than 100.'" *State of Louisiana, By & Through its Div. of Admin. v. I3 Verticals Inc.*, 81 F.4th 483, 486 (5th Cir. 2023) (quoting 28 U.S.C. § 1332(d)(5)(B) and citing *Mississippi ex rel. Hood v. AU Optronics Corp.*, 571 U.S. 161, 169 (2014)). Because CAFA's hundred-member threshold "goes to subject-matter jurisdiction," the Fifth Circuit has considered it even when raised for the first time on appeal. *Id.* at 487 (applying state law to determine whether local government entities were persons capable of suit and therefore countable as members of the proposed plaintiff class).

Sometimes the initial pleading is not removable under CAFA, but an amended pleading or other document later makes the case removable. A defendant then has 30 days to file its notice of removal. *Cobalt Int'l Energy, Inc. v. Alterra Am. Ins. Co.*, 88 F. App'x 254, 257

(5th Cir. 2019) (per curiam) (unpublished) (citing 28 U.S.C. § 1446(b)(3)). When a newly-added defendant has the right to remove, it should file its own notice of removal. Joinder in another defendant's previously filed notice of removal will not suffice if that other notice turns out to have been untimely. *See id.* at 257–58.

Under 28 U.S.C. § 1453(c), courts of appeals may accept appeals from orders granting or denying remands of CAFA class actions but must decide those appeals under a strict statutory time frame. *See, e.g.*, *City of Walker*, 877 F.3d at 566–67 (reviewing CAFA and federal-officer bases for removal, but not federal question jurisdiction); *Louisiana v. Am. Nat. Prop. & Cas. Co.*, 746 F.3d 633, 636 (5th Cir. 2014) (leave to appeal remand order granted because case presented an important CAFA-related question and the record was sufficiently developed); *Frazier*, 455 F.3d at 544 (reciting grant of leave to appeal under § 1453); *Braud v. Transp. Serv. Co.*, 445 F.3d 801, 803 n.1 and 2 (5th Cir. 2006) (explaining procedure for § 1453 appeal); *Patterson v. Dean Morris, L.L.P.*, 444 F.3d 365, 370 (5th Cir. 2006) (statutory period for rendering appellate judgment in § 1453 CAFA appeal runs from the date the court granted permission to appeal, not from the date of the petition for appeal).

Such discretionary appeals "are not limited to only those issues 'unique or peculiar to CAFA,'" but "the purpose . . . is to 'facilitate the development' of interpretations of CAFA 'without unduly delaying the litigation of class actions.'" *Williams v. Homeland Ins. Co. of New York*, 788 F. App'x 297, 298 (5th Cir. 2019) (per curiam) (unpublished) (citing *Alvarez v. Midland Credit Mgmt., Inc.*, 585 F.3d 890, 894 (5th Cir. 2009)). So, according to *Williams*, "the issues raised by the party seeking permission to appeal must be sufficiently linked to CAFA." *Id.* (citing *Perritt v. Westlake Vinyls Co., L.P.*, 562 F. App'x 228, 230 (5th Cir. 2014) (per curiam) (unpublished); *Berniard v. Dow Chemical Co.*, 481 F. App'x 859, 864 (5th Cir. 2010) (per curiam) (unpublished); and *Wallace v. La. Citizens Prop. Ins. Corp.*, 444 F.3d 697, 700 (5th Cir. 2006)). *See also Patterson*, 448 F.3d at 742 (Because CAFA "explicitly limits the power of removal of class actions" to cases under § 1453, appeals under § 1453(c)(1) are "limited to the context of CAFA," and once the court has determined that CAFA is inapplicable, it need not "reach otherwise non-reviewable remand decisions."); *Stewart v. Entergy Corp.*, 35 F.4th 930, 934–35 (5th Cir. 2022) *related second appeal dismissed for lack of jurisdiction*, No. 22-30132, 2022 WL 17579883, at *1 (5th Cir. Dec. 12, 2022) (declining to *extend BP P.L.C. v. Mayor of Baltimore* , 593 U.S. 230 (2021) to appellate review of CAFA remand orders and reaffirming that §1453(c) "does not grant us jurisdiction to consider non-CAFA-related grounds for removal").

Alvarez, which vacated a previously granted permission to appeal after the appellants dropped their CAFA-based arguments, likewise recognized the constraints of the short timeframe for these discretionary interlocutory appeals. 585 F.3d at 894. ("We recognize that § 1453(c) does not limit our discretionary appellate jurisdiction to matters unique or peculiar to CAFA. However, . . . Congress placed very short time limits on our determination of such appeals."). *Alvarez* weighed the costs of an early and fastmoving appeal against the benefits of deciding the issues presented. *Id.* ("[I]n exercising our discretion to hear such appeals we must weigh the time taken from earlier filed appeals to tend to the CAFA appeal against the benefit of hearing such an appeal at this juncture. Part of this weighing necessarily involves consideration of the unique nature of the issues presented in the proposed appeal.").

The Fifth Circuit has held that appellants may rely on 28 U.S.C. §§ 1291 or 1453(c), however, when they appeal a remand order under CAFA's statutory exception found at 28 U.S.C. § 1332(d)(4)(A), known as the "local controversy" exception. *Cheapside Minerals, Ltd. v. Devon Energy Prod. Co., L.P.*, 94 F.4th 492, 495–97 (5th Cir. 2024). Because final orders remanding cases under CAFA's local controversy exception are based on abstention principles—not on lack of subject matter jurisdiction or a procedural defect—28 U.S.C. § 1447(d) does not block a § 1291 appeal. *Id.* Nor is such a § 1291 appeal bound by the CAFA time limits. *Id.* For more discussion of the local controversy exception and CAFA's other exceptions, refer to the next subheading.

The Fifth Circuit reviews de novo an order remanding a lawsuit removed under CAFA. *See, e.g.*, *Robertson*, 814 F.3d at 239; *Turner*; 33 F.4th at 216.

CAFA Exceptions
CAFA jurisdiction has three chief exceptions. First, under CAFA's "local controversy" exception, a district court must decline to exercise jurisdiction over a class action when (1) "greater than two-thirds of the members of all proposed plaintiff classes in the aggregate are citizens of the State in which the action was originally filed"; (2) at least one defendant is a citizen of the State of original filing, from whom "significant relief" is sought and whose "alleged conduct forms a significant basis" for the class claims; (3) "principal injuries" were incurred in the State of original filing; and (4) no other class action asserting the "same or similar factual allegations" has been filed against any defendant within three years before the date of original filing. *See* 28 U.S.C. § 1332(d)(4)(A); *13 Verticals*, 81 F.4th at 486 ("significant relief" and "significant basis" requirements); *Stewart v. Entergy Corp.*, 35 F.4th 930, 932 & n.1 (5th Cir. 2022); *Hollinger v. Home State Mut. Ins. Co.*, 654 F.3d 564, 570 (5th Cir. 2011); *Opelousas Gen. Hosp. Auth. v. FairPay Sol., Inc.*, 655 F.3d 358, 363 (5th Cir. 2011) (per curiam) (recognizing CAFA jurisdiction when alleged conduct of local defendant did not form significant basis for claims of proposed class); *City of Walker*, 877 F.3d at 568–69 (affirming remand under local controversy exception when earlier-filed class action was not sufficiently similar to currently proposed class action to support federal jurisdiction). *Dixon v. D.R. Horton, Inc. - Gulf Coast*, No. 23-30800, 2024 WL 125730, at *2 (5th Cir. Jan. 11, 2024) (unpublished) (per curiam) (determination that two-thirds of putative class were Louisiana citizens not clearly erroneous when (1) class was defined as purchasers of homes located in Louisiana, (2) homeownership was indicium of domicile, (3) all homes were in Louisiana, and (4) plaintiffs presented evidence that over 80 percent of homeowners in one parish claimed a homestead exemption, taken together with (5) presumption of continuing domicile).

In *13 Verticals*, the Fifth Circuit explained that plaintiffs' complaint allegations may establish that an in-state defendant's conduct forms a "significant basis" of their claims by providing information about the in-state defendant's conduct relative to that of the other defendants, distinguishing the in-state defendant's conduct, and estimating the conduct attributable to the in-state defendant versus the others. *13 Verticals*, 81 F.4th at 490 (citing *Opelousas*, 655 F.3d at 361–62).

To determine whether plaintiffs also seek "significant relief" from an in-state defendant, the court does not consider "how much the in-state defendant can actually pay." *13 Verticals*, 81 F.4th at 492. "All that matters is what the plaintiffs seek in damages—not whether there's any likelihood that they will obtain what they seek." *Id.* at 493 (holding "significant relief" requirement satisfied when complaint alleged that all class members were harmed by in-state defendants' conduct, in-state defendants were solely responsible for more than half of time period of continuing injury, and at least half of damages sought were from in-state defendants). The Fifth Circuit has also held that the allegation that the in-state defendant was "jointly, severally, and solidarily liable to all potential class members for all damages" satisfied the "significant relief" requirement. *Dixon,* 2024 WL 125730, at *3.

The "principal injuries" prong of the exception "qualitatively and comparatively evaluates the types of injury, not the quantity of plaintiffs who were injured." *Cheapside Minerals*, 94 F.4th at 499–501. It requires that "all plaintiffs sustain their principal injuries in the forum state and nowhere else." *Id.* at 501 (vacating remand order and directing that case be reinstated in federal court when, although most plaintiffs sustained "principal injury" of financial harm in Texas, others did not. *Id.* at 502.).

Second, under CAFA's "home-state" exception, a district court must decline to exercise jurisdiction when "two-thirds or more of the members of all proposed plaintiff classes in the aggregate, and the primary defendants, are citizens of the State in which the action was originally filed." 28 U.S.C. § 1332(d)(4)(B); *see also Stewart*, 35 F.4th at 932 & n.1; *Madison,*

11 F.4th at 327 (quoting the statute); *Hollinger*, 654 F.3d at 570 (same); *Preston v. Tenet Healthsystem Mem'l Med. Ctr., Inc.*, 485 F.3d 804, 811 (5th Cir. 2007) (same).

The phrase "the primary defendants" means "all primary defendants" and "indicates a chief defendant or chief class of defendants." *See Watson*, 821 F.3d at 641–42 (limiting "primary defendants" to defendants that had primary role in alleged constitutional violations). An intervenor against whom the plaintiff has not yet asserted a claim can still be a primary defendant when it is the "real target" of the litigation and the thrust of the suit is to gain access to its deep pockets; whether the defendant is vicariously or secondarily liable is relevant but not controlling. *Madison*, 11 F.4th at 328–29.

Third, under CAFA's discretionary exception, sometimes called the "interests-of-justice" exception, a district court *may*, "in the interests of justice and looking at the totality of the circumstances," decline jurisdiction "over a class action in which greater than one-third but less than two-thirds of the members of all proposed plaintiff classes in the aggregate and the primary defendants are citizens of the State in which the action was originally filed," after considering a list of statutory factors. *See* 28 U.S.C. § 1332(d)(3); *Preston*, 485 F.3d at 810–11 (recognizing that CAFA's discretionary exception affords "greater latitude to remand class actions," but holding that the court "does not wield unfettered discretion" because "Congress provided a list of factors to guide the district court's consideration").

In the Fifth Circuit, the burden of proving CAFA exceptions falls on the party *objecting* to federal jurisdiction. *See I3 Verticals*, 81 F.4th at 489; *Madison*, 11 F.4th at 327; *Stewart*, 35 F.4th at 932 (party seeking remand bears burden to establish citizenship requirements of CAFA exceptions by preponderance of evidence); *Hollinger*, 654 F.3d at 571 (5th Cir. 2011) (placing burden to prove CAFA local-controversy and home-state exceptions on defendants seeking dismissal of class action brought in federal court); *Frazier*, 455 F.3d at 546 (placing burden to prove CAFA exceptions on plaintiffs seeking remand of class action removed to federal court); *City of Walker*, 877 F.3d at 567 (same).

CAFA exceptions are construed narrowly. *Cheapside Minerals*, 94 F.4th at 50. The Fifth Circuit "resolve[s] lingering doubts" about the applicability of the CAFA exceptions in favor of exercising federal jurisdiction. *Arbuckle*, 810 F.3d at 342. "If the applicability of an exception is not shown with reasonable certainty, federal jurisdiction should be retained." *Id.* at 338. This "reasonable certainty" requirement equates to a "preponderance of the evidence" burden of proof. *See I3 Verticals*, 81 F.4th at 489–90.

The Fifth Circuit has addressed how courts should determine citizenship of natural persons for purposes of the CAFA exceptions, *see Stewart*, 35 F.4th at 933–34; *Hollinger*, 654 F.3d at 571 (citing *Preston*, 485 F.3d at 797–98), and the circuit reviews a "district court's factual finding as to the citizenship of the parties for clear error." *Preston*, 485 F.3d at 809. The Fifth Circuit also has recognized that state defendants have no citizenship for purposes of the CAFA local controversy and home state exceptions. *See Frazier*, 455 F.3d at 547 (declining to treat Louisiana State environmental department as Louisiana citizen).

The "primary defendants" in a CAFA class action must not be "states, state officials, or other government entities." *See Arbuckle*, 810 F.3d at 337 (citing 28 U.S.C. § 1332 (d)(5)(A)). To avoid CAFA jurisdiction under § 1332(d)(5)(A) when the "primary defendants" are states, *all* of the primary defendants must be states; this interpretation avoids "creat[ing] a loophole" for plaintiffs to escape CAFA jurisdiction "by naming a state as a primary defendant in an action largely targeting non-states." *Id.* (footnote omitted).

The Fifth Circuit has reviewed de novo remands under CAFA's local controversy and home state exceptions. *See I3 Verticals*, 81 F.4th at 489; *Madison*, 11 F.4th at 327; *Williams v. Homeland Ins. Co. of N.Y.*, 657 F.3d 287, 290 (5th Cir. 2011); *City of Walker*, 877 F.3d at 567. *See also Stewart*, 35 F.4th at 932 (reviewing jurisdictional determination de novo but factual findings on citizenship for clear error). A remand order under CAFA's discretionary exception has been reviewed for abuse of discretion. *See Preston*, 485 F.3d at 809.

CAFA "Mass Actions"

CAFA also expanded federal jurisdiction over certain "mass actions" that involve multiple plaintiffs but are not brought as class actions. *See* 28 U.S.C. § 1332(d)(11); *see also Robertson*, 814 F.3d at 239 (citing *Mississippi ex rel. Hood v. AU Optronics Corp.*, 134 S. Ct. 736, 739–40 (2014)). CAFA's mass action jurisdiction applies when 100 or more persons propose to try their claims for monetary relief jointly on the grounds that their claims involve common questions of law or fact and certain other requirements are met. *See* 28 U.S.C. § 1332(d)(11); *Lester v. Exxon Mobil Corp.*, 879 F.3d 582, 591 (5th Cir. 2018) (holding that a motion to consolidate and transfer related state court suits can make a removable mass action, even when one of the underlying suits was commenced prior to CAFA's 2005 effective date). Plaintiffs can avoid mass action jurisdiction under CAFA by filing separate complaints, each naming fewer than 100 plaintiffs, so long as "the plaintiffs have not proposed that those actions be tried jointly or otherwise consolidated" for trial. *Eagle U.S. 2, L.L.C. v. Abraham*, 627 F. App'x 351, 353 (5th Cir. 2015) (per curiam) (unpublished).

Under express statutory exceptions, CAFA mass action jurisdiction does not apply to claims that were "joined upon motion of a defendant," *see* 28 U.S.C. § 1332(d)(11)(B)(ii)(II), or "consolidated or coordinated solely for pretrial proceedings," *see id.* at § 1332(d)(11)(B)(ii)(IV). Nor does mass action jurisdiction apply when "all of the claims . . . are asserted on behalf of the general public" under a "State statute specifically authorizing" that. *See id.* § 1332(d)(11)(B)(ii)(III).

As the Fifth Circuit explained in *Bonin v. Sabine River Auth. of Louisiana*, "federal jurisdiction over a mass action additionally requires that the suit satisfy three other prerequisites. First, there must be 'minimal diversity' such that 'any member of a class of plaintiffs is a citizen of a State different from any defendant." 961 F.3d 381, 386 (5th Cir. 2020) (citing 28 U.S.C §§ 1332(d)(2)(A), (d)(11)(A)). "Second, the aggregate amount in controversy must exceed $5 million." *Id.* (citing 28 U.S.C. §§ 1332(d)(2), (d)(6), (d)(11)(A)). "And third, 'at least one plaintiff's claim [must] satisf[y] the $75,000 individual amount in controversy' requirement." *Id.* (citing *Robertson,* 814 F.3d at 239 (5th Cir. 2015) and 28 U.S.C. §§ 1332(a), (d)(11)(B)(i)) (alterations in original)).

To prevent remand of a case removed as a CAFA mass action, the defendant must therefore demonstrate two amounts in controversy: CAFA's $5 million aggregate amount *and*, for at least one plaintiff, the $75,000 individual amount in controversy ordinarily required for diversity jurisdiction. *See* 28 U.S.C. § 1332(d)(2), (d)(11)(B)(i); *see also Hood ex. rel. Mississippi v. JP Morgan Chase Co.*, 737 F.3d 78, 85 (5th Cir. 2013). In a mass action, CAFA jurisdiction exists only over those plaintiffs whose claims satisfy the $75,000 jurisdictional amount. 28 U.S.C. § 1332(d)(11)(B)(i).

By an express statutory exception, CAFA's mass action jurisdiction does not extend to claims that arise from a single event in the State of filing. *See* 28 U.S.C. § 1332(d)(11)(B)(ii)(I); *Bonin*, 961 F.3d at 386 ("The exception provides that 'the term "mass action" shall not include any civil action in which É all of the claims in the action arise from an event or occurrence in the State in which the action was filed, and that allegedly resulted in injuries in that State or in States contiguous to that State.'") (citing 28 U.S.C. § 1332(d)(11)(B)(ii)(I)). This exception "contemplates a *single* event or occurrence" but is not limited "to incidents that occur at a discrete moment in time." *See Rainbow Gun Club, Inc. v. Denbury Onshore, L.L.C.*, 760 F.3d 405, 409 (5th Cir. 2014) (emphasis in original). In the Fifth Circuit, the exception also can apply when a "pattern of conduct" consistently leads to a "single focused event that culminates in the basis of the asserted liability." *Id.* at 412. The in-state element of the exception is not met by an "event that occurs on both sides of the border between two states, which leads to claims in both states," because such an event "is not local to either of those states." *Bonin,* 961 F.3d at 387.

Like other cases where CAFA confers jurisdiction, CAFA "mass actions 'may be removed by any defendant without the consent of all defendants.'" *Bonin,* 961 F.3d at 387 (citing 28 U.S.C. § 1453(b) and *Frazier*, 455 F.3d at 546–47).

b. Personal Jurisdiction

The Fifth Circuit has not yet decided how the Supreme Court's jurisdictional holding in *Bristol-Myers*—that a state court could not exercise specific jurisdiction in a mass tort action over an out-of-state defendant with respect to nonresidents' claims for out-of-state injuries and conduct, *see Bristol-Myers Squibb Co. v. Superior Court of California, San Francisco Cty.*, 582 U.S. 255, 264–66, 269 (2017)—would apply to class actions in federal court. *See Cruson v. Jackson Nat'l Life Ins. Co.*, 954 F.3d 240, 247–51, n.4, 7 (5th Cir. 2020) (declining to decide personal jurisdiction defense for the first time on appeal but holding it preserved for decision on remand). *See also Douglass v. Nippon Yusen Kabushiki Kaisha*, 46 F.4th 226, 236 (5th Cir. 2022) (en banc), *cert. denied sub nom. Douglass v. Kaisha*, 143 S. Ct. 1021, 215 L. Ed. 2d 188 (2023) (various opinions with differing perspectives on the interplay between the Fifth Circuit's jurisdictional holding in that case and *Bristol-Myers*).

c. Standing

Who May Bring a Class Action—Requirements

"Plaintiffs' standing . . . 'is an inherent prerequisite to the class certification inquiry.'" *Angell v. GEICO Advantage Ins. Co.*, 67 F.4th 727, 733 (5th Cir. 2023) (quoting *Bertulli v. Indep. Ass'n of Cont'l Pilots*, 242 F.3d 290, 294 (5th Cir. 2001)). As the Fifth Circuit explained in *Chavez v. Plan Benefit Services, Inc.*, the "Supreme Court has repeatedly explained that 'Article III does not give federal courts the power to order relief to any uninjured plaintiff, class action or not,'" and plaintiffs must "demonstrate standing for each claim that they press and for each form of relief that they seek." 108 F.4th 297, 307 (5th Cir. 2024) (*Chavez II*), *cert. denied sub nom. Plan Benefit Services v. Chavez*, No. 24-426, 2024 WL 5011734 (U.S. Dec. 9, 2024) (quoting *TransUnion LLC v. Ramirez*, 594 U.S. 413, 431 (2021)).

To determine standing, the Fifth Circuit follows the three requirements laid out by the Supreme Court. "'[A] plaintiff must show (i) that he suffered an injury in fact that is concrete, particularized, and actual or imminent; (ii) that the injury was likely caused by the defendant; and (iii) that the injury would likely be redressed by judicial relief.'" *Id.* (quoting *TransUnion LLC v. Ramirez*, 594 U.S. 413, 423 (2021)); *see also Chavez II*, 108 F.4th at 307 (similar, quoting *Thole v. U.S. Bank N.A.*, 590 U.S. 538, 540 (2020)).

As the Fifth Circuit has further explained:

> first and foremost, there must be alleged (and ultimately proved) an injury in fact—a harm suffered by the plaintiff that is concrete and actual or imminent, not conjectural or hypothetical. Second, there must be causation—a fairly traceable connection between the plaintiff's injury and the complained-of conduct of the defendant. And third, there must be redressability—a likelihood that the requested relief will redress the alleged injury.

Servicios Azucareros de Venezuela, C.A. v. John Deere Thibodeaux, Inc., 702 F.3d 794, 799–800 (5th Cir. 2012) (quoting *Steel Co. v. Citizens for a Better Env't*, 523 U.S. 83, 102–04 (1998)). These three requirements—injury in fact, causation, and redressability—together form the core of the Constitutional case-or-controversy requirement; the burden of establishing them falls on the party invoking federal jurisdiction. *See id.* at 800 (quoting *Steel Co.*, 523 U.S. at 103–04); *see also Chavez II*, 108 F.4th at 307 ("Plaintiffs carry this burden throughout the litigation proceedings."); *James v. Hegar*, 86 F.4th 1076, 1081 (5th Cir. 2023); *In re Deepwater Horizon*, 739 F.3d 790, 799 (5th Cir. 2014) (identifying elements of Article III standing as "injury in fact, the injury's traceability to the defendant's conduct, and the potential for the injury to be redressed by the relief requested"). These standing requirements "are equally applicable in class actions," where the named plaintiffs must allege and show that they personally have been injured, not that other, absent class members have suffered injury. *Singh v. RadioShack Corp.*, 882 F.3d 137, 150–51 (5th Cir. 2018) (three elements of constitutional standing, plus prudential standing rules, apply). *See also Braidwood Mgmt., Inc. v. Equal Employment Opportunity Comm'n*, 70 F.4th 914, 924 (5th Cir. 2023); *Nwaorie v. United States*, No. 19-20706, 2023 WL 3034261, at *5 (5th Cir. Apr. 21, 2023) (per curiam) (unpublished) (holding that named plaintiff who never submitted to challenged government policy and thus lacked actual or imminent injury could not seek redress for others who did submit); *Perez v. McCreary, Veselka, Bragg & Allen, P.C.*, 45 F.4th 816, 821 (5th Cir. 2022) (requiring named plaintiff to show on appeal, for each claim asserted and form of relief sought, "injury in fact that is concrete, particularized, and actual or imminent," that was "likely caused by the defendant," and "would likely be addressed by judicial relief") (citing *TransUnion*, 594 U.S. at 423; *Flecha v. Medicredit, Inc.*, 946 F.3d 762, 769 (5th Cir. 2020) (observing that "if the class representative lacks standing, then there is no Article III suit to begin with" (citations omitted)). The Fifth Circuit has also held that concrete injury is lacking when class plaintiffs "suffered no physical harm" and "offered no plausible theory of economic harm." *Earl v. Boeing Co.*, 53 F.4th 897 (5th Cir. 2022). ("At bottom, plaintiffs complain of a past risk of physical injury to which they were allegedly exposed because of defendants' fraud. But because that risk never materialized, plaintiffs have suffered no injury in fact and lack Article III standing.").

The Supreme Court expounded further on the injury-in-fact requirement in *Spokeo, Inc. v. Robins*, 578 U.S. 330, 334, 339–342 (2016). Reaffirming that an injury in fact must be both "concrete *and* particularized," to confer standing, the Supreme Court explained that a plaintiff cannot satisfy the injury-in-fact requirement when he alleges a "bare procedural violation" of a statute "divorced from any concrete harm." *Id.* at 339–42 (emphasis in original). *See also TransUnion*, 594 U.S. 413; *Frank v. Gaos*, 586 U.S. 485, 491–93 (2019). "[A]concrete injury is one that is 'real, and not abstract.'" *Chavez II*, 108 F.4th at 307 (quoting *Spokeo*, 578 U.S. at 340). Applying *Spokeo*, the Fifth Circuit has dismissed an ERISA class claim for lack of a concrete injury; the court concluded that the "bare allegation" of a violation of a claimed statutory right was "insufficient to meet the injury-in-fact prong of Article III standing" when the class representative's "'concrete interest' in the plan—his right to payment—was not alleged to be at risk." *Lee v. Verizon Commc'ns, Inc.*, 837 F.3d 523, 529–30 (5th Cir. 2016) (internal quotations omitted). Applying *TransUnion*, the Fifth Circuit has held that a named plaintiff's receipt of a collection letter for a time-barred debt did not confer standing when she could not show a concrete injury. *Perez*, 45 F.4th at 822 (5th Cir. 2022) ("So *TransUnion* is clear: A plaintiff always needs a concrete injury to bring suit, and injuries are concrete only if they bear a 'close relationship' to injuries that courts have traditionally recognized as concrete.").

The Fifth Circuit has explained that a plaintiff's injury is sufficiently "particularized" to confer standing only when it affects the plaintiff in a "personal and individual way." *See Abbott v. BP Expl. & Prod., Inc.*, 851 F.3d 384, 388 (5th Cir. 2017) (citing, *inter alia*, *Spokeo*, 136 S. Ct. at 1548); *see also Chavez II*, 108 F.4th at 307. *Abbott* held that plaintiffs—businesses, residents, and visitors who anticipated that they could be injured by a potential oil spill—lacked sufficiently particularized injuries when "[t]hese alleged injuries could occur to anyone who uses the Gulf regularly, works near the Gulf, or lives or owns property near the Gulf, i.e., millions of people." 851 F.3d at 388.

"When multiple laws cause the same harm, that injury may not be traceable or redressable when only one of those laws is challenged," although there are exceptions. *See generally Leal v. Becerra*, No. 21-10302, 2022 WL 2981427, at *2 (5th Cir. July 27, 2022) (per curiam) (unpublished) (remanding challenge to ACA for further consideration of standing).

Class plaintiffs seeking prospective injunctive or declaratory relief "must demonstrate 'continuing harm or a real and immediate threat of repeated injury in the future.'" *James*, 86 F.4th at 1081 (quoting *Soc'y of Separationists, Inc. v. Herman*, 959 F.2d 1283, 1285 (5th Cir. 1992)) (holding that past unconstitutional takings of property did not confer standing for prospective relief). "The threat of future injury must be 'certainly impending'; mere allegations of possible future injury will not suffice." *Id.* (quoting *Clapper v. Amnesty Int'l USA*, 568 U.S. 398, 409 (2013)). As the Fifth Circuit has explained, "if Plaintiffs allege no impending future injury, . . . prospective relief in no way redresses Plaintiffs' alleged injuries." *Id.* at 1082; *see also Nwaorie*, 2023 WL 3034261, at *5 (named plaintiff whose seized property had been returned alleged only "a past injury" insufficient to pursue equitable relief on behalf of proposed class whose property had not been returned). Taking actions and incurring costs "out of fear of a future injury . . . do not suffice." *James*, 86 F.4th at 1082.

A named plaintiff seeking a declaratory judgment can demonstrate standing based on a credible threat of future government enforcement in violation of asserted constitutional rights. *See Braidwood Mgmt.*, 70 F.4th at 928 (holding that named plaintiffs had established standing when there were "sufficiently concrete facts, clear harms hanging over plaintiffs' heads, and a prior prosecution with an almost identical set of facts," *id.* at 929 n.27).

In its 2023 *Angell* decision, the Fifth Circuit declined to decide whether a proposed class representative's standing should be addressed only as to the individual named plaintiff, leaving any remaining analysis comparing the plaintiff's injury to that of the class to the Rule 23 inquiry (in what the court termed the "class certification approach"), or instead whether the injuries or interests of the named plaintiff must be compared with those of the putative class to determine whether the plaintiff's harms are "sufficiently analogous to those suffered by the rest of the class" to give the named plaintiff enough "personal stake in the adjudication of the class members' claims" (in what the court termed the "standing" approach). *See* 67 F.4th at 733–35 (holding that named plaintiffs had demonstrated standing under either approach); *see also Chavez II*, 108 F.4th at 307–08, 312–14 (acknowledging three variations of the standing approach, as well as the class certification approach, but not selecting among them because named plaintiffs had satisfied any of these approaches).

"In addition to these constitutional requirements," class plaintiffs "must not run afoul of prudential standing rules." *Singh*, 882 F.3d at 151 (holding that ERISA class plaintiffs who were not participants in Puerto Rico plan and therefore suffered no concrete injury related to that plan lacked standing to challenge it).

Absent Class Member Standing

The Fifth Circuit has yet to adopt a standard for absent class member standing, according to the court's last word on the issue. *See Flecha v. Medicredit, Inc.*, 946 F.3d 762, 768–69 (5th Cir. 2020). ("Our court has not yet decided whether standing must be proven for unnamed class members, in addition to the class representative." *Id.* at 768.). The *Flecha* majority acknowledged the significance of the issue in that case, where "[c]ountless unnamed class members lack[ed] standing," but did not reach it because the proposed class failed in any event under Rule 23. *See id.* ("[T]he Supreme Court has repeatedly instructed that we should first decide whether a proposed class satisfies Rule 23, before deciding whether it satisfies Article III." *Id.* at 768.). The concurring judge in *Flecha* took the view that the Supreme Court requires jurisdiction to be determined first and so would have decided the case on the basis of the unnamed class members' lack of Article III standing. *See* 946 F.3d at 770–71 (Oldham., J., concurring).

In a 2014 *Deepwater Horizon* opinion, the Fifth Circuit acknowledged two competing approaches to absent class member standing at the class certification stage—one exemplified by the Seventh Circuit's *Kohen* decision and the other by the Second Circuit's *Denney* decision—but declined to decide which "articulated the correct test." *In re Deepwater Horizon*, 739 F.3d 790, 800–02 (5th Cir. 2014) (comparing *Kohen v. Pacific Inv. Mgmt. Co.*, 571 F.3d 672 (7th Cir. 2009) with *Denney v. Deutsche Bank AG*, 443 F.3d 253 (2d Cir. 2006)). As the Fifth Circuit explained, the *Kohen* test focuses only on the standing of the named plaintiffs at the class certification stage and ignores the absent class members. *See id.* at 800–01. By contrast, the *Denney* approach requires that the class "be defined in such a way that anyone within it would have standing" but does not insist upon *evidence* of absent class member standing at the class certification stage. *Id.* at 801.

In an earlier case—*Mims v. Stewart Title Guar. Co.*—the Fifth Circuit stated that "[c]lass certification is not precluded simply because a class may include persons who have not been injured by the defendant's conduct." 590 F.3d 298, 308 (5th Cir. 2009) (citing *Kohen*, 571 F.3d 672). But in its *Deepwater Horizon* decision, the Fifth Circuit observed that it was "perhaps unclear whether our circuit has already adopted the *Kohen* test in *Mims*" and went on to describe Judge Clement's use of the *Denney* approach in a case decided after *Mims*. *See In re Deepwater Horizon*, 739 F.3d at 802 (comparing *Mims*, 590 F.3d 298 with *In re Deepwater Horizon*, 732 F.3d 326, 340–42 (5th Cir. 2013)). Ultimately, in *Deepwater Horizon*, the Fifth Circuit saw no need to choose between the *Kohen* and *Denney* tests because the defendant's standing challenge would have failed under either test in that case. 739 F.3d at 802 (concluding that "both the named plaintiffs and the absent class members [in] the class definition include only persons . . . who can allege causation and injury in accordance with Article III" standing); *see also In re Deepwater Horizon*, 785 F.3d 1003, 1008 (5th Cir. 2015) (later appeal summarizing the Court's earlier standing decision).

Deepwater Horizon examined standing only at the class certification stage. But had the class been certified "for further proceedings on the merits rather than for settlement," the Fifth Circuit observed that the district court would have had to have applied a stricter evidentiary standard to determine the absent class members' Article III standing on summary judgment or at trial. *See* 739 F.3d at 806. In a later opinion addressing the implementation of the *Deepwater Horizon* settlement, the Fifth Circuit concluded that the causation requirement of Article III standing was satisfied for purposes of the court-approved settlement, because the parties had explicitly agreed to accept a claimant's certification as a substitute for evidence tracing his injury to the defendant's conduct. *See In re Deepwater Horizon*, 744 F.3d 370, 376 (5th Cir. 2014); *see also In re Deepwater Horizon*, 753 F.3d 509, 515–16 (5th Cir. 2014) (on panel rehearing); *cf. In re Deepwater Horizon*, 928 F.3d 394, 400 (5th Cir. 2019) (class settlement "compensates only those who suffered actual losses," because district court lacked authority to approve settlement of class that included members who had not sustained losses).

d. Mootness Doctrine

In *Campbell-Ewald Co. v. Gomez*, the Supreme Court held that "an unaccepted settlement offer or offer of judgment" cannot moot a plaintiff's claim, siding with the Fifth Circuit and other circuits that had so held. 577 U.S. 153, 160–65, 136 S. Ct. 663, 669–72 (2016) (citing, *inter alia*, *Hooks v. Landmark Indus., Inc.*, 797 F.3d 309, 315 (5th Cir. 2015)). "In *Campbell-Ewald*, the Court relied on 'basic principles of contract law' to conclude that a 'Rule 68 offer of judgment, once rejected, ha[s] no continuing efficacy' and 'does not moot a plaintiff's case.'" *Sandoz v. Cingular Wireless, L.L.C.*, 700 F. App'x 317, 322 (5th Cir. 2017) (per curiam) (unpublished) (citing *Campbell-Ewald*, 136 S. Ct. at 670, 672)).

The Supreme Court did not decide in *Campbell-Ewald*, however, "whether the result would be different if a defendant deposits the full amount of the plaintiff's individual claim in an account payable to the plaintiff, and the court then enters judgment for the plaintiff in that amount." 136 S. Ct at 672. Before *Campbell-Ewald*, the Fifth Circuit had held that a defendant's tendering full corrective relief to the named plaintiffs before they moved for class certification mooted their claims for injunctive relief. *See Fontenot v. McCraw*, 777 F.3d 741, 747–49 (5th Cir. 2015). In post-*Campbell-Ewald* decisions, the district courts in the Fifth Circuit have reached diverse results. In *Ponsurayamas v. Teppo*, No. 3:15-cv-02345-N, slip op. at 7 (N.D. Tex. Aug. 10, 2016), for example, the district court concluded that an unconditional tender of complete relief by check mooted FLSA claims. Another court—distinguishing *Fontenot*—held that a plaintiff still had a live claim after he had rejected a tender of monetary relief that did not include attorneys' fees. *See Pankowski v. Bluenrgy Group Ltd.*, Civil Action No. H-15-1668, 2016 WL 7179122; at *3–4 (S.D. Tex. Dec. 9, 2016); *see also Williams v. Lakeview Loan Servicing LLC*, No. 4:20-CV-01900, 2023 WL

6282829, at *5–7 (S.D. Tex. Sept. 26, 2023), *reconsideration denied*, *Williams v. Lakeview Loan Servicing LLC*, No. 4:20-CV-01900, 2024 WL 4867836 (S.D. Tex. Feb. 13, 2024) (claim not mooted when defendant had unilaterally credited refund to plaintiff's account balance without offering plaintiff choice to receive the funds in another form); *Naranjo v. Nick's Mgmt., Inc.*, 652 F. Supp. 3d 737, 745–47 (N.D. Tex. 2023) (not reaching issue whether defendant's deposit of full amount sought could moot a case when plaintiff had rejected defendant's check that applied damages offset and was not for total amount sought); *Cunningham v. Kitchen Collection, LLC*, No. 4:17-cv-00770, 2018 WL 5728930 at *2–3 (E.D. Tex. Aug. 14, 2018), *report and rec. adopted*, 2018 WL 4328474 at *1 (E.D. Tex. Sept. 10, 2018) (holding that defendant's tender of damages did not moot case when calculation of damages was disputed). A district court in the Fifth Circuit has also held that *Campbell-Ewald* does not keep the claim alive when a plaintiff rejects a binding insurance appraisal award. *Yount v. Travelers Pers. Ins. Co.*, No. SA-23-CV-00150-JKP, 2024 WL 131380, at *8 (W.D. Tex. Jan. 11, 2024).

Recognizing mootness as "a jurisdictional inquiry," the Fifth Circuit has held that, "[a]s a general rule, 'a purported class action becomes moot when the personal claims of all named plaintiffs' have been satisfied prior to certification of a class, since . . . there is no longer an Article III 'case or controversy' for the court to resolve." *Ward v. Hellerstedt*, 753 F. App'x 236, 241 (5th Cir. 2018) (per curiam) (unpublished) (quoting *Murray v. Fid. Nat'l Fin., Inc.*, 594 F.3d 419, 421 (5th Cir. 2010)). *See also Manzo-Hernandez v. Saucedo*, No. 21-40034, 2021 WL 5627068, at *3–4 (5th Cir. Nov. 30, 2021) (per curiam) (unpublished) (dismissing appeal when district court had denied class certification without prejudice and named plaintiffs whose individual claims were moot had not appealed denial).

"Potential class actions involving claims that are 'inherently transitory' fall within an exception to the general mootness rule," however, "since such claims would otherwise likely evade review." *Ward*, 753 F. App'x at 242. In such cases, the trial court will not have time to rule on a motion for class certification before the named plaintiff's individual interest expires, and so "a class certification order is deemed to relate back to the time of the filing of the original complaint." *Id.* To decide whether a claim is inherently transitory, the Fifth Circuit considers as pertinent factors whether "the challenged conduct giving rise to the claim is of a fleeting or temporary nature; uncertainty exists at the outset as to the duration of each plaintiff's exposure to the allegedly harmful conduct; it is unlikely that any given individual plaintiff could see his claim to fruition prior to the claim becoming moot; and there exists a constant group of people suffering the harm alleged by the plaintiffs." *Id.* (applying narrow "inherently transitory" exception to claims of county jail detainees awaiting admission to State mental health facilities). *But see Manzo-Hernandez*, 2021 WL 5627068, at *3–4 (declining to apply "inherently transitory" exception when motion for class certification had been denied and not appealed).

The general rule that a proposed class action becomes moot when the named plaintiff's claim becomes moot "does not apply 'where the named class action plaintiff's claim becomes moot after the class was certified.'" *See Gonzalez v. Gillis*, No. 21-60634, 2023 WL 3197061, at *4–5 n.7 (5th Cir. May 2, 2023) (unpublished) (citing *Fontenot v. McCraw*, 777 F.3d 741, 748 (5th Cir. 2015)). The rule also does not apply to a proposed class action "where a class certification motion was 'diligently filed and pursued at the time the named plaintiff's claim [became] moot' and the defendants had mooted the named plaintiff's claim and could 'pick off successive plaintiffs' claims.'" *See id.* (alterations in original, citing *Fontenot*, 777 F.3d at 750–51 (as cleaned up)) (acknowledging mootness exception but holding it inapplicable where plaintiff had never moved for class certification). *See also Serrano v. Customs & Border Patrol, U.S. Customs & Border Prot.*, 975 F.3d 488, 492 & n.1 (5th Cir. 2020) (per curiam) (holding that return of seized property after named plaintiff had moved for class certification did not moot claims because "'a suit brought as a class action should not be dismissed for mootness upon tender to the named plaintiffs of their personal claims, at least when . . . there is pending before the district court a timely filed and diligently pursued motion for class certification'" (quoting *Zeidman v. J. Ray McDermott & Co.*, 651 F.2d 1030, 1051 (5th Cir. 1981))); *Murray v. Fid. Nat'l Fin., Inc.*, 594 F.3d 419, 420–23 (5th Cir. 2010) (refusing to extend exception to new, would-be named plaintiffs whose claims were mooted while motion to add them was pending in case that was nonjusticiable as to original named plaintiffs).

In an en banc holding, the Fifth Circuit has also recognized that an intervening change in a challenged state law can render a proposed class action moot. *Daves v. Dallas Cty., Tex.*, 64 F.4th 616, 633–35 (5th Cir. 2023) (en banc) (holding moot constitutional challenge to bail procedures after intervening state law change).

3. PLEADING CONSIDERATIONS

Counsel should consult the district court's local rules for pleading requirements in a proposed class action. *See, e.g.*, Local Civil Rules of the United States District Court for the Eastern District of Louisiana, LR 23.1(A) (setting out four requirements for class action complaint); Local Civil Rules of the United States District Court for the Northern District of Texas, LR 23.1 (requiring separate class allegations).

The Fifth Circuit permits district courts to determine class allegations "on the pleadings and before discovery is complete when it is apparent from the complaint that a class action cannot be maintained." *Elson v. Black*, 56 F.4th 1002, 1006 (5th Cir. 2023) ("An order striking class allegations is functionally equivalent to an order denying class certification." (quoting *Microsoft Corp. v. Baker*, 582 U.S. 23, 34 n.7, 137 S. Ct. 1702, 1711 n.7 (2017))).

4. PREREQUISITES FOR CLASS CERTIFICATION

Under Rule 23, a plaintiff seeking class certification must first meet the four prerequisites of Rule 23(a): (1) numerosity, (2) commonality, (3) typicality, and (4) adequacy. Fed. R. Civ. P. 23(a). The plaintiff's claim also must satisfy one of the four subparts of Rule 23(b). *See* Fed. R. Civ. P. 23(b)(1)(A); 23(b)(1)(B); 23(b)(2); 23(b)(3); *see Sampson v. United Services Auto. Ass'n*, 83 F.4th 414, 418 (5th Cir. 2023); *Braidwood Mgmt., Inc. v. Equal Employment Opportunity Comm'n*, 70 F.4th 914, 933 (5th Cir. 2023) (named plaintiffs must meet Rule 23 requirements "for each defined class"); *Ahmad v. Old Republic Nat'l Title Ins. Co.*, 690 F.3d 698, 702 (5th Cir. 2012); *Ward v. Hellerstedt*, 753 F. App'x 236, 243 (5th Cir. 2018) (per curiam) (unpublished). A final implicit requirement is that the class be adequately defined and clearly ascertainable. *See Seeligson v. Devon Energy Prod. Co.*, 761 F. App'x 329, 333 (5th Cir. 2019) (per curiam) (unpublished), *on remand*, 2020 WL 636224 (N.D. Tex. Feb. 11, 2020), *leave for second appeal denied*, 804 F. App'x 304 (5th Cir. 2020) (per curiam) (unpublished); *John v. Nat'l Sec. Fire & Cas. Co.*, 501 F.3d 443, 445 (5th Cir. 2007).

Rule 23 "governs whether a proposed class falls within the limited exception to the usual rule that litigation is conducted by and on behalf of the individual named parties only." *Ibe v. Jones*, 836 F.3d 516, 528 (5th Cir. 2016) (quoting *Califano v. Yamasaki*, 442 U.S. 682, 700–01 (1979)); *see also Sampson*, 83 F.4th at 418 (similar, quoting *Comcast Corp. v. Behrend*, 569 U.S. 27, 33 (2013)). "Class certification requires that plaintiffs' claims 'can be proved on a classwide basis.'" *Id.* (quoting *Wal-Mart Stores, Inc. v. Dukes*, 564 U.S. 338, 356 (2011)). "A district court must conduct a rigorous analysis of the Rule 23 prerequisites before certifying a class." *Castano v. Am. Tobacco Co.*, 84 F.3d 734, 740 (5th Cir. 1996); *see also Prantil v. Arkema Inc.*, 986 F.3d 570, 574 (5th Cir. 2021); *Mitchell v. State Farm Fire & Cas. Co.*, 954 F.3d 700, 709 (5th Cir. 2020); *Cruson v. Jackson Nat'l Life Ins. Co.*, 954 F.3d 240, 253 (5th Cir. 2020); *Flecha v. Medicredit, Inc.*, 946 F.3d 762, 766–67 (5th Cir. 2020) ("Courts must enforce the requirements of Rule 23 vigorously." *Id.* at 766.); *Madison v. Chalmette Ref., L.L.C.*, 637 F.3d 551, 554 (5th Cir. 2011) (grounding rigorous analysis requirement in due process concerns inherent in certification decision). "The party seeking certification bears the burden of proof." *Castano*, 84 F.3d at 740; *see also Elson v. Black*, 56 F.4th 1002, 1006 (5th Cir. 2023) (quoting *Cruson*, 954 F.3d at 253); *Mitchell*, 954 F.3d at 709 (quoting *Castano*, 84 F. 3d at 740); *Cruson*, 954 F.3d at 253.

To satisfy this burden, the party seeking class certification must be prepared to prove—not merely plead—"'that there are *in fact* sufficiently numerous parties, common questions of law or fact, typicality of claims or defenses, and adequacy of representation' and to satisfy at least one of Rule 23(b)'s provisions 'through evidentiary proof.'" *Ward*, 753 F. App'x at 243–44 (quoting *Comcast Corp. v. Behrend*, 569 U.S. 27, 33 (2013)) (emphasis in original)); *see also Sampson*, 83 F.4th at 418 (party seeking to maintain class action "'must affirmatively demonstrate his compliance with Rule 23,'" meaning he must "'be prepared to prove' that the requirements of Rule 23 are met 'in fact,' not under 'a mere pleading standard'") (citing *Comcast*, 569 U.S. at 33)); *Flecha*, 946 F.3d at 766–67 (holding that "the conditions of Rule 23 'do not set forth a mere pleading standard,'" but a "'party seeking class certification must affirmatively demonstrate his compliance with the rule'" (quoting *Wal-Mart Stores, Inc. v. Dukes*, 564 U.S. 338, 350, (2011)); *Unger v. Amedisys Inc.*, 401 F.3d 316, 321–25 (5th Cir. 2005) (holding that the "plain text of Rule 23 requires the court to 'find,' not merely assume, the facts favoring class certification," *id.* at 321); *Cruson,* 954 F.3d at 253 (same). The court must base its ruling on certification issues on "admissible evidence." *Unger*, 401 F.3d at 325.

Expert testimony offered in support of class certification must meet the reliability standards of *Daubert v. Merrell Dow Pharm., Inc*., 509 U.S. 579 (1993). *See Prantil*, 986 F.3d at 575–76. ("[T]he *Daubert* hurdle must be cleared when scientific evidence is relevant to the decision to certify." *Id.* at 575.) The "metric of admissibility" is "the same for certification and trial." *Id.* "[I]f an expert's opinion would not be admissible at trial, it should not pave the way for certifying a proposed class." *Id.* at 576 (holding that district court should not have hesitated "to apply *Daubert*'s reliability standard with full force"). *See also Georgia Firefighters' Pension Fund v. Anadarko Petroleum Corp.*, 99 F.4th 770, 774 (5th Cir. 2024) ("*Daubert* . . . applies with the same rigor at the class certification stage as at trial."). In applying *Daubert* with full force at class certification, the Fifth Circuit shares the majority view espoused by the Third, Seventh, and Eleventh circuits.

To conduct a rigorous analysis of the Rule 23 prerequisites, trial courts must "take a 'close look' at the parties' claims and evidence." *Unger*, 401 F.3d at 321. The court must "'look beyond the pleadings to understand the claims, defenses, relevant facts, and applicable substantive law in order to make a meaningful determination of the certification issues.'" *Ward*, 753 F. App'x at 244 (quoting *Yates v. Collier*, 868 F.3d 354, 362 (5th Cir. 2017)); *see also Braidwood Mgmt.*, 70 F.4th at 934 n.37 (quoting *Yates*, 868 F.3d at 362); *Prantil*, 986 F.3d at 574 ("Additionally, the district court must consider 'how a trial on the merits would be conducted if the class were certified.'" (footnote omitted)). "[T]o satisfy the rigor requirement, a district court must detail with specificity its reasons for certifying." *Chavez v. Plan Benefit Servs., Inc*., 957 F.3d 542, 546 (5th Cir. 2020) (*Chavez I*). "It must explain and apply the substantive law governing the plaintiffs' claims to the relevant facts and defenses, articulating why the issues are fit for classwide resolution." *Id.* "The court should respond to the defendants' legitimate protests of individualized issues that could preclude class treatment." *Id.*; *see also Angell*, 67 F.4th at 741 (quoting *Chavez I*, 957 F.3d at 546). "And its analysis must stay close to the facts and law of the case, spurning reliance on generalizations about what types of disputes may be fit for a class." *Chavez I*, 957 F.3d at 546. "The court must rigorously consider both Rule 23(a)'s prerequisites and the Rule 23(b) class type." *Id.* This rigorous analysis "ensures effective appellate review" and recognizes that a "'class action is an exception to the usual rule that litigation is conducted by and on behalf of the individual named parties only.'" *Id.* at 547 (quoting *Comcast Corp. v. Behrend*, 569 U.S. 27, 33 (2013)). As the court explained in *Chavez I*, "creative uses are perilous," because "certification can coerce a defendant into settling," and it also "fundamentally alters" the rights of class members. *Id.* "No less than due process is implicated, so a careful look is necessary."

Id.; *see also Sampson*, 83 F.4th at 418 (quoting *Chavez I*, 957 F.3d at 547).

"To assist the court in this process it may sanction controlled discovery at the certification stage." *Unger*, 401 F.3d at 321. The court must specifically analyze how the plaintiff has met the Rule 23 requirements and give written reasons for certification. *See Ward*, 753 F. App'x at 244. And, to protect unnamed potential class members, the court must conduct its own thorough inquiry, even when the parties have stipulated to certification or have not contested all of the Rule 23 requirements. *See id.*

The court may consider merits questions only to the extent "'that they are relevant to determining whether the Rule 23 prerequisites for class certification are satisfied.'" *Id.* (quoting *Amgen Inc. v. Conn. Ret. Plans & Tr. Funds*, 568 U.S. 455, 466 (2013)). *See also Cleven v. Mid-Am. Apartment Communities, Inc.*, 20 F.4th 171, 176 (5th Cir. 2021) (reviewing district court's statutory construction because proper construction was "a necessary antecedent to the predominance issue" on class certification). There is no requirement, however, that "'significant (or even complete) merits discovery must occur before class certification,'" as "'delaying certification until late in the case is contrary to the sequencing set forth in Rule 23.'" *In re Par.*, 81 F.4th 403, 419 (5th Cir. 2023) (quoting Robert H. Klonoff, *The Decline of Class Actions*, 90 Wash. U. L. Rev. 729, 756 (2013)).

The Fifth Circuit reviews a class certification decision "for abuse of discretion[,] and the legal questions implicated . . . are reviewed de novo." *Ibe*, 836 F.3d at 528; *see also Sampson*, 83 F.4th at 418–19; *Chavez II*, 108 F.4th at 305–06; *Braidwood Mgmt.*, 70 F.4th at 923; *Angell*, 67 F.4th at 736; *Cleven*, 20 F.4th at 175–76; *Prantil*, 986 F.3d at 574; *Mitchell*, 954 F.3d at 709. Thus, "[i]f the district court has applied the correct legal standard," the Fifth Circuit "review[s] its analysis and order certifying a class for an abuse of discretion." *Ward*, 753 F. App'x at 241. The abuse of discretion standard recognizes "the essentially factual basis of the certification inquiry and of the district court's inherent power to manage and control pending litigation." *Ahmad*, 680 F.3d at 701–02 (internal quotation marks, footnotes, and citation omitted). But the district court's discretion must be exercised within the framework of Rule 23. *See Castano*, 84 F.3d at 740. "If the 'district court premises its legal analysis on an erroneous understanding of governing laws, it has abused its discretion.'" *Ahmad*, 680 F.3d at 702 (quoting *Regents of the Univ. of Cal. v. Credit Suisse First Boston*, 482 F.3d 372, 380 (5th Cir. 2007)). "'A trial court abuses its discretion when its ruling is based on an erroneous view of the law or a clearly erroneous assessment of the evidence.'" *Ward*, 753 F. App'x at 241 (quoting *Yates*, 868 F.3d at 359). The court's analysis in a Rule 23(f) class certification appeal must begin "'with the elements of the underlying cause of action.'" *Flecha v. Medicredit, Inc.*, 946 F.3d 762, 766 (5th Cir. 2020) (quoting *Erica P. John Fund, Inc. v. Halliburton Co.*, 563 U.S. 804, 809 (2011)). "After all, 'a court must understand the claims, defenses, relevant facts, and applicable substantive law in order to make a meaningful determination of the certification issues.'" *Id.* (quoting *Castano*, 84 F.3d at 744). "Absent such knowledge, it will be 'impossible' for a court to determine, inter alia, (1) whether the issues for trial will be individualized or common to all putative class members, (2) whether the issues presented by the class representative will be typical of class members, and (3) whether the common issues at trial will predominate over individualized issues" *Id.* (quoting *Castano*, 84 F.3d at 745).

a. Rule 23(a) Prerequisites

Numerosity

Rule 23(a)(1) requires a class to be "so numerous that joinder of all members is impracticable." To establish numerosity, "a plaintiff must ordinarily demonstrate some evidence or reasonable estimate of the number of purported class members." *Zeidman v. J. Ray McDermott & Co.*, 651 F.2d 1030, 1038 (5th Cir. 1981). In *Mullen v. Treasure Chest Casino, LLC*, the Fifth Circuit held that the district court did not abuse its discretion when it found numerosity satisfied by a class of 100–150 members. 186 F.3d 620, 624–25 (5th Cir. 1999) ("Although the number of members in a proposed class is not determinative of whether joinder is impracticable . . . the size of the class in this case—100 to 150 members—is within the range that generally satisfies the numerosity requirement."); *see also Ibe v. Jones*, 836 F.3d 516, 530 (approving, as not clearly erroneous, district court's conclusion that proposed class of 42 members failed numerosity).

The "proper focus," however, "is not on numbers alone, but on whether joinder of all members is practicable in view of the numerosity of the class and all other relevant factors." *Phillips v. Joint Legislative Comm. on Performance & Expenditure Review of the State of Miss.*, 637 F.2d 1014, 1022 (5th Cir. 1981); *see also In re TWL Corp.*, 712 F.3d 886, 894 (5th Cir. 2013) ("[C]ourts must not focus on sheer numbers alone.") (quoting *Pederson v. La. State Univ.*, 213 F.3d 858, 868 n.11 (5th Cir. 2000)). The relevant factors include, for example, "the geographical dispersion of the class, the ease with which members may be identified, the nature of the action, and the size of each plaintiff's claim." *Zeidman*, 651 F.2d at 1038. Because of the many factors to consider, "no definitive pattern has emerged under Rule 23(a)(1) in terms of the number of purported class members." *Id.*

Even when numerosity is uncontested, the district court must "identify the approximate number of potential class members" and any other factors that bear on the numerosity determination, and it must "explain the effect of those factors on its conclusion." *Ward*, 753 F. App'x at 244 n.16.

Commonality

To certify a Rule 23 class, there must be "questions of law or fact common to the class." Fed. R. Civ. P. 23(a)(2).

The Supreme Court clarified this commonality requirement in *Wal-Mart Stores, Inc. v. Dukes*, 564 U.S. 338, 350 (2011). Under *Wal-Mart*, the class's claims "must depend upon a common contention" that "is capable of classwide resolution—which means that determination of its truth or falsity will resolve an issue that is central to the validity of each one of the claims in one stroke." *Id.; see also Braidwood Mgmt.*, 70 F.4th at 935–36 & n.46 (quoting *Wal-Mart*, 564 U.S. at 350 and noting linkage between commonality analysis and class definition); *Chavez I*, 957 F.3d at 547–48 (5th Cir. 2020) (applying *Wal-Mart); Flecha v. Medicredit, Inc.*, 946 F.3d 762, 767 (5th Cir. 2020) (same); *Ward*, 753 F. App'x at 245 (same); *M.D. ex rel. Stukenberg v. Perry*, 675 F.3d 832, 837 (5th Cir. 2012) (same).

Wal-Mart thus "heightened the standards for establishing commonality." *Perry*, 675 F.3d at 839. After *Wal-Mart*, the "commonality requirement demands more than the presentation of questions that are common to the class because any competently crafted class complaint literally raises common questions." *Id.* at 840 (quotations omitted). Merely "alleging a violation of the same legal provision by the same defendant" is not enough. *Id.* Nor is the commonality test any longer met "when the proposed class merely establishes that there is at least one issue whose resolution *will affect all or a significant number* of the . . . class members." *Id.* (quotations omitted). Proffered common questions that attempt "to aggregate several amorphous claims of systemic or widespread conduct into one 'super-claim'" will not do either. *Id.* at 844.

"Accordingly, what is significant with respect to a commonality determination is 'not the raising of common questions—even in droves—but, rather the capacity of a class-wide proceeding to generate common answers apt to drive the resolution of the litigation.'" *Ward*, 753 F. App'x at 245 (quoting *Yates*, 868 F.3d at 361). "[A] single common question of law or fact is sufficient if it meets the foregoing criteria." *Id.* But "considering dissimilarities among claimants is essential to determining whether even a single common question exists." *Id.* at 246. The court's commonality analysis therefore must "consider and discuss the facts of [the] case, as well as the elements of Plaintiffs' claims." *Id.* (vacating class certification for lack of rigorous commonality analysis).

That is, because "dissimilarities within the proposed class . . . have the potential to impede the generation of common answers," the district court must explain its reasoning on commonality "with specific reference to the 'claims, defenses, relevant facts, and applicable substantive law' raised by the class claims." *Perry*, 675 F.3d at 843 (first quoting *Wal-Mart*, 564 U.S. at 350; then quoting *McManus v. Fleetwood Enters., Inc.*, 320 F.3d 545, 648 (5th Cir. 2003)); *see also Flecha*. 946 F.3d at 767 ("'Dissimilarities within the proposed class are what have the potential to impede the generation of common answers.'" (quoting *Wal-Mart*, 564 U.S. at 350)); *Chavez*, 957 F.3d at 548–49 and n.18 (rejecting commonality analysis as too brief and conclusory when the district court had not identified common question with specificity, had "neglect[ed] to consider asserted differences among class members," and had not explained why differences in benefit plans were "immaterial by reference to the facts, allegations, and law of ERISA").

If the common questions identified by the district court "are not common to the class, or if they are based on incorrect legal conclusions or factual findings," then class certification is an abuse of discretion. *Seeligson v. Devon Energy Prod. Co.*, 761 F. App'x 329, 335 (5th Cir. 2019) (on panel rehearing) (per curiam) (unpublished) (reversing class certification and remanding to determine whether additional evidence would show that breach of duty to market, and any resulting damages, could be evaluated classwide for mineral leases, or instead required individual analysis, *see id.* at 336–37), *on remand*, 2020 WL 636224 (N.D. Tex. Feb. 11, 2020) (certifying class), *leave for second appeal denied*, 804 F. App'x 304 (5th Cir. 2020) (per curiam) (unpublished).

In another post-*Wal-Mart* opinion, the Fifth Circuit found commonality satisfied by a class settlement, emphasizing that "the principal requirement of *Wal-Mart* is merely a single common contention that enables the class action 'to generate common *answers* apt to drive the resolution of the litigation.'" *In re Deepwater Horizon*, 739 F.3d 790, 811 (5th Cir. 2014). "[E]ven a single common question will do under *Wal-Mart*. . . ." *Id.* at 812 (quoting *Wal-Mart*, 564 U.S. at 359). Moreover, *Wal-Mart*'s requirement that the plaintiff "demonstrate that class members 'have suffered the same injury'" is one that "can be satisfied by an instance of the defendant's injurious conduct, even when the resulting injurious effects—the damages—are diverse." *Deepwater Horizon*, *Id.* at 810–12 (quoting Wal-Mart, 564 U.S. at 349–50). And finally, for purposes of commonality, "district courts do not err by failing to ascertain at the Rule 23 stage whether the class members include persons . . . who have suffered no injury at all." *Id.* at 811.

Typicality

Rule 23 also requires the "claims or defenses of the representative parties" to be "typical of the claims or defenses of the class." Fed. R. Civ. P. 23(a)(3). The test for typicality "focuses on the similarity between the named plaintiffs' legal and remedial theories and the theories of those whom they purport to represent." *Mullen v. Treasure Chest Casino, LLC*, 186 F.3d 620, 625 (5th Cir. 1999) (quoting *Lightbourn v. County of El Paso*, 118 F.3d 421, 426 (5th Cir. 1997)); *see also Ibe v. Jones*, 836 F.3d 516, 528–29 (5th Cir. 2016). Typicality "does not require a complete identity of claims. Rather, the critical inquiry is whether the class representative's claims have the same essential characteristics of those of the putative class." *Stirman v. Exxon Corp.*, 280 F.3d 554, 562 (5th Cir. 2002) (quoting *James v. City of Dall.*, 254 F.3d 551, 571 (5th Cir. 2001)) (holding typicality was not satisfied when plaintiff asserted royalty underpayment claims for different types of leases, which were treated differently under Texas law). To put it another way, "factual differences will not defeat typicality" when "the claims arise from a similar course of conduct and share the same legal theory." *Id.* (quoting *James*, 254 F.3d at 571); *see also Angell*, 67 F.4th at 737 (affirming typicality finding when defendant had not provided concrete examples of how different legal questions would be implicated by failure to pay different types of fees under insurance policies). The proper test is whether the plaintiff's "*claims* are typical, not whether she is." *Id.* A finding of typicality does not necessarily follow from a finding of commonality, however, and an appropriate typicality analysis "must be conducted not with respect to *any* potential claimant, but with respect to '*the* representative parties.'" *Ward*, 753 F. App'x at 248 (citing

Rule 23(a) (emphasis in original)).

By contrast, when a plaintiff *fails* to prove commonality, her claims cannot be typical of the claims of the class, because there "is no common issue uniting the putative class." *Flecha v. Medicredit, Inc.*, 946 F.3d 762, 768 (5th Cir. 2020) (holding that plaintiff's "failure to prove commonality also establishes her failure to prove either typicality or predominance").

Adequacy

The final prerequisite under Rule 23(a) is that the "representative parties will fairly and adequately protect the interests of the class." Fed. R. Civ. P. 23(a)(4). In the Fifth Circuit, "[a]dequacy encompasses three separate but related inquiries":

(1) "the zeal and competence of the representative[s'] counsel";
(2) "the willingness and ability of the representative[s] to take an active role in and control the litigation to protect the interests of absentees"; and
(3) the risk of "conflicts of interest between the named plaintiffs and the class they seek to represent."

Slade v. Progressive Sec. Ins. Co., 856 F.3d 408, 412 (5th Cir. 2017) (quoting *Feder v. Elec. Data Sys. Corp.*, 429 F.3d 125, 130 (5th Cir. 2005)); *see also Feder*, 429 F.3d at 130 (holding that the adequacy requirement "serves to uncover conflicts of interest between the named plaintiffs and the class they seek to represent"); *Horton v. Goose Creek Indep. Sch. Dist.*, 690 F.2d 470, 484 (5th Cir. 1982) (mandating inquiry into zeal and competence of counsel and class representative's willingness and ability to control litigation).

The named plaintiffs' adequacy is not presumed but must be demonstrated. *See Berger v. Compaq Comput. Corp.*, 257 F.3d 475, 481–82, 484 (5th Cir. 2001). "Indeed, a district court can only appropriately assess such factors as 'the willingness and ability of the representatives to . . . control the litigation and to protect the interests of absentees' with reference to one or more specific claimants, as opposed to any claimant that could fall within the putative class." *Ward*, 753 F. App'x at 248 (quoting *Slade*, 856 F.3d at 412).

The adequacy requirement serves to protect the due process rights of all members of the class who will be bound by the judgment. *See Berger*, 257 F.3d at 480. This is because "members of a certified class are . . . bound by the resulting judgment . . . when they are adequately represented by the class representative and the other requirements of [Rule] 23 are met." *Taylor v. United Parcel Serv., Inc.*, 554 F.3d 510, 517 (5th Cir. 2008).

Although "class representatives need not be legal scholars . . . plaintiffs do need to know more than that they were involved in a bad business deal." *Id.* at 483 (internal quotation omitted). "Class action lawsuits are intended to serve as a vehicle for capable, committed advocates to pursue the goals of the class members through counsel, not for capable, committed counsel to pursue their own goals through those class members." *Id.* at 484.

"[I]ntraclass conflicts may negate adequacy under Rule 23(a)(4)." *Langbecker v. Elec. Data Sys. Corp.*, 476 F.3d 299, 315 (5th Cir. 2007). The Fifth Circuit has recognized that when a class representative proposes to waive some of the class's claims, her "decision risks creating an irreconcilable conflict of interest with the class." *Slade*, 856 F.3d at 412. Determining whether a class representative's waiver of a claim on behalf of her proposed class defeats adequacy "requires an inquiry into, at least: (1) the risk that unnamed class members will forfeit their right to pursue the waived claim in future litigation, (2) the value of the waived claim, and (3) the strategic value of the waiver." *Id.* at 413 (remanding adequacy question for consideration of these factors). *See also Angell*, 67 F.4th at 737–39 (applying *Slade* factors to affirm adequacy finding, concluding that "strategic value" of waiver was "considerably greater" than waived claims' "inherent worth," *id.* at 739); *Cruson v. Jackson Nat'l Life Ins. Co.*, 954 F.3d 240, 258 (5th Cir. 2020) (leaving for district court to consider on remand the effect of plaintiffs' concession that they would no longer seek certain types of "complicated" damages); *Prudhomme v. Gov't Emps. Ins. Co.*, No. 21-30157, 2022 WL

510171, at *1–2 (5th Cir. Feb. 21, 2022) (per curiam) (unpublished) (holding that when some class members benefitted from allegedly unlawful conduct, this undermined "class-wide theory of liability and . . . doomed adequacy," rejecting contrary reading of *Slade*).

For securities class actions governed by the Private Securities Litigation Reform Act of 1995 (PSLRA), "the adequacy standard must reflect . . . Congress's emphatic command that competent plaintiffs, rather than lawyers, direct such cases." *Berger*, 257 F.3d at 483–84 (applying "PSLRA's requirement that securities class actions be managed by active, able class representatives who are informed and can demonstrate they are directing the litigation"); *see also Feder*, 429 F.3d at 130 (citing *Berger*, 257 F.3d at 483 and *Berger v. Compaq Comput. Corp.*, 279 F.3d 313, 313–14 (5th Cir. 2002)).

b. Rule 23(b) Requirements

Rule 23(b)(1)(A) Classes

Rule 23(b)(1)(A) authorizes class certification when separate actions would create a risk of "inconsistent or varying adjudications with respect to individual class members that would establish incompatible standards of conduct for the party opposing the class." Fed. R. Civ. P. 23(b)(1)(A). The Fifth Circuit has expressed doubt as to "whether a b(1)(A) class can be maintained if damages are the primary remedy sought," explaining that "classic Rule 23(b)(1) class actions . . . are based on situations 'in which different results in separate actions would impair the opposing party's ability to pursue a uniform course of conduct.'" *Langbecker*, 476 F.3d at 318 (quoting Charles Alan Wright, et al., 7AA Fed. Prac. & Proc. Civ. § 1773 (2005 ed.)).

The Fifth Circuit has also recognized that certification under (b)(1)(A) is seldom appropriate for claims seeking "monetary compensation because no inconsistency is created when courts award varying levels of money damages to different plaintiffs." *Casa Orlando Apartments, Ltd. v. Fed. Nat'l Mortg. Ass'n*, 624 F.3d 185, 197 (5th Cir. 2010). Similarly, when state laws are diverse and could lead to varying judgments, "dissimilar outcomes that result from differing state laws are insufficient to justify class certification." *Id.* at 198. And when plaintiffs seek only injunctive relief, separate actions with varying results would not necessarily establish incompatible standards of conduct for the defendant. *See id.* at 197–98. An incompatible judgment would arise, however, "if one court *required*" a defendant to take an action, "while another court *prevented*" that same action. *Id.* at 198.

While (b)(1)(A) certification "focuses on class action suitability from the defendant's perspective," the defendant's consent to certification is not required: "nothing in the plain text of Rule 23 . . . permits a defendant's veto over (b)(1)(A) certification." *Id.* at 196–97.

Rule 23(b)(1)(B) Classes

Rule 23(b)(1)(B) class actions are appropriate when separate actions would create a risk of "adjudications with respect to individual class members that, as a practical matter, would be dispositive of the interests of other members not parties to the individual adjudications or would substantially impair or impede their ability to protect their interests." Fed. R. Civ. P. 23(b)(1)(B). "Rule 23(b)(1)(B) prevents the prejudicing of parties after the initial suit when subsequent suits involve the same subject matter." *Chavez II*, 108 F.4th at 314–15. It "stops one party from collecting damages at the expense of other parties and protects later parties from being bound by the judgment of a case in which their interests were not adequately represented." *Id.*

A "'limited fund' action, which aggregates numerous claims against a fund insufficient to satisfy them all," is a type of class action "traditionally encompassed by Rule 23(b)(1)(B)." *In re Katrina Canal Breaches Litig.*, 628 F.3d 185, 191 (5th Cir. 2010). In reviewing such cases, the Fifth Circuit has relied on the Supreme Court's decision in *Ortiz v. Fibreboard Corp.*, 527 U.S. 815 (1999), which outlined three "'presumptively necessary' characteristics of a traditional limited fund." *Katrina Canal Breaches*, 628 F.3d at 192–93 (quoting *Ortiz*, 527 U.S. at 842). Those characteristics are:

- "the totals of the aggregated liquidated claims and the fund available for satisfying them, set definitely at their maximums, demonstrate the inadequacy of the fund to pay all the claims,"
- "the whole of the inadequate fund [is] to be devoted to the overwhelming claims," and
- "the claimants identified by a common theory of recovery [are] treated equitably among themselves."

Id. at 193 (citations omitted) (quoting *Ortiz*, 527 U.S. at 838, 839).

In *Katrina Canal Breaches*, the Fifth Circuit rejected a proposed Rule 23(b)(1)(B) settlement class for failure to satisfy the third characteristic. *Id.* at 194. The settlement "punt[ed] the difficult question of equitable distribution" and lacked any procedures to resolve how "differently situated claimants" would be treated "with fairness as among themselves." *Id.*

Noting concerns over protection of jury trial and due process rights, the Fifth Circuit also observed that it remains an open question whether a mandatory limited fund rationale could ever constitutionally be applied to a Rule 23(b)(1)(B) settlement class of tort claimants. *See id.* at 191–92.

In *Chavez II*, where the Fifth Circuit granted class certification under Rule 23(b)(3), the court denied certification under Rule 23(b)(1)(B), emphasizing that the "Supreme Court has cautioned against certification under Rule 23(b)(1)(B)" and noting "the many concerns that follow mandatory opt-ins associated with class certification under Rule 23(b)(1)(B)." 108 F.4th at 315–16 (5th Cir. 2024) (citing *Ortiz*, 527 U.S. at 845–48). Because the claims in *Chavez II* were primarily for damages, and it was "not evident that individual adjudications would substantially impair the interests of members not parties to the individual adjudications," Rule 23(b)(1) certification was improper. *Id.* A Rule 23(b)(3) class, preserving "the ability of individual class members to opt out and pursue separate remedies," was the appropriate vehicle. *Id.* at 315.

The Fifth Circuit has cautioned against skimping on the required analysis even for a traditional Rule 23(b)(1)(B) type of class. "Even if a proposed class appears, at first glance, to be an historical example of a 23(b)(1)(B) class, the court must look closely at the facts to ensure that separate adjudications as to each class member would indeed impair nonparties' ability to protect their interests. [T]he Rule does not tolerate a fleeting analysis that assumes that a given class is appropriate just because it appears to be a classic (b)(1)(B) class." *Chavez I*, 957 F.3d at 549–50 (footnote and citations omitted) (vacating Rule 23(b)(1)(B) class for lack of a "case-specific inquiry" into these requirements).

Rule 23(b)(2) Classes

In a Rule 23(b)(2) class, "the party opposing the class has acted or refused to act on grounds that apply generally to the class, so that final injunctive relief or corresponding declaratory relief is appropriate respecting the class as a whole." Fed. R. Civ. P. 23(b)(2). A Rule 23(b)(2) class thus "requires common behavior by the defendant toward the class." *Yates v. Collier*, 868 F.3d 354, 366 (5th Cir. 2017) (quoting *In re Rodriguez*, 695 F.3d 360, 365 (5th Cir. 2012). "While (b)(2) classes are not exclusively reserved for civil rights disputes, this class type is especially suited for those plaintiffs." *Casa Orlando*, 624 F.3d at 200–01 (citing Fed. R. Civ. P. 23(b)(2) advisory committee's note to 1966 Amendment).

The most recent Fifth Circuit Rule 23(b)(2) cases apply a three-part test articulated in *Maldonado v. Ochsner Clinic Found.*: "To qualify for class-wide injunctive relief" under Rule 23(b)(2), "class members must have been harmed in essentially the same way, and injunctive relief must predominate over monetary damage claims. Additionally, the injunctive relief sought must be specific." 493 F.3d 521, 524 (5th Cir. 2007) (citations omitted); *see also Prantil*, 986 F.3d at 580; *Yates*, 868 F.3d at 366; *Ward*, 753 F. App'x at 249 (same three-part test as *Maldonado*).

Note, however, that other Fifth Circuit cases have expressed the Rule 23(b)(2) test in different ways. *See, e.g.*, *Bolin v. Sears, Roebuck & Co.*, 231 F.3d 970, 975 (5th Cir. 2000) ("Rule 23(b)(2) contains two requirements: (1) behavior generally applicable to the class as a whole; (2) injunctive relief predominates over damages sought."); *Casa Orlando*, 624 F.3d at 198 (same); *M.D. ex rel. Stukenberg v. Perry*, 675 F.3d 832, 845 (5th Cir. 2012) (applying two-part test for class seeking injunctive relief: "(1) the 'class members must have been harmed in essentially the same way'" and "(2) 'the injunctive relief sought must be specific,'" *id.* (quoting *Maldonado*).

The first requirement under *Maldonado* is that class members have been harmed in essentially the same way. As the Supreme Court explained in *Wal-Mart*, Rule 23(b)(2) "applies only when a single injunction or declaratory judgment would provide relief to each member of the class. It does not authorize class certification when each individual class member would be entitled to a *different* injunction or declaratory judgment against the defendant." *Wal-Mart Stores, Inc. v. Dukes*, 564 U.S. 338, 360 (2011). The key to Rule 23(b)(2) is thus "'the indivisible nature of the injunctive or declaratory remedy warranted—the notion that the conduct is such that it can be enjoined or declared unlawful only as to all of the class members or as to none of them.'" *Ward*, 753 F. App'x at 249 (quoting *Wal-Mart*). Accordingly, "the relief sought must . . . affect the entire class at once." *Perry*, 675 F.3d at 845 (quoting *Wal-Mart*, 564 U.S. at 361–62).

Rule 23(b)(2) therefore "seeks to redress what are really group as opposed to individual injuries. The uniformity of the injury across the class is what renders the notice and opt-out provisions of [Rule 23(b)(3)] unnecessary." *Casa Orlando*, 624 F.3d at 198 (citing *Bolin*, 231 F.3d at 975 n.22). "Rule 23(b)(2) certification is also inappropriate when the majority of the class does not face future harm." *Maldonado*, 493 F.3d at 525.

Rule 23(b)(2)'s focus on injunctive and declaratory relief "presumes a class best described as a homogenous and cohesive group with few conflicting interests among its members." *In re Monumental Life Ins. Co.*, 365 F.3d 408, 415 (5th Cir. 2004) (internal quotation marks omitted). "Once monetary damages enter the picture, however, class cohesiveness is generally lost." *Id.*

Thus, the second requirement for a Rule 23(b)(2) class is that the "predominant relief sought" must be "injunctive or declaratory," and any requested monetary relief must be merely "incidental to requested injunctive or declaratory relief." *Allison v. Citgo Petroleum Corp.*, 151 F.3d 402, 411, 415 (5th Cir. 1998). This 23(b)(2) requirement, which "focus[es] on uniform relief flowing from defendants' liability, serves essentially the same functions as the procedural safeguards and efficiency and manageability standards mandated in (b)(3) class actions." *Langbecker v. Elec. Data Sys. Corp.*, 476 F.3d 299, 316 (5th Cir. 2007) (internal quotations and citations omitted); *see also Klier v. Elf Atochem N. Am., Inc.*, 658 F.3d 468, 471 (5th Cir. 2011) (recognizing that "where the predominant relief sought is an award of money damages," Rule 23(b)(2) does not apply and class certification must proceed, if at all, "through the (b)(3) gate, with its . . . opt-out provisions").

In the Fifth Circuit, monetary relief is incidental when damages "flow directly from liability to the class *as a whole* on claims forming the basis of the injunctive or declaratory relief." *Allison*, 151 F.3d at 425. "Ideally," incidental relief should encompass only those damages "to which class members automatically would be entitled once liability to the class . . . as a whole is established." *Id.* at 415. Incidental "damages should at least be capable of computation by means of objective standards and not dependent in any significant way on the intangible, subjective differences of each class member's circumstances." *Id.* "Liability for incidental damages should not require additional hearings to resolve the disparate merits of each individual's case," nor should it "entail complex individualized determinations." *Id.* The Supreme Court cited the Fifth Circuit's *Allison* opinion in *Wal-Mart* but refrained from deciding "whether there are any forms of 'incidental' monetary relief that are consistent with . . . Rule 23(b)(2) . . . and that comply with the Due Process Clause." 564 U.S. at 365–67.

Before *Wal-Mart*, the Fifth Circuit had recognized the potential for "hybrid" class actions under Rule 23(b)(2)—that is, class actions seeking both individual monetary relief for certain class members and classwide injunctive or declaratory relief—so long as the district court ordered the same opt-out and notice protections in the hybrid class that the absent class members would have had in a Rule 23(b)(3) class. *See Ayers v. Thompson*, 358 F.3d 356, 375–76 (5th Cir. 2004) (citation omitted). The Fifth Circuit has not yet had occasion to consider how the Supreme Court's treatment of the fundamental differences between (b)(2) and (b)(3) classes in *Wal-Mart*, *see* 564 U.S. at 360–66, might affect the "hybrid" class contemplated by *Ayers*.

The third requirement for a Rule 23(b)(2) class in the Fifth Circuit is that the injunctive relief sought must be specific. To satisfy this requirement, plaintiffs "must 'give content to the injunctive relief they seek so that final injunctive relief may be crafted to describe in *reasonable detail* the acts required." *Ward*, 753 F. App'x at 249 (quoting *Yates*, 868 F.3d at 367). "[M]ore is needed than a common failure by the defendant and the prospect that all class members could realize some benefit if the defendant is compelled to act or desist." *Prantil*, 986 F.3d at 580–81 (holding that proposed medical monitoring and property remediation injunctions discussed in "broad strokes" did not satisfy requirement of reasonable specificity). While plaintiffs "are not required to spell out every jot and tittle of injunctive relief at the class certification stage, they must be able to explain how a court could define or enforce meaningful injunctive relief." *Ward,* 753 F. App'x at 249 (internal quotations and citations omitted). At a minimum, plaintiffs must "describe in some kind of detail from what actions or inactions Defendant should be restrained;" a general request to restrain the defendant from violating constitutional protections is insufficient. *Id.*

The Fifth Circuit has curtailed injunctive relief that is deemed overbroad in Rule 23(b)(2) class actions. *See M.D. by Stukenberg v. Abbott*, 907 F.3d 237, 271–288 (5th Cir. 2018) (vacating and remanding permanent injunction for modification). Recognizing that institutional reform injunctions "are disfavored, as they 'often raise sensitive federalism concerns' and they 'commonly involve[] areas of core state responsibility,'" *id.* at 271 (quoting *Horne v. Flores*, 557 U.S. 433, 448 (2009)), the Court held that "remedies fashioned by the federal courts to address constitutional infirmities 'must directly address and relate to the constitutional violation itself,'' and that "'decrees exceed appropriate limits if they are aimed at eliminating a condition that does not violate the Constitution or does not flow from such a violation.'" *Id.* (quoting *Milliken v. Bradley*, 433 U.S. 267, 282 (1977); *see also M.D. by Stukenberg v. Abbott*, 929 F.3d 272, 276 (2019).

Relief cannot go beyond what is minimally required to achieve constitutional compliance, and it must be narrowly tailored. *Stukenberg*, 907 F.3d at 272 (vacating injunctive provisions that "fail to address the specific problems giving rise to the constitutional violation" or that "aim too high," reflecting "best practices" that go beyond what is minimally required to comport with the Constitution). But a "court may require remedial measures that the Constitution does not of its own force initially require." *Id.* (internal quotation omitted). And "an injunctive remedy 'does not fail narrow tailoring simply because it will have positive effects beyond the plaintiff class." *Id.* (citing *Brown v. Plata*, 563 U.S. 493, 531 (2011)). Thus, if injunctive provisions "are necessary to achieve constitutional compliance, they are not *per se* improper on the basis that they achieve 'collateral' benefits not directly related to the appropriately identified systemic defect." *Id.*

Although the Fifth Circuit has "recognized the increased utility of intervention in a class without opt-out rights," it has rejected would-be intervenors in a Rule 23(b)(2) class who could neither "identify a unique interest of their own" nor specify "a future detrimental preclusive effect." *Guenther v. BP Ret. Accumulation Plan*, 50 F.4th 536, 547 (5th Cir. 2022).

Rule 23(b)(3) Classes

Class certification under Rule 23(b)(3) imposes two additional requirements beyond those of Rule 23(a): predominance and superiority. *See Chavez II*, 108 F.4th at 316. "Questions of law or fact common to class members [must] predominate over any questions affecting only individual members, and a class [must be] superior to other available methods for fairly and efficiently adjudicating the controversy." Fed. R. Civ. P. 23(b); *see also Angell*, 67 F.4th at 736; *Cleven v. Mid-Am. Apartment Communities, Inc.*, 20 F.4th 171, 176 (5th Cir. 2021). Members of a certified 23(b)(3) class must be given the "best notice . . . practicable under the circumstances" and the opportunity to opt out of the class. *See* Fed. R. Civ. P. 23(c)(2)(B)(v) and (vi). Rule 23 does not authorize an "opt-in" class. *See Ackal v. Centennial Beauregard Cellular L.L.C.*, 700 F.3d 212, 216–19 (5th Cir. 2012).

The Fifth Circuit has a well-developed jurisprudence on the Rule 23(b)(3) requirements of predominance and superiority. The predominance requirement, "although similar to the commonality requirement of Rule 23(a), is far more demanding because it tests whether proposed classes are sufficiently cohesive to warrant adjudication by representation." *Steering Comm. v. Exxon Mobil Corp.*, 461 F.3d 598, 601–02 (5th Cir. 2006) (internal quotations omitted); *see also Chavez II*, 108 F.4th at 316; Cruson *v. Jackson Nat'l Life Ins. Co.*, 954 F.3d 240, 253–54 (5th Cir. 2020); *Crutchfield v. Sewerage & Water Bd. of New Orleans*, 829 F.3d 370, 375–76 (5th Cir. 2016). Accordingly, "'Rule 23(a)(2)'s 'commonality' requirement is subsumed under, or superseded by, the more stringent Rule 23(b)(3) requirement that questions common to the class 'predominate over' other questions.'" *Elson v. Black*, 56 F.4th 1002, 1006 (5th Cir. 2023) (quoting *Amchem Prod., Inc. v. Windsor*, 521 U.S. 591, 609 (1997)).

"'The predominance inquiry asks whether the common, aggregation-enabling, issues in the case are more prevalent or important than the non-common, aggregation-defeating, individual issues.'" *Sampson v. United Services Auto. Ass'n*, 83 F.4th 414, 418 (5th Cir. 2023) (quoting *Tyson Foods Inc. v. Bouaphakeo*, 577 U.S. 442, 453 (2016)). "When one or more of the central issues in the action are common to the class and can be said to predominate, the action may be considered proper under Rule 23(b)(3) even though other important matters will have to be tried separately, such as damages or some affirmative defenses peculiar to some individual class members." *Id.*

To determine whether questions common to the class predominate, the court must "inquire how the case will be tried." *Ibe v. Jones*, 836 F.3d 516, 529 (5th Cir. 2016); *see also Prantil*, 986 F.3d at 574, 578–80 (vacating class certification when district court had failed to give adequate consideration to administration of proposed bifurcated trial); *Madison v. Chalmette Ref., L.L.C.*, 637 F.3d 551, 556 (5th Cir. 2011) (reversing class certification where district court had failed to seriously consider "the administration of the trial," instead "adopt[ing] a figure-it-out-as-we-go-along approach"). "In order to predominate, common issues must constitute a significant part of the individual cases." *Ibe*, 836 F.3d at 529 (internal quotation marks and citations omitted); *see also Chavez II*, 108 F.4th at 316. The district court cannot just "assume[] that because . . . common issues would play a part in every trial, they must be significant." *Castano v. Am. Tobacco Co.*, 84 F.3d 734, 745 (5th Cir. 1996).

Instead, the court must "identify[] the substantive issues that will control the outcome, assess[] which issues will predominate, and then determin[e] whether the issues are common to the class." *Ibe*, 836 F.3d at 529; *Seeligson*, 761 F. App'x at 338; *see also Chavez II*, 108 F.4th at 316 (explaining that this process prevents the class from degenerating into a series of individual trials); *Castano*, 84 F.3d at 744 ("[A] court must understand the claims, defenses, relevant facts, and applicable substantive law in order to make a meaningful determination of the certification issues."). "Assessing predominance 'calls upon courts to give careful scrutiny to the relation between common and individual questions in a case.'" *Cruson*, 954 F.3d at 253 (quoting *Tyson Foods, Inc. v. Bouaphakeo*, 577 U.S. 442, 453, 136 S. Ct. 1036, 1045 (2016)). "An individual question is one where members of a proposed class will need to present evidence that varies from member to member, while a common question is one where the same evidence will suffice for each member to make a prima facie showing" or "the issue is susceptible to generalized, class-wide proof." *Id.* (internal quotations and citations omitted); *see also Angell*, 67 F.4th at 739; *Chavez II*, 108 F.4th at 317 (common question whether Master Trust Agreements operated as plaintiffs asserted "unequivocally dominate[d] any potential individualized inquiries."

The district court must balance the common issues against the individualized issues. "[T]he predominance of individual issues necessary to decide an affirmative defense may preclude class certification." *Id.* at 256 (internal quotations and citations omitted) (vacating class certification when erroneous predominance analysis failed to consider individualized evidence relevant to affirmative defenses of waiver and ratification, *id.* at 246); *see also Seeligson*, 761 F. App'x at 338 (abuse of discretion to certify class without considering whether statute of limitations and tolling questions would raise individual issues affecting predominance). "[C]lass issues do not predominate when 'transaction-by-transaction' determinations are required." *Ticknor v. Rouse's Enters., L.L.C.*, 592 F. App'x 276, 278 (5th Cir. 2014) (per curiam) (unpublished) (quoting *Mims v. Stewart Title Guar. Co.*, 590 F.3d 298, 307 (5th Cir. 2009)).

The Fifth Circuit has held that Rule 23(c)(4), which authorizes a class action only "with respect to issues," does not lessen the plaintiff's burden to show predominance. "The proper interpretation of the interaction between subdivisions (b)(3) and (c)(4) is that a cause of action, as a whole, must satisfy the predominance requirement . . . and that (c)(4) is a housekeeping rule that allows courts to sever the common issues for a class trial." *Castano*, 84 F.3d at 745 n.21. Therefore "a district court cannot manufacture predominance through the nimble use of . . . (c)(4)." *Id.* If Rule 23(c)(4) "allow[ed] a court to sever issues until the remaining common issue predominate[d] over the remaining individual issues, [it] would eviscerate the predominance requirement." *Id.* "[T]he result would be automatic certification in every case where there is a common issue." *Id. See also Crutchfield*, 829 F.3d at 378 ("Even though trial courts have flexibility in crafting bifurcated proceedings once a case is certified, the predominance inquiry that is a prerequisite to certification requires assessing all the issues in a case."); *Chavez II*, 108 F.4th at 318–20 (affirming Rule 23(b)(3) class certification but remanding with instructions for district court "to consider whether severing liability from individual damage issues and trying them separately may be appropriate" under Rule 23(c)(4)–(5)).

To meet their burden to establish predominance, plaintiffs seeking certification of a multistate class action based on state law claims must present a choice-of-law analysis that allows the court to decide whether variations in state laws will "swamp any common issues and defeat predominance." *See Spence v. Glock*, 227 F.3d 308, 311 (5th Cir. 2000) (reversing class certification where district court "did not perform an adequate choice of law analysis," *id.* at 316); *see also Elson*, 56 F.4th at 1006–07 (holding that plaintiffs seeking class certification had not met their burden "to assure the district court that . . . differences in state law would not predominate over issues individual to each plaintiff in the litigation"); *Cruson*, 954 F.3d at 246 ("[W]e conclude that the district court erred in its predominance analysis by failing to assess how state-law variations may impact adjudication of the [contractual] breach question."); *Castano*, 84 F.3d at 741–44; *Casa Orlando Apts., Ltd. v. Fed. Nat'l Mort. Ass'n*, 624 F.3d 185, 194–96 (5th Cir. 2010) (holding that variations in state laws on fiduciary duty and unjust enrichment defeated predominance). In *Cruson*, a breach-of-contract case, the Fifth Circuit held insufficient a "chart addressing state laws on certain interpretation issues," when plaintiffs "provided no analysis of state-law variations on the use of extrinsic evidence." 954 F.3d at 254–55, n.13.

The Fifth Circuit has consistently held that "a fraud class action cannot be certified when individual reliance will be an issue." *See Slade v. Progressive Sec. Ins. Co.*, 856 F.3d 408, 415 (5th Cir. 2017) (collecting cases); *see also Elson*, 56 F.4th at 1006–07 (holding that different reliance requirements of state laws defeated predominance). In certain securities fraud cases, reliance can be rebuttably presumed; but without that presumption, a suit "cannot proceed as a class action," because each plaintiff "would have to prove reliance individually, so common issues would not 'predominate' individual issues, as required by Rule 23(b)(3)." *See Halliburton Co. v. Erica P. John Fund, Inc.*, 573 U.S. 258, 281–83, 134

S. Ct. 2398, 2416 (2014).

To invoke this rebuttable presumption in a securities case, "Plaintiffs must prove '(1) that the alleged misrepresentation was publicly known; (2) that it was material; (3) that the stock traded in an efficient market; and (4) that the plaintiff traded the stock between the time the misrepresentation was made and when the truth was revealed.'" *Georgia Firefighters' Pension Fund v. Anadarko Petroleum Corp.*, 99 F.4th 770, 773 (5th Cir. 2024) (quoting *Goldman Sachs Grp., Inc. v. Ark. Tchr. Ret. Sys.*, 594 U.S. 113, 118 (2021)). "The defendant may rebut the presumption by demonstrating that the 'alleged misrepresentation did not actually affect the market price of the stock.'" *Id.* (quoting *Goldman Sachs*, 594 U.S. at 119).

In a split decision en banc, the Fifth Circuit has held that RICO pyramid scheme plaintiffs did not have to prove individual reliance to establish proximate cause, and therefore individual issues of causation did not defeat predominance. *See Torres v. S.G.E. Mgmt., L.L.C.*, 838 F.3d 629 (5th Cir. 2016) (en banc); *see also Vine v. PLS Fin. Servs., Inc.*, 807 F. App'x 320, 329–30 (5th Cir. 2020) (per curiam) (unpublished) (applying *Torres* exception in fraud class action where jury could reasonably infer that borrowers believed District Attorney's letter based on defendant's misrepresentations in affidavits submitted to DA).

The Fifth Circuit has long held that "where individual damages cannot be determined by reference to a mathematical or formulaic calculation," predominance of common issues may be lacking, because individual damages issues may overwhelm "any common issues shared by the class." *Steering Comm.*, 461 F.3d at 602; *see also O'Sullivan v. Countrywide Home Loans, Inc.*, 319 F.3d 732, 744–45 (5th Cir. 2003). Although the Supreme Court included "general language" in *Tyson Foods v. Bouaphakeo* to the effect that individualized damages calculations will not preclude a finding of predominance, *see* 577 U.S. 442, 453–54 (2016), the Fifth Circuit has not treated that statement as altering the Fifth Circuit's prior holdings. Thus, "class treatment may not be suitable where the calculation of damages is not susceptible to a mathematical or formulaic calculation, or where the formula by which the parties propose to calculate individual damages is clearly inadequate." *Ibe v. Jones*, 836 F.3d 516, 529 (5th Cir. 2016) (holding that individual damages issues would defeat predominance when plaintiffs in breach-of-contract case "incurred vastly different expenses," "necessitat[ing] mini-trials to adjudicate damages for each," *id.* at 531); *see also Chavez II*, 108 F.4th at 317–18 (predominance satisfied when plaintiffs' plan to use "an arithmetic, formulaic method" to prove excessiveness of plan fees sufficiently protected defendants' due process rights); *Angell*, 67 F.4th at 739–40 (predominance satisfied when the "need for individual calculation [was] relatively minor when compared to the common issues that predominate"; plaintiffs could "articulate a reasonably ascertainable" formula to calculate sales tax damages "for almost 97% of the class without resort to individualized review" and plaintiffs' expert had provided a table to calculate class members' other damages from vehicle title and registration fees); *Earl v. Boeing Co.*, 21 F.4th 895, 898–99 (5th Cir. 2021) (substantial predominance questions raised by need for individual damages calculations in airline ticket price case); *Cruson*, 954 F.3d at 257–58 (predominance lacking when plaintiffs sought two forms of damages but put forward an expert model calculating only one); *Mitchell v. State Farm Fire & Cas. Co.*, 954 F.3d 700, 710–12 (5th Cir. 2020) (predominance satisfied when plaintiff's proposed damage formula was adequate, and calculation of damages using defendant's software would be feasible); *Vine,* 807 F. App'x at 329 (predominance satisfied where fees set by statute made "requests for actual economic damages . . .'fairly uniform'" from database table).

"What matters for class certification is not whether Plaintiffs' damages model is correct, but whether Plaintiffs' damages model can be applied in a uniform manner across the class." *Sampson*, 83 F.4th at 421. But "[a] district court's wide discretion to choose an imperfect estimative-damages model at the certification stage does not carry over from the context of damages to the context of liability." *Id.* at 422–23 (holding predominance not satisfied when plaintiffs could not establish the fact of an insurer's underpayment by classwide proof). The Fifth Circuit also has explained that it is possible to satisfy the predominance requirement in a mass tort class action, if "virtually every issue prior to damages is a common issue," despite the need for "individualized damages calculations." *See In re Deepwater Horizon*, 739 F.3d 790, 815–16 (5th Cir. 2014) (footnote omitted). Acknowledging the Supreme Court's holding in *Comcast Corp. v. Behrend* that a court should not certify a Rule 23(b)(3) class premised "on a formula for classwide measurement of damages whenever the damages measured by that formula are incompatible with the class action's theory of liability," 133 S. Ct. 1426 (2013), the Fifth Circuit concluded that this holding had "no impact" when "predominance was based not on common issues of damages but on the numerous common issues of liability." *Id.* at 815.

And where predominance is based on the commonality of *both* "liability and damages," the court still must "ask whether in operation the commonality is undone by the damages theory." *Ludlow v. BP, P.L.C.*, 800 F.3d 674, 683 n.36 (5th Cir. 2015); *see also Crutchfield v. Sewerage & Water Bd. of New Orleans*, 829 F.3d 370, 378–79 (5th Cir. 2016) (rejecting certification of mass tort claims seeking "different damages caused by different acts committed by different defendants at different times over a five-year period").

For Rule 23(b)(3)'s superiority analysis, the pertinent factors include:

> (A) the class members' interests in individually controlling the prosecution or defense of separate actions; (B) the extent and nature of any litigation concerning the controversy already begun by or against class members; (C) the desirability or undesirability of concentrating the litigation of the claims in the particular forum; and (D) the likely difficulties in managing a class action.

In re TWL Corp., 712 F.3d 886, 895 (5th Cir. 2013). These factors are not, however, exhaustive. *Id.* The superiority analysis is "a comparative process," in which the court "ought to assess the relative advantages of alternative procedures for handling the total controversy." *Id.* at 896 (quotations omitted). It is "fact-specific and will vary depending on the circumstances of any given case." *Id.*; *see also Ibe*, 826 F.3d at 529–30.

For example, the Fifth Circuit considers whether individual suits are feasible, taking into account whether "individual damage claims are high," whether "punitive damages are available," and whether fee-shifting statutes allow for the recovery of attorneys' fees. *See Castano*, 84 F.3d at 748 ("The most compelling rationale for finding superiority in a class action—the existence of a negative value suit—is missing in this case."); *see also Ticknor v. Rouse's Enters., L.L.C.*, 592 F. App'x 276, 279 (5th Cir. 2014) (per curiam) (unpublished) (recognizing "that the availability of attorney's fees and punitive damages is a common basis for finding non-superiority, as the aggregation of claims is not necessary to facilitate suits"); *Mitchell*, 954 F.3d at 712 (district court "did not abuse its discretion in finding that the negative-value nature of the claims . . . establishes superiority" when over 10,000 claims in the proposed class were too small for separate litigation). But the Fifth Circuit has also recognized that a negative-value suit is not automatically entitled to class certification, even when legitimate claims might "go unheard." *Flecha*, 946 F.3d at 769. "[S]uperiority is only one of the numerous conditions that must be met before a class may be certified under Rule 23." *Id.* at 770. "Nor is class certification the only solution to a negative value suit. The ability of prevailing parties to recover attorney fees . . . may also help solve the problem." *Id.* at 770, n.1.

The Fifth Circuit also has cautioned that certification of an "immature tort"—one without a prior track record of individual trials—should be avoided because it "results in a higher than normal risk that the class action may not be superior to individual adjudication." *Castano*, 84 F.3d at 747; *see also id.* at 749–50. Class size is also "a relevant, though not dispositive, consideration." *Ticknor*, 592 F. App'x at 279.

Finally, the Fifth Circuit has recognized that predominance and superiority are interrelated: "An incorrect predominance finding also implicates the court's superiority analysis: The greater the number of individual issues, the less likely superiority can be established." *Castano*, 84 F.3d at 745 n.19; *see also Steering Comm. v. Exxon Mobil Corp.*, 461 F.3d 598,

604–05 (5th Cir. 2006) ("[T]he predominance of individual issues relating to the plaintiffs' claims . . . detracts from the superiority of the class action device in resolving these claims."). Variations in state law, for example, can be important to both the predominance and the superiority analysis. *See Castano*, 84 F.3d at 741 ("[A] district court must consider how variations in state law affect predominance and superiority.").

c. Manageability

The Fifth Circuit treats manageability as part of the superiority analysis. *See, e.g.*, *Robinson v. Texas Auto Dealers Ass'n*, 387 F.3d 416, 425–26 (5th Cir. 2004) (reversing class certification where district court's superiority analysis had failed to consider "how it would manage the gigantic plaintiff class" and the several hundred defendants, each with the "absolute right to individually defend itself"). Meaningful consideration of trial administration is also crucial to the predominance analysis, however. *See, e.g.*, *Prantil*, 986 at 578 ("[T]he district court's certification order did not discuss the considerations affecting the administration of trial, and it concluded that common questions would predominate without adequately addressing [defendant's] arguments that causation, injury, and damages would be highly individualized."); *Madison v. Chalmette Refining, L.L.C.*, 637 F.3d 551, 556–57 (5th Cir. 2011) (reversing class certification when trial court had not analyzed how it would administer the trial but had simply concluded that common liability issues could be tried in a single class action trial with damages issues reserved for individual treatment); *see also Chavez II*, 108 F.4th at 318–20 (affirming class certification over predominance challenge, but remanding with instructions for district court to consider further how trial would be administered).

The Fifth Circuit acknowledges bifurcation of liability and damages as a tool for the district court's management of complex litigation. *See Prantil*, 986 F.3d at 582; *Chavez II*, 108 F.4th at 318–20 (collecting cases and instructing district court to consider bifurcation on remand). But the Fifth Circuit has also recognized boundaries to the court's discretion. *See Prantil*, 986 F.3d at 578 (vacating class certification when "district court's discussion of trial administration was limited to observing that it was amenable to Plaintiffs' proposal to bifurcate the trial of liability and damages" but "did not discuss the manner in which [court] would conduct the liability phase or how it would implement Plaintiffs' proposed 'bellwether trials' at the damages phase").

The Fifth Circuit has also cautioned against the use of bifurcated trial plans to make a class action manageable when there is a risk that "the court will be forced to bifurcate issues in violation of the Seventh Amendment." *Castano*, 84 F.3d at 750–51. When there is a risk that a second jury will "impermissibly reconsider[ ] the findings of a first jury," that risk "weigh[s] heavily in favor of individual trials," rather than class treatment. *See id.* at 750. The Fifth Circuit also has made clear that a "district court cannot manufacture predominance through the nimble use of management tools." *Ibe v. Jones*, 836 F.3d 516, 531 (5th Cir. 2016) (internal quotation marks omitted) (citing *Castano*, 84 F.3d at 745 n.1).

Confronting mass tort cases, the Fifth Circuit has focused on the trial plan—not only the pragmatic questions of how large numbers of claims could be managed at trial but also the jurisprudential questions of how they could be tried consistent with Due Process, the Seventh Amendment, Separation of Powers, the "case-or-controversy" requirement of Article III, and the application of substantive law as mandated by *Erie* and the Federal Rules Enabling Act. *See, e.g.*, *Castano*, 84 F.3d at 746–52; *Cimino v. Raymark Indus., Inc.*, 151 F.3d 297 (5th Cir. 1998); *In re Fibreboard*, 893 F.2d 706 (5th Cir. 1990); *Jenkins v. Raymark Indus., Inc.*, 782 F.2d 468 (5th Cir. 1986).

Settlement classes need not be manageable for trial, however, because "the existence of a settlement agreement allows the district court to dispense altogether with . . . the likely difficulties in managing a class action." *Deepwater Horizon*, 739 F.3d at 818 (citing *Amchem Prods., Inc. v. Windsor*, 521 U.S. 613, 623 (1997)). "[W]hen confronted with a request for settlement-only class certification, a district court need not inquire whether the case, if tried, would present intractable management problems . . . for the proposal is that there be no trial." *Id.*

d. Ascertainability

"The Fifth Circuit has also articulated an 'ascertainability' requirement for Rule 23 class actions." *Braidwood Mgmt.*, 70 F.4th at 933 & n.36 (recognizing that requirement extends to Rule 23(b)(2) class actions). To maintain a class action, "the class sought to be represented must be adequately defined and clearly ascertainable." *Union Asset Mgmt. Holding AG v. Dell Inc.*, 669 F.3d 632, 639 (5th Cir. 2012) (internal quotation marks and citation omitted); *see also A. A. by & through P.A. v. Phillips*, No. 21-30580, 2023 WL 334010, at *2–3 (5th Cir. Jan. 20, 2023) (per curiam) (unpublished) (citation omitted); *Frey v. First Nat. Bank Sw.*, 602 F. App'x 164, 168 (5th Cir. 2015) (per curiam) (unpublished) (quotation omitted).

"To be ascertainable, the class must be susceptible to a precise definition to properly identify those entitled to relief, those bound by the judgment, and those entitled to notice." *A.A.*, 2023 WL 334010, at *2 (internal quotation marks and citation omitted). But "the court need not know the identity of each class member before certification; ascertainability requires only that the court be able to identify class members at some stage of the proceeding." *Frey*, 602 F. App'x at 168 (quotation omitted); *Seeligson v. Devon Energy Prod. Co.*, 761 F. App'x 329, 33 (5th Cir. 2019) (on panel rehearing) (per curiam) (unpublished), *on remand*, 2020 WL 636224 (N.D. Tex. Feb. 11, 2020), *leave for second appeal denied*, 804 F. App'x 304 (5th Cir. 2020) (per curiam) (unpublished). Further, "the possibility that some may fail to prevail on their individual claims will not defeat class membership" for lack of ascertainability. *In re Rodriguez*, 695 F.3d 360, 370 (5th Cir. 2012) (quotation omitted); *see also A. A.*, 2023 WL 334010, at *2.

Courts should not, however, certify classes with overbroad definitions, for example definitions based on the class members' state of mind or otherwise impermissibly vague or imprecise. *See Braidwood Mgmt.*, 70 F.4th at 935 & n.33 (5th Cir. 2023) (rejecting definitions that would require case-by-case determinations of class membership); *A. A.*, 2023 WL 334010, at *2 ("The order defining the class should avoid subjective standards (e.g., a plaintiff's state of mind) or terms that depend on resolution of the merits (e.g., persons who were discriminated against). There can be no class action if the proposed class is amorphous or imprecise." (internal quotation marks and citations omitted)).

In *A. A.*, the Fifth Circuit held the class unascertainable when the definition used a term that was "too vague to identify class members," *id.* at *3, explaining that "the touchstone of ascertainability is whether the class is sufficiently definite so that it is administratively feasible for the court to determine whether a particular individual is a member," *id.* at *2 (internal quotation marks and citations omitted). As the Fifth Circuit has instructed, "we police the definitions of class actions; otherwise, it would be impossible for future parties and courts to determine the scope and preclusive effect of any judgment." *Braidwood Mgmt.*, 70 F.4th at 935–36.

The Fifth Circuit has "rejected a rule against fail-safe classes," that is, classes "whose membership can only be ascertained by a determination of the merits . . . because the class is defined in terms of the ultimate question of liability." *Id.* at 369–70. The court has cautioned, however, that an appropriate class definition does not mean "there [are] any common class-wide questions, that these questions would predominate trial, or that mere membership in the class [is] sufficient to establish liability en masse." *Benavides v. Chicago Title Ins. Co.*, 636 F.3d 699, 702–03 (5th Cir. 2011).

The Fifth Circuit has approved dismissal of class allegations "[w]here it is facially apparent from the pleadings that there is no ascertainable class." *John v. Nat'l Sec. Fire & Cas. Co.*, 501 F.3d 443, 445 (5th Cir. 2007). The Fifth Circuit has also warned that a district court "should not dismiss an action purely because the proposed class definition is too broad." *Braidwood Mgmt.*, 70 F.4th at 934 & n.37.

5. TYPES OF CLASSES

a. On Plaintiff's Motion

Plaintiff Classes

"Under Rule 23, a class may be certified if it satisfies the requirements of Rule 23(a) and fits into one of the three categories outlined in Rule 23(b)." *Casa Orlando Apts., Ltd. v. Fed. Nat'l Mortg. Ass'n*, 624 F.3d 185, 190 (5th Cir. 2010). That is, to obtain class certification, a plaintiff must satisfy Rule 23(a)'s "four threshold requirements, as well as the requirements of Rule 23(b)(1), (2), or (3)." *Ludlow v. BP, P.L.C.*, 800 F.3d 674, 682 (5th Cir. 2015) (citations omitted).

"Rule 23 does not set forth a mere pleading standard." *Ibe v. Jones*, 836 F.3d 516, 528 (5th Cir. 2016) (quoting *Wal-Mart Stores, Inc. v. Dukes*, 564 U.S. 338, 350 (2011)). "The party seeking class certification bears the burden of demonstrating that the requirements of Rule 23 have been met." *Id.* at 528. "The plain text of Rule 23 requires the court to 'find,' not merely assume, the facts favoring certification." *Unger v. Amedisys Inc.*, 401 F.3d 316, 321 (5th Cir. 2005).

Movants for class certification should consult the local rules for any district-specific requirements. *See, e.g.*, Local Court Rules of the United States District Court for the Western District of Texas, LR CV-23 and Appendix A (detailed requirements for motion to certify).

Defendant Classes

Rule 23(a) provides that "[o]ne or more members of a class may . . . be sued as representative parties on behalf of all members" if the other prerequisites for a Rule 23 class action are met.

The Fifth Circuit gives close scrutiny to the question whether a representative of a defendant class—especially one effectively chosen by the plaintiffs—can satisfy the requirements of Rule 23(a). In *Greenhouse v. Greco*, a case challenging the segregation of parochial schools, the Fifth Circuit upheld the dismissal of defendant class representatives for failure to meet the Rule 23(a) requirements of commonality, typicality, and adequacy. 617 F.2d 408 (5th Cir. 1980). Having decided the case on Rule 23(a) grounds, the court expressly declined to reach "the more troublesome issue" of whether Rule 23(b)(2) authorizes defendant classes at all. *See id.* at 413 n.6. The Fifth Circuit noted that Rule 23(b)(2)'s "literal language . . . indicates that it is not an appropriate basis for certification of a defendant class." *Id.* This is because for a (b)(2) class, the party opposing the class must be the one who has acted or refused to act on grounds generally applicable to the class, making injunctive relief appropriate with respect to the class as a whole. *See id.*; *see also Mayo v. Hartford Life Ins. Co.*, 214 F.R.D. 465, 470–71 (S.D. Tex. 2002) (doubting legal viability of proposed defendant class). The *Greenhouse* court went on to describe the limited situations in which courts have certified Rule (b)(2) classes, however: "cases allowing certification of a defendant class under Rule 23(b)(2) generally involve actions to enjoin a group of local public officials from enforcing a locally administered state statute or similar administrative policies." 617 F.2d 413 n.6 (citations omitted).

A district court within the Fifth Circuit has certified a Rule 23(b)(1)(A) defendant class of public officials over the objection of the defendants, but the subsequent Fifth Circuit appeal did not encompass this class certification holding. *See Tex. Med. Providers Performing Abortion Servs. v. Lakey*, 806 F. Supp. 2d 942, 955 (W.D. Tex. 2011) (certifying defendant class of Texas prosecutors under Rule 23(b)(1)(A) on motion of plaintiffs challenging Texas abortion statute), *vacated in part on other grounds*, 667 F.3d 570 (5th Cir. 2012) (reversing grant of preliminary injunction on the merits), *on remand*, No. A-11-CA-486-SS, 2012 WL 373132, at *6 (W.D. Tex. Feb. 6, 2012) (granting defendants summary judgment on merits).

In *Kerney v. Fort Griffin Fandangle Association*, the Fifth Circuit upheld a Rule 23.2 defendant class action brought against the members of an unincorporated association. 624 F.2d 717, 719–20 (5th Cir. 1980). Although treating the constitutional challenge in that case as premature, *Kerney* emphasized that due process protections must be afforded members of defendant classes. *Id.* at 721. "Both rules 23 and 23.2 expressly contemplate the possibility of defendant class actions and require that the representative parties fairly and adequately protect the interest of the class members." *Id.* And beyond this threshold determination of adequacy, the court has the "power and the duty to ensure that all defendants be given adequate notice of the action and an opportunity to present individual defenses if desired." *Id.*

b. On Defendant's Motion

A Rule 23(b)(2) defendant class was certified by agreement in *Baker v. Wade*, where the plaintiff sought to have a Texas criminal statute declared unconstitutional. 743 F.2d 236, 239 (5th Cir. 1984), *rehearing en banc granted and new opinion issued in Baker v. Wade*, 769 F.2d 289 (5th Cir. 1985) (en banc), *overruled on other grounds by Lawrence v. Texas*, 529 U.S. 558 (2003). In *Baker*, the defendant class consisted of all district, county, and city attorneys in the State who were responsible for enforcing the challenged Texas statute. *Id.* When the original representatives of the defendant class elected not to appeal an adverse decision at the district court level, another member of the defendant class sought to intervene to defend the statute, arguing that the defendant class representatives' failure to appeal had made their representation inadequate. *Id.* at 243. The original *Baker* panel recognized that "[d]efendant class actions embody a potential for unfairness to absent class members because the *plaintiff* makes an initial choice of class representative" but denied intervention. *Id.* at 244 (footnote omitted), *rehearing en banc granted and modified*, 769 F.2d 289 (5th Cir. 1985) (en banc). On rehearing en banc, however, the Fifth Circuit granted the intervention request, holding that the interests of the defendant class "were inadequately represented by those who failed to pursue the appeal." 769 F.2d at 292.

In 2018, a district court in the Fifth Circuit rejected an attempt by a *defendant* (who had been sued individually) to certify a defendant class. *Mary Kay Inc. v. Reibel*, 327 F.R.D. 127 (N.D. Tex. 2018).

c. Counterclaim Classes

Counsel should consult local rules in the district courts for pleading requirements governing counterclaim or cross-claim classes. *See, e.g.*, Local Civil Rules of the United States District Court for the Eastern District of Louisiana, LR 23.1(C).

6. CASE MANAGEMENT

a. Appointing and Substituting Counsel

When a court certifies a class, it must appoint class counsel, considering the four factors set out in Rule 23(g):

- the work counsel has done in identifying or investigating potential claims in the action;
- counsel's experience in handling class actions, other complex litigation, and the types of claims asserted in the action;
- counsel's knowledge of the applicable law; and
- the resources that counsel will commit to representing the class.

Fed. R. Civ. P. 23(g). In addition to these factors, a court "may consider any other matter pertinent to counsel's ability to fairly and adequately represent the interests of the class." *Id.* The Fifth Circuit has not elaborated on Rule 23(g). *See Esquivel v. Kendrick*, No. 22-50979, 2023 WL 5584168, at *2 (5th Cir. Aug. 29, 2023) (per curiam) (unpublished) (noting that "Rule 23(g) addresses the appointment of class counsel following class certification or in the interim before class certification is determined," and holding rule inapplicable where *pro se* plaintiff never sought class certification). Analyzing adequacy under Rule 23(a), however, the Fifth Circuit "mandates an inquiry into the zeal and competence of the representative's counsel." *Horton v. Goose Creek Indep. Sch. Dist.*, 690 F.2d 470, 484 (5th Cir. 1982).

Although district courts "normally enjoy substantial latitude in deciding motions for substitution of counsel," in the Fifth Circuit, "[m]ere dissatisfaction with class counsel's strategy or obtained results does not adequately support a motion for substitution of counsel." *Gates v. Cook*, 234 F.3d 221, 228 (5th Cir. 2000). "In long-standing class actions, in particular, significant administrative difficulties could arise from frequent or competing motions for substitution or intervention." *Id.* The Fifth Circuit has held substitution of counsel to be justified, however, when supported by a large majority of the class, when class counsel has substituted his own subjective judgment for that of the class on major questions of litigation, and when warranted by class counsel's record of nonfeasance and mishandling. *See id.* at 229–230.

b. Discovery Issues

The Fifth Circuit has encouraged district courts to allow discovery on the issue of class certification. *See, e.g.*, *Madison v. Chalmette Ref., L.L.C.*, 637 F.3d 551, 553 (5th Cir. 2011); *Gene & Gene, L.L.C. v. BioPay, L.L.C.*, 624 F.3d 698, 703 n.3 (5th Cir. 2010) (explaining that under Rule 23 advisory committee notes, "it is appropriate to conduct controlled discovery into the 'merits,' limited to those aspects relevant to making the certification decision on an informed basis"); *Unger v. Amedisys, Inc.*, 401 F.3d 316, 319–321 (5th Cir. 2005) (holding that "findings must be made based on adequate admissible evidence to justify class certification" and recognizing that "to assist the court in this process it may sanction controlled discovery at the certification stage").

This is consistent with the Fifth Circuit's direction in *Castano* that "to determine whether the requirements of Rule 23 have been met," district courts are permitted to look past the pleadings. *See* 84 F.3d at 744. "Going beyond the pleadings is necessary, as a court must understand the claims, defenses, relevant facts, and applicable substantive law in order to make a meaningful determination of the certification issues." *Id.*; *see also Madison*, 637 F.3d at 555; *Sampson*, 83 F.4th at 418 (5th Cir. 2023) (recognizing that Rule 23 does not impose a mere pleading standard, and plaintiff must be prepared to prove that the requirements of Rule 23 are met in fact).

At the class certification stage, however, merits questions are considered only insofar as they bear on the class certification requirements. "Rule 23 grants courts no license to engage in free-ranging merits inquiries at the certification stage. Merits questions may be considered to the extent—but only to the extent—that they are relevant to determining whether the Rule 23 prerequisites for class-certification are satisfied." *Amgen Inc. v. Conn. Ret. Plans & Trust Funds*, 568 U.S. 455, 466 (2013). The Fifth Circuit has also recognized that "Rule 23 is not a context where courts must assiduously separate certification from merits issues; they will often be deeply intertwined," and a serious concern about classwide proof "cannot be ignored by simply describing it as a 'merits' issue." *Sampson*, 83 F.4th at 421 (citing *Comcast*, 569 U.S. at 33–34).

Local Rules may also provide guidance on class discovery. *See, e.g.*, Local Uniform Civil Rules of the United States District Courts for the Northern District of Mississippi and the Southern District of Mississippi, L.U. CIV. R 23 ("Until the issue of class certification has been decided, counsel must give priority to discovery directed to the class issue.").

c. Timing of Class Certification

Rule 23 requires the district court to determine whether to certify a class action "[a]t an early practicable time." Fed. R. Civ. P. 23(c)(1)(A). The Fifth Circuit has cautioned against "litigation tactics that drag out class action proceedings." *In re Par.*, 81 F.4th 403, 419 (5th Cir. 2023) ("The fact that plaintiffs choose to join as a putative class rather than sue individually should not unreasonably extend the timeline for resolving the matter."). But the timing of class certification does not detract from the requirement that "[a] district court must conduct a rigorous analysis of the Rule 23 prerequisites before certifying a class." *See Castano v. Am. Tobacco Co.*, 84 F.3d 734, 740 (5th Cir. 1996). Counsel should consult local rules and case management orders for specific timing requirements. *See, e.g.*, Local Civil Rules of the United States District Court for the Eastern District of Louisiana LR 23.1(B) (timing of class motion to be directed by case management order); Local Uniform Civil Rules of the United States District Courts for the Northern District of Mississippi and the Southern District of Mississippi L.U.CIV.R. 23 (similar); Local Civil Rules of the United States District Court for the Northern District of Texas LR 23.2 (requiring class certification motion within 90 days of filing a class action complaint or at such other time as presiding judge directs).

The Fifth Circuit has not been hospitable to repeated attempts at class certification after initial failures. For example, after class denials, the Fifth Circuit has not required district courts to allow renewed motions for class certification under different theories. *See Ludlow v. BP, P.L.C.*, 800 F.3d 674, 691–92 (5th Cir. 2015) ("[W]e cannot conclude that the district court abused its discretion in refusing—after issuing two thorough and well-reasoned opinions—to give the plaintiffs a third bite at the apple."). The Fifth Circuit has come to the same conclusion when the original motion inadequately briefed critical issues. *See Bell v. Ascendant Sols., Inc.*, 422 F.3d 307, 316 (5th Cir. 2005) ("Nor are we persuaded that we should require that [the plaintiffs] get a second bite at the class certification apple; inadequate briefing on an issue critical to class certification for which a party bears the burden of proof is no basis for us to order a repechage round."). And after reversing class certification on interlocutory appeal under Rule 23(f), the Fifth Circuit has disapproved of a district court's decision to reopen discovery and recertify the class, admonishing that "Rule 23(f) is not an interlocutory tool to clarify issues and provide a roadmap for litigants to reformulate their arguments." *See Gene & Gene, L.L.C. v. BioPay, L.L.C.*, 624 F.3d 698, 703 (5th Cir. 2010). In *BioPay*, the Fifth Circuit had expected "a merits determination and disposition of [the plaintiff's] individual claim" on remand, not "a renewed foray" into class certification. *See id.* at 703–04. After deciding a class certification appeal, however, the Fifth Circuit may choose to remand for further consideration. *See, e.g., Chavez I*, 957 F.3d at 551 (vacating class certification but expressing no view on whether a class should be certified and placing "no limit on the matters the court may consider in further proceedings"), *on remand*, *Chavez v. Plan Benefit Services, Inc*, No. 1:17-CV-659-LY, 2022 WL 1493605, at *24 (W.D. Tex. Mar. 29, 2022) (certifying class), *aff'd sub nom. Chavez v. Plan Benefit Services, Inc.*, 77 F.4th 370 (5th Cir. 2023), *opinion withdrawn and superseded on reh'g,* 108 F.4th 297 (5th Cir. 2024), *and aff'd in part, rev'd in part and remanded sub nom. Chavez v. Plan Benefit Services, Inc.* (*Chavez II*), 108 F.4th at 320 (reversing Rule 23(b)(1) class, affirming Rule 23(b)(3) class, and remanding for further proceedings with instructions to consider trial administration).

As for a defendant's attempts to decertify a certified class, even after a Rule 23(f) affirmance of class certification on interlocutory appeal, Rule 23(c) gives the district court authority on remand to alter, amend, or even decertify the class if subsequent discovery shows decertification to be proper. *See BioPay*, 624 F.3d at 703 (citing Fed. R. Civ. P. 23(c)(1)(C)); *see also Angell*, 67 F.4th at 739 n.6 ("[T]he district court may of course decertify the class if evidence supporting [defendant's] arguments is unearthed at a later date.").

The Fifth Circuit has also recognized that an MDL court can manage its docket to limit the filing of new class actions in a complex MDL when the court had previously allowed multi-plaintiff complaints and class action settlements. *In re Deepwater Horizon*, 713 F. App'x 360, 363 (5th Cir. 2018) (per curiam) (unpublished).

And the Fifth Circuit has held that the filing of a putative class action does not "universally estop all separate but related actions from proceeding to the merits until the class-certification process concludes in the putative class action." *In re Par.*, 81 F.4th at 407 (denying mandamus when district court "did not abuse its wide case-management discretion" in authorizing trial of related but unconsolidated individual case before class certification decision). The Fifth Circuit held that such trials do not implicate the prohibition on "one-way intervention," which applies when members can sign on to a class judgment after a decision on the merits. *See id.* at 412–14. Nor could such trials have an issue-preclusive effect on the claims of the proposed class. *See id.* at 415–16. The Fifth Circuit instead likened such trials to "the results of test plaintiffs in a bellwether trial, which are to be used for informational purposes only, not for issue preclusion." *Id.* at 416 (internal quotation marks and citation omitted).

For guidance on the application of the doctrines of preclusion and comity when a decision on class certification is relitigated in a different court, see the Supreme Court's decision in *Smith v. Bayer Corp.*, 564 U.S. 299 (2011).

d. Multidistrict Litigation Issues

The Fifth Circuit has recognized that an individual case pending in an MDL does not thereby become "part of a class action lawsuit, or a single, representative proceeding." *In re Taxotere (Docetaxel) Prods. Liab. Litig.*, 994 F.3d 704, 707 n.1 (5th Cir. 2021).

The Fifth Circuit has held that the transferee court in a Multidistrict Litigation (MDL) case should apply the transferor court's interpretation of federal law when addressing forum non conveniens. *See In re Ford Motor*, 591 F.3d 406, 413 n.15 (5th Cir. 2009). In later cases, the Fifth Circuit has declined to reach the question whether the same principle applies to questions of personal jurisdiction in an MDL transfer case. *See In re Chinese-Manufactured Drywall Prods. Liab. Litig.*, 742 F.3d 576, 586 (5th Cir. 2014) ("[W]e need not reach the issue of which circuit's law should apply because . . . the outcome is the same."); *In re Chinese-Manufactured Drywall Prods. Liab. Litig.*, 753 F.3d 521, 540 (5th Cir. 2014) (same).

The Fifth Circuit has affirmed a district court's "broad discretion and inherent authority to manage its docket," allowing an MDL court to restrict new class action filings "years into a complex MDL." *In re Deepwater Horizon*, 713 F. App'x 360, 361–63 (5th Cir. 2018) (per curiam) (unpublished).

The district courts in the Fifth Circuit have employed a variety of methods to manage MDL cases after class certification has been denied. *See, e.g.*, *In re Vioxx Prods. Liab. Litig.*, 388 F. App'x 391 (5th Cir. 2010) (per curiam) (unpublished); *In re FEMA Trailer Formaldehyde Prods. Liab. Litig.*, 628 F.3d 157 (5th Cir. 2010).

The MDL litigation over the Deepwater Horizon oil spill in the Gulf of Mexico and its resulting class settlement have been the subject of dozens of Fifth Circuit opinions. *See, e.g.*, *In re Deepwater Horizon*, 739 F.3d 790 (5th Cir. 2014 (affirming approval of class settlement); *In re Deepwater Horizon*, 744 F.3d 370 (5th Cir. 2014) (holding implementation of settlement's causation framework not defective under Article III), *order on panel rehearing*, 753 F.3d 509 (5th Cir. 2014); *In re Deepwater Horizon*, 795 F.3d 986 (5th Cir. 2015) (deciding scope of judicial review of claims determinations under court supervised settlement program); *In re Deepwater Horizon*, 819 F.3d 190 (5th Cir. 2016) (declining to recognize plaintiff as having opted out of class settlement); *Holmes Motors, Inc. v. BP Expl. & Prod., Inc.*, 829 F.3d 313 (5th Cir. 2016) (interpreting an unambiguous term in settlement agreement); *In re Deepwater Horizon*, 858 F.3d 298 (5th Cir. 2017) (interpreting ambiguous provisions of settlement agreement); *In re Deepwater Horizon*, 928 F.3d 394 (5th Cir. 2019) (applying mandate rule to reverse district court's application of settlement agreement that deviated from prior Fifth Circuit decision).

In the *Chinese Drywall* MDL, the Fifth Circuit has enforced express waivers of appeal rights in class settlements. *See In re Chinese-Manufactured Drywall Prod. Liab. Litig.*, 959 F.3d 658, 659 (5th Cir. 2020) (per curiam) (dismissing appeal); *In re Chinese-Manufactured Drywall Prod. Liab. Litig.*, 794 F. App'x 387, 389 (5th Cir 2019) (per curiam) (unpublished) (same).

The district courts within the Fifth Circuit have developed significant bodies of case law in MDL actions. *See, e.g.*, *In re Chinese-Manufactured Drywall Prod. Liab. Litig.*, 424

F. Supp. 3d 456, 495–506 (E.D. La. 2020) (deciding attorneys' fees in common fund settlement).

7. CLASS NOTICE

Rule 23 outlines different notice rules for different types of classes.

For Rule 23(b)(1) or (b)(2) classes, "the court may direct appropriate notice to the class." Fed. R. Civ. P. 23(c)(2)(A).

For a Rule 23(b)(3) class, or a proposed Rule 23(b)(3) class settlement, the "court must direct to class members the best notice that is practicable under the circumstances, including individual notice to all members who can be identified through reasonable effort." Fed. R. Civ. P. 23(c)(2)(B). Rule 23(c)(2)(B) "expresses an unambiguous requirement that individual notice . . . be provided to those class members who are identifiable through reasonable effort." *In re Nissan Motor Corp. Antitrust Litig.*, 552 F.2d 1088, 1097 (5th Cir. 1977). After its 2018 amendment, Rule 23(c)(2)(B) expressly provides for (b)(3) class notice by "electronic means," (such as email), when appropriate. *See* Fed. R. Civ. P. 23(c)(2)(B) and Advisory Committee notes to 2018 amendment, ¶ 3–7).

As a general rule, "a judgment in a class action will bind the members of the class," but "*absent* class members may collaterally attack a class action judgment for lack of notice and due process." *In re Deepwater Horizon*, 819 F.3d 190, 198–99 (5th Cir. 2016). *Deepwater Horizon* recognized that an absent class member's "actual notice through his counsel . . . satisfies due process," *id.* at 199, but did not reach the question when constructive notice also satisfies due process, *see id.* at 199, n.7. The Fifth Circuit has held, however, that constructive notice is "a poor substitute for actual notice," to be "used only when circumstances make it impracticable to gain the names and addresses of class members and notify them individually of the action's pendency." *Nissan*, 552 F.2d at 1097 (quotation omitted).

Rule 23 sets out specific information that must be included in a (b)(3) class notice, Fed. R. Civ. P. 23(c)(2)(B)(i)–(vii). The same requirements apply to notice of a Rule 23(b)(3) class settlement. Fed. R. Civ. P. 23(c)(2)(B). "Under Rule 23(c)(2)(B), '[t]he notice must clearly and concisely state in plain, easily understood language . . . the nature of the action,' 'the definition of the class certified,' 'the class claims, issues, or defenses,' and other items of information relating to opting out, making objections, and the consequences of the judgment." *In re Deepwater Horizon*, 739 F.3d 790, 819 (5th Cir. 2014). It is not necessary for class members to "be made cognizant of every material fact that has taken place prior to the notice," however. *Id.* at 819.

To satisfy due process, the class notice must convey the required information "in objective, neutral terms, that, insofar as possible, may be understood by the average absentee class member." *Nissan*, 552 F.2d at 1104. "The usual rule is that a plaintiff must initially bear the cost of notice to the class" as part of "the ordinary burden of financing his own suit." *In re Nissan*, 552 F.2d at 1101.

For settlement classes, Rule 23(e) also provides that a court must "direct notice in a reasonable manner to all class members who would be bound by the proposal" before approving a settlement. Fed. R. Civ. P. 23(e)(1)(B); *see also In re Katrina Canal Breaches Litig.*, 628 F.3d 185, 197 (5th Cir. 2010).

A "court-approved settlement entered in a properly certified class action generally will bind an absent class member." *Claunch v. FIA Card Servs., N.A.*, 608 F. App'x 262, 263 (5th Cir. 2015) (per curiam) (unreported) (quotation omitted). "For absent class members to be bound, due process requires that they receive notice and an opportunity to participate in the litigation." *Id.* In *Claunch*, the Fifth Circuit held that individually mailed notice satisfied due process; it was not determinative that the class member said that he did not actually receive the mailing. *See id.* at 264.

In a Rule 23(b)(1)(B) class settlement, the Fifth Circuit has held that the settlement notice should "satisfy the broad reasonableness standards imposed by due process." *Katrina*

Canal Breaches, 628 F.3d at 197 (citation and internal quotation marks omitted). "Notice of a mandatory class settlement, which will deprive class members of their claims, therefore requires that class members be given information reasonably necessary for them to make a decision whether to object to the settlement." *Id.* This "knowledge critical to an informed decision" includes, for example, the risk that a class member may receive no direct distribution of funds and the facts about attorneys' fees. *See id.* at 197–99.

Practitioners should also consult local rules for provisions regarding class notice procedures. *See, e.g.*, Local Civil Rules of the United States District Court for the Northern District of Texas LR 23.3 (procedures for class notice responses).

8. SUBCLASSES

Rule 23 provides that "when appropriate, a class may be divided into subclasses that are each treated as a class under this rule." Fed. R. Civ. P. 23(c)(5). The Supreme Court has held that "it is not the District Court that is to bear the burden of constructing subclasses. That burden is upon the [plaintiff] and it is he who is required to submit proposals to the court." *U.S. Parole Comm'n v. Geraghty*, 445 U.S. 388, 408 (1980).

Each subclass must independently meet the requirements for certification. *Johnson v. Am. Credit Co. of Georgia*, 581 F.2d 526, 532 (5th Cir. 1978) ("A subclass then, must independently meet all of rule 23's requirements for maintenance of a class action."); *see also Elson*, 56 F.4th at 1007 (recognizing plaintiffs' "duty to show each subclass independently satisfied the Rule 23 requirements"); *M.D. ex rel. Stukenberg v. Perry*, 675 F.3d 832, 848 (5th Cir. 2012) (instructing that on remand, the district court should "perform a rigorous analysis regarding whether the class claims of each of the subclasses meet[] the requirements of Rule 23"). As the court explained in *Elson*, "'[s]ubclass' is not a magic word that remedies defects of predominance. The burden is on Plaintiffs to demonstrate to the district court how certain proposed subclasses would alleviate existing obstacles to certification." 56 F.4th at 1007–08 (citing *Allison*, 151 F.3d at 420 n.15, and *Spence*, 227 F.3d at 313).

The Fifth Circuit has observed that while "the creation of subclasses is sometimes necessary . . . to avoid a fundamental conflict" under Rule 23(a)(4), "there is no need to create subclasses to accommodate every instance of differently weighted interests." *In re Deepwater Horizon*, 739 F.3d 790, 813 (5th Cir. 2014) (internal quotation and footnote omitted) (holding that subclassing by geographic region was not required for class settlement of only federal claims).

Approving a Rule 23(b)(3) class certification in *Chavez II*, the Fifth Circuit remanded the case to the district court with instructions to consider trial administration, including possible Rule 23(c)(5) subclasses. 108 F.4th at 318–20 (observing that a "class may be divided into subclasses for adjudication of damages" but expressing no view on the "ultimate decision whether to divide this large, complex litigation into smaller, more manageable pieces").

9. OPT-OUTS

Members of a Rule 23(b)(3) class must be given the opportunity to opt out of a class action. The Fifth Circuit applies an abuse of discretion standard to review a "district court's determination of whether a member of a class action proposed for settlement . . . has opted out of that class." *In re Deepwater Horizon*, 819 F.3d 190, 195 (5th Cir. 2016). While not speaking definitively as to when a nonconforming attempt to opt out can be treated as effective, the Fifth Circuit has referenced cases where a "reasonableness" standard was applied. *Id.* at 196.

Deepwater Horizon held that the plaintiff had failed to opt out when his conduct was not an "informal but unequivocal expression of a desire to opt out" or "the submission of an imperfect opt out request," but more "resemble[d] an after-the-fact attempt to depict completely distinct litigation conduct in another sphere as expressing a desire to opt out." *Id.* at

197. In *Lester v. Wells Fargo Bank, N.A.*, the Fifth Circuit held that affidavits describing the mailing of an opt-out form were sufficient to preclude summary judgment when it was "difficult to imagine how" the plaintiff "could prove that she placed the opt-out form in the mail other than to swear that she did so." 805 F. App'x 288, 289–93 (5th Cir. 2020) (unpublished).

When a settlement class member has missed the deadline to opt out, the Fifth Circuit has reviewed the district court's denial of the untimely opt-out request for abuse of discretion, applying four factors for excusable neglect: "(1) why the movant missed the deadline; (2) the length of the delay; (3) prejudice; and (4) evidence of good faith." *In re Deepwater Horizon*, 988 F.3d 192, 200–01 (5th Cir. 2021) (per curiam) (footnote omitted) (rejecting argument that filing of individual complaint counted as implicit attempt to opt out and considering five-month delay after deadline prejudicial to settling defendant's finality interest).

The Fifth Circuit has described the practical incentives against opting out of class actions. "One reason that people choose not to opt out of class actions is that if they bring their own suits, they take on more risk. A plaintiff on his or her own must front the lawsuit's cost but will only possibly obtain relief." *In re Par.*, 81 F.4th at 414 n.8. "If he or she instead rides along in a class action, then his or her downside risk is mitigated by not having to front the cost." *Id.*

10. ABSENT CLASS MEMBERS

a. Communication with Absent Class Members

In *Gates v. Cook*, the Fifth Circuit reversed a district court's ban on contact between members of a prisoner settlement class and their proposed substitute counsel. 234 F.3d 221 (5th Cir. 2000). Although district courts in the Fifth Circuit "enjoy wide latitude" in managing class actions, the courts "must seek to avoid impinging on class members' constitutional rights" to "speech, association, and access to counsel of their choice." *Id.* at 227. "No-contact" orders therefore "must be based on a clear record and 'specific findings that reflect a weighing of the need for a limitation and the potential interference with the rights of the parties.'" *Id.* (citing *Gulf Oil Co. v. Bernard*, 452 U.S. 89, 101 (1981)). "A limiting order must be narrowly drawn to minimize prior restraints on speech, association, and inmates' rights to counsel." *Id.*

Applying the Supreme Court's decision in *Gulf Oil Co. v. Bernard*, 452 U.S. 89 (1981), district courts within the Fifth Circuit have recognized each side's right to communicate with putative class members and have required a clear record of abusive communications before restricting free speech rights. *See, e.g.*, *Lynch v. Tesla, Inc.*, No. 1:22-CV-00597-RP, 2022 WL 4295295, at *3–4 (W.D. Tex. Sept. 16, 2022) (ordering employer that had solicited misleading severance agreements from terminated employees to notify them of lawsuit's existence, but refusing to order cessation of all communications with terminated employees); *Matson v. NIBCO Inc.*, No. 5-19-CV-00717-RBF, 2021 WL 2374312, at *4–8 (W.D. Tex. June 10, 2021) (in settlement class, ordering curative notice, invalidating opt outs, and providing second opportunity to opt out when communications from counsel for objector and competing class action were found to have been misleading and coercive); *e.g.*, *Peralez v. Express Drilling Fluids Inc.*, No. 2:18-CV-00032, 2018 WL 2985884, at *6 (S.D. Tex. Apr. 10, 2018) (denying protective order that would have restricted FLSA defendants' speech when plaintiffs alleged retaliatory firing but did not allege that defendants had contacted any plaintiff or potential plaintiff about lawsuit); *Richard v. Flowers Baking Co.*, No. 6:15-CV-02557, 2016 WL 3039714, at *2–3 (W.D. La. May 24, 2016) (allowing FLSA defendant to contact putative class members to request that they sign amended distributor agreement with arbitration clause but revising proposed wording of request); *McWilliams v. Advanced Recovery Sys., Inc.*, 176 F. Supp. 3d 635 (S.D. Miss. 2016) (prohibiting further communications from outside lawyers who had solicited members of certified class, ordering curative notice to class concerning that solicitation, and requiring soliciting lawyers to pay attorney's fees and costs incurred by both class and defense counsel); *Mejia v. Bros. Pe-*

troleum, L.L.C., No. 12-2842, 2015 WL 631346, at *3–4 (E.D. La. Feb. 13, 2015) (recognizing court's authority to limit defendant's *ex parte* contact with proposed or certified class members if contact would undermine purposes of Rule 23, but finding such an order not justified by evidence presented in that case); *Crutchfield v. Sewage & Water Bd. of New Orleans*, No. CV 13-4801, 2014 WL 12658406, at *4 (E.D. La. July 28, 2014) (permitting third party to contact putative class members with settlement offers, but requiring accompanying notice with specific content); *In re Katrina Canal Breaches Consol. Litig.*, No. CV 05-4182, 2008 WL 4401970, at *3, *5 (E.D. La. 2008) (requiring defendant and its investigators to provide specified information in their contacts with putative class members and to log such contacts). *See also Castaneda v. Empath, LLC*, No. CV 19-131-JWD-EWD, 2019 WL 2904311, at *2 (M.D. La. July 5, 2019) (collecting cases).

In *Lynch*, the district court employed a two-part test: "First, the court determines whether there is a need for a restriction on speech by evaluating whether the party's speech is misleading, coercive, or an attempt to undermine the collective action. Second, if such a need exists, the court tailors appropriate injunctions and sanctions in light of First Amendment concerns." 2022 WL 4295295, at *3.

Counsel considering communication with absent class members should also consult the applicable local rules for the district. *See, e.g.*, Local Civil Rules of the United States District Court for the Eastern District of Louisiana, LR 23.1(D) (providing procedures for motions to prohibit communications with class members and requiring attorneys to retain copies of all communications with the class).

Consideration should also be given to whether ethics rules that prohibit opposing counsel from communicating with represented parties may have any application in the circumstances of the case. *See Tellis v. LeBlanc*, No. 18-CV-0514, 2019 WL 1103420, at *1 (March 8, 2019) (prohibiting, under Rule 4.2 of the Louisiana Rules of Professional Conduct, defendants' communications with members of proposed inmate class who had a present attorney-client relationship with plaintiffs' counsel and ordering defense counsel to make certain disclosures before interviewing unrepresented members of proposed class due to coercive nature of prison environment).

b. Discovery Regarding Absent Class Members

Although absent class member discovery is not common, district courts within the Fifth Circuit have permitted it in appropriate circumstances. *See, e.g.*, *S. Ave. Partners LP v. Blasnik*, No. 3:09-CV-00765-M-BK, 2013 WL 11089796 (N.D. Tex. Sept. 19, 2013); *City of San Antonio, Texas v. Hotels.com, L.P.*, No. SA-06-CA-381-OG, 2008 WL 11334563 (W.D. Tex. Dec. 30, 2008); *Transamerican Ref. Corp. v. Dravo Corp.*, 139 F.R.D. 619 (S.D. Tex. 1991).

11. DAMAGES

a. Proof

The Fifth Circuit has applied the Supreme Court's *Comcast* decision to hold that "when plaintiffs argue that damages can be decided on a class-wide basis, plaintiffs must put forward a damages methodology that maps onto plaintiffs' liability theory." *Slade v. Progressive Sec. Ins. Co.*, 856 F.3d 408, 410–11 (5th Cir. 2017) (citing *Comcast Corp. v. Behrend*, 569 U.S. 27, 133 S. Ct. 1426 (2013)). That is, "what *Comcast* demands is [a] fit between plaintiffs' class-wide liability theory and plaintiffs' class-wide damages theory." *Id.* Therefore, "'a model purporting to serve as evidence of damages must measure only those damages attributable to the theory of liability on which the class action is premised.'" *Id.* at 411 (quoting *Deepwater Horizon*, 739 F.3d at 817) (holding that when "[p]laintiffs' damages theory aligns with [their] liability theory," their "damages methodology does not preclude class treatment"). *See also Chavez II*, 108 F.4th at 317–18 (approving "arithmetic, formulaic" method of proof when aligned with Supreme Court's admonition that model must measure only damages attributable to class theory) (citing *Comcast*, 569 U.S. at 35–37); *Prantil v. Arkema Inc.*, 986 F.3d 570, 578 (5th Cir. 2021) (vacating class certification and criticizing "figure-it-out-as-we-go-along" approach when district court had "acknowledged that Plaintiffs' mass appraisal approach to property damages was untenable after their expert was disqualified" but then "did not discuss how this difficulty might affect an eventual damages phase in the proceedings"); *Cruson v. Jackson Nat'l Life Ins. Co.*, 954 F.3d 240, 246 (5th Cir. 2020) (holding that the plaintiffs had "failed to offer a damages model adequate to support class treatment").

"Stated another way, the theory of damages 'must be consistent with [the] liability case, and the district court is required to 'conduct a rigorous analysis [at the class certification stage] to determine whether that is so.'" *Ludlow v. BP, P.L.C.*, 800 F.3d 674, 683 (5th Cir. 2015) (citing *Comcast*, 133 S. Ct. at 1433–34 and rejecting damages model in Rule 10b-5 case that was not "susceptible of measurement across the entire class for purposes of Rule 23(b)(3), as required by *Comcast*," *id.* at 689–90).

The Fifth Circuit has held that "compensatory damages for emotional distress and other forms of intangible injury will not be presumed from mere violation of constitutional or statutory rights." *Allison v. Citgo Petroleum Corp.*, 151 F.3d 402, 417 (5th Cir. 1998). "Specific individualized proof is necessary, and testimony from the plaintiff alone is not ordinarily sufficient." *Id.* "Compensatory damages may be awarded only if the plaintiff submits proof of actual injury, often in the form of psychological or medical evidence, or other corroborating testimony from a third party." *Id.* In *Allison*, the Fifth Circuit held that "the very nature of these damages . . . necessarily implicates the subjective differences of each plaintiff's circumstances; they are an individual, not class-wide, remedy." *Id.* Because the Fifth Circuit most often addresses class action damages in the context of the Rule 23(b)(3) predominance requirement, consult the Rule 23(b)(3) section above for additional discussion of damages issues.

12. SETTLEMENTS

a. Drafting Considerations

The Fifth Circuit permits a negotiated amount of attorneys' fees in a class settlement. *See Ayers v. Thompson*, 358 F.3d 356, 374–75 (5th Cir. 2004).

b. Preliminary Approval

The 2018 amendments to Rule 23(e) require that parties proposing a class settlement "provide the court with information sufficient to enable it to determine whether to give notice of the proposal to the class." Fed. R. Civ. P. 23(e)(1)(A). If the parties have shown that the court will likely be able to approve the settlement proposal and certify the settlement class, the court must then direct notice to all class members. *See id.* 23(e)(1)(B). These rule changes formalized the process for preliminary approval of a class settlement in federal court.

District courts within the Fifth Circuit—both before and after the rule changes—have considered motions for preliminary approval of a class settlement before they ordered class notice and set the fairness hearing for final approval of the settlement. *See, e.g.*, *In re Deepwater Horizon*, 739 F.3d 790, 796 (5th Cir. 2014), (reciting settlement-approval proceedings in district court); *Transamerica Ref. Corp. v. Dravo Corp.*, 952 F.2d 898, 899 (5th Cir. 1992) (same); *Hays v. Eaton Grp. Attorneys, LLC*, No. CV 17-88-JWD-RLB, 2019 WL 427331 (M.D. La. Feb. 4, 2019) (granting preliminary approval of settlement under amended Rule 23(e), ordering notice, scheduling final approval hearing, and setting dates for class members to opt-out, object, or return a claim form); *Gomez v. Niemann & Heyes, L.L.P.*, No. 1:16-CV-119, 2017 WL 1685022 (W.D. Tex. Jan. 25, 2017) (preliminary approval order); *Jones v. Singing River Health Sys.*, No. 1:14CV447-LG-RHW, 2016 WL 6106518, at *5 (S.D. Miss. Jan. 20, 2016) (recognizing preliminary approval as first step in review of class action settlement proposal, to be followed by final approval after fairness hearing); *Bach v. Amedisys, Inc.*, No. 3:10-cv-00395-BAJ-SCR, 2014 WL 12607789 (M.D. La. Apr. 14, 2014) (on motion for preliminary approval, considering the class settlement, whether to preliminarily certify class for settlement purposes, and whether settlement was sufficient to warrant issuance of class notice).

The Fifth Circuit has held that a district court did not abuse its discretion in denying preliminary settlement approval when the plaintiffs did not submit additional evidence to show that the settlement amount was adequate in light of a "$46.2 to $79.2 million gap between the settlement amount and the claimed losses." *Ortiz v. Am. Airlines, Inc.*, 5 F.4th 622, 631 (5th Cir. 2021) ("Before approving a settlement, a court 'must be assured that the settlement secures an adequate advantage for the class in return for the surrender of litigation rights against the defendants.'" (quoting *In re Katrina Canal Breaches Litig.*, 628 F.3d 185, 195 (5th Cir. 2010))).

c. Objectors

Rule 23(e)(5) provides that "[a]ny class member may object" to a proposed class settlement that requires court approval. Fed. R. Civ. P. 23(e)(5). Thus, "[a]ny class member has standing to object to a class settlement." *Union Asset Mgmt. Holding AG v. Dell, Inc.*, 669 F.3d 632, 638 (5th Cir. 2012). *Cf. Garcia v. Matson*, No. 21-51151, 2022 WL 6935303, at *2 (5th Cir. Oct. 12, 2022) (per curiam) (unpublished) (allowing objector's appeal of fairness and adequacy of class settlement fund but holding that issue of intra-class conflicts was waived when objector had not briefed on appeal district court's adverse standing ruling).

The 2018 amendments to Rule 23(e)(5) impose new requirements on objectors, however. They must obtain court approval of any payment made in connection with an objection. Fed. R. Civ. P. 23(e)(5)(B) and (C). And they must state their objections with specificity. Fed R. Civ. P. 23(e)(5)(A). Indeed, even before the 2018 amendments, the Fifth Circuit required an objection to a class settlement based on Constitutional grounds, such as lack of due process, to be specific or risk waiver. "Litigants must allege constitutional violations with factual detail and particularity." *Silvercreek Mgmt., Inc. v. Banc of America Sec., LLC*, 534 F.3d 469, 473 (5th Cir. 2008) (internal quotation marks omitted) (citing *Newby v. Enron Corp.*, 394 F.3d 296, 309 (5th Cir. 2004)).

A district court may require an objector to provide proof of class membership, such as "proof of residency, property ownership, or business operations." *See In re Deepwater Horizon*, 739 F.3d 790, 808–09 (5th Cir. 2014). Rule 23(d) authorizes such an instruction in the district court's preliminary approval order. *See id.* at 809 (recognizing proof-of-membership requirement as "legitimate exercise of [the court's] discretion under Rule 23(d)(1)(A) and Rule 23(d)(1)(C) to 'issue orders that[] . . . determine the course of proceedings' and 'impose conditions . . . on intervenors' in a class action"). Accordingly, the district court also has discretion to find that objectors who have failed to satisfy the court's instructions have "forfeited and waived their objections by disobeying the reasonable requirements of the Preliminary Approval Order." *Id.* (holding timely but incomplete objections were waived). *See also Feder v. Elec. Data Sys. Corp.*, 248 F. App'x 579, 580–81 (5th Cir. 2007) (per curiam) (unpublished).

The Fifth Circuit has overturned a district court's requirement that a class settlement objector post a $150,000 cost bond on appeal. *See Vaughn v. Am. Honda Motor Co.*, 507 F.3d 295 (5th Cir. 2007) (reducing the amount of the bond to $1,000).

The Fifth Circuit has held that an objector's appeal of a class settlement in bankruptcy was mooted when the objector appealed only the settlement approval order and did not appeal a subsequent bankruptcy confirmation order that incorporated and implemented the class settlement. *Matter of Life Partners, Inc.*, 708 F. App'x 831 (5th Cir. 2017) (per curiam) (unpublished).

Non-settling defendants lack standing to object to final approval of a class settlement unless they are prejudiced by it, such as when the settlement purports to strip them of rights to contribution or indemnity. *See, e.g.*, *In re Beef Indus. Antitrust Litig.*, 607 F.2d 167, 172–73 (5th Cir. 1979); *Transamerican Ref. Corp. v. Dravo Corp.*, 952 F.2d 898, 899 (5th Cir. 1992).

The Fifth Circuit applied the Rule 24(a) standard for intervention as of right when it permitted the state of Texas to intervene post-judgment in a class action to challenge a distribution of settlement funds that the state sought as unclaimed or abandoned property. *See In re Lease Oil Antitrust Litig.*, 570 F.3d 244 (5th Cir. 2009).

The Fifth Circuit has held that a court lacked jurisdiction to approve a post-bankruptcy class settlement of claims not preserved by proof of claim in bankruptcy. *Matter of Chesapeake Energy Corp.*, 70 F.4th 273, 281–83 (5th Cir. 2023) (vacating court-approved class settlement and remanding with instructions to dismiss for lack of jurisdiction).

d. Final Approval Factors

"Through the procedural mechanism of a class settlement, defendants are entitled to settle claims pending against them on a class-wide basis, even if a court believes those claims may be meritless, provided that the class is properly certified under Rules 23(a) and (b) and the settlement is fair under Rule 23(e)." *In re Deepwater Horizon*, 739 F.3d 790, 807 (5th Cir. 2014) (quotation marks omitted). *See also* Fed. R. Civ. P. 23, Advisory Committee notes to 2018 amendment (Court must evaluate class settlement proposal for fairness and also determine "whether it can certify the class under the standards of Rule 23(a) and (b) for purposes of judgment based on the proposal."). Under the 2018 amendments to Rule 23(e), the settling parties must also identify "any agreement" made in connection with their proposed settlement. Fed. R. Civ. P. 23(e)(3).

Rule 23(e) requires all class settlements to be "'fair, reasonable, and adequate,'" *id.* at 820 (quoting Fed. R. Civ. P. 23(e)), to "protect the nonparty members of the class," *id.* "By entering into class-wide settlements, defendants obtain releases from all those who might wish to assert claims, meritorious or not." *Deepwater Horizon*, 739 F.3d at 807 (quotation marks omitted). "[A] settlement can be approved despite opposition from class members, including named plaintiffs," however. *Ayers v. Thompson*, 358 F.3d 356, 373 (5th Cir. 2004) (citations omitted).

Rule 23(e) permits the court to approve a class settlement only after considering a list of core concerns:

> (A) the class representatives and class counsel have adequately represented the class;
> (B) the proposal was negotiated at arm's length;
> (C) the relief provided for the class is adequate, taking into account:
>   (i) the costs, risks, and delay of trial and appeal;
>   (ii) the effectiveness of any proposed method of distributing relief to the class, including the method of processing class-member claims;
>   (iii) the terms of any proposed award of attorney's fees, including timing of payment; and
>   (iv) any agreement required to be identified under Rule 23(e)(3); and
> (D) the proposal treats class members equitably relative to each other.

Fed. R. Civ. P. 23(e)(2).

This list of considerations was added to Rule 23(e) effective December 2018. Previously, the Fifth Circuit had applied the six factors set forth in the Court's 1983 *Reed v. Gen. Motors Corp.* decision:

- the existence of fraud or collusion behind the settlement;
- the complexity, expense, and likely duration of the litigation;
- the stage of the proceedings and the amount of discovery completed;
- the probability of plaintiffs' success on the merits;
- the range of possible recovery; and
- the opinions of the class counsel, class representatives, and absent class members.

See Reed v. Gen. Motors Corp., 703 F.2d 170, 172 (5th Cir. 1983); *Union Asset Mgmt. Holding AG v. Dell, Inc.*, 669 F.3d 632, 639 (5th Cir. 2012).

The final approval considerations now listed in Rule 23(e)(2) are similar, but not identical, to the *Reed* factors. The Fifth Circuit has not yet spoken definitively as to how much of the *Reed* analysis survives or how the Rule 23(e) considerations affect the fairness analysis, but the Fifth Circuit has approved a district court's analysis that engaged with both sets of factors. *See Garcia*, 2022 WL 6935303, at *3 (under "highly deferential" standard of review, seeing no abuse of discretion in "well-reasoned analysis" of adequacy of settlement fund). And district courts in the Fifth Circuit have continued to take into account both the Rule 23(e) considerations and the *Reed* factors. *See, e.g.*, *Armstrong v. Kimberly-Clark Corp.*, No. 3:20-CV-3150-M, 2024 WL 1123034, at *4 (N.D. Tex. Mar. 14, 2024) (using Rule 23(e)(2) and *Reed* factors to "support a conclusion that the Settlement is fair, reasonable, and adequate"); *Celeste Neely*, No. 4:21-CV-307-SDJ, 2022 WL 17736350, at *3 (E.D. Tex. Dec. 16, 2022) ("In addition to the nonexclusive Rule 23 factors, courts in this circuit often consider the *Reed* factors in evaluating the fairness, reasonableness, and adequacy of a proposed class settlement."); *Kostka v. Dickey's Barbecue Restaurants, Inc.*, No. 3:20-CV-03424-K, 2022 WL 16821685, at *10 (N.D. Tex. Oct. 14, 2022), *report and recommendation adopted*, No. 3:20-CV-03424-K, 2022 WL 16821665 (N.D. Tex. Nov. 8, 2022) (considering "Rule 23 requirements as informed by the *Reed* factors"); *Matson v. NIBCO Inc.,* No. 5-19-CV-00717-RBF, 2021 WL 4895915, at *9 (W.D. Tex. Oct. 20, 2021), *affirmed sub nom. Garcia v. Matson*, 2022 WL 6935303 (combining Rule 23 and *Reed* factors because they "overlap"); *In re Chinese-Manufactured Drywall Prod. Liab. Litig.*, 424 F. Supp. 3d 456, 485 (E.D. La. 2020) ("[T]he Court will consider the Rule 23 requirements as informed by the *Reed* factors."); *Hays*, 2019 WL 427331 at *9 (preliminary approval of class settlement combining Rule 23(e) considerations and *Reed* factors, recognizing "overlap" between the two sets of factors); *Al's Pals Pet Care v. Woodforest Nat'l Bank*, No. 4:17-CV-3852, 2019 WL 387409 at *3 (S.D. Tex. Jan. 30, 2019) (granting final approval of class settlement after considering Rule 23(e)(2) criteria as well as "*Reed* factors"). *See* Fed. R. Civ. P. 23, Advisory Committee notes to 2018 amendment, ¶¶ 18-20 (While goal of 2018 amendment is "not to displace any factor" previously generated by the different circuits, new list focuses "on the core concerns of procedure and substance that should guide" the approval decision, and amendment "directs the parties to present the settlement to the court in terms of a shorter list of core concerns.").

A settlement should not be "the product of collusion between the parties." *Deepwater Horizon*, 739 F.3d at 820 (quoting *Newby v. Enron Corp.*, 394 F.3d 296, 301 (5th Cir. 2004). Under the *Reed* factors, "[a]bsent a showing of fraud or collusion, the most important factor [was] the probability of the plaintiffs' success on the merits." *Smith v. Crystian*, 91 F. App'x 952, 955 n.3 (5th Cir. 2004) (per curiam) (unpublished) (citation omitted). "[E]ven if the monetary and compensatory relief provided by the settlement [was] not comparable to the relief provided in other cases," a settlement could be approved when the amounts of those other awards were "discounted by the probability" of a loss, such as might result from a statute-of-limitations bar. *See id.* at 955. *See also Garcia*, 2022 WL 6935303, at *3 (affirming class settlement that met or exceeded settlement achieved in similar class action after five more years of litigation, that paid same percentage of losses to different types of class members, that did not pay attorney's fees out of settlement fund, that allowed opt outs, and that made limited warranty program available to class separate from settlement fund).

Applying the third *Reed* factor—the stage of proceedings and amount of discovery completed—the Fifth Circuit has approved a class settlement reached without formal discovery in a securities case when "class counsel had conducted informal discovery by hiring private investigators and experts" and the parties were well informed about the merits.
See Dell, 669 F.3d at 639.

Objectors "have a right to be heard" at a fairness hearing on a proposed class settlement, *id.*, *see also* Rule 23(e)(2), but the Fifth Circuit has admonished that the required hearing "is not a full trial." *Id.* 669 F.3d at 641. "The court does not need to open to question and debate every provision of the proposed compromise;" it may limit the hearing "to whatever is necessary to aid it in reaching an informed, just and reasoned decision." *Id.* at 641 (internal quotation marks and citation omitted) (holding three-hour hearing with argument and cross-examination was sufficient). Moreover, "a district court is not required to hold a hearing on . . . attorneys' fees in a class action." *Id.* at 642.

The Fifth Circuit "reviews the approval of a class-action settlement agreement for abuse of discretion." *Id.* at 638. In an unpublished opinion, the Fifth Circuit has doubted whether a class settlement proposal, once denied, "may ever be resurrected on appeal," but in any event found no reversible error in the district court's denial of a proposed class settlement. *Bates v. Ford Motor Co.*, 174 F.3d 198 (5th Cir. 1999) (per curiam) (unpublished).

The Fifth Circuit has rejected the argument that a receivership settlement involving a large sum of money to be distributed to investor claimants was an "illicit" or "de facto" class settlement subject to Rule 23. *Zacarias v. Stanford Int'l Bank, Ltd.*, 945 F.3d 883, 903–04 (5th Cir. 2019), *cert. denied sub nom. Rupert v. Janvey,* 141 S. Ct. 950, 208 L. Ed. 2d 492 (2020), and *cert. denied sub nom. Zacarias v. Janvey*, 141 S. Ct. 952, 208 L. Ed. 2d 492 (2020) (noting "kinship" at high level between receivership and investor class action in that "both offer . . . litigation in an aggregative form").

e. *Cy Pres*

The Fifth Circuit has explained some courts' use of *cy pres* distributions to dispose of unclaimed class action settlement funds: "When modern large-scale class actions are resolved via settlement, money often remains in the settlement fund even after initial distributions to class members have been made because some class members either cannot be located or decline to file a claim." *Klier v. Elf Atochem N. Am., Inc.*, 658 F.3d 468, 473 (5th Cir. 2011). "Federal district courts often dispose of these unclaimed funds by making what are known as *cy pres* distributions." *Id. Cy pres* is an "equitable doctrine that has been imported into the class-action context from the field of trust law." *Id.* In a class action, *cy pres* "is . . . a way for a court to put any unclaimed settlement funds to their next best compensation use, e.g., for the aggregate, indirect, prospective benefit of the class." *Id.* at 474 (internal quotation marks and footnote omitted).

In *Klier*, the Fifth Circuit disapproved a district court's *cy pres* distribution as contrary to the terms of the settlement agreement. The class settlement "did not authorize the district court to make a charitable gift of the unused . . . funds." *Id.* at 478. Instead, the Fifth Circuit read the settlement to require the district court to reallocate settlement funds, which had not been used by one subclass, to the members of another subclass—so long as further class member distributions were feasible and equitable. *See id.* at 477, 479.

In reaching this result, the Fifth Circuit recognized two core principles that limit the application of *cy pres* in class actions: First, Rule 23—a procedural rule that cannot change the substantive law—"must be applied with the interests of absent class members in close view." *Id.* at 474. Second, the property interests generated by a class settlement, like other property rights, are constitutionally protected. *Id.* at 474. From these two principles, the *Klier* court derived the rule that "a *cy pres* distribution to a third party of unclaimed settlement funds is permissible 'only when it is not feasible to make further distributions to class members.'" *Id.* at 475 (citation and footnote omitted). "Where it is still logistically feasible and economically viable to make additional pro rata distributions to class members, the district court should do so, except where an additional distribution would provide a windfall to class members with liquidated-damages claims that were 100 percent satisfied by the initial distribution." *Id.* (footnote omitted).

The *Klier* opinion also rejected the idea that unused funds belonging to the class under the settlement agreement can constitute "unclaimed or abandoned property available to be claimed by the state or others via escheat or otherwise." *See Klier*, 658 F.3d at 479, n.31. In an earlier decision, *All Plaintiffs v. All Defendants*, the Fifth Circuit had vacated a *cy pres* distribution when the state of Texas claimed custody of uncashed settlement checks. *See* 645

F.3d 329 (5th Cir. 2011). It is doubtful, however, whether the Fifth Circuit's rationale in *All Plaintiffs* survived the Texas Supreme Court's contrary decision in *Highland Homes Ltd. v. State*, 448 S.W.3d 403 (Tex. 2014).

Klier also determined that when a district court "resort[s] to the *cy pres* doctrine for the distribution of unclaimed class-action settlement funds," its ruling is reviewed for an abuse of discretion. *See Klier*, 658 F.3d at 474. But the district court's interpretation of whether and how an unambiguous settlement agreement provides for allocation of unclaimed funds is reviewed de novo. *See id.*

The concurring opinion in *Klier* expressed severe reservations about the use of *cy pres* in any class action and counseled against it. Pointing out that the *Klier* defendant had waived any claim to the unused settlement funds in that case, the concurrence suggested that "if the defendant had not waived its right to request a refund, it would have been entitled to the excess." 658 F.3d at 480 (Jones, C.J., concurring). Because the concurrence viewed the use of *cy pres* in class actions as "inherently dubious," and perhaps a violation of the Constitution or the Rules Enabling Act, it warned that district courts should not award surplus settlement funds to charities: "The preferable alternative . . . is to return any excess funds to the defendant." *Id.* at 480–82 (Jones, C.J., concurring).

Relying on the *Klier* concurrence, the Fifth Circuit has criticized a district court's order placing contempt fines and attorney's fees in trust for foster children as "reminiscent of the invocation of *cy pres* in the class action settlement context," observing that such arrangements "raise constitutional concerns because they transform the judicial process from a bilateral private rights adjudicatory model into a trilateral process." *M. D. by Stukenberg v. Abbott*, 119 F.4th 373, 383 (5th Cir. 2024) (cleaned up) (quoting *Klier*, 658 F.3d at 481 (Jones, C.J., concurring)) (dictum).

After granting certiorari in a Ninth Circuit case to review whether a *cy pres* settlement was fair, reasonable, and adequate, the United States Supreme Court ultimately did not reach the *cy pres* question, instead vacating and remanding the case for further proceedings on standing. *Frank v. Gaos*, 586 U.S. 485 (2019). Justice Thomas, in dissent, would have reached the merits and reversed the *cy pres* class settlement. *Id.* at 494–95 (Thomas, J., dissenting).

Assuming that a *cy pres* distribution is permissible and feasible, a settlement class notice must clearly inform class members if there is a real possibility of a *cy pres* distribution "in lieu of any direct distribution of funds to the class members." *In re Katrina Canal Breaches Litig.*, 628 F.3d 185, 197–98 (5th Cir. 2010) (holding settlement notice "hinting" about *cy pres* to be inadequate when possibility of *cy pres* distribution was "a key aspect of the settlement that might have led more members to object").

f. Interpretation of Class Settlement Agreements

"A district court's interpretation of a settlement agreement is a question of law, which [the Fifth Circuit] review[s] de novo." *In re Deepwater Horizon*, 732 F.3d 326, 332 (5th Cir. 2013); *see also Klier*, 658 F.3d at 474 (reviewing de novo district court's interpretation of "unambiguous settlement agreement"). "The terms of the settlement agreement are always to be given controlling effect." *Id.* at 476 (footnote omitted). "Because the district court's authority to administer a class action settlement derives from Rule 23, the court cannot modify the bargained-for terms of the settlement agreement." *Id.* at 475 (footnote omitted). And "while the settlement agreement must gain the approval of the district judge, once approved its terms must be followed by the court and the parties alike." *Id.* (footnote omitted). Where a settlement provision "is ambiguous, such that its construction turns on a consideration of extrinsic evidence," the Fifth Circuit reviews the district court's interpretation for "clear error." *In re Deepwater Horizon*, 858 F.3d 298, 302 (5th Cir. 2017).

In *Deepwater Horizon*, the settlement provided for a court-supervised settlement program to resolve class members' claims, with several layers of potential appeals: Denials by claims administrators were appealable to appeals panels, followed by discretionary review by the district court. *See In re Deepwater Horizon*, 785 F.3d 986 (5th Cir. 2015). Within this settlement structure—which has become the subject of numerous appellate decisions—the Fifth Circuit has reviewed the district court's denial of discretionary review for abuse of discretion, asking "whether the decision not reviewed . . . actually contradicted or misapplied the Settlement Agreement, or had the clear potential to contradict or misapply" it. *See, e.g., Claimant ID 100250022 v. B.P. Expl. & Prod., Inc.*, 847 F.3d 167, 169 (5th Cir. 2017) (citing *Holmes Motors, Inc. v. BP Expl. & Prod., Inc.*, 829 F.3d 313, 315 (5th Cir. 2016)).

When the appeal involves purely legal questions of contract interpretation, however, even an abuse-of-discretion review is "effectively de novo," because "a district court by definition abuses its discretion when it makes an error of law." *In re Deepwater Horizon*, 785 F.3d 1003, 1011 (5th Cir. 2015) (internal quotation marks and citations omitted). *See generally In re Deepwater Horizon*, 928 F.3d 394, 397 (5th Cir. 2019) (observing that disputes over class settlement agreement's "seemingly simple formula" for calculating business economic loss "have generated an entire body of federal common law in this Circuit").

The Fifth Circuit has "acknowledged that a district court has inherent power to recognize . . . and when necessary enforce settlement agreements reached by the parties," including the power to conduct an independent investigation to determine whether the court has been the victim of fraudulent claims. *In re Deepwater Horizon*, 643 F. App'x 377, 380 (5th Cir. 2016) (per curiam) (unpublished) (internal quotation marks and citation omitted). The Fifth Circuit reviews the district court's exercise of this inherent power for abuse of discretion. *See id.* (holding, in context of court-supervised settlement program, that district court did not abuse its discretion in finding fraud in claims submission and ordering restitution of settlement funds previously paid out, *id.* at 381).

When a class settlement expressly waives the right to appeal determinations made by the district court in a settlement program, the Fifth Circuit has enforced that waiver. *See In re Chinese-Manufactured Drywall Prod. Liab. Litig.*, 959 F.3d 658, 659 (5th Cir. 2020) (per curiam) (dismissing appeal when settlement agreement explicitly waived appellate rights by providing that MDL court's determination of any dispute under settlement agreement "shall be final with no appeal"); *In re Chinese-Manufactured Drywall Prod. Liab. Litig.*, 794 F. App'x 387, 389 (5th Cir 2019) (per curiam) (unpublished) (same); *In re Chinese-Manufactured Drywall Prods. Litig.*, 16 F.4th 1181, 1183–86 (5th Cir. 2021) (enforcing class settlement's waiver of appeal rights beyond district court for settlement-administrator decisions, explaining that "forgoing the chance at error correction in this court is the tradeoff for the finality, expedience, and perhaps larger overall settlement that the appeal waiver achieved").

13. FEES AND COSTS

"In a class action settlement, the district court has an independent duty . . . to the class and to the public to ensure that attorneys' fees are reasonable and divided up fairly among plaintiffs' counsel." *In re High Sulfur Content Gas. Prods. Liab. Litig.*, 517 F.3d 220, 227–28 (5th Cir. 2008). This is true even when the settlement creates a separate fund to pay attorneys' fees. *See id.* The court's "close scrutiny" of fee awards protects the absent class members from "unjust or unfair settlements;" minimize[s] conflicts "between the attorney and the class, between the named plaintiffs and the absentees and between various subclasses;" and "guards against the public perception that attorneys exploit the class action device to obtain large fees at the expense of the class." *Id.* at 228 (quotations omitted). "To fulfill its duty, the district court must not cursorily approve the attorneys' fee provision of a class action settlement or delegate that duty to the parties." *Id.* at 228 (internal quotation omitted). "[T]he district court's responsibility to address attorneys' fees is [not] circumscribed when the parties agree to the amount of fees." *Strong v. BellSouth Telecomms., Inc.*, 137 F.3d 844, 849 (5th Cir. 1998). "[T]hat the defendant will pay the attorneys' fees from its own funds likewise does not limit the court's obligation to review the reasonableness of the agreed-to fees." *Id.*

The district court's award or denial of attorneys' fees is reviewed for abuse of discretion. *See id.* at 850. The court's findings of fact supporting the award are reviewed for clear error. *See id.*

Regarding the timing of attorney fee motions in class actions, Rule 23(h), which requires them to be filed "'at a time the court sets,'" trumps Rule 54 to the extent inconsistent. *See Morrow v. Baker*, No. 21-40922, at *4 (5th Cir. Feb. 15, 2023) (per curiam) (unpublished) (quoting Rule 23(h)), *on remand, Morrow v. Washington*, No. 2:08-CV-00288-JRG, 2023 WL 5435610 (E.D. Tex. Aug. 23, 2023), *appeal pending after remand sub nom. Morrow v. Jones*. "Under Rule 23(h), parties must file motions for attorneys' fees before the deadline to object to the settlement." *Clearman v. Kochanowski*, No. 21-20518, 2022 WL 2163781, at *2 (5th Cir. June 15, 2022) (per curiam) (unpublished).

The district court's duty of active judicial oversight over class actions extends to fee awards, which "'are a powerful influence on the way attorneys initiate, develop, and conclude class actions.'" *See Morrow*, 2023 WL 2009926, at *5 (quoting Rule 23 advisory committee's notes to 2003 amendment). "Consequently, '[a]ctive judicial involvement in measuring fee awards is singularly important to the proper operation of the class-action process'; therefore, 'the district court must ensure that the amount and mode of payment of attorney fees are fair and proper.'" *Id.* (quoting advisory committee notes). In the appeal pending after remand in *Morrow*, the Fifth Circuit has ordered briefing on the question whether class members who have no direct financial interest in the size of an attorney fee award lack Article III standing to appeal the fee award, leaving only class counsel with standing to appeal it. *See Morrow v. Jones*, No. 23-40546 (5th Cir., appeal docketed Sept. 22, 2023) (Court Directive issued July 12, 2024, ECF No. 94).

The Fifth Circuit uses the "lodestar method" to assess attorneys' fees in class action suits. *Strong*, 137 F.3d at 850. "The district court must first determine the reasonable number of hours expended on the litigation and the reasonable hourly rate for the participating attorney." *Id.* "The lodestar is then computed by multiplying the number of hours reasonably expended by the reasonable hourly rate." *Id.* "The district court may adjust the lodestar upward or downward" after a review of 12 factors. *Id.*

These factors, set out in the Fifth Circuit's decision in *Johnson v. Georgia Highway Express, Inc.*, are (1) the time and labor required, (2) the novelty and difficulty of the questions, (3) the skill requisite to perform the legal service properly, (4) the preclusion of other employment by the attorney due to acceptance of the case, (5) the customary fee, (6) whether the fee is fixed or contingent, (7) time limitations imposed by the client or the circumstance, (8) the amount involved and the results obtained, (9) the experience, reputation, and ability of the attorneys, (10) the "undesirability" of the case, (11) the nature and length of the professional relationship with the client and (12) awards in similar cases. 488 F.2d 714, 717–19 (5th Cir. 1974), abrogated by *Blanchard v. Bergeron*, 489 U.S. 87 (1989); *see also Union Asset Mgmt. Holding A.G. v. Dell, Inc.*, 669 F.3d 632, 642 n.25 (5th Cir. 2012). Further, the district court must "explain how each of the *Johnson* factors affects its award." *High Sulfur*, 517 F.3d at 228.

The Fifth Circuit also has considered the effect of the Supreme Court's attorney fee decision in *Perdue v. Kenny A.* on some applications of the *Johnson* factors. In *Perdue*, a civil rights class action, the Supreme Court reversed a fee award of the lodestar amount plus a 75 percent enhancement. 559 U.S. 542 (2010). *Perdue* reaffirmed that under the federal fee-shifting statutes, courts can award an increase over lodestar for superior attorney performance "in extraordinary circumstances" but also emphasized the "strong presumption that the lodestar is sufficient." *Id.* at 546. Importantly, "factors subsumed in the lodestar calculation" cannot be used to increase an award above the lodestar. *Id.* To obtain such enhancement, the party seeking fees must "identify[] a factor that the lodestar does not adequately take into account" and "prov[e] with specificity that an enhanced fee is justified." *Id.*

Explaining these rulings in *Combs v. City of Huntington, Texas*, the Fifth Circuit extracted the following principles:

- "[T]he district court should begin by calculating the lodestar: the reasonable hours expended multiplied by a reasonable rate."
- "The district court may then determine whether any other considerations counsel in favor of enhancing or decreasing the lodestar."
- "In light of the 'strong presumption' that the lodestar represents a sufficient fee, enhancements must necessarily be rare."
- "[S]uperior results are relevant only to the extent it can be shown that they are the result of superior performance."
- "However, in considering whether to decrease the lodestar, the district court must consider the plaintiff's degree of success."
- "[I]n a private civil rights suit, a district court must consider any disparity between the amount of damages sought and the amount of damages awarded," but "there is no *per se* requirement of proportionality" between the two.

829 F.3d 388, 394–96 (5th Cir. 2016) (internal quotations, footnotes, and citations omitted) (concluding that the district court had not erred in *reducing* the plaintiff's attorney's fees *below* the lodestar, when she had succeeded on only one of her claims and received only a fraction of the damages she sought, *see id.* at 390). *See also Fessler v. Porcelana Corona De Mexico, S.A. DE C.V.*, 23 F.4th 408, 413 (5th Cir. 2022) (abuse of discretion when "district court failed to account for counsel's time spent on unsuccessful claims and failed to compare the relief sought to that actually awarded").

The Fifth Circuit also has approved the use of the "percentage method" to award attorneys' fees in a common-fund settlement—one where a settlement fund is to be allocated among the class members and their attorneys—so long as the percentage award is cross-checked with the *Johnson* factors to ensure that it is reasonable. *See Dell*, 669 F.3d 632, 642–44 (5th Cir. 2012) (affirming 18 percent attorneys fee award). In the percentage method, "the court awards fees as a reasonable percentage of the common fund." *Id.* at 642. "Part of the reason behind the near-universal adoption of the percentage method in securities cases is that the PSLRA contemplates such a calculation." *Id.* at 643 (footnote omitted). The percentage method also "brings certain advantages," the Fifth Circuit explained in *Dell*, when it "allows for easy computation, . . . aligns the interests of class counsel with those of class members, and . . . [is] the method . . . chose[n] in the [plaintiffs'] retainer agreement." *Id.*

The Fifth Circuit has set standards for how a district court should allocate fees among class counsel. *See Torres v. SGE Mgmt., L.L.C.*, 945 F.3d 347, 349 (5th Cir. 2019), (requiring application of *Johnson* factors to dispute over attorney fee allocation), *appeal after remand sub nom. Clearman v. Kochanowski*, No. 21-20518, 2022 WL 2163781, at *2 (5th Cir. June 15, 2022) (per curiam) (unpublished) (holding that attorney fee determination under Rule 23 is exclusive province of federal district court, not bound by "outside agreements and state court settlements"). *In re High Sulfur Content Gas Products Liability Litigation* vacated a fee allocation when the district court had accepted, without close scrutiny, the recommendation of a committee of class counsel who themselves had a financial interest in the fee awards. Identifying a series of errors in the district court's fee allocation process, the Fifth Circuit concluded that the district court's flawed procedures had violated basic standards of transparency and fairness. *See* 517 F.3d at 227; *see also id.* at 223–24, 230–35.

Specifically, the district court should not have sealed the record "to discourage internecine fee sharing disputes among the plaintiffs' lawyers." *Id.* at 230. Nor should it have required immediate distribution of fee awards, thereby "discourag[ing] the court from trying to unscramble an unfair or erroneous initial allocation." *Id.* at 231. And although a hearing on attorneys' fees was not required, once the court decided to hold one, the hearing should not have been *ex parte*: Any hearing had to be fair and comport with the due process requirements of notice and an opportunity to be heard. *See id.* at 231. Finally, just as the court should not have imposed a gag order to prevent the attorneys from comparing their awards, the court should not have limited its own review to prevent comparisons of the various attorneys' contributions. *Id.* at 232.

14. APPELLATE ISSUES

a. Standing to Appeal

In *Devlin v. Scardelletti*, the Supreme Court held that an absent class member who has objected to settlement approval at the fairness hearing can appeal without first having formally intervened. 536 U.S. 1, 14 (2002) (holding that objector, who had no ability to opt out of the Rule 23(b)(1) settlement class, would otherwise be deprived of the power to protect his interest in a settlement that would ultimately bind him).

The Fifth Circuit has relied on *Devlin* to hold that "[a]ny class member has standing to object to a class settlement." *Union Asset Mgmt. Holding AG v. Dell, Inc.*, 669 F.3d 632, 638–39 (citing *Devlin v. Scardelletti*, 536 U.S. 1, 6–7 (2002)) (not requiring class member appellant to have filed proof of claim in order to have standing). A non-named class member can waive his right to appeal, however, "by filing an untimely, procedurally deficient objection" in the district court. *See Farber v. Crestwood Midstream Partners L.P.*, 863 F.3d 410, 417 (5th Cir. 2017). Normal waiver rules on appeal also apply. *See Garcia*, 2022 WL 6935303, at *2 (briefing waiver of district court's adverse standing ruling defeated intra-class conflict argument).

In a Rule 23(f) interlocutory appeal, the Fifth Circuit will consider whether the named plaintiff lacks Article III standing as part of the court's obligation to assure itself of its own jurisdiction. *See Perez v. McCreary, Veselka, Bragg & Allen, P.C.*, 45 F.4th 816, 822–23 (5th Cir. 2022).

In an appeal pending as of early 2025, the Fifth Circuit has ordered briefing on the question whether class members who have no direct financial interest in the size of an attorney fee award lack Article III standing to appeal the fee award, leaving only class counsel with standing to appeal it. *See Morrow v. Jones*, No. 23-40546 (5th Cir., appeal docketed Sept. 22, 2023) (Court Directive issued July 12, 2024, ECF No. 94).

b. Interlocutory Review

Under Rule 23(f), a court of appeals "may permit" an interlocutory appeal "from an order granting or denying class action certification." Fed. R. Civ. P. 23(f). A Rule 23(e)(1) order giving notice after preliminary approval, however, is not appealable. *See id.*

"[C]ourts of appeals wield unfettered discretion" to grant permission to appeal under Rule 23(f). *Microsoft Corp. v. Baker*, 582 U.S. 23, 31 (2017) (internal quotation marks and citations omitted). As the Supreme Court explained in *Microsoft*, the Federal Rules Advisory Committee has offered some guidance on when permission for an interlocutory appeal is most likely to be granted: "when the certification decision turns on a novel or unsettled question of law, or when the decision on certification is likely dispositive of the litigation, as in a death-knell or reverse death-knell situation." *Id.* at 32 (internal quotation marks and citation omitted). "Even so, the Rule allows courts of appeals to grant or deny review on the basis of *any* consideration." *Id.* at 32–33 (internal quotation marks omitted, citing Fed. R. Civ. P. 23, Advisory Committee's note to 1998 amendment). *See also Prantil v. Arkema Inc.*, 986 F.3d 570, 575 (5th Cir. 2021) (explaining that Rule 23(f) discretionary appeal "was a response to the determinative character of the certification decision" and the "need for developing a jurisprudence of federal class actions").

The Fifth Circuit likewise has not articulated standards under which it will grant a Rule 23(f) permission to appeal, although it has recognized the advisory committee guidance as observed with approval in *Baker*. *See Seeligson v. Devon Energy Prod. Co., L.P.*, 804 F.

App'x 304, 305 (5th Cir. 2020) (per curiam) (unpublished) ("Although courts of appeals possess 'unfettered discretion' to authorize the interlocutory appeal of a district court's class-certification order, that discretion is best exercised 'when the certification decision turns on a novel or unsettled question of law [or] is likely dispositive of the litigation.'" (citing *Microsoft*, 582 U.S. at 32, 137 S. Ct. at 1709–10 (2017) (quoting Fed. R. Civ. P. 23(f) Committee Note))). *See also Hernandez v. Abbott*, 733 F. App'x 212, 213 (5th Cir. 2018) (per curiam) (unpublished) ("This court has wide discretion under [Rule 23] to permit an appeal from an order denying class certification.").

A study of Rule 23(f) filings between 2006 and 2013 found that the Fifth Circuit was the Circuit most receptive to Rule 23(f) jurisdiction, granting 46.4 percent of the 23(f) petitions in the study period and an even greater percentage of defendants' petitions. The Fifth Circuit granted 69.2 percent of defendants' petitions and 28.6 percent of plaintiffs' petitions during the study period. *See* John H. Beisner, et al., *Study Reveals US Courts of Appeal Are Less Receptive to Reviewing Class Certification Rulings* (May 1, 2014), https://www.jdsupra.com/legalnews/study-reveals-us-courts-of-appeal-are-l-52418.

The Fifth Circuit has emphasized that Rule 23(f) limits interlocutory appeal to orders that either grant or deny class certification. *See, e.g.*, *Ludlow v. BP, P.L.C.*, 800 F.3d 674, 691–92 (5th Cir. 2015) ("[a]n order denying leave to file an amended motion for class certification does not fall into [that] narrow category"); *McNamara v. Felderhof*, 410 F.3d 277, 281 (5th Cir. 2005) (concluding that order reaffirming district court's prior ruling on class certification was not an order granting or denying class certification). Defendants can raise the issue of standing, "despite the limited nature of a Rule 23(f) appeal," however, because "[s]tanding is an inherent prerequisite" to every class certification. *See Bertulli v. Indep. Ass'n of Cont'l Pilots*, 242 F.3d 290, 294 (5th Cir. 2001). Moreover, the Fifth Circuit has recognized as proper a consolidated appeal of a class certification order and an order denying a motion to dismiss when the respective procedures under Rule 23(f) and 28 U.S.C. § 1292(b) have been followed and permission for both appeals granted. *Mitchell v. State Farm Fire & Cas. Co.*, 954 F.3d 700, 704 n.2 (5th Cir. 2020).

In *Microsoft*, the Supreme Court resolved the question whether plaintiffs, having been denied class certification, and having been denied permission to appeal under Rule 23(f), can nonetheless obtain immediate appeal by stipulating to a voluntary dismissal of their claims "with prejudice" while retaining the right to revive those claims upon reversal. They cannot. Such a "voluntary dismissal . . . does not qualify as a 'final decision'" under 28 U.S.C. § 1291. *See Microsoft*, 582 U.S. at 27.

In *Nutraceutical Corp. v. Lambert*, the Supreme Court held that the Rule 23(f) time limit for seeking permission to appeal (although not jurisdictional) is not subject to equitable tolling. 139 S. Ct. 710, 715 (2019). *See also M.D. ex. rel. Stukenberg v. Perry*, 547 F. App'x 543 (5th Cir. 2013) (per curiam) (unpublished) (Rule 23(f) time limit is strict and may not be extended). An untimely Rule 23(f) petition, however, does not preclude an appeal of the class certification order after final judgment. *M.D. by Stukenberg v. Abbott*, 907 F.3d 237, 248 n.15 (5th Cir. 2018) ("[B]ecause an interlocutory appeal is permissive rather than mandatory, the [defendant] retains the right to challenge the class certification following the ultimate disposition of the case on the merits.").

In deciding whether to stay district court proceedings while a Rule 23(f) appeal is pending, the Fifth Circuit considers four factors: "(1) whether the movant makes a strong showing that it is likely to succeed on the merits; (2) whether the movant will be irreparably injured without a stay; (3) whether other interested parties will be irreparably injured by a stay; and (4) where the public interest lies." *Earl v. Boeing Co.*, 21 F.4th 895, 898 (5th Cir. 2021) (citing *Nken v. Holder*, 556 U.S. 418, 426 (2009)) (staying discovery when pending appeal raised substantial question on Rule 23 predominance and all four factors favored stay).

Rule 23 arguments that are not adequately briefed on appeal are waived. *Id.* at 270–71.

15. TOLLING STATUTES OF LIMITATIONS

"Class action lawsuits, like any other lawsuit, are subject to statutes of limitation and repose that limit the time within which a suit must be brought." *Hall v. Variable Annuity Life Ins. Co.*, 727 F.3d 372, 375 (5th Cir. 2013).

But federal courts also recognize that the members of a proposed class should not have to file duplicative individual lawsuits to protect themselves in case the statute of limitations expires and class certification is later denied. Thus, seeking "to balance the competing interests of class action litigation (efficiency and economy)" with "those of statutes of limitation (protection against stale claims)," federal courts have developed a class action tolling jurisprudence. *See Odle v. Wal-Mart Stores, Inc.*, 747 F.3d 315, 320 (5th Cir. 2014); *Hall*, 727 F.3d at 375; *see generally Am. Pipe & Constr. Co. v. Utah*, 414 U.S. 538 (1974); *Crown, Cork & Seal Co. v. Parker*, 462 U.S. 345 (1983).

The resulting rule, sometimes called "*American Pipe* tolling" after the leading Supreme Court case, "is that the filing of a class action tolls the running of a statute of limitations for all asserted members of the class." *Odle*, 747 F.3d at 320 (internal quotation marks and citation omitted); *see also Zaragoza v. Union Pac. R.R. Co.*, 112 F.4th 313, 315 (5th Cir. 2024) ("American Pipe tolling equitably freezes the statute of limitations for all putative or certified class members during the pendency of a class action.").

In *Zaragoza*, the Fifth Circuit looked to the class definitions in a prior class action's operative complaint, and later in the prior class certification order, to determine that the plaintiff was first a putative and then a certified member of the prior class and therefore entitled to tolling. *Id.* at 315–16. "Prior to class certification, the pertinent class definition in a class action is drawn from the plaintiffs' operative complaint(s)." *Id.* at 319. Those pleaded class definitions are "not disturbed by precertification motions practice during the life cycle of a class action." *Id.* Once "a district court certifies a class, the certified class definition supersedes any previously articulated ones" and persists through appeal "until the class is decertified or the case is otherwise resolved." *Id.* Assessing the plaintiff's claims, the court concluded that the class definition certified by the prior court included the plaintiff, or at least did not unambiguously exclude him, and therefore his claims were tolled. *Id.* at 322.

Of course, the filing of a class action cannot resurrect claims that have already expired. *See Beavers v. Metro. Life Ins. Co.*, 566 F.3d 436, 441 (5th Cir. 2009). And *American Pipe* "tolling . . . does not continue indefinitely." *Odle*, 747 F.3d at 320. If the district court denies certification—or if it certifies the class but later decertifies it—tolling ceases, even though those rulings might potentially be reversed on appeal. *See id.*; *Hall*, 727 F.3d at 378.

When tolling has ceased, proposed class members must intervene or they must file individual lawsuits to protect themselves; even when the district court later certifies a class on remand after appeal, they cannot resurrect their time-barred claims. *See Salazar Calderon v. Presidio Valley Farmers Ass'n*, 863 F.2d 384, 390 (5th Cir. 1989) (per curiam); *Rotstain v. Mendez,* 986 F.3d 931, 937–38 (5th Cir. 2021) (assessing timeliness of intervention motion from date class certification was denied, when intervenors "knew or should have known that their interests were not protected by the existing parties"). *But see Odle*, 747 F.3d at 320 (holding that "tolling did not cease" upon remand by appellate court when remand instructions did not constitute a "final adverse determination").

Note that although a member of a class that has been *denied certification* cannot rely on tolling on appeal, a member of a *still-certified* class can rely on tolling on appeal of a *merits* dismissal. *See Taylor v. United Parcel Serv., Inc.*, 554 F.3d 510, 521 (5th Cir. 2008).

There are other important limits on *American Pipe* tolling. It does not apply to statutes of repose, as the Supreme Court held in *California Public Employees' Retirement System v. ANZ Securities, Inc.*, 582 U.S. 497, 510 (2017) ("[T]he object of a statute of repose, to grant complete peace to defendants, supersedes the application of a tolling rule based in equity," including *American Pipe* tolling.).

Resolving a circuit split in 2018, the Supreme Court sided with the Fifth Circuit and other circuits when it held that *American Pipe* tolling does not apply to successive class actions. Thus, upon denial of certification, a putative class member may not maintain "a follow-on class action past expiration of the statute of limitations." *China Agritech, Inc. v. Resh*, 584 U.S. 732, 736 (2018); *see also In re Chinese-Manufactured Drywall Prod. Liab. Litig.*, 854 F. App'x 570, 572 (5th Cir. 2021) (per curiam) (unpublished) (refusing to allow plaintiff to "piggyback on" earlier class action to avoid expiration of limitations); *Salazar-Calderon v. Presidio Valley Farmers Ass'n*, 765 F.2d 1334, 1351 (5th Cir. 1985) (refusing to allow putative class members to "piggyback one class action onto another and thus toll the statute of limitations indefinitely").

Another limitation is that *American Pipe* tolling applies in state courts only to the extent that the states have adopted it. Thus, state courts are free to apply their own tolling rules when they decide whether a federal class action has a tolling effect. *See Newby v. Enron*, 542 F.3d 463, 472 (5th Cir. 2008) (concluding that Texas courts likely will not allow a *federal* class action to toll a state statute of limitations).

And, finally, because federal courts in diversity actions "apply not only state statutes of limitation but also any accompanying tolling rules," the Fifth Circuit will not apply the federal *American Pipe* tolling rule in a diversity case when the governing state law would *not* toll limitations. *See Vaught v. Showa Denko K.K.*, 107 F.3d 1137, 1145 (5th Cir. 1997); *see also Weatherly v. Pershing, L.L.C.*, 945 F.3d 915, 918–25 (5th Cir. 2019) (holding that Florida does not recognize class action tolling when a Florida statute "laid out an exclusive list of tolling exceptions" and class actions were "not on the list," *id.* at 918); *Boone v. Citigroup, Inc.*, 416 F.3d 382, 393–94 (5th Cir. 2005) (holding that earlier class action in Arizona federal court did not toll limitations for Mississippi state law claims later asserted in another federal court).

16. ARBITRATION ISSUES

Under the Supreme Court's holding in *AT&T Mobility LLC v. Concepcion*, the Federal Arbitration Act preempts any state laws that require an arbitration agreement to make classwide arbitration available. *See* 563 U.S. 333, 352 (2011). The effect of *Concepcion* is to make class action waivers in arbitration agreements enforceable, even when state law would forbid such waivers.

In *Epic Systems Corp. v. Lewis*, the Supreme Court resolved a circuit split and sided with the Fifth Circuit, holding that arbitration agreements must be enforced as written, and nothing in the National Labor Relations Act displaces the Federal Arbitration Act. 584 U.S. 497 (2018), *affirming Murphy Oil USA, Inc. v. N.L.R.B.*, 808 F.3d 1013, 1016 (5th Cir. 2015). The Supreme Court's 2019 decision in *New Prime Inc. v. Oliveira* held that an independent-contractor interstate truck driver fell under an exception to court authority to order arbitration under the federal act. 586 U.S. 105, 121 (2019). The Fifth Circuit has applied the reasoning of that case, and the Supreme Court's later decision in *Southwest Airlines v. Saxon*, 596 U.S. 450, 456 (2022), to hold that local delivery drivers are not excepted from arbitration. *See Lopez v. Cintas Corp.*, 47 F.4th 428, 432 (5th Cir. 2022).

As for class arbitrability, the Fifth Circuit has held that it "is a gateway issue for courts, not arbitrators, to decide, absent clear and unmistakeable language to the contrary." *2020 Commc'ns Inc. v. Crawford*, 930 F.3d 715, 717 (5th Cir. 2019); *cf. Sun Coast Res., Inc. v. Conrad*, 956 F.3d 335, 338–39 (5th Cir. 2020) (issue of whether class arbitrability was for the court forfeited when party submitted arbitrability to the arbitrator and did not challenge arbitrator's authority to decide it in a timely fashion before the district court).

The Supreme Court has held that "[c]ourts may not infer from an ambiguous agreement that parties have consented to arbitrate on a classwide basis." *Lamps Plus, Inc. v. Varela*, 587 U.S. Ct. 176, 189 (2019). Nor may courts compel classwide arbitration when an agreement is silent on the availability of classwide arbitration. *Stolt-Nielsen S.1. v. Animal Feeds Int'l Corp.*, 559 U.S. 662, 675–76 (2010); *see also Lamps Plus*, 139 S. Ct. at 1412. Furthermore, the Fifth Circuit has observed that an arbitration clause requiring "an individual, one-on-one arbitration" rules out class actions, among other things. *See In re A&D Interests, Inc.*, 33 F.4th 254, 258 (5th Cir. 2022). The Fifth Circuit has distinguished *Lamps Plus*, however, when an unambiguous arbitration agreement unequivocally incorporated a mediation provider's rules, and those rules in turn used "clear and unmistakable" language to delegate the question of arbitrability to the arbitrator, not the court. *Work v. Intertek Res. Sols., Inc.*, 102 F.4th 769, 771–72 (5th Cir. 2024). When the mediation rules delegated questions of arbitrability to the arbitrator, that included whether class arbitration was available. *Id.* at 770.

The Fifth Circuit's analysis on whether a claim must be arbitrated is the subject of numerous recent opinions based on contract terms and other facts, legal theories, and procedural postures. *See, e.g., Newman v. Plains All Am. Pipeline, L.P.*, 23 F.4th 393 (5th Cir. 2022) ("[D]eciding an arbitration agreement's enforceability between parties remains a question for courts," because when "a court decides whether an arbitration agreement exists, it necessarily decides its enforceability between parties."), *rehearing and rehearing en banc denied*, 44 F.4th 251 (5th Cir. 2022) (Jones, J. dissenting from denial of en banc rehearing); *Bowles v. OneMain Fin. Group, L.L.C.*, 954 F.3d 722 (5th Cir. 2020) (applying test distinguishing between contract formation and enforcement). The Fifth Circuit case law, as well as the governing Supreme Court authorities, should be consulted. *See, e.g., Morgan v. Sundance, Inc.*, 596 U.S. 411, 418 (2022) (rejecting arbitration waiver test that required prejudice and ruling that court "must hold a party to its arbitration contract just as the court would to any other kind" but "may not devise novel rules to favor arbitration over litigation"); *Henry Schein, Inc. v. Archer and White Sales, Inc.*, 586 U.S. 63, 65 (2019) ("When the parties' contract delegates the arbitrability question to an arbitrator, the courts must respect the parties' decision as embodied in the contract.").

The Fifth Circuit has recognized that a defendant who did not sign a contract to arbitrate can nonetheless compel arbitration in a number of circumstances. State law governs such questions. *See, e.g., Hays v. HCA Holdings, Inc.*, 838 F.3d 605 (2016) (applying Texas law of "direct benefits estoppel" and "intertwined claims estoppel" to affirm order compelling arbitration); *Crawford Prof'l Drugs, Inc. v. CVS Caremark Corp.*, 748 F.3d 249 (5th Cir. 2014) (applying Arizona equitable estoppel law to affirm order compelling arbitration). *See also GE Energy Power Conversion France SAS, Corp. v. Outokumpu Stainless USA, LLC*, 140 S. Ct. 1637, 1643–48 (2020). *But see Newman v. Plains All Am. Pipeline, L.P.*, No. 21-51089, 2022 WL 1114407, at *1 (5th Cir. Apr. 14, 2022) (per curiam) (unpublished) ("[b]ecause the arbitration agreement that the Plaintiffs signed governs only employment disputes arising with" their employer, neither employer nor employer's client could force them to arbitrate claims brought against employer's client).

The Fifth Circuit also has applied state law to determine whether there was a meeting of the minds on an arbitration agreement, *see O'Shaughnessy v. Young Living Essential Oils, L.C.*, 810 F. App'x 308, 311–13 (5th Cir. 2020) (per curiam) (unpublished) (applying Utah law); to decide whether an arbitration agreement is unconscionable, *see Crawford*, 748 F.3d at 249 (applying Arizona law), or to decide questions of an agent's authority to agree to arbitration, *see Gross v. GGNSC Southaven, L.L.C.*, 817 F.3d 169 (5th Cir. 2016) (applying Mississippi law on actual and apparent authority).

When a defendant has waived an arbitration provision, the Fifth Circuit has held ineffective a class-action waiver found only within that arbitration provision, based on the wording and structure of the contract. *See Vine v. PLS Fin. Servs., Inc.*, 807 F. App'x 320, 328–29 (5th Cir. 2020) (per curiam) (unpublished) (holding most plausible interpretation of class-action waiver in middle of arbitration provision was as part of arbitration procedure, not as independent waiver of class action outside of arbitration, and noting contrast with jury-trial waiver in same contract).

A district court within the Fifth Circuit has given a defendant permission to contact proposed class members in an FLSA case to request them to sign an amended agreement that includes an arbitration clause. *See Richard v. Flowers Baking Co.*, No. 6:16-CV-02557 2016 WL 3039714 (W.D. La. May 24, 2016) (approving proposed notice with added language).

17. CLASS-SPECIFIC ETHICAL CONSIDERATIONS

The Fifth Circuit has held that class counsel's conduct may warrant substitution of counsel when the original counsel's resources are stretched too thin to actively litigate the class claims, when his dual representation of two classes has resulted in a conflict of interest that has impaired his advocacy, when he has failed to give the class adequate notice of a settlement and the opportunity to object to it, and when he has publicly disclosed confidential communications from a class member. *See Gates v. Cook*, 234 F.3d 221, 229–30 (5th Cir. 2000).

A district court within the Fifth Circuit has relied on a formal ABA ethics opinion for the proposition that "the Model Rules of Professional Conduct generally do not prohibit counsel for either plaintiff or defendant from communicating with putative class members," but has ordered a defendant and its investigators to provide certain specific information whenever they contact putative class members, to refrain from attempts at influencing class members, and to file court notices logging their future class member contacts. *See In re Katrina Canal Breaches Consol. Litig.*, No. 05-4182, 2008 WL 4401970, at *3, *5 (E.D. La. Sept. 22, 2008) (also requiring curative measures when defendant's investigators had removed clocks from homes of putative class members after Hurricane Katrina). *But see Tellis*, 2019 WL 1103420 at *1 (prohibiting, under Louisiana ethics rule, defendants' communications with certain members of proposed inmate class who had present attorney-client relationships with plaintiffs' counsel).

A district court within the Fifth Circuit has held that solicitations seeking to "raid a certified class" violated Rule 23 and ethics rules, justifying a protective order that imposed curative measures and attorneys' fees on the soliciting lawyers. *See McWilliams v. Advanced Recovery Systems, Inc.*, 176 F. Supp. 3d 635, 643–45 (S.D. Miss. 2016).

SIXTH CIRCUIT

Districts of Kentucky, Michigan, Ohio, and Tennessee

Potter Stewart U.S. Courthouse
100 East Fifth Street
Cincinnati, OH 45202

By James A. King and McDaniel M. Kelly
Porter, Wright, Morris & Arthur LLP

1. INTRODUCTION

The Sixth Circuit consists of the states of Kentucky, Michigan, Ohio, and Tennessee. Of the 16 active judges on the Sixth Circuit at the time of this printing, six are from Ohio, five are from Michigan, three hail from Tennessee, and two are from Kentucky. In addition, 14 senior judges regularly hear cases on appeal to reduce the workload of the active judges. They are assisted by district court judges sitting by designation.

The Sixth Circuit has issued a number of interesting decisions pertaining to class actions. For example, in *In re Whirlpool Corp. Front-Loading Washer Products Liability Litigation*, 678 F.3d 409 (6th Cir. 2012) (*Whirlpool I*), the Sixth Circuit considered whether consumers who purchased Whirlpool washing machines that developed mold and mildew that could not be easily corrected could establish a class. Judge Stranch, writing for the panel, held that a class could be established. The class, numbering in the thousands, was sufficiently numerous; questions of whether design defects in the washing machines proximately caused mold and mildew to grow and whether Whirlpool adequately warned consumers of this propensity were liability issues common to the plaintiff class; the named plaintiffs were typical of proposed class members, as they had purchased Whirlpool washing machines for domestic purposes and experienced problems with mold; common questions predominated over individual ones; and the class action mechanism was the superior method to resolve the claims.

The Supreme Court, however, granted certiorari, vacated the judgment, and remanded the case for further consideration in light of *Comcast Corp. v. Glazer*, 133 S. Ct. 1426 (2013). *Glazer* involved the certification of a liability and damages class under Rule 23(a) and (b)(3). The plaintiffs' expert had calculated damages for the class using a model that did not isolate the damages resulting from the one theory of antitrust impact that the district court had allowed to proceed. The Supreme Court reversed. Analyzing *Glazer* in *In re Whirlpool Corp. Front-Loading Washer Products Liability Litigation*, 722 F.3d 838, 851 (6th Cir. 2013) (*Whirlpool II*), the Sixth Circuit held that the case was different from the one at bar, because in *Whirlpool*, the district court certified only a liability class and reserved issues relating to damages. The court in *Whirlpool II* reached the same decision as in *Whirlpool I*.

The Sixth Circuit also recently had the opportunity to confront interesting questions regarding the "local controversy" exception to the Class Action Fairness Act (CAFA) as it relates to the Flint Water Crisis. In *Mason v. Lockwood, Andrews & Newnam, P.C.*, 842 F.3d 383 (6th Cir. 2016), the court held that remand of the action was appropriate under the local controversy exception where more than two-thirds of the proposed plaintiff class were citizens of the state of Michigan, rejecting arguments that much of the plaintiff class were not domiciled in Michigan and noting that the class consisted of property owners in Flint, Michigan, a "strong indicator of domicile." 842 F.3d at 395. In contrast, in *Davenport v. Lockwood, Andrews & Newnam, Inc.*, 854 F.3d 905 (6th Cir. 2017), the court found the local controversy exception inapplicable because pursuant to 28 U.S.C. § 1332(d)(4)(A)(ii), other similar class actions had been filed within the preceding three years.

In more recent years, the Sixth Circuit in *Nessel ex rel Michigan AmeriGas Partners, L.P.*, 954 F.3d 831 (6th Cir. 2020), held that a representative action brought in state court by the state attorney general against a propane distributor, alleging that the distributor's pricing practices violated several aspects of the Michigan Consumer Protection Act (MCPA), was not a "class action" within meaning of the Class Action Fairness Act (CAFA). The action was therefore not removable under CAFA, because the action was not brought under applicable federal class action law or any similar state statute or rule. The Michigan Attorney General had alleged that Section 10 of the MCPA authorized her to bring the action in state court, and AmeriGas subsequently removed the case to federal court. The district court, however, reasoned that because Section 10 of the MCPA did not meet the typicality, commonality, adequacy, and numerosity requirements needed to certify a class, the lawsuit did not qualify as a class action and remanded the action to state court. The Sixth Circuit affirmed, first determining that CAFA's definition of class action unambiguously required class actions to meet Rule 23 of the Federal Rules of Civil Procedure, or a similar state statute's standards. Section 10 did not function as a state equivalent to Rule 23 because, among other things, it did not require that the Attorney General be a member of the harmed class, which failed to meet the typicality requirement.

2. JURISDICTIONAL PREREQUISITES

a. CAFA Requirements

Congress enacted CAFA in 2005, "provid[ing] the federal district courts with 'original jurisdiction' to hear a 'class action' if the class has more than 100 members, the parties are minimally diverse, and the 'matter in controversy exceeds the sum or value of $5,000,000,'" aggregating the claims of individual members of the proposed class. *Standard Fire Ins. Co. v. Knowles*, 568 U.S. 558, 133 S. Ct. 1345, 1348 (2013) (quoting 28 U.S.C. § 1332(d)(2), (d)(5)(B)). "Among other things, CAFA amended the federal diversity statute to provide federal jurisdiction in class actions where the amount in controversy exceeds $5,000,000 and there is some diversity of the parties. The presence of such 'class-action diversity' may also be the basis for removing an action from state court to federal court." *In re UPS Supply Chain Sols., Inc.*, No. 08-0513, 2008 WL 4767817, at *1 (6th Cir. Oct. 27, 2008) (internal citations omitted).

Timing. In removing under CAFA, the defendant "has the burden of demonstrating, by a preponderance of the evidence, that the amount in controversy requirement has been met." *Smith v. Nationwide Prop. & Cas. Ins. Co.*, 505 F.3d 401, 404 (6th Cir. 2007) (internal quotation marks omitted). Defendants removing under CAFA must comply with the time limits of the general removal statute, 28 U.S.C. § 1446. The one-year deadline for removing cases under diversity jurisdiction, however, does not apply to cases removed under CAFA. *See* 28 U.S.C. § 1453. Under § 1446(b)(1), a defendant has 30 days to file a notice of removal "after the receipt by the defendant . . . of a copy of the initial pleading setting forth the claim for relief." However, "if the case stated by the initial pleading is not removable," § 1446(b)(3) provides that "a notice of removal may be filed within 30 days after receipt by the defendant, through service or otherwise, of a copy of an amended pleading, motion, order or other paper from which it may first be ascertained that the case is one which is or has become removable."

In *Graiser v. Visionworks of Am., Inc.*, 819 F.3d 277, 285 (6th Cir. 2016), the Sixth Circuit held that in CAFA cases, the 30-day clocks of § 1446(b) begin to run only when the defendant receives a document from the plaintiff from which the defendant can unambiguously ascertain CAFA jurisdiction. In that decision, the Sixth Circuit stated that "a defendant does have a duty to apply a reasonable amount of intelligence to its reading of a plaintiff's complaint or other document," but is "not required to search its own business records or perform an independent investigation into a plaintiff's indeterminate allegations to determine removability." *Id.* (internal quotation marks and emphasis omitted). Finally, the Sixth Circuit also held that "once a defendant ascertains that a case is removable under CAFA, a defendant may remove the case—within the time constraints of § 1446(b)(1) and (b)(3) discussed above—even if the case was originally removable under a different theory of federal jurisdiction." *Id.* at 287.

Exceptions. There are "home-state" and "local controversy" exceptions found in § 1332(d)(4). Those exceptions require a court to decline jurisdiction when "greater than two-thirds of the members of all proposed plaintiff classes in the aggregate are citizens of the State in which the action was originally filed" and certain other requirements are met or when "two-thirds or more of the members of all proposed plaintiff classes in the aggregate, and the primary defendants, are citizens of the State in which the action was originally filed." 28 U.S.C. § 1332(d)(4). The local controversy and home state exceptions do not deprive a court of jurisdiction, however; the statute speaks only of a district court's declining jurisdiction if the exceptions apply. *Clark v. Lender Processing Servs.*, 562 F. App'x 460, 465 (6th Cir. 2014).

Citizenship. Removal under CAFA allows for federal jurisdiction over "class actions on behalf of 100 or more people and in request of $5 million or more in damages so long as 'any member of a class of plaintiffs is a citizen of a State different from any defendant.'" 28 U.S.C. §§ 1332(d)(2)(A), (d)(5), (d)(6). In *Roberts v. Mars Petcare US, Inc.*, 874 F.3d 953 (6th Cir. 2017), the Sixth Circuit considered whether a court should take into account a corporation's citizenship based on place of incorporation *and* principal place of business when determining whether a class action should be removed to federal court under CAFA. The Sixth Circuit held that a corporation cannot just ignore one of its places of citizenship in order to have the litigation tried in another court. To do so would undo "decades of precedent by re-envisioning the core concept of corporate citizenship." *Id.* at 957. The plaintiff in *Roberts* filed the class action "on behalf of Tennessee citizens in Tennessee state court against Mars Petcare US, a citizen of Tennessee and Delaware," alleging violations of the Tennessee Trade Practices Act. *Id.* at 955. Mars Petcare US ("Mars") claimed that its Tennessee citizenship did not matter and removed the case to federal court, relying on its Delaware citizenship. *Id.* The Sixth Circuit held that Mars could not rely on its state of corporation while ignoring its principal place of business for diversity purposes. *Id.* Therefore, the Sixth Circuit reversed the district court's denial of the plaintiff's motion to remand to state court. *Id.*

Final considerations. In addition, the Sixth Circuit has held that CAFA does not authorize removal by an additional counterclaim defendant, *see In re Morgan & Pottinger, P.S.C.*, No. 10-0309, 2010 WL 9476582, at *1 (6th Cir. June 16, 2010) and that, although CAFA does not "specifically address whether a district court may retain jurisdiction following the denial of class certification . . . denial of class certification does not divest federal courts of jurisdiction." *Metz v. Unizan Bank*, 649 F.3d 492, 500 (6th Cir. 2011) (internal quotation marks omitted). "[A] contrary reading of CAFA would mean that a district court would be unable to revisit an order denying class certification because it would no longer have subject matter jurisdiction." *Id.* at 501.

b. Standing

Who May Bring a Class Action?

"The Article III standing requirements apply equally to class actions. The class representative must allege an individual, personal injury in order to seek relief on behalf of himself or any other member of the class." *Sutton v. St. Jude Med. S.C., Inc.*, 419 F.3d 568, 570 (6th Cir. 2005). The Sixth Circuit follows the Supreme Court's maxim that "[w]e have an obligation to assure ourselves of litigants' standing under Article III." *Fednav, Ltd. v. Chester*, 547 F.3d 607, 614 (6th Cir. 2008) (quoting *DaimlerChrysler Corp. v. Cuno*, 547 U.S. 332, 340 (2006) (internal quotation marks omitted).

Standing has three elements. "First, the plaintiff must have suffered an 'injury in fact'—an invasion of a legally protected interest which is (a) concrete and particularized, and (b) actual or imminent, not conjectural or hypothetical." *Lujan v. Defenders of Wildlife*, 504 U.S. 555, 560, (1992) (internal citations and quotation marks omitted). Second, the injury must be "fairly traceable to the challenged action of the defendant." *Id.* (internal alterations omitted). Third, it must be likely that the injury will be "redressed by a favorable decision." *Id.* at 561.

Potential class representatives must demonstrate "individual standing vis-a-vis the defendant; [they] cannot acquire such standing merely by virtue of bringing a class action." *Fallick v. Nationwide Mut. Ins. Co.*, 162 F.3d 410, 423 (6th Cir. 1998). Named plaintiffs cannot establish standing by relying on the injury of another. *Hadley v. Chrysler Grp., LLC*, 624 F. App'x 374, 378 n.5 (citing *Simon v. E. Ky. Welfare Rights Org.*, 426 U.S. 26, 40 n.20 (1976) ("That a suit may be a class action, however, adds nothing to the question of standing, for even named plaintiffs who represent a class must allege and show that they personally have been injured, not that an injury has been suffered by other, unidentified members of the class to which they belong and which they purport to represent.")). The fact that plaintiffs are no longer employees of the defendant has been held not to deprive them of standing to represent a class consisting of current and prospective employees. *Cross v. Nat'l Trust Life Ins. Co.*, 553 F.2d 1026, 1030–31 (6th Cir. 1977).

With respect to whether an injury is "actual or imminent," in a recent data breach case, the Sixth Circuit commented that although "it might not be literally certain that Plaintiffs' data will be misused, there is a sufficiently substantial risk of harm that incurring mitigation costs is reasonable. Where Plaintiffs already know that they have lost control of their data, it would be unreasonable to expect Plaintiffs to wait for actual misuse—a fraudulent charge on a credit card, for example—before taking steps to ensure their own personal and financial security," *Galaria v. Nationwide Mut. Ins. Co.*, 663 F. App'x 384, 388 (6th Cir. 2016) (internal quotation marks and citation omitted); *see also Sutton v. St. Jude Med. S.C., Inc.*, 419 F.3d 568, 574 (6th Cir. 2005) (holding that an increased risk of future harm resulting from being implanted with defendant's device satisfied the injury requirement).

Absent Class Member Standing

As noted above, a potential class representative must demonstrate individual standing vis-a-vis the defendant; he cannot acquire such standing merely by virtue of bringing a class action. *Fallick v. Nationwide Mut. Ins. Co.*, 162 F.3d at 423. "Once [a plaintiff's individual] standing has been established, whether a plaintiff will be able to represent the putative class, including absent class members, depends solely on whether he is able to meet the additional criteria encompassed in Rule 23 of the Federal Rules of Civil Procedure." *Id.*; *see also Smith v. Sterling Infosys.-Ohio, Inc.*, 2016 WL 6092551, at *2 (N.D. Ohio Oct. 19, 2016) (declining to dismiss claims of absent class members due to lack of standing). "Thus, in order to satisfy [*Fallick*], the Court must conduct a 'rigorous' analysis under Rule 23 to ascertain whether plaintiff can represent the class." *Sterling Infosys.*, 2016 WL 6092551, at *3.

c. Mootness Doctrine

If the plaintiff ceases to have standing such that a live case or controversy no longer exists, the case becomes moot. *See Spencer v. Kemna*, 523 U.S. 1, 7 (1998). An exception to the mootness doctrine exists for cases that are capable of repetition, yet evading review. *Fed. Election Comm'n v. Wis. Right to Life, Inc.*, 551 U.S. 449, 462 (2007). This exception applies if the challenged action is too brief to be litigated fully before it concludes and if "there is a reasonable expectation that the same complaining party will be subject to the same action again." *Id.* at 462. The party asserting the exception bears the burden of proof. *Lawrence v. Blackwell*, 430 F.3d 368, 371 (6th Cir. 2005). Recurrence of the issue need not be more probable than not; instead, the controversy must be capable of repetition. *See id.*; *see also Barry v. Lyon*, 834 F.3d 706, 715 (6th Cir. 2016) (concluding that plaintiff could reasonably expect to encounter additional difficulties with federal Supplemental Nutritional Assistance Program benefits, based on the repeated problems he had faced in the past, including unjustified terminations or threats of termination, such that claims were capable of repetition yet evading review).

3. PREREQUISITES

Although district courts "may not inquire into the merits of the class representatives' underlying claims," district courts must nevertheless consider the factual particularities of the claims in determining whether class certification is appropriate. *Reeb v. Ohio Dep't of Rehab. & Corr.*, 81 F. App'x 550, 555 (6th Cir. 2003). "The Supreme Court's recent opinions in *Amgen* [*Inc. v. Connecticut Retirement Plans & Trust Funds*, 133 S. Ct. 1184 (2013)] and [*Wal-Mart Stores, Inc. v.*] *Dukes* [564 U.S. 338 (2011)] now clarify that some inquiry into the merits may be necessary to decide whether the Rule 23 prerequisites are met. *Amgen*, however, admonishes district courts to consider at the class certification stage only those matters relevant to deciding if the prerequisites of Rule 23 are satisfied." *Whirlpool II*, 722 F.3d at 851.

Both the Supreme Court and the Sixth Circuit require that a district court conduct a "rigorous analysis" of the Rule 23(a) requirements before certifying a class. *Gen. Tel. Co. v. Falcon*, 457 U.S. 147, 161 (1982); *Sprague v. Gen. Motors Corp.*, 133 F.3d 388, 397 (6th Cir. 1998) (en banc). Satisfying Rule 23(a) requires something more than mere repetition of the rule's language; "[t]here must be an adequate statement of the basic facts to indicate that each requirement of the rule is fulfilled." *In re Am. Med. Sys., Inc.*, 75 F.3d 1069, 1079 (6th Cir. 1996) (internal quotation marks omitted). To obtain class certification, the plaintiffs must show that "(1) the class is so numerous that joinder of all members is impracticable; (2) there are questions of law or fact common to the class; (3) the claims or defenses of the representative parties are typical of the claims or defenses of the class; and (4) the representative parties will fairly and adequately protect the interests of the class." Fed. R. Civ. P. 23(a). These four requirements—numerosity, commonality, typicality, and adequate representation—serve to limit class claims to those that are fairly encompassed within the claims of the named plaintiffs because class representatives must share the same interests and injury as the class members. *Whirlpool II*, 722 F.3 at 850.

a. Rule 23(a) Requirements

Numerosity

The Sixth Circuit has commented that "no strict numerical test exists to define numerosity under Rule 23(a)(1)," but that "'substantial' numbers of affected consumers are sufficient to satisfy this requirement." *Whirlpool II*, 722 F.3d at 852. If there are more than several hundred members of the proposed class, this number generally satisfies the requirements of Rule 23(a)(1). *See Bacon v. Honda of Am. Mfg., Inc.*, 370 F.3d 565, 570 (6th Cir. 2004); *see also Bittinger v. Tecumseh Prods. Co.*, 123 F.3d 877, 884 n.1 (6th Cir.1997) (joinder of parties impracticable for class with over 1,100 members and "[t]o reach this conclusion is to state the obvious."). "The key to determining whether the numerosity requirement of Rule

23(a)(1) is satisfied rests on the impracticability of joining potential class members." *Boggs v. Divested Atomic Corp.*, 141 F.R.D. 58, 63 (S.D. Ohio 1991). This analysis does not require that joinder be shown to be impossible, "but only that plaintiff will suffer a strong litigational hardship or inconvenience if joinder is required." *Id.*

Commonality

"Commonality traditionally refers to characteristics of the class as a whole." *Food Lion, LLC v. Dean Foods Co.*, 312 F.R.D. 472, 483 (E.D. Tenn. 2016). The Sixth Circuit requires plaintiffs to "show that class members have suffered the same injury" to satisfy the commonality requirement. *Whirlpool II*, 722 F.3d at 852. "Their claims must depend upon a common contention . . . of such a nature that it is capable of classwide resolution—which means that determination of its truth or falsity will resolve an issue that is central to the validity of each one of the claims in one stroke." *Id.* In other words, "a common question, for purposes of Rule 23(a), is one that is likely to 'generate common *answers*' class-wide." *Doster v. Kendall*, 48 F.4th 608, 612 (6th Cir. 2022) (*quoting Wal-Mart Stores, Inc. v. Dukes*, 564 U.S. 338, 350 (2011)). "Unlike Rule 23(b)(3), which also requires that such common questions predominate over individual questions, the existence of significant common legal or factual issues is enough to satisfy Rule 23(a)(2)'s threshold commonality requirement." *Boggs*, 141 F.R.D. at 64. In analysing a proposed class, courts must ask "whether the proposed class action beats the conventional approach of resolving disputes on a case-by-case basis in terms of efficiency and administrability." *Tarrify Props., LLC v. Cuyahoga Cnty*, 37 F.4th 1101, 1106 (6th Cir. 2022). If, however, the plaintiffs' claims share a "common legal question central to the validity of each putative class member's claims," then commonality will be found. *See Hicks v. State Farm Fire Cas. Co.*, 965 F.3d 452, 459 (6th Cir. 2020). This is true even if "a party concedes [the common] issue, or the issue is resolved in the plaintiffs' favor." *Id.*

Typicality

Typicality "refers to the individual characteristics of the named plaintiff in relation to the class." *Food Lion*, 312 F.R.D. at 483 (internal quotation omitted). "Typicality is met if the class members' claims are fairly encompassed by the named plaintiffs' claims." *Whirlpool II*, 722 F.3d at 852. The typicality requirement "insures that the representatives' interests are aligned with the interests of the represented class members so that, by pursuing their own interests, the class representatives also advocate the interests of the class members." *Id.* at 852–53. "As with the commonality requirement, substantial identity between the operative facts of the named plaintiffs and the class in general is not necessary." *Bentley v. Honeywell Int'l, Inc.*, 223 F.R.D. 471, 482 (S.D. Ohio 2004); *see also Wilkof v. Caraco Pharm. Labs., Ltd.*, 280 F.R.D. 332, 339 (E.D. Mich. 2012) ("If the class representative and the class members have claims based on the same legal or remedial theory, typicality is not defeated, even if the claims are not identical."). The Sixth Circuit has held that where the plaintiffs' claims depends on each individual's unique interactions with the defendant, the typicality requirement is lacking. *See, e.g., Sprague v. Gen. Motors Corp.*, 133 F.3d 388, 399 (6th Cir.1998); *see also Bradberry v. John Hancock Mut. Life Ins. Co.*, 222 F.R.D. 568, 571 (W.D. Tenn. 2004) (citing cases for the proposition that "cases involving sales through non-uniform oral presentations and issues of reliance are generally unsuited for class certification" because, among other things, typicality is defeated).

The concepts of commonality and typicality "tend to merge in practice because both of them serve as guideposts for determining whether . . . maintenance of a class action is economical and whether the named plaintiff's claim and the class claims are so interrelated that the interests of the class members will be fairly and adequately protected in their absence." *Whirlpool II*, 722 F.3d at 853 (internal quotation marks omitted).

Adequacy

"Commonality and typicality tend to merge with the requirement of adequate representation, although the latter factor also brings into play any concerns about the competency of class counsel and any conflicts of interest that may exist." *Whirlpool II*, 722 F.3d at 853 (internal quotation marks omitted). The Sixth Circuit

> use[s] a two-prong test to determine whether the class representatives will fairly and adequately protect the interests of the class under Rule 23(a)(4): 1) The representative must have common interests with unnamed members of the class, and 2) it must appear that the representatives will vigorously prosecute the interests of the class through qualified counsel.

Vassalle v. Midland Funding LLC, 708 F.3d 747, 757 (6th Cir. 2013) (internal quotation marks and brackets omitted); *see also Beattie v. CenturyTel, Inc.*, 511 F.3d 554, 562 (6th Cir. 2007) ("The adequacy inquiry under Rule 23(a)(4) serves to uncover conflicts of interest between named parties and the class they seek to represent. A class representative must be part of the class and possess the same interest and suffer the same injury as the class members." (internal quotation marks omitted)). "Only when attacks on the credibility of the representative party are so sharp as to jeopardize the interests of absent class members should such attacks render a putative class representative inadequate." *Vassalle*, 708 F.3d at 757 (internal quotation marks omitted).

In addition, the Sixth Circuit reviews "the adequacy of class representation to determine whether class counsel are qualified, experienced and generally able to conduct the litigation." *Id.* (internal quotation marks omitted). Where "plaintiffs' attorney is an experienced practitioner in [the] area [at issue]" because of the "numerous class action cases in which counsel has participated," adequacy of representation is satisfied. *Beattie*, 511 F.3d at 563.

b. Rule 23(b) Requirements

"In addition to fulfilling the four prerequisites of Rule 23(a), the proposed class must also meet at least one of the three requirements listed in Rule 23(b)." *Whirlpool II*, 722 F.3d at 850. A party seeking to certify a class must "satisfy through evidentiary proof at least one of the provisions of Rule 23(b)." *Comcast Corp. v. Behrend*, 559 U.S. 27, 33 (2013). That "evidentiary proof," however, is not required to be admissible. In *Lyngaas v. Curaden AG*, 992 F.3d 412 (6th Cir. 2021), the Sixth Circuit joined the Eighth and Ninth Circuits "that such 'evidentiary proof' need not amount to admissible evidence, at least with respect to nonexpert evidence." *Id.* at 428-29. According to the Sixth Circuit, class certification, unlike summary judgment, is "inherently tentative" and that the evidence necessary to support a case evolves as litigation progresses. *Id.* at 429. The trial court's decision certifying the class was upheld because there was sufficient reliable evidence that could later be admitted with proper authentication to support certification under 23(b)(3). *Id.* at 430.

Rule 23(b)(1)(A) Classes

"Rule 23(b)(1)(A) allows for class certification when "prosecuting separate actions by or against individual class members would create a risk of . . . inconsistent or varying adjudications with respect to individual class members that would establish incompatible standards of conduct for the party opposing the class." *Pipefitters Local 636 Ins. Fund v. Blue Cross Blue Shield of Mich.*, 654 F.3d 618, 633 (6th Cir. 2011) (ellipsis in original). A class action is appropriate under this subsection when "the party is obliged by law to treat the members of the class alike," such as when the class involves a utility company's interactions with its customers or how the government imposes a tax. *Amchem Prod., Inc. v. Windsor*, 521 U.S. 591, 614 (1997). Certification is not appropriate simply because "some plaintiffs may be successful in their suits against a defendant while others may not." *In re Bendectin Prod. Liab. Litig.*, 749 F.2d 300, 305 (6th Cir. 1984) (citations omitted)"). In addition, class certification under Rule 23(b)(1)(A) is not proper where plaintiffs seek predominantly money damages and not equitable relief. *See Yost v. First Horizon Nat'l Corp.*, No. 08-2293-STA-CGC, 2011 WL 2182262, at *5 (W.D. Tenn. June 3, 2011).

Rule 23(b)(1)(B) Classes

Rule 23(b)(1)(B) allows certification when prosecuting separate actions by or against individual class members would create a risk of "adjudications with respect to individual class members that . . . would be dispositive of the interests of the other members not parties to the individual adjudications or would substantially impair or impede their ability to protect their interests." This provision "seeks to protect against situations where the individual members would be prejudiced by individual actions as opposed to class treatment of the dispute such as determination of the distribution of a limited fund, or shareholder's suits for remedies not falling within Rule 23.1 or multi-forum patent infringement suits." *Employers Ins. of Wausau v. Fed. Deposit Ins. Corp.*, 112 F.R.D. 52, 56 (E.D. Tenn. 1986). The Advisory Committee Notes for Rule 23(b)(1)(B) provide that certification under this subsection is particularly appropriate in cases charging a "breach of trust by a [fiduciary to] a large class of [beneficiaries], and which requires an accounting or like measures to restore the subject of the trust." Fed. R. Civ. P. 23, Adv. Comm. Notes. "Under Rule 23(b)(1)(B), procedural fairness concerns for the proposed class members can also arise *absent* certification." *In re Nortel Networks Corp. ERISA Litig.*, No. 3:03-MD-01537, 2009 WL 3294827, at *15 (M.D. Tenn. Sept. 2, 2009) (emphasis in original). "If individual adjudications would be dispositive of the interests of other Plan Participants, it would be better for those Plan Participants to be members of a class, where they can be divided into subclasses if multiple theories arise, and enjoy adequate representation."

Rule 23(b)(2) Classes

Rule 23(b)(2) allows for class action certification when "the party opposing the class has acted . . . on grounds that apply generally to the class, so that final injunctive relief or corresponding declaratory relief is appropriate respecting the class as a whole." *See Reeb v. Ohio Dep't of Rehab. & Corr.*, 435 F.3d 639, 656 (6th Cir. 2006). A (b)(2) class is mandatory, with no opportunity to opt out and no right to notice. The relief the proposed class seeks, therefore, "must perforce affect the entire class at once." *Dukes*, 564 U.S. at 361-62. Class certification "does not extend to cases in which the appropriate final relief relates exclusively or predominantly to money damages." Fed. R. Civ. P. 23(b)(2) advisory committee's note; *accord Reeb*, 435 F.3d at 651 (holding that Title VII cases in which plaintiffs seek individual compensatory damages are not appropriately brought as class actions under Rule 23(b)(2) because such individual claims for money damages will always predominate over requested injunctive or declaratory relief); *see also Coleman v. Gen. Motors Acceptance Corp.*, 296 F.3d 443, 448 (6th Cir. 2002) (citing *Allison v. Citgo Petrol. Corp.*, 151 F.3d 402, 414–15 (5th Cir. 1998), approvingly for the proposition that "the predomination requirement of Rule 23(b)(2) serves essentially the same functions as the procedural safeguards and efficiency and manageability standards mandated in (b)(3) class actions").

The primary relief sought in Rule 23(b)(2) classes is declaratory or injunctive relief. *See Weathers v. Peters Realty Corp.*, 499 F.2d 1197, 1200 (6th Cir. 1974). The nature of this primary relief "does not require that the class be as narrowly confined as under either (b)(1) or (b)(3)." *Id.* Rule 23(b)(2), however, "does not authorize class certification when each individual class member would be entitled to a different injunction or declaratory judgment against the defendant" and "does not authorize class certification when each class member would be entitled to an individualized award of monetary damages." *Davis v. Cintas Corp.*, 717 F.3d 476, 490 (6th Cir. 2013) (citing *Dukes*, 564 U.S. 338 at 360). To be certified under (b)(2), case law has suggested that a proposed class be "cohesive," *see Romberio v. UnumProvident Corp.*, 385 F. App'x 423, 433 (6th Cir. 2009), and that the interests of the class members must be "homogenous." *See, e.g., Coleman*, 296 F.3d at 447.

Plaintiffs have the burden to prove the requisite elements of class certification under Rule 23(b)(2). *Burkhead v. Louisville Gas & Elec. Co.*, 250 F.R.D. 287, 290 (W.D. Ky. 2008).

Rule 23(b)(3) Classes

Rule 23(b)(3) tests "whether proposed classes are sufficiently cohesive to warrant adjudication by representation" but is far more demanding than the commonality, typicality, and adequacy inquiries of Rule 23(a). *See Amchem*, 521 U.S. at 623–24. "Federal Rule of Civil Procedure 23(b)(3) requires that the court finds that the questions of law or fact common to class members predominate over any questions affecting only individual members, and that a class action is superior to other available methods for fairly and efficiently adjudicating the controversy." *Pipefitters Local 636 Ins. Fund v. Blue Cross Blue Shield of Mich.*, 654 F.3d 618, 630 (6th Cir. 2011) (internal quotation marks omitted). The rule is designed to "achieve economies of time, effort, and expense, and promote . . . uniformity of decision as to persons similarly situated, without sacrificing procedural fairness or bringing about other undesirable results." *Id.* (internal quotation marks omitted).

The rule itself lists a non-exhaustive list of factors as "pertinent" to a 23(b)(3) analysis: (A) the class members' interests in individually controlling the prosecution or defense of separate actions, (B) the extent and nature of any litigation concerning the controversy already begun by or against class members, (C) the desirability or undesirability of concentrating the litigation of the claims in the particular forum, and (D) the likely difficulties in managing a class action. "Rule 23(b)(3), designed to accommodate claims for money damages, requires notice to the class members, including the member's right to opt out of the class, *see* Fed. R. Civ. P. 23(c)(2)(B), and specifies the factors that a court needs to consider in determining whether common issues predominate. *See* Fed. R. Civ. P. 23(b)(3)." *Reeb*, 435 F.3d at 645–46.

Predominance. To satisfy Rule 23(b)(3), the questions in a class action that are subject to generalized proof, and thus applicable to the class as a whole, must predominate over questions that are subject only to individualized proof. *See Beattie*, 511 F.3d at 560. "[C]ommon issues may predominate when liability can be determined on a class-wide basis, even when there are some individualized damage issues." *Id.* at 564 (6th Cir. 2007) (internal quotation marks omitted). In antitrust cases, the Sixth Circuit has noted that "[p]redominance is a test readily met." *See In re Scrap Metal Antitrust Litig.*, 527 F.3d 517, 532, 535 (6th Cir. 2008). "Courts have fairly consistently found . . . that common issues regarding the existence and scope of the conspiracy," which are issues concerning the conduct of the defendants, "predominate over other questions affecting only individual [class] members in antitrust price fixing cases." *In re Southeastern Milk Antitrust Litig.*, 2010 WL 3521747, at *9 (E.D. Tenn. Sept. 7, 2010). The Sixth Circuit has noted that simply because affirmative defenses "may affect different class members differently," this "does not compel a finding that individual issues predominate over common ones." *Young*, 693 F.3d at 544 (internal quotation marks omitted); *see also Zehentbauer Family Land, LP v. Chesapeake Expl., L.L.C.*, 935 F.3d 496 (6th Cir. 2019) (class of landowners in oil-and-gas-lease dispute properly certified where plaintiffs asserted that defendants used a "netback breach," deducting post-production costs from royalty payments and leaving plaintiffs with less than what was due under the lease agreements; netback breach theory would resolve the claims of each class member without there being too individualized a calculation). However, predominance becomes problematic when "a controlling issue requires individualized determinations" the matter is "ill-equipped for classwide proof." *Tarrify Props., LLC*, 37 F.4th at 1107 (holding that a district court reasonably rejected class-certification when resolution of the controlling issue required individualized inquiries into the fair market value of each class member's property at the time of transfer).

The Sixth Circuit has adopted the "broad view" followed by the Second, Fourth, Seventh, and Ninth Circuits in certifying issues for class treatment under Rule 23(c)(4) even though the class itself lacked predominance on issues of liability. Rule 23(c)(4) provides, "[w]hen appropriate, an action may be brought or maintained as a class action with respect to particular issues." Fed. R. Civ. P. 23(c)(4). Under the "broad view" of Rule 23(c)(4), the court applies the predominance and superiority requirements of Rule 23(b)(3) after common issues have been identified for class treatment. This view allows courts to apply Rule 23(c)(4) even if predominance has not been established for the claims at issue. In *Martin v. Behr Dayton Thermal Products., LLC*, 896 F.3d 405 (6th Cir. 2018), *cert. denied*, 139 S.Ct. 1319 (2019), the court was persuaded by the "broad view," finding that the "narrow view" subscribed to by the Fifth and Eleventh Circuits would require predominance for the entire class, which in turn "would undercut the purpose of Rule 23(c)(4)." *Id.* at 413.

Superiority. To determine whether a class action is the superior method for fair and efficient adjudication, the district court should consider the difficulties of managing a class action. *Beattie*, 511 F.3d at 567. The district court should also compare other means of disposing of the suit to determine whether a class action "is sufficiently effective to justify the expenditure of the judicial time and energy that is necessary to adjudicate a class action and to assume the risk of prejudice to the rights of those who are not directly before the court." *Pipefitters*, 654 F.3d at 630 (internal quotation marks omitted). "Additionally, the court should consider the value of individual damage awards, as small awards weigh in favor of class suits." *Id.* at 631; *cf. Beattie*, 511 F.3d at 567 (holding that possible recovery of roughly $124.68 per class member was too small to encourage individuals to bring suit, thereby making a class action a superior method of adjudicating the dispute). "Where many individual inquiries are necessary, a class action is not a superior form of adjudication. However, where a threshold issue is common to all class members, class litigation is greatly preferred." *Young v. Nationwide Mutual Insurance Co.*, 693 F.3d 532, 545 (6th Cir. 2012); *accord Daffin v. Ford Motor Co.*, 458 F.3d 549, 554 (6th Cir. 2006) (finding that class litigation is superior when a threshold issue of contract interpretation applies equally to the whole class); *see also Vassalle v. Midland Funding LLC*, 708 F.3d 747, 758 (6th Cir. 2013) (where most class members had limited resources; the case was far more procedurally advanced than other actions bringing similar claims; a threshold issue—whether the defendant was liable under the FDCPA—was common to all class members; but unnamed class members had an interest in individually controlling the defense of the defendant's state court judgments against them, and the class members could have collected damages under state law claims that would exceed the value of monetary relief in this settlement; therefore, Sixth Circuit found that the class action was not the superior method of resolving the controversy).

c. Manageability

"To determine whether a class action is the superior method for fair and efficient adjudication, the district court should consider the difficulties of managing a class action." *Pipefitters*, 654 F.3d at 630 (considering manageability in context of discussing Rule 23(b)(3) classes and superiority requirement). "The district court should also compare other means of disposing of the suit to determine if a class action is sufficiently effective to justify the expenditure of the judicial time and energy that is necessary to adjudicate a class action and to assume the risk of prejudice to the rights of those who are not directly before the court." *Id.* (internal quotation marks omitted). "Additionally, the court should consider the value of individual damage awards, as small awards weigh in favor of class suits." *Id.* at 631.

d. Ascertainability

Rule 23(a) has no express ascertainability requirement, but many courts, including the Sixth Circuit, have held that it is an implicit requirement of class certification. "In our circuit, the ascertainability inquiry is guided by *Young v. Nationwide Mutual Insurance Co.*, 693 F.3d 532 (6th Cir. 2012)." *Rikos v. Proctor & Gamble Co.*, 799 F.3d 497, 525 (6th Cir. 2015) (declining to follow *Carrera v. Bayer Corp.*, 727 F.3d 300 (3d Cir. 2013), "given the strong criticism it has attracted from other courts"). In *Young*, the Sixth Circuit adopted the ascertainability requirement, noting that certification necessitated "a class description [that is] sufficiently definite so that it is administratively feasible for the court to determine whether a particular individual is a member." 693 F.3d at 538. *Young*'s reasoning was recently reaffirmed in *Tarrify Props., LLC v. Cuyahoga County*, 37 F.4th 1101, 1106 (6th Cir. 2022) ("If 'mini-trials' become necessary to determine who is in and who is out, the class-action vehicle imposes inefficiencies rather than ameliorates them.").

In *Young*, the named plaintiffs sued their respective insurance companies, alleging "that their insurer charged them a local government tax on their premiums when either the tax was not owed or the tax amount owed was less than the insurer billed." 693 F.3d at 535. The district court certified a class of "[a]ll persons in the Commonwealth of Kentucky who purchased insurance from or underwritten by [Defendant insurer] . . . and who were charged local government taxes on their payment of premiums which were either not owed, or were at rates higher than permitted." *Id.* at 536 (second alteration in original).

On appeal, the insurance companies argued "that the class definition [was] not administratively feasible" because the plaintiffs' class description was not "sufficiently definite so that it [would be] administratively feasible for the court to determine whether a particular individual is a member." *Id.* at 538. The Sixth Circuit rejected this argument, noting that "[f]or a class to be sufficiently defined, the court must be able to resolve the question of whether class members are included or excluded from the class by reference to objective criteria." *Id.* (internal quotation marks omitted). The *Young* plaintiffs had presented such a class, because class membership could be determined by reviewing factors such as "the location of the insured risk/property" and "the local tax charged and collected from the policyholder." *Id.* at 539; *see also Rikos*, 799 F.3d at 526 (reasoning that the proposed class was defined by objective criteria—anyone who purchased the nutritional supplement at issue in California, New Hampshire, Illinois, North Carolina, or Florida—and that the "single state sub-classes can be determined with reasonable—but not perfect—accuracy"); *Am. Copper & Brass, Inc. v. Lake City Indus. Prod., Inc.*, 757 F.3d 540, 545 (6th Cir. 2014) (noting that objective data such as tax numbers can satisfy the ascertainability requirement and citing *Young*, 693 F.3d at 538 for the proposition that class membership is determined "by reference to objective criteria").

Young, however, involved a Rule 23(b)(3) class, 693 F.3d at 536, as have the other cases in which the Sixth Circuit analyzed this requirement. *See, e.g.*, *Tarrify Props.*, 37 F.4th at 1106; *Hicks*, 965 F.3d at 463–65; *Rikos*, 799 F.3d at 524–26; *Am. Copper & Brass*, 757 F.3d at 545. Whether ascertainability is a requirement for Rule 23(b)(2) actions went unanswered in the Sixth Circuit until 2016. In the case of *Cole v. City of Memphis*, 839 F.3d 530 (6th Cir. 2016), the Sixth Circuit held, as a matter of first impression, that ascertainability of class members is not an additional requirement for certification of a class seeking only injunctive and declaratory relief. It noted that "three of our sister circuits have held that 'ascertainability' is inapplicable to Rule 23(b)(2)." *Cole*, 839 F.3d at 541 (citing *Shelton v. Bledsoe*, 775 F.3d 554 (3d Cir. 2015), *Shook v. El Paso Cty*, 386 F.3d 963 (10th Cir. 2004); *Yaffe v. Powers*, 454 F.2d 1362 (1st Cir. 1972). "In the Rule 23(b)(3) context, ascertainability aids the inherent efficiencies of the class device by ensuring administrative feasibility, and as we read our own precedent and the precedent of other courts, ascertainability is a requirement tied almost exclusively to the practical need to notify absent class members and to allow those members a chance to opt-out and avoid the potential collateral estoppel effects of a final judgment." *Id.* But "administering a (b)(3) class is a more procedurally complicated task than overseeing a (b)(2) class," of which the main purpose is to "provide relief through a *single* injunction or declaratory judgment." *Id.* at 541–42. After examining the Advisory Committee Notes to Rule 23(b)(2), which noted that Rule 23(b)(2) is an appropriate device to use "even if [the action directed toward the class] has taken effect or is threatened only as to one or a few members of the class" and that "illustrative" examples of a (b)(2) class are civil rights actions where members of the class "are incapable of specific enumeration," such as the case at bar, the Sixth Circuit held that ascertainability was "inappropriate" in the context of a Rule 23(b)(2) class.

4. CASE MANAGEMENT

a. Appointing Counsel

Upon certifying a class, the court is required under Rule 23(g)(1) to appoint class counsel. Fed. R. Civ. P. 23(g)(1). Rule 23(g)(1)(A) and (B) prescribe the criteria and procedures for appointing class counsel. The court must consider the work counsel has done in identifying and investigating the claims in the case; the experience of counsel with class actions, complex litigation, and the kinds of claims alleged in the action; counsel's knowledge of the applicable law; the resources that counsel has available to commit in representing the class; and any other matters that bear on the counsel's ability to fairly and adequately represent the class. *Willis v. Big Lots, Inc.*, 242 F.Supp.3d 634, 659 (S.D. Ohio 2017).

Counsel must, therefore, be able to provide adequate representation "to meet the demands of maintaining the action." *Cmty. Refugee & Immigration Servs. v. Registrar, Ohio Bureau of Motor Vehicles*, 334 F.R.D. 493, 506 (S.D. Ohio Feb. 20, 2020). "[C]lass counsel must be qualified, experienced, and generally able to conduct the litigation." *Id.* Past misconduct, such as unethically soliciting prospective clients, may render counsel unsuitable to represent a class. *See, e.g., Compressor Eng'g Corp. v. Thomas*, 329 F.R.D. 511, 527 (E.D. Mich. 2016).

b. Discovery Issues

In most cases, discovery is necessary on issues affecting class certification. *See Phillips v. Philip Morris Cos., Inc.*, No. 5:10CV1741, 2013 U.S. Dist. LEXIS 91189, at *6–7 (N.D. Ohio June 28, 2013) ("Courts universally recognize that some discovery is necessary prior to a determination of class certification."). Although Rule 23 contemplates an early ruling on class certification, "this does not mandate precipitate action. The court should defer decision on certification pending discovery if the existing record is inadequate for resolving the relevant issues." *In re Am. Med. Sys., Inc.*, 75 F.3d 1069, 1086 (6th Cir. 1996) (quoting *Chateau de Ville Prods., Inc. v. Tams-Whitmark Music Library, Inc.*, 586 F.2d 962, 966 (2d Cir. 1978)). The need for precertification discovery, however, "is subject to court-imposed limitations, and any such limitations are within the sound discretion of the trial court." *Philip Morris*, 2013 U.S. Dist. LEXIS 91189, at *7. Nevertheless, when fashioning these limitations courts within the Sixth Circuit are generally reluctant to go so far as to impose a complete stay. *See, e.g., Nichols v. State Farm Mut. Auto. Ins. Co.*, No. 2:22-cv-16, 2022 U.S. Dist. LEXIS 72551, *6 (S.D. Ohio Apr. 20, 2022) (denying a motion to stay discovery pending resolution of a motion to dismiss for lack of standing).

For example, depending on the issues and complexity of the case, courts may bifurcate discovery between certification issues and those concerning the merits. *Manual for Complex Litigation* § 21.14 (4th ed. 2004). *McGlone v. Centrus Energy Corp.*, No. 2:19-cv-2196, 2021 U.S. Dist. LEXIS 176058, at *14–15 (S.D. Ohio Sept. 16, 2021) ("[I]t is not uncommon for courts in this Circuit to order [bifurcated] discovery" at the class certification stage). Whether to bifurcate class certification and merits discovery rests within the trial court's discretion. *See Ballard v. Kenan Advantage Group*, No. 5:20cv0142, 2020 U.S. Dist. LEXIS 129549, at *2 (N.D. Ohio July 20, 2020). Factors to consider include

> (1) expediency, meaning whether bifurcated discovery will aid the court in making a timely determination on the class certification motion; (2) economy, meaning "the potential impact a grant or denial of certification would have upon the pending litigation," and whether the definition of the class would "help determine the limits of discovery on the merits;" and (3) severability, meaning whether class certification and merits issues are closely enmeshed.

Id. (quoting 3 *Newberg on Class Actions* § 7:17 (5th ed.)). While the court has wide latitude in deciding if discovery should be bifurcated, courts within the Sixth Circuit have denied bifurcation when considerable overlap exists between class certification and merits-based discovery. *See Chenault v. Beiersdorf, Inc.*, No. 1:20-cv-174, 2020 U.S. Dist. LEXIS 153068, at *6 (S.D. Ohio Aug. 24, 2020).

In *Nash v. City of Oakwood*, 90 F.R.D. 633 (S.D. Ohio 1981), the district court limited discovery to class certification issues. "The Court is . . . of the opinion that discovery, at this juncture, should be directed to, and thereby limited, as much as possible, to determining the maintainability of this cause as a class action." *Id.* at 636; *see also Philip Morris*, 2013 U.S. Dist. LEXIS 91189, at *12–13 (recognizing a court's discretion to limit precertification discovery, but overturning magistrate judge's discovery order as too limiting); *Kane v. Nat'l Action Fin. Servs., Inc.*, No. 11-11505, 2012 U.S. Dist. LEXIS 66219, at *16–20 (E.D. Mich. May 11, 2012) (allowing certain precertification discovery on matters relevant to prerequisites for certification under Rule 23); *McGlone*, 2021 U.S. Dist. LEXIS 176058, at *15–22 (rejecting plaintiff's challenge to bifurcation seeking discovery on causation because causation is a merits issue).

c. Timing of Class Certification

Rule 23(c)(1)(A) provides that "[a]t an early practicable time after a person sues or is sued as a class representative, the court must determine by order whether to certify the action as a class action." Fed. R. Civ. P. 23(c)(1)(A). The Sixth Circuit has held that the district court must conduct "a rigorous analysis" at an "early practicable time" to determine class certification. *Davis v. Cintas Corp.*, 717 F.3d 476, 484 (6th Cir. 2013). "Ordinarily, this means that the class determination should be predicated on evidence presented by the parties concerning maintainability of the class action." *Whirlpool II*, 722 F.3d at 851. As recognized in *Wal-Mart Stores, Inc. v. Dukes*, 564 U.S. 338 (2011), and *General Telephone Co. of the Southwest v. Falcon*, 457 U.S. 147 (1982), the court's analysis may probe the pleadings and overlap with the merits of the plaintiffs' claims. *See Pilgrim v. Universal Health Card, LLC*, 660 F.3d 943, 949 (6th Cir. 2011). Merits questions may be considered, however, only to the extent they are relevant to the requirements of class certification under Rule 34. *Whirlpool II*, 722 F.3d at 751.

A district court enjoys discretion in determining whether and when to certify a case. *Reeb v. Ohio Dep't of Rehabilitation & Correction*, Belmont Corr. Inst. 435 F.3d 639, 643 (6th Cir. 2006). "Determining when that early practicable time should be, however, is not an exact science, particularly while the contours of a case are still taking shape." *Grae v. Corr. Corp. of Am.*, 330 F.R.D. 481, 492 (M.D. Tenn. 2019). Nothing in the rules says that the court must await a motion by the plaintiff to decide whether a class should be certified. *Pilgrim*, 660 F.3d at 949. As such, "[e]ither plaintiff or defendant may move for a determination of whether the action may be certified under Rule 23(c)(1)." *Id.* (quoting 7AA Charles Alan Wright, Arthur R. Miller, & Mary Kay Kane, *Federal Practice & Procedure* § 1785 (2005)).

It is well settled that "a district court is not required to rule on a motion for class certification before ruling on the merits of a case." *Miami Univ. Wrestling Club v. Miami Univ.*, 302 F.3d 608, 616 (6th Cir. 2002). Various courts have decided dispositive motions, including motions for summary judgment, before entertaining class certification. *Coalition to Defend Affirmative Action v. Regents of the Univ. of Michigan*, 539 F. Supp. 2d 960, 973 (E.D. Mich. 2008); *see Lee v. Javitch, Block & Rathbone, LLP*, 522 F. Supp. 2d 945, 947 (S.D. Ohio 2007) ("The Court has discretion to address the parties' summary judgment motions prior to determining the appropriateness of class certification."). A dismissal before certification is res judicata as to class representatives, but it has no effect on the putative class members. *Coalition*, 539 F. Supp. 2d at 974.

d. Multidistrict Litigation Issues

Not infrequently, the existence of similar class action lawsuits in other state or federal courts will raise questions about the timing, scope, and propriety of class certification. The Manual for Complex Litigation identifies the following possible scenarios:

- Multiple cases with similar class allegations, each of which might be appropriately certified under Rule 23 but which may overlap or conflict if more than one is certified;
- Cases alleging a nationwide class and cases seeking multistate or single-state class certification pending in different courts at the same time;
- Cases filed as class actions in federal and state courts relating to the same type of transactions and involving some or all of the same parties;
- Cases filed by the same lawyers seeking to represent an overlapping or duplicative class of plaintiffs in order to obtain the most favorable forum;
- Cases filed by different lawyers competing for the fastest and most favorable rulings on class certification and appointment as class counsel;
- Multiple individual actions or other forms of aggregate litigation pending in state and federal courts, raising the same issues and involving some or all of the same parties; or
- Prior unsuccessful class certification efforts in state or federal courts.

Manual for Complex Litigation at § 21.25. Potential issues include whether and how to proceed with class certification, whether an MDL proceeding is appropriate, the scope of the class definition, claim preclusion, comity and coordination with other courts, and the Anti-Injunction Act.

When a class action is consolidated into an MDL action, a court may appoint both lead and liaison counsel to help manage the litigation. *See In re Cardinal Health, Inc. ERISA Litig.*, 225 F.R.D. 552, 555 (S.D. Ohio 2005). Complex cases involving large numbers of parties and multiple class actions also may require appointment of interim lead counsel under Rule 23(g)(3) before a class is certified. *In re Am. Honda Motor Co., Inc. CR-V Vibration Marketing & Sales Practices Litig.*, No. 2:15-md-2662, 2015 U.S. Dist. LEXIS 182559, at *6 (S.D. Ohio Dec. 18, 2015). "[D]esignation of interim counsel clarifies responsibility for protecting the interests of the class during precertification activities, such as making and responding to motions, conducting any necessary discovery, moving for class certification, and negotiating settlement." *Id.* at *6–7 (quoting *Manual for Complex Litigation* at § 21.11). Courts use the same standards for appointing interim lead counsel as for appointing permanent class counsel. *Id.* at *7.

The Sixth Circuit also recently addressed whether certification of a "negotiation class" in an MDL case is appropriate in *City of North Royalton v. McKesson Corp.*, 976 F.3d 664 (6th Cir. 2020). The opioid MDL involved over 1,300 public-entity-led lawsuits, primarily by cities and counties. *Id.* at 667. In an attempt to facilitate a global settlement, the district court certified a "negotiation class" consisting of "all cities and counties throughout the United States for purposes of negotiating a settlement between class members and opioid manufacturers, distributors, and pharmacies." *Id.* The Sixth Circuit noted that this novel type of class differed from litigation classes because it "[wa]s designed to attempt to reach a settlement while the individual MDL cases continued along their respective litigation paths." *Id.* at 668. Similarly, it also differed from a settlement class in that the class certification and opt-out process would occur prior to a settlement being reached, with no guarantee of a second opportunity to opt-out after a settlement was reached. *Id.* at 668–70. The Sixth Circuit rejected the certification, holding that a "negotiation class" was beyond the scope of Rule 23 and may not be created outside the ordinary rule-making process. *Id.* at 672–77 ("Perhaps in due course the Rules Advisory Committee and Judicial Conference will recommend revising Rule 23 to sanction the negotiation class, which the Supreme Court and Congress may then approve. Until that time, however, this novel mechanism is beyond the

Rule's scope.").

5. CLASS NOTICE

Notice is an important feature of class actions. The Sixth Circuit has explained that class notice must be "reasonably calculated under all the circumstances, to apprise interested parties of the pendency of the action and afford them an opportunity to present their objections." *In re Scrap Metal Antitrust Litig.*, 527 F.3d 517, 535 (6th Cir. 2008) (quoting *Mullane v. Central Hanover Bank & Trust Co.*, 339 U.S. 306, 314 (1950)). "To comport with the requirements of due process, notice must be 'reasonably calculated to reach interested parties.'" *Fidel v. Farley*, 534 F.3d 508, 514 (6th Cir. 2008) (quoting *Karkoukli's, Inc. v. Dohany*, 409 F.3d 279, 283 (6th Cir. 2005)). Notice affords class members an opportunity to participate in the litigation or opt out and ensures that class representatives and class counsel are working in the best interest of the class.

Rule 23 identifies three situations in which notice is required: when a class is certified under Rule 23(b)(3); when a settlement is proposed that would bind the class, Fed. R. Civ. P. 23(e)(1); and when a motion for an award of attorney's fees is made, Fed. R. Civ. P. 23(h)(1). While notice is mandatory for classes certified under Rule 23(b)(3), "the court *may* direct appropriate notice" for classes certified under Rule 23(b)(1) or (b)(2). Fed. R. Civ. P. 23(c)(2)(A) (emphasis added). Rule 23(c)(2)(B) sets out the notice requirements for 23(b)(3) classes. It instructs the court to "direct to class members the best notice that is practicable under the circumstances. . . ." Fed. R. Civ. P. 23(c)(2)(B). As for class settlements, the court "must direct notice in a reasonable manner. . . ." Notice "in a reasonable manner" also is required for attorney's fees claims. Fed. R. Civ. P. 23(h)(1).

Class Certification Notice. Issues related to class notice often center on the requirements for certified classes. For Rule 23(b)(3) classes, "the best notice . . . practicable" must include "individual notice to all members who can be identified through reasonable effort." Fed. R. Civ. P. 23(c)(2)(B). *Id.* The Supreme Court has held that "the import of this language is unmistakable. Individual notice must be sent to all class members whose names and addresses may be ascertained through reasonable effort." *Eisen v. Carlisle & Jacquelin*, 417 U.S. 156, 173 (1974). This requirement cannot be waived, even when the plaintiff argues that providing individual notice to each member of a large class would be "prohibitively" expensive. *Id.* at 176. When the names and addresses of class members are known, courts often direct notice by mail. Other approaches, including the use of the internet, television, radio, newspapers, and other print media, also can be used. Internet postings, for example, are increasingly common. They can be utilized to compliment other forms of notice. For instance, a 2013 opinion from the Southern District of Ohio found that class notice met the requirements of Fed. R. Civ. P. 23(c)(2)(B) where "[t]he Parties engaged in extensive efforts to obtain accurate mailing addresses for Class Members" and "established a website containing copies of the class notice[.]" *Johnson v. Midwest Logistics Systems, Ltd.*, No. 2:11-CV-1061, 2013 U.S. Dist. LEXIS 74201, at *8 (S.D. Ohio May 25, 2013). In general, the precise manner of notice is flexible and will be decided on a case-by-case basis.

Two overarching goals for any notice are to reach a high percentage of class members and that it be read. The Federal Judicial Center recommends that class counsel be required to submit a "notice plan" that sets out "steps to update addresses before mailing, including postal service change-of-address records, and third-party address databases if the list is very old." Federal Judicial Center, Judges' Class Action Notice and Claims Process Checklist and Plain Language Guide (Guide), at 2–3 (2010). The types of questions the plan should address include whether the notice will reach the demographics and geographic coverage of the class, whether individual notice is necessary, what percentage of the class is expected to receive the notice, whether non-English should be used in the notice, and whether class members will have sufficient time to act on rights after receiving notice. *Id.* at 2–4. The plan also should require further efforts to "re-mail notices that are returned as undeliverable[.]" *Id.* at 3. "Key documents" (such as the complaint and answer) should be available on a neutral website. *Id.* at 4.

Rule 23(c) also identifies requirements for the content of a class certification notice. The notice must "clearly and concisely state in plain, easily understood language" the following information:

(i) the nature of the action;
(ii) the definition of the class certified;
(iii) the class claims, issues, or defenses;
(iv) that a class member may enter an appearance through an attorney if the member so desires;
(v) that the court will exclude from the class any member who requests exclusion;
(vi) the time and manner for requesting exclusion; and
(vii) the binding effect of a class judgment on members under Rule 23(c)(3).

Fed. R. Civ. P. 23(c)(2)(B). The Federal Judicial Center's website has a page dedicated to class action notices, which includes model notices for a securities class action, a products liability class action, and an employment discrimination class action. *See* Federal Judicial Center, Class Action Notices Page, https://www.fjc.gov/content/301253/illustrative-forms-class-action-notices-introduction (last visited Oct. 13, 2023). The website contains many helpful resources, such as a Notice Checklist and a Plain Language Guide, Notes for Use by Attorneys and Judges, and an Overview of Methodology.

Notice should be given promptly after the certification order. *Manual for Complex Litigation* at § 21.31. If a settlement is near, delaying notice of class certification until after settlement is common. *Id.* That way, notice of the certification and the settlement can be combined, thereby lessening the costs.

Under Fed. R. Civ. P. 23(d), "a district court . . . [may] require a defendant's cooperation in identifying the class members to whom notice must be sent." *Oppenheimer Fund, Inc. v. Sanders*, 437 U.S. 340, 355 (1978) (footnote omitted). *See, e.g.*, *Misch v. Community Mutual Ins. Co.*, No. C-1-94-428, 1995 U.S. Dist. LEXIS 5059, at *5 (S.D. Ohio Feb. 15, 1995) (certifying a class and directing the defendant to provide Plaintiff with a list of the class members' names and last known addresses). The defendant also may be required to "enclose class notices in [its] own periodic mailings to class members in order to reduce the expense of sending the notice. . . ." *Oppenheimer Fund, Inc.* 437 U.S. at 355 n.22. The court may "exercise its discretion" to require this kind of help when "the defendant may be able to perform [the] task with less difficulty or expense than could the representative plaintiff." *Id.* at 356.

Nonetheless, "[t]he usual rule," as expressed by the Supreme Court in *Eisen*, "is that a plaintiff must initially bear the cost of notice to the class. . . . [T]he plaintiff must pay for the cost of notice as part of the ordinary burden of financing his own suit." *Eisen*, 417 U.S. at 178–79; *see also Griffith v. Javitch, Block & Rathbone, LLP*, 241 F.R.D. 600, 601 (S.D. Ohio 2007) ("the costs of class notice normally are borne by Plaintiff . . . especially . . . when there has been no ruling on the merits of any claim"). Even when the defendant has been directed to provide information or other cooperation in notifying the class members, the plaintiff should bear the cost unless "the expense involved may be so insubstantial as not to warrant the effort required to calculate it and shift it to the representative plaintiff." *Oppenheimer*, at 359. *Cf. Alzawkari v. American SS. Co.*, No. 88-1897, 1989 U.S. App. LEXIS 9993 (6th Cir. June 12, 1989) (upholding the district court's decision to require the defendant to bear the cost of compiling the names and addresses of the class members and the district court's finding that the cost would not be substantial).

Settlement Notice. Settlement notice is required if a settlement will bind the class. Fed. R. Civ. P. 23(e)(1). Rule 23(e)(1) provides that notice must be given "in a reasonable manner to all class members." While courts have wide discretion in determining what constitutes reasonable notice, the Federal Judicial Center recommends that notices "be delivered or communicated to class members in the same manner as certification notices." *Manual for Complex Litigation* at § 21.312. The court will order when the notice should be given as part of the settlement approval process. The notice should identify the time and place of the public hearing on the proposed settlement and the procedures for objecting, opting out, and making an appearance. The contents also should be designed to inform each class member of what the settlement means and the consequences of a dismissal of the action. The notice also should include, among other things, the terms of the settlement, a statement that it will bind all class members, a definition of the class and any subclasses, and a description of how funds will be allocated and distributed.

The Class Action Fairness Act of 2005 contains additional notice requirements for class action settlements. The Act requires within 10 days after a proposed settlement is filed with the court that each participating defendant serve notice of settlement-related papers on designated state officials for each state in which a class member resides and on designated federal officials. 28 U.S.C. § 1715. The notice must contain certain specified information. The statute provides that final approval of the settlement may not be given earlier than 90 days after the notice is served.

Attorney's Fees Notice. Like the settlement notice, notice of any fee motion in a class action must be made in a "reasonable manner." Fed. R. Civ. P. 23(h)(1). Members of the class have an interest in how class counsel will be paid—whether out of the class fund or directly by another party. If a settlement needs to be approved by the court, notice of a fee application often is combined with notice of the proposed settlement. The notice should afford any class member an opportunity to object to the application. Information in the notice should contain information about the motion, including where to obtain a copy, the amount of fees claimed, and when and where a hearing will be held on the motion.

6. SUBCLASSES

When appropriate, a court may divide a class into subclasses, which are "each treated as a class" under Rule 23. Fed. R. Civ. P. 23(c)(5). Consistent with its inherent power to manage and control litigation, a district court has discretion to certify subclasses, and it may do so *sua sponte* or at the request of a party. *U.S. Parole Comm'n v. Geraghty*, 445 U.S. 388, 407–08 (1980); *Butler v. Sterling, Inc.*, No. 98-3223, 2000 U.S. App. LEXIS 6419, at *7 (6th Cir. Mar. 31, 2000). Subclasses are appropriate "whenever a distinct segment of the class presents special factual circumstances, . . . different causes of action, . . . or special legal or equitable prayers for relief." *Heit v. Van Ochten*, No. 1:96-CV-800, 2001 U.S. Dist. LEXIS 532, at *5 (W.D. Mich. Jan. 12, 2001); *see also Hicks v. State Farm Fire & Cas. Co.*, 965 F.3d 452, 459–60 (6th Cir. 2020) ("A class may be certified based on a predominant common issue even though other important matters will have to be tried separately, such as damages or some affirmative defences particular to some individual class members.").

The requirement that subclasses are "treated as a class" means that each subclass must be independently certifiable. *See, e.g.*, *Kendrick v. Std. Fire Ins. Co.*, No. 06-141-BLD, 2010 U.S. Dist. LEXIS 135694, at *24–25 (E.D. Ky. Sept. 30, 2010) (citing *Manual for Complex Litigation* at § 21.23); William Rubenstein, *Newberg on Class Actions*, § 4.80 (5th ed. 2015). As the *Manual for Complex Litigation* advises, "[e]ach ... subclass must independently satisfy all the prerequisites of Rules 23(a) and (b)." *Manual for Complex Litigation* at § 21.23. In other words, a subclass, like a class, must "fulfill[] the four prerequisites of Rule 23(a) . . . [and] must also meet at least one of the three requirements listed in Rule 23(b)." *In re Biery*, 543 B.R. 267, 279–80 (Bankr. E. D. Ky. 2015) (quoting *Whirlpool II*, 722 F.3d at 850). As the Sixth Circuit has admonished, "subclasses are not [a] substitute for full compliance with Rule 23." *Sprague v. Gen. Motors Corp.*, 133 F.3d 388, 399 n.9 (6th Cir. 1998). Subclassing will not make an otherwise unmanageable class action manageable. *See Forsher v. J.M. Smucker Co.*, 612 F. Supp. 3d 714, 728 (N.D. Ohio 2020) (creation of subclasses to address express warranty laws of 44 separate states was unmanageable).

"The necessity of a large number of subclasses may indicate that common questions do not predominate" under Rule 23(b)(3). *Manual for Complex Litigation* at § 21.23. Some courts have adopted the view that "creative subclassing and bifurcation procedures cannot be used to remedy a lack of predominance," while others "see no such barrier and allow subclassing as long as common issues predominate over the subclasses." *Randleman v. Fid. Nat'l Title Ins. Co.*, 646 F.3d 347, 356 (6th Cir. 2011). The Sixth Circuit, however, has not yet weighed in on this issue. *Id.*

7. OPT-OUTS

A prospective plaintiff has the right to opt out of class actions other than those certified under Rules 23(b)(1) or 23(b)(2). Fed. R. Civ. P. 23(c)(2)(A). *See Doster v. Kendall*, 54 F.4th 398, 440 (6th Cir. 2022) (explaining that there is no *automatic* right to opt out of a Rule 23(b)(2) class action, but the district court may allow it). This opt out right is significant in several respects. Those who are not members of the class do not have standing to object. *Tennessee Ass'n of Health Maint. Orgs., Inc. v. Grier*, 262 F.3d 559, 566 (6th Cir. 2001). Class members who opt out of a class action are no longer class members and, therefore, may not object to a settlement by which they are not bound. *Olden v. LaFarge Corp.*, 472 F. Supp. 2d 922, 930–31 (E.D. Mich. 2007). Because opting out and objecting are mutually exclusive options for class members, a class member may not file a "contingent opt-out" request, seeking to opt out of the settlement if the court overrules the objection. *Id.* at 930. However, a class member who opted out at one stage of the litigation may opt back in to participate in a settlement. *Gardner v. LaFarge Corp.*, 472 F. Supp. 2d 922, 942 (E.D. Mich. 2007). Alternatively, a class member who opts out is not bound by a settlement and, therefore, is free to pursue recovery outside the class.

8. ABSENT CLASS MEMBERS

a. Communication with Absent Class Members

Courts have discretion to limit communications with absent class members by plaintiffs, defendants, and their respective counsel. But in exercising that discretion, courts must tread a fine line so as not to infringe on a party's First Amendment rights. Communication with absent class members is treated as commercial speech and therefore subject to the balancing test set forth in *Central Hudson Gas & Elec. Corp. v. Public Service Comm'n*, 447 U.S. 557 (1980). *See Frye v. Baptist Mem. Hosp., Inc.*, No. 07-2708, 2008 U.S. Dist. LEXIS 41511, *15–16 (W.D. Tenn. May 20, 2008). "An order limiting communications between the parties and potential class members should be based on a clear record and specific findings that reflect a weighing of the need for a limitation and the potential interference with the rights of the parties." *Williams v. United States Dist. Court*, 658 F.2d 430, 436 (6th Cir. 1981) (quoting *Gulf Oil Co. v. Bernard*, 452 U.S. 89, 101 (1981)).

On one hand, "[c]ourts have found a need to limit communications with absent class members where the communications were misleading, coercive, or an improper attempt to undermine Rule 23 by encouraging class members not to join the suit." *Lewis v. Huntington Nat'l Bank*, 789 F. Supp. 2d 863, 871 (S.D. Ohio 2011) (quoting *Belt v. Emcare Inc.*, 299 F. Supp. 2d 664, 667–68 (E.D. Tex. 2003)). On the other, "[a] defendant is allowed to engage in 'self-serving advocacy' so long as the statements are not inaccurate or misleading." *Potts v. Nashville Limo & Transp., LLC*, No. 3:14-cv-1412, 2016 U.S. Dist. LEXIS 53217, *55 (M.D. Tenn. Apr. 19, 2016) (quoting *Keystone Tobacco Co., Inc. v. U.S. Tobacco Co.*, 238 F. Supp. 2d 151, 157 (D.D.C. 2002)). In general, "an order limiting communications regarding ongoing litigation between a class and class opponents will satisfy first amendment concerns if it is grounded in good cause and issued with a heightened sensitivity for First

Amendment concerns." *Frye*, 2008 U.S. Dist. LEXIS 41511, at *16 (quoting *Kleiner v. First Nat'l Bank*, 751 F.2d 1193, 1205 (11th Cir. 1985)). "Courts examine four criteria to determine good cause in this context: the severity and likelihood of the perceived harm, the precision with which the order is drawn, the availability of a less onerous alternative, and the duration of the order." *Lewis*, 789 F. Supp. 2d at 871 (quoting *Belt*, 299 F. Supp. 2d at 667–68).

On the plaintiffs' side, websites, mass mailings, and other communications soliciting putative class members are permissible so long as they do not contain deceptive or misleading statements. *See, e.g.*, *Frye*, 2008 U.S. Dist. LEXIS 41511, at *17. Defendants, in turn, are generally permitted to interview and gather information from absent class members on the condition that they similarly refrain from deceptive communications. *See, e.g.*, *Lewis*, 789 F. Supp. 2d at 871 (in putative class action under Fair Labor Standards Act, refusing to prohibit a defendant from distributing and collecting non-misleading acknowledgments from potential class members (i.e., the defendant's employees) that requested information on the amount of overtime worked). Courts have shown a greater willingness to intervene, however, when it comes to unsupervised settlement communications with absent class members, as such communications create an acute danger of coercion and abuse. In one particularly egregious case involving claims under the Fair Labor Standard Act, the Middle District of Tennessee imposed a communications ban, among other remedial measures, following revelations that the defendant had pressured one of its employees to agree to release his claims in exchange for a $50 settlement and, during settlement discussions with the defendant's former employees, had made misleading statements regarding the strength and extent of the plaintiffs' claims, the legal effect of the settlement agreements, and the former employees' right to discuss the proposed settlements with plaintiffs' counsel. *Potts*, 2016 U.S. Dist. LEXIS 53217, at *53–57.

b. Discovery Regarding Absent Class Members

As a general rule, absent class members are not subject to discovery. *Stephenson v. Family Solutions of Ohio*, No. 1:18-cv-2017, 2022 U.S. Dist. LEXIS 35063, at *15 (N.D. Ohio Feb. 28, 2022). Courts reason that "because absent class members are 'parties' to the action, 'to permit extensive discovery [of them] would defeat the purpose of class actions which is to prevent massive joinder of small claims.'" *Garden City Emps. Ret. Sys. v. Psychiatric Solutions, Inc.*, No. 3:09-00882, 2012 U.S. Dist. LEXIS 145807, at *7 (M.D. Tenn. Oct. 10, 2012) (quoting *McCarthy v. Paine Webber Grp., Inc.*, 164 F.R.D. 309, 313 (D. Conn. 1995)). *See also Stephenson*, 2022 U.S. Dist. LEXIS 35063, at *16 (requiring absent class members to respond to discovery may impermissibly turn a class action into an "opt-in" procedure). Consequently, "a party that seeks to take discovery from an unnamed, or 'absent,' class member has the burden to show the necessity of the proposed discovery." *Khaliel v. Norton Healthcare, Inc.*, No. 3:08-CV-69-C, 2012 U.S. Dist. LEXIS 181850, at *3 (W.D. Ky. Nov. 20, 2012).

More specifically, "[t]he court should only allow discovery of absent class members upon a showing of 'particularized need,' which generally requires a demonstration that the discovery is addressed to common issues (as opposed to individual issues), that it is not designed to force class members to opt out, and that it would not impose an undue burden or require the deponent to seek legal or technical assistance to respond." *Id.* (quoting *Groth v. Robert Bosch Corp.*, No. 1:07-CV-962, 2008 U.S. Dist. LEXIS 52328, at *3 (W.D. Mich. July 9, 2008)); *see also Stephenson*, 2022 U.S. Dist. LEXIS 35063, at *18 (noting that some courts in the Sixth Circuit have applied different standards, but all standards require some element of necessity, limitation to common issues/questions, and avoidance of burden on the absent class members). In ordering discovery from absent class members, courts have adopted the test for particularized need contained in the *Manual for Complex Litigation*: "Discovery of unnamed members of a proposed class requires a demonstration of need. If precertification discovery of unnamed class members is appropriate, the court should consider imposing limits beyond those contemplated by the Federal Rules of Civil Procedure." *In re. Sonic Corp. Customer Data Sec. Breach Litig.*, No. 1:17-md-2807, 2020 U.S. Dist. LEXIS 7657, at *3 (N.D. Ohio Jan. 16, 2020) (citing *Manual for Complex Litigation* at § 21.14); *see also In re Polyurethane Foam Antitrust Litig.*, No. 1:10 MD 2196, 2014 U.S. Dist. LEXIS 27116, at *7 (N.D. Ohio Feb. 26, 2014) (adopting the *Manual*'s "particularized-need" rule and requiring any party that seeks discovery of an absent class member to first obtain the court's approval); *J.B.D.L. Corp. v. Wyeth-Ayerst Labs., Inc.*, No. C-1-01-704, 2004 U.S. Dist. LEXIS 32274, at *14 (S.D. Ohio June 7, 2004) ("Discovery from absent class members of a class should be sharply limited and allowed only on a strong showing of justification.").

When a party moves under Fed. R. Civ. P. 26(c) for a protective order to prohibit discovery from absent class members, the particularized-need requirement comes into conflict with the general rule that the burden of demonstrating good cause for the issuance of a protective order falls on the movant. But "since the [particularized-need requirement] is a gateway rule to discovery in class actions, it would seem to trump the burden imposed by Rule 26(c) on the moving party. . . ." *In re Skelaxin Antitrust Litig.*, 292 F.R.D. 544, 550 (E.D. Tenn. 2013).

9. DAMAGES

a. Relationship to Liability

The Supreme Court held in *Comcast Corp. v. Behrend*, 569 U.S. 27, 133 S. Ct. 1426, 185 L. Ed. 2d 515 (2013), that class certification in an antitrust action was improper because the plaintiffs' damages model did not match the liability case, i.e., the model "failed to measure damages resulting from the particular antitrust injury on which petitioners' liability ... is premised." *Id.* at 35–36. The Sixth Circuit has applied *Comcast* outside of the antitrust context. *E.g.*, *Rikos v. P&G Co.*, 799 F.3d 497, 523–24 (6th Cir. 2015). For example, in a case involving alleged damages arising from miscalculated oil and gas royalty payments, the Sixth Circuit affirmed class certification but instructed the trial court to "ensure that, if the plaintiffs prevail on the merits, any damages calculations match the sole remaining theory of liability." *Zehentbauer Family Land, LP v. Chesapeake Expl., LLC*, 935 F.3d 496, 510 (6th Cir. 2019).

b. Proof

As in individual actions, "damages need not be 'exact'" in the class action context. *In re Polyurethane Foam Antitrust Litig.*, 314 F.R.D. 226, 267 (N.D. Ohio 2014) (quoting *Comcast Corp. v. Behrend*, 133 S. Ct. 1426, 1433 (2013)). Rather, proof of damages "will be enough if the evidence show[s] the extent of the damages as a matter of just and reasonable inference, although the result be only approximate." *Id.* (quoting *Story Parchment Co. v. Paterson Parchment Paper Co.*, 282 U.S. 555, 563 (1931)). The "approximate" standard "embodies the principle that a too-demanding damages standard would act as an 'inducement to make wrongdoing so effective and complete in every case so as to preclude any recovery, by rendering the measure of damages uncertain.'" *Id.* at 267–68 (quoting *Bigelow v. RKO Radio Pictures, Inc.* 327 U.S. 251, 264 (1946)); *see also In re Scrap Metal Antitrust Litig.*, 527 F.3d 517, 535 (6th Cir. 2008) ("we have never required a precise mathematical calculation of damages before deeming a class worthy of certification"); *Owner-Operator Indep. Drivers Ass'n v. Arctic Express, Inc.*, 288 F. Supp. 2d 895, 907 (S.D. Ohio 2003) ("The Plaintiffs need not prove the amount of damages with mathematical certainty" but rather need only "set forth evidence sufficient to allow the Court to make a reasonable estimate of damages.").

The presence of "'some individualized damages issues' will not preclude class certification if common issues otherwise predominate." *In re: Polyurethane Foam Antitrust Litig.*, 314 F.R.D. at 268 (quoting *Beattie v. CenturyTel, Inc.*, 511 F.3d 554, 564 (6th Cir. 2007)). Still, "if damages are not susceptible to computation using a 'mathematical or formulaic' calculation, class treatment may be inappropriate." *Id.* (quoting *Bell Atl. Corp. v. AT&T Corp.*, 339 F.3d 294, 307 (5th Cir. 2003)). Suggesting an even higher standard is the Supreme Court's holding in *Comcast* that a damages model must establish that "damages are capable of measurement on a classwide basis." *Comcast*, 133 S. Ct. at 1433. However, the Sixth Circuit has held that this aspect of the *Comcast* decision "has limited application" where the determinations on liability and damages have been bifurcated pursuant to Fed. R. Civ. P. 23(c)(4). *Whirlpool II*, 722 F.3d at 860. Thus, in *Whirlpool II*, in which the district court had certified only a liability class and reserved all issues concerning damages for individual determination, the Sixth Circuit held that the need for individual damages calculations did not preclude certification under Rule 23(b)(3). *Id.* at 861.

Quoted with equal frequency is the *Comcast* Court's holding that "a model purporting to serve as evidence of damages in [a] class action must measure only those damages attributable to [the plaintiffs'] theory [of liability]." *Comcast*, 133 S. Ct. at 1433; *see, e.g.*, *In re Carpenter Co.*, No. 14-0302, 2014 U.S. App. LEXIS 24707, *9 (6th Cir. 2014). However, the Sixth Circuit has narrowly construed this holding as well. In the antitrust context, the Sixth Circuit has held that this prong of *Comcast* applies only where, as in *Comcast*, "multiple theories of liability exist, those theories create separable anticompetitive effects, and the combined effects can result in aggregated damages." *In re VHS of Michigan, Inc.*, 601 F. App'x 342, 344 (6th Cir. 2015). Where, on the other hand, "there is no chance of aggregated damages attributable to rejected liability theories, the Supreme Court's concerns do not apply." *Id.*; *see also In re Carpenter Co.*, 2014 U.S. App. LEXIS 24707, at *9–10 (finding no violation of *Comcast* where "district court ensured that each of the classes' [damages] models adhered to the theories of their cases, translating their legal theories of their harmful events to the economic impact of those events").

c. Distribution

Damages in a class action are frequently determined on a classwide, or "aggregate," basis. *In re Scrap Metal Antitrust Litig.*, 527 F.3d 517, 534 (6th Cir. 2008). Where aggregate damages are awarded, those damages must then be allocated in some manner to the class members. Importantly, "though questions of allocation will likely require individualized analysis, that is typical of aggregate litigation, and does not cause individual issues to predominate over common questions" so as to preclude class certification. *In re Polyurethane Foam Antitrust Litig.*, 314 F.R.D. 226, 269–70 (N.D. Ohio 2014). However, where allocation issues are so complex to essentially require a "mini-trial" for each class member, a court may properly decline certification due to manageability concerns. *See, e.g.*, *Dubose v. City of Morristown*, No. 2:07-CV-115, 2007 U.S. Dist. LEXIS 99897, *15–16 (E.D. Tenn. Aug. 31, 2007), magistrate's report and recommendation adopted at 2007 U.S. Dist. LEXIS 78989 (refusing to certify class seeking damages for police beatings because "[a]llowing an administrator to determine how much should be paid to any given class member in effect requires . . . mini-trials" that "would be disastrously wasteful of judicial resources and defeat[] the very purpose of Rule 23").

In determining the appropriate method of distribution, "[c]ourts generally consider plans of allocation that reimburse class members based on the type and extent of their injuries to be reasonable." *In re Packaged Ice Antitrust Litig.*, No. 08-MDL-01952, 2011 U.S. Dist. LEXIS 150427, at *65 (E.D. Mich. Dec. 13, 2011) (quoting *Meijer Inc. v. 3M*, No. 04-5871, 2006 U.S. Dist. LEXIS 56744, *56 (E.D. Pa. Aug. 14, 2006) (in turn quoting *In re Ikon Office Solutions Sec. Litig.*, 194 F.R.D. 166, 184 (E.D. Pa. 2000))). One of the simplest methods of distribution is the pro rata, or proportional, method, which is typically employed in antitrust and securities suits and "divide[s] the common fund on a pro rata basis among all who timely file eligible claims, thus leaving no unclaimed funds." *Id.* at *66 (quoting 3 *Newberg on Class Actions*, § 8:45 (4th ed. 2011)). For example, in price-fixing cases that employ the *pro-rata* method, "each claimant[']s share [is] calculated based on the ratio that the claimant['s] total purchases of [product] from any of the Defendants bears to the total purchases of all [class members]' purchases during the [class] period. . . ." *Id.* at *64–65.

Where, for whatever reason, a classwide recovery is not capable of distribution to class members or remains unclaimed, courts resort to what is alternately termed "fluid recovery" or the "*cy pres*" doctrine. The latter is Latin for "as near as possible," which, in the class action context, "refers to the parties' plan for the 'next best use' of the . . . funds that cannot be distributed to class members or remains unclaimed following the distribution." *Knuckles v. Mary Jane Elliott, PC*, No. 15-10175, 2016 U.S. Dist. LEXIS 94858, *5 n.2 (E.D. Mich. July 20, 2016) (quoting *Nachshin v. AOL, LLC*, 663 F.3d 1034, 1038 (9th Cir. 2011)). *Cy pres* payments "can be approved when actual funds are 'non-distributable,' or 'where the proof of individual claims would be burdensome or distribution of damages costly.''" *Id.* (quoting *Nachshin*, 663 F.3d at 1038 (in turn quoting *Six Mexican Workers v. Ariz. Citrus Growers*, 904 F.2d 1301, 1305 (9th Cir. 1990))). Similarly, "'[f]luid recovery refers to the distribution of unclaimed or unclaimable funds to persons not found to be injured but who have interests similar to those of the class.'" *In re Scrap Metal Antitrust Litig.*, 527 F.3d at 534 (quoting *In re NASDAQ Market-Makers Antitrust Litig.*, 169 F.R.D. 493, 525 (S.D. N.Y. 1996)). Examples "'include distribution of damages through price reductions rather than by cash to individual plaintiffs; distribution of settlement or damage funds left unclaimed by individuals to nonprofit organizations or to states for uses intended to benefit class members; and distribution of damages calculated on a classwide basis to individual plaintiffs or through various indirect means.'" *Id.* (quoting *Schwab v. Philip Morris USA, Inc.*, No. CV 04-1945, 2005 U.S. Dist. LEXIS 27469, *5–6 (E.D.N.Y. 2005)).

10. SETTLEMENTS

"The claims, issues, or defenses of a certified class—or a class proposed to be certified for purposes of settlement—may be settled, voluntarily dismissed, or compromised only with the court's approval." Fed. R. Civ. P. 23(e). To bind class members, a settlement must be "fair, reasonable, and adequate." Fed. R. Civ. P. 23(e)(2). The proponent of the settlement has the burden of proving its fairness. *Greenberg v. Proctor & Gamble Co. (In re Dry Max Pampers Litig.)*, 724 F.3d 713, 719 (6th Cir. 2013) (citing 4 *Newberg on Class Actions* § 11:42 (4th ed.)). In the Sixth Circuit, the following factors guide the court's determination as to whether a class action settlement is "fair, reasonable, and adequate":

> (1) the risk of fraud or collusion; (2) the complexity, expense and likely duration of the litigation; (3) the amount of discovery engaged in by the parties; (4) the likelihood of success on the merits; (5) the opinions of class counsel and class representatives; (6) the reaction of absent class members; and (7) the public interest.

International Union, United Auto., Aerospace, & Agric. Implement Workers of Am. v. General Motors Corp. (UAW), 497 F.3d 615, 631 (6th Cir. 2007). In addition, courts may consider "whether the settlement gives preferential treatment to the named plaintiffs" or to class counsel, but "only perfunctory relief to unnamed class members." *In re Dry Max Pampers Litig.*, 724 F.3d at 718 (quoting *Vassalle v. Midland Funding LLC*, 708 F.3d 747, 755 (6th Cir. 2013)). The court also considers the "federal policy favoring settlement of class actions." *UAW*, 497 F.3d at 632 (citing *In re Warfarin Sodium Antitrust Litig.*, 391 F.3d 516, 535 (3d Cir. 2004)).

The most important factor a court is to consider in reviewing a settlement is the likelihood of success on the merits. *Doe v. Déjà Vu Consulting, Inc.*, 925 F.3d 886, 895 (6th Cir. 2019) (citing *Poplar Creek Dev. Co. v. Chesapeake Appalachia, L.L.C.*, 636 F.3d 235, 245 (6th Cir.

2011)). "[A]ll class action settlements involve a balancing of competing interests. When extinguishing the claims of a large class of people—some of whom may not even be aware that a pending lawsuit affects their rights—courts are required to closely analyze whether the claims that the unnamed class members are giving are worth the benefits they may receive." *Id.*

A district court enjoys broad discretion in approving a class action settlement and assessing the weight and applicability of these various factors. *Granada Invest., Inc. v. DWG Corp.*, 962 F.2d 1203, 1206 (6th Cir.1992). As such, a district court's approval of a settlement is reviewed for abuse of discretion. *Déjà Vu Consulting*, 925 F.3d at 894. Here, the district court abuses its discretion if it fails to undertake its own analysis of how the proposed settlement would be fair to the unnamed class members and "merely recite[s] the respective arguments of the objectors and parties, and then offer[s] up platitudes about the risks of litigation generally." *Shane Grp., Inc. v. Blue Cross Blue Shield*, 825 F.3d 299, 309 (6th Cir. 2016).

To approve a class action settlement, the district court must undertake the analysis under Rule 23 that would otherwise be required to certify a class. *See Vassalle*, 708 F.3d at 756. This involves a three-step process, including: (1) preliminary approval of the proposed settlement; (2) notice and an opportunity for the class members to object; and (3) final approval after a fairness hearing. *Thacker v. Chesapeake Appalachia, L.L.C.*, 259 F.R.D. 262, 270 (E.D. Ky. 2009) (citing *Tenn. Ass'n of Helath Maint. Orgs., Inc. v. Grier*, 262 F.3d 559, 56566 (6th Cir. 2001)).

a. Preliminary Approval

The first step for a court's review and approval of a class action settlement is preliminary approval of the proposed settlement, the proposed class, and the class notice. During this threshold inquiry, the court must "determine whether the proposed settlement is 'within the range of possible approval.'" *In re Packaged Ice Antitrust Litig.*, No. 08-MD-01952, 2010 U.S. Dist. LEXIS 77645, at *35 (E.D. Mich. Aug. 2, 2010) (quoting *Gautreaux v. Pierce*, 690 F.2d 616, 621 n.3 (7th Cir. 1982)). The purpose of preliminary approval is to ascertain whether there is a reason to notify the class of the settlement and to proceed with a fairness hearing. *Id.* (quoting *Gautreaux*, 690 F.2d at 621 n.3); *see also Manual for Complex Litigation, Fourth*, § 13.14 (2004). "At the stage of preliminary approval, the questions are simpler, and the court is not expected to, and probably should not, engage in analysis as rigorous as is appropriate for final approval." *In re Skechers Toning Shoe Prods. Liab. Litig.*, No. 3:11-MD-2308-TBR, 2012 U.S. Dist. LEXIS 113641, at *20 (W.D. Ky. Aug. 13, 2012) (citing *Manual for Complex Litigation, Fourth*, § 21.662 (2012)).

Generally, preliminary approval is "based upon the court's familiarity with the issues and evidence, as well as the arms-length nature of the negotiations prior to the proposed settlement, ensuring that the proposed settlement is not illegal or collusive." *Thacker*, 259 F.R.D. at 270 (citing *In re Dun & Bradstreet Credit Servs. Customer Litig.*, 130 F.R.D. 366, 370 (S.D. Ohio 1990)). A proposed settlement should receive preliminary approval if the court finds that "the proposed settlement falls within the range of possible approval, does not disclose grounds to doubt its fairness, and includes no obvious deficiencies." *International Union, UAW v. Ford Motor Co.*, Nos. 05-74730, 06-10331, 2006 U.S. Dist. LEXIS 70471, 2006 WL 1984363, at * 11 (E.D. Mich. July 13, 2006).

b. Objections

After notice of a proposed settlement, "[a]ny class member may object. . . ." Fed. R. Civ. P. 23(e)(5). The right to object is "an important component of providing legitimacy to the class action process. . . . [T]he representative plaintiffs (and their counsel) and the defendants (and their counsel) are all jointly urging the court to approve the proposed settlement, meaning the court is not presented with a familiar adversarial discussion of the pros and cons of the settlement." William B. Rubenstein, *Newberg on Class Actions*, § 13:20 (5th ed. 2016).

Nevertheless, the court is "not required to respond to every particular objection as long as it afforded adequate process to determine that the settlement is fair, reasonable, and adequate." *Pelzer v. Vassalle*, 655 F. App'x 352, 363 (6th Cir. 2016) (holding that the district court "must have implicitly rejected" objections based on the court's statement that it had reviewed all the briefing).

In a multiple defendant class action, a non-settling defendant does not have standing to object to the fairness, reasonableness, or adequacy of another defendant's settlement unless that settlement prejudices the legal rights of the non-settling defendant. *Hyland v. Home-Services of Am., Inc.*, No. 3:05-CV-612-R, 2012 U.S. Dist. LEXIS 4818, at *17–18 (W.D. Ky. Jan. 17, 2012); *Geyer v. USX Corp.*, 896 F. Supp. 1440, 1446 (E.D. Mich. 1994).

An objector may obtain discovery only if he makes a colorable showing that the settlement should not be approved. *UAW*, 497 F.3d at 635–36; *Geier v. Alexander*, 801 F.2d 799, 809 (6th Cir. 1986).

c. Final Approval

Final approval of a class action settlement comes after a fairness hearing, in which class members have a right to participate. *UAW*, 497 F.3d at 635 (citations omitted). At the fairness hearing, the parties must present sufficient evidence to allow the district court to review the terms of the settlement and determine that it is fair, reasonable, and adequate applying the factors set forth in *UAW*. *Id.* (citing *In re General Tire & Rubber Co. Sec. Litig.*, 726 F.2d 1075, 1084 n.6 (6th Cir. 1984)). Class members may object to the settlement on the record. *Id.* (quoting Fed. R. Civ. P. 23(e)(5)). In determining whether a class action settlement is fair, reasonable, and adequate, the district court has broad discretion and need not conduct the proceeding as if it were a full-blown trial on the merits or according to the Rules of Evidence. *Id.* (quoting *Tennessee Ass'n of Health Maint. Orgs. v. Grier*, 262 F.3d 559, 567 (6th Cir. 2001)). In giving final approval to a class action settlement, the district court does not resolve factual disputes; it ensures that the settlement is fair, reasonable, and adequate. *Id.*

d. *Cy Pres*

The term *cy pres* derives from the Norman French expression *cy pres comme possible* ("as near as possible") and "is an equitable doctrine with roots in trusts and estates law." *In re Polyurethane Foam Antitrust Litig.*, 178 F. Supp. 3d 621, 622–23 (N.D. Ohio 2016) (quoting 4 *Newberg on Class Actions,* § 12.32 (5th ed.)). From those origins, courts have imported the doctrine into the class action context. *Id.* "A *cy pres* award is 'used to distribute unclaimed portions of a class-action judgment or settlement funds to a charity that will advance the interests of the class.'" *Gascho v. Global Fitness Holdings, LLC*, 822 F.3d 269, 278 n.3 (6th Cir. 2016) (quoting *Black's Law Dictionary* (10th ed. 2014)). The Sixth Circuit has not meaningfully addressed the scope of the doctrine. *In re Polyurethane Foam Antitrust Litig.*, 178 F. Supp. 3d at 622. Increasingly, however, appellate courts follow the American Law Institute's *Principles of the Law of Aggregate Litigation* (2010), which provides principles and guidance for, among other things, the resolution of class actions, including the use of *cy pres*. *See In re Polyurethane Foam Antitrust Litig.*, 168 F. Supp. 3d 985, 1005 (N.D. Ohio 2016) (citing *Klier v. Elf Atochem N. Am., Inc.*, 658 F.3d 468 (5th Cir. 2011); *Oetting v. Green Jacobson, P.C. (In re BankAmerica Corp. Sec. Litig.)*, 775 F.3d 1060 (8th Cir. 2015)).

Settlement funds are property of the class; therefore, a *cy pres* distribution of unclaimed settlement funds is permissible "only when it is not feasible to make further distributions to class members." *Klier*, 658 F.3d at 475 (quoting ALI *Principles*, § 3.07 cmt. a). "Where it is still logistically feasible and economically viable to make additional pro rata distributions to class members, the district court should do so, except where an additional distribution would provide a windfall to class members with liquidated-damages claims that were 100 percent satisfied by the initial distribution." *In re Polyurethane Foam Antitrust Litig.*, 168 F. Supp.

3d at 1005 (quoting *Klier*, 658 F.3d at 475).

In other words, *cy pres* may be used when money may not feasibly be awarded to the beneficiaries of the settlement class. *In re Polyurethane Foam Antitrust Litig.*, 168 F. Supp. 3d at 1005 (quoting *Klier*, 658 F.3d at 475). For example, it may not be economical to distribute small class awards to individual beneficiaries. *Id.*

> In large class actions, substantial administrative costs attend the distribution of settlement funds. As the settlement funds are disbursed and the amount still available for distribution to the class declines, there comes a point at which the marginal cost of making an additional pro rata distribution to the class members exceeds the amount available for distribution. It is only at this point that a district court has discretion to order a *cy pres* distribution.

Klier, 658 F.3d at 475 (internal citation omitted). *Cy pres* is preferable to escheat to the government or reversion to the defendant. *Rosser v. A & S Contr., Inc.*, No. 2:15-cv-00711, 2017 U.S. Dist. LEXIS 23377, at *4 (S.D. Ohio Feb. 17, 2017) (citing *ALI Principles*, § 3.07 cmt. b).

After distribution to class members, "a *cy pres* distribution puts settlement funds to their next-best use by providing an indirect benefit to the class." *In re Polyurethane Foam Antitrust Litig.*, 168 F. Supp. 3d at 1005 (quoting *Klier*, 658 F.3d at 475). The Sixth Circuit has not weighed in on the circuit split over whether *cy pres* recipients must be disclosed in a class notice. *Compare Dennis v. Kellogg Co.*, 697 F.3d 858, 862–63, 867 (9th Cir. 2012) (reversing final approval of class action settlement for failure to identify *cy pres* recipients), *with Baby Prods. Antitrust Litig.*, 708 F.3d 163, 180 (3d Cir. 2013) (reversing final approval because too large a portion of settlement funds was designate for *cy pres* distribution, but no listing of specific recipients is necessary), *and BankAmerica Corp. Sec. Litig.*, 775 F.3d 1060, 1066 (8th Cir. 2015) (noting that unless the amount of funds available for *cy pres* is *de minimis*, a *cy pres* proposal should be disclosed in the settlement notice so that class members may object).

A *cy pres* recipient should not have a previous relationship with the parties or the court to avoid creating the appearance of impropriety. *In re Polyurethane Foam Antitrust Litig.*, 178 F. Supp. 3d at 623 (citing *Nachshin v. AOL, LLC*, 663 F.3d 1034, 1038 (9th Cir. 2011)). When selecting *cy pres* recipients, the court should solicit suggestions for appropriate beneficiaries from the parties, though the final selection remains within the discretion of the court. *ALI Principles*, § 3.07 cmt. b.

11. FEES AND COSTS

Rule 23(h) provides that "[i]n a certified class action, the court may award reasonable attorney's fees and nontaxable costs that are authorized by law or by the parties' agreement." Fed. R. Civ. P. 23(h).

a. Fees

"When awarding attorney's fees in a class action, a court must make sure that counsel is fairly compensated for the amount of work done as well as for the results achieved." *Rawlings v. Prudential-Bache Props., Inc.*, 9 F.3d 513, 516 (6th Cir. 1993). "These two measures of the fairness of an attorney's award—work done and results achieved—can be in tension with each other." *Gascho v. Global Fitness Holdings, LLC*, 822 F.3d 269, 279 (6th Cir. 2016). Within the Sixth Circuit, courts have broad discretion to select the appropriate methodology to achieve these goals and may employ a lodestar computation, a percentage of the fund calculation, or both—using one as a cross-check on the other. *Id.* at 278, 279. The lodestar method better accounts for the amount of work done, whereas a percentage calculation more accurately reflects the results achieved. *Rawlings*, 9 F.3d at 516. In some cases, courts in the Sixth Circuit will conduct a cross-check between both methods; however, the Sixth Circuit has held that such cross-checks are not required. *See, e.g.*, *Waid v. Snyder (In re Flint Water Cases)*, 63 F.4th 486, 499 (6th Cir. 2023) (citing *Linneman v. Vita-Mix Corp.*, 970 F.3d 621, 628 (6th Cir. 2020)).

In arriving at a fee award, the court must identify the factors that support the award. *Moulton v. U.S. Steel Corp.*, 581 F.3d 344, 352 (6th Cir. 2009) (quoting *Rawlings*, 9 F.3d at 516). The relevant factors include:

> (1) the value of the benefit rendered to the plaintiff class; (2) the value of the services on an hourly basis; (3) whether the services were undertaken on a contingent fee basis; (4) society's stake in rewarding attorneys who produce such benefits in order to maintain an incentive to others; (5) the complexity of the litigation; and (6) the professional skill and standing of counsel involved on both sides.

Id. (quoting *Bowling v. Pfizer, Inc.*, 102 F.3d 777, 780 (6th Cir. 1996)). These factors are also known as the "Ramey factors." *See Ramey v. Cincinnati Enquirer, Inc.*, 508 F.2d 1188 (6th Cir. 1974).

Regardless of whether the court uses a lodestar or percentage approach, it "must ensure . . . that the final award is 'reasonable' under the circumstances." *Linneman v. Vita-Mix Corp.*, 970 F.3d 621, 624(6th Cir. Aug. 12, 2020) (internal quotations and citations omitted). The court must also "provide a reasonably specific explanation of this factor to allow for adequate appellate review." *Id.* at 633 (internal quotations omitted). When assessing the reasonableness of a fee award, the "most critical factor" for the court to consider "is the degree of success obtained." *Id.* (citations omitted). Analysis of this factor will typically require the court to make specific findings about the value of the settlement, including consideration of the evidence presented by the parties. *Id.* Other factors may also bear on reasonableness. For example, a fee award may be unreasonable if plaintiff's counsel earlier rejected a reasonable offer to settle his fees and instead "ke[pt] his meter running." *Id.* And pre-litigation measures taken by defendant to remedy the alleged harm may also bear on reasonableness. *Id.* at 634.

Lodestar Calculation

Under the lodestar method, the court multiplies the number of hours "reasonably expended" on the litigation by a "reasonable hourly rate." *Building Serv. Local 47 Cleaning Contractors Pension Plan v. Grandview Raceway*, 46 F.3d 1392, 1401 (6th Cir. 1995). Under this method, an attorney must document the hours charged in "sufficient detail and probative value to enable the court to determine with a high degree of certainty that such hours were actually and reasonably expended" in the litigation. *Imwalle v. Reliance Med. Prods., Inc.*, 515 F.3d 531, 553 (6th Cir. 2008). At minimum, the general subject matter for each charge should be documented. *Id.*

To determine the reasonable hourly rate, courts look to "the prevailing market rate in the relevant community." *Adcock-Ladd v. Secretary of Treasury*, 227 F.3d 343, 350 (6th Cir. 2000) (quoting *Blum v. Stenson*, 465 U.S. 886, 895 (1984). To determine the prevailing market rate, courts look to awards in analogous cases, bar association guidelines, the submissions of the parties, and the court's own knowledge and experience. *Van Horn v. Nationwide Prop. & Cas. Ins. Co.*, 436 F. App'x 496, 499 (6th Cir. 2011). The "relevant community" is the venue of the court, not an out-of-town lawyer's typical jurisdiction where that "home rate" exceeds local rates in the court's venue. *Hudson v. Reno*, 130 F.3d 1193, 1208 (6th Cir. 1997). In other words, the venue of the court determines the maximum reasonable hourly rate. *Adcock-Ladd*, 227 F.3d at 350. The appropriate rate is the market rate sufficient to encourage competent representation. *Gonter v. Hunt Valve Co.*, 510 F.3d 610, 618 (6th Cir. 2007). Counsel seeking fees bear the burden of submitting evidence, in addition to counsel's own affidavit(s), that shows the requested hourly rate is reasonable. *Linneman*,

970 F.3d at 630.

After this initial lodestar calculation, the court "may then, within limits, adjust the 'lodestar' to reflect relevant considerations peculiar to the subject litigation." *Adcock-Ladd*, 227 F.3d at 349. But adjustments to the lodestar "are proper only in certain 'rare' and 'exceptional' cases, supported by both 'specific evidence' on the record and detailed findings." *Id.* at 350 (quoting *Pennsylvania v. Delaware Valley Citizens' Council for Clean Air*, 478 U.S. 546, 565 (1986)). Enhancing the lodestar with a separate "multiplier" can adjust for the risk an attorney assumed in undertaking a case, the quality of the attorney's work, and the public benefit achieved. *Gascho*, 822 F.3d at 279 (quoting *Rawlings*, 9 F.3d at 516). But the Sixth Circuit has emphasized that a multiplier should only be awarded "in the rarest circumstances," such as a billing rate that does not measure an attorney's true market value, exceptionally protracted litigation that required an extraordinary outlay of expenses, or an exceptional delay in the payment of fees. *Linneman*, 970 F.3d at 632.

The factors affecting this multiplier are the 12 listed in *Johnson v. Georgia Highway Express, Inc.*, 488 F.2d 714, 717–19 (5th Cir. 1974). *Adcock-Ladd*, 227 F.3d at 349. They are:

> (1) the time and labor required by a given case; (2) the novelty and difficulty of the questions presented; (3) the skill needed to perform the legal service properly; (4) the preclusion of employment by the attorney due to acceptance of the case; (5) the customary fee; (6) whether the fee is fixed or contingent; (7) time limitations imposed by the client or the circumstances; (8) the amount involved and the results obtained; (9) the experience, reputation, and ability of the attorneys; (10) the "undesirability" of the case; (11) the nature and length of the professional relationship with the client; and (12) awards in similar cases.

Reed v. Rhodes, 179 F.3d 453, 471–72 n.3 (6th Cir. 1999) (citing *Johnson*, 488 F.2d at 717–19). "Some of those factors ordinarily may be considered only when resolving the basic lodestar fee, and thus cannot be used to augment that lodestar." *Adcock-Ladd*, 227 F.3d at 349 n.8 (citing *Delaware Valley Citizens' Council*, 478 U.S. at 565). Upward or downward adjustments to the lodestar may be appropriate. *Van Horn*, 436 F. App'x at 499 (citing *Geler v. Sundquist*, 372 F.3d 784, 792 (6th Cir. 2004)).

The benefits of the lodestar method include providing greater accountability. *Gascho*, 822 F.3d at 279 (quoting *Rawlings*, 9 F.3d at 516). In addition, the lodestar method promotes efficiency by encouraging lawyers to assess the value of work on a case. *Id.* Its drawback is that it is time-consuming for courts to administer. *Id.* at 280 (quoting *Rawlings*, 9 F.3d at 516).

Percentage of the Fund

"When conducting a percentage of the fund analysis, courts must calculate the ratio between attorney's fees and benefit to the class." *Gascho*, 822 F.3d at 282. In other words, attorneys' fees are the numerator, and the dollar value of the total benefit to the class (plus attorneys' fees and the cost of settlement administration) is the denominator. *Id.* Determining the denominator must use a method that gives appropriate consideration to all cash and non-cash components of a settlement, which depends on the facts and circumstances of each particular case. *Id.* The Sixth Circuit has held that what matters is the benefit available to the class, regardless of whether class members exercise it. *Id.* at 282. Therefore, even if unclaimed funds or settlement amounts revert to the defendant, the value of claims paid is not the proper measure of the benefit to the class. *Id.* at 282–87.

The advantages of the percentage of the fund method include its ease of calculation. *Gascho*, 822 F.3d at 279 (quoting *Rawlings*, 9 F.3d at 516). In addition, "it establishes reasonable expectations on the part of plaintiffs' attorneys as to their expected recovery; and it encourages early settlement, which avoids protracted litigation." *Id.* On the other hand, it can provide an incentive for too little recovery, because an early settlement provides a larger fee in terms of the time invested, and it can generate a windfall for class counsel. *Id.*

Clear-Sailing Provisions

A clear sailing clause is an agreement by the defendant not to oppose class counsel's application for attorneys' fees up to a particular amount. *Gascho*, 822 F.2d at 274. A class action settlement that contains a clear sailing provision triggers heightened scrutiny by the district court to "scrutinize closely" the relationship between attorneys' fees and the benefits to the class. *Id.* at 291. Although some circuits disfavor clear sailing agreements, the Sixth Circuit has held that approval of a class action settlement containing such a clause, without more, is not an abuse of discretion. *Id.*

Objectors

"Fees and costs may be awarded to the counsel for objectors to a class action settlement if the work of the counsel produced a beneficial result for the class." *Olden v. Gardner*, 294 F. App'x 210, 221 (6th Cir. 2008). In awarding fees to class counsel for the work done for the benefit of all class members, including objectors, courts in the Sixth Circuit must assess reasonableness using the same *Ramey* factors, and may apply either the lodestar or percentage-of-the-fund methodology. *See, e.g.*, *Waid*, 63 F.4th at 495–96 (6th Cir. 2023).

b. Expenses

"[A] litigant who recovers a common fund for the benefit of persons other than himself is entitled to recover some of his litigation expenses from the fund as a whole." *Hadix v. Johnson*, 322 F.3d 895, 898 (6th Cir. 2003) (citing *Boeing Co. v. Van Gemert*, 444 U.S. 472, 478 (1980)). "Necessary and reasonable costs" may be recovered. *Lankford v. Reladyne, LLC*, No. 1:14-cv-682, 2016 U.S. Dist. LEXIS 85003, at *17 (S.D. Ohio June 29, 2016) (citing *Harris v. Marhoefer*, 24 F.3d 16, 19 (9th Cir. 1994)).

12. APPELLATE ISSUES

a. Standard of Review

Appellate review of an order to certify a class is narrow and very limited. *Hicks v. State Farm Fire & Cas. Co.*, 965 F.3d 452, 456 (6th Cir. 2020) (internal quotations and citations omitted). To reverse a decision to certify a class, the appellant must "make[] a strong showing that the district court's decision amounted to a clear abuse of discretion." *Id.* (citations omitted). A trial court abuses its discretion if it "relies on clearly erroneous findings of fact, applies the wrong legal standard, misapplies the correct legal standard when reaching a conclusion, or makes a clear error of judgment." *Zehentbauer Family Land, LP v. Chesapeake Expl., LLC*, 935 F.3d 496, 502 (6th Cir. 2019).

b. Standing to Appeal

To have standing to appeal a class action, an individual must be a member of the class who would be bound by the court's decision. *See Devlin v. Scardelletti*, 536 U.S. 1, 10 (2002). In *Devlin*, the Supreme Court analyzed whether a petitioner had standing to appeal a court's order in the context of a class action settlement. *Id.* The petitioner in the action was an unnamed member of a certified class who had not successfully intervened in the action. *Id.* at 3. The petitioner sought to appeal the settlement that was approved over his objection at the fairness hearing on the matter. *Id.* The Supreme Court held that the petitioner could appeal because he was "a member of the class bound by the judgment." *Id.* at 7. Further, the settlement decision was a "final decision of petitioner's right or claim sufficient to trigger his right to appeal." *Id.* at 9 (internal citations omitted). By objecting at the fairness hearing, the petitioner had preserved his right to appeal. *Id.* at 10.

In *Fidel v. Farley*, 534 F.3d 508 (6th Cir. 2008), the Sixth Circuit further addressed the issue of an individual's standing to appeal in the class action context. In *Fidel*, the petitioner was an unnamed member of the class who failed to receive timely notice regarding the class action. *Id.* at 511. Because he did not receive timely notice, he was unable to object at the fairness hearing held regarding the settlement. *See id.* The Sixth Circuit considered the issue of whether the petitioner still had standing to appeal, despite not objecting at the fairness hearing, and the court held that because he was bound by the settlement, he is a party with standing to appeal. Based on these opinions, any member of a class who would be bound by the court's decision would be considered a party with rights to appeal a court's class action decision.

In *Waid v. Snyder (In re Flint Water Cases)*, 63 F.4th 486 (6th Cir. 2023), certain class objectors sought to challenge the common benefit assessment structure, under which class counsel and certain individuals' counsel were awarded attorneys' fees. The Sixth Circuit explained that, because the objectors would be no better off with or without the challenged aspects of the common benefit assessments, the objectors lacked standing to appeal those assessments. *Id.* at 503. Additionally, standing could not be manufactured by an objector's individual counsel's claims that he would pass on any reduction in class or liaison counsel's common benefit fees to his clients. *Id.* at 505 (citing *Clapper v. Amnesty Int'l USA*, 568 U.S. 389, 402 (2013)).

c. Interlocutory Review

Federal Rule of Civil Procedure 23(f), which became effective in 1998, allows for interlocutory appeals of class action orders. Pursuant to the rule, "the court of appeals is given unfettered discretion whether to permit the appeal, akin to the discretion exercised by the Supreme Court in acting on a petition for certiorari." Fed. R. Civ. P. 23(f) Advisory Committee Notes (1998). Further, the Advisory Committee anticipated each circuit would develop standards for granting review. *Id.*

The Sixth Circuit first discussed the standard it would employ under Rule 23(f) in detail in *In re Delta Air Lines*, 310 F.3d 953, 957–60 (6th Cir. 2002). The *Delta* court examined the various standards used in other circuits and stated three important premises upon which their review of interlocutory appeals would be founded. *Id.* at 959–60. First, the court could examine "any pertinent factor" and would not create "any hard-and-fast test." *Id.* Second, a Rule 23(f) appeal would not be routine, and third, the "merits of a class certification decision must weigh into the initial determination of whether to grant the interlocutory appeal." *Id.*

Delta and its progeny also articulated specific factors that the Sixth Circuit has repeatedly used to evaluate petitions for interlocutory appeals under 23(f):

(1) whether the petitioner is likely to succeed on appeal under the deferential abuse-of-discretion standard;
(2) whether the cost of continuing the litigation for either party presents such a barrier that subsequent review is hampered;
(3) whether the case presents a novel or unsettled question of law; and
(4) the procedural posture of the case before the district court.

E.g., *In re VHS of Michigan, Inc.*, 601 F. App'x 342, 343 (6th Cir. 2015); *In re HCA Holdings, Inc.*, No. 14-0511, 2015 U.S. App. LEXIS 3015, *3–4 (6th Cir. Feb. 26, 2015); *In re Carpenter Co.*, No. 14-0302, 2014 U.S. App. LEXIS 24707, *6–8 (6th Cir. Sept. 29, 2014). By way of example, the Sixth Circuit has granted petitions for interlocutory review when "there is limited authority on the issues, and no binding authority from our court," *In re Wayne County*, No. 20-0101, 2020 U.S. App. LEXIS 23300 (6th Cir. July 23, 2020); when the permissibility of a certain class-action procedure was both a novel issue and an issue that was relevant to class litigation in general, *In re Nat'l Prescription Opiate Litig.*, No. 19-0306, 2019 U.S. App. LEXIS 33629 (6th Cir. Nov. 18, 2019); and when potentially enormous discovery costs resulting from the decision to certify class could prevent appellate review of an unsettled issue, *In re State Farm Fire & Cas. Co.*, No. 19-0503, 2019 U.S. App. LEXIS 20035 (6th Cir. July 3, 2019). The Sixth Circuit most recently granted interlocutory review of a class certification order that raised questions of standing, specificity of relief, and whether the Sixth Circuit requires 23(b)(2) classes to be "cohesive." *See In re E.I. Dupont de Nemours & Co. C-8 Pers. Injury Litig.*, No. 22-0305, 2022 U.S. App. LEXIS 25452 (6th Cir. Sept. 9, 2022).

The Sixth Circuit has held that it lacks jurisdiction over appeals of class-action settlements where the trial court has not yet determined the amounts of attorneys' fees to be paid, because the appellate court's examination of the reasonableness of the settlement will depend in part on how class members and their counsel will divide the proceeds. *Shane Grp., Inc. v. Blue Cross Blue Shield of Mich.*, Nos. 19-2260, 19-2261, 19-2336, 2020 U.S. App. LEXIS 26817 (6th Cir. Aug. 21, 2020).

In contrast, when the district court has awarded attorneys' fees *after* deciding the merits of the case, and the fee order resolves all attorneys' fees claims, the appellate court has independent jurisdiction over the appeal from the fee award and the appellant need not also challenge the underlying settlement approval or merits judgment. *Waid*, 63 F.4th at 502.

13. TOLLING STATUTE OF LIMITATIONS

The U.S. Supreme Court held in *American Pipe & Constr. Co. v. Utah*, 414 U.S. 538, 554 (1974) that "the commencement of a class action suspends the applicable statute of limitations as to all asserted members of the class who would have been parties had the suit been permitted to continue as a class action." The statute is tolled until a court decides the suit is not appropriate for class action treatment. *Id.* The court reasoned that this policy would avoid multiplicity of activity and increase efficiency because individuals would not need to file multiple suits or intervene to protect their rights. *Id.*

Subsequently, the *American Pipe* doctrine was extended by the Supreme Court in *Crown, Cork & Seal, Co., Inc. v. Parker*, 462 U.S. 345, 346–47 (1983) when it held that "all members of the putative class [may] file individual actions in the event that class certification is denied, provided . . . that those actions are instituted within the time that remains on the limitations period." *Crown* explained that tolling of the statute of limitations extends to all putative class members, regardless of whether those members are seeking to intervene or initiate their own suit. *Id.* at 348. Much like in *American Pipe*, similar policy concerns of efficiency and judicial economy were rationales for the Court's decision.

a. Sixth Circuit Clarification of *American Pipe*

The Sixth Circuit has further clarified *American Pipe*'s tolling authority. In *Wyser-Pratte Mgmt. Co. v. Telxon Corp*, 413 F.3d 553 (6th Cir. 2005), the Court examined the issue of whether plaintiffs who file actions *before* the court rules on class certification also are able to take advantage of the *American Pipe* tolling doctrine. The Court declined to extend tolling to these plaintiffs, stating that judicial economy was the basis for the *American Pipe* decision and "[t]he purposes of *American Pipe* tolling are not furthered when plaintiffs file independent actions before decision on the issue of class certification, but are when plaintiffs delay until the certification issue has been decided." *Id.* at 569. Moreover, the Court said that this will prevent the court from being burdened with separate lawsuits that could "evaporate once a class has been certified." *Id.* (quoting *In re WorldCom, Inc. Sec. Litig.*, 294 F. Supp. 2d 431, 452 (S.D.N.Y. 2003)). *Wyser-Pratte* was recently upheld as controlling law, despite other circuits' decisions to the contrary, in the Sixth Circuit case *Stein v. Regions Morgan Keegan Select High Income Fund, Inc.*, 821 F.3d 780, 788–89 (6th Cir. 2016).

As for the process of tolling, the Sixth Circuit uses the suspension approach. Under this approach, "Section 1367 (d) suspends the running of the statute of limitations" and the clock is stopped while the court considers the issue of class action certification and "for thirty days after the claim is dismissed." *Vertrue v. Vertrue, Inc. (In re Vertrue Mktg. & Sales Practices Litig.)*, 719 F.3d 474, 481–82 (6th Cir. 2013). Therefore, unnamed plaintiffs who wish to pursue claims after class certification is denied may file within the longer of 30 days or the time period remaining under the applicable statute of limitations.

The Sixth Circuit has further clarified that after a court denies certification of a class, an unnamed plaintiff may file either an individual lawsuit or a new class action, taking advantage of the *American Pipe* tolling doctrine. *Phipps v. Wal-Mart Stores*, 792 F.3d 637, 653–54 (6th Cir. 2015). In *Phipps*, a nationwide action by plaintiffs against Wal-Mart was originally denied, and the court examined whether a subsequent timely filed class action requesting to certify a class of plaintiffs within a region against Wal-Mart was permitted. *Id.* The Court held that while issues may arise whether "a follow-on class action or particular issues raised within it are precluded by earlier litigation," no issues are raised by the statute of limitations. *Id.*

Phipps also clarified an earlier decision that prevented the refiling of a subsequent class action that was not filed within the statute of limitations, even with the *American Pipe* tolling. *See Andrews v. Orr*, 851 F.2d 146 (6th Cir. 1998). The *Phipps* court distinguished *Andrews* by stating *Andrews* was limited to class actions that were not timely filed. *Phipps*, 792 F.3d at 652. Therefore, both new class actions and individual actions may be filed after a court denies certification of a class, so long as they are within the filing window.

b. Statute of Repose

The Circuit Courts were split on the issue of whether the American Pipe decision tolls statutes of repose in addition to statutes of limitation. The Sixth Circuit followed the view first articulated by the Second Circuit that American Pipe does not apply to statutes of repose. *See Stein v. Regions Morgan Keegan Select High Income Fund, Inc.*, 821 F.3d 780, 792–95 (6th Cir. 2016) citing *Police & Fire Ret. Sys. of City of Detroit v. IndyMac MBS, Inc.*, 721 F.3d 95 (2d Cir. 2013). Stein held that statutes of repose are inconsistent with tolling principles because the purpose of statutes of repose are to "clearly [] serve as a cutoff." *Stein*, 821 F.3d at 793 quoting *Lampf, Pleva, Lipkind, Prupis & Petigrow v. Gilbertson*, 501 U.S. 350, 363 (1991) (internal citations omitted). *Stein* reasoned that *IndyMac* and its holding are more consistent with the Supreme Court's decision in *CTS Corp. v. Waldburger*, 134 S. Ct. 2175, 2183 (2014) which stated that "a statute of repose is a judgment that defendants should 'be free from liability after the legislatively determined period of time, beyond which the liability will no longer exist *and will not be tolled for any reason*.'"

To resolve the circuit split over the statute of repose, the U.S. Supreme Court granted certiorari in *California Public Employees' Retirement System v. ANZ Securities, Inc.*, 137 S. Ct. 811 (2017), *cert. granted*, 85 U.S.L.W. 3344 (U.S. Jan. 13, 2017) (No. 16-373). On June 26, 2017, the Court issued a ruling, holding 5 to 4 that the "equitable tolling" of *American Pipe* is inapplicable to statutes of repose. *Id.*, 137 S. Ct. 2042. Writing for the majority, Justice Kennedy held that the case was governed by the Court's 2014 opinion in *Waldburger*. The statute at issue in the case—Section 13 of the Securities Act of 1933, 15 U.S.C. §77m—establishes two distinct deadlines for claims alleging misrepresentations in connection with the issuance of securities: a one-year deadline running from the "discovery of the untrue statement" and a later three-year deadline running from the date on which the statement is made. Relying on *Waldburger*, the Court found that statutes of repose are intended to afford "complete peace" to defendants and thus supersedes any tolling based on equity.

14. ARBITRATION ISSUES

Many consumer and employment contracts require the parties to submit any disputes to arbitration. One question that sometimes arises is whether the consumer or employee can seek to arbitrate the dispute on a classwide basis. The answer usually depends on the language of the arbitration agreement. Although the task of construing the contract often falls to the arbitrator, "the question whether an arbitration agreement permits classwide arbitration is a gateway matter, which is reserved 'for judicial determination unless the parties clearly and unmistakably provide otherwise.'" *Reed Elsevier, Inc. v. Crockett*, 734 F.3d 594, 599 (6th Cir. 2013).

Arbitration agreements can either authorize classwide arbitrations, be silent on the issue, or waive any right to classwide arbitration. Given the "momentous consequence" to the parties of requiring classwide arbitration, the Sixth Circuit prohibits classwide arbitration if the agreement is silent. *Reed Elsevier, Inc.*. 734 F.3d at 599–600 (citing *Stolt-Nielsen S.A. v. AnimalFeeds Int'l Corp.*, 559 U.S. 662, 685 (2010)). Courts also typically enforce class arbitration waivers, even if the costs of individual arbitration outweigh the plaintiff's potential recovery. *Am. Express Co. v. Italian Colors Rest.*, 133 S. Ct. 2304 (2013). The current legal framework therefore generally permits the party drafting the agreement to prohibit the classwide arbitration of disputes.

The plaintiff may seek to avoid this result by challenging the arbitrability of the dispute. "[I]f the making of the arbitration agreement . . . is in issue," then the court must decide whether it is enforceable before compelling arbitration. Federal Arbitration Act, 9 U.S.C. § 4. An agreement is "in issue" when "the party opposing arbitration . . . show[s] a genuine issue of material fact as to the validity of the agreement to arbitrate." *Great Earth Cos. v. Simons*, 288 F.3d 878, 889 (6th Cir. 2002). For example, an arbitration agreement may be invalid and unenforceable if there is insufficient consideration, or if one party can unilaterally modify the rules governing the arbitration. *Walker v. Ryan's Family Steak Houses, Inc.*, 400 F.3d 370, 379–81 (6th Cir. 2005). The Sixth Circuit has held that agreements to arbitrate employment claims are only enforceable if the employee knowingly and voluntarily waived his right to pursue those claims in court. *Morrison v. Circuit City Stores, Inc.*, 317 F.3d 646, 668 (6th Cir. 2003) (en banc). If there is "clear and unmistakable" evidence that the parties have agreed to arbitrate the question of arbitrability, however, then this threshold question will be decided by an arbitrator rather than by a court. *Blanton v. Domino's Pizza Franchising LLC*, 962 F.3d 842, 844–45 (6th Cir. 2020).

SEVENTH CIRCUIT

Districts of Illinois, Indiana, and Wisconsin

Everett McKinley Dirksen United States Courthouse
219 S. Dearborn Street, Room 2722
Chicago, IL 60604

By Adam J. Levitt, John E. Tangren, Amy E. Keller, Daniel R. Ferri,
Michelle Locascio, Jessica Holmes, and Julia Veeser
DiCello Levitt LLP

1. INTRODUCTION

The Seventh Circuit, comprised of district courts in the states of Illinois, Indiana, and Wisconsin, sits in Chicago, Illinois. There are 11 seats on the Circuit Court, not including those who have elected senior status but continue to hear appeals. The Seventh Circuit is routinely at the forefront of technology in the courtrooms—developing the Electronic Discovery Pilot Program Committee in 2009 to "conduct a multi-year, multi-phase process to develop, implement, evaluate, and improve pretrial litigation procedures that would provide fairness and justice to all parties while seeking to reduce the cost and burden of electronic discovery consistent with Rule 1 of the Federal Rules of Civil Procedure."[1] Subcommittees of the Program Committee also have developed model rules, webinars, and other useful materials available on the Program Committee's website.[2]

The Seventh Circuit grants oral argument in a high percentage of its cases—usually among the highest of any of the circuits. Audio recordings of those arguments are available on the court's website within a day of the case being argued.[3]

The Seventh Circuit's approach to class certification recognizes that the class action device is a practical and necessary way to allow for lawsuits demanding corporate accountability. The Seventh Circuit recently rejected an invitation by defendants to apply the Supreme Court's *Comcast v. Behrend* holding, 569 U.S. 27, 133 S. Ct. 1426 (2013), in a way that would curb consumer class litigation.

> It would drive a stake through the heart of the class action device, in cases in which damages were sought rather than an injunction or a declaratory judgment, to require that every member of the class have identical damages. If the issues of lia-

[1] *See* Seventh Circuit Council on eDiscovery and Digital Information, About the Council, https://www.ediscoverycouncil.com/about-us (last accessed Dec. 1, 2021).

[2] Seventh Circuit Council on eDiscovery and Digital Information, Resources, https://www.ediscoverycouncil.com/content/resources (last accessed Dec. 1, 2021).

[3] Seventh Circuit Court of Appeals, Public Access to Oral Argument recordings, media.ca7.uscourts.gov/oralArguments/oar.jsp. Opinions also are available when decided. Seventh Circuit Court of Appeals, Public access to Opinions and Nonprecedential Dispositive Orders, media.ca7.uscourts.gov/opinion.html.

> bility are genuinely common issues, and the damages of individual class members can be readily determined in individual hearings, in settlement negotiations, or by creation of subclasses, the fact that damages are not identical across all class members should not preclude class certification. Otherwise defendants would be able to escape liability for tortious harms of enormous aggregate magnitude but so widely distributed as not to be remediable in individual suits. As we noted in *Carnegie v. Household Int'l., Inc.*, 376 F.3d 656, 661 (7th Cir. 2004), "the more claimants there are, the more likely a class action is to yield substantial economies in litigation. It would hardly be an improvement to have in lieu of this single class 17 million suits each seeking damages of $15 to $30. . . . The *realistic* alternative to a class action is not 17 million individual suits, but zero individual suits, as only a lunatic or a fanatic sues for $30" (emphasis in original). The present case is less extreme: tens of thousands of class members, each seeking damages of a few hundred dollars. But few members of such a class, considering the costs and distraction of litigation, would think so meager a prospect made suing worthwhile.

Butler v. Sears, Roebuck and Co., 727 F.3d 796, 801 (7th Cir. 2013).

On the other hand, the Seventh Circuit applies a great deal of scrutiny to class settlements, especially when it comes to the valuation of benefits available to the class and calculation of attorneys' fees, making consumer class actions more difficult to settle and more open to objection. *See In re Southwest Airlines Voucher Litig.*, 799 F.3d 701 (7th Cir. 1995); *Redman v. RadioShack Corp.*, 768 F.3d 622 (7th Cir. 2014).

This chapter provides an overview of class action litigation in the circuit—from pleading a case (including defining the class) through certification, settlement, and final disposition. The chapter aims to set out the basic and developing law surrounding the class action prerequisites, in addition to highlighting circuit-specific nuances relating to the Rule 23 analysis that may be relevant when practicing in the Seventh Circuit.

2. JURISDICTIONAL ISSUES

a. CAFA Requirements

The Class Action Fairness Act of 2005 (CAFA) generally extends federal diversity jurisdiction to any class action with at least 100 class members where there is minimal diversity and the amount in controversy exceeds $5 million. 28 U.S.C. § 1332(d); *Johnson v. Diakon Logistics, Inc.*, 44 F.4th 1048, 1050 (7th Cir. 2022), *reh'g denied*, No. 21-2886, 2022 WL 4290757 (7th Cir. Sept. 16, 2022); *Miller v. Sw. Airlines Co.*, 926 F.3d 898, 905 (7th Cir. 2019). CAFA applies only to plaintiff classes, not defendant classes. *Id.* § 1332(d); *Saskatchewan Mut. Ins. Co. v. CE Design, Ltd.*, 865 F.3d 537, 540–41 (7th Cir. 2017); *Travelers Prop. Cas. v. Good*, 689 F.3d 714, 723 (7th Cir. 2012). Issues under CAFA typically arise in the context of a plaintiff's motion to remand a case originally filed in state court but removed to federal court. In such cases, the removing party bears the burden of establishing that CAFA's requirements are met. *Roppo v. Travelers Com. Ins. Co.*, 869 F.3d 568, 578 (7th Cir. 2017); *Tri-State Water Treatment, Inc. v. Bauer*, 845 F.3d 350, 352 (7th Cir. 2017).

An action qualifies as a "class action" under CAFA if it is "filed under rule 23 of the Federal Rules of Civil Procedure or similar State statute or rule of judicial procedure." 28 U.S.C. § 1332(d)(1)(B). This determination is made at the time of removal, and a plaintiff may not avoid removal by amending to omit class allegations. *In re Burlington Northern Santa Fe Ry. Co.*, 606 F.3d 379, 380–81 (7th Cir. 2010). Even where a plaintiff sues in its individual capacity, the Seventh Circuit has included any claims that arise out of the plaintiff's duties as a class representative within CAFA's definition of a "class action." *See Addison Automatics, Inc. v. Hartford Cas. Ins. Co.*, 731 F.3d 740, 742–44 (7th Cir. 2013) (holding that plaintiff's individual declaratory judgment action seeking to enforce settlement against insurer was a "class action" for CAFA purposes). However, an action brought by a state in its *parens patriae* role on behalf of its residents is not considered a class action. *LG Display Co. v. Madigan*, 665 F.3d 768, 770–74 (7th Cir. 2011).

CAFA also defines as "class actions" certain cases involving "monetary relief claims of 100 or more persons" that "are proposed to be tried jointly." 28 U.S.C. § 1332(11)(B)(i). The proposal for a joint trial must be made by the plaintiffs rather than defendants or the court. *Koral v. Boeing Co.*, 628 F.3d 945, 946–47 (7th Cir. 2011); *see also Anderson v. Bayer Corp.*, 610 F.3d 390, 393–94 (7th Cir. 2010) (holding that related cases may not be aggregated for CAFA purposes). A plaintiffs' motion to consolidate related cases was held to be an "implicit" proposal for a joint trial in *In re Abbott Laboratories, Inc.*, 698 F.3d 568, 573 (7th Cir. 2012), as was filing the claims of more than 100 plaintiffs in a single complaint in *Bullard v. Burlington Northern Santa Fe Ry. Co.*, 535 F.3d 759, 762 (7th Cir. 2008).

In attempting to establish that the amount in controversy exceeds $5 million, a defendant must provide "a good faith estimate that is 'plausible and adequately supported by the evidence.'" *Roppo*, 869 F.3d at 578 (quoting *Blomberg v. Serv. Corp. Int'l*, 639 F.3d 761, 763 (7th Cir. 2011)); *see also Ware v. Best Buy Stores, L.P.*, 6 F.4th 726, 733 (7th Cir. 2021) ("entirely speculative" inferences that the amount in controversy exceeds $5 million under CAFA is not enough). A defendant may rely upon "the complaint's allegations, the plaintiff's informal estimates, affidavits from employees or experts, or other sources" as evidence to support the amount-in-controversy requirement. *Schutte v. Ciox Health, LLC*, 28 F.4th 850, 854 (7th Cir. 2022). The estimate may include all potential damages, except for those that would be "legally impossible" to recover. *Keeling v. Esurance Ins. Co.*, 660 F.3d 273, 274 (7th Cir. 2011); *ABM Sec. Servs., Inc. v. Davis*, 646 F.3d 475, 478 (7th Cir. 2011). The Seventh Circuit has followed the Supreme Court in holding that a named plaintiff may not stipulate to damages less than $5 million to avoid CAFA's reach. *Johnson v. Pushpin Holdings, LLC*, 748 F.3d 769, 772 (7th Cir. 2014) (citing *Standard Fire Ins. Co. v. Knowles*, 133 S. Ct. 1345, 1349 (U.S. 2013)).

Section 1332(d) carves out a few exceptions to the general scope of CAFA jurisdiction. The home-state exception, otherwise known as the abstention doctrine, exempts certain cases where over two-thirds of the class members and the "primary defendant" are citizens of the same state. 28 U.S.C. § 1332(d)(4); *Sudholt v. Country Mut. Ins. Co.*, 83 F.4th 621, 626 (7th Cir. 2023); *Johnson*, 44 F.4th at 1050–51. The local controversy exception requires a district court to decline to exercise jurisdiction of a class action that asserts "the same or similar factual allegations against any of the defendants on behalf of the same or other persons." 28 U.S.C. § 1332(d)(4). Importantly, courts may raise abstention under CAFA on their own. *See City of East St. Louis, Ill. v. Netflix, Inc.*, No. 22-2905, __ F.4th __, 2023 WL 6782279, at *2 (7th Cir. Oct. 13, 2023) (referencing *Mullen v. GLV, Inc.*, 37 F.4th 1326, 1328 (7th Cir. 2022)). In determining what constitutes a "primary" defendant, the Seventh Circuit "requires an assessment of the plaintiff's complaint as a whole—its factual allegations, claims, and requests for relief—with an eye toward examining whether the defendant in question is a principal focus of the class action." *Sudholt*, 83 F.4th at 629 (finding that "more than one defendant or indeed every named defendant can [qualify as a primary defendant] in a particular case").

The securities exception excludes from federal jurisdiction "any class action that solely involves a claim . . . concerning a covered security . . . or that relates to the rights, duties . . ., and obligations relating to or created by or pursuant to any security." 28 U.S.C. § 1332(d)(9)(A), (C). For purposes of this exception, the definition of *security* is "broad" and includes a variety of financial products. *See, e.g.*, *Lincoln Nat. Life Ins. Co. v. Bezich*, 610 F.3d 448, 449–51 (7th Cir. 2010) (holding that variable life insurance policy is included in the definition of *security*). The corporate governance/internal affairs exception applies to cases "relat[ing] to the internal affairs or governance of a corporation or other form of business enterprise and arises under or by virtue of the laws of the State in which such corporation or business enterprise is incorporated or organized." 28 U.S.C. § 1332(d)(9)(B). The Seventh Circuit, in reliance upon CAFA's legislative history, interpreted the internal affairs exception as a means to "withhold federal jurisdiction over[] class actions concentrated on matters of corporate governance, where uniform and definitive interpretations of the legal duties governing management of the enterprise facilitate commercial activity." *Sudholt*, 83 F.4th at 626. Importantly, the court rejected the notion that the "internal-affairs exception applies only to claims against current—but not former—directors and officers." *Id.* at 628 ("We see no indication that Congress intended for employment status to serve as the gating mechanism for applying CAFA's internal-affairs exception."). The party invoking one of these exceptions bears the burden of establishing its requirements. *See Schutte*, 28 F.4th at 858 (placing burden on party seeking remand under local controversy exception); *Myrick v. WellPoint, Inc.*, 764 F.3d 662, 664–65 (7th Cir. 2014) (placing burden on party seeking remand under home state exception); *Hart v. FedEx Ground Package Sys., Inc.*, 457 F.3d 675, 679–82 (7th Cir. 2006) (same); *Appert v. Morgan Stanley Dean Witter, Inc.*, 673 F.3d 609, 619 (7th Cir. 2012) (same for securities exception). The Seventh Circuit has characterized these exceptions as "narrow," *Appert*, 673 F.3d at 618, and has generally held them inapplicable. *See Schutte*, 28 F.4th at 859–60 (precluding application of local controversy exception where, despite differing legal theories, the factual allegations between the cases were the same); *LaPlant v. Northwestern Mut. Life Ins. Co.*, 701 F.3d 1137, 1141–42 (7th Cir. 2012) (holding that case potentially arising under multiple states' laws and seeking to enforce contractual rights did not fall under corporate governance exception); *Appert*, 673 F.3d at 619–22 (holding securities exception inapplicable where claims did not relate directly to a covered security); *Katz v. Gerardi*, 552 F.3d 558, 563 (7th Cir. 2009) (holding that units of real estate investment trust did not qualify as securities to qualify for the securities exception).

If grounds for CAFA jurisdiction do not exist in an initial state court complaint, parties may remove a class action 30 days after receiving "an amended pleading, motion, order, or other paper" that establishes such grounds. 28 U.S.C. § 1446(b)(3). A paper does not start the 30-day clock running unless it "affirmatively and unambiguously specifies" that the CAFA requirements are met. *Walker v. Trailer Transit, Inc.*, 727 F.3d 819, 825 (7th Cir. 2013) (allowing removal of action 30 days after responses to requests for admission confirmed that damages could exceed $5 million). However, if a defendant "independently discovers" that the case is removable under CAFA, "it may remove the case at whatever point it deems appropriate, regardless of whether the window for removal on another basis already opened and closed." *Railey v. Sunset Food Mart, Inc.*, No. 21-2533, 2021 WL 4808222, at *3 (7th Cir. Oct. 15, 2021). Only original defendants may remove a class action filed in state court under CAFA; defendants added to the complaint as a counterclaim defendant may not. *Tri-State*, 845 F.3d at 351–57 (7th Cir. 2017); *First Bank v. DJL Properties, LLC*, 598 F.3d 915, 916–18 (7th Cir. 2010).

b. Standing

Article III of the Constitution requires the named plaintiffs in a class action to show that they are alleging a "concrete and particularized injury that is fairly traceable to the challenged conduct, and is likely to be redressed by a favorable judicial decision." *Lewert v. P.F. Chang's China Bistro, Inc.*, 819 F.3d 963, 966 (7th Cir. 2016); *see also Spokeo, Inc. v. Robins*, 578 U.S. 330 (2016) ("To establish injury in fact, a plaintiff must show that he or she suffered 'an invasion of a legally protected interest' that is 'concrete and particularized' and 'actual or imminent, not conjectural or hypothetical.'") (quoting *Lujan v. Defenders of Wildlife*, 504 U.S. 555, 560 (1992)). Moreover, "standing is not dispensed in gross; rather, plaintiffs must demonstrate standing for each claim that they press and for each form of relief that they seek." *Dinerstein v. Google, LLC*, 73 F.4th 502, 511 (7th Cir. 2023) (quoting *TransUnion LLC v. Ramirez*, 594 U.S. __, 141 S. Ct. 2190, 2208 (2021)). Plaintiffs bear the burden of establishing their Article III standing. *Lewert*, 819 F.3d at 966. To meet this burden, plaintiffs are entitled to rely on the allegations of their complaint, unless there is a factual challenge to standing. *Id.; Robertson v. Allied Sols., LLC,* 902 F.3d 690, 693 (7th Cir. 2018) (reversing dismissal for lack of jurisdiction based upon plaintiff's allegations to support Article III standing, but noting that "we must still examine whether [defendant's] violations . . . caused . . . any concrete injury").

The Supreme Court explained in *Spokeo* that the "concreteness" requirement for an Article III injury in fact is distinct from the "particularity" requirement. *Spokeo*, 578 U.S. 339–40. "Concreteness" is satisfied if the alleged injury is "real," that is, "actually exist[s]." *Id.* The inquiry when reviewing a plaintiff's alleged injury for concreteness asks whether the plaintiff has identified a close historical or common law analogue for their asserted injury. *Dinerstein*, 73 F.4th at 511 (citing *TransUnion*, 141 S. Ct. at 2204); *see also Pierre v. Midland Credit Mgmt., Inc.*, 29 F.4th 934, 938 (7th Cir. 2022) (when reviewing a plaintiff's alleged injury for concreteness, "[h]istory and tradition remain our ever-present guides"). Both "tangible" and "intangible" injuries may actually exist, and thus, either may satisfy the requirement. *Id.* at 340–41. Tangible injuries, such as monetary loss and physical harm, are "perhaps easier to recognize." *Id.* Various intangible injuries can also be concrete, including reputational harms, disclosure of private information, and intrusion upon seclusion. *TransUnion*, 141 S. Ct. at 2204. Alleging a mere *risk* of harm, however, without more is not enough to satisfy the concreteness requirement. *See Pierre*, 29 F.4th 934, 939 (quoting *TransUnion*, 141 S. Ct. at 2210 (clarifying that "a risk of harm qualifies as a concrete injury only for claims for 'forward-looking, injunctive relief to prevent the harm from occurring'")); *See also Dinerstein*, 73 F.4th at 518 ("[A] plaintiff cannot base an injury in fact solely on the defendant's gain."). In other words, a risk of harm will only be concrete if a plaintiff can establish that the risks "have in fact materialized." *See TransUnion*, 141 S. Ct. at 2210–11; *see also Dinerstein*, 73 F.4th at 516 (finding plaintiff in consumer fraud class action related to unauthorized disclosure of anonymized medical records did not establish standing because the impending risk of patient reidentification could not materialize where Google explicitly agreed not "to identify any individual").

Similarly, when plaintiffs allege emotional harm, such allegations must be concrete enough to show "that their 'emotional response led to actionable injury.'" *Florence v. Order Express*, No. 22-C-7210, 2023 WL 3602248, at *6 (N.D. Ill. May 23, 2023) (quoting *Pucillo v. Nat'l Credit Sys., Inc.*, 66 F.4th 634, 639 (7th Cir. 2023)). Likewise, the Seventh Circuit, in explicit tension with the Fifth Circuit, finds that a breach of contract alone—without any actual harm—is purely an injury in law, not an injury in fact, and it therefore falls short of the Article III requirements for a suit in federal court. *Dinerstein*, 73 F.4th at 516. For products cases, district courts in the Seventh Circuit have made clear that the harm must be related to the product purchased by the actual class representative; a named plaintiff cannot establish standing related to products that she did not purchase. *Jackson v. Dole Packaged Foods, LLC*, No. 22-cv-1448, 2022 WL 18027600, at *2 (S.D. Ill. Dec. 30, 2022) (citing *Payton v. Cty. of Kane*, 308 F.3d 673, 682 (7th Cir. 2002)). Additionally, class representatives must have individual claims to pursue claims on behalf of absent class members. *Bryant v. All Ways Auto Transp., LLC*, No. 22-cv-00906, 2022 WL 17338295, at *6 (N.D. Ill. Nov. 30, 2022).

Furthermore, Plaintiffs must allege something more than the mere violation of a statute in order to satisfy Article III standing. *See Larkin v. Fin. Sys. of Green Bay, Inc.*, 982 F.3d 1060, 1066 (7th Cir. 2020) (finding that the violation of a substantive right conferred by the FDCPA does not by itself guarantee the plaintiff's standing). In another action alleging a violation of a statute (this time, the Real Estate Settlement Procedures Act, 12 U.S.C. § 2605(e)(1)(B)), where plaintiffs alleged harm in the form of damage to their credit and higher payments and greater interest rates, that was enough to meet "the minimal requirements for pleading even if it strikes us 'that actual proof of those facts is improbable, and that a recovery is very remote and unlikely.'" *Diedrich v. Ocwen Loan Servicing, LLC*, 839 F.3d 583, 590 (7th Cir. 2016) (citing *Bell Atlantic Corp. v. Twombly*, 550 U.S. 544, 570 (2007)).

See also Ewing v. MED-1 Sols., LLC, 24 F.4th 1146, 1149–50 (7th Cir. 2022) (finding statutory violations by debt collector resulting in intangible reputational injury sufficient to confer standing).

In *Robertson v. Allied Solutions, LLC*, 902 F.3d 690 (7th Cir. 2018), the Seventh Circuit clarified that harm may occur "not only when a plaintiff complains of being deprived of some benefit, but also when a plaintiff complains that she was deprived of a chance to obtain a benefit." *Id.* at 697. Likewise, in the information privacy context, the Seventh Circuit has held that, where there are recognized risks associated with the dissemination of biometric information, conduct that denies a plaintiff the opportunity to approve of the collection and usage of such information may constitute injury sufficient to confer Article III standing. *See Bryant v. Compass Grp. USA, Inc.*, 958 F.3d 617, 624, 626 (7th Cir. 2020). Importantly, to pursue a claim for injunctive relief, a plaintiff has standing only if there is a chance that the plaintiff could be harmed by defendant's conduct in the future. *Troutt v. Mondelez Global LLC*, No. 21-cv-01279, 2022 WL 16552956, at *6 (S.D. Ill. Oct. 31, 2022) (citing Camasta v. Jos. A. Bank Clothiers, Inc., 761 F.3d 732, 741 (7th Cir. 2014)).

Finally, the Seventh Circuit will readily reverse a class certification decision with instructions to the district court to dismiss the case if standing is derived merely from "regret or disappointment," *Eike v. Allergan, Inc.*, 850 F.3d 315, 318 (7th Cir. 2017). Similarly, the Seventh Circuit will uphold the district court's denial of class certification where standing is solely grounded in the plaintiff's "confusion" or perceived intimidation. *Brunett v. Convergent Outsourcing, Inc.*, 982 F.3d 1067, 1068–69 (7th Cir. 2020), *reh'g denied* (Jan. 11, 2021). The Seventh Circuit clarified, however, that confusion can be enough to confer standing when a plaintiff demonstrates that the confusion led her to take some detrimental step. *Smith v. GC Servs. L.P.*, 986 F.3d 708, 710 (7th Cir. 2021) (noting that a plaintiff cannot establish an Article III injury absent an allegation that she took a detrimental step, such as paying money she did not owe, after being confused); *see also Mack v. Resurgent Cap. Servs., L.P.*, 70 F.4th 395, 406–08 (7th Cir. 2023) (finding that where a plaintiff "spent extra money not to clear up her confusion but in order to preserve her right to seek validation," the money spent on additional postage constituted an action to the plaintiff's detriment, which provided the plaintiff with Article III standing). Furthermore, the Seventh Circuit has held that there is no Article III standing if the alleged misconduct is a bare procedural violation and there is no allegation that the misconduct harmed the concrete interest that a statute was intended to protect. *Casillas v. Madison Ave. Assocs., Inc.*, 926 F.3d 329, 339 (7th Cir. 2019); *Thornley v. Clearview AI, Inc.*, 984 F.3d 1241, 1246–47 (7th Cir. 2021).

c. Mootness

In *Campbell-Ewald Co. v. Gomez*, 577 U.S. 153 (2016), the Supreme Court described another way in which Article III standing can be jeopardized: "If an intervening circumstance deprives the plaintiff of a 'personal stake in the outcome of the lawsuit,' at any point during the litigation, the action can no longer proceed and must be dismissed as moot." *Id.* at 161–62 (quoting *Genesis Healthcare Corp. v. Symczyk*, 569 U.S. 66, 133 S. Ct. 1523, 1528 (2013)). For instance, a voter's challenge to an allegedly unconstitutional statute was mooted by an amendment to the statute. *Zessar v. Keith*, 536 F.3d 788, 793–95 (7th Cir. 2008).

A common "intervening circumstance" that can strip Article III standing is when a named plaintiff accepts an offer of judgment as to "all claims brought under this lawsuit." *Wright v. Calumet City, Ill.*, 848 F.3d 814, 816 (7th Cir. 2017); *see also Wrightsell v. Cook Cty., Ill.*, 599 F.3d 781, 784 (7th Cir. 2010) ("[Plaintiff's] settlement, including his explicit waiver of a right to appeal, has removed him from the case."). Even if a plaintiff's settlement expressly attempts to preserve the right to appeal an adverse class certification decision, a settlement may deprive the plaintiff of further Article III standing. *Muro v. Target Corp.*, 580 F.3d 485, 489–92 (7th Cir. 2009). However, the Seventh Circuit recently clarified that standing *is* preserved where the settlement agreement expressly reserves the rights of named plaintiffs to pursue an incentive award on appeal, because the prospect of an incentive award is enough to keep the claim justiciable for the named plaintiff. *Scott v. Dart*, 99 F.4th 1076, 1082–83 (7th Cir. 2024) (citing *Espenscheid v. DirectSat USA, LLC*, 688 F.3d 872, 876–77 (7th Cir. 2012), and *Wright v. Calumet City*, 848 F.3d 814, 819 (7th Cir. 2017)). Article III standing also remains where the plaintiff declines a settlement offer. *Campbell-Ewald*, 136 S. Ct. at 672; *see also Chapman v. First Index, Inc.*, 796 F.3d 783, 786–88 (7th Cir. 2015) (anticipating the *Campbell-Ewald* decision and holding the same).

A class action case also may be protected from being dismissed as moot if it falls within the "inherently transitory" exception. This exception ensures that in those cases in which "it is uncertain that any member of the class would maintain a live controversy long enough for a judge to certify a class," the court may retain jurisdiction to adjudicate the claims of a class constantly in flux. *Olson v. Brown*, 594 F.3d 577, 580–84 (7th Cir. 2010) (holding that suit for injunctive relief on behalf of a class of prisoners not rendered moot even though plaintiff had been transferred out of prison).

3. GUIDELINES FOR DEFINING THE CLASS

In *Mullins v. Direct Digital, LLC*, 795 F.3d 654 (7th Cir. 2015), the Seventh Circuit described "three common problems" with class definitions. *Id.* at 659.

First, a class definition must not be too vague, meaning it must "generally need to identify a particular group, harmed during a particular time frame, in a particular location, in a particular way." *Id.* at 660. In *Steimel v. Wernert*, 823 F.3d 902 (7th Cir. 2016), a class defined as "persons . . . who require more [state-provided Medicaid] services than are available" was held to be impermissibly vague because it was impossible to identify who was in the class. *Id.* at 918.

Second, a class definition must be defined by objective criteria rather than subjective criteria, "such as by a person's state of mind." *Mullins*, 795 F.3d at 660. For example, an employment discrimination class defined to include all those who suffered adverse employment actions "because of their race" was impermissible because it is "impossible to determine who is in the class until the case ends." *Bolden v. Walsh Constr. Co.*, 688 F.3d 893, 895 (7th Cir. 2012).

Third, "classes that are defined in terms of success on the merits—so-called 'fail-safe' classes—also are not properly defined." *Mullins*, 795 F.3d at 660. A class may not be defined "so that whether a person qualifies as a member depends on whether the person has a valid claim"—this is known as a "fail-safe" class. *Messner v. Northshore Univ. HealthSystem*, 669 F.3d 802, 825 (7th Cir. 2012). For example, in *McCaster v. Darden Rests., Inc.*, 845 F.3d 794 (7th Cir. 2017), the Seventh Circuit rejected as a "fail-safe" class, defined by reference to "who did not receive all earned vacation pay benefits." *Id.* at 799. At the same time, however, "[a]ll class definitions allude to the merits, in that they assume either implicitly or explicitly that the defendant's conduct has adversely affected the defined group of people," *Abbott v. Lockheed Martin Corp.*, 725 F.3d 803, 810 (7th Cir. 2013), and classes defined by reference to objective criteria are likely to be upheld. *Id.* at 810 (upholding class definition that includes all plan members whose accounts underperformed an objective index); the Seventh Circuit liberally permits modifications to a class definition to cure any defects. "If the evidence calls into question the propriety of defining a class in a particular way, then the definition must be modified or subclasses certified." *Fonder v. Sheriff of Kankakee Cty.*, 823 F.3d 1144, 1147 (7th Cir. 2016). Problems with class definitions "can and often should be solved by refining the class definition rather than by flatly denying class certification on that basis." *Messner*, 669 F.3d at 825.[4]

[4] Although not an overt requirement, as a practice pointer, the class definition in either a motion for class certification or settlement agreement should match the class definition in the complaint; therefore, attorneys should seek leave to file an amended complaint to ensure that the definitions match. *Cf.* Jamison v. First Credit Servs., Inc., 290 F.R.D. 92, 103 (N.D. Ill. 2013) (noting that "[t]he Seventh Circuit has not addressed the scope of the Court's discretion to modify a class definition at the certification stage," but gathering cases discussing whether an amended complaint is necessary).

4. CLASS CERTIFICATION PREREQUISITES

"To be certified, a proposed class must satisfy the requirements of Federal Rule of Civil Procedure 23(a), as well as one of the three alternatives in Rule 23(b)." *Messner v. Northshore Univ. HealthSystem*, 669 F.3d 802, 811 (7th Cir. 2012). "The party seeking certification bears the burden of demonstrating that certification is proper by a preponderance of the evidence." *Scott v. Dart*, 99 F.4th 1076, 1088 (7th Cir. 2024) (quoting *Bell v. PNC Bank, Nat. Ass'n*, 800 F.3d 360, 373 (7th Cir. 2015)); *see also Messner*, 669 F.3d at 811 ("each disputed requirement" must be "proven by a preponderance of evidence").

The Seventh Circuit has repeatedly expressed concern over the power of class certification to force a defendant to settle on disadvantageous terms, even when the underlying claims have little merit. *See, e.g.*, *Creative Montessori Learning Ctrs. v. Ashford Gear LLC*, 662 F.3d 913, 915 (7th Cir. 2011); *CE Design Ltd. v. King Architectural Metals, Inc.*, 637 F.3d 721, 723 (7th Cir. 2011); *Szabo v. Bridgeport Machines, Inc.*, 249 F.3d 672, 675 (7th Cir. 2001). Accordingly, the court has emphasized that district courts must apply a rigorous analysis to ensure satisfaction of the class certification prerequisites. *Chicago Teachers Union, Local No. 1 v. Bd. of Educ. of City of Chi.*, 797 F.3d 426, 433 (7th Cir. 2015); *Creative Montessori Learning Ctrs.*, 662 F.3d at 916; *CE Design*, 637 F.3d at 723. A district court must "make whatever factual and legal inquiries are necessary to ensure that requirements for class certification are satisfied before deciding whether a class should be certified, even if those considerations overlap the merits of the case." *Am. Honda Motor Co. v. Allen*, 600 F.3d 813, 815 (7th Cir. 2010) (citing *Szabo,* 249 F.3d at 676).

"A district judge may not duck hard questions by observing that each side has some support, or that considerations relevant to class certification also may affect the decision on the merits." *West v. Prudential Sec., Inc.*, 282 F.3d 935, 938 (7th Cir. 2002). Nor may a district court simply accept the truth of the matters as asserted by a plaintiff. *See Messner*, 669 F.3d at 811. Rather, a district court judge must receive evidence and resolve any material factual disputes before certifying a class. *Id.* Moreover, "when an expert's report or testimony is critical to class certification . . . a district court must conclusively rule on any challenge to the expert's qualifications or submissions prior to ruling on a class certification motion." *Am. Honda Motor Co.*, 600 F.3d at 815–16 (internal citations omitted).

Although courts may reach issues related to the merits of a case when deciding a motion for class certification, the determination of class certification does not hinge on the merits of a plaintiff's claims. *See Simpson v. Dart*, 23 F.4th 706, 711 (7th Cir. 2022) ("Likelihood of success on the merits is not among" the "four—and only four—requirements for class certification."); *Schleicher v. Wendt*, 618 F.3d 679, 685 (7th Cir. 2010) (consideration of the merits is "limited to those aspects of the merits that affect the decisions essential under Rule 23"); *Payton v. Kane*, 308 F.3d 673 (7th Cir. 2002) ("a determination of the propriety of class *certification* should not turn on likelihood of success on the merits"); *Messner*, 669 F.3d at 811 ("[T]he court should not turn the class certification proceedings into a dress rehearsal for a trial on the merits.").

a. Rule 23(a) Requirements

Numerosity (Fed. R. Civ. P. 23(a)(1))

While there is no "magic number," generally a class of at least 40 plaintiffs is sufficient to meet the numerosity requirement of Rule 23(a). *Mulvania v. Sheriff of Rock Island Cty.*, 850 F.3d 849, 859–60 (7th Cir. 2017); *see also Williams v. Matteson Sports Bar*, No. 21-CV-04043, 2024 WL 1195722, at *2 (N.D. Ill. Mar. 20, 2024) (proposed class of 33 members failed numerosity); *K. C. v. Individual Members of Med. Licensing Bd. of Indiana*, 345 F.R.D. 328, 334 (S.D. Ind. 2024) (numerosity satisfied where class and subclass containing roughly 50 members from different organizations was large enough to make joinder extremely inconvenient). To satisfy the numerosity requirement, a plaintiff does not need to establish the precise number of class members. *Macial v. Coronet Ins. Co.*, 880 F.2d 954,

957 (7th Cir. 1989); *see also Arnold Chapman & Paldo Sign & Display Co. v. Wagener Equities Inc.*, 747 F.3d 489, 492 (7th Cir. 2014) ("a class can be certified without determination of its size, so long as it's reasonable to believe it large enough to make joinder impracticable and thus justify a class action suit"). A finding of numerosity can be based on common sense assumptions. *Barragan v. Evanger's Dog & Cat Food Co.*, 259 F.R.D. 330, 333 (N.D. Ill. 2009). However, "mere allegations that a class action would make litigation easier for a plaintiff are not enough to satisfy Rule 23(a)(1). *Anderson v. Weinert Enters., Inc.*, 986 F.3d 773, 777 (7th Cir. 2021). Likewise, a plaintiff cannot rely merely on speculation or conclusory allegations as to the size of the class or the impracticability of joinder. *Macial*, 880 F.2d at 957. *See also Daley v. Jones Motor Co., Inc.*, 743 F. App'x 35, 38 (7th Cir. 2018) (finding that the Court "cannot simply ignore. . . evidence and pretend that. . . [an] unfounded assertion that there are at least 100 class members is true").

Commonality (Fed. R. Civ. P. 23(b)(2))

To satisfy the commonality requirement, a plaintiff need only show a single common question of law or fact. *Bell*, 800 F.3d at 374. But plaintiffs cannot rely on a mere pleading standard; "instead a prospective class 'must be prepared to prove that there are *in fact* . . . common questions of law or fact.'" *Phillips v. Sheriff of Cook County.*, 828 F.3d 541, 551–52 (7th Cir. 2016) (quoting *Wal-Mart Stores, Inc. v. Dukes*, 564 U.S. 338, 350 (2011)). Accordingly, "[a] determination of commonality often requires a precise understanding of the nature of the plaintiffs' claims." *Id.* at 552. And the court's analysis may "entail some overlap with the merits of the underlying claim." *Id.* at 550 (quoting *Wal-Mart*, 564 U.S. at 351)).

"What matters to class certification . . . [is] the capacity of a classwide proceeding to generate common answers apt to drive the resolution of [the] litigation." *Bell*, 800 F.3d at 374 (quoting *Wal-Mart*, 564 U.S. at 350). Thus, a plaintiff must show common contention that is capable of classwide resolution. *Id.* "[C]lass-wide resolution means that determining the truth or falsity of the common contention will resolve an issue that is central to the validity" of the claim. *Id.* It is not enough to show that all plaintiffs suffered as a result of a violation of the law. *Id.* "The 'critical point is the need for *conduct* common to members of the class.'" *Scott*, 99 F.4th at 1088 (quoting *Suchanek, v. Sturm Foods, Inc.*, 764 F.3d 750, 756 (7th Cir. 2014); *see also In re IKO Roofing Shingle Prods. Liab. Litig.*, 757 F.3d 599, 602 (7th Cir. 2014). "Where the same conduct or practice by the same defendant gives rise to the same kind of claims from all class members, there is a common question." *Id.* at 1091; *see e.g., Ross v. Gossett*, 33 F.th 433, 437–39 (7th Cir. 2022) (upholding district court finding that commonality requirement satisfied in Eight Amendment discrimination case where defendants "acted pursuant to a common policy and implemented the same or similar procedures."). However, where the defendant's conduct or practice results in different experiences encountered by the members of a proposed class, the Seventh Circuit will not find a common question. *See Howard v. Cook Cty. Sheriff's Off.*, 989 F.3d 587, 598–605 (7th Cir. 2021) (denying class certification where class of female jail employees who were sexually harassed by male inmates experienced differences in severity and type of harassment).

In the employment context, where a case involves the exercise of discretion on the part of the employer, the "plaintiff must demonstrate that the exercise of discretion is tied to a specific employment practice, and that the subjective practice at issue affected the class in a uniform manner." *Chicago Teachers Union*, 797 F.3d at 437 (quoting *Scott v. Family Dollar Stores, Inc.*, 733 F.3d 105, 113 (4th Cir. 2013)). "[D]iscretionary decisions can be the source of a common claim if they are, for example, the outcome of employment practices or policies controlled by higher-level directors, if all decision-makers exercise discretion in a common way because of a company policy or practice, or if all decision-makers act together as one unit." *Chicago Teachers Union*, at 438.

There need not be commonality of damages. *IKO Roofing*, 757 F.3d at 602. The Seventh Circuit recognizes that if this were the case, then "class actions about consumer products [would be] impossible." *Id.* Indeed, the Seventh Circuit also recognizes the difference between *injury* versus *damages*—and that while all class members must be *injured*, not every class member needs to have sustained damages. *Butler*, 727 F.3d at 800–02 (differentiating between injury and damages); *Kohen v. Pacific Inv. Mgmt. Co.*, 571 F.3d 672, 675 (7th Cir. 2009) (recognizing that when distributing a judgment, "[s]ome of the class members, discovering that they were not injured at all, will not submit a claim, and others will submit a claim that will be rejected because the claimant cannot prove damages").[5]

Typicality (Fed. R. Civ. P. 23(a)(3))

The typicality requirement of Rule 23(a)(3) is "meant to ensure that the named representative's claims 'have the same essential characteristics as the claims of the class at large.'" *Lacy v. Cook Cnty.*, 897 F.3d 847, 866 (7th Cir. 2018) (internal quotation mark omitted) (quoting *Oshana v. Coca-Cola Co.*, 472 F.3d 506, 514 (7th Cir. 2006)); *see also Scott v. Dart*, 99 F.4th 1076, 1991–92 (7th Cir. 2024). A plaintiff's claim is typical if it arises from the same event or practice or course of conduct that gives rise to the claims of other class members and [is] based on the same legal theory." *Lacy*, 897 F.3d at 866 (alteration in original) (quoting *Rosario v. Livaditis*, 963 F.2d 1013, 1018 (7th Cir. 1992)).

The typicality requirement is closely related to both the commonality requirement of Rule 23(a)(2) and the adequacy requirement of Rule 23(a)(4). *See Rosario*, 963 F.2d at 1018 ("The question of typicality in Rule 23(a)(3) is closely related to the preceding question of commonality."); *Mace v. Van Ru Credit Corp.*, 109 F.3d 338, 341 (7th Cir. 1997) ("The typicality and commonality requirements of the Federal Rules ensure that only those plaintiffs or defendants who can advance the same factual and legal arguments may be grouped together as a class."); *Robinson v. Sheriff of Cook Cnty.*, 167 F.3d 1155, 1157 (7th Cir. 1999) ("[I]f [a plaintiff's] claim is atypical, he is not likely to be an adequate representative; his incentive to press issues important to the other members of the class will be impaired."); *Abbot v. Lockheed Martin Corp.*, 725 F.3d 803, 813 (7th Cir. 2013) (referencing "intra-class conflicts of the sort that defeats both the typicality and adequacy of representation requirements of Rule 23(a)").

Where classes are defined in a manner that is overly broad, they have been held to fail the typicality requirement. For example, in *Oshana*, the plaintiff asserted a consumer fraud claim based on Coca-Cola allegedly misleading consumers to believe that saccharin was not used as a sweetener in fountain Diet Coke. 472 F.3d at 509. The Seventh Circuit held that the plaintiff failed to satisfy the typicality requirement because her class included all purchasers of fountain Diet Coke, regardless of whether they were exposed to Coca-Cola's allegedly misleading advertising or whether they knew that fountain Diet Coke contained saccharin. *Id.* at 514. Likewise, in *Retired Chi. Police Ass'n v. City of Chi.*, 7 F.3d 584 (7th Cir. 1993), the Seventh Circuit held that the class proposed by plaintiffs, who were annuitants of the Chicago police department pension fund, failed to satisfy the typicality requirement because it was broadly defined to encompass other annuitants of other pension funds and there was no evidence that all of these various groups had been exposed to the same alleged misrepresentations. *Id.* at 597–98.

The typicality requirement does not require "all class members [to] suffer the same injury as the named class representative." *Rosario*, 963 F.2d at 1018. For example, in *Rosario*, the plaintiffs brought claims on behalf of a class of students who attended defendant's beauty schools, which provided less than adequate training. *Id.* at 1016. Although certain class members testified that they were satisfied with the education the schools provided, the court held that this did not defeat typicality because having been in the same position as the plaintiffs with respect to the accused conduct, these satisfied class members still had the same

[5] Although the issue was premature for decision in *Tyson Foods, Inc. v. Bouaphakeo*, 577 U.S. 422, 459–61 (2016), the Supreme Court seems to suggest that the issue of whether certain class members were not entitled to damages is a question for the distribution of any aggregate damages award, not whether certification is appropriate.

claims as plaintiffs. *Id.* at 1018. The fact that they left beauty school satisfied more likely indicated that they suffered less injury, not that they suffered no injury. *Id.*

District courts within the Seventh Circuit have stated that unique defenses applicable to certain class members, but not others, may defeat typicality. *See Wright v. Family Dollar, Inc.*, 2010 WL 4962838, at *3 (Nov. 30, 2010) ("Under the typicality analysis, 'a plaintiff against whom the defendants have a defense not applicable to other members of the class is not a proper class representative.'") (quoting *Hardy v. City Optical Inc.*, 39 F.3d 765, 770 (7th Cir. 1994).) However, the Seventh Circuit has stated that the typicality requirement is more properly focused on a defendant's conduct and that any issue of unique defenses is better analyzed under the adequacy requirement. *See Wagner v. NutraSweet Co.*, 95 F.3d 527, 534 (7th Cir. 1996) (stating that typicality "should be determined with reference to the company's actions, not with respect to particularized defenses it might have against certain class members"); *see also CE Design*, 637 F.3d at 724–25 (analyzing the issue of unique defenses under Rule 23(a)(4) and stating that "[Plaintiff] cannot be an adequate representative of the class . . . if it is subject to a defense that couldn't be sustained against other class members").

Adequacy (Fed. R. Civ. P. 23(a)(4))

Rule 23(a)(4) requires a district court to determine the adequacy of the class representatives, which includes both the named plaintiffs and the attorneys of the proposed class. *Greisz v. Household Bank (Illinois), N.A.*, 176 F.3d 1012, 1013 (7th Cir. 1999). "The adequacy of class representatives is an issue that can be examined throughout the litigation." *In re S.W. Airlines Voucher Litig.*, 799 F.3d 701, 715 (7th Cir. 2015).

The determination of whether named plaintiffs will represent the class adequately often requires consideration of whether these plaintiffs have interests that conflict with other class members. *See Randall v. Rolls-Royce Corp.*, 637 F.3d 818, 824 (7th Cir. 2011) ("A class representative's conflict of interest is an independent ground for denial of class certification."); *Donovan v. Est. of Fitzsimmons*, 778 F.2d 298, 307 (7th Cir. 1985) ("[C]lass plaintiffs cannot fairly and adequately protect the interests of the class they seek to represent if they present a claim about which members of the class have antagonistic or conflicting interests."); *Uhl v. Thoroughbred Tech. & Telecomm., Inc.*, 309 F.3d 978, 985 (7th Cir. 2002) (Rule 23(a)(4) requires a court to "ensure that there is no inconsistency between the named parties and the class they represent."). In *Randall*, for example, the court questioned whether the named plaintiffs were adequate representatives because their positions of authority within the company could conceivably allow them to strategically depress the salaries of their female subordinates so as to better their chances of success in the litigation, which concerned allegations that females were systematically paid less than their male counterparts. 637 F.3d at 824. The presence of a conflict, however, does not necessarily destroy class certification. *See Johnson v. Meriter Health Servs. Emp. Ret. Plan*, 702 F.3d 364, 372 (7th Cir. 2012). The Seventh Circuit has noted that even if a conflict materializes, it "'may be possible to resolve [it] by [creating] subclasses and appointing new class representatives' for them." *Santiago v. City of Chi.*, 19 F.4th 1010, 1018–19 (7th Cir. 2021) (quoting *Johnson*, 702 F.3d at 372).

Similarly, a plaintiff may fail to satisfy the adequacy requirement if a court finds that he will not "keep the interests of the entire class at the forefront." *Conrad v. Boiron, Inc.*, 869 F.3d 536, 539 (7th Cir 2017); *see also Stampley v. Altom Transp., Inc.*, 958 F.3d 580, 585–86 (7th Cir. 2020) (upholding class decertification where plaintiff was an inadequate class representative because he "clearly focused on protecting his own claim against a contractual defense, rather than representing the class as constituted."). The Seventh Circuit has recognized that because named plaintiffs are fiduciaries of the class, adequacy might not be met in cases involving low value claims and a small class size, as the transaction costs associated with class wide resolution (notice and attorneys' fees) threaten to swallow the entirety of a potential recovery, leaving no benefit to anyone but the class attorneys. *Conrad*, 869 F.3d at

540–41.

When a named plaintiff's interests in the requested relief are too tenuous, he also may be found not to be an adequate representative. For example, when a named plaintiff sought to represent a class of inmates seeking injunctive relief relating to a jail's policy of not allowing inmates to use crutches, the Seventh Circuit held that the plaintiff was not an adequate representative because he was no longer an inmate and thus had no personal interest in the injunctive relief. *Arreola v. Godinez*, 546 F.3d 788, 799 (7th Cir. 2008); *see also Orr v. Shicker,* 953 F.3d 490, 500 (7th Cir. 2020) (finding inmates who were no longer in custody could not adequately serve as class representatives on behalf of current inmates).

Recognizing a different sort of conflict, the court, in *Randall*, held that plaintiffs were not adequate class representatives because their claims were significantly weaker than those of other class members. 637 F.3d at 824. ("[N]amed plaintiffs who are subject to a defense that would not defeat unnamed class members are not adequate class representatives."). For this reason, a plaintiff's credibility may also be relevant to a court's adequacy determination. While the court has cautioned against defendants "derail[ing] legitimate class actions by conjuring up trivial credibility problems," the court has recognized that a plaintiff may not be an adequate class representative when "there exists admissible evidence so severely undermining plaintiff's credibility that a fact finder might reasonably focus on plaintiff's credibility, to the detriment of the absent class members' claims." *CE Design*, 637 F.3d at 728 (quoting *Dubin v. Miller*, 132 F.R.D. 269, 272 (D. Colo. 1990)). The Seventh Circuit has held that inadmissible attacks on credibility, including a manslaughter conviction, and minor discrepancies revealed during discovery will not render a plaintiff an inadequate class representative. *See Beaton v. SpeedyPC Software*, 907 F.3d 1018, 1028 (7th Cir. 2018). But when discovery reveals that a plaintiff has intentionally lied, or was recklessly indifferent to the truth, about facts concerning the case, a court may find that he does not satisfy the adequacy requirement. *See Physicians Healthsource, Inc. v. Allscripts Health Sol., Inc.*, 254 F. Supp. 3d 1007, 1021–28 (N.D. Ill. 2017).

The Seventh Circuit, however, has not demanded that named plaintiffs be in the exact position as the other class members. *See Phillips v. Asset Acceptance, LLC*, 736 F.3d 1076, 1080 (7th Cir. 2013) ("We are skeptical that Phillips is not an *adequate* representative of the debtors sued more than four but fewer than five years after the creditors' claims accrued, just because her claim is solid whether the statute of limitations is four years or five. To question her adequacy is to be unrealistic about the role of the class representative in a class action suit. The role is nominal." (emphasis in original)).

Class counsel may not satisfy the adequacy requirement where there are serious doubts about the counsels' integrity and thus legitimate questions as to whether they will litigate the case in the interests of the class, as opposed to the interests of the lawyers who will receive a substantial share of any judgment or settlement. *Creative Montessori Learning Ctrs.*, 662 F.3d at 917–18. This is consistent with the court's recognition that the named plaintiffs are often "nominal," and class counsel may be incentivized to "sell out" the class in exchange for a settlement that disproportionately rewards the class lawyers. *Id.* Apart from any questions of honesty and integrity, class counsel may fail the adequacy requirement when they are found to be inept. *See Greisz*, 176 F.3d at 1014 (finding class counsel inadequate where counsel had "filed untimely appeals, failed to protect the right of clients to opt out of doomed class actions, engaged in flagrant forum shopping, made exorbitant settlement demands, filed frivolous motions, displayed a lack of familiarity with procedural rules—and in the end always lost").

b. Rule 23(b) Requirements

Even if plaintiffs establish that all the requirements set forth in Rule 23(a) are satisfied, to maintain a class action, they also must establish that one of the Rule 23(b) requirements is satisfied.

Rule 23(b)(1)(A) and (B) Classes

"Rule 23(b)(1) provides for a non-opt-out class action where individual actions could 'establish incompatible standards of conduct for the party opposing the class" or "as a practical matter, would be dispositive of the interests of the other members not parties to the individual adjudications." *Neil v. Zell*, 275 F.R.D. 256, 260 (N.D. Ill. 2011) (quoting Fed. R. Civ. P. 23(b)(1)). Rule 23(b)(1)(A) applies to actions in which there is a risk of "incompatible standards of conduct for the party opposing the class," and Rule 23(b)(1)(B) applies to actions that would be dispositive of the interests of class members that are not party to the individual adjudication. Fed. R. Civ. P. 23(b)(1).

The Seventh Circuit has cautioned against the overuse of the Rule 23(b)(1) class actions because there is no right to opt-out of the class, and thus there is a risk of depriving unnamed class members of their right to a day in court. *See Spano v. The Boeing Co.*, 633 F.3d 574, 587 (7th Cir. 2011) ("Too liberal an application of the mandatory-class device risks depriving people of one of their most important due process rights: the right to their own day in court."); *see also Jefferson v. Ingersoll Int'l Inc.*, 195 F.3d 894, 898 (7th Cir. 1999) (stating in the context of Rule 23(b)(2): "When substantial damages have been sought, the most appropriate approach is that of Rule 23(b)(3), because it allows notice and an opportunity to opt out.").

In the ERISA context, class actions for breach of the fiduciary duty owed to an ERISA plan frequently have been certified pursuant to Rule 23(b)(1), "because recovery for a breach of the fiduciary duty owed to an ERISA plan . . . will inure to the plan as a whole, and because defendant-fiduciaries are entitled to consistent rulings regarding operation of the plan." *Neil*, 275 F.R.D. at 267. However, the Seventh Circuit rejected application of Rule 23(b)(1) in an ERISA action in which the plaintiffs defined the class too broadly. *Spano*, 633 F.3d at 588. The class in *Spano* was defined so that it encompassed ERISA plan members who appeared to have benefited from the defendants having offered an allegedly imprudent investment option. *Id.* at 587. Because the class members thus did not have identical interests with respect to the investment option in question, the Seventh Circuit concluded that there was no reason to believe that the disposition of one class member's claim would necessarily be dispositive of the interests of other class members, as was necessary for certification pursuant to Rule 23(b)(1)(B). *Id.* at 588. The court further concluded that the requirements for Rule 23(b)(1)(A) were not met because there was no reason that defendants could not offer the investment option in question to some of the plan members and not others. *Id.* Thus, as is evident from *Spano*, certification under Rule 23(b)(1), will likely be "confined to those cases where there are no, or few, individual questions." *Doe v. Guardian Life Ins. Co.*, 145 F.R.D. 466, 477 (N.D. Ill. 1992).

The fact that a defendant may be found liable to some class members and not others is insufficient to make adjudication appropriate under Rule 23(b)(1)(A). *See Bowe Bell + Howell Co. v. Immco Employees' Ass'n*, 2005 WL 1139645, at *4–5 (N.D. Ill. May 11, 2005) (denying class certification pursuant to Rule 23(b)(1)(A) where there were factual variations among class members). "[D]ifferent results do not 'trap [a defendant] in the inescapable legal quagmire of not being able to comply with one such judgment without violating the terms of another.'" *Vulcan Golf, LLC v. Google Inc.*, 254 F.R.D. 521, 537 (N.D. Ill. 2008) (alteration in original) (quoting *Walker v. Houston*, 341 F. Supp. 1124, 1131 (S.D. Tex. 1971)). Rather, a "[p]laintiff must demonstrate potential rulings are inconsistent by placing 'the party opposing the class in a position of being unable to comply with one judgment without violating the terms of another judgment.'" *Bowe Bell + Howell Co.*, 2005 WL 1139645, at *4–5 (quoting 5 *Moore's Federal Practice*, § 23.41[3][a]).

For certification pursuant Rule 23(b)(1)(B), resolution of certain class members' claims must be dispositive of, or substantially impede, the claims of other class members; the stare decisis effect of an earlier adjudication is insufficient. *See Bowe Bell + Howell Co.*, 2005 WL 1139645, at *4–5 (denying class certification pursuant to Rule 23(b)(1)(B) where there were factual variations among the class members and "the application of the doctrine of *stare decisis* is the only possible effect of a ruling in favor of Plaintiff"). Certification pursuant to Rule 23(b)(1)(B) may be appropriate where there is a common fund that may limit recovery to individual plaintiffs. *See Est. of VanDam ex rel. Horizon Trust & Inv. Mgt., N.A. v. Daniels*, 278 F.R.D. 415, 425–26 (S.D. Ind. 2011) (certification pursuant to Rule 23(b)(1)(B) "tends to arise in cases where, as here, there is a common fund that may limit recovery to individual plaintiffs"); *Hawkins v. Securitas Sec. Servs. USA, Inc.*, 280 F.R.D. 388, 396 (N.D. Ill. 2011) ("[t]he Seventh Circuit has made clear that Rule 23(b)(1) . . . is inappropriate in damage actions not involving a limited fund") (citing *Crawford v. Equifax Payment Servs., Inc.*, 201 F.3d 877, 882 (7th Cir. 2000)).

Rule 23(b)(2) Classes

A case may be certified as a class action under Rule 23(b)(2) where the "party opposing the class has acted or refused to act on grounds that apply generally to the class, so that final injunctive relief or corresponding declaratory relief is appropriate respecting the class as a whole." Fed. R. Civ. P. 23(b)(2). "Colloquially, 23(b)(2) is the appropriate rule to enlist when the plaintiffs' primary goal is not monetary relief, but rather to require the defendant to do or not do something that would benefit the whole class." *Chicago Teachers Union*, 797 F.3d at 441.

"Rule 23(b)(2) provides for binding litigation on all class members without guarantees of personal notice and the opportunity to opt out of the suit." *Lemon v. Int'l Union of Operating Eng'rs, Local No. 139, AFL-CIO*, 216 F.3d 577, 580 (7th Cir. 2000); *see also Senegal v. JPMorgan Chase Bank, N.A.*, 939 F.3d 878, 880 (7th Cir. 2019) (class members "cannot opt out of Rule 23(b)(2) classes, for the relief is indivisible"). Thus, its application is only appropriate when "the interests of the class members are cohesive and homogenous such that the case will not depend on the adjudication of facts particular to any subset of the class nor require a remedy that differentiates materially among class members." *Lemon*, 216 F.3d at 580. "[B]ecause individual claims for compensatory or punitive damages typically require judicial inquiry into the particularized merits of each individual plaintiff's claim," the application of Rule 23(b)(2) does not extend to cases where the appropriate final relief is exclusively or predominantly monetary damages. *Id.*; *see also Wal-Mart*, 564 U.S. at 360–61 (Rule 23(b)(2) "does not authorize class certification when each class member would be entitled to an individualized award of monetary damages."). This remains true even where the plaintiffs seek uniform, class-wide equitable relief in addition to damages. *Lemon*, 216 F.3d at 580.

Where plaintiffs seek both equitable relief and monetary damages, Rule 23(b)(2) is only applicable when the monetary damages are incidental to the equitable relief. *Id.* at 580–81. Incidental damages "flow directly from liability to the class as a whole on the claims forming the basis of the injunctive or declaratory relief." *Id.* at 581 (quoting *Allison v. Citgo Petroleum Corp.*, 151 F.3d 402, 415 (5th Cir. 1998)). "Incidental damages do not depend 'in any significant way on the intangible, subjective differences of each class member's circumstances' and do not 'require additional hearings to resolve the disparate merits of each individual's case.'" *Id.* (quoting *Allison*, 151 F.3d at 415). Thus, where the "calculation of monetary relief will be mechanical, formulaic, a task not for a trier of fact but for a computer program," certification under Rule 23(b)(2) may still be available. *Johnson*, 702 F.3d at 372.

Where plaintiffs seek both equitable relief and monetary damages and the monetary damages are not incidental, a district court has the option of certifying a Rule 23(b)(2) class for the portion of the case addressing equitable relief and a Rule 23(b)(3) class for the portion of the case addressing damages. *Lemon*, 216 F.3d at 580–82; *see also Pella Corp. v. Saltzman*, 606 F.3d 391, 395 (7th Cir. 2010) (affirming a district court's decision to split a class comprising purchasers of defective windows into two groups and certifying those who had paid for replacement windows pursuant to 23(b)(3) and certifying those who had not replaced their windows pursuant to 23(b)(2)). Moreover, when a declaratory order can settle an issue for all plaintiffs, certification for Rule 23(b)(2) still may be appropriate, even though it might be necessary to hold separate hearings to determine the monetary relief to which each class member is entitled. *See Chi. Tchrs. Union*, 797 F.3d at 442–43 ("a determination of liability in this case (i.e., a finding that the reconstitution practice discriminated against African Americans) might require later determinations of individual relief, but would resolve all questions of liability").

Rule 23(b)(3) Classes

Predominance of Common Questions

Rule 23(b)(3) requires "that the questions of law or fact common to class members predominate over any questions affecting only individual members, and that a class action is superior to other available methods for fairly and efficiently adjudicating the controversy." Fed R. Civ. P. 23(b)(3). "There is no mathematical or mechanical test for evaluating predominance." *Messner*, 669 F.3d at 814. "It is not determined simply by counting noses: that is, determining whether there are more common issues or more individual issues, regardless of relative importance." *Parko v. Shell Oil Co.*, 739 F.3d 1083, 1085 (7th Cir. 2014). The analysis aims to determine whether a proposed class is "sufficiently cohesive to warrant adjudication by representation." *Id.* (quoting *Amchem Prod., Inc. v. Windsor*, 521 U.S. 591, 623 (1997)).

"[N]ot every issue must be amenable to common resolution; individual inquiries may be required after the class phase." *Beaton*, 907 F.3d at 1029–30. Indeed, liability with regards to all class members need not be resolved in a single stroke. *Id.* Individual inquires, including those relating to liability, can be handled through such mechanisms as affidavits and proper auditing procedures. *Id.* at 1030; *see also Scott*, 99 F.4th at 1092 ("[W]here a common issue exists such that its resolution is unlikely to be enhanced by repeated proceedings, then it makes good sense, especially when the class is so large, to resolve that issue in one fell swoop while leaving the remaining, claimant-specific issues to individual follow-on proceeding." (cleaned up)).

But predominance is not satisfied if "resolving a common issue will not greatly simplify the litigation to judgment or settlement. . . ." *Parko*, 739 F.3d at 1085. Plaintiffs must show that there is a common question that predominates over individual questions, but "need not prove that the answer to that question will be resolved in its favor." *Bell*, 800 F.3d at 376; *see also Amgen Inc. v. Conn. Ret. Plans and Trust Funds*, 568 U.S. 455 (2013) ("Rule 23(b)(3) requires a showing that *questions* common to the class predominate, not that those questions will be answered, on the merits, in favor of the class.") (emphasis in original). However, "[m]ere *assertion* by class counsel that common issues predominate is not enough." *Parko*, 739 F.3d at 1085 (emphasis in original). Rather, when factual disputes bear on the issue of predominance, the court must receive evidence and resolve the dispute. *Id.*; *see also Eddlemon v. Bradley Univ.*, 65 F.4th 335, 338–41 (7th Cir. 2023) (vacating and remanding the district court's class certification order because the court failed to "rigorously analyze" the commonality and predominance of the plaintiff's claims).

Individualized Damages and "Uninjured" Class Members

"Damages are but one element that [courts in the Seventh Circuit consider] in determining predominance under Rule 23(b)(3)." *Kleen Prods. LLC v. Int'l Paper*, 306 F.R.D. 585, 601 (N.D. Ill. 2015) "It is well established that the presence of individualized questions regarding damages does not prevent certification under Rule 23(b)(3)." *Messner*, 669 F.3d at 815. "This is particularly so where the calculation of damages will be mechanical and formulaic, a task not for a trier of fact but for a computer program." *Balderrama-Baca v. Clarence Davids & Co.*, 318 F.R.D. 603, 613 (N.D. Ill. 2017) (cleaned up). Indeed, "[i]t is routine in class actions to have a final phase in which individualized proof must be submitted." *Suchanek*, 764 F.3d at 756.

Pursuant to the Supreme Court's decision in *Comcast Corp.*, 133 S. Ct. 1426, the calculation of damages must be tied to the theory of liability. *IKO Roofing*, 757 F.3d at 602–03. This does not mean, however, that damages must be uniform across a class for certification to be granted pursuant to Rule 23(b)(3). *Id.* For example, in *IKO Roofing*, which involved allegations of defective roof tiles, the Seventh Circuit recognized that certification would be appropriate where damages were either (a) uniform across a class based on a theory that the proper measure of damages was the difference between the market price of tile as represented and the price of defective tile as sold or (b) buyer-specific based on a theory that only those purchasers whose tiles actually failed were entitled to damages. *Id.* In either case, damages would be tied to the theory of liability. But in the latter case, where damages were buyer-specific, class certification would be limited to questions of liability. *Id.*

A class may be certified even if it encompasses members who were not harmed by the alleged conduct. *See Bell*, 800 F.3d at 380 ("A class will often include persons who have not been injured by the defendant's conduct, but this possibility or, indeed inevitability, does not preclude class certification."). "If, however, a class is defined so broadly as to include a great number of members who for some reason could not have been harmed by the defendant's allegedly unlawful conduct, the class is defined too broadly to permit certification." *Messner*, 669 F.3d at 824. The distinction, therefore, is "between class members who *were not* harmed and those who *could not* have been harmed." *Id.* at 825 (emphasis in original). This distinction is well illustrated by *Bell v. PNC Bank*, which involved plaintiffs' allegations that PNC had an official policy of denying overtime pay. 800 F.3d at 365. The Seventh Circuit explained that a class could be certified even if it included employees who were never harmed by that policy because they never worked beyond their 40-hour work week. *Id.* at 380. But, said the court, it would not be appropriate for the class to include managerial employees, because they are exempt from overtime hour laws and *could not* have been harmed by the policy. *Id.*

Multistate Certification

Generally, "[n]o class action is proper unless all litigants are governed by the same legal rules." *In re Bridgestone/Firestone, Inc.*, 288 F.3d 1012, 1015 (7th Cir. 2002). When plaintiffs bring state law claims on behalf of a class encompassing individuals from multiple states, choice-of-law rules will be applied to determine whether all class members' claims will be governed by the same legal rules. *Id.* The choice-of-law rules come from the state in which the federal court sits. *Id.* Indiana applies the law of the place where the harm occurred. *Id.* Illinois applies the most significant relationship test, under which the law of the place of injury controls unless Illinois has a more significant relationship with the occurrence and with the parties. *Esser v. McIntyre*, 661 N.E.2d 1138, 1141 (Ill. 1996). In Wisconsin, the law of the forum applies unless non-forum contacts are of greater significance. *Henderson v. U.S. Bank, N.A.*, 615 F. Supp. 2d 804, 808–09 (E.D. Wis. 2009). Where plaintiffs assert claims pursuant to state consumer protection law and the place of injury determines the applicable law, the laws of the various states where the plaintiffs live are likely to govern. *In re Bridgestone/Firestone, Inc.*, 288 F.3d at 1018.

The Seventh Circuit has refused to certify classes in which the laws of multiple states would need to be applied to class members' claims on the grounds that the application of various laws defeats predominance and would result in an unmanageable class. *See id.* at 1018 ("Because these claims must be adjudicated under the law of so many jurisdictions, a single nationwide class is not manageable."); *Thorogood v. Sears, Roebuck & Co.*, 547 F.3d 742, 746 (7th Cir. 2008) ("Our plaintiff wants to litigate in a single federal district court half a million claims wrested from the control of the courts of the 29 jurisdictions in which those claims arose and the laws of which govern the claimants' entitlement to and scope of relief. The instructions to the jury on the law it is to apply will be an amalgam of the consumer protection laws of the 29 jurisdictions, and procedural rules by which particular jurisdictions expand or contract relief will be ignored."); *see also Carnegie v. Household Int'l, Inc.*, 220 F.R.D. 542, 548 (N.D. Ill. 2004), *aff'd*, 376 F.3d 656 (7th Cir. 2004) ("[T]he four state-law claims discussed here present such unwieldy issues that a nationwide class action cannot be the most efficient method of resolving them.").

However, multistate classes can be certified through the use of subclasses. For example, in *Pella*, the Seventh Circuit affirmed the certification of six state subclasses wherein the consumer protection acts of the six states had nearly identical elements. 606 F.3d at 396. Moreover, "if the applicable laws 'can be sorted into a small number of groups, each containing materially identical legal standards, then certification of subclasses embracing each of the dominant legal standards can be appropriate.'" *Village of Bedford Park v. Expedia, Inc. (WA)*, 309 F.R.D. 442, 446 (N.D. Ill. 2015) (quoting *Klay v. Humana, Inc.*, 382 F.3d 1241, 1262 (11th Cir. 2004)). But "'[t]he burden of showing uniformity or the existence of only a small number of applicable standards,' however, 'rests squarely with the plaintiffs.'" *Id.* (quoting *Klay*, 382 F.3d at 1262).

Superiority of Class Adjudication

As with predominance, Rule 23's superiority prong is intended to ensure that "a class action [will] achieve economies of time, effort, and expense, and promote . . . uniformity of decision as to persons similarly situated, without sacrificing procedural fairness or bringing about other undesirable results." *Cunningham Charter Corp. v. Learjet, Inc.*, 258 F.R.D. 320, 332 (S.D. Ill. 2009) (emphasis in original) (quoting *Amchem Prods. Inc.*, 521 U.S. at 615).

The superiority analysis is guided by the four factors set out in Rule 23(b)(3): (A) The class members' interests in individually controlling the prosecution or defense of separate actions, (B) the extent and nature of any litigation concerning the controversy already begun by or against class members, (C) the desirability or undesirability of concentrating the litigation of the claims in the particular forum, and (D) the likely difficulties in managing the class action. *See, e.g.*, *Barnes v. Air Line Pilots Ass'n, Int'l*, 310 F.R.D. 551, 562 (N.D. Ill. 2015). The superiority analysis considers "both the costs *and benefits* of the class device." *Mullins v. Direct Digital, LLC*, 795 F.3d 654, 663–64 (7th Cir. 2015) (emphasis in original).

With respect to class members' interest in individually controlling the prosecution or defense of their claim, the Seventh Circuit has recognized that a central purpose of the class action mechanism "is to overcome the problem that small recoveries do not provide the incentive for any individual to bring a solo action prosecuting his or her rights." *Mace v. Van Ru Credit Corp.*, 109 F.3d 338, 344 (7th Cir. 1997). "A class action solves this problem by aggregating the relatively paltry potential recoveries into something worth someone's (usually an attorney's) labor." *Id.* Indeed, consumer class actions are a "crucial deterrent against the proliferation of bogus products whose sticker price is dwarfed even by a court filing fee (now $400 for a civil case in federal district court). Though punitive damages may also deter, few litigants would risk filing suit on the off-chance that punitive damages would be recovered after years of litigation." *Beaton*, 907 F.3d at 1031.

In evaluating class members' monetary interests in individually controlling an action, the Seventh Circuit has suggested that a potential recovery of $1,000 is insufficient to tilt this factor in favor of individual adjudication. *Mace*, 109 F.3d at 344 ("True, the FDCPA allows for individual recoveries of up to $1000. But this assumes that the plaintiff will be aware of her rights, willing to subject herself to all the burdens of suing and able to find an attorney willing to take her case."). On the other hand, where the potential recovery was $50,000, plus attorneys' fees and costs, the Seventh Circuit held that this fact weighed against class certification. *Andrews v. Chevy Chase Bank*, 545 F.3d 570, 577 (7th Cir. 2008) (rejecting assertion that class adjudication was the "only realistic means for recovery").

The fourth factor stated in Rule 23(b)(4), the likely difficulties in managing a class action, is closely tied to issues of commonality and predominance. *See Messner*, 669 F.3d at 814 at n.5 ("There are so many common issues of law and fact relating to the issue of [defendant's] liability . . . that the superiority requirement likely poses no serious obstacle to class certification here."); *Barnes*, 310 F.R.D. at 562 ("'[T]he likely difficulties in managing a class action' in this case are minimal given the predominance of common issues . . . ."); *Hale v. State Farm Mut. Auto. Ins. Co.*, 2016 WL 4992504, *10 (S.D. Ill. Sept. 16, 2016) ("[B]ecause common issues of law and fact predominate, and trying these claims individually would result in a substantial amount of repetition and wasted resources, proceeding as a class action is the superior form of adjudication for this case."). Thus, even when class adjudication would result in the "need for careful administration and individualized assessment of relief," class adjudication still may be superior if litigating claims separately "risks inconsistent determinations on common issues" and "would require multiple courts to evaluate the same evidence and analyze the same policies and practices in what would amount to a wastefully inefficient enterprise." *Cancel v. City of Chi.*, 254 F.R.D. 501, 512 (N.D. Ill. 2008).

Rule 23(c)(4) Issue Classes

"When appropriate, an action may be brought or maintained as a class action with respect to particular issues." Fed. R. Civ. P 23(c)(4). The party seeking certification of a Rule 23(c)(4) issue class must first show that the class meets Rule 23(a)'s prerequisites to certification. *Jacks v. DirectSat USA, LLC*, --F.4th--, 2024 WL 4380256, at *6 (7th Cir. Oct. 3, 2024). Then, they must show that the issue class meets the requirements of Rule 23(b)(3). Specifically, "as part of satisfying its burden under Rule 23, a party seeking certification of an issue class under Rule 23(c)(4) must show that common questions predominate in the resolution of the specific issue or issues that are the subject of the certification motion." *Id.* at *7. The party need not show that individual issues predominate "as to the cause of action, taken as a whole." *Id.* (internal quotation marks omitted). "[I]n addition to demonstrating that common questions predominate as to each issue to be certified, a party seeking certification under Rule 23(c)(4) must show that certifying the proposed issues would be the most practical and efficient way to resolve the litigation." *Id.* at *8. Thus, "the superiority requirement functions as a backstop against inefficient use of Rule 23(c)(4) because it ensures that courts will not rely on issue certification where there exist only minor or insignificant common questions." *Id.* (cleaned up).

c. Class Definiteness

The Seventh Circuit recognizes "an implicit requirement under Rule 23 that a class must be defined clearly and that membership be defined by objective criteria . . . ." *Mullins*, 795 F.3d at 657. A class must not be defined too vaguely because a "court needs to be able to identify who will receive notice, who will share in any recovery, and who will be bound by a judgment." *Id.* at 660. "To avoid vagueness, class definitions generally need to identify a particular group, harmed during a particular time frame, in a particular location, in a particular way." *Id.* Further, "classes that are defined by subjective criteria, such as by a person's state of mind, fail the objectivity requirement." *Id.* "Plaintiffs can generally avoid the subjectivity problem by defining the class in terms of conduct (an objective fact) rather than a state of mind." *Id.* Finally, "classes that are defined in terms of success on the merits—so-called 'fail-safe classes'—also are not properly defined." *Id.* "The key to avoiding this problem is to define the class so that membership does not depend on the liability of the defendant." *Id.*

The Seventh Circuit, however, has rejected the heightened "ascertainability" requirement recently imposed on class certification by some courts, including the Third Circuit (*see, e.g.*, *Carrera v. Bayer Corp.*, 727 F.3d 300 (3d Cir. 2013)). *Mullins*, 795 F.3d at 661–63. Specifically, in *Mullins*, the Court rejected the argument that Rule 23 requires plaintiffs to set forth an administratively feasible mechanism, apart from self-identification (through affidavit or otherwise) by class members, for determining whether putative class members fall within the class. *Id.* at 662. The court explained that such a rule would "not further any interest of Rule 23 that is not already adequately protected by the Rule's explicit requirements." *Id.* Indeed, such a rule would "render[] the manageability criterion of the superiority requirement superfluous" and "conflict[] with the well-settled presumption that courts should not refuse to certify a class merely on the basis of manageability concerns." *Id.* at 663. Moreover, it would effectively bar low-value consumer class actions and other class actions where class members are unlikely to have retained proof of purchase and thus foreclose precisely those cases in which "there realistically is no other alternative to class treatment." *Id.* at 663–64.

d. Timing of Class Certification

Pursuant to Fed. R. Civ. P. 23(c)(1)(A), "[a]t an early practicable time after a person sues or is sued as a class representative, the court must determine by order whether to certify the action as a class action." The timing for the determination of class certification should be informed by the need for courts to "engage in a 'rigorous analysis'—sometimes probing beyond the pleadings—before ruling on certification." *Damasco v. Clearwire Corp.*, 662 F.3d 891, 896–97 (7th Cir. 2011) (quoting *Wal-Mart*, 564 U.S. at 350–51).[6] "Although discovery may in some cases be unnecessary to resolve class issues, in other cases, a court may abuse its discretion by not allowing for appropriate discovery before deciding whether to certify a class." *Id.* at 897 (citation omitted).

"Normally the issue of certification should be resolved [prior to an adjudication on the merits] . . . ." *Thomas v. UBS AG*, 706 F.3d 846, 849 (7th Cir. 2013). However, when a "suit can quickly be shown to be groundless, it may make sense for the district court to skip certification and proceed directly to the merits." *Id.* Because a court has an independent obligation to decide whether an action brought on a class basis is to be so maintained, "a court may deny class certification even before the plaintiff files a motion requesting certification." *Kasalo v. Harris & Harris, Ltd.*, 656 F.3d 557, 563 (7th Cir. 2011). However, because there is a general aversion to striking class allegations at the pleading stage, "a court should address class allegations at the pleading stage only 'when the pleadings are facially defective and definitively establish that a class action cannot be maintained.'" *Murdock-Alexander v. Tempsnow Emp. and Placement Servs., LLC*, 2016 WL 6833961, at *4 (N.D. Ill. Nov. 21, 2016) (quoting *Wright*, 2010 WL 4962838, at *1).

So long as a named plaintiff has not accepted the defendant's offer, a defendant may not preempt a class certification motion through a Rule 68 offer of judgment in an amount greater than the named plaintiff's maximum possible recovery, even if the defendant has deposited the proffered money with the court pursuant to Rule 67. *Fulton Dental, LLC v. Bisco, Inc.*, 860 F.3d 541, 546–47 (7th Cir. 2017.) "[A]s long as the proposed class representative has not lost on the merits before a class certification motion is filed, it is not barred from seeking class treatment." *Id.* at 546.

5. INTERLOCUTORY APPEAL (FED. R. CIV. P. 23(F))

"[N]o 'bright-line' test or 'catalog of factors' governs the wisdom of interlocutory appeal under Rule 23(f)." *Reliable Money Order, Inc. v. McKnight Sales Co.*, 704 F.3d 489, 497 (7th Cir. 2013). But in *Blair v. Equifax Check Servs., Inc.*, 181 F.3d 832 (7th Cir. 1999), the Seventh Circuit set forth three categories of cases for which interlocutory appeal pursuant to Rule 23(f) is likely appropriate. *Id.* at 834–35. First, the court recognized that interlocutory appeal may be appropriate in cases where the "denial of class status sounds the death knell of the litigation, because the representative plaintiff's claim is too small to justify the expense of litigation." *Id.* at 834. Second, interlocutory appeal may be appropriate when class certification has been granted because "a grant of class status can put considerable pressure on the defendant to settle, even when the plaintiff's probability of success on the merits is slight." *Id.* "Many corporate executives are unwilling to bet their company that they are in the right in big-stakes litigation, and a grant of class status can propel the stakes of a case into the stratosphere." *Id.*; *see also In re Bridgestone/Firestone*, 288 F.3d at 1015–16 ("Aggregating mil-

---

[6] Note that pursuant to *Chapman*, the requirement of filing a preemptive motion for class certification as previously required by *Damasco* to withstand mootness challenges is no longer required in the Seventh Circuit. *Chapman*, 796 F.3d at 787.

lions of claims on account of multiple products manufactured and sold across more than ten years makes the case so unwieldy, and the stakes so large, that settlement becomes almost inevitable—and at a price that reflects the risk of a catastrophic judgment as much as, if not more than, the actual merit of the claims. Permitting appellate review before class certification can precipitate such a settlement is a principal function of Rule 23(f).”). For the Seventh Circuit to grant interlocutory appeal of a case that falls into either of these first two categories, “the appellant must demonstrate that the district court’s ruling on class certification is questionable.”

Finally, interlocutory appeal may be appropriate where it “may facilitate the development of the law.” *Blair*, 181 F.3d at 835. “Because a large proportion of class actions settles or is resolved in a way that overtakes procedural matters, some fundamental issues about class actions are poorly developed.” *Id.* Interlocutory appeal allows the Seventh Circuit the chance to weigh in on these issues. *Id.*; *see also In re Bridgestone/Firestone*, 288 F.3d at 1015–16 (“The district court’s conclusion that one state’s law would apply to claims by consumers throughout the country—not just those in Indiana, but also those in California, New Jersey, and Mississippi—is a novelty, and, if followed, would be of considerable import to other suits.”). “When the justification for interlocutory review is contributing to development of the law, it is less important to show that the district judge’s decision is shaky.” *Id.*

Rule 23(f) appeals are limited to “those issues related to [the] class certification decision.” *DeKeyser v. Thyssenkrupp Waupaca, Inc.*, 860 F.3d 918, 922–23 (7th Cir. 2017) (quoting *Andrews v. Chevy Chase Bank*, 545 F.3d 570, 576 n.2 (7th Cir. 2008)). Parties cannot use Rule 23(f) to appeal issues unrelated to the soundness of a class certification decision, even if those issues appear in the district court’s class certification order. *Id.*

6. CLASS NOTICE (FED. R. CIV. P. 23(C)(2))

For Rule 23(b)(3) classes, Rule 23(c)(2)(B) requires the “best notice that is practicable under the circumstances, including individual notice to all members who can be identified through reasonable effort.” The rule does not insist on actual notice to all class members in all cases. It recognizes it might be *impossible* to identify some class members for purposes of actual notice. *Mullins*, 795 F.3d at 665 (citing Geoffrey C. Shaw, Note, *Class Ascertainability*, 124 Yale L.J. 2354, 2367–69 (2015)). While actual individual notice may be the ideal, due process does not always so require. *In re AT&T Mobility Wireless Data Servs. Sales Tax Litig.*, 789 F. Supp. 2d 935, 968 (N.D. Ill. 2011).

Courts may direct notice via alternative means such as through third parties, paid advertising, and/or posting in places frequented by class members, all without offending due process.[7] *See Hughes v. Kore of Indiana Enterprise, Inc.*, 731 F.3d 672, 676–77 (7th Cir. 2013). “As long as the alternative means satisfy the standard of Rule 23(b)(3), there is no due process violation. . . . Due process simply does not require the ability to identify all members of the class at the certification stage.” *Mullins*, 795 F.3d at 665. When class notice is issued, the Seventh Circuit has held that district courts have discretion to shift the cost of class notice to the defendant even though plaintiffs ordinarily bear the initial cost of class notice. *See Bakov v. Consol. World Travel, Inc.*, 68 F.4th 1053, 1060 (7th Cir. 2023) (finding that the district court’s cost allocation did not constitute an abuse of discretion because the court

[7] Although notice via U.S. mail was required previously when class members’ names and addresses were known, *Eisen v. Carlisle & Jacquelin*, 417 U.S. 156, 174–75 (1974), the Advisory Committee on Civil Rules noted, when proposing the now-adopted amendments to Rule 23, including providing clarity that “technological change [since *Eisen*] has introduced other means of communication that may sometimes provide a reliable additional or alternative method for giving notice. . . . [C]ourts and counsel have begun to employ new technology to make notice more effective.” Federal Rules of Civil Procedure, 2018-2019 Amendments to the Federal Rules of Civil Procedure Approved, available at www.federalrulesofcivilprocedure.org/2018-2019-amendments-to-the-federal-rules-of-civil-procedure-approved.

properly revisited class certification in response to changed law, which effectively expanded the class scope).

Notice is not required for classes certified pursuant to Rule 23(b)(1) or 23(b)(2). *See Randall v. Rolls-Royce Corp.*, 637 F.3d 818, 826 (7th Cir. 2011) ("It is only when the primary relief sought is injunctive, with monetary relief if sought at all mechanically computable, that elaborate notice is not required."). There is no opt out right in such cases, and notice costs, "moreover, could easily cripple actions that do not seek damages." Fed. R. Civ. P. 23(c)(2) Adv. Com. Notes to 2003 amendment. *See also Johnson*, 702 F.3d at 370–71 ("there is no requirement of notice, or even of permitting opt outs, in a Rule 23(b)(2) class action. Notice to class members *may* be required by the district court. Fed. R. Civ. P. 23(c)(2)(A). But unlike the case of a (b)(3) class action, *see* Fed. R. Civ. P. 23(c)(2)(B), notice is not mandatory. And when it is ordered, the purpose usually is to enable class members to challenge the class representatives or otherwise intervene in the suit, rather than to allow them to opt out."); *Schrader v. Selective Serv. Sys. Local Bd. No. 76 of Wis.*, 329 F. Supp. 966, 967 (D. Wis. 1971).

7. DISCOVERY OF ABSENT CLASS MEMBERS

In *Brennan v. Midwestern United Life Ins. Co.*, 450 F.2d 999 (7th Cir. 1971), the Seventh Circuit held that "under certain circumstances," absent class members may be subject to discovery. *Id.* at 1004. Weighing against such discovery, the court noted "Rule 23's general policy of permitting absent class members to remain outside the principal action" and held that such discovery should not be permitted "as a matter of course." *Id.* at 1005. However, this policy may be outweighed "[i]f discovery from the absent member is necessary or helpful to the proper presentation and correct adjudication of the principal suit." *Id.* In any event, "adequate precautionary measures" should be "taken to insure that the absent member is not misled or confused." *Id.* at 1005. A party seeking such discovery must establish "that the requested information is actually needed in preparation for trial and that discovery devices are not used to take unfair advantage of 'absent' class members." *Id.* at 1006. "Moreover, adequate notice must be given so that such persons are fully informed of the discovery order and the possible consequences of their noncompliance with it." *Id.*

8. CLASS ACTION SETTLEMENTS (FED. R. CIV. P. 23(E))

a. Preliminary Approval

Rule 23 of the Federal Rules of Civil Procedure—and, more specifically, Rule 23(e) related to the settlement, voluntary dismissal, or compromise of class actions—was amended in December 2018. Although the new language of the Rule contemplates that the court need consider "information sufficient to enable it to determine whether to give notice of the [proposed settlement] to the class," Fed. R. Civ. P. 23(e)(1)(A), courts in the Seventh Circuit still refer to this step as the "preliminary approval" process. *See Abante Rooter and Plumbing, Inc. v. Oh Ins. Agency, et al.*, No. 15-cv-09025, 2019 WL 2366475, at *1 (N.D. Ill. May 29, 2019).

"Federal Rule of Civil Procedure 23(e) requires court approval of any settlement that effects the dismissal of a class action." *In re Nat'l Collegiate Athletic Ass'n Student-Athlete Concussion Injury Litig.*, 314 F.R.D. 580, 588 (N.D. Ill. 2016) (*NCAA Concussion Litig.*) (quoting *Reynolds v. Beneficial Nat'l Bank*, 288 F.3d 277, 279 (7th Cir. 2002)). "A district court may approve a class action settlement if it finds it to be fair, adequate, and reasonable." *Wong v. Accretive Health, Inc.*, 773 F.3d 859, 862 (7th Cir. 2014) (citing Fed. R. Civ. P. 23(e)(2)). When parties seek preliminary approval of a class action settlement agreement and certification of a settlement class, the district court must undertake two essential inquiries.

First, "the court must conduct an independent class certification analysis." *Am. Int'l Grp., Inc. v. ACE INA Holdings, Inc.*, Nos. 07 C 2898, 09 C2026, 2011 WL 3290302, at *3 (N.D. Ill. July 26, 2011). *See also Abante*, 2019 WL 2366475, at *1 (performing a "preliminary evaluation of the Settlement," to ensure that the "Court will likely be able to: (i) approve the proposal under Fed. R. Civ. P. 23(e)(2); and (ii) certify the Settlement Class for purposes of judgment on the proposal"). "This analysis 'demand[s] undiluted, even heightened, attention' when applied to classes for which certification is sought for settlement purposes only." *Id.* (quoting *Amchem Prods., Inc. v. Windsor*, 521 U.S. 591, 620 (1997)); *see also Uhl v. Thoroughbred Tech. & Telecomms., Inc.*, 309 F.3d 978, 985 (7th Cir.2002). "This need for heightened attention is necessary because, when parties jointly seek approval of a class action settlement, the adversarial relationship between the plaintiffs and defendant may fall away, and potential conflicts of interest between class counsel and the class members may arise." *NCAA Concussion Litig.*, 314 F.R.D. at 588 (citing *Redman v. RadioShack Corp.*, 768 F.3d 622, 629 (7th Cir.2014); *Mirfasihi v. Fleet Mortg. Corp.*, 356 F.3d 781, 785 (7th Cir. 2004)). The Seventh Circuit has gone so far as to describe "the district judge as a fiduciary of the class, who is subject therefore to the high duty of care that the law requires of fiduciaries." *Pearson v. NBTY, Inc.*, 772 F.3d 778, 780 (7th Cir. 2014) (quotation omitted).

"Second, the district court must determine whether the proposed settlement is 'within the range of possible approval.'" *NCAA Concussion Litig.*, 314 F.R.D. at 588 (quoting *Gautreaux v. Pierce*, 690 F.2d 616, 621 n.3 (7th Cir.1982)). The purpose of this inquiry "is to ascertain whether there is any reason to notify the class members of the proposed settlement and to proceed with a fairness hearing." *Id.* At this initial stage, the court is not "resolving the merits of the controversy or making a precise determination of the parties' respective legal rights." *E.E.O.C. v. Hiram Walker & Sons, Inc.*, 768 F.2d 884, 889 (7th Cir. 1985).

If the district court finds that the certification of the settlement class is appropriate and the proposed settlement is within the range of possible approval, the court will then order the plaintiffs to provide notice of the settlement to the class "in a reasonable manner" so that the class members can raise any objections to the settlement. *NCAA Concussion Litig.*, 314 F.R.D. at 588 (citing Fed. R. Civ. P. 23(e)(1)). Notice, pursuant to the recent amendments to Rule 23, must be the "best . . . that is practicable under the circumstances, including individual notice to all members who can be identified through reasonable effort. The notice may be by one or more of the following: United States mail, electronic means, or other appropriate means." Fed. R. Civ. P. 23(c)(2). Once the class is provided with notice of the settlement and an opportunity to object, the court conducts a final approval hearing to determine whether the settlement is "fair, reasonable, and adequate." Fed. R. Civ. P. 23(e)(2). If the district court is satisfied that the settlement meets these criteria, it will grant final approval of the settlement, which binds the defendant and all class members to the terms of the settlement. *NCAA Concussion Litig.*, 314 F.R.D. at 589.

At the preliminary approval stage, the extent of the district court's inquiry into the appropriateness of class certification and the reasonableness of the settlement terms depends, as it must, on the circumstances of the individual case. Where the size of the class is small, the cost of notice minimal, and the issues discrete, the court may be able to determine that class certification is proper and the settlement is "within the range of possible approval" with "minimal fuss." *Id.* But where the putative class members range in the millions, the parties have completed extensive discovery, substantive objections are raised at the preliminary stage, and the costs and efforts to provide notice are substantial, it may be advisable for the court to engage in a more piercing and thorough analysis of the issues in the first instance, rather than waiting until the final approval hearing, to promote the "just, speedy, and inexpensive" resolution of the case. *Id.* (citing Fed. R. Civ. P. 1).

b. Notice and Objections

Notice

The court evaluates counsel's proposed notice plan at preliminary approval. The notice must comport with the requirements of due process and, in a Rule 23(b)(3) case, constitute the "best notice that is practicable." *See* Part 6, *supra*.

Objections

"Federal courts naturally favor the settlement of class action litigation." *Schulte*, 805 F. Supp. 2d at 578 (quoting *Isby v. Bayh*, 75 F.3d 1191, 1199 (7th Cir. 1996)). Nevertheless, the Seventh Circuit recognizes the inherent tension that exists between the lawyers' and class members' interests:

> What we said was that the structure of class actions under Rule 23 of the federal rules gives class action lawyers an *incentive* to negotiate settlements that enrich themselves but give scant reward to class members, while at the same time the burden of responding to class plaintiffs' discovery demands gives defendants an *incentive* to agree to early settlement that may treat the class action lawyers better than the class. Class action attorneys have an "inherent motivation" to enrich themselves at the expense of the class (and with the connivance of defendants), but motivation is not a synonym for action; any actual corruption or selling out is gauged case by case.

Thorogood v. Sears, Roebuck & Co., 627 F.3d 289, 293–94 (7th Cir. 2010). Recognizing this tension, the Seventh Circuit scrutinizes settlements—along with any objections—closely. And as of late, the Seventh Circuit has given a lot of deference to meritorious objections. "[A]ppellate correction of a district court's errors is a benefit to the class. Because only parties may appeal, it is vital that district courts freely allow the intervention of unnamed class members who object to proposed settlements and want an option to appeal an adverse decision." *Crawford v. Equifax Payment Servs., Inc.,* 201 F.3d 877, 881 (7th Cir. 2000).[8]

> Enter the objectors. Members of the class who smell a rat can object to approval of the settlement. *See, e.g., Reynolds v. Beneficial National Bank, supra,* 288 F.3d at 287–88; Edward Brunet, *Class Action Objectors: Extortionist Free Riders or Fairness Guarantors*, 2003 U. Chi. Legal F. 403, 411–12. If their objections persuade the judge to disapprove it, and as a consequence a settlement more favorable to the class is negotiated and approved, the objectors will receive a cash award that can be substantial, as in *In re Trans Union Corp. Privacy Litigation,* 629 F.3d 741 (7th Cir.2011).

Eubank v. Pella Corp., 753 F.3d 718, 720 (7th Cir. 2014). To have standing to object to a class settlement, an objector must be a class member. *Douglas v. The W. Union Co.*, 955 F.3d 662, 663 (7th Cir. 2020) (dismissing the objector's appeal for lack of jurisdiction where objector was not a class member).[9]

Frivolous Objections

Although the Seventh Circuit carefully scrutinizes settlements, protecting the rights of absent class members to object and appeal, it recognizes that some objections simply lack mer-

[8] Conditional certification is part in parcel of any preliminary approval motion, and the "Supreme Court has held that objectors who are members of a certified class . . . need not formally intervene." In re Lawnmower Engine Horsepower Mktg. & Sales Pracs. Litig., 733 F. Supp. 2d 997, 1016 (E.D. Wis. 2010).

[9] Note that if an appellant is not a member of a class, and does not seek to intervene, then that appellant does not have standing to appeal. Shakman v. Clerk of the Circuit Court of Cook Cty., 969 F.3d 810, 813–14 (7th Cir. 2020).

it and may be advanced solely for the personal gain of the attorney (i.e., to extract a side deal to withdraw the objection, allowing for the settlement to go forward). For example, the Seventh Circuit has remarked that an objector's unfamiliarity with the basic components of a settlement supported the district court's finding that an objector "was put forward by his attorneys solely to enable them to collect fees in this action." *Vollmer v. Publishers Clearing House*, 248 F.3d 698, 709 (7th Cir. 2001); *see also Pearson v. Target Corp.*, 893 F.3d 980, 986 (7th Cir. 2018) (characterizing "selfish" settlements by objectors as a "serious problem"). The court may review any number of sources in evaluating the objection—including information to establish that the objector is a "serial" objector or "professional" one. *Id.* at 710. Further, where an objector secures no real benefit for the plaintiff class, the court will deny any petition for attorneys' fees. *Kolinek v. Walgreen Co.*, 311 F.R.D. 483, 504 (N.D. Ill. 2015), *appeal dismissed* (Jan. 27, 2016), *appeal dismissed* (Feb. 1, 2016), *appeal dismissed* (Feb. 3, 2016).

As most frivolous objections are brought for the sole purpose of extracting a fee, the recent amendments to Rule 23 were aimed at curbing such objections by requiring court approval prior to the dismissal of any objection or the issuance of any "side payment":

> But some objectors may be seeking only personal gain, and using objections to obtain benefits for themselves rather than assisting in the settlement-review process. At least in some instances, it seems that objectors—or their counsel—have sought to obtain consideration for withdrawing their objections or dismissing appeals from judgments approving class settlements. And class counsel sometimes may feel that avoiding the delay produced by an appeal justifies providing payment or other consideration to these objectors.[10]

Now, individuals bringing objections to class settlements must bear in mind that court approval is required for payment in connection with any such objection. "Unless approved by the court after a hearing, no payment or other consideration may be provided in connection with: (i) forgoing or withdrawing an objection, or (ii) forgoing, dismissing, or abandoning an appeal from a judgment approving the proposal." Fed. R. Civ. P. 23(e)(5)(B).[11]

Recently, the Seventh Circuit held that "settling an objection that asserts the class's rights in return for a private payment to the objector is inequitable and that disgorgement is the most appropriate remedy." *See Pearson v. Target Corp.*, 968 F.3d 827 (7th Cir. 2020) (*Pearson III*).

Meritorious Objections

Nonfrivolous or meritorious objections seek to increase the value of the settlement. *Vollmer v. Selden*, 350 F.3d 656, 660 (7th Cir. 2003). Some examples of meritorious objections that the Seventh Circuit has held could derail a settlement include the following:

- Where class members are not informed of a potential conflict of interest (such as familial or co-counsel relationship) between the class representative and class

---

[10] Federal Rules of Civil Procedure, 2018-2019 Amendments to the Federal Rules of Civil Procedure Approved, *available at* www.federalrulesofcivilprocedure.org/2018-2019-amendments-to-the-federal-rules-of-civil-procedure-approved.

[11] In a RICO case filed in the Northern District of Illinois, *Edelson PC v. The Bandas Law Firm PC*, No. 16 C 11057 (N.D. Ill.), the plaintiff alleged that various law firms had assisted a professional objector in a scheme to extort fees from class action settlements in lieu of proceeding with a frivolous appeal. 2018 WL 723287, at *1. The court noted, "[a]ssuming the truth of the allegations in the complaint, Defendants have engaged in a pattern of reprehensible conduct that has harmed plaintiff and others and benefits no one other than Defendants themselves." 2018 WL 3496085, at *11. The court cited to the then-pending amendments to Rule 23 as a means to curb this type of conduct in the future. *Id.* Final judgment of an injunction was issued in that matter, preventing The Bandas Law Firm, P.C., and Christopher Bandas from, among other things, objecting in a class action settlement without fulfilling a number of criteria. 2019 WL 272812 (N.D. Ill. Jan. 17, 2019).

counsel. *See, e.g., Eubank*, 753 F.3d at 723–24.

- Where class counsel is involved in disciplinary proceedings that could impact his ability to negotiate a fair settlement. *Eubank*, 753 F.3d at 724.
- An advance in an attorneys' fee award before notice is sent to the settlement class. *Id.*
- Complicated individual class member prove-up processes that could discourage filing or pursuing claims under the settlement. *Id.* at 725.
- Complicated and confusing class notices that do not provide all relevant and pertinent information. *Id.* at 725–26.
- A vast disparity between a settlement's "valuation" and the actual claims payout. *Id.*
- The potential for collusion or a "reverse auction." *Reynolds*, 288 F.3d at 283.
- "Clear sailing" and "kicker" provisions in attorneys' fees awards in settlement agreements; however, recognizing that these are not per se reasons to upend a settlement. *In re Sw. Airlines Voucher Litig.*, 799 F.3d 701, 712 (7th Cir. 2015).
- Failure to submit a motion for an award of attorneys' fees and costs prior to the deadline for objecting. *Redman v. RadioShack Corp.*, 768 F.3d 622, 637–38 (7th Cir. 2014).
- A large disparity between relief available to the class and class counsel's fees; moreover, counting the costs of administration as part of the value received from the settlement by members of the class. *Id.* at 639; *Pearson*, 772 F.3d at 781.
- Valuation of settlement value when the class members receive coupons. *Redman*, 768 F.3d at 638.
- Counting the amount of a *cy pres* award as a benefit to class members. *Pearson*, 772 F.2d at 781.

c. Final Approval

A court may approve a settlement that would bind class members only if, after proper notice and a public a hearing, the court determines that the proposed settlement is "fair, reasonable, and adequate." Fed. R. Civ. P. 23(e)(2). Under Seventh Circuit law, a district court must, in evaluating the fairness of a settlement, consider "the strength of plaintiffs' case compared to the amount of defendants' settlement offer, an assessment of the likely complexity, length and expense of the litigation, an evaluation of the amount of opposition to settlement among affected parties, the opinion of competent counsel, and the stage of the proceedings and the amount of discovery completed at the time of settlement." *Synfuel Techs., Inc. v. DHL Express (USA), Inc.*, 463 F.3d 646, 653 (7th Cir. 2006) (quoting *Isby v. Bayh*, 75 F.3d 1191, 1199 (7th Cir. 1996)); *In re Advocate Aurora Health Pixel Litig.*, 2024 WL 3357730, at *7 (E.D. Wis. July 10, 2024); *see also Kolinek*, 311 F.R.D. at 493. These criteria are not viewed individually for purposes of approval; rather, courts in the Seventh Circuit "view them in their entirety in evaluating their fairness." *Isby*, 75 F.3d at 1199 (quotations omitted).

Courts in the Seventh Circuit recognize that a settlement is a compromise, and courts need not—and indeed should not—"reject a settlement solely because it does not provide a complete victory to the plaintiffs." *In re AT & T*, 270 F.R.D. at 347. This is especially true when complete victory would most surely bankrupt the prospective judgment debtor. *In re Capital One Tel. Consumer Prot. Act Litig.*, 80 F. Supp. 3d at 790 (N.D. Ill. 2015), *appeal dismissed* (May 5, 2015), *appeal dismissed* (June 8, 2015), *appeal dismissed* (June 26, 2015). And this is also true even when a settlement figure is lower than the anticipated potential recovery as a result of a potential defense available to the defendant that would leave Plaintiffs with nothing. *See Kaufman v. Am. Express Travel Related Servs. Co., Inc.*, 877 F.3d 276, 285 (7th Cir. 2017) (upholding final settlement approval where "Plaintiffs would likely receive nothing" if the court reversed the district court's decision and sent the action to arbitration in line with defendants' arbitration defense).

Strength of Plaintiffs' Case Compared to the Amount of Defendants' Settlement Offer
"The 'most important factor relevant to the fairness of a class action settlement' is the first one listed: 'the strength of plaintiff's case on the merits balanced against the amount offered in the settlement.'" *Synfuel*, 463 F.3d at 653 (quoting *In re Gen. Motors Corp. Engine Interchange Litig.*, 594 F.2d 1106, 1132 (7th Cir. 1979)). Furthermore, "[i]n conducting this analysis, the district court should begin by 'quantifying the net expected value of continued litigation to the class.' To do so, the court should 'estimate the range of possible outcomes and ascribe a probability to each point on the range.'" *Id.* (quoting *Reynolds v. Beneficial Nat'l Bank*, 288 F.3d 277, 284–85 (7th Cir. 2002)); *see also In re Capital One*, 80 F. Supp. 3d at 788; *Mirfasihi v. Fleet Mortg. Corp.*, 450 F.3d 745, 749 (7th Cir. 2006).

Risk, Expense, Complexity, and Duration of Further Litigation
When litigation "would require the resolution of many difficult and complex issues, . . . entail considerable additional expense, . . . [and] likely involve weeks, perhaps months, of trial time," settlement is appropriate. *Isby*, 75 F.3d at 1199–200 (quotations omitted). In fact, "[t]he Seventh Circuit has recognized the 'overriding public interest in favor of settlements' in the class action context, as they 'minimize[] the litigation expenses' of both parties and also 'reduce[] the stain such litigation imposes on already scarce judicial resources.'" *Roberts v. Graphic Packaging Int'l, LLC*, No. 3:21-cv-00750, 2024 WL 3373780, at *3 (S.D. Ill.) (quoting *Armstrong v. Bd. of Sch Dirs. Of the City of Milwaukee*, 616 F.2d 305, 312–13 (7th Cir. 1980) (citations and quotations omitted), overruled on other grounds by *Felzen v. Andreas*, 134 F.3d 873, 875 (7th Cir. 1998)). When the district court is able to conclude that the settlement represents "an outcome at least comparable, if not far superior, to that which plaintiffs might achieve by proceeding to trial," the district court does not abuse its discretion in approving such a settlement. *Isby*, 75 F.3d at 1199–200 (quotations omitted). "Settlement allows the class to avoid the inherent risk, complexity, time, and cost associated with continued litigation." *Schulte*, 805 F. Supp. 2d at 586 (recognizing settlement to be superior to years of expensive discovery and protracted litigation).

Reaction of the Class
"Although our review of a district court's approval of a class action settlement is limited to whether there was an abuse of discretion . . . we insist that district courts exercise the highest degree of vigilance in scrutinizing proposed settlements of class actions." *Synfuel*, 463 F.3d at 652 (citations and quotations omitted). "In the past, [the Seventh Circuit has] gone so far as to characterize the court's role as akin the high duty of care that the law requires of fiduciaries." *Id.* (quotations omitted). As part of this duty, the Seventh Circuit has instructed district courts to, among other things, "evaluate the amount of opposition to a settlement among affected parties in deciding whether to approve a class action-settlement." *Schulte*, 805 F. Supp. 2d at 586 (citing *Synfuel*, 463 F.3d at 653). When a small number of class members objects or opts out, that is strong circumstantial evidence in favor of the settlement. *Schulte*, 805 F. Supp. 2d at 586.

Opinion of Competent Counsel
"The opinion of competent counsel is relevant to the question whether a settlement is fair, reasonable, and adequate under Rule 23." *Schulte*, 805 F. Supp. 2d at 586 (citing *Synfuel*, 463 F.3d at 653). In particular, the district court examines class counsel's experience in complex and class litigation and whether the settlement was negotiated at arm's length. *Mangone v. First USA Bank*, 206 F.R.D. 222, 226 (S.D. Ill. 2001) (settlement proposal arrived at after negotiations by fully informed, experienced, and competent counsel may be presumed to be fair and adequate) (citations omitted). If class counsel is experienced and there is no indication that the settlement was the result of collusion, then approval of the settlement agreement is appropriate. *Schulte*, 805 F. Supp. 2d at 586–87.

Extent of Discovery and Stage of Proceedings
The final factor is the stage of proceedings and the amount of discovery completed. *Synfuel*,

463 F.3d at 653. "Courts are to consider this factor in order to determine 'how fully the district court and counsel are able to evaluate the merits of plaintiffs' claims.'" *Kolinek*, 311 F.R.D. at 495–96 (citing *Armstrong v. Bd. of Sch. Dirs. of City of Milwaukee*, 616 F.2d 305, 325 (7th Cir. 1980)). *See, e.g.*, *Isby*, 75 F.3d at 1200 ("while settlement discussions began at an early stage in the litigation, [the court] was satisfied that the discovery and investigation conducted by Class Counsel prior to entering into settlement negotiations was 'extensive and thorough,' dating at least as far back as ten months prior to the filing of the complaint").

d. Other Threshold Issues

The Seventh Circuit's scrutiny of class settlements extends not only to the requirements of Rule 23(e), but also to threshold issues involving the strength of plaintiffs' claims. As articulated in *Casillas v. Madison Avenue Associates, Inc.*, 926 F.3d 329, 331 (7th Cir. 2019), "[t]he bottom line of our opinion can be succinctly stated: no harm, no foul." In *Casillas*, when the district court was considering preliminary approval of a class action settlement in a Fair Debt Collection Practice Act case, it asked the parties to brief whether the alleged debtor, who had alleged only a statutory violation of the Act, had asserted the type of injury-in-fact to establish Article III standing. The district court dismissed the action based upon the Seventh Circuit's *Groshek v. Great Lakes Higher Educ. Corp.* decision, 865 F.3d 884 (7th Cir. 2018), finding that a statutory violation, alone, was insufficient to confer standing and, accordingly, subject matter jurisdiction. *Casillas v. Madison Ave. Assocs., Inc.*, No. 1:16-CV-1774-WTL-DML, 2017 WL 6517568, at *3 (S.D. Ind. Sept. 22, 2017). The decision was affirmed by the Seventh Circuit. 926 F.3d 329 (7th Cir. 2019).

The Supreme Court grappled with similar issues in *Frank v. Gaos*, 586 U.S. 485, 139 S. Ct. 1041 (2019), where it had originally granted *certiorari* to determine the propriety of *cy pres* settlements, but ultimately vacated a decision affirming approval of the settlement, and remanded the case "to address the plaintiffs' standing" in light of the Supreme Court's most recent case on class action standing, *Spokeo, Inc. v. Robins*, 578 U.S. 330 (2016).

e. *Cy Pres*

"*Cy pres* (properly *cy pres comme possible,* an Anglo–French term meaning 'as near as possible') is the name of the doctrine that permits a benefit to be given other than to the intended beneficiary or for the intended purpose because changed circumstances make it impossible to carry out the benefactor's intent." *Pearson*, 772 F.3d at 784. Accordingly, "[*c*]*y pres* . . . recovery is a procedural device that distributes money damages either through a market system (e.g., by reducing charges that were previously excessive) or through project funding (the project being designed to benefit the members of the class)." *Simer v. Rios*, 661 F.2d 655, 675 (7th Cir. 1981). *Cy pres* recovery "is used where the individuals injured are not likely to come forward and prove their claims or cannot be given notice of the case." *Id.* at 675. "*Cy pres* recovery is thus ideal for circumstances in which it is difficult or impossible to identify the persons to whom damages should be assigned or distributed." *Mace v. Van Ru Credit Corp.*, 109 F.3d 338, 345 (7th Cir. 1997); *Kolinek*, 311 F.R.D. at 498. "A *cy pres* award is supposed to be limited to money that can't feasibly be awarded to the intended beneficiaries, here consisting of the class members." *Pearson*, 772 F.3d at 784. *Cy pres* distributions in the settlement context typically occur after multiple distributions to settlement class members—first based on claims and another round based on a pro rata basis, with any remaining money distributed to another fund *cy pres*. *Schulte v. Fifth Third Bank*, 805 F. Supp. 2d 560, 568 (N.D. Ill. 2011).

The Seventh Circuit scrutinizes *cy pres* awards in settlements—especially when settlements that do not provide another opportunity for class members to submit claims or for a second distribution to the class members *cy pres*. For example, in a recent settlement in the Seventh Circuit involving glucosamine supplements, the Seventh Circuit questioned what value a *cy pres* distribution would provide to the class when class members were victims of alleged consumer fraud.

> Since the joint problems that glucosamine is supposed to alleviate are the domain of orthopedic medicine, the choice of an orthopedic institute as a recipient of money left over after all approved class members' claims are paid is consistent with *cy pres*. But there is no validity to the $1.13 million *cy pres* award in this case. Notice costing $1.5 million reached 4.72 million class members. Granted, doubling the expenditure would not have doubled the number of class members notified. The 4.72 million who received postcards were all those whom Rexall knew (through pharmacy loyalty programs and the like) to have bought its glucosamine pills, while notice by publication or via the Internet tends to be ineffectual when the class consists of consumers. But the claims process could have been simplified. Or knowing that 4.72 million people had bought at least one bottle of its pills, Rexall could have mailed $3 checks to all 4.72 million postcard recipients. The Orthopedic Research and Education Foundation seems perfectly reputable, but it is entitled to receive money intended to compensate victims of consumer fraud only if it's infeasible to provide that compensation to the victims—which has not been demonstrated.

Pearson, 772 F.3d 784. But if the settlement does not necessarily "contemplate a *cy pres* award," but instead "binds the parties to distribute unclaimed money to class members who do cash their checks unless doing so is not feasible," such activity is in accordance with Seventh Circuit precedent. *Kolinek*, 311 F.R.D. at 498–99.

9. FEES AND COSTS

"In a certified class action, the court may award reasonable attorney's fees and nontaxable costs that are authorized by law or by the parties' agreement." Fed. R. Civ. P. 23(h). "[T]he Court's determination of whether the proposed settlement is both fair and reasonable also includes an evaluation of the reasonableness of the attorneys' fees sought." *Donaldson v. MBR Cent. Ill. Pizza, LLC*, No. 18-cv-3048, 2019 WL 4447969, at *2 (C.D. Ill. Sept. 17, 2019).

a. Fees

In the Seventh Circuit, "there are two acceptable methods of calculating attorney's fees in class action cases. . . . Under the lodestar method, the Court determines the reasonable amount of hours expended by counsel and counsel's reasonable hourly rate. . . . The Court then considers whether a multiplier is necessary in light of the risk that counsel assumed in bringing this kind of case. . . . Under the percentage method, the Court fixes attorney's fees as a percentage of the total recovery paid to the class." *Eubank v. Pella Corp.*, No. 06-cv-4481, 2019 WL 1227832, at *6 (N.D. Ill. Mar. 15, 2019) (internal citations omitted).

The Common Fund Doctrine

"Once a settlement has been reached in a class action, the attorneys for the class petition the court for compensation from the settlement or common fund created for the class's benefit. This method of payment is an exception to the 'American Rule' which requires each party to bear its own expenses." *Sutton v. Bernard*, 504 F.3d 688, 691–92 (7th Cir. 2007) (citing *Florin v. Nationsbank of Ga., N.A.*, 34 F.3d 560, 562–63 (7th Cir. 1994); *Skelton v. Gen. Motors Corp.*, 860 F.2d 250, 252 (7th Cir. 1988)). Also known as the common fund doctrine, this payment scheme "is based on the equitable notion that those who have benefited from litigation should share in its costs." *Skelton*, 860 F.2d at 252 (internal quotations omitted).

The Seventh Circuit recognizes that in a common fund settlement, courts must "do their best to award counsel the market price for legal services, in light of the risk of nonpayment and the normal rate of compensation in the market at the time." *Camp Drug Store, Inc. v. Cochran Wholesale Pharmaceuticals, Inc.*, 897 F.3d 825, 832–33 (7th Cir. 2018) (quoting *In re Synthroid Mktg. Litig.*, 264 F.3d 712, 718 (7th Cir. 2001) (*Synthroid I*). In *Synthroid,* the Seventh Circuit held that the "market rate for legal fees depends in part on the risk of nonpayment a firm agrees to bear, in part on the quality of its performance, in part on the amount of work necessary to resolve the litigation, and in part on the stakes of the case." *Synthroid I*, 264 F.3d at 721; *see also In re Stericycle Securities Litig.*, 35 F.4th 555 (7th Cir. 2022) (quoting *Taubenfeld v. Aon Corp.*, 415 F.3d 597, 599 (7th Cir. 2005)) (district courts can also "recreate the market by considering factors such as actual fee contracts that were privately negotiated for similar litigation, information from other cases, and data from class-counsel auctions."). The Seventh Circuit has further explained that "[t]he object in awarding a reasonable attorney's fee . . . is to give the lawyer what he would have gotten in the way of a fee in arm's length negotiation, had one been feasible." *In re Cont'l Ill. Sec. Litig.*, 962 F.2d 566, 572 (7th Cir. 1992). *See also In re Trans Union Corp. Priv. Litig.*, 629 F.3d at 744 (recognizing that "[s]uch [an] estimation is inherently conjectural").

With that said, district courts within the Seventh Circuit caution that courts "must be aware of the potential conflict of interest between class counsel and the class that arises when class counsel asks for fees to be paid out of a common fund, because every dollar the attorneys receive is a dollar that the class does not." *In re Advoc. Aurora Health Pixel Litig.*, No. 22-CV-1253-JPS, 2024 WL 3357730, at *9 (E.D. Wis. July 10, 2024) (quoting *In re TikTok, Inc., Consumer Priv. Litig.*, 617 F. Supp. 3d 904, 939 (N.D. Ill. 2022)). Accordingly, evaluating the reasonableness of a fee request requires the Court to "compare attorney fees to what is actually recovered by the class." *In re Sears, Roebuck & Co. Front-Loading Washer Prods. Liab. Litig.*, 867 F.3d 791, 793 (7th Cir. 2017).

"It has long been the law in the Seventh Circuit that in common fund cases . . . district courts have discretion to choose either the lodestar *or* a percentage approach to calculating fees." *In re Capital One*, 80 F. Supp. 3d at 794 (emphasis added, citing *Florin*, 34 F.3d at 566 ("It bears reiterating here that we do not believe that the lodestar approach is so flawed that it should be abandoned. . . . We therefore restate the law of this circuit that in common fund cases, the decision whether to use a percentage method or a lodestar method remains in the discretion of the district court. We recognize here . . . that there are advantages to utilizing the percentage method in common fund cases because of its relative simplicity of administration."). "The Seventh Circuit has noted advantages and disadvantages to both approaches. The chief advantage of the percentage approach is simplicity of administration . . . . The chief advantage of the lodestar approach is accountability." *In re Trans Union Corp.*, No. 00 C 4729, 2009 WL 4799954, at *9 (N.D. Ill. Dec. 9, 2009) (internal citations omitted).

Percentage Approach

In the percentage approach, the Seventh Circuit instructs the district courts that the "ratio that is relevant to assessing the reasonableness of the attorneys' fee that the parties agreed to is the ratio of (1) the fee to (2) the fee plus what the class members received." *Redman*, 768 F.3d at 633.[12] In determining a reasonable fee, the court "must balance the competing goals of fairly compensating attorneys for their services rendered on behalf of the class and of protecting the interests of the class members in the fund." *In re Capital One*, 80 F. Supp. 3d at

[12] In "coupon settlements" in particular, 28 U.S.C. § 1712(a) is clear that "[i]f a proposed settlement in a class action provides for a recovery of coupons to a class member, the portion of any attorney's fee award to class counsel that is attributable to the award of the coupons shall be based on the value to class members of the coupons that are redeemed." "To protect against . . . abusive settlements, § 1712(a) requires that any percentage-of-recovery award in a coupon settlement be based upon a percentage of the value of the coupons actually redeemed by class members, not the nominal value of the coupons merely available to the class." In re Sw. Airlines Voucher Litig., 799 F.3d 701, 708 (7th Cir. 2015).

788–99 (citing *Skelton*, 860 F.2d at 258, *cert. denied*, 493 U.S. 810 (1989)). "Administration and notice costs, although paid through the settlement fund, are not benefits to the class and thus not part of 'what the class members received.'" *In re Capital One*, 80 F. Supp. 3d at 795 (citing *Redman*, 768 F.3d at 630).

To award a percentage of the fund as attorneys' fees, district courts in the Seventh Circuit must first subtract attorneys' fees, administration and notice costs, named plaintiff service awards, and any pre-distribution *cy pres* awards. *In re Capital One*, 80 F. Supp. 3d at 795. Then the district courts must determine whether the percentage sought is within the approximate market rate at the "outset of the litigation had negotiations between Class Counsel and 'clients having a real stake' been feasible." *Id.* at 795–96. Although there is no particular preference for determining the marketing fee, the Seventh Circuit has explained that it is possible to learn about "similar bargains" and set forth three "guides" or "benchmarks" to help district courts estimate the market fee: (1) actual fee contracts between plaintiffs and their attorneys, (2) data from similar common fund cases where fees were privately negotiated, and (3) information from class counsel auctions. *Synthroid I*, 264 F.3d at 719. District courts in the Seventh Circuit have used these guideposts to estimate that market rate in percentage fee awards. *In re Capital One*, 80 F. Supp. 3d at 796; *In re AT & T Mobility Wireless Data Services Sales Tax Litig.*, 792 F. Supp. 2d 1028, 1033–34 (N.D. Ill. 2011); *In re Trans Union Corp. Privacy Litig.*, 2009 WL 4799954, at *10–13 (N.D. Ill. Dec. 9, 2009), *rev'd on other grounds*, 629 F.3d 741 (7th Cir. 2011).

Fee Contracts Between Plaintiffs and Their Attorneys

Courts examining this factor find that while "such agreements, where they exist, can '*define* the market,'" *In re Trans Union*, 2009 WL 4799954, at *11 (quoting *Synthroid I*, 264 F.3d at 720 (emphasis in original)), such agreements can provide little guidance on how to compute fees for consumer class actions. This is because no member of the class has a "stake to drive a hard- or any-bargain with the lawyer" in a consumer class action, because any fee negotiation would be with the *class's* money. *Id.* at *11. The Seventh Circuit, however, has "recognized that sliding scale fee arrangements . . . are often the product of arms-length negotiations ex ante." *In re Stericycle Sec. Litig.*, 35 F.4th 555, 562 (7th Cir. 2022).

Data from Similar Common Fund Cases

"[A]wards in other class actions generally (even where no fees were negotiated *ex ante*) may provide some marginally useful information about hypothetical market negotiations, because they may influence the expectations of lawyer and client engaging in the hypothetical negotiation." *In re Trans Union*, 2009 WL 4799954, at *11. "Because data from pre-suit negotiations and auctions tend to be sparse . . . district courts have also examined empirical data analyzing fee awards in other class actions where fees were awarded at the end of the case." *In re Capital One*, 80 F. Supp. 3d at 796. Although courts recognize that empirical studies may not be reflective of the market price at the time the cases were filed, they are instructive for determining "the price at which national class action lawyers are willing to provide their services going forward." *In re Capital One*, 80 F. Supp. 3d at 796–97; *In re Trans Union,* 2009 WL 4799954, at *11 (noting awards in class actions generally may influence expectations of a lawyer and client engaging in negotiation).

Based on studies of fee awards in other cases, the market rate for class cases—although dependent on the *type* of action and overall size of the fund—ranges between 20 percent to approximately 30 percent. *In re Trans Union*, 2009 WL 4799954, at *12; *see also Taubenfeld v. Aon Corp.*, 415 F.3d 597, 598–600 (holding that district court was within its discretion in awarding lead counsel 30 percent of a $7.25 million settlement fund); *Kolinek*, 311 F.R.D. at 501 (finding that market rate of 30 percent is a reasonable base fee); *Bridgeview Health Care Ctr., Ltd. v. Jerryclark*, No. 09 C 5601, 2015 WL 4498741, at *2 (N.D. Ill. July 23, 2015) (awarding one-third of common fund in TCPA class action); *Saf-T-Gard Int'l, Inc. v. Seiko Corp. of Am.*, No. 09 C 0776 (N.D. Ill. Jan. 14, 2011) (awarding one-third of common fund in multimillion dollar TCPA class action). Courts in the Seventh Circuit regularly allow attorneys to recoup one-third of the first $10 million of the class action settlement fund. *See, e.g.*, *Craftwood Lumber Co. v. Interline Brands, Inc.*, No. 11 C 4462, 2015 WL 1399367, at *4 (N.D. Ill. Mar. 23, 2015) (awarding plaintiffs' counsel a sliding scale contingency fee including 30 percent of the first 10 million dollars of the settlement); *In re Capital One*, 80 F. Supp. 3d at 804–05 (finding that before considering possible risk adjustments, 30 percent is the reasonable base market rate for the first $10 million of recovery).

Information from Class Counsel Auctions

The Seventh Circuit has described class counsel auctions as follows:

> [T]he word "auction" is an imprecise description of the process that judges have used to choose lead counsel in class actions. Judges don't look for the lowest bid; they look for the best bid-just as any private individual would do in selecting a law firm, an advertising firm, or a construction company. Bidding law firms provide the judge with firm profiles, testimonials of former clients, predictions of expected recovery, fee proposals, and arguments on why their firm provides good value. The judge in turn acts as an agent for the class, selecting the firm that seems likely to generate the highest recovery net of attorneys' fees.

Synthroid I, 264 F.3d at 720 (internal citations omitted). Auctions are typically utilized in securities and antitrust cases to select class counsel via a competitive process. *See In re Comdisco Sec. Litig.*, 141 F. Supp. 2d 951 (N.D. Ill. 2001); *In re Bank One Shareholders Class Actions,* 96 F. Supp. 2d 780 (N.D. Ill. 2000); *In re Amino Acid Lysine Antitrust Litig.*, 918 F. Supp. 1190 (N.D. Ill. 1996).[13] The "bid" is not necessarily binding; courts may increase the fees if the action involves additional work.

Courts acknowledge that data on these "auctions" is sparse—especially because these auction arrangements are not used in the consumer class action context. *In re Capital One*, 80 F. Supp. 3d at 796, 800. However, one district court in 2006 gathered such information related to securities cases. *In re Cabletron Sys., Inc. Sec. Litig.*, 293 F.R.D. 30, 44–45 (D.N.H. 2006). Courts in the Seventh Circuit recognize that "the fee structures in auction cases . . . are, at best, only illustrative. Each case has unique facts and risk factors." *In re Trans Union*, 2009 WL 4799954, at *13; *see also In re Broiler Chicken Antitrust Litig.*, 80 F.4th 797, 802 (7th Cir. 2023) ("Nevertheless, we have explained that auction bids are properly considered when deciding what bargain the parties would have struck *ex ante*.") Given the difficulty in assessing fees *ex ante*, the Seventh Circuit has suggested that it could be best to determine a fee schedule when appointing class counsel. *Silverman v. Motorola Sol'ns, Inc.*, 739 F.3d 956, 957–58 (7th Cir. 2013). Ultimately, however, "[w]hen reviewing awards set after the fact, the court of appeals asks whether the district judge has abused her discretion." *Id.* at 958.

Lodestar Method

As noted above, courts in the Seventh Circuit may engage in either a percentage or lodestar method to calculate fees. *See City of Burlington v. Dague*, 505 U.S. 557, 562 (1992) ("The 'lodestar' figure has . . . become the guiding light of our fee-shifting jurisprudence. We have established a 'strong presumption' that the lodestar represents the 'reasonable' fee . . . ."); *Florin*, 34 F.3d at 566 ("in common fund cases, the decision whether to use a percentage method or a lode-star method remains in the discretion of the district court"); *Reid v. Unilever United States, Inc.*, No. 12 C 6058, 2015 WL 3653318, at *5 (N.D. Ill. June 10, 2015), *aff'd sub nom. Martin v. Reid*, 818 F.3d 302 (7th Cir. 2016) ("In a statutory fee-shifting case, the court determines a reasonable amount of attorneys' fees by applying the lodestar method.").

---

[13] Judge Milton I. Shadur presided over these cases.

The lodestar approach can either be the sole method a court uses to determine the fees (such as in cases involving a fee-shifting statute) or a "cross-check" on fees awarded using the percentage methodology.[14] *In re Trans Union Corp.*, 2009 WL 4799954, at *17. "In a lodestar analysis, counsel is entitled to a reasonable, market-based rate, not the highest rates that lawyers can cherry-pick from the market." *Id.* at *19 (using the *Laffey* Matrix, adjusting for the Chicago market, to perform a lodestar cross-check to percentage of fund awarded).

"The starting point for determining fees based upon lodestar is calculated by multiplying the number of hours of work spent on the matter by the hourly market rates of the individuals. The lodestar amount is then subject to such adjustment as facts and circumstances may require." *Turner v. Beneficial Nat. Bank*, 405 F. Supp. 2d 929, 931 (N.D. Ill. 2005) (citations omitted). Courts focus on "whether the claimed hours were 'reasonably expended.'" *Id.* (citing *Hensley v. Eckerhart*, 461 U.S. 424, 434 (1983) ("Counsel for the prevailing party should make a good faith effort to exclude from a fee request hours that are excessive, redundant, or otherwise unnecessary, just as a lawyer in private practice is obligated to exclude such hours from his fee submission.")). Courts consider factors such as the role attorneys have within the case, evidenced by whether a notice of appearance was entered and whether their signature appears on submission(s), and raise concerns when high rates are charged by nonlead attorneys. *See In re Advoc. Aurora Health Pixel Litig.*, No. 22-CV-1253-JPS, 2024 WL 3357730, at *19 (E.D. Wis. July 10, 2024) ("[T]he Court shares [defendant's] concerns about the high rates that several of the non-lead attorneys charged, especially since Plaintiffs' counsel has made no attempt at explaining whether their hourly rates are reasonable.").

Courts in the Seventh Circuit also compare the plaintiffs' damages and the resultant attorneys' fees, recognizing that attorneys' fees that are "a large multiple of the amount awarded should cause the court to pause and reflect on the fee requested." *Dominguez v. Quigley's Irish Pub., Inc.*, 897 F. Supp. 2d 674, 686 (N.D. Ill. 2012). However, the Seventh Circuit has repeatedly rejected the notion that fees must be calculated proportionally to damages. *Id. See also Koch v. Jerry W. Bailey Trucking, Inc.*, 51 F.4th 748, 758 (7th Cir. 2022) (noting that, while "a court may . . . consider the ratio of damages and fees as one factor when contemplating a reduction", the "fee award does not need to be proportionate to the amount of damages recovered").

Initial Lodestar Analysis

Courts in the Seventh Circuit may consider several factors when evaluating whether attorneys' fees for class counsel are being sought at class expense: clear sailing clauses, kicker clauses, ease of claims submission, relief to the class, and length of time before settling the case.

First, the court looks to whether a clear sailing clause exists. *In re: Sears, Roebuck and Co. Front-Loading Washer Prods. Liab. Litig.*, Nos. 06 C 7023, 07 C 0412, 08 C 1832, 2016 WL 4765679, *7 (N.D. Ill. Sept. 13, 2016) (quoting *Redman*, 768, F.3d at 767). "The concern is that a defendant likely would not agree to a clear-sailing clause without some concession by class counsel—'namely a reduction in the part of the settlement that goes to the class members, as that is the only reduction class counsel are likely to consider.' While clear-sailing clauses are not unlawful per se, 'such a clause should be subjected to intense critical scrutiny by the district court.'" *Id.* (quoting *Redman*, 768 F.3d at 637).

Second, the district court should scrutinize "kicker clauses," which provide that "if the judge reduces the amount of fees that the proposed settlement awards to class counsel, the savings shall enure not to the class but to the defendant." *Pearson*, 772 F.3d at 786. Describing the kicker clause as a "gimmick for defeating objectors," "the obvious benefit of a kick-

[14] *But see* Williams v. Rohm and Haas Pension Plan, 658 F.3d 629, 636 (7th Cir. 2011) ("consideration of a lodestar check is not an issue of required methodology"); Will v. Gen. Dynamics Corp., No. 06-CV-698, 2010 WL 4818174, at *3 (S.D. Ill. Nov. 22, 2010) ("The use of a lodestar cross-check in a common fund is unnecessary, arbitrary, and potentially counterproductive.").

er clause to the *defendant* is matched by a hidden benefit to *class counsel*—counsel are more likely to get the agreed-upon fee award, because no class member has 'standing to object.'" *In re Sears*, 2016 WL 4765679, at *7 (quoting *Pearson*, 772 F.3d at 786). *See also In re Sw. Airlines*, 799 F.3d at 705 ("'kicker' clauses [are] designed to shield the fee award from challenge").

Third, the district court should ensure that the claims process is straightforward and does not discourage claims from being filed. *See In re Sears*, 2016 WL 4765679, at *7 (claim submission rate of approximately 16 percent, along with ease of filing claim form, demonstrated that the claims submission was not overly complicated so as to suppress claims).

Fourth, the district court determines the type and breadth of recovery received by the class members. While "complete relief" is unnecessary, "complete relief for the class is the model of an adequate settlement. The class members will receive everything they reasonably could have hoped for." *In re Sw. Airlines*, 799 F.3d at 711.

Fifth, the district court considers the length of time it took the lawyers to negotiate a settlement to ensure that the settlement agreement is not merely a "rush . . . in order to maximize class counsel's fees." *In re Sears*, 2016 WL 4765679, at *8; *see also Pearson*, 772 F.3d at 779–81 (parties settled eight months after filing and agreed that defendants would not oppose plaintiffs' counsel's fee request of $4.5 million, suggesting a conflict of interest between counsel and the class).

Based on an analysis of the above three factors, the district court can determine whether or not collusion between class counsel and the defendants exist so as to determine whether use of the lodestar method is appropriate.

Adjustment of Lodestar

After an analysis to determine whether the lodestar method is appropriate, the court may look to other factors to determine whether the lodestar should be adjusted up or down. "After calculating the lodestar, the Court may, in its discretion, increase or reduce the lodestar amount by considering a variety of factors, including: the time and labor required; whether the attorney's fee is fixed or contingent; the amount involved and the results obtained; and the experience, reputation, and ability of the attorneys." *Reid, et al. v. Unilever U.S., Inc., et al.*, No. 12 C 6058, 2015 WL 3653318, at *24 (N.D. Ill. June 10, 2015) (citing *Hensley*, 461 U.S. at 430 n.3). *See also Koch*, 51 F.4th at 756 ("district courts have broad discretion to assess the reasonableness of an attorney's fees and cut hours that they find to be unjustified."). "[A] multiplier of 1.6 . . . is well within the band of lodestar multipliers accepted within the Seventh Circuit. *In re TikTok*, 617 F. Supp. 3d at 943 ("In practice, most multipliers fall between one and four." (collecting cases))."

A district court need not consider every factor, and its fee award is reviewed for an abuse of discretion. *See Americana Art China Co., Inc. v. Foxfire Printing and Packaging, Inc.*, 743 F.3d 243, 246–47 (7th Cir. 2014) ("[T]he district court did not consider the ultimate outcome *at all* in calculating at a reasonable fee under the lodestar method. It considered only the lodestar amount submitted by counsel and the risk multiplier warranted by the contingent nature of the case. It did consider the paucity of the class recovery as compared to the requested fee award when deciding whether to apply the lodestar method, as opposed to the percentage method, in the first place. But that is exactly what we have suggested a district court *should* do."). *See also Standard Iron Works v. ArcelorMittal*, No. 08 C 5214, 2014 WL 7781572, at *6 (N.D. Ill. Oct. 22, 2014) (basing its lodestar multiplier analysis on risk: "Class Counsel bore all the risk of litigating this complex case (including millions of dollars in litigation expenses) with no guarantee of reimbursement. Having shouldered these risks, and having achieved outstanding results for the Class, Class Counsel have earned their requested multiplier.").

"The standard is whether the fees are reasonable in relation to the difficulty, stakes, and outcome of the case." *Gastineau v. Wright*, 592 F.3d 747, 748 (7th Cir. 2010) (citation omitted). However, the presumption is that "the lodestar includes most, if not all, of the relevant factors constituting a 'reasonable' attorney's fee." *Perdue v. Kenny A. ex rel. Winn*, 559 U.S. 542, 553 (2010) (citation omitted); *Hensley*, 461 U.S. at 434 n.9 ("many of these factors usually are subsumed within the initial calculation of hours reasonably expended at a reasonable hourly rate"). The party seeking fees "has the burden of identifying a factor that the lodestar does not adequately take into account and proving with specificity that an enhanced fee is justified." *Perdue*, 559 U.S. at 546. Although the Supreme Court "has never sustained an enhancement of a lodestar amount for performance," it has "repeatedly said that an enhancement may be awarded in 'rare' and 'exceptional' circumstances." *Id.* at 552 (citation omitted).

The Seventh Circuit, when considering the reasonableness of an attorney fee reduction, has taken issue with time entries in connection with work product that does not benefit the class as well as time entries that are both vague and duplicative. In *Koch*, 51 F.4th at 755–56, for example, the Seventh Circuit found the district court properly cut time from class counsel's lodestar related to: (i) supplemental briefing defending adequacy as class counsel, "particularly when [class counsel] was ultimately unsuccessful in maintaining certification"; (ii) "vague billing statements" that did not adequately describe the work performed and duplicative time that lacked an adequate explanation; and (iii) multiple rounds of summary judgment "briefing that was not complex enough to justify the billed hours" because "the second motion for summary judgment was mostly a copy of the original."

Lodestar Method in Coupon or Voucher Settlements

Although "coupon" settlements are not automatically disfavored in the Seventh Circuit, courts scrutinize them heavily, especially when calculating the "value" of the benefit the coupons provide to the class as part of an attorneys' fee calculation. *Redman*, 768 F.3d at 637. Although 28 U.S.C. § 1712(a) provides that the percentage of the fund method in such cases should be based on the value of coupons actually used, "[s]ubsection (a) does not, however, prohibit the use of the lodestar method for coupon settlements that do not provide injunctive relief." *In re Sw.*, 799 F.3d at 708, 710 ("We hold that § 1712 permits a district court to use the lodestar method to calculate attorneys' fees to compensate class counsel for the coupon relief obtained for the class. When a district court considers using the lodestar method in this manner, it will need to bear in mind the potential for abuse posed by coupon settlements and should evaluate critically the claims of success on behalf of a class receiving coupons.").

b. Expenses

Class counsel are entitled to be reimbursed their reasonable costs and expenses in litigating an action to settlement or judgment; however, the Seventh Circuit has explained that district courts must exercise their discretion to "disallow particular expenses that are unreasonable whether because excessive in amount or because they should not have been incurred at all." *Schulte*, 805 F. Supp. 2d at 600 (quoting *Zabkowicz v. W. Bend Co., Div. of Dart Indus., Inc.*, 789 F.2d 540, 553 (7th Cir.1986)). Courts may require class counsel to submit more detailed assessment of costs and expenses; however, "[i]f counsel submit bills with the level of detail that paying clients find satisfactory, a federal court should not require more." *Synthroid I*, 264 F.3d at 772. "[A] summary document containing the amount of detail that generally accompanies a bill of costs submitted under Fed. R. Civ. P. 54(d) and 28 U.S.C. § 1920 will suffice to enable the Court to perform its oversight function." *Schulte*, 805 F. Supp. 2d at 600. However, the Seventh Circuit does not allow for recovery of research costs under 28 U.S.C. § 1920 because such costs are not specifically enumerated in the statute. *Craftwood II, Inc. v. Generac Power Sys., Inc.*, 63 F.4th 1121, 1129–30 (7th Cir. 2023) (citing *Haroco, Inc. v. Am. Nat'l Bank & Trust Co.*, 38 F.3d 1429, 1440 (7th Cir. 1994). Instead, the Seventh Circuit considers research costs a form of attorneys' fees that are not separately recoverable expenses.[15] *Id.*

c. Incentive Awards

The Seventh Circuit adopts the majority approach in allowing for named plaintiffs to receive incentive awards. "Consistent with historical practice, our precedent, and the majority view on the issue, we conclude that incentive awards to named plaintiffs are permitted so long as they comply with the requirements of Rule 23." *Scott v. Dart*, 99 F.4th 1076, 1088 (7th Cir. 2024) (finding that the common fund doctrine did not prohibit named plaintiff from receiving incentive award in class action alleging that county and its sheriff provided pretrial detainees inadequate dental care).

10. ARBITRATION

Despite *AT&T Mobility LLC v. Concepcion*, 563 U.S. 333, 352 (2011), in which the Supreme Court held that the Federal Arbitration Act (FAA) preempts state doctrines invalidating arbitration clauses, traditional principles of contract formation may still render an arbitration clause unenforceable. For example, where a consumer has no reasonable notice that it is agreeing to contractual terms, an arbitration clause may not be enforced. *See Sgouros v. Transunion Corp.*, 817 F.3d 1029, 1033–36 (7th Cir. 2016) (holding that clicking on a button labeled "I Accept" did not provide reasonable notice). Similarly, class arbitration clauses are only enforceable if the parties affirmatively consent to the procedure. *See Herrington v. Waterstone Mortg. Corp.*, 907 F.3d 502, 505 (7th Cir. 2018) ("Because class arbitration 'fundamental[ly] changes' the nature of the proceeding, 'the parties' mere silence on the issue of class-action arbitration' does not signify assent") (quoting *Stolt-Nielsen S.A. v. AnimalFeeds Int'l Corp.*, 559 U.S. 662, 686–87 (2010)).

While the Seventh Circuit previously relied on the National Labor Relations Act (NLRA) to invalidate arbitration waivers, this is no longer the case. Rejecting Seventh Circuit precedent, the Supreme Court held that arbitration clauses that require individual arbitration in class action cases are enforceable under the FAA, regardless of allowances set out within the NLRA. *Epic Sys. Corp. v. Lewis*, 138 S. Ct. 1612, 1616 (2018). Specifically, the court reasoned that an arbitration agreement does not violate the NLRA's protection of "other concerted activities for . . . mutual aid or protection" when it requires plaintiffs to pursue employment-related claims in single-claimant arbitrations. *Id.* at 1624–29. Simply put, the Supreme Court's ruling clarified that a waiver of the right to proceed in a class or collective arbitration is valid. *Id.*

The Seventh Circuit's case law exhibits some tension in the construction it places on arbitration clauses themselves. In *Gore v. Alltel Commc'ns, LLC*, 666 F.3d 1027 (7th Cir. 2012), the court held that "any doubt concerning the scope of the arbitration clause is resolved in favor of arbitration as a matter of federal law." *Id.* at 1032. However, in *Andermann v. Sprint Spectrum L.P.*, 785 F.3d 1157, 1159 (7th Cir. 2015), the court resisted adopting a "presumption" in favor of arbitration: "[I]t's not clear why, so far as eliciting the meaning of a given arbitration clause is concerned, such as clause should be distinguished from any other clause in a contract." *Id.* at 1159. The *Andermann* court explained that "judges should not allow any preference they might have for judicial resolution of a legal dispute to override the parties' dispute-resolution preferences as embodied in an arbitration clause." *Id.* at 1159–60.

[15] The Seventh Circuit has noted that unrecoverable research costs under 28 U.S.C. § 1920 include charges for PACER, Westlaw, and Lexis. *Craftwood II*, 63 F.4th 1121, 1129–30.

EIGHTH CIRCUIT

Districts of Arkansas, Iowa, Minnesota, Missouri, Nebraska, North Dakota, and South Dakota

Thomas F. Eagleton Courthouse
111 South 10th Street
St. Louis, MO 63102

By Christopher E. Roberts
Butsch Roberts & Associates LLC

1. INTRODUCTION

The Eighth Circuit Court of Appeals includes the federal district courts of Arkansas, Iowa, Minnesota, Missouri, Nebraska, North Dakota, and South Dakota. The Eighth Circuit has two offices—one in St. Louis, Missouri, and one in St. Paul, Minnesota. The St. Louis location is where the Clerk of the Court and most of the case managers are located. The Eighth Circuit consists of eleven active judges and one senior judge as of the date of this publication. As for appointments for the last two presidential terms, as of the time of publication, four of the Eighth Circuit's eleven active judges were appointed by President Trump. None of the Eighth Circuit's judges were appointed by President Biden.

The Eighth Circuit has offered opinions on a litany of class action–related issues. The Eighth Circuit's precedent concerning these issues is discussed in this chapter. This chapter provides an overview of the most recent cases since the last edition of this publication and the current state-of-the-law on class-action related issues in the Eighth Circuit.

2. JURISDICTIONAL PREREQUISITES

a. Standing Considerations

Like any other case in federal court, Article III standing requirements are important in class action litigation. Standing is important in all aspects of class action litigation—from the point suit is filed until a judgment is entered or a settlement is reached.

A plaintiff must have Article III standing to pursue a case. To establish Article III standing, the plaintiff must show that he has suffered some actual or threatened injury that can be traced to the allegedly illegal conduct and that is capable of being redressed. *Oetting v. Norton*, 795 F.3d 886, 889 (8th Cir. 2015); *see generally Spokeo, Inc. v. Robins*, 136 S. Ct. 1540, 1547 (2016).

Class action practitioners should not confuse the ability of a plaintiff to succeed on a claim with standing to sue. The fact that some plaintiffs may be unable to succeed on their claims does not necessarily mean that they lack standing to sue. *Stuart v. State Farm Fire and Cas. Co.*, 910 F.3d 371, 377 (8th Cir. 2018). So long as the theory plaintiff pleads creates a sufficient interest for standing purposes, the ultimate merits of the plaintiff's claim are not considered when analyzing standing. *Id.* In other words, a failure on the merits does not affect a class member's individual standing. *Vogt v. State Farm Life Ins. Co.*, 963 F.3d 753, 766 (8th Cir. 2020).

The named plaintiff should also be part of the class allegedly damaged. A class action case may be dismissed where the named plaintiff complains of damage to a class or classes and the plaintiff is not part of the class. *See Oetting,* 795 F.3d at 889–90; *compare with Golan v. Veritas Ent., LLC*, 788 F.3d 814 (8th Cir. 2015) (reversing district court's dismissal of case because class plaintiffs had Article III standing).

Moreover, a district court may not certify a class that includes members who lack standing. *Avritt v. Reliastar Life Ins. Co.*, 615 F.3d 1023, 1034 (8th Cir. 2010); *In re Zurn Pex Plumbing Prods. Liab. Litig.*, 644 F.3d 604, 616 (8th Cir. 2011); *Halvorson v. Auto-Owners Ins. Co.*, 718 F.3d 773, 778 (8th Cir. 2013); *Johannessohn v. Polaris Indus. Inc.*, 9 F.4th 981, 987 (8th Cir. 2021). Therefore, a class may be certified only where each class member can "show an injury in fact that is traceable to the defendant and likely to be redressed in a favorable decision." *Halvorson*, 718 F.3d at 778. Again, practitioners should not confuse standing with proving damages or the merits of a case.

The *Johannessohn* case illustrates this principle. The plaintiffs in *Johannessohn* sought to certify classes of all persons who purchased certain ATV models. *Johannessohn*, 9 F.4th at 987. However, the record showed that not all of the ATVs had the manufacturing defect that formed the basis of the lawsuit. *Id.* Some of the ATVs simply had a "risk" of a defect. *Id.* The *Johannessohn* court therefore held that not all of the class members had Article III standing because some class members did not have "manifest defects" with their ATVs. *Id.* at 988. The *Johannessohn* court therefore refused to certify the class because the class was not "defined in such a way that anyone within it would have standing." *Id.*

A district court must also make sure a plaintiff has Article III even if the parties have reached a settlement of a class action. *Schumacher v. SC Data Ctr., Inc.*, 912 F.3d 1104 (8th Cir. 2019). This is because "an approved settlement takes the form of a judgment of the court, and without both Article III power and proper subject matter jurisdiction, the court cannot act." *Id.* at 1105. It is reversible error for a court to approve a settlement without first assessing the plaintiff's standing. *Id.*

b. Diversity Jurisdiction

Subject matter jurisdiction based on diversity of citizenship exists where the amount in controversy exceeds $75,000 and the parties are citizens of different states. 28 U.S.C. §1332(a)(1). As claims cannot be aggregated to exceed the $75,000 amount in controversy and in light of the Class Action Fairness Act's jurisdictional requirements (discussed below), federal subject matter jurisdiction of a class action or a class action-related case is not usually based on diversity jurisdiction. *See generally Crawford v. F. Hoffman-La Roche Ltd.*, 267 F.3d 760, 765 (8th Cir. 2001) (claims cannot be aggregated to exceed the $75,000 amount in controversy). Class action practitioners, however, should not lose sight of diversity jurisdiction. *American Family Mut. Ins. Co. v. Vein Ctrs. for Excellence, Inc.*, 912 F.3d 1076 (8th Cir. 2019) is instructive.

The insurer in *American Family* filed a declaratory judgment action in federal court disputing its obligation to defend its insured in a class action. *Id.* at 1079. The plaintiff in the class action case moved to dismiss the action claiming that the amount in controversy did not exceed $75,000. *Id.* at 1079–80. The class action plaintiff claimed the insurer improperly aggregated the class members' claims to satisfy the amount in controversy. *Id.* The class action plaintiff essentially alleged diversity jurisdiction did not exist because its individual claim did not exceed $75,000.

The *American Family court* rejected the class action plaintiff's argument. The court noted that in a declaratory judgment action, the amount in controversy ordinarily equals the probable costs of defense and indemnification of underlying litigation less any applicable deductible. *Id.* at 1081. The *American Family* court therefore concluded that the insurer's single indemnity obligation satisfied the amount in because the class action plaintiff had filed a motion for summary judgment in the class case seeking damages of over $17 million and because it would have likely cost more than $75,000 to defend the class action case. *Id.* Thus, the amount in controversy was satisfied because the insurer was not aggregating claims to meet the amount in controversy but was considering a single claim by its insured. *Id.*

Traditional diversity jurisdiction, while not frequently invoked in class cases, is therefore important to keep in mind for class action practitioners.

c. Class Action Fairness Act (CAFA)

The Class Action Fairness Act (CAFA) allows a party to remove a case to federal court if three requirements are satisfied: the amount in controversy exceeds $5 million, there is minimal diversity among the parties and there are at least 100 class members. 28 U.S.C. § 1332(d). Citizenship is determined "as of the date of the filing of the complaint." 28 U.S.C. § 1332(7). Class action practitioners should be aware that minimal diversity may be satisfied where "any member of a class . . . is a citizen if a state from any defendant." 28 U.S.C. § 1332(d)(2)(A). This is important because diversity may be satisfied even if the named plaintiff and defendant are from the same state if the class definition includes persons from other states. A class defined as including only citizens of a state is considered by the Eighth Circuit, however, as necessarily excluding persons who are not citizens of that state as of the time of the filing. *Doe v. SSM Health Care Corp.*, 126 F.4th 1329, 1333–34 (8th Cir. 2024).

Minimal diversity and the number of class members are not the most disputed issues under CAFA. Instead, disputes over removal under CAFA usually focus on the $5 million amount-in-controversy requirement. The amount in controversy is the issue most frequently addressed by the Eighth Circuit. A district court's interpretation of CAFA is subject to de novo review. *See generally Westerfeld v. Indep. Processing, LLC*, 621 F.3d 819, 822 (8th Cir. 2010).

CAFA Removal Timing

CAFA jurisdictional issues usually arise shortly after a plaintiff files a class action complaint. This is because a case usually must be removed "within 30 days after the receipt by the defendant, through service or otherwise, of a copy of the initial pleading setting forth the claim for relief upon which such action or proceeding is based." 28 U.S.C. § 1446(b)(1). The court's jurisdiction under CAFA should be determined when the action is commenced, or, more commonly, at the time of removal. *Brown v. Mortg. Elec. Registration Sys., Inc.*, 738 F.3d 926, 932 (8th Cir. 2013); *Hargis v. Access Capital Funding, LLC*, 674 F.3d 783, 789 (8th Cir. 2012). Notably, the one-year limitation to remove a case to federal court does not apply to class actions brought under CAFA. *Reece v. Bank of New York Mellon*, 760 F.3d 771, 775–76 (8th Cir. 2014).

For instance, there are situations where a case may be removed under CAFA after the 30-day window (and even after the general one-year limitation to remove a case). If the initial pleading does not establish CAFA jurisdiction, the defendant may remove the case under CAFA within 30 days of receiving an "amended pleading, motion, order or other paper from which it may first be ascertained that the case is one which is or has become removable." 28 U.S.C. § 1446(b)(3). There is no one-year limitation in the rule. Notably, however, a second attempt to remove under this section in a given case "requires a different factual basis underlying a new theory of removal." *City of Creve Coeur, Missouri v. DirecTV, LLC*, 58 F.4th 1013, 1017 (8th Cir. 2023).

A document qualifies as an other paper if it is the first such document from which the defendant can *unambiguously ascertain* that the CAFA jurisdictional requirements have been satisfied. *Gibson v. Clean Harbors Envtl. Servs., Inc.*, 840 F.3d 515, 521 (8th Cir. 2016) (emphasis added). Oral statements that are later transcribed satisfy the other paper requirement. *Atwell v. Boston Sci. Corp.*, 740 F.3d 1160, 1162 (8th Cir. 2013). An other paper does not include a decision in a separate case with different parties. *Dahl v. R.J. Reynolds Tobacco Co.*, 478 F.3d 965, 969 (8th Cir. 2007). Nor does another paper include discovery responses from the same plaintiff in a similar class action case against a different defendant. *Dalton v. Walgreen Co.*, 721 F.3d 492, 494 (8th Cir. 2013).

The *Gibson* case highlights the other paper principles and the Eighth Circuit's inclination to exercise CAFA jurisdiction.

Gibson involved a putative class action lawsuit in which plaintiffs' counsel sent a letter to defense counsel recommending a total payment of $6.5 million to resolve the case. *Id.* at 517–18. The letter was based on an estimate of the number of class members and the estimated amount of damages. *Id.* Thirty days passed after the defendant received the letter, and the defendant did not remove the case. *See id.* at 518. More than 30 days after sending its settlement demand letter, the plaintiffs sent an expert report to the defendant that set forth the scientific methodology for determining the geographic scope of the class. *Id.* at 518. The defendant removed the case within 30 days of receiving the expert report under the other paper provision of CAFA. *Id.*

The *Gibson* court concluded that the 30-day clock did not run from the date the defendant received the settlement demand, but from the date the defendant received the expert report. *Id.* at 519–22. The court reached this conclusion because the expert report was a scientific report from which the defendant could unambiguously ascertain that the CAFA jurisdictional requirements were satisfied, whereas the settlement letter only recommended a resolution for $6.5 million and was not based on scientific evidence. *Id.* at 522. Ultimately, the *Gibson* court concluded that this approach strikes the appropriate balance between competing interests: it discourages the use of indeterminate allegations by plaintiffs in their filings and other papers and it eliminates the incentive for defendants to file protective removals. *Id.* at 520.

As discussed below, the Eighth Circuit's inclination to exercise CAFA jurisdiction is based on the parties' burdens of proof of establishing that CAFA jurisdiction does or does not exist. This inclination is also based on the goal of furthering Congress's intent of opening the doors of federal court to corporate defendants out of the concern that meritless class action suits would damage the economy.

The Burden of Proving CAFA Jurisdiction Does or Does Not Exist

The party invoking CAFA jurisdiction has the burden of proving that jurisdiction exists by a preponderance of the evidence. *See generally Lizama v. Victoria's Secret Stores, LLC*, 36 F.4th 762, 765 (8th Cir. 2022); *Bell v. Hershey Co.*, 557 F.3d 953, 958 (8th Cir. 2009). The removing party must show that a "factfinder might legally conclude the amount in controversy" is satisfied. *Lizama*, 36 F.4th at 765. The amount is not in controversy if no "factfinder could legally award it." *Id.*; *see also Brunts v. Walmart, Inc.*, 68 F.4th 1091, 1094 (8th Cir. 2023).

If a preponderance of the evidence establishes that CAFA jurisdiction exists, the burden then shifts to the party seeking remand to establish that the damages do not exceed $5 million or that an exception to CAFA applies. *Westerfeld*, 621 F.3d at 823. The district court should not resolve any doubts about jurisdiction in favor of remand when analyzing whether CAFA jurisdiction exists. *Id.* Rather, all doubts should be resolved *against* the party seeking remand. *Id.; see also Leflar v. Target Corp.*, 57 F.4th 600, 603–04 (8th Cir. 2023). While doubts are resolved against remand, the district court need not accept "speculative" bases for the amount in controversy being satisfied. *Lizama*, 36 F.4th at 766.

The party invoking CAFA does not have to prove to a legal certainty that the amount in controversy exceeds $5 million. *Bell*, 557 F.3d at 957. Instead, the invoking party simply must show that the finder of fact *might* conclude the damages exceed $5 million, not that the damages *are* greater than $5 million. *Id.* at 959; *Hartis v. Chicago Title Ins. Co.*, 694 F.3d 935, 944–45 (8th Cir. 2012); *Grawitch v. Charter Commcn's Broad., Inc.*, 750 F.3d 956, 959 (8th Cir. 2014). In other words, a party seeking removal under CAFA need not confess liability but only show that the damages at issue might exceed $5 million. *Hartis*, 694 F.3d at 946. The burden of showing that over $5 million is in controversy is simply a pleading requirement, not a demand for proof. *Id.* at 945 (quoting *Spivey v. Vertue, Inc.*, 528 F.3d 982, 986 (7th Cir. 2005)). Courts can, in some instances, consider total amount of sales where a case challenges the sales of a product or service. *Brunts*, 68 F.4th at 1094–95.

While the party invoking CAFA needs to show the amount of damages *might* exceed $5 million, the district court has discretion to determine whether the damages *plausibly* exceed $5 million. *Penrod v. K&M Eng'g, Inc.*, 14 F.4th 671, 673 (8th Cir. 2021). The *Penrod* case provides a good example of where a circumstance in which the Eighth Circuit held the amount in controversy did not *plausibly* exceed $5 million.

The plaintiffs in *Penrod* sought to represent a class of persons who purchased allegedly defective oil filters. *Id.* at 672–73. The plaintiffs estimated that 2.5 million oil filters were sold during the class period. *Id.* at 673. The plaintiffs also estimated that only 750 of the oil filters, or less than 3/100ths of 1 percent actually failed. *Id.* While the plaintiffs alleged that all of the oil filters were at risk of failing, the Eighth Circuit noted that purchasing a product at risk of failing is not sufficient to confer standing. *Id.* at 674. Rather, the product had to actually fail or be sure to fail. *See id.* Thus, the damages caused by each oil filter would have to be $6,666.67 to confer CAFA jurisdiction. *Id.* at 673. The Eighth Circuit affirmed the district court's determination that these damage amounts were implausible because two of the plaintiffs simply sustained oil leaks on the tires of their vehicles. *Id.* at 675. As such, the Eighth Circuit affirmed the district court's dismissal of the case for lack of jurisdiction. *Id.* at 676.

If the party invoking CAFA jurisdiction meets its preponderance burden, it becomes difficult for the rebutting party to persuade a district court to remand the case to state court. If the preponderance standard concerning damages is met, the burden shifts to the party seeking remand to establish "a legal certainty" that the claim is less than $5 million. *Bell*, 557 F.3d at 956. In other words, the rebutting party must establish that it is "legally impossible" for the damages to exceed $5 million if the removing party satisfies the preponderance burden. *Dammann v. Progressive Direct Ins. Co.*, 856 F.3d 580, 584 (8th Cir. 2017); *Raskas v. Johnson & Johnson*, 719 F.3d 884, 888 (8th Cir. 2013). The probability of success of the claim cannot be considered under this standard. *See generally Pirozzi v. Massage Envy Franchising, LLC*, 938 F.3d 981, 984 (8th Cir. 2019). This extremely high standard is applied to the party seeking remand to further Congress's intent behind CAFA of opening "federal courts to corporate defendants out of concern that the national economy risked damage of from a proliferation of meritless class action suits." *Bell*, 557 F.3d at 957 (citing Pub. L. No. 109-2,§2(a)(2)(B), §2(a)(4)(A)).

CAFA jurisdiction, however, does not exist where the plaintiff lacks Article III standing. *Wallace v. ConAgra Foods, Inc.*, 747 F.3d 1025, 1032–33 (8th Cir. 2014). Thus, while CAFA jurisdiction is liberally construed, CAFA does not "extend federal jurisdiction to state claims." *Id.* at 1032. The appropriate remedy in cases in which Article III standing does not exist is to remand the case to state court. *See id.* at 1033; *see also St. Louis Heart Ctr., Inc. v. Nomax, Inc.*, 899 F.3d 500, 505 (8th Cir. 2018) (applying principle to a case not related to CAFA).

Items Considered and Not Considered in Determining Whether CAFA Jurisdiction Exists

The Eighth Circuit reviews the pleadings (usually the complaint) and affidavits to determine whether a preponderance of the evidence establishes that the amount in controversy exceeds $5 million. As part of its review of the pleadings, the Eighth Circuit also considers whether the complaint involves a class action as defined by CAFA.

Pleadings

The starting point of most cases is the filing of a complaint. As such, it is no surprise that review of the complaint is the starting point for the Eighth Circuit to determine whether the $5 million threshold is satisfied. The Eighth Circuit pays close attention to the language of the complaint to determine whether removal under CAFA is appropriate. It is therefore critical for plaintiff's counsel to draft their complaint carefully and for defendant's counsel to closely scrutinize the complaint.

The *Hartis* case provides a good example of how the Eighth Circuit will closely scrutinize the complaint to determine whether the $5 million threshold is met. *Hartis v. Chicago Title Ins. Co.*, 694 F.3d 935 (8th Cir. 2012). The complaint in *Hartis* alleged that the class representative was overcharged a total of $24 for recording fees at two real estate closings. *Id.* at 945. The complaint alleged that these overcharges were commonly paid to the defendant and that damages would be calculated the same way for the class members. *Id.* The complaint also alleged that there were over 70,000 transactions in Missouri and that the defendant conducted real estate closings in 16 other states. *Id.*

In concluding that the case involved over $5 million in damages, the *Hartis* court simply multiplied the average amount of overcharges in the class representative's transactions by the number of transactions in Missouri. *Id.* The *Hartis* court then multiplied the Missouri figure by the number of states at issue to conclude that the possible damages exceeded $5 million. *Id.*

As CAFA jurisdiction is analyzed at the time of removal, the Eighth Circuit analyzes the operative complaint in effect at the time of removal to determine whether CAFA jurisdiction exists. *Brown v. Mortg. Elec. Registration Sys., Inc.*, 738 F.3d 926, 931–32 (8th Cir. 2013); *Hargis v. Access Capital Funding, LLC*, 674 F.3d 783, 789–90 (8th Cir. 2012); *see also Fochtman v. Hendren Plastics, Inc.*, 47 F.4th 638, 642–43 (8th Cir. 2022). A plaintiff will not succeed in avoiding CAFA jurisdiction by subsequently amending the complaint to limit the scope of the class or asserting that the class is limited in scope despite the language in the complaint. *Hargis*, 674 F.3d at 789–90; *Brown*, 738 F.3d at 932.

Only statutory attorneys' fees requested in a complaint may be considered in determining whether the amount in controversy exceeds $5 million. *Hartis v. Chicago Title Ins. Co.*, 656 F.3d 778, 781–82 (8th Cir. 2009). A request for "reasonable" attorneys' fees not based on statute should not be considered by the district court when determining whether the $5 million damage threshold is met. *Id.*

A request for punitive damages also may be considered in determining the amount in controversy. *Hurst v. Nissan N. Am., Inc.*, 511 F. App'x 584, 586–87 (8th Cir. 2013) (unpublished); *Raskas v. Johnson & Johnson*, 719 F.3d 884, 887–88 (8th Cir. 2013); *Pirozzi v. Massage Envy Franchising, LLC*, 938 F.3d 981, 984 (8th Cir. 2019). However, punitive damages may not be considered in determining the amount in controversy if state law prohibits the recovery of punitive damages. *Hurst*, 511 F. App'x at 586–87. This is true even if a plaintiff requests punitive damages if the applicable state law does not allow for the recovery of punitive damages. *Id.* Similarly, a court cannot consider punitive damages in determining the amount in controversy if the plaintiff does not request punitive damages in the complaint even if the applicable law allows for punitive damages to be recovered. *Waters v. Ferrara Candy Co.*, 873 F.3d 633, 635 (8th Cir. 2017).

There are also items the court cannot consider when determining whether the CAFA amount-in-controversy is satisfied. For example, a defendant cannot aggregate the amounts in controversy between multiple similar class action lawsuits involving the same defendant to meet the $5 million CAFA threshold. *Marple v. T-Mobile Cent. LLC*, 639 F.3d 1109 (8th Cir. 2011). Class action practitioners, however, should not view the *Marple* case as a license to create smaller classes to avoid CAFA jurisdiction. In reaching its holding, the *Marple* court determined that there was no indication that the plaintiff artificially divided the lawsuit to avoid CAFA and that the plaintiff's litigation strategy was driven by her decision to mirror the separate lawsuits filed by the defendant. *Id.* at 1111. The *Marple* court suggested that it may have reached a different conclusion if the suit had been drafted in a manner to avoid CAFA jurisdiction. *See id.* at 1110–11.

Affidavits/Declarations

Affidavits or declarations in support of removal under CAFA must be considered by the district court even if they are not submitted at the time of removal. *Pudlowski v. The St. Louis Rams, LLC*, 829 F.3d 963, 964–65 (8th Cir. 2016); *see also Leflar v. Target Corp.*, 57 F.4th 600, 605 (8th Cir. 2023). Affidavits concerning CAFA jurisdiction must be considered even when they are first submitted to the court in a defendant's opposition to a motion to remand rather than the defendant's removal papers. *Pudlowski*, 829 F.3d at 964–65.

Moreover, affidavits will be considered in the court's CAFA analysis, even where the plaintiff contends the damage amounts in the affidavit are overinclusive. *Raskas v. Johnson & Johnson*, 719 F.3d 884, 887–88 (8th Cir. 2013). The affidavit in *Raskas* included the total amount of sales for a product to establish the jurisdictional amount although the plaintiff contended he was seeking a lesser amount than the total sales. *Id.* at 887. The *Raskas* court rejected the overinclusive argument and noted that other circuits had rejected similar arguments because the propriety of all the defendant's transactions was put into question and because the amount in controversy is merely an estimate of the total amount in dispute. *Id.*

The district court, however, has authority to closely scrutinize affidavits submitted. *See Waters v. Ferrara Candy Co.*, 873 F.3d 633, 635 (8th Cir. 2017). An affidavit supporting the amount in controversy should be based on specific factual allegations combined with reasonable deductions, reasonable inferences, or other reasonable extrapolations. *Id.* An affidavit that is vague or speculative may be disregarded or afforded little weight by the court in conducting its CAFA analysis. *See id.* While a district court has authority to closely scrutinize affidavits or declarations submitted, the district court must accept the allegations if they "are made in good faith" because declarations are simply pleadings and not considered to be a demand for proof. *Brunts v. Walmart, Inc.*, 68 F.4th 1091, 1094 (8th Cir. 2023) (internal citation and quotation omitted).

Stipulations That Limit Damages

The Supreme Court held in *Standard Fire Ins. Co. v. Knowles*, 568 U.S. 588, 596 (2013), that a plaintiff's stipulation to damages of less than $5 million before class certification does not resolve the amount in controversy question under CAFA. *See Faltermeier v. FCA US LLC*, 899 F.3d 617, 621–22 (8th Cir. 2018). Such a stipulation does not resolve the amount in controversy question because the stipulation cannot bind absent class members. *Id.*

While the *Knowles* court did not consider whether a stipulation limiting the recovery of attorneys' fees would be considered in determining the CAFA amount in controversy, the Eighth Circuit recently addressed this issue. *Faltermeier v. FCA US LLC*, 899 F.3d 617 (8th Cir. 2018). In adopting the reasoning of *Knowles*, the *Faltermeier* court held that a stipulation limiting the recovery of attorneys' fees would also not resolve the CAFA amount in controversy analysis. *Id.* at 621–22. Notably, *Faltermeier* was a case brought under a fee-shifting statute. The *Faltermeier* court recognized that there is no reason to apply a different rule to a stipulation limiting the amount of attorneys' fees to defeat CAFA jurisdiction. *Id.* at 621. Thus, it is proper for a district court to conduct its own analysis of what it believes will be the ultimate amount of attorney's fees awarded in its CAFA analysis in a case brought under a fee-shifting statute. *See id.*

Whether the Case Is a Class Action Under CAFA

The Eighth Circuit also will review the pleadings to determine whether the action is a "class action" as defined by CAFA. CAFA jurisdiction exists in class action cases. 28 U.S.C. § 1332(d)(2). CAFA defines a class action as "any civil action filed under Rule 23 of the Federal Rules of Civil Procedure or similar State statute or rule of judicial procedure authorizing an action to be brought by one or more representative persons as a class action." 28 U.S.C. § 1332(d)(1)(B). As discussed below, the Eighth Circuit has exercised CAFA jurisdiction in a case that was not explicitly filed as a class action where a separate proceeding was based on an underlying class action judgment.

CAFA jurisdiction may exist in a subsequent action to enforce a class action judgment even if the subsequent action does not explicitly reference a state statute or state equivalent of Rule 23. *Williams v. Employers Mut. Cas. Co.*, 845 F.3d 891, 898–902 (8th Cir. 2017); *see also Brown v. Mortg. Elec. Registration Sys., Inc.*, 738 F.3d 926, 931 (8th Cir. 2013) (case considered a class action under CAFA where a state law claim did not require certification, but the state supreme court required the claim to use the state court equivalent of Rule 23 as a procedural guide).

The *Williams* case concerned an equitable garnishment action to enforce a class action judgment against an insurance carrier. *Williams*, 845 F.3d at 895–96. The equitable garnishment action invoked the state equitable garnishment statute but did not explicitly invoke the state corollary to Rule 23. *Id.* at 901–02. The *Williams* court held that while the state equitable garnishment statute did not authorize a party to bring a class action, the proceeding was only brought because of the plaintiff's status as a class representative of the state corollary to Rule 23 and necessarily implicated class-related issues. *Id.* at 901. The *Williams* court therefore considered the equitable garnishment action to be a class action under CAFA and that the district court properly exercised jurisdiction under CAFA. *Id.* at 902.

While not a traditional CAFA "exception," practitioners should be aware that state-enforcement actions may not be subject to CAFA. *See Minnesota by Ellison v. Am. Petroleum Inst.*, 63 F.4th 703 (8th Cir. 2023). *Ellison* involved a suit brought by the Minnesota Attorney General against a "litany of fossil fuel producers," alleging consumer fraud and violations of state consumer protection statutes. *Id.* at 707–08. The defendants removed the case, in part, under CAFA. *Id.* at 708.

The defendants argued that the statute under which the Attorney General exercised its authority qualified the case as a "class action" under CAFA. *Id.* at 716. Specifically, the defendants argued that the statute under which the Attorney General derived its authority to file suit was a "similar state statute" under CAFA's definition of a "class action." *Id.* (citing 28 U.S.C. § 1332(d)(2)).

The *Ellison* court rejected this argument. The *Ellison* court held that the case did not qualify as a "class action" or a "mass action" under CAFA because state actions to enforce consumer protection laws are not necessarily "class actions" or "mass actions" that qualify for CAFA removal. *Id.* at 716–17. Specifically, the *Ellison* court noted that the statute under which the Attorney General derived its authority did not contain requirements similar to Rule 23. *Id.* The court therefore held that a state's authority to act on behalf of its citizens "is not the same as a class action, even when the State seeks recovery for and on behalf of its citizens' injuries." *Id.* at 716.

d. CAFA Exceptions

Local Controversy Exception

While CAFA has multiple jurisdictional exceptions, the exception most frequently addressed by the Eighth Circuit is the local controversy exception. The Eighth Circuit narrowly construes the local controversy exception. This is because "CAFA reflects Congress's desire from broad diversity jurisdiction over class actions. *Hargett v. RevClaims, LLC*, 854 F.3d 962, 962 (8th Cir. 2017). If the removing party establishes by a preponderance of evidence that CAFA jurisdiction exists, a heavy burden then shifts to the party to show that the local controversy exception applies. *Id.*; *Westerfeld v. Indep. Processing, LLC*, 621 F.3d 819, 822–23 (8th Cir. 2010). Any doubt against whether the local controversy exception applies is resolved *against* the party seeking remand. *Westerfeld*, 621 F.3d at 822; *Hood v. Gilster-Mary Lee Corp.*, 785 F.3d 263, 265 (8th Cir. 2015).

The local controversy exception to CAFA provides that a district court must decline jurisdiction when certain requirements are met. These requirements are (1) "greater than two-thirds of the members of all proposed plaintiff classes are citizens of the State in which the action was originally filed," (2) there is at least one defendant "from whom significant relief is sought by members of the plaintiff class" and "whose alleged conduct forms a significant basis for the claims asserted by the proposed plaintiff class" who is a citizen of the state in which the class action was originally filed, (3) the principal injuries were incurred in the state in which the action was filed, (4) and no other class action alleging similar facts was filed in the three years prior to the commencement of the current class action. 28 U.S.C.§1332(d)(4)(A); *Westerfeld*, 621 F.3d at 822 (8th Cir. 2010); *see also Kitchin v. Bridgeton Landfill, LLC*, 3 F.4th 1089, 1094 (8th Cir. 2021) (petition for certiorari pending at the time of publication). The two-thirds requirement is determined as of the date of filing of the complaint, amended complaint, pleading, motion, or other paper, indicating the existence of federal jurisdiction. 28 U.S.C. § 1332(d)(7).

The two-thirds citizenship may be shown by using affidavit evidence, statistically significant surveys showing two-thirds of the class are local citizens or by defining the class to include only local citizens. *Hood*, 785 F.3d at 266 (following the Seventh Circuit's approach). Class action practitioners should be careful not confuse residency with citizenship of a state. The *Hood* court noted that residence is not the same as citizenship and that providing the last known addresses of the putative class members was insufficient to establish that the two-thirds citizenship requirement was satisfied. *Id.* at 265–66 n.1. While residency is fluid, citizenship requires permanence. *Hargett v. RevClaims, LLC*, 854 F.3d 962, 965 (8th Cir. 2017). Unlike citizenship, residency does not require an intent to make a place home. *Id.*

In deciding whether the conduct forms a "significant basis" of the plaintiff's claims, the Eighth Circuit requires district courts to substantively analyze and compare the "local defendant's alleged conduct to the alleged conduct of all the Defendants." *Kitchin v. Bridgeton Landfill, LLC*, 3 F.4th 1089, 1094 (8th Cir. 2021) (petition for certiorari pending at the time of publication). To establish a "significant basis," the local defendant's conduct must be "an important ground for the asserted claims in view of the alleged conduct of all the Defendants." *Id.* at 1094. Thus, if the local defendant's conduct is indistinguishable from the other defendants' conduct, or the same as the other defendants' conduct, then the "significant basis" requirement may not be satisfied. *Id.* at 1095.

The "significant basis" prong may be shown through extrinsic evidence. *See Atwood v. Peterson*, 936 F.3d 835, 838–41 (8th Cir. 2019). This is because, "when a question of the District Court's jurisdiction is raised, the court may inquire by affidavits or otherwise, into the facts as they exist." *Id.* at 840 (quoting *Land v. Dollar*, 330 U.S. 731, 735 n.4 (1947)). As such, a defendant can provide affidavits to establish "the real target" of the litigation. *Id.* at 840. The defendants in *Atwood* submitted affidavits establishing that some of the named individual defendants had no decision-making authority regarding the misconduct at issue. *Id.* at 838–40. The *Atwood* court considered these affidavits and concluded that the non-diverse defendants were not defendants from whom "significant relief" was sought and held the local controversy exception did not apply. *Id.* at 840.

e. Appealing CAFA Jurisdictional Orders

Appellate courts may "accept an appeal from an order of a district court granting or denying a motion to remand a class action." 28 U.S.C. § 1453(c)(1); *see also Hargett v. RevClaims, LLC*, 854 F.3d 962, 965 (8th Cir. 2017); *Leflar v. Target Corp.*, 57 F.4th 600, 602–03 (8th Cir. 2023). An appeal under CAFA is discretionary and is therefore governed by Federal Rule of Appellate Procedure 5 concerning discretionary appeals. *Froud v. Andarko E & P Co. Ltd. P'ship*, 607 F.3d 520, 522 (8th Cir. 2010). This means that class action practitioners who wish to appeal a remand order under CAFA must provide a reason why the appeal should be allowed. *Id.*

Class action practitioners should be careful not to confuse the fact that a case is pled as a class action to mean that CAFA jurisdiction exists. Where a class action case is removed under traditional diversity jurisdiction (i.e., the parties are diverse and the amount in controversy exceeds $75,000), the Eighth Circuit does not have appellate jurisdiction over a district court's order granting or denying a motion to remand. *Saab v. Home Depot U.S.A., Inc.*, 469 F.3d 758, 759–60 (8th Cir. 2006). This is because the traditional diversity statute does not allow an appellate court to accept an appeal of a denial of a motion to remand. *Id. However,* cases removed under CAFA provide an exception to this rule. *Id.*

3. RULE 23 REQUIREMENTS

a. General Principles

The plaintiff bears the burden of initially showing the class certification is warranted. *Day v. Celadon Trucking Servs., Inc.*, 827 F.3d 817, 830 (8th Cir. 2016). The Eighth Circuit has not explicitly stated the evidentiary burden that plaintiff must satisfy to establish that class certification is warranted. It is possible that the burden is a preponderance of the evidence since the district court must make a *limited* preliminary inquiry, looking behind the pleadings, to determine whether the elements of class certification are satisfied. *See Blades v. Monsanto Co.*, 400 F.3d 562, 566 (8th Cir. 2005) (emphasis added).

Ultimately, a district court has broad discretion to decide whether class certification is proper. *See generally Cody v. City of St. Louis*, 103 F.4th 523, 528 (8th Cir. 2024); *Ebert v. General Mills, Inc.*, 823 F.3d 472, 477 (8th Cir. 2016); *Smith v. ConocoPhillips Pipe Line Co.*, 801 F.3d 921, 925 (8th Cir. 2015); *Prof'l Firefighters Ass'n of Omaha, Local 385 v. Zalewski*, 678 F.3d 640, 645 (8th Cir. 2012). The district court's decision to certify a class is reviewed for an abuse of discretion. *See generally McKeage v. TMBC, LLC*, 847 F.3d 992, 999 (8th Cir. 2017); *see also Vogt v. Progressive Cas. Ins. Co.*, --F.4th--, 2025 WL 583348, at *1 (8th Cir. Feb. 24, 2025). The district court only abuses its discretion if it rests its conclusions on clearly erroneous factual findings or if its decision relies on erroneous legal conclusions. *In re Wholesale Grocery Prods. Antitrust Litig.*, 946 F.3d 995, 1004 (8th Cir. 2019) (internal quotation and citation omitted). The district court's factual findings concerning class certification are reviewed under the clearly erroneous standard. *Ebert*, 823 F.3d at 477; *Stuart v. State Farm Fire and Cas. Co.*, 910 F.3d 371, 375 (8th Cir. 2018).

While a district court has broad discretion to certify a class, its discretion is more limited when addressing issues of law. Issues of law involved in the district court's class certification decision are reviewed de novo. *See generally McKeage*, 847 F.3d at 999; *In re St. Jude Med. Inc.*, 425 F.3d 1116, 1119 (8th Cir. 2005); *Blades v. Monsanto Co.*, 400 F.3d 562, 566 (8th Cir. 2005).

The Interplay Between Merits and Class Certification Issues

While the evidence concerning Rule 23 requirements may overlap with the merits of the case, "the district court should not resolve the merits of the case at class certification." *In re Zurn Pex Plumbing Prods. Liab. Litig.*, 644 F.3d 604, 617 (8th Cir. 2011). This is because the decision to certify a class is not "a conclusive judgment on the merits." *Id.* at 613. Instead, Rule 23(c)(1)(C) allows the district court to alter or amend an order granting or denying class certification at any time before final judgment. Fed. R. Civ. P. 23(c)(1)(C). Thus, a district court can later deny class certification or grant summary judgment for a defendant if the court finds liability in favor of a defendant after certifying a class. *In re Zurn Pex Plumbing Prods. Liab. Litig.*, 644 F.3d at 617. In fact, it is the district court's "duty to assure that a class once certified continues to be certifiable under Rule 23(a)." *Petrovic v. Amoco Oil Co.*, 200 F.3d 1140, 1145 (8th Cir. 1999).

However, a class certification decision may be improper if a class definition depends on a determination of an issue of law that the district court wrongly decides or analyzes. *See Luiken v. Domino's Pizza, LLC*, 705 F.3d 370, 372–75 (8th Cir. 2013). In other words, while the merits of the case are not specifically considered at the class certification stage, the district court must consider "what the parties must prove" when deciding whether class certification is appropriate. *Elizabeth M. v. Montenez*, 458 F.3d 779, 786 (8th Cir. 2006); *see also Ford v. TD Ameritrade Holding Corp.*, 995 F.3d 616, 620 (8th Cir. 2021).

This is a subtle distinction, but practitioners should not confuse this principle with meaning that the district court can decide the merits at the class certification stage. Examples of this principle are discussed in the predominance and commonality sections. Of course, there are always exceptions to the rule, as the Eighth Circuit once decided the merits of a case when considering a Rule 23(f) petition and directed the district court to dismiss the case entirely. *See In re State Farm Fire Cas. Co.*, 872 F.3d 567 (8th Cir. 2017).

Class Definitions

Class action practitioners must also pay close attention to how a proposed class is defined. For example, a district court may not certify a class that includes members who lack standing. *Avritt v. Reliastar Life Ins. Co.*, 615 F.3d 1023, 1034 (8th Cir. 2010); *In re Zurn Pex Plumbing Prods. Liab. Litig.*, 644 F.3d at 616; *Halvorson v. Auto-Owners Ins. Co.*, 718 F.3d 773, 778 (8th Cir. 2013). Therefore, a class may be certified only where each class member can show an injury in fact that is traceable to the defendant and likely to be redressed in a favorable decision. *Halvorson*, 718 F.3d at 778.

The class should also not be defined as a fail-safe class. A fail-safe class is a class which the class is defined to preclude membership unless a putative member would prevail on the merits. *Orduno v. Pietrzak*, 932 F.3d 710, 716 (8th Cir. 2019). A class should therefore not be defined to include a merits determination. For example, class action practitioners should avoid defining a class that mirrors the elements of the underlying cause of action.

Courts will not certify a fail-safe class because doing so would allow putative class members to seek a remedy but not be bound by an adverse judgment. *Id.* In other words, the class members in a fail-safe class would win by being class members, but, if they lose, they would not be included in the class and therefore not bound by an adverse judgment. *Id.*

Notably, a class is not necessarily considered fail-safe even if some class members are determined at trial to not have sustained damages. *See Vogt v. State Farm Life Ins. Co.*, 963 F.3d 753, 768 (8th Cir. 2020). In this scenario, the trial court can avoid issues with a fail-safe class by amending the class definition before trial to exclude class members without damages. *Id.*

The District Court Must Conduct a Rigorous Analysis of the Class Certification Requirements

Ultimately, the district court must conduct a "rigorous analysis" to ensure that all the Rule 23 requirements are satisfied. *See generally Comcast Corp.* v. *Behrend*, 569 U.S. 27, 33; *Smith*, 801 F.3d 921, 925 (8th Cir. 2015). The rigorous analysis standard applies to Rule 23(a), (b) and ascertainability. *Id.*; *Sandusky Wellness Ctr., LLC v. Medtox Scientific, Inc.*, 821 F.3d 992, 996 (8th Cir. 2016) (applying standard to ascertainability). A rigorous analysis requires the "district court to state its reasons for certification in terms specific enough for meaningful appellate review." *In re Target Corp. Customer Data Sec. Breach Litig.*, 847 F.3d 608, 612 (8th Cir. 2017). This means that the district court must state with specificity how the facts apply to each element of Rule 23. *Id.* Failing to do so is reversible error. *Id.*

A rigorous analysis also requires district courts to consider the elements of the underlying cause of action and how the elements of Rule 23 apply to the cause of action. *Cody v. City of St. Louis*, 103 F.4th 523, 530–31 (8th Cir. 2024); *see also Ford v. TD Ameritrade Holding Corp.*, 115 F.4th 854, 859 (8th Cir. 2024). Failing to apply Rule 23 to the elements of the cause of action is potentially reversible error. *Cody*, 103 F.4th at 531.

The Eighth Circuit also recognizes that a trial court may decertify a class it later determines to not satisfy the elements of class certification. *See generally Stuart v. Global Tel*Link Corp.*, 956 F.3d 555, 559–60 (8th Cir. 2020). Presumably, this is because a trial court's class certification order may be altered or amended before final judgment. Fed. R. Civ. P. 23(c)(1)(C). The trial court's ruling on decertification is also reviewed under the abuse of discretion standard. *Id.* at 560.

For similar reasons, Rule 23(c)(1)(C) also provides district court discretion to reconsider its previous denial of a motion for class certification. *Cody*, 103 F.4th at 529. A district court only abuses its discretion in reconsidering its previous denial of class certification if its findings are based on erroneous legal conclusions or factual findings. *Id.*

These standards and principles govern all the Eighth Circuit's decisions concerning the Rule 23 class certification requirements.

Striking Class Allegations Before Class Certification

Federal courts are split as to whether a district court can grant a Rule 12(f) motion to strike class allegations before the filing of a motion for class certification. The Eighth Circuit has held that such motions are permitted in limited circumstances. *Donelson v. Ameriprise Fin. Servs., Inc.*, 999 F.3d 1080, 1092 (8th Cir. 2021) (Petition for certiorari pending at the time of publication). The limited circumstance in which class allegations can be stricken at the pleading stage is when "it is apparent from the pleadings that the class cannot be certified because unsupportable class allegations" would require a defendant to defend against claims that "cannot be sustained." *Id.*

b. Rule 23(a) Requirements

Numerosity

The first requirement in deciding whether class certification is appropriate is that the class be so numerous that joinder of all members is impracticable. Fed. R. Civ. P. 23(a)(1). This requirement is not usually difficult to satisfy.

There is no bright line rule in the Eighth Circuit for how many class members are necessary to satisfy the numerosity requirement. *Boyd v. Ozark Air Lines, Inc.*, 568 F.2d 50, 54–55 (8th Cir. 1977). Rather, the numerosity requirement is determined based on the facts of each case. *Id.* at 54. The relevant facts of each case relate to the number of class members, the nature of the case, the size of the individual claims, the inconvenience in trying individual cases, and other factors that bear upon the practicability of joining all of the putative class members. *Paxton v. Union Nat'l Bank*, 688 F.2d 552, 559–60 (8th Cir. 1982).

While determining whether the numerosity requirement is satisfied depends on the facts and circumstances of each case, the Eighth Circuit has found the numerosity requirement satisfied in a class of 20 people. *Arkansas Educ. Ass'n v. Bd. Of Educ. Of Portland, Ark. Sch. Dist.*, 446 F.2d 763, 765–66 (8th Cir. 1971). Thus, it is not surprising that numerosity is not a frequently contested requirement of class certification in the Eighth Circuit.

Commonality

Rule 23(a)(2) requires a plaintiff to show that there are "questions of law or fact common to the class." Fed. R. Civ. P. 23(a)(2). Commonality is not required as to every question of law so long as the "legal question linking the class members is substantially related to the resolution of the litigation." *DeBoer v. Mellon Mortg. Co.*, 64 F.3d 1171, 1174 (8th Cir. 1995) (quotation and citation omitted).

Ultimately, commonality depends on whether a class action can "generate common answers to drive the resolution of the litigation." *Powers v. Cred. Mgmt. Servs., Inc.*, 776 F.3d 567, 571 (8th Cir. 2015) (quoting *Wal-Mart Stores, Inc. v. Dukes*, 564 U.S. 338, 350 (2011)). Thus, the common answers should not depend on varied circumstances, but should be able to be determined in "one stroke." *Luiken v. Domino's Pizza, LLC*, 705 F.3d 370, 376 (8th Cir. 2013).

The commonality requirement is satisfied when the plaintiff establishes that the class members suffered the same injury. *Smith v. ConocoPhillips Pipe Line Co.*, 801 F.3d 921, 925 (8th Cir. 2015) (quoting *Wal-Mart Stores, Inc.*, 564 U.S. at 350). For example, commonality is readily satisfied where the case is based on a uniform contract and is based on the same law to interpret the contract. *See generally Meek v. Kansas City Life Ins. Co.*, 126 F.4th 577, 584 (8th Cir. 2025). Commonality also exists where a defendant engages in a uniform practice that injures the class members in the same way, even if class members received different services or contracts. *McKeage v. TMBC, LLC*, 847 F.3d 992, 999 (8th Cir.

2017); *see also DeBoer*, 64 F.3d at 1174. However, even if the alleged misconduct is uniform, if the injury to the class members resulting from the misconduct is not uniform, the commonality requirement is not satisfied. *Webb v. Exxon Mobil Corp.*, 856 F.3d 1150, 1155–57 (8th Cir. 2017).

Class action practitioners should be aware of the distinction between a nonuniform injury and varying damages stemming from a uniform injury. Different injuries and different damages are not synonymous. Varying damages that result from the same injury cannot be used as a basis to defeat class certification. *See Meek*, 126 F.4th at 584; *Custom Hair Designs by Sandy v. Central Payment Co., LLC*, 984 F.3d 595, 601–02 (8th Cir. 2020); *Stuart v. State Farm Fire and Cas. Co.*, 910 F.3d 371, 376 (8th Cir. 2018); *Day v. Celadon Trucking Servs., Inc.*, 827 F.3d 817, 833–34 (8th Cir. 2016). The critical inquiry is whether there is a way of measuring varying damages on a classwide basis. *Meek*, 126 F.4th at 584. If damages can be measured on a classwide basis, class certification may be proper even if damages vary between class members. *Id.*

As discussed earlier, the district court should analyze what the parties need to prove to establish liability in determining whether class certification is appropriate. *ConocoPhillips* provides an example of such a circumstance applied to the commonality analysis.

The plaintiff in *ConocoPhillips* asserted a nuisance claim based on an environmental contamination. *Smith*, 801 F.3d at 925–27. The *ConocoPhillips* court analyzed the common law concerning nuisance and concluded that the law required actual contamination to prove nuisance rather than a fear of contamination. *Id.* at 927. Since not all of the properties included in the class were contaminated, the *ConocoPhillips* court concluded that the commonality requirement was not met. *Id.* at 925–27. *ConocoPhillips* highlights the subtle distinction between deciding the merits at class certification and analyzing what evidence is necessary to establish liability in determining whether class certification is proper.

Typicality

Rule 23(b)(3) requires that the representative's claims and defenses be typical of the claims and defenses of the class. Fed. R. Civ. P. 23(b)(3).

The typicality requirement is satisfied if "there are other members of the class who have the same or similar grievances as the plaintiff." *Donaldson v. Pillsbury Co.*, 554 F.2d 825, 830 (8th Cir. 1977). The typicality requirement is "fairly easily" met if other class members have claims similar to those of the plaintiff and seek the same relief. *DeBoer v. Mellon Mortg. Co.*, 64 F.3d 1171, 1174 (8th Cir. 1995); *Postawko v. Mo. Dep't of Corrections*, 910 F.3d 1030, 1039 (8th Cir. 2018). Variations in the facts of individual claims will not defeat typicality if "the claim arises from the same event or course of conduct as the class claims and gives rise to the same legal or remedial theory." *Alpern v. UtliCorp United, Inc.*, 84 F.3d 1525, 1540 (8th Cir. 1996).

The class representative's claim in *Alpern* was held to be typical of the putative class members' claims. *Id.* at 1540–41. *Alpern* was a securities fraud class action. *Id.* at 1528. The defendant claimed that typicality was not met because the class representative purchased securities from a different plan than other class members. *See id.* at 1540–41. The *Alpern* court rejected this argument and held that typicality was satisfied because the same set of events leading up to the [alleged misconduct] underlie the claims of the other putative class members. *Id.* at 1540. The representative's claims were also typical because the representative's claim invoked the same legal theory. *Id.*

However, a common legal theory alone "does not establish typicality when proof of a violation requires individualized inquiry." *Elizabeth M. v. Montenez*, 458 F.3d 779, 787 (8th Cir. 2006); *see also Parke v. First Reliance Standard Life Ins. Co.*, 368 F.3d 999, 1004–05 (8th Cir. 2004). Similarly, typicality is defeated when the class representative is subject to a "unique defense that threatens to play a major role in the litigation." *In re Milk Prods. Antitrust Litig.*, 195 F.3d 430, 437 (8th Cir. 1999).

The *Montenez* court held that the class representative's claim was not typical. The representative's claim was not typical because the proof needed to establish the merits of the representative's claim and each class member's claim varied greatly depending on the legal status of the person against whom the claim was made (i.e., a fellow resident or defendant's employee). *Elizabeth M.*, 458 F.3d at 787.

Adequacy

Rule 23(a)(4) requires that the representative party or parties "fairly and adequately protect the interests of the class." Fed. R. Civ. P. 23(a)(4). The adequacy requirement applies to class representatives and their counsel. *See generally Amchem Prods., Inc. v. Windsor,* 521 U.S. 591, 626 n.20 (1997); *Hervey v. City of Little Rock,* 787 F.2d 1223, 1230 (8th Cir. 1986). To determine whether the Rule 23(a)(4) requirements are satisfied, the district court must balance "the convenience of maintaining a class action and the need to guarantee adequate representation to the class members." *Wright v. Stone Container Corp.*, 524 F.2d 1058, 1061 (8th Cir. 1975).

While adequacy is not usually as heavily litigated as other Rule 23 requirements, the district court still must closely scrutinize the adequacy requirements to "ensure due process for absent class members." *Rattray v. Woodbury Cty., IA*, 614 F.3d 831, 835–36 (8th Cir. 2010). The district court must provide specific reasons for why a class representative is adequate to represent the class. *In re Target Corp. Customer Data Sec. Breach Litig.*, 847 F.3d 608, 612 (8th Cir. 2017). In other words, the district court should rigorously analyze this requirement and avoid making conclusions that simply repeat the language of Rule 23(a). *Id.*

Two requirements must be satisfied to meet the Rule 23(a)(4) adequacy requirement. First, the representative's interest must align with the interests of the class. *Paxton v. Union Nat'l Bank*, 688 F.2d 552, 559–60 (8th Cir. 1982). There must be no conflict of interest between the class representative and the putative class members. *See generally In re Target Corp. Customer Data Sec. Breach Litig.*, 892 F.3d 968, 973–76 (8th Cir. 2018) (no conflict where representatives represented a class based on a single incident even though some class members had verified losses and others did not).

Second, the representative must "vigorously pursue" the putative class members' interests. *In re Milk Prods. Antitrust Litig.*, 195 F.3d 430, 437 (8th Cir. 1999); *Paxton*, 688 F.2d at 562–63; *Darms v. McCulloch Oil Corp.*, 720 F.2d 490, 493 (8th Cir. 1983). The district court must analyze these requirements to make sure no conflicts of interest exist between the class representative and the putative class members. *In re Target Corp. Customer Data Sec. Breach Litig.*, 847 F.3d at 613–14. Again, these requirements apply to the class representative and their counsel.

Adequacy does require the interests of the class representative (and counsel) to be perfectly symmetrical. *Vogt v. State Farm Life Ins. Co.*, 963 F.3d 753, 767 (8th Cir. 2020). Adequacy may even be satisfied where the damage theory maximizes damages more for certain class members than others. *Id.* at 768. Adequacy will not be satisfied only in circumstances where the "intra-class conflict must be so substantial as to overbalance the common interests of the class members as a whole." *Id.* The alleged conflict must be concrete and not based on speculation. *Id.* at 767–68.

The Eighth Circuit has provided guidance as to the circumstances in which a class representative's interests may not align with the interests of the class, so as to defeat adequacy. For example, a class representative who is no longer a part of the class members he or she seeks to represent is not an adequate representative. *Bishop v. Comm. On Prof'l Ethics and Conduct of Iowa State Bar Ass'n*, 686 F.2d 1278, 1289 (8th Cir. 1982). The inadequate class representative in *Bishop* was a former attorney who at the time of class certification was no longer practicing law and who could no longer practice law in the state. *Id.* Yet, the class representative sought to represent a class of lawyers who sought to advertise their legal services. *Id.* The *Bishop* court concluded that the class representative therefore could not adequately represent the class members' interests. *Id.*

Similarly, a class representative who does not seek to represent the interests of all the putative class members also is an inadequate class representative. *In re Milk Prods. Antitrust*

Litig., 195 F.3d at 437. The representative in *In re Milk Products Antitrust Litigation* only wished to represent small convenience stores even though the proposed class included large grocery stores that would be part of the defined class. *Id.* The Eighth Circuit concluded that the representative did not satisfy the adequacy requirement because the representative did not desire to represent all the interests of those who were included in the defined class. *Id.*

Class representatives, through counsel, who delay moving for class certification or delay amending the complaint to allege class allegations when class allegations are readily apparent also are not adequate representatives. *Rattray*, 614 F.3d at 835–36. The *Rattray* court concluded that the proposed representative was inadequate in such circumstances because the representative was not vigorously pursuing the class members' interests. *Id.*

Unsurprisingly, a class representative also must have standing to assert the claims at issue to be considered an adequate representative. *Golan v. Veritas Ent., LLC*, 788 F.3d 814, 821 (8th Cir. 2015). Class members who lack standing to assert the pertinent claims are inadequate class representatives. *See generally Hall v. Lhaco, Inc.*, 140 F.3d 1190, 1196–97 (8th Cir. 1998).

c. Rule 23(b) Requirements

Rule 23(b) sets forth the different types of class actions that may be maintained if the Rule 23(a) requirements are met. *See* Fed. R. Civ. P. 23(b)(1)–(3). The two most common types of class actions analyzed by the Eighth Circuit are Rule 23(b)(2) and Rule 23(b)(3) classes.

Rule 23(b)(2) Classes

While Rule 23(b)(2) classes are not litigated as frequently as Rule 23(b)(3) classes, their usage is becoming more commonplace. *See Ebert v. General Mills, Inc.*, 823 F.3d 472, 480 (8th Cir. 2016). A Rule 23(b)(2) class seeks injunctive or declaratory relief because "the party opposing the class has acted or refused to act on grounds that apply generally to the class." Fed. R. Civ. P. 23(b)(2).

Rule 23(b)(2) classes are not generally permissible where "each class member would be entitled to an individualized award of monetary damages." *Id.* (quoting *Wal-Mart Stores, Inc. v. Dukes*, 564 U.S. 338, 360–61 (2011)). The injuries to be addressed in Rule 23(b)(2) classes are "group, as opposed to individual injuries." *In re St. Jude Med., Inc.*, 425 F.3d 1116, 1121 (8th Cir. 2005); *Ford v. TD Ameritrade Holding Corp.*, 115 F.4th 854, 860 (8th Cir. 2024). The primary relief sought in a Rule 23(b)(2) class must therefore be "declaratory or injunctive." *In re St. Jude Med., Inc.*, 425 F.3d at 1121; *see also Ahmad v. City of St. Louis, Missouri*, 995 F.3d 635, 644 (8th Cir. 2021).

However, a Rule 23(b)(2) class may be certified where monetary damages are incidental to the requested injunctive relief. *Paxton v. Union Nat'l Bank*, 688 F.2d 552, 563 (8th Cir. 1982). The Eighth Circuit has suggested, however, that a hybrid Rule 23(b)(2) and (b)(3) class, with injunctive relief and monetary damages available, could be certified. *See Harris v. Union Pac. R.R. Co.*, 953 F.3d 1030, 1034–39 (8th Cir. 2020).

A Rule 23(b)(2) class need not establish the predominance and superiority requirements of a Rule 23(b)(3) class. *Ebert*, 823 F.3d at 480. The critical requirement of a Rule 23(b)(2) class is that the class must be "cohesive." *Id.*; *Ford*, 115 F.4th at 860; *Postawko v. Mo. Dep't of Corrections*, 910 F.3d 1030, 1039 (8th Cir. 2018). Cohesiveness means that the requested relief must "affect the entire class at once." *Ebert*, 823 F.3d at 480. (quoting *Wal-Mart Stores, Inc.*, 564 U.S. at 361–62). In other words, Rule 23(b)(2) applies only where "a single injunction or declaratory judgment would provide relief to each member of the class." *Postawko*, 910 F.3d at 1039–40 (quoting *Wal-Mart*, 564 U.S. at 360).

While predominance and superiority need not be established, the cohesiveness analysis is more stringent than the predominance and superiority requirements. *Id.*; *see also Ford*, 115 F.4th at 860; *Ahmad*, 995 F.3d at 644. This is because unlike Rule 23(b)(3), Rule 23(b)(2) does not have a provision for unnamed class members to "opt-out of the litigation."

Avritt v. Reliastar Life Ins. Co., 615 F.3d 1023, 1035 (8th Cir. 2010). Cohesiveness does not exist if individualized proof is required to resolve the pertinent issues. *Ebert*, 823 F.3d at 481; *see also Avritt*, 615 F.3d at 1036; *Donelson v. Ameriprise Fin. Servs., Inc.*, 999 F.3d 1080, 1093 (8th Cir. 2021).

For example, the Eighth Circuit held that a Rule 23(b)(2) class was not cohesive because the district court could not determine whether a company's policy was "unlawfully discriminatory under the ADA without considering whether it is job related and consistent with business necessity in each situation." *Harris*, 953 F.3d at 1038. In other words, even though the same policy applied, because the discriminatory nature of the policy could only be determined by applying the policy to each worker's particular circumstances, the class could not be certified. *See id.* at 1038–39.

The Eighth Circuit has also held that cohesiveness is not established if the plaintiffs attempt to aggregate multiple discrete claims without "demonstrating that the class members have been harmed in the same way." *Ahmad*, 995 F.3d at 644. In other words, cohesiveness may not be established where each claim "requires different proof to establish" the alleged violation or if the injunctive relief sought does not "relate to a single policy regarding one particular injury." *Id.*

On the other hand, cohesiveness exists if liability turns on a single question that uniformly applies to all class members. *Avritt*, 615 F.3d at 1036 (citing *DeBoer v. Mellon Mortg. Co.*, 64 F.3d 1171, 1173 (8th Cir. 1995)). Cohesiveness may also exist where the relevant misconduct is based on a uniform application of a policy. *Postawko*, 910 F.3d at 1040.

While the cohesiveness requirement of Rule 23(b)(2) is more stringent than the predominance and superiority requirements of Rule 23(b)(3), the Eighth Circuit generally finds that cohesiveness exists where predominance and superiority exist. *See Avritt*, 615 F.3d at 1036. Similarly, the Eighth Circuit generally finds that cohesiveness does not exist where predominance and superiority are lacking. *See id.*

Rule 23(b)(3) Classes

Rule 23(b)(3) classes are the most common type of classes litigated before the Eighth Circuit. Unsurprisingly, there is no shortage of case law in the Eighth Circuit concerning the requirements of Rule 23(b)(3). Predominance and superiority are the focus of Rule 23(b)(3).

Predominance

Predominance is usually the most contested element of class certification. Notably, while the commonality requirement is related to predominance and is "subsumed" within predominance, the predominance requirements are more demanding. *Meek v. Kansas City Life Ins. Co.*, 126 F.4th 577, 583 (8th Cir. 2025). To certify a class, the court must find that the questions of law or fact common to class members predominate over any questions affecting only individual members. Fed. R. Civ. P. 23(b)(3).

The ultimate purpose of a class action lawsuit is to "conserve the resources of the court and the parties by permitting an issue that may affect every class member to be litigated in an economical fashion." *Ebert v. General Mills, Inc.*, 823 F.3d 472, 477 (8th Cir. 2016). The predominance inquiry focuses on achieving this objective. *See id.* at 479–80.

When considering predominance, the court does not "conclude whether the theory of liability is viable." *Custom Hair Designs by Sandy v. Central Payment Co., LLC*, 984 F.3d 595, 601 (8th Cir. 2020). Rather, predominance is defeated "only if the theory of liability is a highly individualized question." *Id.*

The fundamental requirement of predominance is that the defendant's liability should be able to be established with common evidence rather than the court having to consider evidence of the circumstances of each class member's claim. *Avritt v. Reliastar Life Ins. Co.*, 615 F.3d 1023, 1029 (8th Cir. 2010); *Blades v. Monsanto Co.*, 400 F.3d 562, 566 (8th Cir. 2005); *see also Orduno v. Pietrzak*, 932 F.3d 710, 716 (8th Cir. 2019). Predominance is defeated where the evidence necessary to establish liability varies between class members. *Avritt,* 615 F.3d at 1029; *Blades*, 400 F.3d at 566–71; *Halvorson v. Auto-Owners Ins. Co.*, 718

F.3d 773, 778 (8th Cir. 2013). Predominance is satisfied where a prima facie showing of liability is based on the same evidence for each class member. *See id.*; *see also Perras v. H&R Block*, 789 F.3d 914, 916 (8th Cir. 2015). This requirement is necessary to avoid individual questions overwhelming questions common to the class. *Ebert*, 823 F.3d at 478–79) (quoting *Amgen, Inc. v. Conn. Ret. Plans and Trust Funds*, 133 S. Ct. 1184, 1196 (2013); *see also Webb v. Exxon Mobil Corp.*, 856 F.3d 1150, 1156–57 (8th Cir. 2017).

Defendants often argue that predominance is defeated because the class members are subject to affirmative defenses that require an individualized inquiry. However, the relevance of such defenses must be subjected to the same rigorous analysis as plaintiffs' claims. *In re Zurn Pex Plumbing Prods. Liab. Litig.*, 644 F.3d 604, 619 (8th Cir. 2011); *Barfield v. Sho-Me Power Elec. Coop.*, 852 F.3d 795, 806 (8th Cir. 2017). A defendant raising such arguments must therefore present evidence of the alleged defenses. *Barfield*, 852 F.3d at 806.

However, an affirmative defense can be used a basis to defeat predominance in a very narrow circumstance. That narrow circumstance is where the affirmative defense is unusually important to the case and requires the application of an individualized and subjective inquiry to each class member. *See Stuart v. Global Tel*Link Corp.*, 956 F.3d 555, 559–60 (8th Cir. 2020). While an affirmative defense could be used to defeat predominance in extremely limited circumstances, it is the defendant's burden to prove that an affirmative defense is a barrier to class certification.

When considering whether predominance is satisfied, the relevant question is not whether the plaintiffs have already proven their claims through common evidence, it is whether questions of law or fact capable of resolution through common evidence predominate over individual questions. *In re Zurn Pex Plumbing Prods. Liab. Litig.*, 644 F.3d at 619. To achieve this end, the district court must conduct a limited preliminary inquiry, looking behind the pleadings, to determine whether the general allegations are true, [whether] common evidence could suffice to make out a prima facie case for the class. *Blades*, 400 F.3d at 566; *In re Zurn Pex*, 644 F.3d at 619.

Ebert is an environmental contamination case that provides an excellent example of when predominance is defeated because a class action is not an efficient way for the court to adjudicate the case. The *Ebert* court held that liability could only be resolved by analyzing whether the contamination (if any) threatened or existed on each individual property and whether the contamination was caused by the defendant. *Id.* at 479. This analysis would not rely on common evidence but would require an individualized inquiry for each property as to the source of contamination for each property, whether features of the property make the property susceptible to contamination, whether each property is contaminated, and whether mitigation occurred at each property. *Id.* at 479. Ultimately, the individualized extent of inquiry for each property made the case unsuitable for class certification under Rule 23(b)(3). *Id.* at 480.

While *Ebert* provides a quintessential example of when predominance is defeated, the Eighth Circuit also provides guidance of other circumstances in which predominance is satisfied and defeated.

Predominance Is Satisfied Where Liability Derives from a Standard Form Contract That Is Governed by a Single State's Law

Predominance is satisfied in cases where liability derives from a standard form contract. Form contracts present a classic case for treatment as a class action. *McKeage v. TMBC, LLC*, 847 F.3d 992, 999 (8th Cir. 2017); *see also Stuart v. State Farm Fire and Cas. Co.*, 910 F.3d 371 (8th Cir. 2018) (predominance satisfied in a case based on a form contract governed by a single state's law). Notably, the language of the form contract in *McKeage* stated that Missouri law governed the transactions although many of the class members entered into the contracts outside Missouri. *McKeage*, 847 F.3d at 999. Thus, regardless of the state in which the contract was signed, it was proper for the district court to certify a nationwide class. *See id.*

The result in *McKeage* may have been different if the controlling law of each contract was based on the law of the state in which each contract was entered into. The Eighth Circuit has held that predominance is defeated where the law that applies to each class member's contract is dependent on the applicable law of each state of each class member. *Perras v. H&R Block*, 789 F.3d 914, 918 (8th Cir. 2015); *see also Webb v. Exxon Mobil Corp.*, 856 F.3d 1150, 1155–56 (8th Cir. 2017) (district court did not abuse its discretion in decertifying class where class membership would depend on analyzing multiple states' laws); *Hale v. Emerson Elec. Co.*, 942 F.3d 401, 403–04 (8th Cir. 2019).

The district court in *Perras* held that predominance was defeated because the district court would have to interpret all 50 states' consumer protection statutes to determine liability for the class members. *Perras*, 789 F.3d 914 at 918. The *Perras* court affirmed the district court's decision to deny class certification and held that questions of law common to the class members did not predominate over individual questions of law in such circumstances. *Id.*

In *Hale*, the Eighth Circuit reversed the trial court's order granting class certification for reasons like those set forth in *Perras*. *Hale*, 942 F.3d 401, 403–04. The defendant in *Hale* was alleged to have engaged in deceptive advertising from its Missouri headquarters. *Id.* at 402–03. The district court certified a nationwide class under Missouri's consumer protection statute because all the class members' claims would be governed by Missouri law. *Id.* at 402. The Eighth Circuit reversed and held common issues did not predominate. The court reached this conclusion because the only relevant action taking place in Missouri was the design of the advertisement and the laws of the states in which the transactions took place needed to be analyzed. *Id.* at 404.

The *Custom Hair Designs by Sandy v. Central Payment Co., LLC* case provides another good example of when predominance is satisfied. While the pricing terms and fees varied among the class members in *Custom Hair Designs by Sandy*, the relevant contract terms were uniform. *Custom Hair Designs by Sandy*, 984 F.3d 595, 601 (8th Cir. 2020). The Eighth Circuit therefore held predominance was satisfied because the misconduct at issue arose from the same contract.

Ultimately, predominance will be a more difficult hurdle if multiple states' laws need to be analyzed. However, if a single state's laws need to be analyzed, even for a nationwide class, the predominance may be readily satisfied.

Predominance Can Be Satisfied Even Where Class Members' Damage Amounts Vary

Class action practitioners should not confuse varying damages among class members or having to conduct individualized damage inquiries among class members to mean that common evidence cannot be used to establish liability. In other words, a class can be certified even if the class members' damages vary so long as common evidence can be used to establish the underlying liability. *Stuart v. State Farm Fire and Cas. Co.*, 910 F.3d 371, 376 (8th Cir. 2018) (liability based on form contracts); *Day v. Celadon Trucking Servs., Inc.*, 827 F.3d 817, 833–34 (8th Cir. 2016) (liability based on statutory violations).

Even an individualized inquiry regarding the amount of each class member's damages will not defeat predominance if the damages are based on the same operative law. *See id.* The *Day* court recognized that predominance was satisfied because liability was based on the same statute and that the plaintiff's damages model was consistent with its liability theory of the case. *Day*, 827 F.3d at 833. Thus, the *Day* court recognized that while the class members' damages varied, common evidence could be used to establish liability and class certification was proper. *Id.*

While the class members' damages varied in the *Ebert* case discussed earlier, predominance was not defeated because the class members had different damage amounts. Instead, unique evidence for each class member rather than common evidence would be required to establish liability. *Ebert v. General Mills, Inc.*, 823 F.3d 477, 480 (8th Cir. 2016). This is a critical distinction that should not be lost on class action practitioners.

Predominance Is Defeated If a Reasonableness Inquiry Must Be Made to Establish Liability

Predominance is not satisfied if liability for each class member depends on a "reasonableness" inquiry. *Avritt v. Reliastar Life Ins. Co.*, 615 F.3d 1023, 1031–32 (8th Cir. 2010); *Luiken v. Domino's Pizza, LLC*, 705 F.3d 370, 373–74, 377; *Halvorson v. Auto-Owners Ins. Co.*, 718 F.3d 773, 775–80 (8th Cir. 2013); *see also Powers v. Cred. Mgmt. Servs., Inc.*, 776 F.3d 567, 574–75 (8th Cir. 2015); *In re State Farm Fire and Cas. Co.*, 872 F.3d 567, 576 (8th Cir. 2017); *Stuart v. Global Tel*Link Corp.*, 956 F.3d 555, 560–61 (8th Cir. 2020). This is because a reasonableness inquiry often requires looking at the context and individual circumstances of each transaction. *See Luiken*, 705 F.3d at 374–78. The *Halvorson* and *Luiken* cases highlight these principles.

The plaintiff in *Halvorson* sought to certify a class based on an insurance company's failure to pay certain reasonable charges required by the company's policy. *Halvorson*, 718 F.3d at 775–76. The *Halvorson* court held that determining whether a charge was reasonable depended on a review of different injuries for class members and different medical providers charging different amounts for their services. *Id.* at 780. Predominance was therefore defeated because the reasonableness of any claim payment may have to be individually analyzed. *Id.*

Luiken is an example of when the Eighth Circuit looked at the evidence plaintiff needed to prove its case, rather than deciding the merits, to conclude that class certification was improper. *Luiken* involved a class of delivery drivers who alleged their employer violated a state statute by wrongfully withholding gratuities from them. *Luiken*, 705 F.3d at 372–73. The state statute relied upon by the plaintiff class required a reasonableness inquiry to determine whether the gratuity was wrongfully withheld as a payment for a personal service. *Id.* at 372–78. The *Luiken* court concluded that predominance was defeated because liability was dependent on the varied context of the transactions made it unreasonable for some customers to construe the delivery charges as a payment for personal services, thereby preventing one-stroke determination of a classwide question. *Id.* at 378.

Predominance Is Defeated If Liability Depends on Reliance or a Scienter Element

A class that requires each class member to prove reliance on a representation is not suitable for class certification. *See In re St. Jude Med., Inc.*, 522 F.3d 836, 838 (8th Cir. 2008); *see also Vogt v. Progressive Cas. Ins. Co.*, --F.4th--, 2025 WL 583348, at *1 (8th Cir. Feb. 24, 2025); *Johannessohn v. Polaris Indus., Inc.*, 9 F.4th 981, 985–86 (8th Cir. 2021); *Donelson v. Ameriprise Fin. Servs., Inc.*, 999 F.3d 1080, 1093 (8th Cir. 2021). This is because individual evidence, rather than common evidence, is necessary to make a prima facie case for the class. *In re Zurn Pex Plumbing Prods. Liab. Litig.*, 644 F.3d 604, 619 (quoting *Blades v. Monsanto Co.*, 400 F.3d 562, 566 (8th Cir. 2005)). In other words, predominance is defeated where reliance is required to establish liability because evidence varies between class members as to the representations that were made to the class member and the degree to which the class members relied on these representations. *In re St. Jude Med., Inc.*, 522 F.3d at 838.

The Eighth Circuit has also held that class certification is not proper if there is not a uniform causal connection between a defendant's misrepresentations and the class members' damages – even if reliance need not be proved. *Hudock v. LG Electronics of U.S.A., Inc.*, 12 F.4th 773, 776–77 (8th Cir. 2021). The plaintiffs in *Hudock* brought a class action lawsuit under various state consumer protection statutes. *Id.* at 775. The plaintiffs alleged defendant overstated the "refresh rate" for the televisions it sold. *Id.* While reliance was not required to establish the various state consumer protection claims, the *Hudock* court reversed the district court's order granting class certification. *Id.* The *Hudock* noted that the "refresh rate" was immaterial for certain consumers and other consumer did not see or rely on the misrepresentations. *Id.* at 777. As such, the *Hudock* court held that the "causal nexus between the alleged misrepresentations" and damages required individualized inquiries, meaning that common issues did not predominate. *Id.*

Moreover, predominance is defeated if a scienter requirement is necessary to establish liability. *See McCrary v. Stifel, Nicolaus & Co., Inc.*, 687 F.3d 1052, 1059 (8th Cir. 2012); *see also Orduno v. Pietrzak*, 932 F.3d 710, 716 (8th Cir. 2019) (predominance not satisfied where the statute required plaintiff to prove the defendant "knowingly" used personal information "for a purpose not permitted by law"). To establish liability, the plaintiff in *McCrary* needed to prove that a broker acted willfully and with reckless disregard for the interest of his or her clients. *McCrary*, 687 F.3d at 1059. As proving liability with a scienter requirement would require a highly individualized inquiry for each transaction at issue and also was dependent on the class members' reliance on the alleged misrepresentations, the *McCrary* court held that predominance was not satisfied. *Id.*

Superiority

To certify a Rule 23(b)(3) class, the district court must also find that a class action is superior to other available methods for fairly and efficiently adjudicating the controversy. Fed. R. Civ. P. 23(b)(3). Superiority may be satisfied where each class member's claim is small. For example, the Eighth Circuit found superiority to be satisfied where the class members' claims are generally small and unlikely to be pursued individually. *Stuart v. State Farm Fire and Cas. Co.*, 910 F.3d 371, 377 (8th Cir. 2018).

The Eighth Circuit suggests that it will consider the potential recovery to each class member in an individual case compared to a class case in determining whether a class action is the superior method the adjudicate the case. *See Powers v. Cred. Mgmt. Servs., Inc.*, 776 F.3d 567, 572 (8th Cir. 2015). The *Powers* court noted that a class action may not be superior to an individual case where total damages are capped by statute and each individual class member may have a stronger claim if they were to proceed individually. *Id.* This determination appears to address whether a class action is the superior method for fairly adjudicating the case compared to adjudicating the case individually as is required under the superiority analysis. *See id.*

The Eighth Circuit also considers the potential confusion to a jury and challenges in trial management when deciding whether the class action mechanism is the superior method by which to adjudicate a case. *See Johannessohn v. Polaris Indus., Inc.*, 9 F.4th 981, 986 (8th Cir. 2021). The *Johannessohn* court affirmed the trial court's decision that superiority was not satisfied because a jury would have to apply the laws of four different states to over 40 types of products. *Id.* The *Johannessohn* court held superiority was not satisfied because "the putative classes . . . seek to consolidate too many claims with too many variables" and the litigation would be "unmanageable." *Id.*

d. Manageability

The court also must consider the likely difficulties in managing a class action when determining whether class certification is proper. Fed. R. Civ. P. 23(b)(3)(D). The manageability analysis ultimately ties into the predominance and superiority requirements. *Barfield v. Sho-Me Power Elec. Coop.*, 852 F.3d 795, 806 (8th Cir. 2017) (quoting Fed. R. Civ. P. 23(b)(3)(D)).

The Eighth Circuit has provided examples of manageable and unmanageable cases. A case is not manageable when individualized issues frequently arise. *In re St. Jude Med., Inc.*, 425 F.3d 1116, 1121–22 (8th Cir. 2005). This is because there is little benefit from an efficiency standpoint in proceeding as a class action when the court must frequently address individual issues. *See id.* Also, a "fail-safe class," one that is defined to preclude membership unless the member prevails on the merits, is unmanageable "because the court cannot know to whom notice should be sent." *Orduno v. Pietrzak*, 932 F.3d 710, 716 (8th Cir. 2019); *Ford v. TD Ameritrade Holding Corp.*, 995 F.3d 616, 624 (8th Cir. 2021). On the other hand, a case is manageable where class membership is identified using forms and sworn statements. *Barfield*, 852 F.3d at 806.

e. Ascertainability

While ascertainability is not an explicit requirement of Rule 23, the Eighth Circuit requires that a class be adequately defined and clearly ascertainable. *Ihrke v. Northern States Power Co.*, 459 F.2d 566, 573 n.3 (8th Cir. 1972). The Eighth Circuit, however, does not follow the heightened ascertainability standard that has been adopted by other Circuits. *See Sandusky Wellness Ctr., LLC v. Medtox Scientific, Inc.*, 821 F.3d 992, 995–98 (8th Cir. 2016). To this end, ascertainability is not a separate, preliminary requirement in a class action case. *Id.* at 996. Rather, ascertainability is subject to the same rigorous analysis requirements of Rule 23. *Id.*

Ascertainability is satisfied if class membership can be determined by objective criteria. *Id.* at 996–98. The ascertainability requirement has been found to be satisfied where reviewing a defendant's files according to objective criteria identifies class members. *McKeage v. TMBC, LLC*, 847 F.3d 992, 999 (8th Cir. 2017). For example, ascertainability has been held to be satisfied where objective criteria identified the phone numbers that received a fax in violation of the Telephone Consumer Protection Act. *Sandusky Wellness Ctr., LLC*, 821 F.3d at 996–98.

4. CLASS NOTICE

a. Notice of a Class Action Lawsuit and Intervention Issues

Rule 23(d)(1) permits a court to issue various orders to protect class members. Fed. R. Civ. P. 23(d)(1)(B). The most typical order a court issues under this rule is an order requiring notice of the class action lawsuit be provided to the class members. The notice should provide the class members an opportunity to advise the court if they believe class counsel's representation is fair and adequate, an opportunity to intervene in the case and present claims or to otherwise become part of the case. Fed. R. Civ. P. 23(d)(1)(B)(iii). The notice should also advise that a class member may enter an appearance through an attorney if the member so desires. Fed. R. Civ. P. 23(c)(2)(B)(iv).

The Eighth Circuit looks to Federal Rule 24 to determine whether to permit a class member to intervene as a matter of right. *See Swinton v. SquareTrade, Inc.*, 960 F.3d 1001, 1004 (8th Cir. 2020) (citing Fed. R. Civ. P. 24(a)); *Nat'l Parks Conservation Ass'n v. United State Envtl. Prot. Agency*, 759 F.3d 969, 975 (8th Cir. 2014). Thus, the court must permit anyone to intervene who (1) files a timely motion to intervene; (2) 'claims an interest relating to the property or transaction that is the subject of the action'; (3) is situated so that disposing of the action may, as a practical matter, impair or impede the movant's ability to protect that interest; and (4) is not adequately represented by the existing parties. *Id.*

Allowing a class member who contests the adequacy of the class representative and/or class counsel to represent the class to opt out of the class is not a sufficient reason to deny a class member's request to intervene in the case. *Smith v. SEECO, Inc.*, 865 F.3d 1021, 1024–25 (8th Cir. 2017). Otherwise, the notice requirement of Rule 23(c)(2)(B)(iv) which advises the class member that they may enter an appearance in the case would be rendered meaningless. *See id.*

The notice requirement, however, does not mean that the court must always allow a class member to intervene in the case. *See Smith v, SEECO, Inc.*, 922 F.3d 398, 403 (8th Cir. 2019) (noting district court denied motion to intervene based on adequacy concerns and Eighth Circuit denied mandamus) (decision affirmed on other grounds). Thus, while unsettled, the Eighth Circuit may allow district courts to deny motions to intervene in certain circumstances.

The Eighth Circuit recently affirmed a district court's denial of a class member's motion to intervene. *See Swinton*, 960 F.3d 1001. The *Swinton* case provides a good framework for how the Eighth Circuit analyzes motions to intervene in class action cases.

The plaintiff in *Swinton* filed a class action complaint concerning the defendant's business practices. *Id.* at 1003. The plaintiff's complaint was nearly identical to a previous class action lawsuit filed by the intervenor. *Id.* The plaintiff settled the case, and the intervenor's case was made part of the settlement class. *Id.* The intervenor sought to intervene alleging, among other things, that the plaintiff was an inadequate representative because the plaintiff did not oppose the defendant's motion to compel arbitration and because the plaintiff allegedly used his case as a reverse auction to settle the case for a lesser amount. *Id.* at 1005–06.

The *Swinton* court determined that there was no dispute the first two Rule 24(a) elements were satisfied and that the third element was also satisfied. The third element was determined to be satisfied because the class member's interest would be resolved by the settlement. *Id.* The *Swinton* court therefore recognized that simply because the class member could opt out of the settlement did not mean the class member's interests could not be adversely affected. *Id.* (citing *Smith v. SEECO, Inc.*, 865 F.3d 1021, 1024–25 (8th Cir. 2017)). As the class member's interests could be adversely affected, the third element was satisfied.

Ultimately, the *Swinton* court held that intervention was not proper because the class representative adequately represented the intervening class member's interests. *Id.* at 1005. The *Swinton* court reached this conclusion for multiple reasons.

First, the court noted it must presume there is adequate representation when the persons attempting to intervene are members of a class already involved in the litigation. *Id.* (quoting *Jenkins by Jenkins v. Missouri*, 78 F.3d 1270, 1275 (8th Cir. 1996)). Thus, because the intervenor was intervening as a class member and not as a class representative, the court presumed the plaintiff was an adequate class representative. *Id.* Second, the *Swinton* court noted that a difference of opinion as to litigation strategy did not overcome the presumption of adequate representation. Third, the court noted that while a collusive reverse auction would satisfy the inadequate representation prong, the intervenor did not provide sufficient evidence of a collusive reverse auction. *Id.* The Eighth Circuit therefore affirmed the district court's order denying the motion to intervene.

b. Notice of Settlement

Rule 23(e) provides that the court must direct notice [of a proposed settlement] in a reasonable manner to all class members who would be bound by the proposal. Fed. R. Civ. P. 23(e). The driving purpose of this requirement is due process—that is, giving the settlement class members proper notice of the settlement and a fair opportunity to voice their objections to the settlement. *See Grunin v. Int'l House of Pancakes*, 513 F.2d 114, 120–21 (8th Cir. 1975); *DeBoer v. Mellon Mortg. Co.*, 64 F.3d 1171, 1176 (8th Cir. 1995). There is no formula for what constitutes proper notice. Rather, the notice must be the best practical notice under the circumstances. *Pollard v. Remington Arms Co., LLC*, 896 F.3d 900, 905 (8th Cir. 2018).

District courts are afforded great discretion as to how to direct class notice appropriately to the settlement class members. *See id.; see also Jones v. Monsanto Co.*, 38 F.4th 693, 698 (8th Cir. 2022). Notice to the settlement class members has been held to be proper if the class members are notified by mail and through a printing in a national publication. *DeBoer*, 64 F.3d at 1176. However, notice by mail alone may be sufficient notice if publication notice would not be productive. *Grunin*, 64 F.3d at 121–22. The Eighth Circuit has held that class notice is sufficient even if it does not provide all the details of the settlement so long as the notice provides sufficient information to the class members to make a determination as to whether they should object to the settlement. *In re UnitedHealth Grp., Inc. S'holder Derivative Litig.*, 631 F.3d 913, 917–18 (8th Cir. 2011).

The Rule 23(e) class notice requirement may be satisfied even if there is a low claim submission rate if the best practical notice under the circumstances is provided to the class. *Pollard*, 896 F.3d at 905 (approving notice with a claim rate of 0.29%); *Keil v. Lopez*, 862 F.3d 685, 697 (8th Cir. 2017) (noting that a claim rate of 3 percent is not unusual in consumer class actions "and does not suggest unfairness");.*see also* Fed. R. Civ. P. 23(c)(2)(B) (for settlement purposes, the court must direct to class members the best notice that is practicable under the circumstances).

Pollard provides a good example of an acceptable notice plan that resulted in a low claims rate. The parties in *Pollard* submitted multiple notices of settlement in *Pollard*. *Id.* at 904–05. Notice was initially provided through a press release, direct notice, short form notice, long form notice, notice through a settlement website and via social media and the internet. *Id.* at 904. The initial notice resulted in a claim submission rate of 0.1%. *Id.* at 905. In light of the low claim rate, the district court directed the parties to provide supplemental notice via a targeted social media campaign, a targeted radio campaign, e-mail notification to certain class members, additional postcard mailings and posters being displayed at various retailers. *Id.* While the claim submission rate at the time of final approval was only 0.29% the *Pollard* court affirmed the district court's approval of the settlement and the notice provided to class members because the notice was the best practical notice under the circumstances. *Id.*

Pollard also establishes that the Eighth Circuit will consider the practical reasons for a low claim submission rate. For example, the benefit to class members could be *de minimis*, thereby reducing the incentive for class members to make claims. *Id.* at 906 n.2. Perhaps a class member might not believe the effort needed to submit a claim is worth their time. *Id.* at 906. Or perhaps a class member does not want to reveal their class membership to others for privacy reasons. *Id. Pollard* ultimately teaches that a low claim submission rate does not necessarily mean class notice is inadequate.

5. SETTLEMENTS

The Eighth Circuit gives considerable deference to a district court's decision to approve a settlement, even over a class member's objections. *See generally Marshall v. Nat'l Football League*, 787 F.3d 502, 508 (8th Cir. 2015). This deference is reflected in the Eighth Circuit's precedent concerning the approval of class action settlements.

a. Approval of Settlements

Class action settlement agreements are presumed to be valid. *In re Uponor, Inc., F1807 Plumbing Fittings Prods. Liab. Litig.*, 716 F.3d 1057, 1063 (8th Cir. 2013). Approval of class action settlements are guided by the principle that a class action settlement is a private contract negotiated between the parties. *In re Wireless Tel. Fed. Cost Recovery Fees Litig.*, 396 F.3d 922, 934 (8th Cir. 2005); *Marshall v. Nat'l Football League*, 787 F.3d 502, 509 (8th Cir. 2015). The Eighth Circuit's role in reviewing a class action settlement is to ensure that the agreement is not the product of fraud or collusion and that, taken as a whole, it is fair, adequate and reasonable to all concerned. *Id.*

District courts are afforded great discretion in approving class action settlements and a district court's decision to approve a settlement will only be reversed if the court abuses its discretion. *See generally Pollard v. Remington Arms Co., LLC*, 896 F.3d 900, 907 (8th Cir. 2018); *Keil v. Lopez*, 862 F.3d 685, 693 (8th Cir. 2017); *In re BankAmerica Corp. Sec. Litig.*, 350 F.3d 747, 752 (8th Cir. 2003); *Elliott v. Sperry Rand Corp.*, 680 F.2d 1225, 1227 (8th Cir. 1982). The district court is afforded great discretion because the district court is in the best position to evaluate the settlement as it is intimately familiar with the case. *Id.*

A district court, however, can only approve a class action settlement that is fair, reasonable and adequate. Fed. R. Civ. P. 23(e)(2); *see generally Grunin v. Int'l House of Pancakes*, 513 F.2d 114, 123 (8th Cir. 1975). District courts must consider numerous factors before determining whether a settlement is fair, reasonable, and adequate. These factors include the merits of the plaintiff's case, weighed against the terms of the settlement; the defendant's financial condition; the complexity and expense of further litigation; and the amount of opposition to the settlement. *See generally Van Horn v. Trickey*, 840 F.2d 604,

607 (8th Cir. 1988).

The Merits of Plaintiff's Case Weighed Against the Terms of the Settlement

The merits of the plaintiff's case weighed against the terms of the settlement is the most important factor in determining whether the settlement is fair, reasonable, and adequate. *See generally Van Horn v. Trickey*, 840 F.2d 604, 607 (8th Cir. 1988). This factor strongly supports approval of a settlement in circumstances in which the law concerning the viability of the underlying legal theory is uncertain. *DeBoer v. Mellon Mortg. Co.*, 64 F.3d 1171, 1177 (8th Cir. 1995).

DeBoer concerned a case in which there was a circuit split regarding the legal viability of the underlying cause of action. *Id.* There also was a recent district court decision that dismissed a similar cause of action that likewise was the basis of the underlying legal theory in *DeBoer*. *Id.* Therefore, the *DeBoer* court held that these facts weighed in favor of approving the settlement because of the uncertainty of the viability of the underlying legal theory of the case. *Id.*

Moreover, this factor supports approval of a settlement where there are potential difficulties: establishing damages for each class member, establishing manageability, defeating statute of limitation issues, establishing causation or establishing standing. *See In re Target Corp. Customer Data Sec. Breach Litig.*, 892 F.3d 968, 978 (8th Cir. 2018); *Keil v. Lopez*, 862 F.3d 685, 695 (8th Cir. 2017), *Pollard*, 896 F.3d at 907.

The Defendant's Financial Condition

While the defendant's financial condition is a factor to be considered by the district court when deciding whether a class action settlement should be approved, it is not usually a significant factor in the court's approval analysis. For instance, the fact that a defendant could pay more than it is required to pay under the terms of the settlement is not a sufficient basis, standing alone, for a district court to disapprove of a settlement. *Petrovic v. Amoco Oil Co.*, 200 F.3d 1140, 1152 (8th Cir. 1999). The defendant's financial condition is a neutral factor if its financial condition is stable. *See Huyer v. Njema*, 847 F.3d 934, 939 (8th Cir. 2017); *see also In re Target Corp. Customer Data Sec. Breach Litig.*, 892 F.3d 968, 978 (8th Cir. 2018). Logically, this factor also is likely to weigh in favor of approval if the defendant is in financial straits.

The Complexity and Expense of Further Litigation

The Eighth Circuit recognizes that class actions place an enormous burden on costs and expense upon the parties. *Schmidt v. Fuller Brush Co.*, 527 F.3d 532, 535 (8th Cir. 1975). Thus, the complexity and expense of further litigation factor is unlikely to weigh against approval of a settlement.

While this factor is unlikely to weigh against approval of a settlement, several circumstances support approval of a settlement. The prospect of a lengthy and costly trial or extensive litigation supports approval. *Huyer v. Njema*, 847 F.3d 934, 939 (8th Cir. 2017). Cases involving multiple complex legal issues support approval. *Marshall v. Nat'l Football League*, 787 F.3d 502, 512–13 (8th Cir. 2015); *In re Target Corp. Customer Data Sec. Breach Litig.*, 892 F.3d 968, 978 (8th Cir. 2018). Cases that potentially involve lengthy appeals that could delay the case for many years also support approval. *See In re Wireless Tel. Fed. Cost Recovery Fees Litig.*, 396 F.3d 922, 933 (8th Cir. 2005).

The Amount of Opposition to the Settlement

The amount of opposition to the settlement also is unlikely to weigh against approval of a settlement. The Eighth Circuit recognizes that district courts have a duty to the silent majority as well as the vocal minority when approving a settlement. *See In re Wireless Tel. Fed. Cost Recovery Fees Litig.*, 396 F.3d 922, 933 (8th Cir. 2005). Eighth Circuit precedent is consistent with this principle.

The Eighth Circuit has affirmed approval of settlements where a significant percentage of the class objected to the settlement. For example, the Eighth Circuit affirmed approval of a settlement where 45 percent of the class members objected to the settlement. *Van Horn*, 840 F.2d at 606–08. It also has affirmed approval of a settlement where all the named plaintiffs objected to the settlement and 26 percent of the class members objected to the settlement. *Elliott*, 680 F.2d at 1226–28. Unsurprisingly, the Eighth Circuit also has affirmed approval of settlements with smaller percentages of objections. *Petrovic v. Amoco Oil Co.*, 200 F.3d 1140, 1152 (8th Cir. 1999) (fewer than 4 percent of class members objecting); *Marshall v. Nat'l Football League*, 787 F.3d 502, 513–14 (8th Cir. 2015) (less than 10 percent opted out and less than one-tenth of 1 percent objected to the settlement); *Keil v. Lopez*, 862 F.3d 685, 698 (8th Cir. 2017) (approving settlement where 14 class members out of 105,173 claimants objected).

b. Objectors

Article III Standing, Mootness, and Appellate Standing

A person or an entity objecting to a class action settlement must satisfy Article III standing requirements. *Huyer v. Van de Voorde*, 847 F.3d 983, 986 (8th Cir. 2017). To satisfy Article III standing requirements, an objector must sustain an injury in fact resulting from the proposed settlement. *Id.* An objector lacks Article III standing if the objector is not a member of a subclass that is impacted by the objection or where the relief requested by the objector would decrease the objector's compensation or relief. *Id.* at 986–87.

Similarly, if the objection at issue does not come to fruition in the settlement, then the objection may be moot. *In re Gen. Am. Life Ins. Co. Sales Practices Litig.*, 302 F.3d 799, 901 (8th Cir. 2002). For example, the objector in *In re Gen. Am. Life Ins. Co. Sales Practices Litig.* challenged the fairness of the settlement because the settlement authorized certain claims to receive a zero score, which would entitle the class member to zero compensatory relief. *Id.* The claims administrator, however, submitted an affidavit to the court stating that no class members received a zero score. *Id.* Thus, the objection was deemed moot because the issue presented by the objection never came to fruition. *Id.*

Standing, however, is not a significant hurdle for an objector to overcome. An objector may have standing based on a potential harm. For example, a class member has standing where he or she alleges they would have obtained a more favorable result than the settlement provided. *See Rawa v. Monsanto Co.*, 934 F.3d 862, 867–68 (8th Cir. 2019); *Keil v. Lopez*, 862 F.3d 685, 699 (8th Cir. 2017).

An objector must not only satisfy Article III's standing requirements but also have appellate standing. An objector who fails to object to a settlement timely in accordance with a district court's order waives his or her right to appeal the settlement agreement. *In re UnitedHealth Grp., Inc. S'holder Derivative Litig.*, 631 F.3d 913, 916–17 (8th Cir. 2011). The objector in the *UnitedHealth* case filed an objection 20 days after the objection deadline and less than 24 hours before the settlement hearing. *Id.* at 917. The Eighth Circuit affirmed the district court's holding that the objection was untimely and concluded that the objector therefore waived his right to appeal the district court's order. *Id.* at 916–17.

Appeal Bonds

One strategy class action practitioners use to prevent an objection from going through the appellate process (thereby significantly delaying the case) is to request that the district court require the objector to post a large appeal bond that accounts for the resulting delay of the case. However, the Eighth Circuit only requires an objector to post an appeal bond that covers the direct costs of the appeal. *In re Target Corp. Customer Data Sec. Breach Litig.*, 847 F.3d 608, 615 (8th Cir. 2017). Direct or recoverable costs are costs permitted by an applicable statute or federal rule. *Id.* at 614–15.

The costs of delay of a case are not typically authorized by statute and are not authorized by federal rule. Thus, an objector is not required to post an appeal bond that represents the costs associated with the delay of the case while it is being decided on appeal. *Id.*; *see also In re Uponor, Inc., F1807 Plumbing Fittings Prods. Liab. Litig.*, 716 F.3d 1057, 1062 (8th Cir.

2013).

Due Process
Objectors are provided appropriate due process if they are given an opportunity to be heard at the settlement approval hearing and have an opportunity to submit memoranda and argument to the district court concerning the fairness of the settlement. *DeBoer v. Mellon Mortg. Co.*, 64 F.3d 1171, 1176 (8th Cir. 1995); *In re U.S. Bancorp Litig.*, 291 F.3d 1035, 1038 (8th Cir. 2002). A due process objection may be considered waived on appeal if the objector reiterates their objections to the settlement on appeal. *Id.*

c. Attorneys' Fees

The Eighth Circuit affords great deference to a district court's award of attorneys' fees. The district court's award will be reversed only if the award constitutes an abuse of discretion. *See Petrovic v. Amoco Oil Co.*, 200 F.3d 1140, 1156 (8th Cir. 1999). The court should simply provide a concise but clear explanation of its reasons for the fee award. *Rawa v. Monsanto Co.*, 934 F.3d 862, 870 (8th Cir. 2019) (internal quotation and citation omitted); *see also Vines v. Welspun Pipes, Inc.*, 2023 WL 4247395, at *1–2 (June 29, 2023) (unpublished opinion) (affirming district court's order awarding $1 in attorney fees because of counsel's improper conduct where the court provided an explanation for its award).

The district court also is given great latitude to determine whether the amount of attorneys' fees is determined through a lodestar or percentage of the benefit approach. *In re Life Time Fitness, Inc., Tel. Consumer Protection Act (TCPA) Litig.*, 847 F.3d 619, 622–23 (8th Cir. 2017); *Galloway v. Kansas City Landsmen, LLC*, 833 F.3d 969, 972–73 (8th Cir. 2016). Notably, a district court is not required to use a lodestar cross-check if a percentage of the fund methodology is used. *See In re Life Time Fitness, Inc., Tel. Consumer Protection Act (TCPA) Litig.*, 847 F.3d at 623 (citing *Petrovic*, 200 F.3d at 1157). The determination to use a lodestar or percentage of the benefit approach is a decision ultimately made by the court, not class counsel. *Galloway*, 833 F.3d at 973.

The Eighth Circuit has affirmed significant fee awards. It has affirmed an attorneys' fee award of 36 percent of a settlement fund. *In re U.S. Bancorp Litig.*, 291 F.3d 1035, 1038 (8th Cir. 2002). It also has suggested that a 38 percent fee award would not be unreasonable in a case in which it awarded 33 percent of the settlement fund. *Huyer v. Buckley*, 849 F.3d 395, 399 (8th Cir. 2017). The *Huyer* court further noted that courts "have frequently awarded attorneys' fees ranging up to 36%." *Id.* These percentages do not appear to be dependent on the amount of the attorneys' fees awarded as the Eighth Circuit also has approved an attorneys' fee award of $20 million, which amounted to 33 percent of the settlement fund. *Caligiuri v. Symantec Corp.*, 855 F.3d 860, 865–66 (8th Cir. 2017). Notably, the Eighth Circuit recently held that it would not require courts to "award a reduced percentage in megafund cases." *In re T-Mobile Customer Data Sec. Breach Litig.*, 111 F.4th 849, 860 (8th Cir. 2024). Rather than adopting such a "per se" rule, the Eighth Circuit holds that fee awards should be determined by the propriety of the fee based on "case-specific circumstances." *Id.*

The district court also is given deference as to what is included as part of the benefit in calculating the percentage of the benefit approach. For example, a district court does not abuse its discretion by including the cost of class administration as part of the benefit. *In re Life Time Fitness, Inc., Tel. Consumer Protection Act (TCPA) Litig.*, 847 F.3d at 623; *Huyer*, 849 F.3d at 398; *In re Target Corp. Customer Data Sec. Breach Litig.*, 892 F.3d 968, 976 (8th Cir. 2018).

Moreover, a district court may even account for work performed in prior-related litigation in awarding attorneys' fees. *Jones v. Monsanto Co.*, 38 F.4th 693, 700–01 (8th Cir. 2022); *see also Miller v. Dugan*, 764 F.3d 826, 832 (8th Cir. 2014). A district court may consider such work if the work resulted in work product used in the current case and the time is sufficiently connected to the issues in the current case. *Jones*, 28 F.4th at 700–01. Moreover, a court may look favorably upon this approach where the current case avoids a duplication of efforts from the prior case. *Id.*

However, a district court may abuse its discretion if it orders attorneys' fees to be paid from a common fund where a contractual fee-shifting provision exists. *McKeage v. TMBC, LLC*, 847 F.3d 992, 1002–04 (8th Cir. 2017). Requiring fees to be paid strictly from a common fund without considering the contractual fee-shifting provision may be improper because it nullifies the class members' contractual right to recover attorneys' fees as the prevailing party. *Id.* at 1004. The same principle also applies regarding costs. *McKeage v. Bass Pro Outdoor World, LLC*, 943 F.3d 1148, 1152 (8th Cir. 2019).

Of course, some district courts exercise their discretion to calculate fees using the lodestar approach. A district court that elects to use a lodestar approach, however, must first give class counsel a fair opportunity to submit their time records before making a fee award. *Johnston v. Comerica Mortg. Corp.*, 83 F.3d 241, 247 (8th Cir. 1996). Failing to do so may constitute reversible error. *See id.* Moreover, a court using the lodestar approach may commit reversible error by considering the number of hours reasonably worked and the applicable rate. *See Vines v. Welspun Pipes, Inc.*, 9 F.4th 849, 855–56 (8th Cir. 2021).

A lodestar crosscheck "is sometimes warranted to double-check the result of the percentage of the fund method." *Petrovic*, 200 F.3d at 1157. A lodestar crosscheck is particularly helpful "when a megafund case settles quickly given the potential for a windfall." *In re T-Mobile Customer Data Sec. Breach Litig.*, 111 F.4th at 862. For example, the *T-Mobile* court held that a 9.6 multiplier was too high in light of the quick settlement achieved and the relatively little work performed on the case.

While considerable deference is given to a district court's award of fees, the Eighth Circuit suggests that settlement provisions with clear sailing provisions concerning attorneys' fees should be subject to more scrutiny. *See Galloway*, 833 F.3d at 971 n.1. A clear sailing provision is a provision in which a defendant agrees not to contest a plaintiff's request for attorneys' fees (or other monetary awards) up to a certain amount. *Id.* While clear sailing provisions are subject to more scrutiny, they are not per se unlawful. *See In re Target Corp. Customer Data Sec. Breach Litig.*, 892 F.3d 968, 979 (8th Cir. 2018). Clear sailing provisions are closely scrutinized because they heighten the potential for class action settlement abuse as they present the opportunity for class counsel to trade relief for the class for their own benefit. *Id.* at 971 n.1.

d. Costs

Like its analysis of a district court's award of attorneys' fees, the Eighth Circuit also affords great deference to the district court's determination as to what costs may be awarded to class counsel. *In re UnitedHealth Grp., Inc. S'holder Derivative Litig.*, 631 F.3d 913, 918 (8th Cir. 2011). For example, it is not an abuse of discretion for a district court to award class counsel online research costs as part of a negotiated settlement. *Id.* at 919.

e. Class Representative Service Awards

A trial court's award of a class representative service award is also given considerable deference. Such awards are reviewed for an abuse of discretion. *See generally Caligiuri v. Symantic Corp.*, 855 F.3d 860, 867 (8th Cir. 2017); *McDonald v. Edward D. Jones & Co., L.P.*, 791 F. App'x 638, 640 (8th Cir. 2020) (unpublished opinion). Notably, the fact that a class representative receives a service award does not generally create a conflict of interest between the representative and the class members. *McDonald*, 791 F. App'x at 640.

f. *Cy Pres*

The term *cy pres* derives from the French expression *cy pres comme possible*, which means as near as possible. *In re Airline Ticket Comm'n Antitrust Litig.*, 268 F.3d 619, 625 (8th Cir. 2001) (internal quotation and citation omitted). The doctrine originated as a rule of construction to save a testamentary charitable gift that would otherwise fail, allowing the next best use of the funds. *Id.*

Cy pres is traditionally used only in a class action case to distribute unused or unclaimed funds where class members are difficult to identify or where they change constantly. *Powell v. Georgia-Pacific Corp.*, 119 F.3d 703, 706 (8th Cir. 1997). The Eighth Circuit keeps the meaning and purpose of *cy pres* in mind when determining whether a *cy pres* distribution is appropriate. Importantly, *cy pres* terms are to be given controlling effect when they are part of a settlement agreement approved by the district court. *Rawa v. Monsanto Co.*, 934 F.3d 862, 871 (8th Cir. 2019).

Cy Pres Distributions Are Not Proper If It Is Feasible to Make Additional Distributions to the Class Members

Cy pres distributions must be made only if it is not feasible to make further distributions to the class members. *In re BankAmerica Sec. Litig.*, 775 F.3d 1060, 1064–65 (8th Cir. 2015). Additional distributions to the class members are feasible where the administrative cost is minimal compared to the amount of the remaining benefit and it is not difficult to identify and locate the class members to whom the distributions will be made. *Id.*

Making additional distributions, however, does not necessarily require that class members "receive the full amount of unliquidated damages claimed in the complaint before *cy pres* distribution." *Jones v. Monsanto Co.*, 38 F.4th 693, 699 (8th Cir. 2022). Rather, when damages are unliquidated, and the parties disagree on liability and damages, the distribution class members are entitled to receive is the amount each class member would be entitled to receive under the settlement. *Id.*

Cy Pres Need Not Be Excluded from the Value of the Settlement When Calculating Attorneys' Fees from a Common Fund

In a common fund settlement, the amount of *cy pres* need not be excluded from the value of the settlement for purposes of calculating the attorneys' fees. *Jones*, 38 F.4th at 700. This is because the *cy pres* amounts were made available to the class. In other words, there is no fault of class counsel for class members in a claims-made settlement not submitting enough claims to exhaust the fund. *Id.*

The District Court Must Thoroughly Investigate Whether the Cy Pres Recipient Is the Next Best Recipient of the Settlement Funds

A *cy pres* distribution must be made to a recipient who is tailored to the interests of the class and the purposes of the underlying litigation. *In re BankAmerica Sec. Litig.*, 775 F.3d 1060, 1067 (8th Cir. 2015). In other words, the *cy pres* recipient should relate directly to the lawsuit at issue and ultimately settled by the parties. *In re Airline Ticket Comm'n Antitrust Litig.*, 307 F.3d 679, 683 (8th Cir. 2002). This means that the district court must analyze and determine that the *cy pres* recipient is the next best recipient of the funds, after the class members. *In re BankAmerica Sec. Litig.*, 775 F.3d at 1067. Ideally, the recipient's interests will be related to the issues presented in the case. *See id.*

The court must conduct a thorough investigation to determine whether the *cy pres* recipient is appropriate. *Id.* The investigation should consider whether the distribution will benefit the geographic region in which the class members reside or will benefit those in the origin of the nationwide class. *Powell*, 119 F.3d at 706–07; *In re Airline Ticket Comm'n Antitrust Litig.*, 268 F.3d at 626.

6. APPEALING CLASS CERTIFICATION-RELATED ORDERS

a. Rule 23(f) Appeals of Class Certification Orders

A party may appeal a district court's order granting or denying class certification within 14 days of the order being entered (45 days if the United States is a party). Fed. R. Civ. P. 23(f). Being an interlocutory order, there is no right to appeal a district court's class certification order. Rather, Rule 23(f) allows a party to seek permission to appeal the order. *Id.* This is commonly referred to as a 23(f) petition or appeal.

The appeal of a class certification order is narrow and is limited the propriety of the district court's decision to certify the class. *Postawko v. Mo. Dep't of Corrections*, 910 F.3d 1030, 1041 (8th Cir. 2018). A 23(f) appeal must therefore not include challenges to the underlying merits of the case. *Id.*

Class action practitioners should be aware that the 14-day period to petition for permission to appeal a district court's class certification order is strictly enforced. *In re Wholesale Grocery Prods. Litig.*, 849 F.3d 761, 766 (8th Cir. 2017). Rule 23(f) only applies to orders granting or denying class certification, not motions to reconsider a prior class certification ruling. *See id.* (holding the court had no discretion to consider a Rule 23(f) petition because Rule 23(f) did not apply to the district court's order denying a request to consider certifying a narrower class). This is because expanding the applicability of Rule 23(f) to such motions would render the 14-day requirement of Rule 23(f) meaningless. However, Rule 23(f) may apply where the court modifies its class certification order to expand a previously defined class. *Glover v. Standard Fed. Bank*, 283 F.3d 953, 958–59 (8th Cir. 2002).

b. Appealing Orders Denying Motions to Intervene

As earlier discussed, class members may move to intervene in the case. Class action practitioners should be aware of appellate issues that arise when the district court denies a class member's motion to intervene. The Eighth Circuit reviews a district court's intervention determination under a *de novo* standard of review. *Swinton v. SquareTrade, Inc.*, 960 F.3d 1001, 1003 (8th Cir. 2020). The intervenor's allegations are accepted as true and construes the motion in favor of the prospective intervenor. *Id.* at 1003–04 (internal quotation and citation omitted).

Class members whose motions to intervene in a case are denied have 30 days to appeal the order denying the motion to intervene. *Smith v. SEECO, Inc.*, 922 F.3d 398, 404–05 (8th Cir. 2019). The appealing party must also have Article III standing to pursue the appeal. *Id.* at 404 n.4. For example, a person who opts out of a class lacks Article III standing to challenge a court's order denying a motion to intervene because they are not negatively affected by the ruling.

c. Appealing Class Certification Orders as Part of an Appeal of a Final Judgment

A court's ruling on class certification can be appealed as part of an appeal of a final judgment. *Vogt v. State Farm Life Ins. Co.*, 963 F.3d 753, 765–66 (8th Cir. 2020). While a court's final judgment is separate from a court's ruling on class certification, the Eighth Circuit considers a trial court's class certification ruling to be appealable because it is a predicate to the underlying judgment. *Id.* This is because an appeal of a final judgment is understood to bring up for review all the previous rulings and orders that led up to and served as a final predicate for [the] final judgment. *Id.* (internal quotation and citation omitted). The Eighth Circuit therefore considers a ruling on class certification as serving as a predicate for a final judgment.

7. DISMISSAL OF CLASS ACTIONS

A case in which a class has been certified may only be voluntarily dismissed with the court's approval. Fed. R. Civ. P. 23(e). This is a different requirement than the voluntary dismissal standards set forth in Rule 41. Rule 41 allows a case to be voluntarily dismissed without a court order in certain circumstances such as when all parties sign and file a stipulation for dismissal. Fed. R. Civ. P. 41(e)(1)(A)(ii). However, it is critical for class action practitioners to remember that the Rule 23(e) requirement for court approval of dismissal *only* applies when a class has been certified.

The Eighth Circuit addressed the applicability of Rule 23(e)'s voluntary dismissal standards in *Adams v. USAA Cas. Ins. Co.*, 863 F.3d 1069 (8th Cir. 2017). The plaintiffs in *Adams* filed a class action lawsuit in state court and the defendants removed the case to federal court. *Id.* at 1073. The parties litigated the case in federal court, mediated the case multiple times and eventually agreed to settlement terms. *Id.* The parties agreed as part of the settlement to file a joint stipulation to dismiss the federal court case and seek approval of the settlement in state court. *Id.* The federal district court entered the dismissal order. *Id.* at 1074. Notably, the federal court had not certified a class when its dismissal order was entered.

The federal district court learned about the state court settlement shortly after the state court granted final approval of the settlement. *Id.* The district court entered an order imposing Rule 11 sanctions against plaintiffs' and defendants' counsel because the court believed counsel were improperly forum shopping and had improperly used federal jurisdiction as a bargaining chip in their negotiations. *Id.* at 1075.

The *Adams* court reversed the district court's order imposing sanctions. The *Adams* court noted that many courts held that where no class has been certified, voluntary dismissal of a putative class action is governed not by Rule 23, but by Rule 41. *Id.* at 1082. Moreover, the *Adams* court held that CAFA did not dictate a different result. *Id.* As such, counsels' conduct was not sanctionable because they had a strong argument that voluntary dismissal of a case not yet certified was governed by Rule 41, which permits parties to stipulate dismissing the case without the court's approval. *Id* at 1083.

8. TOLLING THE STATUTE OF LIMITATIONS

The U.S. Supreme Court allows the tolling of the statute of limitations for class members' claims when the putative class members are included or proposed to be included in a class action that is not permitted to proceed as a class action. *American Pipe & Const. Co. v. Utah*, 414 U.S. 538 (1974). Specifically, the *American Pipe* court held that "the commencement of a class action suspends the applicable statute of limitations as to all asserted members of the class who would have been parties had the suit been permitted to continue as a class action." *Id.* at 554. The Supreme Court has since clarified that the *American Pipe* rule does not allow the tolling of successive class actions. *See China Agritech, Inc. v. Resh*, 138 S. Ct. 1800 (2019). The Eighth Circuit has not yet had an opportunity to apply *China Agritech*.

Ultimately, a plaintiff is entitled to tolling until there is a class certification ruling that "definitively excludes" the plaintiff from the class sought to be certified. *DeGeer v. Union Pac. R.R. Co.*, 113 F. 4th 1035, 1039 (8th Cir. 2024). Where a class definition does not unambiguously exclude a plaintiff, the Eighth Circuit rules favors tolling. *Id.* at 1041.

Class action practitioners, however, should not consider all the putative class members' claims to be tolled simply by virtue of the class representative being a proposed member of a previous class case that was not allowed to proceed as a class action. The Eighth Circuit narrowly applies the *American Pipe* rule. The Eighth Circuit holds that the statute of limitations is tolled under the *American Pipe* rule only if the claims filed in a later action are the same as those pleaded in the putative class action. *Zarecor v. Morgan Keenan & Co., Inc.*, 801 F.3d 882, 888 (8th Cir. 2015). Thus, the statute of limitations will not be tolled for a putative class member who files a subsequent suit where different causes of action are pled even if the causes of action are based on the same factual issues. *Id.* at 887–88. In other words, the causes of action in the more recently filed case must be identical to the causes of action in the previously filed case for the *American Pipe* rule to allow tolling of the statute of limitations.

The *American Pipe* rule also does not allow for the tolling of state law claims where there is no state law equivalent of *American Pipe*. *Thomas v. U.S. Bank NA ND*, 789 F.3d 900, 902–03 (8th Cir. 2015). If the applicable state law does not provide an *American Pipe* equivalent, the Eighth Circuit will analyze the applicable state law to determine whether the statute of limitations can be tolled in a subsequently filed class action case that was not permitted previously to proceed as a class action. *Id.* at 903. The *Thomas* court found no state law equivalent to *American Pipe* and analyzed the applicable state Supreme Court precedent that did not allow for tolling. *Id.*

9. CLASS ACTION ARBITRATION ISSUES

a. Does a Court or Arbitrator Decide Whether an Arbitration Agreement Authorizes Class Arbitration?

The Eighth Circuit has addressed the issue of whether a court or an arbitrator should determine whether an arbitration agreement authorizes class arbitration. *Catamaran Corp. v. Towncrest Pharmacy*, 864 F.3d 966, 969 (8th Cir. 2017).

This was an issue of first impression in the Eighth Circuit. *Id.* The *Catamaran* court concluded that a court should decide whether the agreement authorizes class arbitration. *Id.*

In reaching this conclusion, the *Catamaran* court first analyzed whether the availability of class arbitration is a substantive or procedural question. *Id.* at 970–71. The court concluded that this was a substantive question because of four distinct differences between bilateral and class arbitration.

First, the benefits of arbitration are substantially lessened in a class arbitration proceeding. *Id.* at 971. Specifically, the benefits of bilateral arbitration such as lower costs, speed, and efficiency are not present in class arbitration because class arbitration requires the kind of formality seen in class-action litigation. *Id.*

Second, confidentiality in class arbitration is lost or becomes more difficult. *Id.* The benefit of confidentiality in bilateral arbitration is lost or diminished in class arbitration because of the formalities required to be followed in class action case. *Id.* at 972.

Third, class arbitration brings the bet-the-company stakes of class action litigation into the realm of arbitration without the safety net of multi-layered judicial review. *Id.* For instance, a class action case that is litigated in the courts is subject to appellate review, including issues of law that may be reviewed de novo. *Id.* On the other hand, the Federal Arbitration Act provides courts limited grounds to vacate or even modify an arbitration award. *Id.* Thus, a class action that is arbitrated could allow errors to go uncorrected in multi-layered judicial review. *Id.*

Finally, the *Catamaran* court noted that due process concerns are raised in class arbitration. *Id.* The required formalities of affording class members notice, providing the class members an opportunity to be heard, and allowing the members to opt out of the class increase the costs and decrease the efficiencies of arbitration. *Id.* Considering these four differences, the *Catamaran* court held that the availability of class arbitration was not a procedural question, but a substantive question for the court to decide.

The *Catamaran* court also held that even though the question of class arbitration lies with the courts, parties to an agreement may nonetheless commit the question to an arbitrator. *Id.* However, the agreement to commit the question to an arbitrator must be clear and unmistakable and cannot simply incorporate an arbitration association's rules. *Id.* at 972–73. Absent such clear and unmistakable language, the court must decide whether an agreement authorizes class arbitration. *Id.*

b. Does an Arbitration Agreement Silent on Class Arbitration Permit Class Arbitration?

The Eighth Circuit implicitly recognizes that an arbitration agreement that is silent on class arbitration does not permit class arbitration. *See Catamaran Corp. v. Towncrest Pharmacy*, 946 F.3d 1020 (8th Cir. 2020).

Ultimately, the district court in *Catamaran* held that the arbitration agreement did not authorize class arbitration, and the case came back before the Eighth Circuit. *See id.* The Eighth Circuit affirmed the district court holding that class arbitration was not available because the agreements at issue were silent on class arbitration and the agreements were not inconsistent with individual arbitration. *Id.* at 1024.

c. Does Moving to Strike Class Allegations Waive the Right to Compel Arbitration?

The Eighth Circuit recognizes that a party who moves to strike class allegations at the same time they seek to compel arbitration does not waive its right to compel arbitration. *Donelson v. Ameriprise Fin. Servs., Inc.*, 999 F.3d 1080, 1087–88 (8th Cir. 2021). This is because a party seeking to strike allegations is not requesting a decision on the merits but is seeking a determination of whether the allegations in the complaint should proceed as individual or class claims. *Id.* Notably, the defendant in *Donelson* responded to the complaint by immediately filing a motion to strike class allegations and a motion to compel arbitration. *See id.* at 1086.

Practitioners who seek to compel arbitration and strike class allegations should make sure to do so in immediately in response to the lawsuit. The *Donelson* court noted that a party could waive its right to arbitrate by invoking the "litigation machinery" through engaging in discovery or not moving to compel arbitration in a timely manner. *Id.* at 1087–88. In other words, had the defendant in *Donelson* first moved to strike the class allegations and then subsequently moved to compel arbitration, the defendant may have then waived its right to arbitrate.

NINTH CIRCUIT

Districts of Alaska, Arizona, California, Guam, Hawaii, Idaho, Montana, Nevada, Northern Mariana Islands, Oregon, and Washington

The James R. Browning Courthouse
95 7th Street
San Francisco, CA 94103

By Jordan Elias and Trevor Tan
Girard Sharp LLP[1]

1. INTRODUCTION

The Ninth Circuit, the largest of the federal courts of appeal, continues to play a leading role in the development of class action law. Size and diversity distinguish this far-flung court and account for much of its strengths. Together with the immigration and criminal cases that fill its dockets, a steady stream of class actions, many arising under California law, occupy the 51 judges—28 of whom are active and receive litigants' en banc petitions.

Ninth Circuit judges are known for their collegial—and comparatively informal—approach, both internally and externally, to deciding cases. Oral arguments are videotaped and viewable on the court's website.[2] Once a panel opinion has issued, it is disseminated to all other judges, who may offer comments via email if they believe a point of law is flawed or incomplete. Thus, instead of granting en banc review, the court may simply amend a decision to prevent a misalignment in its case law.[3] Further, despite being reversed in the Roberts Court's signature class action case, *Wal-Mart Stores, Inc. v. Dukes*,[4] as well as in other recent Supreme Court class action decisions,[5] the Ninth Circuit's reputation as a "cowboy"

---

[1] Views and commentary are the authors' only. The authors thank Adam Polk, Namita Dhawan, and Jordan Isern for their contributions to this chapter.

[2] *See* https://www.ca9.uscourts.gov/media.

[3] *See, e.g.*, In re Century Aluminum Co. Sec. Litig., 729 F.3d 1104, 1105 (9th Cir. 2013) (amending decision affirming dismissal of putative securities class action, to ensure consistency with Starr v. Baca, 652 F.3d 1202 (9th Cir. 2011)).

[4] 564 U.S. 338 (2011).

[5] *See* TransUnion LLC v. Ramirez, 141 S. Ct. 2190 (2021) (class members whose inaccurate credit reports were not shown to have been disseminated to a third party lacked Article III standing to recover out of a class-wide verdict); Nutraceutical Corp. v. Lambert, 139 S. Ct. 710 (2019) (equitable tolling does not apply to 14-day deadline for seeking immediate appeal from order granting or denying class certification); China Agritech, Inc. v. Resh, 138 S. Ct. 1800 (2018) (*American Pipe* tolling applies only to subsequent individual actions, not to subsequent putative class actions); Microsoft Corp. v. Baker, 137 S. Ct. 1702 (2017) (plaintiff cannot convert order denying class certification into final, appealable judgment by voluntarily dismissing claims).

court is mostly undeserved.[6] As the composition of the bench has evolved, the court has policed class action settlements with increasing vigilance,[7] and demonstrated a strict constructionist bent in other recent decisions affecting class action practice. For instance, in *Sonner v. Premier Nutrition Corporation*, 971 F.3d 834 (9th Cir. 2020), the court held that a plaintiff cannot obtain the equitable remedy of restitution unless the plaintiff has no adequate remedy at law.

This chapter provides an overview of class action basics in the circuit, from pleading a case (including defining the class) through certification, settlement, and final disposition. We discuss the law surrounding the Rule 23 prerequisites while also addressing a wide range of procedural issues that have arisen in class actions in the Ninth Circuit. Along the way, we highlight circuit-specific nuances that may be relevant when litigating class actions in federal court on the West Coast.

The Ninth Circuit has issued many recent decisions relevant to class action practice. This chapter devotes special attention to developments in the court's jurisprudence that have already influenced how class actions are pleaded, prosecuted, defended, and resolved. By way of summary:

- In a prominent antitrust case, *Olean Wholesale Grocery Cooperative, Inc. v. Bumble Bee Foods LLC*, a Ninth Circuit panel held that an certified class can contain no more than a *de minimis number* of uninjured members, and suggested that five to six percent of the class represents the upper bound of *de minimis*.[8] The full court reheard the case en banc and, in April 2022, rejected the "argument that Rule 23 does not permit the certification of a class that potentially includes more than a de minimis number of uninjured class members."[9] Another key precedent in this area is *Torres v. Mercer Canyons Inc.,* where the court held that a class may properly contain uninjured members but that concerns arise if "large numbers" of putative class members were "never exposed" to the allegedly unlawful conduct.[10]
- The court held in *Sali v. Corona Regional Medical Center* that evidence need not be admissible to inform the analysis of the Rule 23 requirements, but suggested that a *Daubert* analysis was still appropriate for expert testimony.[11] In a later decision, *Grodzitsky v. America Honda Motor Company, Inc*., the court presumed that a *Daubert* analysis of expert evidence may be properly conducted as part of deciding class certification.[12] The Ninth Circuit clarified in *Lytle v. Nutramax Laboratories, Inc.* that whether a "full" or more "limited" *Daubert* inquiry is required at class certification depends on "what aspect of FRCP 23 is being addressed" and "the timing of the class certification decision."[13]
- The court reviews predominance findings—the engine of most certification decisions outside the employment law context—for an abuse of discretion, although more searching scrutiny may apply to findings regarding questions of law. For example, the court in *Stromberg v. Qualcomm Inc.* reversed a multi-state class certification, holding that California antitrust law could not be applied to claims arising

---

[6] *See, e.g.*, dailycaller.com/2017/02/12/the-9th-circuits-reversal-rate-has-nothing-to-do-with-liberal-judges.

[7] *See, e.g.*, In re Bluetooth Headset Prod. Liab. Litig., 654 F.3d 935 (9th Cir. 2011); Allen v. Bedolla, 787 F.3d 1218 (9th Cir. 2015); Koby v. ARS Nat'l Servs., Inc., 846 F.3d 1071 (9th Cir. 2017); Roes, 1-2 v. SFBSC Mgmt., LLC, 944 F.3d 1035 (9th Cir. 2019); Briseño v. Henderson, 998 F.3d 1014 (9th Cir. 2021).

[8] 993 F.3d 774, 792 (9th Cir.), *reh'g en banc granted*, 5 F.4th 950 (9th Cir. 2021).

[9] 31 F.4th 651, 669 (9th Cir. 2022) (en banc).

[10] 835 F.3d 1125, 1136–37 (9th Cir. 2016).

[11] 909 F.3d 996, 1003–07 (9th Cir. 2018).

[12] 957 F.3d 979, 985 (9th Cir. 2020).

[13] 114 F.4th 1011, 1030–31 (9th Cir. 2024).

from transactions in other states whose laws do not confer indirect purchaser standing.[14]

- Proper construction of Rule 23 continues to be a main theme in the Ninth Circuit's class action decisions. In *Briseno v. ConAgra Foods, Inc.*, the court rejected the notion that, to obtain certification, a plaintiff must establish a reliable and administratively feasible way to identify putative class members; ascertainability analysis instead focuses on the class definition.[15] Subsequently in *Walker v. Life Insurance Company of the Southwest*, the court affirmed a class certification but held that, because *Briseno* was narrowly focused on whether there is a standalone administrability requirement, the district court should not have relied on *Briseno* in rejecting the defendant's predominance arguments.[16] *Briseno* later settled, but the court reversed approval in a cutting 2021 opinion.[17]
- A string of noteworthy recent Ninth Circuit decisions on class action settlements suggests practices to follow and to avoid when negotiating a resolution. Sitting en banc in *In re Hyundai & Kia Fuel Economy Litigation*, the court reinstated a false advertisement settlement and provided guidance on the analysis that applies when litigants propose a nationwide class action settlement of state law claims.[18] In *Campbell v. Facebook, Inc.*, the court addressed standing issues in upholding a settlement limited to injunctive relief related to Facebook's alleged scanning of private user messages. Rejecting an objector's arguments, the court concluded that the settlement provided some value to class members who, by comparison, gave up very little.[19] The court also rejected a class settlement in *Briseno*, holding that all settlements—not merely those reached before a trial class has been certified—should be scrutinized for indicia of potential collusion.[20] The court likewise rejected a settlement in *McKinney-Drobnis v. Oreshack*, holding that the vouchers made available to class members were coupons and there were signs of collusion.[21] And in *Chambers v. Whirlpool Corporation*, although the court let stand a settlement offering coupons to most purchasers of allegedly faulty dishwashers, the court vacated the award of attorneys' fees, holding that the district court's use of the lodestar-multiplier method resulted in an excessive fee given that the coupons likely would provide only minimal benefits.[22]
- The Ninth Circuit also has scrutinized judgments entered in class actions that proceeded to trial. In its 2022 decision in *Wakefield v. ViSalus, Inc.*, the court vacated a $925 million jury award against a weight loss products marketing company, instructing the district court to consider "the magnitude of the aggregated award in relation to the [Telephone Consumer Protection Act's] goals of compensation, deterrence, and punishment and to the proscribed conduct" and holding that in certain "extreme situations" an aggregate statutory damages award may be so "gravely disproportionate" to the legal violation that the award becomes "unconstitutionally excessive" even if the underlying statutory penalty is constitutional.[23]
- In a 2023 decision, *Lowery v. Rhapsody International, Inc.*, the court held that—at

---

[14] 14 F.4th 1059, 1072–74 (9th Cir. 2021).

[15] 844 F.3d 1121, 1124 nn. 3–4, 1133 (9th Cir. 2017).

[16] 953 F.3d 624, 633 (9th Cir. 2020).

[17] 998 F.3d 1014 (9th Cir. 2021).

[18] 926 F.3d 539, 556–72 (9th Cir. 2019) (en banc).

[19] 951 F.3d 1106, 1122 (9th Cir. 2020).

[20] 998 F.3d 1014, 1025 (9th Cir. 2021).

[21] 16 F.4th 594 (9th Cir. 2021).

[22] 980 F.3d 645, 657 (9th Cir. 2020).

[23] 51 F.4th 1109, 1123–24 (9th Cir. 2022).

least in Copyright Act class actions—"[e]xcept in extraordinary cases, a fee award should not exceed the value that the litigation provided to the class."[24] Plaintiffs' lawyers in *Lowery* obtained approximately $50,000 for class members but asked for a $6 million fee, which the district court reduced to $1.7 million. The Ninth Circuit found an abuse of discretion where this award amounted to 30 times the benefit the class received.

2. JURISDICTIONAL ISSUES

a. CAFA Requirements

Under 28 U.S.C. § 1331, any class claim arising under federal law can be brought in federal court. *Merrell Dow Pharms. Inc. v. Thompson*, 478 U.S. 804, 807–08 (1986). The only other route to federal court is through diversity or supplemental jurisdiction. The Class Action Fairness Act of 2005 (CAFA) broadened federal diversity jurisdiction to encompass cases in which (1) there are 100 or more class members; (2) at least one class member is diverse from at least one defendant; and (3) there is more than $5 million in controversy, exclusive of interest and costs. 28 U.S.C. § 1332(d).

Though CAFA's intent and effect were to expand federal jurisdiction, in the context of a removal motion, the bulk of the circuit courts of appeals—including the Ninth Circuit—have unanimously concluded that the defendant must show that CAFA applies to obtain removal to federal court. *See, e.g.*, *Kuxhausen v. BMW Fin. Servs. N.A. LLC*, 707 F.3d 1136, 1141 (9th Cir. 2013) (holding that "even under CAFA . . . 'the burden is on the party removing the case from state court to show the exercise of federal jurisdiction is appropriate.'") (quoting *Lewis v. Verizon Communications, Inc.*, 627 F.3d 395, 399 (9th Cir. 2010)). The burden then flips if the plaintiff seeks a remand. *See Serrano v. 180 Connect, Inc.*, 478 F.3d 1018, 1024 (9th Cir. 2007) (plaintiff bears burden of showing a CAFA exception applies).

When CAFA is litigated, it tends to be on a motion by plaintiffs to remand a case to state court after defendants have removed it to federal court. Recurring issues in such motions include whether the defendant has demonstrated that CAFA's amount-in-controversy requirement is met or whether the plaintiff has shown that one of CAFA's labyrinthine exceptions applies.

Amount in Controversy

Generally, when the face of a state-court complaint is unclear or ambiguous as to whether CAFA's $5 million amount-in-controversy requirement is met, a defendant seeking to remove the case to federal court bears the burden of establishing that the amount in controversy exceeds the jurisdictional threshold by a preponderance of the evidence. *Fritsch v. Swift Transp. Co. of Ariz., LLC*, 899 F.3d 785, 793 (9th Cir. 2018). A defendant is afforded some "latitude when analyzing the amount in controversy" because of the early stage of the litigation. *Jauregui v. Roadrunner Transp. Servs., Inc.*, 28 F.4th 989, 994 (9th Cir. 2022). The Ninth Circuit in *Salter v. Quality Carriers, Inc.* clarified that when a plaintiff makes only a "facial" attack on a defendant's jurisdictional allegations, the defendant need not present evidence in support of its jurisdictional allegations. 974 F.3d 959, 962–65 (9th Cir. 2020). Instead, it need only offer plausible allegations satisfying the jurisdictional requirements and may rely on "reasonable assumptions." *Id.* at 965. This is because in making a facial attack, a plaintiff argues that the jurisdictional allegations are insufficient even when taken as true. *Id.* at 964. If, however, a plaintiff makes a "factual" attack challenging the jurisdictional allegations, the defendant must present competent evidence under the same evidentiary standard that applies to a motion for summary judgment. *Id.* In *Salter*, the court vacated the dis-

[24] 75 F.4th 985, 994 (9th Cir. 2023).

trict court's order remanding a putative wage-and-hour class action to state court. The plaintiff did not challenge the defendant's "essential assumptions or show[] that any one was unreasonable." *Id.* at 965. Thus the plaintiff made only a facial attack, and the district court erred in faulting the defendant for relying on a short declaration from one of its employees to support its jurisdictional allegations where no evidence at all was required.

In another 2020 decision, the Ninth Circuit held that when a defendant relies on the possibility of punitive damages to meet the amount-in-controversy requirement for CAFA removal, the defendant must show that the punitive damages amount "is reasonably possible" (as opposed to likely or probable). *Greene v. Harley-Davidson, Inc.*, 965 F.3d 767, 769, 772 (9th Cir. 2020). One way for a defendant to meet this burden "is to cite a case based on the same or a similar statute in which the jury or court awarded punitive damages based on the punitive-compensatory damages ratio relied upon by the defendant in its removal notice." *Id.* at 772. In *Greene*, the district court required the defendant not only to cite a prior case showing that the punitive damages ratio is possible, but also to explain why the cited case resembled the case at hand. *Id.* at 773. The Ninth Circuit explained that the district court's approach was improper because it required the defendant to show the likelihood of the plaintiff prevailing on punitive damages and overlooked the difficulty in comparing cases when discovery had not yet begun. *Id.*

Intrastate Class Action Exceptions

CAFA contains several important exceptions allowing for intrastate class actions to be heard in state court: "(1) the local controversy exception and (2) the home state exception (sometimes called the 'home state controversy exception')." *Adams v. W. Marine Prod., Inc.*, 958 F.3d 1216, 1220 (9th Cir. 2020). "[U]nder the local controversy exception, a district court 'shall' decline to exercise jurisdiction when more than two-thirds of the putative class members are citizens of the state where the action was filed, the principal injuries occurred in that same state, and at least one significant defendant is a citizen of that state." *Id.* In addition, "[t]he home state exception accords two bases for remand: one mandatory and the other within the district court's discretion." *Id.* at 1220. Under the mandatory exception, a court must decline to exercise jurisdiction if "two-thirds or more of the members of all proposed plaintiff classes in the aggregate, and the primary defendants, are citizens of the State in which the action was originally filed." 28 U.S.C. § 1332(d)(4)(B). The discretionary exception allows a district court to decline to exercise jurisdiction in the interests of justice "when more than one-third of the putative class, and the primary defendants, are citizens of the state where the action was originally filed." *Adams*, 958 F.3d at 1220 (quoting 28 U.S.C. § 1332(d)(3)) (emphasis omitted).

If the requirements for CAFA jurisdiction are met, the party seeking remand has the burden of showing that an exception applies by a preponderance of the evidence. *Id.* at 1222 The Ninth Circuit has held that this means there must be at least "some facts in evidence" to support the application of a local or state controversy exception. *Mondragon v. Cap. One Auto Fin.*, 736 F.3d 880, 884 (9th Cir. 2013). Notably, even a stipulation with a defendant that "at least two-thirds" of putative class members had last known addressees in California is insufficient when there is no other supporting evidence in the record. *King v. Great Am. Chicken Corp, Inc.*, 903 F.3d 875, 879–81 (9th Cir. 2018). In *King*, the court explained that assuming there were 6,000 class members, the local controversy exception's requirement of more than two-thirds of class members meant that there must be at least 4,001 class members who were California citizens. *Id.* at 879. Accepting that 67 percent of potential class members had last-known addresses in California suggested there were 4,020 California citizens, leaving "a cushion of only 19 class members." *Id.* However, in the face of evidence that at least some former employees had since become citizens of other states and the likelihood that some employees were citizens of other states while temporarily residing in California, the "narrow cushion provided by the stipulation," without more, was insufficient to support the conclusion that more than two-thirds of class members were California citizens.

Id. at 879–80.

The Ninth Circuit addressed the local controversy exception at length in *Coleman v. Estes Express Lines, Inc.*, 631 F.3d 1010 (9th Cir. 2011). For this exception to apply, among other conditions, at least one defendant "from whom significant relief is sought"—and "whose alleged conduct forms a significant basis of the claims"—must be a citizen of the state in which the case was originally filed. 28 U.S.C. § 1332(d)(4)(A)(i)(II). In affirming the district court's remand order in *Coleman*, the Ninth Circuit held that these CAFA-specific jurisdictional questions are to be judged solely by reference to the face of the complaint, without considering any record evidence. 631 F.3d at 1015–17. The court explained that the statutory references to "sought" and "alleged" point to an assessment of complaint allegations rather than extrinsic evidence and that courts have long assessed federal subject matter jurisdiction using the "well-pleaded complaint" rule. *Id.* at 1016. Also, when it occurs, jurisdictional fact-finding focuses on issues regarding the amount in controversy and the citizenship of parties, which are typically less fact-intensive than the "significant basis" and "significant relief" elements of CAFA's local controversy exception. *Id.* at 1016–17.

In the 2020 *Adams* case, the defendant appealed after the district court remanded a wage-and-hour class action to state court under the home state controversy exception. 958 F.3d at 1218. The Ninth Circuit explained the plaintiff had presented evidence that over 90 percent of putative class members had last-known California mailing addresses as well as her declaration that when she was hired, she had to certify her California citizenship and that her role as store manager required asking applicants if they were California citizens. *Id.* at 1222. Explaining that a plaintiff seeking remand need not show the citizenship of each class member "with certainty beyond a reasonable doubt" and that the preponderance of evidence standard is not "exceptionally difficult" to meet, the *Adams* court held that the district court "reasonably inferred from the facts in evidence that it was more likely than not that more than one-third of class members were California citizens." *Id.* at 1223. The court reasoned that in contrast to the "narrow cushion" in *King*, the evidence that 90 percent of class members had last-known mailing addresses in California supplied a "substantial cushion" even if some class members were not actually California citizens because 90 percent is "far greater than the one-third . . . required for remand." *Id.* at 1222–23.

Personal Jurisdiction

In *In re Bristol-Myers Squibb Co. v. Superior Court of California*, 582 U.S. 255 (2017) (*BMS*)—the Supreme Court held that the Fourteenth Amendment's Due Process Clause prohibited a California state court from exercising personal jurisdiction over nonresident plaintiffs' claims in a mass action against an out-of-state company. Since then, various lower courts have opined on whether and how *BMS* applies to class actions. In 2021 the Ninth Circuit weighed in with its opinion in *Moser v. Benefytt, Inc.*, a proposed Telephone Consumer Protection Act (TCPA) class action brought by a California plaintiff against Benefytt, a Florida company. Benefytt did not move to dismiss for lack of personal jurisdiction but instead opposed certification of two nationwide classes by arguing that the California court would lack personal jurisdiction over the claims of non-California class members under *BMS*. *Moser v. Benefytt, Inc.*, 8 F.4th 872, 874 (9th Cir. 2021). The district court did not address the personal jurisdiction argument, finding instead that the defendant waived it by not raising the argument at the motion to dismiss phase. The Ninth Circuit reversed, holding that under the circumstances of *Moser*—where the named plaintiff was a California resident—the defendant could not have plausibly moved to dismiss for lack of personal jurisdiction, so the failure to so move could not be construed as a waiver under Rule 12. The court explained that the unnamed, nonresident putative class members were not yet parties to the case, rendering the defense unavailable at the pleadings stage. *Id.* at 877.

The Ninth Circuit's reasoning in *Moser* regarding the party status of absent class members in relation to *BMS* generally tracks the reasoning of other circuits that have delved into this complex issue. *See Lyngaas v. Curaden AG*, 992 F.3d 412 (6th Cir. 2021); *Mussat v. IQVIA, Inc.*, 953 F.3d 441 (7th Cir. 2020); *Molock v. Whole Foods Mkt. Grp., Inc.*, 952 F.3d

293 (D.C. Cir. 2020); *Cruson v. Jackson Nat'l Life Ins. Co.*, 954 F.3d 240 (5th Cir. 2020).

b. Standing

With respect to standing, the Ninth Circuit has made clear that its "law keys on the representative party, not all of the class members. . . . In a class action, standing is satisfied if at least one named plaintiff meets the requirements." *Stearns v. Ticketmaster Corp.*, 655 F.3d 1013, 1021 (9th Cir. 2011) (quoting *Bates v. United Parcel Serv., Inc.*, 511 F.3d 974, 985 (9th Cir. 2007) (en banc)), *cert. denied*, 566 U.S. 962 (2012), *abrogated on other grounds by Comcast Corp. v. Behrend*, 569 U.S. 27 (2013). Issues concerning absent class member standing are discussed in the sections below addressing the predominance requirement.

Sometimes the question of whether the plaintiff has Article III standing overlaps with the merits of her claims. When a defendant makes a factual challenge to a plaintiff's standing under Rule 12(b)(1), the plaintiff then has the burden of supporting her jurisdictional allegations with competent evidence. *Bowen v. Energizer Holdings, Inc.*, No. 23-55116, — F.4th —, 2024 WL 4352496, at *5 (9th Cir. Oct. 1, 2024). If jurisdiction turns on disputed factual issues but those issues are not "intertwined with the merits of the claim," then the district court is allowed to resolve the factual dispute. *Id.* (citation omitted). If, however, jurisdiction is intertwined with an element of the plaintiff's claim, then the district court must treat the Rule 12(b)(1) like a summary judgment motion and leave any disputed issues of material fact for the trier of fact. *Id.*

One hot-button issue concerns the type of injury a plaintiff asserting an invasion of statutory rights must have sustained to establish Article III standing. On remand from the Supreme Court, the Ninth Circuit held in *Robins v. Spokeo, Inc.* that an alleged statutory violation—there, of the Fair Credit Reporting Act—is sufficiently concrete to confer Article III standing if the relevant provisions "protect . . . concrete interests (as opposed to purely procedural rights)" and the alleged violation "actually harm[s], or present[s] a material risk of harm to," those concrete interests. *Robins v. Spokeo, Inc.*, 867 F.3d 1108, 1113 (9th Cir. 2017).

Along similar lines, in 2020, the Ninth Circuit recognized that a claim of unjust enrichment can form the basis for Article III standing even where the alleged harm to class members is intangible. *See In re Facebook Inc. Internet Tracking Litig.*, 956 F.3d 589 (9th Cir. 2020). Citing California law "that individuals maintain an entitlement to unjustly earned profits," the court held that plaintiffs had "adequately pleaded an entitlement to Facebook's profits from users' personal data sufficient to confer Article III standing." *Id.* at 600.

In another Facebook case, *Campbell v. Facebook, Inc.*, the Ninth Circuit held that plaintiffs had standing to sue Facebook for alleged violations of the Electronic Communications Privacy Act (ECPA) and the California Invasion of Privacy Act (CIPA). 951 F.3d 1106, 1112 (9th Cir. 2020). The plaintiffs claimed Facebook used website links included in private messages without users' consent. *Id.* at 1111. The district court approved a settlement, and on appeal, the Ninth Circuit first addressed the threshold question of whether the plaintiffs had Article III standing. The court concluded that they did, explaining that the plaintiffs had shown a concrete and particularized injury because, although a violation of a "bare procedural right" without a concrete harm does not establish Article III standing, the ECPA and CIPA protect substantive rights. *Id.* at 1118–19. According to the *Campbell* court, these statutes are analogous to and "reflect statutory modernization of the privacy protections available at common law" and therefore codify the substantive right to privacy. *Id.* at 1117. And, when a statute "identifies a *substantive* right that is infringed any time it is violated, a plaintiff bringing a claim under that provision 'need not allege any further harm to have standing.'" *Id.* at 1117 (quoting *Eichenberger v. ESPN, Inc.*, 876 F.3d 979, 983–84 (9th Cir. 2017)). The court also rejected the argument that the plaintiffs lacked standing to enjoin Facebook's messaging practices because most of the challenged practices had ended before the plaintiffs filed suit. The court explained that Facebook continued to access private messages and use the data, creating both a continuing harm and a likelihood of future harm. *Id.* at 1120. The court further concluded that the plaintiffs' claims were not moot because Facebook had not proven that its allegedly wrongful behavior could not reasonably be expected to recur. *Id.*

By contrast, in *Bassett v. ABM Parking Services, Inc.*, the court held that a plaintiff lacked standing to maintain FCRA claims based on allegations that a garage issued a receipt displaying his credit card expiration date: "Like the dissemination of an incorrect zip code, it is difficult to see how issuing a receipt to only the card owner and with only the expiration date, 'without more, could work any concrete harm.'" 883 F.3d 776, 783 (9th Cir. 2018) (quoting *Spokeo, Inc. v. Robins*, 578 U.S. 330, 342 (2016)).

Ramirez v. TransUnion LLC, 953 F.3d 1008 (9th Cir. 2020), involved the post-trial posture. There, a plaintiff sued the credit reporting agency TransUnion under the FCRA on behalf of a class individuals after TransUnion erroneously placed alerts on their credit reports falsely suggesting they had been placed on a national security alert list, labelled them as terrorists, drug traffickers, and other national security threats, and then sent them confusing and incomplete mailings about how to dispute or remove the alerts. A jury returned a verdict in favor of the certified class for about $8 million in statutory damages and $52 million in punitive damages. *Id.* at 1022. Prior to trial, the parties stipulated that there were 8,185 affected consumers, including the plaintiff. While the evidence showed that the credit reports of 1,853 class members were requested by a third party, there was no evidence that TransUnion furnished the credit reports of the remaining 6,332 class members to a third party. *Id.* Relying on *Spokeo*, TransUnion argued that none of the class members had standing because they had not suffered a concrete injury, but the Ninth Circuit disagreed, reasoning that all class members "suffered a material risk of harm to their concrete interests protected by [the FCRA] as a result of TransUnion's failure to follow reasonable procedures to assure maximum possible accuracy" of their credit reports. *Id.* at 1025. TransUnion thereby created a significant risk for all class members that a third party would learn of the false or embarrassing information, often without their knowledge. *Id.* at 1027.

A divided Supreme Court reversed. *TransUnion LLC v. Ramirez*, 141 S. Ct. 2190, 2200 (2021). In doing so, the Court first explained that while "Congress may create causes of action for plaintiffs to sue defendants who violate those legal prohibitions or obligations. But under Article III, an injury in law is not an injury in fact. Only those plaintiffs who have been *concretely harmed* by a defendant's statutory violation may sue that private defendant over that violation in federal court." *Id.* at 2205 (emphasis in original). To hold otherwise, the Court reasoned, would allow Congress to authorize "any citizen to bring a statutory damages suit against virtually any defendant who violated virtually any federal law" and thereby infringe on the powers of the Executive Branch while allowing unaccountable private parties to enforce laws. *Id.* at 2206.

The Supreme Court reached different conclusions with respect to the 1,853 class members whose reports were released to third parties and the remaining class members. Analogizing their claims to the tort of defamation, the majority had no trouble concluding that the 1,853 class members had suffered a concrete injury from having their erroneous credit reports published to third parties. *Id.* at 2208–09. But the remaining class members did not suffer a concrete harm for purposes of Article III standing, the Court held, because the evidence did not show that their credit reports were disclosed to a third party. *Id.* at 2209–10. The majority also rejected the contention that these class members had standing based on the risk of future harm, agreeing with TransUnion "that in a suit for damages, the mere risk of future harm, standing alone, cannot qualify as a concrete harm—at least unless the exposure to the risk of future harm itself causes a *separate* concrete harm." *Id.* at 2211 (emphasis in original).

Joined by three other Justices, Justice Thomas dissented, arguing that the majority's decision was inconsistent with the history of Article III and long-standing jurisprudence on standing. *Id.* at 2216–21 (Thomas, J., dissenting). He further argued that "TransUnion's misconduct here is exactly the sort of thing that has long merited legal redress" and the type of conduct the FCRA was intended to curb. *Id.* at 2221. Justice Kagan also wrote a separate dissent, which Justices Breyer and Sotomayor joined. *Id.* at 2225–26 (Kagan, J., dissenting).

After *TransUnion*, in connection with a class action settlement, the Ninth Circuit held that class member standing turns on the plaintiffs' allegations and the extent of the record. In *In re Apple Inc. Device Performance Litigation*, the court rejected a challenge to the inclusion of class members who may have suffered no damages in a settlement negotiated prior to class certification or summary judgment. 50 F.4th 769, 781 (9th Cir. 2022). The plaintiffs' allegation "that all putative class members experienced throttling from Apple's allegedly unlawful intrusion into their phones" was sufficient to establish standing for all settlement class members because the assertion had neither been proven nor disproven. *Id.*

The Ninth Circuit has reaffirmed after *TransUnion* that even the loss of a small amount of money for a short period is not "too trifling" of a concrete injury to deprive plaintiffs of Article III standing. *Van v. LLR, Inc.*, 61 F.4th 1053, 1064 (9th Cir. 2023). In *Van*, a class of Alaska purchasers sued LuLaRoe, an online retail platform, for improperly taxing purchasers based on the location of the retailer, rather than of the purchaser. LuLaRoe had refunded all the improperly collected sales tax, and "the only remaining injury suffered by class members for which they remain[ed] uncompensated is 'the lost time value of money' for the period between the improper charge and the refund." *Id.* at 1063. LuLaRoe had not repaid the interest on the improperly collected tax, and the plaintiffs used the unpaid interest "as a proxy for and method of quantifying" the value of their lost money and time. *Id.* Although many class members were owed only a few cents and some a mere fraction of a cent in interest, the court, citing *TransUnion*, held that "[a]ny monetary loss, even one as small as a fraction of a cent, is sufficient to support standing." *Id.* at 1064.

In another consequential standing case, *Davidson v. Kimberly-Clark Corporation*, the Ninth Circuit clarified what a plaintiff asserting false advertising must allege to have Article III standing to pursue injunctive relief. 889 F.3d 956 (9th Cir. 2018), *cert. denied*, 139 S. Ct. 640 (2018). Reasoning that knowledge of past falsity "does not equate to knowledge" of future falsity, the court rejected the argument that a plaintiff lacks standing because, aware of the misleading representations, he or she does not face actual or imminent future harm. *Id.* at 969–70 & n.5 (noting that this holding parts company with the holdings of several other circuits). The court explained that a threat of harm may arise if, despite wishing to buy the allegedly falsely advertised product in the future, the consumer will refrain from making that purchase in consequence of being unable to rely on the product's advertising. *Id.* at 969–70. The court further reasoned that its conclusion upholds the primary objective of the consumer fraud laws: protecting against future injury. *Id.* at 970.

The Ninth Circuit has also addressed the standing of non-lead or former plaintiffs to appeal. In *Habelt v. iRhythm Technologies, Inc.*, a divided panel held that being a former plaintiff does not, by itself, confer standing to appeal. 83 F.4th 1162 (9th Cir. 2023). Appellant Mark Habelt, an investor, filed a securities fraud complaint against iRhythm and its former CEO. After his case was consolidated with several other related cases, Habelt did not seek appointment as lead plaintiff under the Private Securities Litigation Reform Act of 1995 and did not participate in the litigation once another plaintiff was appointed. Although the lead plaintiff filed an amended complaint with Habelt's name on the caption, the amended complaint did not mention Habelt or contain any allegations specific to him. After the district court granted the defendant's motion to dismiss, Habelt—but not the lead plaintiff—appealed.

Writing for the majority, Judge Thomas concluded that Habelt lacked standing to appeal because he was not a party to the litigation. *Id.* at 1165–66. The majority reasoned that the case caption is probative but not dispositive: "the more important indication . . . are the allegations in the body of the complaint." *Id.* at 1166 (internal quotation marks and citation omitted). Habelt was not a party because the operative complaint did not even mention him.

Id. Nor did being a putative class member confer standing to appeal because absent class members do not acquire party status until a class is certified. *Id.* The court allowed that a nonparty may appeal in "exceptional circumstances," such as where the nonparty participated in the case or the equities compel hearing the appeal. *Id.* at 1167.

In dissent, Judge Bennett contended that Habelt should be considered a party entitled to appeal because he initiated the litigation by filing the first complaint, he remained on the caption of the operative complaint, his own claims were covered by its substantive allegations, and he never manifested a clear intent to remove himself as a party. *Id.* at 1169–70. The dissent also would have granted Habelt appellate standing as a nonparty because he participated in the litigation and equity favored permitting his appeal, including because he did not receive clear notice of having lost his party status and right to appeal. *Id.* at 1171–74.

c. Mootness

Sometimes during a class action, the class representative's situation changes such that his or her claims arguably become moot. The Ninth Circuit has outlined parameters for evaluating whether a class representative whose claims have been mooted may nonetheless continue to pursue claims on behalf of a class: (1) the class was properly certified or the class representative is appealing the denial of class certification; (2) the class representative was a member of the class with standing to sue at the time class certification was granted or denied; (3) the unnamed class members must have a live interest throughout the duration of the case; and (4) the court determines the class representative will adequately pursue the interest of the class even if his or her own interest has expired. *Johnson v. City of Grants Pass*, 72 F.4th 868, 884 n.18 (9th Cir. 2023) (citations omitted).

Another mootness question is: Can a defendant moot a class claim by offering to provide the named plaintiff all the relief sought in the complaint? In *Campbell-Ewald Co. v. Gomez*, 577 U.S. 153 (2016), the Supreme Court answered "no." Prior to class certification in *Campbell-Ewald*, a TCPA action, the defendant, Campbell, proposed to settle plaintiff Gomez's individual claim and filed an offer of judgment under Rule 68. *Id.* at 157–58. Gomez never accepted the offer. Campbell nonetheless moved to dismiss the complaint, maintaining that it had mooted the suit and no Article III claim or controversy remained. *Id.* at 158–59. The district court granted the motion, but the Ninth Circuit reversed. The Supreme Court then affirmed, holding that "an unaccepted settlement offer or offer of judgment does not moot a plaintiff's case" because "[a]n unaccepted settlement offer—like any unaccepted contract offer—is a legal nullity, with no operative effect." *Id.* at 162 (quoting *Genesis Healthcare Corp. v. Symczyk*, 569 U.S. 66, 81 (2013) (Kagan, J., dissenting)).

Mootness law in the Ninth Circuit has continued to evolve since *Campbell-Ewald*. In *Chen v. Allstate Insurance Co.*, 819 F.3d 1136 (9th Cir. 2016), the court was called upon to decide whether a defendant can moot a class action with a Rule 68 offer of judgment and deposit of the full settlement value of the named plaintiff's claims into an escrow account "pending entry of a final District Court order or judgment" directing payment of the tendered funds. *Id.* at 1141. 819 F.3d 1136. The Ninth Circuit held that such an offer would not moot the class action, for two reasons: (1) even assuming the defendant's offer mooted the named plaintiff's claims, he would still be permitted to move for class certification, based on *Pitts v. Terrible Herbst Inc.*, 653 F.3d 1081 (9th Cir. 2011) (recognizing an exception to mootness for class claims); and (2) the named plaintiff's claims were not yet moot because the funds had only been placed in an escrow account; he had not yet accepted the defendant's offer. *Chen*, 819 F.3d at 1148–49. But in *Brady v. Autozone Stores, Inc.*, the Ninth Circuit held that a class representative who settles his or her individual claim must "do more than expressly leave class claims open to avoid mootness. A class representative must also retain—as evidenced by an agreement—a financial stake in the outcome of the class claims." 962 F.3d 1172, 1175 (9th Cir. 2020). Accordingly, where a class representative voluntarily settles an individual claim, he or she must retain a concrete financial stake in the claims of the absent class members to avoid mooting their claims for purposes of that controversy.

Non-CAFA Cases
Assuming the other jurisdictional requirements are met, CAFA covers any "class action" or "any civil action filed under Rule 23 of the Federal Rules of Civil Procedure or similar State statute or rule of judicial procedure authorizing an action to be brought by 1 or more representative persons as a class action." 28 U.S.C. § 1332(d)(1)(B). The Ninth Circuit has held that to be considered a "class action" under CAFA, a state statute must provide for statutory requirements similar to Rule 23's numerosity, commonality, typicality, and adequacy elements and contain procedures for class certification. As a result, certain "representative actions" such as *parens patriae* lawsuits are not "class actions" for CAFA purposes. *Washington v. Chimei Innolux Corp.*, 659 F.3d 842, 848–50 (9th Cir. 2011).

Given the prevalence of wage-and-hour litigation under California's Private Attorneys' General Act of 2004 (PAGA), it should be noted that the PAGA actions are "not sufficiently similar to Rule 23 to establish the original jurisdiction of a federal court under CAFA." *Baumann v. Chase Inv. Servs. Corp.*, 747 F.3d 1117, 1124 (9th Cir. 2014). Relying on *Baumann*, in *Canela v. Costco Wholesale Corporation,* the Ninth Circuit again held that a state action filed under PAGA was not a "similar statute or rule to federal rule of civil procedure" within the meaning of section 1332 and thus did not fall under CAFA's jurisdiction because PAGA neither "closely resembles" Rule 23 nor is it similar to Rule 23 in "substance or in essentials." 871 F.3d 845, 851 (9th Cir. 2020); *see Hamilton v. Wal-Mart Stores, Inc.*, 39 F.4th 575, 583 (9th Cir. 2022) ("Rule 23 class actions and PAGA actions are so conceptually distinct that class action precepts generally have little salience for PAGA actions."). PAGA contains none of Rule 23's requirements of numerosity, commonality, or typicality; it does not afford protection to putative class members under Rule 23; it gives no opportunity for employees to opt out; and employees retain rights to pursue other remedies, which are typically precluded by a class judgment. *Id.* at 851.

Magnuson-Moss Warranty Act Class Actions
The Magnuson-Moss Warranty Act or MMWA provides that any class action under the act must have at least one hundred named plaintiffs. 15 U.S.C. § 2310(d)(3). Some district courts previously held that CAFA—which does not require naming 100 plaintiffs—allows federal courts to exercise jurisdiction over MMWA class actions even when the plaintiffs number less than 100. *See, e.g.*, *Keegan v. Am. Honda Motor Co., Inc.*, 838 F. Supp. 2d 929, 954 (C.D. Cal. 2012); *Morgan v. Apple Inc.*, No. 17-CV-05277-RS, 2018 WL 2234537, at *8 (N.D. Cal. May 16, 2018). Those holdings are now bad law: the Ninth Circuit held in 2020 that "CAFA may not be used to evade or override the MMWA's specific numerosity requirement" given that "CAFA allows certain claims to proceed under diversity jurisdiction, while the MMWA provides for a distinct claim to be brought in federal court for certain state-law warranty violations." *Floyd v. Am. Honda Motor Co.*, 966 F.3d 1027, 1034–35 (9th Cir. 2020). Because the MMWA and CAFA are not irreconcilable—"the MMWA simply prevents claims under that Act from proceeding in federal court absent the satisfaction of certain jurisdictional prerequisites"—"courts can easily give effect to that command and apply CAFA in all other cases." *Id.* at 1035.

Class Actions Subject to the Private Securities Litigation Reform Act
Securities class actions in federal court are "governed by the three-step process set out in the Private Securities Litigation Reform Act (PSLRA), 15 U.S.C. § 78u-4." *In re Mersho*, 6 F.4th 891, 896 (9th Cir. 2021). Under the first step, "notice of the action must be posted so purported class members can move for lead plaintiff appointment." *Id.* at 899. In the second step, the district court determines which movant will make the "most adequate plaintiff"—i.e., the plaintiff "most capable of adequately representing the interests of class members." *Id.* (quoting 78u-4(a)(3)(B)(i)). The court must apply a presumption that the movant with the largest financial interest (financial loss), who makes a *prima facie* showing of meeting the

adequacy and typicality requirements of Rule 23, is the "most adequate" plaintiff. *Id.* In the third step, other movants may attempt to rebut the presumption and show that the plaintiff will not fairly and adequately protect the interests of the class. *Id.* at 899. But if the presumption is not rebutted, the court must select the most adequate plaintiff as the lead plaintiff. *Id.*

One issue that has arisen across the circuits is whether and under what circumstances it is permissible for a group of investors to collectively seek appointment as PSLRA lead plaintiff. In *Mersho*, the Ninth Circuit confirmed that it is permissible to group investor claims in connection with seeking to be appointed lead counsel in a PSLRA case. There, a group of individuals seeking to be lead plaintiff as a group filed a mandamus petition after the district court declined to appoint them, citing "misgivings" as to how the plaintiffs had found each other. *Id.* at 900. The Ninth Circuit granted the petition, holding that the district court had failed to "give effect to the presumption" at the third step by requiring them to demonstrate their adequacy and how they would work together, "even though the burden should have shifted to the competing movants to show inadequacy." *Id.* at 901. While a district court may consider the "pre-litigation relationship or cohesion" of PSLRA movants, it must substantiate a finding that related concerns demonstrate their inadequacy. *Id.* at 902.

3. DEFINING THE CLASS

Any order certifying a class "must define the class" under Rule 23(c)(1)(B). The Rule 23 policies of finality and efficiency animate the often-challenging task of suitably defining a class. In the Ninth Circuit, a class definition is adequate if it is "objective and definitive" and "reasonably co-extensive" with the theory of liability in the case. *Briseno*, 844 F.3d at 1126 n.6; *Torres*, 835 F.3d at 1136–37. For instance, a class may be defined as those employed by the defendant, or those who purchased certain goods or securities, during a discrete time period. The class definition should be clear to laypersons—definitions "that are difficult to follow or understand will leave absent class members unsure of their standing in regard to the litigation" and interfere with the defendant's repose in a preclusive final judgment. 3 William B. Rubenstein, *Newberg on Class Actions* § 7:27 (5th ed. 2013). Thus, "[u]nder the law of this circuit, it is enough that the class definition describes 'a set of common characteristics sufficient to allow' an individual to determine whether she is a class member with a potential right to recover." *Krueger v. Wyeth, Inc.*, 310 F.R.D. 468, 475 (S.D. Cal. 2015) (citation omitted).

In defining a proposed class, it is important to tailor the definition to the claims and underlying facts to avoid including large numbers of unaffected persons in the class. *See Torres*, 835 F.3d at 1138 ("What is critical is that Plaintiffs' theory of . . . injury . . . actually maps onto the membership of the class. In other words, class membership must fit the theory of legal liability."). Plaintiffs also should take care not to propose a "fail-safe class" in which membership is defined in terms of liability or violation itself, "such that the definition presupposes success on the merits." *Melgar v. CSK Auto, Inc.*, 681 F. App'x 605, 607 (9th Cir. 2017). A fail-safe definition is unfair to the defendant, as class members who lose on the merits could nevertheless pursue a follow-on suit because the defeat would eliminate the class as defined. *See, e.g.*, *Brazil v. Dell Inc.*, 585 F. Supp. 2d 1158, 1167 (N.D. Cal. 2008) (striking a fail-safe definition that referenced "falsely advertised" products). One of the reasons a certified class may include some uninjured persons, *see Torres*, 835 F.3d at 1136–37, is that excluding them would often require an impermissible fail-safe definition. *See Rodman v. Safeway, Inc.*, No. 11-cv-03003-JST, 2014 WL 988992, at *15 (N.D. Cal. Mar. 10, 2014). Nor may class membership be defined subjectively or in terms of class members' mental states, which would make it too "easy to fade in or out of the class depending on the outcome." *Xavier v. Philip Morris USA Inc.*, 787 F. Supp. 2d 1075, 1089 (N.D. Cal. 2011).

Under the Ninth Circuit's 2017 *Briseno* decision, neither "ascertainability" nor "administrative feasibility" is a Rule 23 requirement. 844 F.3d at 1124, 1133. The plaintiffs in

Briseno were purchasers of Wesson brand cooking oil products that were labelled "100% Natural." 844 F.3d at 1123. They alleged that the "100% Natural" representation was false or misleading because the oils were made from genetically modified organisms, or GMOs, and therefore are not natural. *Id.* The plaintiffs sought to certify a class of all persons in 11 states who purchased the oils. *Id.* at 1123–24. ConAgra opposed class certification on the grounds that, absent identifying records, there was no administratively feasible way to identify class members given that consumers could not be expected to identify themselves reliably. *Id.* at 1124. The district court rejected ConAgra's argument and granted certification in relevant part. *Id.*

The Ninth Circuit affirmed, holding (1) the plain language of Rule 23 contains no explicit administrative feasibility requirement, and (2) no implicit administrative feasibility requirement is necessary to ensure that a certified class functions as intended. *Id.* at 1133. The Ninth Circuit expressly disagreed with the Third Circuit's endorsement of such a requirement, reasoning that Rule 23's existing manageability criteria already address this subject and should not be displaced by an atextual requirement. The court instead reaffirmed the core "principle that a class definition must be objective and definite." *Id.* at 1126 n.6. Among the significant holdings of *Briseno* are the following:

- Rule 23(b)(3)'s manageability factor requires that courts consider "the likely difficulties in managing a class action," offsetting the need for an independent administrative feasibility requirement to assess the burdens of trying a Rule 23(b)(3) class action.
- Notice of a Rule 23(b)(3) class action need not be provided to every class member; the rule requires only "the best notice that is practicable under the circumstances."
- Concerns about fraudulent claims infringing a defendant's due process rights do not justify an administrative feasibility requirement because plaintiffs already bear the burden of demonstrating compliance with Rule 23 and defendants can oppose plaintiffs' showings at every stage of the case, including by challenging "the claims of absent class members if and when they file claims for damages."

Id. at 1129–30.

The Ninth Circuit has since characterized *Briseno* as being "narrow in focus" and principally directed at the concern "that a standalone [administrability] requirement would improperly bar certification in cases like *Briseno*, where administrability is difficult to demonstrate but for which the class action remains the only realistic way to litigate the case." *Walker v. Life Ins. Co. of the Sw.*, 953 F.3d 624, 633 (9th Cir. 2020). In *Walker*, the court held that class membership may be considered as part of predominance analysis, while rejecting "a one-size-fits-all approach to class-member identification." *Id.* at 632. The court limited its holding to the following: "[i]n UCL cases, (1) exposure [to the alleged unfair or deceptive practices] is relevant to predominance, but only to establish reliance, and (2) a district court does not err *per se* by not considering the class-membership question under the predominance prong." *Id.*

4. DISCOVERY TO LOCATE LEAD PLAINTIFFS

If a district court determines that a plaintiff's claims are governed by the laws of his home state and the state prohibits class actions, may the plaintiff seek discovery from the defendant in order to find a new lead plaintiff? In *In re Williams-Sonoma, Inc.*, a divided Ninth Circuit panel concluded that Rule 26(b)(1) does not allow such discovery, vacating the district court's discovery order directing the defendant to produce a list of California customers. 947 F.3d 535, 537 (9th Cir. 2020). The plaintiff, a Kentucky resident, brought suit under California law claiming that the defendant misrepresented the thread count of its bed sheets. The district court ruled that the law of Kentucky, whose consumer statutes do not permit class actions, governed but granted the plaintiff's request for discovery to help locate a California plaintiff. *Id.* at 537–38. The defendant petitioned for a writ of mandamus. The Ninth Circuit granted the petition, concluding that "Rule 26(b)(1) limits the scope of discovery to 'nonprivileged matter that is relevant to any party's claim or defense'" and that the Supreme Court has concluded class member discovery "is not relevant within the meaning of that rule." *Id.* at 539 (citing *Oppenheimer Fund, Inc. v. Sanders*, 437 U.S. 340, 350–53 (1978)). The majority also noted that subsequent amendments to Rule 26(b)(1) have restricted the scope of discovery, and the fact that no class had been certified (unlike in *Oppenheimer*) further weighed against the plaintiff's request. *Id.* Dissenting, Judge Paez noted the extraordinary nature of mandamus relief and took issue with the majority's reading of *Oppenheimer*, opining that the Supreme Court "did not hold that plaintiffs cannot seek the identities and contact information of absent class members for a different purpose before the class is certified, as here." *Id.* at 541 (Paez, J., dissenting). The dissent also opines that even if Rule 26 did not authorize the district court's discovery order, Rule 23 did. *Id.* at 542-43.

5. PREREQUISITES TO CLASS CERTIFICATION

Under Rule 23, plaintiffs bear the burden of showing that they have met each of the four requirements of Rule 23(a) and at least one subsection of Rule 23(b). *Berger v. Home Depot USA, Inc.*, 741 F.3d 1061, 1067 (9th Cir. 2014) (citing *Zinser v. Accufix Research Inst., Inc.*, 253 F.3d 1180, 1186 (9th Cir. 2001)). The Supreme Court's class action jurisprudence makes clear that plaintiffs "must actually prove—not simply plead—that their proposed class satisfies each requirement of Rule 23, including (if applicable) the predominance requirement of Rule 23(b)(3)." *Halliburton Co. v. Erica P. John Fund, Inc.*, 573 U.S. 258, 275 (2014) (citing *Comcast*, 569 U.S. 31–32; *Wal-Mart Stores, Inc. v. Dukes*, 564 U.S. 338, 350–51 (2011)); *see also Olean*, 31 F.4th at 665 (plaintiff must establish that Rule 23's requirements are met by a preponderance of the evidence); *Miles v. Kirkland's Stores Inc.*, 89 F.4th 1217, 1222 (9th Cir. 2024) ("[A] party cannot plead or speculate her way to class certification. She must marshal facts showing, by a preponderance of the evidence, that class issues predominate."). Although "class-certification analysis must be 'rigorous' and may 'entail some overlap with the merits of the plaintiff's underlying claim,' Rule 23 grants courts no license to engage in free-ranging merits inquiries at the certification stage. Merits questions may be considered to the extent—but only to the extent—that they are relevant to determining whether Rule 23 prerequisites for class certification are satisfied." *Amgen Inc. v. Conn. Ret. Plans & Trust Funds*, 568 U.S. 455, 465–66 (2013) (quoting *Wal-Mart*, 564 U.S. at 351). These analytical principles apply to both Rule 23(a) and 23(b). *See Comcast*, 569 U.S. at 33.

In the Ninth Circuit, the fact that an expert opinion offered in support of certification clears the "scientifically reliable and relevant" hurdle of *Daubert v. Merrell Dow Pharmaceutical, Inc.*, 509 U.S. 579 (1993), does not necessarily mean the expert opinion satisfies the "rigorous analysis" that Rule 23 requires. *Ellis v. Costco Wholesale Corp.*, 657 F.3d 970, 982 (9th Cir. 2011). At class certification, a court must determine whether the expert's evidence supporting certification is persuasive following a rigorous analysis. *Id.* at 983–84. As part of that analysis, the court may be required to resolve factual disputes between the plaintiffs' and defendants' experts if those disputes go to whether or not common questions predominate or injury to the class "as a whole" can be shown using common evidence. *Id.*; *but see Torres*, 835 F.3d at 1134–36 (affirming determination that common questions relating to the existence of an unfair or deceptive practice predominated over questions particular to individual class members' alleged injuries).

In *Olean*, a panel of the Ninth Circuit addressed a putative class action alleging that packaged tuna producers engaged in an antitrust price-fixing conspiracy. 993 F.3d at 781. Plaintiffs' expert testimony primarily relied on statistical evidence in the form of a regression model seeking to prove that class members were harmed by the conspiracy. *Id.* at 782. The defendants disputed that evidence; their expert determined that a higher percentage of class members were unharmed. *Id.* at 782–83. After declining to resolve the discrepancies, the district court certified the class, stating that the evidentiary issues were "not fatal to a finding of classwide impact" but were instead "ripe for use at trial." *Id.* at 783. On appeal, the panel found that the district court abused its discretion because, by not addressing the statistical discrepancies and determining whether there were too many uninjured class members, the district court failed to resolve all factual and legal disputes relevant to class certification. *Id.* at 791. The court thus held that a district court must find, by a preponderance of the evidence, that a plaintiff has established "predominance" under Rule 23(b)(3) and the "determination cannot be outsourced to a jury." *Id.* at 784, 791–82.

The full Ninth Circuit granted the plaintiffs' petition for rehearing en banc and—over two dissenters—held that the district court had not abused its discretion in concluding that the plaintiffs had presented sufficient evidence showing that whether class members were harmed was capable of being established on a common basis. 31 F.4th 651 (9th Cir. 2022) (en banc). The court explained that a district court's obligation to conduct a "rigorous" assessment includes weighing competing expert testimony and resolving disputes over expert testimony and "historical facts" only if they are "necessary to ensure that Rule 23(b)(3)'s requirements are met" and that with regard to the predominance inquiry, "a district court is limited to resolving whether the evidence establishes that a common question is capable of class-wide resolution, not whether the evidence in fact establishes that plaintiffs would win at trial." *Id.* at 666–67. The en banc majority held that, in certifying the classes under Rule 23(b)(3), the district court properly resolved the disputes between the parties' experts and weighed the evidence presented as to whether antitrust impact could be determined on a class-wide basis. *Id.* at 676. Further, the district court did not abdicate its responsibilities when it declined to determine whether all class members were in fact harmed by the alleged conspiracy, as "all that was necessary at the certification stage" was to determine whether the plaintiffs' expert's regression model "was capable of showing that . . . class members suffered antitrust impact on a class-wide basis, notwithstanding [the defendants' expert's] critique." *Id.* at 680–81 (emphasis omitted). In other words, a district court's obligation is to resolve the parties' disputes to the extent necessary to determine whether the class certification prerequisites are met, but the persuasiveness of that evidence in relation to the merits is left for the trier of fact. *Id.*

Under Rule 23(a), a class may be certified only if (1) it is so numerous that joinder of all members is impracticable, (2) there are questions of law or fact common to the class, (3) the claims or defenses of the representative parties are typical of the claims or defenses of the class, and (4) the representative parties will fairly and adequately protect the interests of the class. Fed. R. Civ. P. 23(a). In addition to establishing the Rule 23(a) prerequisites, the plaintiff must establish at least one of the Rule 23(b) grounds for maintaining a class action: (1) there is a risk of substantial prejudice from separate actions; (2) declaratory or injunctive relief benefiting the class as a whole would be appropriate; or (3) common questions of law or fact predominate and a class action is superior to other available methods of adjudication. Fed. R. Civ. P. 23(b).

a. Rule 23(a) Requirements

Numerosity (Fed. R. Civ. P. 23(a)(1))

The general rule is that a "class of 41 or more is usually sufficiently numerous" to make joinder impracticable. 5–23 *Moore's Federal Practice—Civil* § 23.22 (2016). The question is not "whether joinder is a literal impossibility. Rather, the question is whether joinder of all class members is practicable—i.e., reasonably capable of being accomplished." *A. B. v. Hawaii State Dep't of Educ.*, 30 F.4th 828, 837 (9th Cir. 2022) (quotation marks and citation omitted). The Ninth Circuit has stated that "[n]umerosity is far from clear" with a proposed "class size in the neighborhood of 40 to 50 members." *Williamson v. Geisler*, 644 F. App'x 777, 777 (9th Cir. 2016).

A plaintiff cannot rely on allegations or unsupported conclusions to show numerosity, and while a court may make reasonable inferences, "courts have also rejected tenuous chains of inferences" to prove numerosity. *Miller v. RP On-Site, LLC*, No. 19-CV-02114-LHK, 2020 WL 6940936, at **4–9 (N.D. Cal. Nov. 25, 2020); *see Floyd v. Saratoga Diagnostics, Inc.*, No. 20-CV-01520-LHK, 2021 WL 2139343, at *3 (N.D. Cal. May 26, 2021) (courts "may make common-sense assumptions and reasonable inferences") (citation omitted).

Further, "[a]lthough the absolute number of class members is not the sole determining factor, where a class is large in numbers, joinder will usually be impracticable." *Jordan v. Cty. of L.A.*, 669 F.2d 1311, 1319 (9th Cir. 1982), *vacated on other grounds*, 459 U.S. 810 (1982); *see also id.* (court was "inclined to find the numerosity requirement in the present case satisfied solely on the basis of the number of ascertained class members, *i.e.*, 39, 64, and 71"). With smaller proposed classes, however, "the number of class members does not weigh as heavily in determining whether joinder would be infeasible. . . . [and] other factors such as the geographical diversity of class members, the ability of individual claimants to institute separate suits, and whether injunctive or declaratory relief is sought, should be considered in determining impracticability of joinder." *Id.*

In determining whether a class is sufficiently numerous, a court may consider future class members and the fact that class composition may change over time suggests that joinder of all members is impracticable. *A.B.*, 30 F.4th at 838.

Commonality (Fed. R. Civ. P. 23(b)(2))

Under Rule 23(a)(2), plaintiffs must demonstrate that at least one common question of fact or law is common to the class and that a class action may "generate common *answers* apt to drive the resolution of the litigation." *Wal-Mart*, 564 U.S. at 350 (emphasis in original) (citation omitted). For purposes of establishing commonality, "[t]he existence of shared legal issues with divergent factual predicates is sufficient, as is a common core of salient facts coupled with disparate legal remedies within the class." *Hanlon v. Chrysler Corp.*, 150 F.3d 1011, 1019 (9th Cir. 1998); *Abdullah v. U.S. Sec. Assocs., Inc.*, 731 F.3d 952, 957 (9th Cir. 2013). Ultimately, the "claims must depend upon a common contention . . . of such a nature that it is capable of classwide resolution—which means that determination of its truth or falsity will resolve an issue that is central to the validity of each one of the claims in one stroke." *Wal-Mart*, 564 U.S. at 350.

Rule 23(a)(2) "has been construed permissively." *Hanlon*, 150 F.3d at 1019. Not all questions of law and fact need to be common. Instead, "[o]nly one significant issue of law or fact need be demonstrated." *Yamada v. Nobel Biocare Holding AG*, 275 F.R.D. 573, 577 (C.D. Cal. 2011) (citation omitted); *accord In re High-Tech Emps. Antitrust Litig.*, 985 F. Supp. 2d 1167, 1180 (N.D. Cal. 2013); *In re TFT-LCD (Flat Panel) Antitrust Litig.*, 267 F.R.D. 583, 593 (N.D. Cal. 2010). *In re Dynamic Random Access Memory (DRAM) Antitrust Litig.*, No. M 02-1486 PJH, 2006 WL 1530166, at *3 (N.D. Cal. June 5, 2006).

Analysis of the commonality requirement often figures centrally in proposed class actions under employment law. For example, in *Ellis v. Costco*, the court reversed certification and directed the district court to conduct a rigorous analysis of whether Costco's alleged policy of gender discrimination was common to the class claims: "If there is no evidence that the entire class was subject to the same allegedly discriminatory practice, there is no question common to the class. In other words, the district court must determine whether there was 'significant proof that [Costco] operated under a general policy of discrimination.' . . . If no such *nationwide* discrimination exists, Plaintiffs would face an exceedingly difficult challenge in proving that there are questions of fact and law common to the *nationwide* class." 657 F.3d at 983–84 (emphasis in original) (quoting *Wal-Mart*, 564 U.S. at 353). By contrast, the Ninth Circuit affirmed class certification in other employment cases based on its conclusion that common questions of law or fact existed. *See, e.g.*, *Vaquero v. Ashley Furniture Indus., Inc.*, 824 F.3d 1150, 1153–54 (9th Cir. 2016); *Jimenez v. Allstate Ins. Co.*, 765 F.3d 1161, 1164–66 (9th Cir. 2014).

Typicality (Fed. R. Civ. P. 23(a)(3))

Under Rule 23(a)(3), the representative party must have claims or defenses that are "typical of the claims or defenses of the class." Fed. R. Civ. P. 23(a)(3). The typicality inquiry considers the degree of similarity among named plaintiffs' asserted injuries and legal claims and those of the group they propose to represent. *Ellis*, 657 F.3d at 984–85. "Under the rule's permissive standards, representative claims are 'typical' if they are reasonably co-extensive with those of absent class members; they need not be substantially identical." *Hanlon*, 150 F.3d at 1020. A named plaintiff's claim therefore is typical if it "arise[s] from the same event, practice or course of conduct that gives rise to the claims of the absent class members" and is "based on the same legal or remedial theory." *DRAM*, 2006 WL 1530166, at *4 (citation omitted). Typicality is ordinarily present in antitrust cases alleging market-wide restraints. *See, e.g.*, *In re Citric Acid Antitrust Litig.*, No. 95-1092, C-95-2963 FMS, 1996 WL 655791, at *3 (N.D. Cal. Oct. 2, 1996).

The typicality inquiry focuses on the conduct of the defendants, and "[e]ven relatively pronounced factual differences will generally not preclude a finding of typicality where there is a strong similarity of legal theories." *Wood v. Betlach*, 286 F.R.D. 444, 448 (D. Ariz. 2012) (citation omitted). In *DRAM*, for instance, the court rejected the defendants' position that the plaintiffs' claims were atypical on the asserted grounds that there were different types of DRAM purchased, different categories of customers, and different sales channels. 2006 WL 1530166, at *4–6. Hence, "[t]he typicality requirement does not mandate that the products purchased, methods of purchase, or even damages of the named plaintiffs must be the same as those of the absent class members. Instead, the overarching scheme is the linchpin of plaintiffs' complaint, regardless of the product purchased, the market involved or the price ultimately paid." *TFT-LCD*, 267 F.R.D. at 593–94 (internal quotation marks, citations, and alterations omitted).

Typicality is not present, however, if unique defenses threaten to become the focus of the litigation. *Ellis*, 657 F.3d at 984 (holding that "a named plaintiff's motion for class certification should not be granted if there is a danger that absent class members will suffer if their representative is preoccupied with defenses unique to it") (quoting *Hanon v. Dataproducts Corp.*, 976 F.2d 497, 508 (9th Cir. 1992) (internal quotation marks omitted). While often raised as an adequacy challenge, an argument that a plaintiff "will be preoccupied with unique defences falls within our typicality caselaw." *DZ Rsrv. v. Meta Platforms, Inc.*, 96 F.4th 1223, 1239 (9th Cir. 2024). A challenge to a proposed class representative's credibility is not sufficient to destroy typicality where he or she is not a serial litigant and there is no evidence suggesting the representations they are making in the case are false. *Id.*

Typicality was deemed lacking in one notable antitrust components case. *In re Graphics Processing Units Antitrust Litig.*, 253 F.R.D. 478 (N.D. Cal. 2008). The class representatives purchased single GPUs pursuant to non-negotiable contracts but purported to represent a class including wholesalers, who purchased "a vast array of products on individually negotiated terms" through separate distribution channels. *Id.* at 489–90. Because the "wholesale purchasers . . . came to the negotiating table in a fundamentally different position than the representative plaintiffs," the claims of the latter were not typical of the class. *Id.* ("The representative plaintiffs simply do not have the appropriate incentive to establish antitrust violations with respect to all of the absent class members. To prove their claims, the named plaintiffs will have to show that the list prices that they paid for their graphics cards were artificially inflated by defendants. Proof that defendants conspired to fix those prices would hardly prove that defendants also conspired to fix the non-list prices for the transactions entered into with absent wholesale purchasers.").

Adequacy (Fed. R. Civ. P. 23(a)(4))

The adequacy requirement set forth in Rule 23(a)(4) aims "to ensure that the interests of the named representatives align with those of the rest of the class." *Larson v. Trans Union, LLC*, No. 12-CV-05726-WHO, 2015 WL 3945052, at *11 (N.D. Cal. June 26, 2015). Courts in the Ninth Circuit ask two questions to test the adequacy of a class representative: "(1) do the named plaintiffs and their counsel have any conflicts of interest with other class members; and (2) will the named plaintiffs and their counsel prosecute the action vigorously on behalf of the class?" *Staton v. Boeing Co.*, 327 F.3d 938, 957–58 (9th Cir. 2003); *see also Ellis*, 657 F.3d at 985 ("Adequate representation depends on, among other factors, an absence of antagonism between representatives and absentees, and a sharing of interest between representatives and absentees."); *Crawford v. Honig*, 37 F.3d 485, 487 (9th Cir. 1994) (emphasizing "the qualifications of counsel for the representatives, an absence of antagonism, a sharing of interests between representatives and absentees, and the unlikelihood that the suit is collusive") (quoting *Brown v. Ticor Title Ins. Co.*, 982 F.2d 386, 390 (9th Cir. 1992)). However, "[o]nly conflicts that are fundamental to the suit and that go to the heart of the litigation" defeat a plaintiff's adequacy. *In re Online DVD-Rental Antitrust Litig.*, 779 F.3d 934, 942 (9th Cir. 2015) (quoting 1 William B. Rubenstein, *Newberg on Class Actions* § 3.58 (5th ed. 2011)).

Under Rule 23(c)(1)(B), "[a]n order certifying a class action . . . must appoint class counsel under Rule 23(g)." In appointing class counsel, the court considers: "(i) the work counsel has done in identifying or investigating potential claims in the action, (ii) counsel's experience in handling class actions, other complex litigation, and claims of the type asserted in the action, (iii) counsel's knowledge of the applicable law, (iv) the resources counsel will commit to representing the class." Fed. R. Civ. P. 23(g)(1)(A); *see Fendler v. Westgate-Cal. Corp.*, 527 F.2d 1168, 1170 (9th Cir. 1975) (the inquiry looks to the "the zeal and competence of the counsel and party who wish to prosecute the action").

An influential Ninth Circuit case on adequacy of representation is *Walters v. Reno*, 145 F.3d 1032 (9th Cir. 1998). The suit alleged that certain federal governmental procedures violated the due process rights of a Rule 23(b)(2) class of illegal aliens. *Id.* at 1036. The court affirmed a permanent injunction requiring the government to revise two misleading immigration forms, among other mandatory steps. In so ruling, the court rejected the government's contention that the class representatives were inadequate because, having been granted immunity, they admitted to forging documents. *Id.* at 1046. The court explained that these admissions had "no bearing on the class representatives' abilities to pursue the class claims vigorously and represent the interests of the absentee class members." *Id.* Indeed, the results obtained spoke for themselves: the government's adequacy challenge was "particularly weak in light of the fact that the class representatives have been so successful in their efforts to obtain relief for the entire class." *Id.*

b. Rule 23(b) Requirements

Even if plaintiffs establish that all the requirements set forth in Rule 23(a) are satisfied, to maintain a class action, they also must establish that at least one of the Rule 23(b) requirements is satisfied.

Rule 23(b)(1)(A) and (B)

Subdivisions (b)(1)(A) and (b)(1)(B) of Rule 23 are intended for circumstances in which "individual adjudications would be impossible or unworkable[.]" *Wal-Mart*, 564 U.S. at 361.

Rule 23(b)(1)(A) provides for class treatment if individual actions would create a risk of "inconsistent or varying adjudications with respect to individual class members that would establish incompatible standard of conduct" for the defendant. Fed. R. Civ. P. 23(b)(1)(A).

The phrase "incompatible standards of conduct" refers to a situation where "different results in separate actions would impair the opposing party's ability to pursue a uniform continuing course of conduct." 7A Charles Alan Wright, Arthur R. Miller, and Mary Kay Kane, *Federal Practice and Procedure* § 1773 at 431 (2d ed. 1986). Accordingly, Rule 23(b)(1)(A) is designed to "eliminate the possibility of adjudications in which the defendant will be required to follow inconsistent courses of continuing conduct." *La Mar v. H & B Novelty & Loan Co.*, 489 F.2d 461, 466 (9th Cir. 1973). Rule 23(b)(1)(A) certification is thus inappropriate where the proposed class or subclass seeks primarily monetary damages. *In re First Am. Corp. ERISA Litig.*, 258 F.R.D. 610, 622 (9th Cir. 2009) (citing *Zinser*, 253 F.3d at 1193).

While "23(b)(1)(A) considers possible prejudice to a defendant, . . . 23(b)(1)(B) looks to prejudice to the putative class members." *Kanawi v. Bechtel Corp.*, 254 F.R.D. 102, 111 (N.D. Cal. 2008). Certification is appropriate under Rule 23(b)(1)(B) if the prosecution of individual actions would increase the likelihood that "adjudications with respect to individual class members . . . would be dispositive of the interests of the other members not parties to the individual adjudications or would substantially impair or impede their interests." Fed. R. Civ. P. 23(b)(1)(B).

The leading case on Rule 23(b)(1)(A) is *Ortiz v. Fibreboard Corp.*, 527 U.S. 815 (1999), in which the Supreme Court rejected a settlement of asbestos claims. Interpreting the subdivision, the Court stated that: "Classic examples of such a risk of impairment may, for example, be found in suits brought to reorganize fraternal benefit societies, actions by shareholders to declare a dividend or otherwise to fix their rights, and actions charging a breach of trust by an indenture trustee or other fiduciary similarly affecting the members of a large class of beneficiaries, requiring an accounting or similar procedure to restore the subject of the trust. In each of these categories, the shared character of rights claimed or relief awarded entails that an individual adjudication by a class member disposes of, or substantially affects, the interests of absent class members." *Id.* at 833–34 (internal quotation marks, citations, and alterations omitted); *see also Zinser*, 253 F.3d at 1196 (noting that class actions are permitted under Rule 23(b)(1)(B) if separate actions "inescapably will alter the substance of the rights of others having similar claims.") (citation omitted).

Principles of fairness and equity dictate that limited fund class actions—class actions where the fund is insufficient to pay all claims—are particularly amenable to mandatory class treatment under Rule 23(b)(1)(B). *See Ortiz*, 527 U.S. at 834–37. Absent such treatment, individuals could separately sue and recover a disproportionate share of the limited fund. *Id.* at 836–37. Even so, to obtain certification of a Rule 23(b)(1)(B) class under a limited fund theory, plaintiffs must demonstrate that "the assets potentially available to claimants are so limited that separate actions inescapably will alter the rights of other claimants." *Zinser*, 253 F.3d at 1197 (internal quotation marks omitted).

Rule 23(b)(2)

An injunctive class may be certified under Rule 23(b)(2) if "the party opposing the class has acted or refused to act on grounds that apply generally to the class, so that final injunctive relief or corresponding declaratory relief is appropriate respecting the class as a whole." Fed. R. Civ. P. 23(b)(2). In the unanimous Part III of the Supreme Court's *Wal-Mart* decision, the Court opined: "The key to the (b)(2) class is 'the *indivisible* nature of the injunctive or declaratory remedy warranted—the notion that the conduct is such that it can be enjoined or declared unlawful only as to all of the class members or as to none of them.' In other words, Rule 23(b)(2) applies only when a single injunction or declaratory judgment would provide relief to each member of the class. It does not authorize class certification when each individual class member would be entitled to a *different* injunction or declaratory judgment against the defendant." 564 U.S. at 360 (first emphasis added) (citation omitted).

An injunctive relief class must still satisfy the requirements of Rule 23(a). *See Black Lives Matter Los Angeles v. City of Los Angeles*, 113 F.4th 1249, 1265 (9th Cir. 2024). The plaintiff must also establish his or her standing by a preponderance of the evidence. *DZ*

Rsrv., 96 F.4th at 1240 (citing *Olean*, 31 F.4th at 664–65). "In order to establish standing for injunctive relief, 'a plaintiff must show that he is under threat of suffering "injury in fact" that is concrete and particularized; the threat must be actual and imminent, not conjectural or hypothetical; it must be fairly traceable to the challenged action of the defendant; and it must be likely that a favorable judicial decision will prevent or redress the injury.'" *Id.* at 1240 (quoting *Summers v. Earth Island Inst.*, 555 U.S. 488, 493 (2009)). "A plaintiff typically loses standing to challenge a policy affecting businesses when the plaintiff has ceased operating an affected business, unless the challenged policy caused the business's closure." *Id.* at 1241.

A plaintiff seeking certification under Rule 23(b)(2) need not show predominance of common issues or that a class action is a superior form of adjudication as required under Rule 23(b)(3). Rather, "[i]t is sufficient if class members complain of a pattern or practice that is generally applicable to the class as a whole. Even if some class members have not been injured by the challenged practice, a class may nevertheless be appropriate." *Walters*, 145 F.3d at 1047. "The rule does not require [courts] to examine the viability or bases of class members' claims for declaratory or injunctive relief, but only to look at whether class members seek uniform relief from a practice applicable to all of them." *Rodriguez v. Hayes*, 591 F.3d 1105, 1125 (9th Cir. 2010); *see also Zinser*, 253 F.3d at 1195. In addition, the plaintiff should "describe[] the general contours of an injunction" sought on behalf of the class. *B.K. by next friend Tinsley v. Snyder*, 922 F.3d 957, 972 (9th Cir. 2019) (quoting *Parsons v. Ryan*, 754 F.3d 657, 689 n.35 (9th Cir. 2014)).

Rodriguez involved a class of individuals who were detained without bond pending immigration proceedings. The plaintiffs moved to certify a Rule 23(b)(2) class, seeking individual bond hearings for all class members, with the government bearing the burden of proof. Defendants challenged class certification under Rule 23(b)(2), arguing that some class members may not have been entitled to bond hearings under mandatory detention rules, while others were subject to regulations governing burden. But the Ninth Circuit rejected defendants' arguments, holding that Rule 23(b)(2) "does not require us to examine the viability or bases of class members' claims for declaratory and injunctive relief, but only to look at whether class members seek uniform relief form a practice applicable to all of them." 591 F.3d at 1125.

As *Rodriguez* suggests, 50 years after Rule 23(b)(2) took effect, its paradigmatic use remains the civil rights injunction. *See* Fed. R. Civ. P. 23(b)(2) Adv. Comm. Notes to 1966 Amendment ("Action or inaction is directed to a class within the meaning of this subdivision even if it has taken effect or is threatened only as to one or a few members of the class, provided it is based on grounds which have general application to the class. Illustrative are various actions in the civil-rights field where a party is charged with discriminating unlawfully against a class, usually one whose members are incapable of specific enumeration."). In *Rodriguez*, however, the Supreme Court reversed a subsequent Ninth Circuit decision that upheld a permanent injunction forbidding the government from detaining aliens for more than six months absent clear and convincing evidence that further detention is justified and requiring bond hearings at six-month intervals for each alien so detained. *Jennings v. Rodriguez*, 138 S. Ct. 830, 839 (2018). The Court directed the Ninth Circuit to consider whether class certification under Rule 23(b)(2) remained appropriate, commenting that if "some members of the certified class may not be entitled to bond hearings as a constitutional matter," "then it may no longer be true that the complained-of conduct is such that it can be enjoined or declared unlawful only as to all of the class members or as to none of them." *Id.* at 851–52 (internal quotation marks and citations omitted).

The Ninth Circuit also has made clear that a district court may provisionally certify a class when issuing a preliminary injunction. *See Al Otro Lado v. Wolf*, 952 F.3d 999, 1005 n.4 (9th Cir. 2020) (citing *Meyer v. Portfolio Recovery Assocs., LLC*, 707 F.3d 1036, 1041–43 (9th Cir. 2012)). The court explained in *Meyer* that "[t]he plain language of FRCP 23(b)(2) does not restrict class certification to instances when final injunctive relief issues; it only requires that final injunctive relief be appropriate." 707 F.3d at 1043.

Rule 23(b)(3)

Predominance of Common Questions

Rule 23(b)(3) provides for a class action upon a finding that "questions of law or fact common to class members predominate over any questions affecting only individual members, and that a class action is superior to other available methods for fairly and efficiently adjudicating the controversy." Fed. R. Civ. P. 23(b)(3). "Rule 23(b)(3) focuses on the relationship between the common and individual issues," *Hanlon*, 150 F.3d at 1022, and is "even more demanding" than the other class certification prerequisites. *Comcast*, 569 U.S. at 34. The predominance "inquiry tests whether proposed classes are sufficiently cohesive to warrant adjudication by representation." *Amchem Prods., Inc. v. Windsor*, 521 U.S. 591, 623 (1997). It "asks whether the common, aggregation-enabling, issues in the case are more prevalent or important than the non-common, aggregation-defeating, individual issues." *Tyson Foods, Inc. v. Bouaphakeo*, 577 U.S. 442, 453 (2016) (citation omitted). In other words, "predominance does not require that all questions be common" although "predominance is necessarily satisfied if all questions are common." *DZ Rsrv.*, 96 F.4th at 1238 (citation omitted).

The predominance inquiry proceeds in three steps: (1) the court identifies "which questions are central to the plaintiffs' claim"; (2) the court next determines which questions are common and which are individualized; and (3) the court then must analyze whether the common questions predominate over the individual ones. *Id.* at 1233.

Although the plaintiff has the burden of showing that common issues predominate, "a plaintiff need not rebut every individualized issue that could possibly be raised," for requiring "such proof would be akin to demanding proof that 'plaintiffs would win at trial.'" *Van*, 61 F.4th at 1067 (quoting *Olean*, 31 F.4th at 667). "Instead, a plaintiff must merely demonstrate by a preponderance of the evidence that a common question of law or fact exists—an issue that is capable of class-wide resolution." *Id.* If the plaintiff meets this burden, "the defendant must invoke individualized issues and provide sufficient evidence that the individualized issues bar recovery on at least some claims, thus raising the spectre of class-member-by-class-member adjudication of the issue." *Id.* at 1067 (citation omitted). Upon such a showing, the court must determine whether the defendant's evidence means that individualized questions will overwhelm the common ones, defeating predominance. *Id.* (citing *Olean*, 31 F.4th at 669); *see DZ Rsrv.*, 96 F.4th at 1233 ("[P]redominance is not more demanding because the common issues must in some way be 'more common' than would be required under Rule 23(a)(2). Rather, predominance is more demanding because not only must there be common issues, but the common issues must predominate.").

Individualized Damages

A class action plaintiff must show that damages are capable of being measured on a class-wide basis. *Comcast*¸ 569 U.S. at 34. The Ninth Circuit has, however, held that in moving for class certification, a plaintiff does not need to "actually prove that classwide damages exist in order to obtain class certification." *Lytle*, 114 F.4th at 1025. Therefore, a plaintiff "may rely on an unexecuted damages model to demonstrate that damages are susceptible to common proof so long as the district court finds, by a preponderance of the evidence, that the model will be able to reliably calculate damages in a manner common to the class at trial." *Id.* at 1024.

"Although uncertain damages calculations do not alone defeat certification, . . . at the class-certification stage (as at trial), any model supporting a plaintiff's damages case must be consistent with its liability case." *Nguyen v. Nissan N. Am., Inc.*, 932 F.3d 811, 817 (9th Cir. 2019) (emphasis and internal quotation marks omitted) (citing *Comcast*, 569 U.S. at 35). Further, as pattern jury instructions reflect, although damages must not be speculative, they also "need not be proven with exact certainty." *Edwards v. Nat'l Milk Producers*

Fed'n, No. C 11-04766 JSW, 2014 WL 4643639, at *6 (N.D. Cal. Sept. 16, 2014); *see* 3 Kevin F. O'Malley et al., *Federal Jury Practice and Instructions* § 128:60 (6th ed. 2008 & Supp. 2010) ("Damages must be reasonable. . . . You are not permitted to award speculative damages."). Provided they are reliable as applied in a particular case, standard techniques for calculating damages suffice. *See, e.g.*, *Lytle*, 114 F.4th 1033; *In re Rubber Chems. Antitrust Litig.*, 232 F.R.D. 346, 353 (N.D. Cal. 2005); *DRAM*, 2006 WL 1530166, at *10; 3 Alba Conte & Herbert B. Newberg, *Newberg on Class Actions* § 10.3 (4th ed. 2002) ("Aggregate class proof of monetary relief may also be based on sampling techniques or other reasonable estimates, under accepted rules of evidence.") (citing Fed. R. Evid. 703, 1006).

The eventual need to determine individual class member damages does not preclude certification. "Rule 23 specifically contemplates the need for . . . individualized claim determinations after a finding of liability." *Briseno*, 844 F.3d at 1131; *see also Blackie v. Barrack*, 524 F.2d 891, 905 (9th Cir. 1975) (explaining that "[t]he amount of damages is invariably an individual question and does not defeat class action treatment"); *Tyson Foods*, 577 U.S. at 453 (holding that a class action "may be considered proper under Rule 23(b)(3) even though other important matters will have to be tried separately, such as damages or some affirmative defenses") (citation omitted).

A classwide damages model must not sweep beyond the plaintiff's liability theories. *See Nguyen*, 932 F.3d at 817; *Leyva v. Medline Indus. Inc.*, 716 F.3d 510, 514 (9th Cir. 2013) (citing *Comcast*, 569 U.S. at 31–38). But the existence of individualized damages questions does not, by itself, preclude certification. *Vaquero v. Ashley Furniture Indus., Inc.*, 824 F.3d 1150, 1155 (9th Cir. 2016); *Pulaski & Middleman, LLC v. Google, Inc.*, 802 F.3d 979, 987–88 (9th Cir. 2015) (differences in "[d]amages calculations alone cannot defeat class certification.") (citing *Yokoyama v. Midland Nat'l Life Ins. Co.*, 594 F.3d 1087, 1094 (9th Cir. 2010)). That some class members were harmed more than others is insufficient by itself to defeat certification—plaintiffs "need not prove, at the class certification stage, that every single class member was in fact injured in a specific way." *In re Cathode Ray Tube (CRT) Antitrust Litig.*, No. C007-5944-SC, 2013 WL 5391159, at *5–6 (N.D. Cal. Apr. 11, 2014); *see also DRAM*, 2006 WL 1530166, at *8–10.

In the antitrust context, as well, "variations in products and complexities in a distribution chain do not preclude an estimation of whether an overcharge impacted end purchasers." *TFT-LCD*, 267 F.R.D. at 603; *accord In re Static Random Access Memory (SRAM) Antitrust Litig*, 264 F.R.D. 603, 614 (N.D. Cal. 2009) ("[C]ontentions of infinite diversity of product, marketing practices, and pricing have been made in numerous cases and rejected.") (citation omitted).

The Ninth Circuit also noted that "[d]istrict courts are well-equipped to deal with issues of individualized calculations in the wage-and-hour context, and may use 'any of the practices developed to deal with Rule 23 classes facing similar issues.'" *Senne v. Kansas City Royals Baseball Corp.*, 934 F.3d 918, 950 (9th Cir. 2019) (citations omitted). In *Bowerman v. Field Asset Services, Inc.*, however, the Ninth Circuit decertified a wage-and-hour class "because any common question as to misclassification is outweighed by the individual questions going to injury and damages." 60 F.4th 459, 469 (9th Cir. 2023). The district court had based its predominance finding on the analysis of the plaintiffs' expert, who opined that individualized injury and damage assessments "would not be prohibitively cumbersome." *Id.* But after the district court questioned the reliability of his damage model, the plaintiffs withdrew the expert such that "class members were left relying on individual testimony to establish the existence of an injury and the amount of damages." *Id.* Because the individualized testimony would have effectively required hundreds of "individualized mini-trials" to determine both liability and damages, common issues did not predominate. *Id.* at 470. Hence the case was distinguishable from *Senne* and other wage-and-hour cases where plaintiffs submitted representative evidence that applied to all class members. *Id.*

Uninjured Class Members

One hotly contested question in complex class actions is whether a class may contain persons who escaped injury from the defendant's challenged conduct. In *Torres*, the Ninth Circuit cast its lot with the other circuits that have answered "yes." The court held that "even a well-defined class may inevitably contain some individuals who have suffered no harm as a result of a defendant's unlawful conduct." 835 F.3d at 1136 (citing 1 William B. Rubenstein, *Newberg on Class Actions* § 2:3 (5th ed. 2011); *Messner v. Northshore Univ. HealthSystem*, 669 F.3d 802, 823 (7th Cir. 2012)). Conversely, the court allowed that predominance might be defeated if "large numbers of class members . . . were never *exposed* to the challenged conduct to begin with." *Torres*, 835 F.3d at 1136 (emphasis in original).

Recent Supreme Court precedent tends to support these *Torres* holdings—though Chief Justice Roberts made clear in his *Tyson Foods* concurrence that class members should never receive windfall recoveries. 577 U.S. at 466 (Roberts, C.J., concurring) (declaring that "Article III does not give federal courts the power to order relief to any uninjured plaintiff, class action or not."). The Court cemented this holding in *TransUnion*: "Every class member must have Article III standing in order to recover individual damages." 141 S. Ct. at 2208. The post-judgment scenario in *TransUnion* differs, of course, from the pretrial posture, and requiring a plaintiff to show prior to trial that every class member was injured would force the plaintiff prove his or her case to establish standing. In *Tyson Foods* and again in *TransUnion* the Supreme Court left unaddressed the question of whether a certified class may include uninjured persons. In *Tyson Foods*, however, the Court allowed a certified class to pursue distribution of an aggregate damages award in spite of the defendant's claim that some uninjured employees would benefit. 577 U.S. at 461. Additional guidance is found in *Halliburton*, where the Court reaffirmed the fraud-on-the-market presumption of reliance in securities fraud actions, together with the defendant's ability to rebut this presumption. 573 U.S. at 258. The Court reasoned that even though rebuttal evidence "has the effect of leav[ing] individualized questions of reliance in the case, there is no reason to think that these questions will overwhelm common ones and render class certification inappropriate under Rule 23(b)(3). That the defendant might attempt to pick off the occasional class member here or there through individualized rebuttal does not cause individual questions to predominate." *Id.* at 276 (quotation marks omitted). Thus, the Supreme Court in *Halliburton* contemplated—and effectively approved—the inclusion of some uninjured class members so long as common issues predominate in the case as a whole.

Even before *Torres*, courts in the Ninth Circuit held that the potential inclusion of uninjured class members in the class definition is no bar to certification. In *Rodman v. Safeway*, for example, the court rejected the notion that a class definition must exclude all uninjured persons, a position the court concluded would require impermissible merits fact-finding at class certification or an impermissible fail-safe class definition. 2014 WL 988992, at *15 (citing *Wolin v. Jaguar Land Rover N. Am., LLC*, 617 F.3d 1168, 1173 (9th Cir. 2010) ("[N]either the possibility that a plaintiff will be unable to prove his allegations, nor the possibility that the later course of the suit might unforeseeably prove the original decision to certify the class wrong, is a basis for declining to certify a class which apparently satisfies the Rule.") (quoting *Blackie*, 524 F.2d at 901). Consistent with *Torres*, the court in *Rodman* held: "The fact that a Proposed Class 'will often include persons who have not been injured by the defendant's conduct . . . does not preclude class certification,' but it is also the case that 'a class should not be certified if it is apparent that it contains a *great many* persons who have suffered no injury at the hands of the defendant.'" 2014 WL 988992, at *16 (emphasis in *Rodman*) (citation omitted).

A Ninth Circuit panel squarely addressed the issue of uninjured class members in *Olean*, noting in part that a "key factual determination" is whether the plaintiffs' statistical evidence reveals too many uninjured class members. 993 F.3d at 791. The plaintiffs' and defendants' experts disagreed about the number of uninjured class members; plaintiffs' expert claimed about 5.5 percent of the class was uninjured, while defendants' expert claimed the number was closer to 28 percent. *Id.* at 782–83. The district court declined to resolve the issue at the certification stage, instead reasoning that the plaintiffs' statistical evidence was at least plausible and leaving the matter for the jury to resolve. The panel decision found an abuse of discretion, as courts must determine that predominance and superiority are met before certifying a class. *Id.* at 793. The court further held that the number of uninjured class members must be *de minimis*, and although it declined to "adopt a numerical or bright-line rule," it suggested that 5 to 6 percent of the class represents the outer bound of a *de minimis* number. *Id.* at 791–92. Because the district court declined to resolve the competing expert claims regarding the number of uninjured class members, this number may have been more than *de minimis*. *Id.* at 793.

After granting en banc review, the full Ninth Circuit rejected the *de minimis* standard as "inconsistent with Rule 23(b)(3), which requires only that the district court determine after rigorous analysis whether the common question predominates over any individual questions, including individualized questions about injury or entitlement to damages." *Olean Wholesale Grocery Coop., Inc. v. Bumble Bee Foods LLC*, 31 F.4th 651, 669 (9th Cir. 2022) (en banc). In response to the dissent's contention that Rule 23 requires only a *de minimis* number of uninjured class members and that the majority was creating a circuit split, the en banc majority reasoned that "we are bound to apply Rule 23(b)(3) as written, regardless of policy preferences. And contrary to the dissent's assertion, our conclusion that courts must apply Rule 23(b)(3) on a case-by-case basis, rather than rely on a per se rule that a class cannot be certified if it includes more than a *de minimis* number of uninjured class members, is consistent with the approach taken by our sister circuits. *Id.* at 669 n.13. The court explained that in the two cases cited by the dissent, neither the D.C. Circuit nor the First Circuit adopted "a per se rule" requiring no more than a *de minimis* number of uninjured class members. *Id.* Rather, those courts concluded that under the specific facts before them, the need to identify uninjured class members defeated predominance and rendered class-wide adjudication unmanageable. *Id.* (citing *In re Rail Freight Fuel Surcharge Antitrust Litig.-MDL No. 1869 (Rail Freight II)*, 934 F.3d 619 (D.C. Cir. 2019), and *In re Asacol Antitrust Litig.*, 907 F.3d 42 (1st Cir. 2018)). After the Ninth Circuit issued its en banc decision, the defendant in the *Olean* case petitioned unsuccessfully for a writ of certiorari. *See* 143 S. Ct. 424 (2022).

After *Olean*, a defendant still may defeat predominance by raising "the spectre of class-member-by-class-member adjudication" for determining whether a person's claim has merit. In *Van*, the Ninth Circuit considered the defendant's evidence that 18 of the 13,680 discounts "provided to class members were . . . for the purpose of offsetting" the improper sales tax. 61 F.4th at 1068. While the district court in certifying a class had found the number of discounts "de minimis," the Ninth Circuit remanded, concluding that the defendant's "evidence . . . was sufficient to prove that an inquiry into the circumstances and motivations behind each of the 13,680 discounts might be necessary." *Id.* at 1068–69. The court reasoned that "[w]hen a defendant substantiates such an individualized issue in this way, the district court must determine whether the plaintiff has proven by a preponderance of the evidence that the [common] questions of law or fact . . . predominate over any questions affecting only individual members." *Id.* at 1069.

Multistate Certification

Whether a class action may proceed under the laws of several states depends primarily on whether there are material differences among the elements of the respective state laws. *See Am. Law Inst., Principles of the Law of Aggregate Litigation* § 2.05(b) (2010); *see White v. Symetra Assigned Benefits Serv. Co.*, 104 F.4th 1182, 1199 (9th Cir. 2024) ("The need to apply the law of different states raises questions of whether individualized issues predominate and how a matter can be fairly managed as a class action."). In *Hanlon*, the Ninth Circuit concluded that "idiosyncratic differences between state consumer protection laws are not sufficiently substantive to predominate over the shared claims" proposed to be settled. 150 F.3d at 1022–23. Notwithstanding *Hanlon*, if state consumer protection statutes or other state laws would apply in materially different ways to the facts of a case, multistate certification may be inappropriate.

In *Mazza v. American Honda Motor Company*, the Ninth Circuit evaluated whether the district court properly certified a nationwide class under California law in a false advertising case based on Honda's allegedly misleading descriptions of certain features of its Acura RL vehicle. 666 F.3d 581 (9th Cir. 2012). In holding that California law could not apply nationally, the court noted that certain applicable consumer protection statutes—like California's—contain no scienter requirement, while others do. *Id.* at 591. "California also requires named class plaintiffs to demonstrate reliance, while some other states' consumer protection statutes do not." *Id.* The court concluded that "these are not trivial or wholly immaterial differences. In cases where a defendant acted without scienter, a scienter requirement will spell the difference between the success and failure of a claim. In cases where a plaintiff did not rely on an alleged misrepresentation, the reliance requirement will spell the difference between the success and failure of the claim." *Id.* Accordingly, the *Mazza* court held that these "variances in state law overwhelm common issues and preclude predominance for a single nationwide class." *Id.* at 596. The *Mazza* court also deemed class certification inappropriate because "many class members were never exposed to the allegedly misleading advertisements, insofar as advertising of the challenged system was very limited." *Id.* at 595. The court did not address whether grouping state laws with substantially similar elements and designating corresponding subclasses would render certification permissible. *See, e.g.*, *Senne*, 934 F.3d at 928–37 (analyzing choice of law issues at length in connection with class certification); *Ellsworth v. U.S. Bank, N.A.*, No. C 12-02506 LB, 2014 WL 2734953, at *21 (N.D. Cal. June 13, 2014) (finding that "the contract laws of the various states are capable of being organized into groups with similar legal regimes" and that "common issues predominate in each subclass"); *see also Aldapa v. Fowler Packing Co., Inc.*, 323 F.R.D. 316, 326–27 (E.D. Cal. 2018) (discussing the law of subclassing under Rule 23(c)(5) and noting in part that "subclasses may be used to more efficiently resolve common issues during the proceeding") (citing, *inter alia*, *Am. Timber & Trading Co. v. First Nat'l Bank of Or.*, 690 F.2d 781, 787 n.5 (9th Cir. 1982)).

The Ninth Circuit has since made clear that *Mazza* is not limited to state statutes prohibiting unfair or deceptive acts or practices. In *Stromberg v. Qualcomm Inc.*, the court vacated certification of a nationwide class of up to 250 million class members under the Sherman Act and California antitrust law. 14 F.4th 1059 (9th Cir. 2021). By way of background, after the Supreme Court held that indirect purchasers cannot seek damages for Sherman Act violations in *Illinois Brick Company v. Illinois*, 431 U.S. 720 (1977), many states enacted so-called *Illinois Brick* repealer statutes allowing indirect purchasers to pursue antitrust damages suits under state law. In total, 35 states and the District of Columbia have such repealer laws—e.g., California's Cartwright Act—while 15 states do not. *Id.* at 1064. Applying California's choice-of-law rules in *Qualcomm*, the district court concluded that the plaintiffs could bring claims on behalf of a nationwide class under the Cartwright Act even though the non-repealer states' antitrust laws materially differ from the Cartwright Act. *Id.* at 1065–66. The district court reasoned that California has a strong interest in having its laws applied because the defendant Qualcomm is a California business, whereas the non-repealer states lack an interest in protecting a non-resident business or having their laws applied to disadvantage their own citizens. *Id.*

On appeal, the Ninth Circuit concluded that the district court had misapplied California's choice-of-law rules with respect to both the repealer and non-repealer states. *Id.* at 1068–74. The court explained that the district court failed to account for variations even in the antitrust laws of the *Illinois Brick* repealer states and therefore misapplied the first step in California's choice of law analysis. *Id.* at 1068–69. Moreover, while California has an interest in applying its laws to a resident corporation, other states have an interest in regulating their markets and commerce within their borders. *Id.* at 1069. According to the *Qualcomm* court, "[n]on-repealer states' *Illinois Brick* laws are designed to regulate antitrust enforcement by allocating recoverable antitrust damages in a way those states think best promotes market competition." *Id.* The district court's focus on harm to resident consumers was too narrow because "the relevant interests are about harm to the competitive process and in-state business activity." *Id.* at 1072. In addition, the decision of those states without repealer laws reflect a "state calculation that antitrust enforcement is best served by having indirect purchasers realize the benefit of antitrust enforcement outside of court processes" and a policy of seeking to attract more businesses to their state. *Id.* Citing *Mazza*, the court held that because the place of the wrong occurred where consumers purchased their phones, the non-repealer states had an interest in having their own laws applied to the plaintiffs' claims. *Id.* at 1073–74. While leaving open whether "a single class of all repealer state Plaintiffs could be certified under Rule 23(b)(3)," the Ninth Circuit directed the district court to redo its choice-of-law analysis to avoid "impair[ing] non-repealer state policy by allowing California to set antitrust enforcement policy for the entire country." *Id.* at 1074.

Affirmative Defenses

The Ninth Circuit addressed how affirmative defenses may interact with the predominance analysis in *True Health Chiropractic, Inc. v. McKesson Corp.*, 896 F.3d 923 (9th Cir. 2018), a TCPA case. The court first recognized that "[d]efenses that must be litigated on an individual basis can defeat class certification." *Id.* at 931 (citing *Wal-Mart*, 564 U.S. at 367); *see also Hanon*, 976 F.2d at 508 (affirming denial of class certification based on atypicality and deeming certification "inappropriate where a putative class representative is subject to unique defenses which threaten to become the focus of the litigation.") (quoting *Gary Plastic Packaging Corp. v. Merrill Lynch, Pierce, Fenner & Smith, Inc.*, 903 F.2d 176, 180 (2d Cir. 1990)). "[C]ourts have been nearly unanimous," however, "in holding that possible differences in the application of a statute of limitations to individual class members, including the named plaintiffs, does not preclude certification of a class action." *Tait v. BSH Home Appliances Corp.*, 289 F.R.D. 466, 486 (C.D. Cal. 2012) (citation omitted).

Turning to the defendant's assertion of a TCPA consent defense in *True Health Chiropractic*, the Ninth Circuit found the predominance analysis "strongly affect[ed]" by the defendant's burden of proof on that defense: "Since [the defendant] bears the burden, we assess predominance by analyzing the consent defenses [the defendant] has actually advanced and for which it has presented evidence. . . . But we do not consider the consent defenses that [the defendant] might advance or for which it has presented no evidence." 896 F.3d at 931–32. Under *True Health Chiropractic*, therefore, a defendant cannot defeat predominance simply by pointing to a defense and arguing that it raises individualized issues. Instead, just as a plaintiff must show that common questions predominate by a preponderance of the evidence, so must a defendant present sufficient evidence to succeed with an argument that its affirmative defense causes individual questions to predominate.

In addition, at class certification, a district court does not necessarily have to narrow the class period based on the applicable statute of limitations. *See Owino v. CoreCivic, Inc.*, 60 F.4th 437 (9th Cir. 2022). The *Owino* plaintiffs were individuals incarcerated in private immigration detention facilities who alleged that the corporate owner of the facilities used forced labor and paid inadequate compensation in violation of federal and state human trafficking and labor laws. *Id.* at 441. After the district court certified three classes, the defendant argued on appeal that one of the classes should have been narrowed based on the statute of limitations for the state law claim. *Id.* at 445. The Ninth Circuit agreed with the district court that narrowing the class based on the statute of limitations was premature at the class certification stage without more discovery. *Id.* The court noted that the Ninth Circuit and other circuits have held that a statute of limitations problem does not automatically defeat predominance—and "this principle is applicable to certification more broadly" and not just to the predominance inquiry because the district court is free to modify a certification order later in the case. *Id.* at 445–46.

Superiority of Class Adjudication

The superiority inquiry "requires determination of whether the objectives of the particular class action procedure will be achieved in the particular case." *Hanlon*, 150 F.3d at 1023. The inquiry asks whether class treatment will "achieve economies of time, effort, and expense, and promote . . . uniformity of decision as to persons similarly situated, without sacrificing procedural fairness or bringing about other undesirable results." *Amchem*, 521 U.S. at 615 (1997) (quoting Fed. R. Civ. P. 23(b)(3) Adv. Comm. Notes to 1966 Amendment); *see also Valentino v. Carter-Wallace, Inc.*, 97 F.3d 1227, 1234 (9th Cir. 1996) ("Where class-wide litigation of common issues will reduce litigation costs and promote greater efficiency, a class action may be superior to other methods of litigation."). Rule 23(b)(3) sets forth several nonexclusive factors relevant to the superiority analysis: "(A) the class members' interests in individually controlling the prosecution or defense of separate actions; (B) the extent and nature of any litigation concerning the controversy already begun by or against class members; (C) the desirability or undesirability of concentrating the litigation of the claims in the particular forum; and (D) the likely difficulties in managing a class action." Fed. R. Civ. P. 23(b)(3).

A determination that claims are too small, as a practical matter, to be litigated individually supports a finding of superiority. *See Valentino*, 97 F.3d at 1234–35 (holding that "[a] class action is the superior method for managing litigation if no realistic alternative exists."); *Chavez v. Blue Sky Nat. Bev. Co.*, 268 F.R.D. 365, 379 (N.D. Cal. 2010) (finding that "the class action is superior to maintaining individual claims for a small amount of damages"). Where, however, one of the superiority factors weighs strongly against certification, the court may deny the motion even if all the other class certification requirements are satisfied. For example, if the class is limited to a subset of affected persons or if certification would complicate ongoing litigation in another forum, a class action may not be a superior means of resolving the overall controversy. *Compare, e.g.*, *Campos v. W. Dental Servs., Inc.*, 404 F. Supp. 2d 1164, 1172–73 (N.D. Cal. 2005) (declining to certify a class limited to individuals residing in a particular California county because to do so would "lead to piecemeal litigation," a result "inconsistent with the policy behind both the FDCPA and class actions"), *with McCurdy v. Prof'l Credit Serv.*, No. 6:15-CV-01498-AA, 2016 WL 5853721, at *5 (D. Or. Oct. 3, 2016) ("I will not deny certification based on the mere possibility another class action will be filed."); *see also Zinser*, 253 F.3d at 1192 ("If each class member has to litigate numerous and substantial separate issues to establish his or her right to recover individually, a class action is not superior."); *Brown v. Federal Express Corp.*, 249 F.R.D. 580, 587 (C.D. Cal. 2008) (superiority not met because "[w]ithout a viable method of common proof for evaluating the ability of 5,500 class members to take breaks as required by law, the Court will be mired in over 5,000 mini-trials regarding individual job duties and expectations").

While litigation relating to manageability is commonplace, courts seldom deny class certification purely on manageability grounds. And when they do, it is generally because of case-specific problems like intractable conflict-of-law issues or difficulties in providing class notice. *See* 2 William B. Rubenstein, *Newberg on Class Actions* §§ 4:72–4:73 (5th ed. 2012). Given the array of case management tools at the district courts' disposal, the Ninth Circuit, like several other circuits, recognizes a presumption against denial of certification for manageability reasons alone. *Briseno*, 844 F.3d at 1128.

c. Evidence at Class Certification

Whether evidence submitted at class certification must be admissible for district courts to consider has been a contentious issue in the Ninth Circuit. In *Sali v. Corona Regional Medical Center*, the court held that "[i]nadmissibility alone is not a proper basis to reject evidence submitted in support of class certification," and directed the lower court to consider a declaration prepared by a paralegal employed by the plaintiffs' lawyers. 909 F.3d 996, 1004–06 (9th Cir. 2018). The court reasoned that because a class certification decision is inherently provisional, "[a]pplying the formal strictures of trial to such an early stage of litigation makes little common sense." *Id.* at 1004. Just as the standing inquiry looks to different sources as litigation progresses, so does the class certification inquiry precede trial, at which evidence must be admissible to come before the fact finder. *Id.* at 1006. Given that parties typically litigate class certification before discovery has closed, "there is bound to be some evidentiary uncertainty," and in *Sali* the district court "rejected evidence that likely could have been presented in an admissible form at trial." *Id.* at 1005–06 (citation omitted). Nonetheless, the Ninth Circuit stopped short of holding that the quality of evidence does not matter at class certification: "[A]n inquiry into the evidence's ultimate admissibility should go to the weight that evidence is given at the class certification stage." *Id.* at 1006.

The court in *Sali* also noted that its holding, concerning the treatment of evidence at class certification, sides with the Eighth Circuit over a stricter approach required by the Fifth Circuit and suggested by the Seventh and Third Circuits. *Id.* at 1005–06; *see also B.K. v. Snyder*, 922 F.3d 957, 974 (9th Cir. 2019) ("At this 'tentative, preliminary, and limited' stage we have held strictly admissible evidence is not required, and we have indicated that plaintiffs can meet their evidentiary burden in part through allegations when the allegations are detailed and supported by additional materials.") (internal citation omitted)). Judge Bea, joined by four other Ninth Circuit judges, dissented from denial of rehearing en banc in *Sali*, declaring in part that the panel's holding "doesn't pass the straight-face test." 907 F.3d 1185 (9th Cir. 2018).

As for expert testimony at class certification, the majority opinion in *Sali* stated that "in evaluating challenged expert testimony in support of class certification, a district court should evaluate admissibility under the standard set forth in *Daubert*. But admissibility must not be dispositive." 909 F.3d at 1006 (internal citation omitted). The Ninth Circuit itself previously suggested that conducting a *Daubert* admissibility analysis is appropriate at class certification, in *Ellis v. Costco Wholesale Corp.*, 657 F.3d 970, 982 (9th Cir. 2011). After *Sali*, too, the court presumed that such an analysis may be properly conducted at class certification when affirming the exclusion of expert evidence in *Grodzitsky v. America Honda Motor Co.*, 957 F.3d 979, 984–86 (9th Cir. 2020).

In *Olean Wholesale Grocery Coop., Inc. v. Bumble Bee Foods LLC*, the Ninth Circuit suggested that plaintiffs must satisfy Rule 23(b)(3) through "admissible evidence," without mentioning *Sali* or the apparent inconsistency. 31 F.4th 651, 665 (9th Cir. 2022). *Olean* concerned, in part, whether the district court abused its discretion in failing to resolve disputes in expert evidence related to the propriety of class certification.

Citing *Sali*, the Ninth Circuit reiterated again in *Lytle v. Nutramax Laboratories, Inc.* that "there is no requirement that the evidence relied upon by Plaintiffs to support class certification be presented in an admissible form at the class certification stage." 114 F.4th at 1024–25. The likelihood a piece of common proof will not be admissible at trial simply weighs against a finding that common issues will predominate. *Id.* at 1025.

In *Lytle*, the Ninth Circuit also directly addressed the "unsettled question" about "[t]he manner and extent to which the *Daubert* framework applies at the class certification stage" and whether district courts must conduct a "full" or "more limited" *Daubert* inquiry. *Id.* at 1030. A "full" inquiry considers whether the expert's testimony is qualified to testify and weighs the reliability of the testimony while a "limited" inquiry focuses not on admissibility, but the weight the testimony is entitled to for evaluating the requirements of class certification. *Id.* at 1030 & n.6. Noting that "[o]ur own precedent has somewhat oscillated between these two approaches," the panel unanimously held that "the distinction between a 'full' and 'limited' *Daubert* inquiry is a function of what aspect of FRCP 23 is being addressed." *Id.* Where an expert's testimony goes to issues of commonality and predominance, for instance, "such *Daubert* factors as peer review of the proffered model may be highly relevant, while others, such as known error rate, may be more applicable to the later-executed results of the test." *Id.* In addition, the extent of the *Daubert* analysis also turns on when class certification is being decided: "If discovery has closed and an expert's analysis is complete and her tests fully executed, there may be no reason for a district court to delay its assessment of ultimate admissibility at trial. By contrast, where an expert's model has yet to be fully developed, a district court is limited at class certification to making a predictive judgment about how likely it is the expert's analysis will eventually bear fruit." *Id.* at 1031.

d. Timing of Class Certification

Rule 23(c)(1)(A) directs the court to rule on class certification "[a]t an early practicable time after a person sues or is sued as a class representative." Fed. R. Civ. P. 23(c)(1)(A). The court normally sets the due date for moving for certification in its scheduling or standing order. The current "early practicable time" standard is a relaxation of the former rule, which required class certification motions to be brought "as soon as practicable." The Advisory Committee noted that allowing for more time before the certification decision furthered several goals, "including: (1) enabling discovery relevant to certification; (2) helping a court to 'determine how the case will be tried,' (3) permitting a court to consider dispositive motions without binding the class; and (4) giving more leeway to consider counsel's adequacy under Rule 23(g)." *Id.* (citing Fed. R. Civ. P. 23(C)(1)(A) advisory committee note (2003)); *see also* Federal Judicial Center, *Manual for Complex Litigation* § 21.133 (4th ed. 2004) (observing that "local rules specify[ing] a short period" for moving for class certification "may be inconsistent with Rule 23(c)(1)(A)'s emphasis on the parties' obligation to present the court with sufficient information to support an informed decision on certification. Parties need sufficient time to develop an adequate record.").

For many years, an anomalous local rule in the Central District of California provided that any motion for class certification had to be filed "[w]ithin 90 days after service of a pleading purporting to commence a class action[.]" C.D. Cal. L.R. 23-3. Federal judges in that district regularly entered stipulations relieving litigants of the need to abide by that tight time frame. The Ninth Circuit eventually struck down this local rule, deeming it impracticable and inconsistent with Rule 23. *ABS Entm't, Inc. v. CBS Corp.*, 908 F.3d 405 (9th Cir. 2018). In *ABS*, the parties twice stipulated to extend the 90-day deadline to allow for discovery in support of class certification. *Id.* at 426. But the district court denied each stipulation, struck plaintiffs' timely class certification motion for technical deficiencies, and struck the class allegations as untimely. *Id.* at 411–12, 426–27. On appeal, the Ninth Circuit held that these decisions reflected an abuse of discretion. *Id.* at 427. The court reasoned that local rules specifying an unreasonably short period to move for class certification are inconsistent with the parties' obligation to provide the court with sufficient evidence to support an informed decision on class certification. *Id.* The court accordingly held the local rule "incompatible with Federal Rule of Civil Procedure 23." *Id.*

In keeping with the more relaxed timing of current Rule 23(c)(1)(A), the Ninth Circuit recognizes that "[u]nder the proper circumstances—*where it is more practicable to do so* and where the parties will not suffer significant prejudice—the district court has discretion to rule on a motion for summary judgment before it decides the certification issue." *Saeger v. Pac. Life Ins. Co.*, 305 F. App'x 492, 493 (9th Cir. 2008) (emphasis added) (quoting *Wright v. Schock*, 742 F.2d 541, 543–44 (9th Cir. 1984)). Of course, a defendant who loses at summary judgment suffers prejudice, and a defendant who prevails without a certified class is prejudiced to the extent the judgment will not preclude subsequent class claims. In practice, if the defendant elects to move for summary judgment before a class is certified, it will not be heard to complain of prejudice resulting from the timing of its choice.

For their part, plaintiffs should not wait too long to move for certification, lest defendants present the court with an affirmative motion to deny class certification. *See Vinole v. Countrywide Home Loans, Inc.*, 571 F.3d 935, 939–40 (9th Cir. 2009). Regardless of the timing of a certification motion, defendants increasingly file motions to strike class allegations early in the case. Courts in the Ninth Circuit have generally viewed such motions as being premature. *See, e.g.*, *Degenhart v. AIU Holdings, Inc.*, No. C10-5172RBL, 2010 WL 4852200, at *2–3 (W.D. Wash. Nov. 26, 2010); *In re Wal-Mart Stores, Inc. Wage & Hour Litig.*, 505 F. Supp. 2d 609, 616 (N.D. Cal. 2007); *see also Guido v. L'Oreal, USA, Inc.*, No. CV 11-1067 CAS JCX, 2013 WL 454861, at *11 (C.D. Cal. Feb. 6, 2013) (stating that "plaintiffs' allegations do not show that it would be impossible for plaintiffs to satisfy the typicality requirement, and hence a motion to strike would be inappropriate").

6. RULES ENABLING ACT

"Rule 23 . . . and the Rules Enabling Act, 28 U.S.C. § 2072(b), forbid using the class action procedure to expand or modify substantive rights." *Wit v. United Behav. Health*, 79 F.4th 1068, 1084 (9th Cir. 2023); *see also Dukes*, 564 U.S. at 367 ("[T]he Rules Enabling Act forbids interpreting Rule 23 to 'abridge, enlarge or modify any substantive right,' 28 U.S.C. § 2072(b)[.]"). The class certification in *Wit* violated the Rules Enabling Act, the Ninth Circuit held.

In *Wit*, healthcare plan members sued United Behavior Health on behalf of three classes, alleging improper denial of healthcare benefits under the Employee Retirement Income Security Act of 1974 (ERISA). Each class was defined to include members "whose request for coverage . . . was denied . . . in whole or in part" based on certain terms in the defendant's internal administrative guidelines. *Id.* at 1076–77. The district court certified all three classes and later entered judgment against the defendant, which appealed. *Id.* at 1080–81.

The Ninth Circuit reversed, deeming the classes overinclusive. Although the plaintiffs did not challenge all the provisions in the defendant's guidelines, "the classes were not limited to those claimants whose claims were denied based only on the challenged provisions of the Guidelines"; as a result, the classes included members who were not entitled to a complete review of their claims under ERISA. *Id.* at 1085–86. Therefore, the class certification decision applied Rule 23 "in a way that enlarged or modified Plaintiffs' substantive rights in violation of the Rules Enabling Act[.]" *Id.* at 1086.

By contrast, the court in *DZ Reserve* held in a fraud case that not applying California's presumption of reliance across the class "would thus amount to abridging a substantive right, as the presumption would apply in individual cases but not in federal class actions." 96 F.4th at 1237–38.

7. INTERLOCUTORY APPEAL (FED. R. CIV. P. 23(F))

The leading Ninth Circuit case on Rule 23(f) is *Chamberlan v. Ford Motor Co.*, 402 F.3d 952 (9th Cir. 2005) (per curiam), where the court established parameters for ruling on petitions for interlocutory review of class certification orders. While instructing that immediate review "should be a rare occurrence," the court identified three (non-exhaustive) situations in which such review might be warranted:

> (1) there is a death-knell situation for either the plaintiff or defendant that is independent of the merits of the underlying claims, coupled with a class certification decision by the district court that is questionable; (2) the certification decision presents an unsettled and fundamental issue of law relating to class actions, important both to the specific litigation and generally, that is likely to evade end-of-the-case review; or (3) the district court's class certification decision is manifestly erroneous.

402 F.3d at 959. Even so, "[t]he kind of error most likely to warrant interlocutory review will be one of law, as opposed to an incorrect application of law to facts." *Id.* For this reason, "[i]t is difficult to show that a class certification order is manifestly erroneous unless the district court applies an incorrect Rule 23 standard or ignores a directly controlling case. Class certification decisions rarely will involve legal errors, however, simply because class actions typically involve complex facts that are unlikely to be on all fours with existing precedent." *Id.* at 962 (citations omitted).

Under Rule 23(f), a petition to appeal must be filed "within 14 days after the order is entered." Fed. R. Civ. P. 23(f). While the rule does not address the effect, if any, on the deadline from motions for reconsideration, several circuits held that a motion for reconsideration filed within 14 days of the certification order tolls the deadline for filing a Rule 23(f) petition. In 2017, the Ninth Circuit agreed and further held that the filing deadline can be equitably tolled if the movant "took some other action similar to filing a motion for reconsideration within the fourteen-day deadline, such as a letter or verbal representation conveying an intent to seek reconsideration and providing the basis for such action." *Lambert v. Nutraceutical Corp.*, 870 F.3d 1170, 1178 (9th Cir. 2017). The Supreme Court reversed, holding that equitable tolling does not apply to the deadline for petitioning for discretionary review of a class certification order. *Nutraceutical Corp. v. Lambert*, 139 S. Ct. 710 (2019). The Court also clarified that a reconsideration motion has no tolling effect but found "no occasion to address the effect of a motion for reconsideration filed within the 14-day window." *Id.* at 717 & n.7.

Thereafter, in *Walker v. Life Insurance Company of the Southwest*, the Ninth Circuit held that "litigants may not repeatedly extend Rule 23(f)'s stringent deadlines by re-noticing denied reconsideration motions." 953 F.3d at 636. The plaintiffs filed a motion for reconsideration, which the district court denied without prejudice for failure to satisfy a local meet-and-confer requirement. *Id.* at 635. The district court's denial triggered the 14-day period for appealing a certification order. *Id.* But instead of appealing the order, the plaintiffs re-noticed their reconsideration motion. *Id.* The Ninth Circuit held that the district court's order allowing the plaintiffs to re-notice the motion did not "translate into the additional right to file a Rule 23(f) appeal petition beyond the fourteen-day period." *Id.*

In *Microsoft v. Baker*, 582 U.S. 23 (2017), the Supreme Court reversed the Ninth Circuit with the holding that plaintiffs cannot obtain immediate interlocutory review of an order denying class certification by voluntarily dismissing their case with prejudice (but reserving the ability to revive their claims if the order is reversed). The Supreme Court disapproved of this course of action by plaintiffs, concluding that it "subverts the final-judgment rule," would "invite[] protracted litigation and piecemeal appeals" and cannot supplant discretionary review of class certification orders under Rule 23(f). *Id.* at 37.

8. CLASS NOTICE (FED. R. CIV. P. 23(C)(2))

Notice in a Rule 23(b)(3) class action must be "the best practicable"—"reasonably calculated, under all circumstances, to apprise interested parties of the pendency of the action and afford them an opportunity to present their objections." *Phillips Petroleum Co. v. Shutts*, 472 U.S. 797, 812 (1985) (citations omitted). "The notice should describe the action and the plaintiffs' rights in it." *Id.* The rule provides, in relevant part:

> The notice must clearly and concisely state in plain, easily understood language:
> (i) the nature of the action; (ii) the definition of the class certified; (iii) the class claims, issues, or defenses; (iv) that a class member may enter an appearance through an attorney if the member so desires; (v) that the court will exclude from the class any member who requests exclusion; (vi) the time and manner for requesting exclusion; and (vii) the binding effect of a class judgment on members under Rule 23(c)(3).

Fed. R. Civ. P. 23(c)(2)(B). What's more, "an absent plaintiff [must] be provided with an opportunity to remove himself from the class by executing and returning an 'opt out' or 'request for exclusion' form to the court." *Shutts*, 472 U.S. at 812.

Due process does not require that all class members actually receive the notice. *Silber v. Mabon*, 18 F.3d 1449, 1453–54 (9th Cir. 1994). While direct notice via U.S. mail historically has outperformed all other forms of notice, direct notice via email is increasingly used, particularly in cases involving digital technology. *See, e.g.*, *In re Online DVD-Rental*, 779 F.3d at 941, 946 (settlement notice was first emailed to 35 million class members and then sent via U.S. mail to over 9 million class members whose email addresses generated bounce-back messages); *McCrary v. Elations Co.*, No. EDCV 13-0242 JGB (SPx), 2016 WL 769703, at *7 (C.D. Cal. Feb. 25, 2016) (notice was sent via U.S. mail and email to potential class members); *In re Magsafe Apple Power Adapter Litig.*, No. 5:091-cv-01911-EJD, 2015 WL 428105, at *10 (N.D. Cal. Jan. 30, 2015) (emails, the primary notice vehicle, were sent to 5,523,878 class members). When it is infeasible to notify class members directly, "notice by publication in a periodical, on a website, or even at an appropriate physical location is sufficient to satisfy due process." *Briseno*, 844 F.3d at 1129.

The 2018 amendments to Rule 23 add "electronic means" as a potentially acceptable notice method. Embracing the trend toward targeted digital notice, the Ninth Circuit held in a settlement opinion that mailed notice fell short of the "best practicable" notice and that targeted ads should have been used given the circumstances of the case. *Roes, 1-2 v. SFBC Mgt., LLC*, 944 F.3d 1035 (9th Cir. 2019). The court recognized that, even when email addresses are unavailable, "technological developments are making it ever easier to target communications to specific persons or groups and to contact individuals electronically at little cost." *Id.* at 1047.

For classes certified under Rules 23(b)(1) or 23(b)(2), notice is optional rather than mandatory: "the court may direct appropriate notice to the class." Fed. R. Civ. P. 23(c)(2)(A). There is no opt-out right in such cases, and notice costs, "moreover, could easily cripple actions that do not seek damages." Fed. R. Civ. P. 23(c)(2) Adv. Com. Notes to 2003 amendment.

9. DISCOVERY OF ABSENT CLASS MEMBERS

The Supreme Court has made clear that "[u]nlike a defendant in a normal civil suit, an absent class action plaintiff is not required to do anything. He may sit back and allow the litigation to run its course, content in knowing that there are safeguards provided for his protection." *Shutts*, 472 U.S. at 809–10. Indeed, "a primary purpose of the class suit is to promote efficiency by enabling representatives to litigate." 1 William B. Rubenstein, *Newberg on Class Actions* § 1:5 (5th ed. 2011); *see also Wal-Mart*, 564 U.S. at 349 (2011) ("Rule 23(a) ensures that the named plaintiffs are appropriate representatives of the class whose claims they wish to litigate."). Because discovery of absent class members would undermine the efficiencies of representative class litigation, such discovery is "highly irregular" and disfavored in the Ninth Circuit. *In re Worlds of Wonder Sec. Litig.*, No. C-87-5491 SC (FSL), 1992 WL 330411, at *6 (N.D. Cal. July 9, 1992); *see generally McPhail v. First Command Fin. Planning, Inc.*, 251 F.R.D. 514, 517 (S.D. Cal. 2008) (discussing why "[d]iscovery from absent class members is ordinarily not permitted").

10. CLASS ACTION SETTLEMENTS (FED. R. CIV. 23(E))

Proposed class action settlements take effect only upon approval by the court. *See* Fed. R. Civ. P. 23(e)(2) (requiring that a binding class settlement be "fair, reasonable, and adequate"). District courts enjoy discretion in deciding whether to approve proposed - settlements of class claims. *Churchill Vill., L.L.C. v. Gen. Elec.*, 361 F.3d 566, 575 (9th Cir. 2004). Settlement approval procedures under Rule 23(e)—which was substantially amended in 2018, as discussed in subsection 8(c)(vi) below—comprise two distinct steps: (1) preliminary approval of the proposed settlement, which includes a "preliminary determination" of the merits of the settlement and the propriety of certifying the proposed class (if a class has not been certified at the time of settlement), together with assessment of a notice plan and (2) final approval of the proposed settlement following a fairness hearing and the court's determination of whether the settlement is "fair, reasonable, and adequate." *Hawthorne v. Umpqua Bank*, No. 11-cv-06700-JST, 2014 WL 4602572, at *4 (N.D. Cal. Sept. 15, 2014) (quoting Federal Judicial Center, *Manual for Complex Litigation* § 21.632 (4th ed. 2004); *see also* 4 William B. Rubenstein, *Newberg on Class Actions* § 13:1 (5th ed. 2014).

The Ninth Circuit has recognized "an overriding public interest in settling and quieting litigation . . . particularly . . . in class action suits." *Van Bronkhorst v. Safeco Corp.*, 529 F.2d 943, 950 (9th Cir. 1976); *see also Class Plaintiffs v. City of Seattle*, 955 F.2d 1268, 1276 (9th Cir. 1992). The court thus "maintains a 'strong judicial policy' that favors the settlement of class actions." *Lilly v. Jamba Juice Co.*, No. 13-cv-02998-JST, 2015 WL 1248027, at *6 (N.D. Cal. Mar. 18, 2015) (quoting *Class Plaintiffs*, 955 F.2d at 1276).

When a proposed settlement would release damages claims, the proposed class must be sufficiently cohesive to warrant certification under Rule 23(b)(3), with the caveat that the manageability criteria of Rule 23(b)(3)(D) drop out of the certification analysis. *Amchem*, 521 U.S. at 620 ("Confronted with a request for settlement-only class certification, a district court need not inquire whether the case, if tried, would present intractable management problems, for the proposal is that there be no trial. But other specifications of the Rule—those designed to protect absentees by blocking unwarranted or overbroad class definitions—demand undiluted, even heightened, attention in the settlement context.") (citation omitted).

In early 2018, the Ninth Circuit invoked *Amchem* in a controversial split decision overturning approval of a nationwide false advertising settlement. *In re Hyundai & Kia Fuel Econ. Litig.*, 881 F.3d 679 (2018). The majority agreed with settlement objectors that the district court "abused its discretion by failing to conduct a choice of law analysis or rigorously analyze potential differences in state consumer protection laws before certifying a single nationwide settlement class under Rule 23(b)(3)." *Id.* at 701–02. Judge Nguyen dissented. *Id.* at 707–19 (Nguyen, J., dissenting).[25]

The full court granted the settling parties' request for rehearing, and issued its highly anticipated en banc decision on June 6, 2019. *In re Hyundai & Kia Fuel Econ. Litig.*, 926 F.3d 539 (9th Cir. 2019) (en banc). *Hyundai* provides the Ninth Circuit's definitive guide to a recurring legal topic of importance: class certification under Rule 23(b)(3) in the settlement context.

Judge Nguyen, now writing for the en banc majority, rejected the panel opinion's holding that manageability concerns arising from state law variations can preclude certification of a settlement class. After restating the deferential standard of review that applies to class settlement appeals, the court reiterated *Amchem*'s teaching that litigation classes and settlement classes are different in kind—trial "manageability is not a concern in certifying a settlement class where, by definition, there will be no trial." *Id.* at 556–57. Consequently, "[a] class that is certifiable for settlement may not be certifiable for litigation if the settlement obviates the need to litigate individualized issues that would make a trial unmanageable." *Id.* at 558. Instead of manageability, the predominance analysis for settlement purposes centers on assessments of (1) the definition of the class (or subclasses) in relation to the operative facts, to guard against an overbroad or unwarranted release of liability, and (2) class cohesion based on whether the settled claims involve common legal or factual questions that preexist the settlement. *Id.* at 557–58 (construing *Amchem*).

Applying these criteria to the proposed class of vehicle purchasers and lessors in *Hyun-*

[25] After the *Hyundai* panel issued its split decision, one of the authors of this chapter published an article in the ABA's Class Actions and Derivative Suits committee newsletter criticizing the reasoning of the majority opinion. *See* Jordan Elias & Adam E. Polk, *Tilting at Windmills: Nationwide Class Settlements After In re Hyundai and Kia Fuel Economy Litigation*, American Bar Association (Feb. 28, 2018), available at https://www.americanbar.org/groups/litigation/committees/class-actions/articles/2018/winter2018-in-re-hyundai-kia-fuel-economy-litigation.

dai, the en banc court held predominance satisfied. The class was cohesive, the court explained, because its "members were exposed to uniform fuel-economy misrepresentations and suffered identical injuries within only a small range of damages," and "no material conflicts existed among class members." 926 F.3d at 559. The preexisting common questions included whether the representations at issue were false and misleading, and if so, whether the defendants knew that. *Id.* Differences relating to how individual class members were exposed to the representations, and in their rights and potential remedies under various state laws, were irrelevant because they mostly implicated trial manageability issues. *Id.* at 560–63. The court thus reaffirmed its holding in *Hanlon* that "idiosyncratic differences between state consumer protection laws" do not defeat predominance in a case like *Hyundai*, where "the class claims turn on the [defendants'] common course of conduct." *Id.* at 563. In addition, the *Hyundai* objectors failed to establish that California law would not apply classwide. *Id.* at 561–66.

Having dispensed with the concerns about differently situated used car purchasers and diverging state laws that animated the *Hyundai* panel opinion, the en banc court turned to factors traditionally addressed at settlement approval: (1) the sufficiency of the proposed notice; (2) whether the proposed claim forms were adequate; and (3) whether there was evidence of collusion between class counsel and the defendants. *Id.* at 567–72. Deferring to the district court's "careful findings" that the proposed settlement was fair, adequate, and reasonable—a conclusion reached after "multiple status conferences and . . . rounds of briefing"—the en banc court affirmed approval of the settlement along with the award of attorneys' fees. *Id.* at 572. Judge Ikuta's dissent was joined in full by two other judges and in part by one judge. *Id.* at 572–82 (Ikuta, J., dissenting).

The Ninth Circuit has also indicated that where parties settle prior to class certification, courts apply "a higher standard of fairness and a more probing inquiry than may normally be required under Rule 23(e)." *Dennis v. Kellogg Co.*, 697 F.3d 858, 864 (9th Cir. 2012) (internal quotation marks and citation omitted). Courts "must be particularly vigilant not only for explicit collusion, but also for more subtle signs that class counsel have allowed pursuit of their own self-interests and that of certain class members to infect the negotiations." *Bluetooth*, 654 F.3d at 947. Commonly referred to as the *Bluetooth* factors, these warning signs include: (1) when counsel receive a disproportionate distribution of the settlement, or class counsel are well compensated even though the class receives little or nothing; (2) when the parties negotiate "clear sailing" provision wherein the defendant agrees not to challenge class counsel's fee application; and (3) when the agreement includes a "reversion" or "kicker" providing that any reduction in attorney's fees reverts to the defendant rather than for the benefit of the class. *Id.* In *Briseño v. Henderson*, the Ninth Circuit clarified that the *Bluetooth* factors also apply to post-class certification settlements. 998 F.3d 1014, 1023 (9th Cir. 2021).

At the same time, a concurrence in an earlier case notes that "[e]arly dispute resolution is salutary, and we should not encourage the unnecessary expense, delay, and uncertainty caused by lengthy litigation when the parties are prepared to compromise. Nor should we hold . . . that a prompt settlement necessarily suggests a failure to prosecute or defend the action with due diligence and reasonable prudence. To the contrary, an early resolution may demonstrate that the parties and their counsel are well prepared and well aware of the strength and weaknesses of their positions and of the interests to be served by an amicable end to the case." *Molski v. Gleich*, 318 F.3d 937, 959 (9th Cir. 2003) (Graber, J., concurring), *overruled on other grounds by Dukes v. Wal-Mart Stores, Inc.*, 603 F.3d 571 (9th Cir. 2010).

a. Preliminary Approval

At the preliminary approval stage, the court's task is to determine whether the settlement falls "within the range of possible approval." *Lilly*, 2015 WL 1248027, at *6 (quoting *Tableware*, 484 F. Supp. 2d at 1080). In general, preliminary approval is appropriate when the terms of the proposed settlement are "sufficient to warrant public notice and a hearing." Federal Judicial Center, *Manual for Complex Litigation* § 13.14 (4th ed. 2004). As the Ninth Circuit remarked in a widely cited decision: "Settlement is the offspring of compromise; the question we address is not whether the final product could be prettier, smarter or snazzier, but whether it is fair, adequate and free from collusion." *Hanlon*, 150 F.3d at 1027; *see also Dyer v. Wells Fargo Bank, N.A.*, No. 13-cv-02858-JST, 2014 WL 1900682, at *6 (N.D. Cal. May 12, 2014) ("The proposed settlement need not be ideal, but it must be fair and free of collusion, consistent with a plaintiff's fiduciary obligations to the class."). Accordingly, preliminary approval should be granted when "the proposed settlement appears to be the product of serious, informed, non-collusive negotiations, has no obvious deficiencies, does not improperly grant preferential treatment to class representatives or segments of the class and falls within the range of possible approval." *Tableware*, 484 F. Supp. 2d at 1079 (citation omitted).

A district court commits reversible error if it applies a presumption that a proposed class settlement reached prior to class certification is fair and reasonable. *In re Apple Inc. Device Performance Litig.*, 50 F.4th 769, 776 (9th Cir. 2022). The Ninth Circuit has "actually required that courts do the opposite—by employing extra caution and more rigorous scrutiny—when it comes to settlements negotiated prior to class certification," *Roes, 1-2 v. SFBSC Mgmt., LLC*, 944 F.3d 1035, 1049 (9th Cir. 2019), particularly because the certification inquiry tests the cohesion of the proposed class. Although district courts have "commonly applied" a presumption of fairness, the Ninth Circuit deemed this approach "erroneous" if applied to pre-certification settlements. *Id.* at 1049 n.12. Furthermore, "even in post-class certification settlements" the court "must scrutinize attorneys' fees for potential collusion that shortchanges the class." *Briseno v. Henderson*, 998 F.3d 1014, 1031 (9th Cir. 2021).

To determine whether a settlement falls within the range of possible approval, the court "must consider plaintiffs' expected recovery balanced against the value of the settlement offer." *In re High-Tech Emp. Antitrust Litig.*, No. 11-cv-02509-LHK, 2014 WL 3917126, at *3 (N.D. Cal. Aug. 8, 2014) (citation omitted). Settlement relief, moreover, "cannot be assessed in a vacuum. Rather, the settlement's benefits must be considered by reference to what the class actually gave up by settling." *Campbell v. Facebook, Inc.*, 951 F.3d 1106, 1123 (9th Cir. 2019) (citation omitted). The court should not approve a settlement releasing a defendant from future claims unless, at a minimum, the released claims derive from the same factual predicate alleged in the complaint. *See In re Hewlett-Packard Co. S'holder Deriv. Litig.*, No. 3:12-cv-06003-CRB, 2015 WL 1153864, at *5 (N.D. Cal. Mar. 13, 2015) (citing *Hesse v. Sprint Corp.*, 598 F.3d 581, 590 (9th Cir. 2010)). And the court "must also consider whether class members were required to release claims that were more meritorious than the theories Plaintiffs pursued in this litigation." *Campbell*, 951 F.3d at 1124.

A proposed plan for allocating settlement proceeds among class members, too, must be "fair, reasonable and adequate." *In re: Cathode Ray Tube (CRT) Antitrust Litig.*, MDL No. 1917, 2016 WL 6778406, at *3 (N.D. Cal. Nov. 16, 2016) (citation omitted). Courts in the Ninth Circuit have recognized "that an allocation formula need only have a reasonable, rational basis, particularly if recommended by experienced and competent counsel." *Hendricks v. StarKist Co.*, No. 13-CV-00729-HSG, 2015 WL 4498083, at *7 (N.D. Cal. July 23, 2015) (citation omitted); *see, e.g.*, *Jabbari v. Wells Fargo & Co.*, No. 15-CV-02159-VC, 2018 WL 11024841, at *3 (N.D. Cal. June 14, 2018); *In re Aftermarket Auto. Lighting Prod. Antitrust Litig.*, No. 09 MDL 2007-GW(PJWx), 2014 WL 12591624, at *4 (C.D. Cal. Jan. 10, 2014).

b. Notice and Objections

Notice

Importantly, the court evaluates counsel's proposed notice plan at preliminary approval. As discussed above, the notice must comport with the requirements of due process and, in a Rule 23(b)(3) case, constitute the "best notice that is practicable."

Objections

After the court provides notice of a proposed settlement, "[a]ny class member may object[.]" Fed. R. Civ. P. 23(e)(5). Absent class members' right to object has been called "an important component of providing legitimacy to the class action process. . . . [T]he representative plaintiffs (and their counsel) and the defendants (and their counsel) are all jointly urging the court to approve the proposed settlement, meaning the court is not presented with a familiar adversarial discussion of the pros and cons of the settlement." 4 William B. Rubenstein, *Newberg on Class Actions* § 13:20 (5th ed. 2014).

Though Rule 23 expressly permits objections, there is a widespread problem with frivolous objections made for improper purposes that "benefit only the objectors and their attorneys (e.g., by seeking additional compensation to withdraw even ill-founded objections)." Federal Judicial Center, *Manual for Complex Litigation* § 21.133 (4th ed. 2004); *see, e.g.*, *Nwabueze v. AT&T Inc.,* No. C 09-01529SI, 2013 WL 6199596, at *3 (N.D. Cal. Nov. 27, 2013) (finding that "[t]he true basis for" an objection "appears to be obtaining additional money . . . rather than a concern for the fairness, adequacy, and reasonableness of the Settlement."). "Professional objectors" make a living objecting to settlements and extorting money from settling parties in exchange for withdrawing the objections along with the threat of appealing settlement approval and delaying relief. The Federal Judicial Center therefore advises courts to "[w]atch out . . . for canned objections from professional objectors who seek out class actions to extract a fee by lodging generic, unhelpful protests." Federal Judicial Center, *Managing Class Action Litigation: A Pocket Guide for Judges* 15 (2d ed. 2009); *see, e.g.*, *Spann v. J.C. Penney Corp.*, 211 F. Supp. 3d 1244, 1260 n.11 (C.D. Cal. 2016) (criticizing "serial objectors"), *appeal dismissed*, No. 16-56474, 2016 WL 9778633 (9th Cir. Nov. 7, 2016).

Despite the potential for abuse, objections are permitted by Rule 23 and may prove meritorious, even leading to settlement enhancements. Where a meritorious objection benefits the class (e.g., by increasing the common fund), the attorney representing the objector may be entitled to a fee from the fund. *See Rodriguez v. Disner*, 688 F.3d 645, 658–59 (9th Cir. 2012) ("Under certain circumstances, attorneys for objectors may be entitled to attorneys' fees from the fund created by class action litigation. . . . [Where] these objections result in an increase to the common fund, the objectors may claim entitlement to fees on the same equitable principles as class counsel. Conversely, objectors who do not increase the fund or otherwise substantially benefit the class members are not entitled to fees, even if they bring about minor procedural changes in the settlement agreement.") (internal quotation marks and citations omitted).

c. Final Approval

District courts within the Ninth Circuit consider several nonexclusive factors in determining whether or not to grant final approval to a proposed class action settlement: "the strength of the plaintiffs' case, the risk, expense, complexity, and likely duration of further litigation; the risk of maintaining class action status throughout the trial; the amount offered in settlement; the extent of discovery completed and the stage of proceedings; the experience and views of counsel; the presence of a governmental participant; and the reaction of the class members to the proposed settlement." *Hanlon*, 150 F.3d at 1025.

Before delving into these factors, the court must first determine that the proposed settlement was reached at arm's length. *City of Seattle*, 955 F.2d at 1290 ("Before approving a class action settlement, the district court must reach a reasoned judgment that the proposed agreement is not the product of fraud or overreaching by, or collusion among, the negotiating parties'") (citation omitted). That the settlement was negotiated by experienced counsel tends to support a finding of fairness. *See, e.g.*, *Rodriguez v. West Pub'g Corp.*, 563 F.3d 948, 965 (9th Cir. 2009) ("We put a good deal of stock in the product of an arms-length, non-collusive, negotiated resolution"); *Nat'l Rural Telecoms. Coop. v. DIRECTV, Inc.*, 221 F.R.D. 523, 528 (C.D. Cal. 2004) ("'Great weight' is accorded to the recommendation of counsel, who are most closely acquainted with the facts") (citation omitted).

Strength of Plaintiffs' Case

In evaluating the fairness of a proposed settlement, the court "must . . . assess the plaintiffs' claims in determining the strength of their case relative to the risks of continued litigation[.]" *Lane v. Facebook, Inc.*, 696 F.3d 811, 823 (9th Cir. 2012) (citation omitted). "Approval . . . is appropriate when plaintiffs must overcome significant barriers to make their case." *Dyer v. Wells Fargo Bank, N.A.*, 303 F.R.D. 326, 331 (N.D. Cal. 2014) (citing *Chun-Hoon v. McKee Foods Corp.*, 716 F. Supp. 2d 848, 851 (N.D. Cal. 2010)). The risks created by affirmative defenses, for instance, may be relevant. Significant risks to the viability of the class claims weigh in favor of final approval. *Dyer*, 303 F.R.D. at 331 (citing *Moore v. Verizon Commc'ns Inc.*, No. C 09-1823 SBA, 2013 WL 4610764, at *5 (N.D. Cal. Aug. 28, 2013) (finding that the relative strengths and weaknesses of plaintiffs' case favored settlement where plaintiffs admitted they would face obstacles in obtaining class certification and in proving liability and damages)).

Risk, Expense, Complexity, and Duration of Further Litigation

"Difficulties and risks in litigating weigh in favor of approving a class settlement." *Dyer*, 303 F.R.D. at 331 (citing *Rodriguez*, 563 F.3d at 966). This factor subsumes practical risks, like those that may result from insurance coverage limitations or the defendant's financial condition. *See Booth v. Strategic Realty Trust, Inc.*, No. 13-cv-04921-JST, 2015 WL 6002919, at *5 (N.D. Cal. Oct. 15, 2015) ("One of the policies is a 'wasting' policy from which SRT pays its defense costs, which would only increase if litigation were to continue. Accordingly, the Court concludes that the class members' risk of not being able to fully recover damages from Defendants, even assuming that Plaintiffs succeeded in proving liability, favors approval") (citation omitted); *Schwarm v. Craighead*, 814 F. Supp. 2d 1025, 1029–33 (E.D. Cal. 2011) (finding that the defendant's declaration of bankruptcy supported settlement approval); *Torrisi v. Tucson Elec. Power Co.*, 8 F.3d 1370, 1376 (9th Cir. 1993) (similar).

Risk of Maintaining Class Action Status Through Trial

A substantial risk of maintaining class action status through trial also favors settlement approval. *See Zubia v. Shamrock Foods Co.*, No. CV 16-03128 ABA (GRx), 2017 WL 10541431, at *12 (C.D. Cal. Dec. 21, 2017) ("[U]ncertainty surrounding class certification" favored settlement approval); *Custom LED, LLC v. eBay, Inc.*, No. 12-cv-00350-JST, 2014 WL 2916871, at *4 (N.D. Cal. June 14, 2014) ("[B]oth parties recognize that eBay will actively oppose certification of the class if the settlement is not approved. As such, the Court finds that the potential difficulties associated with obtaining class certification weigh in favor of approving the settlement.") (citing *McKee Foods*, 716 F. Supp. 2d at 851 (where a class had been certified but both sides pointed to the risk of decertification, this factor supported settlement approval)); *cf.* Fed. R. Civ. P. 23(c)(1)(C) (the court has discretion to alter or amend a certification order before judgment).

Extent of Discovery and Stage of Proceedings

To negotiate a fair and reasonable settlement, "the parties [must] have sufficient information to make an informed decision about settlement." *Linney v. Cellular Alaska P'ship*, 151 F.3d 1234, 1239 (9th Cir. 1998); *accord In re Mego Fin. Corp. Sec. Litig.*, 213 F.3d 454, 459 (9th Cir. 2000). When litigation has advanced to the point where the parties have a "clear view of the strengths and weaknesses of their cases," the extent of discovery completed and the stage of proceedings support final settlement approval. *See McKee Foods*, 716 F. Supp. 2d at 852; *Edwards v. First Am. Corp.*, No. CV07-03796-SJO-FFMx, 2016 WL 8999934, at *6 (C.D. Cal. Oct. 4, 2016).

Reaction of the Class
"Class members' positive reaction to a settlement weighs in favor of settlement approval; 'the absence of a large number of objections to a proposed class action settlement raises a strong presumption that the terms of a proposed class settlement . . . are favorable to the class members.'" *Dyer*, 303 F.R.D. at 332 (quoting *In re Omnivision Tech., Inc.*, 559 F. Supp. 2d 1036, 1043 (N.D. Cal. 2008)); *see also Johnson v. Quantum Learning Network, Inc.*, No. 15-CV-05013-LHK, 2017 WL 747462, at *2 (N.D. Cal. Feb. 27, 2017) ("The lack of objections and the low rate of opt-outs (less than 1%) are 'indicia of the approval of the class.'") (citations omitted).

2018 Amendments to Rule 23(e)
Significant amendments to the settlement provisions of Rule 23 went into effect in December 2018. The amendments provide formal guidance for settlement approval, permit more flexibility in giving notice to class members, attempt to deter bad-faith objectors, and clarify that no appeal may be taken from an order granting or denying preliminary approval.

Before these amendments, Rule 23 did not recognize the preliminary approval process, notwithstanding its widespread use. Rule 23(e) now contains specific procedural and substantive requirements for preliminary approval. Under Rule 23(e)(1)(B), to grant preliminary approval and direct notice to the class, the court must find that the parties have shown that it "will likely be able to" approve the settlement under Rule 23(e)(2) and certify the proposed settlement class upon final approval. Rule 23(e)(2) sets forth specific factors for determining whether to approve a settlement: whether (1) the class representative and class counsel have adequately represented the class; (2) the settlement was negotiated at arm's length; (3) the relief to the class is adequate in light of such factors as the litigation risks, the effectiveness of any proposed claims procedure, and the terms of any proposed award of attorneys' fees; and (4) the settlement treats all class members equitably relative to each other. The Civil Rules Advisory Committee Note explains that these factors are not intended to be exhaustive or to displace any of the traditional factors for determining whether a settlement is fair, reasonable, and adequate. *See Torrisi v. Tucson Elec. Power Co.*, 8 F.3d 1370, 1375–76 (9th Cir. 1993).

The amendments also change the procedure that applies when a case settles before a class has been certified. Before the amendments, most courts in that situation would conditionally certify a class for settlement purposes only and appoint a class representative and class counsel to represent the settlement class. After the amendments, as the Advisory Committee Note explains, "[t]he ultimate decision to certify the class for purposes of settlement cannot be made until the hearing on final approval of the proposed settlement." Thus, Rule 23(e)(1)(B) focuses on whether the court "will likely be able" to certify the class upon final approval.

Since these amendments they took effect, some courts have applied "the framework set forth in Rule 23, while continuing to draw guidance from the Ninth Circuit's factors and relevant precedent." *Hefler v. Wells Fargo & Co.*, No. 16-CV-05479-JST, 2018 WL 6619983, at *4 (N.D. Cal. Dec. 18, 2018); *see, e.g., In re Chrysler-Dodge-Jeep Ecodiesel Mktg., Sales Practices, & Prod. Liab. Litig.*, No. 17-MD-02777-EMC, 2019 WL 536661, at *8–10 (N.D. Cal. Feb. 11, 2019) (considering the Rule 23(e)(2) factors together with the preexisting standards and forgoing conditional certification where no class had been previously certified). Other courts have continued to apply the traditional factors without directly addressing the factors outlined under Rule 23(e)(2). *See, e.g., Vikram v. First Student Management, LLC*, No. 17-CV-04656-KAW, 2019 WL 1084169, at *1 (N.D. Cal. Mar. 7, 2019) (applying only the traditional factors, granting provisional certification, and appointing class representative and class counsel); *Syed v. M-I LLC*, No. 1:14-CV-00742 WBS BAM, 2019 WL 1130469, at *9 (E.D. Cal. Mar. 12, 2019) (similar).

With regard to notice, while Rule 23(c)(2)(B) still requires "the best notice that is practicable" in cases certified under Rule 23(b)(3), the amendments recognize that email or other electronic methods may provide the most effective way to notify class members in some cases. As such, Rule 23(c)(2)(B) now states, without giving preference to any form of notice, that notice may be accomplished through "electronic means, or other appropriate means," in addition to U.S. mail.

The 2018 amendments also respond to the continuing problem of bad-faith objectors filing objections and appeals in the hopes of extracting a payoff from class counsel. Rule 23(e)(5) requires an objector to state specific grounds for the objection and to explain whether the objection applies only to the objector or to the class or a subset thereof. And although the court no longer needs to approve the withdrawal of an objection, the court now must approve any payment or other consideration furnished in exchange for withdrawing an objection or dismissing an appeal.

Finally, Rule 23(f) was amended in 2018 to clarify that no appeal can be taken from an order granting or denying preliminary approval. Such a ruling does not grant or deny class certification, and therefore provides no grounds for an immediate appeal under subdivision (f).

d. *Cy Pres*

A class action settlement that provides for a charitable award to an organization can be fair, reasonable, and adequate under Rule 23(e)(2), but the award must be narrowly tailored to the objectives of the class in the relevant litigation. *Koby v. ARS Nat'l Servs.*, 846 F.3d 1071, 1080 (9th Cir. 2017) (holding that "*cy pres* awards [must] be tethered to the objectives of the underlying statutes or the interests of class members."). On behalf of a nationwide class of 4 million individual debtors, the plaintiffs in *Koby* pursued claims against ARS National Services, Inc., for allegedly unlawful debt collection practices. *Id.* at 1073–74. The statute at issue in the case—the Fair Debt Collection Practices Act—allows for statutory damages of $1,000 for named plaintiffs, but caps damages for the class at the lower of $500,000 or 1 percent of the defendant's net worth. *Id.* at 1074. In *Koby*, ARS represented that its net worth was $3.5 million and argued that the maximum recovery for the class of 4 million would therefore be only $35,000. *Id.* at 1074–75. Given the practical problems with distributing "less than a penny" to each class member, ARS agreed to settle the claims by (a) stopping its unlawful debt collection practices and (b) disbursing $35,000 to a San Diego veterans' organization. *Id.* Plaintiffs agreed to a release forfeiting the class members' right to seek damages from ARS based on its alleged conduct. *Id.* at 1080. A magistrate judge approved the settlement as fair, reasonable, and adequate. *Id.* at 1075.

The Ninth Circuit reversed. The court concluded that the injunctive relief in the settlement conferred no value upon the class: It only benefited future debtors contacted by ARS, who were not included in the class definition. *Id.* at 1079. The court then addressed whether the *cy pres* award, in and of itself, justified the release. Because the $35,000 award to a veterans' organization was not "tethered to the objectives" of the nationwide class, the court found that the award conferred no value on the class. *Id.* at 1080. The court also repudiated the notion that the "trivial" value of the claims rescued the settlement: "The fact that class members were required to give up anything at all in exchange for worthless injunctive relief precluded approval of the settlement as fair, reasonable, and adequate under Rule 23(e)(2)." *Id.* at 1081.

In *Nachshin v. AOL, LLC*, 663 F.3d 1034 (9th Cir. 2011), the court likewise froze distributions to charities whose purposes were insufficiently aligned with the suit's objectives and the interests of the absent class members. The court explained that "[a]lthough the class includes more than 66 million AOL subscribers throughout the United States, two-thirds of the donations will be made to local charities in Los Angeles, California." *Id.* at 1040. The court further commented: "When selection of *cy pres* beneficiaries is not tethered to the nature of the lawsuit and the interests of the silent class members, the selection process may answer to the whims and self-interests of the parties, their counsel, or the court. Moreover, the specter of judges and outside entities dealing in the distribution and solicitation of settlement money may create the appearance of impropriety." *Id.* at 1039; *see also Dennis v. Kellogg Co.*, 697 F.3d 858 (9th Cir. 2012) (in false advertising case, deeming it inappropriate to award settlement residue to unidentified food banks: "appropriate *cy pres* recipients are not charities that feed the needy, but organizations dedicated to protecting consumers from, or redressing injuries caused by, false advertising").

The appearance of unfairness and of arbitrary or corrupt applications of the *cy pres* doctrine led Chief Justice Roberts to write separately in connection with the denial of certiorari to the Ninth Circuit in *Marek v. Lane*, 571 U.S. 1003 (2013). The Chief described how the settlement with Facebook over alleged privacy violations yielded no money for the affected individuals and no injunction prohibiting the challenged practice. Instead, $3.5 million went to class counsel, while $6.5 million went to a new privacy issues nonprofit—on whose board Facebook would sit. The Chief wrote that he agreed with the denial of certiorari because the challenges were to particular settlement features. But the Chief also warned that "[i]n a suitable case," the Supreme Court "may need to clarify the limits on the use of such [*cy pres*] remedies," alluding to "fundamental concerns surrounding the use of such remedies in class action litigation, including when, if ever, such relief should be considered; how to assess its fairness as a general matter; whether new entities may be established as part of such relief; if not, how existing entities should be selected; what the respective roles of the judge and parties are in shaping a *cy pres* remedy; how closely the goals of any enlisted organization must correspond to the interests of the class; and so on." *Id.*

According to the ALI, *cy pres* awards are appropriate "only when direct distributions to class members are not feasible—either because class members cannot be reasonably identified or because distribution would involve such small amounts that, because of the administrative costs involved, such distribution would not be economically viable." Am. Law Inst., *Principles of the Law of Aggregate Litigation* § 3.07, cmt. b (2010). Most commonly, *cy pres* awards simply distribute unclaimed settlement funds (known as the "residue") after an initial distribution. *See Six (6) Mexican Workers v. Arizona Citrus Growers*, 904 F.2d 1301, 1304–09 (9th Cir. 1990). Again, however, the Ninth Circuit has made it clear that any such award must provide the "next best" distribution to paying class members directly and should not benefit a group "too remote from the plaintiff class." *Id.* at 1308–09.

As foreshadowed by the Chief Justice's statement in *Marek*, the Supreme Court granted certiorari to the Ninth Circuit in another recent case presenting *cy pres* issues, *Frank v. Gaos*, 138 S. Ct. 1697 (2018). In the underlying decision, the Ninth Circuit approved of *cy pres* distributions of about $5.3 million in settlement funds where the class included nearly 130 million individuals, such that even the "[o]bjectors d[id] not contend that it would have been feasible to make a 4-cent distribution to every class member." *In re Google Referrer Header Privacy Litig.*, 869 F.3d 737, 741–42 (9th Cir. 2017). Dissenting in part, Judge Wallace expressed concern that class counsel had attended three of the educational institutions slated to receive *cy pres* awards. *Id.* at 749 (Wallace, J., concurring in part and dissenting in part). The Supreme Court, after holding argument, requested supplemental briefing on whether any named plaintiff had standing to sue Google for its alleged unauthorized disclosure of search terms.

The Court then issued a per curiam opinion that avoided reaching the *cy pres* issue, instead remanding for further consideration of the plaintiffs' standing under *Spokeo*. *Frank v. Gaos*, 139 S. Ct. 1041 (2019). Justice Thomas dissented, stating that he would have reversed approval because the settlement provided the class members with "no damages and no other form of meaningful relief. . . . Whatever role *cy pres* may permissibly play in disposing of unclaimed or undistributable class funds, *cy pres* payments are not a form of relief to the absent class members and should not be treated as such (including when calculating attorney's fees)." *Id.* at 1047 (Thomas, J., dissenting) (internal citation omitted).

After *Frank*, the Ninth Circuit again "reject[ed] the suggestion that a district court may not approve a class-action settlement that provides monetary relief only in the form of *cy pres* payments to third parties." *In re Google Inc. Street View Elec. Commc'ns Litig.*, 21

F.4th 1102, 1113 (9th Cir. 2021). In a decade-long case over Google's collection of Wi-Fi data involving a 60 million-person class—but only a $13 million settlement fund—the Ninth Circuit held that the use of *cy pres* payments was appropriate because it was not possible for any claimants (or the settlement administrator) "to determine with any degree of probability whether they are class members." *Id.* at 1115. The court also rejected the argument that class certification is inappropriate when it is impossible to distribute funds to class members, for class members still benefit, albeit indirectly, from the *cy pres* distribution given the requirement that the award must have a "direct and substantial nexus to the interests of absent class members" even if the settlement "also provides a diffuse benefit to society at large." *Id.* at 1116 (citation omitted). While one of the objectors claimed that the settlement also violated his First Amendment rights by distributing funds to organizations adverse to his own interests, the court was unpersuaded, pointing out that any class member holding such a view can simply opt out. *Id.* at 1118.

11. RECENT SETTLEMENT OPINIONS

The Ninth Circuit has closely scrutinized recent proposed class settlements—particularly injunctive-relief-only and coupon settlements—for unfairness and possible signs of collusion.

In *Campbell v. Facebook*, the Ninth Circuit upheld a settlement between Facebook and a class of its users whose privacy was allegedly violated when using the website. 951 F.3d at 1128. The settlement provided only injunctive relief, including requiring Facebook to make certain disclosures regarding its message monitoring practices. *Id.* at 1111. The settlement further provided that class counsel would apply for $3.89 million in attorneys' fees and costs, an award Facebook would not contest. *Id.* Class members would release their declaratory and injunctive relief claims and the named plaintiffs would release their damage claims. *Id.* at 1115–16. The Ninth Circuit rejected the objector's contention that the settlement provided only "worthless" injunctive relief, explaining that the provision requiring Facebook to publish a disclosure was not "worthless" because it provided class members with additional relief beyond what Facebook had already promised to do. *Id.* at 1123. In addition, the class members did not need to receive much for the settlement to pass muster because they gave up very little—the claims were relatively weak and the releases were narrow in scope. *Id.* at 1123–24. Although the Ninth Circuit in *Campbell* declined to resolve whether the *Bluetooth* factors apply to cases that settle after a class has been certified, the court concluded that the settlement was not the product of collusion, observing that the litigation proceeded nearly to the end of discovery before settling, the settlement was the result of multiple in-person, arms'-length mediations, and the value of what the class members received was proportional to what they gave up and the award of fees to class counsel. *Id.* at 1125–27. Finally, while the Ninth Circuit disagreed with the district court's statement that a "clear sailing" provision is not a concern with an injunctive-relief-only settlement, that error was harmless absent evidence suggesting the class could have received "meaningfully more injunctive or declaratory relief" if the settlement had allowed Facebook to oppose the fee application. *Id.* at 1127.

After declining to do so in *Campbell*, the Ninth Circuit in *Briseño v. Henderson* clarified that district courts must scrutinize fee arrangements in post-certification settlements for collusion using the *Bluetooth* factors. 998 F.3d 1014, 1019 (2021). In *Briseño*, a class of plaintiffs sued ConAgra, then owner of Wesson Oil, for allegedly marketing its olive oil as "100% Natural" despite the fact that it contained genetically modified organisms (GMOs). *Id.* After the court certified a class, the parties reached a settlement which required ConAgra to pay claims submitted by class members and stop advertising its oil as "natural." *Id.* at 1020. ConAgra also agreed not to contest a request for up to $6.85 million in attorneys' fees and expenses. *Id.* The Ninth Circuit held that the settlement contained all three red flags of potential collusion under *Bluetooth*. *Id.* at 1026.

First, plaintiffs' counsel received a disproportionate distribution of the settlement. Although the parties estimated the settlement was worth $95 million in value to the class, ConAgra ended up paying out less than $1 million. *Id.* at 1026. Class counsel, however, received almost $7 million. *Id.* "This gross disparity in distribution of funds between class members and their class counsel raises an urgent red flag demanding more attention and scrutiny." *Id.* Second, the parties agreed to a "clear sailing arrangement" by which ConAgra agreed not to challenge the agreed-upon fee. *Id.* at 1026–27. Third, the settlement contained a reversion clause providing that the defendant, not class members, would receive the remaining funds if attorneys' fees were reduced. *Id.* at 1027. In reversing the settlement approval, the court also concluded that the district court had failed to recognize that the injunctive relief was worthless: not only had ConAgra already agreed to stop marketing the oil as 100% natural two years before the settlement, but ConAgra also had sold Wesson Oil, so the new owner could resume labelling it as 100 percent natural at will. *Id.* at 1028.

In *Kim v. Allison (Kim I)*, the court similarly reversed approval of a settlement, finding that the district court underrated the strength of plaintiff's claims, overstated the settlement's worth, and failed to adequately scrutinize the settlement for possible collusion. 8 F.4th 1170, 1179 (9th Cir. 2021). In *Kim I*, a plaintiff filed a putative class action against the owner of the Tinder dating app, alleging that Tinder violated California law by reducing prices for subscribers under 30. *Id.* at 1174. The parties reached a settlement providing for, among other things, in-app perks and injunctive relief. *Id.* at 1176. The agreement also contained a "clear sailing provision"—the defendant agreed not to challenge class counsel's request for fees of $1.2 million. *Id.* at 1177. Six class members objected to the settlement, but the district court approved it and awarded the requested attorneys' fees. *Id.* at 1176–78.

The Ninth Circuit reversed, holding that the approval of the settlement and attorneys' fees reflected an abuse of discretion. *Id.* at 1179. The court found that the district court substantially underrated the strength of the plaintiff's claims and overstated the settlement's value. *Id.* In addition, the in-app perks were worth little because 44% of the class had stopped using Tinder, and those still looking for love (or a hook-up) through Tinder already received many in-app perks. *Id.* Moreover, the court held that the district court failed to adequately scrutinize "the combination of a clear-sailing provision and an attorneys' fee award that outstripped the likely financial benefit to the class." *Id.* at 1179. The district court did not support its conclusion that the fees were proportionate to the benefit to the class; it instead calculated the value of the settlement using an unrealistic claims rate and an unsupported injunctive-relief valuation. *Id.* Finally, the Ninth Circuit vacated the award of $1.2 million in fees because the district court failed to substantiate its valuation of the injunctive relief and, in any event, should have excluded the injunctive relief from its valuation of the settlement for purposes of determining a reasonable fee. *Id.* at 1181.

After remand, the parties reached an amended settlement agreement, which the district court approved over objections that the plaintiff was inadequate because she was subject to binding arbitration. *See Kim v. Allison (Kim II)*, 87 F.4th 994, 999 (9th Cir. 2023). On appeal, the Ninth Circuit again reversed, explaining that the district court had "conflated a class representative's adequacy with her typicality." *Id.* at 1000. Adequacy is focused on potential conflicts between the named plaintiff while the more "permissive" typicality standard focuses on whether the plaintiff's claims are reasonably co-extensive with the class so "[w]hile a lack of typicality can indicate that a class representative may be inadequate, the two inquiries are not the same." *Id.* (citation omitted). Because the *Kim* plaintiff faced a binding arbitration agreement, she had a conflict of interest since she was strongly incentivized to settle even if it was at the expense of a broad release for thousands of class members who may not be bound by arbitration. *Id.* at 1001. The *Kim II* court also concluded that the plaintiff and her counsel were not adequate because they had not vigorously represented the class, having taken only minimal discovery and offering only a belated and cursory opposition to the defendant's motion to compel arbitration, revealing an unwillingness to "maximize her leverage at the negotiating table." *Id.* at 1002–03.

In *Lowery v. Rhapsody Int'l, Inc.*, 75 F.4th 985 (9th Cir. 2023), the Ninth Circuit held that, at least in copyright cases, a district court must determine the settlement's actual value to class members in evaluating the reasonableness of a fee request. The lower court approved the plaintiffs' counsel's request of $1.7 million in fees, but on appeal, the Ninth Circuit concluded this amount was unreasonable and disproportionate because class claims amounted to only $52,841.05. *Id.* at 993–94 ("Except in extraordinary cases, a fee award should not exceed the value that the litigation provided to the class.").

The Ninth Circuit has also recently issued several decisions concerning coupon settlements under CAFA, which requires courts to apply heightened scrutiny to such settlements and award attorneys' fees on the redemption value of coupons as opposed to their face value. Although CAFA does not define "coupon," the Ninth Circuit has identified three factors for determining whether settlement relief constitutes a coupon under CAFA: "(1) whether class members have 'to hand over more of their own money before they can take advantage of' a credit, (2) whether the credit is valid only 'for select products or services,' and (3) how much flexibility the credit provides, including whether it expires or is freely transferrable." *In re EasySaver Rewards Litig.*, 906 F.3d 747, 755 (9th Cir. 2018) (quoting *In re Online DVD-Rental Antitrust Litig.*, 779 F.3d 934, 951 (9th Cir. 2015)).

In *Chambers v. Whirlpool Corporation*, the Ninth Circuit affirmed approval of a class settlement agreement providing coupons to purchasers of allegedly defective dishwashers but overturned the attorneys' fees awarded by the district court in a contested fee proceeding. 980 F.3d 645, 655 (2020). The plaintiffs alleged that control boards in their dishwashers were prone to overheating and could start a fire. *Id.* at 654. The settlement provided benefits to both class and non-class members based on the type of control board in the dishwasher, including reimbursement for repairs and revisions to Whirlpool's service procedures; however, a vast portion of the settlement was comprised of coupon benefits. *Id.* at 655. The value of the coupons was disputed: plaintiffs alleged the coupons were worth $116.7 million while defendants argued they were only worth $4.2 million. *Id.* at 655–56. In approving the settlement the district court awarded $14.8 million in attorney's fees. *Id.* at 656.

On appeal, the Ninth Circuit first determined that CAFA's attorney fee provisions, including those governing fees in coupon settlements, preempt any corresponding state law and apply to all federal class actions, including those based on diversity jurisdiction and even where the parties' contract provides that it is governed by state law. *Id.* at 657. Next, the court determined that the district court improperly used the lodestar method to calculate attorneys' fees for the coupon portion of the settlement, as it was required to use either (i) a percentage-of-value calculation for any "portion" of a fee award attributable to coupons under CAFA, or (ii) a lodestar methodology divorced from the coupon portion of the settlement. *Id.* at 657–58. Because the district court did neither, the Ninth Circuit remanded for further proceedings. *Id.* at 669. The court also held that the district court erred in applying an upward multiplier. *Id.* at 665–68. At the same time, the Ninth Circuit upheld approval of the settlement itself because only 0.17% of the class experienced a malfunction, and those class members received a repair or replacement reimbursement, while the vast majority of class members who had not suffered a problem could receive a rebate for a new dishwasher and extended protections. *Id.* at 669.

The Ninth Circuit again considered a coupon settlement in *McKinney-Drobnis v. Oreshack*, 16 F.4th 594 (9th Cir. 2021). The plaintiffs sued Massage Envy, alleging that it had periodically increased membership fees in violation of the membership agreement. Before a class was certified, the parties reached a settlement in which Massage Envy agreed to provide vouchers to class members. On appeal, the court first found that the vouchers would likely require class members to hand over their own money before they take advantage of the settlement because the class members receiving the smallest voucher, in the amount of $36.28, was not enough to purchase most of Massage Envy's services. *Id.* at 604. Second, the vouchers were only valid for "select products or services" because, while Massage Envy offers many products in addition to massages, these products all fall under the same category of health and wellness, are not sold at every Massage Envy location, and are not available online. *Id.* at 604–05. Last, the court noted that the vouchers were flexible because they could be transferred, sold, and aggregated; there were no blackout dates; the vouchers remained valid for more than one year; and the vouchers did not carry a "use it or lose it" restriction. Thus, the third factor weighed against treating the vouchers as coupons. *Id.* at 605. Nevertheless, based on the first two factors, the court deemed the vouchers "coupons" under CAFA. *Id.* And because the district court did not calculate the value of the coupons as required by CAFA, the Ninth Circuit vacated the attorneys' fee award and remanded with instructions to use the value of the redeemed vouchers, rather than that of the vouchers merely claimed, in awarding fees under CAFA. *Id.*

Unlike in *Chambers*, where the Ninth Circuit vacated the fee award but upheld the district court's decision to approve the settlement, in *McKinney* the court reversed on both issues. The court explained that the district court failed to apply the requisite heightened scrutiny under *Bluetooth* to "smoke out potential collusion." *Id.* at 608 (quoting *Henderson*, 998 F.3d at 1023). The *Bluetooth* factors must be considered in addition to the factors laid out in Rule 23(e)—which means consideration of factors relevant to a settlement's fairness cannot cure a district court's failure to guard against signs of collusion. *Id.* at 609. The proposed settlement in *McKinney* contained both "clear sailing" and "reverter" provisions, and "[w]hen a clear sailing provision is paired with a reverter," there is an increased risk that "class counsel will unreasonably raise the amount of requested fees, and the class members will have less incentive to push back because the recovery of any unawarded fees will revert back to the defendants, not the class members." *Id.* at 610. Judge Miller filed a concurrence arguing that the full Court should revisit its guidelines established in *Online DVD-Rental* for what constitutes a "coupon." *Id.* at 612–13.

The Ninth Circuit revisited coupon settlements in *McKnight v. Hinojosa*, 54 F.4th 1069 (9th Cir. 2022). The *McKnight* plaintiffs asserted breach of contract and consumer law claims against Uber for allegedly misrepresenting "its 'Safe Ride Fees' and the safety measures, background checks, and other efforts it takes to provide safety for its customers." *Id.* at 1073. The parties reached a settlement providing for injunctive relief and a $32.5 million non-reversionary settlement fund whereby class members would receive 25 cents for the first Safe Rides Fee they were charged and 5 cents for each subsequent fee, and the average class member was expected to receive $1.07. *Id.* Class members would receive the settlement funds either by submitting a claim or by having the amount credited to their Uber account if they did not submit a form. *Id.* at 1074. Uber agreed to attempt to remit any unused credits after one year to the class member's payment account on file. The district court awarded attorneys' fees amounting to approximately 17.5 percent of the fund after finding CAFA's coupon settlement provisions inapplicable.

Three objectors appealed the fee award, arguing that the district court erred by not applying CAFA's coupon settlement provisions. The *McKnight* court affirmed, applying the *Online DVD-Rental* factors to find the settlement not a coupon settlement. Under the first factor, while most class members' settlement awards were too small to purchase a ride without also paying out of pocket, class members could claim their credit upfront in cash and also stood to receive cash relief if they did not use their credit. *Id.* at 1075–76. The second factor further weighed against finding a coupon settlement because, although Uber's services were not as limited as those in cases like *Chambers* and *McKinney-Drobnis*, the settlement credit was valid only for Uber's services. *Id.* at 1076. The third factor also weighed against finding a coupon settlement because the unused credits became cash after one year without further action by class members. *Id.* at 1077.

12. FEES AND COSTS (FED. R. CIV. P. 23(H))

Rule 23(h) provides that "[i]n a certified class action, the court may award reasonable attorney's fees and nontaxable costs that are authorized by law or by the parties' agreement." Fed. R. Civ. P. 23(h).

a. The Common Fund Doctrine

The common fund doctrine applies in the Ninth Circuit, as elsewhere. *Staton*, 327 F.3d at 267. This doctrine recognizes that to avoid unjust enrichment and ensure equitable apportionment of a common fund, counsel are entitled to be compensated for their efforts in bringing about the fund. *Id.* at 968; *Boeing v. Van Gemert*, 444 U.S. 472, 478 (1980) (holding that "a litigant or lawyer who recovers a common fund . . . is entitled to a reasonable attorney's fee from the fund as a whole."); *In re Wash. Pub. Power Supply System Sec. Litig.*, 19 F.3d 1291, 1300 (9th Cir. 1994) (same).

"Where a settlement produces a common fund for the benefit of the entire class, courts have discretion to employ either the lodestar method or the percentage-of-recovery method." *Bluetooth*, 654 F.3d at 942; *Vizcaino v. Microsoft Corp.*, 290 F.3d 1043, 1047 (9th Cir. 2002). Because the benefit to the class is "easily quantified" in common fund settlements, "courts can 'award attorneys a percentage of the common fund in lieu of the often more time-consuming task of calculating the lodestar.'" *Boring v. Bed Bath & Beyond of Cal. LLC*, No. 12-cv-05259-JST, 2014 WL 2967474, at *2 (N.D. Cal. June 30, 2014) (quoting *Bluetooth*, 654 F.3d at 942). In common fund cases, the "percentage of the fund" is the preferred method for determining reasonable attorneys' fees. *See, e.g.*, *Blum v. Stenson*, 465 U.S. 886, 900 n.16 (1984) (under the common fund doctrine, a "reasonable fee is based on a percentage of the fund bestowed on the class"); *Six Mexican Workers*, 904 F.2d at 1311 ("[A] reasonable fee under the common fund doctrine is calculated as a percentage of the recovery."); *Paul, Johnson, Alston & Hunt v. Graulty*, 886 F.2d 268, 272 (9th Cir. 1989). In *Vizcaino*, while recognizing the propriety of a lodestar cross-check (to be performed in the district court's discretion), the Ninth Circuit criticized lodestar for creating an incentive for counsel "to expend more hours than may be necessary on litigating a case so as to recover a reasonable fee." 290 F.3d at 1050; *see also In re Quantum Health Resources, Inc.*, 962 F. Supp. 1254, 1257 (C.D. Cal. 1997) (noting that lodestar "creates an incentive to keep litigation going in order to maximize the number of hours included in the court's lodestar calculation"); *Bautista v. Harvest Mgmt. Sub LLC*, No. CV 12-10004 FMO (CWx), 2014 WL 12579822, at *13 (C.D. Cal. July 14, 2014) (awarding a 30 percent fee without performing a lodestar cross-check and stating that such a "cross-check is not required in this circuit, and in some cases is not a useful reference point") (citation omitted).

b. Factors Influencing the Award of Fees

For cases in which the district court compensates counsel using the percentage of the fund method, "courts typically calculate 25% of the fund as the 'benchmark' for a reasonable fee award[.]" *Bluetooth*, 654 F.3d at 942; *Hanlon*, 150 F.3d at 1029 ("This circuit has established 25% of the common fund as a benchmark for attorneys' fees."). An award of 25 percent of a common fund is therefore presumptively reasonable. *Ching v. Siemens Indus., Inc.*, No. 11-cv-04838, 2014 WL 2926210, at *7 (N.D. Cal. June 27, 2014).

Under both the percentage and lodestar approaches for determining attorneys' fees, "[t]he ultimate goal . . . is to reasonably compensate counsel for their efforts in creating the common fund." *Omnivision*, 559 F. Supp. 2d at 1047. To ensure that the fee award is reasonable, "[s]election of the benchmark or any other rate must be supported by findings that take into account all of the circumstances of the case." *Vizcaino*, 290 F.3d at 1048. In determining whether a fee award is reasonable, courts consider (1) the results obtained, (2) the risk involved in the litigation, (3) the skill required by and quality of work performed by counsel, (4) the contingent nature of the fee, and (5) awards made in similar cases. *Ching*, 2014 WL 2926210, at *7 (citing *Vizcaino*, 290 F.3d at 1048).

Results Obtained

The quality of the result obtained through the settlement is a major factor to be considered in making a fee award. *Hensley v. Eckerhart*, 461 U.S. 424, 436 (1983) (stating that the "most critical factor is the degree of success obtained."); *Omnivision*, 559 F. Supp. 2d at 1046. As part of this analysis, courts may place a dollar value on nonmonetary consideration: "Incidental or nonmonetary benefits conferred by the litigation are a relevant circumstance" in determining fee awards. *Vizcaino*, 290 F.3d at 1049. For example, in affirming approval of the class settlement in *Linney v. Cellular Alaska Partnership*, 151 F.3d 1234 (9th Cir. 1998), the court concluded that "the value of the injunctive relief ($20.9 million to $34.2 million) far outweighs the value of the settlement fund[.]" *Id.* at 1240.

Risks Involved
The risk of continuing litigation represents the other key factor for determining a reasonable fee. *Vizcaino*, 290 F.3d at 1048. Uncertainty that a recovery would be obtained is highly relevant in assessing risk. *See In re Wash. Pub. Power Supply Sys. Sec. Litig.*, 19 F.3d 1291, 1300 (9th Cir. 1994) (noting that "courts have routinely enhanced the lodestar to reflect the risk of non-payment in common fund cases"); *In re Heritage Bond Litig.*, Nos. 02-ML-1475 DT, et al., 2005 WL 1594403, at *21 (C.D. Cal. June 10, 2005) (stating that "[c]ourts consistently recognize that the risk of non-payment or reimbursement of expenses is a factor in determining the appropriateness of counsel's fee award").

Skill of Counsel and Quality of Work Performed
The skill and quality of legal counsel bear upon a requested fee award as well. *See Vizcaino*, 290 F.3d at 1048; *Heritage Bond*, 2005 WL 1594403, at *19 ("[T]he quality of Class Counsel's effort, experience and skill is demonstrated in the exceptional result achieved."). The quality of opposing counsel is relevant to the analysis of the work done by class counsel. *See Barbosa v. Cargill Meat Solutions Corp.*, 297 F.R.D. 431, 449 (E.D. Cal. 2013).

Contingent Nature of Fee
"Courts have long recognized that the public interest is served by rewarding attorneys who assume representation on a contingent basis with an enhanced fee to compensate them for the risk that they might be paid nothing at all for their work." *Ching*, 2014 WL 2926210, at *8 (citing *Wash. Pub. Power Supply Sys.*, 19 F.3d at 1299; *Vizcaino*, 290 F.3d at 1050; *Omnivision*, 559 F. Supp. 2d at 1047). Similarly relevant to the analysis of a reasonable fee is class counsel's "foregoing [of] other work" as they pursued and negotiated a settlement of the claims. *Online DVD-Rental*, 779 F.3d at 955.

Awards in Similar Cases
Fees awarded in comparable cases may also serve as a reference point for determining a reasonable fee. *See, e.g.*, *Vizcaino*, 290 F.3d at 1050 n.4 ("This award was within the range of fees awarded in settlements of comparable size.").

Reaction of the Class
Just as class members' reaction to a proposed settlement bears on the settlement approval inquiry, so does their reaction to the proposed fee bear on the analysis of what fee is reasonable. *See, e.g.*, *Heritage Bond*, 2005 WL 1594403, at *21 ("The absence of objections or disapproval by class members to Class Counsel's fee request further supports finding the fee request reasonable.").

Lodestar Cross-Check
As noted above, the Court may engage in a lodestar "cross-check" when awarding a fee as a percentage of a common fund. *Vizcaino*, 290 F.3d at 1050–51 & n.5. The purpose of a cross-check is not to recalculate the fee, but to supply a "final check on the reasonableness of the requested fees." *Omnivision*, 559 F. Supp. 2d at 1048. In *Vizcaino*, the court stated that analysis of the "lodestar method is merely a cross-check on the reasonableness of a percentage figure[.]" 290 F.3d at 1050 n.5. To aid in "cross-checking" the reasonableness of a percentage-based fee, class counsel submit records of hours worked on the case and applicable hourly rates. If requested by the court, class counsel also submit records documenting time spent by individual lawyers on specific tasks. *See, e.g.*, *Dyer*, 303 F.R.D. at 333 ("At the

hearing on the instant motion, the Court asked Plaintiffs' Counsel to submit more specific records of hours worked on the case; the Court did not require actual billing statements, but asked Plaintiffs' counsel to at least provide[] summaries of hours worked on particular categories of tasks so that the Court could evaluate whether the hours worked were reasonable.").

c. Fee-Shifting Cases

A court may also award attorneys' fees in a class action pursuant to a fee-shifting provision of the civil rights laws, the Copyright Act, or other statutes. State-law fee jurisprudence governs the determination of a fee award when the plaintiff prevailed under state law. *Vizcaino*, 290 F.3d at 1047 (citing *Mangold v. Cal. Pub. Utils. Comm'n*, 67 F.3d 1470, 1478 (9th Cir. 1995)).

Lowery, 75 F.4th 985, involved claims under the Copyright Act: music copyright holders alleged that a music streaming service provider, Rhapsody International, had infringed their copyrights by reproducing and distributing their musical compositions without an appropriate license. *Id.* at 989. The parties agreed to a settlement under which Rhapsody would pay up to $20 million, but because a separate settlement with an industry trade group had "gutted the potential class, very few class members submitted claims" and Rhapsody only paid about $52,000 to the class. *Id.* at 990.

Although the plaintiffs' attorneys sought $6 million in fees, the district court awarded only $1.7 million. *Id.* at 990–91. The Ninth Circuit reversed, finding an abuse of discretion because "the $1.7 million fee award is more than *thirty times* larger than the amount paid to class members." *Id.* at 990 (emphasis in original). The court stressed the need to consider the settlement's "actual or realistically anticipated benefit to the class" (both monetary and nonmonetary), rather than a maximum hypothetical amount, in determining the reasonableness of a fee award, to "assure that the counsel's fee does not dwarf class recovery." *Id.* at 994 (quoting *Bluetooth*, 654 F.3d at 945). The Ninth Circuit remanded with instructions to "rigorously evaluate the actual benefit provided to the class and award reasonable attorneys' fees considering that benefit." *Id.* at 988.

In holding that "[d]istrict courts awarding attorneys' fees in class actions under the Copyright Act must still generally consider the proportion between the award and the benefit to the class to ensure that the award is reasonable," the court distinguished the objectives of the Copyright Act's fee-shifting provision from those of civil rights fee-shifting statutes designed to promote vindication for victims of civil rights violations, noting that civil rights cases often "provide significant nonmonetary and injunctive relief to plaintiffs." *Id.* at 995. The court also recognized that a fee award exceeding the monetary benefit to the class may be appropriate in certain copyright infringement cases that provide a substantial public benefit. It remains uncertain whether or how *Lowery*'s limitations apply in other federal fee-shifting cases or to claims brought under state fee-shifting statutes.

d. Expenses

"Reasonable costs and expenses incurred by an attorney who creates or preserves a common fund are reimbursed proportionately by those class members who benefit by the settlement." *In re Media Vision Tech. Sec. Litig.*, 913 F. Supp. 1362, 1366 (N.D. Cal. 1995) (citing, *inter alia*, *Mills v. Elec. Auto-Lite Co.*, 396 U.S. 375, 391–92 (1970)). Reimbursement of expenses is appropriate to the extent they were reasonable and necessarily incurred in furtherance of the case prosecution. *Vincent v. Hughes Air W.*, 557 F.2d 759, 769 (9th Cir. 1977); *Omnivision*, 559 F. Supp. 2d at 1048.

e. Incentive Awards

Courts frequently approve "incentive" or "service" award to class representatives in recognition of their efforts on behalf of the class. *See Rodriguez v. West Pub'g Corp.*, 563 F.3d 948, 958 (9th Cir. 2009) (noting that such awards "are fairly typical in class action cases"). In

Staton v. Boeing Company, the Ninth Circuit clarified that "named plaintiffs, as opposed to designated class members who are not named plaintiffs, are eligible for reasonable incentive payments. The district court must evaluate their awards individually, using 'relevant factors includ[ing] the actions the plaintiff has taken to protect the interests of the class, the degree to which the class has benefitted from those actions, . . . the amount of time and effort the plaintiff expended in pursuing the litigation . . . and reasonabl[e] fear[s of] workplace retaliation.'" 327 F.3d 938, 977 (9th Cir. 2003) (quoting *Cook v. Niedert*, 142 F.3d 1004, 1016 (7th Cir. 1998)).

Although courts have approved incentive awards for decades, the propriety of such payments to class representatives has become a hotly contested issue in federal courts. The Eleventh Circuit has held that incentive awards are categorically prohibited under nineteenth century Supreme Court decisions. *See Johnson v. NPAS Sols, LLC*, 975 F.3d 1244, 1255–61 (11th Cir. 2020) (citing *Trustees v. Greenough*, 105 U.S. 527 (1882) and *Central Railroad & Banking Co. v. Pettus*, 113 U.S. 116 (1885)). The Ninth Circuit, however, reiterated in 2022 that incentive awards "cannot categorically be rejected or approved" but are permissible so long as they are reasonable. *In re Apple Inc. Device Performance Litig.*, 50 F.4th 769, 786 (9th Cir. 2022). In rejecting the objector argument in *Apple Device Performance* that incentive awards amount to an impermissible salary under *Greenough* and *Pettus*, the court contrasted typical service awards with *Greenough*, where the Supreme Court disapproved of a 10-year allowance that was the modern-day equivalent of $76,000 per year for "personal services" as well as "personal expenditures" equivalent to $458,000. 50 F.4th at 785–87. While hefty service awards in some cases might be "more aptly analogized to a salary," the district court's decision to award $1,500 to each plaintiff was reasonable under the circumstances, the Ninth Circuit concluded. *Id.* at 786.

When it comes to applying these factors in a typical class action, courts in the Ninth Circuit have coalesced around the propriety of a $5,000 incentive award, subject to inflation. In *In re Mego Financial Corporation Securities Litigation*, which settled for $1.725 million, the Ninth Circuit endorsed payment of $5,000 incentive awards to each of the two class representatives. 213 F.3d 454, 457, 463 (9th Cir. 2000). Likewise, in *Online DVD-Rental*, the court rejected an objector's argument that payment of $5,000 incentive awards rendered the class representatives inadequate. 779 F.3d at 942–43. Based in part on these authorities, "a $5,000 payment is presumptively reasonable," with awards "typically rang[ing] from $2,000 to $10,000." *Bellinghausen v. Tractor Supply Co.*, 306 F.R.D. 245, 266 (N.D. Cal. 2015) (collecting cases); *see also In re Toys R Us-Del., Inc. FACTA Litig.*, 295 F.R.D. 438, 470–72 (C.D. Cal. 2014) (awarding three plaintiffs $5,000 each, "consistent with the amount courts typically award as incentive payments."); *Smith v. Am. Greetings Corp.*, No. 14-CV-02577-JST, 2016 WL 362395, at *10–11 (N.D. Cal. Jan. 29, 2016) (rejecting request for $7,500 awards, explaining that each of the two plaintiffs spent only 20–25 hours on the case, and instead approving awards of $5,000—which "in the Ninth Circuit . . . is presumptively reasonable."); *Roe v. Frito-Lay, Inc.*, No. 14-CV-00751-HSG, 2017 WL 1315626, at *8 (N.D. Cal. Apr. 7, 2017) (awarding $5,000 and explaining that the requested $10,000 would be "substantially disproportionate to class members' anticipated recovery of $193.45").

Higher amounts are sometimes awarded, particularly in employment class actions, where named plaintiffs may risk retaliation or blacklisting. *See, e.g.*, *Buccellato v. AT & T Ops., Inc.*, No. C10-00463-LHK, 2011 WL 4526673, at *4 (N.D. Cal. June 30, 2011) (awarding $20,000 to a named plaintiff whose "initiation of the lawsuit caused him personal exposure and potential adverse consequences with future employers," and who "educat[ed] Class counsel regarding Class Members' job duties and [the defendant's] policies and procedures"); *Hughes v. Microsoft Corp.*, Nos. C98-1646C & C93-0178C, 2001 WL 34089697, at *12–13 (W.D. Wash. Mar. 26, 2001) (approving incentive awards of $65,000 to six class representatives in case arising from alleged denial of employee benefits); *Van Vranken v. Atl. Richfield Co.*, 901 F. Supp. 294, 299–300 (N.D. Cal. 1995) ($50,000 to class representative in non-employment case, for violations of Economic Stabilization Act); *but see Roberts* *v. Marshalls of CA, LLC*, No. 13-CV-04731-MEJ, 2018 WL 510286, at *19 (N.D. Cal. Jan. 23, 2018) (gathering authorities showing that "named plaintiffs in employment class actions regularly receive" awards in "the $5,000 and $10,000 range, if not less").

In other cases, as where plaintiffs were minimally involved, smaller awards may be appropriate. *See, e.g.*, *Davis v. Brown Shoe Co., Inc.*, No. 1:13-cv-01211-LJO-BAM, 2015 WL 6697929, at *12 (E.D. Cal. Nov. 3, 2015) (approving "the lower incentive award of $2,500" to two plaintiffs who spent 15–20 hours on case); *Wilson v. Airborne, Inc.*, No. EDCV 07-770 VAP (OPx), 2008 WL 3854963, at *12–13 (C.D. Cal. Aug. 13, 2008) (awarding $2,500 instead of the requested $10,000 to a plaintiff who was never deposed); *Wolph v. Acer Am. Corp.*, No. C 09-01314 JSW, 2013 WL 5718440, at *6 (N.D. Cal. Oct. 21, 2013) (awarding $2,000 instead of the requested $5,000 to plaintiffs who did "not suggest that they undertook any great risk to either their finances or to their reputation in bringing this [products liability] action").

Ethical pitfalls relating to award size or guarantees dot the landscape of incentive award jurisprudence. In *Staton*, the Ninth Circuit warned that "special 'incentives' in the settlement agreement" may result in class representatives being "more concerned with maximizing those incentives than with judging the adequacy of the settlement as it applies to class members at large." 327 F.3d at 977. Class representatives thus must "disclaim[] any right to a preferred position in the settlement. Were that not the case, there would be considerable danger of individuals bringing cases as class actions principally to increase their own leverage to attain a remunerative settlement for themselves and then trading on that leverage in the course of negotiations." 327 F.3d at 976 (citation omitted). Accordingly, a class representative must be treated the same as other class members for purposes of allocating settlement relief, with any incentive award representing a "bonus" for the class representatives' unique contributions.

To ensure fairness to the class and the class representatives' unconflicted ability to assess a settlement's adequacy, the "proportion of the [incentive] payments relative to the settlement amount," in addition to the absolute amount of payments, bears consideration. *Id.* at 977. In *Bellinghausen*, for example, the district court reduced the requested $20,000 award to $15,000, explaining that $20,000 at "2 percent of the gross settlement funds" was "higher than what other courts have found acceptable" and significantly exceeded both the average and the highest estimated class member recoveries. 306 F.R.D. at 267–68; *see also Alberto v. GMRI, Inc.*, 252 F.R.D. 652, 669 (E.D. Cal. 2008) (criticizing a similarly "explicit disparity and the utter lack of evidence demonstrating the quality of plaintiff's representative service"); *Roe*, 2017 WL 1315626, at *8 (reducing requested award as disproportionate to class member recovery) (citing *Zepeda v. PayPal, Inc.*, No. C 10-1668 SBA, 2017 WL 1113293, at *19 (N.D. Cal. Mar. 24, 2017)); *Radcliffe v. Experian Info. Sols. Inc.*, 715 F.3d 1157, 1165 (9th Cir. 2013) ("There is a serious question whether class representatives could be expected to fairly evaluate whether awards ranging from $26 to $750 is a fair settlement value when they would receive $5,000 incentive awards.").

Radcliffe and *Rodriguez v. West Publishing* present cautionary tales regarding incentive awards. In *Rodriguez*, certain plaintiffs' counsel had promised some class representatives that they would seek incentive awards in amounts tied to the size of the class recovery. 563 F.3d at 957–59. The district court found that these "bounty" agreements created a divergence of interest between the class and its putative representatives, who were consequently inadequate. The Ninth Circuit affirmed the district court's invalidation of the incentive agreements, while also affirming its approval of the settlement agreement. The Ninth Circuit remarked that "[b]y tying their compensation—in advance—to a sliding scale based on the amount recovered, the incentive agreements disjoined the contingency financial interests of the contracting representatives from the class." *Id.* at 959. The court further held that class counsel had improperly "simultaneously represented" parties with conflicting interests due to the incentive agreements, and remanded for reconsideration of how that ethical lapse might affect counsel's entitlement to fees. *Id.* at 958–60, 968. On remand, the district court found that class counsel were not entitled to fees for the period during which the conflict existed. But, rejecting objections that the conflict should have resulted in disqualification, making it improper for class counsel to perform any work for the class after the conflict arose, the district court awarded class counsel fees for the work they performed after the incentive agreements were invalidated. The Ninth Circuit agreed in a follow-on appeal, holding that the "rejection of the incentive awards cured any conflict of interest and that [class counsel's] services thereafter were properly performed and conferred a benefit on the class." *Rodriguez v. Disner*, 688 F.3d 645, 660 n.12 (9th Cir. 2012).

Radcliffe involved another troubling form of agreement connected with incentive awards: The settlement agreement itself provided that class representatives would *only* receive an incentive award if they supported the settlement. 715 F.3d at 1161. The Ninth Circuit held that this provision rendered the class representatives inadequate because it "weigh[ed] on the[ir] independent judgment on whether to support the settlement by calling for the denial of incentive awards if they do not support it." *Id.* at 1165–66 (the provision removed "a critical check on the fairness of the class-action settlement, which rests on the unbiased judgment of class representatives"). Class counsel also were inadequate, for "[a]s soon as the conditional-incentive-awards provision divorced the interests of the class representatives from those of the absent class members, class counsel was simultaneously representing clients with conflicting interests." *Id.* at 1167. On remand, the district court denied a motion to disqualify class counsel, and the Ninth Circuit affirmed. *White v. Experian Info. Sols.*, 993 F. Supp. 2d 1154, 1167 (C.D. Cal. 2014) (reasoning that "[t]he attorneys in question have committed no other ethical violations, have vigorously litigated the claims up to this point, did not enter into the improper award agreements until the eve of settlement, and successfully arranged far-reaching and groundbreaking injunctive relief"), *aff'd sub nom. Radcliffe v. Hernandez*, 818 F.3d 537 (9th Cir. 2016).

13. ARBITRATION ISSUES

Up until 2011, courts declined to enforce class action waivers in consumer contracts of adhesion (including in arbitration agreements) on public policy grounds. The California Supreme Court held that such waivers are unconscionable, and therefore unenforceable, when "found in a consumer contract of adhesion in a setting in which disputes between the contracting parties predictably involve small amounts of damages, and when it is alleged that the party with the superior bargaining power has carried out a scheme to deliberately cheat large numbers of consumers out of individually small sums of money[.]" *Discover Bank v. Super. Ct.*, 113 P.3d 1100, 1110 (Cal. 2005) (citation omitted). But in *AT&T Mobility LLC v. Concepcion*, 563 U.S. 333, 352 (2011), the Supreme Court held that the Federal Arbitration Act (FAA) preempts this "*Discover Bank* rule."

The practical effect of *Concepcion* is that arbitration clauses (and their embedded class action waivers) are routinely enforced throughout the Ninth Circuit. And following the Supreme Court's ruling in *Henry Schein, Inc. v. Archer & White Sales, Inc.*, a court may not rule on threshold issues of arbitrability if the parties have agreed to delegate the question to an arbitrator. 139 S. Ct. 524 (2019). For instance, in *Adams v. Postmates, Inc.*, the parties agreed that apart from the enforceability or unconscionability of the class action waiver, any dispute relating to the enforceability or interpretation of the arbitration provision would be decided by the arbitrator. 823 F. Appx 535 (9th Cir. 2020). Because the parties' dispute did not fall within one of the specified categories, the parties' dispute was reserved for the arbitrator. *Id.* at 536. Even after *Concepcion*, however, arbitration agreements may be challenged on traditional formation grounds. *See Concepcion*, 563 U.S. at 353 (Thomas, J., concurring) (noting that "the FAA requires that an agreement to arbitrate be enforced unless a party successfully challenges the formation of the arbitration agreement, such as by proving fraud or duress.").

In *Norcia v. Samsung Telecommunications Am.*, LLC, 845 F.3d 1279 (9th Cir. 2017), the Ninth Circuit held that no agreement to arbitrate had been formed when a defendant cell phone company placed a warranty brochure containing an arbitration clause within a product box but neither the box nor the cover of the brochure prominently disclosed the clause. Rejecting the defendant's argument that the consumer's use of the phone manifested assent to the arbitration agreement, the court concluded that "no contract is formed 'when the writing does not appear to be a contract and the terms are not called to the attention of the recipient.'" *Id.* at 1289 (citation omitted). The court explained that "Samsung has not pointed to any principle of California law that imposed a duty on [plaintiff] to act in response to receiving the Product Safety & Warranty Information brochure," and that "the outside of the Galaxy S4 box did not notify the consumer that opening the box would be considered agreement to the terms set forth in the brochure." *Id.* at 1286–87. In a companion appeal involving the same defendant, the court applied the same reasoning to reverse an order compelling arbitration. *Dang v. Samsung Elecs. Co., Ltd.*, 673 F. App'x 779 (9th Cir. 2017).

In *Ferguson v. Corinthian Colleges, Inc.*, 733 F.3d 928 (9th Cir. 2013), the court held that the FAA preempts California's *Broughton-Cruz* rule barring the arbitration of claims for public injunctive relief. Applying the Supreme Court's arbitration precedents, the Ninth Circuit explained that the California rule impermissibly disfavors arbitration as a forum for certain relief: "By exempting from arbitration claims for public injunctive relief under the CLRA, UCL, and FAL, the *Broughton-Cruz* rule . . . prohibits outright arbitration of a particular type of claim." *Id.* at 934.

In *Sakkab v. Luxoticca Retail North America, Inc.*, 803 F.3d 425 (9th Cir. 2015), however, the court recognized an exception to the general enforceability of arbitration clauses, holding that the FAA did not preempt the California rule barring waivers of representative claims under the Private Attorneys General Act of 2004 (PAGA), Cal. Lab. Code § 2698, *et seq*. PAGA is a California statute that in some ways resembles the False Claims Act; it empowers employees to sue their employer for broadly applicable labor code violations, with most of the recovery going to the state. *Sakkab*, 803 F.3d at 430 (citation omitted). In finding that arbitration clauses cannot bar PAGA claims, the Ninth Circuit emphasized the difference between a class action claim and a PAGA claim: "Because a PAGA action is a statutory action for penalties brought as a proxy for the state, rather than a procedure for resolving the claims of other employees, there is no need to protect absent employees' due process rights in PAGA arbitrations." *Id.* at 436. In other words, because there are no special procedures tied to PAGA claims—e.g., absent class members do not have notice or opt out rights—a finding that PAGA claims cannot be waived does not interfere with the contracting parties' right to select arbitration or other informal procedures to the same extent as would a finding that class action waivers are unenforceable. *Id.* Similarly, in *McGill v. Citibank, N.A.*, the California Supreme Court held that the FAA does not preempt California's rule against waiver of state statutory claims for public injunctive relief, i.e., injunctive relief that "by and large" benefits the general public. 2 Cal. 5th 945, 955 (2017) (citation omitted).

The Supreme Court's 5–4 decision in *Epic Systems Corporation v. Lewis*, 138 S. Ct. 1612 (2018), called into question the continued viability of these California doctrines. In *Epic Systems*, the Supreme Court held that arbitration provisions in employment contracts must be enforced notwithstanding the National Labor Relations Act's guarantee of workers' right to engage in "concerted activities for the purpose of collective bargaining or other mutual aid or protection." The Court interpreted this guarantee, in light of the surrounding statutory language, as referring to collective bargaining and formation of labor unions, such that the clause could not displace the FAA's command that arbitration agreements be enforced according to their terms. *Id.* at 1625. The Court rejected the employees' argument that the FAA's saving clause applies, explaining that even if their interpretation of the NLRA were correct and could supply a "ground . . . at law" to revoke the contracts, their interpretation targeted arbitration in particular and so could not trigger the saving clause under the reasoning of *Concepcion*. *Id.* at 1622–23.

Nonetheless, in *Blair v. Rent-A-Center, Inc.*, 928 F.3d 819 (9th Cir. 2019), the Ninth

Circuit upheld the *McGill* rule against an FAA preemption challenge. The court concluded that, although *Epic Systems* held that the FAA preempts "defenses that target arbitration either by name or by more subtle methods," the *McGill* rule prohibiting waiver by private parties of public injunctive relief does not target arbitration but instead arises from a neutral provision of the Civil Code (section 3513) that prohibits private waiver of public rights. *Blair*, 928 F.3d at 824–28 (quoting *Epic Systems*, 138 S. Ct. at 1622). So the *McGill* rule, like the *Sakkab* rule, "applies 'equally to arbitration and non-arbitration agreements'" and "expresses no preference as to whether public injunction claims are litigated or arbitrated[;] it merely prohibits the waiver of the right to pursue those claims in any forum." *Blair*, 928 F.3d at 827 (quoting *Sakkab*, 803 F.3d at 432). Nor does *McGill* covertly interfere with arbitration, since it "leaves undisturbed an agreement that both requires bilateral arbitration and permits public injunctive claims." *Blair*, 928 F.3d at 829. Thus, because it neither directly nor indirectly burdens the ability of contracting parties to select arbitration, *McGill* is unaffected by the policies of the FAA. *Id.* at 827–31.

Since *Blair*, the Ninth Circuit has considered what may or may not qualify as public injunctive relief. In *Hodges v. Comcast Cable Communications, LLC*, the Ninth Circuit held that whether the *McGill* rule applies depends on whether the particular injunction sought seeks public injunctive relief. 12 F.4th 1108, 1113 (9th Cir.), *opinion amended and superseded on denial of reh'g*, 21 F.4th 535 (9th Cir. 2021). The panel majority held that "public injunctive relief within the meaning of *McGill* is limited to forward-looking injunctions that seek to prevent future violations of law for the benefit of the general public as a whole, as opposed to a particular class of persons, and that do so without the need to consider the individual claims of any non-party." 12 F.4th at 1115. Judge Berzon dissented, arguing that the majority too narrowly construed California law regarding what relief may have the primary effect of benefiting the public. *See id.* at 1122–26 (Berzon, J., dissenting). A subsequent California Court of Appeal decision endorsed Judge Berzon's dissent over the majority opinion in *Hodges*. *See Vaughn v. Tesla, Inc.*, 87 Cal. App. 5th 208, 231 n.16 (2023).

14. TOLLING AND CLAIM PRECLUSION

The Supreme Court has held that a timely filed class action tolls the statute of limitations for all persons encompassed by the complaint and that if class certification is denied, putative class members may intervene individually to pursue their claims or file a separate individual action. *American Pipe & Constr. Co. v. Utah*, 414 U.S. 538 (1974); *Crown, Cork & Seal Co. v. Parker*, 462 U.S. 345 (1983). After a denial of class certification, however, a putative class member may not file a subsequent *class* action if the statute of limitations has expired. *China Agritech, Inc. v. Resh*, 138 S. Ct. 1800, 1804 (2018).

In *Clemens v. DaimlerChrysler Corporation*, the Ninth Circuit held that *American Pipe*—"which allows tolling within the federal court system in federal question class actions—does not mandate cross-jurisdictional tolling as a matter of state procedure." 534 F.3d 1017, 1025 (9th Cir. 2008). The court concluded that "the weight of authority and California's interest in managing its own judicial system counsel us not to import the doctrine of cross-jurisdictional tolling into California law." *Id.* Thus, a prior nationwide class action filed in Illinois state court did not toll a plaintiff's fraud claim under California law. *Id.* The Ninth Circuit likewise concluded that a class action filed in New Jersey federal court did not toll the statute of limitations as a matter of California law. *See Kwon Yi v. BMW of N. Am., LLC*, 805 F. App'x 459, 462 (9th Cir. 2020); *Smothers v. BMW of N. Am., LLC*, 813 F. App'x 291, 294 (9th Cir. 2020). But *Clemens* does not mean that a class action plaintiff may not seek to invoke state tolling doctrines, such as equitable tolling, at least for individual claims. *See Hatfield v. Halifax PLC*, 564 F.3d 1177, 1188 (9th Cir. 2009).

Another tolling question is: "when does the narrowing of a class definition end *American Pipe* tolling of the statute of limitations for members of a putative or certified plaintiff class?" *DeFries v. Union Pac. R.R. Co.*, 104 F.4th 1091, 1095 (9th Cir. 2024). That case involved a plaintiff who was a putative class member under the original class definition of a class action pending in federal district court in Nebraska, but when plaintiffs' counsel moved for class certification, they narrowed the proposed class definition. *Id.* at 1095. The district court certified the narrowed class, but the Eighth Circuit reversed. *Id.* After the Eighth Circuit's decision, the *DeFries* plaintiff then filed an individual suit in the District of Oregon, raising parallel claims to the Nebraska action and the defendant moved for summary judgment based on the statute of limitations. The district court granted summary judgment and the "central question" on appeal was whether the narrowed class definition included or excluded the plaintiff. *Id.* at 1096. The Ninth Circuit reversed the grant of summary judgment, holding that "a relevant ambiguity in the scope of a class definition should be resolved in favor of allowing a bystander plaintiff to rely on *American Pipe* tolling" and even though the "better reading" of the narrowed definition in the Nebraska litigation excluded persons like the *DeFries* plaintiff, the existence of a "reasonable argument to the contrary" meant the plaintiff was entitled to *American Pipe* tolling. *Id.* at 1104–09.

The claims of class action plaintiffs are also potentially subject to claim preclusion (or res judicata). In *Piatt v. Money Store*, the court ruled that the plaintiffs' claims of improper attorneys' fees were precluded because the claims arose out of the same "transactional nucleus of fact" as a previous case. 819 F. App'x 477, 478–79 (9th Cir. 2020). In both cases, class members sought to recover damages from the same defendants based on improperly charged attorneys' fees related to the same documents. *Id.* at 479. The court concluded that the claims could have been brought in the prior case and were barred by res judicata. *Id.*

15. AGGREGATE DAMAGES

In the rare instance a class action goes to trial, a large class along with a statutory damages claim may result in a significant judgment against the defendant. The Ninth Circuit addressed the issue of whether a large aggregate damages award violates a defendant's substantive due process rights in *Wakefield v. ViSalus, Inc.*, 51 F.4th 1109 (9th Cir. 2022). That case involved 1.8 million robocalls and statutory damages of $500 per violation under the Telephone Consumer Protection Act (TCPA). On appeal, the court vacated a $925 million jury award against a weight-loss products marketing company, instructing the district court to consider "the magnitude of the aggregated award in relation to the [Telephone Consumer Protection Act's] goals of compensation, deterrence, and punishment and to the proscribed conduct" and holding that in certain "extreme situations" an aggregate statutory damages award may be so "gravely disproportionate" to the legal violation that the award becomes "unconstitutionally excessive" even if the underlying statutory penalty is constitutional. *Id.* at 1123–24; *see also Montera v. Premier Nutrition Corp.*, 111 F.4th 1018, 1041 (9th Cir. 2024) (remanding to district court to consider whether $91 million statutory damages award was unreasonable in light of intervening *Wakefield* decision).

TENTH CIRCUIT

Districts of Colorado, Kansas, New Mexico, Oklahoma, Utah, and Wyoming

The Byron White U.S. Courthouse
1823 Stout Street
Denver, CO 80257

By Paul Karlsgodt, Keeley O. Cronin, and Alexis J. Opper[1]
Baker & Hostetler LLP

1. INTRODUCTION

The geographic reach of the Tenth Circuit encompasses the states of Colorado, Kansas, New Mexico, Oklahoma, Utah, and Wyoming. The high plains and mountainous west in the geography of the circuit influences the nature of the disputes presented to the Court. Mineral, oil, and gas, and other property rights disputes are a common feature in the Tenth Circuit, as are disputes involving environmental and public lands issues. The circuit covers many low population density areas, though each of the states within its boundaries has one or more urban areas. As a result of these factors, class action litigation is less common in the Tenth Circuit than in many of the other circuits, and many of the class actions that are brought in the circuit are different from those in other circuits in terms of the factual basis and legal claims presented. On the other hand, the Tenth Circuit includes several major metropolitan areas including Denver, Salt Lake City, Oklahoma City, Albuquerque, and Kansas City, Kansas, so the circuit sees its share of the same kinds of antitrust, consumer, and securities class actions that are filed in other parts of the country. Tenth Circuit decisions and those of the district courts within the Tenth Circuit also tend to take on the Midwest and Western sensibilities of the region, where common sense, pragmatism, and basic fairness are often the preferred guideposts for decision making over intellectualism, idealism, and judicial activism.

2. JURISDICTIONAL ISSUES

a. CAFA Requirements

Diversity

Pursuant to the Class Action Fairness Act of 2005 (CAFA), federal diversity jurisdiction exists for class actions with 100 or more class members where more than $5 million is in controversy and "any member" of the plaintiff class is a citizen of a state different from that of "any defendant." 28 U.S.C.A. § 1332(d). In *Siloam Springs Hotel, L.L.C. v. Century Surety Co.*, the Tenth Circuit relied on the Supreme Court's *Carden* rule in holding that an unin-

[1] Thank you to the various authors for their contributions to previous editions of the Tenth Circuit chapter.

corporated association, such as an LLC, is a citizen of every state of which its owners/members are citizens rather than simply the association's state of organization or primary business operations. 781 F.3d 1233, 1237–38 (10th Cir. 2015) (citing *Carden v. Arkoma Assocs.*, 494 U.S. 185, 195–96 (1990)). In *Conagra Foods, Inc. v. Americold Logistics, LLC*, the Tenth Circuit held that a trust is a citizen of every state in which its beneficiaries are citizens. 776 F.3d 1175, 1179 (10th Cir. 2015).[2]

Local Controversy Exception

CAFA carves out an exception to diversity jurisdiction for matters that are essentially local. *See* 28 U.S.C.A. § 1332(d)(4)(A).[3] This so-called local controversy exception requires federal courts to abstain from jurisdiction where more than two-thirds of the proposed class are citizens of the state in which the action was filed and at least one defendant is a defendant "(aa) from whom significant relief is sought by members of the plaintiff class; (bb) whose alleged conduct forms a significant basis for the claims asserted by the proposed plaintiff class; and (cc) who is a citizen of the State in which the action was originally filed." 28 U.S.C. § 1332(d)(4)(A). In addition, the "principal injuries" arising from the alleged conduct must have been incurred in-state within three years of the filing of the action. *Id.*; *see also Woods v. Standard Ins. Co.*, 771 F.3d 1257, 1265 (10th Cir. 2014).

In *Woods*, the Tenth Circuit took up the second element—whether a defendant's conduct formed a "significant basis" for plaintiffs' claims. Construing that requirement "strictly," the Court held that the plaintiffs failed to plead that the local defendant's conduct formed a "significant basis" for the claims, because her only role in the alleged wrong was her failure to disclose her employer's alleged unlawful practices to state employees. 771 F.3d at 1265 ("[F]or the local controversy exception to apply there must be at least one real defendant . . . whose alleged conduct is central to the class's claims and from whom the class seeks significant relief." (alterations in original) (internal quotation marks and citation omitted)). The Tenth Circuit further clarified that where a suit involves multiple defendants, courts "must compare [each defendant's] conduct with that of the other defendant[s]" to determine the defendant's "significance as a defendant," *Lax v. APP of New Mexico ED, PLLC*, No. 22-2057, 2022 WL 2711230, at *11 (10th Cir. July 13, 2022). In *Fulgenzi v. Smith*, the district court held that the plaintiff failed to establish the "significant relief" requirement, the "significant basis" requirement, or the "no other class action" requirement of the local controversy exception. No. 1:12-cv-1261-RB-RHS, 2014 WL 11497836, at *3 (D.N.M. Nov. 13, 2014). It also noted that the local controversy exception is not jurisdictional and can, unlike subject matter jurisdiction, be waived by failing to raise it in a timely manner. *Id.* at *2.[4]

State Action Exception

CAFA also carves out an exception to federal jurisdiction for "any class action in which—(A) the primary defendants are States, State officials, or other governmental entities against whom the district court may be foreclosed from ordering relief." 28 U.S.C. § 1332(d)(5)(A).

---

[2] *See also* Baker v. PDC Energy, Inc., No. 14-cv-02537-RM-MJW, 2014 WL 7445626 (D. Colo. Dec. 30, 2014) (mailing address alone insufficient to show citizenship); Arguedas v. Seawright, No. CIV-13-00565-KG-KK, 2015 WL 11089508 (D.N.M. June 3, 2015) ("[I]t is very common for district courts to ignore citizenship of parties that are fraudulently joined for the purpose of avoiding diversity federal jurisdiction," but district court is not allowed to "consider the citizenship of a party that has been purportedly fraudulently non-joined solely to defeat diversity of jurisdiction").

[3] The local controversy exception does not apply to "class actions that are based on federal question jurisdiction." Ogden Reg'l Airport Ass'n Inc. v. Ogden City Airport & Ogden City, No. 121CV00075DBBDBP, 2022 WL 103792, at *4 (D. Utah Jan. 11, 2022) (noting that the local controversy exception is "part of CAFA" and is "codified at 28 U.S.C. § 1332(d)(4)," indicating that Congress's intent was to "limit only the jurisdiction district courts otherwise possess under th[e] statute").

[4] *See also* Dutcher v. Matheson, 840 F.3d 1183 (10th Cir. 2016) (failure to establish any of the exceptions to CAFA jurisdiction).

Analyzing the plain language of the statute, the Court in *Woods* concluded that the state action exception requires "all primary defendants to be state entities." 771 F.3d at 1263). The Tenth Circuit reasoned that "use of the definite article, 'the,' before the plural noun, 'primary defendants,'' and the use of the plural verb, 'are,' left no doubt Congress intended the state action provision to preclude CAFA jurisdiction only when all of the primary defendants are states, state officials, or state entities." *Id.*; *see also Dutcher v. Matheson*, 840 F.3d 1183, 1194 (10th Cir. 2016) (quoting *Woods*, 771 F.3d at 1263)). Accordingly, where a state entity is merely one defendant in an action that contains a private co-defendant, the state action exception will not apply.

Home-State Exception

The related "home-state exception," 28 U.S.C.A. §§ 1332(d)(4)(B), requires federal courts to abstain from jurisdiction when two-thirds or more of the members of all proposed plaintiff classes in the aggregate, as well as the "primary defendants," are citizens of the state in which the action was originally filed. In *Reece v. AES Corp.*, the district court held that the plaintiff failed to meet its burden of demonstrating that more than two-thirds of its proposed class members were citizens of the state from whose courts the case was removed. No. CIV-12-0457-JH, 2013 WL 1342379, at *4 (Apr. 2, 2013), *aff'd*, 638 F. App'x 755 (10th Cir. 2016) (unpublished). The plaintiffs had propounded demonstrative exhibits to prove the requisite diversity, including a pie chart purporting to reflect the percentage of "Oklahoma Class Populace" (8 percent) versus the "Non–Oklahoma Class Populace" (92 percent), but the district court declined to take judicial notice of those exhibits. *Id.* Further, the court noted that the proper analysis centers on the citizenship of class members rather than their residence or where they own property. *Id.*; *see also Coffey v. Freeport McMoran Copper & Gold,* 581 F.3d 1240, 1243 (10th Cir. 2009). The plaintiffs were not all citizens but rather a mix of citizens, residents, and property owners, which presented "too many variables" to assume that the pertinent citizenship threshold had been met. *Reece*, 2013 WL 1342379, at *5.[5]

Similarly, in *Nichols v. Chesapeake Operating, LLC*, the Tenth Circuit upheld a district court order finding a proffered putative class member sample and extrapolated statistical analysis insufficient to prove the home-state exception applied. 718 F. App'x 736, 742 (10th Cir. 2018) (unpublished), *cert. denied*, 139 S. Ct. 788 (2019). There, plaintiff, a gas well royalty owner, brought a putative class action suit in state court against Chesapeake, which owned and operated plaintiff's gas wells. *Id.* at 738. After Chesapeake removed the case to federal court based on the CAFA, plaintiff "filed a motion arguing that CAFA's home-state exception required the district court to remand the case to state court." *Id.* (referencing 28 U.S.C. § 1332(d)(4)(B)). In support of this motion, plaintiff proffered proof that he had retained a marketing research firm and private investigator to survey a random sample of 100 out of 28,929 putative class members (13 trusts, 7 entities, and 80 individuals) regarding their citizenship information, which a retained statistician then analyzed to extrapolate a finding that more than 67 percent of the putative class members were Oklahoma citizens. *Id.* at 738–39. Though this offer of proof was unrebutted, the district court "was not persuaded, finding three significant flaws in the evidence": (1) the survey data did not properly account for the components of the trusts' citizenship; (2) the sample included deceased persons whose heirs' citizenship was not considered; and (3) there was an "insufficient basis" underlying certain citizenship determinations made with respect to the sample. *Id.* at 739. For these reasons, the district court denied plaintiff's motion to remand and plaintiff appealed. *Id.*

[5] *See also* Jeter v. Wild West Gas, LLC, No. 12-cv-411-TCK-PJC, 2014 WL 3890308 (N.D. Okla. Aug. 7, 2014) (defendants failed to present a reasonable estimate of the percentage of putative class members that were Oklahoma citizens, rendering the home-state exception inapplicable).

On appeal, plaintiff argued that a rebuttal presumption of citizenship arose from his allegation that the home-state exception applied. *Id.* at 739–41. The court rejected this argument, reasoning that "[t]here is a 'strong preference that interstate class actions should be heard in a federal court if properly removed by any defendant.'"[6] *Id.* at 741 (citing *Dutcher*, 840 F.3d at 1189, 1190). The Tenth Circuit then went on to review the district court's ruling for clear error,[7] ultimately affirming the lower court's holding based on its finding that plaintiff's offer of proof was "extrapolate[ed] from a flawed sample" that was not "statistically viable." *Id.* at 742.

The Discretionary Exception

Another exception to CAFA jurisdiction is set out in 28 U.S.C. § 1332(d), which "permits a district court to decline to exercise jurisdiction over a class action meeting certain citizenship prerequisites 'in the interests of justice and looking at the totality of the circumstances,' based on its consideration of six enumerated factors." *Speed v. JMA Energy Co.*, 872 F.3d 1122, 1125–26 (10th Cir. 2017) (citing § 1332(d)(3)); *see also Dutcher*, 840 F.3d at 1194 ("This exception allows a federal court to decline to exercise jurisdiction over a class action that is otherwise covered by CAFA based on six enumerated factors."). To even raise this exception, plaintiffs must make a threshold showing that "greater than one-third but less than two-thirds of the members of all proposed plaintiff classes in the aggregate and [] the primary defendants are citizens of the State in which the action was originally filed." *Dutcher*, 840 F.3d at 1194 (cleaned up). Once this initial showing is made, a district must conduct the following six-factor analysis to determine whether the discretionary exception applies:

(A) whether the claims asserted involve matters of national or interstate interest;
(B) whether the claims asserted will be governed by laws of the State in which the action was originally filed or by the laws of other States;
(C) whether the class action has been pleaded in a manner that seeks to avoid Federal jurisdiction;
(D) whether the action was brought in a forum with a distinct nexus with the class members, the alleged harm, or the defendants;
(E) whether the number of citizens of the State in which the action was originally filed in all proposed plaintiff classes in the aggregate is substantially larger than the number of citizens from any other State, and the citizenship of the other members of the proposed class is dispersed among a substantial number of States; and
(F) whether, during the three-year period preceding the filing of that class action, 1 or more other class actions asserting the same or similar claims on behalf of the same or other persons have been filed.

Speed, 872 F.3d at 1127–28 (citing 28 U.S.C. § 1332(d)(3)). "No single factor is dispositive; not all need to favor remand for the court to decline jurisdiction." *Id.* at 1128 (citing William B. Rubenstein, *Newberg on Class Actions* § 6:21 (5th ed. 2017)) ("The plaintiff need not satisfy all [six] factors; courts employ a balancing test, taking into consideration the totality of the circumstances." (alteration in original)). Thus, when evaluating whether this exception should apply, district courts are "charged with evaluating the factors in the aggregate." *Id.* In line with this holistic approach, the Tenth Circuit has disaffirmed arguments in favor of a presumption of jurisdiction, holding that while a movant will have the burden to justify remand, there is "no statutory command, nor any sound reason" for a court to "press an additional thumb on the scale" by weighing a "neutral" factor against remand. *Id.* at 1128–29.

---

[6] However CAFA's removal provision, 28 U.S.C. § 1453(b), does not allow a third-party counterclaim defendant to remove the counterclaim against it. Home Depot U.S.A., Inc. v. Jackson, 139 S. Ct. 1743, 1745–46 (2019).

[7] *Nichols*, 718 F. App'x at 741 ("We review for clear error the district court's factual findings concerning the applicability of CAFA's home-state exception.") (citing Middleton v. Stephenson, 749 F.3d 1197, 1201 (10th Cir. 2014); Mondragon v. Capital One Auto Fin., 736 F.3d 880, 886 (9th Cir. 2013)).

Amount in Controversy
CAFA also requires, as a condition for removal or original jurisdiction, that the matter in controversy "exceed[] the sum or value of $5,000,000." 28 U.S.C.A. § 1332(d)(2). Although it is well established that a defendant seeking removal bears some burden to show that it has met the requisite amount in controversy, federal circuits disagree as to the contours of that burden when the plaintiff requests undefined damages or seeks to duck federal jurisdiction by pleading an amount in controversy below the statutory minimum.

The Tenth Circuit has adopted the view that a defendant seeking removal bears the burden of proving by a preponderance of the evidence that the amount in controversy exceeds $5 million, regardless of the amount a plaintiff pleads in the complaint. "When [a] defendant removes an action to federal court under [CAFA], the amount-in-controversy allegation should be accepted when not contested by the plaintiff or questioned by the court." *Phelps Oil & Gas, LLC v. Noble Energy Inc.*, No. 23-1243, 2023 WL 6121016, at *2 (10th Cir. Sept. 19, 2023) (internal quotation marks and citation omitted). On the other hand, "[i]f the defendant's allegation is challenged [] then both sides [must] submit proof and the court decides, by a preponderance of the evidence, whether the amount-in-controversy requirement has been satisfied." *Id.* (internal quotation marks and citation omitted).

In *Frederick v. Hartford Underwriters Insurance Co.*, the court held that defendants seeking removal must prove all jurisdictional facts—including the amount in controversy—by a preponderance of the evidence, which they may show through discovery conducted in the state court, in affidavits, or by reference to the plaintiff's own estimates. 683 F.3d 1242, 1247 (10th Cir. 2012) (citing *McPhail v. Deere & Co.*, 529 F.3d 947, 954 (10th Cir. 2008); *Gibson v. Jeffers*, 478 F.2d 216, 220 (10th Cir. 1973)). Once a defendant meets this burden, remand is appropriate only if the plaintiff can establish that it is "*legally impossible* to recover more than $5,000,000." *Id.* (emphasis added).[8]

In *Hammond v. Stamps.com, Inc.*, the Tenth Circuit appeared to soften the defendant's burden, noting that the jurisdictional question "isn't what damages the plaintiff will *likely* prove but what a factfinder *might* conceivably lawfully award." 844 F.3d 909, 912 (10th Cir. 2016). Thus, the defendants were entitled to CAFA jurisdiction because it was conceivable, albeit perhaps highly improbable, that all 312,000 class members would be entitled to between $31.98 and $300, equating to a possible recovery range of $10–$93 million. *Id.*

---

[8] *See also* Valdez v. Metro. Prop. & Cas. Ins. Co., 867 F. Supp. 2d 1143 (D.N.M. 2012) (holding that a party seeking removal under CAFA need only establish the amount in controversy by a preponderance of the evidence regardless of whether the complaint alleges an amount below the jurisdictional minimum); Parrish v. Range Res. Corp., No. CIV-14-01283-M, 2015 WL 1516424 (W.D. Okla. Apr. 1, 2015) ("[R]emoval is proper because defendants have shown by a preponderance of the evidence that the amount in controversy may exceed 5 million dollars."); Heather v. Air Methods Corp., No. CIV-16-143-R, 2016 WL 7109675 (W.D. Okla. Dec. 6, 2016) (motion to remand denied where plaintiffs alleged defendants failed to show with any particularity that the amount in controversy had been met; particularity requirement is not the law).

b. Personal Jurisdiction

When determining whether a court may exercise specific personal jurisdiction over a defendant, the court is tasked with analyzing the "relationship among the defendant, the forum, and the litigation." *Daimler AG v. Bauman*, 571 U.S. 117, 132–33 (2014). "That relationship does not depend on the makeup of the unnamed class members." *Farmer v. Walmart, Inc.*, No. 2:23-CV-00397-MIS-KRS, 2024 WL 1539789 at *11 (D.N.M. Apr. 9, 2024) (citing *Lyngaas v. Curden Ag*, 992 F.3d 412, 437 (6th Cir. 2021)). "[T]he named representatives must be able to demonstrate either general or specific personal jurisdiction, but the unnamed class members are not required to do so." *Id.* (citing *Mussat v. IQVIA, Inc.*, 953 F.3d 441, 447 (7th Cir. 2020)).

c. Subject Matter Jurisdiction Issues

In cases where plaintiffs bring purely state law claims, they can establish federal jurisdiction under 28 U.S.C. § 1331 if they survive the "creation" test for federal question jurisdiction and "if a federal issue is: (1) necessarily raised, (2) actually disputed, (3) substantial, and (4) capable of resolution in federal court without disrupting the federal-state balance approved by Congress." *Gunn v. Minton*, 568 U.S. 251, 258 (2013). The Tenth Circuit elaborated on this "so-called 'substantial question' branch of federal question jurisdiction," first noting "the long-settled understanding that the mere presence of a federal issue in a state cause of action does not automatically confer federal-question jurisdiction." *Becker v. Ute Indian Tribe of the Uintah & Ouray Reservation*, 770 F.3d 944, 947–48 (10th Cir. 2014) (internal quotations and citation omitted). Second, federal question jurisdiction cannot depend solely on a federal defense, even if the defense is anticipated in the plaintiff's complaint and both parties concede that the federal defense is the only question truly at issue. *Id.* Third, if a claim is not a nearly pure issue of law that could be settled once and for all and would govern numerous cases but is "fact-bound and situation-specific," then federal question jurisdiction will generally be inappropriate. *Id.* (internal quotation marks and citation omitted).

The District of Kansas applied this reasoning in deciding to remand two cases in multidistrict court to state court where the plaintiffs attempted to present a state claim as a question of federal law under the federal common law of foreign relations. *In re Syngenta AG MIR 162 Corn Litig.*, No. 14-md-2591-JWL, 2015 WL 2092435 (D. Kan. May 15, 2015). Similarly, in *Flandro v. Chevron Pipe Line Co.*, the District of Utah remanded a case to state court reasoning that a complaint "contain[ing] factual conclusions made by federal agencies as well as references to federal laws . . . for the purpose of bolstering plaintiffs' state tort causes of action" do not create a "substantial question" of federal law. No. 2:18-cv-697, 2019 WL 1574811, at *5 (D. Utah Apr. 11, 2019).

d. Standing

The Tenth Circuit has held that in class actions, Article III standing is satisfied if at least one named plaintiff meets the standing requirements. *DG ex rel. Stricklin v. Devaughn*, 594 F.3d 1188, 1197 (10th Cir. 2010) ("[O]nly named plaintiffs in a class action seeking prospective injunctive relief must demonstrate standing by establishing they are suffering a continuing injury or are under an imminent threat of being injured in the future." (internal citations omitted)); *Tandy v. City of Wichita*, 380 F.3d 1277, 1283 (10th Cir. 2004) ("To seek prospective relief, the plaintiff must be suffering a continuing injury or be under a real and immediate threat of being injured in the future." (citation omitted)); *Valdez v. Grisham*, No. 22-2112, 2024 WL 2319752, at *2 (10th Cir. May 22, 2024) ("[W]hen analyzing our jurisdiction over a class action suit like this, we do not speculate about the injuries of unnamed class members. We instead focus on named class representatives.").[9] And while Congress

[9] *See also* Morris v. Davita Healthcare Partners, Inc., 308 F.R.D. 360 (D. Colo. 2015) (plaintiffs in putative class action failed to establish standing where they alleged injury based on a dialysis clinic's concealment of information concerning

may create "a statutory right or entitlement the alleged deprivation of which can confer standing to sue even where the plaintiff would have suffered no judicially cognizable injury in the absence of statute," this statutorily created "entitlement doesn't scuttle the need for an injury-in-fact" for every alleged violation of a statute. *Kellogg v. Watts Guerra LLP*, 41 F.4th 1246, 1263 (10th Cir. 2022) (concluding that RICO and the declaratory judgment statutes do not "automatically confer an injury-in-fact") (citing *TransUnion v. Ramirez*, 141 S. Ct. 2190, 2200 (2021)); *see also Laufer v. Looper*, 22 F.4th 871, 878 (10th Cir. 2022) ("Article III standing requires a concrete injury even in the context of a statutory violation." (quoting *Spokeo, Inc. v. Robins*, 578 U.S. 330, 341 (2016)).

A necessary corollary construct of this doctrine, where an individual brings claims that are identical to those in a pending class action, the individual claims can be subsumed within the class complaint, thereby depriving the individual plaintiff of standing to bring the individual claim(s). Illustrating this principle, in *Sanchez v. Brennan*, the plaintiff filed a charge with the EEOC against his employer, the U.S. Postal Service, alleging "racial, retaliatory, and disability discrimination claims." 679 F. App'x 671, 672 (10th Cir. 2017) (unpublished). In accordance with EEOC directives, an administrative judge "entered an order subsuming [the] disability discrimination claim into a pending class action, the Pittman Class Action, which also challenged the Postal Service's overtime practices as to disabled employees." *Id.* Seven years later, the administrative judge and EEOC approved settlement of the Pittman Class Action and class counsel sent the plaintiff a notice of resolution articulating his right to object. *Id.*

Instead of objecting to the settlement however, the plaintiff proceeded to file an unsuccessful administrative appeal with the EEOC and then took his claim to federal district court, reasserting all claims in his EEOC charge. *Id.* at 673–74. Both the district court and the Tenth Circuit upheld the administrative court's decision precluding the individual claim, finding, in relevant part, that the plaintiff had "failed to exhaust his administrative remedies as to any individual claim because he failed to appeal the [] administrative decision to subsume his claim into the Pittman Class Action, and [] didn't participate in the Pittman Class Action settlement." *Id.* at 673. Therefore, there was no subject matter jurisdiction that would allow the courts to exert federal jurisdiction over the claim. *Id.*

e. Mootness

A named plaintiff must not only have standing at the time of filing but also must maintain standing throughout the entire case; if a plaintiff's claim becomes moot at any stage, the court loses subject matter jurisdiction. *See Brown v. Buhman,* 822 F.3d 1151, 1165 (10th Cir. 2016) ("If an intervening circumstance deprives the plaintiff of a personal stake in the outcome of the lawsuit, at any point during litigation, the action can no longer proceed and must be dismissed as moot." (quoting *Campbell-Ewald Co. v. Gomez*, 577 U.S. 153, 160–61 (2016)), *as revised* (Feb. 9, 2016)). In *Campbell-Ewald Co*, the Supreme Court held that a defendant cannot moot a plaintiff's individual claim—or that of the entire class—by making a formal offer of judgment under Federal Rule of Civil Procedure 68 if the plaintiff does not in fact accept the offer. 577 U.S. at 162. This decision accords with earlier cases in the Tenth Circuit holding that class plaintiffs can proceed to certification even when a defendant attempts to moot the plaintiff's claim through a formal offer of judgment (that is rejected by

---

the type of drug used during treatment; plaintiffs now possessed that information and were therefore under no threat of injury); Hapka v. Carecentrix, Inc., No. 16-2372-CM, 2016 WL 7336407 (D. Kan. Dec. 19, 2016) (plaintiff established standing in a data breach case through allegations that the breach put her at increased risk of future identity theft and the fact that someone had already committed tax fraud using her personal information); Farmer v. Walmart, Inc., No. 2:23-CV-00397-MIS-KRS, 2024 WL 1539789, at *6–8 (D.N.M. Apr. 9, 2024) (plaintiff in a putative class action failed to establish standing over claims concerning products that he did not purchase but instead were purchased by putative class members, despite their similarity to products he did purchase).

the plaintiff). For example, in *Lucero v. Bureau of Collection Recovery, Inc.*, the court noted that, upon the filing of a class complaint, a nascent interest attaches to the proposed class so that a rejected offer of judgment for statutory damages and costs made to a named plaintiff does not render the case moot under Article III. 639 F.3d 1239 (10th Cir. 2011).[10]

The Tenth Circuit also has recognized that the mootness doctrine should be applied "less strictly" in class actions and has permitted plaintiffs, under certain circumstances, to maintain standing even where they lack the requisite injury-in-fact. *See Clark v. State Farm Mut. Auto. Ins. Co.*, 590 F.3d 1134, 1138 (10th Cir. 2009) (citing *U.S. Parole Comm'n v. Geraghty*, 445 U.S. 388, 400 (1980)). One such exception is for claims that are "capable of repetition, yet evading review"—for example, where the challenged action will have ceased by the time the claims are adjudicated but there is a reasonable expectation that another party will suffer the same harm in the future. *Id.*; *Milonas v. Williams*, 691 F.2d 931, 937–38 (10th Cir. 1982). A similar exception exists in injunctive relief cases where a defendant "voluntary ceases" the challenged conduct; although injury-in-fact would no longer be present, courts have nonetheless permitted class actions to proceed in order to prevent the defendant from simply resuming the conduct as soon as the litigation is dismissed. *See id.* For example, in *In re HomeAdvisor, Inc. Litigation.*, the court held that although HomeAdvisor ceased the challenged conduct by removing the online profiles of the named plaintiffs from its platform, the voluntary cessation exception applied because HomeAdvisor continued to maintain that its terms and conditions were an enforceable contract giving it a license to use plaintiffs' content. 345 F.R.D. 208, 219–20 (D. Colo. 2024).

3. PLEADING CONSIDERATIONS

"Although not mentioned specifically in Rule 23 itself, a prerequisite to class certification is an appropriate class definition." *Small v. BOKF, N.A.*, No. 13-cv-01125-REB-MJW, 2014 WL 3893052, at *2 (D. Colo. 2014) (quoting *Maez v. Springs Auto. Grp., LLC*, 268 F.R.D. 391, 394 (D. Colo. 2010)); *see also Rhodes v. Nat'l Collection Sys., Inc.*, 317 F.R.D. 579, 582 (D. Colo. 2016). A class definition is considered "critically important" because it serves as the foundation of the class—identifying the persons who are entitled notice and relief, and who will be bound by the final judgment. *In re Motor Fuel Temperature Sales Practices Litig.*, 279 F.R.D. 598, 604 (D. Kan. 2012). "The definition must be precise, objective and presently ascertainable." *Id.*; *see, e.g., Davoll v. Webb*, 194 F.3d 1116, 1146 (10th Cir. 1999) ("[T]he district court has broad discretion to determine whether the class description is sufficiently definite.") (quoting *Moore's Federal Practice* § 23.21[5] at 23–61 (3d ed. 1999)); *Cook v. Rockwell Int'l Corp.*, 151 F.R.D. 378, 382 (D. Colo. 1993) (class definition must be "sufficiently definite so that it is administratively feasible for the court to determine whether a particular individual is a member").

Courts within the Tenth Circuit have required that a class definition not be "self-defeating"—meaning that a court must not be required to examine the merits of the underlying claims to determine who is in the class. *See Morris v. Travelers Indem. Co. of Am.*, No. 05-cv-00727-EWN-BNB, 2006 WL 166597, at *7–8 (D. Colo. Jan. 19, 2006) ("Where such a decision on the merits of a person's claim is needed to determine whether a person is a member of a class, the proposed class action is unmanageable virtually by definition."). Importantly, "the court is not bound by the class definition proposed in the complaint and, thus, may refine the suggested definition if necessary." *Maez v. Springs Auto. Grp., LLC*, 268 F.R.D. 391, 394–95 (D. Colo. 2010) (internal quotation marks and citations omitted); *see also Klassen v. Solid Quote LLC*, 702 F. Supp. 3d 1052, 1059 (D. Colo. 2023) (exercising dis-

[10] *See also* Clark v. State Farm Mut. Auto. Ins. Co., 590 F.3d 1134, 1138 (10th Cir. 2009) (if the named plaintiff's claim becomes moot during the pendency of an appeal challenging the district court's denial of class certification, the appellate court is not divested of jurisdiction) (citing *Geraghty*, 445 U.S. at 404 & n.11)).

cretion to "slightly amend the proposed definition" to cure overbreadth rather than strike the offending pleading and require amendment). Courts within the Tenth Circuit have held that it is appropriate to err on the side of class certification because they have broad discretion to later redefine (or even decertify) the class if necessary. *See Esplin v. Hirschi*, 402 F.2d 94, 99 (10th Cir. 1968); *Heartland Commc'ns, Inc. v. Sprint Corporation*, 161 F.R.D. 111, 115 (D. Kan. 1995) (court can tailor class as necessary by eliminating class members, requiring additional class representatives or modifying class definition).

4. CERTIFICATION OF A QUESTION TO A STATE SUPREME COURT

While federal courts in the Tenth Circuit will not certify a question for ruling by a state supreme court "every time an arguably unsettled question of state law" is presented, when a question arises that "(1) may be determinative of the case at hand and (2) is sufficiently novel that [federal courts] feel uncomfortable attempting to decide it without further guidance," courts will employ their ability to certify a question to a state supreme court. *See, e.g.*, *Pino v. United States*, 507 F.3d 1233, 1236 (10th Cir. 2007) (Judge Neil M. Gorsuch deciding). "Certification is never compelled, even when there is no state law governing an issue." *Boyd Rosene & Assocs., Inc. v. Kansas Mun. Gas Agency*, 178 F.3d 1363, 1365 (10th Cir. 1999). However, "[a] court must consider whether certification will conserve the time, energy, and resources of the parties as well as of the court itself." *Id.*

District courts may—and often do—certify questions of law to state supreme courts even after removal. *See, e.g.*, *Rooftop Restorations, Inc. v. Am. Family Mut. Ins. Co.*, No. 15-cv-2560, 2017 WL 514060, at *4 (D. Colo. Feb. 8, 2017). While litigants should be aware that at least one court within the Tenth Circuit has articulated that "parties seeking a binding state court decision should file their lawsuits in state court, even if they know that the Defendant might remove," even in that case, the court certified a question to the Colorado Supreme Court because the question at issue could only be resolved by what the federal court considered to be "judicial legislation—a task ill-suited to a federal court sitting in diversity." *Nguyen v. Am. Fam. Mut. Ins. Co.*, No. 15-cv-0639-WJM-KLM, 2015 WL 5867266, at *3–5 (D. Colo. 2015) ("Plaintiffs' choice to file in this Court and seek certification . . . smacks of pure gamesmanship, somewhat like a defendant who removes to federal court and then asks that Court to abstain from exercising jurisdiction.").

Alternatively, Tenth Circuit courts will "exercise 'judgment and restraint' before certifying questions . . . when a 'reasonably clear and principled course' presents itself." *Roberts v. C.R. England, Inc.*,
321 F. Supp. 3d 1251, 1260 (D. Utah 2018), *motion to certify appeal denied*, No. 2:12-cv-00302-RJS-BCW, 2018 WL 2386056 (D. Utah Apr. 24, 2018). In particular, where there is "sufficient guidance and authority" enabling a district court to thoroughly analyze a novel, unsettled issue of state law under "controlling federal authority," motions to certify are likely to be denied. *Id.* Litigants should also be advised that where a party "requests certification *after* a ruling . . . the time and resources already expended resolving the matter [will] counsel against certification." *Id.* at 1261.

5. PREREQUISITES FOR CLASS CERTIFICATION

a. Burden of Proof

Federal Rule of Civil Procedure 23 "sets forth the requirements for maintaining a class action." *Black v. Occidental Petroleum Corp.*, 69 F. 4th 1161, 1173 (10th Cir. 2023). "As the proponents of class certification, plaintiffs have the burden to demonstrate 'under a strict burden of proof' that the requirements of Rule 23 are clearly satisfied." *Small*, 2014 WL

3893052, at *1 (citing *Trevizo v. Adams*, 455 F.3d 1155, 1162 (10th Cir. 2006)); *Anderson Living Trust v. WPX Energy Prod., LLC*, 306 F.R.D. 312, 378 (D.N.M. 2014) ("Rule 23 does not set forth a mere pleading standard. A party seeking class certification must affirmatively demonstrate his compliance with the Rule—that is, he must be prepared to prove that there are in fact sufficiently numerous parties, common questions of law or fact, etc."). If a party is able to meet the requirements of Rule 23(a), then the court will look to the category of class action as defined under Rule 23(b) to determine whether "additional prerequisites involving certification of a class" are met. *Versteeg v. Bennett, Deloney & Noyes, P.C.*, 271 F.R.D. 668, 671 (D. Wyo. 2011) (citing *Shook v. El Paso Cty.*, 386 F.3d 963, 968 (10th Cir. 2004)). When ruling on a class certification motion, courts are not required to accept the representations of either party as true; instead, the court must "independently find the relevant facts to a preponderance of the evidence." *Zuniga v. Bernalillo Cty.*, No. CV 11-0877 JB-LAM, 2016 WL 7210148, at *16 (D.N.M. Oct. 25, 2016). Tenth Circuit courts apply Rule 23's standards liberally with "doubtful cases" being resolved in favor of class certification. *See id.* (citing *Esplin*, 402 F.2d at 101). In fact, "the party seeking class certification must prove the requirements 'are *in fact*' satisfied," which requires that "the district court [] conduct a rigorous analysis, often necessarily 'prob[ing] behind the pleadings[,]' to assure itself the requirements for certification are satisfied." *Black*, 69 F.4th at 1174 (internal citations omitted) (alterations in original); *see also Brayman v. KeyPoint Gov't Sols., Inc.*, 83 F.4th 823, 837 (10th Cir. 2023) ("is essential that courts keep in mind that 'Rule 23 does not set forth a mere pleading standard. A party seeking class certification must affirmatively demonstrate his compliance with the Rule—that is, he must be prepared to prove that there are *in fact* sufficiently numerous parties, common questions of law or fact, etc.'" *Wal-Mart Stores*, 564 U.S. at 350, 131 S. Ct. 2541. Under this standard, "the district court has an independent obligation to conduct a 'rigorous analysis' before concluding that Rule 23's requirements have been satisfied.").

b. Choice of Law

"[T]he Court must conduct a choice-of-law analysis at the class certification stage." *In re HomeAdvisor, Inc. Litig.*, 345 F.R.D. at 227. "In a multi-state class action, variations in state law may swamp any common issues and defeat predominance." *Id.* (citing *Goode v. Nuance Commc'ns, Inc.*, 2020 WL 4606848, at *4 (N.D. Okla. May 7, 2020)). It is, therefore, incumbent upon a district court to consider how variations in state law affect predominance and superiority. *Simon v. Metro. Prop. & Cas. Ins. Co.*, No. CIV-08-1008-W, 2012 WL 12931425, at *4 (W.D. Okla. Jan. 12, 2012).

c. Rule 23(a) Requirements[11]

Numerosity

Rule 23(a)(1) requires plaintiffs to show that "the class is so numerous that joinder of all members is impracticable." "To meet this burden, [p]laintiff[s] must produce some evidence or otherwise establish by some reasonable estimate the number of class members who may be involved." *Evans v. Brigham Young Univ.*, No. 1:20-CV-100-TS, 2022 WL 596862, at *3 (D. Utah Feb. 28, 2022) (quoting *Rex v. Owens ex rel. State of Okl.*, 585 F.2d 432, 436 (10th Cir. 1978) (internal quotation marks omitted)). This requires the plaintiff to "present[] some

[11] With respect to putative class or collective actions arising from the Fair Labor Standards Act (FLSA) in the Tenth Circuit, practitioners may need to look beyond the requirements of Rule 23 to determine if a class can be certified. Under the FLSA, the named plaintiff(s) can sue on behalf of themselves and "other employees similarly situated." In re Chipotle Mexican Grill, Inc., No. 17-1028, 2017 WL 4054144, at *1 (10th Cir. Mar. 27, 2017) (citing 29 U.S.C. § 216(b)). In this specific context, to determine which individuals are "similarly situated," the Tenth Circuit has approved three different analyses: "the *ad hoc* approach, the Rule 23 approach, and the spurious approach." *Id.* (citation omitted) (affirming district court's use of ad hoc approach in deciding to join 10,000 opt-in plaintiffs to an underlying collective action brought pursuant to the FLSA).

evidence of established, *ascertainable* numbers constituting the class in order to satisfy even the most liberal interpretation of the numerosity requirement," but it does not require that the class "be so ascertainable that every potential member can be identified at the commencement of the action." *Id.* While other circuits have held that numerosity is presumed at a set number of putative class members, the Tenth Circuit "has never adopted such a presumption." *WPX Energy Prod., LLC*, 306 F.R.D. at 379–80; *Trevizo*, 455 F.3d at 1162. Instead, the Tenth Circuit grants district courts "wide latitude" in making this determination. *Trevizo*, 455 F.3d at 1162 (citing *Johnson by Johnson v. Thompson*, 971 F.2d 1487, 1498 (10th Cir. 1992)); *Jill Adler v. All Hours Plumbing Drain Cleaning 24-7-365, LLC*, No. 2:21-CV-00141, 2022 WL 15513196, at 5 (D. Utah Oct. 27, 2022) ("Because numerosity is a 'fact-specific inquiry,' the court has 'wide latitude' to determine if it is met."). The "nature of the particular case and the nature of the proposed class are key considerations in determining whether joinder of all parties is impractical." *Small*, 2014 WL 3893052, at *2; *WPX Energy Prod., LLC*, 306 F.R.D. at 380 (D.N.M. 2014) (numerosity is a fact-specific inquiry); *Wornicki v. Brokerpriceopinion.com, Inc.*, No. 13-cv-03258-PAB-KMT, 2015 WL 1403814, at *5 (D. Colo. 2015) (same). "Satisfaction of the numerosity requirement does not require that joinder is impossible, but only that plaintiff will suffer a strong litigational hardship or inconvenience if joinder is required." *Lane v. Page*, 272 F.R.D. 558, 569 (D.N.M. 2011) (internal quotation marks and citations omitted); *see also Bustillos v. Bd. of Cnty. Comm'rs of Hidalgo Cty.*, 310 F.R.D. 631, 649–50 (D.N.M. 2015) (quoting *Cook*, 151 F.R.D. at 384).

Commonality and Typicality

Plaintiffs also must prove that "there are questions of law or fact common to the class." Fed. R. Civ. P. 23(a)(2). "Complete identity of legal claims among class members is not required." *Small*, 2014 WL 3893052, at *2. Instead, the commonality requirement demands that Plaintiffs demonstrate that the class has suffered the same injury for the same reason. *See Soseeah v. Sentry Ins.*, 808 F.3d 800, 808–09 (10th Cir. 2015) (citing *Wal-Mart Stores, Inc. v. Dukes*, 564 U.S. 338, 341 (2011)); *Wornicki*, 2015 WL 1403814, at *6 (commonality requires that "a discrete legal or factual question common to the class must exist"). "In other words, the focus of Rule 23(a)(2)'s commonality requirement is not so much on whether there exist common *questions*, but rather on the capacity of a classwide proceeding to generate common *answers* apt to drive the resolution of the litigation." *Brayman v. KeyPoint Gov't Sols., Inc.*, 83 F.4th 823, 837 (10th Cir. 2023) (internal quotation marks and citation omitted); *see also Naylor Farms, Inc. v. Chaparral Energy, LLC*, 923 F.3d 779, 789 (10th Cir. 2019). A question is common when "the same evidence will suffice for each member to make a prima facie showing . . . or when the issue is susceptible to generalized, class-wide proof." *WPX Energy Prod., LLC*, 306 F.R.D. at 386–87 (internal quotations marks and citations omitted).[12] While a single common question will suffice to satisfy Rule 23(a)(2), the question must be one "that is central to the validity of each one of the claims" and capable of "generat[ing] common *answers* apt to drive the resolution of the litigation." *WPX Energy Prod., LLC*, 306 F.R.D. at 380–81; *Wal-Mart*, 564 U.S. at 351; *Naylor Farms, Inc. v. Chaparral Energy, LLC*, 923 F.3d 779, 789 (10th Cir. 2019). The Tenth Circuit further clarified the correct standard courts must apply when considering commonality in *Gordon v. Jordan School District*, No. 21-4044, 2023 WL 34105, at *3 (10th Cir. Jan. 4, 2023). In *Gordon*, the Tenth Circuit held that commonality requires the "presence of only a single legal or factual issue in common among members of the class." *Id.* at *2, *5. The court emphasized that all that is necessary to establish commonality is a single "legal or factual issue in common among" class mem-

[12] In securities fraud litigation, commonality requirements have been applied "permissively" because these types of cases generally involve "allegations of common courses of fraudulent conduct" that are usually sufficient to meet commonality requirements. *WPX Energy Prod., LLC*, 306 F.R.D. at 380.

bers; the presence of other inquiries that may vary from class member to class member does not defeat commonality. *Id.*; *see also Colo. Cross Disability Coal. v. Abercrombie & Fitch Co.*, 765 F.3d 1205, 1216 (10th Cir. 2014) (noting commonality does "not require that every member of the class share a fact situation *identical* to that of the named plaintiff"). However, it is important to note that plaintiffs may not merely show that "common questions apply to the class," plaintiffs are still required to "show the capacity of a class-wide proceeding to generate common *answers* apt to drive the resolution of the litigation." *Sherman v. Trinity Teen Sols., Inc.*, 84 F.4th 1182, 1192 (10th Cir. 2023) (internal quotation mark and citation omitted).

Similarly, Rule 23(a)(3) requires that "the claims or defenses of the representative parties [be] typical of the claims or defenses of the class." Fed. R. Civ. P. 23(a)(3). The typicality element requires that "the claims of the class representative and class members are based on the same legal or remedial theory." *Sherman*, 84 F.4th at 1193 (internal quotation marks and citation omitted). The purpose of the typicality requirement is to ensure that class members are "adequately represented" by thoroughly evaluating and determining whether "the named plaintiff's interests are sufficiently aligned with the class' interests." *Bustillos*, 310 F.R.D. at 651–52. A proposed class representative is not typical if the representative is subject to a unique defense that is likely to become a "major focus of the litigation," or if "most proposed class members would have to show a different injury than [the class representative.]" *N. Brevard Cnty. Hosp. Dist. v. C.R. Bard, Inc.*, 710 F. Supp. 3d 1090, 1104 (D. Utah 2023) (citing *Wesley v. Snap Fin. LLC*, 339 F.R.D. 277, 293 (D. Utah 2021)); *see also Melnick v. TAMKO Bldg. Prod. LLC*, 347 F.R.D. 79, 94 (D. Kan. 2024) (finding no typicality where a "unique defense would [] be a focus in the litigation and could possibly foreclose [class representative's] claim and affect absent class members."). "The typicality requirement is satisfied if there are common questions of law or fact." *Small*, 2014 WL 3893052, at *2 (citing *Milonas v. Williams*, 691 F.2d 931, 938 (10th Cir. 1982); *Adamson v. Bowen*, 855 F.2d 668, 676 (10th Cir. 1988)). Accordingly, the commonality and typicality requirements of Rule 23(a) tend to merge. *Id.* at *2 (citing *Gen. Tel. Co. of Sw. v. Falcon*, 457 U.S. 147, 157 n.13 (1982)).

Adequacy

Plaintiffs must show that the class "representative parties will fairly and adequately protect the interests of the class." Fed. R. Civ. P. 23(a)(4). This requirement "concerns both the competence of the class representative's counsel and the representative's willingness and ability to control the litigation and to protect the interests of the class as a whole." *Small*, 2014 WL 3893052, at *3; *WPX Energy Prod., LLC*, 306 F.R.D. at 383–84. "The Tenth Circuit has identified two questions relevant to the adequacy-of-representation inquiry: (i) whether the named plaintiffs and their counsel have any conflicts with other class members; and (ii) whether the named plaintiffs and their counsel will vigorously prosecute the action on behalf of the class." *Bustillos*, 310 F.R.D. at 652 (citing *Rutter & Wilbanks Corp. v. Shell Oil Co.*, 314 F.3d 1180, 1187–88 (10th Cir. 2002)). The first question involves an inquiry that centers on whether the class representative is in fact part of the putative class and whether he or she "possess[es] the same interest and suffer[ed] the same injury as the class members." *Id.* at 652–53 (internal quotation marks and citation omitted). A class representative has a fundamental conflict with putative class members "where some class members claim an injury resulting from conduct that benefitted other class members." *N. Brevard Cnty. Hosp. Dist.*, 710 F. Supp. 3d at 1104; *see also Melnick*, 347 F.R.D. at 94 ("To defeat class certification, a conflict must be fundamental and go to specific issues in controversy. Class certification will not be defeated by minor conflicts." (internal citations and quotations omitted)). The second inquiry is resolved by analyzing an attorney's "experience and competence." *Bustillos*, 310 F.R.D. at 652.

d. Rule 23(b) Requirements

In addition to satisfying the requirements of Rule 23(a), a putative class action also must meet the requirements of at least one subsection of Rule 23(b). Fed. R. Civ. P. 23(b); *Small*, 2014 WL 3893052, at *3.

Rule 23(b)(1)(A) and (B) Classes

Rule 23(b)(1) provides that a class can be maintained when "prosecuting separate actions" would create a risk of "(A) inconsistent or varying adjudications with respect to individual class members that would establish incompatible standards of conduct for the party opposing the class" or "(B) adjudications with respect to individual class members that, as a practical matter, would be dispositive of the interests of the other members not parties to the individual adjudications or would substantially impair or impede their ability to protect their interests." Fed. R. Civ. P. 23(b)(1)(A)–(B). The threshold inquiry in determining whether a putative class can be certified under Rule 23(b)(1) is whether separate actions would result should the action not be certified. *Nat'l Union Fire Ins. Co. of Pittsburgh, Pa. v. Midland Bancor, Inc.*, 158 F.R.D. 681, 686 (D. Kan. 1994). Classes can be certified under Rule 23(b)(1) only in "very particular circumstances." *WPX Energy Prod., LLC*, 306 F.R.D. at 384–85.

To fall within the requirements of Rule 23(b)(1)(A), the possibility of inconsistent judgments on identical questions of law must be "more than [a] mere possibility." *Midland Bancor, Inc.*, 158 F.R.D. at 687 (finding that defendant insurer's putative class did not meet the requirements of Rule 23(b)(1)(A) where defendant contended only that "if there were separate suits, it might win some and lose others," finding that "Rule 23(b)(1)(A) is not intended to address this type of risk").

> While Clause (A) of Rule 23(b)(1) deals with the risk of inconsistent or varying adjudications to the party opposing the class . . . Clause (B) addresses the risk of separate adjudications to individual members of the class . . . An example of class certification under Clause (B) is a case in which numerous parties are making claims against a fund that is insufficient to satisfy all claims, and thus satisfaction of one claim would impair the interests of other claimants.

Id. at 687.

The Tenth Circuit's most in-depth analysis of class certification under Rule 23(b)(1) was in the bankruptcy context. In *In re Integra Realty Resources, Inc.*, 354 F.3d 1246 (10th Cir. 2004), the court considered an appeal of a bankruptcy court's decision to certify a defendant class of investors under Rule 23(b)(1)(A) and (B). The defendant class members had been corporate shareholders to whom a portion of a business had been spun off prior to the business's having experienced financial difficulties, ultimately culminating in a bankruptcy filing. *Id.* at 1252–54. The Tenth Circuit held that the bankruptcy court had not abused its discretion by certifying a mandatory defendant class under Rule 23(b)(1)(B) rather than an opt out class under Rule 23(b)(3).[13] *Id.* at 1263–64. It reasoned that because the bankruptcy trustee's suit as against the first defendant or group of defendants could be dispositive of the claims against the remaining defendants, class certification under Rule 23(b)(1)(B) was necessary to ensure adequate representation of all defendants. *Id.* at 1264. The court thus distinguished the First Circuit's decision in *Tilley v. TJX Cos.*, 345 F.3d 34, 42 (1st Cir. 2003), finding that there was more than a "mere possibility" of a *stare decisis* effect since the issue of whether the spinoff was unlawful would be completely independent of the identity of any individual defendant shareholder. *Integra Realty Res., Inc.*, 254 F.3d at 1263–64. The Tenth

[13] The Tenth Circuit disagreed with the trial court's decision to also certify the defendant class under Rule 23(b)(1)(A), disagreeing that an order recovering some of the shares but not others would necessarily create mutually conflicting obligations. *See* In re Integra Realty Res., Inc., 354 F.3d 1246, 1264 (10th Cir. 2004).

Circuit held that the fact that the bankruptcy trustee sought a monetary recovery from the defendant class members did not prevent class certification under Rule 23(b)(1), notwithstanding case law suggesting that class actions seeking monetary damages are only certifiable under Rule 23(b)(3). *Id.* at 1264–65. The court reasoned that the fact the outcome of the proceeding may require the defendants to pay money did not mean the trustee's claims were claims for "money damages" of the type that would preclude certification under sections of the rule other than Rule 23(b)(3). *Id.* at 1265 (rejecting argument that pursuant to *Phillips Petroleum Co. v. Shutts*, 472 U.S. 797 (1985), certification of mandatory defendant class would violate due process).

In *Boughton v. Cotter Corp.*, 65 F.3d 823, 827 n.2 (10th Cir. 1995), the lower court had found that plaintiffs' claims for medical monitoring arising from exposure to uranium mill emissions failed to meet the standards for a limited fund under Rule 23(a)(1)(B). On appeal, the Tenth Circuit concluded that the plaintiff had waived any right to contest that conclusion, so it did not evaluate the standards applicable to a Rule 23(a)(1)(B) limited fund class. *Id.* at 827. The Tenth Circuit also found that the plaintiffs' argument that the defendant would be bound by determinations on common issues reached in a bellwether trial of the claims of selected plaintiffs constituted an implied waiver of any argument that failure to certify a class would lead to inconsistent adjudications, as required for a class under Rule 23(a)(1)(A). *See id.*

Many of the Tenth Circuit opinions addressing classes certified under Rule 23(b)(1) have involved the question of notice to class members. In *Pelt v. Utah*, the Tenth Circuit noted that though notice is required only in class actions certified under Rule 23(b)(3), "notice also will usually be provided in Rule 23(b)(1) and (b)(2) actions, at the discretion of the court." 539 F.3d 1271, 1284 (10th Cir. 2008). And in *Elliott Industries Ltd. Partnership v. BP America Production Co.*, the court recognized that an absent class member's failure to intervene prior to a final judgment in the district court was reasonable because the class had been certified in part under Rule 23(b)(1), which provided no right to opt out. 407 F.3d 1091, 1104 & n.5 (10th Cir. 2005); *see also Skinner v. Uphoff*, 175 F. App'x 255, 257–58 (10th Cir. 2006) (unpublished) (holding that a district court did not abuse its discretion in deciding not to give notice in a class action certified under Rule 23(b)(2) and addressing the advisory committee notes regarding factors to be considered in giving notice to a class certified under Rule 23(b)(1) or (b)(2)). In *Southern Ute Indian Tribe v. Amoco Production Co.*, a case against a defendant class certified under Rule 23(b)(1) and (b)(2), the court reversed a trial court's order requiring the plaintiff to pay 25 percent of the named defendant's costs in obtaining a list of interest holders of mineral rights. 2 F.3d 1023 (10th Cir. 1993). The court noted that the lists had already been compiled as part of its normal business operations, the defendants for the most part favored the creation of a defendant class, and the defendants would benefit from the notice. *Id.* at 1030–31.

The only other discussion by the Tenth Circuit of the specific rules underlying certification under Rule 23(b)(1) comes from a dissent authored by Judge Tacha in *Shook v. El Paso County*, 386 F.3d 963 (10th Cir. 2004), addressing the propriety of a district court considering specific criteria of one of the subsections of Rule 23(b), such as the manageability factor specified in Rule 23(b)(3), in evaluating whether a class action could be certified under another of the three subsections of Rule 23(b). *See Shook*, 386 F.3d at 975 (Tacha, C.J., dissenting in part and concurring in part) ("The majority's reading collapses the differences between a Rule 23(b)(1), (b)(2) and (b)(3) class, allowing a district court to consider any criteria under any of the subsections for any type of class. Such a reading is not in line with the structure of Rule 23(b) and is thus contrary to standard statutory construction." (citing *United States v. Rodgers*, 461 U.S. 677, 706 (1983))). However, the majority opinion in *Shook* expressly did not reach a conclusion whether a class should be certified under any subsection of Rule 23(b), concluding instead that the case should be remanded to the district court for a determination. *See id.* at 973–74.

Rule 23(b)(2) Classes
Under Rule 23(b)(2), a class can be certified if "the party opposing the class has acted or refused to act on grounds that apply generally to the class, so that final injunctive relief or corresponding declaratory relief is appropriate respecting the class as a whole." "Class actions under (b)(2) are broadly available, but are only capable of seeking injunctive or declaratory relief, and not damages." *WPX Energy Prod., LLC*, 306 F.R.D. at 385. "[V]ague, partially formulated request[s] for injunctive relief" are insufficient to meet Rule 23(b)(2)'s requirements. *N. Brevard Cnty. Hosp. Dist.*, 710 F. Supp. 3d at 1114–15 (citing *In re EpiPen (Epinephrine Injection, USP) Mktg., Sales Pracs. & Antitrust Litig.*, No. 17-MD-2785-DDC-TJJ, 2020 WL 1180550, at *59 (D. Kan. Mar. 10, 2020)). Moreover, a plaintiff seeking injunctive relief on behalf of a purported class is not certifiable under Rule 23(b)(2) if the requested relief "would effectively result in individualized monetary damages for each of the putative class members." *Melnick*, 347 F.R.D. at 112. "[M]any courts have found Rule 23(b)(2) well suited for cases where the composition of a class is not readily ascertainable. . . ." *Shook*, 386 F.3d at 972. Accordingly, class definitions are given more leeway in the Rule 23(b)(2) context. *See Shook v. Bd. of Cty. Comm'rs of Cty. of El Paso*, 543 F.3d 597, 611 (10th Cir. 2008) (explaining that difficulties in identifying class members do not defeat class certification under Rule 23(b)(2) because, among other things, notice is optional for (b)(2) classes); *Zapata v. IBP, Inc.*, 167 F.R.D. 147, 156 (D. Kan. 1996) ("Greater precision is required in defining a class when compensatory relief is sought, rather than injunctive or declaratory relief."); *Shook*, 386 F.3d at 972 (quoting *Yaffe v. Powers*, 454 F.2d 1362, 1366 (1st Cir. 1972) ("Notice to the members of a (b)(2) class is not required"; thus, the "class need not [] be precisely delimited.")).

Rule 23(b)(3) Classes
Classes maintained under Rule 23(b)(3) have been considered "[f]ar and away the most controversial class action category." *WPX Energy Prod., LLC*, 306 F.R.D. at 384–85. Classes maintained under Rule 23(b)(3) "can be brought for class-wide damages, injunctive relief, declaratory relief, or any combination thereof." *Id.* at 385. Certification of a class under Rule 23(b)(3) is appropriate if "the court finds that the questions of law or fact common to class members predominate over any questions affecting only individual members, and that a class action is superior to other available methods for fairly and efficiently adjudicating the controversy." *Small*, 2014 WL 3893052, at *3 (quoting Fed. R. Civ. P. 23(b)(3)). Rule 23(b)(3) provides that courts should consider four factors: (1) "the class members' interests in individually controlling the prosecution or defense of separate actions;" (2) "the extent and nature of any litigation concerning the controversy already begun by or against class members;" (3) "the desirability or undesirability of concentrating the litigation of the claims in the particular forum; and" (4) "the likely difficulties in managing a class action." Fed. R. Civ. P. 23(b)(3). Tenth Circuit courts will generally consider these four requirements within the context of a "predominance" and "superiority" inquiry. *See Bustillos*, 310 F.R.D. at 654. However, each of these four factors is probative in analyzing whether a putative class should be certified under Rule 23(b)(3). *Id.*

Predominance
"Predominance focuses on the question of liability. [I]f the liability issue is common to the class, common questions are held to predominate over individual questions." *Small*, 2014 WL 3893052, at *3 (internal quotation marks and citations omitted). "While Rule 23(a)(2) requires only that the class share at least one common question of law or fact, Rule 23(b)(3) 'calls upon courts to give careful scrutiny to the relation between common and individual questions in a case.'" *Curran v. Progressive Direct Ins. Co.*, 345 F.R.D. 498, 507 (D. Colo. 2023) (citing *Sherman*, 84 F.4th at 1194). The predominance inquiry requires courts to first "characterize the issues in the case as common or not, and then *weigh which* issues predominate." *CGC Holding Co., LLC v. Broad & Cassel*, 773 F.3d 1076, 1087 (10th Cir. 2014).

To satisfy this requirement, "a plaintiff must show that common questions subject to generalized, classwide proof *predominate* over individual questions." *Naylor Farms, Inc. v. Chaparral Energy, LLC*, 923 F.3d 779, 789 (10th Cir. 2019). Where a legal question requires the same evidence or is susceptible to proof on a generalized classwide basis, common questions will be deemed to exist. *WPX Energy Prod., LLC*, 306 F.R.D. at 386–87. Conversely, when each member of a putative class would need to offer varying evidence to prove their claims, individualized questions will be deemed to exist. *Id.* "The fact that damages may have to be ascertained on an individual basis is not, standing alone, sufficient to defeat class certification." *Naylor Farms*, 923 F.3d at 798 (internal quotations marks and citation omitted). "Instead, material differences in damages determinations will only destroy predominance if those individualized issues will overwhelm . . . questions common to the class." *Id.* (internal quotation marks and citation omitted) (omission in original). Similarly "the assertion of an [individualized] affirmative defense does not necessarily preclude a predominance finding. Instead, the question is whether the common issues predominate over the individualized issues." *Melnick*, 347 F.R.D. at 108.

Use of Statistical Sampling to Prove Damages

In the wake of the U.S. Supreme Court's landmark decision in *Wal-Mart Stores, Inc. v. Dukes*, 564 U.S. 338 (2011), courts within the Tenth Circuit have grappled with the predominance analysis as it pertains to the use of statistical sampling methods to prove damages on a classwide basis. The *Wal-Mart* decision was noteworthy, among other reasons, for its disapproval of the lower court's "novel" plan to conduct a "Trial by Formula," wherein damages would be determined for a sample set of class members and then applied by extrapolation to the rest of the class "without further individualized proceedings." *564 U.S.* at 367; *see also Lyall v. City of Denver*, No. 16-cv-2155-WJM-CBS, 2017 WL 2167031, at *7 (D. Colo. Apr. 27, 2017). Proceeding in that fashion, the Court held, would have violated the Rules Enabling Act and precluded Wal-Mart from "litigat[ing] its statutory defenses to individual claims." *Wal-Mart*, 564 U.S. at 367.

The Tenth Circuit confronted the proof-by-sampling issue in *Dow Chem. Co. v. Seegott Holding, Inc. (In re Urethane Antitrust Litig.)*, 768 F.3d 1245 (10th Cir. 2014), an antitrust class action brought by purchasers of polyurethane chemicals alleging Dow chemical company conspired to manipulate prices of those chemicals. In *In re Urethane Antitrust Litigation*, the district court certified the class at trial and a jury issued a $400,049,039 verdict for the plaintiffs. *Id.* at 1249, 1253, 1255, 1268. On appeal, Dow argued that certification violated *Wal-Mart* because the plaintiffs impermissibly utilized statistical extrapolation to calculate price impact and damages for the class. *See id.* at 1249. Specifically, the plaintiffs' expert extrapolated damages for the entire class by estimating price overcharges based on a comparison between the chemicals' actual price versus what would have existed in a competitive market. *See id.* The court, in affirming the district court's certification order, explained that *Wal-Mart's* prohibition against "Trial by Formula" applied only to proof of liability, not damages, and the *Urethane* plaintiffs proved liability through common evidence. *Id. at* 1256–57. In so doing, the Court signaled that *Wal-Mart* may have limited reach in the Tenth Circuit and that the door to utilizing expert-backed damages calculation models is still open for plaintiffs seeking to show predominance of common issues. *See Rodarte v. Bd. of Cnty. Comm'rs of Bernalillo Cty.*, No. 14-cv-193-JAP-SCY, 2014 WL 10298032, at *7 (D.N.M. Oct. 20, 2014) (finding predominance in Fair Labor Standards Act (FLSA) case where each class member's individual damages could be computed based on the number of shifts they worked and their hourly wages, noting that a damages formula can account for any individualized variances, or the court can simply bifurcate any trial into liability and damages portions); *N. Brevard Cnty. Hosp. Dist.*, 710 F. Supp. 3d at 1108–12 (finding no common proof as to impact or injury in antitrust case, where regression model and average overcharge benchmarks were not capable of showing whether any individual class member paid an overcharge, let alone that all of them had been overcharged, but instead, assumed average overcharges could be applied uniformly across the class).

Treatment of Comcast Corp. v. Behrend

Comcast Corp. v. Behrend, 569 U.S. 27, 31–32 (2013), was another Supreme Court case affecting the landscape in the Tenth Circuit surrounding the role of damages calculation models in the predominance analysis. *Comcast* was an antitrust case in which the Supreme Court reversed class certification because the plaintiffs' damages methodology failed to reflect the one theory of antitrust impact that had been accepted by the district court. *Id.* at 1433–35. The Supreme Court held that to prove predominance of common issues, plaintiffs must show that a sufficient nexus exists between their theory of liability and their theory of damages—and that courts must conduct a "'rigorous analysis' to determine whether that is so." *Id.* at 1433 (quoting *Dukes*, 564 U.S. at 351–52).

In the *Urethane Antitrust Litigation*, the defendants challenged the plaintiffs' use of an expert to establish predominance because, in the defendants' view, the plaintiffs' theory of price impact did not match the theory they advanced at trial for liability (a nationwide conspiracy to fix prices). *See* 768 F.3d at 1249, 1259. But the Tenth Circuit held that it was within the district court's discretion to determine, in light of testimony by the plaintiffs' expert, that there indeed was such a fit. *Id.* at 1259. Other courts in the Tenth Circuit have followed suit, rejecting *Comcast* arguments by defense counsel and suggesting that the case has a limited reach. *See, e.g.*, *Wallace B. Roderick Revocable Living Trust v. XTO Energy, Inc.*, 725 F.3d 1213, 1220 (10th Cir. 2013) (even after *Comcast*, "there are ways to preserve the class action model in the face of individualized damages" (citation omitted)); *Roberts v. C.R. England, Inc.*, 318 F.R.D. 457, 516–17 (D. Utah 2017) (finding predominance of common issues where plaintiffs' theory of liability was consistent with and corresponded to models capable of reasonably predicting classwide damages based on specific data). Furthermore, the cases suggest that, as a practical matter, proving predominance of common issues based on classwide proof is not the insurmountable obstacle that defense counsel would like it to be. *See, e.g.*, *Sibley v. Sprint Nextel Corp.*, 315 F.R.D. 642, 662 (D. Kan. 2016) (to satisfy the predominance inquiry for class certification, "there must be a single or common method that can be used to measure and quantify the damages of each class member"); *In re: Syngenta AG MIR 162 Corn Litig.*, No. 14-MD-2591-JWL, 2016 WL 5371856, at *9 (D. Kan. Sept. 26, 2016) (rejecting argument, under *Comcast*, that a classwide damage model is required for certification). *But see Stender v. Archstone-Smith Operating Trust*, No. 07-cv-02503-WJM-MJW, 2015 WL 5675304, at *11 (D. Colo. Sept. 28, 2015) (declining to certify class as to damages, since damages calculations by plaintiffs' expert "turn[ed] on several momentous assumptions, to the point where there can be no confidence that his final figures are anywhere close to the harm the Class allegedly suffered"); *Wallace B. Roderick Revocable Living Trust v. XTO Energy, Inc.*, 725 F.3d 1213, 1220 (10th Cir. 2013) (reversing certification order and remanding to the district court, directing the district court to "consider the extent to which material differences in damages determinations will require individualized inquiries" in light of *Dukes* and *Comcast*).

Statute of Limitations Tolling and Predominance

District courts in the Tenth Circuit have taken divergent approaches as to whether statute of limitations defenses and related tolling arguments create individualized issues that preclude class certification under Rule 23. For example, the U.S. District Court for the District of New Mexico has held that statute of limitation defenses and related tolling arguments do not preclude class certification based on individualized issues because those defenses and related tolling arguments, as applied, could either be considered on a common basis or, if individualized evidence was necessary, the amount of individualized evidence was still manageable. *Anderson Living Trust v. WPX Energy Prod., LLC*, 306 F.R.D. 312, 457–58 (D.N.M. Jan. 6, 2014); *Daye v. Cmty. Fin. Serv. Ctr., LLC*, 313 F.R.D. 147, 168 n.11 (D.N.M. 2016) ("Although a necessity for individualized statute-of-limitations determinations invariably weighs against class certification under Rule 23(b)(3), we reject any per se rule that treats the presence of such issues as an automatic disqualifier."). By contrast, in *Miller v. Farmers Insurance Group*, the U.S. District Court for the Western District of Oklahoma concluded that because statute of limitations defenses require the court to determine who knew about claims practices and when they knew it, which triggers the beginning of a statute of limitations period, individualized issues raised by those defenses will predominate over common issues and make class certification inappropriate. No. CIV-10-466-F, 2012 WL 8017244, at *16–17 (W.D. Okla. Mar. 22, 2012). As the district courts in the Tenth Circuit currently stand, this issue remains intensely case-by-case and fact-specific.

Superiority

Superiority requires that "class resolution must be superior to other available methods for the fair and efficient adjudication of the controversy." *Wornicki*, 2015 WL 1403814, at *6 (internal quotation marks omitted) (citing *Amchem Prod., Inc. v. Windsor*, 521 U.S. 591, 615 (1997)). Superiority likely exists where a putative class is made up of claims involving small dollar amounts that "individual class members would be unlikely or unable . . . to pursue on their own." *Rhodes*, 317 F.R.D. at 585–86 (citations omitted); *Small*, 2014 WL 3893052, at *3 (finding that the superiority requirement of Rule 23(b)(3) was satisfied where the majority of plaintiffs' claims involved low dollar amounts that plaintiffs would be reluctant to pursue on their own); *Melnick*, 347 F.R.D. at 109 (finding that where recovery "could be measured in the thousands and tens of thousands for each class member . . . [p]laintiffs' contention that class members would lack the incentive to proceed individually is without merit"). "The proposed class members' emotional connection to the case may also be relevant [to the superiority inquiry]: the stronger the attachment, the more reticent the court should be to certify the case." *Bustillos*, 310 F.R.D. at 655 (citations omitted). In Rule 23(b)(3) in particular, the ability of putative members to opt out of the class is a powerful factor weighing in favor of superiority. *Abraham v. WPX Prod. Prods., LLC*, 317 F.R.D. 169, 240 (D.N.M. 2016) ("In evaluating the (b)(3)(A) and (b)(3)(B) factors, the court must keep in mind a powerful fact that counsels strongly in favor of finding superiority: (b)(3) class actions give all proposed class members the opportunity to opt out of inclusion in the class." (*citing* Fed. R. Civ. P. 23(c)(2)(B))); *see also Bustillos v. Bd. of Cty. Comm'rs of Hidalgo Cty.*, 310 F.R.D. 631, 672 (D.N.M. 2015).

Manageability and Ascertainability

In determining whether to certify a class under Rule 23(b)(3), courts also examine whether the class is manageable and ascertainable. The "manageability factor encompasses the whole range of practical problems that may render the class action format inappropriate for a particular suit." *WPX Energy Prod., LLC*, 306 F.R.D. at 411 (internal quotation marks and citation omitted). The core inquiry in determining whether a class is sufficiently manageable is individualization—"a court must consider . . . the extent to which the court will be able to manage the class action, if certified, through pre-trial litigation and trial, accurately adjudicating the class's claims—in particular the individual issues—and fairly distributing relief among the class members." *Id.*; *see also Yazzie v. Ray Vickers' Special Cars, Inc.*, 180 F.R.D. 411, 417 (D.N.M. 1998) ("In this case, the class is manageable, no other suits are being maintained, and the concentration of actions in this forum is judicially efficient."). Where the court must contend with variations in the laws of different states, a class may be unmanageable. *In re HomeAdvisor, Inc. Litig.*, 345 F.R.D. at 237 (finding plaintiffs failed "to show how the Court could manage a nationwide class, applying the laws of all fifty states, as well as nine state classes").

"It is unsettled whether ascertainability is a separate and distinct requirement for class certification under Rule 23(b)(3)." *In re EpiPen (Epinephrine Injection, USP) Mktg., Sales Pracs. & Antitrust Litig.*, 2020 WL 1180550, at *9. Courts within the Tenth Circuit have acknowledged that although there is a circuit split regarding the "proper standard for determining whether a class is ascertainable . . . the majority of district courts in the Tenth Circuit" apply a "stringent standard for ascertainability" requiring that class members be "ascertained in an economical and administratively feasible manner and [that] class members be identified without extensive and individualized fact-finding or 'mini-trials.'" *Banks v. Cent. Refrigerated Servs., Inc.*, No. 2:16-cv-356-DAK, 2017 WL 1683056, at *4 (D. Utah May 2, 2017) (citing *Carrera v. Bayer Corp.*, 727 F.3d 300, 307 (3d Cir. 2013) (citations omitted)); *see also Melnick*, 347 F.R.D. at 92 n.21 (D. Kan. 2024) (finding proposed class definition did not meet ascertainability requirements because definition was unwieldy and amorphous and it was unclear how proposed class members would be identified).[14]

e. Issue Classes

As an alternative to class certification, "when appropriate, an action may be brought or maintained as a class action with respect to particular issues." Fed. R. Civ. P. 23(c)(4); *see also Martinez v. FedEx Ground Package Sys., Inc.*, No. CV 20-1052 SCY/LF, 2023 WL 7114678, at *14 (D.N.M. Oct. 27, 2023). Issue classes advance judicial economy "by allowing adjudication of issues common to the class even when the entire case does not satisfy the requirements to proceed as a class action." *Melnick*, 347 F.R.D. at 110 (citing *Black*, 69 F.4th at 1188). "[C]ertification of an issue class under Rule 23(c)(4) is appropriate if the issue class itself satisfies the requirements of Rules 23(a) and 23(b)." *Black*, 69 F.4th at 1188. Accordingly, for an issue class to be certified pursuant to Rule 23(b)(3), "the contemplated issue class must meet all the requirements of Rule 23(a) and the predominance and superiority requirements of Rule 23(b)(3)." *Id.* Meeting the superiority requirement depends on whether "the resolution of the issue class will 'materially advance' resolution of the dispute." *Id.* (citing *In re Motor Fuel Temperature Sales Pracs. Litig.*, 292 F.R.D. 652, 665 (D. Kan. 2013)); *see also Morris v. Davita Healthcare Partners, Inc.*, 308 F.R.D. 360, 379 (D. Colo. 2015).

6. CASE MANAGEMENT

a. Appointing Counsel

Under Federal Rule of Civil Procedure 23(a)(4), a class action may be maintained only if "representative parties will fairly and adequately protect the interests of the class." In assessing the adequacy of representation, historically, the Tenth Circuit has identified two questions relevant to the inquiry: "(i) whether the named plaintiffs and their counsel have any conflicts with other proposed class members; and (ii) whether the named plaintiffs and their counsel will vigorously prosecute the action on the class' behalf." *Daye v. Cmty. Fin. Serv. Ctr., LLC*, 313 F.R.D. at 179 (citing *Rutter & Wilbanks Corp. v. Shell Oil Co.*, 314 F.3d 1180, 1187–88 (10th Cir. 2002)); *Disability Law Ctr. v. Utah*, No. 2:15-cv-00645-RJS, 2016 WL 5396681, at *6 (D. Utah Sept. 27, 2016).

Under the first requirement, courts consider whether the named plaintiffs are a "part of the class and 'possess[] the same interest and suffer[] the same injury' as the putative class members." *Daye*, 313 F.R.D. at 179 (quoting *E. Tex. Motor Freight Sys. Inc. v. Rodriguez*, 431 U.S. 395, 403 (1977)). Courts also consider other factors such as whether the named plaintiffs' interests coincide with the proposed class members' interests, whether they seek any separate individual relief, and whether any intra-class conflicts exist. *Id.*

Rule 23(g) encapsulates the second requirement, which is less objective than the first. In assessing whether counsel will "vigorously prosecute" the action on the class's behalf, courts consider the factors set forth in 23(g), such as the attorneys' experience litigating the subject claims, particularly in the context of class actions; whether that experience occurred in the same forum (state versus federal); and any other related experience, such as author-

[14] While the majority of courts within the Tenth Circuit apply this standard, the Tenth Circuit has not adopted a specific approach. Evans v. Brigham Young Univ., No. 1:20-CV-100-TS, 2022 WL 596862, at *3 (D. Utah Feb. 28, 2022).

ship in the area of law at issue. *See* Fed. R. Civ. P. 23(g). Ethical violations or other misconduct are also highly pertinent to whether the attorney will adequately represent the class. *In re HomeAdvisor, Inc. Litig.*, 345 F.R.D. at 238. In *In re HomeAdvisor, Inc. Litigation,* the U.S. District Court for the District of Colorado adopted the "serious doubt" test, reasoning that class counsel's discovery violations "while troubling, do not raise 'serious doubt' about the adequacy of [counsel] to loyally represent the class." *Id.* at 239.

b. Discovery Issues

In the Tenth Circuit, courts apply a six-factor test to assess whether good cause exists to reopen discovery. The test, set forth in *Smith v. United States*, 834 F.2d 166 (10th Cir. 1987), requires courts to consider:

> 1) whether trial is imminent, 2) whether the request is opposed, 3) whether the non-moving party would be prejudiced, 4) whether the moving party was diligent in obtaining discovery within the guidelines established by the court, 5) the foreseeability of the need for additional discovery in light of the time allowed for discovery by the district court, and 6) the likelihood that the discovery will lead to relevant evidence.

Id. at 169. The U.S. District Court for the District of New Mexico applied the *Smith* test to determine whether discovery should be "reopened" on class certification issues. *See Anderson Living Trust v. WPX Energy Prod., LLC*, 308 F.R.D. 410, 415 (D.N.M. 2015). The court noted, however, it was "not certain" that "the *Smith* standard really applie[d]" because the court was "not truly 'reopening' discovery" since discovery on the merits had not yet begun. *Id.* at 440. While the court noted that it was still applying Rule 16's general good cause rule—which the *Smith* factors effectively replace in motions to reopen discovery—the court found the factors "highly instructive" given the plaintiffs' "run-of-the-mill motion to reopen discovery" and thus applied them nonetheless. *Id.* at 441.

In disputes over jurisdictional discovery, courts are allowed greater discretion in resolving disputes. *Compare Baker v. PDC Energy, Inc.*, No. 14-cv-02537-RM-MJW, 2014 WL 6910207, at *1 (D. Colo. Dec. 9, 2014) (applying a two-factor test to determine whether to allow discovery into the home state exception under the Class Action Fairness Act), *with Dutcher v. Matheson*, 16 F. Supp. 3d 1327 (D. Utah 2014) (generally analyzing whether to allow discovery into the home-state exception under the Class Action Fairness Act). In *Dutcher*, the Tenth Circuit did not find an abuse of discretion where the District Court of Utah provided a general analysis to resolve the jurisdictional discovery issue that arose there, nor did it indicate that the two-factor test applied in *Baker* and other federal courts is required to avoid an abuse of discretion. 840 F.3d at 1195.

c. Timing of Class Certification

In *Gagnon v. Merit Energy Co., LLC*, No. 14-cv-00832-PAB-KLM, 2015 WL 3961174, at *1 (D. Colo. June 29, 2015), the court denied as premature the plaintiffs' motion for summary judgment that was brought on behalf of a class that had not yet been certified. The court agreed with the defendant that plaintiffs' motion impermissibly sought to modify the jointly proposed scheduling order without having shown good cause to do so. *See id.* at *2 (citing Fed. R. Civ. P. 16(b)(4)). Though the plaintiffs argued that defendant already had all of the discovery necessary to respond to their motion and that they had provided defendants the opportunity to take discovery on other relevant issues, the court held that (1) expert discovery needed to be conducted before the defendants could respond to plaintiffs' motion; and (2) that plaintiffs' "willingness to comply with discovery that is contrary to the scheduling order does not constitute good cause for a motion for summary judgment that requires deviation from the court-ordered discovery plan." *Id.*

7. FEES AND COSTS

Under 28 U.S.C. § 1447(c), a court may award costs and attorneys' fees where a party removes a case to federal court when it was not objectively reasonable to do so at the time. *Martin v. Franklin Capital Corp.*, 546 U.S. 132, 136 (2005). If the decision was objectively reasonable at the time of the removal, a court may award fees and costs only under unusual circumstances. *See, e.g.*, *Baker v. PDC Energy, Inc.*, No. 14-cv-02537-RM-MJW, 2014 WL 7445626, at *3–5 (D. Colo. Dec. 30, 2014) (denying plaintiff's request for attorneys' fees and costs incurred as a result of removal where plaintiff had previously "conceded" that defendant could remove where it noted that defendant may move to amend its notice of removal on the basis of putative class members' citizenship). District courts retain discretion to consider whether unusual circumstances warrant a departure from the rule in a given case. *Martin*, 546 U.S. at 141. For instance, "a plaintiff's delay in seeking remand or failure to disclose facts necessary to determine jurisdiction may affect the decision to award attorney's fees." *Id.*

For cases that are already in federal court based on diversity, "attorney fees are a substantive matter controlled by state law." *Nieberding v. Barrette Outdoor Living, Inc.*, 129 F. Supp.3d 1236, 1248 (D. Kan. 2015). In cases in which a "common fund" is created from which the class members obtain the settlement benefit, the Tenth Circuit has recognized that attorneys' fees may appropriately be awarded from that fund. *See Farley v. Family Dollar Stores, Inc.*, No. 12-cv-00325-RM-MJW, 2014 WL 5488897, at *3 (D. Colo. Oct. 30, 2014) (citing *Gottlieb v. Barry*, 43 F.3d 474, 482 (10th Cir. 1994)). In such cases, attorneys' fees that constitute approximately one-third of the total common fund settlement have been found to be reasonable awards. *See id.* at *4 (finding the requested fee that was 30.3 percent of the total settlement "reasonable"); *Nieberding*, 129 F. Supp.3d at 1249 (holding that reducing the attorneys' fee award to "one third of the total common fund" was a "reasonable and appropriate" award).

In common fund cases, the "hybrid" approach that combines the percentage of the fund method with the twelve factors originally developed in *Johnson v. Georgia Highway Express, Inc.*, 488 F.2d 714, 717–19 (5th Cir. 1974), is used to determine attorneys' fees. *Farley*, 2014 WL 5488897, at *3. The *Johnson* factors are:

> the time and labor required, the novelty and difficulty of the question presented by the case, the skill requisite to perform the legal service properly, the preclusion of other employment by the attorneys due to acceptance of the case, the customary fee, whether the fee is fixed or contingent, any time limitations imposed by the client or the circumstances, the amount involved and the results obtained, the experience, reputation and ability of the attorneys, the 'undesirability' of the case, the nature and length of the professional relationship with the client, and awards in similar cases. . . . [T]he weight given to different factors may vary in common fund, as opposed to statutory fee shifting cases.

Id. (alterations in original) (quoting *Gottlieb*, 43 F.3d at 482 n.4).

When applying these factors, a district court "may exercise its judgment in assigning different relative weights to the factors, and may determine one factor is not applicable or give greater weight to one factor over another, where the bases for doing so are clearly reflected in the record." *Id.* (citing *Brown v. Phillips Petro. Co.*, 838 F.2d 451, 451, 456 (10th Cir. 1988)).

8. INTERLOCUTORY APPEAL (FED. R. CIV. P. 23(F))

Although the Tenth Circuit has held that it has "unfettered" discretion to grant petitions for interlocutory review of certification orders under FRCP 23(f), *Vallario v. Vandehey*, 554

F.3d 1259, 1262 (10th Cir. 2009), the court is typically reluctant to employ that discretion. Numerous decisions have noted the court's general resistance to interlocutory review of class certification on the grounds that such review "disrupt[s] and delay[s] the proceedings below." *Carpenter v. Boeing Co.*, 456 F.3d 1183, 1189 (10th Cir. 2006). Accordingly, the Court has cautioned that it should "exercise restraint in accepting Rule 23(f) petitions." *Downes v. Rivera*, No. 15-705, 2015 WL 9022001, at *1 (10th Cir. Dec. 8, 2015).

The Tenth Circuit has not defined a unified test for determining which appeals to accept, but in *Carpenter v. Boeing*, it "set forth a set of principles that may prove useful in evaluating the merits of a Rule 23(f) petition." *Downes*, 2015 WL 9022001, at *1. First, "appeal might be permitted when the class certification decision sounds the 'death-knell' for the entire case." *Id.* Second, appeal may be appropriate when the class certification order implicates unresolved legal issues and may facilitate development of the law. *Id.* Third, a court may grant permission to appeal when the district court's decision is manifestly erroneous." *Id.* (citations omitted). Finally, the Tenth Circuit cautioned that courts should not use this category to "micromanage class actions," but may invoke it only where "the deficiencies of a certification order are both significant and readily ascertainable." *Vallario*, 554 F.3d at 1263–64 (citation omitted).

These factors were reaffirmed by a recent Tenth Circuit decision, *C.R. England, Inc. v. Roberts*, wherein the court held that the decision of whether to grant a Rule 23(f) petition is "purely discretionary," but ultimately applied and denied the defendants-petitioners' petition for failure to establish factors set out in *Carpenter* and *Vallario*. No. 17-600, 2017 WL 3611971, at *1 (10th Cir. Mar. 27, 2017) (denying defendants-petitioners' Rule 23(f) petition for failure to establish that "the district court's class certification decision was based upon manifest error," "that permissive interlocutory review [was] necessary to address 'an unresolved issue of law relating to class actions that is likely to evade end-of-case review' or to avoid a 'death knell' situation" (citation omitted)); *see also Pfizer, Inc. v. All Plaintiffs*, No. 20-603, 2020 WL 4048681, at *2 (10th Cir. May 26, 2020) (finding that although the petitioners had presented "persuasive arguments" for interlocutory review, the district court had conducted the required "rigorous analysis" and its findings were well-supported and therefore, "[t]he petitioners have not convinced us that interrupting the district court proceedings with an interlocutory appeal at this time is necessary or warranted").

9. CLASS NOTICE AND OPT-OUT PROCEDURES

Rule 23(c)(2)(A) provides that if a class is certified under (b)(1) or (b)(2), "the court ***may*** direct appropriate notice to the class." (emphasis added). However, classes certified under section (b)(3) always require notice to all proposed class members and putative class members must be given the opportunity to opt out of the class. *Id.* at 23(c)(2)(B); *WPX Energy Prod., LLC*, 306 F.R.D. at 384–85. Practitioners should be mindful, however, that notice provided to (b)(3) members must be "the best notice that is practicable under the circumstances, including individual notice to all members who can be identified through reasonable effort." Fed. R. Civ. P. 23(c)(2)(B). To attack the notice procedure, a party should be prepared to show that "some other method of notification offers a better means of notifying the class." *LaVigne v. First Cmty. Bancshares, Inc.*, 330 F.R.D. 293, 297 (D.N.M. 2019) (internal citation omitted). Merely arguing that the class is not ascertainable is "not a reason to deny class notice." *Id.*

In *Murphy v. LenderLive Network, Inc.*, No. 13-cv-03135-RBJ, 2014 WL 5396165, at *6 (D. Colo. Oct. 22, 2014), the court held that the proposed opt out procedures contained in class notice were overly burdensome because it required class members who wished to opt out to pay the cost of a certified mailing. The court stated that "[t]he type of mail should not be used to gain a strategic advantage. It should be a means of giving class members a relatively easy method for communicating their wishes." *Id.* The court also held that it was improper to set the opt out deadline as the date of receipt—rather than the date of mailing. *Id.*

Cf. Nieberding v. Barrette Outdoor Living, Inc., No. 12-cv-2353-DDC-TJJ, 2015 WL 2218965, at *2 (D. Kan. May 12, 2015) (setting class members' deadline to opt out as "postmarked" by a certain date); *Helmer v. Goodyear Tire & Rubber Co.*, No. 12-cv-00685-RBJ, 2014 WL 4436406, at *2 (D. Colo. Sept. 9, 2014) (holding that "[a]ny member of the class who wishes to be excluded from the class must send a written request for exclusion to the Class Counsel *so that it is postmarked before the close of the opt out period.*" (emphasis added)).

The notice requirement also extends to claims for attorneys' fees, which "must be made by motion . . . Notice of the motion must be served on all parties and, for motions by class counsel, directed to class members in a reasonable manner." Fed. R. Civ. P. 23(h)(1). In *Chieftain Royalty Co. v. SM Energy Co.*, the court held that, although class-wide notice had been provided for the first motion to approve attorneys' fees for class counsel, class members were entitled to notice on the renewed motion because class members maintained their interest in the payment of class counsel. 100 F.4th 1147, 1157 (10th Cir. 2024). The court noted that the renewed motion was distinct from the first motion because it sought a different percentage of the class action settlement for attorney fees, and provided evidence in support for the first time. *Id.* at 1157–58. Accordingly, the court directed the district court to "direct notice of the 2018 attorneys' fees motion to the class in a reasonable manner that provides a meaningful opportunity to object to the motion and its supporting documentation." *Id.* at 1160.

"In addition to the requirements of Rule 23, the Due Process Clause in the Fifth Amendment of the United States. Constitution guarantees unnamed class members the right to notice of class certification or settlement." *Lengel v. HomeAdvisor, Inc.*, No. 15-cv-2198-KHV, 2017 WL 1338839, at *3 (D. Kan. Apr. 12, 2017) (citing U.S. Const., amend. V; *DeJulius v. New Eng. Healthcare Empls. Pension Fund*, 429 F.3d 935, 943–44 (10th Cir. 2005)). "The legal standards for satisfying Rule 23(c)(2)(B) and . . . due process are coextensive and substantially similar." *Id.*

10. SUBCLASSES

Several courts within the Tenth Circuit have "determined that the plaintiffs in a putative class action 'may only assert a state law claim if a named plaintiff resides in, does business in, or has some other connection to that state.'" *Roco, Inc. v. EOG Res., Inc.*, No. 14-1065-JAR-KMH, 2014 WL 5430251, at *3 (D. Kan. Oct. 24, 2014) (citing *Thomas v. Metro. Life Ins. Co.*, 540 F. Supp. 2d 1212, 1226–27 (W.D. Okla. 2008), *aff'd*, 631 F.3d 1153 (10th Cir. 2011); *Smith v. Pizza Hut, Inc.*, No. 09-1632-CMA, 2011 WL 2791331, at *9–10 (D. Colo. July 14, 2011). *But see Beer v. XTO Energy, Inc.*, CIV-07-798-L, 2009 WL 764500 (W.D. Okla. Mar. 20, 2009) (finding standing in royalty dispute involving royalty owners in Kansas and Oklahoma despite the lack of a class representative from Kansas) (citations omitted).

In *Roco*, the plaintiff brought a class action for underpaid royalty payments on behalf of royalty owners in Kansas. 2014 WL 5430251, at *1. Plaintiff later sought leave to amend its petition to add a new putative subclass of royalty owners in Oklahoma. *Id.* The U.S. District Court for the District of Kansas rejected the defendant's argument that each named plaintiff needed to establish standing as to each and every claim asserted in the complaint—i.e., that the plaintiff for each subclass establish standing as to both the Kansas and Oklahoma subclasses. *Id.* at *3. The court held instead that "a claim cannot be asserted on behalf of a class unless *at least one* named plaintiff has suffered the injury that gives rise to that claim." *Id.* That is, "[a]s long as at least one plaintiff has standing with respect to each claim alleged in the [complaint], it will satisfy the injury requirement of standing." *Id.*

Likewise, the court denied the defendant's motion to sever and transfer the Oklahoma claims under Federal Rule of Civil Procedure 21, which gives district courts the "discretion to sever any claim against a party and proceed with the claim or claims separately." *Id.* at *6. This discretion requires courts to consider "the convenience of the parties, avoiding prejudice, promoting expedition and economy, and the separability of law and logic." *Id.* The court in *Roco* held that severance and transfer of the Oklahoma claims to a federal district court in Oklahoma was inappropriate where the claims "share[d] a common nucleus of operative facts and law" and severance and transfer would "create an additional case in a different venue with identical factual claims and several identical legal issues" and would not be more convenient for the parties. *Id.* at *6–7.

11. COMMUNICATIONS WITH ABSENT CLASS MEMBERS

It is well settled in the Tenth Circuit that, prior to class certification, defendants may communicate *ex parte* settlement offers directly to absent class members without providing the court or opposing counsel notice, provided the communication is not "abusive" or coercive. *Jin Nakamura v. Wells Fargo Bank, Nat'l Ass'n*, No. 17-4029-DDC-GEB, 2018 WL 994706, at *4 & n.5 (D. Kan. Feb. 21, 2018) (collecting cases). Illustrative here, *Jin Nakamura* involved a putative class action suit arising from Wells Fargo's alleged unlawful "repossession of 1,150 servicemembers' vehicles without court orders in violation of . . . the Servicemembers Civil Relief Act." *Id.* at *1. Prior to class certification, Wells Fargo sent settlement offers and corresponding release agreements to absent class members that failed to make any mention of the class action lawsuit. *Id.* at *1–2. To cure this deficiency, Wells Fargo sent revised settlement communications that included information about the class suit including "Plaintiff's counsel's contact information and a Wells Fargo-controlled toll-free number" to field questions. *Id.* at *3. With respect to servicemembers who had already accepted the settlement agreement and executed a release, Wells Fargo sent a supplemental letter providing them an opportunity to rescind their release and be part of the proposed class while retaining any settlement monies received. *Id.*

Plaintiff's counsel then moved the court to blanketly order corrective notices and invalidate all executed releases, arguing that the settlement communications were "secretive, confusing and misleading." *Id.* at *4. The court denied Plaintiff's motion, finding the *ex parte* communications lawful because the "class ha[d] not been certified, a Rule 23(c)(2) certification notice ha[d] not been approved or issued, and not only [was] there no order banning Wells Fargo from contacting putative class members, but the law d[id] not preclude such actions." *Id.* at *5. The court further dismissed Plaintiff's argument that the communications were "secretive and deceptive," reasoning that Plaintiff had cited "no authority to support Wells Fargo had a duty to mention or even disclose the letters before mailing." *Id.* at *6.

12. TOLLING OF STATUTE OF LIMITATIONS FOR OPT IN PLAINTIFFS IN FLSA COLLECTIVE ACTIONS

Tolling of the statute of limitations for plaintiffs opting into collective actions brought under the FLSA is treated differently than the tolling of the statute of limitations for Rule 23 class actions. The commencement of a class action under Rule 23 tolls the statute of limitations for putative class members. *Joseph v. Wiles*, 223 F.3d 1155, 1167–68 (10th Cir. 2000), *abrogated by California Pub. Employees' Ret. Sys. v. ANZ Sec., Inc.*, 137 S. Ct. 2042 (2017). "Unlike Rule 23 class actions, the commencement of an FLSA collective action does not toll the statute of limitations for putative class members." *Avendano v. Averus, Inc.*, No. 14-cv-01614-CMA-MJW, 2015 WL 1529354, at *9 (D. Colo. Mar. 31, 2015) (citing 29 U.S.C. § 256(b)). Unless the court orders tolling of the applicable statute of limitations, each putative opt in class member's limitations period continues to run. *Id.*

The Tenth Circuit has not addressed the specific application of equitable tolling to FLSA claims. That said, federal district courts in the Tenth Circuit have opined that equitable tolling is appropriate when a putative class member's failure to meet a statute of limitations deadline arose from circumstances beyond that litigant's control.

> Early notice to Opt-in Plaintiffs in a collective action such as this is favored, however, and nothing in the record of this case shows that any potential opt-in plaintiff was deceived, misled, lulled into inaction, or otherwise faced extraordinary circumstances that made it impossible for them to file a timely FLSA claim. Plaintiff's argument is ultimately rooted in the assumption that potential opt-in plaintiffs could not know about the facts that are the basis of their possible FLSA claim until they receive notice of a collective action. Generally, however, potential opt-in plaintiffs are presumed to be aware of the facts and circumstances of their employment . . . and it is those facts and circumstances that allegedly form the basis of each plaintiff's FLSA claim . . . Generally, their claims accrue when they gain knowledge of these facts.

Id. (omissions in original) (internal quotation marks and citation omitted).

Moreover, a court may grant equitable tolling during the time that a court decides certification of an FLSA collective action matter where undue delay arising from the court's deliberation of a motion for certification constitutes an "extraordinary circumstance." *See Abrams v. City of Albuquerque*, Civ. No. 10-0872-MV/RHS, 2014 WL 11497810, at *8–9 (D.N.M. June 26, 2014) (internal quotation marks and citation omitted). The *Abrams* court stated that "[t]he relevant inquiry [for equitable tolling] thus becomes whether the facts demonstrate that the delay during the Court's review of [a motion for certification] was undue or otherwise extraordinary." *Id.* at *10–11 (concluding that a twenty-month delay was extraordinary and tolling the statute of limitations for putative opt in plaintiffs from the date the plaintiffs filed their second FLSA collective action complaint through the date collective action notice was issued to the putative opt in class members).

13. CLASS ACTION SETTLEMENTS IN THE TENTH CIRCUIT

Federal Rule of Civil Procedure 23(e) provides that parties may settle, voluntarily dismiss, or compromise certified class claims only with the court's approval. The court may approve a settlement only after conducting a hearing and upon finding that it is "fair, reasonable, and adequate." Fed. R. Civ. P. 23(e)(2); *See e.g., Elna Sefcovic, LLC v. TEP Rocky Mountain, LLC*, 807 F. App'x 752, 757 (10th Cir. 2020) (unpublished) (internal quotation marks and citation omitted).

a. Stages of Class Settlement Approval

Tenth Circuit courts engage "in a two-step process to ensure the fairness of any class action settlement." *Rhodes v. Olson Assocs., P.C.*, 308 F.R.D. 664, 666 (D. Colo. 2015) (citing *Newberg on Class Actions* § 13:12 (5th ed.)); *Stanforth v. Farmers Ins. Co. of Ariz.*, No. CIV-09-1146, 2014 WL 11497806, at *3 (D.N.M. Jan 10, 2014). First, courts will make a preliminary determination about the "fairness, reasonableness, and adequacy of the settlement terms." *Rhodes*, 308 F.R.D. at 666; *Cisneros v. EP Wrap-It Insulation, LLC*, No. 19-500 GBW/GJF, 2021 WL 2953117, at *5 (D.N.M. July 14, 2021). The purpose of this first preliminary assessment is not to make a final determination about settlement terms, but instead to determine whether the class should be given notice of the settlement agreement. *Rhodes*, 308 F.R.D. at 666. Accordingly, the standard imposed at the preliminary approval stage is "less demanding" than the standard imposed in coming to a final fairness determination—the second stage in class settlement approval. *Id.* Nonetheless, where class settlement is sought prior to or concurrently with class certification, Tenth Circuit courts will be "'even more scrupulous than usual' when examining the fairness of the proposed settlement." *In re*

Motor Fuel Temperature Sales Practices Litig., 271 F.R.D. 263, 270 (D. Kan. 2010).

"The Court will ordinarily grant preliminary approval where the proposed settlement appears to be the product of serious, informed, non-collusive negotiations, has no obvious [] deficiencies, does not improperly grant preferential treatment to class representatives or segments of the class and falls within the range of possible approval." *In re Motor Fuel Temperature Sales Practices Litig.*, No. 07-MD-1840-KHV, 2011 WL 4431090, at *5 (D. Kan. Sept. 22, 2011) (internal quotation marks and citation omitted); *see also Cisneros*, 2021 WL 2953117, at *6–7. This standard is heightened, however, when a court undertakes to make a final determination about the fairness of a proposed class settlement at the second phase of class settlement approval—the final fairness hearing. This hearing takes place after a proposed class settlement has been given preliminary approval and the class has been given notice. *See Rhodes*, 308 F.R.D. at 666. "[C]lass objectors (if any) may provide testimony [at the final fairness hearing], and the [c]ourt again decides whether the settlement is fair, reasonable, and adequate." *Id.* "In evaluating the fairness of settlements, courts should not decide the merits of the lawsuit or substitute its own judgment for that of the parties," but the court must "independently analyze the evidence before it in making its determination." *Farley v. Family Dollar Stores, Inc.*, No. 12-cv-00325, 2014 WL 5488897, at *2 (D. Colo. Oct. 30, 2014) (citations omitted); *Lucas v. Kmart Corp.*, 234 F.R.D. 688, 693 (D. Colo. 2006).

Objectors and Class Members Who Choose to Opt Out

"Once a [class] settlement [] has been achieved, Rule 23 mandates that notice be sent to the absent class members and that they be given the opportunity to object to the terms of the settlement or, in most cases, to opt out of the class." *Newberg on Class Actions* § 13:20; Fed. R. Civ. P. 23(e)(1)(B) ("The court must direct notice in a reasonable manner to all class members who would be bound by the proposal."). But notice under Rule 23(e) is a "less stringent notice standard than Rule 23(c)(2)(B)," requiring only "notice in a reasonable manner to all class members who would be bound by the proposed settlement." *Marquez v. Midwest Div. MMC, LLC*, No. 19-2362-DDC-ADM, 2022 WL 4355298, at *19 (D. Kan. Sept. 20, 2022) (internal quotation marks and citation omitted). Procedural protections providing objectors the right to state their objections to the court are intended to provide an opportunity for the court to be part of a meaningful "adversarial discussion of the pros and cons of settlement," which may not otherwise be presented where the named parties are "all jointly urging the court to approve" the settlement. *Id.* (citing Theodore Eisenberg and Geoffrey P. Miller, *The Role of Opt-Outs and Objectors in Class Action Litigation: Theoretical and Empirical Issues*, 57 Vand. L. Rev. 1529, 1531 (2004)); *see also Tennille v. W. Union Co.*, 785 F.3d 422, 433–41 (10th Cir. 2015) (analyzing the arguments of a dozen unnamed class member objectors but ultimately finding that a district court did not abuse its discretion in approving a class settlement).

Class members can also choose to opt out under Rule 23, effectively removing themselves from the class. *Newberg on Class Actions* § 13:23. A class member who opts out does not have standing to object to the class settlement. *Id.* Class members have the choice to either "object or opt out, but they cannot do both . . . Nor may class members 'contingently opt out. . . .'" *Id.* (internal citation omitted). After all, class members who choose to exercise their right to opt out are immune to the preclusive effect of any class settlement; therefore, they cannot complain about its terms. *Id.*; *see also Jones v. I.Q. Data Intern., Inc.*, 2015 WL 5704016, at *3 (approving proposed class settlement and finding that the settlement was not binding on the "individuals who validly and timely excluded themselves from the settlement").

Conversely, objectors, who are parties to the settlement, do have a right to not only challenge a class settlement's terms in the trial court, but also to pursue appeals challenging the propriety of settlement and class certification. *Harper v. C.R. England, Inc.*, No. 17-4008, 2018 WL 3860471, at *8 (10th Cir. Aug. 14, 2018) (holding that objectors had the right to appeal class certification and remanding case because lower court's decision to certify class was conclusory and truncated, depriving the appellate court of its ability to analyze whether the district court had abused its discretion in granting certification).

b. The Tenth Circuit's Class Settlement Approval Analysis

The Tenth Circuit has established the following four factors for analyzing the fairness, reasonableness, and adequacy of a class action settlement:

> (1) whether the proposed settlement was fairly and honestly negotiated; (2) whether serious questions of law and fact exist, placing the ultimate outcome of the litigation in doubt; (3) whether the value of an immediate recovery outweighs the mere possibility of future relief after protracted and expensive litigation; and (4) the judgment of the parties that the settlement is fair and reasonable.

Nieberding v. Barrette Outdoor Living, Inc., 129 F. Supp. 3d 1236, 1245 (D. Kan. 2015) (citing *Rutter & Wilbanks Corp. v. Shell Oil Co.*, 314 F.3d 1180, 1188 (10th Cir. 2002)).

Prong 1: Whether Settlement Was Fairly and Honestly Negotiated

"When examining whether a settlement was fairly and honestly negotiated, district courts within the Tenth Circuit often examine whether the parties 'have vigorously advocated their respective positions throughout the pendency of the case'" and whether the rights of class members have been adequately considered during settlement negotiations. *See, e.g., Key v. Butch's Rat Hole & Anchor Service, Inc.*, No. CIV 17-1171 RB/KRS, 2022 WL 457915, at *2 (D.N.M. Feb. 15, 2022); *Acevedo v. Sw Airlines Co.*, No. 1:16-CV-00024-MV-LF, 2019 WL 6712298, at *2 (D.N.M. Dec. 10, 2019), *report and recommendation adopted*, No. 1:16-CV-00024-MV-LF, 2020 WL 85132 (D.N.M. Jan. 7, 2020); *O'Dowd v. Anthem, Inc.*, No. 14-cv-02787-KLM-NYW, 2019 WL 4279123, at *13 (D. Colo. Sept. 9, 2019); *Lane v. Page*, 862 F. Supp. 2d 1182, 1245 (D.N.M. 2012); *Lane v. Page*, 862 F. Supp. 2d 1182, 1245 (D.N.M. 2012). In making this determination, courts emphasize the necessity to negotiate in good faith and at arm's length. *See, e.g., Acevedo*, 2019 WL 6712298, at *2–4; *O'Dowd*, 2019 WL 4279123, at *13; *Wilkerson v. Martin Marietta Corp.*, 171 F.R.D. 273, 284 (D. Colo. 1997); *Tripp v. Rabin*, No. 14-cv-2646-DDC-GEB, 2016 WL 3615572, at *3 (D. Kan. July 6, 2016). For instance, courts recognize that extensive discovery taken in the case and/or briefing summary judgment or class certification prior to negotiation offer counsel knowledge of the strengths and weaknesses of their respective clients' cases and the benefits of settling the matter. *Nieberding* 129 F. Supp. 3d at 1245–46. Moreover, courts will ensure that the settlement is not a product of collusion and instead derived from "vigorous advocacy" through "well-briefed" motions by knowledgeable and experienced class counsel. *Rhodes*, 308 F.R.D. at 667. Courts also recognize that formal negotiation before a mediator or third party also facilitates fair and honest negotiations. *Nieberding*, 129 F. Supp. 3d at 1245; *Farley*, 2014 WL 5488897, at *2 (finding settlement agreement was fairly and honestly negotiated where (1) the "parties extensively litigated th[e] action, engaging in motions practice and comprehensive discovery, before commencing settlement discussions," (2) the lawyers involved were experienced, and (3) the negotiations were undertaken with the "assistance of a knowledgeable and qualified employment mediator"); *Tripp v. Rabin*, No. 14-cv-2646-DDC-GEB, 2016 WL 3615572, at *3 (D. Kan. July 6, 2016) (finding parties fairly and honestly negotiated the proposed settlement where the "parties conducted discovery, engaged in contested class certification briefing, and mediated the case").

Prong 2: Whether Serious Questions of Law and Fact Exist

In assessing the second factor—whether serious questions of law and fact exist—the existence of undecided and consequential motions, such as summary judgment motions or class certification or appeals from orders granting or denying the same, mitigate in favor of settlement because they "project meaningful doubt about the ultimate outcome of the case."

Nieberding, 129 F. Supp. 3d at 1246; *see also, e.g.*, *Lucas v. Kmart Corp.*, 234 F.R.D. 688, 694 (finding, at the preliminary approval stage, that serious questions of law and fact existed where (1) if the case were litigated, an appellate court could reverse or modify class certification, (2) there were "numerous contested factual issues," and (3) the parties disputed the implications of key case law—all of which "could have had a serious impact on the results for either side"); *Farley*, 2014 WL 5488897, at *3 (finding that serious questions of law and fact existed where there were disputes about whether the parties had entered into a contract central to Plaintiffs' claims and uncertainties about damages).

Prong 3: Whether the Value of an Immediate Recovery Outweighs the Mere Possibility of Future Relief

These same issues could play a part in assessing the fourth factor, whether the value of an immediate recovery outweighs the mere possibility of future relief. Additionally, courts will compare the potential litigation expenses moving forward in relation to the proposed settlement relief offered. For instance, the costs of appeals, discovery, expert discovery, briefing class certification or summary judgment motions, and trial all reduce the value of the class members' recovery, depending on which stage of litigation the case has reached by the time of settlement. *See Nieberding*, 129 F. Supp. 3d at 1246. Part of the analysis here also may include a court's assessment of the settlement amount per class member relative to the harm alleged, in addition to the timeliness of the proposed schedule for settlement payments. *Id.*; *Farley*, 2014 WL 5488897, at *3 (finding third prong of fairness analysis was met where the proposed "settlement provide[d] the Class Members with a certainty of approximately $1.5 [m]illion in payment [at the time of settlement], as compared with the uncertainty of whether they w[ould] receive any payment after additional litigation . . . on [the] merits").

Prong 4: Whether Parties Consider the Settlement to Be Fair and Reasonable

Finally, the settlement to be both fair and reasonable. *Tripp*, 2016 WL 3615572, at *4; *Nieberding*, 129 F. Supp. 3d at 1246. In making this determination, courts will consider whether plaintiffs are represented by experienced class counsel. *See, e.g.*, *Tripp*, 2016 WL 3615572, at *4 (finding that fourth prong of fairness analysis weighed in favor of preliminary class settlement approval where plaintiff was "represented by experienced class counsel" and believed the settlement to be fair, reasonable, and adequate). Courts also will look for any evidence of collusion or fraud that would call into question the fairness of the settlement. *Nieberding*, 129 F. Supp. 3d at 1246. And courts will examine the scope of the released claims in the context of the settlement agreement to determine for themselves whether the parties are justified in considering the settlement to be fair and reasonable. *Id.*

c. Subject Matter Jurisdiction at the Settlement Phase

Courts may engage, *sua sponte*, in an analysis of subject matter jurisdiction when determining whether the court may approve a class action settlement agreement. *See Suaverdez v. Circle K Stores, Inc.*, No. 20-cv-01035-RM-NYW, 2021 WL 1698197, at *1 (D. Colo. Apr. 29, 2021) (raising *sua sponte*, "whether [the court] ha[d] subject matter jurisdiction" over the proposed settlement); *see also Amazon, Inc. v. Dirt Camp, Inc.*, 273 F.3d 1271, 1276 (10th Cir. 2001) (reiterating the well-established principle that a "court has an independent obligation to examine its own jurisdiction" at every stage of the case). In particular, some courts will consider the question of whether the amount in controversy exceeded the CAFA jurisdictional minimum of $5 million, particularly when the settlement amount may be much less. *See, e.g.*, *Nieberding*, 129 F. Supp. 3d at 1241–43 (conducting amount-in-controversy analysis when the gross amount of the settlement was $350,000, or seven percent of CAFA's jurisdictional threshold). In these cases, counsel may want to consider the various factors already discussed that govern jurisdiction under CAFA in case explanation is needed for such an analysis, keeping in mind that courts look to the amount in controversy alleged in the original complaint without considering any reductions in the amount in controversy that may occur after the lawsuit is commenced. *Id.* (citing *St. Paul Mercury Indemn. Co. v. Red*

Cab Co., 303 U.S. 283, 289–90 (1938)).

d. Incentive Awards

An incentive award "encourage[s] individuals to undertake the frequently onerous responsibility of [serving as the] named class representative. *Nieberding*, 129 F. Supp. 3d at 1251 (alteration in original) (quoting *Hershey v. ExxonMobil Oil Corp.*, No. 07-1300-JTM, 2012 WL 5306260, at *12 (D. Kan. Oct. 26, 2012)). Before approving a proposed incentive award, courts must first "determine whether [such award is] fair and reasonable." *Cazeau v. TPUSA, Inc.*, No. 2:18-cv-00321-RJS-CMR, 2021 WL 1688540, at *7 (D. Utah, Apr. 29, 2021). In the Tenth Circuit, the appropriateness of an incentive award to a class representative is governed by three factors: "(1) the actions the class representative took to protect the interests of the class; (2) the level of benefit that the class received from the class representative's actions; and (3) the quantity of time and effort the class representative spent in pursuing the litigation." *Nieberding*, 129 F. Supp. 3d at 1251 (citing *Freebird Inc. v. Cinemax Energy, Co.*, 264 P.3d 500, 511 (2011) (citing *In re U.S. Bancorp Litig.*, 291 F.3d 1035, 1038 (8th Cir. 2002); *Cook v. Niedert*, 142 F.3d 1004, 1016 (7th Cir. 1998)); *Jerry v. Newfield Expl. Mid-Continent, Inc.*, No. 11-cv-755-GKF-PJC, 2015 WL 12743740, at *3 (N.D. Okla. July 29, 2015) (awarding a $5,000 incentive award for each of three class representatives)); *see also Ramos v. Banner Health*, No. 15-cv-2556-WJM-RNR, 2021 WL 2823079, at *9–10 (D. Colo. July 7, 2021). Courts within the Tenth Circuit are well within their discretion to deny or reduce incentive awards determined to be "excessive under the circumstances of [the] action." *See e.g., Ramos*, 2021 WL 2823079, at *10; *Elston v. Horizon Global Americas, Inc.*, No. 19-2070-KHV, 2020 WL 6318660, at *11 (D. Kan. Oct. 28, 2020) (reducing incentive award based on plaintiff's failure to "show[] any basis for an enhanced incentive award").

In September 2020, the Eleventh Circuit held that, in class action settlements, incentive awards "that compensate[] a class representative for his time and reward[] him for bringing a lawsuit" are prohibited under U.S. Supreme Court precedent. *Johnson v. NPAS Sols, LLC*, 975 F.3d 1244, 1260 (11th Cir. 2020). Though the Tenth Circuit has yet to "squarely address[] the argument presented in *Johnson*–namely, that Supreme Court precedent precludes the award of effectively all service or incentive awards in class-action cases," *Hunter v. CC Gaming, LLC*, No. 19-CV-01979-DDD-KLM, 2020 WL 13444208, at *7 (D. Colo. Dec. 16, 2020), incentive awards must nonetheless be "proportional to the contribution of the plaintiff," *McClintock v. Continuum Producer Servs., L.L.C.*, No. 6:17-cv-00259-JAG, 2020 WL 3022744, at *3 (E.D. Okla. June 4, 2020). And incentive awards also must be substantiated by adequate factual material in the record supporting the three factors. In *Chieftain Royalty Co. v. Enervest Energy Institutional Fund XIII-A, L.P.*, two objectors appealed the approval of a class settlement that, in part, provided for one-half percent ($260,000) of a common settlement fund to be allocated to the named plaintiff as an incentive award. 888 F.3d 455, 464 (10th Cir. 2017). In considering the merits of the appeal, the Tenth Circuit acknowledged that incentive awards are commonplace, with 28 percent of settled class actions including a grant of an incentive award that is, on average, .16 percent of the class recovery. *Id.* at 464 (citing Theodore Eisenberg & Geoffrey P. Miller, *Incentive Awards to Class Action Plaintiffs: An Empirical Study*, 53 UCLA L. Rev. 1303 (2006) (Empirical Study)). However, the court went on to find that two grounds were offered in support of the incentive, neither of which was supported by evidence in the record. *Id.* at 468–69.

First, the named plaintiff, a licensed attorney, argued that he was entitled to an incentive award because of the "risk or burden" he incurred as a result of the litigation. *Id.* at 464. In support of this first argument, he claimed that the litigation had impacted his ability to do business, impaired his ability to interact with oil and gas companies as well as attorneys representing them, demanded 200 to 300 hours of his time, and was likely to require another 50 to 100 hours of his time. *Id.* at 464–65. The appellate court found this proffered support insufficient, dismissing "the presentation of risk and burden" as "quite weak." *Id.* at 467.

Next, the court dismissed the named plaintiff's second argument, that the incentive award was justified to fairly compensate him for the services he rendered. *Id.* at 468–69. Applying *Erie*, the court determined that it should look to state law to determine the propriety of the incentive award on this ground, but there was no state law on point. *See id. at 468*. While the court found robust jurisprudence in other jurisdictions supportive of approving an incentive award on the basis of time and effort invested, the court emphasized that any "award should be proportional to the contribution of the plaintiff," and the "weight of authority [] disfavors percentage based awards." *Id.* (citing *Newberg on Class Actions* § 17:16 (4th ed. 2002) ("Percentage-based awards are disfavored, if not altogether forbidden."). Based on this authority, the court held that appropriate measure of incentive award should be determined by calculating "a reasonable rate for reasonable time expended on services rendered that were helpful to the litigation and did not duplicate what could be performed less expensively by counsel." *Id.* at 469. Finding insufficient facts in the record to make this calculation, the court ultimately reversed and remanded the case for further fact-finding. *Id.* at 470.

e. Attorneys' Fees

In diversity cases under CAFA, attorneys' fees are a substantive matter controlled by state law. *Nieberding v. Barrette Outdoor Living Inc.*, 129 F. Supp. 3d 1236, 1248 (D. Kan. 2015) (citing *Combs v. Shelter Mut. Ins. Co.*, 551 F.3d 991, 1001 (10th Cir. 2008)). However, when federal law governs, federal courts exercise their "general equitable powers" to determine reasonable attorneys' fees in the context of class settlement. *Oppenlander v. Standard Oil Co. (Indiana)*, 64 F.R.D. 597, 605 (D. Colo. 1974). "There is no fixed standard or guide by which [Tenth Circuit courts] determine reasonable attorney fees, but the entire litigation must be considered and evaluated to arrive at a just allowance fair to all parties." *Id.* "To date, [the Tenth Circuit has] not adopted a benchmark percentage for attorneys' fees from common fund settlements." *Voulgaris v. Array Biopharma, Inc.*, 60 F.4th 1259, 1263 (10th Cir. 2023). Instead, courts must ensure that "awards across a range of percentages [are] reasonable." *Id.* at 1263–64; *see also Charlie v. Rehoboth McKinley Christian Health Care Servs.*, No. CV 21-652 SCY/KK, 2023 WL 4591167, at *3 (D.N.M. July 18, 2023) ("Attorneys' fees must be reasonable, regardless of whether the attorneys are paid by hour or percentage," which requires that "the reasonableness of their fees should be considered with reference to the overall settlement amount."); *Fager v. CenturyLink Commc'ns, LLC*, 854 F.3d 1167, 1177 (10th Cir. 2016).

The courts' obligation to ensure attorneys' fees are reasonable extends to contingency fee agreements as well. *In re Syngenta AG MIR 162 Corn Litig.*, 61 F.4th 1126, 1225 (10th Cir. 2023). In *re Syngenta*, the Tenth Circuit affirmed the Kansas district court's conclusion that contingent fee contracts do not dictate the reasonableness of an attorneys' fees award. *Id.* Instead, because district courts have the "inherent power to review contract-fee contracts," coupled with Fed. R. Civ. P. 23(h), courts have the power to "modify the contingent-fee contracts," where necessary. *Id.* at 1185–90. Some of the factors that Tenth Circuit courts will consider in conducting this analysis include (1) "benefits conferred upon class members," (2) "results achieved," (3) "the magnitude, complexity, and uniqueness of the litigation," (4) "the court's knowledge of the nature, extent[,] and quality of services rendered by counsel," (5) the "time and effort expended by counsel in the litigation," (6) "advance fee arrangements, if any, between counsel and members of the class," (7) "public policy considerations," and (8) the "extent and basis of [any] objections to allowance of attorneys' fees." *Id.* (capitalization removed). "The trial judge may exercise its judgment in assigning different relative weights to the factors and may determine one factor is not applicable or give greater weight to one factor over another, where the bases for doing so are clearly reflected in the record." *Farley v. Family Dollar Stores, Inc.*, No. 12-cv-00325, 2014 WL 5488897, at *3–4 (D. Colo. Oct. 30, 2014) (ultimately approving a "gross [class] settlement amount of $2,300,000.00, with payments of . . . attorney's fees and costs in the amount of $698,049.32 . . . and $60,950.68 in costs"); *Bridgeview Health Care Ctr., Ltd. v. Jerryclark*, No. 09 C

5601, 2015 WL 4498741, at *3 (N.D. Ill. July 23, 2015) (attorneys' fees of $1,295,000, amounting to 35 percent of the $3,700,000 settlement proceeds, in addition to litigation expenses in the amount of $38,132.92, awarded to class counsel); *Nieberding*, 129 F. Supp. 3d at 1245 (in a settlement resulting in a $350,000 common fund, the court approved $73,899.25 to pay the claims administrator and $35,426.26 in expenses but reduced the amounts requested in fees and the incentive award from $125,829.42 and $7,000 to $118,587.24 and $3,500, respectively). And where a settlement agreement includes a "kicker" or "clear-sailing" agreements, court have "a heightened duty" to "make findings as to the defendant's total liability to the class under the settlement—i.e., the value of the settlement—and the estimated financial impact on the defendant based on the terms of the settlement and in light of then-prevailing information on the class participation rate" before approving an award of attorneys' fees. *In re Samsung Top-Load Washing Machine Mktg., Sales Prac. and Products Liab. Litig.*, 997 F.3d 1077, 1094 (10th Cir. 2021).

While attorneys' fee award calculations under these factors are largely left to the discretion of trial court, that discretion has its limits. "The 'lodestar method' is the accepted analysis for determining a reasonable fee amount for a prevailing party in federal court." *Kerner v. City & Cty. of Denver*, 733 F. App'x 934, 936 (10th Cir. 2018) (unpublished) (citing *Gisbrecht v. Barnhart*, 535 U.S. 789, 801–02 (2002)). Thus, the starting place for a federal court to calculate a reasonable fee award is multiplying the "reasonable number of hours expended on the litigation by a reasonable hourly rate. . . ." *Id.* In at least one case, the Tenth Circuit has found that district courts cannot "abdicate [their] responsibility" to completely and independently complete this calculation, meaning that the court cannot, for instance, "avoid performing its own lodestar analysis (or perform only part of the lodestar analysis) and then adopt the fee amount that the losing party left unchallenged." *Id.* at 937 ("[T]he district court abused its discretion by failing to conduct a full lodestar analysis."); *cf. In re Motor Fuel Temperature Sales Practices Litig.*, 872 F.3d 1094, 1121 (10th Cir. 2017) (holding that while the appellate court may not have "agree[d] with the decision the district court ultimately reached," it would not find that the district court abused its discretion in approving attorneys' fee award as part of class settlement where it considered the factors relevant to that exercise), *cert. denied sub nom, Speedway LLC v. Wilson*, 138 S. Ct. 1299, 200 L. Ed. 2d 502 (2018).

Though the lodestar method will generally be the analysis of choice in the Tenth Circuit, where a class settlement involves a common fund, the Tenth Circuit prefers the percentage-of-the-fund approach. *Chieftain Royalty Co.*, 888 F.3d at 458 (citing *Newberg on Class Actions* § 15:63 (5th ed. 2016)); *see also Rothe v. Battelle Memorial Inst.*, No. 1:18-cv-03179-RBJ, 2021 WL 2588873, at *7–8 (D. Colo. June 24, 2021) ("The Tenth Circuit favors the common fund approach, as opposed to the lodestar method, because a percentage of the common fund is less subjective than the lodestar plus multiplier approach, matches the marketplace most closely, and is the better suited approach when class counsel was retained on a contingent fee basis[.]" (collecting cases)); *Gottlieb v. Barry*, 43 F.3d 474, 483 (10th Cir. 1994). Notwithstanding this preference, *Erie* may demand a different result. Where state law governs the award of attorneys' fees, as is the case with "substantive attorney fees" that are "tied to the outcome of the litigation," state law will "also govern[] how to calculate the amount." *Chieftain Royalty Co.*, 888 F.3d at 461 (quotation marks omitted) (award and calculation of substantive attorneys' fees was controlled by state law in diversity case therefore state statute requiring application of the lodestar method, not the percentage-of-the-fund approach, was applied to determine reasonable fee award).

Courts within the Tenth Circuit are mindful that a "request for attorneys' fees generally should not result in a second major litigation." *Voulgaris,* 60 F.4th at 1262; *Orchestrate HR, Inc. v. Blue Cross & Blue Shield of Kansas, Inc.*, No. 19-4007-DDC, 2023 WL 6216307, at *8 (D. Kan. Sept. 25, 2023). But the courts are also cognizant that Rule 23's allowance of objectors to class action settlements, by its nature, may result in "some litigation when class counsel requests fees." *Id.* If an objection is made to a request for attorneys' fees, courts within the Tenth Circuit will review the fees request consistent with the factors laid out *supra. Voulgaris*, 60 F.4th at 1262. However, the individual challenging an award of attorneys' fees, "whether a defendant, class member, objector, or attorney," must be actually aggrieved in order to have standing to appeal. *Shields L. Grp., LLC v. Stueve Siegel Hanson LLP*, 95 F.4th 1251, 1287 (10th Cir. 2024) (noting that while class members have standing to appeal an attorneys' fees award if the class recovery and attorneys' fees are paid from a common fund, . . . they generally do not have standing to appeal an attorneys' fees award when the award comes from a separate fund," because "modifying the fee award would not actually benefit the objecting class member" (internal citations and quotations omitted)).

f. *Cy Pres*

"The *cy pres* doctrine is an equitable doctrine which "allows a court to distribute unclaimed or non-distributable portions of a class action settlement fund to the 'next best' class of beneficiaries." *Peace Officers' Annuity & Benefit Fund of Ga. V. DaVita Inc.*, No. 17-cv-0304-WJM-NRN, 2021 WL 1387110, at *6 (D. Colo. Apr. 13, 2021) (quoting *Tennille v. W. Union Co.*, 809 F.3d 555, 560 n.2 (10th Cir. 2015)); *see also In re Thornburg Mortg., Inc. Sec. Litig.*, 885 F. Supp. 2d 1097, 1105 (D.N.M. 2012). A court may not approve a *cy pres* award if it lacks jurisdiction over the dispute or if no named plaintiff has standing. *Frank v. Gaos*, 586 U.S. 485, 492–93 (2019). The Tenth Circuit does not look favorably upon the doctrine of *cy pres*. *In re Thornburg*, 885 F. Supp. 2d at 1105. As one court put it, Tenth Circuit courts generally hold that "*cy pres* awards are a bad idea and inappropriate, because they inject a third party into the litigation, do not adequately reflect the best interests of absent class members, create an appearance of impropriety, and are not the best use of the Court's time and resources." *Id.* at 1111. *Cy pres* awards are thus viewed with extreme scrutiny in the Tenth Circuit. *See id.* ("*Cy pres* moves the focus too much away from the class members' welfare, which the Court must jealously protect if the class action device is to remain a legitimate means of advancing justice. The Court can be cautious and prudent in using the class action device without touching the extreme limits of what the judiciary can do."); *In re Motor Fuel Temperature Sales Practices Litig.*, 286 F.R.D. 488, 504 (D. Kan. 2012) (denying preliminary approval of *cy pres* clause); *Lowery v. City of Albuquerque*, No. CIV-09-0457-JB-WDS, 2013 WL 1010384, at *41 n.5 (D.N.M. Feb. 27, 2013); *but see Tennille v. W. Union Co.*, 785 F.3d 422, 429 (10th Cir. 2015) (affirming class action settlement providing that "any of the settlement fund remaining after paying all the claims class members file . . . will [be] place[d] . . . in a *cy pres* fund to be distributed by the district court at its discretion"). In evaluating a settlement agreement that provides for *cy pres*, the district court must conduct an analysis of whether the provision, in the context of the overall settlement, makes it "fair, reasonable, and adequate." *Allred v. ReconTrust Co., N.A.*, 787 F. App'x 994, 996 (10th Cir. 2019) (unpublished) (citation omitted). The failure to do so is an abuse of discretion. *Id.* at 996–97 (vacating district court's unilateral decision to award cy pres funds to the United States and remanding for the purpose of evaluating the parties' agreement to pay the funds to the State of Utah).

14. ARBITRATION ISSUES

a. Arbitration and Waiver

The Tenth Circuit "has a well-established procedure for determining whether a party has waived its right to compel arbitration." *In re Cox Enter., Inc. Set-top Cable Television Box Antitrust Litig.*, 790 F.3d 1112 (10th Cir. 2015). As described in *Peterson v. Shearson/Am. Express, Inc.*, 849 F.2d 464 (10th Cir. 1988), the Tenth Circuit considers six factors to determine waiver:

> (1) whether the party's actions are inconsistent with the right to arbitrate; (2) whether the litigation machinery has been substantially invoked and the parties

> were well into preparation of a lawsuit before the party notified the opposing party of an intent to arbitrate; (3) whether a party either requested arbitration enforcement close to the trial date or delayed for a long period before seeking a stay; (4) whether a defendant seeking arbitration filed a counterclaim without asking for a stay of the proceedings; (5) whether important intervening steps [e.g., taking advantage of judicial discovery procedures not available in arbitration] had taken place; and (6) whether the delay affected, misled, or prejudiced the opposing party.

Id. at 467–68 (alteration in original) (internal quotation marks omitted) (quoting *Reid Burton Constr. Inc. v. Carpenters Dist. Council of S. Colorado*, 614 F. 2d 698, 702 (10th Cir. 1980)). The *Cox* court determined that a defendant failing to bring up the presence of arbitration agreements until after certification was inconsistent with an intent to arbitrate and resulted in waiver of the ability to assert arbitration. 790 F.3d at 1120–21. And the Tenth Circuit has held that issues "concerning the formation of an arbitration contract cannot be delegated to an arbitrator," and "must always be decided by a court, regardless of whether the alleged agreement contained a delegation clause or whether one of the parties specifically challenged such a clause." *Fedor v. United Healthcare*, 976 F.3d 1100, 1105–06 (10th Cir. 2020) (citing *Rent-A-Center, West, Inc. v. Jackson*, 561 U.S. 63, 72 (2010); *Granite Rock Co. v. Int'l Brotherhood of Teamsters*, 561 U.S. 287, 297 (2010)).

b. Arbitration and Collective Bargaining Agreements

In the context of arbitration provisions contained in collective bargaining agreements (CBA) (union context), the Tenth Circuit enforced arbitration of a class claim where the arbitration provision in the applicable CBA did not distinguish between class and individual disputes, concluding that the arbitration agreement covered all claims except those specifically excluded in the arbitration provision terms. *Soc'y of Prof'l Eng'g Employees in Aerospace v. Spirit Aerosystems, Inc.*, 541 F. App'x 817, 820 (10th Cir. 2013) (unpublished).

c. Clarity of Agreement to Arbitrate

Under Tenth Circuit law, it is important that arbitration provisions be clear and consistent, particularly if multiple arbitration agreements between parties apply. *Ragab v. Howard*, 841 F.3d 1134, 1138 (10th Cir. 2016) (concluding that conflicting details in multiple arbitration agreements agreed to by parties indicated that there was no meeting of the minds with respect to arbitration, and, as a result, motion to compel arbitration was properly denied); *see also Cavlovic v. J.C. Penney Corp.*, 884 F.3d 1051, 1058 (10th Cir. 2018) (affirming district court's order ruling that J.C. Penney could not invoke an arbitration clause in a contract because the agreement did "not evidence a clear intent to provide J.C. Penney—a third party—with the right to demand arbitration. . . ."). The Supreme Court has held that a court may not compel arbitration on a classwide basis when an agreement is "silent" or "ambiguous" as to the availability of such arbitration. *Lamps Plus, Inc. v. Varela*, 139 S. Ct. 1407, 1415 (2019).

d. Arbitration Agreements with Class/Collective Action Waiver

The Supreme Court has held that class and collective action waiver provisions are enforceable in the context of workplace agreements. *Epic Sys. Corp. v. Lewis*, 584 U.S. 497 (2018). In *Epic*, an employer and employee entered into a contract providing they would arbitrate any disputes between them. *Id.* at 497–98. Nonetheless, after the employee was terminated, he sought to litigate FLSA claims against his former employer through a federal class action. *Id.* at 503–04. Plaintiff argued the Federal Arbitration Act's "saving clause" invalidated the class action waiver provision because it allegedly violated the National Labor Relations Act. *Id.* The Supreme Court disagreed. It held that while the savings clause invalidated arbitration agreements extracted by fraud, duress, or unconscionability—i.e., contract related defenses—it did not apply to defenses relating "only to arbitration or that derive their meaning from the fact that an agreement to arbitrate is at issue." *Id.* at 508. Therefore, because plaintiff only raised arbitration related defenses, not contract related defenses, the class action waiver provision was not invalidated by the saving clause. *Id.* at 508–09.

Courts in the Tenth Circuit have previously ruled along similar lines. *See Pollard v. ETS PC, Inc.*, 186 F. Supp. 3d 1166 (D. Colo. 2016) (granting motion to compel individual arbitration where class action arbitration waiver existed in arbitration agreement); *Bell v. Ryan Transp. Serv., Inc.*, 176 F. Supp. 3d 1251 (D. Kan. 2016) (same); *Dish Network L.L.C. v. Ray*, 900 F.3d 1240, 1252 (10th Cir. 2018) (rejecting argument that where an arbitration agreement is silent on the matter, it lacks the requisite consent for class or collective arbitration, and instead affirming lower court's ruling that the "arbitrator . . . did not manifestly disregard Colorado law when he concluded that he was authorized to conduct class arbitration by the broad language of the Agreement [at issue] in combination with the requirement that arbitration be conducted pursuant to the AAA's Employment Dispute Rules"). However, the Tenth Circuit takes a critical eye to class action waivers and has cautioned courts against upholding class action waivers carte blanche. Recently the Tenth Circuit affirmed a trial court's decision to strike down a remedies limitation provision, which included a class action waiver, concluding that because the provision prevented the plaintiff "from effectively vindicating his statutory remedies" available under ERISA, the arbitration provision violated "effective vindication exception" or prospect-waiver doctrine. *Harrison v. Envision Mgmt. Hold., Inc.*, 59 F.4th 1090 (10th Cir. 2023). The court's ruling in *Harrison* reflected its reluctance to reduce parties' substantive rights in arbitration, a reluctance mirrored across the country. *See id; see also Stanton v. Cash Advance Centers, Inc.*, No. 21-CV-00285-SRB, 2022 WL 715491 (W.D. Mo. 2022), *appeal dismissed*, 59 F.4th 932 (8th Cir. 2023); *Orozco v. Gruma Corp.*, 2021 WL 4847014 (E.D. Cal. 2021), *appeal dismissed*, 2022 WL 17081065 (9th Cir. 2022).

15. APPEALABILITY OF CLASS CERTIFICATION

Beyond interlocutory appeals under 28 U.S.C. § 1292(b) and Rule 23(f) petitions, *see supra* Part 8, Plaintiffs seeking to appeal the denial of class certification must "litigate 'their individual claims on the merits to final judgment,' and then appeal the order denying class certification under 28 U.S.C. § 1291." *Anderson Living Tr. v. WPX Energy Prod., LLC*, 904 F.3d 1135, 1139 (10th Cir. 2018). "Final judgment" is only obtained where the litigations ends "on the merits and leaves nothing for the court to do but execute the judgment." *Id.* (internal quotation marks and citation omitted). Known as the "finality principle," this doctrine aims to prevent "piecemeal, pre-judgment appeals" that undermine judicial efficiency. *Id.* (named plaintiffs voluntarily dismissed their claims after entering into individual settlement agreements and then attempted to appeal class certification denial, arguing that the order on class certification and the stipulated judgment "merged" to form a final, appealable order, but Tenth Circuit ruled it lacked jurisdiction because no final judgment had issued); *Medina v. Allen*, No. 23-4057, 2024 WL 1006791, at *3 (10th Cir. Mar. 8, 2024) (finding that where certification was denied and named plaintiffs claims became moot, district and appellate courts were deprived of jurisdiction to rule on the merits of the claims of the unnamed, uncertified class members).

ELEVENTH CIRCUIT

Districts of Alabama, Florida, and Georgia

Elbert P. Tuttle Courthouse
56 Forsyth Street, N.W.
Atlanta, GA 30303

By Kenneth S. Byrd and Betsy Sugar, Lieff Cabraser Heimann & Bernstein, LLP,
and Beau D. Hollowell, Frantz Ward LLP

1. INTRODUCTION

Based in Atlanta, with satellite offices in Miami, Jacksonville, and Montgomery, the Eleventh Circuit's jurisdiction includes the nine federal district courts in Alabama, Florida, and Georgia, and seats 12 active and nine senior judges. The Honorable Judge Nancy G. Abudu was appointed in May 2023. The nine districts were originally part of the Fifth Circuit, but became the Eleventh Circuit in 1981. Fifth Circuit decisions before that "split" remain part of Eleventh Circuit jurisprudence. As of September 2021, there is one vacant seat.

As of September 30, 2024, more than 164,000 federal cases are pending within the districts in the Eleventh Circuit, amounting to about one-third of all cases pending in the entire federal judiciary (*see* www.uscourts.gov/data-news/data-tables/2024/09/30/judicial-business/c-1, last checked Feb. 13, 2025). This large share was due to the nearly 300,000 cases previously pending in the Northern District of Florida where the largest-ever (in terms of cases filed) MDL sits with District Judge Casey Rodgers, *In re: 3M Combat Arms Earplug Product Liability Litigation*, MDL No. 2885. These numbers have dropped this year by roughly 140,000 terminated cases after Judge Rodgers landed the plane on a $6 billion global settlement to resolve the MDL in 2023.

In late 2023, the Eleventh Circuit fully interpreted the 2018 amendment to Rule 23(e)(2) regarding class settlements in conjunction with its own prior *Bennett* settlement factors. *Ponzio v. Pinon*, 87 F.4th 487 (11th Cir. 2023); *see Bennett v. Behring Corp.*, 737 F.2d. 982, 986 (11th Cir. 1984). In *Ponzio*, the Court held that the 2018 amendment is not meant "to displace" the *Bennett* factors previously identified by the Eleventh Circuit in reviewing class action settlement agreements, but rather to focus the court and the lawyers on the four core concerns of procedure and substance that should guide the decision whether to approve the proposal. *Ponzio*, 87 F.4th at 494–95 (citing Fed. R. 23(e)(2)). Rule 23(e)(2) provides the primary considerations, but the Eleventh Circuit Court held that the *Bennett* factors "can, where appropriate, complement those core concerns." *Id.* at 595.

As to class actions, the Eleventh Circuit continues to tackle matters of standing. The Court itself may have put it best: "In opinion after opinion, one standing issue continues to arise—what it takes to show concrete harm." *Hunstein v. Preferred Collection & Mgmt. Servs.*, 48 F.4th 1236, 1239 (11th Cir. 2022) (en banc). And the U.S. "Supreme Court has since ratified our approach." *Id.* That requires discussion of *TransUnion*. In *TransUnion*, the Supreme Court considered the standing of a certified class that sued a credit reporting agency under the Fair Credit Reporting Act. *TransUnion LLC v. Ramirez*, 141 S. Ct. 2190 (2021). The credit agency improperly identified the class members as potential terrorists in their credit reports, but a subset of the class stipulated that their reports had not been disseminated to anyone. The Court determined that those class members who so stipulated had not suffered a "concrete injury" and therefore lacked Article III standing. *Id.* However, the Court stressed that "certain harms readily qualify as concrete injuries," the "most obvious" being "traditional tangible harms, such as physical harms and monetary harms." *Id.* at 2204 (emphasis added).

In 2023, the Eleventh Circuit provided further clarification of *TransUnion* and *Cordoba*. In *Drazen v. Pinto*, the full Eleventh Circuit held that a single unwanted text is enough to confer Article III standing to assert a claim under the Telephone Consumer Protection Act. *Drazen v. Pinto*, 74 F.4th 1336, 1343 (11th Cir. 2023) (confirming test for whether statutory harm constitutes injury in fact is whether "'harm has a close relationship to a harm that has traditionally been regarded as providing a basis for a lawsuit in English or American courts'") (citation omitted).

As to its posture toward class actions, the Eleventh Circuit is rigorous in its review. For example, the Eleventh Circuit's decision in *Johnson v. NPAS Sols., LLC*, continues to reverberate around the class action community when it denied a service award to the named plaintiff although such awards are "'fairly typical in class actions.'" 975 F.3d 1244, 1259 (11th Cir. Sept. 17, 2020). It noted: "Although it's true that such awards are commonplace in modern class-action litigation, that doesn't make them lawful, and it doesn't free us to ignore Supreme Court precedent forbidding them." *Id.* at *28. The appellate court applied to two U.S. Supreme Court decisions to support its position. *Id.* at 1255 (citing *Trustees v. Greenough*, 105 U.S. 527 (1882), *Central Railroad & Banking Co. v. Pettus*, 113 U.S. 116 (1885)).

The Eleventh Circuit is also careful when considering grants of class-action certifications as well. For example, in 2009, the Court inquired whether a category of employees admitted by defendants to number "'in the thousands'" nationwide still may not be numerous enough to create a Florida class of 40. *Vega v. T-Mobile USA, Inc.*, 564 F.3d 1256, 1267 (11th Cir. 2009). At other times, the appellate court has challenged plaintiffs over the adequacy of representation prong, such as in a 2003 decision that vacated and remanded a Southern District of Florida ruling because of potential disparate economic outcomes among the class representatives and unnamed class members. *Valley Drug Co. v. Geneva Pharm., Inc.*, 350 F.3d 1181, 1189–94 (11th Cir. 2003) ("A fundamental conflict exists where some party members claim to have been harmed by the same conduct that benefitted other members of the class."); *cf. In re Equifax*, 999 F.3d at 1275–76 (affirming certification of settlement class under abuse of discretion standard when all class member "claims arise out of the same unifying event" even if some class members have statutory claims with various values). In September 2021, the court ruled that individual questions defeated class certification in a case brought by police officers related to allegedly defective straps on their bulletproof vests. *Ohio State Troopers Ass'n v. Point Blank Enters.*, No. 20-13588, 2021 U.S. App. LEXIS 29112 (11th Cir. Sept. 27, 2021) (inquiry into use of the vests and whether each person actually experienced the vest is needed).

The Eleventh Circuit also has issued rulings favorable to class certification. For instance, in 2009's *Williams v. Mohawk Indus., Inc.*, it reversed a Northern District of Georgia decision denying class certification, agreeing with the proposed employee class that "their injury is subject to common proof because every employee was damaged by the illegal hiring by Mohawk, irrespective of an employee's job description or location." 568 F.3d 1350, 1359 (11th Cir. 2009). In 2016, the Eleventh Circuit affirmed certification of a class of motor-vehicle purchasers against a manufacturer for consumer fraud claims as common issues related to false safety ratings information on their vehicles' window stickers predominated over individual ones. *Carriuolo v. Gen. Motors Co.*, 823 F.3d 977 (11th Cir. 2016).

The Eleventh Circuit's analysis of U.S. Supreme Court decisions did not find any major sea shift in existing class-action jurisprudence. For example, in 2016, the Eleventh Circuit sided with plaintiffs in holding that "Comcast did not alter the black-letter rule that individual damages do not always defeat predominance." *Brown v. Electrolux Home Prods., Inc.*, 817 F.3d 1225, 1238–39 (11th Cir. 2016). Its trial court has noted that *Electrolux* can be "a significant legal hurdle" for class plaintiffs. *Montoya v. PNC Bank, N.A.*, No. 14-20474-CIV-Goodman, 2016 U.S. Dist. LEXIS 50315, *37 (S.D. Fla. April 13, 2016).

The Eleventh Circuit also has considered the Supreme Court's *Spokeo* decision in a couple cases; in a 2016 decision, it found a plaintiff had standing against a defendant who sent a disclosure that failed to meet a federal statute. *Church v. Accretive Health, Inc.*, 654 F. App'x 990 (11th Cir. 2016). The Eleventh Circuit noted that *Spokeo* concentrated not on whether the injury was particularized, but rather whether it was concrete. A few months later, the Eleventh Circuit considered whether a plaintiff had standing against a bank that failed to comply with a state statute requiring it to record the satisfaction of mortgages. *Nicklaw v. CitiMortgage, Inc.*, 839 F.3d 998 (11th Cir. 2016). The Eleventh Circuit ruled that the plaintiff did not suffer a concrete injury, even if the defendant violated the statute, because his complaint lacked allegations, for example, that he lost money or that his credit suffered. *Id.* at 1003. Per *Spokeo*, the appellate court recognized that a plaintiff has standing for "intangible injuries," but the injury "must actually exist." *Id.* at 1002.

But in a 2020 decision, a dissenting opinion from the Eleventh Circuit noted that "[s]ome district courts in our circuit eventually came to the opposing conclusion [than *Church*] regarding Article III standing and violations of the FACTA[,]" and that "[t]he same is true of the cases from our sister circuits...." *Muransky v. Godiva Chocolatier, Inc.*, 979 F.3d 917, 961 (11th Cir. 2020) (J. Jordan, dissenting) (citations omitted). The majority, however, held that that a consumer's receipt "violated the law because it contained too many digits, [plaintiff] has alleged no concrete harm or material risk of harm stemming from the violation." *Id.* at 936. From there, the court dismissed the case "[b]ecause this amounts to nothing more than a 'bare procedural violation, divorced from any concrete harm'...." *Id.* Thus, [t]his Court has rejected the assertion that the allegation of a statutory violation alone is sufficient to confer standing." *Banks v. Sec'y of HHS*, No. 21-11454, 2021 U.S. App. LEXIS 22086, *6 (11th Cir. July 26, 2021) (citing *Muransky*, at 924).

Like other circuits, the Eleventh Circuit reviews a district court's grant of class certification for an abuse of discretion. However, in the Eleventh Circuit, an abuse of discretion is a "continuum," and "in the context of class actions, review for abuse of discretion often 'does not differ greatly from review for error.'" *Electrolux*, 817 F.3d at 1233. And it cautioned in *Klay v. Humana, Inc.*, "[W]ith great power comes great responsibility; the awesome power of a district court [to certify a class action] must be exercised within the framework of rule 23." 382 F.3d 1241, 1251 (11th Cir. 2004).

2. JURISDICTIONAL PREREQUISITES

a. CAFA Requirements

Congress enacted the Class Action Fairness Act (CAFA) in 2005, granting federal courts jurisdiction over class actions in which the amount in controversy exceeds $5 million and there is minimal diversity (at least one plaintiff and one defendant are from different states). 28 U.S.C. § 1332(d); *Evans v. Walter Indus. Inc.*, 449 F.3d 1159 (11th Cir. 2006); *see also Kress Stores of P.R., Inc. v. Wal-Mart P.R., Inc.*, 2024 U.S. App. LEXIS 28656, at *23 n.6, *29 (1st Cir. Nov. 12, 2024) (citing *Evans* favorably for its comparative test. In addition, CAFA's "mass action" provisions extend federal diversity jurisdiction to certain actions brought individually by large groups of plaintiffs. 28 U.S.C. § 1332(d)(11); *Lowery v. Ala. Power Co.*, 483 F.3d 1184, 1198 (11th Cir. 2007). A "mass action" is deemed to be a "class action" for purposes of CAFA and federal jurisdiction if (1) the action proposes "monetary relief claims of 100 or more persons" and (2) the "plaintiffs' claims involve common questions of law or fact." *Lowery* at 1202. As an aside, The Eleventh Circuit in *Lowery* noted that, unlike the class action provisions of CAFA, the mass action provision appears to be limited to only suits seeking monetary relief and thus jurisdiction would not extend to cases seeking solely equitable relief. *Id.* at 1202 n.45.

Combining CAFA's "mass action" and "class action" provisions, the Eleventh Circuit in *Lowery* set forth the following requirements for a federal court to obtain original or removal jurisdiction over a "mass action." "These requirements are (1) an amount-in-controversy requirement of aggregate of $5 million in claims, (2) a diversity requirement of minimal diversity, (3) a numerosity requirement that the action involve monetary claims of 100 or more plaintiffs, and (4) a commonality requirement that plaintiffs' claims involve common questions of law or fact." *Pretka v. Kolter City Plaza II, Inc.*, 608 F.3d 744, 751 (11th Cir. 2010); *Lowery* at 1202–03; *Hamilton v. Crete Carrier Corp.*, 2024 U.S. Dist. LEXIS 153313, at *5 n.4 (M.D. Fla. Aug. 27, 2024) ("indeed, with limited exception, CAFA's removal provision expressly adopts the procedures of the general removal statute, 28 U.S.C. § 1446") (citing *Pretka* at 756–57, 757 n.11).

CAFA does not require that any individual plaintiff's claim exceed $75,000. *Cappuccitti v. DirecTV, Inc.*, 623 F.3d 1118, 1122 (11th Cir. 2010); *see Bland v. Urology of Greater Atlanta, LLC*, 2024 U.S. Dist. LEXIS 118794, at *8 (N.D. Ga. Mar. 14, 2024) (citing *Cappuccitti* at 1123 n.8. If the jurisdictional amount necessary for federal question jurisdiction under CAFA is stated clearly on the face of the documents before the court or is readily deducible from them, then the court has jurisdiction. *Id.* at 1123, n.8 (citing *Lowery*, 483 F.3d at 1211); *Fox v. Ritz-Carlton Hotel Co., LLC*, 977 F.3d 1039, 1045 (11th Cir. 2020) (citing *Cappuccitti* at 1122 n.8); *Hung Cavalieri v. Avior Airlines C.A.*, 25 F.4th 843, 850 (11th Cir. 2002) (finding "[i]t is for a later stage in the litigation for the district court to make the factual determination on whether there is indeed jurisdiction in this case") (citing *Cappuccitti* at 1122 n.8); *Killick v. Harbor Freight Tools USA Inc.*, 2022 U.S. Dist. LEXIS 171523, at *8 (N.D. Fla. Aug. 23, 2022) ("courts also may consider cover sheets attached to a complaint or filed in conjunction with a complaint") (citing *Cappuccitti* at 1122 n.8)). In *Cappuccitti*, the district court had subject matter jurisdiction over a class of satellite television subscribers as an original action, although the plaintiffs did not allege an amount in controversy over $75,000 for any class member, but the putative class exceeded 100 persons, and the amount in controversy, in the aggregate, exceeded $5 million, exclusive of interest and costs. *Cappuccitti* at 1122–23.

In 2019, the Eleventh Circuit reiterated that the "pertinent question is what is in controversy in the case, not how much the plaintiffs are ultimately likely to recover as a result of the lawsuit." *Anderson v. Wilco Life Ins. Co.*, 943 F.3d 917, 925 (11th Cir. 2019) (quoting *Pretka*, 608 F.3d at 751). In 2020, the Eleventh Circuit ruled that a district court erred when it ruled it lacked subject matter jurisdiction over two counts because it could not determine whether the $5 million threshold was met in a case alleging 49 restaurants improperly charged automatic gratuity and sales tax to over hundreds of thousands of customers. *Fox v. Ritz-Carlton Hotel Co.*, 977 F.3d 1039 (11th Cir. 2020). To overturn the Southern District of Florida, the Eleventh Circuit stated: "Even though class members may have overpaid only some percentage of the total bill each time they ate at the hotel's Florida restaurants, added up over hundreds of thousands of customers across four years at ten Ritz-Carlton hotels and forty-nine restaurants, we do not need to suspend reality to conclude that the overpayment was more than $5 million." *Id.* at *6.

Under CAFA, the defendant carries the burden of proof to establish jurisdiction in removal actions. *Pretka*, 608 F.3d at 752. Where the plaintiff has not pled a specific amount of damages, a removing defendant must prove by a preponderance of the evidence that the amount in controversy exceeds the jurisdictional requirement. If the jurisdictional amount is not facially apparent from the complaint, the court should look to the notice of removal and may require evidence relevant to the amount in controversy—focusing on the amount in controversy at the time the case was removed. *Id.* at 751–56 (finding a developer defendant met its burden of proving the amount in controversy exceeded $5 million through declarations); *Otoh v. Fannie Mae*, No. 22-13279, 2023 U.S. App. LEXIS 18341, at *3 (11th Cir. July 19, 2023) ("the removing defendant may direct the court to additional evidence beyond the complaint") (citing *Pretka*, 608 F.3d at 751). Notably, in *Miedema v. Maytag Corp.*, 450 F.3d 1322 (11th Cir. 2006), the Eleventh Circuit upheld a district court's decision to remand a case because, even after supporting affidavits, the amount in controversy was uncertain. *Miedema* at 1332. The *Miedema* opinion noted that CAFA is silent on whether a district court should resolve doubts in favor of finding jurisdiction. *Id.* at 1328. "The rule of construing removal statutes strictly and resolving doubts in favor of remand, however, is well-established." *Id.* In 2023's *Otoh* decision, the Eleventh Circuit affirmed that the amount in controversy exceeded $75,000 based on documents showing the total value of the property and the remaining principal on the loan at issue. *Otoh*, 2023 U.S. App. LEXIS 18341, at *4.

CAFA does have an exception to federal jurisdiction for cases that are truly local in nature. 28 U.S.C. § 1332(d)(4)(A). The "local controversy exception" is a "narrow one, with all doubts resolved 'in favor of exercising jurisdiction over the case.'" *Evans v. Walter Indus. Inc.*, 449 F.3d 1159, 1163 (11th Cir. 2006) (citing S. Rep. No. 109-14 at 42, *U.S. Code Cong. & Admin. News* 3, 40). The plaintiff bears the burden of proof of establishing they fall within the exception. *Id.* at 1163. In *Evans*, plaintiffs (property owners, lessees, licensees of properties on which numerous defendants deposited waste substances over 85-year period) failed to meet their burden of showing whether (1) more than two-thirds of the class members were Alabama citizens and (2) at least one defendant from whom "significant relief" is sought and whose conduct forms a "significant basis" for the claims asserted is a citizen where the action was originally filed. The plaintiffs, the Eleventh Circuit concluded, were unable to provide a credible estimate of the percentage of Alabama class members, nor did they provide "any enlightenment" with respect to the significance of the relief sought against one Alabama defendant or its comparative significance relative to the relief sought from the other 17 named co-defendants. *Id.* at 1166–68; *but see Toll v. Fla. Power & Light Co.*, 701 F. Supp. 3d 1286, 1296 (S.D. Fla. Nov. 12, 2023) ("Eleventh Circuit cautions district courts to resolve all doubts in favor of exercising federal jurisdiction over class actions, the Court declines to invoke the local controversy exception here.") (citing *Evans*, 449 F.3d at 1163).

In 2020, the Eleventh Circuit overruled a lower court decision to dismiss a case for failing to reach the required amount under CAFA. *Fox v. Ritz-Carlton Hotel Co., L.L.C.*, 977 F.3d 1039, 1048 (11th Cir. 2020). It instructed (1) "[t]he district court can make common-sense inferences about the jurisdictional amount from the fact of the complaint, but it cannot speculate or hypothesize about facts that are not in the record[;]" *Id.* (citing *Pretka*, 608 F.3d at 752, 770); (2) "the amount-in-controversy inquiry [is not] a discussion on 'how much the plaintiffs are ultimately likely to recover,' which is not the proper jurisdictional measure under the Class Action Fairness Act." *Id.* (citing *Anderson*, 943 F.3d at 925).

In a March 2020 decision, the Eleventh Circuit interpreted CAFA's use of "an event or occurrence," which the statute leaves undefined. *Spencer v. Specialty Foundry Prods.*, 953 F.3d 735, 740 (11th Cir. 2020). It held "that the local-event exception applies to a singular harm-causing moment in time as well as contextually connected series of incidents that culminates in that harm-causing event or occurrence." *Id.* at 743. Further, "a large number of defendants acted separately to generate the alleged harm is not dispositive of the local-event exception." *Id.* (citing *Adams v. Int'l Paper Co.*, No. 1:17-cv-105, 2017 U.S. Dist. Lexis 71693, 2017 WL 1828908, *7 (S.D. Ala. May 5, 2017)). But it found that plaintiff's failure to allege a single culminating event without a showing that the defendants' conduct "came together to create one event or occurrence" did not satisfy the local-event exception. *Id.* at 743–44; *but see Adams v. Adient United States LLC*, 2021 U.S. Dist. LEXIS 252083, at *41 (W.D. Tenn. Sept. 30, 2021) (finding that local event or occurrence exclusion does not apply).

b. Standing

Who May Bring a Class Action

The Eleventh Circuit "review[s] standing determinations de novo." *Calderon v. U.S. Bank Nat'l Ass'n*, 860 F. App'x 686, 687 n. 1 (11th Cir. 2021) (citing *A&M Gerber Chiropractic LLC v. Geico Gen. Ins. Co.*, 925 F.3d 1205, 1210 (11th Cir. 2019)).

The Eleventh Circuit "start[s] from the basic principle that at the class certification stage only the named plaintiffs need have standing." *Green-Cooper v. Brinker Int'l, Inc.*, 73 F.4th 883, 888 (11th Cir. 2023) (citing *Cordoba v. DirectTV, LLC*, 942 F.3d 1259, 1264 (11th Cir. 2019)). In 2019, the Eleventh Circuit determined that not every class member must have standing: the "plaintiff need not prove that every member of the proposed class has Article III standing prior to certification, and in some cases a court might reasonably certify a class that includes putative members who might not have satisfied the requirements of *Lujan* and decide to deal with the problem later on in the proceeding, but before it awarded any relief." *Cordoba v. DirectTV, LLC*, 942 F.3d 1259, 1277 (11th Cir. 2019).

In June 2021, the U.S. Supreme Court passed on deciding "the distinct question whether every class member must demonstrate standing before a court certifies a class." *TransUnion LLC v. Ramirez* (2021), 141 S. Ct. 2190, 2208 n.4 (emphasis in original) (citing *Cordoba*, at 1277). In July 2022, the Eleventh Circuit provided further clarification of *TransUnion* and *Cordoba*. *Drazen v. Pinto*, 41 F.4th 1354, 1361 (11th Cir. 2022), *reh'g en banc granted, opinion vacated,* 61 F.4th 1297 (11th Cir. March 13, 2023). Simply, "*TransUnion* has affirmed the reasoning of *Cordoba*." *Id.* When considering standing for certification purposes, *Cordoba* and *TransUnion* "merge[] … to lead us to the following conclusion: when a class seeks certification for the sole purpose of a damages settlement under Rule 23(e), the class definition must be limited to those individuals who have Article III standing. If every plaintiff within the class definition in the class action in *TransUnion* had to have Article III standing to recover damages after trial, logically so too must be the case with a court-approved class-action settlement." *Id.* Thus, "*TransUnion* says that we can't award damages to plaintiffs who do not have Article III standing." *Id.* at 1362.

The *Drazen* decision answered that unnamed plaintiffs with no standing in the Eleventh cannot be part of a nationwide class even though they might have standing in another circuit. *Id.* at 1361. "We cannot, therefore, check our Article III requirements at the door of the class action. Any class definition that includes members who would never have standing under our precedent is a class definition that cannot stand." *Id.* at 1362 (vacating and remanding class certification and its settlement to redefine the class). Without individual standing to raise a legal claim, a named representative does not have the requisite typicality to raise the same claim on behalf of class. *Prado-Steiman ex rel. Prado v. Bush*, 221 F.3d 1266, 1279 (11th Cir. 2000). "It is well-settled that 'if none of the named plaintiffs purporting to represent a class establishes the requisite of a case or controversy with the defendants, none may seek relief on behalf of himself or any other member of the class.'" *A&M Gerber*, at 1211 (citing *O'Shea v. Littleton*, 414 U.S. 488, 494 (1974) (other citations omitted)). Thus, the "class representative must have individual standing to raise class claims." *Id.* at 1211 (citing *Prado-Steiman*, at 1279–80).

To establish standing under Article III, plaintiff must show that he or she has suffered an injury-in-fact, must demonstrate a causal connection between asserted injury-in-fact and challenged action of the defendant, and must show that the injury will be redressed by a favorable decision. *Shotz v. Cates*, 256 F.3d 1077, 1081 (11th Cir. 2001); *Kennedy v. Floridian Hotel, Inc.*, 998 F.3d 1221, 1229 (11th Cir. 2021) (same) (quoting *Shotz*, at 1081). A party has standing to seek injunctive relief only if the party alleges a real and immediate—as opposed to a merely conjectural or hypothetical—threat of future injury. *Id.*

In 2016, the Supreme Court in *Spokeo, Inc. v. Robins*, 136 S. Ct. 1540, 1545, 1548 (2016), elaborated on injury-in-fact, affirming that a plaintiff must show he or she suffered an "invasion of a legally protected interest" that is "concrete and particularized" and "actual or imminent, not conjectural or hypothetical." *Spokeo* at 1548. Soon after the Supreme Court's decision, the Eleventh Circuit considered the Supreme Court's *Spokeo* decision in *Church*, 654 F. App'x at

993. In *Church*, the Eleventh Circuit found that *Spokeo* concentrated not on whether the injury was particularized but rather whether it was concrete. *Id.* (citing *Spokeo* at 1550). In the case, the plaintiff alleged that defendant sent her a letter that failed to comply with a federal statute. The appellate court held that plaintiff suffered a concrete injury "because she did not receive the allegedly required disclosures," an invasion of her rights "that Congress has elevated to the status of a legally cognizable injury" through the statute. *Id.* at 995. In July 2023, however, the Eleventh Circuit vacated *Church* as inconsistent with *TransUnion*. *Davis v. Pro. Parking Mgmt. Corp.*, No. 22-14026, 2023 WL 4542690, at *3 (11th Cir. July 14, 2023). The court ultimately concluded that a plaintiff establishes an injury-in-fact by merely asserting a statutory right. *Id.*

In May 2017, the Eleventh Circuit considered *Nicklaw v. CitiMortgage, Inc.*, 839 F.3d 998 (11th Cir. 2016), rehearing en banc denied, 855 F.3d 1265 (May 1, 2017). The plaintiff alleged that the defendant bank failed to comply with a state statute requiring the bank to record the satisfaction of mortgages. Per *Spokeo*, the appellate court recognized that a plaintiff has standing for "intangible injuries," but the injury "must actually exist." *Id.* at 1002 (stating "a plaintiff who alleges a violation of a statutory right to receive information alleges a concrete injury.") (quoting *Spokeo*, at 1540). But the appellate court found that the plaintiff did not suffer a concrete injury, even if the defendant violated the statute. *Id.* at 1002. His complaint lacked allegations, for example, that he lost money or that his credit suffered. *Id.* at 1003.

In January 2018, the Eleventh Circuit found that the plaintiffs did not allege a concrete and particularized interest related to a local school board's alleged policy. *Baxter v. VSC LLC*, No. 8:17-cv-1718-T-17TGW, 2018 U.S. Dist. LEXIS 41650, *13 (M.D. Fla. March 13, 2018) (citing *L.M.P. on behalf of E.P. v. School Bd. of Broward Cty., Fla.*, 879 F.3d 1274 (11th Cir. 2018)). But a few months later, the Middle District of Florida found that "if the plaintiff in that TCPA case suffered a concrete injury because his fax line was occupied while an unsolicited fax was being sent, then the plaintiffs here suffered a concrete injury when the use and enjoyment of their phones were interrupted by the unwanted calls." *Id.* at *14. In 2019, the Eleventh Circuit found that a plaintiff had standing when he suffered a heightened risk of identity theft when retailer printed more digits of his credit card than the law allows. *Muransky v. Godiva Chocolatier, Inc.*, 922 F.3d 1175 (11th Cir. 2019).

The Eleventh Circuit addressed standing in a section 1983 case after public high school students brought an action against the Birmingham police and board of education for excessive force for permitting student resource officer' use of incapacitating chemical spray on students. *See J W v. Birmingham Bd. Of Educ.*, 904 F.3d 1248 (11th Cir. 2018). The students had been sprayed or exposed to spray in their vicinity at various times over a three-year period. Among other claims, the students sought class claims on behalf of current and future students for injunctive relief to prevent the use of spray and to enforce training on the conduct. *See id.* at 1265–73. The Court said the student would have to show a sufficient likelihood (a "real and immediate threat") that the spray would be used on the student (known as "K.B.") in an unconstitutional way—not merely a way that would be permitted under the Fourth Amendment. *See id.* at 1267. The Court noted that the Supreme Court has stated whether a suit is a class action "adds nothing to the question of standing, for even named plaintiffs who represent a class must allege and show that they personally have been injured." *Id.* at 1272 (quoting *Spokeo* at 1547 n.6). The Court refused standing for the class claims saying the student was required to show a real and immediate threat as opposed to a threat of "future" injury. *See id.*

In *Cordoba v. DirectTV, LLC*, the Eleventh Circuit determined that consumers who did not request to be placed on provider's do-not-call list lacked the standing to maintain a Telephone Consumer Protection Act claim related to the regulations governing the do-not-call list. 942 F.3d 1259, 1268–72 (11th Cir. 2019). While the court found that consumers who did request to be on the no-call list had standing, it found that absent class members who had not requested placement on the list would not have an injury that would be "fairly traceable to challenged action of the Defendant." *Id.* at 1271–72. "There's no remotely plausible causal chain linking the failure to maintain an internal do-not-call list to the phone calls received by class members who *never* said to [the provider] they didn't want to be called again." *Id.* at 1272 (emphasis in original).

In *Fox v. Ritz-Carlton Hotel Co., L.L.C.*, a customer at three of the many Ritz-Carlton Hotels in Florida sued the hotel for charging him an automatic gratuity made illegal by Florida statute. 977 F.3d 1039 (11th Cir. 2020). Although only a patron at three of the hotel's restaurants, he sued on behalf of a class of customers who paid the gratuity at the hotel's 49 other Florida restaurants during a four-year period. *Id.* at *14. He argued that the injuries were identical because the Ritz-Carlton employed the same practices at each of its restaurants during that time. *Id.* The Eleventh Circuit warned not to "conflate the requirements of individual standing with those for a class representative." *Id.* Although the plaintiff could not sue individual claims at the restaurants he did not frequent, the appellate court reminded that "class representative standing does not necessarily require that the class representative suffer injury at the same place and on the same day as the class members." *Id.* (citing *Mills*, 511 F.3d at 1307). It held that he had standing as a class representative because he and the class members "have the same interest and suffer the 'same injury.'" *Id.* (citing *Prado*, 221 F.3d at 1279); *see also Kurimski v. Shell Oil Co.*, No. 21-80727-CV, 2021 U.S. Dist. LEXIS 215967, *12 (S.D. Fla. Nov. 5, 2021) (finding "[p]ayment of an allegedly unauthorized premium constitutes an economic injury" where plaintiff was charged an unknown fee for using her debit card for gasoline) (citing *Fox*); *but see In re Zantac (Ranitidine) Prods. Liab. Litig.*, No. 2924 20-MD-2924, 2020 U.S. Dist. LEXIS 245338, *59 (S.D. Fla. Dec. 31, 2020) (distinguishing *Fox* as *Zantac*'s nationwide class with 183 named plaintiffs under law of all 50 states "markedly different" than Fox's "one named plaintiff suing one defendant under one state's law.") (citing *Fox*, at 1047).

In 2020, the Eleventh Circuit considered standing under its precedent and *Spokeo* in two FDCPA cases. In the first case, the appellate court found no concrete injury-in-fact for the plaintiffs' theory that the collection letters posed a risk to them of making a payment or potentially exposing a consumer to a lawsuit. *Trichell v. Midland Credit Mgmt.*, 964 F.3d 990, 1002 (11th Cir. 2020). The court also explored rulings from the Sixth and Second Circuits that did find sufficient harm (in disagreement with the Eleventh), but found "the approach of the Seventh and D.C. Circuits is more faithful to Article III"—and the Eleventh's rulings. *Id.* at 1002. (In 2021, the U.S. Supreme Court quoted the Eleventh Circuit favorably: "As Judge Katsas has rightly stated, 'we cannot treat an injury as 'concrete' for Article III purposes based only on Congress's say-so.'" *TransUnion LLC v. Ramirez* (2021), 141 S.Ct. 2190, 2205 (quoting *Trichell*, at 999 n.2).

In *Cooper v. Atl. Credit & Fin., Inc.*, the court found no *Spokeo* injury-in-fact for the plaintiff's "confusion about her statutory rights resulting in her not disputing the debt, that her confusion would have resulted in her utilizing one of the payment options in the second letter despite the debt being invalid, that her confusion would have resurrected any previously invalid debt, or that the confusion would have resulted in any other negative consequences." 822 F. App'x 951, 955 (11th Cir. 2020). It stated that *Cooper*'s theory "is much more attenuated than" the plaintiffs' injuries in *Trichell*: "*Cooper* does not allege any particularized injury; she simply does not say she was affected in any meaningful way by the letter." *Id.* (citations omitted).

In 2021, the Eleventh Circuit considered another injury-in-fact case, *In re Equifax Customer Data Sec. Breach Litig.*, 999 F.3d 1247, 1257 (11th Cir. 2021). In this data breach case, an objector argued that the plaintiffs lacked Article III standing because the plaintiffs may not have had their identifies stolen, and therefore could not suffer an injury-in-fact or have their injuries redressed by the settlement. *Id.* at 1261. The appellate court rejected those arguments. It reaffirmed its earlier decisions that "[e]conomic injuries are 'certainly concrete" and so is identify theft and wasted time, because when facing "a sufficient risk of harm, the time, money, and effort spent mitigating that risk are also concrete injuries." *Id.* at 1262 (internal citations). Without an actual injury, the injury must be imminent, meaning "certainly impending." *Id.* (citing *Clapper v. Amnesty Int'l USA*, 568 U.S. 398 (2013)). That doesn't require "literally pending that the injury will come about, but there must be a substantial risk. *Id.* (citing *Clapper*, at 414 n.5). With hackers obtaining names, dates of birth, Social Security numbers, addresses, driver's license numbers, credit card numbers, and tax identification numbers, there was a plausible injury-in-fact because the thieves could create fake identities to fraudulently obtain loans and tax refunds as well as destroy a person's credit score. *Id.* at 1262. This was "material" and "substantial." *Id.* Although no theft was actually necessary, the case was bolstered by the fact that several plaintiffs did have their identidies stolen and suffered various injuries. *Id.* at 1262–63. With this, it ruled that "[p]laintiffs have easily shown an injury-in-fact." *Id.* at 1263.

In 2021, the appellate court explained that a plaintiff can establish a concrete injury for Article III standing when his personal information is subject to a data breach and he experiences "misuse" of his data in some way. *Tsao v. Captiva MVP Rest. Partners, LLC*, 986 F.3d 1332, 1333–34 (11th Cir. 2021) (discussing that evidence of a data breach is not enough without allegations of "substantial risk" of future identity theft or that identity theft was "certainly impending") (citing *Clapper*, 568 U.S. at 409).

In a 2022 en banc decision, the Eleventh Circuit "reiterated the Supreme Court's guidance from *Spokeo, Inc. v. Robins* that one way to evaluate such alleged statutory harms was by comparing them to traditional common-law claims." *Hunstein v. Preferred Collection & Mgmt. Servs.*, 48 F.4th 1236, 1240–41 (11th Cir. 2022) (en banc) (citing *Muransky v. Godiva Chocolatier*, Inc., 979 F.3d 917, 926 (11th Cir. 2020) (citing *Spokeo*, 578 U.S. at 340—41)). In this case, the plaintiff "experienced a nearly inevitable frustration of modern American life—an expensive medical bill." *Id.* at 1240. When the plaintiff failed to pay the bill, the hospital turned the debt over to a collection service that, in turn, hired a mail vendor to send information to the plaintiff to collect the debt. The plaintiff claimed that the debt collection service violated the Fair Debt Collection Practices Act when it provided the mail vendor with his information. A panel found that his injury was concrete, even if it was neither tangible nor a "risk of real harm," since it was akin to an invasion-of-privacy tort, such as public disclosure of private facts. *Id.* at 1241. But then *TransUnion* was decided, and that decision was vacated for a new one: reaching the same result. *Id.* That led to the en banc decision in 2022, which considering standing "in light of *Spokeo*, *Muransky*, and *TransUnion*." *Id.*

That en banc decision found no standing, remanding with instructions to dismiss the case without prejudice, because there was no concrete harm but rather only a statutory violation: "'an injury in law is not an injury in fact.'" *Id.* at 1242 (citing *TransUnion*, 141 S.Ct. at 2205). It reiterated that "the Supreme Court has cautioned that Congress 'may not simply enact an injury into existence, using its lawmaking power to transform something that is not remotely harmful into something that is.'" *Id.* at 1243 (quoting *TransUnion*, at 2205). But it did so with respect "between appropriately respecting congressional judgment and properly maintaining the boundaries of Article III jurisdiction ...." *Id.* With support from the Supreme Court, it notes that when a statutory violation has harm with a close relationship to harm traditionally regarded in the common law, that "generally causes harm concrete enough to support standing." *Id.* (citing *TransUnion*, at 2204). The fit "need not be perfect" *Id.* at 1244, but there must be "commonalities between the harms." *Id.* (citing *Muransky*, at 926). Several Supreme Court cases support the court's decision, including *TransUnion*, *Thole v. U.S. Bank N.A.*, and other "[c]ases since *Spokeo*" as well as the Eleventh Circuit's *Muransky*. *Id.* at 1244–45.

For the case itself, the court found that although "congressional intent does not automatically transform every arguable invasion of privacy into an actionable, concrete injury[,]" it found that the plaintiff "has alleged only a legal infraction—a 'bare procedural violation'—and not a concrete harm, we lack jurisdiction to consider his claim." *Id.* at 1248. Although no appellate court has yet to cite to the September 2022 *Hunstein* decision, district courts in the Third, Fourth, Seventh, and Eleventh already have.

In April 2023, the Eleventh Circuit considered a proposed settlement class regarding "brain performance supplements" allegedly marketed with false and misleading statements. *Williams v. Reckitt Benckiser LLC*, 65 F.4th 1243, 1247 (11th Cir. 2023). The court vacated and remanded a certification of a settlement class, noting that the named plaintiffs failed to establish an actual or imminent injury because none of the plaintiffs had concrete plans to purchase the supplements again. *Id.* at 1255. The court concluded that the named plaintiffs failed to establish "any 'continuing, present adverse effects' associated with prior purchases." *Id.* (quoting *Lujan v. Defs. of Wildlife*, 504 U.S. 555, 564 (1992).

In July 2023, the court found that allegations in a data breach case that one's personal information was "exposed for theft and sale on the dark web" was "critical." *Green-Cooper*, 73 F.4th at 889–90. It distinguished *Tsao* when there were allegations that the information was posted for sale, establishing "a present injury—credit-card data and personal information floating around on the dark web—and a substantial risk of future injury—future misuse of personal information associated with the hacked credit card." *Id.* at 890 ("hold[ing] that this is a concrete injury that is sufficient to establish Article III standing").

In July 2023, the Eleventh Circuit found that a person who receives a single unwanted, illegal text suffers a concrete injury. *Drazen*, 74 F.4th 1336 (11th Cir. 2023). In 2024, the Middle District of Florida considered the *Drazen* case in the context of a phone call to the plaintiff. *Simpson v. J.G. Wentworth Co.*, 2024 U.S. Dist. LEXIS 11395 (M.D. Fla. Jan. 23, 2024). It offered that because of *Drazen*, "the simple receipt of an unwanted phone call causes a concrete injury." *Id.* at *8 (citing *Drazen*, at 1346). And it noted that the TCPA accomplished the same for unwanted telemarketing texts and phone calls. *Id.* (citing *Drazen*, at 1345).

In February 2024, the Eleventh Circuit considered a proposed class settlement against a sunglasses manufacturer for allegedly deceptive warranty and repair policies. *Smith v. Morelli*, 93 F.4th 1206, 1208 (11th Cir. 2024). The court vacated the district court's settlement approval, concluding that "none of the named plaintiffs alleged any threat of future injury, let alone that the threat was real and immediate" given that none of the named plaintiffs had broken sunglasses in need of repair under the defendant's warranty policy. *Id.* at 1212. The court further explained that "a district court abuses its discretion in approving a class action settlement when the named plaintiffs lack Article III standing to pursue injunctive relief, yet the district court considers the injunctive relief when determining whether the settlement is fair, reasonable, and adequate." *Id.* at 1212–13 (citing *Williams*, 65 F.4th at 1253–57).

The Eleventh Circuit has developed a string of benefit-of-the-bargain cases too. *See Doss v. General Mills, Inc.*, 816 Fed App'x 312, 314 (11th Cir. 2020). It recognizes that "[a] person experiences an economic injury when, as a result of a deceptive act or an unfair practice, she is deprived of the benefit of her bargain." *Id.* (citing *Carriuolo*, 823 F.3d at 986–87) (class members suffered benefit-of-bargain injury when purchasing a car represented to have safety ratings it did not have). Under this theory, the defective product still retains some value, so the "'benefit-of-the-bargain damages are less than the entire purchase price of the product.'" *Id.* (quoting *Debernardis v. IQ Formulations, LLC*, 942 F.3d 1076, 1084 (11th Cir. 2019)). The exception to that is "when the 'product is rendered valueless as a result of a defect.'" *Id.* (quoting *Debernardis*, at 1084). In that scenario, the "damages will be equal to the entire purchase price of the product." *Debernardis*, at 1084 (citing *Rollins, Inc. v. Heller*, 454 So. 2d 580, 585 (Fla. Dist. Ct. App. 1984)). In *Doss*, the Eleventh Circuit affirmed dismissal because the plaintiff failed to show that the defect was so harmful that it made the product "presumptively unsafe and therefore worthless." *Doss*, at 314; *see Deluna v. Am. Journey (PET), LLC*, No. 21-60483-CIV-SINGHALF/Valle, 2021 U.S. Dist. LEXIS 210618 (S.D. Fla. Oct. 29, 2021) (dismissing mislabeled dog food case) (citing *Doss*, at 314); *see Sabater v. Am. Journey (PET), LLC*, No. 21-60409-CIV, 2021 U.S. Dist. LEXIS 209489 (S.D. Fla. Oct. 29, 2021) (same) (citing *Doss*, at 314); *see Malgeri v. Vitamins Because LLC*, No. 19-22702-CIV-Williams, 2022 U.S. Dist. LEXIS 200228 (S.D. Fla. Sept. 30, 2022) (dismissing case because named plaintiffs were not physically harmed by defendant's vitamins or tested the product) (citing *Doss*); *but see Carder v. Graco Children's Prods.*, No. 220-CV-00137-LMM, 2021 U.S. Dist. LEXIS 165492 (N.D. Ga. Aug. 31, 2021) (distinguishing *Doss* because *Doss* plaintiff had not purchased the product but its plaintiffs had purchased the subject booster seat product) (citing *Doss*, at 313–14). Several cases cite to *Yachera v. Westminster Pharmaceuticals, LLC* to "address how a plaintiff may establish injury in fact when all subject products are defective." *Malgeri*, at *23 (citing *Yachera*, 447 F. Supp. 3d 1251 (M.D. Fla. 2020)).

Absent Class Member Standing

In *In re Checking Account Overdraft Litig.*, the Eleventh Circuit addressed the issue in the context of a defendant seeking to force arbitration against putative class members. 780 F.3d 1031 (11th Cir. 2015). In that case, plaintiffs alleged excessive overdraft fees on credit card transactions and moved for class certification. After lengthy discovery and proceedings, Wells Fargo sought to dismiss absent class members in favor of enforcing arbitration provisions based on a Supreme Court opinion issued during the case. *Id.* at 1036. Defendant argued that if the class was certified, the bank would be estopped to assert its contractual rights to arbitration. The district court ruled that defendant waived its right to compel arbitration against the named plaintiffs, noting that if it certified the class, the class would be fixed with a definition and this would resolve the arbitration issue, if any, of class members at that time.

The Eleventh Circuit concluded that the named plaintiffs lacked Article III standing to seek affirmance of the district court's provisional holding that if a class was certified, Wells Fargo would be estopped from asserting its rights to arbitration. The court found that absent class certification, there is no justiciable controversy between Wells Fargo and the unnamed putative class members. *Id.* at 1037. "In the absence of both live claims and cognizable plaintiffs, the District Court's pronouncement purporting to definitively foreclose the arbitration of the hypothetical claims that might be raised in the future by hypothetical plaintiffs cannot be regarded as anything but an impermissible 'advisory opinion . . .'" *Id.*

The Eleventh Circuit noted that third-party standing could potentially be found if the party asserting the right had a close relationship with the person who actually possesses the right and if the possessor of the right is somehow hindered in his or her own ability to protect his or her own interests. *Id.* at 1038–39 (citing *Kowalski v. Tesmer*, 543 U.S. 125, 129–30 (2004)). However, even assuming the named plaintiffs had a sufficiently close relationship with the unnamed putative class members to assert rights on their behalf, the named plaintiffs had not explained how unnamed putative class members would be hindered in their ability to assert their own rights. More fundamentally, the court noted, the named plaintiffs had no cognizable stake in outcome of question as they had already received favorable ruling as to whether bank waived its rights to compel arbitration against them. *Id.* at 1039.

In 2018, the *Wells Fargo* case found its way back to the Eleventh Circuit and the Court determined that Wells Fargo could compel arbitration against the absent class members after the case was certified. *See Gutierrez v. Wells Fargo Bank, NA*, 889 F.3d 1230 (2018) (further discussion in Arbitration section below).

The Eleventh Circuit's district courts have considered whether named plaintiffs in a consumer class action have standing to pursue claims against non-purchased products if the products are sufficiently similar and part of the same product line. In *Garcia v. Kashi Co.*, 43 F. Supp. 3d 1359 (S.D. Fla. 2014), the district court restricted the products at issue in the class, relying in part on *Prado-Steiman*, 221 F.3d 1266, 1279–80. It held that named plaintiffs lacked standing to challenge a non-purchased product because there is no injury-in-fact as to that product, even if plaintiffs had purchased substantially similar products. *See Garcia*, at 1392–93.

In a FLSA case, *Mickles v. Country Club, Inc.*, 887 F.3d 1270 (11th Cir. 2018), the Eleventh Circuit considered an issue of first impression. *Zuliani v. Santa Ana, LLC*, No. 17-62080-CIV-MORENO-SELTZER, 2018 U.S. Dist. LEXIS 89209, *2–3 (S.D. Fla. May 25, 2018) (citing *Mickles*). It found that opt-in plaintiffs became parties to the case when they filed a written consent to become a party plaintiff and could then appeal the court's dismissal with prejudice of their claims. *Id.* at 1280; *see also Zuliani*, at *3–4 (citing *Mickles*). Further, it found that the opt-in plaintiffs could then "go forward with [their] individual cases since discovery has been completed[, and . . . were] entitled to statutory tolling of their claims beginning on the dates they filed their written consents." *Id.* at 1281.

c. Mootness Doctrine

In *Campbell-Ewald Co. v. Gomez*, the Supreme Court held that a defendant cannot moot a plaintiff's individual claim—or that of the entire class—by making a formal offer of judgment under Fed. R. Civ. P. 68 if the plaintiff does not accept the offer. 136 S. Ct. 663 (2016). This decision is in accord with a 2014 case from the Eleventh Circuit, *Stein v. Buccaneers Ltd. P'ship*, 772 F.3d 698 (11th Cir. 2014). In *Stein*, recipients of unsolicited faxes sought damages on behalf of a putative class under the Telephone Consumer Protection Act. Defendant issued an offer of judgment shortly after removing the case to federal court, offering to pay the named plaintiffs in full. The *Stein* court distinguished decades-old cases and held that the offer of full relief to named plaintiffs did not moot the putative class action, although the offer preceded any class-certification motion, so long as the named plaintiffs diligently pursued class certification. *Stein*, 772 F.3d at 707. To act diligently, a named plaintiff need not file a class-certification motion with the complaint or prematurely, the court held. "It is enough that the named plaintiff diligently takes any necessary discovery, complies with any applicable local rules and scheduling orders, and acts without undue delay," the *Stein* court ruled. *Id.* Thus, the *Stein* decision "expanded Zeidman's mootness exception to include cases in which the named plaintiff is picked off before he's even moved for class certification." *Sos v. State Farm Mut. Auto. Inc., Co.*, No. 21–11769, 2023 U.S. App. LEXIS 22986, at *36–37 (11th Cir. Aug. 30, 2023) (citing *Stein*).

3. PLEADING CONSIDERATIONS

Counsel should consult the district court's local rules for pleading requirements in a proposed class action. *See, e.g.*, Local Civil Rule 23.1 Class Actions, of the U.S. District Court for the Southern District of Florida.

4. PREREQUISITES

The initial burden of proof to establish the propriety of class certification rests with the advocate of the class. *Rutstein v. Avis Rent-A-Car Sys., Inc.*, 211 F.3d 1228, 1233 (11th Cir. 2000). All else being equal, the presumption is against class certification, because the party seeking class certification has the burden of proof. *See Electrolux*, 817 F.3d 1225, 1233. A plaintiff seeking to represent a proposed class must establish that the proposed class is "adequately defined and clearly ascertainable." *Little v. T-Mobile USA, Inc.*, 691 F.3d 1302, 1304 (11th Cir. 2012). If a district court determines this requirement has been met, then it moves on to examining Rule 23(a). A class action may be maintained only when it satisfies all the requirements of Fed. R. Civ. P. 23(a) and at least one of the alternative requirements of Rule 23(b). *Carriuolo*, 823 F.3d 977, 984. The district court must conduct a "rigorous analysis" to determine whether the movant carries the burden, which frequently entails overlap with the merits of the plaintiff's underlying claims. *Electrolux*, at 1234 (citing *Comcast Corp. v. Behrend*, 133 S. Ct. 1426, 1432 (2013) (*quoting Wal-Mart Stores, Inc. v. Dukes*, 131 S. Ct. 2541, 2551 (2011))). The district court can consider the merits only to the extent they are relevant to determining whether Rule 23's prerequisites are satisfied. But if a question of fact or law is relevant to that determination, then the district court has a duty to decide it and not accept it as true or construe it in anyone's favor. *Electrolux*, at 1234 (citing *Comcast*, at 1432–33).

The Eleventh Circuit reviews a district court's grant of class certification for an abuse of discretion. However, the Court has noted that abuse of discretion is a "continuum" and "in the context of class actions, review for abuse of discretion often 'does not differ greatly from review for error.'" *Electrolux*, 817 F.3d 1225, 1233 (citing *Abrams v. Interco Inc.*, 719 F.2d 23, 28 (2d Cir. 1983) (Friendly, J.)). The Court has stated: "[W]ith great power comes great responsibility; the awesome power of a district court [to certify a class action] must be 'exercised within the framework of rule 23.'" *Id.* at 1233 (citing *Klay*, 382 F.3d 1241, 1251). Regardless of the parties' positions on each element, the district court has an independent obligation to conduct its own rigorous analysis as to whether each of the prerequisites of Rule 23 have been satisfied before certifying a class. *See Valley Drug*, 350 F.3d 1181, 1184.

a. Rule 23(a) Requirements

Numerosity

Rule 23(a)(1) requires that the class be "so numerous that joinder of all members is impracticable." Rule 23(a)(1) Fed. R. Civ. P. Although a plaintiff is not required to establish the exact number of class members, "mere speculation and unsubstantiated allegations" as to numerosity are insufficient to satisfy Rule 23. *See Vega*, 564 F.3d 1256, 1266–67 (finding district court abused its discretion by finding the numerosity requirement satisfied when it assumed T-Mobile sales associates numbers in the state of Florida to be "an exercise in sheer speculation."); *see also Grimes v. Rave Motion Pictures Birmingham, LLC*, 264 F.R.D. 659, 668 (N.D. Ala. 2010).

There is no bright-line number of plaintiffs to satisfy the numerosity requirement, but "generally less than twenty-one is inadequate, more than forty adequate, with numbers between varying according to other factors." *Cox v. Am. Cast Iron Pipe Co.*, 784 F.2d 1546, 1553 (11th Cir. 1986). Other factors the court looks to include analyzing the size of the class, the ease of identifying its numbers and determining their addresses, the facility of making service on them if joined, and their geographic dispersion. *See Kilgo v. Bowman Transp., Inc.*, 789 F.2d 859, 878 (11th Cir. 1986); *Mills v. Foremost Ins. Co.*, 269 F.R.D. 663, 670 (M.D. Fla. 2010).

Commonality

Commonality pertains to the class's characteristics as a whole, whereas typicality pertains to the individual characteristics of the named plaintiff in relation to the class. *Piazza v. Ebsco Indus., Inc.*, 273 F.3d 1341, 1346 (11th Cir. 2001). To meet Rule 23(a)(2)'s commonality requirement, the moving party must demonstrate that the issues are susceptible to classwide proof. *Mohawk*, 568 F.3d 1350, 1355. There must be a common contention—"its truth or falsity will resolve an issue that is central to the validity of each one of the claims in one stroke." *Carriuolo*, 823 F.3d 977, 984 (quoting *Wal-Mart*, 131 S. Ct. 2541, 2551); *see also Sos*, 2023 U.S. App. Lexis 22986, at *53 (citing *Carriuolo*, 823 F.3d at 988). Rule 23 does not require that all questions of law and fact be common. "'[E]ven a single [common] *question*' will do." *Wal-Mart*, 131 S. Ct. at 2556; *Sos*, 2023 U.S. LEXIS 22986, at *52 (quoting *Wal-Mart*).

In January 2018, the Eleventh Circuit reversed a district court's decision denying class certification in a consumer case. *Venerus v. Avis Budget Car Rental, LLC*, 723 F. App'x 807 (11th Cir. 2018). The district court held that the class was not held together by a common question because each customer's contract included a voucher with a rental receipt that provided different rate codes, coverages, and additions depending on the options each customer selected. *Id.* at 815. The appellate court found that "[w]hile form contracts are ideal for class treatment," they are not necessary. *Id.* Rather, class certification is appropriate as long as "[t]he material terms at issue are the same—the renters were promised something they did not receive, which is apparent from the uniform part of the contract." *Id.* at 816.

Typicality

Though the issues of commonality and typicality require separate inquiries, the proof required for each tends to merge. A class may be certified only if "the claims or defenses of the representative parties are typical of the claims or defenses of the class." Fed. R. Civ. P. 23(a)(3). The claim of a class representative is typical if "the claims or defenses of the class and the class representative arise from the same event or pattern or practice and are based on the same legal theory." *Mohawk*, 568 F.3d at 1357 (quoting *Kornberg v. Carnival Cruise*

Lines, Inc., 741 F.2d 1332, 1337 (11th Cir. 1984). "A class representative must possess the same interest and suffer the same injury as the class members in order to be typical under Rule 23(a)(3)." *Id.* (quoting *Murray v. Auslander*, 244 F.3d 807, 811 (11th Cir. 2001)). When there is a strong similarity of legal theories, the typicality requirement can be satisfied even if there are substantial factual differences. *Id.* at 1356.

Adequacy

The final requirement of Rule 23 is referred to as the "adequacy-of-representation" requirement, and it requires the representative party in a class action to protect fairly and adequately the interests of those he or she purports to represent. This determination encompasses two separate inquiries: (1) whether any substantial conflicts of interest exist between the representatives of the class and (2) whether the representative will prosecute the action adequately. *Valley Drug*, 350 F.3d 1181, 1189. If substantial conflicts of interest exist among a class, class certification is inappropriate. *Id.* (remanding for further proceedings and calling into question whether this prerequisite was met where some class members claim to have been harmed by the same conduct that benefited other members of the class); *see also Pickett v. Iowa Beef Processors*, 209 F.3d 1276 (11th Cir. 2000) (reversing class certification decision by district court where the class definition included cattle producers who claimed to have been harmed by contracts and marketing agreements that some unnamed class members benefited from). However, the existence of "minor" conflicts alone will not defeat class certification. *Valley Drug*, 350 F.3d at 1189. To thwart certification, the conflict must be a "fundamental" one going to the specific issues in controversy. *Id.* In 2023, the Eleventh Circuit followed this line of reasoning when it looked at an objection to a class settlement based on adequacy, where the same named plaintiffs and class counsel represented the injunctive class and the damages class. *In re Blue Cross Blue Shield Antitrust Litig., MDL 2406*, 85 F. 4th 1070, 1091 (11th Cir. 2024). The court found that its precedents "do not categorically prohibit the same plaintiffs and counsel from representing an injunctive relief and a damages class."

b. Rule 23(b) Requirements

A class action may be maintained only when it satisfies all the requirements of Fed. R. Civ. P. 23(a) and at least one of the alternative requirements of Rule 23(b). *Carriuolo*, 823 F.3d 977, 984.

Rule 23(b)(1)(A) and (b)(1)(B) Classes

Rule 23(b)(1) class certification is permitted when separate actions by individual class members would create a risk of either (A) inconsistent or varying adjudication with respect to individual class members that would establish incompatible standards of conduct for the party opposing the class or (B) adjudications with respect to individual class members that, as a practical matter, would be dispositive of the interests of the other members not parties to the individual adjudications or would substantially impair or impede their ability to protect their interests.

The Eleventh Circuit holds that because the risk that judicial action will create incompatible standards of conduct is low when a party seeks compensatory damages, only actions seeking declaratory or injunctive relief can be certified under Rule 23(b)(1)(A). *See Babineau v. Fed. Express Corp.*, 576 F.3d 1183, 1195 (11th Cir. 2009) (holding that certification of a class seeking injunctive relief stopping defendant from accepting labor from hour employees without pay when "the primary remedy sought in this case is unquestionably monetary relief for past failure to compensate employees") (citing *Cohen v. Office Depot, Inc.*, 204 F.3d 1069, 1078 fn. 7 (11th Cir. 2000) (holding that Rule 23(b)(1)(A) certification was improper when plaintiffs requested both compensatory damages and injunctive relief)). For example, the Southern District of Alabama certified a plaintiff class of persons who wished to obtain same-sex marriage licenses against a defendant class of Alabama probate judges in Alabama under Rule 23(b)(1). *Strawser v. Strange*, 307 F.R.D. 604 (S.D. Ala. 2015). The district court found that plaintiffs "do not seek compensatory damages and it is clear that the prosecution of separate actions by individuals would create a risk of inconsistent and varying adjudications." *Id.* at 614.

As to Rule 23(b)(1)(B), it is settled that the possibility that an action will have either precedential or *stare decisis* effect on later cases is not sufficient to satisfy the rule. *See Cohen*, 204 F.3d at 1078 n.7 (citing *In re Dennis Greenman Sec. Litig.*, 829 F.2d 1539, 1545 (11th Cir. 1987)). The traditional and most common use of class action certification under this rule is a "limited fund" case where claims are aggregated against a res or preexisting fund that is insufficient to satisfy all claims. *See Greenman*, 829 F.2d at 1546 (refusing certification under Rule 23(b)(1)(B) because the district court did not indicate the receivership fund it sought to certify initially was intended to be the sole source of recovery for plaintiffs).

In *Juris v. Inamed Corp.*, 685 F.3d 1294 (11th Cir. 2012), the Eleventh Circuit addressed a challenge from absent class members to an agreed limited fund certification of settlement under Rule 23(b)(1)(B) for defective breast implant claims. The absent class member attempted to undo the settlement's preclusive effect on her claims, arguing, in part, that the certification under Rule 23(b)(1)(B) was improper. The Eleventh Circuit duly noted the Supreme Court's decision in *Ortiz v. Fibreboard Corp.*, 527 U.S. 815 (1999) (overturning a certification under Rule 23(b)(1)(B) of a limited fund that purported to settle asbestos-related claims)[1] and elaborated on the three "'common characteristics' consistent with the 'historical limited fund model.'" *Juris*, 685 F.3d at 1334. The first and most distinctive characteristic, under *Ortiz*, "is that the totals of the aggregated liquidated claims and the fund available for satisfying them, set definitively at their maximums, demonstrate the inadequacy of the fund to pay all the claims." *Id.* (quoting *Ortiz* at 838). The second historical characteristic is that "the whole of the inadequate fund was to be devoted to the overwhelming claims." *Id.* (quoting Ortiz at 839). The third characteristic is that "the claimants identified by a common theory of recovery were treated equitably among themselves." *Id.* These characteristics should be treated as "presumptively necessary, and not merely sufficient," to justify certification of a Rule 23(b)(1)(B) limited fund class. *Id.* (quoting *Ortiz* at 842).

In *Juris*, however, the Eleventh Circuit said the absent class member could not belatedly challenge the certification. *Juris* at 1340–41 ("The issue is not whether we would on direct appeal vacate certification under the strict Rule 23 guidelines later announced in *Ortiz* or whether Rule 23(b)(1)(B) should be used to settle aggregated tort claims in a post-*Ortiz* world."). The Eleventh Circuit observed that the *Ortiz* decision "ultimately leaves open the question of whether—even if the three essential premises are supported—a mandatory, limited fund class settlement can ever be used to resolve tort claims." *Id.* at 1334.

Rule 23(b)(2) Classes

Rule 23(b)(2) provides that a class can be certified for purposes of seeking injunctive or declaratory relief if "'the party opposing the class has acted or refused to act on grounds that apply generally to the class, so that final injunctive relief or corresponding declaratory relief is appropriate respecting the class as a whole.' 'The key to the (b)(2) class is the indivisible nature of the injunctive or declaratory remedy warranted.'" *Lakeland Reg'l Med. Ctr. v. Astellas US LLC*, 763 F.3d 1280, 1291 (11th Cir. 2014) (quoting *Wal-Mart*, 131 S. Ct. 2541, 2557). Thus, "Rule 23(b)(2) applies only when a single injunction or declaratory judgment would provide relief to each member of the class." *Id.*

Monetary damages are "legal relief that can only be awarded in a Rule 23(b)(2) class action when the damages sought are incidental to the claims for equitable and declaratory relief." *Mohawk*, 568 F.3d 1350, 1359 (citing *Cooper v. S. Co.*, 390 F.3d 695, 720 (11th Cir.

---

[1] The Supreme Court's decision in *Ortiz* came roughly six months after the district court judge in the underlying MDL had completed the certification of the class fund under Rule 23(b)(1)(B).

2004)). In *Mohawk*, employees alleged that their employer violated RICO by hiring illegal aliens, thereby depressing wages in violation of Georgia's racketeering statutes. The district court denied class certification, finding commonality and typicality were not satisfied. Thus, the district court also denied the injunctive relief the employees sought under a state law claim as to a "hybrid class" under Rule 23(b)(2) and Rule 23(c)(4), which permits certification "with respect to particular issues." *See* Fed. R. Civ. P. 23(c)(4). The Eleventh Circuit has explained that a "hybrid class action" may be certified in some cases:

> It is possible to create hybrids in given cases. Since in theory there should be no hard requirement that (b)(2) be mutually exclusive, and since subpart (c)(4)(A) allows an action to be maintained 'with respect to particular issues,' the fact that damages are sought as well as an injunction or declaratory relief should not be fatal to a request for a (b)(2) suit, as long as the resulting hybrid case can be fairly and effectively managed.

Mohawk, at 1360 (citing *Holmes v. Cont'l Can Co.*, 706 F.2d 1144, 1158 n.10 (11th Cir. 1983) (quoting 3B J. Moore, *Moore's Federal Practice* ¶ 23.40[4], at 23–308 (2d ed.1981))).

In *Mohawk*, the Eleventh Circuit disagreed with the district court's Rule 23(b)(3) analysis and its commonality and typicality analysis: "the flawed analysis of commonality by the district court infected its consideration of a hybrid class action." *Id.* The Eleventh Circuit remanded the case and stated that if the district court determines that common issues predominate and certifies a class for damages under subsection (b)(3), the district court must consider whether to certify a class under subsection (b)(2) with respect to the employees' claim for equitable relief. *Id.*

When certifying a class of persons who wished to obtain same-sex marriage licenses, the Southern District of Alabama stated for its Rule 23(b)(2) analysis that defendant's alleged conduct of failure to issue marriage licenses "is directed against a specific class of people, same-sex couples, and is uniform in its application." *Strawser*, 307 F.R.D. at 614. The court found that all plaintiff class members "have been harmed by being denied the ability of obtaining a marriage license and their injury can be properly addressed by class-wide injunctive relief. Thus, the case falls squarely within the ambit of Rule 23(b)(2)." *Id.*

Rule 23(b)(3) Classes

The Eleventh Circuit has observed that Rule 23(b)(3) "requires findings *both* (1) 'that the questions of law or fact common to class members predominate over any questions affecting only individual members,' and (2) 'that a class action is superior to other available methods for fairly and efficiently adjudicating the controversy.'" *Vega v. T-Mobile USA, Inc.*, 564 F.3d 1256, 1277 (11th Cir. 2009) (emphasis in original); *Equifax*, 999 F.3d at 1274–75 (citing *Vega*, at 1265); *Baker v. State Farm Mut. Auto. Ins.*, No. 21-14197, 2022 U.S. App. LEXIS 22978, *5 (11th Cir. 2022) (citing *Vega*, at 1265). Rule 23(b)(3) "sets forth four specific (though non-exclusive) considerations pertinent to these findings:

> (A) the class members' interest in individually controlling the prosecution or defense of separate actions;
> (B) the extent and nature of any litigation concerning the controversy already begun by or against class members;
> (C) the desirability or undesirability of concentrating the litigation of the claims in the particular forum; and
> (D) the likely difficulties in managing a class action.

Id. at 1277 (quoting Fed. R. Civ. P. 23(b)(3)).

The predominance requirement in Rule 23(b)(3) is far more demanding than the commonality requirement of Rule 23(a) and "tests whether proposed classes are sufficiently cohesive to warrant adjudication by representation." *Carriuolo*, 823 F.3d at 985 (11th Cir. 2016). The Eleventh Circuit has adopted the following "rule of thumb" in determining whether common questions predominate over the individual ones:

> [I]f common issues truly predominate over individualized issues in a lawsuit, then the addition or subtraction of any of the plaintiffs to or from the class [should not] have a substantial effect on the substance or quantity of evidence offered. . . . If, on the other hand, the addition of more plaintiffs leaves the quantum of evidence introduced by the plaintiffs as a whole relatively undisturbed, then common issues are likely to predominate.

Electrolux, 817 F.3d at 1235 (citing *Vega*, 546 F.3d at 1270 (quoting *Klay*, 382 F.3d at 1255)).

The Eleventh Circuit has added that predominance "requires a qualitative assessment too; it is not bean counting," and the "relative importance" of the common versus individual questions also matters. *Brown*, 817 F.3d at 1235 (citing *Butler v. Sears, Roebuck & Co.*, 727 F.3d 796, 801 (7th Cir. 2013)); *see also Rutstein*, 211 F.3d at 1234 (explaining that predominance "can only be determined after considering what value the resolution of the class-wide issue will have in each class member's underlying cause of action").

In August 2022, the Eleventh Circuit considered a diminishing value case against a national vehicle insurer. *Baker v. State Farm*, 2022 U.S. App. LEXIS 22978. The plaintiff sought to certify a class of policyholders who had their vehicle losses assessed by a court-approved diminution-in-value formula. *Id.* at *2–3. The Middle District of Georgia denied class certification, and the Eleventh Circuit affirmed that decision.

The appellate court began by noting that "'a district court must conduct a rigorous analysis of the Rule 23 prerequisites before certifying a class'" and that it "'can and should consider the merits of the case to the degree necessary to determine whether the requirements of Rule 23 will be satisfied.'" *Id.* at *6–7 (quoting *Vega*, at 1265).

The Eleventh Circuit determined that the case needed "individualized inquiries" because "the central liability question ... requires a finding that each putative class member received a lower reimbursement for his diminished value claim than the contract entitled him to." *Id.* at *12. It found that the expert did identify some fundamental flaws to the formula but that his sample was too small (75 cases from an unstated number of class members) and not representative of the class that would vary based on vehicle makes, model years, mileage, severity levels, and repair costs. *Id.* at *13.

In *Electrolux*, class members brought claims against a manufacturer of smelly, moldy washing machines. While similar claims in other federal circuits against other manufacturers of moldy washers had survived class certification, the Eleventh Circuit disagreed with a district court's assessment of predominance as to some of the claims against the Electrolux manufacturer and remanded to the district court to reconsider some of the analysis. The Eleventh Circuit concluded that the district court abused its discretion in finding predominance was satisfied as to Texas and California consumer protection claims because the elements of causation require individual proof. *Electrolux*, 817 F.3d at 1237. The court also overturned the class certification of the warranty claims because the district court had not first resolved questions of state law concerning issues such as pre-suit notice, opportunity to cure, and manifestation of the defect. The court stated that answering those questions would help the district court determine what the law is in California and Texas, "which in turn would help it identify the overall mix of individual versus common questions for purposes of predominance." *Id.* at 1238. The court expressed no view on how the district court would answer those questions or ultimately rule on certification.

In *Electrolux*, the Eleventh Circuit also expounded on the Supreme Court's 2013 ruling in *Comcast*, 133 S. Ct. 1426. The Eleventh Circuit noted that *Comcast* "did not alter the black-letter rule that individual damages do not always defeat predominance." *Electrolux*, at

1239. Individual damages will defeat predominance only if computing them "will be so complex, fact-specific, and difficult that the burden on the court system would be simply intolerable." *Id.* at 1240 (quoting *Klay*, 382, F.3d at 1260). Finally, before remanding the issues of predominance back to the district court, the Eleventh Circuit noted that the district court was correct in holding that individual affirmative defenses ordinarily do not defeat predominance. *Id.*

In *Carriuolo*, the Eleventh Circuit found that common issues predominated over individual ones in a class action involving claims by motor vehicle purchasers against the manufacturer alleging unjust enrichment and violation of the Florida Deceptive and Unfair Trade Practices Act (FDUTPA). *Carriuolo*, 823 F.3d 977. The Eleventh Circuit upheld certification of the class, in part, because a plaintiff asserting a FDUTPA claim need not show "actual reliance on the representation or omission at issue," so the mental state of each class member was irrelevant. *Id.* at 984; *see Marrache v. Bacardi U.S.A., Inc.*, No. 20-10677, 2021 U.S. App. LEXIS 33175 (11th Cir. Nov. 08, 2021) (dismissing class complaint alleging FDUTPA and unjust enrichment claims for their purchases of Bombay Sapphire Gin related to its marketing and labelling of "grains of paradise").

In *Fitzpatrick v. Gen. Mills, Inc.*, the Eleventh Circuit, however, remanded a case certified by the district court under the FDUTPA about the nutritional benefits of a yogurt because the class definition included all persons who purchased the yogurt "to obtain its claimed digestive health benefit." 635 F.3d 1279 (11th Cir. 2011). The court said this additional language did take into account individual reliance on the health claims. *Fitzpatrick*, at 1282. The Eleventh Circuit said without the extra language, the class could be certified and sent it back to the district court for further consideration. *Id.*

In 2019's *Cordoba v. DirectTV, L.L.C.*, the Eleventh Circuit noted that whether absent class members can establish standing may be "exceedingly relevant" to the predominance analysis. 942 F.3d 1259, 1273 (11th. Cir. 2019). In *Cordoba*, consumers alleged violations of the TCPA on behalf of a putative class of consumers who were on a do-not-call list. *Id.* at 1271. But the Eleventh Circuit noted a problem will necessarily arise, because, at some point, before it can award any relief, the district court will have to determine whether each member of the class has standing. *Id.* at 1274. The Court said the record on appeal was lacking as to how many class members asked the provider not to call them anymore as the class representative did. *Id.* at 1275. In addition, how do class members intend to prove that they made these requests, the Court asked. *Id.* As a result, the Court determined that the class definition was likely overbroad and sent the case back to the district court for a further predominance analysis. *Id.* at 1276–77.

Notably, in late 2019, the Eleventh Circuit reversed a district court's refusal to certify a class under the predominance analysis, finding that a district court can also abuse its discretion when it improperly categorizes a question as presenting an individual issue, when it actually poses a common question. *Sellers v. Rushmore Loan Mgmt. Services, L.L.C.*, 941 F.3d 1031, 1040–44 (11th Cir. 2019). In *Sellers*, former debtors who had received a discharge of their personal liability on home mortgage debts in bankruptcy pursued claims under the Fair Debt Collection Practices Act against the defendant for its post-discharge collection letters. *Id.* The district court had determined that questions in the case raised individualized issues, including whether the bankruptcy code precluded or preempted the plaintiffs' claims. *Id.* at 1040. The district court thus determined common questions did not predominate. The Eleventh Circuit reversed, ruling that the legal question of whether the bankruptcy code precludes or displaces any remedy under the FDCPA was a common question to all class members. *Id.* at 1042.

The second prong of Rule 23(b)(3) requires a court to determine whether "a class action is superior to other available methods for fairly and efficiently adjudicating the controversy." The focus of this analysis in the Eleventh Circuit is on the relative advantages of a class action over whatever other form of litigation might realistically be available to plaintiffs. *Sacred Heart Health Sys., Inc. v. Humana Military Healthcare Servs.*, 601 F.3d 1159, 1183–

84 (11th Cir. 2010). As a result, the predominance analysis has a "tremendous impact on the superiority analysis" for the simple reason that the more common the issues, the more desirable a class action. *Id.* at 1184 (citing *Klay*, 382 F.3d at 1269). The converse also is true in that the less common the issues, the less desirable a class action. *Id.*

In *Carriuolo*, the Eleventh Circuit found that more than 1,000 individual claims over vehicle window stickers with false safety ratings would lead to claims too small for a separate action by each class member. *Carriuolo*, 823 F.3d at 989. Thus, because common questions of law and fact predominate, classwide adjudication appropriately conserves judicial resources and advances society's interests in judicial efficiency. *Id.* The Eleventh Circuit also has noted that the creation of a number of subclasses in a Rule 23(b)(3) case may defeat the superiority requirement by splintering the proposed class and diminishing the value of a class action. *Id.* (citing *Manual for Complex Litigation* 21.23 (4th ed. 2004)). A class action containing numerous uncommon issues may become unmanageable quickly. *Sacred Heart*, 601 F.3d at 1184.

c. Manageability and Ascertainability[2]

Before establishing the explicit requirements of Rule 23(a), the Eleventh Circuit imposes an implicit requirement that the proponent of a class must first establish that the proposed class is "adequately defined and clearly ascertainable." *See Little*, 691 F.3d at 1303–04. To establish ascertainability, the plaintiff must propose an "administratively feasible" method by which class members can be identified. *Karhu v. Vital Pharm., Inc.*, 621 F. App'x 945, 947 (11th Cir. 2015) (holding plaintiff failed to meet burden of showing ascertainability by simply proposing to use defendant's sales data where defendant sold primarily to distributors and retailers).

However, the Court has now noted that its precedents do not mandate "proof of administrative feasibility." *See Cherry v. Dometic Corp.*, 986 F.3d 1296, 1302–03 (11th Cir. 2021). A class is "clearly ascertainable" if we are certain that its membership is "capable of being" determined. *Id.* at 1303. "But membership can be capable of determination without being capable of *convenient* determination. Administrative feasibility is not an inherent aspect of ascertainability." *Id.*

The identification of class members should be "a manageable process that does not require much, if any, individual inquiry." *Bussey v. Macon Cnty. Greyhound Park, Inc.*, 562 F. App'x 782, 788 (11th Cir. 2014) (revising class definition to cover only loyalty-card-using gamblers who lost money during a season rather than during a specific game because plaintiffs had not provided any indication that they have or could obtain data about losses at a game level). A plaintiff cannot establish ascertainability simply by asserting that class members can be identified using the defendant's records without showing the records are useful for identification purposes and identification will be administratively feasible. *Karhu*, at 948. Similarly, while a plaintiff can potentially satisfy the requirement by proposing that class members self-identify, it also must be shown that self-identification is administratively feasible and not otherwise problematic. *Id.*

The district court must be satisfied that this requirement can be met even before delving into the rigorous analysis of the Rule 23 elements. *Id.* If a plaintiff fails to demonstrate that the putative class is clearly ascertainable, then class certification is properly denied. *See Walewski v. Zenimax Media, Inc.*, 502 F. App'x 857, 861 (11th Cir. 2012); *see also Roberson v. Health Career Inst. LLC*, 2024 U.S. Dist. LEXIS 149707, at *22 (S.D. Fla. Aug. 21, 2024) (citing *Walewski*, at 861); *Nguyen v. Raymond James & Assocs.*, 2022 U.S. Dist. LEXIS 187653, at *24 (M.D. Fla. Aug. 12, 2022) (citing *Walewski*). However, the Court has now noted that its precedents do not mandate "proof of administrative feasibility." *See*

[2] The "manageability" of a class action is often analyzed through the superiority requirement of Rule 23(b)(3). *See, e.g., Sacred Heart*, at 1184.

Cherry v. Dometic Corp., 986 F.3d 1296, 1302–03 (11th Cir. 2021). A class is "clearly ascertainable" if we are certain that its membership is "capable of being" determined. *Id.* at 1303. "But membership can be capable of determination without being capable of *convenient* determination. Administrative feasibility is not an inherent aspect of ascertainability." *Id.*

5. TYPES OF CLASSES

a. Defendant Classes

In *Strawser v. Strange*, a district court decision certified not only a plaintiff class of persons who wished to obtain same-sex marriage licenses but also a defendant class of probate judges in Alabama. *Strawser I*, 307 F.R.D. 604. The plaintiffs moved for a class of plaintiffs and a class of defendants, and both were certified. *Id.* As to the class of defendants, the court observed that there are 68 probate judges in Alabama, all of which had refused, or may in the future refuse, to issue marriage licenses to same-sex couples and refused to recognize same sex marriages. *Id.* at 611. As to numerosity, the court found that although the members of the defendant class were readily identifiable, the joinder of all of them is impractical. *Id.* The court observed that one of the primary reasons for certifying a class is its efficiency. *Id.* The court found the class of defendants met the commonality requirements, because the resolution of the common question will be resolved as to all members "in one stroke." *Id.* at 612. The defendant judges all operate under the same statutory framework and have the same ministerial duties, the court found as to typicality. *Id.* As to adequacy, the court rejected defendant's argument that there was no unified position of the 68 judges. *Id.* at 613. However, the court noted, "the issuance of marriage licenses is a purely ministerial act" and it is their common obligation to carry out their ministerial duties. *Id.* The court proceeded to certify the class of defendants under Rule 23(b)(1) and Rule 23(b)(2). Later, one of the named defendant probate judges, Judge Don Davis, attempted to withdraw because he did not want to continue to represent the class of defendants. The court refused the request, finding that Rule 23(a)(4) "does not require a willing representative, [but] merely an adequate one." *Strawser II*, 190 F. Supp. 3d 1078, 1080 (quoting *Nat'l Broad. Co., Inc. v. Cleland*, 697 F. Supp. 1204, 1217 (N.D. Ga. 1988)). The court went on to state that:

> "In contrast with representatives of plaintiff classes, named defendants almost never choose their role as class champion [as] it is a potentially onerous one thrust upon them by their opponents." *Marcera v. Chinlund*, 595 F.2d 1231, 1239 (2d Cir.), vacated on other grounds sub nom. *Lombard v. Marcera*, 442 U.S. 915, 99 S. Ct. 2833, 61 L.Ed.2d 281 (1979). "But courts must not readily accede to the wishes of named defendants in this area, for to permit them to abdicate so easily would utterly vitiate the effectiveness of the defendant class action as an instrument for correcting widespread illegality." *Id.* This Court previously found that Judge Davis is adequate to represent the Defendant Class. After reviewing Judge Davis' motion and amended motion, the Court finds that Judge Davis has not provided any justification to reconsider that decision. The Court also finds no justification for permitting counsel to withdraw as Defendants' Class Counsel.

Id. at 1080.

6. CASE MANAGEMENT

a. Appointing Counsel

Federal Rule of Civil Procedure 23(g)(1) outlines the considerations pertinent to the appointment of lead counsel at the time a class is certified and applies equally to the appointment of interim lead counsel before certification. *See* Fed. R. Civ. P. 23(g)(1); *see also In re Disposable Contacts Lens Antitrust*, No. 3:15-md-2626 2015 WL 10818781 (M.D. Fla. Oct. 7, 2015). Under that rule, courts must consider four factors in appointing lead counsel: (1) the work counsel has done in identifying or investigating potential claims in the action; (2) counsel's experience in handling class actions, other complex litigation, and claims of the type asserted in the action; (3) counsel's knowledge of the applicable law; and (4) the resources counsel will commit to representing the class. Fed. R. Civ. P. 23(g)(1)(A)(i–iv).

The Eleventh Circuit has rarely elaborated on Rule 23(g). However, if the discussion of adequacy of counsel arises at all, it is more likely to occur in the context of the "adequacy" inquiry in Rule 23(a)(4). *See London v. Wal-Mart Stores Inc.*, 340 F.3d 1246, 1253–55 (11th Cir. 2003) (finding Rule 23(a)(4) not met where the class representative had too many close financial ties to counsel and the counsel's fees would likely far exceed the representative's recovery). Since Rule 23(g) was added in 2003, courts have been slow in shifting the analysis of adequacy of counsel from Rule 23(a)(4) to Rule 23(g), but district courts are beginning to take note that the entire discussion of adequacy of counsel should take place separately under Rule 23(g) analysis. *See, e.g., Braggs v. Dunn*, 317 F.R.D. 634, 666, n.43 (M.D. Ala. 2016).

b. Discovery Issues

The district court has broad discretion under Rule 26 to compel or deny discovery. *Josendis v. Wall to Wall Residence Repairs, Inc.*, 662 F.3d 1292, 1306 (11th Cir. 2011). The Eleventh Circuit reviews a district court's discovery rulings for an abuse of that discretion. *Id.* (citing *Sanderlin v. Seminole Tribe of Fla.*, 243 F.3d 1282, 1285 (11th Cir. 2001)). "Discretion" means the district court has a "range of choice" and that an appellate court will not disturb its decision as long as it remains within that range and is not "influenced by any mistake of law." *Id.* at 1306 (quoting *Guideone Elite Ins. Co. v. Old Cutler Presbyterian Church, Inc.*, 420 F.3d 1317, 1324 (11th Cir. 2005)).

While the Eleventh Circuit has pointed out the discretion of the district court in discovery rulings, it has cut off a district court from granting post-removal discovery for the purpose of establishing jurisdiction because "sound policy and notions of judicial economy and fairness" cut against it. *Lowery*, 483 F.3d 1184, 1215–16 (instructing the district court to refrain from post-removal discovery to establish jurisdiction under CAFA). The *Lowery* court noted that a defendant's request for discovery to prove its removal jurisdiction assertions "is tantamount to an admission that the defendants do not have a factual basis for believing that jurisdiction exists." *Id.* at 1217. A district court should not "insert itself into the fray," and granting leave for a defendant to conduct discovery or engaging in its own discovery "impermissibly lightens the defendant's burden of establishing jurisdiction." *Id.* at 1218.

The Eleventh Circuit generally encourages discovery prior to making class certification rulings. *See Mills v. Foremost Ins. Co.*, 511 F.3d 1300, 1309 (11th Cir. 2008) (holding the district court's ruling on class certification was premature, noting that often a district court will need to go beyond the pleadings and permit some discovery and/or an evidentiary hearing to determine whether a class may be certified) (citing *Gen. Tel. Co. of the Sw. v. Falcon*, 457 U.S. 147, 160 (1982)). Practitioners should seek early case management orders from the court permitting necessary time for discovery. In *Walewski*, 502 F. App'x 857, 860, the Eleventh Circuit upheld a district court's denial of class certification and denial of the plaintiff's belated request for discovery. In that case, local rules in the Middle District of Florida provided that a plaintiff seeking to pursue a class action must move for class certification within 90 days of filing the complaint. *Id.* The plaintiff not only filed his motion for class certification late but also did not move for discovery before the case management hearing and only requested discovery after the magistrate recommended that certification be denied. The Eleventh Circuit held that because the plaintiff failed to comply with local rules, the district court did not abuse its discretion in denying the late request for discovery. *Id.*

It is worth noting that the Eleventh Circuit has stated that a district court was within its discretion to strike a motion for summary judgment filed prior to discovery on the merits when the parties had agreed to bifurcate class and merits discovery. *Kelsey v. Withers*, 718 F. App'x 817 (2017). The district court's discretion in this area is reviewed under an abuse of discretion standard. *Id.* at 819.

As to absent class member discovery, the Eleventh Circuit has not looked at the issue recently. However, plaintiffs in the circuit rely on *Cox*, 784 F.2d 1546, for the proposition that discovery of absent class members is rarely approved in the Eleventh Circuit. *See, e.g.*, *Collins c. Int'l Dairy Queen*, 190 F.R.D. 629, 630 (M.D. Ga. 1999) (refusing defendants' request for discovery of absent class members).

c. Timing of Class Certification

Rule 23(c) instructs that the district court must at an early practicable time determine by order whether to certify the action as a class action. *Mills*, 511 F.3d 1300, 1309. Practitioners should look to local rules for class certification timing issues. *See, e.g.*, *Walewski*, 502 F. App'x 857, 860.

d. Multidistrict Litigation Issues

Of note is a recent Eleventh Circuit case involving tobacco cases removed under CAFA into federal court as part of the "Engle progeny" litigation. Originally a state class action that was later decertified, Engle progeny cases were being tried against Big Tobacco throughout state and federal courts in Florida with certain common issues previously decided prior to decertification. In one of the federal trials addressing due process and preemption issues, the Eleventh Circuit observed, *in dicta*, the ability of courts to develop their own rules to protect against the relitigation of common issues or the piecemeal resolution of disputes. *See Graham v. R.J. Reynolds Tobacco Co., et al.*, 857 F.3d 1169, 1184 (11th Cir. 2017). The en banc Eleventh Circuit opinion noted that Engle was not the first time a defendant's common liability was established through a class action and given binding effect in subsequent individual damage actions. *Id.* (citing *Electrolux*, 817 F.3d 1225, 1239 (discussing several "tools to decide individual damages" in a class action, including "(1) bifurcating liability and damage trials with the same or different juries; (2) appointing a magistrate judge or special master to preside over individual damages proceedings; [and] (3) decertifying the class after the liability trial and providing notice to class members concerning how they may proceed to prove damages))."

In *Checking Account*, numerous class actions around the country were centralized into an MDL, where the district court judge certified subclasses to address variations in state law. *Checking Account*, 307 F.R.D. 630, 654. Defendant argued that the court should not certify subclasses represented by different plaintiffs from varying underlying actions prior to the MDL. *Id.* Instead, the defendant argued that the cases should be remanded to its originating jurisdiction at the close of pretrial proceedings before any certification. The district court disagreed and remanded discrete subclasses for trial, noting that both the MDL and Rule 23 mechanisms aim to promote a just and efficient resolution of cases. *See id.* at 654.

7. CLASS NOTICE AND OPT-OUT MATTERS

The notice provisions of Rule 23 are meant to protect the due process rights of absent class members. *Juris*, 685 F.3d 1294, 1317. The rule sets forth "different notice requirements to different kinds of cases and even to different phases of the same case." *Id.* (citing *Battle v. Liberty Nat'l Life Ins. Co.*, 770 F. Supp. 1499, 1515 (N.D. Ala. 1991), *aff'd*, 974 F.2d 1279 (11th Cir. 1992). The rule itself does not require notice in Rule 23(b)(1) and (b)(2) class actions. *See* Fed. R. Civ. P. 23(c)(2)(A)–(B). Instead, in these "mandatory" class actions, Rule 23 allows courts to exercise their discretion to provide appropriate notice "to protect class members and fairly conduct the action." *Juris*, at 1317 (citing Fed. R. Civ. P. 23(c)(2)(A), 23(d)(1)(B)); *see also* 3 William B. Rubenstein et al., *Newberg on Class Actions* § 8:5 (4th ed. 2011) ("('[T]he court may make appropriate orders requiring notice to some or all of the members regarding the pendency of the class, proposed judgment or settlement, soliciting input on the adequacy of class representation, opportunity to intervene or present claims or defenses, and the like.') 'Regardless of the category under which a class suit may be or potentially may be certified, however, Rule 23(e) requires that absent class members be informed when the lawsuit is in the process of being voluntarily dismissed or compromised.'" *Juris*, at 1317 (citing *Newberg on Class Actions* § 8:17; *see* Fed. R. Civ. P. 23(e)(1))). Under certain circumstances, even when notice is not provided for under Rule 23, due process may receive notice of the pendency of the proceeding. *Id.* (citing, *e.g.*, *Johnson v. Gen. Motors Corp.*, 598 F.2d 432, 437 (5th Cir. 1979)). The Eleventh Circuit has held that due process will require at least some notice to potential absent class members prior to class certification under Rule 23(b)(1)(B). *Id.* at 1318 (citing *In re Temple*, 851 F.2d 1269, 1272 (11th Cir. 1988)).

As to the sufficiency of the contents of the notice, the Eleventh Circuit has stated in part:

> Surely the best notice practicable under the circumstances cannot stop with . . . generalities. It must also contain an adequate description of the proceedings written in objective, neutral terms, that, insofar as possible, may be understood by the average absentee class member. . . .
>
> Absentee class members will generally have had no knowledge of the suit until they receive the initial class notice. This will be their primary, if not exclusive, source of information for deciding how to exercise their rights under [R]ule 23. . . . Not only must the substantive claims be adequately described but the notice must also contain information reasonably necessary to make a decision to remain a class member and be bound by the final judgment or opt out of the action.

Twigg v. Sears, Roebuck & Co., 153 F.3d 1222, 1227 (11th Cir. 1998) (concluding that prior class judgment could not bar absent member's claims because even if absent class member had received the notices, their language was insufficient to notify him that claims like his were being litigated in the action) (quoting *In re Nissan Motor Corp. Antitrust Litig.*, 552 F.2d 1088, 1103–05 (5th Cir. 1977)). The Eleventh Circuit has observed that the notice should give "'information reasonably necessary to make a decision [whether] to remain a class member and be bound by the final judgment or opt out of the action,' though the notice need not include 'every material fact' or be 'overly detailed.'" *Faught v. Am. Home Shield Cor.*, 668 F.3d 1233, 1239 (11th Cir. 2011); *see also Adams v. S. Farm Bureau Life Inc. Co.*, 493 F.3d 1276, 1286 (11th Cir. 2007) (finding 48-page notice was sufficient where it was written understandably; set forth specific types of relief available; described how to opt out; explained members would be bound by settlement and release; and included toll-free numbers for further information).

Rule 23(c)(2)'s requirement is that an opt-out class-action notice be given to all class members as soon as practical was intended by Congress to prevent "one-way intervention." *See London*, 340 F.3d 1246, 1252. One-way intervention occurs when potential members of a class action are allowed to await final judgment on the merits "in order to determine whether participation [in the class] would be favorable to their interests." *Id.* (quoting *Am. Pipe & Constr. Co. v. Utah*, 414 U.S. 538, 547 (1974)).

8. SUBCLASSES

Rule 23(c)(5) provides that "when appropriate, a class may be divided into subclasses that are each treated as a class under this rule." The Eleventh Circuit has observed that if applicable state laws can be sorted into a small number of groups, each containing materially identical legal standards, then certification of subclasses embracing each of the dominant legal standards can be appropriate. *Klay*, 382 F.3d 1241, 1262. However, a court must be careful not to certify too many groups. *Id.*; *see also Sacred Heart*, 601 F.3d 1159, 1183–84 (holding that the creation of a number of subclasses in a Rule 23(b)(3) suit may defeat the superiority requirement); *but see Checking Account*, 307 F.R.D. 630, 655 (certifying several subclasses to address variations in state law under Rule 23, finding "these subclasses are reasonable and manageable because they group together materially identical claims to be pursued by qualified representatives who have demonstrated their firm commitment to seek relief both for themselves and for the similarly situated Wells Fargo customers").

9. DAMAGES

a. Proof

"'[D]amages [must be] capable of measurement on a classwide basis.'" *Carriuolo*, 823 F.3d 977, 988 (citing *Behrend*, 133 S. Ct. 1426, 1433).

In this Circuit, "the presence of individualized damages issues does not prevent a finding that the common issues in the case predominate." *Electrolux*, 817 F.3d at 1239 (11th Cir. 2016) (citation omitted). This is "[t]he 'black letter rule' recognized in every circuit. . . ." *Id.* (citing William B. Rubenstein, *Newberg on Class Action* 4:54 (5th Ed.)). Individual damages "are sometimes easy to resolve because the calculations are formulaic." *Id.* (citing *Klay*, 382 F.3d 1241, 1259–60). The appellate court has found exceptions to the rule though—such as, "if computing them 'will be so complex, fact-specific, and difficult that the burden on the court system would be simply intolerable'" and if the individual damages "are accompanied by 'significant individualized questions going to liability.'" *Id.* at 1240 (citations omitted).

In the Third Circuit's view, "*Comcast* did not change the law about the effect of individual damages on predominance." *Electrolux*, at 1238. Rather, "*Comcast* simply requires that 'any model supporting a plaintiff's damages case must be consistent with its liability case.'" *Carriuolo*, at 988 (quoting *Comcast*, at 1433). And a failure to conduct a "rigorous analysis" is an abuse of discretion per the *Comcast* decision. *See Bussey v. Macon Cnty. Greyhound Park, Inc.*, 562 F. App'x 782, 790 (11th Cir. 2014).

b. Distribution

Although the Eleventh Circuit favors settlement of class cases, it will set aside a settlement if the distribution plan is invalid as a matter of law. *Leverso v. Southtrust Bank*, 18 F.3d 1527, 1531 (11th Cir. 1994) (vacating approval of distribution plan and remanding for modification) (citation omitted).

In a 2012 case, the appellate court considered the interplay between a class member's share and the *cy pres* distribution. *Nelson v. Mead Johnson & Johnson Co.*, 484 F. App'x 429 (11th Cir. 2012). Over objection, the Southern District of Florida approved a settlement in which a *cy pres* distribution occurred only if the claims were less than a certain sum—in this case, $8 million. Since each class member would receive full compensation before the *cy pres* distribution, the appellate court found that the district court did not abuse its discretion when it granted approval of the settlement. *Id.* at 435. In 2021, the Middle District of Florida approved the parties agreed-upon cy pres recipients and awards in a consumer class case. *Esposito v. I.q Data Int'l*, No. 2:18-cv-437-JES-NPM, 2021 U.S. Dist. LEXIS 76587, *3–4 (M.D. Fla. Apr. 21, 2021).

Punitive damages go to the class in a common and undivided interest, as "the failure of one plaintiff's claim will increase the share of successful plaintiffs." *Tapscott v. MS Dealer Serv. Corp.*, 77 F.3d 1353, 1359 (11th Cir. 1996) (*abrogated on other grounds by Cohen v.*

Office Depot, Inc., 204 F.3d 1069 (11th Cir. 2000)).

10. SETTLEMENTS

The circuit's case law sets forth a two-step process for the district court to approve of a class action settlement. *Leidel v. Project Investors, Inc.*, No. 9:16-cv-80060, 2016 U.S. Dist. LEXIS 150009, *2 (S.D. Fla. Oct. 26, 2016) (citing *Fresco v. Auto Data Direct, Inc.*, No. 03-cv-61063, 2007 U.S. Dist. LEXIS 37863, *4 (S.D. Fla. May 14, 2007)). The first step is preliminary approval, which "requir[es] the Court to 'make a preliminary determination on the fairness, reasonableness, and adequacy of the settlement terms.'" *Id.* (citing *Fresco*, at *4). After notice to the class with an appropriate amount of time and opportunity for objectors, the second step is final approval of the settlement. *Id.* (citing *Smith v. Wm. Wrigley Jr. Co.*, No. 09-cv-60646, 2010 U.S. Dist. LEXIS 67832, *2 (S.D. Fla. June 15, 2010)).

To approve a class settlement prior to the 2018 amendment to Rule 23(e)(2), the "district court had to find that a class action settlement was 'fair, adequate and reasonable and is not the product of collusion between the parties.'" *Carter v. Forjas*, 701 F. App'x 759, 766 (11th Cir. 2017) (quoting *Bennett v. Behring Corp.*, 737 F.2d 982, 986 (11th Cir. 1984)). Since its amendment in 2018, Rule 23(e)(2) has set out four concerns the district court must consider in making this determination.

In late 2023, the Eleventh Circuit interpreted the 2018 amendment to Rule 23(e)(2) in conjunction with its own *Bennett* factors in *Ponzio v. Pinon*, 87 F.4th 487 (11th Cir. 2023); *see Bennett v. Behring Corp.*, 737 F.2d. 982, 986 (11th Cir. 1984). In *Ponzio*, the Court held that the 2018 amendment is not meant "to displace" the *Bennett* factors previously identified by courts in reviewing class action settlement agreements, but rather to focus the court and the lawyers on the four core concerns of procedure and substance that should guide the decision whether to approve the proposal. *Ponzio*, 87 F.4th at 494–95 (citing Fed. R. 23(e)(2)). Rule 23(e)(2) provides the primary considerations, but the Eleventh Circuit held that the *Bennett* factors "can, where appropriate, complement those core concerns. *Id.* at 595. The additional *Bennett* factors are: "(1) the likelihood of success at trial; (2) the range of possible recovery; (3) the point on or below the range of possible recovery at which a settlement is fair, adequate and reasonable; (4) the complexity, expense and duration of litigation; (5) the substance and amount of opposition to the settlement; and (6) the stage of proceedings at which the settlement was achieved." *Bennett*, 737 F.2d at 986. In *Ponzio*, the Court said that *Bennett* factors (1), (2), (4), and (6), for example, can inform whether the relief provided to the class is adequate (core concern three). *Ponzio*, 87 F.4th at 495. And *Bennett* factors (3) and (5) can inform "whether the proposal treats class members equitably relative to each other (core concern four)." *Id.* The "proponents of class action settlements bear the burden of developing a record demonstrating that the settlement distribution is fair, reasonable and adequate." *Id.*

Under the *Bennett* factor review, "a court considers the likelihood of success at trial and the range of possible recovery, as well as the complexity and expense of the litigation and the stage of the proceedings at which the settlement is reached, among other factors." *U.S. v. Everglades Coll., Inc.*, 855 F.3d 1279, 1287 (11th Cir. 2017) (citing *Day v. Persels & Assocs., LLC*, 729 F.3d 1309, 1326 (11th Cir. 2013)). The court may rely on the judgment of the parties' attorneys and "should be hesitant to substitute its own judgment for that of counsel." *Greco v. Ginn Dev. Co., LLC*, 635 F. App'x 628, 632 (11th Cir. 2015) (citations omitted). But the courts give no deference to the settling parties because the court's purpose "is to protect absent class members from an unfair bargain," *Everglades*, at 1287 (citing *Amchem*, 521 U.S. 591), and therefore does not need to approve it just because the parties agreed to it. *Palmer v. Dynamic Recovery Solutions, LLC*, No. 6:15-cv-59, 2016 WL 2348704, *3 (M.D. Fla. May 04, 2016) (citations omitted).

Thus, the appellate court will overturn a district court's decision "'only upon a clear showing of abuse of discretion.'" *Greco*, at 631 (quoting *Cont'l Can*, 706 F.2d 1144, 1147). An abuse of discretion occurs only when the court "'applies an incorrect legal standard, applies the law in an unreasonable or incorrect manner, follows improper procedures in making a determination, or makes findings of fact that are clearly erroneous.'" *Id.* (quoting *Aycock v. R.J. Reynolds Tobacco Co.*, 769 F.3d 1063, 1068 (11th Cir. 2014) (quoting *Brown v. Ala. Dep't of Transp.*, 597 F.3d 1160, 1173 (11th Cir. 2010))). "This deferential standard applies not only because settlements are favored, but also because '[t]rial courts generally have a greater familiarity with the factual issues and legal arguments in the lawsuit, and therefore can make an evaluation of the likely outcome were the lawsuit to be fully tried.'" *Id.* (citation omitted).

The Eleventh Circuit has also analyzed some public policy considerations in class settlements. For example, it explored future claims releases in a class settlement and found that public policy "does not categorically prohibit releases of future antitrust claims." *In re Blue Cross Blue Shield Antitrust Litig. MDL 2406*, 85 F.4th 1070, 1088 (11th Cir. 2024). Likewise, as to adequacy of counsel in class settlements, the Eleventh Circuit has stated that its precedents "do not categorically prohibit the same plaintiffs and counsel from representing an injunctive relief and a damages class." *Id.* at 1091.

In 2024, the Eleventh Circuit looked at coupon settlements under the Class Action Fairness Act (CAFA). It took its third review of a class settlement in *Drazen v. Pinto*, 106 F.4th 1302 (11th Cir. July 16, 2024), focusing on whether the settlement qualified as a "coupon" settlement, because the settlement gave class members a "voucher" option in addition to a cash option. At issue in *Drazen* was a class action settlement of claims made under the Telephone Consumer Protection Act of 1991 (TCPA). The plaintiffs alleged that GoDaddy violated the TCPA by using an automatic telephone dialing system (ATDS) to make telephone calls or send text messages to their telephone numbers or cell phones and those of the putative class. The first swipe at the settlement involved standing matters, where, ultimately, the full Eleventh Circuit held that even a single unwanted text is enough to confer Article III standing to assert a claim under the TCPA. *Drazen v. Pinto*, 74 F.4th 1336, 1342 (11th Cir. 2023). After establishing standing, the settlement made its way back to the Eleventh Circuit after *Pinto* continued to object. After two hearings (vacating and narrowing the initial broad novel rulings written by Senior Judge Gerald Tjoflat), the court ultimately determined that the settlement's use of vouchers as one payment option qualified as a "coupon" under CAFA even though there was also a cash option. *Drazen v. Pinto*, 106 F.4th 1302 at 1342–49 (11th Cir. 2024). Thus, the Eleventh Circuit found the district court abused its discretion by calculating attorney fees as a percentage of possible relief to the class, rather than another method. *Id.* at 1349–51. As noted in more detail below, the court concluded "attorney's fees for coupon settlements under CAFA may be based on the value of the coupons that are redeemed, the lodestar method, or a combination of both." *Id.* at 1350.

As to service awards for class representatives, the Eleventh Circuit's decision in *Johnson v. NPAS Sols., LLC*, continues to cause waves when it denied a service award to the named plaintiff, although such awards are "'fairly typical in class actions.'" 975 F.3d 1244, 1259 (11th Cir. Sept. 17, 2020). It noted: "Although it's true that such awards are commonplace in modern class-action litigation, that doesn't make them lawful, and it doesn't free us to ignore Supreme Court precedent forbidding them." The appellate court applied to two U.S. Supreme Court decisions to support its position. *Id.* at 1255 (citing *Trustees v. Greenough*, 105 U.S. 527 (1882), *Central Railroad & Banking Co. v. Pettus*, 113 U.S. 116 (1885) (citation omitted)).

The Eleventh Circuit reaffirmed this ruling again in June 2021 when it reversed a district court's decision awarding an incentive award and remanded the case for the sole purpose of vacating the award. *In re Equifax Customer Data Sec. Breach Litig.*, 999 F.3d 1247, 1257 (11th Cir. 2021). As of August 2021, the Northern District of Alabama has found that this is still "something of an open question" as the Eleventh Circuit's *Johnson* decision was a divided panel, and although an Eleventh Circuit judge upheld that ruling in a subsequent trial court decision, an en banc appeal is now pending (and is still pending as of November 2021). *Phillips v. Hobby Lobby Stores*, No. 2021 U.S. Dist. LEXIS 157862, at *12 (N.D. Ala. Aug. 20, 2021). *See also Dickenson v. NPAS Solutions, LLC*, Case No. 9:17-cv-80393-RLR (11th Cir.).

A practice tip is to include a severability provision stating that the settlement should remain in effect even if the district court doesn't approve the incentive awards. *Poblano v. Russell Cellular Inc.*, No. 8:19-cv-265-T-KKM-AAS, 2021 U.S. Dist. LEXIS 10896, at **3–4 (M.D. Fla. June 10, 2021) (declining to approve settlement that requested incentive award without severability provision that was imperative in *Equifax* settlement); *Phillips*, at *12 ("current best practice appears to be to approve the settlement except for the incentive award, but retain jurisdiction to allow Plaintiff to renew the request if [*Johnson*] is reversed").

Other circuits have considered this issue as well with mixed results:

- Second Circuit: finding that *Greenough* and *Pettus* do not prevent award of a service payment. *Melito v. Experian Marketing Solutions, Inc.*, 923 F.3d 85, 96 (2d Cir. 2019).
    - New York, Southern District: precedent "authorize[s the court] to approve such a payment." *Knox v. John Varvatos Enters.*, 520 F. Supp. 3d 331, 349 (S.D.N.Y. 2021) (citing *Melito*); *Hart v. BHH, LLC*, No. 15cv4804, 2020 U.S. Dist. LEXIS 173, at *13 (S.D.N.Y. Sept. 22, 2020) (affirming award but recognizing the "issue is deserving of congressional attention").
- Third Circuit:
    - Pennsylvania, Eastern District: "not deviat[ing] from that precedent here" to affirm service award. *Wood v. Saroj & Manju Invs. Phila. LLC*, No. 19-2820-KSM, 2020 U.S. Dist. LEXIS 243700, at *12 n.8. (E.D. Pa. Dec. 28, 2020).
    - New Jersey, District Court: awarding service award. *Somogyi v. Freedom Mortg. Corp.*, 495 F. Supp. 3d 337, 345 (D.N.J. 2020).
- Seventh Circuit:
    - Illinois, Northern District: "The [c]ourt has considered *Johnson* … and its reasoning regarding incentive award and declines to follow it…." *Wickens v. Thyssenkrupp Crankshaft Co, LLC*, No. 1:19-cv-6100, 2021 U.S. Dist. LEXIS 17884, at *6 (N.D. Ill. Jan. 26, 2021) (citing *In re Continental Illinois Sec. Litig.*, 962 F.2d 566, 571 (7th Cir. 1992); *Schulte v. Fifth Third Bank*, 805 F. Supp. 2d 560, 600 (N.D. Ill. 2011)).
    - Michigan, Eastern District: reducing $10,000 request to $1,000. *Garner Props. & Mgmt., LLC of Inkster*, 333 F.R.D. 614, 628 (E.D. Mich. 2020).
- Eighth Circuit:
    - Missouri, Western District: finding that "the Eighth Circuit has expressly recognized the value of incentive awards." *Vogt v. State Farm Life Ins. Co.*, No. 2:16-cv-04170-NKL, 2021 U.S. Dist. LEXIS 12776, at *10 (W.D. Mo. Jan. 25, 2021) (citing *Tussey v. ABB, Inc.*, 850 F.3d 951, 962 (8th Cir. 2017)).
- Ninth Circuit:
    - California, Northern District: rejecting an objector's argument "that incentive awards are unlawful under 'binding circuit precedent,' but cites an Eleventh Circuit case that is not binding and is contrary to Ninth Circuit precedent." *Izor v. Avacus Data Sys.*, No. 19-cv-01057-HSG, 2020 U.S. Dist. LEXIS 239999 (N.D. Cal. Dec. 21, 2020) (citations omitted); *In re Lithium Ion Batteries Antitrust Litig.*, No. 13-MD-02420-YGR-DMR, MDL No. 2420, 2020 U.S. Dist. LEXIS 233607, at *102 n.24 (N.D. Cal. Dec. 10, 2020) ("reasonable service awards have long been approved in

the Ninth Circuit") (citations omitted); *Grace v. Apple, Inc.*, No. 17-cv-00551-LHK, 2021 U.S. Dist. LEXIS 66294, at *21 (N.D. Cal. March 31, 2021) (same).

A court has noted that "[t]his issue is deserving of congressional attention," since Rule 23 has never referenced service awards, no statute has ever created them or "abrogate[d] the holdings of *Pettus* or *Greenough*," and the awards exist only because "they are judicially forged." *Hart*, 2020 U.S. Dist. LEXIS 173634, at **13–14 n.2 (citations omitted).

a. Preliminary Approval

The purpose of this step is to determine "whether the proposed settlement appears to be 'the result of informed, good-faith, arms'-length negotiation between the parties and their capable and experienced counsel' and not 'the result of collusion." *Leidel*, 2016 U.S. Dist. LEXIS 150009, at *3 (quoting *Torres v. Bank of Am.* (*In re Checking Account*) (*Checking Acc't Litig.*), 830 F. Supp. 2d 1330, 1341 (S.D. Fla. 2011)). When certifying a class for settlement purposes only, "certification requires 'heightene[d] attention . . . to the justification for binding the class members.'" *Fata v. Pizza Hut of Am.*, No. 6:14-cv-376, 2016 U.S. Dist. LEXIS 153035, at *6–7 (M.D. Fla. Oct. 31, 2016) (quoting *Amchem*, 521 U.S. at 620). In that light, the settlement must "represent[] a bona fide end to the adversarial process or the collusive exploitation of the class action mechanism to the detriment of absent class members." *Palmer*, 2016 WL 2348704, at *3 (citations omitted).

In 2017, the Eleventh Circuit permitted plaintiffs who had filed a prior class action related to unsolicited fax advertisements to intervene in a new identical case filed three years later apparently to undercut the first case and settle the claims for a reduced amount, referred to by the intervenors as a "reverse auction." *See Technology Training Assoc., Inc. v. Bucaneers Ltd. Partnership*, 874 F.3d 692 (11th Cir. 2017). The Court said the district court should permit the intervenors to intervene because their interests are not being adequately represented by the new existing parties. *See id.*

The party seeking class certification must affirmatively demonstrate all the Civil Rule 23(a) factors and at least one subsection of Rule 23(b). *Id.* at *2. For preliminary approval, the court also designates class representatives and class counsel and sets the matter for a final approval hearing. *Leidel*, 2016 U.S. Dist. LEXIS 150009, at *7. It also approves class notice. *Id.* at *8.

When evaluating the fairness, adequacy, and reasonableness of a settlement, the Eleventh Circuit has enumerated the six *Bennett* factors noted above for its district courts. *Ponzio v. Pinon*, 87 F.4th 487 (11th Cir. 2023); *see Bennett v. Behring Corp.*, 737 F.2d. 982, 986 (11th Cir. 1984); *Palmer*, 2016 WL 2348704, at *2 (citing *Faught*, 668 F.3d at 1240). Those factors "are neither determinative nor exhaustive," so the Eleventh Circuit has offered additional factors:

- an unjustifiably burdensome claims procedure,
- unduly preferential treatment of the class representative,
- the terms of settlement in similar cases,
- an unreasonably high award of attorney's fees to prevailing class counsel, and
- impermissibly broad releases of liability.

Palmer, 2016 WL 2348704, at *2 (citations omitted).

"The proponents of a settlement bear the burden of proving its fairness, adequacy, and reasonableness." *Id.* at *3 (citing *Faught*, at 1239).

b. Objectors

Civil Rule 23(e)(5) permits any class member to object. The courts examine class settlement in light of objections and are to "provide a reasoned response to those objections." *Greco*, 635 F. App'x at 632 (citation omitted). In 2023, the Eleventh Circuit analyzed objections to several class action settlements under the newly amended 2018 Rule 23(3)(2). In *Ponzio*, objectors to a proposed settlement agreement to address defective paint on certain automobiles claimed that it left 80 percent of the class members without any benefits. *Ponzio*, 87 F.4th 487, 491–92. The Eleventh Circuit said while proponents of the settlement bear the burden of developing a record demonstrating the settlement is fair, reasonable, and adequate, "objectors to the settlement have some obligations of their own." *Id.* at 499. Rule 23(e)(5)(A) requires that they "state with specificity" the grounds for an objection. *Id.* at 500. This means that objections "must provide sufficient specifics to enable the parties to respond to them and the court to evaluate them." *Id.* (citing Fed. R. Civ. P. 23(e)(5)(A) (Advisory Committee's Note to 2018 Amendment)). When the objections are factual in nature, they cannot be conclusory," the Court added. *Id.* Once proper objections are lodged by an objector, the proponents of the settlement must show that the matters do not affect the fairness, reasonableness, or adequacy of the agreement. *Id.* at 500. In upholding the settlement, the Court detailed why objectors to the car paint settlement (plaintiffs with a separately filed class action on the same defect in another jurisdiction) had used a demonstrably flawed calculation as the basis of its objection. *Id.* at 500–01.

The Eleventh Circuit upheld a $2.67 billion class action settlement of an antitrust action brought against Blue Cross Blue Shield Association, alleging Sherman Act violations. *In re Blue Cross Blue Shield Antitrust Litig., MDL 2406*, 84 F.4th 1070 (11th Cir. 2023). The Court rejected appeals by numerous objectors, including Home Depot and others, and affirmed the district court's approval of the settlement after two fairness hearings. The Court rejected objections that the same plaintiffs and plaintiffs' counsel should not represent the injunctive relief class and the damages class. *Id.* at 1091. The Court found the district court did not abuse its discretion in finding no conflict for having shared class representatives and counsel. *Id.* at 1091–92. The Court also rejected an objection that the settlement did not treat class members equally, noting that Rule 23(e)(2) "requires equity, not equality, and treating class members equitably does not necessarily mean treating them all equally." *Id.* at 1093.

However, in another 2023 case, the Court did agree with objectors to a class settlement, finding that a district court's approval of a class settlement providing injunctive relief sought by named plaintiffs who lacked Article III standing to seek injunctive relief was legal error and thus an abuse of discretion. *Williams v. Reckitt Benckiser, LLC*, 65 F.4th 1243, 1256–57 (11th Cir. 2023) (finding named class members who previously bought a brain performance supplement and alleged misleading statements about its efficacy did not have standing to bring injunctive relief with no proof they planned to buy the same product in the future).

In a 2021 decision in which 388 people from the 147 million class members (that include the Federal Trade Commission, the Consumer Financial Protection Bureau, and the attorneys generals for 48 states, the District of Columbia, and Puerto Rico all supported the settlement) objected, and pursued the Northern District of Georgia's approval of the settlement to the appellate court, the Eleventh Circuit reaffirmed that "[o]ften time objectors play a 'beneficial role in opening a proposed settlement to scrutiny and identifying areas that need improvement.'" *In re Equifax Customer Data Sec. Breach Litig.*, 999 f3d 1247, 1256–57 (11th Cir. 2021) (citing David F. Herr, Annotated Manual for Complex Litigation § 21.643 (4th Ed. 2021)). "And because objectors have the right to object, it is our obligation to closely review the issues they present." *Id.*

To prevail, objectors "must show how the settlement, viewed as a whole, fails to satisfy the criteria for settlement approval." *In re Domestic Air Transp. Antitrust Litig.*, 148 F.R.D. 297, 330 (N.D. Ga. 1993). Unless the objectors produce "a beneficial effect upon the progress of the litigation," they are "not generally entitled to an award of counsel fees." *Id.* (citation omitted). To receive a fee and expenses, the objectors need not win their objection, but must benefit the class and assist the court with its review of the settlement. *Id.* (awarding the objectors fees and expenses equal to 0.26 percent of median value of the common fund). While considering an award of fees and expenses, the district court also should consider whether the objector has "an ulterior motive in objecting to the settlement, rather than opting out." *Greco*, at 633 (citing *In re Prudential Ins. Litig.*, 148 F.3d 283, 318 (3d Cir. 1998) (considering that the most vociferous objectors were persons enlisted by counsel seeking control of the litigation)).

c. Final Approval

Before final approval, the district court will host a fairness hearing to determine several issues: (1) whether the settlement is fair, reasonable, and adequate; (2) whether the court should dismiss the case with prejudice against all class members who have not opted out; (3) what amount to award class counsel in fees and expenses; and (4) what amount to grant the named plaintiffs as a service award. *Largess v. U.S. Bank N.A.*, No. 1:14-cv-21252, 2016 U.S. Dist. LEXIS 119720, *4 (S.D. Fla. Aug. 30, 2016).

The standard on appeal is an abuse of discretion. *Day*, 729 F.3d at 1327 (citing *Indigo Room, Inc. v. City of Fort Myers*, 710 F.3d 1294, 1299 (11th Cir. 2013)). As it relates to factual findings, the district court abuses it discretion only if it was clearly erroneous. *Id.* (citing *Indigo Room*, at 1299). One example is a factual finding that had no support in the record. *Id.* (citing *U.S. v. Newman*, 614 F.3d 1232, 1238–39 (11th Cir. 2010)).

d. *Cy Pres*

The Eleventh Circuit permits *cy pres* distribution of unclaimed settlement funds. *Nelson*, 484 F. App'x at 435 (11th Cir. 2012) (citing *In re Pharm. Indus. Average Wholesale Price Litig.*, 588 F.3d 24, 34 (1st Cir. 2009)); *Nelson v. Greater Gadsden Hous. Auth.*, 802 F.2d 405, 409 (11th Cir. 1986). But the court must approve it. *In re Charter Secs. Litig.*, No. 3:84-cv-448, 2016 U.S. Dist. LEXIS 35362, *4 (M.D. Fla. Mar. 17, 2016) (citing *Nelson*, 484 F. App'x at 435).

The court should distribute the funds "for a purpose as near as possible to the legitimate objectives underlying the lawsuit, the interests of class members, and the interests of those similarly situated.'" *Lacour v. Whitney Bank*, No. 8:11-cv-1896, 2014 U.S. Dist. LEXIS 3228, *3 (M.D. Fla. Jan. 10, 2014) (quoting *Checking Acc't Litig.*, 830 F. Supp. 2d at 1355 (other citations omitted)). When considering the *cy pres* recipient, "the recipient should reasonably approximate the interest of class members based on a number of non-exclusive factors." *Id.* at *4 (listing the factors) (citations omitted). The best application is to use the funds "for purposes closely related to their origin," but "the courts' broad equitable powers now permit the use of funds for other public service organizations.'" *Id.* at *5 (citations omitted). It is also common for the court to choose organizations geographically close to it. *Id.* at *6 (citations omitted). *Cy pres* recipients tend to be "'worthy charities, especially to charities whose purposes harmonize with the underlying lawsuit.'" *Id.* at *3 (quoting *Checking Acc't Litig.*, at 1354).

The Eleventh Circuit also has affirmed a district court's decision to disburse unclaimed compensatory damages through the use of fluid recovery, similar to a *cy pres* award. *Poertner v. Gillette Co.*, 618 F. App'x 624, 629 (11th Cir. 2015) (citing *Greater Gadsden*, 802 F.2d at 409).

11. FEES AND COSTS

a. Fees

Civil Rule 23(h) authorizes courts to "award reasonable attorney's fees and non-taxable costs that are authorized by law or by the parties' agreement." In this circuit, district courts have "'great latitude in formulating attorney's fees awards subject only to the necessity of explaining its reasoning so that [the Eleventh Circuit] can undertake [their] review.'" *Carter v. Forjas*, 701 F. App'x 759, 767 (11th Cir. 2017) (quoting *Waters v. Int'l Precious Metals Corp.*, 190 F.3d. 1291, 1293 (11th Cir. 1999)). The appellate court reviews its district court's decisions under an abuse of discretion standard. *Id.*

In common fund settlements, it is appropriate to award nontaxable costs and reasonable attorney's fees "'based upon a reasonable percentage of the fund established for the benefit of the class.'" *Cotter v. Checkers Drive-In Restaurants, Inc.*, No. 8:19-cv-1386-VMC-CPT, 2021 U.S. Dist. LEXIS 160592, *32 n.5 (M.D. Fla. Aug. 25, 2021) (quoting *Camden I Condo. Ass'n Inc. v. Dunkle*, 946 F.2d 768, 774 (11th Cir. 1991)). In 2021, the Eleventh Circuit "clarified that ... '[t]he percentage method therefore remains the proper method to apply when awarding attorney's fees in common-fund settlement case.'" *Id.* at *32 n.5 (M.D. Fla. Aug. 25, 2021) (quoting *In re Equifax*, 999 F.3d at 1279). The "'percentage applies to the total fund created, even where the actual payout following the claims process is lower.'" *Id.* at *33 (quoting *Pinto v. Princess Cruise Lines, Ltd.*, 513 F. Supp. 2d 1334, 1339 (S.D. Fla. 2007) (citing *Waters*, at 1295–96 (11th Cir. 1999) (other citations omitted).

For those percentage-of-the-fund cases, "'there is no hard and fast rule mandating a certain percentage," but "an award of one-third of the common fund is 'consistent with the trend in this Circuit.'" *Id.* at 33 (quoting *Hanley v. Tampa Bay Sports & Ent. LLC*, No. 8:19-cv-550-CEH-CPT, 2020 WL 2517766, *6 (M.D. Fla. April 23, 2020)). That's an increase from years past: in 2015, the Eleventh Circuit noted that 25 percent was the "benchmark" for attorneys' fee awards for common fund cases, *Poertner*, 618 F. App'x at 628 (quoting *Camden I Condo. Ass'n v. Dunkle*, 946 F.2d 768, 770 (11th Cir. 1991)), but later clarified in 2017, that it has "identified twenty to thirty percent of the common fund as a 'benchmark' for an attorney's fee award." *Carter*, 701 F. App'x at 767 (citing *Waters*, at 1294). Though in 2022, it stated that "Eleventh Circuit precedent generally only allows district courts to award 25% of the common fund to class counsel as attorneys' fees." *Arkin v. Pressman*, Nos. 21-11019, 21-11502, 2022 U.S. App. LEXIS 18205, *3 (11th cir. 2022) (citing *Faught*, 668 F.3d at 1242 (11th Cir. 2011) (recognizing the 25% common fund award benchmark). But "[t]here is no hard and fast rule mandating a certain percentage of a common fund. . . ." *Camden I*, at 774.

From there, the appropriate percentage varies based on the court's consideration of the 12 factors from *Johnson v. Georgia Highway Express, Inc.*, 488 F.2d 714 (5th Cir. 1974), *abrogated on other grounds by Blanchard v. Bergeron*, 489 U.S. 87 (1989), "as well as '[o]ther pertinent factors,' including 'any non-monetary benefits conferred upon the class by the settlement [] and the economics involved in prosecuting a class action,' in determining the reasonableness of a fee award." *Poertner*, at 628–29 (quoting *Camden I*, at 775). The *Johnson* factors include:

- the time and labor required;
- the difficulty of the issues;
- the skill required;
- the preclusion of other employment by the attorney because he accepted the case;
- the customary fee in the community;
- whether the fee is fixed or contingent;
- time limitations imposed by the client or circumstances;
- the amount involved and the results obtained;
- the experience, reputation, and ability of the attorneys;
- the undesirability of the case;
- the nature and length of the professional relationship with the client; and
- awards in similar cases.

Faught, 668 F.3d at 1242–43 (citations omitted).

When considering what percentage to award, the circuit's courts consider the monetary and nonmonetary relief along with the *cy pres* award. *Poertner*, at 628. For example, in 2017, the Eleventh Circuit found no abuse of discretion when the district court found that on top of $30 million cash option, an enhanced warranty on defendant's products was "itself a significant tangible benefit" worth over $200 million. *Carter*, 701 F. App'x at 767.

The lodestar method "tak[es] the number of hours reasonably expended on the litigation multiplied by a reasonable hourly rate." *Alhassid v. Bank of Am., N.A.*, 688 F. App'x 753, 757 (11th Cir. 2017) (citing *Hensley v. Eckerhart*, 461 U.S. 424, 433–34 (1983)). Once the court has calculated the lodestar amount, courts are to give that amount a strong presumption. *Id.* at 758 (finding that the district court does not have to accept defendant's requests for reduction to a voluminous request of over 100 pages of statements for fees over 1,700 hours of legal work) (citation omitted). The Eleventh Circuit has held that the hourly rate for purposes of the lodestar calculation should be tied to the "going rate" in the community and the "relevant market" to consider is the place where the case is filed. *Sos v. State Farm Mut. Auto. Inc., Co.*, No. 21–11769, 2023 U.S. App. LEXIS 22986, at *68 (11th Cir. Aug. 30, 2023) (finding the district court abused its discretion in applying a "national market" approach rather than using the relevant area, Central Florida).

The Supreme Court holds "that the lodestar should only be altered 'in those rare circumstances in which [it] does not adequately take into account a factor that may properly be considered in determining a reasonable fee.'" *Yellow Pages Photos, Inc., v. Ziplocal, LP*, 846 F.3d 1159, 1164 (11th Cir. 2017) (quoting *Perdue v. Kenny ex rel. Winn*, 559 U.S. 542, 554 (2010) (other citation omitted)). The Eleventh Circuit has noted that the circumstances for adjusting the lodestar amount higher or lower are "severely limited." *Id.* (quoting *Resolution Trust Corp. v. Hallmark Builders, Inc.*, 996 F.2d 1144, 1150 (11th Cir. 1993)); *see also Sos v. State Farm Mut. Auto. Inc., Co.*, at *4 (11th Cir. 2023) (finding the district court's application of the maximum multiplier of 2.5 was an abuse of discretion because the record did not support a finding that success was unlikely at the outset of the case). The court may adjust the amount downward for partial success, but "'must compare the amount of damages sought to the amount awarded[,]'" *Alhassid*, at 758 (citing *Gray ex rel. Alexander v. Bostic*, 720 F.3d 887, 894 (11th Cir. 2013)), including "all distinct measures of success when determining whether success was limited." *Id.* (citation omitted). "But, the Supreme Court has frowned on a strictly mathematical approach calculating attorney's fees based on a ratio of total claims to successfully litigated ones. . . ." *Yellow Pages*, at 1164 (citation omitted). "A comparison of damages sought to the damages received is an appropriate measurement of the relative success of litigation." *Id.* (citing *Popham v. City of Kennesaw*, 820 F.2d 1570, 1580–81 (11th Cir. 1987)).

A conclusory statement that the fee is reasonable is not enough either. *See Danubis Group, LLC v. Landmark Am. Ins. Co.*, 685 F. App'x 792 (11th Cir. 2017) (affirming lower court decision on fees based on specific findings) (citing *Norman v. Hous. Auth. of Montgomery*, 836 F.2d 1292, 1304 (11th Cir. 1988)). In that vein, counsel should maintain proper records detailing the time and general subject matter of the time with sufficient particularity. *Alhassid*, at 757–58 (citing *Norman*, 836 F.2d at 1303). The district court need not give applications an hour-by-hour review, as it is "both impractical and a waste of judicial resources" and the appellate court has approved "across-the-board percentage cuts to the number of hours claimed." *Id.* at 758 (citing *Loranger v. Stierheim*, 10 F.3d 776, 783 (11th Cir. 1994)). If the trial court excludes time, the Eleventh Circuit asks that it "identify the hours excluded and explain why those hours were disallowed." *Id.* (citing *Villano v. City of Boynton Beach*, 254 F.3d 1302, 1311 (11th Cir. 2001)).

Most recently, the Eleventh Circuit considered calculating attorney's fees for a "coupon settlement" under CAFA. *Drazen*, 106 F.4th at 1349–50. The Court defined a coupon as a "voucher, certificate, or form that can be exchanged for one or more goods or services, or for a discount on one or more goods or services, thus aligning our interpretation with those of the Fourth and Second Circuits." *Id.* at 1349. The Court determined that the district court calculating attorney's fees as a percentage of possible recovery was an abuse of discretion as the wrong legal standard. *Id.* at 1351. Aligning with sister circuits other than the Ninth Circuit, the Court concluded "attorney's fees for coupon settlements under CAFA may be based on the value of the coupons that are redeemed, the lodestar method, or a combination of both." *Id.* at 1350. Thus, a court may not rely on total possible recovery under a coupon settlement when approving attorney's fees, but rather it must first estimate the value of coupons likely to be redeemed. *Id.* The Court noted that in many cases, it will be reasonable for a district court to entertain fee motions "only after the coupons' expiration date so that it knows for certain the value of the coupons that *were* actually redeemed." *Id.* at 1350 (emphasis in original).

b. Clear-Sailing Provision and Kicker Clause

A clear sailing provision is "an 'agreement[] whereby the defendant agrees not to contest class counsel's fee petition as long as it does not exceed a specified amount.'" *Poertner*, 618 F. App'x at 630, n.6. The Eleventh Circuit has remarked that "[s]ome courts and commentators have noted that clear sailing clauses could allow 'a defendant to pay class counsel excessive fees and costs in exchange for counsel accepting an unfair settlement on behalf of the class.'" *Id.* (quoting *In re Bluetooth Headset Prods. Liab. Litig.*, 654 F.3d 935, 947 (9th Cir. 2011)).

A "kicker" clause reverts all fees not awarded to the defendants, rather than to the class or any *cy pres* fund. *Id.* (citing *Bluetooth*, at 947). These "clauses are potentially problematic because they deprive the class of benefits that the defendant is willing to pay." *Id.* (citing *Bluetooth*, at 949).

In a recent case, the Eleventh Circuit found that the inclusion of both clauses in a settlement agreement were not "'subtle signs' that objectively the class is not getting as good of a deal as it could. . . ." *Id.* at 630. But it cautions that when such clauses do exist, the district court should maintain its "active supervisory role." *Waters*, 190 F.3d 1291, 1300.

c. Expenses

Similar to fees, the Eleventh Circuit permits recovery of fair, reasonable, and justified litigation costs. *Poertner*, 618 F. App'x at 631; *Nelson*, 484 F. App'x at 433.

12. APPELLATE ISSUES

a. Standing to Appeal

"The general rule is 'only parties to a lawsuit, or those that properly become parties, may appeal an adverse judgment.'" *Carter*, 701 F. App'x at 764 (quoting *Marino v. Ortiz*, 484 U.S. 301, 304 (1988) (per curiam)). But in 2002, the Supreme Court held that a class member who intervened by objecting at a fairness hearing to the settlement had standing to appeal. *Devlin v. Scardelletti*, 536 U.S. 1, 14 (2002). The Eleventh Circuit has consistently followed this precedent. *U.S. v. Alabama*, 271 F. App'x 896, 898–99 (11th Cir. 2008) (finding non-named class members who filed timely objections to settlement agreements have prudential standing) (citing *Devlin*, at 2013), but has held that nonintervening objectors who were excluded from the class definition have no standing to appeal the trial court's denial of their objections. *AAL High Yield Bond Fund v. Deloitte & Touche LLP*, 361 F.3d 1305, 1309 (11th Cir. 2004). Thus, unnamed class members "who have timely objected to a class settlement may appeal the denial of their objections without first moving to intervene." *Day*, 729 F.3d at 1320 (quoting *AAL*, at 1309). This aligns with its sister circuits as well. *Id.* (citations omitted).

In a 2015 case, the defendant argued that objectors who never formally intervened in the case lacked standing to appeal a Rule 23(b)(3) class settlement. *Poertner*, 618 F. App'x at 628. The defendant opposed the objectors, arguing that only class members of a Rule 23(b)(1) class could appeal a settlement's approval because, under the Supreme Court's decision in *Devlin* permitting objection appeals only from those class members who have no other way to avoid being bound by the settlement. *Id.* at 627. The Eleventh Circuit rejected that argument, permitting the objectors standing to appeal settlement approval for both Rule

23(b)(1) and 23(b)(3) classes. *Id.* at 628. This is consistent with the First, Sixth, Seventh, Ninth, and Tenth Circuits. *Id.* at 627–28 (citations omitted).

In a 2015 case, the defendant opposed class certification and conditionally moved to compel arbitration of the unnamed putative class members' claims. *Checking Acc't Litig.*, 780 F.3d 1031. The Eleventh Circuit held that the court lacked jurisdiction to consider the defendant's motion to compel arbitration of the class members' claims because without class certification, the defendant and the putative class members lack a justiciable controversy. *Id.* at 1037 ("because the unnamed putative class members are not yet before the court, any claims that they might have against [the defendant] necessarily exist only by hypothesis"); *see Day*, 729 F.3d at 1316 ("absent class members are not 'parties' whose consent is required for a magistrate judge to enter a final judgment").

But an unnamed class member has standing to appeal the district court's denial of his or her untimely opt out request. *In re Healthsouth Corp. Secs. Litig.*, 334 F. App'x 248, 252–53 (11th Cir. 2009). Finally, in 2017, the Eleventh Circuit found that objecting class members, who did not opt out of the class, have standing to appeal. *Carter*, 701 F. App'x 759.

b. Interlocutory Review

Federal Civil Rule 23(f) allows for interlocutory appeals of class certification orders.

The rule also sets a 14-day deadline from the date of the district court's class certification order to appeal. If the appeal is untimely, the appellate court lacks jurisdiction to consider it. *Jenkins v. BellSouth Corp.*, 491 F.3d 1288, 1290 (11th Cir. 2007). The "window closes quickly to promote judicial economy." *Id.* The Eleventh Circuit has held that a party can toll that deadline by filing a motion for reconsideration with the district court. *Id.* (citing *Shin v. Cobb Cnty. Bd. of Educ.*, 248 F.3d 1061, 1064–65 (11th Cir. 2001)). But the district court cannot circumvent the deadline by vacating and reentering its order to restart the clock. *Id.* at 1289 (finding that a district court cannot "sponsor a revival of a right to seek an interlocutory appeal of its decision about class certification as frequently and spontaneously as an evangelical preacher leads a revival for a congregation").

As for discovery, this interlocutory appeal does not automatically stay the district court case. This circuit acknowledges that Rule 23(f) "'contemplates that in most cases discovery (at the very least, merits discovery) will continue notwithstanding the pendency of an appeal of the class certification order.'" *Local 703, I B of T Grocery & Food Emps. Welfare Fund v. Regions Fin. Corp.* (*Local 703*), No. 12-cv-14168, 2012 U.S. App. LEXIS 18603, *3 (11th Cir. Sept. 4, 2012) (quoting *Prado-Steiman ex rel. Prado v. Bush*, 221 F.3d 1266, 1273 n.8 (11th Cir. 2000)). The requesting party must show that it will suffer irreparable harm if the court does not stay discovery. *Id.* at *2 (citing *Prado-Steiman*, at 1273 n.8). "[M]ere litigation expense, even substantial and unrecoupable cost, does not constitute irreparable injury." *Id.* at *3 (citing *F.T.C. v. Standard Oil Co. of California*, 449 U.S. 232, 244 (1980)).

The Eleventh Circuit reviews certification decisions for an abuse of discretion, but that standard "does not differ greatly from review for error." *Electrolux*, 817 F.3d at 1233 (vacating district court order for applying wrong standard for predominance requirement) (citation omitted). Basically, the Eleventh Circuit "will only find an abuse of discretion if the District Court applies the wrong legal standard, follows improper procedures in makings its determination, bases its decision on clearly erroneous findings of fact, or applies the law in an unreasonable or incorrect manner." *Local 703*, 762 F.3d at 1253 (citation omitted). It reviews interpretations of the Civil Rules under a de novo standard. *Pickett*, 209 F.3d 1276, 1279 (citation omitted).

Rule 23(f) does not permit the appellate court to review the merits of the case, only the certification order. *Id.* at 1279; *Carter v. West Publ'g Co.*, 225 F.3d 1258, 1262 (11th Cir. 2000) (citing *Pickett*). The Eleventh Circuit holds that standing is part of Rule 23(a)'s adequacy requirement and therefore is proper for a Rule 23(f) appeal. *West Publ'g*, at 1263. This includes statute of limitations issues as well. *Id.* at 1267.

In *Prado*, the Eleventh Circuit engaged in a detailed review of the standards for a Rule 23(f) review. *See Prado*, 221 F.3d at 1271–78. Ultimately, the Court in *Prado* set the following "guideposts" that may be utilized in determining whether to grant an interlocutory appeal under Rule 23(f). "First, and most important," the Eleventh Circuit will "examine whether the district court's ruling is likely dispositive of the litigation by creating a 'death knell' for either plaintiff or defendant." *Id.* at 1274. Other considerations include (1) whether the petitioner has shown a *substantial* weakness in the class certification decision, such that the decision likely constitutes an abuse of discretion; (2) whether the appeal will permit the resolution of an unsettled legal issue that is important to the particular litigation as well as important in itself; (3) the nature and status of the litigation before the district court ("Some cases plainly will be in a better pre-trial posture for interlocutory appellate review than others."); and (4) the likelihood that future events may make immediate appellate review more or less appropriate. *Id.* at 1274–76.

The *Prado* court added that it was not creating any bright-line rules or rigid categories for accepting or denying Rule 23(f) petitions, noting the decisions are "highly discretionary." *Id.* at 1276. It reiterated that interlocutory appeals are inherently disruptive, time-consuming, and expensive and that the court should use restraint in accepting the petitions. *Id.* at 1276–77. Acknowledging the instant case may not raise the kind of issues that ordinarily meet the guideposts above, the Eleventh Circuit nevertheless granted the petition and vacated the class certification. *Id.* at 1277–83 (noting in part that the lawsuit has tremendous importance to thousands of developmentally disabled persons in Florida who have a critical need for prompt delivery of services and public interest in determining promptly the scope of state financial obligations).

The appellate court recognizes that class certification causes settlement pressures for the losing party, and "such pressures were the main reason behind the enactment of Rule 23(f). . . ." *Klay*, 382 F.3d at 1275. But it does not allow defendants "to rely upon it as the basis for overturning the underlying certification ruling." *Id.*

13. TOLLING STATUTE OF LIMITATIONS

The U.S. Supreme Court held that the filing of a class action suspends the statute of limitations for all putative class members. *Am. Pipe & Constr. Co. v. Utah*, 414 U.S. 538 (1974). Almost ten years later, the Eleventh Circuit acknowledged that the Supreme Court extended its ruling "to would-be class members who filed separate actions after the denial of class certification." *Dusek v. JPMorgan Chase & Co.*, 832 F.3d 1243, 1247 (11th Cir. 2016) (citing *Crown, Cork & Seal Co., Inc. v. Parker*, 462 U.S. 345, 353–54 (1983)).

In a well-known case from 1994, the Eleventh Circuit considered whether a pending class case that was certified and then later vacated tolled the statute of limitations for the class members. *Griffin v. Singletary*, 17 F.3d 356 (11th Cir. 1994); *see also China Agritech, Inc. v. Resh*, 138 S. Ct. 1800, 1806 (2018) (citing *Griffin*). It held that a pending class case did *not* toll the statute of limitations for later class actions, but it did for individual cases. *Id.* at 357. Thus, one class action cannot "piggy back" onto another class to toll the statute of limitations for the second class action. *Id.* at 359. It eliminates "endless rounds of litigation in the district court. . . ." *Id.*

Although the Third, Sixth, Seventh, Eighth, and Ninth Circuits have either distinguished, criticized, or rejected *Griffin*, the Eleventh Circuit affirmed *Griffin* in 2015 based on its prior-precedent rule. *Ewing Indus. Corp. v. Bob Wines Nursery, Inc.*, 795 F.3d 1324 (11th Cir. 2015), *cert. denied*, 136 S. Ct. 1379 (2016). The district court in *Ewing* held that a pending class action did not toll the statute of limitations for a later class action seeking to represent the same class. *Id.* at 1325. The Eleventh Circuit affirmed. *Id.* It explained that the *Griffin* decision does not permit a piggyback class action no "matter whether the first purported class action fails due to the inadequacy of the class representative or due to defects in the class itself." *Id.* at 1327. Thus, "the Eleventh Circuit maintains a 'no piggyback rule' for class actions." *Barkley v. Pizza Hut of Am., Inc.*, No. 6:14-cv-376, 2015 WL 12826455, *1 (Oct. 15, 2015, M.D. Fla.) (citing *Griffin*, at 359, *Ewing*, at 1327–28).

For individual claims, the Eleventh Circuit recognized that *American Pipe* tolls the statute of limitations "as of the date the complaint is filed, and it remains tolled until the court rejects class certification or the case comes to an end." *Davis v. Coca-Cola Bottling Co. Consol.*, 516 F.3d 955, 968 (11th Cir. 2008) (citing *Am. Pipe*, at 552–53). If the case is dismissed, the class members "must seek to intervene or file a separate action[,]" *Fox v. Tyson Foods, Inc.*, 519 F.3d 1298, 1303 (11th Cir. 2008) (citation omitted), but must do so promptly. *Bost v. Fed. Express Corp.*, 372 F.3d 1233, 1242 (11th Cir. 2004) ("[e]quitable tolling is inappropriate when a plaintiff did not file an action promptly or failed to act with due diligence"), *cert. denied*, 543 U.S. 1020 (2004). But "[d]ue diligence, though necessary, is not sufficient to prevail on the issue of equitable tolling." *Moore v. Chamberlain*, 559 F. App'x 969, 970 (11th Cir. 2014) (citing *Bost*, at 1479).

14. ARBITRATION ISSUES

The enforceability of a class-action waiver is a question of law that the Eleventh Circuit will review de novo. *Davis v. Oasis Legal Fin. Operating Co., LLC*, 936 F.3d 1174, 1178 (11th Cir. 2019) (citing *Cruz v. Cingular Wireless, LLC*, 648 F.3d 1205, 1210 (11th Cir. 2011)). The Eleventh Circuit has found that the Federal Arbitration Act "creates a 'presumption of arbitrability.'" *Mason v. Midland Funding LLC*, 815 F. App'x 320, 323–24 (11th Cir. 2020) (quoting *Dasher v. RBC Bank (USA)*, 745 F.3d 1111, 1115 (11th Cir. 2014)). "Consistent with the FAA's text, 'courts must rigorously enforce arbitration agreements according to their terms. . . .'" *Walthour v. Chipio Windshield Repair, LLC*, 745 F.3d 1326, 1329 (11th Cir. 2014) (quoting *Am. Express Co. v. Italian Colors Rest.*, 133 S.Ct. 2304, 2309 (2013)). "Any doubts concerning the scope of arbitrable issues—that is, doubts over whether an issue falls within the ambit of what the parties agreed to arbitrate—should be resolved in favor of arbitration." *Earth Sci. Tech, Inc. v. Impact UA, Inc.*, 809 F. App'x 600, 604 (11th Cir. 2020) (quoting *JPay, Inc. v. Kobel*, 904 F.3d 923, 929 (11th Cir. 2018)).

"'[W]hile doubts concerning the scope of an arbitration clause should be resolved in favor of arbitration, the presumption does not apply to disputes concerning whether an agreement to arbitrate has been made.'" *Mason*, 815 F. App'x at 323–24 (quoting *Dasher*, 745 F.3d at 1116). "Rather, the threshold question of whether an arbitration agreement exists at all is 'simply a matter of contract.'" *Id.* (quoting *First Options of Chicago, Inc. v. Kaplan*, 514 U.S. 938, 943 (1995)).

The Eleventh Circuit has "identified three distinct types of challenges to motions to compel arbitration:

> (1) A challenge to the validity of the arbitration clause standing alone;
> (2) A challenge to the validity of the contract as a whole; and
> (3) A challenge to the very existence of the contract."

Reiterman v. Abid, 26 F.4th 1226, 1231 (11th Cir. 2022) (quoting *Wiand v. Schneiderman* 778 F.3d 917, 924 (11th Cir. 2015) (citing *Buckeye Check Cashing, Inc. v. Cardegna*, 546 U.S. 440, 444–45 n.1 (2006))).

In 2014, the Eleventh Circuit dismissed a FLSA case, as it enforced collective action waivers contained in the plaintiff-employee's arbitration agreement. *Id.* at 1335–36. Specifically, it found that the waivers were permissible because Congress failed to explicitly exempt FLSA cases from arbitration. *Id.* at 1336. In 2011, a class of cell phone users argued that Florida's consumer statutes and public policy prohibited the enforcement of an arbitration provision to exculpate the defendant from liability. *Cruz v. Cingular Wireless, LLC*, 648 F.3d 1205, 1212 (11th Cir. 2011). The Eleventh Circuit rejected that argument and dismissed the complaint. *Id.* at 1216.

In 2017, the Eleventh Circuit reaffirmed that a nonparty to an arbitration agreement "may force arbitration if the relevant state contract law allows him or her to enforce the agreement to arbitrate. *Variable Annuity Life Ins. Co. v. Laferrera*, 680 F. App'x 880, 883 (11th Cir. 2017) (applying Alabama law to deny arbitration "because the description of the parties subject to the agreements is 'so restrictive as to preclude arbitration' by non-parties") (quoting *Lawson v. Life of the S. Ins. Co.*, 648 F.3d 1166, 1170 (11th Cir. 2011)); *Kroma Makeup EU, LLC v. Boldface Licensing + Branding, Inc.*, 845 F.3d 1351, 1354 (11th Cir. 2017) (finding Florida law requires the nonparty to show that the other party is relying on the agreement to assert claims and that the scope of the arbitration clause covers the dispute) (citing *Lawson*, at 1170–71)); *Drayton v. Toyota Motor Credit Corp.*, 686 F. App'x 757 (11th Cir. 2017) (determining that equitable estoppel was not appropriate in Florida case because plaintiff was not seeking liability against defendant under terms of agreement); *Branch v. Ottinger*, 477 F. App'x 718, 720 (11th Cir. 2012) (recognizing that Georgia law requires the claims against the nonparty "be directly based on the contract containing the arbitration clause").

In late 2024, in *Lubin v. Starbucks Corp.*, 2024 WL 5113125 (11th Cir. Dec. 16, 2024), the Eleventh Circuit rejected an employer's attempt to compel arbitration of claims brought by a former employee's husband, where he had not signed an agreement with the employer and his claims were not sufficiently related to his wife's employment agreement. That case arose from a putative action against Starbucks, alleging the company did not provide adequate health notifications under COBRA. *Id.*

In 2018, the Eleventh Circuit recently reversed a district court and permitted Wells Fargo to compel arbitration against unnamed putative class members after the class was certified. *Gutierrez v. Wells Fargo Bank, NA*, 889 F.3d 1230 (11th Cir. 2018). In doing so, the Court said Wells Fargo did not act inconsistently with its arbitration rights as to unnamed plaintiffs, because the bank stated expressly that it did not plan to seek arbitration with named plaintiffs while explaining that it was not in position to assert its arbitration rights against unnamed plaintiffs but wished to preserve those rights for when the matter became ripe for court to consider them. *See id.*; *see also Lambert v. Signature Healthcare, LLC*, 2022 U.S. App. LEXIS 18787 (11th Cir. July 8, 2022) (reversing Florida district court that found an arbitration agreement in employment contract both procedurally and substantively unconscionable under Florida law) (citing *Guitierrez*).

In *JPay, Inc. v. Kobel*, the Eleventh Circuit looked at a matter of first impression: whether the availability of class arbitration was a substantive, gateway question, that was presumptively for a Court to decide. 904 F.3d 923 (11th Cir. 2018). The court determined it was a gateway question for the Court to presumptively decide, but found that the parties had clearly expressed their intent to submit the question of whether the arbitration can proceed on a class basis to the arbitrator, overcoming the presumption that the Court would decide. *See id.* In 2020, the appellate court reinforced its *JPay* decision, holding "that where parties expressly incorporate the AAA rules into an arbitration provision, 'this alone serves as a clear and unmistakable delegation of questions of arbitrability to an arbitrator.'" *WasteCare Corp. v. Harmony Enters.*, 822 F. App'x 892, 895–96 (11th Cir. 2020) (quoting *JPay*, 904 F.3d at 936 (other citations omitted)); *see also Attix v. Carrington Mortg. Servs., LLC*, 35 F.4th 1284 (11th Cir. 2022) (reversing trial court's denial of motion to compel arbitration and remanding with instructions to compel arbitration).

The Eleventh Circuit has also declined to compel arbitration in certain circumstances. In 2016, the appellate court affirmed the denial of a motion to compel because it construed an ambiguous arbitration clause in favor of the party that did not draft it and because the clause required the parties to arbitrate in an unavailable forum. *Parm v. Nat'l Bank of Cal., N.A.*, 835 F.3d 1331, 1337–38 (11th Cir. 2016); *see also Tuckman v. JPMorgan Chase Bank, N.A.*, 2021 U.S. App. LEXIS 22876 (11th Cir. Aug. 3, 2021) ("turn to the merits issue only if we conclude that the delegation provision is invalid or unenforceable.) (citing *Parm*).

The court of appeals affirmed the denial of a defendant's motion to compel when a prior agreement with an arbitration clause was superseded by a newer agreement that did not contain one. *Dasher v. RBC Bank (USA)*, 745 F.3d 1111 (11th Cir. 2014). The Eleventh Circuit found its opinion consistent with the Second and Sixth Circuits. *Id.* at 1123.

In March 2022, the court reaffirmed its ruling in *Dasher*. *Reiterman v. Abid*, 26 F.4th 1226, 1232—33 (11th Cir.). In *Reiterman*, the appellate court remanded to the district court for it to determine contract issues before considering whether it should compel arbitration. *Id.* at 1233. In that case, the issue was whether chose to rescind their agreement entirely while *Dasher* considered whether the parties replaced the earlier contract with a later one. *Id.* The appellate court saw "no reason the two situations should be treated differently; in both cases, the existence of the earlier contract is called into doubt, not its validity." *Id.* Thus, "the 'threshold question of whether an arbitration agreement exists at all is 'simply a matter of contract.'"

Although the courts enforce arbitration provisions, parties can waive its right to arbitration "'if, under the totality of the circumstances, the party has acted inconsistently with the arbitration right and, in so acting, has in some way prejudiced the other party.'" *Grigsby & Assocs. v. M Sec. Inv.*, 635 F. App'x 728, 731 (11th Cir. 2015) (quoting *S&H Contractors, Inc. v. A.J. Taft Coal Co.*, 906 F.2d 1507, 1514 (11th Cir. 1990)); see also Bennett v. Sys. & Servs Techs., 2022 U.S. Dist. Lexis 84445 (Fla. M.D. May 10, 2022) ("Waiver is inherently case-specific.") (citing *Grigsby*). For example, a defendant waived arbitration rights when it ignored correspondence from plaintiff seeking arbitration and forced plaintiff to incur litigation costs for more than eight months in the district court and then later in a bankruptcy proceeding. *Robinson v. Alston*, 596 F. App'x 871, 873 (11th Cir. 2015). In another case, the defendant waived arbitration when it failed to pursue a delegation clause directing an arbitrator to decide the validity of an arbitration agreement. *Checking Acc't Overdraft Litig.*, 754 F.3d 1290. Rather, defendant choose to take plaintiff for "two trips around the pretrial-motion-and-appeal carousel," (*id.* at 1296), "after it had asked the district court to decide arbitrability—and lost." *Id.* at 1298 (citations omitted). The appellate court ruled that defendant forced plaintiff to incur "precisely the kind of litigation costs that the delegation provision intended to alleviate." *Id.* at 1296.

But a plaintiff can revive a defendant's waived arbitration rights in limited circumstances by, say, filing an amended complaint that asserts new claims or changes the scope or theory of plaintiff's claims. *Garcia v. Wachovia Bank, N.A.*, No., 1:09-MD-02036, 2016 WL 6082035, *7–8 (S.D. Fla. Oct. 17, 2016) (citing *Krinsk v. SunTrust Banks, Inc.*, 654 F.3d 1194, 1200 (11th Cir. 2011)); *Collado v. J.&G. Transp., Inc.*, 820 F.3d 1256, 1261 (11th Cir. 2016). In *Krinsk v. SunTrust Banks, Inc.*, a defendant litigated the matter for nine months—contested class certification and class discovery—before requesting arbitration. 654 F.3d 1194 (11th Cir. 2011). The Southern District of Florida held that defendant waived its right to compel arbitration. The Eleventh Circuit reversed. The amended complaint alleged "revised, but mostly similar, claims" and "greatly enlarged the potential size of the putative class . . . [to] thousands—if not tens of thousands" of potential class members. *Id.* at 1199. The appellate court ruled that even if defendant had waived its right to compel arbitration to original complaint's claims, the amended complaint's "vast augmentation of the putative class so altered the shape of litigation" that the defendant's right to arbitration was revived. *Id.* at 1204.

But in *Collado*, the Eleventh Circuit found that although an amended complaint adding a new state law claim did not revive the defendant's right to arbitrate the initial federal law claims, the defendant could seek compel arbitration of the later-added state claim. 820 F.3d at 1261; *Plaintiffs' S'holders Corp. v. S. Farm Bureau Life Ins. Co.*, 486 F. App'x 786 (11th Cir. 2012) (holding that defendant waived arbitration to plaintiff's original claims even if it could compel arbitration on plaintiff's new cause of action in its Second Amended Complaint).

In *American Family Life Assurance Co. v. Hubbard*, the Eleventh Circuit denied plaintiff's procedure and substantive unconscionability arguments to avoid an arbitration agreement. 759 F. App'x 899 (11th Cir. 2019). First, Georgia law doesn't find the lack of mutual obligations to arbitrate as substantively unconscionable. *Id.* It was not moved that the plaintiff had to incur their party's arbitrator's fees and expenses because there was no evidence they were prohibitively expensive. *Id.* at 906. It again "warned that 'speculative fear of high fees is insufficient.'" *Id.* at 906 (quoting *Escobar v. Celebration Cruise Operator, Inc.*, 805 F.3d 1279, 1291 (11th Cir. 2015)). It also found that a confidentiality provision did not make the provision unconscionable under Georgia law. *Id.*

Most recently in September 2024, the Eleventh Circuit considered whether statutory challenges to the FAA can be decided by an arbitrator rather than a court. *Steines v. Westgate Palace, L.L.C.*, 113 F.4th 1335, 1341 (11th Cir. 2024). The Court concluded, "the question of whether the FAA has been overridden by another act of Congress cannot be delegated to an arbitrator." *Id.* at 1342–43.

FEDERAL CIRCUIT

Veterans Claims Court, Court of Federal Claims, Court of International Trade, and Administrative Agencies

717 Madison Place, N.W.
Washington, DC 20439

By Catherine Ross Dunham
Professor of Law at Elon University School of Law

1. INTRODUCTION

The U.S. Court of Appeals for the Federal Circuit is headquartered in Washington, D.C. The court was created by Congress with passage of the Federal Courts Improvement Act of 1982, which merged the U.S. Court of Customs and Patent Appeals and the appellate division of the U.S. Court of Claims, making the judges of the former courts into circuit judges. The court sits primarily in Washington, D.C., but also sits from time to time in locations other than Washington, and its judges can and do sit by designation on the bench of other courts of appeals and federal district courts. The Federal Circuit may have a total of 12 active circuit judges sitting at any given time. As with other Article III federal judges, the Federal Circuit judges are nominated by the President, must be confirmed by the Senate, and serve lifetime appointments subject to the standard of "good behaviour."

The Federal Circuit is unique among the courts of appeals as it is the only court that has its jurisdiction based wholly upon subject matter rather than geographic location. The Federal Circuit has jurisdiction generally as specified in 28 U.S.C. § 1295. Subject to its jurisdictional grant, the Federal Circuit Court hears certain appeals from all the U.S. District Courts, appeals from certain administrative agencies, and appeals arising under certain statutes. The court hears appeals from the following U.S. tribunals: the Court of Federal Claims; the Court of Appeals for Veterans Claims; the Trademark Trial and Appeal Board; the Patent Trial and Appeal Board; the Boards of Contract Appeals for the Armed Services, Civilians and the Postal Service; the Merit Systems Protection Board; the International Trade Commission; and the Court of International Trade. In addition, the Federal Circuit Court hears appeals from the U.S. District Courts on matters related to patents.

The Federal Circuit has added to class action precedent in several important ways. First, many class action appeals in the Federal Circuit address the sustainability of a class action under Rule 23 of the Rules of the Court of Federal Claims (RCFC) that mirrors Rule 23 of the Federal Rules of Civil Procedure (FRCP) but also differs in several significant ways, most significantly in the lack of any mandatory class action options and the absence of an opt out class under the RCFC Rule 23.

RCFC Rule 23 provides:

(a) Prerequisites. One or more members of a class may sue as representative par-

> ties on behalf of all members only if: (1) the class is so numerous that joinder of all members is impracticable; (2) there are questions of law or fact common to the class; (3) the claims or defenses of the representative parties are typical of the claims or defenses of the class; and (4) the representative parties will fairly and adequately protect the interests of the class.
>
> (b) Class Actions Maintainable. A class action may be maintained if RCFC 23(a) is satisfied and if . . . (2) the United States has acted or refused to act on grounds generally applicable to the class; and (3) the court finds that the questions of law or fact common to class members predominate over any questions affecting only individual members, and that a class action is superior to other available methods for fairly and efficiently adjudicating the controversy. The matters pertinent to these findings include: (A) the class members' interests in individually controlling the prosecution of separate actions; (B) the extent and nature of any litigation concerning the controversy already begun by class members; . . . and (D) the likely difficulties in managing a class action.

The U.S. Court of Federal Claims and the Federal Circuit have held that RCFC Rule 23 differs from FRCP Rule 23 in two important respects: "(1) [RCFC 23] has been modified to reflect the court's jurisdiction, in particular, the narrow circumstances in which the court will afford declaratory or injunctive relief, and (2) it allows only 'opt-in,' but not 'opt-out,' class actions." *Rasmuson v. United States*, 91 Fed. Cl. 204, 210 (2010) (quoting *King v. United States*, 84 Fed. Cl. 120, 122 n.2 (2008)). The criteria set forth in RCFC Rule 23(a) and (b) can be grouped into five categories: (i) **numerosity**—a class so large that joinder is impracticable; (ii) **commonality**—in terms of the presence of common questions of law or fact, the predominance of those questions, and the treatment received by the class members at the hands of the United States; (iii) **typicality**—that the named parties' claims are typical of the class; (iv) **adequacy**—relating to fair representation; and (v) **superiority**—that a class action is the fairest and most efficient way to resolve a given set of controversies. The predominance inquiry of FRCP Rule 23(b)(3) has been incorporated into the commonality inquiry under RCFC Rule 23(a) even though it is stated as a separate requirement under RCFC Rule 23(b). The same is true regarding the superiority requirement that, although included in RCFC Rule 23(b), has been included in the five-element analysis employed by the Federal Court of Claims and Federal Circuit when analyzing class actions filed under RCFC Rule 23. RCFC Rule 23 borrows nearly verbatim the FRCP Rule 23 language, but the criteria from FRCP Rule 23 have been modified to reflect the Court of Claims' focus on awarding damages rather than issuing injunctive or declaratory relief. *Quinault Allottee Ass'n & Individual Allottees v. United States*, 453 F.2d 1272 (Ct. Cl. 1972).

In reviewing class action precedent from the Federal Circuit, this chapter will address primarily precedent involving RCFC Rule 23. Periodically, the Federal Circuit does review class action cases involving patent litigation and other topics that flow from the U.S. District Courts to the Federal Circuit based on the subject matter of the appeal. However, the bulk of the class action case law from the Federal Circuit involves cases filed in the Federal Court of Claim; thus, RCFC Rule 23 plays a prominent role in the Federal Circuit's class action jurisprudence. Also, the subject matters involved in Federal Circuit class action case review are limited, focused primarily on wage and hour cases from the VA Board of Appeals, Tucker Act cases, cases involving takings of real property under the "Rails-to-Trails" Act and other federal statutes involving the taking of real and personal property, and cases involving the law related to Indian tribes. The following discussion describes key principles practitioners can glean from class action decisions of the Federal Circuit and its trial level tribunals.

2. RECENT DECISIONS

In June 2023, the Court of Federal Claim issued a decision that denied class certification because the prerequisites for commonality, typicality, and superiority as set forth in RCFC Rule 23 were not met. *See Arnhold v. United States*, 166 Fed. Cl. 499 (2023). In *Arnhold*, owners of property near a small landing strip on Whidbey Island, Washington (OLF Coupeville), filed a putative class action against the United States, claiming they suffered a Fifth Amendment taking and the United States breached its contract with property owners arising from alleged destruction of or substantial interference with the use and enjoyment of their real property by increased operations of the Navy's fighter jets from the landing strip and the Naval Air Station (NAS) over and around their property. The property owners moved for class certification defining themselves as "all property owners whose use and enjoyment of their real property was destroyed or substantially interfered with on and after March 12, 2019, by the increased operations of the Navy's EA-18g Growler fighter jets from NAS Whidbey Island and OLF Coupeville over and around Plaintiffs' property" and proposed three subclasses representing three different geographically and temporally defined groups within the class of affected property owners. The Court examined the "five requirements" of RCFC Rule 23(a) and determined that the plaintiffs had satisfied the numerosity requirement but failed to satisfy the commonality, typicality, adequacy, and superiority requirements. As to commonality, the Court found that the common questions identified by the plaintiffs could not generate common answers. The Court relied on precedent from similar "avigation" cases, which found that avigation easement claims cannot be resolved in a "one size fits all" manner as each element of the takings claim must be established for each property owner. The Court's analysis of commonality was repeated in its analysis of the other requirements as the plaintiffs were unable to demonstrate a cohesive class when the members of the putative class experienced the harm differently depending on their proximity to the NAS and the length of time they had owned their property, relative to the NAS increased flight activity in and around OLF Coupeville. The court reached its conclusion that the class action framework was not the "fairest and most efficient method to proceed with [the] litigation" thus not superior to other methods of litigating the controversy, "without needing to consider plaintiffs' expert's proposed methodology for assessing damages."

In *Oztimurlenk v. United states,* 162 Fed. Cl. 658 (2022), nurses currently and formerly employed by the Department of Veterans Affairs (VA) brought a putative class action against the United States alleging they were deprived of overtime pay for work performed outside of their regularly scheduled tours of duty. The Federal Court of Claim denied class certification, finding that the nurses' claims failed to satisfy the commonality, numerosity, and superiority requirements of RCFC Rule 23. The Court in *Oztimurlenk* reviewed in detail the analysis required under RCFC Rule 23, comparing the requirements of RCFC Rule 23 to FRCP Rule 23 and noting key differences between the two similar rules, such as the opt-out, opt-in distinction. The Court relied on *Wal-Mart v. Dukes*, 564 U.S. 338 (2011), a FRCP Rule 23 case, to clarify that RCFC Rule 23 "does not set forth a mere pleading standard" that allows the Court to "look beyond the pleadings and seek to develop an understanding of the relevant claims, defenses, facts, and substantive law." As to the numerosity requirement, the Court looked beyond just a numerical analysis, finding that the "count of potential class members speaks to the practicability of joining all of them." Again, relying on *Dukes*, the Court found that commonality was not satisfied as the putative class members could not identify a central question that was resolvable "in one stroke." The Court reasoned that there is no way to resolve on a class wide basis whether an individual nurse worked overtime at all and, even if that question were capable of class wide resolution, the question of damages for each opt-in plaintiff would "overwhelm any common question."

Significant in *Oztimurlenk* is the Court's detailed examination of FRCP Rule 23, and in particular the *Dukes* case, as precedent for a class certification analysis under RCFC Rule 23. The Court analyzes the predominance requirement of FRCP Rule 23(b)(3) as if it were part of the RCFC Rule 23 commonality analysis. RCFC Rule 23(a) does not include a separate predominance prerequisite but rather includes a predominance requirement under RCFC Rule 23(b). The Court correctly notes that the requirements of RCFC Rule 23(a) and (b) form a conjunctive list but the RCFC Rule 23 itself does not merge the analysis of commonality and predominance. Judge Solomson's decision in *Oztimurlenk* raises the question of whether the Federal Court of Claim is attempting to incorporate the Supreme Court's *Dukes* approach, which is largely considered a deterrence to class litigation based on its merger of the commonality requirement of FRCP Rule 23(a) and the predominance requirement of FRCP Rule 23(b)(3) only, into the RCFC Rule 23 class action analysis.

Approximately one month after *Oztimurlenk*, Judge Dietz denied class certification in a lawsuit filed as a putative class action by Fisher on behalf of users of the Public Access to Court Electronic Records (PACER) system. *See Fisher v. United States*, 163 Fed. Cl. 178 (2022). The complaint alleged claims for breach of contract, breach of implied covenant of good faith and fair dealing, and illegal exaction. Fisher, on behalf of "all PACER users who . . . accessed a U.S. District Court, Bankruptcy Court, or the U.S. Court of Federal Claims and were charged for at least one docket report due to a systemic flaw in PACER's billing codes" filed this action alleging that the government overcharged PACER users for accessing federal dockets online. The Government conceded that Fisher had satisfied the requirements of RCFC Rule 23(a) (numerosity, commonality, typicality, adequacy, and superiority) but argued that the putative class action did not meet the RCFC Rule 23(b) requirement of predominance. The Court cited *Oztimurlenk* and the standard for predominance imported from *Wal-Mart v. Dukes*, furthering the meshing of the commonality and predominance requirements in the RCFC Rule 23 context. In *Fisher*, the Court found that the putative class action did not meet the predominance standard as any resolution of class claims would require an individual inquiry into per occurrence determinations of damages. The plaintiff offered expert evidence of methodologies for avoiding individual damages determinations, but the Court was "not convinced that Mr. Fisher's proposed methodologies [were] capable of establishing class wide harm and damages." Based on the same reasoning, the Court also found that Fisher had failed to establish that a class action would be a superior method of litigating the controversy because of the "highly individualized questions of harm and damages presented by this case."

In late 2022, the court of claims issued an unreported decision, *Greene v. United States*, 2022 WL 17547204 (Dec. 9, 2022), which denied class certification because the plaintiffs were proceeding pro se and therefore could not serve as adequate representatives of the class under RCFC Rule 23(a). The plaintiffs—Greene, Byrd, Jackson, Smallen, Wilson, and Day—were granted leave to proceed *in forma pauperis*, then filed a motion for appointment of counsel that was before the court along with the plaintiffs' motion for class certification. The plaintiffs filed a lawsuit seeking compensatory and punitive damages for wrongful incarceration. The putative class would include "members/descendants of the Cherokee Nation and/or those freedmen subject to treaties between [the] Cherokee Nation and the United States," whose incarceration under Oklahoma state law constituted "unlawful violations of Cherokee treaty rights." The court first denied the plaintiffs' motion for appointment of counsel, leaving plaintiffs to proceed pro se on behalf of the putative class. The court then analyzed whether the proposed class action would meet the RCFC Rule 23(a) requirements, specifically Rule 23(a)(iv) (adequacy), which requires that the putative class representative will fairly represent the proposed class. Relying on precedent from putative class actions brought by prisoners proceeding pro se, the court held that "because all plaintiffs in the case are proceeding *pro se*, the adequacy requirement of RCFC 23 is not met." The court further clarified that because plaintiff is acting pro se and lacks formal legal training, he has failed to demonstrate "that he can fairly represent the alleged rights of a class of individuals."

3. OTHER CLASS CERTIFICATION DECISIONS

Owners of bump-type-stock devices, which allow semi-automatic weapons to fire continuous rounds, filed a putative class action against the United States arguing that the applicable law, which would classify such weapons as "machine guns" thus outlawing their possession and sale, amounts to a taking in violation of federal law and the Fifth Amendment of the U.S. Constitution. In *McCutchen v. United States*, 14 F.4th 1355 (Fed. Cir. 2021), the Federal Circuit affirmed the Federal Court of Claim's decision to dismiss plaintiff's putative class action for failure to state a legally cognizable claim under Court of Federal Claims Rule 12(b)(6), holding that the owners of bump-type-stock devices lacked a property right in continued possession or transfer of the devices. The Federal Circuit's decision rested on the "inhere in title" exception to a government taking as specifically applied to personal property. The "inhere in title" exception rests on the threshold requirement that a plaintiff in a takings case identify a legally cognizable property interest. The Federal Circuit concluded that "given the preexisting federal statutory prohibition on possession or transfer of 'machine guns' ... plaintiffs lacked a property right in what they allege was taken – continued possession or transferability of their bump-stock-type devices."

The United States Court of Federal Claim denied class certification under RCFC Rule 23 in a proposed class action filed by registered nurses from the VA Medical Center in Richmond, Virginia and hybrid health care workers from the VA Medical Center in Hines, Illinois in *Crowley v. United States*, 2021 WL 2525838 (Jan. 25, 2021). The Court found that the plaintiffs had failed to carry their burden in establishing that all the RCFC Rule 23 requirements are met. The Court chided plaintiffs for "relying on quotes from other cases without analysis" and for "relying on general assertions that the requirements are met." The Court agreed with plaintiffs that some requirements were met but denied certification because plaintiffs arguments were not "robust enough" to allow the Court to fully analyze the certification requirements.

In contrast, the United States Court of Appeals for Veteran's Claims certified a class of claimants "who received an adverse benefits decision under the Caregiver Program, exhausted the administrative review process within the VHA, and have not been afforded the right to appeal to the Board of Veteran's Appeals." *Beaudette v. McDonough*, 34 Vet. App. 95 (2021). In *Beaudette*, the plaintiff sought relief for himself and others similarly situated who were afforded no administrative appeal at the Board of Veteran Affairs after being denied benefits under the Caregivers and Veterans Omnibus Health Services Act of 2010, Pub. L. No. 111-163, Title I, 124 Stat. 1130, 1132–40 (codified principally at 38 U.S.C. §1720G). The Court determined the VA had wrongfully denied claimants the right to seek Board review. Plaintiff's class description included people who had not sought Board review but the Court discerned no failure to exhaust administrative remedies because any attempt by proposed class members to obtain Board review would be futile given the lack of process. The Secretary contested only the typicality requirement of class certification based on the argument that the requirement that appeals be "on the merits" indicates each claim will differ and plaintiffs did not allege an agency error in common. The Court disagreed, finding that the main substantive issue in the case was whether Board review was available under the Caregiver Program, an issue typical of all past claimants who were not permitted Board review.

In 2021, the Court of Federal Claim issued three decisions approving settlements in equal pay class actions. In *Kandel v. United States*, 2021 WL 2627135 (June 25, 2021), the Court approved a settlement in a two-class class action involving claimants who claimed they were entitled to payment for accrued and accumulated, unused annual leave equal to the pay they would have received had they worked their regular and customary hours per 5 U.S.C. § 5551. The Court found the settlement agreement was "fair, reasonable and adequate" under RCFC Rule 23(a)(2) weighing the factors set forth in the Rule. The Court found the settlement agreement was the result of "conscientious, arms-length negotiation between the parties." Four days later, in *Gallimore v. United States*, 2021 WL 2661421 (June 29, 2021), the Court of Federal Claim again approved a Settlement Agreement in a class action brought by census workers who claimed they performed non-overtime work on a Sunday but did not receive Sunday premium pay under 5 U.S.C. § 5546(a). Following RCFC Rule 23(a)(2), the Court again found that the settlement agreement was the result of "dedicated, arms-length negotiation between the parties" noting that the class members will receive 88.5% of the back pay they are owed, based on the relevant payroll data. The Court again approved settlement in an equal pay class action in *Austin v. United States*, 2021 WL 4006026 (September 2, 2021) wherein nurses and other health care workers working for the VHA and VA claimed they were entitled to additional pay for services performed on a federally recognized holiday. Relying on RCFC Rule 23, the Court again found the settlement was "fair, reasonable and adequate" noting the "extensive settlement negotiations" between counsel for both parties which led to a one hundred percent recovery to each claimant.

In August 2020, the Federal Circuit heard a challenge to subject matter jurisdiction in *National Veteran Legal Services Program v. United States,* 968 F.3d 1340 (Fed. Cir. 2020). The case involved a class action brought by three national nonprofit organizations against the United States alleging that fees incurred by use of PACER (Public Access to Court Electronic Records) exceeded the amount that lawfully could be charged under 28 U.S.C. § 1913. Plaintiffs alleged that each individual download of a public record through PACER gave rise to a separate "illegal exaction" claim in violation of the statute. The plaintiffs sought return or refund of PACER fees collected over the previous six years, asserting subject matter jurisdiction under the Little Tucker Act, 28 U.S.C. § 1346. The district court certified a class consisting of all individuals and entities who had paid PACER fees between April 21, 2010, and April 21, 2016, excluding federal government entities and present class counsel. The parties filed cross motions for summary judgment, disagreeing on the applicability of 28 U.S.C. § 1913 to the plaintiffs' claims. The government challenged the court's jurisdiction under the Little Tucker Act. After denying in part and granting in part each movant's motions for summary judgment, the court stayed further proceedings and allowed cross appeals. On appeal, the government argued the trial court lacked subject matter jurisdiction over plaintiffs' illegal exaction claim because 28 U.S.C. § 1913 does not provide a cause of action with a monetary remedy. The Court of Appeals for the Federal Circuit disagreed with the government's argument, specifically holding that the "sole certified class claim here asserts that the value sued for—the excessive PACER fees remitted—was improperly collected" in contravention of a federal statute thus "[p]laintiffs' complaint states a claim over which the district court had jurisdiction under the Little Tucker Act."

In 2019, the Federal Circuit addressed the issue of whether a settlement agreement had been abandoned in the context of a rails-to-trails class action against the government. *Haggart v. United States*, 943 F.3d 943 (Fed. Cir. 2019). The issue on appeal involved a settlement agreement between the landowners and the government that was approved by the Court of Federal Claims in 2013 and then vacated by the Federal Circuit because the "class counsel withheld critical information necessary for class members to make an informed decision." The matter was remanded back to the Court of Federal Claims for further action. The Court of Federal Claims held a hearing, ultimately granting class counsel's Motion to Enforce the Settlement Agreement. The government argued that class counsel had "abandoned" the settlement agreement and filed a motion for reconsideration. The Court of Federal Claims denied the government's motion and issued an opinion approving the settlement agreement as procedurally and substantively fair in January 2018. On appeal, the government argued that the Court of Federal Claims erred in finding that the parties did not abandon the settlement agreement. Specifically, the government argued that class counsel's conduct on remand was inconsistent with any intent to preserve the settlement agreement. At various times during the remand proceedings, class counsel reported on ongoing communications with class members, relating that he was meeting with class members to ascertain whether they would accept individual settlement amounts and otherwise support the settlement. In the course of relating those conversations to the trial court, class counsel at times referred to efforts to "resurrect" the settlement agreement and determine whether the agreement was "still in tact." The Federal Circuit found that class counsel's conduct in the course of the remand proceedings "evidenced an effort to address various legal and factual uncertainties surrounding the Settlement Agreement," rather than being conduct inconsistent with an intent to be bound by the settlement agreement. The Federal Circuit held that the Court of Federal Claims did not err in finding that the government failed to meet its burden of demonstrating the parties abandoned the settlement agreement.

In 2017, the Federal Circuit issued an important decision in *Monk v. Shulkin*, Nos. 2015-7092, 2015-7106, 2017 U.S. App. LEXIS 7329, at *2 (Fed. Cir. Apr. 26, 2017*)*, holding expressly that the Veterans Court has the "authority to certify a class for class action and to maintain similar aggregate resolution procedures." The case reviewed the appeal of Monk from adverse decisions at the Veterans Court regarding the delay in payment of his VA benefits and a decision to deny Monk's request that his action be certified as a class action as other veterans were similarly situated, experiencing delays in the payment of VA benefits. The Veterans Court denied the request for class certification based on its practice not to allow class actions in Veterans Court, and Monk appealed that ruling. In addition to a full discussion of mootness that is discussed below, the Federal Circuit evaluated the Veterans Court authority to certify class actions and the reasons the class action procedure would be positive if employed in Veterans Court. FRCP Rule 23 does not apply in Veterans Court, but the Federal Circuit found that the Veterans Court had authority to certify a class action under the All Writs Act, 28 U.S.C. §1651(a) and under the Veterans' Judicial Review Act (VJRA), Pub. L. 100-687, Div. A, Title III, 301(a), §§ 4052, 4061, and 4066, 102 Stat. 4113, 4113, 4115–16 (1988). The court referenced other veterans' class actions from the district courts, noting that these actions had met the requirements under FRCP Rule 23. *See, e.g.*, *Johnson v. Robinson*, 415 U.S. 361 (1974); *Wayne State Univ. v. Cleland*, 590 F.2d 627 (6th Cir. 1978), and *Giusti-Bravo v. United States Veterans Admin.*, 853 F. Supp. 34 (D.P.R. 1993). The *Monk* court further held that class actions in the VA context can "help the Veterans Court exercise [its] authority by promoting efficiency, consistency, and fairness, and improving access to legal and expert assistance by parties with limited resources." *Monk* at *18–19. In support of its holding, the court discussed three reasons class actions are appropriate in Veterans Court: (1) the use of an aggregate procedure may reduce the delays in Veterans Court, the very subject of Monk's litigation; (2) the use of class actions may allow for more consistent adjudication in Veterans Court as aggregate litigation is more likely to produce precedential opinions (whereas now the Veterans Court produces only a small number of precedential opinions per year); and (3) "class action suits could be used to compel correction of systemic error and to ensure that like veterans are treated alike." *Monk* at *20.

For practitioners in the Federal Circuit and the Veterans Court, the *Monk* decision is important as it now allows practitioners to serve clients in aggregate litigation, thus permitting similarly situated veterans to proceed together. The use of aggregate litigation in this context speaks to the original goals of class action litigation—to allow those with limited access and resources to join in pursuit of a common resolution. The decision also will keep viable veteran-based class actions in Veterans Court where there is experience relating to veterans' claims, thus enabling overall system efficiency and the best results for the litigants.

4. JURISDICTIONAL PREREQUISITES

a. Subject Matter Jurisdiction

The Court of Federal Claim addressed subject matter jurisdiction under the Tucker Act in a putative class action brought by Plaintiff Rodgers, *pro se* and purporting to represent a class of individuals injured in the United States foster care system, against the United States through the Department of Health and Human Services, judges, court officials, social workers, police officers, attorneys, adoption agencies, volunteers, counties, and their agencies. *Rodgers v. United* States, 153 Fed. Cl. 538 (2021). The Court examined the subject matter jurisdiction of the Court of Claim, specifically jurisdiction under the Tucker Act, in response to the government's motions to dismiss under Court of Federal Claim Rules 12(b)(1) and 12(h)(3) noting that the United States Court of Federal Claim is a court of limited subject matter jurisdiction. The Tucker Act, which serves as a waiver of sovereign immunity, placed within the Court of Claim's jurisdiction "any claim against the United States founded either upon the Constitution, or any act of Congress or any regulation of an executive department, or upon any express or implied contract with the United States, or for liquidated or unliquidated damages in cases not sounding in tort." 28 U.S.C. § 1491(a)(1). The Tucker Act is a jurisdictional statute which does not create any right of action against the United States. To proceed against the government under the Tucker Act, the plaintiff must demonstrate that the substantive law relied on can be interpreted as mandating compensation by the United States government. Plaintiff Rodgers argued subject matter jurisdiction under 28 U.S.C. §1331 and §1332, overlooking the fact that these statutes confer subject matter jurisdiction on the Federal District Courts and not the Federal Court of Claim. The plaintiff further argued subject matter jurisdiction under the Class Action Fairness Act (CAFA), 28 U.S.C. §§1711–1715. The Court of Claim found no basis for subject matter jurisdiction under CAFA since CAFA jurisdiction is derived from jurisdiction under 28 U.S.C. §1332 which does not apply to the Federal Court of Claim. The Court also noted that plaintiff's claim failed as she attempted to bring the action in her own name, pro se, and as class representative for other members of the putative class. A pro se plaintiff is not permitted to represent class members under RCFC 83.1(a)(3) which requires Plaintiff to be a member in good standing of the relevant bar if she will be representing other parties in the litigation.

The Federal Circuit decided two similar cases involving legal malpractice suits against law firms that handled patent litigation cases by former clients who alleged that the lawyers made errors in patent prosecution and litigation. *See Air Measurement Tech. Inc. v. Akin Gump Strauss Hauer & Feld, L.L.P.*, 504 F.3d 1262 (Fed. Cir. 2007), and *Neoro Repair, Inc. v. The Nath Law Group*, 781 F.3d 1340 (Fed. Cir. 2015). The subject matter jurisdiction issue in both cases centered on whether the federal patent issues that formed the core inquiry in the legal malpractice lawsuits created a federal issue such that subject matter jurisdiction was proper in federal court under *Grable and Sons Metal Products, Inc. v. Darue Engineering & Manufacturing*, 545 U.S. 308 (2005).[1] In *Air Measurement Technologies*, the court held that "where, as here, establishing patent infringement is a necessary element of a malpractice claim stemming from alleged mishandling of patent prosecution and earlier patent litigation, the issue is substantial and contested, and federal resolution of the issue was intended by Congress, there is 'arising under' jurisdiction" under 28 U.S.C. §1338 and *Grable Air Measurement Technologies*, 504 F.3d at 1273. In contrast, under similar facts, the court in *Neuro Repair* found that the federal patent issue was disputed but not substantial, as required under *Grable*. The court further held that if the federal courts hear attorney malpractice claims that do not raise substantial issues of federal law, the federal courts "would usurp the important role of [the]state courts in regulating the practice of law within their boundaries and disrupt [] the federal-state balance approved by Congress." *See Neuro Repair*, 781 F.3d at 1348.

[1] These cases are not class action cases but are included here as the *Grable* arising under theory is often used in class action and mass tort cases to remove cases from state court to federal court, such as has been done in the VW litigation. In the VW litigation, federal courts have removed cases finding a federal issue based on the plaintiffs' allegations that the EPA emissions violations form the factual core of the VW emissions litigation.

b. CAFA Requirements

It is worth noting that there are no Federal Circuit cases regarding the Class Action Fairness Act (CAFA), 28 U.S.C. § 1332(d). This gap is most likely due to the relatively recent enactment of CAFA in 2005, the low volume of FRCP Rule 23 class actions appealed to the Federal Circuit, the dominant role of the RCFC Rule 23 in Federal Circuit class action appeals, and the prevalence of federal question cases heard in the Federal Circuit.

c. Standing

In May 2017, the Federal Circuit reviewed an appeal by Starr International, the largest shareholder in AIG at the time of the 2008 economic collapse, alleging that the action taken by the federal government to bolster AIG constituted an unconstitutional taking. *Starr Int'l Co., Inc. v. United States*, 856 F.3d 953 (Fed. Cir. 2017). Starr sued on behalf of all AIG shareholders, seeking relief based on economic losses caused by the government's acquisition of equity and subsequent reduction in the value of AIG stock. The Court of Claims determined that the government's action was an illegal exaction in violation of the Federal Reserve Act and the Fifth Amendment but declined to grant relief to the plaintiff shareholders. On appeal, the government argued that the plaintiff shareholders lacked standing to sue as the action was a derivative action which belonged to the corporation not its shareholders.[2] The Federal Circuit reversed the Court of Claim on the issue of standing finding that the government's acquisition of equity did not constitute a physical seizure of the plaintiff's AIG stock, thus Starr and other shareholders did not have standing to sue the federal government.

Considerations of standing in the Federal Circuit overlap with discussions of the tolling of the statute of limitations in class action litigation. For that reason, the tolling discussion and the standing discussion are combined here for ease of understanding and reduced duplication. The Federal Circuit has authored several important decisions on the issues of standing and the tolling of the applicable statute of limitations as those issues relate to class action litigation: *Arctic Slope Native Ass'n Ltd. v. Sebelius*, 583 F.3d 785 (Fed. Cir. 2009); *Bright v. United States*, 603 F.3d 1273 (Fed. Cir. 2010); and *Ramona Two Shields v. United States*, 820 F.3d 1324 (Fed. Cir. 2016).

The plaintiffs in *Ramona Two Shields v. United States* brought claims on behalf of themselves and others similarly situated seeking redress for the U.S. government's alleged mishandling of oil and gas leases on Indian allotment land. *Ramona*, 820 F.3d 1324 (Fed. Cir. 2016). The lawsuit was based on a previous action brought by 300,000 Native Americans against the government for similar claims of financial mismanagement. The previous opt-out litigation settled, resulting in a $3.4 billion settlement ratified by Congress in the Claims Resolution Act of 2010 and referred to as the *Cobell* settlement. *See Cobell v. Salazar*, No. 96-1285, 2011 WL 10676927 (D.D.C. July 27, 2011). In *Ramona Two Chiefs,* the question was whether the court had jurisdiction over these new claims or whether all claims were extinguished in 1996 action. The Federal Circuit held that "that exact alignment of injury is not required between class representatives and other class members. *Id.* The question, instead, is whether the claims of the class representatives and other class members 'implicate a significantly different set of concerns.'" *Ramona Two Shields*, 820 F.3d at 1331 (quoting *Gratz v. Bollinger*, 539 U.S. 244, 265, 123 S. Ct. 2411, 156 L. Ed. 2d 257 (2003)). In its decision, the Federal Circuit court found that the present suit raised the same concerns as were resolved through the *Cobell* litigation and settlement; thus, plaintiff class members in this suit did not have standing to pursue their claims.

In *Birdbear v. United States*, several members of the Three Affiliated Tribes of the Fort Bernhold Indian Reservation who are beneficial owners of allotted reservation land held in

[2] The derivative lawsuit argument was one of several standing arguments raised by the government and based on federal and Delaware law.

trust for them by the United States filed suit against the United States, alleging the government breached its fiduciary duty owed to plaintiffs with respect to the approval and management of mineral leases on the allotted land. 162 Fed. Cl. 225 (2022). The United States filed motions for summary judgment arguing, among other things, that the applicable six-year Statute of Limitations barred some or all of plaintiffs' claims. The plaintiffs argued first that their claims are not barred by the Statute of Limitations because the Statute of Limitations was tolled by the filing of a class action in the long-running litigation summarized in *Cobell v. Salazar*, 679 F.3d 909 (D.C. Cir. 2012), and discussed above. The Court of Claim examined the procedural history of the *Cobell* litigation and first determined that the specific breach claims at issue in *Birdbear* were not raised in the original *Cobell* class complaint. The claims were addressed in the 2010 amended complaint but those claims did not relate back to the original complaint so, to the extent the limitations period is tolled for those breach claims (identified in *Birdbear* as Count 1), that tolling period would begin when the *Cobell* amended complaint was filed. The plaintiffs further argued that the claims in Count 1 are not time barred as they involve continuing violations. The Court rejected the plaintiffs' position, relying on *Shoshone Indian Tribe of the Wind River Rsvr. v. United States*, 672 F.3d 1021 (Fed. Cir. 2012), to find that the plaintiffs did not meet their burden of establishing that the secretary breached a continuing duty to remove the lessees. The Court resolved this issue by finding that "the statute of limitations bars the claims in Count 1, except as to those leases entered on or after September 15, 2009."

In *Bright v. United States*, plaintiffs were named parties in a putative class of landowners seeking compensation under the Fifth Amendment pursuant to the Tucker Act, 28 U.S.C. § 1491(a)(1) for the alleged taking of their property interests under the "Rails-to-Trails" Act. 603 F.3d 1273 (Fed. Cir. 2010). The standing issue on appeal related to the tolling of the applicable statute of limitations as applied to class members who wanted to opt in to the litigation (as is allowed under RCFC Rule 23) after the expiration of the applicable statute of limitations. Specifically, the question before the court was when a class action complaint is filed in the Court of Federal Claims within the six-year limitations period by one named plaintiff, are putative class members permitted to opt in after expiration of the limitations period, when class certification was sought prior to expiration of the limitations period, but the complaint was not amended to add other named plaintiffs as putative class members until after expiration of the limitations period. The Court held that "when a class action complaint is filed in the Court of Federal Claim and class certification is sought prior to expiration of the . . . limitations period, the limitations period is tolled" and the putative class members are allowed to opt in to the class per RCFC Rule 23. *See Bright*, 603 F.3d at 1274. As the opt in plaintiffs were allowed to join the putative class action despite expiration of the statute of limitations on their individual claims, they had standing to join the litigation.

The Federal Circuit addressed the issues of statutory and equitable tolling of the statute of limitations (thus standing to sue) in a class action brought by Indian tribes and tribal healthcare providers against the Indian Health Services (IHS) related to the payment of contract support costs incurred in providing healthcare services to tribal members. *Arctic Slope Native Ass'n, Ltd. v. Sebelius*, 583 F.3d 785 (Fed. Cir. 2009). The claims in this litigation were contract claims filed under the Contract Disputes Act (CDA), 41 U.S.C. § 605(a), which includes a six-year statute of limitations for filing claims under the CDA. The *Arctic Slope* class action included putative class members who had stayed their claims pending the resolution of other class action lawsuits involving the payment of benefits by the IHS. *See Cherokee Nation of Okla. v. Leavitt*, 543 U.S. 631 (2005), and *Pueblo of Zuni v. United States*, 243 F.R.D. 436 (D.N.M. 2007). Those putative class members argued that the six-year statute of limitations in the CDA was tolled for them, as class members, when the original claims were made in *Arctic Slope* litigation even though some putative class members were not part of the original suit. The lower tribunal, the Civilian Board of Contract Appeals, disagreed and dismissed the case. The class members appealed to the Federal Circuit and raised the issues of whether statutory and equitable tolling applied to save their claims.

The Federal Circuit held that the six-year time limit for filing a claim with a contracting officer was not subject to statutory class action tolling as the putative class members seeking the benefit of statutory tolling in *Arctic Slope* failed to make a timely presentment of their claims to a contracting officer and would not have been eligible to be class members if the *Pueblo of Zuni* and *Cherokee Nation* cases had continued as class actions. However, the court concluded that the six-year time period was subject to equitable tolling and remanded the case to the Board to determine whether, on the facts of these cases, the appellants had established their entitlement to suspension of the limitations period.

On remand, the Board denied the *Arctic Slope* plaintiffs' (ASNA) claims based on the equitable tolling argument under the CDA and the plaintiffs again appealed to the Federal Circuit. *Arctic Slope Native Ass'n, Ltd. v. Sebelius*, 699 F.3d 1289 (Fed. Cir. 2012). The Federal Circuit reversed the Board's ruling and remanded the case back to the Board for further proceedings. In considering the arguments for equitable tolling, the court recognized equitable tolling applies where the litigant proves "(1) that he has been pursuing his rights diligently, and (2) that some extraordinary circumstance stood in his way and prevented timely filing." *Arctic Slope*, 699 F.3d at 1295 (quoting *Holland v. Florida*, 560 U.S. 631, 130 S. Ct. 2549, 2553, 177 L. Ed. 2d 130 (2010). The exercise of equity powers must be made on a case-by-case basis, and equitable relief is typically extended only sparingly. *See Cloer v. Sec'y of Health & Human Servs.*, 654 F.3d 1322, 1344–45 (Fed. Cir. 2011) (en banc). Equitable tolling does not apply to garden variety claims of excusable neglect, such as an attorney miscalculation leading to a missed deadline. *Holland*, 130 S. Ct. at 2564. Based on this precedent, the court held that equitable tolling applied to the ASNA plaintiffs as they relied on other pending litigation by Indian tribe plaintiffs against the IHS in deciding they were not required to present claims to the contracting officer within the six-year limitations period. The court found that this reliance constituted an "extraordinary circumstance" sufficient to warrant equitable tolling of the filing deadline. Further, the court found that the other tribal litigation put the government on notice of the general nature and legal theory underlying ASNA's claims. The court was careful to limit its application of equitable tolling in this circumstance to the unique facts and circumstances at issue in the tribal class actions against IHS, noting that the decision "that equitable tolling applies is informed by these unique facts and extraordinary circumstances, taken together with the obligations flowing from the special relationship between the government and Indian tribes." *Arctic Slope*, 699 F.3d at 1298.[3]

Finally, *Block v. Sec'y of Veteran Affairs*, 641 F.3d 1313 (Fed. Cir. 2011), is an unusual Federal Circuit court case dealing with the issue of equitable tolling related to Vietnam Veterans and Agent Orange exposure and the resulting government action and litigation. This case originated with a class action pleading filed in the U.S. District Court for the District of Columbia in 1979, arguing that the "Agent Orange Program Guide" published in 1979 violated the rule making process of the APA and violated the plaintiffs" due process rights. The original case amassed a complex procedural history, ending with the Supreme Court's denial of plaintiff-petitioners petition for a writ of certiorari in 2009. In this case, the same plaintiff filed a petition to obtain judicial review of the same 1979 publication. The petition for review was filed in 2010, but the court found that any right of action accrued in 1979 when the Agent Orange Program Guide became final. Petitioners then contended they were entitled to equitable tolling because their complaint in the district court was pending from the day it was filed in 1979 until 2009, creating an "extraordinary circumstance" for purposes of equitable tolling. When the initial complaint in the case was filed in 1979, there was no statutory basis for any court to hear the petitioners' procedural challenges to the Agent Orange Pro-

[3] The ASNA cases should be read narrowly on the issue of equitable tolling. The Supreme Court did not find for the tribal plaintiffs on the issue of equitable tolling under different facts in *Menominee Indian Tribe v. United States*, 136 S. Ct. 750 (2016).

gram Guide. For that reason, the district court in which petitioners filed their challenge to the Agent Orange Program Guide did not have jurisdiction to address the procedural objections raised in the petition. The filing of the district court action therefore did not toll the running of the statute of limitations. The petitioners contended that the long delay in the resolution of their original lawsuit should not create a time bar to relief, but the court found that the long delay also could not have the effect of creating a cause of action that did not exist at the time the claim was originally filed. In a narrow decision, the Federal Circuit held that the petitioners' action was not timely; thus, the request for review of the publication was not within the jurisdiction of the court.

d. Mootness Doctrine

The Court of Appeals for Veteran's Claims considered the "inherently transitiory" and "picking-off" exceptions to the mootness doctrine in a case brought by a veteran who received his requested relief while the class action was pending. The plaintiff argued the class should still go forward because the inherently transitory exception and the related picking off exception to mootness applied to the injuries sustained by the proposed class members. *Hamill v. McDonough*, 37 Vet. App. 65 (2023). The Court disagreed, holding that neither mootness doctrine exception applied. The plaintiff's litigation was thus mooted. The Court clarified that the "inherently transitory exception" applies to classes comprised of claims that are "unavoidably time sensitive" and "acutely suspectable to mootness." The purpose of the exception is to assure that the short-lived nature of the claim does not shield the defendant from aggregate litigation. The Court found this exception inapplicable as the alleged injury here—the VA's inaction related to a request to revisit a COD (character of discharge) determination—is not, by its nature, transitory. Likewise, the Court found the picking off exception to mootness did not apply as that exception applies to prevent the defendant from resolving the plaintiff's claim to close off the possibility of aggregate litigation. Since no litigation was pending when the VA settled Mr. Hamill's claim, the picking off exception did not apply.

In *Doblin v. McDonough*, 34 Vet. App. 334 (2021), the plaintiff, a veteran, filed a motion for class certification requesting the Court certify a class consisting of "claimants with active appeals that have been adjudicated by the Board of Veterans' Appeals in the Legacy appeals system and returned to the Board in the VAIMA system but have not been returned to their original places on the docket or been afforded expeditious treatment by the Board." In his lawsuit, plaintiff challenged the Board's first-come first-served docketing system of the Rapid Appeals Modernization Program (RAMP), claiming that the order of appeals should be controlled by 38 C.F.R. § 20.902(a) rather than by RAMP. The plaintiff argues that, because of this error, his appeal has been unduly delayed and therefore seeks relief for himself and others similarly situated. The Court first determined that the plaintiff's claim fails as a matter of law because: (1) the RAMP Act clearly applies to plaintiff, (2) plaintiff completed a RAMP opt-in form that adopts the RAMP appeal process for his appeal, and (3) there is no indication the Board has unduly delayed processing plaintiff's appeal. As the plaintiff's claim fails as a matter of law, the claims of a putative class are moot. "[I]f the theory of relief that the putative class representative proceeds under fails as a matter of law, the Court can deny the class certification as moot because the claim of any other putative class member would fail for the exact same reason." The Court found that because plaintiff failed to show that 38 C.F.R. § 20.902(a) applies to RAMP appeals and his appeal has not been unduly delayed, plaintiff's claim is denied on grounds that would apply to any member of the putative class, so the motion for class certification must also be dismissed.

In *Charleston Area Medical Center, Inc. v. United States*, 940 F.3d 1362 (Fed. Cir. 2019), the Court of Appeals for the Federal Circuit affirmed the trial court in holding that when the trial court ruled that the class plaintiffs were taxpayers for purposes of calculating the proper rate of interest on income tax refunds, entering judgment on the pleadings for the government, the trial court also correctly ruled the motion for class certification was moot.

The Federal Circuit court relied on *Greenlee County v. United States*, 487 F.3d 871 (Fed. Cir. 2007), which held that, as to certification motions before the district courts, the appellate court has "repeatedly found on appeal that issues related to class certification were moot in light of our resolution against the plaintiff of a motion to dismiss or for summary judgment." In *Charleston Area Medical Center*, the appellate court "saw no reason to apply a different rule when it is the Claims Court that finds the issue moot." The taxpayers further argued that the Supreme Court's holding in *Eisen v. Carlisle & Jacqueline,* 417 U.S. 156 (1974), required the trial court to resolve the issue of plaintiffs' motion to certify the class before resolving questions on the underlying merits of the claim, in this case whether the taxpayers were corporate or nonprofit taxpayers for purposes of applying the appropriate tax refund interest rate. The Court of Appeals rejected this contention, noting that the weight of authority interpreting *Eisen* and Federal Rule of Civil Procedure Rule 23 "supports our conclusion that it was within the discretion of the Court of Federal Claims to find the class certification motion moot."

In *Russell v. United States*, 661 F.3d 1371 (Fed. Cir. 2011), the court remanded a putative class action to the district court for further consideration on the issue of mootness. Plaintiff Russell filed a class action complaint against the United States, seeking relief for himself and a class of similarly situated persons regarding interest charges the government had assessed on military credit accounts against him and the other putative class members. Prior to ruling on Mr. Russell's motion for class certification, the district court dismissed his individual action as moot on the ground that the government, by issuing a payment to Mr. Russell during the pendency of the lawsuit, had satisfied his individual claim. Russell argued that the amount paid by the government was insufficient to moot his case as it did not account for other costs and fees, including attorneys' fees. As to plaintiff Russell's individual claim, the court held "[t]he law is clear that when a court seeks to determine whether a plaintiff's claim is moot because the claim has been satisfied, the proper focus is on whether the plaintiff's principal claim has been resolved, not on whether ancillary expenses, such as court costs, sunk litigation costs, and attorney's fees, have been paid or have accrued." *Russell*, 661 F.3d at 1375. However, the plaintiff argued that the resolution of his individual claim did not impede the continuance of the class action. Plaintiff Russell argued that the government should not be able to "pick off" class representatives in a putative class action by offering individual relief to the class members rather than relief to the entire putative class. The mootness argument turned on timing, with Plaintiff arguing that it does not matter whether class certification has been granted by the time of the offer to the class representative. If class certification has not been granted at the time of the offer, the act of certification should relate back to the filing of the class action complaint. If the decision to certify relates back to the original filing of the complaint, the mootness of an individual claim should not result in dismissal of the class complaint. The Federal Circuit avoided a definitive ruling on mootness in this context and remanded the case to the district court for further findings on mootness in response to information that the government had paid partial claims to some putative class members as the action was pending.

In *Evans v. United States*, 694 F.3d 1377 (Fed. Cir. 2012), the Federal Circuit addressed the issue of mootness as it relates to factually similar class actions pending when one action results in an appellate decision unfavorable to the class. The question in *Evans* was whether the Federal Circuit decision in *Bright v. United States*, 603 F.3d 1273 (Fed. Cir. 2010), mooted other pending class actions based on claims under the Fifth Amendment Takings Clause and the Tucker Act, 28 U.S.C. § 2501, for alleged takings under the "Rails-to-Trails" Act.[4] The *Evans* case, like many other pending cases, was a "protective action"

[4] The "Rails-to-Trails" Act has spawned considerable litigation under the Fifth Amendment takings clause as railway easements have been closed around the nation to allow for walking trail use of abandoned railway property. The takings issues arise as most railway easements occupy land owned under a fee simple absolute with a reversionary provision

filed under the authority of the Little Tucker Act, 28 U.S.C. § 1346.

The issue before the Federal Circuit was, in view of *Bright* and the court's remand to the Court of Federal Claims for trial of the takings issues that underlie the "Rails-to-Trails" takings cases, whether the determination of the ultimate law of the case is advanced or hindered by having these "protective" suits no longer relevant but pending. Although there are exceptions to the general rule that when a case becomes moot on appeal, the court is to vacate the decisions below with instructions to dismiss, *see U.S. Bancorp Mortg. Co. v. Bonner Mall P'ship*, 513 U.S. 18, 29, 115 S. Ct. 386, 130 L. Ed. 2d 233 (1994) (vacatur inappropriate because parties settled while appeal was pending); *Karcher v. May*, 484 U.S. 72, 83, 108 S. Ct. 388, 98 L. Ed. 2d 327 (1987) (denying vacatur when a case is moot only because the losing party failed to pursue appeal), the Federal Circuit did not find the exceptions applicable here. The court held "it is clear beyond peradventure that [the protective suits] can play no useful role in the resolution of the merits case before the Court of Federal Claims, which is the only case that now matters in this litigation" and dismissed *Evans* and the other "protective actions" under the "Rails-to-Trails" Act without prejudice. *Evans*, 694 F.3d at 1381–82.

In *Monk v. Shulkin*, the Federal Circuit considered mootness when the named plaintiff in a putative class action had his claims adjudicated while appealing the Veterans Court's refusal to certify the class action. *Monk*, 2017 WL 1487283. The government asserted that the Federal Circuit lacked subject matter jurisdiction as the plaintiff Monk had received full relief on his pending claim for veteran's benefits. The Federal Circuit cited the Supreme Court's decision in *U.S. Parole Comm'n v. Geraghty*, 445 U.S. 388 (1980), that held that a "class [action] does not become moot upon expiration of the named plaintiff's substantive claim, even though class certification has been denied." *Geraghty*, 445 U.S. at 404. The Secretary argued that *Geraghty* and other precedent were inapplicable because those decisions were based on FRCP Rule 23, which does not apply in Veterans Court. The Federal Circuit rejected this reasoning and further found that because the plaintiff's claim had become moot after class certification was sought and denied in Veterans Court, the fact that the claim was paid did not moot the claims of the "[t]housands of veterans seeking benefits [and] still awaiting results of their appeals." *Monk*, 2017 WL 1487283, at *4. The Federal Circuit found that the case was not moot because it was "capable of repetition, yet evading review." *Geraghty*, 445 U.S. at 398. "Where the named plaintiff does have a personal stake at the outset of the lawsuit, and where the claim may arise again with respect to that plaintiff; the litigation then may continue notwithstanding the named plaintiff's current lack of a personal stake." *Monk*, 2017 WL 1487283, at *4.

In 2010, the Federal Circuit authored an unpublished opinion in *Biopolymer Engineering, Inc. v. Immunocorp*, 390 F. App'x 989 (Fed. Cir. 2010), on the issue of whether a negotiated settlement can moot the appeal of summary judgment. In *Biopolymer*, which involved patent enforcement litigation originating in the district court, the parties reached a negotiated settlement while an appeal was pending on a summary judgment ruling in favor of defendants finding noninfringement. Plaintiff Bioploymer Engineering (Biothera) asserted that the summary judgment appeal was not moot because a real controversy existed as to whether defendants' products infringed the subject patent. Biothera argued that the pending appeal

---

stating that when the railway easement ceases to be used as a railway easement, the land shall revert back to the fee simple owner of the encumbered land in the form of fee simple absolute ownership. The "Rails-to-Trails" Act allows the government, on its own or with partners, to set aside the railway easement in favor of a new easement for walking trials, thus taking the reversionary interest and resulting fee simple absolute ownership away from the property owner and subjecting the property to a new easement. For this deprivation of fee simple absolute title, the landowners allege a taking requiring just compensation pursuant to the Fifth Amendment. The Federal Court of Claims has reviewed many "Rails-to-Trails" Act class actions wherein groups of adjacent landowners create a putative class for purposes of determining just compensation. The *Bright* decision in 2010 is one of the few Federal Circuit opinions in a "Rails-to-Trails" case.

would ultimately decide the legal rights between Biothera and the defendants, regardless of the settlement. The court held that Biothera had not shown that any claim for relief was contingent on the court's determination and the case did not present a "definite and concrete [case or controversy], touching the legal relations of parties having adverse legal interests." *Biopolymer Engineering*, 390 F. App'x at 991 (quoting *Aetna Life Ins. Co. v. Haworth*, 300 U.S. 227, 240–41 (1937)).

In *Lohmann v. United States*, 154 Fed. Cl. 355 (2021), the Court of Federal Claims addressed the issue of mootness in a RCFC Rule 23 class action wherein the plaintiff's claim became moot before the court ruled on a pending certification motion. The mootness issue arose after Reserve Component (RC) soldiers brought a putative class action to recover per diem payments allegedly owed under federal regulations addressing payments to RC soldiers who served multiple temporary tours of duty. Prior to the plaintiffs motion for class certification, the Army Board for the Correction of Military Records (ABCMR) determined RC soldiers were eligible for per diem allowances in the relevant time periods. The government argued that the ABCMR determination mooted any live controversy in the putative class action. Having no precedent on the issue under RCFC Rule 23, the Court looked to FRCP Rule 23 and the general rule that "a class action must be dismissed for mootness when the personal claims of the named plaintiffs are satisfied and no class has been properly certified." *Lohmann*, 154 Fed. Cl. 355 (quoting *Clark v. State Farm Mut. Auto Ins. Co.*, 590 F.3d 1134, 1138 (10th Cir. 2009). The plaintiff argued the mootness-avoidance exception that allows the certification to "relate back" to the filing of the complaint. *See Sosna v. Iowa*, 419 U.S. 393, 402 n.11 (1975). After a thorough review of the mootness-avoidance doctrines applicable to FRCP Rule 23, the Court of Federal Claims found the plaintiff had not shown that an exception would allow them to proceed under either FRCP Rule 23 or FRFC Rule 23. Notably, the Court declined to "break new ground" on the issue of mootness-avoidance under FRFC Rule 23 specifically.

5. PLEADING CONSIDERATIONS

The Federal Court of Claim addressed the interplay between a proposed stay of proceedings and amended pleadings in *Braswell v. United States*, 155 Fed. Cl. 148 (2021). The Court of Claim addressed the government's request for a stay of its motion to dismiss pending review of a similar case brought by other and current federal employees alleging the same violations of the same pay statutes at the Federal Circuit (*see Adams v. United States*, 152 Fed. Cl. 350 (2021). In both cases, plaintiff employees sought extra pay due to workplace exposure to the virus that causes COVID-19 under relevant federal statutes and the Fair Labor Standards Act (FLSA). Plaintiffs opposed the government's request for a stay arguing the stay would interfere with the ability of similarly situated federal employees to file the consent forms necessary to commence their actions under FLSA. The plaintiffs argued that the government's stay, if granted, should not stay other actions, notably the plaintiff's motion for class certification. The Court found that plaintiffs could be prejudiced by having the motion for class certification stayed as those plaintiffs with FLSA claims must file those claims subject to a two-year statute of limitations, thus allowing existing plaintiffs to file amended complaints after the stay is lifted will not remove the prejudice from putative class members who might join the litigation after a class is certified and noticed. Noting that the decision not to grant the government's request for a stay is not the most efficient, the Court still denied the stay as to putative class members with FLSA claims, holding that a stay of the government's motion to dismiss would not preclude employees from filing class certification motions with respect the FLSA claims.

The Federal Circuit heard three cases in 2017 and 2018 involving new actions filed based on a breach of contract theory related to prior class action settlement agreements. In each case, the defendants argued that the lawsuits failed to state a claim for relief for breach of contract as the settlement agreements at issue were not contracts, thus not subject to suit for breach. In *Ingraham Regional Medical Center v. United States*, the hospital brought a putative class action against the federal government asserting breach of contract claims related to underpayments per the TRICARE military health care system, administered by the Department of Defense. 874 F.3d 1341 (Fed. Cir. 2017). The crux of plaintiff's contract-based lawsuit was that the Department of Defense had failed to follow the terms of a release agreed to by plaintiffs as part of a 2011 review and adjustment process related to payments under TRICARE. The Department argued that the Release served to eliminate any and all claims arising from the underpayment dispute, thus plaintiff's lawsuit failed to state a claim. The Federal Circuit held otherwise, finding that the Release cannot be used to bar claims based on the Department's failure to follow the terms of the Release itself, rather only to bar claims based on underpayments that preceded the Release. Similarly, in *LaBatte v. United States*, the Federal Circuit Court of Appeals allowed a Native American famer to sue under a breach of contract theory alleging the government failed to follow the terms of a class action settlement agreement in a discrimination lawsuit brought by a class of Native American farmers against the Department of Agriculture. 899 F.3d 1373 (Fed. Cir. 2018). The Court held that the government could not use finality terms in the class action settlement agreement to bar a breach of contract lawsuit based on a failure to follow the terms of the settlement agreement, noting the Court's previous rulings which clarify that a waiver of appeal does not stop a party from suing for breach of contract when the settlement agreement is not followed. In contrast, in an unpublished opinion, the Federal Circuit did not allow a breach of contract claim to go forward in a case where an African American debtor who was part of a class action against the Department of Agriculture sued under the settlement agreement. *Slaughter v. United States*, 733 F. App'x 531 (Fed. Cir. 2018). In *Slaughter*, the claim failed because it was deemed to be untimely and seeking relief outside of the settlement terms.

In *Dimare Fresh, Inc. v. United States*, 808 F.3d 1301 (Fed. Cir. 2015), a putative class of tomato producers appealed the decision of the U.S. Court of Federal Claim dismissing their amended complaint pursuant to Rule 12(b)(6) of the Rules of the United States Court of Federal Claim. The Claim Court dismissed the amended complaint on the ground that press releases issued by the Food and Drug Administration that warned consumers of a possible link between plaintiffs' tomatoes and an outbreak of salmonella did not constitute a regulatory taking. In evaluating the pleadings and the RCFC Rule 12(b)(6) motion to dismiss, the court applied the law applicable to the FRCP Rules 8 and 12(b)(6), including the *Bell Atlantic* plausibility standard, in reviewing the pleadings at issue. *See Bell Atl. Corp. v. Twombly*, 550 U.S. 544, 557, 127 S. Ct. 1955, 167 L. Ed. 2d 929 (2007) (To avoid dismissal for failure to state a claim, a complaint must allege facts "plausibly suggesting (not merely consistent with") a showing of entitlement to relief.). The court found that the government's issuance of press releases, together with a media briefing, warning consumers of possible salmonella in plaintiffs' products did not constitute a regulatory taking under Fifth Amendment jurisprudence; thus, the plaintiffs' claim failed to state a claim for relief.

In *Mercier v. United States*, the trial court dismissed a class action filed on behalf of VA nurses seeking overtime pay under a statutory provision that required the agency to compensate "officially ordered or approved" overtime work. The trial court dismissed the nurses' claim because they did not allege that the agency "expressly directed" their overtime. *See Mercier v. United States*, 114 Fed. Cl. 795, 802 (2014). The nurses appealed the lower court ruling, and the Federal Circuit reviewed de novo the Court of Federal Claim's dismissal of the complaint for failure to state a claim upon which relief may be granted. *Mercier v. United States*, 786 F.3d 971 (Fed. Cir. 2015). The Federal Circuit applied the plausibility standard, stating that "[t]o avoid dismissal, a complaint must allege facts 'plausibly suggesting (not merely consistent with)' a showing of entitlement to relief." *Mercier*, 786 F.3d at 980 (quoting *Cary v. United States*, 552 F.3d 1373, 1376 (Fed. Cir. 2009), and *Bell Atlantic Corp. v. Twombly*, 550 U.S. 544, 127 S. Ct. 1955, 1966, 167 L. Ed. 2d 929 (2007)). The issue leading to the Motion to Dismiss was the plaintiff nurses' interpretation of the statutory language "officially ordered and approved" as it was used in the statute requiring overtime pay. *See* 38 U.S.C. § 7453. The statutory language was the subject of previous litigation, and the lower court dismissed plaintiffs' complaint relying on only one interpretation of the relevant statutory language. The Federal Circuit found that the plaintiff nurses had relied on a valid legal theory when constructing their complaint; thus, the decision by the lower court dismissing the claim was reversed. *Mercier*, 786 F.3d at 982.

6. REQUIREMENTS FOR CLASS CERTIFICATION IN THE FEDERAL CIRCUIT

As was noted in the introduction to this chapter, the Federal Circuit has appellate jurisdiction over certain cases filed in the district courts based on subject matter (e.g., patent litigation) and has appellate jurisdiction over cases filed in certain lower tribunals, most importantly the Federal Court of Claim. Because most class action litigation in the Federal Circuit emanates from the Federal Court of Claim, the relevant rule analysis for determining whether a class action will certify relies on the Rules of the Court of Federal Claims (RCFC), specifically Rule 23. In evaluating opt-in class actions brought under RCFC Rule 23(a) and (b), the court has identified a five-part analysis: (a) **numerosity**—a class so large that joinder is impracticable; (b) **commonality**—in terms of the presence of common questions of law or fact, the predominance of those questions, and the treatment received by the class members at the hands of the United States; (c) **typicality**—that the named parties' claims are typical of the class; (d) **adequacy**—relating to fair representation; and (e) **superiority**—that a class action is the fairest and most efficient way to resolve a given set of controversies.

In *Hamill v. McDonough*, 37 Vet. App. 65 (2023), the Court considered the presumption that a class action in Veterans Court would not be superior to a precedential decision. The Court's discussion is dicta as the class action at issue was mooted (see the reference above in the section on the mootness doctrine); however, the Court offered clarity on the role of the presumption.

> When it reviews an RCA (request for a class action), the Court considers whether the proposed class meets the requirements for class certification laid out in Rule 23 of our Rules of Practice and Procedure [the Federal Rules of Civil Procedure]. The Court also considers whether a class action would be superior to a "precedential decision granting relief on a non-class action basis." Prospective class representatives must make this showing. And it's no small feat because this Court has limited fact-finding abilities, so class actions here are the exceptions, not the rule. To that end, the Court presumes that "classes should not be certified because our ability to render binding precedential decisions ordinarily will be adequate."

See Hamill, 37 Vet. App. at 76–77.

In *King v. United* States, 2022 WL 3716442 (August 29, 2022) the Court of Claims heard a motion for class certification by named Plaintiffs King, Gugliuzza and Dardzinski on behalf of similarly situated vested participants in the New York State Teamsters Pension and Retirement Fund, a pension plan in critical or declining status. The government authorized a reduction in benefits that resulted in a 29 percent reduction in monthly pension benefits to the plaintiffs and other members of the putative class which led to plaintiffs' lawsuit. The government did not oppose the motion for class certification, but the Court noted that under RCFC Rule 23 it must "independently verify that the plaintiffs meet the requirements" of class certification. The Court found that all five requirements for class certification were met, designated the three named plaintiffs as class representatives, and appointed class counsel.[5]

The following sections explore the Federal Circuit jurisprudence, including published cases from the Court of Federal Claim, in the order indicated by RCFC Rule 23.

a. Numerosity

The Court of Claim certified a class action brought by self-administered, self-insured multi-employer health plans against the United States seeking to recover amounts allegedly unlawfully collected under the Affordable Care Act. The defendant did not oppose plaintiffs' certification motion but the Court reviewed all five requirements in detail before certifying the class. On the issue of numerosity, the Court found not only that the hundreds of entities involved satisfied the numerosity requirement but also that the geographical dispersion of class members supported the numerosity requirement.

Issues of numerosity are rarely central to the certification of class actions. However, the issue is discussed in detail regularly in cases in the Federal Court of Claim as many recent class action cases in that court are based on the "Rails-to-Trails" Act, thus often involving small groups of property owners joining together to seek redress for alleged takings of real property along the former railway corridors now converted to walking trails. As the putative classes are generally small in number, the courts have developed a more robust analysis of numerosity in these cases. As an initial matter, the court recognizes that "the numerosity criterion is somewhat peculiar in the context of an opt-in class action." *Geneva Rock Products, Inc. v. United States*, 100 Fed. Cl. 778, 787 (2011). In an opt in class action, each member of the class must opt in, which is a joinder regardless of class status. *See Haggart v. United States*, 104 Fed. Cl. 484 (2012). However, in keeping with FRCP Rule 23 jurisprudence, numerosity in the RCFC Rule 23 context requires that joinder of the parties be impracticable, not impossible. *Geneva Rock*, 100 Fed. Cl. at 787. In determining numerosity under RCFC Rule 23, the courts evaluate several criteria. First, the Federal Circuit has certified class actions with a small number of plaintiffs. *See Stewart v. Abraham*, 275 F.3d 220 (3d Cir. 2001) (class of over 40 plaintiffs meet numerosity and should be certified), and *Douglas R. Bigelow Trust v. United States*, 97 Fed. Cl. 674 (2011) (class of 25 certified). Other decisions consider the size of the class relative to the cost of the litigation. *See Bell v. United States*, 123 Fed. Cl. 390 (2015). "The smaller the size of the claim and the larger the number of persons the less likely it is that, without the benefit of a class action, any plaintiff will recover." *King v. United States*, 84 Fed. Cl. 120, 125 (2008). Other courts have focused on the geographic location of the parties, noting that putative class members would find joinder more difficult if they were geographically dispersed. *See Geneva Rock*, 100 Fed. Cl. at 787. Specific to the "Rails-to-Trails" and takings jurisprudence, the Court of Claim has held that when a large number of putative class members hold a small amount of land, the cost of litigating a takings claim can easily exceed the compensation due. *See Haggart v. United States*, 104 Fed. Cl. 484 (2012).[6]

In sum, the issue of numerosity is more nuanced in the Federal Circuit and the Court of Claim as best arguments for and against this requirement for certification amount to more than merely the practicality of joinder based on the number of members in the putative

---

[5] *See also Carson v. United States*, 2023 WL 8812926 (Dec. 20, 2023) (The Federal Court of Claims certified a class under RCFC Rule 23, finding that all the requirements for class certification were met following an amendment to the class description language adding the word "supervisory" as applied to police officers who did not receive weekend premium pay for work completed during a defined ten-year period).

[6] For more "Rails-to-Trails" cases on numerosity and class certification generally, *see* Curry v. United States, 81 Fed. Cl. 328 (2008); Bell v. United States, 123 Fed. Cl. 390 (2015); Janssen v. United States, No. 09-559 L, 2010 WL 697343 (Fed. Cl. Feb. 24, 2010); Singleton v. United States, 92 Fed. Cl. 78 (2010); and Brown v. United States, 126 Fed. Cl. 571 (2016).

class.[7] *Gross v. United States*, 106 Fed. Cl. 369 (2012), offers an interesting analysis of numerosity in a wage and hour class action. In *Gross*, the Court of Claims denies certification on numerosity, specifically finding that the number of class members is not ascertainable; thus, numerosity is not met. *See Gross*, 106 Fed. Cl. at 377 (class action for monies related to reduced wages paid to employees who were required to work on Sundays but which employees and how many employees were implicated was not provided).[8]

b. Commonality

The commonality requirement under RCFC Rule 23 encompasses three elements: (1) questions of law or fact are common to the class, RCFC 23(a)(2); (2) "the United States has acted or refused to act on grounds generally applicable to the class," RCFC 23(b)(2); and (3) "questions of law or fact common to class members predominate over any questions affecting only individual members," RCFC 23(b)(3). The commonality requirement serves two primary purposes: (1) to ensure "proposed classes are sufficiently cohesive to warrant adjudication by representation" and (2) to prevent certification of a class that will "degenerat[e] into a series of individual trials." *Fauvergue v. United States*, 86 Fed. Cl. 82, 99 (2009) (reversed on other grounds in *Bright v. United States*, 603 F.3d 1273 (Fed. Cir. 2010)), quoting *Barnes*, 68 Fed. Cl. at 496. To meet commonality under RCFC Rule 23, "the questions underlying the claims of the class merely must share essential characteristics, so that their resolution will advance the overall case." *Fauvergue v. United States*, 86 Fed. Cl. 82, 99 (2009), *rev'd sub nom. Bright v. United States*, 603 F.3d 1273 (Fed. Cir. 2010). Overall, the standard for commonality and predominance in the Federal Circuit have not historically been interpreted as hard to meet, particularly when compared with the commonality analysis put forth by the Supreme Court in *Wal-Mart v. Dukes*, 564 U.S. 338 (2010).[9]

In *Fauvergue*, another "Rails-to-Trails" takings case, the commonality issue centered on the difference between the takings claims of landowners who experienced temporary and permanent loss of the reversionary interests in the effected land. *Fauvergue v. United States*, 86 Fed. Cl. 82 (2010). Plaintiffs argued the class shared one core common question: Did a Fifth Amendment taking occur, thereby blocking the landowners' reversionary interests in their land? The court found that common questions existed and further found that the common questions predominated over questions affecting individual members of the class. *Id.* The predominate question applicable to all putative plaintiffs was whether the government committed a taking by blocking their reversionary interests in the property. The court found that the mere fact that plaintiffs may receive different awards of damages based on the nature of the taking does not alter the principal legal question or the core facts of this case. *Id.*

The Court of Federal Claim granted a motion for class certification in a lawsuit brought by self-administered, self-insured multi-employer group health plans against the United States. *Electrical Welfare Trust Fund v. United States*, 160 Fed. Cl. 462 (2022). The plaintiff sought to recover funds that were allegedly illegally collected based on an unlawful interpretation of the Transitional Reinsurance Program (TRP) provision of the Affordable Care Act (ACA). The plaintiff sought to certify a proposed class of "all self-administered, self-insured employee health and welfare benefit plans that are or were subject to the as-

[7] *See* discussion of the numerosity requirement in *Oztimurlenk v. United States,* 162 Fed. Cl. 658 (2022), in the Recent Decisions section above.

[8] For another case where certification fails due to the plaintiff's inability to show that an ascertainable class is sufficiently numerous to meet the Rule 23 requirement, *see RadioShack Corp. v. United States*, 105 Fed. Cl. 617 (2012) (taxpayer failed to satisfy numerosity in attempt to certify a class of similarly situated taxpayers seeking a refund of communications excise taxes).

[9] *See* class certification discussion in *Oztimurlenk v. United states,* 162 Fed. Cl. 658 (2022), in the Recent Decisions section above, particularly the Court's reliance on the *Wal-Mart v. Dukes* decision in *Oztimurlenk* and *Fisher* in its analysis of commonality and predominance.

sessment and collection of the TRC under Section 1341 of the Affordable Care Act for the benefit year of 2014." The Court examined each requirement of RCFC Rule 23(a). As to numerosity, the defendant acknowledged that over 652 entities made a TRC contribution for 2014. Furthermore, the putative class members (the 652 entities) are geographically dispersed, thus making joinder impracticable. The Court found that "common issues predominate," as liability for all class members turns on whether the defendant improperly required the putative class members to pay the TRP contribution for 2014, and each putative class member's damages can be calculated using a common methodology. In keeping with the numerosity and commonality determinations, the Court further found the named plaintiff had claims typical of the class, as the plaintiff's claims were identical to other class claims and a class action is the superior method of litigation as it involves many claimants with identical claims against defendants. "[J]udicial economy is best served by proceeding as a class action rather than via potentially hundreds of individual suits presenting identical questions of law and similar questions of fact."[10]

In *Freund v. McDonough*, 35 Vet. App. 466 (2022), the Court of Appeals for Veterans Claims denied the plaintiffs' motion for class certification, finding plaintiffs failed to satisfy the commonality requirement of RCFC Rule 23(a). The plaintiffs, the brother and surviving spouse of veterans, sought class certification on claims against the Veterans Affairs' (VA) erroneous closure of veterans' pending administrative appeals. The plaintiffs sought certification of a proposed class consisting of "all claimants with a timely perfected legacy appeal: (1) that is an original appeal, (2) that the Secretary has closed, (3) that remains closed, (4) that appears in VACOLS,[11] (5) for which a copy of the Substantive Appeals appears in VBMS,[12] and (6) for which the VA has not issued a rating decision regarding the Substantive Appeals timeliness." The plaintiffs claimed that all members of the putative class were seeking resolution of common legal issues, specifically whether the secretary is withholding agency action and thus violating federal regulations and "fair process" through the no-notice appeal closure process. The Court held that the putative class description itself failed to demonstrate the commonality requirement as there was no requirement that members of the class were subject to the no-notice appeal closure to be included in the class. Furthermore, the nature of the plaintiffs' allegation against the secretary necessitated individual determinations as to actions taken or not taken in each putative class member's appeal. The fact that all putative class members would have had an administrative appeal closed due to the VACOLS system and have a timely substantive appeal on file is not enough to show there is "any common answer to a common question that will allow the Court to resolve the dispute 'in one stroke.'"

In *Kluge v. Department of Homeland Security*, 60 F.4th 1361 (2023), the plaintiff, John Kluge, a commissioned officer in the United States Army Reserve and an employee of the Department of Homeland Security (DHS), appealed from a decision of the Merit Systems Protection Board (MSPB) denying class certification. Mr. Kluge was ordered to report to active duty in January 2011 to support a contingency operation and was absent from his DHS job for approximately six months in 2011. After the first few weeks of this period, Mr. Kluge was on unpaid leave and was not paid by DHS during his Reserve duty, apart from

[10] In 2024, the Court of Federal Claim conducted a fairness hearing on the proposed settlement agreement and evaluated class counsel's request for attorneys' fees in *Electronic Welfare Trust Fund v. United States*, 171 Fed. Cl. 362 (May 16, 2024). The settlement agreement at issue arose after the Federal Court of Claim approved certification of the class in *Electronic Welfare Trust Trust Fund v. United States*, 160 Fed. Cl. 462 (2022) (as discussed above). The Court of Claim held that the class members received fair notice of the proposed settlement; the proposed settlement of $169,022,397.28 was fair, reasonable, and adequate; the proposed allocation of the net settlement fund between the 357 certified class members was fair, reasonable, and adequate. The Court also determined that class counsel's fee request for 25 percent of the common fund, net of expenses was fair, reasonable, and adequate.

[11] "VACOLS is a computerized, automated system in which the VA tracks and monitors activity within legacy appeals."

[12] VBMS is the Veterans Benefits Management System.

one day, July 4, 2011. Mr. Kluge argued he was entitled to differential pay under 5 U.S.C. § 5538 and filed an appeal before the MSPB in 2019 seeking to recover differential pay for himself and similarly situated service members employed by the federal government. The administrative judge denied class certification and Mr. Kluge appealed that decision to the Court of Appeals for the Federal Circuit.

The Court of Appeals first noted that the MSPB is not bound by the FRCP Rule 23; thus the administrative judge reviewing the Board's decision is not required to address any factors identified in FRCP Rule 23. Regarding the issue of whether the putative class action demonstrated commonality, the Court upheld the administrative judge's decision that commonality was not met as the putative class contained employees from various government agencies. Kluge argued that all members of the class shared common questions of fact and law as all government agencies followed the guidance of the Office of Personnel Management (OPM). The Court of Appeals noted that Kluge's own case lacked commonality with the putative class as his employing agency (DHS) failed to rely on OPM guidance in his case.

In a similar case involving wage and hour claims by FBI officers, the Court of Claims found common questions of law and fact predominated over individual issues despite the fact that the class members would receive different awards of damages based on such factors as seniority and pay grade. *King v. United States*, 84 Fed. Cl. 120 (2008). In certifying the class on commonality/predominance grounds, the court found that "the outcome-determinative question is whether or not the government failed to pay FBI police officers in violation of 28 U.S.C. § 540C." *King*, 84 Fed. Cl. at 126. *See also Barnes v. United States*, 68 Fed. Cl. 492, 498 (2005) ("[T]here scarcely would be a case that would qualify for class status in this court [if individual damages were outcome determinative for class certification].""). The court held that to the extent individual damages needed to be calculated, the court could determine a formula. *King*, 84 Fed. Cl. at 126.

In contrast, the Court of Federal Claims determined commonality was not met in *Horvath v. United States*, 149 Fed. Cl. 735 (2020), a putative class action by a Secret Service agent seeking backpay allegedly illegally denied by regulation that was inconsistent with the Federal Employees Pay Act (FEPA), 5 U.S.C. §5542(e). The Court found that commonality failed when the named plaintiff Horvath, after failing to substantiate his own equal pay claim, asked the Court to certify a broader class of plaintiffs of all Secret Service and Diplomatic Security Service special agents who performed protective duties and may have been denied pay. The Court found the broader class could not be certified because Horvath failed to establish any other claimants who were denied pay because of "policy, practice, or unexplained systematic and widespread error," thus failing to meet the requirement of FRFC Rule 23 "to have acted on grounds generally applicable to the class."

In another post-*Wal-Mart* case, the Court of Claims found commonality and predominance based on the standards set forth specifically in *St. Bernard Parish Government v. United States*, 126 Fed. Cl. 707 (2016). In this post-Katrina class action, private and public landowners brought a putative class action against the United States seeking just compensation for takings under the Fifth Amendment for the government's failure to construct and maintain the Mississippi River Gulf Outlet (MR-GO), causing storm surge flooding on their property. *Id.* Although the core issue in all class member claims involved the adequacy of the MR-GO, each class member suffered distinct damages related to flooding and other storm damage. The government argued that an evaluation of liability and damages required review of certain factors, including duration of flooding, the character of the land, and the severity of damage. *Id.* The Court of Claims applied the standard for commonality set forth in *Wal-Mart:* "[w]hat matters to class certification . . . [is] the capacity of a classwide proceeding to generate common *answers* apt to drive the resolution of the litigation." *Wal-Mart,* 564 U.S. at 350, 131 S. Ct. 2541 (quotation omitted) (emphasis in original). *Id.* at 736. The Court of Claims also distinguished the evidence provided by the MR-GO plaintiffs from the evidence offered in support of class certification in *Wal-Mart*. The MR-GO plaintiffs' evidence was taken almost entirely from the Army Corps of Engineers. Thus, the court found, the plaintiffs had sufficiency and reliability distinctly different than that presented in *Wal-Mart.* Relying on the *Wal-Mart* commonality analysis, the court found there were "common answers" to the question of whether the Army Corps' construction, expansion, operation, and failure to maintain the MR-GO caused increased storm surge flooding during Hurricane Katrina and subsequent hurricanes and severe storms, effecting a temporary taking of plaintiffs' properties.[13]

In *Monk v. Wilkie*, 978 F.3d 1273 (Fed. Cir. 2020), the Federal Circuit Court of Appeals upheld denial of class certification in a case involving a putative class action by veterans whose disability claims had not been resolved within one year of filing a notice of disagreement. While the putative class was pending in Veterans Court, Congress enacted legislation called the Veterans Appeals Improvement and Modernization Act of 2017, Pub. L. No. 115-55, §2 (x), 131 Stat. 1105 (2017) intended to resolve issues like the ones described in plaintiff's complaint. Plaintiff argued the Act did not cover legacy appeals and that the class included over 200,000 members with legacy appeals to whom the Act was inadequate and whose claims required judicial intervention. The Court disagreed and found that plaintiff failed to demonstrate commonality or suggest a path for meeting the commonality requirement in the future.

c. Typicality

RCFC Rule 23(a)(3) provides that "the claims or defenses of the representative parties [must be] typical of the claims or defenses of the class." "[T]he analysis of commonality and typicality tends to merge because '[b]oth serve as guideposts for determining whether . . . the named plaintiff's claim and the class are so interrelated that the interests of the class members will be fairly and adequately protected in their absence.'" *Barnes*, 68 Fed. Cl. at 498 (quoting *Gen. Tel. Co. of Southwest v. Falcon*, 457 U.S. 147, 157 n.13, 102 S. Ct. 2364, 72 L. Ed.2d 740 (1982)). "[E]ven if some factual differences exist between the claims of the named representatives," plaintiffs can establish typicality successfully by showing that "the named representatives' claims share the same essential characteristics as the claims of the class at large." *Curry v. United States*, 81 Fed. Cl. 328, 335 (2008). The threshold for plaintiffs to overcome is "also [like the commonality test] not high." *Fisher v. United States*, 69 Fed. Cl. 193, 200 (2006).

In *Fauvergue v. United States*, the defendant argued that the named plaintiffs' takings claims were not "typical" because "[e]ven assuming *arguendo* that Fauvergue's individual claim could be considered typical of the claims of the landowners in Missouri . . . her claim is not typical of the claims of the landowners in Kansas. . .." *Fauvergue v. United States*, 86 Fed. Cl. 82, 100 (2010) (reversed on other grounds in *Bright v. United States*, 603 F.3d 1273 (Fed. Cir. 2010)). Plaintiffs maintained that the notice of taking issued on June 21, 2002 was the basis for all class members' takings claims such that even if the named plaintiff's property-based claims from Missouri tracts on the railbanking trail were not representative of class members with Kansas railbanked property, 10 of the 16 named plaintiffs added to the amended complaint were landowners in Kansas on June 21, 2002. *Id.* Based on the additional Kansas-named plaintiffs included in the amended complaint, the court found the plaintiffs satisfied their burden in proving typicality under RCFC Rule 23(a)(3).

[13] Compare this case to *Brown v. United States*, 126 Fed. Cl. 571 (2016), wherein the Court of Claim did not certify a post-*Wal-Mart* takings case. The Court in *Brown* distinguished its decisions from the "Rails-to-Trails" takings cases prior to *Wal-Mart* and determined commonality was not met as Norfolk Southern Railroad, the easement owner, had acquired the subject property interests through "condemnation, prescription, and various deeds"; thus, "it is not possible to ascertain whether Norfolk Southern acquired an easement—or the scope of any such easement—in one fell swoop as required by *Wal-Mart*." *Brown*, 126 Fed. Cl. at 583. The issue of the method of easement acquisition had not played a role in "Rails-to-Trails" Act class action cases prior to *Brown*.

d. Adequate Representation

A certified class must be "fairly and adequately protect[ed]" by adequate counsel. RCFC Rule 23(a)(4). There are two steps to evaluate adequacy of representation; first, the court must consider whether the proposed class counsel is "qualified, experienced and generally able to conduct the litigation." *Curry*, 81 Fed. Cl. at 336 (quoting *Barnes*, 68 Fed. Cl. at 499); *see also King*, 84 Fed. Cl. at 127. Second, plaintiffs also must show that class members do not "have interests that are 'antagonistic' to one another." *Curry*, 81 Fed. Cl. at 336 (quoting *Barnes*, 68 Fed. Cl. at 499). In *In re Upstream Addicks and Barker (Texas) Flood Control Reservoirs*, 157 Fed. Cl 189 (2021), the Court of Claim heard plaintiffs' motion for class certification which followed bellwether trials finding the government liable for the taking of a non-categorical, permanent flowage easement as a result of government-induced flooding during Hurricane Harvey. After the finding of liability in their favor, plaintiffs' sought certification of a class on the issue of just compensation. The Court found the requirements of numerosity, commonality and typicality were met but found that the requirement of adequate representation was not met. The Court found the bellwether plaintiffs and the putative class members would have antagonistic interests because the bellwether plaintiffs would have no incentive to relitigate liability and would not oppose a motion to dismiss based on collateral estoppel. The Court also noted the role of plaintiffs' delay in seeking class certification as the decision to delay the certification motion until after the bellwether trials created the conflicts between the bellwether plaintiffs and putative class members.

In reviewing cases from the Court of Claim where RCFC Rule 23 certification and the adequacy of representation criteria are at issue, there is no significant jurisprudence finding class counsel inadequate to represent the class. Regarding the second criterion, the defendant in *Fauvergue* raised a "conflict of interest, grounding its challenge on the factual[ ] and legal[ ] distinct[ions]" presented by "any temporary claims that could be pursued by the Kansas landowners." *Fauvergue*, 86 Fed. Cl. at 101. The defendant did not present any other arguments in support of its position. Thus, the court found that "[b]ecause plaintiffs have the same legal and factual claims, the court cannot divine from the facts of record how the adjudication of this case as a class action could affect adversely other potential class members." *Id.*

The Court of Claim addressed the issue of potential conflicts between class counsel and class members when a previously certified class was divided into subclasses. *Sears v. United States*, 124 Fed. Cl. 444 (2015) (a "Rails-to-Trails" takings case discussed here and below in the section on subclassing). The government contended that establishing subclasses created a potential conflict of interest between class counsel and the subclass members as all fees were to be taken from a common fund. *Id.* The government reasoned that if one subclass took its claims to trial, class counsel would generate additional fees that would cause a "disproportionate[] harm" to the settlement subclass because the trial fees would be withdrawn from the same common fund. *Id.* at 450. The Court of Claim found that the settlement subclass would have no additional exposure to attorneys' fees due to the establishment of subclasses. *Id.* In this action, liability was addressed separately by the parties prior to the subclassing. Thus, any increase in fees attributable to a damages trial for one subclass would ultimately be payable under the URA if the subclass proved damages. The government also argued a conflict existed because a subclass trial would delay settlement for the remaining subclasses and class counsel would be conflicted in protecting the interests of both the settling and non-settling subclasses. However, the court has authority to issue a judgment for the settlement subclass independent of a judgment for the other subclass. *See* RCFC 54(b) ("When an action presents more than one claim for relief . . . or when multiple parties are involved, the court may direct entry of a final judgment as to one or more, but fewer than all, claims or parties only if the court expressly determines that there is no just reason for delay."). *Id.* at 451. Thus, the subclassing in *Sears* did not raise issues of adequate representation related to class counsel.

e. Superiority

The final RCFC Rule 23 requirement, superiority, is met when "a class action would achieve economies of time, effort, and expense, and promote uniformity of decision as to persons similarly situated, without sacrificing procedural fairness or bringing about other undesirable results." Fed. R. Civ. P. 23 advisory committee's note (1966 amendment, subdivision (b)(3)). Essentially, under this prong of analysis, the court is obligated to conduct a "cost/benefit analysis, weighing any potential problems with the manageability or fairness of a class action against the benefits to the system and the individual members likely to be derived from maintaining such an action." *Starr Int'l Co. v. United States*, 109 Fed. Cl. 628, 636 (2013) (quoting *Barnes*, 68 Fed. Cl. at 499 (citing *Eisen v. Carlisle & Jacquelin*, 417 U.S. 156, 163–64, 94 S. Ct. 2140, 40 L. Ed.2d 732 (1974))).

In *In re Addicks and Barker (Texas) Flood Control Reservoirs*, discussed above, the Court of Claim found the plaintiffs' putative class failed to meet the superiority requirement for class certification. In regard to the plaintiffs' decision to pursue bellwether litigation prior to seeking class certification, the Court found "it is not fair to the government to bind it to instantaneous class-wide adjudication of potentially thousands of plaintiffs' claims after a trial on liability on the claims of the thirteen bellwether plaintiffs." As the plaintiffs actively engaged in the bellwether approach over years of pretrial litigation and a trial on the issue of liability, the Court found it would be "unfair" to permit plaintiffs to "turn the tables" on defendant after a favorable ruling on liability and expand the scope of the court's liability decisions from thirteen bellwether plaintiffs to thousands of plaintiffs.

In *Jones*, current and former employees of the VA filed a putative class action against the government seeking back pay for regularly scheduled Sunday shifts. *Jones v. United States*, 118 Fed. Cl. 728, (2014). The court found that a class action was the superior mechanism for claims based on the Federal Salary and Fringe Benefits Act, 5 U.S.C. §§ 5544(a) or 5546, but adding claimants from agencies other than the VA who had similar claims under the Act would be "likely to create more problems than their association solves." *Jones*, 118 Fed. Cl. at 734.

In the group of "Rails-to-Trails" takings cases, the Court of Claim generally has found in favor of the plaintiff class members on the issue of superiority. In takings cases, "[u]nder a cost-benefit analysis, the pendulum tips comparatively in favor of class certification." *Fauvergue*, 86 Fed. Cl. at 101. The court has found superiority, even considering the possible distinction of claims between temporary and permanent takings, *see Barnes,* 68 Fed. Cl. at 500–01. In a takings case, the court has found that litigating all putative class members' claims in one action achieves "economies of scale in time, effort, and expense because the court is dealing with common questions of law and fact." *Fauvergue*, 86 Fed. Cl. at 101.

The Court of Claim also has addressed the overlap of the superiority analysis with the numerosity analysis, particularly in takings cases. *See Bell v. United States*, 123 Fed. Cl. 390 (2015). In some cases, the Court of Claim has viewed the numerosity analysis as cabined to the evaluation of the number of putative class members and the impracticability of joinder through another mechanism. However, some courts evaluate the size of the class relative to the value of each class member's claim as a matter of superiority, not numerosity. *See Bell v. United States*, 123 Fed. Cl. 390 (2015). The Court of Claim looks to the Advisory Committee Notes for FRCP Rule 23 for guidance on the issues of numerosity and superiority *Bell*, 123 Fed. Cl. at 396 ("interpretation[s] of the court's rules will be guided by case law and the Advisory Committee Notes that accompany the Federal Rules of Civil Procedure") and has determined that questions about the number of claimants, the amount of compensation for the individual claims, the costs of individual litigation, and the geographic location of the claimants are all considerations of superiority, not numerosity. *See Bell*, 123 Fed. Cl. at 396–401. In land takings cases, the court has found that a class action is not a superior method to pursue the litigation when all of the landowner-claimants have adjacent parcels in the same geographic area and can easily be joined in non-class litigation. *See Brown v. United States*, 126 Fed. Cl. 571 (2016).

f. Subclasses

Class subdivision is appropriate under RCFC Rule 23(c)(5). "When appropriate, a class may be divided into subclasses that are each treated as a class under this rule." *Sears v. United States*, 124 Fed. Cl. 444, 449 (2015). Subclassing under RCFC Rule 23 allows the court to "treat common things in common and to distinguish the distinguishable." *Sears*, 124 Fed. Cl. at 449 (quoting *Jenkins v. United Gas Corp.*, 400 F.2d 28, 35 (5th Cir. 1968)). Subclasses may be certified to provide adequate representation to plaintiffs who have interests that are in some respects adverse to one another or to distinguish groups of plaintiffs by injury sustained or to isolate common issues of law or fact shared by distinct groups of plaintiffs. *Sears*, 124 Fed. Cl. at 449 (citing *Haggart*, 104 Fed. Cl. 484 (2012)). Each subclass must satisfy the requirements of RCFC Rule 23. *Sears*, 124 Fed. Cl. at 449.

The Court of Claim addressed subclassing in two "Rails-to-Trails" Act cases. In *Sears v. United States*, the plaintiff class members, consisting of 269 landowners whose land was subject to a taking when converted from railway easement to a trail, had almost reached a settlement with the government when 21 landowners withdrew from settlement negotiations, thus ending the settlement process. *Id.* The 21 landowners then sought approval for a 21-member "acutely-bisected agricultural-property subclass." *Sears*, 124 Fed. Cl. at 449. The court found the 21-member subclass met the numerosity requirement of RCFC Rule 23 and further found that all remaining factors in the Rule 23 inquiry also were met as the action by the total class of landowners was previously certified, prior to any settlement negotiations. *Id.* at 450. Similarly, the court certified six subclasses on a joint motion by both parties despite the small size of some classes in *Haggart*, 104 Fed. Cl. at 488–89 (numerosity found even when one subclass had 18 members). In *Haggart*, the court found subclassing to be practical as the pending claims of some subclasses needed to be determined first, before the claims of other subclasses, and relying on multiparty litigation would create difficulties in sequencing the resolution of claims. *See id.*

In *Health Republic Insurance Company v. United States*, 2021 WL 2325165 (June 1, 2021), the Court of Federal Claim heard arguments on the parties joint Motion to Divide Dispute Subclass into Two Subclasses, *et al.* This action followed a related decision in *Maine Community Health Options v. United States*, 140 S. Ct. 1308 (2020) which divided a class into three subclasses, one identified as the Dispute Subclass which is the subject of this decision. The Motion sought the Court's approval of subclass division within the already existing Dispute Subclass to allow recovery for one subsection of the Dispute Subclass, known as the Freelancers Subclass (defined as "class members offering Qualified Health Plans under the Patient Protection and Affordable Care Act in the 2014 and 2015 benefit years, whose allowable costs … were more than 103 percent of their target amounts …, and who were previously members of the Dispute Subclass, but have since agreed to a resolution of their dispute with the government with respect to this litigation."). The Court granted the parties' joint motion, allowing the parties to form the Freelancers Subclass and stipulate that the Freelancers Subclass was entitled to payment from the United States in an amount in excess of $23 million.

7. CASE MANAGEMENT

a. Attorneys' Fees

In *Mercier v. United States*, 156 Fed. Cl. 580 (2021), a class action brought by nurses and physician assistants employed by the Department of Veteran's Affairs, which is discussed separately above on the issue of pleading, the Court considered the plaintiffs' motion for final approval of the proposed settlement agreement and approved attorneys' fees and expenses related to the litigation. Plaintiffs based their fee request on the common fund doctrine. "Under that doctrine, 'a litigant or a lawyer who recovers a common fund for the benefit of persons other than himself or his client is entitled to reasonable attorney fees from the fund as a whole.' (quoting *Haggart v. Woodley*, 809 F.3d 1336 (2016). The Supreme Court has held that the requirements of the common fund doctrine are satisfied when each member of a certified class has an undisputed and mathematically ascertainable claim to part of a lump sum judgment collected on each member's behalf. *See Boeing v. Van Gemert*, 444 U.S. 472 (1980). In this case, the class was awarded a lump sum settlement of $160,000,000.00. Each plaintiff was entitled to a proportionate and ascertainable share of that amount, thus a common fund existed in the case. The Court's next step is to determine what fee award is fair to the class members who all take from the common fund. In this case, six named plaintiffs agreed to a 33% contingent fee which, if enforced, would lead to an attorney fee windfall to class counsel. The Court noted that the contingent fee agreement by the named plaintiffs does not bind the Court in its fee determination, even when there are none or few objections to the fee.

The Federal Circuit has held that in common fund cases reasonable attorneys' fees may be calculated using either the percentage or lodestar method. *See Haggart*, 809 F.3d. at 1355. The Federal Circuit has not specified what considerations govern the assessment of reasonable fee requests in common fund cases but several judges on the Federal Circuit have identified a multi-factor test to determine reasonableness. The factors include, (1) the quality of counsel; (2) the complexity and duration of the litigation; (3) the risk of nonrecovery; (4) the fee that likely would have been negotiated between private parties in similar cases; (5) any class members' objections to the settlement terms or fees requested by class counsel; (6) the percentage applied in other class actions; and (7) the size of the award. *Moore v. United States*, 63 Fed. Cl. 781, 787 (2005) (citing Manual for Complex Litig. § 14.121 (4th ed. 2004)). The Court in *Mercier* applied this multi-factor test to determine that a 20% attorney fee was appropriate.

In *Electronic Welfare Trust Fund v. United States*, 171 Fed. Cl. 362 (2024), the Court considered whether the common fund doctrine applied while evaluating a 25 percent attorneys' fee in a $169 million dollar settlement to a 357-member class consisting of self-administered, self-insured employee health and welfare benefit plans who claimed the United States illegally exacted transitional reinsurance contributions from plans contrary to the Affordable Care Act (ACA). The Court followed *Mercier* in finding the common fund doctrine was satisfied because "each member of a certified class has an undisputed and mathematically ascertainable claim to part of a lump-sum judgment recovered on his behalf." The Court then considered whether the common fund doctrine may be applied to allow class counsel to recover attorney fees. The Court noted that class counsel had litigated the class claims throughout the near decade-long dispute entirely on a contingent fee basis, fully bearing the risk of nonrecovery for the class. Class counsel expended more than 9,000 hours on behalf of the class (amounting to lodestar of approximately $6.351 million) and incurred over $500,000 in expenses. In evaluating the class counsel fee request, the Court stated "[r]elevant jurisprudence further supports the proposed fee, especially in view of the temporal length of the dispute, litigation risks borne solely by counsel, and the high 91.25% recovery for the class." Using a lodestar percentage of 6.63, the Court awarded class counsel fees of 25 percent of the settlement amount, approximately $42.120 million.

The Federal Court of Claim held that the common fund doctrine did not apply to fees and expenses awarded under the Equal Access to Justice Act (28 U.S.C. 2412(b). *See Kandel v. United States*, 160 Fed. Cl. 255 (2022) (citing *Athey v. United States*, No. 2020-2291, 2021 WL 4282593 (Fed. Cir. Sept. 21, 2021).

In *Arnold v. United States*, 2022 WL 14198936 (Oct. 24, 2022), a Rails to Trials temporary takings case involving property in parts of Nebraska and Kansas, the plaintiffs moved the Court of Claim for an award of attorneys' fees and litigation expenses under the Relocation Assistance and Real Property Acquisition Policies Act (URA), 42 U.S.C. §4654(c), which allows fee shifting. The Court denied Plaintiffs' requested fee award of $794,577.50 as exceeding the bounds of any objective measure of reasonableness in a 13 owner, 17 parcel class action involving a total of 51.09 acres of land and an aggregate settlement amount of $7595.17. The Court engaged in a detailed analysis of the fees requested, examining the applicable billing rates and analyzing rates and activity under both the percentage and lodestar methods. Relying on the Supreme Court's decision in *Hensley v. Eckhart*, 461 U.S. 424, 435036 (1983) stating, "'the significance of the overall relief obtained by the plaintiff[s] in relation to the hours reasonably expended–also denoted as 'the degree of success obtained'–is 'the most critical factor' in determining reasonable attorney's fees," the Court of Claim found this case to be one of the "rare and exceptional cases" meriting a downward adjustment in fees and expenses. The fees awarded were reduced to $100, 282.47 from the requested $794,577.50.

In a similar Rails-to-Trails case, property owners filed a motion for attorneys' fees and costs under the URA after demonstrating that the United States's conversions of owners' property from railroad rights-of-way to recreational trails constituted a taking as to 145 of 173 parcels. The Court examined the motion in detail, first relying on the lodestar method to calculate allowable hourly rates for attorney fees, which rendered a total fee request of $2,005,360.50. The Court reduced this award by 6 percent ($120,321.63) to account for unsuccessful claims and further adjusted the fee to address disallowed hours stemming from administrative work, block billing, hours billed for travel, excessive, duplicative, or otherwise unnecessary hours, and hours improperly billed for work on other cases. After considering defendant's arguments for reductions (which sought an overall reduction of approximately $1.9 million), the Court awarded a reduced total award of attorneys' fees of $1,553,202.31. The Court performed a similar analysis as to costs and reduced the requested amount of costs from $481,248.10 to $421,836.85 (a reduction of almost $60,000).

In May 2022, the Federal Circuit heard an appeal from a Court of Claims ruling regarding attorneys' fees in the long, procedurally complex, and ongoing takings litigation which began as *Haggart v. United States,* 116 Fed. Cl. 131 (2014) (*Haggart I*). Plaintiff Evans appealed the Court of Claim's award of attorneys' fees, arguing that the URA fee shifting statute required the government to reimburse class members for fees retained by counsel under contingent fee arrangements. The Federal Circuit rejected this argument as inapplicable when the Court had already determined an award of reasonable attorneys' fees using the lodestar method. *See Haggart v. United States*, 2022 WL 1419603 (May 5, 2022).

In a decision related to the *Health Republic* case discussed above, the Court of Federal Claims held the class counsel's request for a five percent attorneys fee to be reasonable. *See Health Republic Insurance Company v. United States*, __ Fed. Cl. __, 2021 WL 4233966 (September 16, 2021). Noting that the Federal Circuit had not mandated the use of one attorney fee calculation method over another, the Court exercised its discretion to choose between the percentage-of-the-fund or lodestar methods in a common fund case. The Court determined that the lodestar method was a poor fit in this common fund case and applied the percentage-of-the-fund method which required the multi-factor analysis applied in *Moore v. United States*, 63 Fed. C. 781 (2005). Weighing the seven factors of *Moore*, the Court found the balance favored the fee request, noting, among other factors, that the Court received only one substantive objection out of hundreds of class members including 34 involved entities.[14] In *Health Republic*, the Court approved an attorney's fee in excess of $184 million.

In contrast, the Court of Federal Claim denied a request for attorneys' fees sought under the Equal Access to Justice Act in *Athey v. United States*, 149 Fed. Cl. 497 (2020). In what the Court described as the "epilogue of protracted class action litigation" the class action plaintiffs sought payment of attorneys' fees after a lump sum settlement between the Department of Veterans Affairs and the class. The fee request was grounded in the Equal Access to Justice Act, 28 U.S.C. § 2412. The Court described its task as requiring it to "juxta-

[14] The decision simultaneously denied class counsel's request for $100,000 incentive awards to plaintiffs Health Republic and Common Ground citing concerns with the propriety of approving incentive fee awards paid from class counsel attorneys' fees under the Model Rules of Professional Conduct.

pose the Class's modest success on the merits" with "firmly rooted jurisprudence governing the payment of attorney fees and expenses where the position of the United States was substantially justified." The decision relies, in part, on the Court's application of RCFC Rule 23(h)(1) requiring notice to members of the class prior to filing the motion seeking an award of attorneys' fees. The class failed to give proper notice under FRFC Rule 23(h). The Court also analyzed the fee request under the Equal Justice to Access Act, which permits attorneys' fees when the position of the United States was not substantially justified and no special circumstances are present which would make the award unjust. The award can be determined to be unjust if the class failed to submit contemporaneous records to support the fee it seeks to recover. Here, the Court found the position of the United States was substantially justified and that the class failed to submit contemporaneous itemized statements to support the fee request, thus denied the class's attorneys' fee request.

The Federal Circuit addressed an attorneys' fee issue in *Keith Manufacturing Co. v. Butterfield*, 955 F.3d 936 (Fed. Cir. 2020). *Keith* was not a class action. It was a patent-based dispute between employer and former employee, but the case addressed a claim for attorneys' fees under FRCP Rule 54. As part of the trial court litigation, the parties had filed a stipulation of dismissal pursuant to FRCP Rule 41(a)(1)(A)(ii), which was silent as to costs and attorneys' fees.[15] The defendant then moved for attorneys' fees under FRCP Rule 54 and the trial court denied the motion, holding that FRCP Rule 54 requires a judgment that the Rule defines as "a decree and any order from which an appeal lies." The issue on appeal was whether the trial court was correct in concluding that the parties' stipulation of dismissal was not a final judgment under FRCP Rule 54. The Federal Circuit noted that the Rule 54 requirement presupposes a relationship between a judgment and its appealability, which exists for the purpose of minimizing piecemeal litigation. The plaintiff argued that the Supreme Court's reasoning in *Microsoft Corp. v. Baker*, __ U.S. __, 137 S. Ct. 1702, 198 L. Ed. 132 (2017), should apply here, thus requiring a final judgment under Rule 54 and 28 U.S.C. §§ 1291 and 1295.[16] The Federal Circuit rejected the trial court's interpretation of Rule 54 and found the reasoning in *Microsoft* inapplicable here. The Federal Circuit found that "[t]he definition of judgment in Rule 54 indicates that some non-appealable orders can still constitute a judgment." Furthermore, the court found that treating a voluntary stipulation with prejudice as a judgment will not invite parties to engage in piecemeal appellate litigation, as was the concern in *Microsoft*. The court also noted that as *Keith* was not a class action, this interpretation of Rule 54 would not undermine class action procedure.

In *Sabo v. United States*, the government appealed a lower court decision allowing for attorney's fees in a class action by service members who suffered PTSD yet were not able to attain disability ratings at or above 50 percent. 717 F. App'x 986 (Fed. Cir. 2017). The class action was settled with plaintiff's counsel filing an application for fees and costs thereafter. The government argued that the application should be denied for two reasons: (1) the application was not timely as it was filed more than 30 days after the Settlement Agreement was originally accepted by the court, and (2) the government's position in the lawsuit was substantially justified thus no fees should be awarded. The lower court granted the application for fees and the government appealed. The Federal Circuit affirmed the lower court's ruling finding that the 30-day timeline begins when the Settlement is final, meaning no further action can or should be taken in the litigation. In this case, the Settlement Agreement contemplated future action by the parties, thus was not final at the time it was approved by the court, therefore the application for attorney's fees was timely. The Federal Circuit also found no abuse of discretion in the court's ruling that the government's positions in defending the action were not substantially justified as the government interpreted regulations regarding disability ratings in a manner contrary to the express terms of the governing statute.

---

[15] A stipulation of dismissal requires no court order and no court approval as *Keith* was not a class action.

[16] *Microsoft Corp. v. Baker* was a class action that analyzed, among other issues, the parties' application for attorneys' fees.

In *Bywaters v. United States*, the plaintiff class included landowners who alleged their lands had been unconstitutionally taken under the "Rails-to-Trails" Act. *Bywaters v. United States*, 670 F.3d 1221 (Fed. Cir. 2012). The case was originally brought in the district court for the Eastern District of Texas where the class action was certified under FRCP Rule 23 and a settlement was approved. The appeal came to the Federal Circuit under subject matter jurisdiction based on the Tucker Act and the Little Tucker Act.[17] The only issue on appeal was the district court's determination of attorneys' fees. As a threshold matter, the court first determined whether it should apply Federal Circuit law or the law of the regional circuit, the Fifth Circuit. The government argued that the district court's award of attorneys' fees was dependent on FRCP Rule 23 and thus implicated procedural issues rather than the merits of a takings claim under the Tucker Act. However, the district court's award of attorneys' fees in the case was based on the mandatory fee-shifting provision of the URA.[18] The Federal Circuit held that government takings claims brought under the Tucker Act or the Little Tucker Act, cases that are within the Federal Circuit's exclusive jurisdiction, are to be interpreted in accordance with the law of the Federal Circuit and not the regional circuit encompassing the district court where the case originated. *Id.*

In *Otay Mesa Property, L.P. v. United States*, 124 Fed. Cl. 141 (2015), another takings case where the plaintiff sought attorneys' fees under the URA, the court assessed whether attorneys' fees were reasonable, as required by the URA. The court used the "lodestar method" to determine reasonable attorneys' fees. The lodestar method involves multiplying "the number of hours reasonably expended on the litigation . . . by a reasonable hourly rate." *Otay Mesa*, 124 Fed. Cl. at 146 (quoting *Hensley v. Eckerhart*, 461 U.S. 424, 433 (1983)). However, strict adherence to the lodestar method is not required. *Id.* "Generally, in determining the amount of reasonable attorneys' fees to award under federal fee-shifting statutes, the district court is afforded considerable discretion." *Bywaters v. United States*, 670 F.3d 1221, 1228 (Fed. Cir. 2012). Along with other factors, a court may consider the degree of success obtained by the plaintiff and adjust the calculation accordingly. *Id.* To make such an adjustment, a court may reduce the number of hours "reasonably expended" on the litigation in its initial calculation of the lodestar figure, but it generally may not engage in a wholesale "reduc[tion of] the lodestar figure itself." *Bywaters*, 670 F.3d at 1232. The party seeking the fees bears the burden of showing that the hourly rate is reasonable. *Otay Mesa*, 124 Fed. Cl. at 147. Rates are presumptively reasonable when they are in line with the prevailing market rate—the rate "prevailing in the community for similar services by lawyers of reasonably comparable skill, experience and reputation." *Id.* (quoting *Blum v. Stenson*, 465 U.S. 886, 896 n.11, 104 S. Ct. 1541, 79 L. Ed. 2d 891 (1984)).

Using these parameters, the court in *Otay Mesa* carefully examined the attorneys' fees, which represented considerable work on complex litigation that resulted in two appeals and ultimately allowed reimbursement for the bulk of the fees paid.[19]

In 2019, the Federal Circuit evaluated an attorneys' fees issue in another Rails-to-Trails takings class action against the United States. *Haggart v. United States*, 943 F.3d 943 (Fed. Cir. 2019). In *Haggart*, the government argued that because the Settlement Agreement awarded "statutory attorney's fees and costs . . . pursuant to the URA" and because the Agreement provided the amounts noted were inclusive of all interest, fees, and litigation expenses that "have been or could be incurred," the court cannot award any URA fees above

[17] 28 U.S.C. §§ 1491 and 1346.

[18] The Uniform Relocation Assistance and Real Property Acquisition Policies Act of 1970, 42 U.S.C. § 4654.

[19] *See also* Martinez v. United States, 94 Fed. Cl. 176, 188 (2010) (Court of Claims allowed award of attorneys' fees for time spent in unsuccessful settlement negotiations, rejecting a "categorical rule against awarding fees expended during settlement negotiations" as such a rule "would 'discourage the pursuit of settlements' on the part of plaintiffs." (citations omitted)).

the amount indicated in the Settlement Agreement.[20] The Court of Federal Claims entered a partial final judgment pursuant to Rule 54(b) as to the principal and interest amounts under the settlement agreement but deferred consideration of the attorneys' fees in the settlement agreement. The Federal Circuit held that the lower court's deferral did not constitute a final judgment; therefore, the Federal Circuit did not have jurisdiction to address the Government's argument regarding attorneys' fees.

In 2017, the Court of Claims heard two Rails to Trails Act cases addressing questions related to fees and costs under a proposed settlement agreement. In *Furlong v. United States*, 131 Fed. Cl. 548 (2017), the Court of Claims granted preliminary approval to a proposed settlement agreement in an RCFC Rule 23 class action brought by 271 plaintiff landowners with parcels adjacent to a 9.14-mile rail corridor in Albany County, New York. The proposed settlement agreement includes over $6 million in compensation, $5.7 million in interest, and $1,305,000 in attorneys' fees, costs, and other expenses. In *Greenwood v. United States*, 131 Fed. Cl. 231 (2017), the Court of Claims again approved a settlement in a Rails-to-Trails Act class action filed under RCFC Rule 23 by the landowners of 78 parcels adjacent to a railroad corridor in Lawrence County, Arkansas. In accordance with RCFC Rule 23, the Court of Claims found the settlement agreement, which allocated approximately $610,000, with interest, to the plaintiff class, as "fair, reasonable and adequate."

---

[20] The Settlement Agreement provided for $2.58 million in attorneys' fees and costs pursuant to the URA.

Printed by Libri Plureos GmbH in Hamburg,
Germany

9 781639 056613